ANNUAL REVIEW OF IRISH LAW 1997

UNITED KINGDOM
Sweet & Maxwell
London

AUSTRALIA
LBC Information Services
Sydney

CANADA AND USA
Carswell
Toronto • Ontario

NEW ZEALAND
Brooker's
Auckland

SINGAPORE AND MALAYSIA
Thomson Information (S.E. Asia)
Singapore

Annual Review
of Irish Law 1997

Raymond Byrne
B.C.L., LL.M., Barrister-at-Law
Lecturer in Law, Dublin City University

William Binchy
B.A., B.C.L., LL.M., Barrister-at-Law
Regius Professor of Law, Trinity College, Dublin

Round Hall Sweet & Maxwell
1998

Published in 1998 by
Round Hall Sweet & Maxwell
Brehon House, 4 Upper Ormond Quay,
Dublin 7

Typeset by
Gough Typesetting Services, Dublin.

Printed by
MPG Books Limited, Cornwall

ISBN 1-85800-119-6

A catalogue record for this book
is available from the British Library.

Table of Contents

Preface

In this eleventh volume in the Annual Review series, our purpose continues to be to provide a review of legal developments, judicial and statutory, that occurred in 1997. In terms of case law, this includes those judgments which were delivered in 1997, regardless of whether they have been (or will be) reported and which were circulated up to the date of the preface. Once again, it is a pleasure to thank those who made the task of completing this volume less onerous.

Once again, we are in the debt of a number of people for providing access to library facilities. In particular, Ms Peggy McQuinn, of the Office of the Supreme Court, Ms Margaret Byrne and Ms Mary Gaynor, of the Library of the Incorporated Law Society of Ireland, and Mr Johnathon Armstrong, of the King's Inns Library, were as helpful as ever with a number of difficult queries from the authors. And once again, Ms Jennifer Aston, Librarian in the Law Library, Four Courts, was also especially helpful in facilitating access to statutory material which is otherwise very difficult to source.

We would also like to express our heartfelt thanks to the staffs of the Dublin City University and Trinity College libraries for their assistance in the research for this volume. This eleventh volume in the Annual Review series also marks a departure from previous years. The authors are delighted to have had the benefit of specialist contributions on Company Law, Communications, Contract Law, Equity, Evidence, Land Law, Practice and Procedure and Restitution included in the volume. The authors continue to take final responsibility for the overall text as in the past, but are especially grateful for the contributions of David Tomkin and Adam McAuley in Company Law, Eamon Hall in Communications, Eoin O'Dell in Contract Law and Restitution, Paul Coughlan in Land Law, Declan McGrath in Evidence, Hilary Delany in Equity and Practice and Procedure.

Finally, we are very grateful to Round Hall Sweet & Maxwell and Gilbert Gough, whose professionalism ensures the continued production of this series.

Raymond Byrne and William Binchy,
Dublin

November 1998

Table of Cases

Other Tables

Table of Irish Statutes

Statutory Instruments

English Stautes

EC Treaties and Conventions

Administrative Law

APPROPRIATION

The Appropriation Act 1997 provided as follows. For the year ended December 31, 1997, the amount for supply grants in accordance with the Central Fund (Permanent Provisions) Act 1965 was £12,103,829,000. Under the Public Accounts and Charges Act 1891, the sum for appropriations-in-aid was £1,115,427,000. The 1997 Act came into effect on its signature by the President on December 19, 1997.

CIVIL SERVICE

Reorganisation   The Public Service Management Act 1997 arose from the then Government's *Strategic Management Initiative* (SMI) document published in 1994. The SMI led to the initiation of a number of efficiency, effectiveness and value for money studies within the public sector. Within that general framework, the 1997 Act provides for a new management structure for Government Departments. The 1997 Act applies without prejudice to the terms of the Ministers and Secretaries Act 1924, as amended, which had provided the legislative background up to 1997. However, the 1997 Act differentiates between the so-called 'core' of a Department and its associated offices. Section 1 of the 1997 Act defines a Department as 'the part of a Department of State [as defined in the 1924 Act] that is staffed by civil servants who exercise functions directly under a Minister of the Government or a Minister of State.' In the context of the Department of Finance, this definition would exclude, for example, the Revenue Commissioners, since they operate as an independent branch within the Department of Finance. In addition, the 1997 Act replaced the title 'Secretary' for the head of a Department with 'Secretary General'. Section 3 of the 1997 Act restates the position under the 1924 Act that the Minister having charge of the Department is responsible for the functions assigned to him or her under the 1924 Act and thus remains responsible for the administration of the Department. Section 4 provides that the Secretary General of a Department is responsible, under the terms of the 1997 Act, for the day-to-day management of Departments, advising Ministers in relation to Departmental matters, arranging cross-departmental relations and ensuring cost effectiveness in delivering 'outputs' which includes the standard of goods and service provided by a Department. The Secretary General is also empowered by section 9 of the 1997 Act to delegate management functions to officers within the Department, which can include delegation of targets concerning the delivery of policy and provision of goods and services in specified areas. The Secretary General is also given power concerning the appointment, performance, discipline and dismissal of staff below the level of Principal Officer. Section 11 of the Act also provides for the appointment of special advisers to Ministers; these had previously been the subject of some criticism at political level. Section 13 provides that the Government may confer corporate status on the Attorney General, the Comptroller and Auditor General, the Director of Public Prosecutions and the Ombudsman, which would allow them to sue and be sued, and in respect of whom there would be perpetual succession. Under the 1924 Act, Ministers already have corporate status as 'corporations sole.' The Public Service Management Act 1997 (Commencement) Order 1997 (S.I. No. 339 of 1997) brought the 1997 Act into force on September 1, 1997.

ETHICS IN PUBLIC OFFICE

Disclosure duty: cesser of office   The Ethics in Public Office Act 1995 (Section 3(1)(B)) Regulations 1997 (S.I. No. 320 of 1997), made under the Ethics in Public Office Act 1995 (1995 Review, 3-4), provides that where a person ceases to be an office holder, the disclosure duty imposed by section 19 of the 1995 Act must be carried out within 30 days of such cesser. The Regulations came into effect on July 21, 1997.

Prescribed public bodies   The Ethics in Public Office (Prescribed Public Body, Designated Directorships and Designated Positions in Public Bodies) Regulations 1997 (S.I. No. 32 of 1997), also made under the 1995 Act, applied the provisions of the Act to persons occupying specified positions in the wider public service and required them to furnish statements of registrable interests with effect from January 15, 1997. The Ethics in Public Office (Prescribed Public Body, Designated Directorships and Designated Positions In Public Bodies) (Amendment) Regulations 1997 (S.I. No. 310 of 1997), also made under the 1995 Act, amended the 1997 Regulations and provided that Airmotive Ireland Holdings Ltd was no longer a public body for the purposes of the 1995 Act, arising from its privatisation.

FREEDOM OF INFORMATION ACT 1997

Introduction and Commencement   The Freedom of Information Act 1997 provides, in general terms, for a right of access to records, whether held in electronic or other form, held by public bodies and to have personal information amended where it is incomplete, incorrect or misleading. The 1997 Act also provides for procedures for obtaining access to information and establishes an independent Information Commissioner to review refusals, delays or editing of information. Significant exemptions from the general right of access are also provided and the 1997 Act did not repeal the Official Secrets Act 1963. As provided for in section 1 of the 1997 Act, its terms came generally into force on April 21, 1998 (one year after its passing), with the exception of the provisions applicable to local authorities and health boards which required a Ministerial Commencement Order to have effect no later than October 21, 1998.

Access to records Section 6 of the 1997 Act provides a legal right for the public to official information and imposes an obligation on public bodies to assist the public when making requests for such information. In general, access will be provided to records created from commencement of the 1997 Act on April 21, 1998, along with access to earlier records, where these are necessary to understand more recent information. In addition the Minister for Finance may, by Regulations, provide general access to records created before the 1997 Act came into force. Personal records may be accessed regardless of when they were created. As regards personnel records of staff in public bodies, access will be available to current records or any earlier records liable to be used in a way that might adversely affect the interests of the member of staff involved.

Section 7 sets out how the right of access is to be exercised and also requires that public bodies acknowledge receipt of requests within two weeks. Section 8 requires that public bodies decide whether to accede to or refuse requests within four weeks of receipt and that they notify the requester accordingly. Where a request is being refused, reasons for refusal must be given, along with a statement setting out rights of review and appeal. Section 9 allows the period within which a decision must be made on a request to be extended by up to four weeks if the request, or related requests, concern such a large number of records that compliance within the specified timeframe is not possible. Section 10 sets out grounds for refusing a request where it would not be practicable to do so or where the request is frivolous or vexatious. Section 11 permits deferral of access to a narrow range of records, such as records held only for the information of the Houses of the Oireachtas, while section 12 provides for different ways in which access can be granted, including by way of computer disk. Where part of a record is exempt, section 13 provides for access to the remainder, where this is practical and does not mislead.

Section 14 provides for internal review against an initial decision by a public body in respect of the following: refusal to grant a request; deferral of

access to a document being prepared for the Houses of the Oireachtas; the
provision of access in a form other than that requested; the granting of access
to part only of a record; a refusal to amend a record relating to personal information, the giving of reasons for a decision; and the charging of a fee or
deposit in respect of the grant of access. Such a review must be undertaken at
a higher level than that at which the original decision was made, and completed within three weeks.

Section 15 requires that a public body must publish information setting
out a general description of its structure, functions and services it provides to
the public as well as a general description of its rules and guidelines used in
implementing its schemes and programmes. In addition it must describe the
classes of records it holds and the arrangements for enabling the public to
access such records. The provision also requires the public body to set out
rights of review and appeal against its decisions generally. Section 16 requires
that each public body publish the rules, procedures, guidelines, interpretations and an index of precedents used by it for the purposes of decisions and
recommendations. Where such material is not published, or, where published,
it is incomplete or inaccurate, the public body concerned is required to ensure
that a person is not prejudiced, due to such failure or error on the part of that
body.

Section 17 confers a legal right on each member of the public to require
that personal information relating to oneself and held by a public body be
amended, where it is incomplete, incorrect or misleading. This is similar to
the right of correction in the Data Protection Act 1988 (1988 Review, 390-
99). Section 18 confers a legal right on each person to reasons for a decision
on a matter particularly affecting that person.

Section 45 sets out legal protections for the granting of access to a record
in accordance with the provisions of the 1997 Act, or in the reasonable belief
that its provisions were complied with.

Exempt records and ministerial certificates   Section 19 provides that access under section 7 of the Act may be refused in respect of matters prepared
for consideration by Government and related briefing material. This protection does not apply where five or more years have elapsed since the relevant
Government decision was made or where the information constitutes factual
material and the decision to which it relates has been made public. This, to
some extent, indicates a liberalisation of the '30 year rule' by which Government records are released and made available under the National Archives
Act 1986.

Section 20 provides that access to records relating to the deliberative processes of a public body may be refused, but only where disclosure would be
contrary to the public interest. This section does not offer protection to factual
information, certain technical reports or reports on the performance or effec-

tiveness of public bodies. Internal rules and guidelines and reasons for decisions are also excluded from the protections afforded to the deliberative processes.

Section 21 provides that records may be protected where disclosure could prejudice the effectiveness of certain operations of a public body. Such operations would include audit, control, examinations or investigative functions of the body. In addition, this provision offers protection in respect of industrial relations functions and negotiating positions of Government and state agencies. Information may be released where the public interest would on balance, be better served by granting than by refusing the request.

Section 22 exempts from disclosure records prepared for court proceedings which would be protected on the grounds of legal professional privilege, on which see now the new Rules of the Superior Courts (No. 7) 1997, discussed in the Practice and Procedure chapter, 593, below. It also exempts any records whose disclosure would constitute contempt of court. Similarly it exempts from production certain matters relating to the proceedings of the Oireachtas and the private papers of elected representatives of the European Parliament and of local or regional authorities are also exempt from disclosure. We may note that the private papers of Members of the Oireachtas are excluded under section 46 of the 1997 Act.

Section 23 provides that information may be protected where its disclosure could prejudice or impair law enforcement functions or public safety. This protection does not extend to information concerning the performance of a body or the success or otherwise of a law enforcement programme or policy where the public interest would be served by such disclosure.

Section 24 provides that information may be withheld where its disclosure could adversely affect defence, security or international relations.

Section 25 outlines the procedures in relation to the issue of Ministerial certificates. Where a Minister is satisfied that information sought is exempt by reference to prejudicing interests in sections 23 or 24, and that the information is of sufficient sensitivity or seriousness to justify him or her doing so, he or she may sign a certificate confirming that the material is exempt. In such cases review is undertaken by other members of the Government rather than by the Information Commissioner. A certificate must be withdrawn where such a review finds insufficient grounds for its use.

Section 26 provides that information may be protected where it has been given to a public body and is subject to an obligation of confidence. This section also provides that a public body should consult with the Information Commissioner prior to entering into classes of confidential agreements. The head has discretion to consider release of the information where, on balance, he or she is of the opinion that it is in the public interest to do so. Prior to making a decision on such release, the consultation procedures in section 29 must be followed.

Section 27 provides that a public body may refuse to grant access to commercially sensitive information to persons other than the individual or company to whom the information relates. The head has discretion to consider release of the information where, on balance, he or she is of the opinion that it is in the public interest to do so. Prior to making a decision on such release, the consultation procedures in section 29 must be followed.

Section 28 protects personal information held by a public body against third party access. Particular procedures are specified in respect of medical or social work information where the head of the body is of the opinion that its disclosure to the person concerned may be prejudicial to his or her health or emotional well-being. In these circumstances, the public body shall, if requested to do so by the person concerned, instead release the record to an appropriate health professional nominated by the requester.

The head has discretion to consider release of the information to a third party where, on balance, he or she is of the opinion that the public interest in disclosure outweighs the right to privacy of the individual concerned or where release of the information would benefit the individual. Prior to making a decision on such release, the consultation procedures in section 29 must be followed.

Section 29 outlines the consultation procedures to be followed if a head proposes to release, in the public interest, information referred to in sections 26, 27 or 28. In that case, the public body is obliged to:

(i)   advise the relevant third party of the intention to release the information and the public interest grounds involved.

(ii) consider the response of the third party prior to deciding on disclosure. and

(iii) allow opportunity for appeal to the Commissioner, if the public body proposes release of the information.

Section 30 deals with information relating to research and natural resources. Information in relation to research may be withheld by a public body if premature disclosure of the information would be likely to expose the body concerned or the persons engaged in the research to serious disadvantage. Information may also be protected where its release could reasonably be expected to prejudice the well-being of a cultural, heritage or natural resource or the habitat or species of flora or fauna. Information may be released where the public interest would on balance, be better served by granting than by refusing the request.

Section 31 protects information where its disclosure could reasonably be expected to have serious adverse effects for the financial interests of the State or the ability of the Government to manage the economy. Information is also protected if premature disclosure could result in undue disturbance of the ordinary course of business of the community or in undue benefit or loss to any person. Information may be released where the public interest would on balance, be better served by granting than by refusing the request.

Section 32 upholds the operation of specific non-disclosure provisions in other legislation. However, general 'catch-all' secrecy provisions, contained in the legislation listed in the Third Schedule to the 1997 Act, are now subject to the particular provisions set out in the 1997 Act. The legislation in the Third Schedule includes many 'regulatory' Acts, such as the Competition Act 1991 and the Irish Medicines Board Act 1993, which typically include non-disclosure provisions. Section 32 of the 1997 Act also provides for periodic review of secrecy provisions in other legislation by a Committee of the Oireachtas.

The head of a public body may refuse to disclose the existence or non-existence of information in certain specific circumstances. This provision may be used to protect information outlined in sections 23(1) (law enforcement), or 24(1) (defence and security) where disclosure of its existence or non-existence would be likely to prejudice the interests protected by those subsections. In addition this provision may be used to protect information referred to in sections 19(1) (matters before government) or 22(1)(a) (parliamentary or court material), where confirmation of its existence or non-existence would be contrary to the public interest.

Finally, section 46 sets out matters which are outside the scope of the 1997 Act. This includes information held by the courts, by a tribunal established with the powers contained in the Tribunals of Inquiry (Evidence) Acts 1921 to 1997, by the Attorney General, the Director of Public Prosecutions, the Comptroller and Auditor General or the Ombudsman. In addition it excludes information which would disclose the identity of a confidential source of information in relation to enforcement of criminal law, records concerning the President, the private papers of a member of the Oireachtas or which is otherwise publicly available.

Information Commissioner   Section 33 of the 1997 Act provides for the establishment of the Office of Information Commissioner. The Ombudsman Act 1980 was amended so as to allow for the appointment of the Ombudsman as Information Commissioner. Section 34 outlines the decisions subject to review by the Commissioner. The Commissioner may, on review, exercise the same powers as the head of a public body and his or her decisions would be binding on the parties concerned, subject to appeal to the High Court under section 42. It also provides that the onus shall be on the public body to show that its original decision to refuse information was justified.

Section 35 allows the Commissioner to require a public body to provide more detailed reasons for refusal to grant a request where he or she is of the view that the details given in a notice under section 8 are inadequate. Such additional information may include particulars taken into account by the public body pertaining to the public interest.

Section 36 provides that the Commissioner shall keep the 1997 Act under review and may carry out investigations into the practices and procedures adopted by public bodies for the purpose of compliance with the provisions of the Act.

Section 37 sets out the powers of the Commissioner to examine documents and summon witnesses. Section 38 provides that the Commissioner shall foster and encourage the publication by public bodies of information of relevance and interest to the public. Section 39 enables the Commissioner to make available information on the practical application of the Act, including particular provisions. Section 40 provides for the preparation of annual and special reports by the Commissioner.

Appeals   Section 41 provides that failure by a public body to reply to a request within the timeframe specified will be deemed to be a refusal. Following from this the requester can proceed further to appeal. Section 42 provides for an appeal to the High Court on a point of law against a decision of the Information Commissioner, or in relation to a matter the subject of a Ministerial Certificate. Precautions against the disclosure of exempt information and stay on certain decisions which may be subject to appeal are set out in sections 43 and 44.

Fees   Section 47 provides that fees may be charged in respect of the location and copying of records, based on a standard hourly rate, to be prescribed by the Minister of Finance. No charges will apply in relation to the location of records in respect of personal information, save where a large number of records are involved. No charges will apply: where the cost of collecting and accounting for the fee would exceed the amount of the fee; where the information would be of particular assistance to the understanding of an issue of national importance; or, in the case of personal information, where such charges would not be reasonable having regard to the means of the requester. A deposit may be charged where the fee involved is likely to exceed £40.

Official secrets legislation   Section 48 provides that a person is deemed to be duly authorised to release official information under the Official Secrets Act 1963 where they do so on the basis of being so authorised under the 1997 Act, or 'reasonably believes that he or she is... authorised by this Act to communicate official information to another person.' The release of information in accordance with the 1997 Act also provides a full defence against prosecution under the 1963 Act. The question as to whether the 1963 Act should be repealed is to be considered by a Committee of the Oireachtas.

GOVERNMENT DEPARTMENTS

A number of Orders were made in 1997 under the Ministers and Secretaries (Amendment) Act 1939 giving effect to changes in the names and titles of Government Departments and Ministers, arising from the change of government in 1997.

Arts, Heritage, Gaeltacht and the Islands   The Arts, Culture and the Gaeltacht (Alteration of Name of Department and Title of Minister) Order 1997 (S.I. No. 306 of 1997) changed the name of the Department of Arts, Culture and the Gaeltacht to the Department of Arts, Heritage, Gaeltacht and the Islands.

Agriculture and Food   The Agriculture, Food and Forestry (Alteration of Name of Department and Title of Minister) Order 1997 (S.I. No. 302 of 1997) changed the name of the Department of Agriculture, Food and Forestry to the Department of Agriculture and Food.

Enterprise, Trade and Employment   The Enterprise and Employment (Alteration of Name of Department and Title of Minister) Order 1997 (S.I. No. 305 of 1997) changed the name of the Department of Enterprise and Employment to the Department of Enterprise, Trade and Employment.

Environment and Local Government   The Environment (Alteration of Name of Department and Title of Minister) Order 1997 (S.I. No. 322 of 1997) changed the name of the Department of the Environment to the Department of the Environment and Local Government.

Health and the Child   The Health (Alteration of Name of Department and Title of Minister) Order 1997 (S.I. No. 309 of 1997) changed the name of the Department of Health to the Department of Health and the Child.

Justice, equality and law reform   The Justice (Alteration of Name of Department and Title of Minister) Order 1997 (S.I. No. 298 of 1997) changed the name of the Department of Justice to the Department of Justice, Equality and Law Reform. The Department also subsumed the functions of the Department of Equality and Law Reform, which had operated between 1993 and 1997.

Marine and natural resources   The Marine (Alteration of Name of Department and Title of Minister) Order 1997 (S.I. No. 301 of 1997) changed the name of the Department of Marine to the Department of Marine and Natural Resources.

Public Enterprise   The Transport, Energy and Communications (Alteration of Name of Department and Title of Minister) Order 1997 (S.I. No. 299 of 1997) changed the name of the Department of Transport, Energy and Communications to the Department of Public Enterprise.

Social, Community and Family Affairs   The Social Welfare (Alteration of Name of Department and Title of Minister) Order 1997 (S.I. No. 307 of 1997) changed the name of the Department of Social Welfare to the Department of Social, Community and Family Affairs.

Tourism, Sport and Recreation   The Tourism and Trade (Alteration of Name of Department and Title of Minister) Order 1997 (S.I. No. 304 of 1997) changed the name of the Department of Tourism and Trade to the Department of Tourism, Sport and Recreation.

NATIONAL ARCHIVES

Exempted records   The National Archives Act 1986 (Prescription of Classes of Records) Order 1997 (S.I. No. 281 of 1997), made under the National Archives Act 1986, deals with the classes of records in respect of which certificates may be issued under section 8 of the 1986 Act, that is, classes of records which are not to be deposited with the National Archives notwithstanding that they are 30 years old. The 1997 Order revoked and replaced the National Archives Act 1986 (Prescription of Classes of Records) Order 1991. The records exempt from production include, for example, pension files in all Departments of State, certain consular files of the Department of Foreign Affairs, records of the Special Criminal Court established in 1939 and High Court office files in matrimonial causes and revenue cases. The 1997 Order provides that records of the Secretary of the Department of the Taoiseach, which were exempt from disclosure under the 1991 Order, are now no longer exempted from production. The 1997 Order came into effect on June 26, 1997 on is signature by An Taoiseach.

SOVEREIGN IMMUNITY

Extradition   In *Schmidt v. Home Secretary*, Supreme Court, April 24, 1997 the Supreme Court upheld the High Court decision in the instant case (1994 Review, 107) that the defendants were entitled to rely on sovereign immunity and to have the service of the plaintiff's proceedings issued against them set aside pursuant to Order 12, rule 26 of the Rules of the Superior Courts 1986. The plaintiff had instituted proceedings claiming damages against the defendants for an alleged breach of his constitutional rights. He had contended that the defendants had conspired against him in order to procure his arrest in the United Kingdom and so facilitate his extradition to the Federal Republic of Germany, where he was wanted in connection with drugs charges. The plaintiff had been contacted in Ireland by a member of the British police force actively engaged in seeking his extradition to Germany and a ruse had been used in order to entice him to come to the United Kingdom. The police officer stated that there had been certain fraudulent dealings with the plaintiff's cheque card and that he was to come to the United Kingdom in order to clear his name; there was in fact no truth in these allegations. The plaintiff had travelled to London where he was arrested and extradited to Germany. He had sought an order of *habeas corpus* prior to his extradition, but that was refused by the House of Lords. The plaintiff had been convicted in Germany, and sentenced to five years imprisonment. The plaintiff then issued the instant proceedings claiming damages against the defendants on foot of their alleged conspiracy to entice him to the United Kingdom in order to facilitate his arrest and extradition to Germany. The defendants claimed sovereign immunity from suit.

As already indicated the plea of sovereign immunity was upheld in the High Court and, on appeal, affirmed by the Supreme Court. The Court held that the actions of the defendants were not civil or commercial activities, and thus did not fall within the areas of activity now regarded as falling outside the ambit of sovereign immunity as discussed in *Government of Canada v. Employment Appeals Tribunal* [1992] 2 I.R. 484; [1992] I.L.R.M. 325 (1991 Review, 90-2). The Supreme Court held that, in acting as he did the police officer who enticed the plaintiff to the United Kingdom had not been engaged on a frolic of his own but was performing the duties and functions of his office as a member of the police squad seeking the plaintiff's extradition. As indicated, the Court thus concluded that Geoghegan J. had been correct in his decision that the defendants were entitled to rely on sovereign immunity and to have the service of the proceedings issued against them set aside. The decision is further discussed in the Conflicts of Law chapter, 159, below.

TRIBUNALS OF INQUIRY

Section 2 of the Tribunals of Inquiry (Evidence) (Amendment) Act 1997 amended section 1 of the Tribunals of Inquiry (Evidence) Act 1921 to provide that a person who produces or sends a document to a tribunal pursuant to an order of that tribunal shall be entitled to the same immunities and privileges as if he or she were a witness before the High Court.

Section 3 amended section 6 of the Tribunals of Inquiry (Evidence) (Amendment) Act 1979 to provide that where a tribunal is of the opinion that, having regard to the findings of the tribunal and all other relevant matters (including the terms of the resolution passed by each House of the Oireachtas relating to the establishment of the tribunal), there are sufficient reasons rendering it equitable to do so, the tribunal, or the chairman, as the case may be, may of either of the tribunal's or the chairman's own motion or on application by any person appearing before the tribunal, order that the whole or part of the costs:

(a) of any person appearing before the tribunal by counsel or solicitor, as taxed by a Taxing Master of the High Court, shall be paid to the person by any other person named in the order

(b) incurred by the tribunal, as taxed as aforesaid, shall be paid to the Minister for Finance by any other person named in the order may order that costs incurred by the tribunal be paid by any person named in the order and that a tribunal may, of its own motion, order the costs of any person appearing before the tribunal to be paid by any person named in the order. The cost provisions only apply in respect of any costs incurred by any tribunal after the coming into force of the 1997 Act.

This provision was included after it was realised during the course of one of the Tribunals appointed during 1997: see Hogan and Morgan, *Administrative Law in Ireland*, 3rd ed. (Round Hall Sweet & Maxwell, 1998), p. 304, n.283. Section 4 provides that where a person fails or refuses to comply with or disobeys an order of a tribunal, the High Court may, on application to it in a summary manner in that behalf by the tribunal, order the person to comply with the order and make such other order as it considers necessary and just to enable the order to have full effect.

The 1997 Act came into effect on December 18, 1997, on its signature by the President.

JUDICIAL REVIEW

Availability for errors within jurisdiction   In *Killeen v. Director of Public Prosecutions* [1998] 1 I.L.R.M. 1 (SC) (discussed in the Criminal Law chapter, 320, below) and *Farrell v. Attorney General* [1998] 1 I.L.R.M. 364 (HC & SC) (discussed in the Coroners chapter, 259, below), the Supreme Court reviewed the case law on errors going to jurisdiction, including the judgment of Henchy J. in *The State (Holland) v. Kennedy* [1977] I.R. 193, which appeared to have followed the views expressed by the Privy Council in *Anisminic Ltd. v. Foreign Compensation Commission* [1969] 2 A.C. 147. Thus, the Court confirmed the modern view of jurisdiction that it did not necessarily follow that a court which started a hearing within jurisdiction will be treated as continuing to act within jurisdiction. A similar view had been expressed by Costello J. in *Ryan v. Compensation Tribunal* [1997] 1 I.L.R.M. 194 (HC), discussed in the 1996 Review, 5-7. The judgment of Costello J. in *Ryan* was not referred to by the Supreme Court in either judgment.

Locus standi   In *Shannon v. McGuinness*, High Court, March 20, 1997, Kelly J. held that the applicants, witnesses in criminal proceedings dismissed in the District Court on the application of the Director of Public Prosecutions, lacked the *locus standi* to challenge that dismissal on judicial review. The background to the application was that the applicants were sisters who were due to be called as witnesses for the prosecution in a case alleging assault against their brother. The case had been brought at the suit of the Director of Public Prosecutions. Simultaneously, their brother had, as common informer, initiated a private prosecution against the applicants alleging assault by them on him. Both criminal proceedings came before the respondent judge of the District Court on the same date. The Director's representative informed the respondent that, on the Director's instructions the charges against the brother were being withdrawn. No reasons were advanced for the Director's decision. The solicitor for the sisters, the applicants, unsuccessfully sought an adjournment of the proceedings, but the respondent indicated that he had no alternative but to dismiss the proceedings. The solicitor for the brother then informed the respondent that, in view of the withdrawal of the prosecutions against him, he did not want to proceed with the common informer proceedings. The respondent dismissed all four summonses.

As already indicated, Kelly J. dismissed the sisters' application for judicial review. He pointed out that the orders which the applicants had sought to challenge were made in criminal proceedings commenced by the Director exercising his statutory powers under the Prosecution of Offences Act 1974. The sole function of the sisters in those proceedings was to attend and give evidence when and if required, and they were not party or privy to the proceedings in any other way. Referring to the leading decision in *Cahill v. Sutton* [1980] I.R. 269, Kelly J. noted that a test for *locus standi* was whether the applicants' interests had been 'adversely affected', or stood 'in real or imminent danger of being adversely affected', by the operation of the orders made in the District Court. In the instant case, although the prosecution brought to an end by the Director displeased the applicants, they could not complain of any legal right of theirs as having been affected adversely.

Kelly J. rejected the argument that, since no evidence had been called, the District Court hearing did not constitute a hearing. He referred to rule 66 of the District Court Rules 1948, which provides that a judge is entitled to dismiss the complaint on the merits or without prejudice to it being made again. The orders in the instant case did not mis-state the position by reciting that 'a complaint was heard', as it reflected the reality that the Director had indicated that he did not wish to continue the prosecution against the brother. Thus, Kelly J. concluded that an order striking out and entitling the Director to proceed with a new charge for the same offence would not reflect reality. However, Kelly J. held that the applicants had not *locus standi* to make such an argument and, in any event he concluded that this was not an appropriate case in which to grant declaratory relief as to do so would neither be just nor convenient, within the meaning of the Supreme Court's decision in *H. v. Director of Public Prosecutions* [1994] 2 I.R. 589; [1994] 2 I.L.R.M. 285 (1994 Review, 208-10).

Public v. private   In *Healy v. Fingal County Council*, High Court, January 17, 1997, Barr J. held that a decision by the respondent Council was not amenable to judicial review as it involved a transaction between a public body and an individual which was private in nature and was unrelated to the public interest or to the exercise of a public function. The applicant was an elected councillor of the Council and had been involved in judicial review proceedings against the Council's predecessor in title in 1992. The application had been dismissed and costs were awarded against the applicants; these were taxed at £13,767 but the applicant had made no attempt to discharge the sum. Ultimately, the Council informed the applicant by letter that an order had been made that payment of allowances and expenses would be withheld from him until the costs due to the Council had been paid and a total of £7,000 in expenses otherwise payable to the applicant had been deducted on foot of this. As indicated Barr J. dismissed the applicant's claim for judicial review. In holding that the Council's decision was not amenable to judicial review, Barr J. applied the test adopted by the Supreme Court in *Beirne v. Garda Commissioner* [1993] I.L.R.M. 1 (1992 Review, 382) that where a transaction between a public body and an individual was private in nature and was unrelated to the public interest, or to the exercise or non-exercise, of a public function, then the only remedy which might be available to an aggrieved body was in private law. Citing the decisions in *Murphy v. Turf Club* [1989] I.R. 171 (1989 Review, 14) and *Browne v. Dundalk UDC* [1993] 2 I.R. 512; [1993] I.L.R.M. 328 (1992 Review, 15), Barr J. noted that there was no public dimension involved in the set off made by the Council against the expenses due by it to the applicant and thus the issue between the parties was not a matter which introduced the requisite public element necessary to justify relief by way of judicial review. Barr J. also commented that no acceptable explanation had been put forward to explain or justify the substantial delay on the applicant's part in seeking relief, and even if the facts had raised an issue which was justiciable on judicial review, he would not have been disposed to extend the time for bring an application under Order 84 of the Rules of the Superior Courts 1986.

By contrast, in *Walsh v. Irish Red Cross Society*, Supreme Court, March 7, 1997, the Supreme Court held that the operation of the Rules of the respondent Society were amenable to judicial review. The Society had been established in 1939 by the Irish Red Cross Society Order 1939, a statutory Order. Article 5 of the 1939 Order provided that 'all Irish citizens shall be eligible for membership'. Article 15 empowered the central council, the governing body of the Society, to make rules, *inter alia*, for the admission of persons to membership. Rule 43 of the rules made by the central council provided that 'a member is an Irish citizen who expresses a wish to become a member of the society and who has paid the appropriate fee'. The applicant had been a member of the Society for many years and a member of the central council for 14 years. A newspaper article, critical of the society, was published in May 1993, and part of the information on which the article was based originated with the applicant. It was claimed by the executive committee of the central council, but denied by the applicant, that the applicant had given an interview to the journalist contrary to an express direction from the executive committee. The applicant was removed from membership of the society by the executive committee's exercise of a power derived from an amendment to rule 43, adopted by the central council in May 1993, after the article had appeared. The relevant part of the amended rule 43 provided that 'the executive committee of central council may, provided due cause is shown, decline to admit any person to membership, or remove any person from membership.' The decision to remove the applicant from membership was taken at a meeting of the executive committee in October 1993, and the reasons given were that the applicant had granted the interview in circumstances where he was specifically requested not to do so, together with his refusal to reveal a source regarding a damaging allegation against the Society.

In the High Court, Geoghegan J. held that the applicant had not been validly removed as a member of the Society and he granted an order of *certiorari* quashing the relevant decision of the executive committee and the confirmation of that decision by the central council. The Court also held that the amendment of rule 43 by the central council did not have retrospective effect and that the society had no power to expel the applicant for matters which arose prior to the amendment of the rule. This decision was upheld by the Supreme Court.

The Court first examined the contention that the decisions of the executive committee and central council were not amenable to judicial review and referred to its decision in *Beirne v. Garda Commissioner* [1993] I.L.R.M. 1 (1992 Review, 382-3) and that of Barr J. in *Murphy v. Turf Club* [1989] I.R. 172 (1989 Review, 14). The Court concluded that an examination of the manner in which the society was established by statutory order, its structure and its operating rules made it clear that membership was not governed by private law but was in the public domain. The Court noted that membership of the Society was not consensual but was a right created by Article 5 of the 1939 order and was open to every citizen who paid the relevant fee. Thus, there was no question of any applicant making an offer which became a contract once the society accepted the application for membership, since there was no right of refusal. Turning to the amended rule 43, the Court stated that the amended rule could not be interpreted as permitting removal for conduct which occurred before the rule was made and thus affirmed the granting of relief in the High Court. Alternatively, the Court considered that the expulsion was also vulnerable on the ground that the Society had taken into account irrelevant factors in its decision, namely, whether the applicant had given an interview to the media.

Finally, we note briefly that, in *Rizk v. Royal College Of Physicians Of Ireland*, High Court, August 27, 1997, Laffoy J. followed the decision of Keane J. in *Rajah v. Royal College of Surgeons* [1994] 1 I.R. 384; [1994]1 I.L.R.M. 233 (1993 Review, 17) in concluding that there was no public law aspect to the applicant's case in which he had sought an explanation as to why he had failed his medical examinations in the respondent college. In the instant case, Laffoy J. declined to grant leave to seek judicial review.

Reasons for decision   In *McCormack v. Garda Síochána Complaints Board* [1997] 2 I.L.R.M. 321 (HC), Costello P. declined to hold that there was a general duty on administrative bodies to give reasons for their decisions, a conclusion in line with recent case law which has taken a case-by-case approach to this matter. The applicant in this case had been convicted of three offences in the Circuit Criminal Court and sentenced to a term of imprisonment. He claimed that the principal evidence against him were three statements which he had made to a named Garda (a notice party in the proceedings). He had lodged an appeal against conviction, averring, *inter alia*, that these statements had been obtained by duress, threat and inducements by the named Garda. The applicant alleged that the Garda had subsequently visited him in prison, under an assumed name, and had advised him to withdraw his appeal against conviction. The applicant later wrote a formal letter of complaint to the relevant Garda Superintendent. He was forwarded an official form of complaint in accordance with the terms of the Garda Síochána (Complaints) Act 1986 which he completed and returned to the Superintendent. As required by the 1986 Act, the complaint was forwarded to the chief executive of the Complaints Board, who is then required to consider whether the complaint is admissible and if he so decides, is required to notify the complainant and the Garda Commissioner. In the instant case, the applicant was informed by letter by the chief executive of the Complaints Board that the complaint was admissible and that a request had been made for the appointment by the Garda Commissioner of an investigating officer. The applicant was later informed by letter that the result of the investigation was that the chief executive of the Complaints Board was of the opinion that neither an offence nor a breach of discipline had been disclosed. The applicant sought the reasons for this decision, but the Board replied that it was not its policy to give reasons on which its decisions were based, that its decisions were recorded in each case but not the reasoning behind them.

It was argued on the applicant's behalf that, once the Board's chief executive found that the allegation was admissible, the Board should have concluded that the conduct disclosed an offence or breach of discipline. Costello P. disagreed with this analysis. He held that the finding of admissibility by the chief executive merely indicated that, if the allegation of misconduct was true, the acts complained of would constitute an offence or breach of discipline. It was not a finding that an offence or breach of discipline had actually occurred. He held that the inference to be drawn form the opinion arrived at by the Board was that the evidence obtained in the investigation contradicted that of the applicant. There was certainly no inference, he concluded, that its opinion must have been an irrational one in the sense that the Board had acted plainly and unambiguously in the face of reason and common sense within the meaning of the decision in *The State (Keegan) v. Stardust Victims Compensation Tribunal* [1986] I.R. 642. He held that it was clear that the Board had arrived at an opinion that neither an offence nor a breach of discipline had been disclosed and having done so it made a decision to take no further action in the matter. There was no basis on which the Court could intervene merely where a different conclusion might have been reached by the Board on the available evidence. The applicant's case, therefore, was interpreted as an argument that the Board had a duty to provide reasons for its opinion that no breach of discipline and no offence had been disclosed.

Costello P. accepted that, even if no duty to give reasons existed, a failure to give reasons could furnish a ground for challenging an administrative decision, citing the well-known decision in *Padfield v. Minister for Agriculture, Fisheries and Food* [1968] A.C. 997. Thus, the refusal to give reasons for a decision might justify the Court in inferring that no valid reasons for the decision existed and that therefore it was arbitrary and irrational, but he held that no such inference could be drawn on the facts of this case. He acknowledged that English case law (such as *R v. Gaming Board for Great Britain, ex p. Benaim* [1970] 2 Q.B. 417) was to the effect that the rules of natural justice did not require that reasons should be given for administrative decisions and that it was necessary for statute to require that tribunals do so. But Costello P. accepted that, in this jurisdiction, the concept of constitutional justice could be extended to require that reasons be given. In this respect, he held that, in considering such an extension of the common law, the court was required to consider first, the nature of the statutory function which the decision maker was carrying out, secondly, the statutory framework in which it was to be found and, thirdly, the possible detriment the claimant might suffer arising from the failure to state reasons.

He referred to previous cases where the courts had held that reasons for a decision were necessary, including *International Fishing Vessels Ltd v. Minister for the Marine* [1989] I.R. 149 (1988 Review, 18), P. & F *Sharpe Ltd v. Dublin City Manager* [1989] I.L.R.M. 149 (1988 Review, 296-301) and *O'Keeffe v. An Bord Pleanála* [1993] 2 I.R. 39; [1992] I.L.R.M. 237 (1991 Review, 16-8). In the instant case, he concluded that the statutory functions of the Complaints Board were different to those considered in these cases; in particular the Board was not carrying out a quasi-judicial function such as a tribunal awarding compensation was performing, nor was it exercising a statutory discretion to permit an economic activity to be pursued or a development of land to take place. Its function was, he held, to reach an opinion on questions of fact after assessing evidence and considering the recommendations of its chief executive. In addition, he also noted that the absence of reasons did not deprive the court of an ability to exercise its supervisory jurisdiction. He was satisfied that the investigating officer had investigated all aspects of the alleged wrongdoing and that there was thus no basis to grant judicial review within the principles laid down in the *Keegan* case.

Similarly, in *Maigueside Communications Ltd v. Independent Radio And Television Commission*, High Court, July 18, 1997, McGuinness J. held that the applicants were not entitled to relief. The applicants had applied to be considered by the respondent Commission, established under the Radio and Television Act 1988, for the award of a broadcasting licence in the Limerick area. The applicants were not on a short-list of four applicants compiled by the Commission and no reasons were furnished as to why hey had been unsuccessful. In refusing the applicants judicial review, McGuinness J. first stated that there was no evidence to support the contention that the applicants had a legitimate expectation to an oral hearing. She referred to the decision of Barr J. in *Egan v. Minister for Defence*, High Court, November 24, 1988 (1988 Review, 28-30) in this respect. McGuinness J. emphasised that the selection of sound broadcasting contractors was a matter for the judgment of the Commission provided that they adhered to the procedures set out in the Radio and Television Act 1988. Citing with express approval the decision of Costello P. in *McCormack v. Garda Síochána Complaints Board* [1997] 2 I.L.R.M. 321 (discussed above), McGuinness J. concluded that the giving of reasons for a decision made by an administrative body was not in all cases necessary. In the instant case, she held that the detriment suffered by the applicants did not arise from the Commission's failure to give the reasons for its decision but from the actual rejection of their applications. On this basis, she refused the relief sought.

Admiralty

ARREST POWER

Meaning of ship: maritime dredger   In *The 'Von Rocks'; Targe Towing Ltd v. Owners And All Persons Claiming An Interest In The Vessel 'Von Rocks'* [1997] 1 I.L.R.M. 542 (HC); [1998] 1 I.L.R.M. 481 (SC) Barr J. held that a maritime dredger known as a backhoe dredger was not a ship within the meaning of the Jurisdiction of Courts (Maritime Conventions) Act 1989, which had implemented in Irish law the Brussels Convention on the Arrest of Seagoing Ships 1952. The decision was reversed on appeal by the Supreme Court.

The plaintiffs had instituted these proceedings in the English High Court against the owners of the 'Von Rocks', a maritime dredger registered in the Swedish Registry of Ships. In November 1996, the Irish High Court made an order ex parte that the 'Von Rocks' be arrested. The defendants applied for an order directing its release on the ground that it was not a ship within the meaning of the 1952 Brussels Convention or the 1989 Act. Evidence was given that the dredger was used primarily to deepen waters in harbours, channels or estuaries. It comprised a platform and three hydraulic legs which may be lowered to hold it in position; it had no bow, stern, anchor, rudder, steering mechanism, wheelhouse or means of self-propulsion. Nor could it carry cargo, spoil or any personnel other than those engaged in dredging. Dredging was carried out by means of an excavator bolted to one end of the platform. The dredging spoil would be poured into an adjacent barge and when all the spoil within the radius of the dredger was removed, the hydraulic legs would be raised, the dredger towed forward and re-positioned. The dredger could be dismantled and transported by road or towed by sea. When under tow, the dredger was unmanned and played no active part in the operation.

Article 2 of the 1952 Brussels Convention provides, *inter alia*, that a ship flying the flag of one of the Contracting States may be arrested in the jurisdiction of any of the Contracting States in respect of any maritime claim. Section 13(2) of the 1989 Act provides that the term 'ship' includes every description of vessel used in navigation', and the term 'vessel' 'includes any ship or boat, or any other description of vessel used in navigation'. Against this background, Barr J. directed the release of the 'Von Rocks'. He opined that the courts should be cautious in extending the definition of 'ship' for the purposes of the 1952 Convention and the 1989 Act. He referred with approval in this context to *Steedman v. Scofield* [1992] 2 Lloyd's Rep. 163 and *Polpen Shipping Co. Ltd v. Commercial Union Assurance Co Ltd* [1943] 1 All E.R. 162. In the instant case, an object which was incapable of self-propulsion or of transporting persons or property or of taking any active part in being towed and whose primary purpose was to form a rigid platform for dredging could not be regarded as being 'used in navigation' and accordingly, was not a ship within the meaning of the 1952 Convention or the 1989 Act.

As we have already indicated, Barr J.'s decision was reversed on appeal by the Supreme Court, which we will discuss in the 1998 Review and this decision is discussed in detail in the Conflicts of Law chapter, 134, below.

Warrant   In *The MV 'Blue Ice'*, High Court, March 21, 1997, Barr J. declined to discharge a warrant for the arrest of a vessel where it was argued that the plaintiff did not have 'good and sufficient reason for having caused the issue and execution of the warrant of arrest' within the meaning of section 47 of the Admiralty Court (Ireland) Act 1867, because the plaintiff had established a fair, stateable case in support of his claim.

The plaintiff had obtained a warrant of arrest for the 'Blue Ice', owned by the defendant. The plaintiff claimed that it had concluded a contract with the defendant for the carriage of frozen meat from Ireland to Russia in the vessel. When the vessel had arrived in Ireland to take delivery of the cargo, the vessel's master had delivered a notice of readiness to the plaintiff confirming that the vessel was ready to load the cargo, but the plaintiff's marine surveyor had discovered that certain certificates relating to the vessel had expired and that the defendant had been unable to obtain temporary certification covering the voyage to Russia. The plaintiff claimed that it had been obliged to charter an alternative vessel at a substantially higher price than that agreed with the defendant. The defendant applied for the discharge of the arrest warrant and submitted that the plaintiff did not have 'good and sufficient reason' within the meaning of section 47 of the Admiralty Court (Ireland) Act 1867 for having caused the issue and execution of the warrant of arrest. The defendant claimed that the plaintiff had insisted that the defendant provide a warranty that there were no outstanding debts on the vessel and no existing or foreseeable disputes which might hinder the performance of the contract; that it had given and then lawfully withdrawn the warranties and that, as a result, no contract of carriage had been concluded between the parties.

Barr J. pointed out that it was not the function of the court, on an application to discharge an arrest warrant, to determine whether the parties had entered into a concluded contract of carriage. He referred to section 47 of the Admiralty Court (Ireland) Act 1867, which provides that the party at whose instance any property is arrested under a warrant of the High Court of admiralty shall be liable to be condemned in all costs and expenses occasioned thereby, and in damages for the detention of the property, unless he shows to the satisfaction of the court that he could not, without such arrest, have obtained bail or other security for the sum in which the cause is instituted, or that he had otherwise good and sufficient reason for having caused the issue and execution of the warrant of arrest. Against this background, Barr J. refused to discharge the warrant of arrest, being satisfied that the plaintiff had discharged its obligation to established a fair, stateable case in support of its claim.

COSTS

Non-disclosure of lodgment   In *The 'La Livia'*, Supreme Court, December 16, 1997, the Supreme Court upheld an order for costs in the following circumstances. The plaintiffs had discovered three wrecks off the Irish coast which formed part of the Spanish Armada. A lengthy trial ensued, both in the High Court and on appeal to the Supreme Court. On appeal, the Supreme Court ordered that the question of costs be remitted to the High Court for determination. The trial judge awarded the plaintiffs their costs for the High Court action against the defendants on a party and party basis. The defendants appealed unsuccessfully to the Supreme Court from that decision.

The Court noted that the issues raised in the High Court were of public importance and that the decisions thereon were of value to the State and the defendants and that the trial judge was entitled to have regard to this in the exercise of his discretion on the award of costs. The Court considered that in view of the defendants' refusal to disclose to the trial judge the amount of any lodgments made, in the particular circumstances of this case the trial judge was entitled to disregard the fact of such lodgment in the exercise of his discretion. While the Court accepted that it could not be suggested that the plaintiffs had been successful in their claim in the substantive action, this was not sufficient to deprive them of their costs or to render them liable to pay the defendants' costs. Finally, the Court accepted that this was an exceptional case and justice required that the plaintiffs should not be at any particular loss because of their efforts in discovering the Armada wrecks and that included the costs of proceedings in connection therewith, even when such proceedings were not successful as they were bona fide and reasonably brought.

DAMAGES

Repairs   In *The 'Striopach'; Mooney v. Irish Geotechnical Services Ltd*, High Court, February 24, 1997 Barr J. considered the general issue of the level of damages to be awarded after a maritime collision involving a yacht.

The plaintiff was the owner of the yacht in question, which had been damaged when struck by a barge owned by the defendant company. The hull of the yacht had been built and fully fitted out in an Irish boat yard in 1981. The plaintiff, an accountant in private practice, had purchased the yacht in 1991 for £21,750. At the time of the collision, the yacht was insured for damage up to a maximum sum of £22,500. The plaintiff ascertained that the cost of fitting out a new hull for the yacht would be £43,000 and that a second hand yacht would cost from ST£20,000 to ST£25,000. He decided against attempting to find a second hand yacht in the United Kingdom as he considered that it would be difficult to find one of comparable quality and that the search would involve the expense of several trips to the United Kingdom. The yacht was ultimately repaired in the boat yard in which it had originally been fitted out at a cost of just over £20,000. The plaintiff did not claim this sum from his insurers but instead borrowed the sum of £20,000. Nor had he obtained estimates for the repairs from any other boat yard. A marine surveyor gave evidence on behalf of the plaintiff that the cost of the repairs was fair and reasonable and estimated that the pre-accident value of the yacht was between £23,000 and £25,000. The plaintiff claimed the cost of the repairs, the sum of £4,350 for net loss of professional income, £1,250 for depreciation, a sum in respect of interest on the money borrowed to pay for the repairs, a sum for inconvenience, together with miscellaneous expenses.

Barr J. awarded the plaintiff damages under most of these headings, but not for interest on the money borrowed to pay for the repairs. On the general issue of the level of damages, Barr J. referred with approval to *Darbishire v. Warren* [1963] 1 W.L.R. 1067 in holding that damage caused to a vessel is to be quantified as the cost of repairing the vessel, unless the cost of repairs greatly exceeds the value of the vessel. He held that the plaintiff had acted reasonably both in having the yacht repaired rather than attempting to find a second hand yacht in the United Kingdom and also in entrusting the repairs to the boat yard which had originally fitted out the yacht rather than seeking estimates from other boat yards and he awarded the plaintiff the cost of repairs. However, Barr J. held that the plaintiff ought to have arranged for his own insurers to pay the cost of repairs rather than borrowing a sum for this purpose and thus the claim for interest on the sum borrowed was not allowed. Although the yacht had been satisfactorily repaired, Barr J. accepted that prospective purchasers were likely to enquire if she had suffered any substantial accidental damage and thus the plaintiff was awarded a sum in respect of the depreciation in value of the yacht as a result of the damage Finally, as the plaintiff was in private practice, Barr J. accepted that it was likely that he had suffered inconvenience and some net loss of earnings as a result of dealing with the consequences of the accident. He awarded £2,500 under these latter heads.

Agriculture

ABATTOIRS

Definition of animal The Abattoirs Act 1988 (Amendment) Order 1997 (S.I. No. 422 of 1997), made under the Abattoirs Act 1988 (1988 Review, 37-8) amended the definition of animal under the 1988 Act, with effect from October 27, 1997. The Abattoirs Act 1988 (Abattoirs) (Amendment) Regulations 1997 (S.I. No. 424 of 1997) also made under the 1988 Act, amended the Abattoirs Act 1988 (Abattoirs) Regulations 1989) (1989 Review, 17) by providing for the construction of abattoirs for the slaughter of ratite birds with effect from October 27, 1997.

Health mark The Abattoirs (Health Mark) (Amendment) Regulations 1997 (S.I. No. 423 of 1997) amended the form of the health mark to be used to certify that certain meat is fit for human consumption under the Abattoirs (Health Mark) Regulations 1992 (1992 Review, 13), with effect from October 27, 1997.

Veterinary examination The Abattoirs Act 1988 (Veterinary Examination) (Amendment) Regulations 1997 (S.I. No. 425 of 1997) amended the Abattoirs Act 1988 (Veterinary Examination) Regulations 1992 (1992 Review, 13) to provide for post-mortem veterinary examinations of ratite birds to establish if their meat is fit for human consumption with effect from October 27, 1997.

ANIMAL DISEASES

Bovine TB and brucellosis The Livestock Marts (Date of Test and Name and Address of Owner) Regulations 1997 (S.I. No. 33 of 1997), made under the Livestock Marts Act 1967, requires that the name and address and date of bovine TB and brucellosis tests be supplied for animals sold at marts, with effect from February 3, 1997.

BSE The Diseases of Animals (Bovine Spongiform Encephalopathy) (Specified Risk Material) Order 1997 (S.I. No. 80 of 1997), made under the Diseases of Animals Act 1966, imposed controls on certain bovine, caprine and ovine material with effect from February 21, 1997. The Diseases of Animals

(Bovine Spongiform Encephalopathy) (Amendment) Order 1997 (S.I. No. 97 of 1997), made under the Diseases of Animals Act 1966, amended the Diseases of Animals (Bovine Spongiform Encephalopathy) Order 1989 (1989 Review, 17) and prohibited the use of poultry offal in animal feedingstuffs with effect from February 18, 1997.

ANIMAL WELFARE

Transport The Diseases of Animals (Protection of Animals During Transport) (Amendment) Order 1997 (S.I. No. 326 of 1997), made under the Diseases of Animals Act 1966, amended the Diseases of Animals (Protection of Animals During Transport) Order 1995 (1995 Review, 10) and gave effect to Directive 95/29/EC. They prescribe rules for watering and feeding intervals, journey times and rest periods for animals during transportation and came into effect on July 28, 1997.

COMMON AGRICULTURAL POLICY

Damages In *Emerald Meats Ltd v. Minister for Agriculture (No. 2)* [1997] 1 I.R. 1; [1997] 2 I.L.R.M. 275 (SC), the Supreme Court upheld an award of damages made by Costello J. in the High Court in 1991 (1991 Review, 199-200). Briefly, the plaintiff company had purchased the importation quotas for non-EC meat from certain meat processors and the Department of Agriculture had been aware of this, designating the plaintiff and other similar companies as 'meat brokers.' Under Regulation (EEC) No. 4024/89, a procedure was introduced by which such quotas could only be allocated to meat importers. The Department of Agriculture declined to designate the plaintiff as a meat importer for this purpose. The plaintiff sought declaratory relief that it was entitled to be considered as a meat importer for the purposes of the 1989 Regulation.

In the High Court, Costello J. had found that the plaintiff was entitled to an import quota under the terms of Regulation (EEC) No. 4024/89. He considered that the central issue in the case was whether the plaintiff had acted as the agent of the meat processors in importing the GATT meat in question. He found that the plaintiff had, in respect of all the consignments, completed the import formalities and put the meat into circulation. In addition, Costello J. held that the description of the plaintiff in the licences as acting 'for and on behalf of' the meat processors was merely a formula and did not have the effect of making the plaintiff an agent. Holding that there was a duty on the Minister to receive and examine applications for import licences and to furnish to the Commission the names of those applicants who in their opinion were entitled to a share in the quota, he also found that the plaintiff was entitled to damages arising from the loss it had suffered as a result of the Minister's failure to carry out that duty.

The defendant's appeal was dismissed by the Supreme Court. Delivering the leading judgment, Blayney J. stated that he was satisfied that on the primary findings of fact made in the High Court, Costello J. had been entitled to draw the inference that there had been no agency in the plaintiff's relationship with the meat processors. It was clear from the time the meat processor sold his quota to the plaintiff that the latter took over completely in that the meat was imported and subsequently disposed of as part of the plaintiff's business and with no connection whatsoever with the meat processor from whom the quota had been purchased

Blayney J. accepted that a 1993 Regulation passed by the Commission in the wake of the High Court judgment in the instant case did not oust the Supreme Court's jurisdiction but it had a definite relevance. He pointed out that it would have been open to the defendant to challenge this regulation for a two-month period immediately after it had been passed and the fact this was not done made it very difficult for the defendant to argue a case which was in direct conflict with what the regulation laid down.

The Supreme Court went on to reject the submission that the plaintiff had not been the importer of GATT meat during 1987 and 1988. Once it was accepted that the plaintiff had been the importer of the meat, it followed that it had been entitled to have its application forwarded by the Minister to the Commission. Blayney J. did not consider that it was necessary to decide whether the Minister had been bound to accept the evidence provided by the customs document for release for free circulation, when it was clear that the Minister had made the wrong decision without giving the plaintiff any opportunity to make its case. In failing to forward the plaintiff's application as importer, the Court agreed that the Minister had been in breach of its duty to the plaintiff arising under the relevant EC Regulation.

The Minister had argued that it was a well established principle of Community law that damages were not recoverable as a general rule against the Community unless there had been a breach of a superior rule of law (citing *Mulder v. Council and Commission* [1992] E.C.R. I-3061) and that on this basis the trial judge had erred in awarding damages to the plaintiff. But Blayney J. pointed out that the plaintiff's action was not against the Community but against a Member State and so the Minister's submissions with regard to damages were not applicable. Blayney J. went on to state that the right to recover damages from a Member State for the breach of an obligation imposed on it by Community law was clearly recognised by decisions such as *Francovich v. Italian Republic* [1991] ECR I-5357, which had been applied by the High Court in *Tate v. Minister for Social Welfare* [1995] 1 I.R. 418; [1995] 1 I.L.R.M.

507 (1995 Review, 458-9). Blayney J. emphasised that the national courts, who are required to apply Community law, had to ensure that those rules had full effect and the full effectiveness of Community rules would be impaired if individuals were unable to obtain compensation when their rights had been infringed by a Member State. It followed that the plaintiff was entitled to claim compensation from the defendants arising from the Minister's failure to carry out the obligation imposed on it by the EC Regulation. See further the discussion in the Torts chapter, 785, below.

On the level of damages, the Supreme Court had been unable to find any authority to support Costello J's finding that general damages should not be awarded against the Minister for a breach of statutory duty. Blayney J. considered that it was difficult to see how the Minister could be liable for special damages and not for general damages as both were equally caused by the wrongful act. He commented that neither the State nor any other public authority enjoyed any special position in the law of torts and in the circumstances the plaintiff was entitled to general and special damages.

Milk quota   In *Duff v. Minister for Agriculture and Food (No. 2)*, High Court, July 10, 1992; Supreme Court, March 4, 1997, the Supreme Court (reversing the High Court) held that the plaintiffs were entitled to damages in the following circumstances.

Regulation (EC) 857/84 concerning the milk super levy provided that there should be a national milk quota and within that quota there should be a national reserve to deal with three special categories one of which being small farmers who following inducements by the State had adopted milk production plans. Article 5 of the 1984 Regulation stated that the special categories had to be allocated out of a special reserve and not otherwise. The Minister for Agriculture and Food did not constitute a national reserve. The plaintiffs, a small group of development farmers, sought a declaration that they were entitled to be allocated an additional reference quantity under the milk super levy and to damages for failure to establish such additional reference quantity. The plaintiffs' case was dismissed in the High Court (1993 Review, 12-15) and they appealed to the Supreme Court. The Court determined that the issue raised questions concerning the validity and interpretation of Regulation (EC) 857/84 and referred certain questions to the Court of Justice under Article 177 of the EC Treaty. The Court of Justice held that Article 3(1) of Regulation 857/84 did not impose on a member state an obligation to grant a special reference quantity to producers; recognised that Member States had a discretion to do so; and when deciding whether or not to allocate specific reference quantities in pursuance of such discretion Member States were obliged to take into consideration the situation of producers with a development plan.

On remittal of the case to the Supreme Court, the Court noted that in the Advocate-General's opinion, he had not excluded the possibility that the plaintiffs may have a remedy in national law, he did not exclude the possibility that principles of Community law, such as legitimate expectation, may be invoked by the plaintiffs so long as there is no discrimination against community funds (as compared to national funds) and so long as the interest of the community are kept in sight. The Court also emphasised that, following the decision of the European Court of Justice, it must be accepted that the Community legislator has power to change European law and the plaintiffs, whose activities are subject to European law, can have no legitimate expectation that the law will not be changed. It must also be accepted that the discretion granted to the Minister under Article 3 (1) of Regulation (EC) 857/84 is a real discretion and that the plaintiffs cannot invoke any principle of European law to require that the discretion be exercised in any particular manner.

Applying these principles, the Court accepted that the Minister had made a mistake of law in that he did not constitute a national reserve at all, he gave away the whole quota to the dairies and the co-operatives, and he was thus not in a position to satisfy his legal obligations to those to whom he had a legal obligation, namely the diseased herd farmers, nor was he in a position to exercise any discretion in relation to the other two categories. As a matter of national law, the Court held that the plaintiffs had a legitimate expectation that the Minister would honour his commitment to them. The Court held that, just as money paid under a mistake of law can be recovered if the responsibility for the mistake lies more on one party than the other and the one responsible for the mistake is in a more powerful position, the plaintiffs are entitled to a remedy at the hands of the Minister for the wrongs they have suffered. Since the plaintiffs had suffered loss and damage as a result of the Minister's mistake of law, it was just and proper in the circumstances that the Minister should pay compensation. The Court remitted the case to the High Court to assess damages.

FOODSTUFFS

Additives The European Communities (Additives in Feedingstuffs) (Amendment) Regulations 1997 (S.I. No. 127 of 1997) further amended the European Communities (Additives in Feedingstuffs) Regulations 1989 in order to give effect to Directives 96/66/EC and 97/6/EC. They further amended the list of additives which are prohibited in animal feedingstuffs with effect from March 31, 1997.

MILK SUPPLY

Elections The National Milk Agency (Election Day) Regulations 1997 (S.I. No. 184 of 1997), made under the Milk (Regulation of Supply) Act 1994 (1994 Review, 17) appointed June 27, 1997 as the election day in respect of the National Milk Agency. The National Milk Agency (Conduct of Elections) Regulations 1997 (S.I. No. 185 of 1997) specified the detailed requirements for the conduct of the election to the National Milk Agency.

PLANT HEALTH

Organisms harmful to plant or plant products The European Communities (Introduction of Organisms Harmful to Plants and Plant Products) (Prohibition) (Amendment) Regulations 1997 (S.I. No. 126 of 1997) further amended the European Communities (Introduction of Organisms Harmful to Plants and Plant Products) (Prohibition) Regulations 1980 to give effect to Directives 96/76/EC and 96/78/EC and Decision 96/301/EC, with effect from March 20, 1997. The European Communities (Introduction of Organisms Harmful to Plants and Plant Products) (Prohibition) (Amendment) (No. 2) Regulations 1997 (S.I. No. 289 of 1997) gave effect to Directive 97/14/EC, amending the importation restrictions on tubers with effect from July 3, 1997.

Plant protection products The European Communities (Authorization, Placing on the Market, Use and Control of Plant Protection Products) (Amendment) Regulations 1997 (S.I. No. 290 of 1997) further amended the European Communities (Authorization, Placing on the Market, Use and Control of Plant Protection Products) Regulations 1994 (1994 Review, 19) to give further effect to Directive 91/414/EEC. The 1994 Regulations, as amended, specify the testing requirements for residues in plant protection policies to be submitted with applications for authorisations for marketing and use of such products. They came into force on July 3, 1997.

RETIREMENT OF FARMERS

The European Communities (Retirement of Farmers) Regulations 1997 (S.I. No. 283 of 1997) further amended the European Communities (Retirement of Farmers) Regulations 1974 by increasing the amount payable under the Framers Retirement Annuity Scheme created by Directive 72/160/EEC. The annuity for a single person was increased from £2,448 to £2485 and for a married person from £3672 to £3727, with retrospective effect from May 1, 1997.

SEED LABELLING

Beet The European Communities (Beet Seed) (Amendment) Regulations 1997 (S.I. No. 55 of 1997) further amended the European Communities (Beet

Seed) Regulations 1981 to give effect to Directive 96/72/EC and to replace the abbreviation 'EEC' with 'EC' on the labelling and packaging of beet seeds, with effect from January 30, 1997.

Cereal The European Communities (Cereal Seed) (Amendment) Regulations 1997 (S.I. No. 243 of 1997) amended the European Communities (Cereal Seed) Regulations 1981, also to give effect to Directive 96/72/EC and to replace the abbreviation 'EEC' with 'EC' on cereal seed labels, with effect from July 1, 1997.

Fodder Similarly, the European Communities (Seed of Fodder Plants) (Amendment) Regulations 1997 (S.I. No. 53 of 1997) amended the European Communities (Seed of Fodder Plants) Regulations 1981, also to give effect to Directive 96/72/EC and to replace the abbreviation 'EEC' with 'EC' on fodder plant seed labels, with effect from January 30, 1997.

Oil and fibre plants The European Communities (Seed of Oil Plants and Fibre Plants) (Amendment) Regulations 1997 (S.I. No. 54 of 1997) amended the European Communities (Seed of Oil Plants and Fibre Plants) Regulations 1981, also to give effect to Directive 96/72/EC and to replace the abbreviation 'EEC' with 'EC' on oil plants and fibre plants seed labels, with effect from January 30, 1997.

Potato Similarly, the European Communities (Seed Potatoes) (Amendment) Regulations 1997 (S.I. No. 252 of 1997) amended the European Communities (Seed Potatoes) Regulations 1980, also to give effect to Directive 96/72/EC and to replace the abbreviation 'EEC' with 'EC' on seed potato labels, with effect from May 28, 1997.

Vegetable Finally, the European Communities (Vegetable Seeds) (Amendment) Regulations 1997 (S.I. No. 56 of 1997) amended the European Communities (Vegetable Seeds) Regulations 1981, also to give effect to Directive 96/72/EC and to replace the abbreviation 'EEC' with 'EC' on vegetable seed labels, with effect from January 30, 1997.

TRADE IN ANIMAL PRODUCTS

Cattle and pigs The European Communities (Trade in Bovine Animals and Swine) Regulations 1997 (S.I. No. 270 of 1997) gave effect to Directives 94/42/EC and 95/25/EC and regulate trade in cattle and swine within the European Community. They came into effect on July 1, 1997.

VETERINARY

Fees   The European Communities (Fees for Health Inspections and Controls of Fresh Meat) (Amendment) Regulations 1997 (S.I. No. 207 of 1997) amended the European Communities (Fees for Health Inspections and Controls of Fresh Meat) Regulations 1995 (1995 Review, 16) and gave effect to Directive 93/118/EEC. They provide for the recovery of real inspection costs incurred in relation to meat inspections, with effect from May 15, 1997.

Registration   The Veterinary Surgeons (Annual Fees) Order 1997 (S.I. No. 131 of 1997), made under the Veterinary Surgeons Act 1931, increased the fee for annual registration of veterinary surgeons to £130 with effect from April 1, 1997.

WILDLIFE

Protection of birds   The European Communities (Wildlife Act 1976) (Amendment) Regulations 1997 (S.I. No. 152 of 1997) amended the categories of dove and pigeon protected by the 1976 Act, with effect from April 26, 1997.

Special areas of conservation (SACs)   The European Communities (Natural Habitats) Regulations 1997 (S.I. No. 94 of 1997) gave effect to Directive 92/43/EEC. They enable the Minister for Arts, Culture and the Gaeltacht to designate areas of land as Special Areas of Conservation (SACs) in order to protect endangered species and the habitats of endangered species as part of an EC network to be known as NATURA 2000. The Regulations provide for a means of compensating landowners for the restrictions imposed by designating land as an SAC. Other relevant Ministers and local authorities must have regard to the Regulations in carrying out their statutory functions, in particular in the context of planning legislation. In this context, the 1997 Regulations amended a number of provisions of the Wildlife Act 1976 and sections 2 and 19 of the Local Government (Planning and Development) Act 1963. The Regulations came into effect on February 26, 1997. The Regulations proved controversial in 1998 when it was proposed that turf cutting on commonage wetland designated as SACs would be prohibited in 1998 and when a compensation package agreed between the Government and landowners was not approved by the European Commission. After some dispute, the Minister acceded to requests that turf cutting on the wetland in question be permitted during 1998 but that it would cease thereafter and after a revised compensation agreement was approved by the European Commission.

Wild birds: special protection areas   The European Communities (Conservation of Wild Birds) (Amendment) Regulations 1997 (S.I. No. 210 of 1997) further amended the European Communities (Conservation of Wild Birds) Regulations 1995 and classified an additional three sites as special protection areas with effect from June 1, 1997.

Aliens and Immigration

DETENTION

Garda station   The Aliens (Amendment) (No.5) Order 1997 (S.I. No. 362 of 1997), made under the Aliens Act 1935, designated certain Garda Stations as places of detention for aliens, with effect from August 30, 1997.

RIGHTS OF RESIDENCE

EU citizens   The European Communities (Right of Residence for Non-Economically Active Persons) Regulations 1997 (S.I. No. 57 of 1997) revoked and replaced the European Communities (Right of Residence for Non-Economically Active Persons) Regulations 1993 (1993 Review, 41) and gave effect to Directives 90/364/EEC, 90/365/EEC and 93/96/EEC. They grant a right of residence to and prescribe residence permits and documents for nationals of European Union Member States who are not economically active in the State. A number of restrictions to the right of residence continue to apply, such as where public health may be affected or where the person cannot establish a means of support. The Regulations came into effect on January 30, 1997. The 1997 Regulations do not apply to citizens of the United Kingdom, who remain covered by the common travel area between the State and the United Kingdom. In addition, the Aliens Order 1946 also continues to apply without prejudice to the 1997 Regulations.

REFUGEES

Commencement of Refugee Act 1996   The Refugee Act 1996 (Sections 1, 2, 5, 22, and 25) (Commencement) Order 1997 (S.I. No. 359 of 1997) brought sections 1, 2, 5, 22 and 25 of the Refugee Act 1996 (1996 Review, 31–8) into force on August 29, 1997.

Dublin Convention   The Dublin Convention (Implementation) Order 1997 (S.I. No. 360 of 1997), made under the Refugee Act 1996 (1996 Review, 31-8), gave effect to the Dublin Convention and provides a procedure for establishing whether applications for asylum should be dealt with in the State or in another Convention country. The Order came into effect on September 1, 1997.

'First safe country' In *Anisimova v. Minister for Justice*, High Court, February 18, 1997; [1998] 1 I.L.R.M. 523 (SC), Morris J. (as he then was) and the Supreme Court held that where an applicant for asylum had already passed through another State willing to consider the application under the United Nations Convention of the Status of Refugees 1951, the applicant's case need not be considered in this State.

The applicant was a Russian national from Moldova. She had come to Ireland via the United Kingdom as she was only able to obtain an entry visa for that country. On arrival in the United Kingdom she went straight to Holyhead in Wales, and from there came to Dublin, spending less than 24 hours in the United Kingdom. On arrival in Ireland she applied for asylum for herself and her daughter. The Department of Justice contacted the United Kingdom authorities who agreed to process the applicant's application should she be sent back there. The office of the United Nations High Commissioner for Refugees was also contacted and they also consented to the applicant being returned to the United Kingdom for her application to be processed there. The Minister decided that Ireland could not process her application as the United Kingdom had been her first country of safe haven, the United Kingdom was a signatory to the 1951 Convention and it was also willing to process her application.

As indicated, Morris J. and, on appeal, the Supreme Court, refused the applicant judicial review of the Minister's decision. In the High Court, Morris J. accepted that, in light of the decision in *Fakih v. Minister for Justice* [1993] 2 I.R. 406; [1993] I.L.R.M. 274 (1992 Review, 22-3), the State was obliged to comply with the 1951 UN Convention, even though it had not been ratified by the State. However, Morris J. did not accept the applicant's contention that the Minister had to examine all the circumstances of the case before exercising its jurisdiction to return an applicant to a host third country. Indeed, he pointed out that the signatories to the 1951 Convention did not surrender their discretionary power to grant or withhold asylum but instead agreed to abide by Article 33 which prohibited refoulement, that is an examination by this State of the application where a third State was available to do so. In the instant case there was a host third country, namely the United Kingdom, and in these circumstances the Minister was precluded from examining the application for asylum irrespective of the applicant's wishes. In those circumstances, the application for judicial review was refused.

In the Supreme Court, Murphy J., speaking for the Court, noted that, while the Minister had accepted the 1951 Convention, this was, however, subject to the qualification that there was an international understanding that a person seeking asylum was under an obligation to seek it in the 'first safe country' where he had an opportunity to do so. Murphy J. added that the correspondence indicated that the Minister had carried out an appropriate inquiry and afforded the applicant an adequate opportunity of being heard in relation to the decision affecting her rights. Indeed, it had been made patently clear by the Minister that no investigation was taking place on the substantive issue of her right to asylum, but that the investigation had centred on the duration of her stay in the United Kingdom. Since the results of this inquiry had been formally put to the applicant in the context of a possible deportation order being made against her and she had been invited to make whatever observations she thought fit and had availed of that opportunity, the Court concluded that the Minister had carried out a proper inquiry as to whether the United Kingdom was the 'first safe country' and thus the requirements of constitutional and natural justice had been complied with.

We note here that the terms of Article 33 of the 1951 Convention have now been effectively replaced, at least as far as European Union Member States are concerned, by the Dublin Convention: see above and the 1996 Review, 31-8.

UNITED KINGDOM

Procedure The Aliens (Amendment) (No. 3) Order 1997 (S.I. No. 277 of 1997), made under the Aliens Act 1935, provided that an immigration officer may examine aliens entering the State from the United Kingdom. The Order came into effect on June 29, 1997.

VISA REQUIREMENTS

Brunei The Aliens (Amendment) Order 1997 (S.I. No. 86 of 1997), made under the Aliens Act 1935, abolished entry visa requirements for nationals of Brunei wit effect from February 17, 1997.

Equador The Aliens (Amendment) (No. 4) Order 1997 (S.I. No. 361 of 1997) imposed entry visa requirements on citizens of Equador, with effect from August 30, 1997.

Hong Kong The Aliens (Amendment) (No. 2) Order 1997 (S.I. No. 280 of 1997) exempted holders of Hong Kong Special Administrative Region passports from the requirement of entry visas, with effect from July 1, 1997 the date on which Hong Kong reverted to the People's Republic of China.

Arts and Culture

FILM

Film board   The Irish Film Board (Amendment) Act 1997 increased the level of expenditure the Irish Film Board may incur in the promotion of the Irish film industry from £15m to £30m: the previous level had been set by the Irish Film Board (Amendment) Act 1993 (1993 Review, 73). The 1997 Act also provided that the appointment of officers and servant shall be subject to the consent of the Minister. The Act came into effect on December 18, 1997, on its signature by the President.

NATIONAL CULTURAL INSTITUTIONS ACT 1997

Introduction to 1997 Act   The National Cultural Institutions Act 1997 is a major piece of legislation which provided for the establishment of new statutory Boards to care for and manage the collections of heritage objects in the National Museum and library material in the National Library. The existing National Museum and National Library and their respective collections had been directly controlled by the Minister for Arts, Culture and the Gaeltacht and the 1997 Act provides for greater autonomy for these institutions. The Act also established a system of indemnity in respect of important cultural exhibitions imported from abroad and for valuable cultural items on long-term loan to the major collecting institutions of the State. It also provided for a register of significant cultural objects whose export from the State would constitute a serious loss to the heritage of Ireland. Measures to protect registered cultural objects include an option, in restricted circumstances, permitting compulsory acquisition of such objects where loss is threatened or safety is jeopardised. The Act extended previous statutory provisions for licensing, prior to export, of certain classes of cultural objects. Additional functions were conferred on the National Gallery of Ireland. The granting of intoxicating liquor on-licences to the Boards of the main collecting institutions, operating refreshment facilities, is also provided for. A new provision extends copyright deposit arrangements under the Copyright Act 1963 in relation to books to other classes of library material, such as videos and other electronically created material. The 1997 Act also involves the first legislative reference to the

Chief Herald of Ireland and provided for the establishment of a Committee on Genealogy and Heraldry.

Commencement The National Cultural Institutions Act 1997 (Commencement) Order 1997 (S.I. No. 222 of 1997) and the National Cultural Institutions Act 1997 (Commencement) (No. 2) Order 1997 (S.I. No. 328 of 1997) brought the Act into force on various dates between June 2, 1997 and January 1, 1998.

Establishment of National Museum and National Library Section 8 sets out the names by which the institutions will be known, namely, the National Museum of Ireland (in the Irish language, Bord Ard-Mhúsaem na hÉireann) and the National Library of Ireland (in the Irish language, Bord Leabharlann Náisiunta na hÉireann). Section 9 provides for the Minister to appoint a day to be the Museum establishment day, and a day to be the Library establishment day, while section 10 formally provides for the establishment of the Museum and Library Boards on the respective establishment days. Each Board is a body corporate with powers to sue and be sued, to acquire, hold and dispose of land (with the consent of the Minister), and any other property.

Powers of National Museum Board Section 11 sets out the functions and powers of the Board of the National Museum. These include caring for and managing the heritage collection for the benefit of the public, increasing and diffusing knowledge of human life in Ireland, of Ireland's natural history and of the relations of Ireland in these respects with other countries. Other powers include engaging in restoration work, organisation of exhibitions, promotion of research, development of contacts with other institutions, participation in international collaborative projects, acceptance of donations, engaging in fundraising activities and promotion of the Museum as an integral part of the national culture.

Powers of National Library Board Section 12 sets out the functions of the Board of the National Library. These include caring for and managing the material in the collection, and establishing a record of library material in relation to Ireland They also include promotion of research, lending of material from the collection, development of the Library as a national centre for research and information services, promotion of the Library as an integral part of the national culture, participation in international collaborative heritage projects, entry into agreements with other libraries and cultural bodies, acceptance of donations and engagement in fund-raising activities.

Genealogical Office and National Library Section 13 provides that the Genealogical Office is a branch of the National Library. The Board is required to ensure that the functions of researching, granting and confirming coats of arms shall be performed by a person designated by the Board, from time to time, using the appellation Chief Herald of Ireland. It also provides for the establishment of a Committee on Genealogy and Heraldry which, although generally answerable to the Board, may regulate its own procedures. As originally drafted, the legislation provided for the abolition of the Genealogical Office through the proposed revocation of the Allocation of Administration (Genealogical Office) Order 1943. The effect would have been to transfer any property or choses in action of the Genealogical Office to the Board. This proposal was abandoned and it was accepted that the Office might become completely autonomous in the future. However, section 13 of the 1997 Act provides that the Board is entitled to any copyright subsisting in coats of arms. On the role of the Genealogical Office and the Chief Herald and the status of coats of arms, see further Andrew Lyall's comprehensive annotation to the 1997 Act, *Irish Current Law Statutes Annotated.*

Bye-laws Section 14 enables both Boards to make bye-laws concerning the care and management of the Museum or Library, regulation of access, the protection of property in the Museum or Library, and the fixing of entry charges to the Museum or Library (subject to the consent of the Minister). It also provides for enforcement of bye-laws, including provision for display of the bye-laws, and a maximum fine of £500 for non-compliance. Moneys accruing to either Board arising from application of the bye-laws, or in the performance of functions, must be disposed of by a Board for the purposes of its functions.

Additional functions Section 15 provides that the Minister may confer additional functions on the Boards.

Collections to be held in authorised repositories Section 16 of the 1997 Act provides that the respective collections of the Museum and Library are, in general, to be held in repositories authorised and listed in the First Schedule to the Act, and that items from the collections may only be removed for specified reasons. It provides for designation by Order of other premises as authorised repositories, and for amendment or revocation of such orders. Finally, a person who unlawfully removes an object from an authorised repository, shall be guilty of an offence and the penalties are also are set out.

Lending by National Museum Section 17 sets out provisions governing the lending of objects in the National Museum's collection. It provides that the Board of the Museum, after consultation with the Heritage Council, shall draw up guidelines under which objects in the collection may be lent to institutions within the State and Northern Ireland. Adequate safety and management conditions must be ensured before items are lent. It is also provided that objects from the Museum may be lent for public exhibition outside of the State and Northern Ireland to various types of institutions, on the basis of reciprocity and that any moneys received shall be used by the Board to enlarge or conserve its collection.

Lending and disposal by National Library   Section 18 sets out provisions for the lending and disposal of material in the collection of the National Library. It permits loans for the purposes of research or exhibition taking into account certain criteria. It also sets out special circumstances in which certain classes of material may be disposed of, provided that the provision is not to be used in contravention of the terms of a donation or bequest and that any moneys accruing from loans or disposals shall be used by the Board to enlarge or conserve its collection.

Composition of Boards   Section 19 sets out the numbers and composition of persons to comprise each Board, the minimum and maximum numbers for the respective Boards, including the chairperson, being 14 to 16 in respect of the Museum and 10 to 12 in respect of the Library. A minimum of Board members from each gender is provided for. Section 20 sets out the terms of office of members of the Boards and provisions governing the resignation, removal, remuneration or disqualification of a Board member. It provides that a person may only serve two consecutive terms. Section 21 provides that the Minister shall appoint a member of the Board to be chairperson of that Board, sets out the term of office and provisions governing the resignation, remuneration, removal or disqualification of the chairperson or a Board member. Section 22 sets out provisions governing meetings of the Boards. Section 23 provides for the establishment from time to time by either the Board of the Library or Museum of advisory committees which may include persons who are not Board members.

Annual grants and other income   Section 27 provides for making of grants of amounts each year towards the expenditure incurred by a Board in the performance of its functions. Section 28 empowers, and sets out basic criteria under which, a Board may accept and invest gifts of money, land and other property.

Directors of Museum and Library Section 29 sets out the respective names, roles and functions of the Directors of the National Museum and National Library. It provides that the Directors of the National Museum and Library shall be the chief executive officers managing those institutions, subject to the control, superintendence and directions of the relevant Board.

Staff of boards   Section 30 provides for appointment of staff of both Boards. It empowers a Board to appoint new members of staff of the Board, with the consent of the Minister and the Minister for Finance. Persons employed exclusively in the National Museum and National Library prior to the establishment of the new Boards were transferred to them on the basis of continuance of their existing terms and conditions of employment.

Annual accounts and reports   Section 35 requires each Board to prepare annual accounts and audits of those accounts for the Minister. The accounts are also audited by the Comptroller and Auditor General. Section 36 requires each Board to make a report in both Irish and English languages to the Minister of its activities during a year and for the Minister's right to information in relation to each Board's activities.

Indemnities in respect of certain cultural objects   Section 43 of the 1997 Act established a procedure for indemnification of a lender of a cultural object where both the lender and object is based outside the State in respect of the loss of, or damage to, such an object while it is on loan to certain institutions for public exhibition. The institutions are listed in a schedule to the Act. Section 44 provides for an upper monetary limit of £150m on total indemnities outstanding above which indemnities may not be given. A lower limit of £1m per indemnity, subject to certain exceptions, is also provided for. Other detailed provisions on indemnities are also included in the 1997 Act.

Provisions in relation to heritage collections   Section 47 of the 1997 Act concerns the lending and acquisition of cultural objects. The section empowers the main collecting institutions to lend to, borrow from, or exchange with each other, any cultural objects in its collection. The Minister may, by agreement, designate by Order other institutions for loans and transfers, as well as revoke such designations.

Register of objects and export   Section 48 provides for the establishment by the Minister of a register of certain classes of cultural objects whose export from the State would constitute a serious loss to Ireland's heritage. The list will be compiled by specific cultural institutions under the Minister's aegis.

Export licensing regime   Section 49 consolidated with amendments, export licensing provisions contained in the Documents and Pictures (Regulation of Export) Act 1945 (the 1945 Act being repealed) and the National Monuments Act 1930. It revised the scope of the licensing requirements and established new categories of cultural objects to which the export licensing provision applies. As with the previous regime, export licences continue to be required for archaeological objects, and revised categories of non-printed documents and paintings. For the first time, cultural objects entered in the register established under section 48 of the 1997 Act, classes of decorative arts objects listed in a schedule to the Act and other classes of cultural objects designated by Order by the Minister are also included. The section also provides for offences and penalties for non-compliance with its provisions. Section 50 sets out provisions governing the licensing of the export of cultural objects. In respect of a registered cultural object that was already in public care for at least five years prior to the coming into force of the 1997 Act the Minister may refuse to grant the export licence. A refusal may also be made in respect of an object which comes into and stays in public care for 10 years after the coming into force of the 1997 Act. As indicated, the Documents and Pictures (Regulation of Export) Act 1945, which permitted copies to be taken are repealed and adapted, and it is provided that the making of such copies shall not constitute infringement of copyright. Other provisions on export restrictions of archaeological objects were re-enacted in the 1997 Act. In cases where the five year or ten year rules do not apply, the applicant will be granted the export licence, subject to a requirement that the licence be issued within one year from the date of application. Section 51 of the 1997 Act provides for delegation of certain of the Minister's functions. Export licensing functions may be delegated to the Board of the Museum, to the Board of Governors and Guardians of the National Gallery, and to the Board of the Library, and in relation to deposit library requirements to the Board of the Library, while simultaneously not taking from the Minister's overall authority and responsibilities.

Acquisition of certain cultural objects   As indicated, the 1997 Act sets out procedures by which acquisition by the State of registered cultural objects in public care may be effected, if necessary on the basis of compulsory acquisition. Section 52 provides that this applies to cultural objects registered under the 1997 Act and which have been in the care of a public institution for at least five years prior to commencement of the 1997 Act. Section 53 provides that where the return of such an object is sought by an owner, the State may acquire the object in the interests of the common good, by means of a 'vesting order', subject to payment of compensation out of moneys provided by the Oireachtas. It also provides that the Minister is required to decide within eight weeks whether it is intended to acquire the object. Section 54 requires that if the object is to be acquired compulsorily the Minister must then publish and serve notice on every owner of the intention to make a vesting order. In the event of a dispute as to compensation, section 59 provides that the claimant may apply to the High Court. The High Court is empowered to decide if a compensation award should be paid and to fix the amount to be paid. In assessing the amount the Court is to take into account if a licence to export the object may be refused.

National Gallery of Ireland   Section 60 of the 1997 Act conferred additional functions on the National Gallery of Ireland under the National Gallery of Ireland Acts 1854 to 1963, including requirements to contribute to an increase and diffusion of knowledge of the visual arts, to dispose of land it has acquired, with the consent of the Minister, and to engage in fund-raising activities. Section 61 also empowers the Gallery to make bye-laws, to borrow money for its activities, to prepare annual reports and accounts and for these to be audited by the Comptroller and Auditor General.

Intoxicating liquor licences   Section 62 provides that certain key collecting institutions may be granted licences permitting them to sell intoxicating liquor to visitors to the premises in respect of a premises vested in the Commissioners of Public Works in Ireland. Procedures for renewing, transferring or extending licences are provided for. Categories of licence holder are confined to those institutions whose premises are specified in the Second Schedule to the 1997 Act. Opening hours are limited to those hours during which the premises is open to members of the public.

Marsh's Library   Section 63 provides for changes to the governance framework of the Board of Marsh's Library, the oldest public library in the State, whose board of governors is appointed under the Marsh's Library Act 1707. The Minister is empowered, with the consent of the Governors and Guardians of Marsh's Library, to appoint two additional persons to the Board, bringing its total membership to eight. On the Library, see Andrew Lyall's annotation to the 1997 Act, *Irish Current Law Statutes Annotated*.

Rates exemption   Section 64 provides that any property occupied by certain cultural institutions and bodies, whose remits come within the sphere of arts and heritage, are exempt from local authority rates.

Copyright deposit requirement extended   The Copyright Act 1963 requires that copyright material in book form be delivered to the National Library within one month of first publication. Section 65 of the 1997 Act extended this requirement to apply to other 'library material', including engravings, play scripts, sound and video recordings, and other non-print forms of material. The word 'published' is defined as meaning when distributed to the public. The Minister is empowered to make Regulations as to the quality and format of library material, and the classes of material not required to be so deposited. A maximum fine of £500 is provided for contravention of this provision. Section 65 also provides that the Minister may, by Order, extend this new deposit provision to the other existing deposit libraries listed in the Copyright Act 1963, as amended by the University of Limerick Act 1989 and the Dublin City University Act 1989. Section 66 of the 1997 Act increases the penalty set out in section 56(5) of the Copyright Act 1963, in respect of books in order to correspond with the £500 penalty level set out in the 1997 Act and also amended the definition of 'publish' in the 1963 Act to coincide with that in the 1997 Act. In his annotation to the 1997 Act, *Irish Current Law Statutes Annotated*, Andrew Lyall argues that the provisions in the 1963 Act, as amended by the 1997 Act may be vulnerable to constitutional challenge on the ground that they constitute an unjust attack on property rights under Article 40.3.1, particularly as they do not provide for any compensation for the confiscation involved.

Heritage Council   Section 67 provides that the Minister may request a Board, the Director of the National Archives or the Governors and Guardians of the National Gallery to make available such advice to the Heritage Council, established by the Heritage Act 1995 (1995 Review, 19) as required to assist it in performing its functions.

Licensing and disposal of archaeological objects   Section 68 amended the National Monuments Act 1930 so that the licensing of an archaeological object is transferred from the Minister for Education to the Board of the Museum. It also confines further a provision in the National Monuments (Amendment) Act 1994 (1994 Review, 4-5) allowing the Director of the National Museum to waive ownership of the State in an archaeological object. Further delegation of powers of designation of places and persons held respectively by the Minister and the Director of the Museum under the 1994 Act is provided for. These powers establish where and by whom newly found archaeological objects may be held temporarily for safekeeping.

Maintenance of premises   Section 70 of the 1997 Act provides that the Commissioners of Public Works in Ireland shall be responsible for maintenance and improvement of any premises occupied by the Board of the Museum and Library.

Prosecution of offences   Section 4 of the 1997 Act provides that summary proceedings for offences under the Act may be prosecuted by the Minister within twelve months of the date of the offence.

Repeals   Section 6 repealed the Dublin Theatres Act 1786, which required that a person operating a theatre obtain a theatre patent, and the Documents and Pictures (Regulation of Export) Act 1946, whose provisions were consolidated with amendments in the 1997 Act.

STOLEN OR ILLEGALLY EXPORTED CULTURAL OBJECTS

The Law Reform Commission, in its *Report on the Unidroit Convention in Stolen or Illegally Exported Cultural Objects* (LRC 55 – 1997), recommends that Ireland should accede to the Convention, which was formulated in 1995. The need for an effective international instrument is clear: from colonial times, rich nations have plundered the cultural treasures of the countries they have dominated, aided, not only by thieves, but also by some high-status auctioneers who on occasions asked less questions about the provenance of their sources of profit than prudence and honesty might have suggested.

The Convention applies to claims 'of an international character' for:

(a) the *restitution of stolen cultural objects*, and
(b) the *return of illegally exported cultural objects*.

A 'cultural object', defined in Article 2 with reference to the Annex to the Convention, is an object which on religious or secular grounds is of importance for archeology, prehistory, history, literature, art or science and belongs to one of the eleven categories listed in the Annex. This is a closed list, so an object which is admittedly of supreme importance to archaeology, for example, but which does not fall within one these eleven categories will come within the scope of the Convention. The list is so comprehensive, however, that it is hard to imagine that this will prove a weakness in the Convention.

The Convention does not seek to define the scope of the expresion 'claims of a an international character.' Clearly claims arising from purely domestic transactions are not covered but, once the cultural object has crossed a frontier, an issue will arise as to whether the claim is of an international character. If an object stolen in one country is taken to another and sold there, subsequently returning to the country of the theft, there are strong arguments that the claim of the original owner is indeed of an international character. This view derives support from the decision of the English Court of Appeal in *Winkworth v Christie, Manson & Woods Ltd.* [1980] 1 All E.R. 1121, which held that the *lex sitae*, Italian law, should apply where cultural objects stolen from an English collector were subsequently sold to an Italian purchaser who later presented them for sale in London. The outcome of the case would be different under the Convention, but the point that the claim is of an international character is strengthened by the fact that, under English (and Irish) private international law, the situation is clearly regarded as being of international rather than domestic dimensions.

The Convention prescribes uniform legal rules regarding restitution and return. Article 3(1) establishes the general principle that *stolen* cultural objects must be returned. This is scarcely revolutionary for common law jurisdictions, whose law places great emphasis on the principle *nemo dat quod non habet*, subject to narrow exceptions. Civil law systems, which afford the *bona fide* purchaser considerably more rights, have had to accommodate their domestic law radically in order to adhere to the Convention.

In general, claims must be taken within three years of the time the claimant came to know of the location of the object and the identity of the possessor, subject to an upper limit of fifty years from the date of the theft. This upper limit does not apply where the cultural object forms an integral part of an identified monument or archeological site or belongs to a public collection. Contracting States are free to impose a seventy-five year limitation or such longer period as is provided in their law; this will override the qualification to the fifty year limit.

A *bona fide* possessor of a stolen cultural object who is required to return it is entitled to 'payment of fair and reasonable compensation' if capable of proving the at it exercised due diligence when acquiring the object: Article 4.

The provisions relating to the return of illegally exported cultural objects are somewhat more gentle than those relating to stolen cultural objects. The Contracting State from which the object was illegally exported may *request* the court or other competent authority of the Contracting State where it has gone to order its return. The latter must make that order if the requesting State establishes that the removal of the object from its territory significantly impairs one or more of the following interests:

(a) the physical preservation of the object or of its context;
(b) the integrity of a complex object;
(c) 'the preservation of information of, for example, a scientific or historical character.'
(d) the traditional or ritual use of the object by a tribal or indigenous community,

or establishes that the object is 'of significant cultural importance for the requesting State': Article 5(3).

Broadly similar time limits apply to requests of this kind as apply to the return of stolen objects: Article 5(5). The *bona fide* reasonable purchaser is entitled to payment by the requesting State of fair and reasonable compensation: Article 6(1). Instead of compensation, and, *in agreement with the requesting State*, the possessor may retain ownership of the object or transfer it to a person of its choice residing in the requesting State 'who provides the necessary guarantees': Article 6(3).

Among the Law Reform Commissioner's recommendations, its proposal (paragraph 6.21) that the claimant should be able to rely on the *location* of the object at the time the claim is initiated is worthy of note. The rationale is essential one of practical convenience based on 'the reluctance of States to ..

enforce' a judgment of foreign jurisdiction: *id*. This consideration would have particularforce for countries outside the remit of the Brussels and Lugano Conventions.

Commercial Law

AGENCY

Commercial agents   The European Communities (Commercial Agents) Regulations 1997 (S.I. No. 31 of 1997) amended the European Communities (Commercial Agents) Regulations 1994 (1994 Review, 25-34) in order to confirm that commercial agents shall be entitled to compensation after termination of an agency agreement pursuant to Article 17 of Directive 86/653/EEC, which the 1994 Regulations had purported to implement, subject to the limitations in Articles 18, 19 and 20 of the 1986 Directive. We commented in the 1994 Review, 25, that the 1986 Directive had been implemented in a most unsatisfactory manner by the 1994 Regulations. Indeed, proceedings had been initiated against the State by the European Commission in respect of failure to implement the Directive, and these continued even after the 1994 Regulations were made. The proceedings were ultimately not proceeded with only after the 1997 Regulations clarified the provisions on post-termination compensation. Although the 1997 Regulations came into effect on January 7, 1997, they have retrospective effect to agreements made on or after January 1, 1994.

BUSINESS NAMES

Fees   Business Names Regulations 1997 (S.I. No. 357 of 1997), made under the Registration of Business Names Act 1963, set out revised fees to be paid in connection with the 1963 Act, with effect from September 15, 1997.

CENTRAL BANK ACT 1997

The Central Bank Act 1997 enacted a range of measures concerning the Central Bank, including payment systems and cross-border credit transfers, the accountability of the Governor of the Central Bank, extension of the Central Bank's supervision and enforcement powers, including the supervision of bureaux de change. A number of specific amendments were enacted to ensure compatibility with some clearly defined provisions of the Treaty on European Union, the Maastricht Treaty (discussed in the 1992 Review, 326-31), in particular those associated with the establishment of the European Central Bank and the introduction of the Euro currency in 1999. The Central Bank Act 1997 (Commencement) Order 1997 (S.I. No. 150 of 1997) brought the Act into force on April 9, 1997. We should note that a proposal to amend the Bills of Exchange Act 1882 and the Cheques Act 1959, to confer legal status on cheques marked 'account payee only', contained in the original legislative proposal, the Central Bank Bill 1996, was not proceeded with.

Regulation of payment systems, including cheque clearance Part II of the 1997 Act (sections 5 to 22) brought the payment or clearing system operated by the main high street banks, including the cheque clearing system, under the direct supervisory control of the Central Bank for the first time. This enabled the institutions other than banks, such as building societies and credit unions, to participate in the new clearing system operated by the Central Bank. Section 6 empowers the Central Bank to become a member of, or be a party to the establishment or operation of, a payment system. Section 7 provides that no new payment system can be established without the prior agreement of the Central Bank. Section 8 deals with existing payment systems and provides that, within three months of the passing of the 1997 Act, the rules of existing payment systems must be approved by the Central Bank or the systems will be deemed to be disestablished. Section 9 provides that the Central Bank may approve the rules of a payment system subject to conditions or requirements and that the application for approval may be in such form as the Central Bank may determine. It also provides that the approval by the Central Bank of the rules of a payment system does not constitute a warranty of the solvency of the system. On the potential tortious implications of the Central Bank's approval of a clearing system, see John Breslin's Annotation to section 9 of the 1997 Act, *Irish Current Law Statutes Annotated*. Section 10 outlines the procedure where the Central Bank proposes to refuse to approve of the rules of a payment system. Section 11 provides that the provisions of section 17 of the Central Bank Act 1971, which relates to the keeping of books and records, shall apply to payment systems and members of payment systems as if they were bank licence holders. Section 12 empowers the Central Bank to direct a system, or any member of a system, to cease activity, or to cease operating as a member of a payment system as the case maybe, in certain circumstances. It also provides for an application to the courts, by the Central Bank (for confirmation of a direction under this section) or by a payment system, or members thereof (for the setting aside of a direction). Section 13 provides for the revocation of approval by the Central Bank of the rules of a payment system in certain circumstances, subject to the agreement of the Minister for Finance. It also sets out the procedure to be followed by the system in these circumstances. Section 14 provides that non-compliance with the provisions on payment systems are offences and also specifies the penalties therefor. On summary prosecution, the maximum penalty is a fine £1,500 and/or 12 months imprisonment, while on indictment the maximum penalty is a fine of £50,000 and/or five years imprisonment. Section 15 allows the Central Bank to impose certain requirements for membership of a payment system. Section 16 of the 1997 Act amends section 26 of the Central Bank Act 1971, which deals with the collection of cheques. The section allows the Central Bank to extend the scope of section 26 of the 1971 Act to other parties or instruments and extends the meaning of licence holder to include a credit institution within the meaning of Reg.2 of the European Communities (Licensing and Supervision of Credit Institutions) Regulations 1992 (1992 Review, 33). Section 18 provides that the Minister for Finance may, after consulting with the Central Bank, prescribe fees to be paid by all entities supervised by the Central Bank under any enactment. Section 19 provides that, once payments have been debited from a credit institution's account in the Central Bank on the instructions of the credit institution concerned, the payment becomes final. Section 20 allows payment instructions and authorisations to and from the Central Bank to be of a form other than in writing. This allows for electronic, or other, transmission of instructions. Section 21 amended section 7 of the Central Bank Act 1942 in order to enable the Central Bank to invest in and to take an active management role in the operation of clearing systems. Section 22 of the 1997 Act empowers the Minister for Finance to make Regulations for the purposes of regulating cross-border credit transfers.

Power of Central Bank to form or acquire company   Section 23 of the 1997 Act empowers the Central Bank to form or acquire subsidiary bodies to exercise its statutory powers, subject to the consent of the Minister.

Functions and duties of governor of bank   Section 24 provides that the Governor shall attend before the Finance and General Affairs Committee of Dáil Éireann and furnish that Committee with any information requested. Section 25 amended section 8 of the Central Bank Act 1942 to empower the Central Bank to assist the Central Statistics Office in the collection, compilation, analysis or interpretation of balance of payments, national accounts or any other financial statistics, including, where appropriate, the actual collection of data for this purpose. Section 26 amends section 19 of the Central Bank Act 1942 (which deals with the appointment and tenure of office of the Governor of the Central Bank) and extends the prohibition on the Governor from being a director of a licensed bank to all commercial credit institutions, financial institutions or insurance undertakings. Section 27 amends section 20 of the Central Bank Act 1942 (which prohibits the holding of shares by the Governor in a bank) and extends that prohibition to credit institutions, financial institutions or insurance undertakings.

Supervision of bureaux de change   Section 29 of the 1997 Act provides that it is an offence to carry on the business of a bureau de change without authorisation from the Central Bank and sets out the procedure involved in the grant or refusal of an authorisation by the Central Bank. It also provides that existing operations have a period of six months after it came into effect to obtain authorisation from the Bank. Section 30 requires bureau de change businesses to comply with any requirement laid down by the Central Bank. Section 31 applies to bureaux de change the provisions of section 17 of the Central Bank Act 1971 (which concerns the keeping of books and records). Section 32 outlines the powers of the High Court to deal with failure by a bureau de change to comply with a requirement or condition of the Central Bank. Proceedings may be held otherwise than in public if the Court determines. Section 33 requires the Central Bank to publish an annual list of bureaux de change and to publish notice of any revocation of an authorisation as soon as possible. Section 34 sets out the various offences for failure to comply with the provisions on bureaux de change and the associated penalties. On summary prosecution, the maximum penalty is a fine £1,500 and/or 12 months imprisonment, while on indictment the maximum penalty is a fine of £50,000 and/or five years imprisonment. Section 35 relates to the revocation of authorisation of a bureau de change by the Central Bank. The Central Bank must seek the consent of the Minister to the revocation unless the revocation has been requested by the person who was authorised or where the revocation is as a consequence of the withdrawal of authorisation by another Member State of the European Community in which the bureau has its head office.

Investment intermediaries   Part VI of the 1997 Act (sections 37 to 49) amended a number of provisions of the Investment Intermediaries Act 1995 in order to confer on the Central Bank the powers of supervision and inspection of investment intermediaries, conferred by the 1995 Act on the Department of Enterprise, Trade and Employment and, in effect, on the industry itself. The powers thus conferred are similar to those already conferred on the Central Bank in connection with the banking sector. The changes effected by the 1997 Act were made in the light of perceived inadequacies in the 'self-regulatory' model contained in the 1995 Act: see the 1995 Review, 42.

Directors of Central Bank   Section 50 of the 1997 Act amended section 24 of the Central Bank Act 1942 (which deals with the tenure of office of directors of the Central Bank) and provides that a uniform term of office of five years from date of appointment will apply to all directors of the Central Bank, other than service directors. Section 51 amended section 28(2) of the Central Bank Act 1942 (which deals with notification to the Minister of Board vacancies) by transferring responsibility for notifying the Minister of vacancies on the Board from the Board to the Secretary of the Central Bank.

Non-disclosure of information by Bank   Section 52 extended the provisions of section 16 of the Central Bank Act 1989 (concerning non-disclosure of information by the Central Bank) to a number of institutions within and outside the State. It also extended the number of situations in which disclosure is permitted.

Duties of auditor   Section 53 of the 1997 Act extends the provisions of section 47 of the Central Bank Act 1989 (concerning the duties of an auditor of a bank to disclose certain financial irregularities to the Central Bank) to financial institutions in the International Financial Services Centre (IFSC), financial futures and options exchanges and moneybrokers.

Notice of liquidation of bank   Section 54 amended section 48 of the Central Bank Act 1989 to facilitate the protection of the payment and banking systems in the event of a liquidation of a licence holder by requiring that the Central Bank be notified of any petition for winding up before the petition is presented.

Acquiring transactions   Section 55 of the 1997 Act extends the provisions of section 75(2) of the Central Bank Act 1989 (which sets out the application of Chapter VI of the 1989 Act dealing with acquiring transactions) to include acquiring transactions entered into with the prior approval of the Central Bank. Section 56 amends section 76 of the Central Bank Act 1989 (which sets out the limitations on the validity of acquiring transactions) by providing that in all cases a person can apply to the High Court to seek relief from the null and void provision where the failure to get the Bank's prior approval for an acquisition arose from inadvertence or oversight and where the circumstances are such that, had the Central Bank been notified in time, it would have given its approval.

Financial services supervision   Section 57 amends section 90 of the Central Bank Act 1989 (which relates to the supervision by the Central Bank of firms established in the International Financial Services Centre) to allow the Central Bank to enforce its supervision from an earlier date specified by the Central Bank. Section 58 amended section 91 of the Central Bank Act 1989 (which deals with orders of the Minister exempting certain financial institutions from the supervisory regime of the Central Bank where there is already adequate supervision provided for) by providing that the Minister for Finance may, by Order, exempt certain firms or services in the IFSC from supervision by the Central Bank. Section 59 amended section 92 of the Central Bank Act 1989 (which empowers the Bank to impose supervisory and reporting requirements) thus allowing the Central Bank to exempt certain firms or services from the application of supervisory requirements in part or in full where the application of such requirements is not practicable or necessary to safeguard the public or the reputation of the International Financial Services Centre (IFSC). Section 60 amended section 3(2) of the Consumer Credit Act 1995 to confirm that activities of firms in the IFSC fall outside the scope of the 1995 Act. Section 61 of the 1997 Act provides that where a company or firm in the IFSC has had its certificate withdrawn, it will, nonetheless, remain subject to supervision and direction by the Central Bank until it has discharged its liabilities in whole or in part to the satisfaction of the Central Bank.

Prospectuses   Section 62 of the 1997 Act amends section 104 of the Central Bank Act 1989, which relates to the publication of prospectuses by the promoters of any new financial futures or options exchange in the State. The amendment empowers the Central Bank to require any such promoter to put a 'health warning' on the prospectus to the effect that, if such be the case, the exchange has not yet been approved by the Central Bank and that such approval should not be taken for granted.

Settlement facilities   Section 63 amends section 139 of the Central Bank Act 1989, which deals with the electronic transfer of certain securities, to enable the Central Bank to engage in the provision of settlement facilities for the buying and selling of securities and other instruments by financial institutions and to act as a depository or custodian of such securities and instruments.

Prohibition on financing of public sector by Central Bank   Sections 50 to 54 of the 1997 Act deleted from certain legislation provisions which conflicted with Article 104 of the Treaty on European Union which prohibits monetary financing of the public sector by central banks. The amendments in question were made to the Bretton Woods Agreement Act 1957, the International Finance Corporation Act 1958, the International Development Association Act 1960, the Multilateral Investment Guarantee Agency Act 1988 and the European Bank for Reconstruction and Development Act 1991. The amendments removed the power of the Central Bank to advance to the Minister for Finance any Irish currency held by the Bank as Irish depository for the international bodies dealt with in these Acts.

Immunity from suit   Section 69 inserts a new section 25A into the Central Bank Act 1989 and provides that no employee or member of the Board of the Central Bank will be liable for damages for anything done or omitted in the discharge of duty unless it is shown that the omission or act was in bad faith. This should be seen in conjunction with section 9 of the 1997 Act, discussed above.

Bank licensing   Section 70 provides for a substantial adjustment of the definition of 'banking business' as set out in section 2 of the Central Bank Act 1971, in order to conform to the wider regulation provided for in the 1997 Act. Section 71 amends section 11 of the Central Bank Act 1971, which deals with the revocation of banking licences, to allow the Central Bank to revoke a banker's licence if the bank organises its business or corporate structure in such a way as to avoid or escape effective supervision by the Central Bank. Section 72 amends section 48 of the Central Bank Act 1971, which allows the Central Bank to issue bonds to licence holders, by extending the facility to issue bonds to all credit institutions. Section 73 amended section 51 of the Central Bank Act 1971 provides relief to the Bank of Ireland from certain restrictions imposed by its Charter and by legislation.

Application for injunctive relief by Central Bank   Section 74 of the 1997 Act empowers the Central Bank to apply to the courts for an injunction in respect of the taking of, or advertising for, deposits by a person not licensed or authorised to do so under the Central Bank Acts, the Building Societies Acts, the Trustee Savings Banks Acts, the ACC Bank Acts or the ICC Bank Acts.

Inspection powers of authorised officers of Bank   Section 75 of the 1997 Act confers substantial powers of inspection of financial institutions on authorised officers of the Central Bank, referred to as 'appropriate persons' in the 1997 Act. These powers were modelled on those contained in the Investment Intermediaries Act 1995. In conjunction with this, section 76 provides that a judge of the District Court may issue a warrant authorising a member of the Garda Síochána and any others named in the warrant to enter a specified premises to search for and take possession of documents which an officer of the Central Bank believes are held on the premises. The warrant will have effect for one month from date of issue and any documents seized may be retained for a period of three months, or until the conclusion of criminal proceedings. It is an offence to obstruct any person in the execution of the warrant. On summary prosecution, the maximum penalty is a fine £1,500 and/or 12 months imprisonment, while on indictment the maximum penalty is a fine of £1,000,000 and/or ten years imprisonment.

Value for money audits   Section 77 provides for the Central Bank to be subject to value-for-money audits under the Comptroller and Auditor General (Amendment) Act 1993 (1993 Review, 147-50).

Building society joint accounts   Section 78 inserted a new section 101A into the Building Societies Act 1989 to provide for more equitable treatment of certain joint account holders as respects voting rights and the issue of free shares in the context of future conversions of building societies into public companies.

National housing programme   Section 79 imposes a requirement on mortgage lenders to supply the Minister for the Environment with information and returns for the purposes of his functions in relation to the national housing programme.

Regulation of powers of trustees of authorised investments   Section 80 of the 1997 Act amends the Trustee (Authorised Investments) Act 1958 to enable the Minister for Finance to impose conditions on the investment powers of trustees. The requirement that Orders made under the 1958 Act take statutory effect only after positive Oireachtas approval has been removed in favour of the standard 'negative' provision that such Orders take effect unless annulled by the Oireachtas.

Deposit guarantee schemes   Section 81 of the 1997 Act amended the European Communities (Deposit Guarantee Schemes) Regulations 1995 (1995 Review, 40) to add to the list of deposit takers excluded from cover by the 1995 Regulations. This mainly involves non-retail deposit takers.

ICC Bank   Section 82 specifies that references to 'the company' in section 3(1) of the ICC Bank Act 1992 or any Regulations made thereunder are to be construed as including any subsidiary of ICC Bank plc.

Securities Settlement Office   Section 83 amended the Stock Transfer Act 1963 by substituting for the 'Gilts Settlement Office' of 'Central Bank of Ireland Securities Settlement Office' and to provide that the Minister may by Regulations change the name of that office.

Establishment of non-EU banks   Section 84 allows banks from States outside the EU to establish representative offices in the State, subject to certain conditions imposed by the Central Bank.

COMPETITION

Decisions of Competition Authority   In *Cronin v. Competition Authority* [1998] 2 I.L.R.M. 51, the Court held that the notification procedure in section 4 of the Competition Act 1991 (1991 Review, 23-6), by which undertakings notify the Competition Authority of agreements regulated by the 1991 Act did not involve a breach of principles of natural justice and fair procedures nor did the powers given to the Authority by section 4 of the 1991 Act constitute an unconstitutional delegation of a legislative function by the Oireachtas.

The case arose against the following background. In March 1992, the Competition Authority placed an advertisement in the newspapers announcing that it had received notification from Texaco (Ireland) Ltd, a wholesale oil products company, of five different types of agreement for the supply of motor fuel. The applicant, a licensee of a Texaco retail petrol outlet, took no steps in relation to this notification. In November 1992, the Authority published a notice to the effect that it had received notification of, *inter alia*, a new licence agreement for Texaco (Ireland) Ltd licensees. Later that month, the applicant wrote to the Authority requesting information concerning this notification. In early December 1992, the Authority replied that details of a notification were confidential, but a draft of the relevant category licence was made available to the applicant later that month. In July 1993, the Authority granted a category licence under section 4(2)(a) of the Competition Act 1991 in respect of the Texaco agreements. The applicant sought to quash this decision by the Authority and also claimed that the powers of the Authority involved an unconstitutional delegation of power and/or that the Minister for Enterprise and Employment had failed in a duty which it was claimed was placed upon him to make Regulations prescribing the procedures to be followed by the Authority. In the High Court, it was held that the procedures adopted by the Authority were fair and reasonable. On appeal, the Supreme Court affirmed.

The Court held that the Competition Authority was an administrative body which formulated its competition policy in the light of the requirements of the common good, the provisions of the 1991 Act and prevailing market conditions. While the Court accepted that the powers contained in section 4(2) of the 1991 Act were extensive and could involve the analysis of very complex questions of fact, the legislative bounds within which these powers must be exercised were clearly laid down and amounted to no more than the implementation of principles and policies contained on the 1991 Act itself. The powers did not thus breach the 'principles and policies' test laid down in *Cityview Press Ltd v. An Chomhairle Oiliúna* [1980] I.R. 280.

Distribution agreement   In *Chanelle Veterinary Ltd. v. Pfizer (Ireland) Ltd.* [1998] 1 I.L.R.M. 161 (HC), O'Sullivan J. held that the defendant company's decision to 'de-list' the plaintiff as a wholesaler of its products was not in breach of the Competition Act 1991 (1991 Review, 23-6).

The plaintiff, a wholesale distribution company of animal health products, including those manufactured by the defendant, an Irish subsidiary of a multinational corporation. In 1995, the plaintiff and four other companies were appointed as wholesale distributors of the defendant's products and its products were only available through these five, the largest wholesalers in the distribution market. The terms of the distributorship included a wholesaler's discount and a rebate scheme for end users who bought through the appointed wholesalers. Relations between the plaintiff and defendant deteriorated, and the plaintiff claimed that the other four wholesalers were being given a greater discount on the defendant's most successful product. A sister company of the plaintiff also developed a competing product to one of the defendant's products in respect of which the patent had come to an end. In 1996, the plaintiff was notified by the defendant that it had been de-listed as an appointed wholesaler.

The plaintiff claimed that the defendant's range of products was an essential part of its business and that it was not viable without access to the defendant's products on the same terms as the other four appointed wholesalers. The plaintiff also argued that the defendant's distribution system was a selective distribution system which operated in a discriminatory manner with anti-competitive effect. As already indicated, O'Sullivan J. dismissed the claim.

He held that there was no question in the instant case of any agreement or concerted practice between the defendant and the other four wholesalers in relation to the de-listing of the plaintiff and it was clear that the de-listing had been a unilateral act. O'Sullivan J. stated that in approaching the question whether an alleged agreement or concerted practice was anti-competitive under section 4 of the 1991 Act, the object of the agreement had first to be examined. If the object did not of its nature restrict competition, the effect of the agreement then had to be considered. He concluded that any agreement involving the de-listing of the plaintiff did not have as its object the prevention, restriction or distortion of competition. He refused to accept that the evidence that the plaintiff was placed at a disadvantage as a competitor established, without more, that the de-listing was in breach of section 4(1) of the 1991 Act. It was necessary to show, he held, that competition had been or would be prevented, restricted or distorted and he was not satisfied that the evidence established that any agreement or concerted practice had or would have this effect.

O'Sullivan J. accepted that the distribution system in the instant case was selective in that four wholesalers were appointed to service the entire country. A selective distribution system properly called also involved the imposition by the supplier upon such distributors of a requirement that they would re-sell only to end users or other appointed wholesalers. Such restriction was justified, he held, only if the system operated in selecting distributors on a qualitative basis and was operated in a non-discriminatory manner, that is, any distributor who wanted to be supplied and who met the qualitative criteria had to be appointed. In the present case, the plaintiff was still entitled to buy from the other wholesalers and would be entitled to the rebate. There was thus no restriction on the number of competitors at the wholesale level as a result of the distribution system operated by the defendant and the appointed wholesalers were free to supply the relevant goods to any other wholesaler. On that basis the question of dominance under section 5 of the 1991 Act did not arise.

Dominant position: arguable case In *Hinde Livestock Exports Ltd v. Pandoro Ltd*, Supreme Court, December 18, 1997, the Supreme Court, reversing the High Court, *sub nom. Gernon v. Pandoro Ltd*, High Court, August 1, 1997, held that the plaintiffs had established an arguable case that the defendant company was in breach of Article 85 of the EC Treaty.

The plaintiffs were hauliers and livestock transporters engaged in exporting live animals from Ireland to the continent. In 1994, the defendant commenced a service of transportation of livestock for breeding, fattening and slaughter purposes by ferry from Rosslare to Cherbourg. In October 1994, the service was limited to the transportation of livestock for breeding purposes only. In March 1997, the service included once again the transportation of livestock for breeding, fattening and slaughter purposes. Three months later, the company informed the Minister for Agriculture that they would be transporting livestock for breeding purposes only. It was accepted that the volume and profitability of the livestock trade was low, but another factor in the defendant's decision had been adverse publicity associated with the live export trade from groups concerned with animal welfare. The plaintiffs instituted proceedings seeking, *inter alia*, declaratory relief that they had a legitimate expectation that the transportation of livestock by the defendant company would include fattening and slaughter purposes and that the defendant was in breach of Article 86 of the EC Treaty in that it had abused a dominant position in the market. They also sought interlocutory injunctive relief pending the trial of the action. In the High Court, Costello P. had refused the interlocutory relief sought, but on appeal the Supreme Court reversed.

Costello P. held that the decision by the company to terminate the service had been made for *bona fide* commercial reasons. He also took the view that there had been no guarantee that the service would last for an indefinite period. As to Article 86 of the EC Treaty, while accepting that its terms were directly applicable in Irish law, he concluded that the defendant had not abused its dominant position as there was an objective justification for its action. Although there had been adverse publicity and opposition to the re-introduction of the trade in livestock between Rosslare and Cherbourg, there was no evidence that the defendant had given in to improper force or pressure. Referring to the decision in *R. v. Chief Constable of Sussex* [1995] 4 All E.R. 364, Costello P. considered that Article 34 of the EC Treaty applies to national measures only and that the plaintiffs had not made out a fair question that Article 34 did not apply to national measures only. Finally, he held that the defendant's action could not be regarded as a quantitative restriction on exports or a measure having equivalent effect.

On appeal, the Supreme Court held that a *prima facie* case had been made out that the defendant was in a dominant position and that, *prima facie*, there had been an abuse of that position. As it concluded that there was a fair question to be tried on the Article 86 point, no view was expressed on the applicability or otherwise of Article 34 of the EC Treaty. The Court referred to the decision of the Court of Justice in Case C-265/95 *Commission v. France*, December 9, 1997, in which the Court had held that the failure of the French government to prevent blockades of French ports by French protesters at the importing of lamb from Irish and United Kingdom ports was in breach of the EC Treaty. The Supreme Court opined in the *Hinde* case that it was not open to a private undertaking to yield too tamely to threats of vandalism or adverse publicity, if that undertaking's prime duty under Community law had been breached. The Court held that in the circumstances the balance of convenience favoured granting the interlocutory injunction sought.

Dominant position: evidential burden   In *Blemings and Ors v. D. Patton Ltd and Ors*, High Court, January 18, 1997, the plaintiffs, all residents of County Monaghan, were a group of 47 chicken producers for the fifth named defendant, Monaghan Poultry Products Ltd (MPP). MPP's place of business was on the outskirts of the town of Monaghan. The plaintiffs claimed that MPP had, through its arrangements with the plaintiffs, abused its dominant position in the market, contrary to section 4 of the Competition Act 1991. The significant features of the arrangements were: the plaintiffs were not permitted to purchase chicken feed other than through MPP; the cost of meal was deducted by MPP from the price paid to the plaintiffs; that the plaintiffs were not paid for 'dead or useless chickens'; and that more favourable prices were offered by MPP to other growers. The parties agreed that the relevant product market was the market for the provision of broiler growing services. Shanley J. also accepted the plaintiffs' expert evidence, given by an economist Dr David Jacobson, that the relevant geographical market was within a 15 miles radius of the MPP factory. He also accepted that there was little competition in the relevant market and that MPP held a dominant position in that market, as the plaintiffs' expert witness had claimed. He also accepted the opinion of the economist that MPP enjoyed the position of a monopsonist, that is, where a company is the sole buyer or seller of goods or services. Nonetheless, Shanley J. concluded that there had been no abuse of a dominant position within section 4 of the 1991 Act. No genuinely comparable prices had been introduced in evidence, he held, such as would satisfy the test laid down in *United Brands and United Brands Continental BV v. Commission* [1978] E.C.R. 207 or *Bodson v. Pompes Funetrees des Regions Libres* [1988] E.C.R. 2479. Thus, he concluded that the different prices offered by MPP had not been shown to place any of the affected growers at a competitive disadvantage. He also held that the requirement that the plaintiffs buy their meal from MPP was objectively justified under the principles established in *Metro-SB-Grossmärkte GmbH & Co KG v. Commission* [1977] E.C.R. 3933 and *Metro-SB-Grossmärkte GmbH & Co KG v. Commission (No. 2)* [1986] E.C.R. 3021. This was because the requirement was directly connected as a result of commercial usage with the broiler growing service. In summary, therefore, although a dominant position was clearly established, Shanley J. concluded that there had been no breach of the 1991 Act.

CONSUMER CREDIT

Local authority housing loans   The Consumer Credit Act 1995 (Section 3) Regulations 1997 (S.I. No. 186 of 1997), made under the Consumer Credit Act 1995 (1995 Review, 24-39), brought housing loans advanced by local authorities within the scope of the 1995 Act with effect from September 1, 1997.

CONSUMER PROTECTION

Concert advertisements   The Consumer Information (Advertisements for Concert or Theatre Performances) Order 1997 (S.I. No. 103 of 1997), made under the Consumer Information Act 1978, provided that certain information relating to admission prices and additional charges, in particular booking fees and charges for bookings by credit cards, must be provided in advertisements for concert or theatre performances. The Order came into effect on May 12, 1997.

Prices: intoxicating liquor   The Retail Prices (Intoxicating Liquor) Order 1997 (S.I. No. 108 of 1997), made under the Prices Act 1958, provided that the prices charged for intoxicating liquor outside of Dublin shall be those displayed on November 4, 1996. The Order, which came into effect on March 11, 1997, was made in the context of a well-publicised dispute between the licensed vintners in Limerick and the Department of Enterprise and Employment as to the appropriate price to charge for alcohol in the wake of an increase in excise duties imposed by the 1997 budget. The making of the 1997 Order ultimately resolved the dispute and it was revoked by the Retail Prices (Intoxicating Liquor) (Revocation) Order 1997 (S.I. No. 426 of 1997).

Prices: petrol   The Retail Prices (Diesel and Petrol) Display Order 1997 (S.I. No. 178 of 1997), made under the Prices Act 1958, prescribe the manner in which the price per litre for diesel and petrol products must be displayed at retail petrol outlets. The Order came into effect on May 19, 1997 and revoked the Retail Prices (Petrol) Display Order 1986. The Consumer Information (Diesel and Petrol) (Reduction In Retail Price) Order 1997 (S.I. No. 179 of 1997), made under the Consumer Information Act 1978, prescribes the manner in which reductions in the retail price of diesel and petrol products must be advertised at retail petrol outlets, with effect from May 19, 1997.

Time share agreements   The European Communities (Contracts for Time Sharing of Immovable Property - Protection of Purchasers) Regulations 1997 (S.I. No. 204 of 1997) gave effect to Directive 94/47/EC. The 1994 Directive and 1997 Regulations concern time share contracts for the sale of immovable property, defined in Regulation 2 of the 1997 Regulations as 'any building or part of a building for use as accommodation.' Regulation 4 of the 1997 Regulations provide that any person seeking information on time share properties must be supplied with a document or brochure, containing a number of matters specified in the Annex to the Regulations. These include a general description of the property, details on the vendor, location of property, its current status in terms of completion or non-completion, associated services and facilities, the price and the right of the purchaser to cancel. Regulation 7 of the 1997 Regulations provides for a general 10 day 'cooling off' period or, in the absence of or the non-provision of information under the Regulations, a 'cooling off' period of three months. These are, in effect, rights to cancel the contract and are stated to be without prejudice to any rights under the European Communities (Unfair Terms in Consumer Contracts) Regulations 1995. Regulation 10 of the 1997 Regulations prohibit the vendor from seeking deposits. Regulation 13 of the 1997 Regulations also provide that failure to comply with the provisions laid down constitutes an offence which may be prosecuted by the Director of Consumer Affairs and for which the maximum penalty is a fine of £1,500. The Regulations came into effect on May 14, 1997.

CREDIT UNION ACT 1997

The Credit Union Act 1997 consolidates and updates the Credit Union Act 1966, which was repealed by the 1997 Act. It deals with registration and membership, extends the range of services a credit union may provide, provides for the management and supervision of credit unions, extending the powers of the Registrar of Friendly Societies, deals with accounts and auditing of unions and the winding up of credit unions. The Credit Union Act 1997 (Commencement) Order 1997 (S.I. No. 403 of 1997) brought the majority of the Act (other than sections 46 to 52, section 68(1)(c), section 120(5) and section 122(1)(f)) into force on October 1, 1997.

Registration and membership   Section 6 sets out the criteria for registration as a credit union. The Registrar of Friendly Societies must be satisfied that the applicant for registration is formed for certain specified purposes, that there be a common bond among the members and that other conditions relating to the rules of the applicant, to minimum membership and to its registered office are fulfilled. Section 7 provides that an application to the Registrar for registration as a credit union must meet certain specified requirements. Section 8 empowers the Registrar to accept or refuse the registration application and provides for the entry of the name of every approved applicant into a register of credit unions to be maintained by the Registrar. A right of appeal to the High Court against every refusal of registration by the Registrar is provided. Section 9 provides that by virtue of its registration, a credit union shall be a body corporate known by its registered name (by which it may sue and be sued) with perpetual succession, a common seal and limited liability. On registration, any property vested in trust for the credit union shall be vested in the credit union, and any legal proceedings by or against the credit union may predate the date of registration. Section 10 contains certain conditions and restrictions relating to the form, use and display of a credit union's registered name. Section 11 provides that a credit union may only change its registered name by resolution at a general meeting and with the Registrar's agreement. A right of appeal to the High Court against a decision of the Registrar to refuse a name change is available. A credit union must change its registered name if so directed by the Registrar. The Registrar is required *inter alia* to enter every new name in the register of credit unions. Section 13 provides *inter alia* that the registered rules of a credit union shall be in such form as the Registrar may determine and that they shall contain the provisions with respect to the matters set out in the First Schedule to the Act or such additional provisions as the Registrar may determine after consultation with the Credit Union Advisory Committee or other expert or knowledgeable bodies.

The First Schedule to the 1997 Act provides that the rules of a credit union shall stipulate: its name; its objects; the place of its registered office; the qualifications for, and the terms of admission to, membership; the provisions for notifying and conducting meetings and for making rules; the mode of appointing/removing officers and their powers and remuneration, where applicable; the maximum amount of shares which may be held by any member; the provisions for withdrawing shares and for the payment of the balance due; the mode and circumstances relating to the making and repayment of loans; the arrangements for custody and use of the credit union's seal; the arrangements for the audit of its accounts; the arrangements for the settlement of credit union/member disputes; the provisions relating to the withdrawal of members, the settlement of the claims of deceased members and of the assignees or trustees of the property of bankrupt members and the payment of nominees.

Section 14 provides *inter alia* that an amendment of its registered rules requires the approval of two-thirds of the members of a credit union present and voting at a general meeting. The Registrar is also required to be satisfied that the proposed amendment is not contrary to the provisions of the Act. A right of appeal to the High Court is provided to a credit union against a decision of the Registrar to refuse to register an amendment of its rules. Section 15 binds a credit union, all its members and all persons claiming through the members to the registered rules of the credit union. However, a member shall not be bound to any amendment of the registered rules which requires him, in the absence of his written consent, to subscribe for more shares, to pay more than the amount unpaid on his shares or otherwise to increase his liability to contribute to the share capital of the credit union. Section 16 requires that a copy of the rules of a credit union be supplied by the credit union to any person who demands it, on payment of a fee not exceeding £1 or any larger prescribed amount. Section 17 provides that in general, the minimum number of members of a credit union shall be 15. The conditions for membership of a credit union include that a person must be a shareholder and qualify under the common bond set out in the credit union's rules. If a member ceases to have the common bond, he or she may retain membership and voting rights and continue saving notwithstanding that he or she is a non-qualifying member. A person under the age of 16 may enjoy, acting through a parent or guardian, all the rights of membership, other than voting rights and the right to act in speci-fied positions of responsibility within the credit union. An incorporated or unincorporated body may be admitted to membership where the majority of its members are eligible for membership. Section 18 provides for a right of appeal to the District Court by any person who has been refused membership of a credit union. Section 19 provides for the expulsion by a credit union of a member and for a right of appeal to the District Court by any person who has been so expelled. A member may withdraw from membership, and the conse-quences for the shares, deposits and liabilities of the expelled or withdrawing member are described in the section. Section 21 provides that a member of a credit union may nominate in writing to the credit union any person or persons to become entitled to the member's property in the credit union on his death. Section 23 provides that, on the death of a member who had not made a nomi-nation under section 21 and whose property in the credit union does not ex-ceed £5,000 or any greater prescribed amount, the board of directors of a credit union may, without letters of administration or probate of any will, dis-tribute the member's property to such persons as appears to the board to be entitled by law to receive it. Section 24 provides that the board of directors of a credit union may make to any person, whom the board judges proper to receive it, a payment of any property held by or on behalf of a member who is incapable, through disorder or disability of mind, of managing his own affairs and in respect of whom no person has been appointed to administer his prop-erty on his behalf.

Operation of credit unions Section 26 provides that a credit union may do anything consistent with the objects for which it was formed. Any act or deed done by a credit union which it had no power to do, but which if it had such power, would have been lawfully and effectively done, shall be effective in favour of a person who dealt with the credit union in good faith. On the appli-cation of a member or the Registrar, the High Court may restrain a credit union from doing any act or thing which it has no power to do. Section 27 provides that a credit union may raise funds through the issue of shares to members (subject to a member's shareholding not exceeding £50,000 or 1% of the credit union's total assets, whichever is the greater) and through the acceptance of deposits from members with a minimum shares balance of £1,000 (subject to a member's deposits not exceeding £20,000). The maximum amounts of a member's shareholdings and deposits may be increased from time to time by Ministerial Order. The aggregate liabilities of a credit union in respect of deposits shall not exceed 75% of its aggregate liabilities in respect of shares, unless the Registrar has granted a dispensation from this requirement. Section 28 provides that shares are to be of £1 denomination, that no share shall be allotted until fully paid in cash, that no certificate denoting ownership of a share shall be issued by a credit union, that all withdrawable shares shall have equal rights, that all non-withdrawable shares shall have equal rights and that the credit union may issue fully paid-up bonus shares to members from any sum standing to the credit of its reserves (other than the reserve required by section 45 of the 1997 Act). Section 29 permits the transfer, without charge, of shares from one member to another with the approval of the board of directors and subject to the limits on shareholdings set out in the Act. A member refused approval by a credit union to transfer shares may appeal to the District Court. Section 30 provides that on the recommendation of the board of directors, a dividend up to a maximum of 10% of the nominal value of shares (or such other percentage as may be prescribed) may be approved at each annual general meeting on all credit union shares out of surplus funds. Section 31 specifies that the board of directors may pay from time to time different rates of interest on deposits, provided that the rate of interest is the same for all deposits of a particular class and that it does not exceed the return received from the employment of such deposits. Section 32 provides that a credit union may require from a member not less than 60 days' notice of his or her intention to withdraw a share and not less than 21 days' notice of his or her intention to withdraw a deposit. The withdrawal of any shares is prohibited while a claim due on account of deposits is unsatisfied. Where a member has an outstanding liability to a credit union, a withdrawal of savings shall not be permitted unless it is approved by the board of directors. However, no withdrawal of savings shall be permitted where the value of the member's savings immediately after the withdrawal would be less than 25% of the outstanding liability or such other percentage as may be set by the Registrar. With the member's written consent, the credit union may withdraw any of his or her shares or deposits and set them off against any indebtedness. Section 33 empowers a credit union to borrow money, subject to its rules, provided that total borrowings (excluding members' shares and deposits) do not exceed 50% of the aggregate of its shares and deposits balances. A credit union proposing to borrow money which would have the effect of raising total borrowings in excess of 25% of the aggregate of its shares and deposits balances must give 28 days' notice of its intention to do so to the Registrar. A transaction involving the lending of funds to a credit union shall not be invalid or ineffectual if the 50% limit has been exceeded, unless the lender was aware of the fact in advance. Section 34 provides that an instrument executed by a credit union constituting a charge on its assets shall not be a bill of sale under the Bills of Sale (Ireland) Acts 1879 and 1883 or that it shall not be invalidated by those Bills where it is recorded with the Registrar. Section 35 provides for the making of loans by a credit union to a member (excluding any member under the age of 18 unless the loan is guaranteed by the member's parent or guardian) for a provident or productive purpose without or with security (which may take the form of a guarantee by a member or a pledge by him of shares or deposits in the credit union) and upon such terms as the credit union's rules may provide. Certain restrictions are also specified. Thus, a credit union is prohibited from making a loan to a member: (a) for a period exceeding 5 years, if, were the loan to be made, the total amount of such loans outstanding by the credit union would then exceed 20% of all outstanding loans; or (b) for a period exceeding 10 years, if, were the loan to be made, the total amount of such loans outstanding by the credit union would then exceed 10% of all outstanding loans; or (c) if the member's indebtedness to the credit union would exceed £30,000 or 1.5% of the total assets of the credit union, whichever is the greater. Section 36 provides that a loan to a member must be approved, in accordance with the credit union's rules, either by a credit officer or by a majority of the members of the credit committee or by a majority of the board of directors. A loan to an officer which exceeds the value of his shares must be approved by two-thirds of the members of a special committee voting by secret ballot. Section 38 limits the rate of interest charged on loans to 1% per month of the amount outstanding and provides *inter alia* that the interest cost must include all the charges made by the credit union in making the loan. However, if a credit union charges or accepts interest at a rate greater than that permitted, all the interest shall be deemed to have been waived and the interest already paid shall be recoverable by the member as a simple contract debt. Section 43 permits a credit union to invest its surplus funds in securities, in other credit unions, in the shares of industrial and provident societies or in such other manner as may be prescribed by the Minister. Surplus funds which are not invested or kept as cash in the credit union shall be kept with a credit institution. Section 44 enables the general meeting of a credit union to approve the establishment and subsequent winding up of a special fund for such social, cultural or charitable purposes as are specified in the resolution. Section 45 provides that a credit union shall establish a reserve by allocating at least 10% of its surplus funds in each financial year. The reserve shall not be capitalised by way of bonus shares or distributed by way of dividends. The basis on which the allocation to the reserve may be increased or reduced is also defined. Section 46 provides that a credit union may participate in a savings protection scheme which is approved by directions given by the Registrar. Such directions may include the structure of the scheme, the size of contributions and the management of the funds. Section 47 requires a credit union to maintain a policy of insurance to protect against loss to members arising from fraud or dishonesty by its officers or voluntary assistants. Section 48 permits a credit union to provide, as principal or agent, additional services for its members. The provision of any type of additional service by a credit union must *inter alia* be permitted by the credit union's rules, be passed by a resolution of not less than two-thirds of the members present and voting at a general meeting and be subsequently approved by the Registrar under section 49. The Registrar may specify such requirements as he considers necessary for credit unions providing additional services, and if these requirements are not met or if the credit union does not begin to provide the services within 12 months of approval by the Registrar, the credit union shall not provide the specified additional services.

Management of credit unions Section 53 of the 1997 Act specifies the general functions of the board of directors of a credit union and establishes certain provisions in relation to the number of directors, the manner of their election, the length of their term of office and those ineligible to be a director. Section 54 requires that subject to an annual minimum of ten regular meetings, the board of directors meet as often as necessary to discharge its business and that the secretary keep minutes of all its meetings. The board is permitted to fill any casual vacancy, and the person appointed shall hold office until the next general meeting at which an election to the board is held. The secretary is required to notify the Registrar and the Supervisory Committee where he becomes aware that the number of directors is or will within one month be less than half the number specified in the registered rules. Section 55 sets out the functions of the board of directors. These include *inter alia* deciding on membership and loan applications, loan and deposit interest rates, the recommended level of dividend, the maximum sum of shares, deposits and loan applicable to every member, the investment of surplus funds, the borrowing of money by the credit union, the auditing of accounts, the arrangements for general meetings and the establishment of appropriate internal structures and procedures to assist in the proper discharge of the business of the credit union. Section 57 requires that a register of directors be kept by the secretary and signed by all directors. The acts of a director shall be valid notwithstanding the later discovery of any defect in his appointment. The Supervisory Committee shall convene a special general meeting to elect a board of directors in certain specified circumstances. Section 58 provides that a credit union shall have a Supervisory Committee which has the general duty of overseeing the performance by the officers of their functions and that one of their number shall be appointed as secretary of the Committee. Section 63 provides that the board of directors shall elect the directors to fill the principal posts of chairman (or president), vice-chairman (or vice-president), treasurer and secretary. Provision is also made for the holder's term of office, the filling of casual vacancies and the issue to the Registrar of notification of such appointments.

Section 67 provides for the appointment by the board of directors of a credit committee to decide on applications for credit, a credit control committee to ensure the repayments of loans in accordance with the loan agreement and a membership committee to consider applications for credit union membership. The Third Schedule to the 1997 Act specifies that the membership of each committee shall comprise a minimum number of members (including at least one director) and that each committee shall regularly meet and report to the board of directors and comply with any board instructions. Section 68 prohibits the payment, either directly or indirectly, of remuneration to officers (other than the treasurer) and committee members, although it permits (with the approval of the board of directors) the payment or reimbursement of expenses necessarily incurred in the course of their duty. Payment of the treasurer's remuneration must *inter alia* be approved in advance by a general meeting. Officers and voluntary assistants may tender for and supply goods or services to the credit union. Section 70 provides that to be effective, conveyances of property or cheques drawn on the credit union's funds must be signed by at least two officers (one of whom shall be a director). Where the registered rules of the credit union contain specific rules on signatures, compliance with section 70 of the 1997 Act does not render invalid any document which fails to comply with the registered rules. Section 71 prohibits officers or voluntary assistants from disclosing any information dealing with the business of the credit union' except in certain specified circumstances. Every officer and voluntary assistant is required to be informed of and acknowledge his obligations under this section when he takes up office. Section 72 provides that a person who has been adjudicated bankrupt and whose bankruptcy still subsists or who has been convicted of an offence in relation to a credit union or an offence involving fraud or dishonesty shall not be involved in the formation, management or operation of a credit union. If a person is adjudicated bankrupt or is convicted of such an offence during his term of office as a director or member of the Supervisory or a principal Committee, he or she is required to resign forthwith.

Meetings and resolutions   Sections 77 to 83 of the 1997 Act provide for the holding of annual general meetings, special general meetings and passing of resolutions.

Control and supervision of credit unions by registrar Sections 84 to 106 describe the detailed powers and functions of the Registrar of Friendly Societies in the supervision of credit unions with a view to the protection of members' funds and the maintenance of the financial stability and well-being of credit unions generally. In exercising his functions, he may consult with the Credit Union Advisory Committee and other expert or knowledgeable bodies in credit union matters. Neither the State nor the Registrar shall be liable for any losses incurred through the insolvency or default of a registered credit union. Section 85 provides that a credit union shall keep an appropriate proportion of its total assets in liquid form and that the Registrar may require one or more credit unions to comply with a specified asset/liability ratio or with specified requirements for the composition of its assets or liabilities. Section 86 provides that the Registrar may give any credit union directions in relation to the content and form of its advertising, including withdrawing or modifying certain advertisements. Section 87 defines the circumstances in which the Registrar may give regulatory directions to a credit union. Any such directions may include prohibiting the raising of funds, the making of payments and the acquisition or disposal of assets or liabilities for a specified period or requiring the realisation within a defined period of certain investments. The Fourth Schedule provides that a credit union may appeal to the High Court against the making of a regulatory direction and that the Registrar may seek the Court's confirmation, extension, revocation or termination of such a direction. The Court may make such order as if deems fit, including an order for the preparation for Court consideration of a scheme for the orderly termination of the credit union's affairs. Where any regulatory directions are in force, the credit union shall *inter alia* take all necessary steps to ensure that its assets are not depleted.

Accounts and audit Sections 107 to 124 deal with the obligations on a credit union to establish and maintain proper accounting records and systems of control such that they give a true and fair view of the state of affairs of the credit union and to take adequate precautions to ensure the safe keeping and storage of the accounting records in whatever form they take.

Disputes and complaints Sections 125 to 127 deal with the resolution of disputes between a credit union and one of its members or any other persons.

Amalgamations and transfers of engagements Sections 128 to 132 deal with the amalgamation of two or more credit unions and sets out the conditions for the formation of a credit union as their successor and also deal with transfer of engagements.

Winding up   Sections 133 to 136 deal with the power of the Registrar to petition the High Court for an order to wind up a credit union in specified circumstances and for its winding up in accordance with the Companies Acts 1963 to 1990, subject to any necessary modifications, as if a credit union were a company limited by shares.

Appointment of credit union administrator   Sections 137 to 141 provide that on the application of the Registrar, the High Court may make an administration order in specified circumstances. An administrator shall *inter alia* carry on the credit union's business as a going concern with a view to re-establishing the proper and orderly regulation and conduct of the credit union.

Appointment of examiner   Sections 142 to 170 provide that the High Court may appoint an examiner to a credit union to examine the state of its affairs, where it appears *inter alia* that the credit union is or is likely to be unable to pay its debts and where it is nevertheless satisfied that there is a reasonable prospect of the survival of the credit union as a going concern. hey also provide for the effect of such appointment.

Offences and civil proceedings   Section 171 stipulates that unless otherwise provided, a credit union or other person guilty of an offence under the Act shall be liable on summary conviction to a fine not exceeding £1,000 and/ or to three months imprisonment, or in the event of conviction on indictment, to a fine not exceeding £5,000 and/or imprisonment for a term of up to two years. Section 172 provides *inter alia* that where an offence under the Act is committed by a credit union or by a body corporate (other than a credit union) with the consent or connivance of, or is attributable to neglect on the part of, officers and other specified persons in the credit union or body corporate, any such person shall be liable to be punished as if guilty of the offence committed by the credit union or by the body corporate. Various other specific offences are also included in the Act.

Credit Union Advisory Committee   Section 180 provides for the establishment of the Credit Union Advisory Committee, its functions, constitution, membership and the payment of expenses to its members.

FINANCIAL SERVICES

Central Bank   The Central Bank Act 1997 is discussed above, 46–53.

Credit unions   The Credit Union Act 1997 is discussed above, 59–67.

ICC bank The ICC Bank (Amendment) Act 1997 amended the ICC (Amendment) Bank Act 1992 (1992 Review, 5) and increased the amount the ICC Bank is authorised to borrow from £1,300m to £2,300m. The Act also increased the bank's share capital. The Act came into force on May 21, 1997. It was stressed during the Act's passage that it was not related to possible plans for its privatisation and/or merging with the TSB Bank Group, with a view to its becoming a 'third banking force.' It seems unlikely at the time of writing (May 1998) that such a proposal will be implemented.

Investment intermediaries The Investment Intermediaries Act 1995 (Determination Committees) Rules of Procedure 1997 (S.I. No. 381 of 1997), made under the Investment Intermediaries Act 1995 (1995 Review, 41-2) prescribed the rules of procedure to be followed by determination committees appointed under section 74 of the 1995 Act, with effect from September 10, 1997.

Stock exchange The Stock Exchange Act 1995 (Determination Committees) Rules of Procedure 1997 (S.I. No. 380 of 1997), made under the Stock Exchange 1995 (1995 Review, 42) prescribed the rules of procedure to be followed by determination committees appointed under section 65 of the 1995 Act. They came into effect on September 10, 1997.

IMPORTS AND EXPORTS

Pathogens The Importation of Pathogenic Agents Order 1997 (S.I. No. 373 of 1997), made under the Diseases of Animals Act 1966 prohibited the importation of pathogenic agents into the State save under licence from the Minister for Agriculture. The Order came into effect on September 22, 1997.

INSURANCE

Agencies The Insurance Act 1989 (Section 49(3)) Regulations 1997 (S.I. No. 465 of 1997), made under the Insurance Act 1989 (1989 Review, 44-7) brought section 49(2) of the 1989 Act into force on January 1, 1998 thereby limiting to four the number of life and non-life agencies which can be held by an insurance agent.

Brokers In *Dawson v. Irish Brokers Association*, Supreme Court, February 27, 1997 the Supreme Court ordered a re-trial concerning a libel award against the defendant association: see the discussion in the Torts chapter, 775, below.

Policy terms In *Carna Foods Ltd v. Eagle Star Insurance Co. (Ireland) Ltd* [1997] 2 I.L.R.M. 499 (SC), the Supreme Court held that principles of contract law precluded the implication of a term into insurance policies to the effect that in the event of a declinature or cancellation the insurers had to state their reasons therefor: see the discussion in the Contract law chapter, 212, below.

Information The European Communities (Non-Life Insurance and Life Assurance) Framework (Amendment) Regulations 1997 (S.I. No. 457 of 1997) amended the European Communities (Non-Life Insurance and Life Assurance) Framework Regulations 1994 (1994 Review, 39-40) and empower the Minister for Enterprise, Trade and Employment to seek information about companies related to insurance companies and to require auditors to furnish information relating to likely breaches of the insurance legislation. They came into effect on December 15, 1997.

INTELLECTUAL PROPERTY

Fees The Patents, Trade Marks, Copyright and Designs (Fees) Order 1997 (S.I. No. 433 of 1997), made under the Patents Act 1992 (1992 Review, 40-6) and the Trade Marks Act 1996 (1996 Review, 70-6) consolidated with amendments the fees payable in respect of patents and trade marks with effect from November 1, 1997.

Copyright: video In *Universal City Studios Inc v. Mulligan* [1998] 1 I.L.R.M. 438 (HC), Laffoy J. held that a videotape came within the definition of a 'cinematograph film' within the meaning of section 18(10) of the Copyright Act 1963. The plaintiff had instituted proceedings against the defendant, claiming that he had copied videotapes in contravention of the plaintiff's copyright under section 18(10) of the 1963 Act. The defendant contended that videos were not 'copies' within the meaning of the 1963 Act in that they were not cinematograph films, and as such that he had not breached its provisions. The matter was tried as a preliminary issue.

Laffoy J. accepted that the type of videotape technology which existed today was not in contemplation by the draftsmen of the 1963 Act when they defined the expression 'cinematograph film'. Nonetheless, she also held that the proper approach was to look at the language of the definition in section 18(10) in the light of the expert evidence as to the nature of a videotape and the process by which a moving picture was produced by it. In this respect, the evidence indicated that in the case of a videotape, a metal particle tape clearly qualified as 'material of any description' within the meaning of section 18(10) of the 1963 Act. While a sequence of visual images was not observable on the tape, the information of the tape represented such a sequence and had been put on the tape with a view to reproducing the sequence. She pointed out that there was no requirement in the definition in section 18(10) that the sequence of visual images should be observable on the material nor was there a requirement that the tape itself should be capable of reproducing the sequence of visual images without the intervention of other technology. Laffoy J. thus concluded that the language of section 18(10) admitted of production or reproduction of visual images by means of videotape technology and, as indicated, concluded that a videotape was a cinematograph film within the meaning of that expression in section 18(10) of the 1963 Act.

INTERNATIONAL TRADE

International development The International Development Association (Amendment) Act 1997 enabled the State to make a payment of sums not exceeding £13m to the International Development Association (as to which see the 1988 Review, 3, the 1990 Review, 4, and the 1993 Review, 9), the sum designated under the most recent multilateral funding of the Association. This represents 0.13% of the total involved in the replenishment, which is for the period July 1996 to June 1999. The Act came into force on its signature by the President on May 7, 1997.

Iraq The European Communities (Trade With Iraq) Regulations 1997 (S.I. No. 370 of 1997) gave full effect to Regulation (EC) No. 2465/96 and generally prohibits trade with Iraq arising from the 1990 Gulf War, subject to certain limitations involving humanitarian aid. The Regulations also prescribe criminal offences and penalties for breaches of their provisions. They came into effect on September 3, 1997 and replaced the European Communities (Trade With Iraq and Kuwait) Regulations 1990, the European Communities (Trade With Iraq and Kuwait) (No. 2) Regulations 1990, the European Communities (Trade With Iraq and Kuwait) Regulations 1991 and the European Communities (Trade With Iraq and Kuwait) (No. 2) Regulations 1991 (1990 Review, 286 and 1991 Review, 203). The Financial Transfers (Iraq) Order 1997 (S.I. No. 449 of 1997), made under the Financial Transfers Act 1992 (1992 Review, 33-5) deals with the exchange control aspects of the trade restrictions and came into effect on November 7, 1997.

Yugoslavia The Financial Transfers (Federal Republic of Yugoslavia (Serbia And Montenegro)) (Revocation) Order 1997 (S.I. No. 448 of 1997), made under the Financial Transfers Act 1992 (1992 Review, 33-5) revoked the Financial Transfers (Federal Republic of Yugoslavia (Serbia and Montenegro)) Regulations 1992 (1992 Review, 34) which had imposed financial sanctions on Yugoslavia. The 1997 Order, which arose from the ending of the war in former Yugoslavia, came into effect on November 7, 1997.

MERGERS AND TAKE-OVERS

Take-over panel The Irish Take-over Panel Act 1997 provided for the establishment of a Take-over Panel to monitor and supervise take-overs and transaction in securities of certain companies. It conferred powers on the Take-over Panel to make Rules as respect take-overs, to make rulings and give directions and also to advise, admonish or censure companies found to be in breach of the envisaged Rules. The Act provided for the appointment of Panel Directors, hearings by the Panel, applications to the High Court for rulings and appeals against Panel decisions. The Irish Take-over Panel Act 1997 (Commencement) Order 1997 (S.I. No. 158 of 1997) brought the Act, other than sections 5(3), 7(1) and (2), and 9 to 15, into force on April 14, 1997. The Irish Take-over Panel Act 1997 (Commencement) (No. 2) Order 1997 (S.I. No. 255 of 1997) brought these remaining sections of the Act into force on July 1, 1997.

METROLOGY (WEIGHTS AND MEASURES)

Metrology service The Metrology Act 1996 (Commencement and Establishment) Order 1997 (S.I. No. 177 of 1997), made under the Metrology Act 1996 (1996 Review, 65-7), brought the 1996 Act into effect on May 12, 1997 and also provided that the Metrology Service stood established on that day.

Winter time The Winter Time Order 1997 (S.I. No. 484 of 1997), made under the Standard Time (Amendment) Act 1971, varies the period of winter time for the years 1998 to 2001. The Order came into effect on December 9, 1997. The change from winter time to summer time will be effected at 1a.m. rather than 2a.m.

PROMPT PAYMENT BY PUBLIC AUTHORITIES

The Prompt Payment of Accounts Act 1997 provides that the public bodies specified in the Schedule to the Act who buy goods or services must pay the supplier of the goods or services within a prescribed payment date. The Act is part of the general *Strategic Management Initiative* document published in 1994 aimed at achieving greater efficiency in the State sector and should also be seen against the background of agreements between the social partners to protect small and medium sized businesses. The Act provides for an interest penalty payable in the event of late payment. During the passing of the Act, it was estimated that it would result in financial costs for public sector organisations in making payments earlier than would otherwise be the case. It was estimated that the cost of eliminating late payment in the public sector was likely to be somewhere between £3.9m and £10m per annum. On the assumption that suppliers were likely to borrow at overdraft rates on foot of late payments, the benefits to suppliers of the 1997 Act were estimated to be somewhere between £7.6m and £19.7m per annum. The Prompt Payment of Accounts Act 1997 (Commencement) Order 1997 (S.I. No. 239 of 1997) brought the Act into force on January 1, 1998.

The list of public bodies covered by the Act, as listed in the Schedule, runs to over 220, and includes Government Departments, State bodies, universities and hospitals. Section 4 of the 1997 Act requires the public sector purchasers listed who obtain goods or services from a supplier to pay for them by the prescribed payment date. Section 1 defines the prescribed payment date as either: (a) the due date specified in any written contract for the sale of goods or supply of services or (b) 45 days after receipt of an invoice. The Minister for Enterprise, Trade and Employment may specify a shorter time period by Order. Where a purchaser does not pay by the prescribed date, an interest penalty must be paid to the supplier on the amount outstanding, for the period between the prescribed payment date and the date on which the payment is made. The interest penalty is not capable of being waived by the supplier and must be paid without a demand for its payment being made by the supplier. The interest ate is set from time to time by Order of the Minister for Enterprise, Trade and Employment under section 10 of the 1997 Act. The Prompt Payment of Accounts Act 1997 (Rate of Penalty Interest) Order 1997 (S.I. No. 502 of 1997) fixed the rate of interest to be charged under section 4 of the 1997 Act at 0.0322% per day (equivalent to 11.75% per annum) and came into effect on January 2, 1998.

Section 5 provides for the return by the purchaser to the supplier of inadequate or inaccurate invoices for correction and allows for extension of the payment period where the invoice is returned within a specified number of days after receipt of the invoice. The purchaser must furnish a written statement identifying the defects in the invoice that prevent payment being made. Section 6 specifies that certain information must be given when paying penalty interest. Any payment which includes an interest payment must be accompanied by a notice stating the amount of the interest payment included and the rate by which, and the period for which, the interest penalty was computed. Section 7 deals provides that where payment is not made on time due to a dispute as to the amount due, the purchaser shall not be liable to pay interest in respect of the goods in dispute provided that (a) the parties agree that the goods are genuinely in dispute or a court or arbitrator so decides and (b) the purchaser pays for the goods, if any, agreed or determined not to be in dispute. Section 8 provides that where there is a dispute relating to the payment of an interest penalty, the supplier may submit the dispute to arbitration. The arbitrator may be appointed by agreement between the parties or, in the absence of such agreement, by the President of the Law Society of Ireland or such other person as the Minister for Enterprise, Trade and Employment may prescribe. The Arbitration Acts 1954 to 1980 will apply to the arbitration. Section 9 deals with prompt payment to sub-contractors. It provides that a main contractor on a public sector contract must provide the same payment period to a sub-contractor as is set down in the main contractor's written contract with the public body, unless otherwise provided in the contract between the main contractor and sub-contractor. Section 11 empowers the Minister, by order, to restrict the payment period to 45 days where he/she is of the opinion that the practices of a purchaser allow the purchaser credit terms that are unreasonable in the circumstances. Section 12 deals with the disclosure of payment practices by public sector purchasers. Where the purchaser is required by statute to publish an annual report, the report must include details of the purchaser's payment practice in the period covered by the report. Where the purchaser is not required to publish an annual report, an annual review of payment practice must be lodged with the Minister and the Minister shall ensure that a copy of the review is laid before the Houses of the Oireachtas. Section 13 provides that an auditor auditing the affairs of a public sector purchaser shall report on whether, in all material respects, the purchaser has complied with the provisions of the 1997 Act.

Section 14 deals with tax clearance certificates and withholding tax. It provides that where a supplier has failed to comply with a request from a purchaser to provide a tax clearance certificate, the Act does not require payment of any amount due to the supplier. It also provides that if a supplier does not furnish a tax clearance certificate within seven days after being so requested, the prescribed payment period shall cease to run from the expiration of that seven day period until the tax clearance certificate has been shown. Section 14 also permits the deduction of withholding tax from any payment.

Communications

Eamonn G. Hall

THE INFORMATION SOCIETY, 1997

Communications law and regulation are entwined with the shaping of the Information Society. During 1997 significant legislative changes occurred in the regulation of the communications sector, particularly in relation to the telecommunication carrier services. Most of these legislative developments emanated from the institutions of the European Union and European Community.

The *Information Society Ireland, Strategy for Action Report* published by the Information Society Steering Committee in 1997 ('the 1997 Report') established by the Minister for Enterprise and Employment, set out many issues of a legal and regulatory nature facing the communications sector – some of which are considered in detail in this chapter. In the preface, Richard Bruton, TD, Minister for Enterprise and Employment, noted that the development and convergence of information and communication technologies had the potential to transform our society, the way we do business, our capacity to engage in life-long learning and the way we deliver public services.

The chairman of the Steering Committee, Vivienne Jupp, noted in her foreword that as the Information Society takes shape, Ireland had a unique window of opportunity: Ireland had the position of carving out for itself a strong and sustainable position as a location with a competitive advantage for information- based services.

Many legal issues were considered in the 1997 Report. The Report emphasised the importance of a predictable legal framework and, in particular, an appropriate legal framework for intellectual property rights and related areas of law. The Report called for a Government strategy updating statutory protection for intellectual property rights; the establishment of statutory protection for new forms of work and organisation, *e.g.* teleworking; the implementation of a range of measures aimed at prevention, detection and prosecution of fraudulent and illegal uses of the new technologies; the assessment and amendment of the law in the area of data protection and privacy; and the impact of the Information Society, in particular on value added taxes and the general tax code as appropriate.

The 1997 Report recommended, in the context of the regulation of Ireland's telecommunications market and the Telecommunications (Miscellaneous Provisions) Act 1996, that the Director of Telecommunications Regulation ('the Director') should be independent and sufficiently empowered to ensure a fair and competitive market in telecommunications infrastructure and service provision in Ireland. Priorities were specified for the Director as including, fair and competitive practices in the telecommunications marketplace; appropriate administrative and licensing procedures in respect of infrastructure provision in advance of liberalisation; fair and transparent rules on interconnection; prices relative to the costs of an efficient operator; appropriate measures to ensure the provision of leased lines of capacity greater that 2 Mbits and an objective management of the radio spectrum to facilitate its optimum use for telecommunications. The Report considered that the Irish Government needed to amend existing legislation and introduce new legislation to develop an appropriate legal framework that would encourage the deployment and use of information and communications technologies in enterprises and in homes. The Report submitted that a small group of legal experts should be commissioned to track legal developments in the United States and in Europe.

The 1997 Report noted that the Copyright Act 1963 did not regulate adequately copyright issues in the Information Age. Immediate attention was demanded for the appropriate transposition of EU Directives on rental and lending rights, databases and cable and satellite deregulation. Further, the 1997 Report demanded that adequate legal and administrative resources should be allocated to the intellectual property unit of the sponsoring Government Department.

In relation to the control of so-called offensive material, the 1997 Report called for specific provisions that would criminalise the collection, storage or use of digitised images that are obscene or pornographic in the context of the Censorship of Films Acts 1923 to 1970, the Video Recordings Act 1989 and the Copyright Act 1963, customs legislation, wireless telegraphy and telecommunications laws.

In particular, the Report urged the Data Protection Act 1988 be amended to give effect to the EU Directive on data protection. On the issue of prevention, detection and prosecution of computer related crime, the Report urged the adoption of the Law Reform Commission's *The Law Relating to Dishonesty Report (1992)* and the updating of legislation prohibiting fraudulent conduct to take account of the Information Age. Further, contractual practices, insurance issues, liability issues and evidentiary matters also needed to be addressed.

The Report in essence set out a vision for Ireland as an information society and the goals necessary to achieve that vision. The Report explored the legal and regulatory issues constituting the forces pushing Ireland towards a future dominated by information and communications technologies. The Report emphasised that citizens, communities, enterprises and government all had a part to play in creating Ireland's information society.

BROADCASTING

Broadcasting Complaints Commission   The eighteenth annual report of the Broadcasting Complaints Commission, a statutory tribunal established pursuant to the Broadcasting Authority Act 1960 as amended by the Broadcasting Authority (Amendment) Act 1976 was published in 1997. The chairperson of the Commission is Ms Geri Silke, Barrister. The report, addressed to the Minister for Arts, Culture and the Gaeltacht, was laid before both Houses of the Oireachtas.

Fourteen formal decisions of the Commission were published in the 1997 annual report. All of the complaints related to radio and television programmes on RTÉ, although the jurisdiction of the Broadcasting Complaints Commission was, pursuant to the Radio and Television Act 1988 (Complaints by Members of the Public) Regulations 1992 (S.I. No. 329 of 1992) extended to any sound broadcasting service or any television programme service provided under the Radio and Television Act 1988. These services are sometimes designated as the independent broadcasting services.

In the *Complaint of Kenneth Ahern*, it was alleged that a particular RTÉ One television programme, 'Questions and Answers', on the topic of the divorce referendum, was not fair to all interests and that the subject matter was not presented in an objective and impartial manner as required by section 18 of the Broadcasting Authority Act 1960 as amended by section 3 of the Broadcasting Authority (Amendment) Act 1976. Mr Ahern stated that four of the five questions addressed by members of the studio audience to the panel on the television programme were asked by persons who were aligned to the pro-divorce side. He argued that this course of action obliged the anti-divorce panellists alone to adopt a defensive posture in answering the questions posed, thereby preventing them from raising issues pertaining to the pro-divorce campaign. Mr Ahern submitted that the producer and presenter of the programme would have been aware of the bias in favour of the pro-divorce interests but proceeded with the presentation knowing that it would not be fair, balanced and impartial. Mr Ahern argued that as the questions were selected by the programme manager before the programme began, the producer had failed to be fair and impartial in the selection of questions and the questioners, because all the questions accepted by the programme presenter emanated from the pro- divorce side.

RTÉ submitted that the programme makers made extensive efforts to structure the programme in an even-handed way. The panel contained two speakers in favour of divorce, Michael Noonan and Peter Ward, and two speakers against divorce, Rosemary Swords and Mr Justice Rory O'Hanlon. The audience was stated by RTÉ to be divided into an equal number people in favour of divorce and an equal number against divorce. RTÉ argued that to submit that the RTÉ programme should have been absolutely balanced was unreasonable and indeed unrealistic in such a lively studio debate involving a panel and some sixty persons. Having viewed the programme on a number of occasions, the Commission considered that there had been no breach of the statutory duty of fairness and impartiality by RTÉ. The Commission considered that there had been ample opportunity for both sides to make their own views known and the Commission dismissed the complaint.

The alleged lack of impartiality in a broadcast on RTÉ 1 news relating to water charges was considered in the *Complaint of R.B. Haslam*. Mr Haslam complained that the anti-water charges lobby was given extensive coverage including two interviews, one with the leader of the anti-water charges campaign and one with a defeated candidate in a by-election who had campaigned on the water charges issue. Mr Haslam submitted that two relevant aspects relating to water charges were not referred to in any way in the programme. The first such matter related to the Local Government (Financial Provisions) (No. 2) Act 1983 which made provision for a waiver in relation to water charges if a person was not in a financial position to pay the charges. Secondly, there was a provision in a recent Government Budget which had allowed charges to be included for income tax relief up to a maximum of £150 per annum. Mr Haslam complained that the programme lacked objectivity and could do serious damage to local authorities in their efforts to collect relevant charges.

The Commission considered that the broadcast was not fair to all interests concerned and in particular was not fair to the interests of local authorities. The Commission accepted that RTÉ did intend to have the Minister for the Environment speak on the programme but this did not occur and he was not replaced by someone who could represent the interests of local authorities. The Commission was further of the opinion that RTÉ did not discharge its responsibilities under the broadcasting legislation and held that the programme was not balanced and presented in an impartial manner.

In the *Complaint of Eamonn Hannan*, the chief executive of the Western Health Board, complained about the Primetime television programme on RTÉ One which was based on a published report on the events that led to the death of Kelly Fitzgerald, a young girl in the West of Ireland, and the role of the Western Health Board in those events. The programme took the form of a summary of a previously transmitted documentary which considered the events surrounding the death of Ms Fitzgerald, and a studio discussion. Mr Hannan complained that sections of the programme were unfair to the Western Health Board and to the relevant staff of the Board and were not presented in an objective and impartial manner, without expression of the RTÉ Authority's own views. Mr Hannan referred to extracts from the introduction by Ms Hilary

Orpen and submitted that they were unfair to the interests of the Western Health Board and that the presentation was not objective and impartial.

In its response, RTÉ denied that the programme was in breach of RTÉ's statutory obligations under the broadcasting legislation and stated that Ms Orpen made repeated efforts to communicate with Mr Hannan of the Western Health Board in order to ascertain his version of events and to offer him an opportunity to participate in the programme but, it was claimed, he had failed to accept any of her telephone calls. In upholding the complaint of Mr Hannan, the Commission considered that RTÉ had failed in its statutory obligations of fairness. It held that the programme was not fair to all interests concerned and, in particular, was not fair to the interests of the Western Health Board. Further the Commission considered that the programme was not presented in an objective and impartial manner.

International issues were considered in the *Complaint of Declan McKenna*. Mr McKenna, on behalf of the Cuba Support Group – Ireland, complained about the 'one-sided' RTÉ news coverage of the shooting down of two aircraft by the Cuban airforce. Mr McKenna also complained about the *Morning Ireland* radio programme on RTÉ 1 in which there were interviews with Bob Dole, then a US Presidential candidate, a number of Cuban Americans in Miami and with US President Clinton. There was no comment from any Cuban source. Mr McKenna submitted that this report contained calls for the overthrow of the Cuban government and that the radio news coverage was biased and did not provide listeners with an accurate, balanced view on the incident.

In its response, RTÉ submitted that the broadcast coverage of the shooting down of two US aircraft must be viewed in the context of how this story developed across radio and television news programming at that time. The *Morning Ireland* editorial staff had commissioned a report from RTÉ's Washington Correspondent on the story, the focus of which was to be on the reaction to the incident on the part of the US Government and Cuban exiles. RTÉ submitted that at the time of commissioning and editing of the report, there was no on-the-record reaction from the Cuban Government which could have been incorporated into the report. The Commission held that both programmes complained of were not fair to all interests concerned. The Commission, upholding the complaint, held that the programmes were not presented in an objective and impartial manner and, therefore, RTÉ was held to be in breach of its statutory obligation of fairness.

The *Complaint of Anthony Coughlan* concerning uncontested party political broadcasts on RTÉ during the divorce referendum was subsequently litigated in the High Court. Mr Coughlan's complaint related to RTÉ's policy of allocating uncontested radio and television broadcasts to the Oireachtas political parties in the course of the divorce referendum and constitutional referenda in general. Mr Coughlan submitted that the RTÉ Authority's statutory obligations under section 17 of the Broadcasting Authority Act 1960 as amended by section 13 of the Broadcasting Authority (Amendment) Act 1976 direct RTÉ, *inter alia*, to uphold the democratic values enshrined in the Constitution, especially those relating to rightful liberty of expression. Mr Coughlan contended that in the context of a constitutional referendum, that obligation required RTÉ to refrain from exercising the permissive power which the Authority possesses under section 18(2) of the Broadcasting Authority Act 1960 to transmit uncontested broadcasts on behalf of political parties.

Mr. Coughlan requested the Broadcasting Complaints Commission to uphold that contention and to direct RTÉ to base its policy upon that contention in future referenda. Mr Coughlan further submitted it was clear that RTÉ was under no statutory obligation to give the political parties uncontested broadcasting facilities in referenda. Referenda were occasions on which the political parties play a different role in the political process from what may be described as candidate elections. In constitutional referenda it is the citizens themselves who are legislating directly. The choice is always a straight one between 'yes' or 'no' to a particular proposition. To grant an uncontested political broadcast facility to a political party was, in effect, it was submitted, to leave it to the leadership of that party to decide the content of the broadcast message. Such content rarely, if ever, reflected the divided views of the party's members and supporters and usually constituted a partisan presentation of the referendum issue in question, according to Mr Coughlan. In a constitutional referendum context, where most or all of the political parties and their leaderships are lined up on one side, this unnecessary and gratuitous practice by RTÉ has, or could have, the effect of using 'State' radio and television to make a one-sided, unbalanced presentation of the referendum issue, which in turn impinges directly and adversely on the rights of citizens to equality and fairness in the referendum process.

Mr. Coughlan submitted that the RTÉ Authority's policy on the divorce referendum had the effect of committing a total of 42.5 minutes of uncontested broadcasting time to the 'Yes' side and 10 minutes to the 'No' campaign between certain dates. Mr Coughlan requested the Broadcasting Complaints Commission to uphold the principle that RTÉ's statutory obligations, in effect, permitted no uncontested broadcasting at all in referenda and so confining the coverage of the issues to current affairs programmes, where the views of the political parties could be quite adequately considered, or else to allocate uncontested broadcast facilities on a 50/50 basis to both 'Yes' and 'No' campaigns divided between non-party groups and political parties whether inside or outside the Oireachtas.

Mr. Coughlan further requested the Commission to hold that RTÉ's policy of gratuitously granting uncontested broadcast facilities to political parties in referenda had the effect of using the 'State' broadcasting system to confer a significant advantage on one side in those referendum contests in certain circumstances. Mr Coughlan also complained that RTÉ's unscheduled second transmission of a broadcast by the Right to Re-marry Group a few days before the referendum without according a counter-balancing repeat facility to the other side, violated the statutory principles of fairness, impartiality and objectivity of the treatment of current affairs in matters of public controversy that RTÉ was obliged to uphold.

RTÉ, in its response to the *Coughlan Complaint*, stated that it recognised the particular character of constitutional referenda. RTÉ submitted that it allocated equal time to the presentation of the arguments in favour of and against the issue to be determined by the people once the relevant bill was passed by the Dáil and Seanad. That policy informed RTÉ's approach to the 1995 Divorce Referendum. RTÉ stated that over the years it had allocated political party broadcasts to qualifying parties in Dáil Éireann in relation to most referenda. Those broadcasts were allocated without regard to the views likely to be expressed therein by the parties. The nature of a political party broadcast was that its contents are determined by the political party concerned. RTÉ stated that it had no role in relation to the content of such broadcasts and never had any such role. The precise allocation of time for a political party broadcast was based on well-established guidelines. Party political broadcasts were transmitted in accordance with section 18(2) of the Broadcasting Authority Act 1960.

RTÉ submitted that section 18(1) of the Broadcasting Authority Act (as amended) as it relates to objectivity, impartiality and fairness does not apply to political party broadcasts. Consequently, these broadcasts have to be left out of an account of any evaluation of RTÉ's discharge of its statutory obligations in the 1995 Divorce referendum. RTÉ referred to the decision of Laffoy J. in *Kenny v. RTÉ*, High Court, November 20, 1995, where Laffoy J. held that RTÉ, having regard to its statutory obligations, was entitled to allocate time for political party broadcasts at the time of a referendum without being obliged to have regard to the content of the views expressed in such broadcasts.

The Commission in its determination held that RTÉ did not breach its statutory obligations in broadcasting the various party political broadcasts. Section 18(2) of the Broadcasting Authority Act 1960 allowed RTÉ to broadcast party political broadcasts in the context of referenda. Accordingly, the Commission dismissed this part of Mr Coughlan's complaint. However, in broadcasting the second transmission of a broadcast by the Right to Re-Marry Group (which was not a party political broadcast) on 19 November 1995, RTÉ did breach its statutory obligations according to the Commission. RTÉ failed to counter-balance this programme by either giving a repeat facility to the opposing side or in some other way addressing the imbalance. The Commission upheld that part of the complaint.

The complainant, Anthony Coughlan subsequently instituted High Court proceedings against the Broadcasting Complaints Commission, RTÉ and the

Attorney General. Carney J. in his judgment on April 24, 1998 upheld certain contentions of Mr Coughlan. The High Court judgment in *Coughlan* will be considered in the 1998 Annual Review.

Government's Proposals for Broadcasting Legislation   During 1997, the Government published its proposals for broadcasting legislation. The publication, *Clear Focus, the Government's Proposals for Broadcasting Legislation*, represented the heads of bill which the Minister for Arts, Culture and the Gaeltacht had brought to the Government and which the Government had agreed should be drafted in a bill to be introduced in the Oireachtas.

The introduction to the Government's paper on broadcasting stated that there had been no fundamental review of the television and radio services since the Broadcasting Authority (Amendment) Act 1976. It was noted that the Radio and Television Act 1988 made no substantial change to the Broadcasting Authority Acts and was in fact modelled on them. The Broadcasting Act 1990 and the Broadcasting Authority (Amendment) Act 1993 addressed specific issues of broadcasting policy without making any fundamental change to overall broadcasting structures.

The Minister noted that the development of digital compression of television signals was the most recent technological advance in broadcasting. Digital transmission would dramatically increase the number, flexibility and technical quality of services available to viewers. All forms of information, whether in the form of moving or still images, sound, text or data, would be made available more widely in an interactive manner. The implementation of digital technology would allow easy inter-working between television terminals, multi-media workstations, personal computers and other information terminals resulting in flexible access to a wide range of information and services. For viewers and listeners, the distinction between telecommunications and broadcasting would become increasingly difficult to determine. These developments had the potential for giving listeners and viewers a variety of choices and increased control over their viewing and listening. Implications for the programme content of this virtually unlimited transmission capacity were stated to be serious. The vast majority of new services would be commercial activities driven ultimately by the profit imperative and funded by means of advertising, subscription and pay-per-view arrangements.

The Minister submitted that from a cultural, social, economic and broadcasting policy perspective, support for public service broadcasting needed to be maintained for the foreseeable future. The ethos of public service broadcasting was therefore to be safeguarded and restated in statutory terms. A balance would have to be struck between the legitimate aspirations of programme makers in addressing a wide audience, attractive to advertisers, and the rights of all citizens in a democratic society to be able to find in the broadcasting schedules, at reasonable times and in reasonable quantity, programming that appeals to their tastes and interests. The Minister emphasised that by the expression 'public service broadcasting' he meant a service provided by a broadcaster or broadcasters in the public service, as distinct from the concept of segments of public service programming within a commercially-run broadcasting service.

The Minister proposed a fundamental change in the broadcasting structures currently in existence. The main features of the proposals included:

- a clear definition of public service broadcasting as a broadcasting service provided by a publicly-owned broadcaster;

- a clear statement in legislation that public service broadcasting is an essential and central part of the mix of broadcasting services in Ireland;

- the establishment of a single regulatory and policy-making body – the Irish Broadcasting Commission – to oversee the broadcasting sector in Ireland (including the regulation of local and community services on cable television and multi-point microwave distribution systems (MMDS), satellite broadcasting, educational television services etc);

- the conversion of the RTÉ Authority into a statutory broadcasting corporation, to be charged with operating the present RTÉ services consistent with the general policy objectives adopted by the new Commission and the new legislation;

- the establishment of Teilifís na Gaeilge as a separate statutory corporation, to be charged with operating Teilifís na Gaelige consistent with the general policy objectives of the Commission and the legislation.

It was proposed that the existing functions of the Independent Radio and Television Commission would be transferred to the new Broadcasting Commission. The Commission would consist of five full-time members including a chairperson, be appointed by the Government after a formal interviewing process and subject to approval by both Houses of the Oireachtas. The chairperson and members would serve for a seven-year term during which time they would not hold any other office or paid employment, to ensure maximum commitment and impartiality.

The main functions of the proposed Broadcasting Commission would include:

- to arrange for the provision of nation-wide broadcasting services, including Irish language broadcasting services to be provided by a State-owned broadcaster or broadcasters;

- to arrange for the provision of broadcasting services other than those provided by State-owned broadcasters, including local, regional and nationwide services, including those provided on cable television and MMDS systems;

- to arrange for the issuing of broadcasting receiving licences and the collection of the licence fee;

- to pay the ongoing Exchequer grant to Teilifís na Gaelige;

- to arrange for the provision and maintenance of a broadcast transmission system or systems commensurate with the development of relevant technologies;

- to provide general advice to the Minister with responsibility for broadcasting and, as necessary, to the Minister for the Public Enterprise on broadcasting issues, including the application of new technology, the performance of RTÉ in meeting its public-service remit, and the contribution of Irish broadcasters to the independent programming, music sectors and economy generally;

- to set general programming standards;

- to draw up and amend, from time to time, codes regulating broadcast advertising and sponsorship;

- to control the amount of time allocated to advertising on all broadcasting services, including the power to prohibit advertisements during certain times and on certain services;

- to perform the investigative functions of the present Broadcasting Complaints Commission and to adopt a more active role in monitoring compliance with codes of programme standards and adherence by broadcasters to contracts and legal obligations.

The Government proposals noted that while the Broadcasting Complaints Commission had performed its functions admirably, it had no powers of a disciplinary nature. The proposed Broadcasting Commission would be empowered to impose (non-monetary) penalties where breaches of duties occur.

The subsequent Minister for Arts, Heritage, Gaeltacht and the Islands in the Fianna Fáil/Progressive Democrats Government, Ms Síle de Valera, published details of the Cabinet's approval for legislation on July 23, 1998. These will be considered in the 1998 Annual Review.

Independent Radio and Television Commission   In *Radio Limerick One Ltd v. Independent Radio and Television Commission,* January 1997, [1997] 2 IRLM 1 (SC) the law pertaining to certiorari, the issue of reasonableness, proportionality, bias, and the test of proportionality applicable to administrative decisions arose in the context of judicial review. This chapter will only consider the issues in that case relating to communications law.

Section 14(4) of the Radio and Television Act 1988 provides that every sound broadcasting contract shall provide that the Independent Radio and Television Commission ('the Commission') may, at its discretion, suspend or terminate a sound broadcasting contract if, *inter alia*, the sound broadcasting contractor has, in the opinion of the Commission, committed 'serious or repeated' breaches of its obligations under the sound broadcasting contract or under the 1988 Act. Section 10(4) of the Radio and Television Act 1988 provides that the total daily times for broadcasting advertisements in a sound broadcasting service provided pursuant to a sound broadcasting contract shall not exceed a maximum of 15% of the total daily time and the maximum time to be given to advertisements in any one hour shall not exceed ten minutes.

The Commission alleged that Radio Limerick One had exceeded the maximum times permitted under section 10 of the 1988 Act for advertisements, by conducting outside broadcasts at shops in Limerick which included extensive references to the products and services available at the shops in question. Radio Limerick One challenged the decision of the Commission to terminate the sound broadcasting contract. The radio station did so by way of judicial review. On October 14, 1996 Smyth J. refused the application for judicial review and the applicant appealed to the Supreme Court. (See Annual Review 1996, 80–81)

The Supreme Court in *Radio Limerick One*, in a judgment delivered by Keane J. (with Hamilton C.J. and Barrington J. concurring) dismissed the appeal of *Radio Limerick One* and held that there had been evidence upon which the Commission was entitled to form the opinion that Radio Limerick One had committed 'serious or repeated breaches' of its obligations under the sound broadcasting contract and under the Radio and Television Act 1988. In reaching its decision, the Commission was also entitled to take into account those breaches which were not serious in nature or which had not since been remedied. In construing the term 'advertisements' under section 10 of the Radio and Television Act 1988 the Supreme Court held that regard must be had to the policy of the legislation so as to ensure a reasonable balance between advertising and the provision of news, entertainment and programmes. On a common-sense approach, outside broadcasts which took the form of programmes containing details of the products and prices of the businesses concerned and the fact that those businesses were selected by the radio station on the basis of the extent to which they contributed to the station's advertising revenues over a given period, constituted advertising. Keane J. considered that he was satisfied that not merely was the Commission entitled to adopt the interpretation that such outside broadcasts constituted advertising but that any other construction of the relevant provisions would seriously frustrate the policy of the legislature. It followed that the decision of the Commission was not vitiated by any error in law which would have entitled the High Court to set it aside.

The issue of advertising was also considered in the judgment of Geoghegan J. in *Murphy v. Independent Radio and Television Commission and the Attorney General* [1997] 2 I.L.R.M. 467. Section 10(3) of the Radio and Television Act 1988 ('the 1988 Act') provides that no advertisement shall be broadcast which is directed towards any religious or political end or which has any relation to an industrial dispute. The Commission refused to permit Mr Murphy to transmit a religious advertisement on a radio station known as 98FM on behalf of the Irish Faith Centre on the ground that it breached section 10(3) of the 1988 Act. Mr Murphy then sought a judicial review quashing that decision. First, Mr Murphy submitted that the advertisement did not breach section 10(3) of the 1988 Act. He claimed that the advertisement was simply a notification of the occurrence of a particular religious event. Secondly, it was submitted that even if the advertisement did breach the sub-section, the sub-section was invalid having regard to the Constitution. In this regard, the applicant submitted that the sub-section breached Article 40.3.1° (vindication of the personal rights of the citizen), Article 40.6.1°.i (freedom of expression) Article 44.2.1 (freedom of conscience and the free profession of practice of religion to every citizen) and Article 44.2.3 which prohibits the imposition by the State of any disabilities or the making of any discrimination on the ground of religious profession, belief or status.

Geoghegan J. refused the application in *Murphy* for judicial review quashing the decision of the Commission. Geoghegan J. held that it was clear from the advertisement that the radio listener was being led to at least favourably consider the proposition that Christ is the son of the living God and that the traditional beliefs about Christ are in fact historical facts. He considered that the advertisement constituted more than a mere notification of an event. He considered that the advertisement clearly infringed Section 10(3) of the 1988 Act. Geoghegan J. considered that the prohibition on the broadcast of the advertisement was not an attack on freedom of conscience or the free practice of religion as guaranteed by Article 44.2.1 of the Constitution. The refusal to broadcast the advertisement did not constitute discrimination on the ground of religious profession, belief or status as prohibited by Article 44.2.3 of the Constitution.

There are not two distinct rights of communication conferred by Article 40.3.1°, on the one hand, and Article 40.6.1°.i, on the other hand. According to Geoghegan J. Article 40.6.1°.i does not confer a new right to communicate but rather gives special protection to a particular form of the right to communicate as conferred by Article 40.3.1°. Geoghegan J. considered that Article 40.3.1° is the constitutional source for the basic right to communicate whether it be information or opinion. As such, the right of the citizen to express freely his or her convictions and opinions contained in Article 40.6.1°.i was merely an aspect of the unenumerated personal right to communicate as contained in Article 40.3.1°. of the Constitution. The decisions in the *Attorney General v. Paperlink Ltd* [1984] I.L.R.M. 373 and *Oblique Financial Services Ltd. v. The Promise Production Co. Ltd* [1994] I.R.L.M. 74 were applied.

Geoghegan J. considered that Article 40.6.1°.i had no particular relevance to the facts of this case. First, the proposed advertisement, although it did implicitly contain matters of opinion had, as its principal source, the communication of information. He considered that Article 40.6.1°.i did not appear to apply to every expression of opinion. For example, it did not appear to apply to the right of a citizen to express private opinions with a view to influencing some other person or persons. Article 40.6.1°.i was mainly directed at protecting the expression of opinions whether deriving from groups or otherwise with a view to influencing public opinion. By its very nature, according to the judge, it involved plurality and the influencing of public opinion. An advertisement on radio was addressed to the individual listener rather than to the public at large and, according to Geoghegan J., Article 40.6.1°.i had no relevance to it.

Article 10(1) of the European Convention of Human Rights which provides that everyone has the right to freedom of expression and that this right includes freedom to hold opinions and receive and impart information and ideas without interference by public authorities regardless of frontiers was raised and considered in *Murphy*. The rights protected by Article 10 of the Convention according to the judge were for the most part protected by Article 40.3.1° of the Constitution and the limitations on the exercise of those rights and the interests of the common good largely corresponded to the limitations expressly permitted by Article 10 of the Convention. Accordingly, in a general sense, there was no inconsistency between the Constitution and Article 10 of the Convention.

Geoghegan J. considered the licensing system of broadcasting adopted by a state can involve restrictions on freedom of expression which go beyond the restrictions permitted in Article10(2) of the Convention. The High Court considered that it was reasonable for the Oireachtas to take the view that in Irish society religious advertising on commercial radio might be undesirable in the public interest. Irish people with religious beliefs tend to belong to particular churches and religious advertising coming from a different church could be offensive to many people and could be interpreted as proselytising. The High Court considered that it was legitimate for the Oireachtas to have regard to these matters. The ban was a reasonable restriction on the right to communicate in the interests of the common good. The ratios in *Informationsverein Lentia v. Austria* (1994) 17 E.H.R.R. 93 and *R. v. Radio Authority, ex parte Bull* [1995] 3 W.L.R. 572 were applied.

Finally, Geoghegan J. considered that the absolute ban on the advertisement of religious matters was not a disproportionate measure. He considered that it would not be possible in practice to devise a form of legislative wording that might have the effect of permitting certain alleged categories of innocuous religious advertising. He considered that the advertisement was directed towards a religious end which could be regarded as potentially offensive to the public.

The plaintiff appealed to the Supreme Court. On 28 May, 1998, the Supreme Court upheld the decision of Geoghegan J. The Supreme Court decision in *Murphy* will be considered in the 1998 Annual Review.

The issues of natural justice and alleged procedural irregularities in relation to the granting of a broadcasting licence by the Independent Radio and Television Commission were considered by the High Court in the case of *Maigueside Communications Limited v. Independent Radio and Television Commission*. Judgment was given by McGuinness J. on July 18, 1997. The High Court considered that the detriment suffered by the applicants did not arise from the Commission's failure to give the reasons for its decision but from the actual rejection of their applications and refused the relief sought.

Intellectual Property   Issues in the context of radio broadcasting and the issue of whether certain action constituted passing off were considered by Costello J. in *Radio Limerick One Limited v. Treaty Radio Limited*. The judgment of Costello J. was given on November 13, 1997. Costello J. held that the defendant did not commit the actionable wrong of passing off as the defendant had not made any representation that its business was part of the business of Radio Limerick One Limited or that it was in any way associated with Radio Limerick One Limited.

Re-transmission of television signals   The issue of the broadcasting re- transmission systems known as multi-point microwave distribution systems (MMDS), the controversy surrounding the licensing of re-transmission of television signals and the so-called deflector systems, were considered by the High Court in *MMDS Television Limited v. South East Community Deflector Association Limited*. Carroll J. delivered judgment in the case on April 8, 1997.

The plaintiffs were holders of licences granted under the Wireless Telegraphy Act 1926 and the Broadcasting and Wireless Telegraphy Act 1988 permitting them to broadcast television services by means of MMDS. The plaintiffs claimed that the licences were exclusive, that they had expended a considerable sum of money to provide television service by way of MMDS and cable and sought injunctive relief against the allegedly unlawful operators of the deflector systems. The central issue in the case was the balance of convenience test and on whether an injunction should be granted. Carroll J. held that the Wireless Telegraphy Act 1926 and the Broadcasting and Wireless Telegraphy Act 1988 conferred rights on individual licence holders as well as protecting the public. The court considered that the adequacy of the criminal sanction imposed by law could be judged by the absence of prosecutions. If a person's right under statute was being eroded by un-checked illegal activity, they were entitled to come into court and submit that the criminal sanction was not just inadequate but was in fact absent. In this context, the court applied the *ratio* in *Parson v. Kavanagh* [1990] I.L.R.M. 560, and *O'Connor v. Williams* [1996] 2 I.L.R.M. 382.

MMDS Television Limited argued that the deflector systems had interfered with their constitutional right to earn a living and the High Court considered that there was a fair issue to be tried between the views expressed in *PMPA v. Attorney General* [1983] I.R. 339 and *Iarnrod Éireann v. Ireland* [1995] 2 I.L.R.M. 161. The High Court considered that damages were not an adequate remedy as the plaintiffs had contended that it was extremely difficult for them to quantify damages because the damage was the loss of potential customers. The High Court considered, on the facts of the case, that the balance of convenience lay with the plaintiffs. The plaintiffs were entitled to bring the application under section 27 of the Local Government (Planning and Development) Act 1976 to restrain unauthorised use. The discretion to be exercised under section 27 of the 1976 Act was covered by the discretion exercised in granting the injunction.

INTERCEPTION

Section 8 of the Interception of Postal Packets and Telecommunications Messages (Regulation) Act 1993 ('the 1993 Act') provides that the President of the High Court shall from time to time after consultation with the Minister for Justice invite a person who is a judge of the High Court to undertake the duty of keeping the operation of the 1993 Act under review and ascertaining whether its provisions have been complied with. The designated judge is to report to the Taoiseach at such intervals (being intervals of not more than twelve months) as the designated judge thinks desirable in relation to the general operation of the Act and from time to time in relation to any matters relating to the 1993 Act which the judge considers should be so reported.

The designated judge is empowered pursuant to the 1993 Act to investigate any case in which an authorisation has been given and is empowered to have access to and may inspect any official documents relating to the authorisation for interception or an application therefor. The Hon. Mr Justice Declan Costello was appointed by the Government at a meeting on September 8, 1993 to be the designated judge under section 8 of the 1993 Act. Reporting to the Taoiseach on July 14, 1997 Costello J. stated that since his last report, (his third report dated July 19, 1996), he had kept the operation of the 1993 Act under review and was satisfied that its provisions were being complied with.

The Secretary to the Government certified that no matter had been excluded from the judge's report and this was so certified pursuant to section 8(8) of the 1993 Act.

Section 111(5) of the Postal and Telecommunications Services Act 1983 ('the 1983 Act') provides that where a licence is granted under section 111 of the 1983 Act to any person to perform any telecommunications function, every provision of the 1983 Act or any other enactment relating to Telecom Éireann which is specified in regulations made by the Minister for Public Enterprise shall, in respect of that function, and subject to such conditions, limitations and modifications as may be prescribed in such regulations, apply to the licensee as it applies to Telecom Éireann.

The Postal and Telecommunications Services Act 1983, (Section 111(5)) Regulations 1997 (S.I. No. 517 of 1997) ('the 1997 Regulations') provided that two sections of the 1983 Act were to apply to Eircell Ltd and ESAT Digifone Ltd in respect of their respective mobile telephony licences. The first section to be applied was section 98 of the 1983 Act. Section 98 of the 1983 Act as amended by section 13 of the Interception of Postal Packets and Telecommunications Messages (Regulation) Act 1993 prohibits the interception of telecommunications messages and the disclosure, existence, substance or purport of any such message which has been intercepted. Further, the use for any purpose of any information obtained from such message is also prohibited. Subject to certain exceptions, a person acting in contravention of the section shall be guilty of an offence. The penalties are specified in section 4 of the 1983 Act. A person who contravenes section 98 of the 1983 Act shall be liable on summary conviction to a fine not exceeding £800 or at the discretion of the court to imprisonment for a term not exceeding 12 months or to both the fine and imprisonment. Upon conviction on indictment, a person is liable to a fine not exceeding £50,000 or, at the discretion of the court, to imprisonment for a term not exceeding five years or to both the fine and imprisonment.

Section 110 of the 1993 Act was the second section which the 1997 Regulations applied to both Eircell Limited and ESAT Digifone Limited. Section 110 of the 1983 Act provides that the Minister for Public Enterprise may issue directions in writing directing Telecom Éireann, An Post and now Eircell Limited and ESAT Digifone to comply with policy decisions of a general kind made by the Government, to do (or refrain from doing) anything which the Minister may specify from time to time as necessary in the national interest. The person who receives such a direction, *e.g.* a direction to intercept communications pursuant to the Interception of Postal Packets and Telecommunications Messages (Regulation) Act 1993, must comply with such a direction and this stipulation is set out in section 110(3) of the 1983 Act.

POSTAL COMMUNICATIONS

Tariffs, terms and conditions of An Post   Pursuant to section 70 of the Postal and Telecommunications Services Act 1983, An Post in its Foreign Parcel Post Amendment (No. 32) Scheme 1997 (S.I. No. 172 of 1997) was authorised to increase its parcel post rates to destinations outside Ireland. The Inland Post Amendment (No. 56) Scheme 1997 (S.I. No. 173 of 1997) authorised An Post to increase certain parcel post rates in Ireland.

SATELLITE SERVICES

The European Communities (Satellite Telecommunications Services) Regulations 1997 (S.I. No. 372 of 1997) ('the 1997 Regulations') made by the Minister for Public Enterprise in exercise of the powers conferred on her by section 3 of the European Communities Act 1972 gave effect to Commission Directive 94/46/EC of October 13, 1994 amending Commission Directive 88/301/EC of May 16, 1988 and Commission Directive 90/388/EC of June 28, 1990 in particular with regard to satellite communications.

The purpose of Commission Directive 94/46/EC is to provide for the liberalisation of the markets for satellite communications services, networks and equipment. The 1997 Regulations provide that the Wireless Telegraphy Acts 1926 to 1972 and the Broadcasting and Wireless Telegraphy Act 1988 were not to apply to the placing on the market of satellite earth station equipment. Satellite earth station equipment is defined in the 1997 Regulations as meaning equipment which is capable of being used for the transmission only or for the transmission and reception, or for the reception only of radio communications signals, by means of satellite or other space-based systems.

Section 87(1) of the Postal and Telecommunications Services Act 1983, which granted certain privileges to Telecom Éireann, was stated in the 1997 Regulations to be construed as not applying to satellite services. In effect, satellite communication services were liberalised by the 1997 Regulations.

TELECOMMUNICATIONS CARRIER SERVICES

Infrastructure Liberalisation   The European Communities (Telecommunications Infrastructure) Regulations 1997 (S.I. No. 338 of 1997) ('the 1997 Regulations') introduced a further measure of liberalisation which, *inter alia*, abolished certain restrictions on the use of cable television networks for the provision of already liberalised telecommunications services and restricted further the statutory privileges of Telecom Éireann as set out in section 87(1) of the Postal and Telecommunications Services Act 1983 ('the 1983 Act') as amended by Regulation 3 of the European Communities (Telecommunications Services) Regulations 1992.

The 1997 Regulations were made pursuant to section 3 of the European Communities Act 1972 and for the purpose of giving effect to Commission Directive 95/51/EC of October 18, 1995, amending Commission Directive 90/388/EEC of 28 June 1990 with regard to the abolition of the restrictions on the use of cable television networks for the provision of already liberalised telecommunications services and Commission Directive 96/19/EC of March 13, 1996, amending Directive 90/388/EEC with regard to the implementation of full competition in telecommunications markets.

The 1997 Regulations provide that no person shall establish in the State a telecommunications network other than in accordance with a licence or otherwise authorised by law. A person who has established a telecommunications network under licence pursuant to section 111 of the 1983 Act is not to operate or allow the operation of that network otherwise than in accordance with the terms and conditions of a licence (Regulation 4).

Every person who establishes or operates a telecommunications network in contravention of the 1997 Regulations is guilty of an offence and is liable on summary conviction to a fine not exceeding £1,500. An offence under this regulation may be prosecuted by the Director of Telecommunications Regulation ('the Director').

The exclusive privilege in relation to telecommunications, in the widest sense of the term, is vested in the Minister for Public Enterprise pursuant to section 4 of the Telegraph Act 1869. The 1997 Regulations provide that each of the following is not to be regarded as a breach of the exclusive privilege granted to the Minister for Public Enterprise pursuant to the 1869 Act. These are:

(a) services and networks provided and maintained by a person solely for his or her own use (including by a business for use between employees for the purposes of the business) and not rendering a service to any other person;

(b) the operation of a broadcasting station under licence granted by the Minister for Public Enterprise pursuant to the Broadcasting Authority Act 1960 or the Radio and Television Act 1988;

(c) radio communications systems provided under licences granted in accordance with the Wireless Telegraphy (Community Repeater Licence) Regulations, 1988 or exempted from licensing in accordance with the Wireless Telegraphy Acts 1926 to 1972; and

(d) a cable television system licensed under the Wireless Telegraphy Acts 1926 to 1972, when used solely for the purposes identified in the licence.

The 1997 Regulations also provide for the award of licences for the establishment of a telecommunications network for the purposes of providing telecommunications services. Regulation 6 of the 1997 Regulations amends section 111 of the 1983 Act by the insertion of certain provisions following sub-section (2C) (inserted by the European Communities (Mobile and Personal Communications) Regulations, 1996 (S.I. No. 123 of 1996)). A licence to establish a telecommunications network as specified and as defined in the 1997 Regulations may be granted on the basis of a declaration by the applicant for the licence that the telecommunications network in respect of which the licence is being sought shall, at all times, comply with conditions prescribed by the Director as being applicable to the provisions of a telecommunications network.

Whenever the Director proposes to refuse to grant a licence or to revoke or suspend, or amend, the terms or conditions of a licence, the Director is obliged by section 111(2D)(1) of the 1983 Act, as amended by the 1997 Regulations, to include a statement for the reasons for the proposal and of the rights of the applicant or holder and the Director must take into account any representations made by the applicant.

An authorised officer of the Director is empowered pursuant to Regulation 6 if he or she reasonably suspects in the context of a licence that an offence has been or is being committed on or at any premises or any other place, or evidence that the offence has or is being committed on or at those premises or that place, to enter the premises or place and make such inspections, tests and measurements of machinery and apparatus and other equipment found on the premises and inspections of such records and other information, in whatever form kept, so found as he or she considers it appropriate. Furthermore, the authorised officer is authorised to take copies or extracts of any record or other information in any form found by him or her on the premises or place. The person in charge of the premises and any person found on the premises by an authorised officer shall give to the officer such information as he or she may reasonably require for the relevant purposes and shall not obstruct him or her in the performance of his functions.

Criminal sanctions are specified in the 1997 Regulations for breach of the licensing provisions or for obstructing or interfering with an authorised officer in the exercise of his or her functions. Furthermore, where an offence is committed by a body corporate and is proved to have been committed with the consent or connivance or attributable to any neglect on the part of any person, being a director, manager, secretary or other officer of the body corporate, or a person, purporting to act in that capacity, that person shall be guilty of an offence and shall be liable to be proceeded against and punished as if he or she were guilty of the offence. The offence is to be punishable on summary conviction and the fine is not to exceed £1,500. Offences in this context may be prosecuted by the Director.

There is a specific provision under regulation 7 of the 1997 Regulations authorising the use of cable television networks for the provision of already liberalised telecommunications services subject to the requirements of the 1983 Act in relation to the licensing of telecommunications networks and telecommunications services.

The Wireless Telegraphy (Wired Broadcast Relay Licence) Regulations 1974 (S.I. No. 67 of 1974) have been amended by regulation 7 of the 1997 Regulations.

Specific provisions are set out in the 1997 Regulations relating to provisions concerning the financial accounts of Telecom Éireann. Telecom Éireann is obliged to operate and maintain a system which ensures the separation of financial accounts in respect of its activity as a provider of telecommunications services, and its activity as a provider of a cable television network. The Director is to ensure compliance with this obligation. Telecom Éireann's failure to comply with this Regulation shall constitute an offence and Telecom Éireann shall be liable on summary conviction to a fine not exceeding £1,500. An offence under this regulation may be prosecuted by the Director.

Monitoring of Telecommunications Services   The European Communities (Telecommunications Services Monitoring) Regulations, 1997 (S.I. No. 284 of 1997) ('the 1997 Regulations') made pursuant to section 3 of the European Communities Act 1972 empower the Director of Telecommunications Regulation to monitor certain telecommunications links to ensure that telecommunications service providers act in compliance with their applicable licence condition. The 1997 Regulations provide for the amendment of section 111 of the Postal and Telecommunications Services Act 1983 ('the 1983 Act') by providing that telecommunications links may be monitored by the Director of Telecommunications Regulation for the purposes of ascertaining whether certain telecommunications services comply in all respects with service conditions prescribed under section 111 of the 1983 Act.

The 1997 Regulations also amended section 98(2A) of the 1983 Act inserted by section 13 of the Interception of Postal Packets and Telecommunications Messages (Regulation) Act 1993 and authorised persons within Telecom Éireann to disclose information concerning the use made of telecommunications services where that disclosure is made, *inter alia*, to an officer of the Minister for Public Enterprise or an authorised officer of the Director of Telecommunications Regulation for the purposes of any monitoring in accordance with section 111(9) of the 1983 Act.

Telecommunications Schemes of Telecom Éireann   Pursuant to section 90 of the Postal and Telecommunications Services Act 1983, Telecom Éireann made several schemes during the year specifying its tariffs and amending terms and conditions of telecommunications services provided to its customers. Most of the schemes related to amendments of the Telecommunications Scheme 1994 (S.I. No. 177 of 1994), the principal telecommunications scheme which sets out the terms and conditions of telecommunications services provided by Telecom Éireann.

The Telecommunications (Amendment) Scheme 1997 (S.I. No. 75 of 1997) authorised Telecom Éireann to 'rebalance' leased line charges. The Telecommunications (Amendment)(No. 2) Scheme 1997 (S.I. 130 of 1997) amended the 1994 Scheme in the context of certain references to Eircell equipment. The Telecommunications (Amendment) (No. 3) Scheme, 1997 (S.I. 246 of 1997) provided for certain volume discounts to certain customers. This scheme also provided for a national virtual private network facility. The Telecommunications (Amendment) (No. 4) Scheme 1997 (S.I. No. 309 of 1997) provided for certain reductions in charges. The Telecommunications (Amendment) (No. 5) Scheme 1997 (S.I. No. 318 of 1997) made provision for a call-forwarding facility for telephone customers generally and provided for relevant charges. The Telecommunications (Amendment) (No. 6) Scheme 1997 (S.I. No. 378 of 1997) made provision for certain modifications to charges for telephone services. The Telecommunications (Amendment) (No. 7) Scheme, 1997 (S.I. No. 379 of 1997) provided for a discount in respect of certain telephone calls. The Telecommunications (Amendment) (No. 8) 1997 (S.I. 485 of 1997) provided for a discount on the annual rental charges for leased lines in certain circumstances. The Telecommunications (Amendment) (No. 9) Scheme, 1997 (S.I. No. 486 of 1997) provided for further volume discounts in relation to telecommunications charges and the Telecommunications (Amendment) (No. 10) Scheme, 1997 (S.I. No. 529 of 1997) provided for chargecard telephone calls.

Telephone Numbers   The issue of Telecom Éireann altering a customer's telephone number in the context of the promotion and marketing of alpha numeric telephone numbers was considered by the High Court in *Zockoll Group Limited v. Telecom Éireann.* The judgment was given by Kelly J. on November 28, 1997. The High Court held that the absolute discretion given to Telecom Éireann to alter subscribers' telephone numbers could only be exercised if it could be shown that the subscriber was in breach of contract with Telecom Éireann or if circumstances existed in which in the interests of some revision of the telecommunications service it is necessary to change the subscriber's telephone number.

Zockoll Group Limited had issued proceedings claiming that Telecom Éireann had wrongfully withdrawn the use of eight alpha numeric telephone numbers. In addition, Zockoll had claimed that in breach of statutory duty, Telecom Éireann had refused to allocate certain additional telephone numbers. Telecom Éireann had submitted that Zockoll Group Limited was brokering telephone numbers in contravention of Articles 9 and 51 of Telecommunications Scheme 1994. Kelly J. granted the plaintiffs the relief sought and held that Zockoll was entitled to have reinstated to them the telephone numbers in question and to have allocated to them the other numbers requested.

Terminal Equipment The European Communities (Telecommunications Terminal Equipment) Regulations 1997, (S.I. No. 73 of 1997) ('the 1997 Regulations') were made by the Minister for Transport, Energy and Communications pursuant to section 3 of the European Communities Act 1972 and for the purpose of giving effect to Council Directive No. 91/263/EEC of April 29, 1991, as amended by Council Directive No. 93/68/EEC of July 22, 1993. These Directives provide for the approximation of laws of EU Member States concerning telecommunications terminal equipment including the mutual recognition of their conformity. Terminal equipment is defined in Regulation 2 of the 1997 Regulations as equipment intended to be connected to the public telecommunications network.

Regulation 4 of the 1997 Regulations provides, *inter alia*, that a person shall not place on the market telecommunications terminal equipment unless each item of equipment is:

(a) accompanied by a declaration made by a manufacturer or a supplier, set out in a prescribed form,

(b) accompanied by an operating manual, and

(c) affixed with the CE mark and a specified symbol in such a way that the symbol follows the CE mark and visually forms an integral part of the total marking.

In the event that terminal equipment is connected to the public telecommunications network and is not being used for its intended purpose, the Minister for Public Enterprise ('the Minister') may by notice in writing, as the Minister may decide, to either the telecommunications operator or the person who, in the opinion of the Minister, bears responsibility for such connections or use, require that any such equipment shall be disconnected from, or cease to be used in conjunction with the public telecommunications network.

Regulation 7 of the 1997 Regulations empowers the Minister to designate a body or bodies established in the European Community to carry out the certification, product checks and associated surveillance tasks set out in the Directive. The Minister is also entitled to designate a test laboratory or test laboratories, established in the Community, for carrying out tests pertaining to the relevant procedures.

The Minister may approve standards for terminal equipment (being standards which implement harmonised standards applicable to terminal equipment) which standards are to be known and referred to as national standards (Regulation 8).

The Minister may appoint such and so many of his officers or other suitably qualified persons to be authorised officers for the purpose of the 1997 Regulations. An authorised officer is empowered to enter at all reasonable times any premises or place in which he or she has reasonable grounds for suspecting that there is telecommunications equipment or terminal equipment and to inspect and take copies of or extracts from books, records or other documents which he finds in the course of his inspections; require any person at the premises or place and the owner or person in charge to give him such information and produce to him or her such books, documents and other records within that person's power of procurement; take possession of and remove for examination and checking by the Minister or a person nominated by the Minister any telecommunications equipment or terminal equipment or part thereof and retain such equipment or part thereof for such time as he considers reasonable for the purposes of his or her functions under the Regulations or the relevant Directive (Regulations 12).

Contravention of the Regulations is a criminal offence. A person who is guilty of an offence under the Regulations shall be liable on summary conviction to a fine not exceeding £1,500 (Regulation 13).

Where the Minister is of the opinion that any terminal equipment or telecommunications equipment is likely to cause death or serious injury or damage to property, he or she may apply to the High Court for an order to prevent the use of such equipment and the Court may grant such an order on such terms and for such period as it thinks proper, having regard to the evidence presented by the Minister (Regulation 14).

There is provision for granting of a search warrant to an authorised officer where the District Court is satisfied by information on oath of an authorised officer or a member of the Garda Síochána that there is reasonable ground for believing that at any specified place, specified vehicle, or specified vessel, relevant apparatus is to be found which does not comply with the provision of the Directive or the provisions of these Regulations. Any person who by act or omission impedes or obstructs an authorised officer, a member of the Garda Síochána or any other person in the exercise of any lawful power shall be guilty of an offence and shall be liable on summary conviction to a fine not exceeding £1,500.

It is intended that the functions of the Minister for Public Enterprise under the 1997 Terminal Equipment Regulations will be transferred to the Director of Telecommunications Regulation. No such transfer was made as of August 1998.

Voice Telephony Regulations   The Minister for Public Enterprise pursuant to section 3 of the European Communities Act 1972 and for the purpose of giving effect to Directive No. 95/62 EC of the European Parliament and of the

Council of 13 December 1995 ('the 1995 Directive') on the application of Open Network Provision to Voice Telephony, made the European Communities (Application of Open Network Provision to Voice Telephony (Regulations) 1997 (S.I. No. 445 of 1997) ('the 1997 Regulations'). The Regulations came into operation on October 31, 1997.

The purpose of the 1995 Directive was to provide for the harmonisation of conditions for open and efficient access to and use of fixed public telecommunications networks and public telephony services together with the availability throughout the Community of a harmonised voice telephony service.

Telecom Éireann is obliged pursuant to Regulation 3 of the 1997 Regulations to provide a fixed public telecommunications network and a voice telephony service in accordance with the provisions of the Regulations. Specifically, Telecom Éireann is to ensure that users can, subject to the Regulations, obtain a connection to the fixed public telecommunications network; ensure that users may, subject to the 1997 Regulations, connect and use terminal equipment which is situated on the customer's premises and adhere to the principle of non-discrimination when it uses the fixed public telecommunications network for providing services which are or may be provided by other service providers.

Publication of and public access to certain information must be complied with by Telecom Éireann. The 1997 Regulations also impose a duty on Telecom Éireann to set targets for supply-time and certain quality-of-service indicators set out in the 1995 Directive.

Telecom Éireann is to ensure that it continues services provided by it for a reasonable period of time and that termination of a service, or a change that materially alters the use that may be made of such service, may not take place other than after consultation by Telecom Éireann with the users affected, and after an appropriate period of notice which is to be specified by the Director of Telecommunications Regulation ('the Director'). Users are to have the right to appeal to the Director in the event of a dispute concerning a termination date decided upon by Telecom Éireann in the context of withdrawal of a particular service (Regulation 6).

Pursuant to Regulation 7 of the 1997 Regulations, Telecom Éireann is to provide a scheme for compensation or refunds if the service quality levels contracted for are not met. Telecom Éireann is to respond without delay to a request for connection to the fixed public telecommunications network and give the customer an estimated date for the provision of the service requested. The Director may require Telecom Éireann to alter the conditions of contracts including conditions relating to limitations for liability. Contracts between Telecom Éireann and customers are to contain particulars of the method of initiating procedures for the settlement of disputes. Section 88(1) of the Postal and Telecommunications Services Act 1983 in relation to limitation of liability is to apply only in respect of voice telephony. With effect from January 1,

2000, this statutory limitation of liability on the part of Telecom Éireann is to be repealed.

Telecom Éireann is to provide, subject to technical feasibility and economic viability, certain advanced telecommunication facilities specified in the 1995 Directive (Regulation 9).

On interconnection, Telecom Éireann is to ensure that it meets reasonable requests for interconnection with the fixed public telecommunications networks from telecommunications organisations providing fixed public telecommunications networks in other Member States whose names have been notified to the Commission of the European Communities by their respective national regulatory authorities as being authorised to interconnect their fixed public telecommunications networks directly with those of telecommunications organisations in other Member States in order to terminate telephony traffic in the State. The same duty applies to Telecom Éireann in respect of operators of public mobile telephony in the State. Telecom Éireann must adhere to the principle of non-discrimination when it enters into interconnection agreements (Regulation 11).

In relation to the issue of tariffs, Telecom Éireann is to ensure that tariffs for the use of fixed public telecommunications network and voice telephony service follow certain basic principles of transparency and cost orientation as set out in Annex 2 to Directive 90/387/EEC.

On cost accounting principles, Telecom Éireann is to operate and maintain a cost accounting system which is suitable for the implementation of the basic principles of transparency and cost orientation. Compliance by Telecom Éireann in the context of a cost accounting system is to be verified by a person or a body independent of Telecom Éireann and selected by Telecom Éireann with the prior approval of the Director (Regulation 13).

Bulk discount schemes offered by Telecom Éireann to customers are to be notified to the Director not later than one week or such other period as may be specified by the Director before they come into effect (Regulation 14).

In the context of itemised billing, Telecom Éireann must, taking into account the state of network development and market demand, set and publish targets for the provision of itemised billing as a facility available to customers on request (Regulation 15).

In the context of directory services, Telecom Éireann is to ensure, subject to any requirements of the law relating to the protection of personal data and privacy, that users of the voice telephony service may obtain directories in either printed or electronic form, and Telecom Éireann is to ensure that such directories are updated at least once a year. Customers have the right to have or not to have an entry in publicly-available directories; public directory information concerning voice telephony services are to be made available upon request on published terms which are fair, reasonable and non-discriminatory (Regulation 16).

Telecom Éireann shall, in so far as reasonably practicable, provide public payphones to satisfy all reasonable demands for such services throughout the State and ensure in so far as reasonably practicable that it is possible to make emergency calls from such telephones. Telephone calls to the single European emergency call number referred to in Council Directive 91/936/EEC of July 29, 1991 are to be free of charge (Regulation 17).

Telecom Éireann is to comply with any conditions drawn up and notified to it by the Director in order to aid disabled users and people with special needs in their use of the voice telephony service (Regulation 18).

The allocation of telephone numbers and changes in a numbering system often cause legal and administrative problems. Regulation 20 of the 1997 Regulations provides that no person should allocate a number or other character to a network termination point on the public telecommunications network other than in accordance with the national numbering scheme. The Director is empowered to attach conditions to the allocation of numbers from the national numbering scheme and such conditions shall be complied with. The Director is under an obligation to ensure that the procedures for allocation of individual numbers and numbering ranges are to be transparent, equitable and timely, and the allocation is to be carried out in an objective, transparent and non-discriminatory manner. The Director is to ensure also that the main elements of the national numbering scheme and all subsequent additions or amendments to it are published, subject only to limitations imposed on the grounds of national security (Regulation 20).

Certain restrictions on access to and use of the public fixed telecommunications network are permissible in order to ensure compliance with so-called 'essential requirements'. Regulation 21 of the 1997 Regulations provides that where a customer's terminal equipment does not comply or no longer complies with its approval conditions, or where it malfunctions in a way which adversely affects the integrity of the network, or where there is a danger of physical injury to persons, Telecom Éireann shall ensure that certain procedures are followed. Service provision may be interrupted by Telecom Éireann until the terminal is disconnected from the network termination point. Telecom Éireann must immediately inform the customer about the interruption giving the reasons for it and, as soon as the customer has ensured that the relevant offending apparatus is disconnected from the network, public service is to be restored.

Regulation 21 also specifies that Telecom Éireann is not to refuse to provide access to the fixed public telecommunications network, nor interrupt nor reduce the availability of the voice telephony service on the grounds of a user's alleged failure to comply with conditions of use, other than in accordance with procedures for this purpose which may be laid down by the Director. The Director, however, is empowered to establish or approve specified measures in the case of defined infringements of the conditions of use. In this context, such procedures must provide for a transparent decision-making process in which due respect is given to the right to the parties concerned and all parties must have an opportunity to state their case. The Director's decision under the procedures are to be substantiated and notified by the Director to the parties within one week of their adoption. The Director is empowered for the purposes of the 1997 Regulations by notice in writing to direct Telecom Éireann to refuse to provide access to the fixed public telecommunications network or interrupt or reduce the availability of the voice telephony service and Telecom Éireann must comply with any directions so made (Regulation 21).

In the context of non-payment of bills by customers, Telecom Éireann is to draw up specified measures which shall be subject to the approval of the Director, to establish procedures to be followed in the event of non-payment of bills, and any consequent service interruption or disconnection. Any service interruption is to be confined to the service concerned as far as it is technically feasible and that due warning is to be given to the customer concerned in advance (Regulation 22).

Telecom Éireann is to provide services according to certain technical standards published in the *Official Journal of the European Communities* in accordance with Article 5(1) of Directive 90/387/EEC, European standards adopted by the European Telecommunications Standards Institute (ETSI), or the European Committee for Standardisation (CEN) and the European Committee for Electrotechnical Standardisation (Cenelec), or in the absence of such standards, international standards or recommendations adopted by the International Telecommunications Union, (ITU) the International Organisation for Standardisation (ISO) or the International Electrotechnical Commission (IEC) or in the absence of such standards, national standards or specifications. Telecom Éireann is to inform customers on request of standards or specifications, including any European or international standards which are implemented through the national standards, in accordance with which the services and facilities are provided (Regulation 23).

The Director is to notify the EC Commission of certain information and Telecom Éireann is obliged to furnish the Director with progress reports. The Director is obliged to keep available and submit to the EC Commission on request details of individual cases where access to the fixed public telecommunications network or voice telephony service or use of the fixed public telecommunications network or voice telephone service have been restricted or denied including the measures taken and the justification for those measures. However, the stipulations mentioned in the foregoing sentence are not to apply to any action taken in the context of enforcement of licensing conditions or to proceedings before a court (Regulation 24).

In the context of conciliation and resolution of disputes, without prejudice to any action that the EC Commission or any Member State may take pursuant to the EC Treaty, and without prejudice to the rights of persons invoking certain procedures and including the right of a person to make a complaint under section 4 of the Ombudsman Act 1980 certain procedures are set out in Regulation 25 of the 1997 Regulations in relation to conciliation and resolution of disputes concerning an alleged infringement of the 1997 Regulations. Any party including customers or other users, having an unresolved dispute with Telecom Éireann concerning an alleged infringement of the provision of the 1997 Regulations shall have a right of appeal to the Director. The Director is to ensure that the procedures established are to be published, easily accessible and, in principle, inexpensive, and is to facilitate the resolution of disputes in a fair, transparent and timely manner. The Director however is not to investigate the dispute if the dispute has been the subject of an investigation under the Ombudsman Act 1980. Where the Director finds that there is a case for further examination, following a receipt of a notification of a dispute, the matter may be referred to the Chairman of the Open Network Provision Committee, the Committee established by Article 9(1) of Council Directive 90/387/EEC of June 28, 1990 (Regulation 25).

The Director is empowered to monitor compliance by Telecom Éireann with these Regulations. The functions of the Director under the 1997 Regulations are deemed to be included in the functions conferred on the Director under the Telecommunications (Miscellaneous Provisions) Act 1996. Telecom Éireann is to furnish the Director with any such information as the Director may reasonably require for the purpose of his or her functions under these Regulations. (Regulation 26).

A person who contravenes the 1997 Regulations is to be guilty of an offence and shall be liable on summary conviction to a fine not exceeding £1,500. Summary proceedings may be brought by the Director and summary proceedings for an offence may be brought within 12 months from the date of the offence.

WIRELESS TELEGRAPHY

Wireless telegraphy is a species of telecommunications and is regulated by the Wireless Telegraphy Acts 1926 to 1972 and the Broadcasting and Wireless Telegraphy Act 1988. Wireless telegraphy is defined in section 2 of the Wireless Telegraphy Act 1926 as amended by section 2 of the Broadcasting and Wireless Telegraphy Act 1988 as meaning:

the emitting and receiving, or emitting only or receiving only, over paths which are not provided by any material substance constructed or arranged for that purpose, of electric, magnetic or electro-magnetic energy of a frequency not exceeding 3 million megahertz, whether or not such energy serves the conveying (whether they are actually received or not) of communications, sounds, signs, visual images or signals, or the actuation or control of machinery or apparatus.

Essentially the wireless telegraphy code regulates the process of communications without wires.

Exemption of Cordless Telephones The Wireless Telegraphy Act 1926 (Section 3) (Exemption of Cordless Telephones) Order 1997 (S.I. No. 410 of 1997) provided for the exemption of digital cordless telephones operating in certain frequency bands as designated by the European Communities (Digital European Cordless Telecommunications – DECT) Regulations 1994 (S.I. No. 168 of 1994) and standards approved under the European Communities (Telecommunications Terminal Equipment) Regulations 1997 (S.I. No. 73 of 1997) from the requirement to be licensed under the Wireless Telegraphy Act 1926. The same exemption also applies to analogue cordless telephones, meaning apparatus for wireless telegraphy consisting of a fixed part that operates in a certain frequency band and one or more portable units that operate in a frequency band between which radio communication can be effected using equipment in conformity with certain specifications specified in the Order.

Mobile Telephony Licence The Wireless Telegraphy (GSM and TACS Mobile Telephony Licence) Regulations 1997 (S.I. No. 468 of 1997) made by the Director of Telecommunications Regulation in the exercise of powers conferred on her by section 6(1) of the Wireless Telegraphy Act 1926 and section 4 of the Telecommunications (Miscellaneous Provisions) Act 1996 with the consent of the Minister for Public Enterprise, provide for the issue of licences for apparatus for wireless telegraphy used solely for the purpose of providing GSM and TACS mobile telephony services and for the regulation of such apparatus for the payment of fees for persons granted licences for that purpose.

The term 'GSM mobile telephony service' means a service consisting of the provision of a pan-European, cellular, digital, land-based, mobile telephony service conforming with the standard known as GSM. TACS mobile telephony service means a service consisting of the provision and operation of cellular, land-based, mobile telephony service in a certain frequency band using analogue technology and conforming with the standard known as Total Access Communications System Mobile Station published by the Radio Communications Agency, London.

The conditions of licences are set out in Regulation 5 of the 1997 Regulations. The apparatus must be used only for the purpose of provision of the service authorised by the licence and must be used only on such radio frequency channels as may be specified in the licence and those channels must be used in an efficient manner. The licensee must ensure that the apparatus is not used in a manner that could infringe the privilege of the Minister for Public Enterprise under the Telegraph Act 1869.

If the Director is satisfied that the use of relevant apparatus is causing, or is likely to cause interference with any other apparatus for wireless telegraphy and gives the licensee appropriate notice, the licensee must ensure that the relevant requirement is complied with. The licensee is not to assign the licence or any of the powers, duties or functions conferred by it or otherwise transfer any of the rights or obligations conferred by it. The licensee must take all reasonable measures to prevent a communication of information which the licensee and employee and agents of the licensee and users of the service are not authorised to receive from being received by means of the apparatus. If such communication is received, the licensee must not, and shall endeavour to ensure that employees and agents of the licensee do not make known its contents, origin or destination or existence or the fact of such receipt, to a person (other than the Director or a member of staff of the Director) or reproduce it in writing or otherwise copy it or make use of it.

The licensee must ensure that the installation of the apparatus is effected and its maintenance and operation are carried on in such manner as to ensure that the safety of persons or property is not endangered. The erection and positioning of apparatus consisting of antennae and support structures of antennae must be effected in accordance with law. Non-ionising emissions from the mobile telephony network operated by the licensee for the purpose of service must be within the limits specified by the guidelines published by the International Non-Ionising Radiation Committee of the International Radiation Protection Association(IRPA) and that it complies with any radiation emission standards adopted and published from time to time by the IRPA and any standards of the European Committee for Electrotechnical Standards and any standards specified by the European Union. Access to the apparatus must be restricted to the licensee, employees or agents of the licensee and persons authorised by or on behalf of the licensee to have such access. In certain circumstances, the Director is empowered to revoke or suspend the licence in certain circumstances.

Certain procedures in relation to refusal to grant, or to revoke or suspend or to amend a term or a condition of a licence are set out in Regulation 6 of the 1997 Regulations. A person may appeal to the High Court against the decision of the Director.

Pursuant to Regulation 7 of the 1997 Regulations, the Director may appoint authorised officers who may enter at all reasonable times any premises where he or she reasonably suspects that any apparatus to which a licence relates is kept or any business relating to a licence is carried on and inspect the premises and any such apparatus found in the premises and any records of whatever form kept so found relating to the apparatus and test any such apparatus; direct any person whom he or she finds on the premises to give to him or her any information in his or her possession or procurement which he or she may reasonably be requested for the purposes of his or her functions and take copies of or extracts from any such records found.

The fees for the licence are specified in Regulation 8 of the 1997 Regulations. Regulation 9 specifies that nothing in the 1997 Regulations shall absolve a licensee from any requirement in law to obtain any consents, permissions, authorisations or other licences that may be necessary for the provision of a mobile telephony service or for the discharge of the obligations, or the exercise of the entitlements of the licensee under the licence.

Company Law

Dr David Tomkin and Adam McAuley

Piercing the corporate veil *Allied Irish Coal Supplies Ltd v. Powell Duffryn International Ltd,.* Supreme Court, December 19, 1997. The facts of this case are set out in 1996 Review, 95–96. A dispute arose between two companies. One alleged the other owed it money. The creditor company was concerned that if successful in its claim, the debtor would have insufficient funds to pay the debt. The creditor sought an order that the holding company should be joined as co-defendant with the debtor. The creditor company argued that the debtor and its holding company were trading as a single economic entity. The creditor company was concerned that the holding company planned a prophylactic sale of its subsidiary. In support of this contention, the creditor company relied on Costello J.'s judgment in *Power Supermarkets Ltd v. Crumlin Investments Ltd* High Court, June 22, 1981.

In the High Court, Laffoy J. refused to allow the holding company to be joined as a co-defendant. To do so would be fundamentally at variance with the principle of separate corporate legal personality and limited liability laid down in *Salomon v. Salomon & Co.* [1897] A.C. 22.

The creditor company appealed to the Supreme Court. In the Supreme Court, Murphy J. stated that *Salomon* permitted shareholders to exclude personal liability in respect of the company's debts, even where those dealing with the company would suffer by such a rule. Murphy J. held that Laffoy J. was correct in adhering to the *Salomon* principle to prevent the holding company's assets being available to answer the liabilities of a subsidiary. It was clear from the facts that in this case, unlike those in the *Power Supermarkets* case, that the holding and subsidiary companies were controlled and managed as separate companies.

Murphy J. found that nothing in the Companies Acts required a company to answer the debts of another in the same group. Murphy J. did not discount the possibility that shareholders – whether corporate or individual – could so conduct the company's business as to render their own assets liable to claims by the company's creditors. Where such a claim was made involving a corporate shareholder, the creditors interested in the holding and subsidiary company's assets had to be afforded the opportunity of being heard. Murphy J. dismissed the creditor's appeal.

Ultra vires and ostensible authority   *Ulster Factors Ltd v. Entonglen Ltd*
High Court, February 21, 1997. Ulster Factors Ltd is a factoring company. It
entered into a factoring agreement with Entonglen Ltd. During the course of
the factoring agreement, an advance was paid not to Entonglen Ltd, but to a
third party, a firm of solicitors.

Entonglen Ltd went into liquidation. The factors sued the liquidator for
the recovery of this advance. The liquidator sought to resist the factor's claim.

The liquidator argued that the advance was *ultra vires*. He argued that
Entonglen Ltd owed no money to the solicitors. It was therefore a gratuitous
payment. The memorandum of Entonglen Ltd did not allow gratuitous payments. Hence the payment was *ultra vires*. The liquidator further argued that
whereas section 8 of the Companies Act 1963 saves some *ultra vires* payments, this particular payment was not saved. This was because in *In re
Frederick Inns Ltd* [1994] 1 I.L.R.M. 387 the Supreme Court held that an
ultra vires payment was not lawful for the purposes of section 8, if made by
directors who knew that their company was insolvent at the time of the payment.

In the High Court, Laffoy J. rejected the liquidator's argument based on
Re Frederick Inns as there was no evidence that when the solicitors were paid,
Entonglen Ltd was insolvent.

The liquidator argued that the directors of Entonglen Ltd, when they requested the factors to use Entonglen Ltd's funds to pay off a third party, had
misapplied company funds. As section 8 could not be used to save the transaction, the money paid was subject to a constructive trust. Had the factors read
Entonglen Ltd's memorandum, they should have appreciated that company
funds were being misapplied. Laffoy J. held that a person becomes a constructive trustee, when he or she receives company funds with actual or constructive knowledge that they are being misapplied. Laffoy J. found that Ulster
Factors Ltd knew nothing of why the payment was made, nor of any possible
misapplication of company funds. The factoring contract expressly permitted
the factors to make payments to third parties. Ulster Factors Ltd had no obligation to inquire why a third party was being paid, nor what for. It was not
obliged to satisfy itself that the payment was *intra vires*. Laffoy J. added that
even if the payment were *ultra vires*, the factors did not have constructive
knowledge that the funds were being misapplied, solely because they failed to
inquire if the payment was or was not *intra vires*.

The second ground advanced by the liquidator for refusing to repay the
money advanced, was that the payment had not been properly authorised. The
liquidator contended that Ulster Factors Ltd had failed to obtain Entonglen
Ltd's authorisation for paying the solicitors. In the High Court, Laffoy J. accepted that the signatures of two directors should have been obtained, not just
one. But Entonglen Ltd admitted that the factors were never told of this.

Ulster Factors Ltd argued that the director had ostensible authority to bind

Entonglen. Laffoy J. applied the four conditions for ostensible authority propounded by Diplock L.J. in *Freeman and Lockyer v. Buckhurst Park Properties (Mangal) Ltd* [1964] 2 Q.B. 480.

First, Laffoy J. held that there had been a representation. There was a verbal agreement that two signatories were required for draw-downs to Entonglen Ltd's account. But in practice, the factors acted on a request by a single officer of the company. Laffoy J. held that Entonglen Ltd had tacitly represented that *all* draw-downs could be effected on the request of one officer by failing to specify that draw-downs to third parties required the authorisation of two officers. The first authorisation was signed by both its financial director and managing director. The factors might have viewed this as a special case, because it was for the credit of a company officer.

Second, Laffoy J. held that the articles accorded the Board actual authority to manage the company's business.

Third, Laffoy J. found that the factors had relied on this representation.

Fourth, there was nothing in Entonglen Ltd's memorandum and articles of association which might prohibit a request for payment to third parties.

Laffoy J. decided that Ulster Factors Ltd was entitled to the sum claimed. As the factoring contract included a "Factor's Discount", Ulster Factors Ltd was entitled to this up to the date of judgment.

The interesting feature of this case is Laffoy J.'s interpretation of *Belmont Finance* as applied in *In re Frederick Inns Ltd*. In *In re Frederick Inns* Blayney J. held that where a constructive trust is created by an *ultra vires* transaction not covered by section 8, knowledge of the memorandum of association's contents is imputed to the constructive trustee. Yet Laffoy J.'s analysis seems to be directed towards ascertaining what *actual* knowledge the factors had. It appears as if Laffoy J. appears to be accepting a narrower version of the *Frederick Inns* decision.

The case involves unusual facts, but those drafting factoring agreements will probably infer that the best way of dealing with draw-downs is to ensure that the bank credits the company bank account and requires the company to operate this account in conformity with the memorandum and articles and all appropriate resolutions. Problems arise when debits and credits are not authorised in the traditional and time honoured way. Whether or not they are initiated electronically or by fax is a different consideration, and the document should now specifically deal with this.

Financial assistance in the purchase of shares   *CH (Ireland) Inc (in liquidation) v. Credit Suisse Canada,* High Court, December 12, 1997. CH company went into liquidation. The liquidator instituted proceedings against Credit Suisse Canada (CSC) claiming that CSC had given CH financial assistance to purchase some of CH's shares. This assistance was given through a series of transactions with a number of different companies. All but one of these transactions took place in December 1989. The last took place in 1991.

The transactions began when CSC made a loan of £18.8 million to a finance company, Castor. Castor used this money to subscribe for shares in its wholly owned subsidiary, CHNB. CHNB used the money to purchase shares in CH. CH deposited the £18.8 million with Credit Suisse Zurich (CSZ), the parent company of CSC. CH indemnified CSZ against any liability on foot of its payment obligation to CSC and pledged the deposited monies as security. CSZ executed a payment obligation in favour of the CSC. This transaction had the effect of guaranteeing the repayment of the loan made by CSC to Castor. The liquidator claimed that the monies paid by CHNB to the CH as a subscription for shares in the company were deposited by the CH effectively as the ultimate security for the monies advance by the CSC to Castor and that this was a breach of section 60 of the Companies Act.

In 1991, CH gave a guarantee to CSZ and CSC. This document guaranteed all liabilities of Castor to either of the banks in very wide terms, including the liability of Castor to repay the £18.8 million advanced to CH by CSC.

In the High Court, McCracken J. considered the test which a court should apply when deciding whether a transaction or a series of transactions breached section 60. McCracken J. adverted to Hoffman J.'s dicta in *Charterhouse Investment Trust Ltd v. Tempest Diesels Ltd* [1986] B.C.L.C. 1. In that case, Hoffman J. warned that the section was a penal one and should not be strained to cover transactions which are not covered by it. Hoffman J. held that the section will be contravened if the only or main purpose of such a transaction is to enable the purchaser to buy shares.

McCracken J. held that the main purpose of CH depositing monies with CSZ was to ensure that CSC, effectively on the direction of CSZ, would advance monies to Castor and then to CHNB to enable it to purchase shares in CH. This transaction violated section 60. However, McCracken J. considered that the CH's guarantee in 1991 did not breach section 60. The main purpose of this guarantee was to try to ensure continued financial support for the entire Castor Group, rather than to give financial assistance for the purchase of shares.

CSC argued that the "transaction" referred to in section 60 must be the entire circular transaction including the advance of the monies by CSC to Castor and the subscription by Castor for shares in CHNB. McCracken J. rejected this interpretation. McCracken J. held that only a transaction directly involving the company can be impugned. In this case, the relevant transaction was the depositing of the monies by or at the direction of the company with CSZ, and the consideration for that deposit, namely the giving of the payment obligation by CSZ to CSC. This transaction assisted CHNB to acquire the shares in CH by ensuring that CSC made finance available.

McCracken J. held that a transaction is only voidable against any person who had notice of the facts which constitute the breach of section 60. McCracken J. stated that the onus was upon CH to prove on the balance of probability that CSC had actual notice of the facts constituting the breach of section 60. CH pointed to the payment instructions given by Castor and CHNB to CSC. These instructions referred to capital subscription. McCracken J. held that the only reasonable meaning of those instructions were, that Castor, being the borrower was in fact directing the monies to be paid to its subsidiary CHNB, as a capital subscription to CHNB. It had to be inferred that CHNB was further directing that the monies be used for a capital subscription to CH. McCracken J. held that the CSC had notice that the monies it advanced to Castor were ultimately to go to CHNB so that it might acquire shares in CH. The monies in question were secured by a payment obligation or guarantee by CSZ. CH in turn secured the monies by depositing them with CSZ.

CSC argued that before it could be held to have been aware of the breach within the terms of section 60, it would have had to be aware both of the facts constituting the breach of section 60 and also of the law relating to section 60. McCracken J. rejected this. Awareness of the facts breaching section 60 is all that is required. There was no requirement that a party had to be aware that the facts in question constituted a breach of the law.

McCracken J. held that there had been a breach of section 60. He said that he could make no order against CSZ, as the proceedings against CSZ had been stayed. All that McCracken J. held he could do was to declare that the transaction was void, in which CH deposited money with CSZ in consideration of the indemnity by CSZ to CSC.

Wrongful dismissal of a director   *Harte v. Kelly,* High Court, July 16, 1997. The plaintiff was an employee, shareholder and director of a company. The plaintiff's employment was terminated, and he was removed as a director. The plaintiff instituted proceedings for wrongful dismissal. The plaintiff sought an interlocutory injunction permitting his continued participation in company management. The defendants resisted the plaintiff's application, claiming that the company would suffer were the court to allow the plaintiff to take part in company management. The defendants argued that the relationship of trust and confidence between the plaintiff and the other directors had completely broken down. The interests of both the company and its employees would suffer if the injunction were granted.

In the High Court, Laffoy J. ordered the company to continue to pay the plaintiff's salary and other employment benefits until the trial of the action. Considering whether the plaintiff could be involved in the management of the company, Laffoy J. decided that there was a broader interest to be considered than merely the interest of shareholders. The court had to have regard to the interest of the employees and of the creditors of the company. These interests might be affected if the court compelled the company to allow the director to resume participation in the company's management. Laffoy J. opined that the plaintiff would not be prejudiced by non-involvement in the company's affairs as a director. Laffoy J. ordered that the plaintiff was to be furnished with quarterly management accounts of the company.

Where a plaintiff and defendant are protagonists in an internal company dispute, those advising should be alert to the court's propensity to take into account not just the rights and wrongs of those in dispute, but the broader interests affected: creditors, employees and those of the company itself.

Appointment and resignation of company directors *Phoenix Shannon p.l.c. v. Purvey*, High Court, March 7, 1997. In 1996, the defendants were co-opted to the board of directors of Phoenix Shannon p.l.c.(Phoenix). Under Phoenix's Articles of Association, these directors held their position until the annual general meeting following their appointment. There was internal conflict between the board members. No annual general meeting was called. In 1997, two of the non co-opted directors decided that as no AGM had been held all the co-opted directors were *deemed* to have resigned, and there was only one board member validly remaining.

Phoenix's Articles provided that if there was only one director of the company, that director could co-opt others to the board. The director who believed himself to be the only valid board member purported to use this power. He co-opted two others to the board. An application was brought to the High Court seeking a declaration that this co-option was valid.

In the High Court, Costello P. found nothing in the company's articles which dealt with the failure to convene annual general meetings. Costello P. refused to hold that if no annual general meeting were held, there was some implied automatic termination procedure. It would have been open to the company to include such provision in its memorandum and articles had it so wished. Costello P. held that the purported co-option was invalid.

Director's duties *Sweeney v. Duggan* [1997] 2 I.L.R.M. 211. The plaintiff was employed by a mining and quarry company. The plaintiff was injured whilst working in the quarry. The plaintiff successfully sued the company and was awarded over £20,000 in damages. Before he got the £20,000, the company went into liquidation. The plaintiff instituted these proceedings against the company and a director/shareholder of the company. The plaintiff claimed that the company as his employer should have taken out employer's liability insurance. The plaintiff brought a similar claim against the principal company director/shareholder. The plaintiff's claim was dismissed in the High Court. He appealed to the Supreme Court.

In the Supreme Court, Murphy J. refused to imply a term into the plaintiff's contract of employment or impose a tortious duty requiring an employer to take out employer's liability insurance. Murphy J. stated that as the company had no such liability, neither could its principal director/shareholder. The piercing of the corporate veil or even its complete removal could not make the principal director/shareholder liable where the company itself was not liable. Murphy J. declined to hold that a relationship between a company director/shareholder and the company's employee obliges the director/shareholder to care for the employee's economic welfare. Even if it did, the duty could not be more onerous and extensive than that owed by the company itself to the employee. The case is discussed in detail in the Torts chapter, 704, below.

Fraudulent, reckless trading proceedings and fiduciary duties of directors *Jones v. Gunn* [1997] 2 I.L.R.M. 245. In this case the plaintiff, a firm of architects, brought proceedings against the defendant company and one of its directors. The company was left with £85,000 to pay its debts. The company owed the firm of architects £35,666, and its bank £95,000. The directors had given personal guarantees to the company's bank. The directors decided to pay the bank, procure the release of their personal guarantees, and thus end their own potential liability. The company ceased trading in 1989, but by the time of the hearing had not been placed in liquidation. The plaintiff claimed these actions of the director constituted reckless and fraudulent trading, and that the director had breached his fiduciary duties to the creditors of the company.

As a preliminary point, this director argued that since the alleged reckless and fraudulent actions were claimed to have occurred prior to the commencement of the Companies Act 1990, there was no case to answer on this ground. The director also argued that no duty outside those prescribed by the Companies Acts could be owed to the creditors.

In the High Court, McGuinness J. considered both these arguments as preliminaries to the trial of the action.

The first issue was whether it was possible for the firm of architects to ground a claim on sections 297A, 298 and 251 of the Companies Act 1963 in respect of events which occurred prior to the coming into force of the Companies Act 1990 on August 1, 1991. Section 251 of the Companies Act 1990 permits fraudulent, reckless trading and misfeasance proceedings to be brought where the company is not in liquidation. Section 251 requires a person seeking to rely upon it to satisfy one of two conditions. Either, it must appear to the court that the company is unable to pay its debts as they fall due and the principal reason why the company is not placed in liquidation is due the insufficiency of its assets. Alternatively that execution or other process issued on a judgment, decree or order of any court in favour of a creditor of the company is returned unsatisfied in whole or in part. This second condition had been satisfied by the architects' obtaining judgment in default and attempting unsuccessfully to execute this judgment.

McGuinness J. held that it was presumed that an Act is prospective not retrospective unless the legislature had declared a contrary intention.

McGuinness J. considered the judgment of Murphy J. in *In re Hefferon Kearns Ltd (No. 1)* [1993] 3 I.R. 177. In this case, a preliminary issue was raised as to whether the new reckless trading provisions could apply retrospectively to events which occurred prior to the coming into force of the 1990 Act. Relying on *Hamilton v. Hamilton* [1982] I.R. 466, Murphy J. held that legislation operated retrospectively where it takes away or impairs any vested right acquired under existing laws or creates a new obligation, or impose a new duty, or attaches a new disability in respect to past transactions. Murphy J. distinguished retrospective legislation from other statutes which took account of past events when applying new law. Murphy J. held that the liability created by the new reckless trading provisions was not retrospective.

McGuinness J. held that the architects were grounding their reckless trading claim on transactions which had occurred prior to the introduction of the 1990 provisions. To allow such a claim would be to apply legislation retrospectively, and McGuinness J. refused to do so.

The architects argued that the same facts would justify their claiming fraudulent trading. It was a precondition of the original fraudulent trading section that the company had to be in liquidation. McGuinness J. found that as the company had not been placed in liquidation, the only means by which the fraudulent trading section could apply was if section 251 of the Companies Act 1990 applied. McGuinness J. held that to operate section 297A(1)(b) in conjunction with section 251 would be to impose personal liability on the director which could not have been imposed upon him under the original section 297 of the 1963 Act. The transactions in question were completed prior to the commencement date of the Companies Act 1990 and therefore the plaintiff's claim under section 297A must fail because it involved retrospection. For this reason also, the architects could not bring misfeasance proceedings under section 298 either.

The firm's last claim was that the director had breached his fiduciary duty owed to the firm as a creditor. McGuinness J. accepted that *In Re Frederick Inns Ltd* [1991] I.L.R.M. 582; [1994] 1 I.L.R.M. 387 it was decided that a director of a clearly insolvent company owed a fiduciary duty to the general body of creditors. This duty prohibits directors from making payments which benefit either themselves personally or loosely connected companies, to the detriment of the general and independent creditors. Therefore, McGuinness J. held that if the architects could prove their allegations, they could claim against the director and company for breach of this fiduciary duty. McGuinness J. decided to proceed to hear evidence in regard to these claims. McGuinness J.'s decision is currently under appeal.

This case emphasises the fundamental importance of equity and common law to the underlying structure of company law. Restrictive considerations such as retrospectivity and other matters of statutory interpretation are irrelevant to judicial application of the common law and equity. In so doing, judges should not be assumed to be circumventing or repairing the deficiencies of the legislative provisions.

The fiduciary duties of directors and constitutional rights of promoters
Crindle Investments, Roche and Roche v. Wymes and Wood, High Court, March 27, 1997. This case arose from the Bula litigation. The plaintiffs were shareholders of both Bula Holdings Ltd and Bula Ltd. The defendants were directors of Bula Holdings Ltd and Bula Ltd. The plaintiffs made two claims. First, the shareholders claimed that the directors had breached their fiduciary duty to the company by bringing and failing to compromise the by now discredited litigation involving Tara and the banks. Secondly, the shareholders claimed that these directors, by taking various proceedings in their personal capacity involving matters which were really to do with the company, had breached the shareholders' constitutional rights.

In the High Court, Murphy J. endorsed the well-know proposition of law that directors of a company owe fiduciary duties to the shareholders of a company collectively. However, particular circumstances may arise where a director may owe additional fiduciary duties to an individual shareholder. If such a situation arises, the existence of the corporate structure does not prevent the particular shareholder from enforcing or relying upon the existence of this fiduciary duty.

A company had been established to develop the Navan ore body. The plaintiffs had joined in this enterprise in their corporate and personal capacities. Murphy J. held that where people have set up a company for an enterprise such as this, the parties intend that their relationships shall be governed by company law. Clear evidence would be necessary to substantiate the existence of obligations beyond those prescribed by legislation or identified by long established legal principles.

Murphy J. held that the course adopted by the directors or two of them was imprudent and possibly even improvident. They should have explored fairly and fully the prospects of settlements. There were various close relationships between some of the shareholders and the directors, but this closeness did not give rise to extra fiduciary duties.

Murphy J. said that even if the directors had any extra fiduciary duty to the shareholders in Bula, this would not of itself have given rise to rights. Had such an extra fiduciary duty been established, all that the plaintiff shareholders could have claimed was that the directors had put themselves in a position where their obligations as directors had conflicted with their personal right to pursue litigation. The Companies Acts, 1963-1990 provided various ways in which a dissatisfied shareholder could seek redress in such circumstances. There was no need to seek recourse to other, possibly innovative, equitable remedies.

Secondly, Murphy J. dealt with the claim that the directors had breached the shareholders' constitutional rights. Murphy J. found that the shareholders had a constitutional property right in the company. The directors also had a constitutional property right in their litigation, and an unenumerated constitutional right of access to the courts. Murphy J. was willing to accept that the directors were pursuing their individual claims and preventing a settlement of the corporate claim to exert leverage. Murphy J. questioned whether this approach breached the shareholders' constitutional rights. Murphy J. answered this question in the negative. The shareholders would have had to show that the directors had done something wrong, before they could be restrained by the court. All those involved had decided to promote the company, Bula, and personally guarantee its debts. In so deciding, they exercised their freedom under the Constitution and set limits to the exercise of their constitutional rights. Indeed so complex were the ensuing relationships that it was difficult if not impossible for them to exercise their individual constitutional rights except in conjunction with their fellow promoters. The route for the vindication of these constitutionally protected rights was through section 205. The facts as presented disclosed nothing constituting oppression or disregard of interests.

This judgment raises three issues.

First, a director does not owe an individual shareholder a particular fiduciary duty, unless the director assumes some extra obligation, or role which adds an element to the relationship.

Second, the courts recognise both the constitutional rights of a company, and the constitutionally protected rights of shareholders in the company. Where a shareholder or director claims these rights are being contravened by another director or possibly another shareholder, Murphy J.'s judgment emphasises that any shareholder dispute should be resolved through existing Companies Acts procedures.

Third, where shareholders are aggrieved at the director's incompetence, improvidence or folly (as opposed to their dishonesty, or oppression) the general meeting and not the courts is the appropriate forum to seek relief. The main remedy is to replace the board of directors.

Section 205 petition and abuse of process   *Horgan v. Murray*, High Court, January 31, 1997; [1998] 1 I.L.R.M. 110 (SC). This case concerned a company with three (sic) shareholders. Its business was run as a consensual partnership. The consensual partnership broke down. One of the shareholders presented a petition for relief against oppression. The petitioner sought to have his shares bought by the other shareholders.

An application was brought by two other shareholders to strike out the petition, claiming abuse of process. They said that Article 6 of the company's Articles of Association provided a mechanism for the valuation of shares on a sale. The shares had to be valued by auditors acting as experts. They expressed themselves willing to allow the shares to be valued as of some date before the oppression was alleged to have commenced. The basis was what would have been the likely course of the business between the chosen date and the date of valuation.

In the High Court, Barron J. stated that before proceedings constitute an abuse of the process of the court, there must be some element of impropriety. Thus, a plaintiff whose valid claim is admitted, who continues proceedings for further relief to which he is not entitled, abuses process. If Article 6 provided a complete remedy, Barron J. held there would be no ground for court proceedings. Barron J. supported his argument by reference to *In Re A Company* [1987] B.C.L.C. 562. There the company's articles set out what should be done in the event of oppression. The petitioner disregarded these provisions and proceeded to court. However, Barron J. found that the English courts had refused to strike out two other petitions in similar circumstances: *In re A Company ex p. Kremer* [1989] B.C.L.C. 365 and *In re A Company ex p. Holden* [1991] B.C.L.C. 597. The English courts refused to strike out or put a stay, because the oppression had impacted on the value of the petitioner's shares, or there was a risk that the petitioner's shareholding would not be fairly valued.

Barron J. stated that the offer of favourable terms to the petitioner in this case was designed to short circuit any claim by him that the valuation was improper.

Barron J. refused to strike the petition out as an abuse of process for four reasons.

First, Article 6 was confined to voluntary sales. Second, since the articles were part of the contractual terms subsisting between the shareholders, these could not be varied by one shareholder without the consent of all others. Third, since the shareholders denied there had ever been oppression, the court's function would be to decide whether there had or had not been such oppression. The court's function was not to value the shares in the same way as the auditors might do. Fourth, the petitioner's claim was equitable, so the price would be fixed on the basis of the court's view of the oppression.

Barron J. pointed out that Blayney J.'s judgment in the Supreme Court in *Irish Press p.l.c. v. Ingersoll Irish Publications Ltd* [1995] 2 I.R. 175; [1995] 2 I.L.R.M. 270 (1995 Review, 90) permitted the price of the oppressed shareholder's shares to include an element of compensation, so long as it was incidental to the main relief. Barron J. held that Article 6 excluded a valuation with this compensation element. Barron J. found no abuse of process. The shareholders appealed.

In the Supreme Court, Murphy J. considered a number of English decisions, including three of Hoffman J. reported under the title of *In Re A Company* [1986] B.C.L.C 362; [1987] B.C.L.C. 94 and [1989] B.C.L.C. 365. The majority of these cases had decided that it was an abuse of process to present a section 205 petition where an offer had been made to buy the petitioner's shares, but yet no oppression had occurred. Oppression was apprehended but had not happened. Oppression may occur where the petitioner is locked into the company and prevented from realising his investment. If such oppression occurred, Murphy J. stated that an Irish court would not strike out the petition as being an abuse of process.

Murphy J. held that the petitioner did not wish to proceed under Article 6. The Article 6 process might involve application to court for directions, and an appeal from the expert's decision. Murphy J. held the petitioner had an arguable case which, if successful, would involve judicial consideration of what constituted an appropriate remedy. He dismissed the respondents' appeal.

Murphy J. introduced a caveat, echoed by O'Flaherty J. Were this litigation to proceed, it would be bitter, expensive and damaging to both sides, irrespective of the outcome. Murphy J. likened section 205 petitions to matrimonial litigation. Both were fuelled by bitterness borne of rejection. In both, the courts found it difficult to persuade the parties to solve their own problems amicably rather than litigate. Murphy J. drew the petitioner's attention to three matters. First, the petition might not succeed. Second, even if successful, the petitioner might not get the relief sought. Third, the offer made by the other shareholders that the shareholding of the petitioner should be valued as if that shareholding formed part of a majority shareholding seemed to offer compensation which if directed by the courts might breach the Supreme Court decision *in Irish Press p.l.c. v. Ingersoll Irish Publications Ltd* [1995] 2 I.R. 175.

O'Flaherty J. dissented. He regarded the amended offer to the petitioner as being preferable to any order which the court could make. The main thrust of O'Flaherty J.'s judgment is directed to the fact that section 205 proceedings are equitable, discretionary, and involve a broader judicial remit than the usual run of adversarial cases. The courts are afforded considerable leeway to strike out redundant proceedings.

O'Flaherty J. advised that if the matter went to trial, the trial judge should attempt to bring the matter to a speedy end without incurring excessive costs so that the remedy which it is agreed on all sides should be available to the petitioner. O'Flaherty J. referred to the other interests which might be affected by this litigation apart from the parties to it. He referred to the companies in their separate and corporate capacities, the company employees, their clients and indeed the public at large.

This judgment shows that it is not possible to provide an article of association dealing with circumstances involving oppression or disregard of interests which excludes court intervention under sections 205 and 213. Nevertheless, the Supreme Court has indicated in the strongest terms possible that parties should only use these sections as a last resort.

Purchasing the shares of an oppressed shareholder   *In Re New-Ad Ad-*

vertising Ltd, High Court, July 1, 1997. In the High Court, Costello P. in a successful section 205 case, gave some indication about how the value of the shareholding should be computed. Costello P. said that the preferred method was to determine the net asset worth at a given date, and add to that a figure representing a review of its dividend policy over a period of three to five years. In this case, there was insufficient evidence to show what the assets of the company were and no dividends had been paid. Costello P. therefore said that it was necessary to establish what the income of the company ought to have been and from this to reconstruct what the net asset position would have been. He did not add in any sum for dividends, as none were declared and paid. On this basis, Costello P. valued the petitioner's shareholding at £67,200, and ordered the majority shareholder to purchase the petitioner's shares at this price.

Security for costs under section 390 of the Companies Act 1963 *Irish Press v. Warburg Pincus & Co* [1997] 2 I.L.R.M. 263. The plaintiff brought a claim for negligent misrepresentation against the defendant, a merchant bank. The defendant sought security for costs for these proceedings under section 390 of the Companies Acts. Under this section, a court may require a plaintiff company to provide security for costs in any proceedings where it has been shown that the plaintiff company will be unable to pay the costs of the defendant, should the defendant be successful. The court may stay all the proceedings until the security is given.

In the High Court, McGuinness J. explained that the court has a discretion to order security for costs. The court must have regard to all the circumstances of the case. A judge considering the security for costs issue is not concerned to assess the merits of the substantive action.

The defendants had to establish that the plaintiff company would be unable to meet the costs if the defendant were successful. If the defendants establish this, and the plaintiff wishes to avoid giving security, it must establish that there are special circumstances justifying refusal of the order granting security for costs.

In granting such an order, the judge is only concerned with security for the hearing, and not for any potential appeals. An appellate court could deal with the issue of security for costs in respect of any appeal to it.

McGuinness J. noted that the courts tended to lean against the making of orders for security for costs. The right of access to courts guaranteed by Article 34.4.3 of the Constitution was one which should be safeguarded. It applied not only to natural persons but to companies.

In this case, McGuinness J. found that while the plaintiff's assets appeared to be diminishing, the plaintiff was not insolvent and continued to hold reasonably substantial assets through its subsidiary companies. McGuinness J. felt that on the balance of the evidence presented the plaintiff was in a position to meet the defendant's costs if the defendant was successful. McGuinness J. refused to order security for costs.

Harrington v. JVC (UK) Ltd Supreme Court, February 21, 1997. In the High Court, O'Hanlon J. ordered that Magna Ltd, the third plaintiff, had to provide security for costs. Magna appealed to the Supreme Court.

In the Supreme Court, O'Flaherty J. held that as Magna was in receivership the defendant was *prima facie* entitled to an order of security for costs. The burden of proof was on Magna to establish that there are special circumstances justifying refusal of the order granting security for costs. Magna claimed that its solvency difficulties were brought about by the conduct of the defendants, the subject matter of the litigation. O'Flaherty J. held that a mere averment such as this was insufficient.

O'Flaherty J. held that there was credible evidence to support the trial judge's finding that Magna had failed to establish special circumstances. O'Flaherty J. refused Magna's appeal.

The constitutionality of section 297   *O'Keeffe v. Ferris* [1997] 2 I.L.R.M. 161. This case concerned an appeal from the High Court's decision, discussed in 1993 Review, 107–108, that fraudulent trading proceedings under section 297 did not amount to a trial of a criminal offence. Therefore, an officer of a company subject to these proceedings was not entitled to the constitutional rights of criminal defendants.

In the Supreme Court, O'Flaherty J. stated that a person could not be made amenable under section 297 unless he or she has actively participated in management decisions designed to defraud creditors. O'Flaherty J. approved Lord Denning M.R.'s interpretation of the English legislative equivalent in *Re Cyona Distributors Ltd* [1967] Ch. 889. There the Master of the Rolls held that the court may make an order against the person who traded fraudulently, requiring that person to pay a fixed sum. This sum must not exceed the total liabilities of the company. This sum may be compensatory, or it may be punitive. The court has complete discretion in directing how this sum is to be applied. The court can order the sum to be paid in discharge of the debt of any particular creditor, class of creditors or paid to the liquidator to swell the general assets of the company. O'Flaherty J. held that section 297(1) did not create a criminal offence. Section 297(3) creates the criminal offence. Section 297(4) allows both civil and criminal proceedings to be brought simultaneously in respect of the same facts. O'Flaherty J. found that section 297 did not contain the ingredients of a criminal offence identified in *Melling v. O'Mathghamhna* [1962] I.R. 1. There was no prosecutor, no offence created, no mode of trial of a criminal offence and no criminal sanction imposed. O'Flaherty J. held that the Oireachtas was entitled to implement this section to protect creditors and others who may fall victim to fraudsters.

O'Flaherty J. recognised that although fraud was an ingredient in many criminal offences, it formed a component of various civil wrongs. In civil fraud cases, the civil burden of proof applied. In such cases where the fraud is serious, the trial judge must ensure that the allegation has been satisfactorily established.

O'Flaherty J. considered the punitive element of section 297. He held that it may take two forms. First, the loss of limited liability for shareholders involved in the management of the company. Second, the court has the discretion to require a fraudulent trader to repay more than he illegally obtained. O'Flaherty J. held that the function of the trial judge is to ensure any sanction is proportionate.

O'Flaherty J. dismissed the appeal.

Restriction of directors   *In Re Outdoor Advertising Services Ltd,* High Court, January 28, 1997. A liquidator brought restriction proceedings against three directors of the company: a husband, wife and a third party.

In the High Court, Costello P. held that a restriction order under section 150 will be made against the directors of a company in liquidation, unless the court is satisfied they have acted "honestly and responsibly" in relation to the conduct of the affairs of the company. The directors must discharge the burden of proof by showing that they did act honestly and responsibly.

Costello P. considered two company cheques signed by two of the company's directors: the wife and third party. The cheques were paid to discharge overdrafts of two companies. These two companies were owned by the husband and wife. Neither of these companies were creditors of Outdoor Advertising Services Ltd. These cheques were signed when the company was insolvent and in negotiations for takeover.

Costello P. found that the husband and wife had failed to establish that they acted honestly and responsibly in relation to the two cheques. The wife accepted that one of the companies was not a creditor of the company. She argued that the liabilities of the two companies were part of the proposed takeover deal. If these two companies fell into insolvency, the takeover would be imperilled. Costello P. found this totally unconvincing. Costello P. believed that the husband and wife were fully aware of the enormous insolvency of the company. Costello P. held that the husband and wife had acted irresponsibly and dishonestly. They caused the company to pay non-creditors, including a director. Costello P. decided that although the husband had not signed the two cheques, he was deliberate and complicit in procuring the signature of his wife and the third director. Costello P. made restriction orders against the husband and wife.

Costello P. examined the position of the third director. Costello P. stated that the third director had agreed to accept the post of managing director of the company. He was described as a director on the company's stationery and in the mandate provided to the company's bankers. However, he was never in fact appointed as a director or a managing director of the company. Costello P. decided that the man ceased to act as a *de facto* director about nine months before the liquidation. Costello P. was satisfied that the man's continued involvement with the company thereafter was not that of a director notwithstanding appearances to the contrary. Costello P. was satisfied that section 150 did not apply to him.

In *Re Ambury Wholesale Electrical Ltd*, High Court, *ex tempore*, June 3, 1997. Shanley J held that there was *prima facie* evidence that the directors have acted irresponsibly when a company is small, and the deficiency in the assets on liquidation is large. There was a heavy burden placed on the directors to prove to the court that they had acted responsibly. The burden of proof that directors must discharge varies depending on the size of the company and the concomitant deficiency: see Brian Walker, 'Creditors' rights to have directors restricted – a new development' in *Commercial Law Practitioner* (1998), Vol. 5, No. 7 (July), pp. 159–163 at 163.

Receiver's duty when selling assets of company   *In Re Edenfell Holdings Ltd*, High Court, July 30, 1997; Supreme Court, April 23, 1998. In 1992, Edenfell Holdings Ltd completed a debenture giving a fixed charge over land. On May 25, 1995, the debenture holder, a bank, appointed a receiver. Edenfell's indebtedness to the bank was approximately £930,000. Edenfell was placed in liquidation on 19 June.

In November, Stormdust Ltd obtained leave to issue proceedings. These claimed that Edenfell had agreed to sell the charged land. In the High Court, McCracken J. held that there was no such valid contract between Stormdust and Edenfell, and he refused Stormdust's application for specific performance. Stormdust appealed McCracken J.'s decision.

By now, Edenfell's indebtedness to the bank was in excess of £1.1 million. Interest was accruing at £2,850 per week. The receiver obtained two offers for the land. The first was a conditional offer of £1.6 million. The second was an unconditional offer of £1.5 million for the land and in addition the offeror was prepared to pay £100,000 to Stormdust to withdraw its appeal to the Supreme Court. The receiver was advised by two auctioneers to accept the £1.5 million offer. The receiver accorded other interested parties the opportunity to make further bids. None better emerged. The receiver signed contracts accepting the £1.5 million offer. Following this, the £1.5 million conditional offeror made an improved counter offer of £1.8 million.

The receiver informed the liquidator of the transaction. The liquidator was concerned whether receiver had obtained the best possible price for the company's asset as required by section 316A of the Companies Act 1963. The matter was referred to the High Court for adjudication.

In the High Court, Laffoy J. explained that section 316A requires that when selling company property, a receiver must exercise all reasonable care to obtain the best price reasonably obtainable for the property at the time of the sale. This is merely a statutory restatement of the common law duty of care owned by a receiver in relation to the sale of property charged by the debenture. Relying on *Holohan v. Friends Provident and Century Life Office* [1966] I.R. 1 Laffoy J. stated that if such sale were in breach of these provisions, its completion could be restrained by injunction.

Laffoy J. found that the receiver had not acted unreasonably in concluding that the unconditional offer was the more attractive offer of the two. However, there was no evidence whatsoever that the receiver gave any consideration as to whether paying £100,000 to Stormdust to procure the withdrawal of its appeal at that juncture was reasonable and prudent. Laffoy J. did accept that Stormdust's appeal did give rise to a number of imponderables. Laffoy J. stated that the receiver should have considered these before accepting the second offer. The £100,000 being paid to Stormdust to withdraw its appeal might be available to Edenfell. The receiver should have considered applying to the court on notice to the liquidator for leave to enter into the arrangement before committing himself to it. Laffoy J. held that the receiver had not exercised all reasonable care to obtain the best price reasonably obtainable for the lands on the date in question. Laffoy J. injuncted the receiver from completing this contract and ordered him to return the deposit to the purchaser.

The receiver appealed against Laffoy J.'s decision. In the Supreme Court, Keane J. upheld the receiver's appeal. On receiving the unconditional £1.5 million offer, the receiver gave other potential buyers an opportunity to improve on the offer. No buyer was prepared to make an unconditional offer in excess of £1.5 million or indeed an unconditional offer of any sort, at least for as long as the litigation remains unresolved. If the receiver had refused the unconditional offer, he could have found himself without a buyer, with ever-increasing interest and costs relating to the appeal. It was accepted that if Stormdust's appeal was unsuccessful, there was no prospect of recovering any costs from Stormdust as it was a shelf company with no assets.

The court could not operate with the benefit of hindsight. The receiver had considered the £1.5 million offer in light of the expert valuer's advice. Having tested the market again unsuccessfully, the receiver was entitled to take the prudent course of accepting the £1.5 million. Keane J. directed that the receiver and the liquidator should complete the conveyance of the land to the buyer.

The Supreme Court judgment emphasises that once a receiver has taken proper professional advice, the court will allow that receiver to make an independent judgment as to the optimal course to take. It does not answer the more difficult problem of how the receiver should proceed if the proposed course of action, while definitely to the advantage of the debenture holder, significantly maximises the loss to the general creditors. This is particularly acute in an environment when banks can and do virtually take all possible security. Some residium should be statutorily available for the benefit of the general body of creditors, as is the case in other jurisdictions.

The appointment of an interim examiner and conferring powers on an examiner *In re Advanced Technology College Ltd,* High Court, March 13, 1997. In this case the High Court considered the test to be applied for the appointment of an interim examiner.

This company ran educational courses. At the time of the petition, approximately five hundred students were enrolled. When the students learned of the college's insolvency, they were concerned lest they could not finish their courses and exams. The students petitioned for the appointment of an interim examiner.

In the High Court, Kelly J. found that the students had established that the college was or was likely to be unable to pay its debts. No resolution subsisted for the winding up of the company and no order had been made for the winding up of the company by the court. Kelly J. then considered whether the students had demonstrated the existence of an identifiable possibility of survival of the company or at least a part of its undertaking as a going concern as required by the Supreme Court in *Re Atlantic Magnetics* [1993] 2 I.R. 561. Kelly J. accepted that creditor petitioners will have greater difficulty in satisfying this test. These petitioners do not have access to the quality and quantity of information available to the company and its directors. However, Kelly J. refused to dilute the test in *Re Atlantic Magnetics* for creditor petitioners.

Kelly J. examined the affidavit evidence presented by the students. The students recognised the need for investment, but failed to identify a potential investor in their affidavit. Kelly J. took the unusual step of allowing oral testimony from one of the deponents, a solicitor. This solicitor claimed that there was one prospective investor, a large company. The contact with the investor was made through the father of one of the students. The investor's name was not given as the company in question did not wish to be identified. It appears that Kelly J. was told a name, but the judgment does not disclose it. The solicitor was unable to give information as to the size or terms of the investment. The directors of the company indicated that they had received approaches from other potential investors. Kelly J. found that on the basis of this evidence the students had demonstrated the existence of an identifiable possibility of survival of the college.

Kelly J. did not expressly identify any difference between the tests for appointing an examiner and an interim examiner. One possible explanation is that an interim examiner may be appointed where this is necessary to preserve the company's viability until the petition may be heard. It was argued that in this case, some students might leave, and the resulting depletion of the student numbers would make it uneconomic for the college to continue. Likewise some staff might leave, and the college would lose its reputation which would affect is ability to attract investors. Kelly J. accepted this and appointed an interim examiner.

The students petitioned that the interim examiner should be accorded powers to deal with a deadline for examination applications. Kelly J. pointed out that under statute, the examiner's role is to report on the company's situation and prospects. The examiner's authority does not initially extend to running the company, although if the examiner applies under section 9, the court may afford him such powers. Only the examiner may so apply. This is not open to petitioners.

Finally, Kelly J. at an earlier hearing, having found the advertisements for the petition failed to refer to the time and venue for its hearing, ordered its readvertisement. Kelly J. held the advertisement of ought at a minimum to specify the time, date and place of hearing. The petitioners appealed Kelly J.'s order. The Supreme Court upheld Kelly J.'s order. The Supreme Court held the purpose of the advertisement was to inform members of the public where and when the application was to be made and its fundamental purpose. An advertisement must state the time, date and place where the application is to be heard.

Despite the clear import of the Supreme Court's decision, the petitioners applied to Kelly J. for leave not to readvertise the petition. They averred that it was unlikely others apart from those already before the court would have any interest in the company. Kelly J. found that since the petitioners had no information as to the number, nature or quantum of other creditors of the company, he was obliged to refuse their petition.

The requirements for a petition for the appointment of an examiner   *In Re Aston Colour Print Ltd,* High Court, February 21, 1997. Under section 3 of the Companies (Amendment) Act 1990, the directors may petition for examinership. In *Aston*, the High Court discussed the procedural requirements for such application.

This company, Aston Colour Print Ltd, was incorporated in 1996. The company had two directors and six shareholders. The directors, shareholders and the financial controller had meetings concerning the company's affairs nearly every week. In January 1997, the company was in serious financial difficulties.

On January 27, a meeting was called to discuss the options available to the company. On the basis of the financial information available, the financial controller informed the directors and shareholders that the company could not continue to trade unless something was done. The meeting canvassed the options of finding a new investor, or petitioning for liquidation or examinership. A petition was presented on the February 5, in the name of the two directors. In the High Court, Shanley J. appointed an interim examiner.

On February 17, the petition came on for plenary hearing. One of the directors objected to the presentation of the petition. Kelly J. directed that both directors were to be cross-examined on their affidavits. A shareholder and the financial controller who attended the January 27 meeting also gave evidence.

In the High Court, Kelly J. found that at the January 27 meeting, no resolution had been proposed or passed to petition for the examinership. This was not unusual. The weekly meetings were informal, and the business was conducted by way of emerging consensus rather than by voting on resolutions. This was an understandable way to run a small business. However, the risk was that the participants might not have agreed the outcome.

Kelly J. attempted to elicit whether the January 27 meeting was technically a board meeting, and if so, whether it had validly resolved to petition for examinership.

Kelly J. concluded that the January 27 meeting was not a board meeting.

Directors must be aware that the meeting they are attending is in fact a board meeting. The financial controller had testified that he did not know that he was attending a board meeting. Likewise, one of the directors did not appreciate that the meeting was not the usual weekly executive meeting but purported to be a board meeting. It was chaired not by the chairman of the board, but by one of the shareholders. The shareholder chairing the meeting assumed he was chairing a shareholder's meeting which subsequently became a board meeting, though Kelly J. questioned somewhat sceptically at what stage the transformation occurred.

Although Kelly J. decided that the January 27 meeting was not a board meeting, he considered whether the meeting had validly resolved to petition for examinership. Kelly J. found that no formal resolution was put or voted on at this meeting. The presentation of an examinership petition is a momentous matter, not just for the company but for the company's creditors and workforce. For this reason, the board must make the decision in a clear fashion. Normally this is done by the tabling and passing of a resolution. Had this course been adopted at the February 27 meeting, Kelly J. believed that one director would have voted against the proposal as he did not want his name associated with a petition to place the company under court protection. Kelly J. dismissed the application, but stated that this did not preclude the presentation of a further petition by a duly authorised party. Though informal running of the internal affairs of a company is in general permissible, where the rights and interests of outsiders are or may be concerned, it is necessary to take the required formal steps, if only for the avoidance of doubt.

The priority of an examiners' costs and expenses   *In Re Springline Ltd* [1998] 1 I.L.R.M. 300. Springline Ltd, initially under court protection went into liquidation. The High Court sanctioned the examiner's costs remuneration and expenses. These totalled just under £55,000. The examiner sought payment from the liquidator. The liquidator refused.

In the High Court, Shanley J. decided that the narrow point for decision was whether the liquidator's costs, remuneration and expenses can be regarded as a company debt or whether it constitutes a different type of debt. If the former, section 29(3) of the Companies (Amendment) Act 1990 accords the examiner's costs and expenses priority over those of a liquidator.

Shanley J. decided that a liquidator's costs, remuneration and expenses cannot be considered a debt or claim against the company. Shanley J. found that the 1963 Act and the Rules of the Superior Courts 1986 provided different approaches to determining on the one hand the debts of the company and on the other the costs, remuneration and expenses of a liquidator. Shanley J. opined that this difference alone did not mean the liquidators costs and expenses was not a company debt.

Shanley J. inferred a more substantive distinction from section 283 of the Companies Act 1963. This provides that all claims against the company, present or future, shall be admissible to proof against the company upon a winding up of the company. Section 75 of the Bankruptcy Act 1988 provides that debts and liabilities "present or future" shall be provable in the bankruptcy or arrangement. Shanley J. held that references to a future claim or future debt did not include the remuneration costs and expenses of a liquidator. Future debts or future claims relate to obligations incurred by the company *before* the date of winding-up. Shanley J. held that a liquidator's remuneration, costs and expenses is an obligation incurred by the company *after* the date of the winding-up and cannot therefore fall into the category of future claims or future debts. They do not fall to be proven as debts in liquidation or as claims in the liquidation in the manner provided for in Order 74 of the rules. Under section 29(3) of the Companies (Amendment) Act 1990 the examiner's priority covered all other claims of the company secured or unsecured. It did not give an examiner priority over the costs expenses and remuneration of a liquidator. Shanley J. was aware of the duty of the courts where interpreting legislation to give effect to the intention of the legislature. However, Shanley J. found that it was impossible to construe section 29(3) of the Companies (Amendment) Act to permit an examiner to be paid ahead of a liquidator without doing violence to the subsection.

The examiner also raised the argument that he was entitled to be paid in priority to the liquidator, because his fees were incurred in preserving, realising and getting in the company's assets. Order 74 rule 128(1) of the Rules of the Superior Court 1986 provides that any fees or expenses properly incurred in preserving or getting in the assets of the company may be paid before the liquidator's expenses and the debts of the company.

Shanley J. rejected this argument. The function of the examiner is to investigate the viability of the company and, in certain circumstances, to formulate proposals for its survival. Shanley J. accepted that while the examiner is performing these functions, it is necessary to preserve the company's assets. Such protection is afforded not by an examiner, but from the fact of court protection and its consequences.

Accordingly, Shanley J. held that the liquidator was right in refusing to pay the examiner his fees and expenses in priority to his own. The examiner appealed to the Supreme Court. On July 22, 1998, Keane J. in the Supreme Court, held that the costs of an examiner must be paid in full out of the company's assets before any of the costs of a liquidator appointed by a court after the examiner had ceased to act. The Supreme Court allowed the appeal from the High Court, holding that section 29(3) of the Companies Act 1990 gives the examiner priority over the costs, expenses and remuneration of the liquidator in the winding-up of a company.

In camera **and section 231**   *In Re Greendale Developments Ltd,* High Court, July 28, 1997. The liquidator of Greendale sought court permission under section 231 to continue two plenary actions, initiated prior to liquidation. The liquidator wished to have this section 231 application heard *in camera*.

In the High Court, Laffoy J. held that there is a constitutional requirement for justice to be administered in public, save where a statutory provision permits *in camera* hearings. No specific statutory provisions existed here. Therefore, the point for determination by Laffoy J. was whether the application by the liquidation constituted the administration of justice.

Laffoy J. considered two of the five characteristics of the administration of justice identified in *McDonald v. Bord na gCon* [1965] I.R. 1. These were the presence of an *inter partes* contest, and the liability of one or other party to liability or penalty. Laffoy J. opined that both were present in a liquidator's application under section 231.

A judgment of the High Court to allow the liquidator to continue proceedings was qualitatively different from the decision by a board of directors of a solvent company to litigate. The latter decision is grounded on the company's interests. In a liquidation, the court's judgment to allow proceedings to go forward will take into account the interests of the creditor or contributory and, in particular, to the protection of his legal entitlement to a distribution from the assets of the company.

Laffoy J. distinguished this case from the situation in *Re Countyglen plc* [1995] 1 I.R. 220. In the *Countyglen* case there was no contest between the parties, whereas section 231 provides the machinery for the commencement of a contest. Once a contest is started, its resolution must be a justiciable issue.

Since Laffoy J. held that the determination of section 231 proceedings constituted the administration of justice, the High Court was obliged to hear such applications in public.

Misfeasance proceedings *In Re Greendale Developments Ltd,* Supreme Court, February 20, 1997. Misfeasance proceedings under section 298 are brought by motion on notice, and come on for hearing relatively quickly. Section 298 allows the High Court to order the directors to repay or restore monies or property of the company which had been either misapplied or retained by the directors or for which the directors had become liable or accountable to the company.

Greendale Developments Ltd was incorporated in 1988. The company had three shareholders: a husband and wife and a third party. The husband and the third party were the directors of the company. The company was formed to carry out a property development on a site in Islandbridge. The company successfully developed this site. Subsequently, a bitter dispute arose between the two directors. The husband sought to wind-up the company on the ground that it was "just and equitable" to do so. The High Court allowed the winding-up petition and appointed a liquidator. The liquidator investigated the company's financial position. As a result of his inquiries, the liquidator believed that the husband owed substantial sums of money to the company. The liquidator was worried that the husband and wife would dissipate personal assets before obtaining a court order requiring the repayment of the money allegedly owing by the husband.

The liquidator instituted misfeasance proceedings under section 298 and sought an injunction restraining the husband and wife from disposing of the proceeds of a house they owned. At the hearing, the liquidator claimed that the husband and wife owed the company over £330,000. The husband and wife disputed the liquidator's claim. In fact, they argued that they were entitled to set off money that the company owed to them against any claim the company might have against them.

According to the directors' compulsory statement of affairs, the company had paid the husband and wife in total £255,893.69. The husband and wife claimed that the company owed them £130,000 in wages. The liquidator disputed this sum and claimed that only £77,800 was owed in wages. The company had made payments to a company controlled by the husband for work done on the Islandbridge site. The husband claimed that Greendale Developments owed his company £108,500. In addition, the company made payments for the benefit of the husband and wife. Some of these sums were not in dispute. Others were. These included a house costing the company over £110,000 but owned by the husband and wife and a credit card bill of over £30,000. The husband claimed that the company was not in a financial position to close the contract for the house and the husband and wife had to buy the house.

In the High Court, Costello P. found that the liquidator had established that the husband owed the company £435,750.06. The husband was not entitled to set off the sums claimed by him against the money due to the company. He ordered the husband to pay in total £437,750 to the liquidator. The President of the High Court made no order against the wife, as she was not an officer of the company for the purposes of section 298. The wife was a promoter of the company. But none of the liquidators' claims against the wife related to transactions performed at the time of the formation of the company or during its promotion. The husband appealed to the Supreme Court.

Four grounds to the husband's appeal are of relevance. First, the company was solvent at all times. Second, the transactions had been assented to by all the shareholders of the company and so no misfeasance proceedings could be brought against the directors. Third, misfeasance proceedings under section 298 were inappropriate. Fourth, the husband was entitled to a right of set-off.

In the Supreme Court, Keane J. stated first that it seemed reasonable to suppose that the company was at the relevant time solvent, as the order for the company's winding had been made not on the basis of its insolvency but on the basis that it was "just and equitable". Keane J. examined the statement of affairs filed by the husband. It showed a surplus of assets and liabilities of £338,664. However, one of the assets consisted of prospective legal claims against the company's legal and financial advisers, estimated at over £3.5 million. The statement also showed that the company owed trade creditors over £60,000 and the Revenue Commissioners £260,000, even though the returns had yet to be submitted to the Revenue Commissioners to date. The liquidation costs and expenses had yet to be factored in. Keane J. concluded that the solvency of the company could not be guaranteed.

Second, Keane J. applied the legal principles laid down in *Buchanan Ltd & Anor. v. Mc Vey* [1954] I.R. 89. In *Buchanan*, Kingsmill Moore J. held that if shareholders informally agree to a certain transaction, it is an act of the company and binds the company. This was subject to two conditions. First, the transaction to which the shareholders agree should be *intra vires*. Second, that the transaction should be honest. Considering the first condition, Keane J. held that Greendale Developments in no way benefitted from these transactions. A company cannot make gratuitous dispositions of its property except where this is incidental to the carrying on of the business. Keane J. held that the transactions in question were *ultra vires* and were made by the company for the benefit of the husband and wife. This "fundamental illegality" could not be cured by the fact that all the shareholders assented to all the agreements in question. Keane J. stated that the position might be different if the transactions were expressly authorised by the memorandum and articles of association of Greendale Developments.

The husband argued that a company may spend money or apply property for purposes which are *ultra vires* the company provided all the shareholders assent to the *ultra vires* transaction. The husband relied upon the decision of Gavan Duffy P. in *Re S M Barker Ltd* [1950] I.R. 123. In this case, three shareholders/directors of a company had sold their shareholding to a group of individuals in a complex and unorthodox manner. The company subsequently went into liquidation. The liquidator brought misfeasance proceedings against the shareholders/directors under the relevant section of the Companies (Consolidation) Act 1908. Keane J. held that the ratio of *Re S M Barker Ltd* was that misfeasance proceedings can only be brought against directors. Such proceedings cannot be brought against shareholders making a profit *qua* shareholders. He refused to uphold the husband's argument.

Third, Keane J. addressed the claim that misfeasance proceedings were inappropriate. Keane J. found that section 298 did not create any new cause of action. It merely provides a summary remedy for the recovery of monies which an officer of the company would be liable to repay or account for the company. The husband attempted again to rely upon *Re S M Barker Ltd* [1950] I.R. 123. Keane J. said that this case did not apply for two reasons. In *Re S M Barker Ltd*, the transactions were carried out by the shareholders and although the transfer of shares occurred in "a bizarre and unorthodox manner" the company had suffered no loss. In this case, the transactions had been carried out by the two directors, not by the shareholders and the shareholders at no time attempted to pass a resolution authorising these transactions. In the present case the company had suffered damage as a consequence of the transactions. Keane J. concluded that the section 298 application brought by the liquidator was appropriate.

Finally, Keane J. examined the husband and wife's claim that they were entitled to set off the sums claimed by the liquidator against certain sums owed by the company to them. In the High Court, Costello P. found that none of the claims justified any set off to the credit of the husband and wife. Keane J. pointed out that it was settled law in England since *In Re Anglo French Co-Operative Society, ex p. Pelly* [1882] 21 Ch. D. 492, that an officer of a company who has been found liable to pay money to the company in misfeasance proceedings is not entitled to set off a debt owing by the company to him against that liability. The reason for the rule was that the right of set off only arose in the case of actions between parties. In addition, it was well established that no right of set off can in any event arise unless the debts could be said to be mutual. In this case, there was clearly no mutuality between the sum sought to be recovered by the liquidator as having been misapplied by the husband in breach of his fiduciary duties as a director to the company and the sums claimed by the husband in respect of certain transactions. The husband could still prove these alleged debts as an unsecured creditor in the liquidation.

Keane J. dismissed the appeal.

European Communities (Public Ltd Companies Subsidiaries) Regulations, 1997 (S.I. No. 67 of 1997) The Second Directive, Formation and Capital of Public Ltd Companies, requires member states to ensure that directors of p.l.c.s, or those companies which translate from private companies to p.l.c.s, should be adequately capitalised. The assumption is that capital is the creditor's buffer. It assumes that if company's shareholders are required to pay cash for part of their shares, a company thus provided with a bare minimum of capital has some consequential viability and a higher likelihood of solvency, a proposition which has never been satisfactorily tested, and whose converse is frequently obviously true.

The 1963 Act provided some instances of capital protection, in particular by providing (subject to exceptions) that a company should not be allowed to buy its own shares, nor lend money to others to do so.

Part XI of the Companies Act 1990 derogated from this principle by allowing certain companies to acquire their own shares. Upon acquisition, these shares are denominated 'treasury shares' and carry no right to dividend or vote, until re-issued for money or money's worth. They then revert to being shares with some or all of the usual characteristics. Though these provisions are unexceptionable, some of the other capital protection provisions are so complex, so frequently avoided, and the avoidance schemes so likely to be judicially impugned that statutory clarification is urgently needed.

The 1990 Act left some gaps. In particular, though the legislation aimed to catch not merely the purchase by a company of its own shares, but also the purchase of any subsidiary company's assets.

The function of this Statutory Instrument is to extend the definition of a subsidiary of a p.l.c., and to apply the rules in Part XI of the 1990 Act to such subsidiaries. The Statutory Instrument fills an apparent gap in the 1990 Act by including in the definition of a subsidiary company of a p.l.c., any company in which the p.l.c. owns shares and with some or all of whose other shareholders the p.l.c. has an agreement by which the p.l.c. is given effective control of the subsidiary's voting rights.

In so doing, this Statutory Instrument provides for directors' obligations to disclose certain acquisitions, and imposes penalties for breaches of these regulations.

Conflicts of Law

ADOPTION

Intercountry adoption   In its *Consultation Paper on the Implementation of the Hague Convention on the Protection of Children and Co-operation in Respect of Intercountry Adoption, 1993*, published in September 1997, the Law Reform Commission provisionally recommends that Ireland implement this Convention by legislation containing regulations setting out the detail of the procedures to be followed by the various authorities. One of the Commissioners, Professor William Duncan, played a leading role in the formulation of the Convention.

The need for the Convention is clear. The practice of intercountry adoption has been fueled by the inequalities between rich and poor countries, the phenomena of war, famine and civil unrest and the dearth of children available for adoption in North America and Western Europe. Every year over twenty thousand children experience intercountry adoption. There is evidence of 'the falsification of birth records, the coercion and bribery of natural parents, and in some cases the sale and abduction of children . . .': *Consultation Paper*, paragraph 3.03.

The Convention seeks to establish open channels of communication between the countries of origin of adopted children and 'receiving countries'. It sets up a framework for regulation and co-operation between states. As the Commission notes, '[i]ts primary, though not exclusive, focus is on the process of adoption, rather than on subsequent recognition': *id.*, paragraph 3.05.

Chapter II of the Convention sets out the requirements for intercountry adoption. The competent authorities of the state of origin must establish that the child is adoptable, determine that an intercountry adoption is in the child's best interests and ensure that those whose consent is necessary for adoption have been counselled and duly informed of the effects of their consent, that they have given their consent freely, without financial inducement, that the child's wishes have been considered and, where his or her consent is required, that it had been given freely, again without financial inducement: Article 4.

The competent authorities of the receiving state must have determined the eligibility and suitability of the prospective adoptive parents: Article 5.

Chapter III requires each contracting state to designate a Central Authority to discharge the wide range of duties which the Convention imposes. Chapter IV prescribes the procedural requirements for intercountry adoptions. If the

Central Authority of the receiving state is satisfied about the eligibility and suitability of the prospective adopters, it must prepare a report on them which it transmits to the Central Authority of the state of origin, which is under a similar obligation in relation to the child. The latter Central Authority must ensure that all necessary consents have been obtained and determine, on the basis of the two reports, whether the envisaged placement is in the child's best interests.

Chapter V prescribes the rules relating to recognition and effects of adoption. These are of considerable breadth. Article 23 requires an adoption certified by the competent authority of the state of the adoption as having been made in accordance with the Convention to be 'recognised by operation of law in the other Contracting States'. The only ground for non-recognition, specified by Article 24, is that the adoption is 'manifestly contrary to public policy, taking into account the best interests of the child'.

Article 26 deals with the principal effects of recognition. It provides that the recognition of an adoption includes recognition of the legal parent-child relationship between the child and his or her adoptive parents, their parental responsibility for the child and the termination of the pre-existing relationship between the child and his or her mother or father, if (as in Ireland, for example) the adoption has this effect in the contracting state where it was made, in which case the child will enjoy in the receiving state and other contracting states where the adoption is recognised rights equivalent to those resulting from adoptions having this effect in these states. Article 26 seeks to provide a *via media* to deal with the fact that many countries have a concept of 'simple' adoption in contradistinction to 'full' adoption (which is the Irish model): see the *Consultation Paper*, paragraph 3.12.

Chapter VI of the Convention contains general provisions, relating to such matters as controls on contact between the prospective adopters and the natural parents before the adoption process is under way (Article 29), the preservation of information as to the child's origin and medical records for subsequent access by the child (Article 30) and the prohibition on the sale of children: Article 32.2 provides that only costs and expenses, 'including reasonable professional fees of persons involved in the adoption', may be charged.

Among detailed provisional recommendations, the Commission proposes that, where Ireland is the State of origin in a Convention adoption, the same criteria for adoptability should be applied to children entrusted to prospective adoptive parents for adoption outside the jurisdiction as are applied to children in domestic adoptions. More controversially, it proposes that, where Ireland is the receiving State under the Convention, the determination by the competent authorities of the state of origin in accordance with Article 4 of the sufficiency of consents should, as a general principle, be accepted by the Irish authorities, whether the adoption is to be effected in Ireland or the state of origin. Irish requirements for parental consent require this to be a fully informed and free one. Some other countries are less fastidious. The Commission acknowledges that care must be taken in all cases to ensure that child is not placed for an intercountry adoption without the consent of the natural parents. It goes on to state (in paragraph 4.45):

> There must be no possibility that lower standards of consent be applied to intercountry adoption than to domestic adoptions. This need not preclude, however, an adaptation of the procedures for the giving of consent to meet the particular needs of intercountry adoption. Since the Convention depends on co-operation between the competent authorities of Contracting States, it would be in accordance with the spirit of the Convention to accept the State of origin's determination of the sufficiency of consents, in all but the most unusual cases.

Undoubtedly it would be a great deal less troublesome to take this approach. In practice, no opposition to it is likely to be heard from those who may suffer from lax foreign requirements on consent. Yet there is something disturbing about the idea that a consent which is less than fully free, judged by our domestic legal requirements, should in at least some instances be acceptable because it is foreign people whose consent is at issue. It is true that Irish courts have in recent years been coy about the idea that our Constitution is capable of giving protection to people outside the jurisdiction or that the humanistic principles on which it is based are universal rather than narrowly territorial in their application to human beings beyond our shores. Yet it was an adoption case in which Hamilton J., as he the was, could say, in *Northampton County Council v. A.B.F.* [1982] I.L.R.M. 162:

> It seems to me . . . that non-citizenship can have no effect on the interpretation of Article 41 or the entitlement to the protection afforded by it . . . The natural law is of universal application and applies to all human persons, be they citizens of this State or not. . . .

It is quite possible for Ireland to make a policy decision to facilitate the recognition of foreign adoptions under the Convention by tolerating less fastidious standards for consent for foreign adoptions than under our own law. Whether this can be done consistently with constitutional requirements we need not here consider; but what is clear beyond argument is that we cannot, as the Commission appears to believe, have it both ways, by accepting foreign determinations of consent which we know are not as demanding as our own while pretending to ourselves that '[t]here must be no possibility that lower standards of consent be applied to intercountry adoption than apply to domestic adoptions'.

ADMIRALTY

In the 1989 Review, 69–73, we analysed the Jurisdiction of Courts (Maritime Conventions) Act 1989, which gives effect in Irish law to (*inter alia*) the 1952 Brussels Convention on the Arrest of Sea Going Ships. For further analysis, see Alan Doherty, 'Ship Arrest in Ireland' (1996) 3 *C.L.P.* 232 (1996). Article 2 of the Convention provides that a ship flying the flag of one of the Contracting States may be arrested in the jurisdiction of any of the Contracting States in respect of any maritime claim. Section 13(2) of the 1989 Act defines 'ship' as including 'every description of vessel used in navigation'. 'Vessel', in turn, is defined in the same subsection as including 'any ship or boat, or any other description of vessel used in navigation.'

In *The "Von Rocks": Targe Towing Ltd v. The Owners and All Persons Claiming an Interest in the Vessel "Von Rocks"* [1997] 1 I.L.R.M. 542; [1997] 1 I.R. 236 (see above, 19), Barr J. had no hesitation in holding that a backhoe dredger, a species of maritime dredger, was not a ship or other vessel within the meaning of the 1989 Act, and that accordingly it should be released forthwith from arrest in respect of a claim for negligence and breach of contract. The Supreme Court, on January 22, 1998, unanimously reversed Barr J. [1998] I.L.R.M. 481. The sharp difference of judicial opinion is worth examining more closely than the somewhat mundane facts might at first suggest, since in both the High Court and the Supreme Court there is a clear appreciation of the wider issues of principle and policy.

In approaching the issue Barr J. stressed the far-reaching consequences of the arrest process for an alleged debtor through interference with the debtor's business by immobilisation of the vessel. It followed that there was 'a strong onus on the person seeking to exercise that remedy to establish that the craft to be arrested is in fact a ship or vessel as defined in the 1989 Act and Arrest Convention.'

The backhoe dredger was primarily used in harbours, channels or estuaries to deepen the water in these locations. When not in operation, it was a floating platform comprising ten individual pontoons bolted together. When in use, it was held in position on the seabed by three spud legs which were capable of being hydraulically lowered and raised. When the legs were lowered to the seabed at the site of dredging, the platform was jacked-up to form a rigid platform; it remained in this state until the legs were withdrawn and the structure floated again. An excavator was bolted to one end of the platform and was used to excavate spoil from the seabed. The spoil was in turn poured into an adjacent barge and taken away from time to time. The backhoe dredger had no bow, no stern, no anchors, no rudder or other means for steering, no keel and no skeg. It had no means of self-propulsion and no wheelhouse. It had a lighting tower and a steel cabin which contained an office and a toilet. It could not carry cargo, spoil or personnel other than those engaged in the dredging operation.

On completion of a contract the backhoe dredger had either to be dismantled and transported by road or to be towed by sea. Extensive preparations were required to make it seaworthy for towing for any significant distance. During this maneuver it was unmanned and 'merely an inert object being towed by a power-driven vessel.'

Barr J. approached the issue of 'look[ing] primarily to the basic nature and purpose of the structure when in operation.' He was satisfied that, while the dredger became a floating object temporarily when its legs were raised and it was towed a few metres forward after it had removed all spoil from a given areas within the radius of its dredging arm, 'negligible movements of that sort' could not reasonably be considered to mean that the dredger was a vessel 'used in navigation', as section 13(2) required. Likewise, an object under tow which took no part in the towing operation *per se* could not reasonably be regarded as being 'used in navigation'. Barr J. was of the view that this phrase:

> necessarily implies some element of participation in the towing operation. In fact the towing of a backhoe dredger would seem to be essentially similar to the towing of a fixed oil rig to or from its drilling station. Such rigs are not ships.

Barr J. derived support from Atkinson J.'s reference, in *Polpen Shipping Co. Ltd v. Commercial Union Assurance Co. Ltd.* [1943] K.B. 161, to the definitions of 'ship' and 'vessel' in section 742 of the Merchant Shipping Act 1894, which are virtually identical to those in the 1989 Act. It seemed to Atkinson J. that 'the dominant idea is something which is "used in navigation" and not merely capable of navigating for the moment.' Thus a flying-boat was not a ship or vessel since its real purpose was to fly and its ability to float and navigate short distances was merely incidental to its real purpose. Applying that reasoning to the instant case, it followed that, even if the backhoe dredger was deemed capable of navigation when being towed for minute distances in the course of dredging or while being towed by sea from site to site, use in navigation by sea was not its real work but was merely incidental to its primary purpose of being a rigid platform for dredging.

Barr J. was also tempted by Sheen J.'s view in *Steedman v. Scofield* [1992] 2 Lloyd's Rep. 163, at 166 that the phrase 'used in navigation' 'conveys the concept of transporting persons or property by water to an intended destination. . . .' One can perhaps question whether this is too narrow a definition. An unmanned vessel on a scientific exploration is surely capable of being 'used in navigation.' As we shall see, the Supreme Court made much of the weakness of this rationale for holding that the dredger was not 'used in navigation'.

Finally, Barr J. found re-enforcement for his conclusion in the narrowness of the definition of ship and vessel in the 1894 and 1989 Acts, in contrast to

section 3(1) of the Sea Pollution Act 1991 and section 2(1) of the Merchant
Shipping (Salvage and Wreck) Act 1993, which included fixed or floating
platforms, fixtures, fitting and equipment. It seemed to him that these extended
statutory definitions, which appeared to capture backhoe dredgers, indicated
that the earlier definitions had not been wide enough to do so.

On appeal, the Supreme Court, on January 22, 1998, reversed Barr J.
Keane J. (Barrington and Lynch JJ. concurring) disagreed with Barr J's view
that a strong onus rested on the plaintiffs to establish that the *Von Rocks* was a
'ship' within the meaning of the relevant legislation. Such a view gave insufficient weight to what must be presumed to be the underlying policy of this
legislation:

> A person or business which extends credit to the owners of a ship may
> find that the only asset to which they can have recourse has left the
> jurisdiction. In contrast, the assets of a debtor within the jurisdiction
> were regarded as being more readily available to satisfy the creditors. In
> an age of greatly enhanced electronic communications, that is not al-
> ways the case and hence the remarkable development of the *Mareva*
> injunction in recent years.

Turning to section 13(2) of the 1989 Act, Keane J. considered that two features of the definition it contained were of importance. First, the word 'includes' indicated that the definition was not intended to be exclusive or
exhaustive. Secondly, the word 'ship', in a somewhat circuitous fashion, was
expressly extended to include a 'boat'. Thus the definition included the hum-
ble rowing boat propelled by oars. Whilst not of immediate relevance, this
reinforced the impression given by the use of the word 'includes' that the
legislature had deliberately adopted a wide-ranging definition of the word
'ship.'

Keane J. observed:

> The authorities, some of which are not easy to reconcile, demonstrate
> that it would be difficult, and not particularly helpful, to attempt to for-
> mulate a general definition of a 'ship' or 'vessel' applicable to every
> case. With that caveat, however, one can as a starting point take it that,
> as an irreducible minimum, the object under consideration must not
> merely be capable of traversing the surface of water, but must spend a
> reasonably significant part of its operative life in such movement.

It was clear that to come within the definition of a 'ship' it was not essential
that the craft under consideration should be capable of self propulsion, 'whether
by oars, sail, steam, nuclear power or whatever.'

Thus, barges which had no motive power of their own and were usually towed had been held to be ships. In *The "Mac"* [1882] Aspinall's Maritime Law Cases, 555, a barge in use on the Thames and called a 'mud hopper' barge, was held by the Court of Appeal to be a 'ship', despite the absence of any means of self propulsion, Brett L.J. observing that:

> the term ['ship or boat'] includes . . . all things which are built in a particular form for the purpose of being used on the water.

It was also clear that the presence of a rudder and the manning of the craft with a crew, while an important factor in determining whether the craft was a 'ship' or 'vessel', was not of itself conclusive. Thus, in *Merchants' Marine Insurance Company Limited v. North of England Protection and Indemnity Association* (1926) 43 T.L.R. 107, the question was whether a floating crane mounted on a pontoon was a 'ship' or 'vessel'. In the Court of Appeal, Bankes L.J. referred to the fact that the crane was not capable of being steered and observed:

> I think that again is only an incident, but I think it is rather an important incident. [The crane] is undoubtedly capable of being moved, but it is obviously so unseaworthy that it can only be moved short distances or comparatively short distances and only when the weather is exactly favourable. It is a most unwieldy structure. . . .

Keane J. contrasted that decision with the Canadian authority of *The Queen v. St. John Ship Building and Dry Dock Company Ltd* (1981) DLR (3d) 353. There a floating crane vessel was also under consideration. It was not self-propelled and it did not appear that it had any form of rudder or steering. Unlike the crane under consideration in the earlier English decision, however, it was capable of reasonably extensive travel on the sea, amounting in one incident to a voyage of approximately three hundred miles. Urie J., having referred to a number of the earlier decisions, including *Merchants' Marine Insurance Company Ltd*, concluded that the craft in question was a ship. He said:

> While it appeared that she was not capable of navigation herself and was not self-propelled, these facts do not detract from the fact that she was built to do something on water requiring movement from place to place.

This case, and the decision of Barr J. in *Hanly v. Kerry County Council*, High Court, March 3, 1986, also made it clear that the fact that the carriage of cargo or passengers was not the exclusive or even the primary object for which the craft was being used was not a decisive consideration. The preponderance of judicial opinion supported the view that, provided the craft was built to do something on water and for the purpose of carrying out that work, was designed and constructed to be capable of traversing significant water surfaces and did in fact regularly so traverse them, it was capable of being classified as a 'ship', in spite of the absence of any form of self-propulsion or steering mechanism, such as a rudder. Thus, in *Hanly*, a mussel raft, consisting of the forehead part of a former naval landing craft with no means of self propulsion save when an outboard motor was attached to it, was held by Barr J. to be a 'ship', although it appeared to have spent most of its life in one location, being navigated by its owner back to the shore by means of an out-board motor at the end of the nine months' mussel season.

Keane J. noted that, in some of the authorities, the expression 'used in navigation' was treated as connoting 'free and ordered movement from one place to another', as Atkinson J. had put it in *Polpen Shipping Company Ltd v. Commercial Union Assurance Company Ltd* [1943] K.B. 161. It was, however, clear from other authorities that the 'free and ordered movement' there referred to did not necessarily postulate the presence in the craft of some form of self propulsion, a rudder or other means of steering or a crew. The free and ordered movement from one part of the water to another might be the result of towing, as in the case of the barges and floating cranes.

Keane J. took issue with Sheen J's suggestion in *Steedman v. Schofield & Anor* [1992] 2 Lloyd's Rep. 163 at 166, that the phrase 'used in navigation' conveys the concept of transporting persons or property by water to an intended destination.

If this view were correct, and a craft designed and constructed for use on the sea which, in the course of its contemplated use, regularly traversed the water, but did not carry cargo or passengers, was not to be regarded as a 'ship', it would follow that objects such as floating cranes or, indeed, vessels used for such purposes as marine exploration could similarly not be regarded as ships. The preponderance of authority seemed to be against that view.

It was questionable whether, to come within the category of a 'ship' the purpose of a craft had to be 'to go from one place to another', as Sheen J. had suggested, Keane J. commented:

> In the case of non commercial craft, it seems somewhat unreal to regard their purpose as being a journey from one point to a specific destination. Yachts which take part in the America's Cup are designed and constructed with a view to testing the excellence of their technology and the seamanship of their crews rather than transporting people from one place to another. On a less exalted level, people will for long continue to derive enjoyment from being on the sea, not because they are accomplishing a journey to an intended destination but simply for the pleasure of – in the well worn phrase from *The Wind in the Willows* – 'messing about in boats'.

Returning to the facts of the instant case, Keane J. acknowledged that *Von Rocks* undoubtedly lacked some of the characteristics one would normally associate with a 'ship'. It was not self-propelled, it normally was not manned by a crew and it had no form of rudder or other steering mechanism. But it was a structure designed and constructed for the purpose of carrying out specific activities on the water and was capable of movement across the water and in fact spent significant periods of time moving across the sea from one contracting site to another. If it was to do its normal work, it had to be in a seaworthy condition and it seemed, the regulatory authorities in Ireland and elsewhere treated it as subject to compliance with the normal requirements as to sea-going vessels. Keane J. was satisfied that, having regard to the non-exhaustive and wide-ranging definitions supplied by the Oireachtas and the policy which must be assumed to underlie the legislation, the *Von Rocks* should be regarded as a 'ship' within the meaning of the Arrest Convention.

DEFAMATION

Defamation in an international context poses difficulties for the law. How are the courts in one country to deal with a situation where the allegedly defamatory communication has been broadcast around the world by satellite or published in a newspaper or book which is sold in may countries? Free speech and the right to a reputation are important, potentially competing, values widely rooted in fundamental constitutional norms. To which country should the courts look for guidance? That of the publisher's place of establishment? Would such a solution not mean that publishers with defamatory intent simply have to seek out free speech havens and publish internationally to their heart's content? Is the country of the place of publication the appropriate one to provide the governing law? Is this a practical or just rule at a time of world-wide transmission? And is it not problematical that a defamed person should have to sue in every country where the publication occurred to obtain, cumulatively, full damages for all of the injury to his or her reputation?

Some of these issues were addressed by the Court of Justice in *Shevill v. Presse Alliance SA (Case C–68/93)* [1995] E.C.R. I–415. It held as follows:

1. On a proper construction of the expression 'place where the harmful event occurred' in Article 5(3) of the [Brussels] Convention . . . the victim of a libel by a newspaper article distributed in several contracting states may bring an action for damages against the publisher either before the courts of the contracting state of the place where the publisher of the defamatory publication is established, which have jurisdiction to award damages for all the harm caused by the defamation, or before the courts of each contracting state in

which the publication was distributed and where the victim claims to have suffered injury to his reputation, which have jurisdiction to rule solely in respect of the harm caused in the state of the court seised.

2. The criteria for assessing whether the event in question is harmful and the evidence required of the existence and extent of the harm alleged by the victim of the defamation are not governed by the Convention but by the substantive law determined by the national conflict of laws rules of the court seised, provided that the effectiveness of the Convention is not thereby impaired.

For a comprehensive analysis of the policy issues raised by the *Shevill* judgment, see T.P. Kennedy and Alan Reed, 'The Europeanisation of Defamation' (1996) 5 *IJEL* 201 at 211–225.

In *Ewins v. Carlton U.K. Television Ltd and Ulster Television plc* [1997] 2 I.L.R.M. 223, analysed by Karen Murray, 'Cross Border Defamation' (1997) 15 *ILT* 157, the plaintiffs sought damages (including aggravated and exemplary damages) for libel arising out of a television documentary made and broadcast in Britain by the first defendant, a British company, and transmitted to viewers in both parts of Ireland by the second defendant. The programme was received within the State in three ways:

(i)   by unavoidable spillage of signal in border areas;
(ii) by extension in other areas by deliberate tuning of aerials to intercept signals from north of the borer or from Wales;
      and
(iii) by lawful distribution of cable companies and deflector systems.

The subject matter of the documentary was a purported account by one Éamonn Collins of his activities and experiences as a member of the Provisional I.R.A. and it contained matters allegedly defamatory of the plaintiffs. The defendants entered conditional appearances challenging the jurisdiction of the court and contending that the British courts were the appropriate forum for the proceedings.

Adopting Carswell L.J.'s reasoning in *Turkington v. Baron St. Oswald and British Broadcasting Corporation*, High Court of Northern Ireland, May 6, 1996, Barr J. considered that 'it would be flying in the face of reality' to avoid the conclusion that the first defendant ought to have realised that the programme would be received by viewers in the State. Under the rule in *Speight v. Gospay*, (1891) 60 L.J. Q.B. 231, the original publisher of a defamatory statement was liable for its republication by another person where, *inter alia*, the republication of the words to a third person was the national and probable consequence of the original result. Thus, if there was harm in the instant case, that harm was done in the State within the meaning of Article 5(3). It followed that the plaintiffs were *prima facie* entitled to maintain their actions against both defendants in the Irish jurisdiction.

Barr J. went on to address the question whether the court had discretion to stay the plaintiffs' action on the ground of *forum non conveniens*. He stated:

> Articles 21 to 23 of the Convention deal with problems arising in connection with actions pending in different contracting states but they are not relevant to the matter under review. In the context of the Convention, it appears that, if the plaintiffs can establish that they are within the ambit of the exception contained in Article 5(3) to the general rule as to jurisdiction, then the court has no power to refuse jurisdiction on the ground of *forum non conveniens*. However, there is a substantial argument in favour of the proposition that, notwithstanding the absence of any specific provision in the Convention or in the enabling Act, the court has an inherent jurisdiction to grant a stay of proceedings to prevent injustice, e.g., where there is evidence that a plaintiff is improperly using the proceedings and terms of the Convention to oppress the defendant, or is guilty of unconscionable conduct. The contra argument is that the motivation of a plaintiff in choosing a particular contracting state for his action is not a matter which the court has jurisdiction to investigate and that, whatever the motivation of a plaintiff may be, the chosen court cannot refuse jurisdiction in the absence of specific authority in the convention and is not obliged to give effect to its provision.

Barr J. did not consider that he had to resolve this issue as the defendants had not advanced evidence to suggest that, in electing to sue them in the Irish jurisdiction, the plaintiffs had been guilty of oppression or unconscionable conduct. Having a choice of jurisdiction, they had been entitled to select that which they perceived to be most advantageous for them. Any consequential disadvantages there might be for the defendants were 'very far from constituting a denial of justice for them.'

Finally Barr J, following what the Court of Justice said in *Shevill*, held that the plaintiffs were not entitled to maintain a claim for damages on a worldwide basis in the instant proceedings. Having elected to sue in the Irish jurisdiction rather than before the courts of the Contracting State where the publisher was established, the plaintiffs' claim for damages was limited to harm done to them in the State on foot of the alleged libel. (It appears that the second and third plaintiffs were not claiming damages on a world-wide basis; whether the first plaintiff was doing so was not clear to Barr J.)

INTERNATIONAL CARRIAGE OF GOODS

The Warsaw Convention In *S. Smyth & Co. Ltd v. Aer Turas Teoranta*, Supreme Court, February 3, 1997, the Court, as matters transpired, was not called to resolve the question whether a claim for negligence in respect of the carriage of goods by air was sustainable outside the scope of the Warsaw Convention of 1929 as amended at the Hague in 1955. The House of Lords, in *Abnett (known as Sikes) v. British Airways plc* [1997] 1 All E.R. 193, had held that the Convention provided the exclusive cause of action and sole remedy for a passenger making a claim for personal injury.

> The domestic courts are not free to provide a remedy according to their own law, because to do this would be to undermine the Convention. It would lead to the setting alongside the Convention of an entirely different set of rules which would distort the operation of the whole scheme.
>   The Convention is, of course, tightly drawn on these matters. This has been done in the interests of the carrier, whose exposure to these liabilities without the freedom to contract out of them was a principal consequence of the system which it laid down. Were remedies outside the Convention to become available, it would encourage litigation in other cases to restrict its application still further in the hope of obtaining a better remedy, against which the carrier would have no protection under the contract. I am in no doubt that the Convention was designed to eliminate these difficulties. I see no escape from the conclusion that, where the Convention has not provided a remedy, no remedy is available.

In *Smyth*, where the plaintiff's claim for negligence in respect of the international carriage of goods by air fell outside the Warsaw Convention, the defendant had not contested the plaintiff's right to make such a claim and therefore it did not become an issue on appeal. The Supreme Court affirmed the High Court's dismissal of the negligence claim: we consider this aspect of the case in the Torts Chapter below, 723-5). Blayney J. (O'Flaherty and Keane JJ. concurring) referred to the *Abnett* decision but left for another day the question whether the Irish court would agree with the construction of the Warsaw Convention which the House of Lords had adopted.

DOMICILE

It is easy to understand why judges, a couple of centuries ago, thought it a good idea to adopt domicile as a connecting link between a person and a particular country's legal system on matters affecting that person in the long term. There is much to be said in favour of having such matters as marital status, adoption, succession to property and even taxation determined by the law of a country where one has one's permanent place of residence. This is the society which may be considered to have the greatest interest and concern in these matters.

The problem with domicile is that, while it works easily when dealing with the choices of autonomous adults, it breaks down when the *propositus* lacks autonomy through mental incapacity or infancy. To remedy these gaps, the courts developed an elaborate scaffolding of concepts, with their associated rules. Thus, one begins with a domicile of origin; one can acquire, on adulthood, a separate domicile – of choice; if this is abandoned, one reverts to one's domicile of origin unless one has acquired a new domicile of choice. Elaborate rules relating to residence and intention apply to these various concepts. The result is an elaborate extravaganza yielding results in particular cases which defy logic, justice and practicality.

In *Proes v. Revenue Commissioners* [1998] 1 I.L.R.M. 333, some of these elaborations were apparent. The essential question concerned the domicile of the appellant, subsequent to the death of her husband in 1982, for the purposes of the revenue legislation. Section 76(1) of the Income Tax Act 1967 provides for payment of income tax on income arising from securities outside the State, but section 76(2) provides that this does not apply to any person who satisfies the Revenue Commissioners that he is not domiciled in the State. The appellant appealed against assessments made by the Revenue Commissioners that she was domiciled within the State from 1982 until 1989. The Appeal Commissioners rejected her appeal and the Circuit Court judge affirmed. The appellant appealed to the High Court by way of case stated.

Costello P. addressed first the facts of the case. The appellant had been born in 1916 in Bandon, of Irish-domiciled parents. She went to South Africa at the age of fifteen, before going to England where she trained as a nurse. In 1940 she married an Englishman. He served in the British navy during the war, his ship being based in Derry. Largely for that reason, the appellant spent most of the war years with her parents in the family home at Bandon and staying with friends in Derry.

Following the war, the appellant's husband was posted abroad in the course of his employment with an international petrol company. The appellant lived at various times in Egypt, Japan, California, Texas, New York and Bermuda. The appellant's children were, however, born in Bandon as she went to her home to have her mother's support at these times.

During this international chapter of her life, the appellant and her husband lived in homes in England for two periods, from 1949 to 1951 and from 1956 to 1962. In both cases, they bought and subsequently sold the house where they lived.

From 1980 to 1982, the appellant and her husband lived in an apartment in

England provided by her husband's employer. Her husband died suddenly in 1982 at the age of sixty-one.

In 1970 the appellant and her husband had bought a house in Kinsale as a holiday home. They had not thought greatly about what they would do on her husband's retirement but would probably have stayed much of the time there, while intending to travel a great deal. As matters transpired, circumstances had prevented them from making any extensive use of it during the period from 1970 until 1982, though they had returned to it for a period of recuperation in 1979 when the appellant's husband had developed heart trouble.

Six months after her husband's death, the appellant was obliged to vacate the apartment. She decided to stay at the house in Kinsale because it was the only place immediately available to her in which to live and put her furniture from the apartment and because she had been strongly encouraged by family and friends not to make any permanent decision as to her future in the immediate period following her husband's death. Her daughters had tried to persuade her to live in London on several occasions but she was happy in Kinsale. She would probably stay in Kinsale as long as her health permitted.

Over a period of time the appellant said that she found living in Kinsale quite agreeable but, until approximately 1991, when she became less able to travel as a result of having broken her leg in a fall, the appellant spent only part of every year at Kinsale. The remainder of the year tended to be spent with one or other of her daughters who were married with their own families in England and more frequently travelling to stay with friends in Portugal, the United States of America and elsewhere. In later years her visits to London diminished and her family came to visit her in Kinsale quite often.

Since 1982, the appellant had always envisaged that, if she ceased to be able to look after herself and live alone, she would return to England to live closer to her daughters to whom she would have to look for support and assistance. While there had been no immediate urgency during most of that period about finding somewhere to live in England, she and her son-in-law made various enquiries with estate agents and visited several houses with a view to making a purchase but none of the houses suited her. The appellant viewed about four houses in four years. In mid-1992 she finally purchased a house in London with the object of having it available to her as a residence. At the time of the Circuit Court judgment, she had not actually resided in the house. She purchased it as a very old house which required extensive refurbishment and builders had been carrying out the necessary works on her behalf since early 1993.

The appellant gave evidence that she was a British subject and held a British passport. Having been born in Ireland in 1916, she became entitled under the provisions of the British Nationality Act 1948 to elect to remain a British subject. She had given notice to the Home Office of her election to remain British in 1951. She regarded all of her affairs as being based in England and looked after for her there by accountants, solicitors and a stockbroker. She was in receipt of an old age pension from the British Department of Social Security. Apart from a current account which she maintained in Ireland for routine household expenses, her main accounts and investments were all maintained with institutions outside Ireland. She had health insurance in Ireland through V.H.I. and also had private health insurance in Britain.

Both her daughters were married to English nationals and were domiciled in England, as were her grandchildren. One of her reasons for keeping on the home in Kinsale and living there was the fact that her children and her grandchildren very much enjoyed visiting Kinsale and spending extensive holiday periods there each year. The house in Kinsale was regarded by the families as a holiday home.

In reply to a question posed by the Circuit Court judge at the conclusion of her evidence as to whether the appellant then considered the Kinsale house as her permanent home, the appellant replied 'yes, for the time being.'

The Circuit Court judge held that the appellant had been domiciled in Ireland during the relevant periods. There was no doubt that she had had an English domicile from the date of her marriage until 1982. There was no question that either the appellant or her husband acquired a domicile in this country by purchase of the house in Kinsale as this had not been intended as anything other than a holiday home up to the death of the appellant's husband in 1982. Although the appellant had resided in Kinsale for a period of over ten years, the judge was satisfied that she had intended to return to England at some future time and if the house she already acquired in London did not turn out to be suitable she would probably acquire some alternative residence.

The judge considered that the issue was whether or not, despite the appellant's evidence as to her intention for the future, her acts belied her intention sufficiently to establish that she nevertheless intended to live indefinitely in Cork. The judge noted that, while it was true that, if the appellant's two daughters had married Irishmen, the position would have been easier to resolve because the appellant would clearly have envisaged remaining permanently in Ireland to be near them, the fact was that her daughters were clearly permanently resident in England. On balance, the length of residence in Cork seemed difficult to ignore and he accordingly determined that the appellant had acquired a domicile of choice in Ireland.

As formulated in the case stated, the question of law for the opinion of the High Court was as follows:

Having regard to the evidence given and the facts found by me as aforesaid and having regard to the submissions of law which were made thereon was I correct in law in determining that the appellant had acquired a domicile of choice in the State by residing in Kinsale since 1982[?]

Costello P. first addressed the legal principles. He recorded the rule that everyone receives at birth a domicile of origin and that this may be displaced by a domicile of choice based on the combination of residence and intention of permanent or indefinite residence. In turn, the domicile of choice may be lost by abandonment where a person ceases to reside in the country of domicile and also ceases to have the intention to return to it as his or her permanent home. When a domicile of choice is abandoned, either (i) a new domicile of choice is acquired or (ii) the domicile of origin revives.

Costello P. considered that section 76(2) of the 1967 Act imposed on the appellant the burden of establishing that she had acquired an English domicile of choice in 1940 and that she had not abandoned it when she returned to Kinsale after her husband's death or subsequently. The Circuit Court judge had been mistaken in seeking to answer the question whether the appellant had acquired a *new domicile of choice* in Ireland; he should have enquired whether her *English domicile of choice had been abandoned*, in which case her Irish domicile of origin revived.

If the right question had been asked, proper weight would have been given to the 'very compelling' evidence that no intention to abandon her English domicile could properly be inferred from the admitted facts. When the appellant came to Kinsale in 1982, she was advised by her family that she should not make any permanent arrangement as to her future in the immediate aftermath of her husband's death. From then on, she envisaged that, if she ceased to be able to look after herself, she would return to live in England close to her two married daughters. She had made enquiries and visited several houses in London with this end in view. She had achieved her goal with the purchase of a house there in 1992. Had the proper test been applied to all the evidence, the inference that would inescapably have arisen was that the appellant had never ceased to have an intention to return to reside permanently in England.

A further weakness in the Circuit Court judge's analysis was his failure to explain how a change of domicile could have occurred in 1982 when the basis of his holding that a change occurred was the length of the appellant's residence within the State *subsequent* to 1982 which, in his view, belied her stated intention to return to England.

Costello P. concluded that the question raised by the Circuit Court judge should be answered by stating that he had been incorrect in law in determining that the appellant had acquired a domicile of choice in the State, that she had acquired an English domicile of choice which she had not abandoned and accordingly that at the relevant times her Irish domicile of origin had not revived.

It must be said that Costello P.'s determination that the appellant had retained her English domicile of choice is convincing: there was a tentative quality to her residence in the State which seems not to have been overridden by the passage of years. Nevertheless Costello P.'s approach to the legal aspects of the case can best be explained by the limitations on the power of the High Court judge on a case stated to disturb conclusions arrived at by the Circuit Court judge unless they are beyond the bounds of reasonableness or are based on a mistaken view of the law: *Ó Cúlacháin v. McMullan Brothers Ltd* [1995] 2 I.L.R.M. 498; *Mara v. Hummingbird Ltd* [1982] I.L.R.M. 421.

Costello P.'s identification of legal error in the Circuit Court judge's formulation of the question in terms of the appellant's acquisition of a new domicile of choice savours of a formalistic critique. The truth of the matter is that, using such a test, the Circuit Court judge had held that the appellant *had* acquired a new domicile of choice. If the vice in his approach was to have failed to address the other possibility that a person may abandon an earlier domicile of choice without acquiring a new domicile of choice, such an error could clearly not have damaged the appellant's interests since her domicile of origin was in any event Irish.

Costello P.'s own formulation of the test appears to be unduly restrictive. It is not the case that the only question relevant to events from 1982 onwards was whether the appellant's English domicile of choice had been abandoned and that, '[i]f it had, then the Irish domicile revives.' An abandonment of an earlier domicile of choice, as Costello P. recognised earlier in his judgment, need not necessarily be followed by the revival of one's domicile of origin. It may be replaced immediately by the acquisition of a new domicile of choice, as the Circuit Court judge found on the evidence. The essential difference of opinion in this case related to the application of the rules regarding domicile to the evidence rather than any real dispute as to what those rules were.

INTERNATIONAL CHILD ABDUCTION

Judicial discretion not to order the return of a child How should a court deal with an important international Convention which has been poorly drafted? The Supreme Court confronted this question in *In Re V.B., a minor and ward of court; B.B. v. J.B.* [1998] 1 I.L.R.M. 136.

The objects of the Hague Convention on Civil Aspects of International Child Abduction, set out in Article 1, are to secure the prompt return of children wrongfully removed to or retained in any Contracting State and to ensure that rights of custody and access under the law of one Contracting State are effectively respected in other Contracting States.

Article 3 provides that the removal or retention of a child is to be considered wrongful where it is in breach of another's rights of custody and these rights were actually exercised at the time of removal or retention or would have been but for the removal or retention.

Article 12 provides as follows:

Where a child has been wrongfully removed or retained in terms of Article 3 and, at the date of the commencement of the proceedings before the judicial or administrative authority of the Contracting State where the child is, a period of less than one year has elapsed from the date of the wrongful removal or retention, the authority concerned shall order the return of the child forthwith.

The judicial or administrative authority, even where the proceedings have been commenced after the expiration of the period of one year referred to in the preceding paragraph, shall also order the return of the child, unless it is demonstrated that the child is now settled in its new environment.

Article 13 provides (in part) as follows:

Notwithstanding the provisions of the preceding Article, the judicial or administrative authority of the requested State is not bound to order the return of the child if the person, institution or other body which opposes its return establishes that:

(a) the person, institution or other body having the care of the person of the child was not actually exercising the custody rights at the time of removal or retention, or had consented to or subsequently acquiesced in the removal or retention; or

(b) there is a grave risk that his or her return could expose the child to physical or psychological harm or otherwise place the child in an intolerable situation.

In considering the circumstances referred to in Article 13, the judicial and administrative authorities are required to take into account the information relating to the social background of the child provided by the Central Authority or other competent authority of the child's habitual residence.

In the instant case, a minor whose habitual residence was English came with her father to Ireland. The mother took proceedings under the Hague Convention, claiming that there had been a wrongful removal of her daughter and seeking her return to England. The father produced strong documentary and oral evidence that the removal had not been wrongful. Barron J., having so found, concluded that, since there had been no wrongful removal, the terms of the Convention did not apply. He limited his order to refusing the application for the return of the child, commenting that there was no bar to subsequent legal proceedings to establish the future care and control of the child.

The Supreme Court held that Barron J. ought to have dealt with the issues of custody and access, as Article 13 imposed a requirement on the court to exercise its discretion in cases where it found that the removal had not been wrongful.

Denham J. acknowledged that Article 13 was drafted in a rather convoluted form. Notwithstanding the mandatory and discretionary powers set out in Article 12 relating to a situation where a child had been wrongfully removed, special situations and defences were established in Article 13. One of these related to the position where there had been consent to the removal:

> This Article must be construed so as not to render it nugatory. It must be capable of applying to both parties in an action. I construe it to mean that the judicial authority is not subject to a mandatory rule in relation to the child if the party opposing the return establishes that the persons having care of the child consented to the removal. If this situation arises the judicial authority is not bound to order the return of the child. Yet the Court, being not bound, has a discretion.

Such discretion was in keeping with the Convention for four reasons. The Convention stressed that the interests of the children were paramount. It sought to secure protection for rights of custody and access. The objects of the Convention set out in Article 1 were to secure the prompt return of children wrongfully removed to or retained in any Contracting State, and to ensure that rights of custody and of access under the law of one Contracting State were effectively respected in the other Contracting States. In considering the circumstances referred to in Article 13 relating to consent to the removal, the judicial authority was required to take into account the information relating to the social background of the child provided by the Central Authority or other competent authority of the child's habitual residence.

Thus it was entirely consistent with the Convention that, even if there was a removal that was not wrongful, the rights of custody and access in both the Contracting States were effectively respected.

Denham J. noted that the discretion under Article 13 had been exercised by Morris J. in *In re P.K. and A.K., infants; N.K. v. J.K.* [1994] 3 I.R. 483 (noted in the 1994 Review, 75–6), where, having found that removal of children from Britain by the father had been with the consent of the mother and that there had been acquiescence to conditions as to access, and accordingly, that he was not bound under Article 12 to order the return of the children to Britain, he held that he had a discretion in the matter.

In the instant case Barron J. had fallen into error of law in failing to exercise his discretion under Article 13 of the Convention. Consequently, the case should be remitted to the High Court for it to exercise a discretion as to whether the child should be returned to England. This exercise in discretion was a matter of balance in which the Court should apply factors relevant under the Hague Convention.

Denham J. provided a non-exhaustive extensive list of the factors to be considered. She stated:

(1) The habitual residence of the child at the time of the removal.
(2) The law relevant to her custody and access.
    These two first factors raise the issue of the comparative suitability of the competing jurisdictions: whether the decisions as to the best interest of the child should be taken in an English or Irish Court: in light of the Hague Convention.
(3) The overall policy of the Convention and its objective to secure protection for rights of access.
    In this lat[t]er regard the fact that the mother of a two year old girl has not had access other than on the day of the Court hearing [to] the child is a relevant consideration, though not decisive on its own.
(4) The object of the Convention to ensure the rights of custody and of access under the law of one Contracting State are effectively respected in the other Contracting States.
(5) The circumstances of the child, information relating to the social background of the child, as stated in the final paragraph of Article 13 of the Hague Convention.
(6) The nature of consent of the appellant. Was it consent to the removal of the child from England for some time or in effect a waiver of custody of the child until she was 16? In this regard the circumstances of the making of the consent are relevant.
(7) The litigation in England and the decision of August 6, 1996 by the English High Court, Family Division, that [the child be made] a Ward of Court, that the respondent return the child to that jurisdiction, and that [the child] reside with the appellant.
(8) The matter of undertakings, which are settled law in this jurisdiction, especially in relation to very young children.

(This list of factors has proved helpful in subsequent litigation: see *In re B.A.D. (an infant); M.D. v. A.T.D.*, High Court, March 6, 1998, a decision of O'Sullivan J. which we shall analyse in the1998 Review).

Lynch and Keane J.J. delivered concurring judgments. Keane J. referred to Article 18 of the Convention, which had not been cited in argument. It states that 'the provisions of this Chapter do not limit the power of a judicial or administrative authority to order the return of the child at any time.' It would seem that this provision was included with the purpose of ensuring that a Convention designed to encourage the prompt return of children wrongfully removed from the state of their habitual residence would not inhibit the capacity of courts to do this when they would, under their national law, have done so in any event. It does not appear that Article 18 throws a great deal of light on the proper interpretation of Article 13.

Acquiescence, risk of harm and undertakings In *A.S. v. P.S.*, Supreme
Court, March 26, 1998, reversing High Court, November 20, 1997, two issues
fell for consideration: the nature of acquiescence, for the purposes of Article
13(a) of the Hague Convention, and the scope of operation of paragraph (b) of
Article 13, which, as we have mentioned, relieves the court of the requested
State from the obligation to return a child to the jurisdiction of the applicant if
the person who opposes the child's return establishes that there is a grave risk
that it would expose the child to physical or psychological harm or otherwise
place the child in an intolerable situation.

The case concerned two young children, aged nine and six, who had been
taken to Ireland by their mother, who was Irish, from England where the children, their mother, and their father, to whom the mother was married, had
been living in the family home. The mother, when she came to Ireland, osten-
sibly on holiday with the children, told her husband that she and the children
were not going to return to England.

The husband delayed for two months before taking proceedings for the
return of his daughters under the Hague Convention. During that period he
was having regular telephone calls and correspondence with the applicant,
seeking to save the marriage and dissuade her from separating from him. His
resort to the proceedings was precipitated by his having been informed by his
mother-in-law that his wife had commenced a relationship with a former boy-
friend.

Geoghegan J. held, on balance, that the husband had acquiesced in his
wife's retention of the children in Ireland, though he acknowledged that it was
'perhaps a fine point [which] might be open to argument. . . .' Geoghegan J.
considered that the husband's concern at the relevant period had been 'the
reconciliation of the parties to the marriage and the restoration of the marriage, not the return of the children to the English jurisdiction as such.' There
had been little to suggest that, in the event of his having to face up to a broken
marriage, he had any particular objection to the children being with their mother
or as to any particular place of residence.

The Supreme Court reversed Geoghegan J. on this issue. Denham J. (Keane
and Barron JJ. concurring), considered it clear that, throughout the relevant
time, the husband had been seeking to reach a reconciliation with his wife,
'which would have the effect of restoring the [wife] and the children to England, their habitual residence.' Viewing the circumstances, including the correspondence, objectively, the husband had not acquiesced in the children
remaining in Ireland and he had taken no action inconsistent with his later
application under the Hague Convention.

In relation to Article 13 (b), the wife had made serious allegations that the
husband was guilty of sexually abusing one of his children. Geoghegan J.
gave credence to these allegations, and refused to order the return of the children, on the basis of the grave risk of exposing them to harm. Geoghegan J.

did not think that the husband's undertaking to vacate the family home was enough to warrant the return of the children. The daughter who had allegedly been sexually abused was now settled in Ireland and Geoghegan J. thought it likely that 'there would be a strong association of ideas in her mind if she was returned to that house in any form and that there must necessarily be a grave risk of serious psychological harm'.

The Supreme Court reversed Geoghegan J. on this issue too. Denham J. stressed that an order for a return of the children to England did not necessarily mean that the children should be returned to their father. The mandatory character of the Convention in its requirement to order the return of children save in the exceptional cases specified in the Convention meant that, if there were reasonable options for achieving their return, they should be considered carefully. In Denham J.'s view, there was:

> . . . no adequate evidence to indicate that to return the child . . . to the house of the family would place her at a grave risk or in an intolerable position. The evidence relates to the presence of the [husband], not the home.

The English courts and other relevant services would be informed of the situation and, while the mother had not always acted in a responsible fashion, other persons would have a responsibility for the children as well. The mother had no authority to permit breaches of any undertakings by any party. If they occurred, 'there would be the most severe sanctions, not the least [of which] would relate to future access to [the child who had allegedly been abused].'

Geoghegan J.'s reluctance to rely on the father's undertakings had been based on Costello J.'s judgment in *R.G. v. B.G.*, High Court, November 12, 1992 but Denham J. considered that the facts of that case were 'entirely different' from those of the instant case, since they involved a grave risk that the mother would be subjected to physical harm even if the father left the family home and that, if this happened, there was a grave risk that the children would also be subject to physical harm, especially when the father was intoxicated. Similarly the facts of *P.F. v. M.F.*, Supreme Court, January 13, 1993 (1993 Review, 125, 134) were distinguishable from the instant case, since in *P.F. v. M.F.* the father was improvident, with a propensity toward violent conduct against the mother, sometimes in the presence of the children, and there was limited evidence of violence by him towards one of the children. For discussion of *P.F. v. M.F.*, see 1993 Review, 125–126.

Strict procedural requirements Article 13 of the Luxembourg Convention requires in paragraph (c) that a request for recognition or enforcement in another contracting state of a decision relating to custody be accompanied, in the case of a decision given in the absence of the defendant or his legal representative, by 'a document which establishes that the defendant was duly served with the document which instituted the proceedings or an equivalent document.' In *P.M. v. V.M. (otherwise known as V.B. or V.McK.)*, High Court, November 3, 1997, Kinlen J. held that the strict requirements of the Convention had not been complied with in this regard where notice of the plenary summonses in custody proceedings in England had not been served on the mother who had taken her child from England to Ireland prior to the making by the English court of an *ex parte* order. All the documents were served on the mother two days thereafter. Kinlen J. held that this was too late. He rejected the argument that proceedings culminating in the *ex parte* order should be characterised as subsidiary proceedings seeking interim relief, severable from the main proceedings.

The Supreme Court affirmed Kinlen J. on February 20, 1998. Hamilton C.J. (Denham and Barrington JJ. concurring) followed Kinlen J.'s analysis closely, in greater detail than Kinlen J.'s judgment, coming to the identical conclusion.

JURISDICTION

Contract In *United Meat Packers (Ballaghadereen) Ltd (In Receivership) v. Nordstern Allegeine Versicherungs AG* [1997] 2 I.L.R.M. 553, the Supreme Court had to deal with 'court applications [which] were excessive and unnecessary': *per* O'Flaherty J. (Barrington and Keane JJ. concurring). The plaintiff had originally sought an order under Order 11, rule 1 (e)(ii) of the Rules of the Superior Courts 1986 to serve notice of proceedings on the defendants, who were German insurers. Rule 1(e)(ii) bases jurisdiction in the case of a contractual claim on the fact that it was 'made by or through an agent trading or residing within the jurisdiction on behalf of a principal trading or residing out of the jurisdiction.' Geoghegan J. had granted the order, which was expressed as having been authorised under rule 1(e), with no greater specificity.

It transpired that this basis could not be sustained. When a number of the defendants resisted a motion for judgment for failure to deliver a defence on the ground that they had had no agent within the jurisdiction, the plaintiff later sought to remedy the position by seeking approval from Carroll J. to serve out of the jurisdiction on the basis of Order 11, rule 1 (e)(iii), which permits such service where the contract is governed by Irish law or the action has been brought in respect of a breach committed within the jurisdiction of a contract wherever made.

Carroll J. declined to give her approval, being of the view that she had to assume that Geoghegan J. had made the order squarely on the agency ground and that she could not assume that another judge would grant service out of the jurisdiction on ground (iii) on the evidence that had been before Geoghegan

J.: [1996] 2 I.L.R.M. 260.

The Supreme Court reversed the decision. O'Flaherty J. considered that the court in the proceedings before Geoghegan J. clearly had had jurisdiction under rule (e). The Supreme Court had power to give leave to amend the proceedings, whether by deletion, as in *Doran v. Power* [1996] I.L.R.M. 55, or by addition, as in the instant case. There was no principled reason for making any differentiation on this point.

As matters had unfolded, the Lugano Convention, which had not entered into force in Ireland when the application was made to Geoghegan J., had come into effect one day before the proceedings were instituted on December 1, 1993. (The Convention had been given force of law in the State by the Jurisdiction of Court and Enforcement of Judgments Act 1993: see the 1993 Review, 118.) The plaintiff, *ex abundante cautela*, had subsequently issued proceedings under Order 11A, which required no prior judicial authorisation. O'Flaherty J. was of the view that these proceedings were now redundant. The plaintiff's advisers had to 'take their best course in regard to that as to how to bring the whole matter into proper order and present it to the High Court judge in due course in an intelligible fashion.' For analysis of the uncertain position regarding the proper procedures to be followed in Lugano Convention cases, see Jonathan Newman, 'Procedural Errors in International Litigation: The *United Meat Packers* Case' (1997) 3 *Bar Review* 87 at 90–91.

Forum non conveniens   In *Intermetal Group Ltd and Trans-World (Steel) Ltd v. Worslade Trading Ltd,* O'Sullivan J. in the High Court on December 12, 1997, and the Supreme Court on appeal on March 6, 1998, had to determine a *forum non conveniens* challenge in the context of substantial international litigation. The plaintiffs were part of the Trans-World Metals group of companies. The first plaintiff was a British Virgin Island company. The defendant, being incorporated under the law of Ireland, had its seat in the State; by virtue of section 13(2) of the Jurisdiction of Courts and Enforcement of Judgments (European Communities) Act 1988, its domicile was Irish for the purposes of that legislation.

The plaintiffs sought (*inter alia*) interlocutory injunctions restraining the defendant from interfering with contracts between Intermetal and a large Russian steel mill, Novolipetzk Iron and Steel Corporation; a similar order in relation to a contract between Intermetal and Trans-World; an order restraining the defendant from inducing breaches of contract between Trans-World and its customers; and a *Mareva*-type order restraining Worslade on a worldwide basis from diminishing its assets below £50 million sterling. The defendant brought a motion seeking a stay on the proceedings on the basis of *forum non conveniens*.

O'Sullivan J. first considered whether the court had any jurisdiction to entertain such an application. The question was the subject of debate and he thought it fair to say that, in the absence of a definitive ruling from the Court of Justice, it would remain debatable. He derived much assistance from the English Court of Appeal decision in *Re Harrods (Buenos Aires) Ltd* [1991] 4 All E.R. 334, to the effect that a residual discretion did survive the Brussels Convention of 1968.

In support of this interpretation, several arguments could be marshalled. The Convention should not readily be construed as inhibiting non-contracting States in cases where the jurisdiction of such States would otherwise plainly be the most appropriate forum. The Convention itself acknowledged that there were exceptions to the domicile rule. The Court should be slow to construe the Convention to inhibit the valuable jurisdiction to stay on grounds of *forum non conveniens* which was designed to promote comity, encourage efficiency, prevent duplication of time and cost and avoid inconsistent judgments.

It would, moreover, be anomalous if the Convention were construed so as to determine the appropriate forum for competing jurisdictions of contracting states but to require entertainment of suit in the domicile of the defendant (without the application of any test of appropriateness) where a non-contracting State was concerned. The purpose of consistency and simplification of judgments in contracting States would not be disturbed by a jurisdiction to stay in favour of non-contracting States.

If the court had no residual discretion, then it would have no discretion to refuse to entertain an action on the grounds of *lis alibi pendens* if the *lis* was pending in the courts of non-contracting State nor any discretion to refuse where the parties had agreed that the courts of a non-contracting State should have exclusive jurisdiction.

O'Sullivan J. acknowledged that there were arguments against this approach. The effect of ordering a stay would be that the plaintiff was being sent away from the courts of *all* contracting States. The plaintiff would be deprived of the legal certainty which Article 2 seemed to offer and also of the opportunity to obtain a judgment which could be enforced under the Convention. Apart from this, the language of Article 2 was simple and mandatory.

O'Sullivan J., accepting that there were powerful arguments on both sides of the controversy, took the view that, in dealing with an interlocutory application of extreme urgency, he could do no more than record his initial view that, on balance, the arguments supporting the retention of a residual discretion were more attractive.

O'Sullivan J. referred to two decisions of the Supreme Court which addressed the question of the test to be used in determining the *forum non conveniens* application. In *Murphy (Joseph) Structural Engineers Ltd v. Maintowoc (UK) Ltd*, Supreme Court, July 30, 1985, Griffin J., after a review of earlier caselaw, observed that the effect of these decisions was:

(1) [that] a mere balance of convenience is not a sufficient ground for

depriving a plaintiff of the advantages of prosecuting his action in
an English court if it is otherwise properly bought, but
(2) that a stay will be granted if,
   (a) continuance of the proceedings will cause injustice to the de-
       fendant, and
   (b) a stay will not cause injustice to the plaintiff.

That fundamental question can generally be answered by an application
of Lord Diplock's restatement of the rules stated by Scott L.J. in the *St.
Pierre* case. I would accept that these are the principles which should
properly be applied in this case.

The restatement by Lord Diplock referred to was as follows:

In order to justify a stay two conditions must be satisfied, one positive
and the other negative:
(a) the defendant must satisfy the court that there is another forum to
    whose jurisdiction he is amenable in which justice can be done be-
    tween the parties at substantially less inconvenience or expense, and
(b) the stay must not deprive the plaintiff of a legitimate personal or
    juridical advantage which would be available to him if he invoked
    the jurisdiction of the English court.

O'Sullivan J. noted that considerations of inconvenience or expense were, at
least generally, relevant. Equally relevant, however, was the principle that the
plaintiff must not be deprived of a legitimate personal or juridical advantage
to him if he invoked the jurisdiction of the Irish court.

   In *Doe v. Armour Pharmaceutical Company Inc* [1994] 3 I.R. 178, Blayney
J. had adopted essentially the test favoured by Lord Salmon in the House of
Lords case of *MacShannon v. Rockware Glass Ltd* [1978] A.C. 795, at 818.
Lord Salmon had there stated:

In an action brought in England when its natural forum is Scotland, I
consider the question as to whether it should be stayed depends on
whether the defendants can establish that to refuse a stay would produce
injustice. Clearly if the trial of the action in England would afford the
Scottish plaintiff no real advantage and would be substantially more
expensive and inconvenient than if it were tried in Scotland, it would be
unjust to refuse a stay. If, on the other hand, a trial in England would
offer the plaintiff some real personal advantage, e.g. if he had come to
live in England, a balance would have to be struck and the Court might
in its discretion consider that justice demanded that the trial should be
allowed to proceed in England. . . . *To my mind the real test of stay or no*

stay depends upon what the Court in its discretion considers that justice demands (emphasis added by O'Sullivan J.).

O'Sullivan J. considered that the reference to justice included considerations of expense and inconvenience since Lord Salmon had said that, if a trial in England would afford the Scottish plaintiff no real advantage and would be substantially more expensive and inconvenient than if it were tried in Scotland, it would be *unjust* to refuse a stay.

O'Sullivan J. noted that, in the English courts, the jurisprudence on this topic had developed a little more since the Supreme Court decision in *Doe v. Armour Pharmaceutical Co. Inc*, to the point where, in *Re Harrods (Buenos Aires) Ltd.*, above, the test appeared to be that the court should look first at the connecting factors (such as convenience, expense, availability of witnesses, governing law, place of residence and place of business) and, if these indicated that the case had its closest and most real connection with the foreign court, the English court would then consider whether or not substantial justice could be obtained in that forum. As this appeared to O'Sullivan J. to be a slightly different formulation of the test than that explicitly approved by Blayney J. in *Doe v. Armour Pharmaceutical Co. Inc* and by Griffin J. in the *Murphy* case. O'Sullivan J. made it clear that he was following the test as indicated in the earlier Supreme Court decisions.

Having considered the evidence and the submissions on both sides, O'Sullivan J. was of the view that a wrong similar to the Irish tort of inducing breach of contract was known to Russian law. He was less sure that justice could be done between the parties in the Russian courts at *substantially* less inconvenience or expense. Many of the witnesses were likely to come from Russia, but not all. Contracts made with the trading partners of Trans-World would be evidenced by witnesses outside of Russia. If it was reasonable to suppose that a Russian court would be in a better position to assess the trustworthiness of Russian-speaking witnesses, then the same could be said of an Irish court in relation to English-speaking witnesses and the position must be neutral in relation to witnesses speaking in 'third country languages'. In relation to inconvenience, it was of the essence of this kind of jurisdiction that the travelling party would have greater inconvenience. That was why the test referred to by Griffin J. referred to *substantially* less inconvenience or expense. In O'Sullivan J.'s view, given that teams of witnesses would come from countries inside and outside of Russia, it could not be said to be clear that substantially less inconvenience or expense would be achieved if the proceedings were conducted in Russia rather than Ireland.

The second part of the test provided that the stay must not deprive the plaintiff of a legitimate personal or juridical advantage which would be available to him if he invoked the jurisdiction of the Irish court. If the stay were granted, the application for an injunction could not be entertained. The matter was extremely pressing and the cost of any delay would be counted in millions of US dollars. If the defendant's application for a stay succeeded, this was an advantage of which the plaintiff would be deprived if he succeeded in the application for an injunction, at least for the time being and quite possibly for the non-disputed balance of the term of the frame agreements which continued to the end of 1997. In all the circumstances O'Sullivan J. did not think it could be said that a continuance of the proceedings would cause injustice to the defendant and he considered it might well be said that the granting of a stay would cause injustice to the plaintiffs, Accordingly, he declined to grant the stay.

Turning to the application for the restraining injunctions, O'Sullivan J. was satisfied that the plaintiffs had established that a serious question arose as to whether the defendant was liable in damages to the plaintiffs. This question arose regardless of whether Irish law or Russian law applied. In this context, O'Sullivan J. noted Keane J.'s observations in *An Bord Tráchtala and Waterford Food plc,* High Court, November 25, 1992 (1993 Review, 139, 580) to the effect that the plaintiffs could succeed if they established that there was:

> a serious issue to be tried as to whether the activities of the defendants in the United Kingdom would, if carried on in this country, amount to the tort of passing off.

A further serious question arose in relation to the extension of some of the frame agreements beyond the end of 1997.

O'Sullivan J. was of the view that damages would not be an adequate remedy and that, even if they were, the defendant had not demonstrated anything like a capacity to meet an award. He was satisfied that the balance of convenience issue should be resolved in favour of the plaintiffs. O'Sullivan J. did not, however, consider it appropriate at this stage in the proceedings to grant the 'very widely-termed relief' sought by the plaintiffs in applying for a *Mareva* type order. Even if its scope were limited, O'Sullivan J. did not have sufficient detail in relation to the defendant's assets to enable him to frame an order.

Accordingly, O'Sullivan J. granted an order restraining the defendant from attempting to procure the breach of any subsisting agreement between Intermetal and NLMK, any agreement between the plaintiffs and any agreement between Trans-World and its customers.

The Supreme Court on appeal affirmed O'Sullivan J. in all respects on March 6, 1998. We shall analyse the judgment of Murphy J. (with which Lynch and Barron JJ. concurred) in some detail in the 1998 Review. We need here note merely a couple of aspects of Murphy J.'s approach.

On the issue of *forum non conveniens*, Murphy J. was satisfied that the approach favoured by Lord Goff in *Spiliada Maritime Corporation v. Cansulex*

[1987] A.C. 460 at 476 was 'fully consistent with the judgment of Mr Justice Blayney in *Doe v. Armour* and represents a correct statement of law in this jurisdiction'. Lord Diplock had stated too narrow a test in *MacShannon*. The proper test was, as Bingham J. had anticipated in *Harrod* and Blayney J. had anticipated in *Doe v. Armour*, the broader principle of 'justice for both parties'. To apply the *Diplock* test might involve refusing a stay on the grounds of relatively minor procedural differences or the perception as to quantum of damages awarded in different jurisdictions.

Murphy J. declined to express a view on whether the Brussels Convention had any application. He noted that the House of Lords in *Harrods* had referred the issue to the Court of Justice but that the reference had been withdrawn when the proceedings were compromised, leaving 'academics' and distinguished authors' to continue to express differing opinions on the issue.

Procedural options   In *Schmidt v. The Home Secretary of the Government of the United Kingdom* [1997] 2 I.R. 121, a decision we analyse in the section on Sovereign Immunity, below 159–62, the Supreme Court left open the question whether liberty may be given to serve a notice of a plenary summons on a defendant out of the jurisdiction pursuant to Order 11, rule 1 of the Rules of the Superior Courts in a case where such service might in any event be effected pursuant to Order 11A of those Rules.

SOVEREIGN IMMUNITY

Enticement in the course of duty   In *Schmidt v. The Home Secretary of the Government of the United Kingdom* [1997] 2 I.R. 121, an attempt by the plaintiff to encourage the court to sidestep the barrier of sovereign immunity proved unsuccessful. The plaintiff, a German national resident since 1989 in Ireland, had been enticed to England by 'deception and lies' of the third defendant, a member of the Extradition Passport and Illegal Immigration Squad of the International and Organised Crime Branch of the Metropolitan Police.

In 1991 an international arrest warrant had been issued by the Mannheim local court in Germany for the arrest of the plaintiff in respect of alleged offences of unlawful importation and supply of controlled drugs from the Netherlands into Germany. Interpol in Weisbaden requested the assistance of the United Kingdom Extradition Squad to effect the arrest and extradition of the plaintiff to Germany.

The third defendant learned that the plaintiff was resident in Waterford and was accustomed to travel to Britain quite frequently. He also had reason to believe that the plaintiff used false documentation showing different identities on his visits to Britain and that it would therefore be difficult to be aware in advance of the plaintiff's arrival so as to effect an arrest of him in the ordinary way.

With the authority of his superior officer, the third defendant devised a ruse to entice the plaintiff to come to discuss certain matters with him in Britain. The third defendant succeeded in getting in contact with the plaintiff in Waterford and with his solicitor in Dublin. He told the plaintiff and his solicitor that he was investigating frauds with cheques and cheque cards in the name of an N. Schmidt and he wished to interview the plaintiff in order to ascertain whether he was involved and if not to eliminate him from his enquiries.

There was no truth whatsoever in these statements. That being so the plaintiff knew that he was not involved in any such fraud and would therefore be able to have himself eliminated from the third defendant's enquiries. Nevertheless he enquired as to what would happen if he refused to travel to Britain and he was told that in such an event it would be normal practice to circulate details regarding the plaintiff on the police national computer as being suspected of an offence and that the plaintiff would be arrested when he first came to the notice of the authorities in Britain.

Since it was important for the plaintiff that he should be able to travel freely between Ireland and Britain, he agreed to travel to London with his solicitor to meet the third defendant there on November 17, 1992. On that morning the third defendant obtained a provisional arrest warrant under Britain's Extradition Act 1989 with a view to the plaintiff's extradition from England to Germany.

When the plaintiff met the third defendant as arranged, he was promptly arrested on foot of the warrant.

The plaintiff thereafter brought an unsuccessful *habeas corpus* proceedings as far as the House of Lords. The plaintiff was extradited to Germany on August 17, 1994 and he was convicted by the Mannheim Landgericht Court of various offences of drug trafficking and sentenced to imprisonment. He was released from prison in October 23, 1995 but remained on probation until his full release date which was in October 1997.

The plaintiff in May 1993 obtained an order from Carney J. on an *ex parte* application giving him liberty pursuant to Order 11, rule 1(f) of the Rules of the Superior Courts 1986 to serve notice of a plenary summons on the second defendant (the Commissioner of the Metropolitan Police) and the third named defendant. The plaintiff's claim was for damages for (*inter alia*) trespass to the person, false imprisonment and deceit, breaches of his constitutional rights pursuant to Articles 40.3.1, 40.3.2 and 40.4.1 of the Constitution, conspiracy to deprive him of his rights of establishment and free movement pursuant to Articles 48, 52, 53 and 54 of the Treaty of Rome, conspiracy to deprive him of his rights of access to the Irish courts pursuant to the European Convention on Extradition, the Extradition Act 1965 and Statutory Instrument No. 9 of 1989, and misfeasance of public office.

On November 22, 1994, Geoghegan J. set aside the earlier order on the basis that the second and third defendants were entitled to sovereign immunity from suit in Ireland and that the plaintiff's claim fell within Order 11A of the Rules of the Superior Courts (relating to claims within the Jurisdiction of Courts and Enforcement of Judgments (European Communities) Act 1988 and the Convention therein incorporated) and that thus Order 11 did not apply.

On the January 19, 1994 the first defendant (the Home Secretary of the Government of the United Kingdom) succeeded in a similar application heard by Murphy J. in having the order of the May 28, 1993 set aside on the ground of sovereign immunity.

The plaintiff's appeal to the Supreme Court was unsuccessful. Lynch J. (Hamilton C.J., O'Flaherty, Barrington and Keane JJ. concurring) considered that the third defendant's conduct could not be regarded as falling outside the scope of his functions or duties so as to render it beyond the mantle of sovereign immunity:

> The misconduct of the third defendant in this case in resorting to deception and lies to induce the plaintiff to travel from Ireland to the United Kingdom is analogous to the case of a member of the Garda Siochána using manifestly excessive force in effecting an arrest. The garda is not employed by the State to use excessive force, but he is employed to arrest persons suspected of criminal conduct. The fact that he used manifestly excessive force does not relieve the State of liability for his misconduct because he was doing that which he was employed to do, namely effecting the arrest of persons reasonably suspected of criminal conduct although doing it in a very wrong way.
>
> So also with the third defendant. In acting as he did in contacting the plaintiff and his solicitor by telephone to Ireland he was not engaged on a frolic of his own. He was purporting and intending to perform and in fact was performing the duties and functions of his office as a member of the said extradition squad. If he had behaved in a perfectly proper way there could be no question of proceedings being taken against him and therefore no question of having to rely on sovereign immunity. It is because he behaved in an improper way that proceedings have been brought against him and sovereign immunity is therefore relied upon by him and the second defendant.

This was sufficient to dispose of the appeal and it was therefore unnecessary for Lynch J. to express any views on the question as to whether or not liberty may be given to serve out of the jurisdiction pursuant to Order 11, rule 1 of the Rules of the Superior Courts in a case where such service might in any event be effected pursuant to Order 11A of those Rules. For discussion of *Schmidt,*

see Jack Anderson, *'Par in Parem Non Habet Imperium* – The Problem of
Foreign Sovereign Immunity: An Irish Perspective' (1997) 15 *ILT* 200 at
203–204.

Officers of the court and private litigation   In *Herron v. Ireland,* Supreme
Court (*ex tempore*), December 5, 1997, the doctrine of sovereign immunity
defeated a claim in the context of child abduction. It appeared that the Irish
courts had had seisin of the case when a young boy, the son of the plaintiff,
had left the State to go to England. Barrington J. (Murphy and Lynch JJ. concurring) noted that '[e]ither he was abducted or was facilitated by his father to
leave this jurisdiction and the father in doing so placed himself in contempt of
the Irish Court and that contempt has never been purged'. The English High
Court and on appeal the Court of Appeal, having consulted the boy (as required by Article 13 of the Hague Convention on Child Abduction) who expressed a very strong preference to remain there, ordered that he not be returned:
[1992] 2 F.L.R. 126.

The plaintiff took proceedings against two officers of the British Administration, the Attorney General and the Official Solicitor.

As to the former, Barrington J. considered it hard to see on the unfolding
of the case how he had had any input whatsoever into the tragic story but in
any event there was no doubt that he was entitled to invoke the doctrine of
sovereign immunity. He had done so, and there was nothing the Irish Court
could do about it but accept that under international law he was entitled to
take this step. Even if the Attorney General had acted *male fide* (and there was
nothing to indicate that he had done so), he would still, in the existing state of
international law, be entitled to invoke the doctrine of sovereign immunity.

The plaintiff's principal attack was directed against the Official Solicitor.
She contended that the litigation was private in character, touching the welfare of her young son. Nonetheless, as Barrington J. observed:

> so far as the Official Solicitor was concerned he was acting as an officer
> of the British courts at the request of the English courts to furnish them
> with his view as an *amicus curiae* as to what should be done in this
> situation. He was also acting as head of the child abduction unit and
> again it appears to be beyond doubt that he acted throughout in his offi-
> cial capacity and he performed a function which was entrusted to him by
> the court. If in the course of doing that he did anything wrong, and again
> this Court is far from suggesting that he did, he is answerable to the
> English courts for doing that but he is not answerable to the Irish courts.

Accordingly, the Supreme Court affirmed the order of the High Court setting
aside the liberty to serve the summons on the British Attorney and the Official
Solicitor.

ENFORCEMENT OF FOREIGN JUDGMENT

Plaintiffs acting in a representative capacity   In *Foskett (Suing on his own behalf and on behalf of Mount Eden Investors Group) v. Deasy*, Supreme Court, June 3, 1997, some clarification was given as to the enforcement of foreign judgments where the plaintiff acts in a representative capacity. The case concerned a bankruptcy adjudication. The person declared bankrupt in the High Court on November 4, 1996 by Shanley J. had been a defendant in proceedings taken in England by investors in a property development in Portugal which had foundered. The plaintiff, Mr Foskett, had sued on behalf of the investors. An English High Court order had appointed him to represent their interests, pursuant to Order 15, rule 13 of the Rules of the Supreme Courts. In due course, the English High Court had made an order requiring the defendant (and another defendant) to pay to Mr Foskett, 'representing all the purchasers', a large sum by way of compensation for breach of trust. That order deemed the earlier order appointing Mr Foskett to represent the investors to be discharged on and from the date of entry of the second order.

This second order was the subject of an order for enforcement made by the Master of the Irish High Court under the provisions of the Jurisdiction of Courts and Enforcement of Judgments (European Communities) Act 1988. Mr Foskett attempted unsuccessfully to execute on foot of the order and later successfully presented the bankruptcy petition to the High Court.

On appeal to the Supreme Court, the appellant argued that Mr Foskett did not have authority to represent the interests of all (or even a majority) of the creditors. Counsel on his behalf argued forcefully and correctly, in the view of Murphy J. (Lynch and Barron JJ. concurring), that a representative order was a matter of procedure which was governed by the *lex fori* and that accordingly an order for that purpose made outside the State would not be operative in proceedings here. He went on to argue that the representative order, even if effective within the State, had been expressly deemed to have been discharged *in futuro* by the English High Court judgment against (*inter alios*) the appellant for breach of trust.

The appeal proved unsuccessful. Murphy J. interpreted the bankruptcy petition and associated correspondence as having been expressed in terms which induced a misunderstanding: while the correspondence described Mr Foskett as suing on his own behalf and on behalf of the investors, the English High Court judgment had in fact ordered payment of the monetary sum to Mr Foskett. Murphy J. stated:

> I suspect that it is unusual to find such an order being made in proceedings in which a plaintiff is suing in a representative capacity. But where it is done (and *EMI Records Ltd v. Riley* [1981] 1 W.L.R. 923 is an example of where it may be done) the consequences must be that the

judgment debt if and when received by the judgment creditor would be held by him or trust for the group or class on whose behalf he had sued. It seems inescapable that the effect of the UK order was to convert the plaintiff therein from a representative into a trustee of any monies received or indeed of the right to receive them. I have no doubt but that when Mr Foskett obtained the order of the Master of the High Court enabling the execution of the UK judgment in this State, [he] was entitled to collect in his own name, albeit as trustee, the monies due to him pursuant to the judgments and orders of the Courts here and in England.

The error (if such it was) in the bankruptcy proceedings had been to describe Mr Foskett as suing on his behalf and on behalf of others of the investors. If it was intended to disclose the beneficial interests in the judgment debt, it would have been more appropriate to say that he was suing as *trustee* for the investors. In Murphy J.'s view, there could not have been in the circumstances any question of Mr Foskett's suing in a representative capacity or requiring any order of the Irish courts for that purpose.

The statement in the petition was in substance correct 'even though the terminology used might lead a lawyer familiar with legal proceedings to believe that the petitioner was acting in a representative capacity where such in reality was not the case.' Murphy J. did not believe that there was such misdescription of the petitioner or his capacity as would warrant setting aside the order made by the High Court and he could not see that any injustice was suffered by the appellant as a result of the misdescription:

> The petition for bankruptcy was a logical consequence of the making of the UK order and its enforcement in this jurisdiction.

Procedural requirements as to service In *Barnaby (London) Ltd v. Mullen* [1997] 2 I.L.R.M. 341, the Supreme Court, with some regret, emphasised the requirement for those seeking to enforce foreign judgments in the State to comply fully with the requirements of Article 31 of the Brussels Convention of 1968, section 5 of the Jurisdiction of Courts and Enforcement of Judgments (European Communities) Act 1988 and Order 42A of the Rules of the Superior Courts 1989, rule 9 of which provides that:

> Notice of an Order granting leave to enforce a judgment under section 5 of the 1988 Act shall be served together with an Order on the person against whom the Order was made by delivering it to him personally, or in such other manner as the Master of the High Court may direct.

In the instant case, the plaintiff had obtained a judgment in England of over a quarter of a million pounds against the defendant. The Master of the High

Court ordered that it be enforced within the State. The order required that a copy be personally served on the defendant. In fact it was served on the defendant's wife at her place of residence. On April 7, 1995 Kinlen J. declared that the Master's order was valid and effective and complied with the Brussels Convention.

Counsel for the plaintiff acknowledged that the Order had never personally been delivered to the defendant. He contended, however, that the service, such as it was, had been effective and that the defendant had unquestionably become aware of the existence of the Order. This was necessarily so as he could not otherwise have instituted proceedings challenging the effectiveness of the Order. Kinlen J. accepted that contention, stating as follows:

> The Court is satisfied that it has discretion to deem service good under its own rules and, in the particular circumstances of this case, the Court is satisfied that there was service on the defendant by service at his family home on his wife and possibly, also by service, as a matter of courtesy, upon his solicitor.

It did not, however, appear from the Order made pursuant to that judgment that Kinlen J. had deemed the service good or purported to amend the Order of the Master as to the mode of service.

The Supreme Court upheld the defendant's appeal. Murphy J. (Hamilton C.J. and Barron J. concurring) understood the judgment of the Court of Justice in *Isabelle Lancray SA v. Peters und Sickert KG* [1990] E.C.R. I–2725 to emphasise the importance of complying with the regulations as to service and not merely meeting the needs of the defendant in the preparation of his or her defence in the proceedings. Undoubtedly they had such a purpose but they were also designed to achieve other crucial goals. It was the fact of service which fixed the *terminus a quo* for the purposes of any appeal by the party affected and the entitlement of the plaintiff to issue execution on a judgment.

It was not feasible for the court to 'deem good' at a subsequent date a form of service which did not comply with that prescribed by the Master originally or in any subsequent Order made by him. If the service was not in compliance with the Master's Order in the first place, the time for an appeal would not have started to run and if deemed good after the expiration of one month the time for appealing would have expired.

In a brief concurring judgment, Hamilton C.J. sought to give some practical guidance on two matters. The defendant had not sworn an affidavit. The Chief Justice regarded this as 'a significant omission . . .' and went on to stress that in circumstances such as arose in the instant case it was 'essential' that the party himself should swear the affidavit dealing with the merits of the case and any facts that might be in controversy which were within his own knowledge.

This requirement is somewhat puzzling. If the suggestion here is that the outcome of the decision would have been different had it been established that the defendant was aware of the service at his wife's residence, it is surely contradicted by Murphy J.'s judgment, with which the Chief Justice concurred.

The second point that Hamilton C.J. had to make was less contentious:

> It was the Order of the Master which directed the personal service of the documentation on [the defendant]. If and when compliance with that Order became impracticable the correct and obvious solution was to apply to the Master for a variation of his Order to permit substituted service thereof. Such an application would have obviated many of the problems which subsequently arose.

Constitutional Law

ADMINISTRATION OF JUSTICE

Reporting restrictions In *Irish Times Ltd v. Ireland* [1997] 2 I.L.R.M. 541 (HC); Supreme Court, March 11, 1998, Morris J. (as he then was) declined to interfere with a trial judge's order placing reporting restrictions on the media in connection with a drugs trial. We should note here that the High Court decision was unanimously reversed on appeal by the Supreme Court in an important decision delivered in March 1998 which we will discuss in the 1998 Review. For the present, we discuss the High Court judgment only.

The trial involved five accused charged with possession of cocaine with intent to supply and the unlawful importation of the drugs into the State. One accused pleaded guilty on arraignment and sentencing as put back to the end of the trial of the other four accused, who had pleaded not guilty. Morris J. noted that the case concerned the largest seizure of cocaine in the State, it was the first prosecution for alleged importation under the Criminal Justice (Drug Trafficking) Act 1996, the accused persons had been in custody awaiting trial for more than five months and were of foreign nationality, the case had attracted significant media interest and there had already been inaccurate reporting in this case. In addition, a drugs case heard before the trial judge shortly before the instant case had to be aborted due to inaccurate media reporting. At the start of the instant trial, the trial judge made an order providing that 'there should be no contemporaneous media reporting of the trial save for the fact that the trial is proceeding in open court, the names and addresses of the accused parties, the nature of the crimes alleged in the indictment... but not referring to the fact that the accused are in custody [and] the fact that the captain of the vessel has pleaded guilty to the charge'. The applicants sought judicial review of the order. The case centred on a number of provisions of the Constitution. These included: Article 34.1, which provides, *inter alia*, that 'save in such special and limited cases as may be prescribed by law, [justice] shall be administered in public'; Article 38.1, which provides that '[n]o person shall be tried on any criminal charge save in due course of law'; and Article 40.6.1°i, which deals with the expression of convictions and opinions. As indicated, Morris J. refused the relief sought.

He accepted that the effect of a ban on contemporaneous reporting was that the trial was not being held 'in public' within the meaning of Article 34.1. While the order placed no prohibition on full reporting after the case had been concluded, the case was not being held in public because the order prohibited publication to the wider public of fair and accurate reports of proceedings. The order in the instant case was quite different from the order made in *R. v. Horsham Justices, ex P. Farquharson* [1982] Q.B. 762, arising from which it had become the common practice of the media not to report matters said in a jury's absence, and to delay reporting where the accused's trial was the first of a series of cases. Such an order and practice recognised the interests of ensuring a fair trial for the accused in accordance with law.

Morris J. then considered whether the more extensive restrictions imposed in the instant case could be justified. In this respect he accepted that a conflict of constitutional rights arose between the accused's right to trial in due course of law under Article 38.1 of the Constitution and the right of the media and the general citizenry to freedom of expression under Article 40.6.1°i. In balancing these two rights, Morris J. noted that the trial judge had clearly found that the accused's right to a fair trial was paramount and ranked higher in the hierarchy of rights to the media's right to contemporaneous reporting. Referring to the Supreme Court's decision in *D. v. Director of Pubic Prosecutions* [1994] 2 I.R. 465; [1994] 1 I.L.R.M. 435 (1994 Review, 200-1), Morris J. agreed that the right to a fair trial was superior to the community's right to have an alleged crime prosecuted and in this respect the general approach of the trial judge had been correct.

As to whether the trial judge had applied the test correctly in the instant case, Morris J. held that the trial judge was entitled to take such measures as were necessary to ensure that the trial over which he was presiding was conducted in a fair manner and in accordance with the Constitution, and to protect that constitutional right. Before a trial judge imposed a ban on reporting, he had to be satisfied that there was a 'real risk of an unfair trial' if contemporaneous reporting were permitted, and that the damage which such improper reporting would cause could not be remedied by the trial judge, either by appropriate directions to the jury or otherwise. Applying these tests to this case, the trial judge was justified in concluding that a real risk existed, bearing in mind the general media publicity already generated by the case, the inaccurate reporting on the case and the aborted drugs trial over which the trial judge had recently presided. The trial judge was thus entitled to conclude that a total ban on contemporaneous reporting was necessary to protect the accused from risk and Morris J. noted that it was not the function of the High Court on judicial review to decide whether it would have arrived at the same conclusion.

As indicated, the High Court decision was unanimously reversed on appeal by the Supreme Court in March 1998, and we will discuss that decision in the 1998 Review.

AMENDMENT TO CONSTITUTION

Amendment in conflict with original text In *Riordan v. Ireland*, High Court, November 14, 1997, the plaintiff had challenged the validity of Fifteenth Amendment to the Constitution Act 1995, which replaced the prohibition on divorce in the original text of Article 41.3.2° with a new Article 41.3.2° empowering the courts to grant divorce: see the 1995 Review, 136-144 and the 1996 Review, 352-7. The plaintiff argued that the Fifteenth Amendment Act was invalid because it was in conflict with the original text of the Constitution. Costello P. curtly rejected the argument. He held that there was a clear constitutional distinction between the power of the Oireachtas to make laws for the State and the power of the people to amend the Constitution. An amendment to the Constitution could not be declared invalid because it infringed some provision of the original text. The plaintiff was thus not entitled to make, and the Court had no jurisdiction to entertain, a challenge to an Act to amend the Constitution where that Act had been duly approved by the people in referendum and signed by the President.

The plaintiff had also raised other, quite unconnected, matters challenging the validity of the appointment of Carroll J. as chair of a Government appointed Commission on Nursing and Moriarty J. as chair of a tribunal of inquiry with the powers of the Tribunals of Inquiry (Evidence Acts 1921 to 1997. Costello P. held that the plaintiff had failed to establish the necessary *locus standi* to invoke the court's jurisdiction to make the declarations sought. Citing the decision in *Cahill v. Sutton* [1980] I.R. 269, he concluded that the plaintiff had not shown that any right of his had been infringed or threatened by the appointments, and had failed to advance any countervailing considerations which would justify a departure from the normal *locus standi* rule.

BREACH OF RIGHT

McDonnell v. Ireland [1996] 2 I.L.R.M. 222 (HC); Supreme Court, July 23, 1997 was a decision which arose almost directly from the Supreme Court's decision in *Cox v. Ireland* [1992] 2 I.R. 503 (1991 Review, 105-7). The applicant in *McDonnell* had been a civil servant in the Department of Posts and Telegraphs from 1963. In May 1974, he was arrested and charged with being a member of an unlawful organisation, the IRA, contrary to the Offences Against the State Act 1939. He was found guilty and sentenced to a term of imprisonment. In July 1974, he was informed that he had forfeited his position in the civil service under the provisions of section 34 of the 1939 Act. He applied to be reinstated but was told in May 1975 that his application could not be favourably considered. In *Cox v. Ireland* [1992] 2 I.R. 503, section 34 of the 1939 Act was found to be invalid having regard to the provisions of the

Constitution and, in the aftermath of this decision, the applicant instituted the present proceedings in which he claimed damages for breach of his constitutional rights resulting from the exercise and implementation of section 34 of the 1939 Act. In the High Court, Carroll J. dismissed the claim on the ground that the action was statute barred under the Statute of Limitations 1957 (see the 1996 Review, 436-9). The applicant's appeal was dismissed by the Supreme Court.

While the Court accepted that the effect of the *Cox* case was that section 34 of the 1939 Act was void *ab initio*, it also held that, in the light of *Murphy v. Attorney General* [1982] I.R. 241, this did not necessarily vest a cause of action in the applicant. Nonetheless, despite this strong view expressed by the Court, it dealt with the applicant's claim on the basis that he had an identifiable cause of action in 1974 because the case had at all times been argued between the parties on the basis that he was entitled to damages for an alleged breach of constitutional rights but that the claim was barred either by virtue of the Statute of Limitations 1957 or by laches.

The Court then considered the nature of an action for infringement of a constitutional right. The Court accepted that being the reference to the Constitution did not preclude its classification as a civil wrong and it could be classified as a civil wrong which is not a breach of contract but which was remediable by an action for unliquidated damages and/or an injunction. Citing the leading decision in *Meskell v. Coras Iompair Éireann* [1973] I.R. 121, the Court held that a constitutional right could be protected by a new form of action in tort provided the form of action thus fashioned sufficiently protected the constitutional right in question. In the context of the instant case, the Court noted that the parties had not been able to identify any ground for supposing that where an action for breach of a constitutional right has all the *indicia* of an action in tort it should have a different limitation period from that applicable to actions in tort generally. The Court recalled the policy considerations which underlie statutes of limitations as outlined in *Tuohy v. Courtney* [1994] 3 I.R. 1; [1994] 2 I.L.R.M. 503 (1994 Review, 336-8). In the instant case, therefore, the Court agreed with Carroll J's conclusion that the applicant's action was statute-barred. See further the discussion in the Limitation of Actions chapter, 543, below. See also the discussion of *H.M.W. v. Ireland* [1997] 2 I.R. 141 in the Torts chapter, 709–14 below.

CABINET CONFIDENTIALITY

The Seventeenth Amendment of the Constitution Act 1997, enacted in the wake of a referendum held in November 1997, inserted a new Article 28.4.3° into the Constitution, providing for limited access to cabinet discussions (the original Article 28.4.3° was consequently renumbered Article 28.4.4°). The provision inserted reads as follows:

> '3° The confidentiality of discussions at meetings of the Government
> shall be respected in all circumstances save only where the High Court
> determines that disclosure should be made in respect of a particular
> matter–
> i. in the interests of the administration of justice by a Court, or
> ii. by virtue of an overriding public interest, pursuant to an application
> in that behalf by a tribunal appointed by the Government or a minister of
> the Government on the authority of the Houses of the Oireachtas to in-
> quire into a matter stated by them to be of public importance.'

The new provision was required in view of the absolute prohibition on disclosure of cabinet discussions laid down in *Attorney General v. Hamilton (No. 2)*
[1993] 2 I.R. 250; [1993] I.L.R.M. 81 (1992 Review, 212-7). During the passage in the Oireachtas of the Bill to amend the Constitution, opposition speakers queried why the proposed amendment did not seek to re-establish what
had been thought to be the position before the *Hamilton* decision, namely that
cabinet discussions could be raised in proceedings before the courts on discovery or before tribunals of inquiry (which was the origin of the *Hamilton*
case). The Government indicated that while such a proposal might be considered in the future, it was confident that the more modest provision contained
in what became the Seventeenth Amendment would prove sufficient at least
as an interim measure. The Government was particularly concerned that the
Amendment would be carried in time to ensure that the workings of a Tribunal of Inquiry into Planning already established by the Oireachtas in 1997
would be able to investigate any relevant cabinet discussions if so required.
The Government also pointed out that the *Report of the Constitution Review
Group* (1996), pp.94-5 had indicated that there were great difficulties in framing a more wide-ranging proposal in this area and that great caution should be
exercised.

CHILDREN

Imprisonment   In *D.G. v. Eastern Health Board* [1998] 1 I.L.R.M. 241 (SC),
the Supreme Court held, by a majority, that the High Court has an inherent
jurisdiction to order the detention of minors in penal institutions albeit in rare
and extreme occasions when the Court is satisfied that it is required for a short
period in the interests of the welfare of the child and where no other suitable
facility is available.

The applicant in the instant case was 17 years of age. He had been in the
care of the Health Board since the age of two and had a history of criminal

activity and violence. He was not mentally ill but had a serious personality disorder, was a danger to himself and others and had failed to co-operate with the Health Board in the carrying out of a psychiatric assessment. Following his release from St. Patrick's Institution, the penal institution in the State for persons over the age of 17, he was homeless and resided on a temporary basis with a priest. There was no secure unit suitable for him in the State and the Health Board had sought to place him in a secure unit in the United Kingdom. The applicant sought an order of *mandamus* directing the Health Board and the State to provide suitable care and accommodation for him. In June 1997, the High Court (Kelly J) made an order that the applicant be detained in St. Patrick's Institution for a period of three weeks and that a full psychiatric assessment be carried out. As indicated, the Supreme Court, by a majority, affirmed this order.

The Court considered that the case raised issues concerning the hierarchy of rights contained in the Constitution, first explicitly discussed *The People v. Shaw* [1982] I.R. 1 and later analysed in *Attorney General v. X* [1992] 1 I.R. 1; [1992] I.L.R.M. 401 (1992 Review, 158-86). See also *Irish Times Ltd v. Ireland* [1997] 2 I.L.R.M. 541 (HC); Supreme Court, March 11, 1998, discussed above, 167–8. In the instant case, the Court held that the High Court has an inherent jurisdiction to order the detention of minors in penal institutions. This jurisdiction should be exercised only in rare and extreme occasions when the Court was satisfied it was required for a short period in the interests of the welfare of the child and where no other suitable facility was available. In the instant case, the Court held that the High Court had exercised its jurisdiction in a manner consistent with the requirements of the applicant's welfare. Delivering a strong dissenting judgment, Denham J. considered that the detention of a minor in a children's residential home for the purpose of providing for his welfare and education was fundamentally different from the detention of a minor in a penal institution. She concluded that to detain the applicant in a penal institution was in breach of the State's duty to provide for his moral welfare and development. She noted that, as an adult, the applicant could not be detained in a penal institution in similar circumstances and it would thus also be in breach of the constitutional guarantee of equality in Article 40.1.

ELECTIONS

Electoral Act 1997   The Electoral Act 1997 constituted a major reform of the electoral law in the State and, in substantial part, proved highly controversial during its passage through the Oireachtas.

Among the points which provoked particular debate were those in Part III of the 1997 Act (sections 16 to 21) which provide for fixed payments by the State to political parties and candidates, those in Part IV (sections 22 to 26) which concern disclosure of donations to parties and candidates for political purposes, those in Part V. (sections 27 to 45) which limit expenditure at general elections by political parties and candidates and those in Part VI (sections 46 to 62) which similarly place limits on expenditure during presidential elections. These provisions had not come into effect when the 1997 General Election was called. Although they came into effect in 1998, since the Government which came to power after the 1997 election appears to oppose these provisions, it remains to be seen whether they will continue to operate, at least in the form in which they appear in the 1997 Act. At the time of writing it appears more likely that a modified version of these provisions will be proposed and we will discuss any such provisions in a future Review.

Other matters included in the 1997 Act proved less controversial and have been brought into force. Thus Part II of the 1997 Act (sections 5 to 15) provided for the establishment of a Constituency Commission, replacing the non-statutory Commission which had been in existence since 1977. The Constituency Commission (Establishment) Order 1997 (S.I. No. 393 of 1997), established the Constituency Commission with effect from September 30, 1997. Part VII of the 1997 Act (sections 63 to 70) also provides for more extensive provision for postal voting than had been in place under the Electoral Act 1992 (1992 Review, 141-4) or the Electoral (Amendment) Act 1996 (1996 Review, 146-7). The 1997 Act provides that postal voting is to be available to persons whose employment prevents them from attending a polling station as well as full-time students. This is in addition to the categories covered by the previous regime such as members of the Defence Forces and those with a physical disability. As for the regime under the 1996 Act, the Registration of Electors Regulations 1997 (S.I. No. 5 of 1997) prescribed the dates for the preparation of the disabled persons postal voters list for 1997/1998. Finally, Part VIII of the 1997 Act (sections 71 to 82) deals with a number of miscellaneous matters, such as appointment of election agents and the expenses of returning officers, free postage for election candidates and arrangements for counting votes.

The provisions of the 1997 Act on disclosure of donations and appointment of election agents, came into force on May 15, 1997 as provided for in section 1(6)(a) of the 1997 Act; those on payments to political parties and reimbursement of election expenses, expenditure by political parties at general elections and at presidential elections came into force on January 1, 1998 as provided in section 1(6)(b). The remainder of the Act requires Commencement Orders to come into force. At the time of writing, the following Orders have been made. The Electoral Act 1997 (Commencement) Order 1997 (S.I. No. 233 of 1997) brought section 77 of the 1997 Act, which deals with the expenses of returning officers, into force on June 1, 1997, in time for the 1997 General Election.

European Parliament   The European Parliament Elections Act 1997 consolidated and updated the legislative provisions on elections to the European Parliament, and is in line with the general provisions contained in the Electoral Act 1992 (1992 Review, 141-4) and the Electoral Act 1997 (see immediately above). It also gives effect to Directive 93/109/EEC and repealed the European Parliament Elections Act 1977. The European Parliament Elections Act 1997 (Commencement) Order 1997 (S.I. No. 163 of 1997) brought the Act into force on April 21, 1997. For further discussion, see the European law chapter, 374, below.

Postal voters   See the discussion of the Electoral Act 1997, 142, above.

Presidential elections   The Presidential Elections (Forms) Regulations 1997 (S.I. No. 29 of 1997), made under the Presidential Elections Act 1993 (1993 Review, 158) prescribed the forms to be used in presidential elections, including the election held in 1997 in which President Mary McAleese was elected in succession to President Mary Robinson.

EQUALITY

Arrest power   In *Molyneux v. Ireland* [1997] 2 I.L.R.M. 241 (HC), Costello P. rejected a challenge to the validity of the arrest powers contained in section 28 of the Dublin Police Act 1842. The gravamen of the claim was that section 28 of the 1842 Act was in breach of the equality guarantee in Article 40.1 in that it applied to an arrest in the Dublin area only. As indicated, the challenge was unsuccessful, but the claim itself is now largely of historical interest only since the powers in the 1842 Act have been superseded by the comprehensive arrest powers in the Criminal Law Act 1997 (see the Criminal Law chapter, 265, below) linked to the changes in the substantive law on assault in the Non-Fatal Offences Against the Person Act 1997 (also discussed in the Criminal Law chapter, 304, below). Nonetheless, the arguments advanced in the *Molyneux* case are worthy of discussion for their illumination of the judicial attitude to claims based on Article 40.1.

The background to the claim was as follows. The plaintiff was alleged to have committed an assault in the Dublin Metropolitan District in July 1992. He was arrested by a Garda under section 28 of the Dublin Police Act 1842, which provides that: 'it shall be lawful for any constable belonging to the said Dublin Police to take into custody without warrant any person within limits of the police district who shall be charged by any other person with committing any aggravated assault, in every case in which such constable shall have good reason to believe that such assault has been committed, although not within view of such constable, and by reason of the recent commission of the offence a warrant could not have been obtained for the apprehension of the offence'. The validity of section 28 of the 1842 Act was tried as a preliminary issue. The plaintiff argued that since the power of arrest in section 28 did not exist outside the Dublin area, all citizens were not being treated equally by the law, thereby infringing Article 40.1, which provides:

> All citizens shall, as human persons, be held equal before the law. This shall not be held to mean that the State shall not in its enactments have due regard to differences of capacity, physical or moral, and of social function.

Costello P. held that the plaintiff's submission was based on a misunderstanding of Article 40.1 and was unsustainable. He accepted that the concepts enshrined in Article 40.1 were ones:

> which, quite literally, are universally recognised. The 1948 UN Declaration of Human Rights refers in its preamble to 'the inherent dignity of all members of the human family' and declares in article 1 that 'all human beings are born free and equal in dignity and rights.

However, Costello P. pointed out that many laws treat people differently, whether by conferring benefits on them or imposing tax burdens on them and such laws could not be taken to breach Article 40.1 or the more concept of equality in international law in the 1948 UN Declaration. Citing the Supreme Court decision on Article 40.1, *Quinn's Supermarkets Ltd v. Attorney General* [1972] I.R. 1, Costello P. stated:

> The guarantee in the Constitution is not a guarantee of absolute equality for all citizens in all circumstances, but is a guarantee of equality as human persons relating to their dignity as human beings and a guarantee against inequalities based on an assumption that some individuals because of their human attributes, ethnic, racial, social or religious background are to be treated as inferior or the superior of other individuals in the community.

Costello P. went on to state that, in a case where different treatment between one group of persons and another was being challenged, the following approach should be taken:

> (a) the category of persons allegedly adversely affected by the law, (ii) the difference of treatment enacted by the law of which complaint is made, (b) the difference of treatment enacted by the law of which complaint is made, and (c) the basis on which the difference of treatment

was enacted. If it appears that the difference of treatment in the impugned law is not related in any way to a difference based on the characteristics or attributes of citizens as human persons, then quite clearly [Article 40.1] is not infringed. But if it is so based then a further examination requires to be undertaken. . . . If . . . the difference of treatment which is challenged can be justified because it is based on the differences referred to in the second paragraph of Article 40.1 then no constitutional invalidity has occurred.

Applying this approach, Costello P. noted that the category of persons affected by section 28 of the 1842 Act were suspects of the crimes referred to in the section who were in the Dublin area. He considered that it was a reasonable inference that the difference in treatment between suspects in the Dublin area and those outside it was based on considerations of public policy relating to the incidence of crime in the Dublin area, the difficulty of apprehending suspects in that area and the need to do so speedily. Thus, the difference in treatment in no way infringed the guarantee of equality in Article 40.1 and he therefore considered that there was no need to examine whether it was justified by the second part of Article 40.1. As we already noted, any general issue raised in *Molyneux* case has been resolved by the enactment of the comprehensive arrest powers in the Criminal Law Act 1997 (see the Criminal Law chapter, 265, below) linked to the changes in the substantive law on assault in the Non-Fatal Offences against the Person Act 1997 (also discussed in the Criminal Law chapter, 304, below).

Employment and equal status legislation   The decision of the Supreme Court in *In re the Employment Equality Bill 1996* [1997] E.L.R. 132 (SC) and in *In re the Equal Status Bill 1997* [1997] E.L.R. 185 (SC) are discussed in the Labour Law chapter, 485, 492, below.

EXPRESSION

Radio broadcasting: religious advertising   The decision of Geoghegan J. in *Murphy v. Independent Radio and Television Commission* [1997] 2 I.L.R.M. 467 is discussed in the Communications chapter, 85, above.

GOVERNMENT

Tánaiste   In *Riordan v. An Tánaiste* [1998] 1 I.L.R.M. 494 (SC), the Supreme Court rejected the plaintiff's contention that the Constitution prohibited the Tánaiste from being absent from the State at the same time as the

Taoiseach. The plaintiff alleged that the Tánaiste had breached his duty under Article 28.6.3° of the Constitution when he was absent from the State on five separate occasions when the Taoiseach was also absent. He argued that on his departure from the State, the Taoiseach ceased to be such, and as such the Tánaiste had to remain in the State so as to discharge the duties and functions, both constitutional and legislative, of the Taoiseach. The claim was dismissed in the High Court and the Supreme Court affirmed.

The Court was of the view that the Constitution did not expressly prohibit the Tánaiste from leaving the State if the Taoiseach was also outside the State. The Court considered that there was no logic in implying a geographical or territorial dimension to the term 'absence' in Article 28.6.3°. When both the wording and the sense of constitutional provisions was clear, the Court concluded that it would be wrong for it to import a facet to the duties of those who have to perform various functions under the Constitution which were neither stated in the document, nor otherwise justified. Indeed, the Court opined that with modern telecommunications and sensible delegation of authority combined with collective responsibility, the Taoiseach could exercise leadership of the government while abroad in most instances.

LIBERTY

Judicial review or inquiry In *McSorley v. Governor of Mountjoy Prison* [1997] 2 I.L.R.M. 315 (SC), the Supreme Court emphasised the limited circumstances in which a Court should order an *ex parte* release of a person under Article 40.4.2°.

The applicants had been arrested and charged with various offences relating to the unlawful possession of a motor car. They admitted the charges before the District Court and were imprisoned. They later applied to the High Court for an enquiry into their detention pursuant to Article 40.4.2° of the Constitution, on the ground that at no time had they been offered either by the Gardaí or the District Court judge the services of a solicitor following their arrest or at their sentencing. This assertion was accepted in the High Court, who ordered their immediate release, relying on the decision in *Sheehan v. Reilly* [1993] 2 I.R. 81; [1993] I.L.R.M. 427 (1992 Review, 152-4). On appeal, the Supreme Court reversed and held that the case should have been dealt with by way of judicial review.

Delivering the leading judgment, O'Flaherty J. cited the Court's decision in *The State (McDonagh) v. Frawley* [1978] I.R. 131 that a person who is detained on foot of a conviction on indictment were to be regarded as being *prima facie* detained in accordance with law within the meaning of Article 40.4 and that it would require the most exceptional circumstances for the court to intervene. He accepted that, if as was conceded in this case the District

Court judge failed to explain the applicants' rights to them, their detention would call for review. However, the failure to afford the District Court judge and the Director of Public Prosecutions an opportunity to make a case was a breach of the requirement of *audi alteram partem*. By contrast with the situation in *Sheehan v. Reilly* [1993] 2 I.R. 81; [1993] I.L.R.M. 427, there was no question but that the applicants were in lawful custody. In those circumstances, the Supreme Court concluded that the District Court judge should have been given the opportunity of offering his observations, and that the correct course for the High Court would have been to give leave to apply for judicial review.

LIFE OF UNBORN

The issue of abortion has been at the centre of legal, social and political debate in Ireland over the past two decades. We welcome the publication in 1997 of an insightful rigorous analysis of the subject by James Kingston, Anthony Whelan and Ivana Bacik, entitled *Abortion and the Law*.

Abortion information   In *Society for the Protection of Unborn Children (Irl) Ltd v Grogan and Ors (No.3)*, Supreme Court, March 6, 1997, the Supreme Court brought some finality to long-running litigation on the dissemination by various student organisations of information concerning abortion services available outside the State. The judgment of Denham J. in the Supreme Court also provides a summary of the many connected cases in this area. *Grogan* should thus also be seen against the general background of the amendments made to Article 40.3 of the Constitution concerning abortion and the right to life of the unborn child, beginning in 1983 and including three referenda in 1992: see the 1992 Review, 154-208. The defendants in *Grogan* had appealed against the judgment of Morris J. in the High Court, delivered on August 7, 1992 which prohibited them, along with anyone having knowledge of the said order, from providing information to persons of the identity and location of clinics where abortions were performed: see the 1992 Review, 186-8. Virtually all the defendants (apart from the 15th named defendant who was a printer) were officers of either the Union of Students of Ireland, the Students' Union of University College Dublin and the Students' Union of Trinity College Dublin. In 1988, the plaintiff society had applied successfully to the courts for injunctive relief to prevent a counselling service operating in the State from providing information related to abortion in their counselling service: see *Attorney General (Society for the Protection of Unborn Children (Irl) Ltd v Open Door Counselling Ltd* [1988] I.R. 593; [1989] I.L.R.M. 19 (1988 Review, 132). In 1989, the plaintiff society sought an interlocutory injunction restraining the defendants from publishing, distributing or printing information relating to abortion clinics in the United Kingdom. The plaintiff claimed that the distribution of this information contravened Article 40.3.3°

of the Constitution which, following the Eighth Amendment to the Constitution in 1983, provided:

> The State acknowledges the right to life of the unborn and, with due regard to the equal right to life of the mother, guarantees in its laws to respect, and, as far as practicable, by its laws to vindicate that right.

In the High Court, Carroll J. referred certain questions to the Court of Justice of the European Communities for a preliminary ruling in accordance with Article 177 of the EC Treaty: see *Society for the Protection of Unborn Children (Irl) Ltd v Grogan and Ors* [1989] I.R. 753 (1989 Review, 102-5). Carroll J. did not in terms refuse the plaintiff society interlocutory relief but it appealed to the Supreme Court against Carroll J.'s failure to grant the said injunction. In December 1989, the Supreme Court allowed the appeal and made the order sought, giving liberty to apply before the trial for a variation of the order in light of the preliminary ruling of the European Court of Justice. In its ruling delivered in October 1991, the Court of Justice found that the performance of an abortion did constitute a 'service' within the meaning of Article 60 of the EC Treaty. However, the Court went on to rule that it was not contrary to community law for a Member State, in which abortion was forbidden, to prohibit student associations from distributing information about the location of abortion clinics in another Member State where abortion was lawfully carried out.

Before the instant proceedings came on for substantive hearing, the provisions of Article 40.3.3° of the Constitution were considered by the Supreme Court in *Attorney General v. X* [1992] 1 I.R. 1 (1992 Review, 154-208). The Court recognised that there could be a conflict between the 'right to life of the unborn' and the 'equal right to life of the mother' and that where there was such a conflict, the Constitution required that its provisions be interpreted harmoniously. The Court determined that the proper test to be applied was that if it was established as a matter of probability that there was a real and substantial risk to the life, as distinct from the health, of the mother, which could only be avoided by the termination of her pregnancy, such termination was permissible having regard to the true interpretation of Article 40.3.3°. The Court concluded that once the termination of the pregnancy was permissible, the mother had the right to all relevant information necessary to enable her to have the pregnancy terminated, including the information which was the subject matter of orders in *Attorney General (Society for the Protection of Unborn Children (Irl) Ltd) v. Open Door Counselling Ltd* [1988] I.R. 593.

In the High Court in the instant proceedings Morris J. held that it had been decided by the Supreme Court in the *Open Door Counselling* case and at the interlocutory stage of the instant proceedings that the distribution and provision of information relating to United Kingdom abortion services was uncon-

stitutional. The defendants had argued that the *X* case had identified a class of
person and a circumstance in which an abortion could be permissible and that
in those circumstances, the communication of information to such a person
was permissible rendering their conduct lawful. However, this submission was
rejected by Morris J. because no case had been made that the conduct of the
defendants related only to people coming within the class identified by the *X*
case, nor, had it been suggested that the defendants had wished to confine
their activities to the distribution of information to that class. Accordingly, a
perpetual injunction was granted.

Before the appeal came on for hearing in the Supreme Court, the law relating to abortion was amended in 1992 by the 14th Amendment of the Constitution: see the 1992 Review, 205-8. This 'information amendment' provided
that the following paragraph be added to Article 40.3.3°:

> This subsection shall not limit freedom to obtain or make available, in
> the State, subject to such conditions as may be laid down by law, infor-
> mation relating to services lawfully available in another State.

The conditions referred to were prescribed by the Regulation of Information
(Services outside the State for Termination of Pregnancies) Bill 1995 which
was referred to the Supreme Court by the President for an opinion as to its
validity pursuant to Article 26 of the Constitution: see *In re the Regulation of
Information (Services outside the State for Termination of Pregnancies) Bill
1995* [1995] 1 I.R. 1 (1995 Review, 145-54). The Court found that the Bill
was constitutional, remarking that if the purpose of travel or the securing of
information was to procure a lawful abortion – one which complied with the
test laid down in *Attorney General v. X* – then neither the travel or the giving
or obtaining of information with regard thereto would be unlawful.

Prior to this, in 1993 the Supreme Court had declined to set aside the
injunction granted to the society against Open Door Counselling, even in the
wake of the 1992 information referendum, which had provided that information could be disseminated: see *Attorney General (Society for the Protection
of Unborn Children (Irl) Ltd v Open Door Counselling Ltd* [1994] 1 I.L.R.M.
256 (1993 Review, 160-5).

In the *Grogan* case before the Supreme Court, the defendants submitted
that while Morris J. had been bound by the Supreme Court decision in the
1988 *Open Door Counselling* case to grant the perpetual injunction in 1992,
the 1988 decision had been wrongly decided by the Supreme Court and should
be overruled. They claimed that the 1988 Supreme Court decision in *Open
Door Counselling* had been based on the premise that abortion could never be
lawful, a conclusion which had been rejected by the Supreme Court in 1992 in
the *X* case. In addition, they submitted that the Supreme Court had failed to
interpret the provisions of Article 40.3.3° harmoniously and had failed to give

due regard to the right to life of the mother along with the right of citizens to express freely their convictions.

The Supreme Court acceded to the application to have the injunction lifted. In this respect, it reviewed its case law on the extent to which it would depart from its previous decisions, a view it had first taken in the seminal decisions *The State (Quinn) v. Ryan* [1965] I.R. 70 and *Attorney General v. Ryan's Car Hire Ltd* [1965] I.R. 642. These had established that the Supreme Court could depart from a previous decision where there was a compelling reason to do so and where it appears that the previous decision was clearly wrong. In *Mogul of Ireland Ltd v. Tipperary (North Riding) County Council* [1976] I.R. 260, Henchy J. had underlined the continued importance of the *stare decisis* principle by noting that even if the Court was of the opinion that an earlier decision was wrong, it might decide in the interests of justice not to overrule it, if it had become inveterate and if, in a widespread way, people had acted on the basis of its correctness to such an extent that greater harm would result from over-ruling it than from allowing it to stand. In a concurring judgment, Keane J. distinguished *Mogul of Ireland* on the basis that since the instant case was concerned with constitutional rights, whereas *Mogul* involved an issue of statutory interpretation only, the need to avoid any possible infringement of constitutional rights of citizens would justify a departure from earlier decisions of the Court.

As to whether the injunction granted in the instant case should be confirmed, the Court crucially held that it had to look at the present state of the law in regard to providing abortion information rather than what it was when the proceedings commenced, applying the approach taken in *Application Des Gaz S.A. v Falks Veritas Ltd* [1974] Ch. 381. On this, the Court noted that there had been two significant changes in the law since the High Court injunction had been granted, namely the Fourteenth Amendment of the Constitution in 1992 and the enactment of the Regulation of Information (Services Outside the State for Termination of Pregnancies) Act 1995. In light of these, the Court concluded that it should not continue the injunction as granted. Citing the decision of Costello J. in *Attorney General v. Paperlink Ltd* [1984] I.L.R.M. 373, the Court noted that the defendants were either complying with the conditions for the dissemination of information as set out in the 1995 Act and were thus protected by the Fourteenth Amendment to the Constitution or they were committing criminal offences. If the latter was the case, the only person who had the right to obtain an injunction against the defendants was the Attorney General.

As to whether this conclusion should lead the Court to holding that the decision in the 1988 *Open Door* case had been wrongly decided, a majority, Hamilton C.J., Blayney and Barrington JJ., held that this was not necessarily so. They considered that *Open Door Counselling* case had been correctly decided on the facts and issues before the Court at the time. They considered that since the issue in that case was between the right to life of the unborn and the right of freedom of expression of the defendants, the Court had been entitled to prefer the right to life of the unborn even if that meant restricting the freedom of expression of the defendants and that no issue had arisen in that case as to the right to life of the mother. Dissenting on this point, Denham and Keane JJ. held that since the decision in *Open Door Counselling* had been based on the premise that abortion could never be lawful and since this was in error, the decision flowing therefrom was flawed and should be overruled. The divergence of views on this aspect of the case reflects a continuing reluctance by members of the Supreme Court since the 1960s to engage in considerable mental gymnastics in order to avoid overtly overruling one of its previous decisions: see Byrne and McCutcheon, *The Irish Legal System*, 3rd ed (Butterworths, 1996). Rather than overruling a previous decision, the majority in the Supreme Court would appear content to conclude that, for example, the *Open Door Counselling* case can be confined to the particular facts on which it was decided; without actually overruling it, the decision is in effect devoid of any value as a precedent.

Right to Life of The Unborn In *A. and B. v. Eastern Health Board* [1998] 1 I.L.R.M. 460, Geoghegan J. in judicial review proceedings, addressed important issues relating to the right to life of the unborn. He did so under the shadow of the Supreme Court decision of *Attorney General v. X* [1992] 1 I.R. 1; [1992] I.L.R.M. 401, which interpreted Article 40.3.3° of the Constitution as authorising abortion based on a danger to the mother's life. In the 1992 Review at 160-186 we criticised the Supreme Court's holding on several grounds: it violated the principle of equality of the right to life as between the mother and her unborn child, contrary to the express language of Article 40.3.3°; it failed to understand the crucial philosophical distinction between a direct attack on life and the loss of life as an indirect and unsought side-effect; it received no evidence as to the distinction between necessary medical treatment of pregnant women and abortion and thus treated the former as legally indistinguishable from the latter; it received no evidence from a psychiatrist, though it authorised abortion on essentially a psychiatric ground; it acted on the basis of a mistaken concession by counsel on behalf of the Attorney General that Article 40.3.3° authorised abortion; and it replaced a coherent philosophy of human dignity and equality by a criterion dependent on the values or attitudes commanding support in certain social quarters and in particular among judges at any particular time.

The facts in *A. and B.,* as in *X.,* were tragic. A thirteen year old girl, C., was brutally raped by an adult and became pregnant as a result. She was a member of the travelling community, one of a family of twelve. She lived 'in particularly squalid conditions which were quite unlike the conditions in which most travelling people lived.'

The alleged rapist was also of the travelling community and a long-standing friend of the family. The girl was severely traumatised by the rape and 'there was a well-founded view that the behaviour of her parents A and B, after the rape did not correspond in various respects to the kind of behaviour one would expect of parents in such appalling circumstances.' It was in this context that temporary care orders were made. With the approval of the parents the girl, C., stayed with a foster mother who had her own family some fifty miles away. C. at all times wanted to have an abortion. For quite some time the parents and particularly the father were not only supportive of the idea of an abortion but were advocating it. They had doubts about this at times, however, and ultimately changed their minds and opposed any idea of termination of pregnancy. The mother was absolutely opposed; the father's opposition was qualified in that he would favour it if otherwise his daughter was going to take her own life.

The Health Board sought an order by the District Court under section 17 (4) of the Child Care Act 1991 directing that C. be permitted to 'proceed to such place as may be appropriate for the purpose of securing treatment, to wit, a termination of her pregnancy', that she be 'afforded the said treatment . . .', and that the Eastern Health Board execute all necessary documents and make all arguments required to facilitate the implementation of the earlier directions. Judge Fahy, having heard evidence from a psychiatrist that C. was likely to commit suicide if she did not have an abortion, made an order to this effect. The parents took judicial review proceedings seeking to have the order quashed.

Several grounds were put forward by the parents. It may be useful to consider those of general import first and then go on to consider those which were specific to the facts of the case.

The parents argued first that the expression 'medical . . . treatment', which is included in section 13(7) of the 1991 Act and incorporated by reference into section 17(4), could never include abortion. Geoghegan J. disagreed. It is worth recording how he disposed of the argument:

> [counsel for C.] has drawn my attention to the fact that in the English Abortion Legislation, termination of pregnancy is regarded as a medical treatment. I do not think much importance can be attached to that as there could have been political and other reasons for such definition. But where a psychiatrist as in this case gives strong evidence to the effect that a child is likely to commit suicide unless she has a termination of pregnancy, that termination of pregnancy which is a medical procedure is clearly in my view also a medical treatment for her mental condition. It is not necessary therefore to consider whether all terminations of pregnancy come within the expression 'medical treatment'. I am satisfied that on the facts of this case it would come within that expression.

Having set out the evidence of the psychiatrist in some detail, Geoghegan J. stated:

> In the light of this evidence coming from a consultant psychiatrist including the advice that she undergo medical procedures involving the termination of her pregnancy because of her suicidal tendencies such medical procedures must, in my view, constitute 'medical treatment' within any normal definition. I am therefore of the opinion that the direction of Judge Fahy did involve medical treatment and came within the statutory provision.

It has to be said that this analysis is less than convincing. It fails to acknowledge, or perhaps even recognise, that language serves more than the function of a passive signpost, directing the reader or listener to a particular objectively discernible destination. Language has far greater potency: it is integrated into human consciousness, values and emotions, not only at the level of the individual but also at the level of society. How society speaks publicly, through its laws, political language and other prestigious communications, affects social and individual values and attitudes and can in turn influence and mould personal conduct.

There is no real argument that a society which tolerates, or even uses, language that demeans particular human beings, encourages attitudes towards those people which can translate into harmful conduct. This century has witnessed the grossest injustices towards stigmatised groups of people. Stigma brings with it its own distinctive labels: kikes, wops, kaffirs, paddies. The labels are not always the major cause of the harmful conduct but they play their part in legitimising it and in making it harder to resist.

The counterpoint to stigmatic language is sanitised language, softening the reality of a particular activity so as to encourage or legitimate its practice.

When it comes to the taking of human life, the desire to use sanitising language may be strong. The very passage from life to death can be so frightening for some people that they resort to 'passing on', 'passing away' or 'losing' a parent or other loved one.

Abortion, the direct intentional taking of the life of an unborn child, can be so disconcerting a concept, since it violates the most basic of human rights, that euphemisms may be attractive. The phrase 'termination of pregnancy', widely used in *A. and B. v. Eastern Health Board*, is one such euphemism. It can be criticised for its inaccuracy, since it is overbroad in embracing situations – notably the birth of a healthy baby – which it is not truthfully intended to connote. The fact that it ignores the life and fate of the unborn child is also a weakness: one cannot resolve the issues of justice and human rights associated with abortion by the device of pretending that abortion does not involve the death of the unborn child as a direct, inevitable and intended result of the process.

These criticisms of the phrase 'termination of pregnancy' are of a different order from those which attach to the characterisation of abortion as 'medical treatment'. The words 'medical treatment' do not merely connote a range of scientific processes impacting of the body. They bear the weight of three millenia of ethics, social philosophy and human solidarity. Our cultural understanding of the purpose of human life and of social organisation is bound up in several simple notions: that life in all its forms has inherent value; that we all have a right to life; that helping people to preserve their life is a moral good, and that those who go to the assistance of people needing medical treatment are engaging in part of this process. Doctors and nurses are highly regarded because of this dimension to their work.

Medical treatment may impact negatively on the patient or, in the case of treatment of a pregnant woman, on the foetus, as an indirect unsought side effect, but we would surely baulk at the idea that a response to a medical condition in one human being, designed to improve that condition, which consists of intentionally and directly causing injury or death to another human being is 'medical treatment' simply because the medical condition of the first human being improves as a result. We are not referring here to the moral character of the action in question (though clearly such action raises stark issues of justice and human rights).

There has been an increasing willingness internationally to contemplate the taking of the lives of disabled newborn children – 'defective neonates'. If we imagine a case where the father of a disabled infant was so depressed as to contemplate committing suicide if the child continued to live, could the decision by a medical team to terminate the child's life be characterised as 'medical treatment'? Would it become so if accompanied by the provision of a course of sedatives for the father to reduce his condition of anxiety? Not all acts designed to improve a person's medical condition can be characterised as medical treatment on account of their purpose. The point is reached where the act is so overloaded with other ethically and socially relevant characteristics as no longer to warrant that description.

Abortion can involve a surgical process and clearly has in some instances potentially damaging medical implications for the mother but it is not itself a medical treatment. If it is accepted that taking the life of a child who has already been born, to improve the medical condition of another person, should not be characterised as 'medical treatment', the principle should also apply to abortion.

As a general observation, it is worth noting how a society in the process of a shift in values finds comfort in sheltering behind the prestige of medical decisionmaking. Everyone now accepts that the 'medicalisation' of contraception in Ireland twenty years ago was a convenient way of disguising the change of attitudes towards contraception. The idea that people wishing to have access to contraceptives should need a doctor's prescription seems fantastic today. It may be predicted that historians will regard the AIDS rationale for the further radical legal extension of access to contraceptives in 1985 as involving a genuine medical concern in a wider cultural process. The characterisation of feeding through a tube as a medical process in *In re a Ward of Court* [1995] 2 I.L.R.M. 161 was helpful to the Supreme Court in its embracing the notion that bringing about death through starvation of a life deemed not worth living was legal acceptable: see the 1995 Review, 156.

Undoubtedly contraception, tubal feeding and, indeed, abortion have a medical dimension but only those engaged in self-delusion will allow themselves use the medical characterisation to hide from their vision the process of replacement of values which this involves. Once that process is completed, the international experience is that the courts that have engaged in it awaken to the new values, embrace them without embarrassment and dispense with the medical characterisation which, having served its purpose, is seen for what it was.

The second crucial issue in *A. and B. v. Eastern Health Board* concerned the effect of the 'travel' amendment in 1992 on the Eighth Amendment and the implications of this for the exercise by a court of its discretion under the Child Care Act 1991, in the light of section 24 which requires the court to have regard to the welfare of the child as 'the first and paramount consideration'.

Counsel for C. argued that the District Judge had power to authorise an abortion outside the jurisdiction in circumstances which did not fall within the decision of *Attorney General v. X* [1992] 1 I.R. 1; [1992] I.L.R.M. 401, where the Supreme Court held, controversially, that the Eight Amendment rendered lawful an abortion where the mother's life, as opposed to health, required it.

Counsel for the child argued that, as a result of the 'travel' amendment, a child in the care of her parents could be taken to England by her parents on one of the grounds for which abortion were carried out there; if this was so, why should a child who was in care 'be disadvantaged and not permitted to do so'?

Geoghegan J. rejected this line of argument. In an important passage, having quoted the 'travel' amendment, which provides that Article 40.3.3° 'shall not limit freedom to travel between the State and another State', he observed that this amendment was:

> framed in negative terms and must, in my view, be interpreted in the historical context in which it was inserted. There was, I think, a widespread feeling in the country that a repetition of the *X* case should not occur in that nobody should be injuncted from actually travelling out of the country for the purpose of an abortion. It must be remembered that three out of the five judges of the Supreme Court took the view that in an appropriate case a travel injunction could be granted. It was in that

context, therefore, that the amendment was made and I do not think it was ever intended to give some new substantial right. Rather, it was intended to prevent injunctions against travel or having an abortion abroad. A court of law, in considering the welfare of an Irish child in Ireland and considering whether on health grounds a termination of pregnancy was necessary, must I believe, be confined to considering the grounds for termination which would be lawful under the Irish Constitution and cannot make a direction authorising travel to another jurisdiction for a different kind of abortion. The amended Constitution does not now confer a right to abortion outside of Ireland. It merely prevents injunctions against travelling for that purpose.

Geoghegan J. considered that this view conformed with what the Supreme Court had held in *In re Article 26 and the Regulation of Information (Services Outside the State for Termination of Pregnancies) Bill 1995* [1995] 1 I.R. 1 at 47; [1995] 2 I.L.R.M. 81, at 110, where Hamilton C.J., for the Court, said that the position set forth in *X* was 'unaltered by either of the provisions of the thirteenth or fourteenth amendment to the Constitution or of the Bill.' He noted that Keane J., *in Society for the Protection of Unborn Children Ireland Ltd v. Grogan (No. 3)*, Supreme Court, March 6, 1997, discussed above, 178, had expressed his support for the views of McCarthy and O'Flaherty JJ. in *X* that the High Court injunction had impermissibly violated the plaintiff's right to travel, Geoghegan J. observed that the fact that there might be different views as to the importance of the constitutional right to travel did not affect the issue of whether the District Court, under the Child Care Act 1991, could actually exercise a jurisdiction authorising travel for an abortion in circumstances where the proposed abortion would not be allowed under Irish law. Geoghegan J. thought that the court would be prevented from doing so by the terms of the right to life of the unborn expressed in the Constitution as unaffected by the 'travel' amendment. The Supreme Court had so held. Having made his view on this issue plain, Geoghegan J. went on to say that, if the Supreme Court took a different interpretation on the scope of the power of the District Court to authorise an abortion abroad, so that the limitation of *X* did not apply, he wished it to be known that he 'would have taken a different view and would have granted the order' authorising an abortion abroad.

Geoghegan J.'s decision is rigorously analysed by James Dalton, 'The C. Case', 1 *Trinity College Law Review* 55 (1998). Mr Dalton identifies 'the ineffectiveness of judicial review as a device for enforcing even minimal standards of fair procedures of lower courts in the abortion context.' He raises the question whether Geoghegan J.'s interpretation of the 'Travel' Amendment from an historical standpoint can be justified.

LOCUS STANDI

Lack of standing In *Riordan v. Ireland*, High Court, November 14, 1997, Costello P. held that the plaintiff had failed to establish the necessary *locus standi* to challenge certain matters on constitutional grounds: see 169, above.

Mootness In *O'Connell v. Minister for Justice*, High Court, July 31, 1997, Geoghegan J. declined to address the constitutionality of section 65 of the Courts of Justice Act 1936 and the Regulations made thereunder providing for court fees on the ground that the applicant did not have the required *locus standi* to challenge the legislation. The applicant had instituted proceedings in the High Court. He applied *ex parte* to the High Court for an order directing that the State waive the court fees on the notice of trial. In August 1994, the High Court assigned the applicant a solicitor and counsel under the Attorney General's scheme (as to which, see Byrne and McCutcheon, *Irish Legal System*, 3rd ed (Butterworths, 1996, p.290), for the purpose of making a formal application for an order waiving the court fees. The applicant borrowed the money to pay the court fees, succeeded in his action and was awarded his costs. The sum due in respect of his costs was paid by May 1996. In July 1996, the applicant obtained leave from the High Court to challenge the constitutionality of section 65 of the Courts of Justice Act 1936 and the Regulations made thereunder providing for court fees. As indicated, Geoghegan J. declined the relief sought.

Following the leading decision in *Cahill v. Sutton* [1980] I.R. 269, he noted that the applicant had exercised his right of access to the courts and recovered all his costs. Accordingly he had no *locus standi* to maintain the proceedings. In addition, he cited the decision in *McDaid v. Sheehy* [1991] 1 I.R. 1; [1991] I.L.R.M. 250 (1990 Review, 464-5) in support of the view that the courts ought not to pronounce on the constitutionality of legislation if to do so would be a moot. Finally, he commented that as legal aid would probably have been available to the applicant, he was precluded from complaining that the imposition of court fees denied him access to the courts. On the general issue of the validity of court fees, see *MacGairbhith v. Attorney General* [1991] 1 I.R. 412; Supreme Court, March 29, 1995 (1991 Review, 98-9 and 1995 Review, 131).

OIREACHTAS

Allowances The Oireachtas (Allowances to Members) (Constituency Telephone Allowance) (Amendment) Regulations 1997 (S.I. No. 201 of 1997), made under the Oireachtas (Allowances to Members) Act 1962, allows for the payment of a party whip allowance to a deputy party whip where the chief whip is a government whip, with effect from January 1, 1997.

Committees   The Committees of the Houses of the Oireachtas (Compellability, Privileges and Immunities of Witnesses) Act 1997 provided for the granting to those Oireachtas Committees, whose terms of reference include provision for the calling of persons, papers and records, of powers of compellability in respect of witnesses and evidence. For a comprehensive discussion of the background to the 1997 Act, and earlier proposals, see Siobhán Gallagher's Annotation, *Irish Current Law Statutes Annotated*. Witnesses giving evidence to such committees, or sending papers and records to such committees, are accorded the same level of privilege as that enjoyed by a witness appearing before the High Court. The Act began its legislative life in 1995, in the aftermath of concerns expressed at the costs, particularly the legal costs, associated with the three-year *Tribunal of Inquiry Into the Beef Processing Industry*, which had reported in 1994. The powers contained in what became the 1997 Act were proposed with a view to ensuring that such inquiries could be conducted by an Oireachtas Committee and would not conflict with the requirements of fair procedures outlined in *In re Haughey* [1971] I.R. 217, the seminal decision on the powers of Oireachtas Committees.

While the 1997 Act was ultimately enacted in 1997 and confers extensive powers comparable to a tribunal of inquiry appointed with the powers in the Tribunals of Inquiry (Evidence) Acts 1921 to 1998. However, the public and political attitude to tribunals of inquiry in 1997 was quite different to that in 1995. During 1997, a series of tribunals of inquiry had been established; the potential for the level of legal costs associated with the Beef Processing Tribunal had been largely circumvented by imposing limited terms of reference and associated time restrictions on the lifetime of such tribunals. Thus, while the 1997 Act may lead to the compelling of witnesses to appear before Oireachtas Committees in the future, it seems unlikely that it will replace the need for the establishment of tribunals of inquiry. Indeed, it is notable that the Tribunals of Inquiry (Evidence) (Amendment) Act 1997 (see 11–12, above, in the Administrative Law chapter) was enacted within months of the Committees of the Houses of the Oireachtas (Compellability, Privileges and Immunities of Witnesses) Act 1997. Nonetheless, it remains important to discuss the provisions of the latter Act. The relevant resolutions of both Houses of the Oireachtas required to bring the Act into force had not been made at the time of writing.

Section 2 provides that only those committees on which power to send for persons, papers and records is conferred by the Oireachtas shall be covered by the Act. Section 3(1), the key section in the 1997 Act, provides that such committees, or their sub-committees, may direct a person: to attend in order to give evidence and to produce or send any document in his or her possession. Section 3(2) provides that the reasonable expenses of a person directed to attend before a committee shall be paid out of moneys provided by the Oireachtas. Section 3(4), (5) and (6) exempts certain office holders and officials from compellability, namely, the President and any officer of the President, members of the judiciary, the Attorney General and any officer of the Attorney General and the Director of Public Prosecutions and any officer of the Director of Public Prosecutions, except in relation to the Committee of Public Accounts and in relation to the general administration of the Office of the Attorney General. Section 3(7) provides that any person who is directed to attend before a committee, and having had tendered to him or her expenses for attendance as would be payable to a witness at the High Court, disobeys the direction or refuses to take an oath or to answer any question or produce any document to which the committee are legally entitled, or does anything which if done in Court would constitute contempt, shall be guilty of an offence. Section 3(10) provides that, if a person gives false evidence before a committee while on oath, he or she shall be guilty of the offence of perjury.

Section 4 provides that a committee may not direct a person to give evidence or produce or send a document which is not relevant to the committee's terms of reference.

Section 5 provides that the following areas are outside of the scope of compellability in all circumstances. These are: discussions at Government meetings or at a committee appointed by the Government whose membership consists of members of the Government together with Ministers of State and/or the Attorney General and/or members of the civil service; matters currently before the Irish courts (though not European courts as had been originally proposed); matters 'adversely affecting' the security of the State (as opposed to matters 'respecting' the security of the State, as had originally been proposed); information which could reasonably be expected to prejudice or impair the preventing, detecting or investigating of offences or apprehending or prosecuting offenders; information kept for purposes of assessing liability for, or for collecting, any tax, duty or other payment to the State, a local authority or a health board; the source of any information contained in a statement by a member of the Oireachtas made in the Oireachtas or at a meeting of an Oireachtas committee, the latter reflecting the views expressed in *Attorney General v. Hamilton (No. 2)* [1993] 3 I.R. 227 [1993] I.L.R.M. 821 (1993 Review, 166-7). See also the Seventeenth Amendment of the Constitution Act 1997, which limited to some extent the *Hamilton* decision, discussed above, 171.

Section 6 of the Act, which deals with the procedures to be followed where claims for non-disclosure or privilege under section 11 of the Act are being sought, was substantially amended during the Oireachtas debate. The original proposed wording exempted from production a wide range of material, including: information given and received in confidence; information relating to the business, profession or occupation of a person (not directly concerned with the proceedings) whose disclosure could be prejudicial to the person in relation to his/her business, profession or occupation; information relating to the family life or other private affairs of a person; or information whose disclosure might be prejudicial to the State in its international relations. As enacted, section 6 merely provides that where the material would be privileged in the High Court under section 11 of the 1997 Act, the committee shall hold its proceedings in private.

The privilege provided by section 11 of the 1997 Act extends to what was formerly referred to as executive privilege, legal professional privilege, sacerdotal privilege, police privilege and the privilege against self-incrimination. This is clearly much less wide-ranging than the matters set out in section 6 of the 1997 Act as originally drafted. Section 12 provides that evidence before a committee shall not be admissible in any criminal proceedings against the person giving such evidence.

Section 13 empowers a committee or sub-committee to make rules and draw up guidelines for its procedures. Section 14 provides that a witness may be required to give evidence on oath and that the clerk to the committee may administer such oath.

Section 15 prohibits a civil servant, a member of the Defence Forces or a member of the Garda Síochána from expressing an opinion on the merits of government policy when appearing before a committee or sub-committee. The provision was strongly criticised by the Opposition during the Oireachtas debate and some amendments were made to the original proposal to ensure that, for example, where a document included some discussion of a civil servant's views on policy, this material would be severed from the document and the remainder made available to the Committee.

Section 16 provides that section 3 of the 1997 Act shall be without prejudice to section 65 of the Court Officers Act 1926 which provides that court documents shall be held in the possession of the appropriate judge. It also provides that the restrictions set out in sections 4 and 5 of the Official Secrets Act 1963, shall not apply to evidence given or a document produced or sent to a committee on direction. A further general provision in the original text of the legislation, which would have precluded disclosure where any statute or rule of law prohibited or restricted the disclosure of information, was deleted from the final version of section 16, on foot of opposition objections to the potentially far-reaching nature of such an exclusion.

Section 17 provides penalties for offences under section 3(8). The penalties for which offenders are liable are: on summary conviction a fine not exceeding £1,500 and/or 12 months imprisonment or on conviction on indictment, a fine not exceeding £20,000 and/or 2 years imprisonment. It also provides that where an offence under this Act is proved to have been committed with the consent, connivance or approval of, or to have been attributable to the wilful negligence of, any person being a director, manager, secretary or other officer of the body corporate, that person as well as the body corporate, shall be guilty of an offence and be liable to be proceeded against and punished.

Delegation   In *O'Neill v. Minister for Agriculture and Food* [1997] 2 I.L.R.M. 435 (SC), the Supreme Court held that the Minister had acted *ultra vires* the Livestock (Artificial Insemination) Act 1947. The 1947 Act controls the practice of artificial insemination of cattle, sheep, goats, swine and horses. In November 1990 the respondent Minister refused to grant the applicant a field service licence under the 1947 Act stating in a letter that having regard to the licences already in existence in the State the Department did not consider that the issue of further licences would, irrespective of its reservations regarding the applicant's proposal, be justified. The applicant sought judicial review on the grounds that the restriction on the numbers of field stations granted was *ultra vires* the provisions of the 1947 Act and contrary to the provisions of the EC Treaty.

The relief was refused in the High Court, but on appeal the Supreme Court reversed. The Court held that the power conferred on a Minister to make law by way of regulation or statutory instrument in any given case is primarily to be determined by the interpretation of the legislation purporting to confer the power, but that Article 15.2 of the Constitution limits the extent to which such law-making power may be delegated. The Court held that there was nothing in the 1947 Act to suggest that the Oireachtas intended that the Minister should divide the country into a number of regions, in respect of each of which only one licence was to be granted, as had been done in by the Minister through administrative decision. The Court thus concluded that in adopting the exclusivity scheme the Minister had acted *ultra vires* the 1947 Act, thus breaching the delegation test in *Cityview Press Ltd v. An Chomhairle Oiliúna* [1980] I.R. 281.

PRESIDENT

Allowance   The Presidential Establishment Act 1938 (Section 193)) Order 1997 (S.I. No. 455 of 1997), made under the Presidential Establishment Act 1938, increased the annual allowance paid to the President with effect from November 11, 1997, thus taking effect on the election of President Mary McAleese, who succeeded President Mary Robinson.

PRESUMPTION OF CONSTITUTIONALITY

Minister for Agriculture, Food and Forestry v. Brennan, High Court, July 11, 1997 arose as a consequence of the decision in *Meagher v. Minister for Agri-*

culture and Food [1994] 1 I.R. 329; [1994] 1 I.L.R.M. 1 (1993 Review, 299-304). The applicant sought an order of *mandamus* directing the respondent judge of the District Court to hear and determine four charges against a named person arising out of alleged breaches of, *inter alia*, the European Communities (Control of Veterinary Medicinal Products and their Residues) Regulations 1988, which had been at issue in the *Meagher* case. The respondent had declined jurisdiction to hear the case and struck out the charges against on the ground that in his opinion the 1988 Regulations had already been found by the High Court in *Meagher* to be *ultra vires* and void. Carroll J. accepted, on the authority of *The State (Llewellyn) v. Ua Donnchada* [1973] I.R. 151, that if the High Court had declared the entire of the 1988 Regulations to be invalid, the respondent would have been bound by that decision until it was reversed. However she noted that there had in fact not been a declaration that the Regulations were in their entirety invalid. As such, the Regulations enjoyed a presumption of constitutionality which the respondent was bound to observe. She therefore concluded that the respondent had no jurisdiction to refuse to hear the case.

PRIVACY

Professional disciplinary tribunal In *Barry v. Medical Council*, High Court, February 11 1997; Supreme Court, December 16, 1997, Costello P. and, on appeal, the Supreme Court, held that the Medical Council was empowered to hold its hearings under the Medical Practitioners Act 1978 in private and that no breach of Article 34 of the Constitution, or of Article 6 of the European Convention on Human Rights 1950 arose from such arrangements.

The applicant, a medical practitioner, had been informed that an inquiry under the 1978 Act into certain allegations against him was to be held in private by the Medical Council. He sought an order of *certiorari* quashing the decision to hold the hearing in private. He relied on a number of provisions of the Constitution and also on Article 6.1 of the European Convention on Human Rights 1950, which provided for a fair and public hearing for every person within a reasonable time by an independent and impartial tribunal established by law. Although it was agreed that the Convention formed no part of Irish law, the arguments concerning Article 6 were considered by Costello P. in the context of his discussion of the constitutional provisions.

Costello P. accepted for the purposes of this case that there was a right to a public hearing before a professional disciplinary body. But he noted that, under the terms of the 1978 Act, any findings of the Medical Council had no legal effect on a doctor's right to practice until confirmed by the High Court. The High Court, if the doctor so applied to it, could cancel or vary the decision of the Medical Council, but in any event if no such application was made, the Medical Council's decision still required confirmation by the High Court.

Costello P. pointed out that Article 6(1) of the European Convention on Human Rights 1950 did not confer an absolute right to a public hearing in all circumstances where the article applied. Thus, the press and public could be excluded from all or part of a trial when 'the protection of the private lives of the parties' so required, and to the extent strictly necessary in the court's opinion 'in special circumstances where publicity would prejudice the interests of justice'.

Citing the decisions in *Re M*. [1984] 2 I.R. 479 and *M. v. Medical Council* [1984] I.R. 485, Costello P. held that in the context of the 1978 Act, the relevant statutory provisions meant that justice was in fact administered in public in the High Court and neither the 1978 Act nor the hearings, if held in camera, rendered the proceedings constitutionally infirm. He held that Article 6 did not require that all stages of proceedings in which rights were determined should be held in public, and in this case the High Court was not merely exercising an appellate jurisdiction but would hear all the evidence as if it were a court sitting at first instance should the doctor object to the Medical Council's decision.

Of course, Costello P. accepted that fair procedures should be applied in making any determination, including whether a hearing should be held in camera. Since the Act was silent as to whether the hearing should be in private or in public the Act was properly construed as conferring a discretion in the matter. The question then arose as to whether that discretion had been validly exercised in the light of the Constitution. He noted that a number of intimate private matters would be disclosed to public scrutiny should the hearings be in public. Costello P. concluded that it had been correctly concluded that, in the instant case, the right to a public hearing was one which should cede place to the rights to privacy of others should a public hearing infringe them. This decision was not unfair merely because it had failed to apply internationally accepted norms.

In upholding Costello P.'s decision, the Supreme Court noted that the purpose of section 45(5) of the 1978 Act was to protect the reputations of those practitioners into whose conduct inquiries had been held, who had not been found guilty of professional misconduct. Such a provision would have been pointless had the inquiry been held in public. While the Court accepted that, by virtue of section 45(5), the Council had a discretion to hold inquiries in private, the section did not require it. If all parties to the inquiry agreed that it be held in public, then the Council had a discretion to do so.

The Supreme Court acknowledged that, when examining the rights conferred by Article 40.3 of the Constitution and those in Article 10 of the Convention on Human Rights , it had to look at the procedure as a whole, and it was not the function of the Supreme Court to rule in advance as to whether any future hearing should be in public or *in camera*.

The Court also reiterated the more traditional view that, as the Convention on Human Rights did not form part of the domestic law of Ireland, it was inappropriate for the Court to decide whether the holding of an inquiry in private violated its provisions. It confined itself to concluding that the decision by the Council to hold the inquiry in private did not violate Article 40.3 of the Constitution.

PROPERTY

Forfeiture In *Gilligan v. Criminal Assets Bureau*, High Court, June 26, 1997, McGuinness J. rejected a challenge to the validity of the forfeiture powers in the Proceeds of Crime Act 1996 (1996 Review, 233-4). In earlier proceedings against the plaintiff, the High Court had made an order pursuant to section 2 of the 1996 Act preventing the plaintiff from dealing with certain property. The grounding affidavit in support of the order was sworn by a Chief Superintendent of An Garda Síochána, and deposed to his belief that the property was directly or indirectly the proceeds of crime.

McGuinness J. held that the procedures set out under the 1996 Act were not criminal in nature. There was no constitutional bar on the determination in civil or other proceedings of matters which might constitute elements of criminal offences. The standard of proof in procedures under the 1996 Act could therefore, she held, be the balance of probabilities. Once it was accepted that proceedings were in fact civil, McGuinness J. held that there was no constitutional infirmity in a procedure whereby the onus was placed on a person seeking property to negative the inference from evidence adduced that a criminal offence has been committed. While she accepted that the Act's provisions might affect property rights, they did not constitute an 'unjust attack'. The State had to show to the court's satisfaction that the property constituted proceeds of crime and therefore that the plaintiff had no title to the property. The right to private ownership could not hold so high a place in the hierarchy of rights that it protected the position of assets illegally acquired and held.

Applying the principle of proportionality discussed in *Cox v. Ireland* [1992] 2 I.R. 503 (1991 Review, 105-7) and *Heaney and McGuinness v. Ireland* [1994] 3 I.R. 593; [1994] 2 I.L.R.M. 420 (1994 Review, 128-33), she concluded that the legislature was justified in enacting the 1996 Act and in restricting certain rights through the operation of the Act. The restriction or impairment of these rights was to some extent balanced by the various safeguards included in the Act. See also the Evidence chapter, 338–9, 417 and 433–5, below.

REFERENDUM

Agents In *Sherwin v. Minister for the Environment*, High Court, March 11, 1997, Costello P. rejected a challenge to validity of the provisions of the Electoral Act 1992 on the appointment of agents by candidates standing for election to Dáil Éireann, though he granted the plaintiff some declaratory relief.

The plaintiff's case arose against the background of the Fifteenth Amendment of the Constitution (No. 2) Bill 1995, which proposed to delete the constitutional prohibition of civil divorce in Article 41 and was supported by all the political parties represented in the Oireachtas. This proposal was adopted after a favourable vote in a referendum under the Referendum Act 1994 and the Constitution was accordingly amended: see the 1995 Review, 136-44. The plaintiff was a member of an organisation which had campaigned against the proposal. In the course of the campaign the plaintiff realised that she had no access to members of the Oireachtas and could not therefore appoint agents or personation agents to represent her organisation. The plaintiff complained to the defendant Minister by letter about section 26 of the 1994 act to the Minister and requested him to rectify the defects she had identified utilising his powers under section 164 of the Electoral Act 1992. The Minister replied that he had no power to adopt the requested measures. After several attempts, the plaintiff had secured from the County Sheriff's office in Dublin a limited number of passes for the counting of votes which were under the Sheriff's control, but claimed that the number of agents who received authorisations for the opposition groups with which she was associated were entirely inadequate to enable a proper supervision of the count to take place.

Section 60 of the 1992 Act allows a candidate or his election agent to appoint agents to be present on the candidate's behalf at the issue of ballot papers to postal voters, in polling stations, at the opening of postal ballot boxes and at the counting of votes. The section also provides for a 'personation agent' to be present in each polling station for the purpose of assisting in the detection of personation. Section 26 of the Referendum Act 1994 provides that only members of the Oireachtas can appoint personation agents and agents to monitor the counting of votes at referenda. Section 164 of the Electoral Act 1992 empowered the Minister for the Environment to alter the provisions of the Act where a 'special difficulty' arose in an election or referendum. The plaintiff argued that the 1994 Act had become unconstitutional in the circumstances surrounding the Fifteenth Amendment, when all the political parties supported the proposed amendment and opposition to it was organised by groups of citizens.

Costello P. accepted that the power conferred on the Minister by section 164 of the 1992 Act was discretionary but could only be exercised when it appeared to the Minister that there was an emergency or special difficulty. Should the Minister conclude that circumstances of a 'special difficulty' existed, he had the power to modify section 26 of the Referendum Act 1994, so as to enable additional agents to be appointed by means other than those provided for, if that was necessary to enable a referendum to be held. The Minister had misconstrued his ministerial powers by deciding that the only way in which he could remedy the plaintiff's grievance was by amending the 1994 Act when section 164 had given him the power to modify the 1994 Act.

However, Costello P. held that it did not follow from this that the 1992 Act was therefore unconstitutional. Section 164 of the 1992 Act contained a statutory mechanism for dealing with special circumstances and a factual development which produced a constitutional defect could be properly regarded as a special circumstance. A statute which contained a built-in remedial mechanism to remedy possible constitutional invalidity was not an unconstitutional statute.

SEPARATION OF POWERS

Oireachtas questions In *O'Malley v. Ceann Comhairle*, Supreme Court, March 14, 1997, the Supreme Court held that the manner in which questions are framed for answer by Ministers of the Government are not justiciable.

The plaintiff had been a member of Dáil Éireann from 1987 to 1989 and at this time became interested in the beef processing industry and in particular the dominant position he considered to be held by the Goodman group of companies in that sector. He accordingly directed a number of questions to the Minister for Industry and Commerce but felt he had not received a full explanation on the points raised and so tabled the question at issue in these proceedings. The Ceann Comhairle, the chair of Dáil Éireann, wrote to the plaintiff stating that he was disallowing part of the question as it would involve repetition in view of the replies to previous questions in the previous month. The plaintiff claimed that the amended version of his question was printed on the Dáil Order Paper and that in his response to the question the Minister stated that he was not in a position to reply to the question. The plaintiff asserted that the question had been changed without reference to him and that this was in breach of Order 33 of the Standing Orders of the House, adopted under Article 15.10 of the Constitution. Order 33 of the Standing Orders of Dáil Éireann provides: 'The Ceann Comhairle shall examine every question in order to ensure that . . . it does not seek information provided within the preceding four months...The Ceann Comhairle...may amend any Question, after consultation with the member responsible for the question, to secure its compliance with Standing Orders.'

In the High Court, it was held that the judicial arm of government had no authority to interfere with the internal affairs of the Dáil. In addition, it was held that the right of any Dáil member to challenge the Ceann Comhairle ceased once the Dáil had been dissolved. As indicated, on appeal, the Supreme Court upheld the High Court decision.

The Court held that the manner in which questions should be framed for answer by Ministers of the Government was so much a matter concerning the internal working of Dáil Éireann that it would seem inappropriate for the Court to intervene except in some very extreme circumstances which it was impossible to envisage. The Court considered that the manner in which questions were framed involved to such a degree the operation of the internal machinery of debate in the House as to remain within the competence of Dáil Eireann to deal with exclusively, having regard to Article 15.10 of the Constitution. Finally, the Court held that, in the instant case, no purpose could be served by granting the order sought as any declaration could not have any effect.

TRIAL OF OFFENCES

Appeal against acquittal   In *Considine v. Shannon Regional Fisheries Board* [1994] 1 I.L.R.M. 499 (HC); [1998] 1 I.L.R.M. 11 (SC), the Supreme Court upheld the decision of Costello J. in the High Court (1993 Review, 170-2).

Costello J. had rejected a challenge to the validity of section 310 of the Fisheries (Consolidation) Act 1959, which provides for an appeal against an acquittal in a summary prosecution under the Act. The first named defendant, the Shannon Regional Fisheries Board, had issued a summons against the plaintiff under the Fisheries (Consolidation) Act 1959, alleging various breaches of the 1959 Act. The summons was dismissed in the District Court and the first named defendant appealed to the Circuit Court under the provisions of section 310 of the 1959 Act, which allows the prosecutor to appeal to the Circuit Court against an acquittal in the District Court of a complaint on a summons. The plaintiff then issued a plenary summons seeking a declaration that section 310 of the 1959 Act was invalid on the ground that it was in conflict with Article 38.1 of the Constitution which provides that 'no person shall be tried on any criminal charge save in due course of law.' The defendants submitted that section 310 of the 1959 Act was valid as being in contemplation of Article 34.3.4° of the Constitution, which provides: 'The courts of first instance shall also include courts of local and limited jurisdiction with a right of appeal as determined by law.' They also relied on the Supreme Court decision in *The People v. O'Shea* [1983] I.L.R.M. 549; [1982] I.R. 384, and argued that Costello J. was bound by that decision. Costello J. agreed, and this view was upheld on appeal by the Supreme Court.

In the Supreme Court, as in the High Court, the views expressed by O'Higgins C.J. in *O'Shea* were quoted with approval, in particular, his view that the appellate jurisdiction of the Supreme Court conferred by Article 34.4.3° was not limited by Article 38.1. While it was accepted that in *O'Shea* the

Supreme Court had not been dealing with Article 34.3.4°, it was accepted that the principle of law established by *O'Shea* could be applied with equal force to Article 34.3.4°. Delivering the Supreme Court's decision in *Considine*, Hamilton C.J. also noted that it had been the case prior to the enactment of the Constitution that appeals against acquittals had been a feature of the legislative landscape, and were thus to be accommodated within the general understanding of the rule against double jeopardy. He referred in this context to the views expressed by Lord Halsbury in *Cox v. Hakes* (1890) 15 App. Cas. 506, and of Palles C.B. in *Great Southern and Western Railway Co v. Gooding* [1908] 2 I.R. 429. Aligning this 'historical' perspective with what he took to be the harmonious approach of O'Higgins C.J. in *O'Shea*, Hamilton CJ (for the Court) concluded that section 310 of the 1959 Act was within the permissible range of laws envisaged by Article 34.3.4° of the Constitution.'

As we noted in the 1993 Review, the decision in *Considine* is of considerable importance for a wide variety of what is sometimes described as 'regulatory' criminal law, such as the 1959 Act. In recent years, the positive right of appeal against acquittals on summary charges has been included in such legislation: see for example, section 52 of the Safety, Health and Welfare at Work Act 1989. The outcome in the Supreme Court in *Considine* clearly supports such provisions.

Children In *Director of Public Prosecutions v. O'Neill* [1998] 1 I.L.R.M. 221 (HC), Smyth J. upheld the constitutional validity of section 5(1) of the Summary Jurisdiction Over Children (Ireland) Act 1884, which provides for the summary trial of young persons charged with an indictable offence where the accused has been informed of his right to trial by jury. It also provides that the trial court is to have regard to the character and antecedents of the person charged. In the instant case, the trial judge expressed concern that if he were to know the legal character and antecedents of the accused person that he might embark upon a trial in a prejudiced position. He also believed that the accused should be innocent until proved guilty, and that the tendering of evidence of character at such an early stage was a wholly inappropriate proceeding in the light of the Constitution.

On case stated, Smyth J. held that the procedure in section 5(1) of the 1884 Act was in the nature of a preliminary investigation, and was clearly not the trial of the offence and it ensured that if given the choice the young person had an appreciation of the possible legal course and consequences of making such choice. Far from infringing the principle of equality before the law in Article 40.1 he held that section 5(1) of the 1884 Act had in-built in it the constitutional concern to ensure that due regard to differences of capacity were observed. He considered that it was consistent with the requirement of a trial in 'due course of law' in accordance with Article 38.1, which required a fair and just balance between the exercise of individual freedom and the requirements of ordered society. Smyth J. considered that the reference in section 5(1) of the 1884 Act to the character and antecedents of the person charged was directed towards his legal character and antecedents.

Finally, Smyth J. had some interesting comments on the constitutional position of the trial judge in the instant case. While the District Court had no jurisdiction to consider the constitutionality of post-1937 laws, he noted that the position was different in the case of pre-1937 laws. If, in appropriate proceedings, the District Court judge was faced with a conflict between a pre-1937 law and the Constitution, Smyth J. held that he was bound to give effect to the higher law, namely the Constitution, by disapplying the pre-1937 law.

Right to silence   In *Rock v. Ireland*, Supreme Court, November 19, 1997, the Supreme Court upheld the constitutional validity of sections 18 and 19 of the Criminal Justice Act 1984, which provides that a court is permitted to draw 'such inferences as appear proper' from the failure or refusal of the accused to account for possession of items in certain circumstances.

The plaintiff had been charged with unlawful possession of forged bank notes contrary to section 8 of the Forgery Act 1913. Sections 18 and 19 of the Criminal Justice Act 1984 permit the court, in determining whether the accused is guilty of an offence to draw 'such inference as appear proper' from the failure or refusal of an accused to account for his possession of items, but an accused may not be convicted of an offence solely on an inference drawn from such failure or refusal. The plaintiff sought a declaration in the High Court that sections 18 and 19 of the 1984 Act were invalid having regard to the Constitution and an order of prohibition. In the High Court, Murphy J. dismissed the claim: see the 1995 Review, 243-4, and as indicated, the Supreme Court affirmed this.

The Court affirmed the view it had taken in *Heaney and McGuinness v. Ireland* [1994] 3 I.R. 593 (HC); [1994] 2 I.L.R.M. 420 (HC); [1996] 1 I.R. 580 (SC); [1997] 1 I.L.R.M. 117 (SC) (1994 Review, 128-33, and 1996 Review, 329-32) that while the right to silence and the presumption of innocence in a criminal trial were implicit in the provisions of the Constitution, the right to silence was not absolute and was subject to public order and morality. Referring to its decision on the shifting of the evidential burden, *O'Leary v. Attorney General* [1995] 1 I.R. 266; [1995] 2 I.L.R.M. 259 (1995 Review, 181), the Court held that the burden of proof which rested on the prosecution in a criminal charge was not in any way affected by the provisions of sections 18 or 19 of the 1984 Act, which merely provided a factor which could be adduced as evidence in the course of the trial. If inferences were properly drawn such inferences amounted to evidence only and could only be used as corroboration of any other evidence in relation to which the failure or refusal was material. The Court thus concluded that sections 18 and 19 did not constitute an attack on, or interference with, an accused person's constitutional right to the presumption of innocence.

The Court considered that, in enacting sections 18 and 19 of the 1984 Act, the Oireachtas had sought to balance the individual's right to avoid self-incrimination with the right and duty of the State to defend and protect the life person and property of all its citizens. The Court held that the central issue was whether the restrictions which sections 18 and 19 placed on the right to silence were any greater than was necessary to enable the State to fulfil its constitutional obligations. In this respect, it noted that sections 18 and 19 contained two important limiting factors, namely, that an inference could not form the basis for a conviction in the absence of other evidence and that only such inferences as 'appear proper' could be drawn. In that light, the Court concluded that the restrictions on the right to silence in sections 18 and 19 were proportionate to the State's interest in instituting criminal prosecutions.

As we noted in the 1995 Review, the decisions in *O'Leary*, *Heaney* and *Rock* may indicate that while the courts retain the language of an accusatorial system of criminal justice in their judgments, the legislative provisions upheld in these decisions indicate that the courts have accepted that elements of the inquisitorial system are not incompatible with their sense of the Irish criminal justice system. See further the discussion of *Rock* in the Evidence chapter, 430–3, below.

Contract Law

Eoin O'Dell, Trinity College, Dublin

CERTAINTY

A contract may be uncertain because it is simply too vague, or because it is incomplete (Treitel *The Law of Contract* (9th ed., Stevens Sweet & Maxwell, London, 1995) p.47; see, generally, Lücke 'Illusory, Vague and Uncertain Contractual Terms' (1977) 6 *Adelaide L Rev* 1).

Vagueness   As to contracts potentially uncertain on the grounds of vagueness, where a phrase is capable of too many meanings, and the intended meaning is not specified or capable of specification by the court, the contract will be void for vagueness (*Scammell v. Ouston* [1941] A.C. 251 (phrase 'on hire-purchase' capable of too many meanings). Nevertheless, the vague language must be 'so obscure and so incapable any definite or precise meaning that the court is unable to attribute to the parties any particular contractual intention' (*Scammell v. Ouston* [1941] A.C. 251 at 268 *per* Lord Wright). Treitel points out that the 'courts do not expect commercial documents to be drafted with strict precision, and will . . . do their best to avoid striking it down on the grounds that it is too vague' (Treitel, *id*; see, generally, *Sammell v. Ouston* [1941] A.C. 251 at 268 *per* Lord Wright; see also *Anangel v. IHI* [1990] 2 Lloyd's Rep. 526 at 546 *per* Hirst J.). Courts therefore seek to avoid 'the reproach of being the destroyer of bargains' (*Hillas v. Arcos* (1932) 147 L.T. 503 at 512 *per* Lord Tomlin). This is particularly so if the parties have acted on an agreement (Treitel, *id*.). Hence, the 'fact that the transaction was performed on both sides will often make it . . . difficult to submit that the contract is void for vagueness or uncertainty. . . . Clearly, similar considerations may sometimes be relevant in partly executed transactions' (*Trentham v. Archital Luxfer* [1993] 1 Lloyd's Rep. 25 at 27 *per* Steyn L.J.). In particular, 'the fact that the transaction is executed makes it easier to imply a term resolving any uncertainty' (*ibid.*). Again, where the vagueness is the product of ambiguity, the courts will admit oral evidence (by way of exception to the parol evidence rule) to resolve that ambiguity and vagueness (*ESB v. Newman* (1933) 67 I.L.T.R. 124).

Incompleteness   As to contracts potentially uncertain on the grounds of incompleteness, a contract may be incomplete due to the absence of an important term or terms. However, simply because a term or terms remain to be agreed, the contract is not necessarily incomplete. For example, there are many situations in which 'parties intend to be bound forthwith even though there are further terms still to be agreed' (*Pagnan SpA v. Feed Products* [1987] 2 Lloyd's Rep. 601 at 619 *per* Lloyd L.J.; citing *Love and Stewart v. Instonve* (1917) 33 T.L.R. 475 at 476 *per* Lord Loreburn). In which case 'there is no legal obstacle which stands in the way of the parties agreeing to be bound now while deferring important matters to be agreed later. It happens every day when parties enter into so-called 'heads of agreement'.' (*Ibid.*; see generally Ellinghaus 'Agreements which defer 'Essential' Terms (1971) 45 *A.L.J.* 4).

Nevertheless, it must be a fine line between a contract uncertain for incompleteness and a contract sufficiently certain to be enforceable on its own terms, even if other terms remain to be agreed. For example, if a price is not agreed, courts will often conclude that the contract is uncertain for incompleteness. In *Peter Lind v. Mersey Docks and Harbour Board* [1972] 2 Lloyd's Rep. 234, negotiations were proceeding for a large building contract, but the parties could not agree on the price. Negotiations continued, but ultimately failed on this issue. The Court of Appeal held that the parties' inability to agree the price was fatal to the conclusion of an agreement. (During the currency of the negotiations, the plaintiffs did work to the value of more than £1m. The defendants wanted this work done, and did not prevent it happening. It was held that the plaintiff was thus entitled to a *quantum meruit*). In *Courtney and Fairbarin v. Tolaini* [1975] 1 All E.R. 716, Courtney by letter seemed to agree to sell certain property, and Tolaini by letter seemed to agree to purchase it. However, neither letter stated a price, and Denning MR in the Court of Appeal held that the absence of agreement on a price or a method to calculate it negatived any agreement. In both of these cases, the question was whether there was a contract in the first place, and the absence of a price precluded it. On the other hand, section 8(3) of the Sale of Goods Act 1893 allows the court to imply a term as to a reasonable price if there is a concluded contract for the sale of goods but no agreement on price. Indeed, Guest (ed.), *Benjamin's Sale of Goods* (5th ed., Sweet and Maxwell, London, 1997) makes it clear that this 'was also the rule at common law . . .' (p.128, para. 2-046; citing *Acebal v. Levy* (1834) 10 Bing 376; *Valpy v. Gibson* (1847) 4 C.B. 837; see also *Hoadly v. McLaine* (1834) 10 Bing 482; 131 E.R. 982). And in *British Bank for Foreign Trade v. Novinex* [1949] 1 K.B. 623 (CA) the performance of a contract on both sides resulted in the implication of a term as to the commission to which the plaintiffs were entitled for introducing the defendants to vendors of oilskin suits.

Such authorities demonstrate that if the absence of the price is not fatal to the agreement (if it is sufficiently certain apart from the issue of the price), then the court can imply a term as to a reasonable price. More generally, as with *Trentham*, above, the context of *Novinex* and *Pagnan* illustrates that uncertainty by incompleteness can be avoided by the implication of terms (on this process, see generally Coote 'Contract Formation and the Implication of Terms' (1993) 6 *J.C.L.* 51, arguing that a possibly contrary *dictum* of Lord Roskill in *Aotearooa International v. Scancarriers* [1985] 1 N.Z.L.R. 513 at 556 (PC) should 'not be allowed to inhibit the implication of terms where the parties have intended to contract' ((1993) 6 *J.C.L.* 51 at 57). Hence, as with contracts potentially uncertain on the grounds of vagueness, the courts can cure potential uncertainty on the grounds of incompleteness by the implication of a term.

Uncertainty The principles of contracts void for uncertainty figured in the judgment of Barron J. in the Supreme Court in *Mackey v. Wilde* [1998] 1 I.L.R.M. 449. The parties were the owners of a joint fishery; the plaintiff sought to reach agreement with the defendant to limit numbers, by which only 25 annual tickets and a few day tickets would be granted by each party. Barron J. (Hamilton C.J. and Barrington J. concurring) held that the word 'few' was too uncertain, and that the contract was therefore void for uncertainty.

> There have been many cases in which the full terms of the contract are not set out precisely, but which have been found to be valid binding agreements. Examples are where a term is implied, where there is a formula for determining the apparent uncertainty with precision or where the term is to be determined on the basis of what is reasonable or by reference to custom or trade usage. Even in some cases, when none of these means can be operated, the agreement will still be upheld where the court is satisfied that the term which is still to be settled is a subsidiary one and the parties intended to be bound in any event by the main agreement ([1998] 1 I.L.R.M. 449 at 455).

This statement of principle is entirely reflexive of the orthodoxy in the previous cases. However, Barron J. continued:

> The essential question is whether the parties have left over some matter to be determined which can only be determined by themselves. So an agreement to enter into an agreement is not a concluded contract (*id*).

This is unfortunate, for two reasons. First, in relation to agreements to agree generally, though some such agreements are inherently uncertain and therefore void, it is not true that all such agreements share this vice. In respect of such contracts to negotiate, on the one hand, in *Hillas v. Arcos* (1932) 147 L.T. 503, Lord Wright thought that 'there is a contract (if there is good consideration) to negotiate, though in the event of repudiation by one party the damages may be nominal . . .'; and *Guardians of Kells Union v. Smith* (1917) 52 I.L.T.R. 65 may provide an Irish example of nominal damages for breach of such a contract. On the other hand, Lord Wright's dictum has not met with much subsequent approval (see, for example, *Courteny & Fairbairn v. Tolaini* [1975] 1 All E.R. 716) even as a matter of Irish law (see *Cadbury Ireland v. Kerry Co-Op* [1982] I.L.R.M. 77 (Barrington J)). Nevertheless, the matter is not entirely settled; in interlocutory proceedings in *Bula v. Tara* [1987] I.R. 95 Murphy J. set out the competing arguments, but concluded that 'resolution must await the full consideration of the facts and the law at the hearing of the action'. Certainly, the issue requires resolution, but a single sentence is hardly adequate. Suppose a contract by which the parties agree that they will deal with each other in good faith in forthcoming negotiations. In this particular context of agreements to negotiate in good faith, the issues of contracts to negotiate have been examined in great detail in many courts in the common law world. For example, the House of Lords in *Walford v. Miles* [1992] A.C. 128 (HL) held that that was less was void, and yet most 'academic commentary supports the possibility of a contract to negotiate in good faith' Paterson 'The Contract to Negotiate in Good Faith: Recognition and Enforcement' (1996) 10 *J.C.L.* 120 at 121 n 9, citing Brown [1992] *JBL* 211; Carter and Furmston (1994–95) 8 *J.C.L.* 1 at 93; Cohen in Beatson and Friedmann (eds.) (*supra*) p.25; Farnsworth (1987) 87 *Col. L. Rev.* 217), and such contracts are enforceable and often enforced in the United States and Australia (the cases are discussed in particular in Paterson and Farnsworth; see in particular the judgment of Kirby P. in *Coal Cliff Collieries Pty v. Sijehama Pty Ltd* (1991) 24 N.S.W.L.R. 1 (NSW CA); see also Stewart 'Good Faith in Contractual Performance and Negotiation' (1998) 72 *ALJ* 370; *Hughes Aircraft Systems International v. Air Services Australia* (1997) 146 A.L.R.1 (FCA; Finn J); noted Furmston (1998) 114 *L.Q.R.* 362. The compatibility of the concept of good faith with Irish law is discussed in the 1993 Review, 177–178; 1995 Review, 178–179). If this latter lead is followed in Ireland, then the contract to negotiate in good faith would form an example of a contract to make a contract which would nonetheless not be void for uncertainty and would be capable of enforcement.

Second, in relation to agreements to agree a specific matter at a later date where, in the words of Barron J. in *Mackey v. Wilde*, 'the parties have left over some matter . . . which can only be determined by themselves', though it is the case that an agreement may be incomplete because it expressly envisages further negotiations on matters not yet resolved, whether the matters left open in fact deprived the contract of binding force 'depends primarily on the intentions of the parties; and inferences as to this intention may be drawn both from the importance of the matter left over for further agreement, and from the extent to which the parties have acted on the agreement' (Treitel, p 52). Thus, though some such agreements to agree a specific matter at a later date may not be enforceable (*May & Butcher v. R* [1934] 2 K.B. 17n (HL)), this is not an invariable conclusion (e.g. *Foley v. Classique Coaches* [1934] 2 K.B. 1; Treitel, pp 53–54). Hence, as was argued above, simply because a term or terms remain to be agreed, the contract is not necessarily incomplete, even if it is a matter which can only be determined by the parties themselves. As Lloyd L.J. observed in *Pagnan SpA v. Feed Products* [1987] 2 Lloyd's Rep. 601, there are many situations in which 'parties intend to be bound forthwith even though there are further terms still to be agreed . . . there is no legal obstacle which stands in the way of the parties agreeing to be bound now while deferring important matters to be agreed later. It happens every day when parties enter into so-called 'heads of agreement'.' ([1987] 2 Lloyd's Rep. 601 at 619). In that case, the parties had agreed 'the cardinal terms' of a contract for the purchase and sale of corn feed pellets: the 'product, price, quantity, period of shipment, range of loading ports and governing contract terms' ([1987] 2 Lloyd's Rep. 601 at 611); but they had not agreed a specific loading port, the rate of loading, and other matters. However, the Court of Appeal, having decided that the cardinal terms were agreed, held that the contract was not uncertain as incomplete.

In *Mackey v. Wilde* itself, Barron J. concluded that 'the agreement was not capable of being saved by any of the means' to which he had referred:

> The parties did not intend to be limited to 25 annual licences without any day tickets. Nor could the number be determined by what is reasonable. Reasonableness in law is an expression capable of certainty. But there can be no certainty here. The learned trial judge had held that ten day tickets would be reasonable. But equally any number between two and ten would have been said to also have been reasonable. When an apparently uncertain term is saved on the basis of what is reasonable, it is because this is imparting certainty, something which cannot be done by choosing which of several correct answers is the correct one. In other words, the court cannot make the agreement for the parties by saying this is reasonable. In the instant case, what the parties have left over, what is meant by the word 'few', is something which only they can settle. It follows that there was no concluded agreement ([1998] 1 I.L.R.M. 449 at 455).

Hence, *Mackey v. Wilde* is a case of uncertainty by vagueness rather than by incompleteness; and it is authority against using a standard of reasonableness to resolve vague terms. On the one hand, it is similar to *Scammell v. Ouston* [1941] A.C. 251 (above). On the other hand, in the leading case of *Hillas v. Arcos* (1932) 147 L.T. 503 (HL) an agreement for the sale of 'fair' timber was upheld as the standard of reasonableness would make that vague term certain. Reasonableness enables the court to arrive at such a definite meaning. The trend of the majority of the cases on the point in most other jurisdictions was against findings of uncertainty: 'the whole thrust of the law today is to attempt to give proper effect to commercial transactions. It is for this reason that uncertainty, a concept so much loved by lawyers, has fallen into disfavour as a tool for striking down commercial bargains' (*Banque Brussels Lambert SA v. Australian National Industries* (1989) 21 N.S.W.L.R. 502 at 523 cited in Buckley (1993) 6 J.C.L. 58 at 58). The many cases, of which *Pagnan* (above) is a good example, in which the courts strain to find certainty, are consistent with this. The implication of terms is another example. The standard of reasonableness to resolve vagueness is entirely consistent with this trend. It is unfortunate that *Mackey v. Wilde* should have taken an opposite view. In the leading Australian case of *Meehan v. Jones* (1982) 149 C.L.R. 571, Gibbs C.J. held that it 'is only if the court is unable to put any definite meaning on the contract that it can be said to be uncertain' ((1982) 149 C.L.R. 571 at 578). He upheld as certain a clause that made the contract subject to 'satisfactory' finance, a clause which if 'understood to import a subjective test . . . is impossible . . . to regard . . . as uncertain. The question whether the purchaser does think the finance is satisfactory is a simple question of fact' (*id*). Furthermore, he held that if 'the test is an objective one, and the question is whether the finance ought reasonably have been regarded as satisfactory, I should not have thought that the clause is too indefinite for the courts to be able to attribute any particular contractual intention to the parties' ((1982) 149 C.L.R. 571 at 579). As Mason J. argued in the same case, to 'say that clauses of this kind are void for uncertainty is to ignore the traditional doctrine that the courts should be astute to adopt a construction which will preserve the validity of the contract' ((1982) 149 C.L.R. 571 at 589). Similarly, in *Mackey v. Wilde*, the question of whether a given number of day tickets constituted a 'few' could have been regarded subjectively as question of fact for the parties, or objectively as a term capable of reasonable interpretation by the court; either interpretation would have preserved the validity of the contract.

It may have been open in *Mackey v. Wilde* to draw a distinction between an uncertain term and an uncertain contract, and to sever the uncertain term to render what remains certain, thereby avoiding uncertainty by vagueness; (and, perhaps, if necessary to imply a term on the business of the business efficacy test, below, to avoid uncertainty by incompleteness). However, courts have been slow to engage in such radical surgery, reserving the scalpel for the excision of meaningless phrases. Treitel puts it this way: if a meaningless phrase 'is simply verbiage, not intended to add anything to an otherwise complete agreement, or if it relates to a matter of relatively minor importance, it can be ignored. But if the parties intend it to govern some vital aspect of their relationship, its vagueness will vitiate the entire agreement' (Treitel, p 48). Allowing for day fishing would have been a vital aspect of the contract, so it would have been difficult to characterise the relevant term as meaningless;

hence, on this test, it is unlikely that the term would have been severable. Nevertheless, the absence of a consideration of this issue is another matter of regret in *Mackey v. Wilde.*

ILLEGALITY

Champerty The law relating to champerty has had a number of recent outings, less successful in England (e.g. *Giles v. Thompson* [1994] 1 A.C. 142 (HL); *Re Oasis Merchandising* [1997] 1 All E.R. 1009 (CA); *Abrahamson v. Thompson* [1997] 4 All E.R. 362 (CA)), more so in Ireland (*McIlroy v. Flynn* [1991] I.L.R.M. 294 (HC; Blayney J) and *Fraser v. Buckle* [1994] 1 I.R. 1; [1994] 1 I.L.R.M. 276 (HC; Costello J); [1996] 1 I.R. 1; [1996] 2 I.L.R.M. 34 (SC)). To maintain an improper claim is contrary to the common law; such maintenance 'may nowadays be defined as improperly stirring up litigation and strife by giving aid to one party to bring or defend a claim without just cause or excuse' (*In Re Trepca Mines* (No 2) [1963] Ch. 199 at 219 *per* Denning MR); where there is a further agreement that the person who renders such aid will receive a share of what is recovered in the action, this is champerty. Hence in the Irish cases, the courts held that an heir-locator who contracted to put potential heirs in contract with inheritances to which they were entitled, in return for a share of the inheritance, could not enforce his contract with the heirs (see (1996) 14 *I.L.T.* (*ns*) 85; Capper (1997) 113 *L.Q.R.* 49). As summed up by Lynch J. in the Supreme Court this year in *O'Keeffe v. Scales*:

> A person who assists another to maintain or defend proceedings without having a *bona fide* interest independent of that other person in the prosecution or defence of those proceedings acts unlawfully and contrary to public policy and cannot enforce an agreement with that other person for any form of benefit . . . if the claim is successfully [maintained or] defended. ([1998] 1 I.L.R.M. 393 at 397 *per* Lynch J., Barrington and Murphy JJ. concurring).

In that case, the Supreme Court properly rejected an ambitious expansion of the doctrine. In an action for breach of contract and negligence brought by the plaintiffs against their former solicitor, one of the heads of claim related to an amount of money due to the plaintiffs' current solicitors which the plaintiffs claim would not have been incurred but for the defendant's breach of contract and negligence. The defendant sought to have the plaintiffs' action stayed or dismissed on the basis that including that head of claim operated to alter the position of the plaintiffs' solicitor 'into a position of maintenance or champerty in that he [wa]s assisting in the promotion or conduct of litigation by the [plaintiffs] from which he ha[d] an interest to receive a share of the award if the respondents [we]re successful . . .' ([1998] 1 I.L.R.M. 393 at 395). Lynch J. concluded from *McIlroy v. Flynn* and *Fraser v. Buckle* that 'the law relating to maintenance and champerty still exists in this state' but held that, while

> the law relating to maintenance and champerty therefore undoubtedly still subsists in this jurisdiction it must not be extended in such a way as to deprive people of their constitutional right of access to the courts to litigate reasonably stateable claims. In the present case unlike *Fraser v. Buckle* or *McIlroy v. Flynn*, the [defendant] seeks to stifle the [plaintiffs'] action before any plenary hearing . . . [even if champertous] I doubt if that would in itself amount to a defence to the [plaintiffs'] action much less entitle the [defendant] to stifle the [plaintiffs'] claim *in limine* on this motion to stay or dismiss . . . [1998] 1 I.L.R.M. 393 at 397–398

On the motion to dismiss see also our Practice and Procedure chapter, below; and in this respect, compare the similar refusal of a stay by the Court of Appeal in *Abrahamson v. Thompson* [1997] 4 All E.R. 362 (CA)). The conclusion in *O'Keefe v. Scales* must be right. It is simply another example of the process charted in recent Reviews (see the 1993 Review, 184–189; 1995 Review, 204–209; 1996 Review, 180–182) by which the courts have, by and large, tended to ameliorate the negative consequences of potential illegality upon the enforceability of contracts. More specifically, take the case of a defendant's breach of contract which causes a plaintiff to incur a debt to a third party, in circumstances where the plaintiff can recover the amount of that debt in an action for breach of contract against the defendant; in principle, if the debt to the third party is a debt to a solicitor incurred for legal services arising out of the breach, nothing changes, and it is still recoverable. If the solicitor's fees would be recoverable if a further firm of solicitors handled the breach of contract action, why should the fact that the plaintiff chooses to remain with that solicitor in the subsequent action for breach of contract in any way alter the fact of that recoverability and now render those fees irrecoverable and the breach of contract action itself unsustainable? There is no good reason. The application in *O'Keeffe v. Scales* was properly dismissed, and the case could proceed to determine whether there was in fact a breach of contract, or negligence, on the part of the defendant, and if so whether it caused the plaintiffs' debts to their current solicitors.

IMPLIED TERMS

Terms may be implied into a contract as a consequence of the parties' (presumed) intentions or as a consequence of the particular nature of the contract.

Terms implied in fact   When a term is implied into a contract as a consequence of the parties' intention, as the Supreme Court made clear in *Tradax v. Irish Grain Board* [1984] I.R. 1, it may be implied into a contract for two related but separate reasons. First, it may have been the intention of the parties that the term be included, but for them, it was 'so obvious that it [went] without saying; so that, if while the parties making their bargain, an officious bystander were to suggest some express provision for it in the agreement, they would testily suppress him with a common 'Oh, of course'.' (*Shirlaw v. Southern Foundries* [1939] 2 K.B. 206 at 227 *per* MacKinnon L.J.; *affd* [1940] A.C. 701). Second, the courts presume that the parties intend that their contract will in fact be operable, and so will imply terms into it necessary to give it effect, thus a term may be implied 'from the presumed intention of the parties with the object of giving the transaction such efficacy as both parties must have intended that at all events it should have'. (*The Moorcock* (1889) 14 PD 64 at 68 *per* Bowen L.J.; *cp. Luxor (Eastbourne) v. Cooper* [1941] A.C. 108 at 137 *per* Lord Wright). Both rules of implication are said to reflect the parties' intentions. The first, the officious bystander test, might be said to reflect their actual intentions; whereas the second, the business efficacy test, reflects the courts' presumption that the parties intended that the contract be operative. In that latter case, though the implication is based upon a presumption as to the parties' intention, the term is implied independently of their actual intentions: hence, as Murphy J. put it *Sweeney v. Duggan* 'a term may be implied independently of the intention of the parties where it is necessary as a matter of law or logic to enable the provisions of the agreement to have operative effect' ([1997] 2 I.R. 531 at 545; [1997] 2 I.L.R.M. 211 at 222). As a consequence, courts have rightly counselled caution in implying terms into contracts (*Tradax v. Irish Grain Board* [1984] I.R. 1 at 14 *per* O'Higgins C.J (Hederman J. concurring); *Grehan v. NEHB* [1989] I.R. 422 at 425 *per* Costello J.).

There are of course alternative means to represent the law embodied in such cases. The position in Australia differs in some significant respects (*BP Refinery (Wessternport) Pty Ltd v. Shire of Hastings* (1977) 180 C.L.R. 266 (PC) 283; *Byrne v. Australian Airlines* (1995) 131 A.L.R.422 (HCA) on which see Tolhurst and Carter (1996–7) 11 *J.C.L.* 76 and *cf.* Swanton (1991) 5 J.C.L. 26 criticising an earlier statement of Deane J. in *Hawkins v. Clayton* (1988) 164 C.L.R. 539 at 570 of what became the majority position in *Byrne*) and Professor Phang in particular has long been a harsh critic of the rationales deployed by the courts in these cases (see, *e.g.* Phang 'Implied Terms Revisited' [1990] J.B.L. 394; 'Implied Terms in English Law – Some Recent Developments' [1993] *J.B.L.* 242; 'Implied Terms, Business Efficacy and the Officious Bystander' [1998] *J.B.L.* 1). But whereas the Australian approach conflates elements of both tests, Phang's work makes it clear that they have separate historical sources and are in modern English usage separate, parallel, tests. Thus, for example, in *Associated Japanese Bank v. Crédit du Nord* [1988] 3 All E.R. 912, Steyn J. treated them as separate tests, declined to imply a term on the basis of the business efficacy test, but did so on the basis of the officious bystander test.

Terms implied as a matter of law   Beyond the officious bystander and business efficacy tests, terms are implied into contracts for other reasons. For example, there are certain categories of contracts in which precedent has decreed that certain terms should be implied. Thus, for example, in many contracts for professional services, the law will imply into the contract a duty to take reasonable care. Most such terms implied by the common law arise because of the nature of the relationship between the parties to the contract: vendor and purchaser of real property, employer and employee, landlord and tenant, and so on. In such situations, the law takes the view that certain terms must be implied into such contracts as a consequence of the particular nature of the contract, and the implication is independent of the intention of the parties. Such terms are understood as *legal incidents* of such contracts, and are implied into *every* contract of that type by virtue of relationship between the parties and independently of the identities and intentions of the parties to any particular contract. It is important, therefore, to distinguish carefully between a term implied in fact on the basis of the business efficacy test and a term implied in law: in the former, *this* term is implied into *this* contract between *these* parties to give effect to *this* contract (on the basis that it is necessary to give effect to these parties' intention that this contract be effective); in the latter, a term is implied into *every* contract of that type by virtue of relationship between the parties and independently of the identities and intentions of the parties to any particular contract.

This distinction is at the heart of the decision of the House of Lords in *Liverpool City Council v. Irwin* [1977] A.C. 239 (HL). The Council were a local authority Housing Authority and thus landlords of a block of flats, where the lifts and waste disposal chutes were inoperable (continually breaking down, tardily and inadequately repaired). Tenants withheld rent to persuade the Council to repair, the Council sought possession for non-payment of rent, and the tenants defended on the basis that the Council was in breach of a term implied to the lease imposing upon them a duty 'to take reasonable care to keep in reasonable repair and usability the common parts of the building'. The House of Lords refused to imply such a term arising from the parties' presumed intentions on the basis of the business efficacy test, but did imply it as a matter of law as arising from the nature of the relationship of landlord and tenant. According to the later case of *Scally v. Southern Health and Social Services Board* [1992] 1 A.C. 29, the latter is 'a standardised term implied by law . . . [as] an incident of all [such] contracts' ([1992] 1 A.C. 294 at 307 *per* Lord Bridge). In *Scally*, it was held that a term that all employees in a certain category had to be notified by their employer of their entitlement to certain benefits was not required on the basis of the business efficacy test but was required on the basis of the *Irwin* test ([1992] 1 A.C. 294 at 306–307). Though Lord Cross in *Irwin* suggested that such a term could be implied because it was reasonable to do so arising out of the nature of the contract, and though Lord Denning championed this view (*Shell v. Lostock* [1977] 1 All E.R. 481), Lord Wilberforce in *Irwin* required that the test be necessary to the relationship embodied in the contract, and this was essentially the position adopted by Lord Bridge in *Scally*. Hence, as a matter of English law, Lord Wilberforce's test of necessity seems to have prevailed.

Implied terms In three cases this year the Supreme Court refused to imply terms into contracts before then. In the first, *Sweeney v. Duggan* [1997] 2 I.R. 531; [1997] 2 I.L.R.M. 211 (SC), decided on 14 February 1997, Murphy J. declined to imply a term on the basis of any of the three tests. The plaintiff had been injured in an employment accident, and had secured judgment for £20,866 against his employer. The employer subsequently went into liquidation, in which the plaintiff would only recover about £4,500 of the award. The plaintiff commenced the present proceedings against the defendant, who owned 18,999 of the 19,000 shares in – and was managing director of – the company, arguing that the company had a duty to insure itself against claims such as that of the plaintiff (or to warn the plaintiff that it had no such insurance), and that the defendant had a duty to ensure that the company had so insured itself (or had so warned the plaintiff). The plaintiff argued that such duty arose in tort, and as a term implied into the contract. Both arguments had failed before Barron J. in the High Court ([1991] 2 I.R. 274; see the 1991 Review, pp 386–387 at 459–460 (concentrating on the tort aspects of the case). On appeal to the Supreme Court (Murphy J.; Hamilton C.J. and Barrington J. concurring) the plaintiff's appeal was dismissed.

In the second, *Carna Foods v. Eagle Star Insurance Co* [1997] 2 I.R. 193; [1997] 2 I.R. 499, decided on May 28, 1997, Lynch J. declined to imply a term on the basis of the officious bystander test. The plaintiffs had argued that there was implied, in their contract of insurance with the defendant, a term by which the defendant had a duty to give reasons if it chose to cancel certain insurance policies and to give notice that it would not renew others. The argument had failed before McCracken J. in the High Court ([1995] 1 I.R. 526; [1995] 2 I.L.R.M. 474; see the 1995 Review, 209–211). On appeal to the Supreme Court (Lynch J., Hamilton C.J. and Keane J. concurring) the plaintiff's appeal was dismissed.

And in the third, *Sullivan v. Southern Health Board* [1997] 3 I.R. 123, decided on 30 July 1997, Murphy J. similarly declined to imply a term on the basis of the officious bystander test. The plaintiff had been appointed consultant in Mallow hospital, pursuant to an agreement by which (a) he would be required to work certain hours, (b) entitled to certain facilities and (c) to certain leave. The hospital had been allowed to run down, and the Board had therefore failed to perform its obligations, and was held liable to the plaintiff in damages both in the High Court (29 July 1993, Keane J.; see the 1993 Review, pp 176–177 (discussing the defendant's argument – dismissed by Keane J. and not pursued on appeal – that the contract had been frustrated) and in the Supreme Court (Murphy J., Lynch and Barron JJ. concurring). The plaintiff argued that it contained a further, implied, term that the Board would employ a second consultant at the hospital; when the second consultant died a permanent replacement was not appointed, and the plaintiff argued that the various temporary provisions made by the Board were inadequate. The High Court had implied such a term into the contract and found that it had been breached. The Supreme Court reversed. Since no damages would be available under that head, and since the facts surrounding the particular award in the High Court and the manner in which it was segregated between special and general damages was unsatisfactory, Murphy J. directed a retrial on the issue of damages. (The remitted High Court action was settled: reporter's note [1997] 3 I.R. 123 at 139).

As to the officious bystander test as it was applied in these cases, in *Carna Foods*, Lynch J. pointed out that 'the evidence before the learned trial judge is quite clearly to the effect that if such a term were sought to be included in the insurance policies at the time when the plaintiffs were seeking insurance the defendants would not have contracted with the plaintiffs at all' ([1997] 2 I.R. 193 at 200; [1997] 2 I.R. 499 at 504). Hence, if:

> 'the officious bystander had interrupted . . . and had asked the defendant 'If you do cancel, will you give your reasons for cancelling?' [the] defendant's answer would have been an emphatic 'No' whereas to imply such a term into the policies the answer would have to be by both parties 'Yes, of course' expressed rather testily to discourage the officious bystander from further interrupting:
>
> > . . .it is not enough for the court to find that such a term would have been adopted by the parties as reasonable men if it had been suggested to them: it must have been a term that went without saying, a term necessary to give business efficacy to the contract . . . (*Trollope and Colls v. North West Metropolitan Hospital Board* [1973] 1 W.L.R. 601 at 609 *per* Pearson L.J.)

These basic principles of law preclude the implication of a term into the policies to the effect that in the event of a declinature or cancellation the defendant must state its reasons therefor ([1997] 2 I.R. 193 at 200; [1997] 2 I.R. 499 at 504–505).

The imagery of the officious bystander was even more elaborate in the subsequent decision of Murphy J. in *Sullivan*. It seemed to him that 'a distinction must be made between a situation which exists and which parties expected to continue on the one hand and a contractual obligation on one or other of them positively to ensure that it does so on the other' ([1997] 3 I.R. 123 at 131). Murphy J. held that 'the argument for implying the term ... was the presumed intention of the parties as that concept was identified in' *The Moorcock* (1889) 14 PD 64 and *Shirlaw v. Southern Foundries* [1939] 2 K.B. 206. 'Clearly that condition is not met where the question posed by the ubiquitous bystander is answered in the negative or even where it is the subject matter of further discussion between the parties' ([1997] 3 I.R. 123 at 132). However, both parties believed that the Board could not fill the second post without the sanction of the Department of Health and Comhairle na nOspidéal. Since that was parties' belief

> it is clear that if one came to write the intervene in the negotiations for the contract that a simple affirmative would not suffice. The script writer would have to anticipate a lengthy debate as to what could or might happen on the death of retirement of either of the two permanent consultants. It might well be that the representative of the Board would offer reassurance to the doctor as to the likelihood of the outgoing permanent consultant being replaced by another holding similar tenure but having regard to the state of his knowledge or belief, nobody could anticipate that he would have unhesitatingly entered into a binding legal commitment to do something which he believed was outside his legal capacity to perform. In the circumstances, I am forced to conclude that this was not a case in which the term on which the plaintiff relies should have been implied ([1997] 3 I.R. 123 at 133).

Hence the damages awarded for breach of that term were not properly awarded. Murphy J. observed that the plaintiff could have made the same argument as a claim for money payable on foot of the contract for payment at the same rate as a locum in addition to his ordinary remuneration for those periods when a second consultant was absent, but held that the matter had neither been pleaded nor argued in this form. In the circumstances, the award of damages for breach of the implied term could not stand.

In both *Carna Foods* and *Sullivan*, the metaphor of the officious bystander is given very wide rein. It is a beguiling metaphor. But, the officious bystander is in danger of becoming over-animated, and should not be pressed too far. As with the principles of interpretation discussed below, it is no more than a judicial tool for the discovery of the intentions of the parties. There is a danger with such beguiling metaphors that their purpose, the end for which they are merely the means, will be lost, so that they become ends in themselves. Such was not the case in either *Carna Foods* or *Sullivan*, but it is a danger of which courts ought to be aware, and against which they must be vigilant. The danger might best be alleviated by the abandonment of the terms of the officious bystander test in favour of a more accurate enquiry: whether the term was so obvious that it went without saying. Though best, it might now be too late for that prescription to be followed. In which case, caution with the metaphor is indicated instead.

A second possible danger is that the beguiling metaphor of the officious bystander would prove too attractive in a particular case that analysis would finish with it; either because it would be treated as the same as the logically independent business efficacy test, or simply because of the dominance of the metaphor, logically alternative tests would not be addressed. For example, in *Carna Foods*, Lynch J. held that 'apart from cases where the law implies some terms into certain kinds of contracts, whether by statute or by common law . . . one can imply a term into a contract *only* when the implied term gives effect to the true intention of all the parties to the contract who might be affected by such implied term' ([1997] 2 I.R. 193 at 199–200; [1997] 2 I.R. 499 at 504; emphasis added). The saver at the beginning of the sentence plainly acknowledges that a term might be implied on the basis of *Liverpool City Council v. Irwin*; but after that, the statement that a term may be implied '*only* . . . [to] give[] effect to the true intention of . . . the parties' is simply not the case. It is true that a term implied on the basis that it was so obvious that it went without saying is one which is implied to give effect to the intention of the parties, but that is not the *only* basis (apart from *Liverpool City Council v. Irwin*) upon which a term may be implied. As was pointed out above, the business efficacy test is an entirely independent test, reflecting not the parties actual intentions but their presumed intention that the contract be workable. As Murphy J. put it in the earlier *Sweeney v. Duggan* 'a term may be implied independently of the intention of the parties where it is necessary as a matter of law or logic to enable the provisions of the agreement to have operative effect' ([1997] 2 I.R. 531 at 545; [1997] 2 I.L.R.M. 211 at 222). That Lynch J. in *Carna Foods* did not expressly address this point may be due to over-attraction of the dangerously beguiling officious bystander test. If so, then the metaphor was so dominant, a logically alternative test was neither admitted nor addressed.

Of course, even if the business efficacy test were to be applied to the facts of *Carna Foods*, it is more than arguable that the provisions of the insurance contracts at issue were perfectly workable – had operative effect – without the implication of a duty to give reasons for cancellation or non-renewal. Furthermore, though he did not expressly address the alternative test, Lynch J. gave reasons in support of his primary conclusion which had that effect. For example, he held that if 'the court were to imply such a term into the contracts of insurance the consequences would be very far reaching' ([1997] 2 I.R. 193 at 202; [1997] 2 I.R. 499 at 506); in particular, he raised the spectre of the insurance company giving as reasons for the termination suspicions which if voiced would be defamatory. If the commerce of insurance contracts in general would be made very difficult by the implication of such a term, it could hardly be said to be necessary to give business efficacy to this particular contract. However, his fears as to possible defamation are misplaced: if the defendant communicates with the plaintiff and not to a third party, there is no publication and no defamation; if there is publication to a third party (for example, a broker through which the plaintiff obtained the insurance) it may be that the publication could be regarded as an occasion of qualified privilege; and since the plaintiff had required the statement as a matter of contract, it may be that the defendant could argue that the plaintiff had consented to it. In any event, there would seem to be no warrant for unclear questions of the law of defamation to preclude the implication of a term if a relevant contractual test is satisfied.

Similarly, in *Sullivan*, Murphy J. concentrated on the script written by the officious bystander. But by failing to consider the separate business efficacy test, that script did not tell the whole story. The question on that test is not so much what did the parties agree, as, assuming that the parties intended that their contract be workable, what must be implied into it to make it workable? Hence, on the facts of *Sullivan*, the question would be: whether it was necessary to imply the term alleged by the plaintiff to give the contract business efficacy, to render it workable? Given that caution which a court must exercise in implying terms, it is likely that a negative answer would have been given to this question as it had been to the question addressed by the court; but this second question ought also to have been addressed and answered.

On the other hand, in Murphy J.'s other discussion of implied terms this year, the earlier *Sweeney v. Brophy*, the analysis is given over in part to the officious bystander test elided into the business efficacy test, and in part to a discussion where the business efficacy test and *Liverpool City Council v. Irwin* both figure. At first, the officious bystander and the business efficacy tests are elided, by making the officious bystander test in *Shirlaw v. Southern Foundries* the basis for the implication of a term on foot of *The Moorcock*, an early leading case on the business efficacy test (see [1997] 2 I.R. 531 at 538; [1997] 2 I.L.R.M. 211 at 216). Nevertheless, when it came to considering whether there was implied into the plaintiff's contract of employment with the company a term that the company had a duty to insure itself against claims brought against it by its employees and that the defendant had a duty to ensure that the company had so insured itself, Murphy J. rejected the claim in language which fulfilled both tests. Thus, when he held that the contract 'would and did operate effectively without any such term' ([1997] 2 I.R. 531 at 540; [1997] 2 I.L.R.M. 211 at 217) he in terms applied the business efficacy test and concluded that it provided no basis for the implication of the term. Furthermore, he went on to hold that 'if one postulated an enquiry by the ubiquitous and officious bystander as to whether such a term should be included I anticipate that it might well have been rejected and certainly would not have been accepted without considerable negotiation and discussion[,] a result which would negative the existence of an implied term' ([1997] 2 I.R. 531 at 540; [1997] 2 I.L.R.M. 211 at 217). This is undoubtedly so; indeed, Murphy J. goes on to provide a script of that possible negotiation. (Similarly, 'a collective agreement negotiated across a broad front for a substantial labour force . . . represented a carefully negotiated compromise between two potentially conflicting objectives . . . It is in the nature of such an agreement that it should be concise and clear . . . Should there be any topic left uncovered by an agreement of that kind, the nature inference . . . is not that there has been an omission so obvious as to require judicial correction, but rather that the topic was omitted advisedly from the terms of the agreement . . .' (*Ali v. Christian Salvesen Food Services* [1997] 1 All E.R. 721, (CA) 726 *per* Waite L.J.)). Hence, the officious bystander test – like the business efficacy test before it – provided no basis for the implication of the term. However, notwithstanding that he had rejected the claim in terms which fulfilled both tests, he concluded this part of his judgment by rejecting 'the contention that the term for which the plaintiff contends could be implied on the basis of the *Moorcock* doctrine' ([1997] 2 I.R. 531 at 541; [1997] 2 I.L.R.M. 211 at 218); again eliding the two separate tests. This elision in *Sweeney* is confusing; greater clarity of analysis would have been achieved had these two bases for implication of terms been kept separate.

Sweeney v. Brophy is however the only one of this year's three cases to consider the implications of *Liverpool City Council v. Irwin*. Murphy J. distinguished between a term implied on the basis of *The Moorcock* and *Shirlaw v. Southern Foundries* on the one hand, and of *Liverpool City Council v. Irwin*, on the other. The latter terms are implied not 'on the basis . . . of the intention of the parties to the contract' but upon a basis 'deriving from the nature of the contract itself' ([1997] 2 I.R. 531 at 538; [1997] 2 I.L.R.M. 211 at 216). Such a term, however, 'must be not merely reasonable but also necessary' ([1997] 2 I.R. 531 at 539; [1997] 2 I.L.R.M. 211 at 217). Hence, on this issue, Irish law has followed the same route as the dominant English approach rather than that advocated by Lord Denning. Further, Murphy J. held that such a term 'cannot be implied if it is inconsistent with the express wording of the contract' ([1997] 2 I.R. 531 at 539; [1997] 2 I.L.R.M. 211 at 217). With respect, this does not necessarily follow. It is clear that a term cannot be implied on the basis of the officious bystander test if the proposed term is inconsistent with the terms of the contract: the issue having been dealt with in one way, the parties could not testily reply 'of course' if the bystander had suggested that it be dealt with in another (or, the issue having been dealt with in one way, plainly it could not be said that an alternative term was so obvious that it went without saying). However, when a term is implied to make the contract work, when it is, in his Lordship's own words in the same case 'implied independently of the intention of the parties where it is necessary . . . to enable the . . . contract to have operative effect' ([1997] 2 I.R. 531 at 545; [1997] 2 I.L.R.M. 211 at 222) it may be necessary to imply one inconsistent with an express term, especially if it is that express term which gives rise to the relevant unworkability (see the 1996 Review, 198). Furthermore, if a term is implied because it is a necessary incident of the particular type of contract of which the instant contract is an example, the term would seem implicable whether or not the instant contract has made provision for the relevant issue, and whether or not that provision is consistent with the implied term. If the term is a legal incident of a particular type of contract, it is implied into every such contract, whatever an individual contract might provide. On the other hand, since such implied terms 'operate as default rules. The parties are free to exclude or modify them' (*Malik v. BCCI* [1997] 3 All E.R. 1 (HL) 15 *per* Lord Steyn; see, generally, Rakoff 'The Implied Terms of Contracts: Of 'Default Rules' and 'Situation Sense'' in Beatson and Friedmann (eds.) *Good Faith and Fault in Contract Law* (Clarendon Press, Oxford, 1995) p 191; and Carswell and Schwarz *Foundations of Contract Law* (New York, 1994) pp 16–29). Nevertheless, given the logic underlying such terms, there may be circumstances in which the default rule cannot be displaced. Furthermore, Murphy J. pointed out that it 'may be difficult to infer a term where it cannot be formulated with reasonable precision' ([1997] 2 I.R. 531 at 540; [1997] 2 I.L.R.M. 211 at 217). Finally, he pointed out that in two English Court of Appeal decisions (*Reid v. Rush & Tompkins* [1990] 1 W.L.R. 212; *Van Oppen & Clarke v. Bedford Charity Trustees* [1990] 1 W.L.R. 235 (and compare *Byrne v. Australian Airlines* (1995) 131 A.L.R.422 (HCA))) the court had declined to imply similar terms into contracts of employment. He therefore seemed to conclude that the term contended for by the plaintiff was not to be implied into his contract of employment with the company on the basis of the nature of the contract as a contract of employment.

However, that conclusion is not entirely clear, since it seems that having elided the officious bystander test into one end of the business efficacy test, he also elided the *Liverpool City Council v. Irwin* test into the other end of the business efficacy test. For example, having referred to *Irwin*, Murphy J. held that '[w]hether a term is implied pursuant to the presumed intention of the parties or as a legal incident of a definable category of contract[,] it must be not merely reasonable but also necessary'. To the extent that this means that a term implied on the basis of *Irwin* must be necessary, this is entirely consistent with the nature of such an implied term. And to the extent that the reference to the 'presumed intention of the parties' is a reference to the business efficacy test, so that a term – implied to make the contract workable – must be necessary, this too is entirely consistent with the nature of such an implied term. (It goes without saying that the reference to the 'presumed intention of the parties' does not reach the business efficacy test, since that is based on the actual but simply unexpressed intention of the parties, and the term which was so obvious that it went without saying might be neither necessary nor reasonable, but just simply one which the parties obviously would have wanted).

A similar elision occurs more seriously at a later point in his judgment. He referred to the two English Court of Appeal decisions which concluded that a duty similar to that contended for on behalf of the plaintiff before him was 'inappropriate for incorporation by law into all contracts of employment . . .' (*Reid v. Rush & Tompkins* [1990] 1 W.L.R. 212 at 227 *per* Ralph Gibson L.J., followed in *Van Oppen & Clarke v. Bedford Charity Trustees* [1990] 1 W.L.R. 235; see [1997] 2 I.R. 531 at 541–542; [1997] 2 I.L.R.M. 211 at 218–220). This was clearly a holding that the terms of the *Liverpool City Council v. Irwin* test had not been satisfied. And yet Murphy J. bolstered that conclusion by reference to the decision of the House of Lords in *Scally v. Southern Health and Social Services Board* [1992] 1 A.C. 294 (see especially [1997] 2 I.R. 531 at 545; [1997] 2 I.L.R.M. 211 at 222). In *Scally*, it was held that a term that all employees in a certain category had to be notified by their employer of their entitlement to certain benefits was not required on the basis of the business efficacy test but was required on the basis of the *Irwin* test. As with *Irwin* itself, the fact that one test was fulfilled and the other not, demonstrates that there are in fact two separate tests. And though *Scally* might be authority against the implication of the term contended for by the plaintiff by means of the business efficacy test, it is not authority against it on the *Irwin* test; in fact, quite the contrary. At best, it seems that Murphy J. elided the conclusion on the *Irwin* test in the Court of Appeal decisions of *Reid* and *Van Oppen* with the conclusion on the business efficacy test in the House of Lords in *Scally*; but that approach would be contestable not only because of that elision, but also because it overlooks the conclusion of the House of Lords in *Scally* on the *Irwin* point. Nevertheless, assuming that there are separate tests, and given that he had earlier concluded that the business efficacy test did not require that the term proposed by the plaintiff be implied, Murphy J's conclusion of this discussion, that 'there is no basis for the implication in the contract of employment between the company and the plaintiff' of that term ([1997] 2 I.R. 531 at 545; [1997] 2 I.L.R.M. 211 at 222), must therefore be understood as a conclusion that the term was not justified on the basis of the *Irwin* test.

In any event, in general, clarity of analysis is not served by eliding the officious bystander test into the business efficacy test and in turn eliding that into the *Liverpool City Council v. Irwin* test. Occasionally, the elision will work no real damage (for example, near the end of his judgment, and still dealing with *Scally*, Murphy J. agreed with Lord Bridge that 'a term may be implied independently of the intention of the parties where it is necessary as a matter of law and logic to enable the provisions of an agreement to have operative effect'([1997] 2 I.R. 531 at 545; [1997] 2 I.L.R.M. 211 at 222). But there is nothing in this aspect of Murphy J.'s discussion of *Scally* to indicate which of the relevant species of implied terms he intended to be encompassed in that statement. The statement is, however, capable of referring to both a term implied for business efficacy reasons and on foot of the *Irwin* test; it ought to be understood as applying to both. In which case, this is an example of where the elision works no real damage). Furthermore, it is true that Lord Wilberforce in *Irwin* and, following him, Murphy J. in *Sweeney v. Duggan* 'preferred to describe the different categories . . . as no more than shades on a continuous spectrum' ([1997] A.C. 239 at 254 *per* Lord Wilberforce; followed [1997] 2 I.R. 531 at 538; [1997] 2 I.L.R.M. 211 at 216 *per* Murphy J). But red, orange, yellow, green, blue, indigo and violet are colours on a continuous spectrum; yet we would not elide one into the other. We would recognise their essential differences. Likewise, the officious bystander test, the business efficacy test and the *Irwin* test may be shades or colours on a continuous spectrum, nonetheless they are separate tests as the colours on the spectrum are separate colours.

Notwithstanding the elisions, at least *Sweeney v. Duggan* considered the possible application of the *Irwin* test to the facts of that case. Of the two later cases, *Carna Foods* and *Sullivan*, the *Irwin* test may have been relevant on the facts of the former. For example, the question may be posed: why is a term that an insurer who cancels of fails to renew an insurance policy must give reasons for this action not implied into every contract of insurance, on the grounds that it is a necessary incident of such contract? If Lynch J's fears that the commerce of insurance contracts in general would be made very difficult by the implication of such a term, it could hardly be said to be necessary on the basis of the *Irwin* test. However, it was pointed out above that such fears – especially those based on possible defamation – do not seem very strong. Further, Lynch J. treated *Sun Fire Office v. Hart* (1889) 14 App. Cas. 98 as authority against the plaintiff's arguments, but, even on the extracts cited by Lynch J., that judgment seems more concerned with the validity of the exercise of the power to terminate than with the subsequent question of whether – even if the power to terminate is validly exercised – the insurer must give reasons for the termination. If that is so, then *Hart* does not preclude the implication of the term as a necessary incident of the contract of insurance. Furthermore, Lynch J. seems to have cited *Hart* for the view that if the contract is validly terminated, the insured got what he paid for, and can protect himself by obtaining insurance elsewhere. On the other hand, without knowing why one insurer refuses to insure, it makes it more difficult to obtain alternative insurance, and if the cure for termination is so to obtain, the duty to give reasons makes it easier to do so. Hence, the argument in favour of the term canvassed in *Carna Foods* seems stronger on the basis of the *Irwin* test than it did in the case itself on the basis of the officious bystander test. Similarly, the plaintiff in *Sullivan* might have sought to argue that the relevant term was implied as a consequence of the very nature of the contract itself, by analogy with *Liverpool City Council v. Irwin* (above), but this would have been most unlikely to succeed.

PRINCIPLES OF INTERPRETATION

In interpreting a contract, 'the task of the court is to decide what the intention of the parties was, having regard to the language used in the contract itself and the surrounding circumstances' (*Kramer v. Arnold* [1997] 3 I.R. 43 at 55 *per* Keane J.). This elusive search for the intention of the parties is the guiding light of all principles of interpretation. The courts have pressed many approaches into service in that search, often contradictory and often without realising the contraction. They are engaged in seeking the objective as opposed to subjective meaning of the words. They express themselves as seeking the natural meaning or the literal meaning, in the first instance; though of course it may be that a natural meaning is not a literal one, or *vice versa*. Such a meaning is often required to reflect common sense, or business common sense, or a commercially sensible construction. Of course, they concede that such a natural or literal meaning would cede to a necessary specialist meaning, or a meaning which arises from the context of the relevant words in the contract, or from the context of the circumstances surrounding the contract, and all of these alternatives might be justified on the basis of one or other of the above species of common sense. If the courts are not to succumb to the danger of getting lost in a post-modern maze of meanings, they should remember that any such rule of construction is the servant and not the master. 'It is not a permissible method of construction to propound a general or generally accepted principle . . . and then . . . to seek to force the provisions of the [contract] into the straitjacket of that principle' (*The Sea Queen* [1988] 1 Lloyd's Rep. 500 at 502 *per* Saville J.; *Cargill International SA v. Bangladesh Sugar and Food Industries Corp* [1998] 2 All E.R. 406 (CA), 413 *per* Potter L.J.); sight should not be lost then of the guiding principle that the interpretation of a contract should reflect the intentions of the parties to that contract.

The general rule in the interpretation of contracts is that 'most expressions do have a natural meaning, in the sense of their primary meaning in ordinary speech . . . [Hence] the inquiry will start, and usually finish, by asking what is the ordinary meaning of the words used' (*Charter Reinsurance v. Fagan* [1996] 3 All E.R. 46 (HL) at 50 *per* Lord Mustill). Presumably, this is because, in the first instance, the parties can be taken to have intended that the words would bear their ordinary meaning. Thus, in *Axa Reinsurance v. Field* [1996] 3 All E.R. 517 (HL), on one insurance policy, a reinsurer was liable for an excess over a stated sum of 'each and every loss . . . arising out of one event'; on another insurance policy, liability was limited in respect of claims 'arising from one originating cause'. For Lord Mustill, the expressions 'cause' and 'event' were 'not at all the same . . . In ordinary speech, an event is something which happens at a particular time, at a particular place, in a particular way. . . . A cause is to my mind something altogether less constricted. It can be a continuing state of affairs; it can be the absence of something happening'

([1996] 3 All E.R. 517 at 526). Hence, the natural meanings of each phrase, their primary meanings in ordinary speech, led to the different interpretations of the relevant clauses.

In *Kramer v. Arnold* [1997] 3 I.R. 43 the Supreme Court was faced with need to interpret the word 'immediately' in a contract for the sale of land. By means of a written agreement, the defendant granted the plaintiff an option to purchase property. The agreement provided that 'immediately the purchase price shall have either been agreed between [the parties or determined by a valuer] . . . [the plaintiff] shall pay to [the defendant's solicitors] as stakeholder by way of deposit a sum equal to 10% of such purchase price'. It also provided that the 'Incorporated Law Society of Ireland General Conditions of Sale (1988 edition) shall apply to the sale . . .' and those conditions in turn provided that 'The failure by [the plaintiff] to pay in full the deposit as hereinbefore specified as payable by him shall constitute a breach of conditions entitling [the defendant] to terminate the sale . . .'. In a valuation dated March 28, 1995 and published to the plaintiff between 5.30pm and 6.00pm on Friday March 31, 1995, the valuer determined the value of the property as £92,000. By fax to the plaintiff's solicitor, on Monday April 3, 1995, the defendant's solicitor pointed out that, by the terms of the agreement, the 10% deposit became payable 'immediately'. On April 12, 1995, the defendant's solicitors sent a letter by hand to the plaintiff's solicitors purporting to terminate the option agreement on the grounds that the deposit had not been 'immediately' paid. On the same day, the plaintiff's solicitors sent a letter by hand to the defendant's solicitors containing a cheque in the amount of the deposit; the defendant's solicitors immediately returned the cheque. In an action by the plaintiff to enforce the option agreement, McGuinness J. in the High Court (November 14, 1996) ordered specific performance. On appeal to the Supreme Court, Keane J. (O'Flaherty and MurphyJJ. concurring) reversed: since the deposit had not been paid immediately (in the circumstances, meaning that it had not been paid as soon as was practicable), the plaintiff was in breach of contract, and the defendant was entitled to terminate the option agreement (compare the cases discussed in Carter 'Two Cases on Time Stipulations in Commercial Contracts' (1992) 5 *J.C.L.* 60).

On the interpretation issue, the defendant had conceded that payment 'immediately' did not require payment on March 28, 1995 when the award was made but not published; that it did not have its literal meaning of 'without any interval of time, however minimal elapsing', since even if the plaintiff had delivered the cheque upon learning of the award, 'some interval of time must necessarily have elapsed'; and that it would have been 'hardly practicable' for the plaintiff to contact the defendant upon receiving the award between 5.30 and 6.00 on 'a Friday evening, at which stage the office of the plaintiff's solicitors would, in the normal way be closed'. ([1997] 3 I.R. 43 at 56). Nevertheless Keane J. held that:

In this case, as in any case where the parties are in disagreement as to what a particular provision of a contract means, the task of the court is to decide what the intention of the parties was, having regard to the language used in the contract itself and the surrounding circumstances ([1997] 3 I.R. 43 at 55)

Hence, 'since the parties chose to use the word 'immediately', it must be given some significance . . . Whether or not the payment of the deposit is properly regarded in law as a condition precedent, a fundamental term of the contract or simply one of the terms of the contract, it was, to put it at its lowest, a stipulate of at least some importance' ([1997] 3 I.R. 43 at 56) and he concluded that:

while the parties in using the word 'immediately' were not imposing on the intending purchaser, the plaintiff, an obligation to pay the deposit within a time limit compliance with which was impossible or even impracticable, they did envisage that the deposit would be paid by him as soon as was practicable after he, or his agent, had received a copy of the award ([1997] 3 I.R. 43 at 56)

This was a conclusion which he tied both to the meaning of the word 'immediately' and 'to the surrounding circumstances' (see *esp.* [1997] 3 I.R. 43 at 58; an interpretation not displaced by the *contra proferentem* rule, since such a rule would not justify a construction 'contrary to the intentions of the parties' ([1997] 3 I.R. 43 at 62)). Hence, it followed that 'the plaintiff was in breach of the agreement in not paying the deposit on Monday the 3rd April, when he could have arranged for the delivery of a cheque to the defendant's solicitor's office' ([1997] 3 I.R. 43 at 59); and on the evidence, the plaintiff had not therefore paid the deposit as soon as was practicable. Since it was 'clear that a condition of this nature is, at the least, a fundamental term of the contract' the breach of which allowed the defendant to terminate the option agreement ([1997] 3 I.R. 43 at 60).

In *Kramer v. Arnold* , Keane J. referred to the attitude of the courts of equity to stipulations as to time for completion of contracts for the sale of land (more liberal than the former common law rules, but the equitable rules have been applied in common law courts since the enactment of the Judicature (Ireland) Act 1877) but held that 'the rules under which particular stipulations are not to be of the essence of the contract have no application to cases in which an option is to be exercised within a specified time or indeed to compliance with any condition precedent to a party's obligations . . . ' ([1997] 3 I.R. 43 at 60). Again, in the Privy Council case of *Union Eagle v. Golden Achievement* [1997] 2 All E.R. 215, a contract for the sale of land provided that time was of the essence of the agreement, and that the purchaser was to complete on or before 5.00 p.m. on September 31 on pain of rescission of the contract by the vendor and forfeiture of the purchaser's deposit. Lord Hoffman held that tender of the purchase price at 5.10 p.m. did not fulfill the terms of the contract, and the vendor was entitled to rescind it and to forfeit the deposit. 'Once 5.00 p.m. had passed, performance of the contract by the purchaser was no longer possible' ([1997] 2 All E.R. 215 at 218 *per* Lord Hoffman); the natural meaning of the clause led to that conclusion, and there was no basis upon which to relieve against the rescission or the forfeiture of the deposit: 'in many forms of transaction it is of great importance that if something happens for which the contract has made express provision, the parties should know with certainty that the terms of the contract will be enforced' (*id*).

Of course, the question may be whether something for which the contract has made express provision has in fact occurred. In *Kramer v. Arnold*, the question was whether the option had been validly exercised by the 'immediate' payment of the deposit. In *Hankey v. Clavering* [1942] 2 K.B. 326 (CA) a lease could be determined if either party served a notice to expire on December 25; and the Court of Appeal held insufficient a notice expiring on December 21; hence, the consequence for which the contract had expressly provided (the determination) did not follow because the fact of which it was the contractual consequence (the valid notice) had not occurred. However, *Hankey v. Clavering* was overruled by the House of Lords in *Mannai Investments v. Eagle Star* [1997] 3 All E.R. 352 by a majority of 3 (Lords Steyn, Hoffman and Clyde) to 2 (Lords Goff and Jauncey). A lease provided that the tenant could determine the lease 'by serving not less than six months notice in writing on the Landlord . . . such notice to expire on the 3rd anniversary of the term commencement date'. The lease had commenced on January 13, 1992, and the tenant sought to determine it by 'giving notice . . . to determine the lease on January 12, 1995'. The landlord claimed that this mistake rendered the notice ineffective, but the majority disagreed. Hence, the consequence for which the contract had expressly provided (the determination) did follow because the fact of which it was the contractual consequence (the valid notice) had in fact occurred.

In both *Hankey v. Clavering* and *Mannai Investments v. Eagle Star*, that for which the contract had made express provision was a notice, itself in need of interpretation. Thus, interpretation was necessary both of the clause in the lease and of the terms of the notice. Lord Goff, dissenting, declined the invitation to overrule *Hankey v. Clavering*, on the ground that the adoption of an alternative test would inevitably lead to uncertainty, whereas the clarity of *Hankey v. Clavering* must have formed the basis of innumerable leases and of the resolution of many disputes in the county court. For him, 'the notice, properly construed, did not comply with the agreement between the parties. The key does not fit the lock, and so the door will not open' ([1997] 3 All E.R. 352 at 357). A latently ambiguous notice might be interpreted to be consistent with the terms of the contract; and it might be plain from the face of the notice that the date is given in error for the true date which the giver of the notice must have intended to specify, as where there is a typographical error. But if the date as given was that which was intended to be given, and it turns out to have been the wrong date, the notice does not comply with terms of the contract, and is thus ineffective. Lord Jauncey agreed (see *esp.* [1997] 3 All E.R. 352 at 365–367).

On the other hand, for the majority, Lord Steyn held that the words of the clause 'do not have any customary meaning in a technical sense. No terms of art are involved. . . . The language . . . must be given its ordinary meaning' ([1997] 3 All E.R. 352 at 368–569). As to the notice, he held that its construction 'must be approached objectively. The issue is how a reasonable recipient would have understood [it] . . . construed taking into account the relevant objective contractual scene' ([1997] 3 All E.R. 352 at 369; applying *Rearden Smith Line v. Hansen-Tagen* [1976] 3 All E.R. 570). In that context, the purpose of the notice is to inform the landlord that the tenant has decided to determine the lease in accordance with the relevant clause. A reasonable recipient of the notice 'would have appreciated that the tenant wished to determine the leases on the third anniversary date but wrongly described it as January 12, instead of January 13. The reasonable recipient would not have been perplexed in any way by the minor error . . .' and the notice would have achieved its intended purpose ([1997] 3 All E.R. 352 at 370). For him *Hankey v. Clavering* no longer represented the law; it had not expressly posed the necessary objective test, and, since it was decided, 'there has been a shift from strict construction of commercial instruments . . . towards commercial interpretation. . . . In contradistinction to this modern approach . . . *Hankey v. Clavering* is rigid and formalistic. Nowadays one expects a notice to determine under a commercial lease to be interpreted not as a 'technical document' but in accordance with business common sense' ([1997] 3 All E.R. 352 at 372). Similarly, Lord Clyde also interpreted the notice by reference to 'the reasonable man exercising his common sense in the context and in the circumstances of the particular case . . . The test is an objective one . . .' ([1997] 3 All E.R. 352 at 383). The intent of the tenant was plain, and the landlord would recognise that the reference to 12 January was to be read as one to January 13.

For Lord Hoffman, it was 'a matter of constant experience that people can convey their meaning unambiguously although they have used the wrong words . . . [and] we adjust our interpretation of what they are saying accordingly'. They may have used the wrong words, as Mrs Malaprop did, from 'an imperfect understanding of the conventional meanings of English words. But the reason for the mistake does not really matter. We use the same process of adjustment when people have made mistakes or descriptions or days or times because they have forgotten or become mixed up. . . . If one applies that kind of interpretation to the notice in this case, there will also be no ambiguity' ([1997] 3 All E.R. 352 at 375): the landlord would understand that the notice refers to the date upon which the lease allow the termination. Thus, the objective interpretation of words proceeds not only upon the basis of their dictionary meanings but also from the context of the background against which the utterance was made: it is 'that background which enables us, not only to choose the intended meaning when a word has more than one dictionary meaning, but also . . . to understand a speaker's meaning, often without ambiguity, when he has used the wrong words' ([1997] 3 All E.R. 352 at 376). (On this admirably post-modern view, compare the work of Stanley Fish: *Is There a Text in This Class? The Authority of Interpretative Communities* (Harvard University Press, 1980); *'Doing What Comes Naturally': Change, Rhetoric and the Practice of Theory in Literary and Legal Studies* (Clarendon Press, Oxford, 1989); and *There's No Such Thing As Free Speech (And it's a Good Thing, Too)* (New York, 1994)). Cases like *Hankey v. Clavering* which applied a contrary rule of construction ('capricious' and 'incoherent' as 'based upon an ancient fallacy which assumes that descriptions and proper names can somehow inherently refer to people or things' ([1997] 3 All E.R. 352 at 379)) are therefore no longer good law. As to Lord Goff's fears of uncertainty, Lord Hoffman did not think that 'overruling the old cases [would] create uncertainty as to what the law is. In fact I think that the present law is uncertain and that only a decision of [the House of Lords], either adopting or rejecting the *Hankey v. Clavering* rule of construction, [would] make it certain' ([1997] 3 All E.R. 352 at 381).

Hence, the speech of Lord Hoffman in *Mannai Investments* interpreting the words of the notice served by the tenant is an excellent example of the principle that the words being interpreted must be understood in context. It is a first cousin of the principle that the words being interpreted 'must be set in the landscape of the instrument as a whole' (*Charter Reinsurance v. Fagan* [1996] 3 All E.R. 46 at 51 *per* Lord Mustill); and the ordinary meaning might be displaced if the relevant phrase is exclusively a specialist term, or, though an ordinary word, it also has a specialist meaning which the context shows was intended. Lord Hoffman's approach in *Mannai Investments* demonstrates that the same principle can be applied to determine that a meaning other than an ordinary literal meaning was objectively the meaning of a clause, and the context which justifies that meaning is not just the instrument as a whole, but also the background circumstances. Hence, as he held in *Charter Reinsurance v. Fagan,* ' in some cases the notion of words having a natural meaning is not a very helpful one. Because the meaning of words is so sensitive to syntax and context, the natural meaning of words in one sentence may be quite unnatural in another. Thus a statement that words have a particular natural meaning may mean no more than that in many contexts they will have that meaning. In other contexts their meaning will be different but no less natural' ([1996] 3 All E.R. 46 at 57). And in others still, as *Mannai Investments* demonstrates, a meaning may be quite unnatural, but still objectively be the meaning of the words.

In *Fagan* itself, in a reinsurance contract where the 'net loss' payable by the reinsurer was the sum 'actually paid' by the reinsured, less certain deductions, Lord Mustill held that 'actually paid' in effect meant 'payable': 'actually' meant 'in the event when finally ascertained' and 'paid' meant 'exposed to liability as a result of the loss insured [another] clause', ([1996] 3 All E.R. 46 at 52–53) so the reinsurer was liable to the reinsured once the reinsured as insurer was exposed to a liability which was actually payable, even though the reinsured had not paid, and could not pay, the relevant inward claims. These were 'far from the ordinary meanings of the words, and they may be far from the meanings which they have had in other policies . . . [But the House of Lords was] called upon to interpret them in a very specialised form of reinsurance . . .'. Lord Hoffman agreed with Lord Mustill 'that the context points to a wish to emphasise the net character of the liability as opposed to what, under the terms of the policies, the liability might have been' ([1996] 3 All E.R. 46 at 58). Hence, for him, '[c]onsiderations of history, language and commercial background therefore led . . . to the conclusion that the word 'actually' . . . is used to emphasise that the loss for which the reinsurer is to be liable is to be net and that the clause does not restrict liability to the amount by which the liability of the reinsured for the loss has been discharged. [He thought] that this is the natural meaning of the clause'.

Thus, for Lord Mustill, his interpretation was not the natural meaning but a specialised one imposed by context; whereas for Lord Hoffman, the meaning in the context was the natural one. On either approach, *Fagan* is an excellent example of a meaning emerging from the specific context of the words and the specific type of contract. As Keane J. put it in *Kramer v. Arnold*, in the interpretation of a contract, the court must have regard to the surrounding circumstances ([1997] 3 I.R. 43 at 55 and 58). Like *Mannai Investments* and *Kramer v. Arnold*, *Fagan* is an excellent illustration that 'modern principles of construction require the court to have regard to the commercial background, the context of the contract and the circumstances of the parties, and to consider whether, against that background and in that context, to give the words a particular or restricted meaning would lead to an apparently unreasonable and unfair result' (*Cargill International SA v. Bangladesh Sugar and Food Industries Corp* [1998] 2 All E.R. 406 (CA), 413 *per* Potter L.J.). More generally, 'if a detailed semantic and syntactical analysis of words in a commercial contract is going to lead to a conclusion that flouts business common sense, it must be made to yield to business common sense' (*Antaios Cia Naviera SC v. Salen Rderierna AB* [1985] A.C. 191 at 201 *per* Lord Diplock). Keane J's interpretation of 'immediately' in *Kramer v. Arnold* to mean 'as soon as was practicable' is certainly of that nature. Hence, as Lord Steyn has observed, 'there has been a shift from strict construction of commercial instruments to what is sometimes called purposes construction of such documents. . . . It is better to speak of a shift towards commercial interpretation. . . . In determining the meaning of the language of a commercial contract, and unilateral contractual notices, the law therefore favours a commercially sensible construction. The reason for this approach is that a commercial construction is more likely to give effect to the intention of the parties. Words are therefore interpreted in the way in which a reasonable commercial person would construe them. And the standard of the reasonable person is hostile to technical interpretations and undue emphasis on niceties of language' (*Mannai Investments v. Eagle Star* [1997] 3 All E.R. 352 at 371–372).

A particularly good example of this emphasis on reality is provided by the treatment in the Supreme Court in *McCabe v. South City and County Investment Co* [1997] 3 I.R. 300; [1998] 1 I.L.R.M. 264 of a *dictum* of Carroll J. *Waterford Glass (Group Services) Ltd v. The Revenue Commissioners* [1990] 1 I.R. 334. Carroll J. had held that the 'court is entitled to look at the reality of what has been done. Just because the parties put a particular label on a transaction the court is not obliged to accept that label blindly' ([1990] 1 I.R. 334 at 337). Murphy J. (Lynch and BarronJJ. concurring) adopted that principle and continued that it is:

> of general application. It is encountered frequently in relation to transactions which might fall into one or other of two categories and the parties to the transaction wish to have the legal rights attaching to one category and the practical advantages of the other. It is understandable that labels have been challenged where they seek to define a lease as a licence (*Irish Shell and BP v. John Costello Ltd* [1981] I.L.R.M. 66); a mortgage as a conveyance (*In re Kent and Sussex Sawmills* [1947] Ch. 177); a fixed charge as a floating charge (see *In re Keenan Bros.* [1985] I.R. 401) or a sale as a retention of title (*Carroll Group Distributors v. G and JF Bourke* [1990] 1 I.R. 481)'. ([1997] 3 I.R. 300 at 305–306; [1998] 1 I.L.R.M. 264 at 269–270).

On the facts, Murphy J. held that the relevant transaction, described as an 'annuity', by which the taxpayer had paid a capital sum to purchase annual payments, generated income liable to tax rather than capital repayments plus interest. This was an eminently sensible and reasonable conclusion on the facts. However, if in *McCabe*, as in any other case, an interpretation once arrived at seems unreasonable, alarms bells should start to ring: '[t]he more unreasonable the result the more unlikely it is that the parties can have intended it, and if they do intend it the more necessary it is that they shall make that intention abundantly clear' (*L Schuler AG v. Wickman Machine Tool Sales Ltd* [1974] A.C. 235 at 251 *per* Lord Reid; *Cargill International SA v. Bangladesh Sugar and Food Industries Corp* [1998] 2 All E.R. 406 (CA), 413 *per* Potter L.J.). In the end, however, this 'practical rule of thumb . . . must however have its limits. There comes a point at which the court should remind itself that the task is to discover what the parties meant from what they have said, and that to force upon the words a meaning which they cannot fairly bear is to substitute for the baring actually made one which the court believes could better have been made. This is an illegitimate role for a court. Particularly in the field of commerce, where the parties need to know what they must do and what they can insist on not doing, it is essential for them to be confident that they can rely on the court to enforce their contract according to its terms' (*Charter Reinsurance v. Fagan* [1996] 3 All E.R. 46 at 54 *per* Lord Mustill). The decision of the Supreme Court in *Kramer v. Arnold* is an excellent example of the court enforcing a contract according to its terms.

REMEDIES

It is axiomatic that when a party performs his obligations under a contract, he cannot be in breach of contract; once the evidence had been evaluated, this was, in the view of Barron J., the position of the defendant in *Atherton Services v. Killeen* (High Court, January 28, 1997). Barron J. was faced with the task first of resolving whether a contract had been agreed between the parties, and thereafter breached, and if so, of determining the appropriate level of damages. He held that a contract had come into existence between the parties, by which the parties valued certain machinery, which would then be sold through main dealers arranged by the plaintiffs, and the proceeds applied to repay money borrowed by the defendant from the plaintiff. In the event of a shortfall, the parties agreed that the loss would be borne as to the first £5,000 by the plaintiffs, and as to the next £10,000 by the defendants. Most of the items were in fact sold, though very few seem to have been sold through a main dealer. Barron J. accepted that the valuations were believed to have been reasonably accurate, but held that since the plaintiff could not 'establish the prices which would have been obtained had the items been sold in accordance with the terms of the agreement, it must accept the valuations in their place. . . . Having regard to the breach by [the plaintiff] to effect sales in the manner agreed, there is no evidence of a shortfall. In these circumstances the plaintiff must accept that no liability on the part of the defendants to meet a shortfall can have arisen. I accept the defendants' submission that they performed their part of the bargain and that no further obligation on their part came into being.'

Damages for mental distress for breach of contract   Where a plaintiff is entitled to damages for breach of contract, he is entitled 'so far as money can do it, to be paced in the same position with respect to damages, as if the contract had been performed' (*Robinson v. Harman* (1841) 1 Ex. 850 *per* Parke B). However, the plaintiff is entitled only to such damages 'as may fairly and reasonably be considered either arising naturally, *i.e.* according to the usual course of things, from such breach of contract itself, or such as may reasonably be supposed to have been in the contemplation of the parties, at the time they made the contract, as the probable result of the breach of it' (*Hadley v. Baxendale* (1854) 9 Ex. 341 *per* Alderson B). Thus, expectation losses are recoverable provided that they are either reasonably foreseeable, or were (or could have been) foreseen by the parties. Though it was at one time thought that these classic formulae precluded the availability of damages for pain and suffering, emotional upset, mental distress, or the like, for breach of contract, the modern position is not so clear. It seems now to be accepted that such damages may be recovered in an action for breach of contract, though the precise basis of such recovery is still decidedly unclear.

The matter figured in two cases this year. In *Smith v. Custom House Docks Development Authority* (High Court, March 20, 1997) McGuinness J. simply assumed their availability; the matter was raised but not resolved in the Supreme Court in *Sullivan v. Southern Health Board* [1997] 3 I.R. 123 (SC, Murphy, Lynch and Barron J.; *rvsg* High Court, July 29, 1993, Keane J.). The plaintiff had been appointed consultant in Mallow hospital, pursuant to an agreement by which (a) he would be required to work certain hours, (b) entitled to certain facilities and (c) to certain leave. The hospital had been allowed to run down, the Board had therefore failed to perform its obligations, and was held liable to the plaintiff in damages both in the High Court and in the Supreme Court. The plaintiff had attempted to quantify his specific losses and had also claimed for the stress and anxiety caused to him in both his professional and domestic life by the persistent failure of the Board to remedy his legitimate complaints. In the High Court, Keane J. had awarded damages under both these heads. In relation to the award of damages for stress and anxiety, Murphy J. in the Supreme Court affirmed that the 'plaintiff is entitled to be compensated for the general and any special damage caused to him' by the Board's breaches ([1997] 3 I.R. 123 at 136). However, in the High Court, Keane J. had accepted an argument that there was implied into the contract a further term that the Board would employ a second consultant at the hospital, but Murphy J. in the Supreme Court rejected it (see the Implied Terms section, above). Since the plaintiff's claim for damages for stress and anxiety was inextricably bound up with his unsustainable claims to damages for' the breach of that alleged implied term (([1997] 3 I.R. 123 at 136–137), and the manner in which the award was segregated between special and general was unsatisfactory, Murphy J. directed a retrial on the issue of damages. (The remitted High Court action was settled: reporter's note [1997] 3 I.R. 123 at 139).

Presumably, the reference to 'general . . . damage' in Murphy J's recognition of the plaintiff's entitlement to compensation 'for the general and any special damage caused to him' is a reference to the plaintiff's claim for damages for stress and anxiety. Similarly, in *Smith v. Custom House Docks Development Authority* (High Court, March 20, 1997) McGuinness J. acceded to the plaintiff's claim for 'general damages for breach of contract'. But this is the language of tort; *quaere* whether that language is appropriate to a claim in contract? Whatever the language, *Sullivan* marks a clear acceptance on the part of the Supreme Court that damages for stress and anxiety are properly available for breach of contract. It also suggests that had the relevant term been implied, then such damages would have been properly awarded; but, beyond that, it indicates no test by which their availability might be determined. It might be thought that the fact that there is no hint of a restriction upon such damages suggests that Murphy J. seemed to accept the general availability of such damages, so that that had the relevant term been implied, such damages would have been properly awarded. However, that may be to read too much into the decision, especially in the light of the history of the availability of such damages for breach of contract. (See Macdonald 'Contractual Damages for Mental Distress' (1994) 7 J.C.L. 134). The story has been that of a general rule against such damages, subject to exceptions, collapsing under the weight of the exceptions when the absence of logic at its foundations has been exposed; the best position is probably that seemingly adopted by McGuinness J. in *Smith* and by Murphy J. in *Sullivan*, but it requires a long journey to reach that destination.

The general rule was that in an action for breach of contract, a plaintiff is not entitled to recover 'damages for the disappointment of mind occasioned by the breach of contract' (*Hamlin v. Great Northern Rly* (1856) 1 H&N 408 at 411; 156 E.R. 1261 at 1262 *per* Pollock CB). In *Addis v. Gramophone Co Ltd* [1909] A.C. 488 (HL) the plaintiff was employed by the defendants as their manager in Calcutta on a salary plus commission. The contract provided for a notice period of six months. The defendants sought to terminate the contract and gave the required six months notice, but immediately installed his successor and prevented the plaintiff from acting as manager. This amounted either to a wrongful dismissal or to a breach of the plaintiff's right to act as manager during the notice period and to earn the best commission he could make. The House of Lords held that the plaintiff's damages for that breach were the six months salary plus commission, but no more. Lord Loreburn LC could not 'agree that the manner of dismal affect[ed] these damages . . . [such damages] cannot include compensation either for the injured feelings of the [plaintiff] or for the loss he may sustain from the fact that his having been dismissed of itself makes it more difficult to obtain fresh employment' ([1909] A.C. 488 at 491). Similarly, Lord James of Hereford held that 'damages on the ground that there has been an aggravation of the injury in consequence of the manner of dismissal' could not be recovered for breach of contract (([1909] A.C. 488 at 492). To like effect, Lord Atkinson characterised the manner of the plaintiff's dismissal as 'harsh and humiliating' but held that he could not 'recover in the shape of exemplary damages for illegal dismissal, in effect damages for defamation' ([1909] A.C. 488 at 493) since 'damages for breach of contract [a]re in the nature of compensation, not punishment' ([1909] A.C. 488 at 494). A plaintiff who seeks exemplary damages should sue in tort; a plaintiff who chooses to sue in contract accepts the consequences of that form of action, one of which is that the plaintiff 'is entitled to be paid adequate compensation in money for the loss of that which he would have received had his contract been kept, and no more' ([1909] A.C. 488 at 496). Indeed, as Lord Shaw of Dunfermline pointed out, if slander or libel accompanies the dismissal, the law still provides a remedy: the plaintiff can still sue for defamation ([1909] A.C. 488 at 503). Finally, Lord Gorell applied traditional remoteness rules, in effect the two limbs of the rule in *Hadley v. Baxendale*. Under the second limb, the loss in respect of which the plaintiff sought damages had not been actually contemplated by the parties; under the first, the plaintiff was entitled to recover the net benefit of having the contract performed but not 'damages for the manner in which his discharge took place' ([1909] A.C. 488 at 501). Lord Collins dissented.

Hence, it would seem that the decision in *Addis* is to the effect that a plaintiff cannot recover damages for damage to the plaintiff's reputation or injury to the plaintiff's feelings arising from the manner of the breach of contract. In particular, it is the leading authority for the general rule that a plaintiff is not entitled to recover damages for mental distress in an action for breach of contract. The leading Irish case is the decision of the former Supreme Court in *Kinlen v. Ulster Bank* [1928] I.R. 171. The plaintiff had a current account in credit, but the bank refused to allow withdrawals or to cash cheques presented by the plaintiff; the bank was thus held to be in breach of contract, and the measure of damages payable was held to be the interest which the plaintiff would have had to pay to borrow the relevant amounts elsewhere. The plaintiff sought damages for injury to reputation and for mental distress. Kennedy C.J. accepted that damages for injury to reputation would be available for the wrongful dishonouring of a trading cheque presented by a third party payee to the bank, but unlike such three party cases, a 'demand made personally by a customer upon his banker is a two-party transaction. The refusal of payment cannot give rise to the implication of defamation . . .' and thus does not injure reputation. On the question of damages for mental distress, Kennedy C.J. held that it was well settled that 'in actions for breach of contract damages may not be given for such matters as disappointment of mind, humiliation, vexation, or the like . . .' ([1928] I.R. 171,184 *per* Kennedy C.J.; citing *Hamlin* and *Addis*). Hence, Kennedy C.J. held that in the case of a breach of a simple contract to pay money 'the measure of damages is a reasonable compensation for the non-performance of the contract . . . by allowing interest on the money [unpaid]'. However, in the case of a special contract 'where the money is to be paid for a special purpose known to the debtor, and injurious consequences of a particular character flow naturally from the non-payment' the plaintiff would be entitled to recover such special damages; but Kennedy C.J. held that no such special damages arose on the facts. Thus, as in *Addis*, the plaintiff failed to recover damages for damage to his reputation or injury to his feelings arising from the breach of contract.

To this general rule, however, there had always been exceptions. In *Addis* itself, Lord Atkinson accepted three ([1909] A.C. 488 at 495) as did Kennedy C.J. in *Kinlen* ([1928] I.R. 171 at 184); more recently, in the High Court of Australia in *Baltic Shipping v. Dillon (The Mikhail Lermontov)* Mason C.J. identified five ((1992–1993) 176 C.L.R. 344 at 362–363, Toohey and GaudronJJ. concurring; see also the judgment of McHugh J. at pp 397–404 tracing the history of the exceptions). The modern development of these exceptions begins with cases involving disastrous holidays. In *Jarvis v. Swans Tours* [1973] 1 All E.R. 71 (CA), the plaintiff booked a holiday through the defendant; it was very disappointing and certainly inferior to what he had expected based on the Swans Tours brochure. Lord Denning MR held that, in 'a proper case damages for mental distress can be recovered in contract . . . One such case is a contract for a holiday, or any other contract to provide entertainment or enjoyment. If the contracting party breaks his contract, damages can be given for the disappointment, the distress, the upset and frustration caused by the breach . . . Here, Mr Jarvis's fortnight winter holiday has been a grave disappointment. . . . He went to enjoy himself with all the facilities which the defendant said he would have. He is entitled to damages for the lack of those facilities, and for his loss of enjoyment.' ([1973] 1 All E.R. 71 at 74). In such a case, the plaintiff's 'expectations have been largely unfulfilled' ([1973] 1 All E.R. 71 at 76 *per* Edmund Davies L.J.), and 'damages for the breach of [the contract] should take such . . . inconvenience or discomfort into account ([1973] 1 All E.R. 71 at 77 *per* Stephenson L.J.). Furthermore, in *Jackson v. Horizon Holidays* [1975] 3 All E.R. 92 (CA) it was held that where the plaintiff booked a holiday for himself, his wife and his children, and the holiday was a disaster, the plaintiff can recover damages not only for his own disappointment and distress but also for that of his wife and children on whose behalf he had made the contract. ('Once recovered, it will be money had and received to their use . . . [so that he must] recompens[e] them accordingly out of what he recovers' [1975] 3 All E.R. 92 at 96 *per* Lord Denning MR). (These cases have been subsequently approved in *Ichard v. Frangoulis* [1977] 2 All E.R. 461 at 462 *per* Peter Pain J.; *Archer v. Brown* [1984] 2 All E.R. 267 at 281–282 *per* Peter Pain J.). And in *Baltic Shipping v. Dillon (The Mikhail Lermontov)* (1992–1993) 176 C.L.R. 344, Mrs Dillon was taking a pleasure cruise aboard the *Mikhail Lermontov* when it struck a shoal, was holed and sank; as a consequence, she lost some of her possessions and suffered some personal injuries. The High Court of Australia held that she was entitled to recover damages for the disappointment and distress occasioned by that shipwreck in breach of a contract the object of which was to provide for enjoyment and relaxation.

However, the cases in which plaintiffs have obtained such damages in actions for breach of contract are not confined to disastrous holidays. For example, in *Heywood v. Wellers* [1976] 1 All E.R. 300 (CA), the plaintiff had instructed the defendant firm of solicitors to seek a full injunction against a man who had stalked and molested her, and who repeatedly broke an interlocutory injunction. The facts amounted to a long tale of the serious mistakes made by the clerk in the firm who was dealing with her case, including negligent advice and his failure to apply for a final injunction or to bring the man's breaches of the interlocutory injunction before the court. In the plaintiff's action against the firm, Denning MR held that their negligence amounted to a breach of contract: 'owing to their want of care she was molested . . . on three or four occasions. This molestation caused her much mental distress and upset. It must have been in their contemplation that, if they failed in their duty, she might be further molested and suffer much upset and distress. This damage she suffered was within their contemplation within the rule in *Hadley v. Baxendale*. . . . Here Wellers were employed to protect her from molestation causing mental distress – and should be responsible in damages for their failure' ([1976] 1 All E.R. 300 at 306–307). And in *Cox v. Philips Industries* [1976] 3 All E.R. 161, the plaintiff had been offered alternative employment in a position of greater responsibility, and to retain his services, his employers, the defendants, agreed to give him a similar position. Some time later, in breach of contract, he was removed to a position of lesser responsibility in which his duties were extremely vague and were never clarified. 'The result of this was that the plaintiff became very depressed, extremely anxious and very frustrated. He began to have periods of sickness and depression' ([1976] 3 All E.R. 161 at 165). Lawson J. held that it was 'a case where in all the circumstances in the contemplation of the parties that, if that promise of a position of greater responsibility was breached, then the effect of that breach would be to expose the plaintiff to the degree of vexation, frustration and distress which he in fact underwent . . . I can see no reason in principle why, if a situation arise which within the contemplation of the parties would have given rise to vexation, distress and general disappointment and frustration, the person who is injured by a contractual breach should not be compensated in damages for that breach' ([1976] 3 All E.R. 161 at 166). Similarly, if it is correct to read the decision of Murphy J. in *Sullivan v. Southern Health Board* as suggesting that had the relevant term been implied such damages would have been properly awarded, then *Sullivan* is a case of this type.

Furthermore, it seems as a matter of Irish law that where a builder fails to provide a house consistent with the terms of the contract or persistently fails adequately to repair it, he will be liable for the physical discomfort and mental distress occasioned by the breach (see *Johnson v. Longleat Property* (High Court, May 19, 1976) where MacMahon J. applied *Jarvis v. Swan Tours*; the contemporary decision of McWilliam J. in *Murphy v. Quality Homes* (High

Court, June 22, 1976) is similar. And see the important analysis of *Johnson* in Clark 'Damages for Loss of Enjoyment and Inconvenience Resulting From Breach of Contract' (1978) XIII *Ir. Jur. (ns)* 186). Similarly, in *Perry v. Sidney Philips* [1982] 3 All E.R. 705 (CA) the plaintiff hired the defendants to survey a house he wished to buy. On foot of their report, he bought it; and soon discovered many defects. Denning MR held that the plaintiff was entitled to damages for the vexation, stress and worry caused by the defendants' breach of contract: if 'a man buys a house for his own occupation on the surveyor's advice that it is sound and then finds out that it is in a deplorably condition, it is reasonably foreseeable that he will be most upset . . . All this anxiety, worry and distress may nowadays be the subject of compensation. Not excessive, but modest compensation' ([1982] 3 All E.R. 705 at 709). Kerr L.J. concurring, held that the vexation and inconvenience were foreseeable physical consequences of the breach, and thus recoverable ([1982] 3 All E.R. 705 at 712).

At this point in the story, the position seems to be one of a general principle (precluding damages in contract for mental distress) the exceptions to which have been expansively applied. More recent English cases have taken a considerably narrower view. In *Bliss v. South East Thames Regional Health Authority* [1987] I.C.R. 700 (CA), the plaintiff was employed by the defendant as a consultant. Following what seemed to be an ongoing deterioration in the plaintiff's state of mind, which seemed to be demonstrated in particular in a course of correspondence over a six month period, the defendant, in April and May 1980, had required the plaintiff to submit to a psychiatric examination and had suspended him from duty for refusing to do so. In July 1981, a Committee of Inquiry having acquitted the plaintiff of the charges against him, the defendant withdrew the requirement of the examination and lifted the suspension. At first instance, it was held the request and suspension were without reasonable cause, and thus constituted a breach of contract, and, following the decision of Lawson J. in *Cox v. Philips Industries*, the plaintiff was awarded damages, *inter alia*, for frustration, vexation and distress from the circumstances of the breach of contract. On appeal, Dillon L.J. affirmed that the defendant was in breach of contract, but held that the views of Lawson J. in *Cox* were 'wrong' ([1987] I.C.R. 700 at 717) so that the plaintiff was not entitled to such damages:

> The general rule laid down by the House of Lords in *Addis v. Gramophone Co Ltd* [1909] A.C. 488 is that where damages fall to be assessed for breach of contract rather than in tort it is not permissible to award general damages for frustration, mental distress, injured feelings or annoyance occasioned by the breach. . . . There are exceptions now recognised where the contract which has been broken was itself a contract to provide peace of mind or freedom from distress: see *Jarvis v. Swans Tours* and *Heywood v. Wellers*. Those decisions do not however cover

this present case.

In *Cox v. Philips Industries* Lawson J. took the view that damages for distress, vexation and frustration, including consequent ill-health, could be recovered for breach of contract of employment if it could be said to have been in the contemplation of the parties that the breach would cause such distress etc. For my part, I do not think that that general approach is open to this court unless and until the House of Lords has reconsidered its decision in the *Addis* case. ([1987] ICR 700 at 717–718).

The earlier Irish decision of McWilliam J. in *Garvey v. Ireland*, High Court, December 19, 1979) seems to be to similar effect. Refusing to follow *Cox*, and accepting the decision in *Addis* instead, he held that 'unless some injury was occasioned to the plaintiff as a result of the wrongful removal from office which could reasonably have been foreseen by the defendants, I am of opinion that he is not entitled to any general damages under this heading'. Furthermore, *Bliss* was followed by the Court of Appeal in *Hayes v. Dodd* [1990] 2 All E.R. 815 (CA). The plaintiffs wished to purchase property to expand their business. The defendants were the plaintiffs' solicitors. The defendants informed the plaintiffs that they would have a right of way over adjoining property which was crucial for the business. The absence of that right of way led to the failure of the business. In the plaintiffs' action for breach of contract, the judge had awarded damages for anguish and vexation, but he was overturned on this by the Court of Appeal. For Staughton L.J., the 'law seem[ed] to be in some doubt', but he was wary of huge awards ([1990] 2 All E.R. 815 at 823). He pointed out that in *Perry v. Sidney Phillips*, Kerr L.J. had held that the vexation and inconvenience were foreseeable *physical consequences* of the breach, and thus recoverable and held that 'damages for mental distress are, for reasons of policy, limited to certain classes of case'. He approved Dillon L.J.'s classification in *Bliss* of contracts 'to provide peace of mind or freedom from distress' (as did Purchas L.J. at [1990] 2 All E.R. 815 at 826) and concluded that it 'may be that the class is somewhat wider than that. But it should not, in my judgment include any case where the object of the contract was not comfort or pleasure, or the relief [of] discomfort, but simply carrying on a commercial activity with a view to profit' [1990] 2 All E.R. 815 at 824). Furthermore, in *Watts v. Morrow* [1991] 4 All E.R. 937 (CA) the plaintiffs hired the defendant to survey a country house they wished to buy, explaining that they wanted a house which, apart from regular maintenance, would not require refurbishment. He advised them that the defects in the house could be dealt with by regular maintenance. They bought it; and soon discovered considerably more – and much more serious – defects that had been outlined in the defendant's report. In their action for breach of contract, the plaintiffs argued that since they both had stressful occupations, weekend relaxation in their country house was essential but was unavailable for the eight months they spent in a veritable building site while their house was being repaired and refurbished. The judge had awarded damages for the 'distress, worry, vexation and inconvenience' but he was overturned on this by the Court of Appeal. For Ralph Gibson L.J., it was clear 'that the plaintiffs were not entitled to recover general damages for mental distress not caused by physical discomfort or inconvenience resulting from the breach of contract' ([1991] 4 All E.R. 937 at 955, upon which basis he explained the decision in *Perry v. Sidney Phillips* by reference to the decision of Kerr L.J. in that case). Furthermore, it would be 'impossible [to] view the ordinary surveyor's contract' as one to provide peace of mind or freedom from distress 'within the meaning of Dillon L.J.'s phrase in *Bliss*' ([1991] 4 All E.R. 937 at 956). Bingham L.J. came to a similar conclusion:

> A contract-breaker is not in general liable for any distress, frustration, anxiety, displeasure, vexation, tension or aggravation which his breach of contract may cause to the innocent party. This rule is not founded on the assumption that such reactions are not foreseeable, which they surely are or may be, but on considerations of policy.

> But the rule is not absolute. Where the very object of a contract is to provide pleasure, relaxation, peace of mind or freedom from molestation, damages will be awarded if the fruit of the contract is not provided or if the contrary result is procured instead. . . . A contract to survey the condition of a house for a prospective purchaser does not, however, fall into this exceptional category. ([1991] 4 All E.R. 937 at 959–560).

However, this storyline of retrenchment has not been much followed outside of England. In New Zealand, Canada, and Australia, the general rule has only reluctantly been accepted, the exceptions have been interpreted widely, and there is a discernible movement to abandon the general rule altogether.

In *Horsburgh v. New Zealand Meat Processors Industrial Union of Workers* [1988] 1 N.Z.L.R. 698, Cooke P. refused to extend *Addis* and awarded damages for mental distress for expulsion from a trade union, on the grounds that a 'reasonably substantial award should be made for knowingly unlawful deprivation of status and interference with the right to work' but was careful to 'refrain from suggesting that damages for mental distress can be awarded in . . . an action for breach of an ordinary commercial contract . . .'. (see [1988] 1 N.Z.L.R. 698 at 701–703). In *Hetherington v. Faudet* [1989] 2 N.Z.L.R. 224 Cooke P. again called *Addis* into question ([1989] 2 N.Z.L.R. 224 at 227). And, in *Whelan v. Waitaki Meats* [1991] 2 N.Z.L.R. 74, in an action by an employee for damages for breach of his contract of employment, Gallen J., after a comprehensive review of the authorities in England, Canada and New

Zealand, and reference to academic discussion, declined to follow *Addis*: to the extent that it stated a rule against general damages for breach of contract, he did 'not think that it can now be said to be a tenable proposition and it is difficult in any event . . . to see why it should be' ([1991] 2 N.Z.L.R. 74 at 88). Hence, 'when parties enter into a contract which affects one of them personally, then that involves consequences which can properly reflect in the award of damages . . .' ([1991] 2 N.Z.L.R. 74 at 89). In the event, Gallen J. found an implied term that the employer would not dismiss the employee in a manner which would occasion distress, and therefore awarded damages to the employee for mental distress from breach of that term. Furthermore, in *Rowlands v. Collow* [1992] 1 N.Z.L.R. 178, Thomas J. followed a similar path, rejected *Hayes v. Dodd*, and argued that 'the rule in *Addis* is contrary to settled principle relating to the assessment of damages, and it is open to the Court to apply that settled principle, certainly in preference to an ailing authority' ([1992] 1 N.Z.L.R. 178 at 206), where the relevant settled principle were the rules relating to causation and remoteness. In particular, Thomas J. rejected the contemporary narrow English position of confining damages for mental distress to particular categories of case:

> limiting damages for mental distress to certain classes of case when the damages would otherwise come within the general principles applicable to damages in contract is both unnecessary and unwise. Rather, the question of whether or not such damages are recoverable should be resolved in terms of the test of remoteness as it might be articulated from time to time. If it is, the damage which has been contemplated should be met by an appropriate award of damages. . . . It may therefore be timely for the Courts to reassert in this context the basic principles relating to remoteness of damages. If this is done the question in relation to all contracts is whether mental distress was a reasonably foreseeable consequence of the breach of contract or was within the reasonable contemplation of the parties in respect of any such breach at the time they entered into the contract. With commercial contracts it is most unlikely that such damage will have been foreseeable or within the parties' contemplation with contracts of a more personal nature, mental distress could well be a foreseeable consequence and within the contemplation of the parties. ([1992] 1 N.Z.L.R. 178 at 207).

Hence, at its high water mark in New Zealand, the trend against *Addis* was to replace it with 'the application of the ordinary principles of remoteness in assessing loss' ([1992] 1 N.Z.L.R. 178 at 208); and on the facts, the test in *Hadley v. Baxendale* was 'readily met' (*id*). And in *Mouat v. Clark Boyce* [1992] 2 N.Z.L.R. 559 (NZ CA), Richardson J. seemed to approve of this development. Nevertheless, there has been a retrenchment in New Zealand parallel to that in England. Thus, for example, in *Mouat v. Clark Boyce*, Cooke P., who had begun the above trend by questioning the authority of *Addis*, revisited the issue, and concluded that, though there are some contract (and other) cases in which foreseeable distress has been an element of the award, nevertheless, the courts

> have stopped short of giving stress damages for breach of ordinary commercial contracts. Such damages may be foreseeable, but I think that the restriction may be seen as justifiable by policy. Stress is an ordinary incident of commercial or professional life. Ordinary commercial contracts are not intended to shelter the parties from anxiety. By contrast one of the very purposes of imposing duties on professional persons to take reasonable care to safeguard the interests of their clients is to enable the clients to have justified faith in them ([1992] 2 N.Z.L.R. 559, 569; this point was not considered on further appeal to the Privy Council ([1993] 4 All E.R. 268 (PC)).

The third judge in the case, Gault J., expressed no opinion on this point. And in the slightly later case of *Watson v. Dolmark Industries* [1992] 3 N.Z.L.R. 311, Cooke P. held that since it was 'a commercial case, so an award for injury to feelings is prima facie inappropriate' [1992] 3 N.Z.L.R. 311 at 316. Most recently, in *Bloxham v. Robinson* [1996] 2 N.Z.L.R. 664n (CA), the Court of Appeal (McKay and TemmJJ.; Thomas J. dissenting) held that the contract-breaker was not liable for any emotional distress caused to the innocent party by his breach of contract because in a commercial case, an award for injury to feelings would be *prima facie* inappropriate, following *Addis*, *Watts v. Morrows* and *Watson v. Dolmark Industries*, and not *Rowlands v. Callow*. It is, however, unfortunate that there is only a note of the judgment.

It would seem therefore that the New Zealand cases present three views: a rigid application of *Addis* and narrow exceptions (*Bloxham*); a critique of *Addis* and its non-application in non-commercial cases (the approach of Cooke P); and the abrogation of *Addis* and the full application the rules of causation and remoteness to the issue of the availability of damages for mental distress (*Rowlands v. Callow*). A similar range of views is to be found in the leading decision in the Supreme Court of Canada: *Vorvis v. Insurance Corp. of British Columbia* (1989) 58 D.L.R. (4th) 193 (see Swan (1990) 16 *Can Bus L.J.* 213). That court had earlier accepted the authority of *Addis* (*Peso Silver Mines v. Cropper* (1966) 58 D.L.R. (2d) 1), but many lower court decisions (collected in Fridman *The Law of Contract in Canada* (3rd ed., 1994) pp 735–744) had found ways to award damages for mental distress; and in *Vorvis*, the foundations of *Addis* were further substantially eroded. For example, the majority (McIntyre J.; Beetz and Lamer JJ. concurring) concluded that both 'aggravated damages' and 'punitive damages' may be awarded in actions for breach of contract in an appropriate case, where the breach of contract resulted in an 'actionable wrong' ((1989) 58 D.L.R. (4th) 193 at 204–207). And, although McIntyre J. purported to accept *Addis* and *Peso* (((1989) 58 D.L.R. (4th) 193 at 209) he also adopted the broad English cases on damages for mental distress (e.g. *Jarvis, Heywood,* and *Cox*: (1989) 58 D.L.R. (4th) 193 at 204). Hence the majority adopted the broader English view rather than the narrower. The minority went even further. Wilson J. (L'Heureux-Dubé J. concurring) separated the issues of damages for mental distress and punitive damages, but rejected the 'actionable wrong' test for both. On the former issue, argued that 'the common denominator' of the cases in which damages for mental distress have been awarded 'is the notion that the parties should reasonably have foreseen mental suffering as a consequence of a breach of the contract at the time the contract was entered into' (1989) 58 D.L.R. (4th) 193 at 213; *cp.* 'the basic principles of contract relating to remoteness of damage' *id* at pp 215–216). Hence, she rejected *Cox, Bliss and Hayes* v. *Dodds* in favour of the principles in *Hadley v. Baxendale*; and would have awarded damages for mental distress on that basis. However, though she accepted that there was a jurisdiction to award punitive damages, she held that the breach was not on the facts sufficient ('shockingly harsh, vindictive, reprehensible and malicious': (1989) 58 D.L.R. (4th) 193 at 224). Hence, on the question of the availability of damages for mental distress, the majority adopted a wide view of cases such as *Jarvis, Heywood,* and *Cox*; the minority went even further, being prepared to impose liability on the basis of the ordinary rules of remoteness. In the more recent *Wallace v. United Grain Growers* [1997] 3 SCR 701 (SCC), Iacobucci J. for the majority (Lamer C.J., Sopinka, Gonthier, Cory, and Major JJ. concurring) affirmed the majority position in *Vorvis*; as it seems did McLachlin J. for the minority (La Forest and L'Heureux-Dubé JJ. concurring).

A similar range of views is to be seen in the High Court of Australia in *Baltic Shipping v. Dillon (The Mikhail Lermontov)* (1992–1993) 176 C.L.R. 344 (HCA), where the plaintiff recovered damages for the disappointment and distress occasioned by the shipwreck of her pleasure cruise ship. Mason C.J. (Toohey and GaudronJJ. concurring) strongly criticised the general bar on the recovery of such damages, and thought that the merits of Wilson J's approach in *Vorvis* were obvious, but concluded that since the plaintiff's distress and disappointment if the defendant does not perform 'are seldom so significant as to attract an award of damages . . . it is preferable to adopt the rule that damages for disappointment and distress are not recoverable unless they proceed from physical inconvenience caused by the breach or unless the contract the object of which is to provide enjoyment, relaxation or freedom from molestation' ((1992–1993) 176 C.L.R. 344 at 356). McHugh J. went further still; for him if the matter 'were free from authority, the object of an award of damages for breach of contract and the principles of causation and remoteness would require the conclusion' that damages mental distress would ordinarily be available, even if 'in most cases, the disappointment would be so negligible that the damage suffered could be regarded as *de minimis* and ignored' ((1992–1993) 176 C.L.R. 344 at 404). He traced *Addis* and its exceptions, and held that even though the rule had stood for almost a century it would still be open to the High Court to hold that damages for mental distress in contract ought to be generally available and not subject to any special rules. However, he declined to make a final decision on the question as counsel for Mrs Dillon had not argued it, and instead held the question over for another occasion, adopting for the purposes of the case before him a test similar to that of the Chief Justice, awarding damages for mental distress for breach of 'breach of an express or implied term [of the contract] that the promisor will provide the promisee with pleasure or enjoyment or personal protection or if it is consequent upon the suffering of physical injury or physical inconvenience' ((1992–1993) 176 C.L.R. 344 at 405). On the other hand, in the same case, Deane and DawsonJJ. (in a joint judgment) '[n]otwithstanding that the [general] rule is based upon pragmatism rather than logic, . . . [we]re unable to agree with the suggestion to be found in some recent judgments that it should now be effectively abolished by judicial decision' ((1992–1993) 176 C.L.R. 344 at 381) and instead adopted a test similar to that of Mason C.J. And Brennan J. went further, strongly defending, on grounds of policy, the approach based upon the general bar moderated by exceptions, so that the general principle 'has no application when . . . 'the disappointment of mind' is itself the 'direct consequence of the breach contract'. In such a case the disappointment is not merely a reaction to the breach and resultant damage but is itself the resultant damage' ((1992–1993) 176 C.L.R. 344 at 369–370).

The cases outside of England do not speak with one voice. But there is nonetheless a broad consistency: *Addis*, if it is accepted, is followed with reluctance; the exceptions have, more often than not, been interpreted widely, and there is a discernible movement to abandon the general rule altogether. More precisely, there is some small degree of support for a rigid application of *Addis* and a small number of narrow exceptions, often expressed for policy reasons (*Bloxham*; Brennan J. in *The Mikhail Lermontov*). But a common position is a wide view of the exceptions (the majority in *Vorvis*; the Supreme Court of Canada in *Wallace*, Deane and DawsonJJ. in *The Mikhail Lermontov*) often as the second best solution of those who would prefer to abolish the rule in *Addis* altogether (Mason C.J. and McHugh J. in *The Mikhail Lermontov*). Another common position among the critics of *Addis* is to confine it to commercial cases, allowing the recovery of damages for mental distress in noncommercial cases (the approach of Cooke P. in New Zealand). And there are the critics who would have no truck with such half-way houses, and would simply apply the rules of causation and remoteness to the issue of the availability of damages for mental distress (Gallen J. in *Rowlands v. Callow*; Wilson J. in *Vorvis*).

Given the divergence of views, this is an issue which will not be resolved solely by reference to precedent. Simply as a matter of Irish law, *Kinlen* and *Garvey* state the uncompromising *Addis* rule, and it may be that *Kelly v. Crowley* does too (on this see below). On the other hand, a wide view of the *Jarvis* exception was taken in the building cases (*Johnson, Murphy*), and in n *Lennon v. Talbot* (High Court, unreported, 20 December 1985) Keane J. perceived no difficulty with awarding (admittedly 'modest') damages for mental distress. The defendant was a car manufacturer; the plaintiffs had been dealers in the defendant's cars. The defendant had wrongfully terminated the dealership agreements with the plaintiffs, and those plaintiffs who claimed damages for the distress and anxiety caused by the defendant's breach of contract were successful, though Keane J. thought the damages 'must inevitably be of a modest order . . .'. And in *Smith v. Custom House Docks Development Authority* (High Court, March 20, 1997, McGuinness J.) awarded general damages for breach of a contract by which the plaintiff had been employed as a quantity surveyor by the defendant on a prominent building project. Any resolution of the issue must therefore revisit the basis in logic and in policy of the general rule and exceptions announced in *Addis*.

As to the precedent upon which the general rule is constructed, *Addis* has not fared well. In *Malik v. BCCI* [1997] 3 All E.R. 1 (HL), it came under a sustained attack on many levels. Lord Steyn observed that the 'true *ratio decidendi* of the House of Lords decision in *Addis v. Gramophone Co Ltd* has long been debated' ([1997] 3 All E.R. 1 at 19) and that the 'speeches are not always easy to follow' ([1997] 3 All E.R. 1 at 20). Further, Lord Nicholls observed that the 'report of the facts in *Addis's* case is sketchy' ([1997] 3 All E.R. 1 at 9) and that the 'House [wa]s not bound by the observations in *Addis* . . .' ([1997] 3 All E.R. 1 at 11). And in the event *Addis* was radically reinterpreted and significantly read down. It is an implied term of every employment contract that the parties will not engage in conduct likely to undermine the mutual trust and confidence required if the employment relationship is to continue (see e.g. Brodie (1996) 25 *ILJ* 121 cited in *Malik*). In *Malik*, Lord Steyn regarded its emergence as a sound development of the law ([1997] 3 All E.R. 1 at 16) and the House of Lords unanimously held that as a consequence of such an implied term, an employer is under a duty not to conduct a dishonest or corrupt business. If the employer does in fact carry on a dishonest and corrupt business, the employee can suffer prejudice to his future employment prospects from having been innocently involved with the dishonest and corrupt business. In *Malik*, two employees of BCCI, which had been carrying on such a business, sought such damages from the liquidator of BCCI. Lord Nicholls held that 'if it was reasonably foreseeable that a particular type of loss of this character was a serious possibility, and loss of this type is sustained in consequence of a breach, then in principle, damages in respect of the loss should be recoverable' ([1997] 3 All E.R. 1 at 7; compare Lord Steyn at p.17g).

The employees had characterised their claim was as one for stigma compensation, which amounted to a claim for damages for injury to professional reputation. Hence, the liquidator argued that such a head of loss was excluded by *Addis* Lord Nicholls observed that the 'case is generally regarded as having decided . . . that an employee cannot recover damages for the manner in which the wrongful dismissal took place, for injured feelings or for any loss he may sustain from the fact that his having been dismissed of itself makes it more difficult for him to obtain fresh employment' ([1997] 3 All E.R. 1 at 8). However, in the view of Lord Nicholls, the observations of Lord Loreborn LC in *Addis* 'cannot be read as precluding the recovery of damages where the manner of dismissal involved a beach of the trust and confidence term and this caused financial loss. *Addis v. Gramophone Co Ltd* was decided in the days before this implied term was adumbrated. Now that this term exists and is normally implied into every contract of employment, damages for its breach should be assessed in accordance with ordinary contractual principles.' ([1997] 3 All E.R. 1 at 9).

Lord Steyn accepted that the majority in *Addis* 'apparently thought that they were applying a special rule applicable to awards for wrongful dismissal. It is, however, far from clear how far the *ratio* of *Addis's* case extends. . . . The actual decision is only concerned with wrongful dismissal. It is therefore arguable that as a matter of precedent the *ratio* is so restricted. But it seems to me unrealistic not to acknowledge that *Addis's* case is authority for a wider principle . . . that damages for breach of contract may only be awarded for breach of contract, and not for loss caused by the manner of the breach . . . *Addis's* case simply decided that the loss of reputation in that particular case could not be compensated because it was not caused by a breach of contract: see Nelson Enonchong 'Contract Damages for Injury to Reputation' (1996) 59 *M.L.R.* 592 at 596' ([1997] 3 All E.R. 1 at 20). Thus, *Addis* does not preclude damages for injury to reputation caused by the breach of contract, and did not bar the claims in *Malik*. Hence, Lord Steyn concluded: '[p]rovided that a relevant breach of contract can be established, and the requirements of causation, remoteness and mitigation can be satisfied, there is no good reason why in the field of employment law recovery of financial loss in respect of damage to reputation caused by breach of contract is necessarily excluded' ([1997] 3 All E.R. 1 at 21).

On its traditional reading, the decision in *Addis* was to the effect that a plaintiff cannot recover damages for damage to the plaintiff's reputation or injury to the plaintiff's feelings arising from the manner of the breach of contract. As explained by Lord Steyn in *Malik*, however, the decision in *Addis* was simply that the loss of reputation in that particular case could not be compensated because it was not caused by a breach of contract; so that, if a loss of reputation was caused by a breach of contract, it could be compensated. By parity of reasoning, therefore, if the decision in *Addis* was simply that the injury to the plaintiff's feelings in that particular case could not be compensated because it was not caused by a breach of contract, if the injury to feelings was caused by a breach of contract, it could be compensated.

Furthermore, Lord Steyn's reinterpretation of *Addis* in *Malik* might be pressed into service to explain the decision of Kennedy C.J. in *Kinlen v. Ulster Bank* [1928] I.R. 171. He accepted that damages for injury to reputation are available for the wrongful dishonouring of a trading cheque presented by a third party payee to the bank, but were unavailable where the plaintiff himself directly presented the cheque to the bank, because there is no injury to the plaintiff's reputation as a matter of fact in such a two-party case. (Drawing an analogy with defamation proper, there is no publication, and thus no injury to reputation). Hence, *Kinlen* simply decided that there was no injury to the plaintiff's reputation flowing from the breach of contract on the facts of the case. As with *Malik*, the loss of reputation in *Kinlen* could not be compensated simply because it was not caused by a breach of contract on the facts, and not because of a general rule against damages for such loss. It follows that if a loss of reputation was caused by a breach of contract, it can be compensated. Furthermore, in *Kinlen*, Kennedy C.J. having excluded damages for mental distress, went on to hold that the plaintiff could have damages 'if he pleads and proves that he has suffered special damage flowing naturally in the circumstances from the banker's breach of contract' ([1928] I.R. 171 at 185); there is almost the implication that damages for mental distress would have been available on the latter test, so that their prior exclusion was simply a conclusion that any mental distress in *Kinlen* could not be compensated because it was too remote on the facts, and not because of a general rule against damages for such loss. It follows that if mental distress is specially foreseen, it too can be compensated. Similarly, in *Garvey v. Ireland* where McWilliam J. purported to follow *Addis*, the *ratio* of his decision was to the effect that 'unless some injury was occasioned to the plaintiff as a result of the wrongful removal from office *which could reasonably have been foreseen by the defendants*, I am of opinion that he is not entitled to any general damages' (emphasis added); from which it follows that if such injury could reasonably have been foreseen by the defendants, the plaintiff would have been entitled to such damages. Thus reinterpreted, far from precluding the availability of damages for mental distress for breach of contract, both *Kinlen* and *Garvey* support the view that such damages are recoverable if the mental distress is actually foreseen by the parties, and is thus within the second limb of the rule in *Hadley v. Baxendale*.

Whether or not *Kinlen* and *Garvey* are capable of such reinterpretation, Lord Steyn in *Malik* demonstrated that *Addis* certainly is. Hence, a leading case in favour of the general rule does not mandate it. On the level simply of precedent, the decision of McWilliam J. in *Garvey* and the decision of Dillon L.J. in *Bliss*, rejecting *Cox* and taking a narrow view of exceptions to the general rule on the basis of *Addis*, must therefore be called into question (as, of course, must those cases following them). This issue was squarely before the Supreme Court in *Sullivan v. Southern Health Board*, as the appellant sought to overturn the award of general damages by reference to *Bliss* and the respondent sought to defend it by reference to *Cox* ([1997] 3 I.R. 123 at 125). If, as argued above, it is correct to read the decision of Murphy J. as suggesting that had the relevant term been implied, such damages would have been properly awarded, then *Sullivan* is consistent with the rejection of *Garvey* and *Bliss*. In any event, it is clear that the classic authorities in favour of the rule that damages for mental distress are not usually available for breach of contract are very tenuous. Hence, many of the modern statements of the rule justify it by reference to policy (*e.g.* Bingham L.J. in *Watts v. Morrow*, Cooke P in *Mouat v. Clark Boyce*). In *The Mikhail Lermontov*, Brennan J. identified that policy as based upon a fear inflated awards:

> The institution of contract, by which parties are empowered to create a charter of their rights and obligations inter se, can operate effectively only if the parties, at the time when they create their charter, can form estimate of liability in the event of default in performance. But no approximate estimate of liability could be formed if the subjective mental reaction of an innocent party to a breach and resultant damage were added on as further damage without proof of pecuniary loss by the innocent party. If the mental reaction to breach and resultant damage were itself a head of damage, the liability of a party in breach would be at large and liable to fluctuation according to personal situation of the innocent party. If a promisor were exposed to such an indefinite liability in the event of breach, the making of commercial contracts would be inhibited, the assignment of a contractual right would carry new risks for the party subject to the reciprocal obligation, and trade and commerce would be seriously impeded. ((1992–1993) 176 C.L.R. 344 at 369)

In this rationale, he was reflecting the views of Lord Atkinson in *Addis* and of Pollock CB in the earlier *Hamlin v. Great Northern Rly* (1856) 1 H&N 408; 156 E.R. 1261. Lord Atkinson saw as the reason for the general rule the 'confusion and uncertainty in commercial affairs' ([1909] A.C. 488 at 495) which would follow from the availability of damages for mental distress for breach of contract. Pollock CB, requiring that damages for breach of contract must be 'capable of being appreciated or estimated', held that such damages for mental distress 'cannot be stated specifically' ((1856) 1 H&N 408 at 411; 156 E.R. 1261 at 1262). Similarly, Staughton L.J. in *Hayes v. Dodd* was 'wary of adopting . . . the United States practice of huge awards . . .' ([1990] 2 All E.R. 815 at 823) which he saw as inherent in such damages.

Thus, the policy identified in the cases as justifying the general rule against damages for mental distress for breach of contract is a fear of high damages, especially, it seems, in commercial cases. However, this may prove too much, since it precludes all such damages, whereas even the modern judgments which articulate this policy use it to justify a very narrow approach to the exceptions to the general rule, confining the availability of damages for mental distress to breaches of a contract where 'the very object of a contract is to provide pleasure, relaxation, peace of mind or freedom from molestation, . . . [and] . . . the fruit of the contract is not provided or if the contrary result is procured instead' (*Watts v. Morrow* [1991] 4 All E.R. 937 at 960 *per* Bingham L.J. approved in *The Mikhail Lermontov* ((1992–1993) 176 C.L.R. 344 at 371 *per* Brennan J., 382 *per* Deane and Dawson JJ.). This is inconsistent: either the rule is justified by the policy, and the exception is precluded; or the exception is admitted and the policy is precluded. If the latter, then the policy underlying the general rule is called into question and an alternative explanation of both the general rule and the exception is required. This is the preferable course since the fear of high damages for mental distress seems misplaced. Although Brennan J. in *The Mikhail Lermontov* feared that 'if the mental reaction to breach and resultant damage were itself a head of damage, the liability of a party in breach would be at large and liable to fluctuation according to personal situation of the innocent party' as McHugh J. pointed out in the same case, 'in most cases, the disappointment would be so negligible that the damage suffered could be regarded as *de minimis* and ignored' ((1992–1993) 176 C.L.R. 344 at 404). Further, the experience of the law of tort is such that damages for pain and suffering can be sufficiently well estimated; if there, so here. Furthermore, if there is reality in the policy of fear of inflated awards, it can be easily addressed by admitting such a head of damages but confining the awards: as Denning MR observed in *Perry v. Sidney Philips* what is to be awarded under this head is '[n]ot excessive, but modest compensation'. Such temperance is not unknown in Irish law: in *Kinlen v. Ulster Bank* Kennedy C.J. accepted, as one of the exceptions to the general rule, that damages for injury to reputation are available for the wrongful dishonouring of a cheque, and stressed that such damages may be 'substantial, though temperate and reasonable' ([1928] I.R. 171 at 183). If the Irish courts can make such a determination here, they can be equally astute to keep such damages 'temperate and reasonable' in the general context of damages for mental distress. Thus, for example, in *Lennon v. Talbot,* High Court, December 20, 1985) Keane J. found that the defendant car manufacturer's breach of contract with the plaintiff car dealers caused some of the plaintiffs distress and anxiety, but held that the damages 'must inevitably be of a modest order . . .'. And in New Zealand, where the courts for a time strained against *Addis* and awarded such compensation, the awards were 'decidedly modest' (*Rowlands v. Collow* [1992] 1 NZLR 178 at 207 *per* Thomas J.). Similarly, as Wilson J. commented in *Vorvis v. Insurance Corp. of British Columbia*, 'the fear of unrealistic or unfair awards for mental distress in breach of contract cases is not really warranted by anything that ha[d] happened to date' in Canada ((1989) 58 D.L.R. (4th) 193 at 218). Since damages for mental distress can be confined to relatively modest sums, the fear of high awards evaporates, and with it the policy justification for the general rule against damages for mental distress for breach of contract.

On the other hand, if high awards of damage for mental distress are appropriate, they ought to be available. Perhaps that is the moral to be drawn from the decision of McGuinness J. in *Smith v. Custom House Docks Development Authority* (High Court, March 20, 1997) in which expectation damages of £30,000 and 'general damages for breach of contract' of £50,000 were awarded. On January 25, 1988, the defendant authority agreed with a development consortium that the consortium would develop the Custom House Docks area according to the terms of a Master Project Agreement Building Programme. The plaintiff had acted as quantity surveyor for the defendant in 1987 and 1988, on an informal basis as and when the defendant required, in particular in connection with developing the building programme and drafting a Monitoring and Action Schedule thereto dealing with monitoring the consortium's work. Seeking to put his employment with the defendant on a more formal basis, on July 21, 1988 the plaintiff sent to the defendant a letter, headed MPA Building Programme, offering to carry out construction management activities on the programme – in effect monitoring the consortium's work on behalf of the defendant – for certain hourly rates, to be increased annually for inflation. On July 23, 1988, the plaintiff sent an alternative proposal to the defendant to supply the same services for a percentage of the construction costs. An hourly rate was acceptable to the defendant; a percentage was not. According to the terms of an internal memorandum, the Development Director of the defendant recommended to the Chairman that the plaintiff's charges 'be accepted as reasonable' and that he be engaged 'for the period of the MPA'. The plaintiff came to understand that the hourly rates in the July 21, 1988 letter were agreed, and issued invoices to the defendant, headed MPA Building Programme, according to the terms of that letter. In November 1988, the defendant negotiated a reduction of the plaintiff's overall level of fees; the plaintiff re-adjusted fees already paid to him to take account of the lower rates, and sent a credit note in the difference to the defendant. Work proceeded at those rates; the defendant allowed one increase for inflation but refused further such increases. Then, in late 1991 and early 1992, the defendant decided to retain another firm of quantity surveyors, commenced a tendering process, and appointed another firm. On 6 March 1992, the defendant orally informed the plaintiff that his services were no longer required, and on May 19, he ceased to carry out any work for the defendant.

The plaintiff argued that he had been appointed on foot of his letter of July 21, 1988; that it was an express or implied term of that contract that his services would be retained for the entire period of the construction and development which was to take place pursuant to the building programme; that the defendant had wrongfully terminated the contract in May 1992 when only 36% of the work specified in the building programme had been completed; and that he was entitled to be compensated for the fact that he should have been employed in the same way for the remaining 64% of the work. The defendant argued that the plaintiff had merely been appointed on an 'as required' basis, since that was the basis of his work in 1987 and 1988, and the Monitoring and Action Schedule to the building programme referred to the monitoring being carried out by 'members of the Authority's own staff, supplemented by specialist advisors as required'.

McGuinness J. felt that it 'was most undesirable that the appointment of the plaintiff to carry out an important part of the crucial work of monitoring the MPA [building programme] should have been carried out in such a confused and informal manner, without any form of advertising or tendering process or any formal written contract or letter of appointment' (pp 28–29). Since there was 'an unresolvable conflict of evidence' as to the terms of the contract, McGuinness held that it fell 'to the court to endeavour to interpret the contract from the documentation available and the surrounding facts' (p 30). She held that, in July 1988, the plaintiff 'intended his proposal to cover the entire MPA Building Programme', pointed to the text of the internal memorandum, and accepted the plaintiff's evidence that 'in persuading him to accept a reduction in fees and, more strikingly, a re-adjustment of fees already paid to him, there was at least an implication and probably a positive assertion that he would have security and continuity of employment'. Furthermore, the relevant sentence in the Schedule referred 'more logically . . . to the fluctuating nature of the plaintiff's work during the period of the MPA' than to his appointment on an 'as required' basis. Hence, McGuinness J. found that 'there was a contract . . . whereby the plaintiff was appointed as a quantity surveying consultant to the . . . [defendant] for the period of the Master Project Agreement . . .'.

The original agreement had provided for a five year period for the project. The plaintiff claimed that 'this 'period' should include all possible time extensions envisaged in the Master Project Agreement. At times he also suggest[ed.] that the 'the period of the MPA' should mean the entire time until all the buildings planned in the original agreement were completed' (p.33). McGuinness J. rejected this interpretation for three reasons: first, because in 'an area so uncertain as the building industry, no employer could conceivably bind himself or herself to such a contract'; second, 'it is impossible to accept a contact that would be potentially infinite in its timespan', and third, the plans for the site had vastly changed since the MPA had been executed in 1988. Instead, she interpreted the phrase 'the period of the MPA' to mean the basic five year period covered by the initial MPA building programme, from January 25, 1988 to January 25, 1993, until which date the plaintiff had a right to continue to be employed as a quantity surveyor by the defendant. As to the level of damages to which the plaintiff was therefore entitled, McGuinness J. rejected as 'bordering on the fanciful' (p.35) calculations starting from the point that 36% of the work in the MPA building programme was completed in May 1982, or based upon possible profits from other jobs which the plaintiff claimed he could have obtained had he not been working for the defendant, both of which calculations resulted 'in a claim in the region of half a million pounds'. Instead, she held that the plaintiff's losses 'must be based on [her] finding that he should have been employed by the defendant to all required quantity surveying work under the original MPA Agreement until it expired in January 1993' including 'the yearly inflation-related increase set out in his original proposal, which could in total 'be expressed in a round figure of £30,000' (pp.35–36). The plaintiff also sought 'general damages for breach of contract', for which McGuinness J. awarded £50,000 in part because 'the termination of his employment must, to some extent have affected [the plaintiff's] general business' and in part for what amounts to mental distress:

> the plaintiff was placed in an extremely awkward position by the behaviour of the defendant. During the early period of 1992 his competitors in the quantity surveying business were well aware that he was about to be dismissed from his employment with the defendant before he had any information on the subject. He was not given any chance whatsoever to tender for the work that was subsequently carried out by [the other quantity surveyors] . . . the plaintiff should at least have been given an opportunity to make his case as to his abilities and resources for carrying out this work and to tender for it.

> Given the nature of Irish business and Irish society generally, I have no doubt that the dismissal of the plaintiff from the defendant's employment must have been something of a 'nine day's wonder' to others in the quantity surveying business and the construction industry generally, particularly in view of the fact that the Custom House Docks Project was so high profile. (pp 36–37).

It might be said that the award of £50,000 was significantly out of line with those many authorities which emphasise that damages for mental distress for breach of contract ought to be temperate and modest, even allowing that that figure also included a sum for the effects the termination had upon the plaintiff's business. On the other hand, it was the view of McGuinness J. that the plaintiff seems to have been sufficiently badly treated by the defendant to justify such an award of 'general damages'; and it might therefore be said that *Smith* illustrates the view that if a high award is justified it should be made, even where such awards in general should be temperate and modest.

The policy against high damages is perceived to be especially strong in precluding such damages in commercial cases. Thus, it might be thought that the rule in *Addis* might be reserved to commercial cases; while effect might be given to the criticisms of the rule in *Addis* above by allowing damages for mental distress for breach of a non-commercial contracts. This would be consistent with the disastrous holiday cases and their ilk, and this is a position at which the New Zealand courts seem to have arrived. There might be said to be some warrant for drawing such a distinction as a matter of Irish law in the judgment of Murphy J. in *Kelly v. Crowley* [1985] I.R. 212, who argued in respect of mental distress arising out breach of contract that 'damage of that nature is not reasonably foreseeable. No doubt all commercial contracts carry a considerable stress . . . but I do not think it gives rise to any additional claim for damage' ([1985] I.R. 212 at 231). This passage implies first, that the reason why the damage was not reasonably foreseeable is because the contract was a commercial contract, so that if it were not a commercial contract such damage could be reasonably foreseeable; and second, that if damage were reasonably foreseeable, then it would have been recoverable. Hence, it might be thought that this *dictum* of Murphy J. in *Kelly v. Crowley* has the potential to distinguish between commercial and non-commercial contract and allow the recovery of damages for mental distress for breaches of the latter contracts.

On the other hand, in *The Mikhail Lermontov*, Mason C.J. (Toohey and Gaudron JJ. concurring) argued that the 'distinction is by no means easy to draw and, in any event, it is not a distinction which should necessarily be decisive in determining whether such damages are available or not' ((1992–1993) 176 C.L.R. 344 at 366; cp. p.381 *per* Deane and Dawson JJ.). The first point, that the distinction is difficult to draw, is weak in so far as it is a distinction which courts are often required to draw (it is required by the Unfair Contract Terms Directive) and one which they have often been prepared to draw in other contexts; for example, in *Cue Club v. Navaro*, Supreme Court, October 23, 1996, where Murphy J. was less inclined to relieve against forfeiture in the case of commercial transactions where the parties were on equal terms. The second point, that it is not a distinction which ought to be decisive in this context, is rather more compelling. If the fear of high awards can be met by confining damages for mental distress for breach of contract to modest sums in most cases, the entire policy fails, and therefore provides no warrant against such damages in any context. Indeed, *Smith v. Custom House Docks Development Authority* is an example of a case in which there was a breach of a commercial contract in circumstances in which McGuinness J. felt that 'general damages for breach of contract' were clearly justified.

The main policy identified in the cases as justifying the general rule against damages for mental distress for breach of contract is a fear of high damages. A related policy emerges from the judgment of Mason C.J. (Toohey and Gaudron JJ. concurring) in *The Mikhail Lermontov*. He maintained an approach based upon the general rule and its exceptions on the ground that a plaintiff's distress and disappointment if the defendant does not perform 'are seldom so significant as to attract an award of damages' ((1992–1993) 176 C.L.R. 344 at 404). On the other hand, McHugh J. in the same case developing an approach based simply the principles of remoteness concluded merely that 'in most cases, the disappointment would be so negligible that the damage suffered could be regarded as *de minimis* and ignored' ((1992–1993) 176 C.L.R. 344 at 404). The approach of McHugh J. is preferable: negligible mental distress can simply be ignored; but it is not a reason to deny compensation where the mental distress is serious. Thus, it would seem that there is no coherent policy justification for the general rule against damages for mental distress for breach of contract. Consequently, as Mason C.J. argued in *The Mikhail Lermontov*:

> The conceptual and policy foundations of the general rule [in *Addis*] are by no means clear. It seems to rest on the view that damages for breach of contract are in essence compensatory and that they are confined to the award of that sum of money which will put the injured party in the *financial* position the party would have been in had the breach of contract not taken place. On that approach, anxiety and injured feelings do not, generally speaking, form part of the plaintiff's compensable loss which flows from a breach of contract. At, bottom, this approach to the problem is based on a policy . . . [which is itself] based on an apprehension that the recovery of compensation for injured feelings will lead to inflated awards of damages in commercial contract cases, if not contract cases generally. . . . [It is] a rule which rests on flimsy foundations and conceptually is at odds with the fundamental principle governing the recovery of damages, . . . (*The Mikhail Lermontov* (1992–1993) 176 C.L.R. 344 at 361–362 *per* Mason C.J. (Toohey and GaudronJJ. concurring); cp. pp.394–397 *per* McHugh J. to like effect (no satisfactory rationale)).

Other policy objections are in the end no more than restatements of the fear of high damages, and are equally suspect. For example, Professor Burrows identifies three further subspecies of objection: first, that it is too harsh on the defendant to pay damages for mental distress; second, that mental distress is incapable of exact proof; and third, that the risk of mental distress is voluntarily assumed by the plaintiff upon entering into the contract (Burrows [1984] *L.M.C.L.Q.* 119 at 132–133). However, as Professor Burrows argues, such damages are no more harsh than ordinary damages compensating pecuniary losses; the difficulties of proof do not preclude tort claims or damages for personal injuries arising out a breach of contract; and, since a contracting party accepts the risk of any consequences of breach only to the extent that he will get sufficient expectation damages for such consequences, why should one consequence sound in such damages when others do not.

It is clear, therefore, that the general rule in *Addis* against damages for mental distress for breach of contract has no coherent policy justification. It was clear above that the authorities which have been said to embody the rule do not compel its acceptance and are all susceptible of reinterpretation in a manner which does not require it. In sum, then, there seems to be no bar to awarding such damages; and the question becomes: if such damages are to be available, and not necessarily trammelled by the *Addis* rule, what is the basis upon which they may be awarded? The courts have adopted various techniques. The first comes from the disastrous holiday cases and their ilk, which establish that where 'the very object of a contract is to provide pleasure, relaxation, peace of mind or freedom from molestation, damages will be awarded if the fruit of the contract is not provided or if the contrary result is procured instead' (*Watts v. Morrow* [1991] 4 All E.R. 937 at 960 *per* Bingham L.J.; approved in *The Mikhail Lermontov* (1992–1993) 176 C.L.R. 344 at 371 *per* Brennan J., 382 *per* Deane and Dawson JJ.). The very object of the contract may emerge from the nature of the contract itself (for example, a contract for entertainment or pleasure, such as a holiday contract) or from a specific, even implied, term. *Whelan v. Waitaki Meats* and *Malik v. BCCI* are of this nature. In such cases, 'the damages flow directly from the breach of contract . . . because the breach results in a failure to provide promised benefits' (*The Mikhail Lermontov* (1992–1993) 176 C.L.R. 344 at 365 *per* Mason C.J.). Hence, it might be said that the very breach of contract itself consists in the mental distress for which the plaintiff is entitled to damages.

In *Sullivan v. Southern Health Board* had there been implied into the contract a term that the Board would employ a second consultant at the hospital, that would have amounted to a term as to the quality of the plaintiff's working conditions. On the test focusing on the objects of the contract or term, whether the plaintiff would be entitled to damages for breach of contract would depend on whether the very breach of the term as to the quality of the plaintiff's working conditions consisted in the mental distress which the plaintiff suffered. But the breach consisted in the failure to employ a second consultant, and though it led to the mental distress, that distress was not of itself of the essence of the very breach of contract in the same way as it is of the essence of a disastrous holiday amounting to a breach of a contract for enjoyment. In this respect, *Sullivan* is like an ordinary contract for professional services which is breached by the failure to provide those services: mental distress may result from the breach, but it is not itself the breach and, damages are not therefore on the *Watts v. Morrow* formulation of the test for damages for mental distress for breach of contract. On this view, there is 'a clear distinction to be drawn between mental distress which is an incidental consequence to the client of the misconduct of litigation by his solicitor, one the one hand, and mental distress on the other hand which is the direct and inevitable consequence of the solicitor's negligent failure to obtain the very relief which it was the sole purpose of the litigation to secure. The first does not sound in damages; the second does' (*Heywood v. Wellers* [1976] 1 All E.R. 300 at 310 *per* Bridge L.J.; cp. *The Mikhail Lermontov* ((1992–1993) 176 C.L.R. 344 at 370–371 *per* Brennan J.; for an example of mental distress to the client which was held to be an incidental rather than direct consequence of solicitors' negligence in breach of contract, see *e.g. Cook v. S* [1967] 1 All E.R. 299 (CA)).

Where the very object of a contract is to provide pleasure, relaxation, peace of mind or freedom from molestation, arguably, it is foreseeable that when the promisor breaches the contract, the promisee will suffer mental distress, either because in such circumstances the mental distress is reasonably foreseeable within the first limb of the rule in *Hadley v. Baxendale* (above), or because it was (or could have been) foreseen by the parties within the second limb of that rule. Thus, the exception to the rule in *Addis* might be explained as being based on the ordinary rules of remoteness; both Mason C.J. and Brennan J. took that line in their judgments in *The Mikhail Lermontov* ((1992–1993) 176 C.L.R. 344 at 363–364, 367–369). Hence, in *Heywood v. Wellers* Denning MR held that it must have been in the contemplation of the solicitors that 'if they failed in their duty, she might be further molested and suffer much upset and distress. This damage she suffered was within their contemplation within the rule in *Hadley v. Baxendale.*' ([1976] 1 All E.R. 300 at 306–307). But mental distress may be reasonably foreseeably or foreseen in many circumstances beyond contracts the objects of which is provide pleasure, relaxation, peace of mind or freedom from molestation. As Mason C.J. (Toohey and GaudronJJ. concurring) pointed out in *The Mikhail Lermontov* 'the remoteness test does not provide a satisfactory explanation for the approach now adopted in England. If that test be the sole determinant for the recovery of damages for disappointment and distress, such damages would generally be recoverable so long as they were not too removed; their availability would not be relegated to an exception to a general rule denying recovery' ((1992–1993) 176 C.L.R. 344 at 364). Thus, the traditional remoteness rules provide a much broader basis upon which to award damages for mental distress than the objects of the contract rule, and therefore provide the second technique adopted by the courts to determine the basis upon which damages for breach of contract for mental distress may be awarded.

In this role, the remoteness rules have a long pedigree. In *Hobbs v. London & South Western Rly Co* (1875) LR 10 Q.B. 111, the plaintiffs had purchased tickets to one railway station but were conveyed to another, and were consequently put to considerable inconvenience walking the long distance home late at night. Cockburn C.J. explained the denial of damages for inconvenience in *Hamlin v. Great Northern Rly* as turning on an application of the *Hadley v. Baxendale* remoteness rules, and explained that 'it did not decide that decide that personal inconvenience, however serious, was not to be taken into account as a subject matter of damage . . . there is no authority that personal inconvenience, where it is sufficiently serious, should not be the subject of damages to be recovered in an action of this kind . . .'. The inconvenience of arriving at the wrong station therefore sounded in damages, but the fact that one of the plaintiffs suffered some ill health as a consequence was too remote (presumably because it was not reasonably foreseeable within the first limb of the rule in *Hadley v. Baxendale*). The strong implication is that if the distress had not been too remote, damages would have been available. On this reading, *Hobbs* demonstrates the view, substantially contemporary with *Addis*, that damages for mental distress for breach of contract were unproblematically available. Indeed, in *Addis* itself, Lord Collins dissented, pointing out that historically such damages were countenanced by English law ([1909] A.C. 488 at 498–499).

Hobbs effects a re-interpretation of the decision in *Hamlin* to parallel the *Malik* re-interpretation of *Addis*. Likewise, in *Kinlen*, Kennedy C.J. excluded damages for mental distress because they did not arise on the facts as a specially foreseen damage: that is, they did not come within the second limb of the rule in *Hadley v. Baxendale*; and it was argued above that had the remoteness rule been fulfilled, damages would have been available. *Garvey v. Ireland* is to similar effect. Hence, it follows on this view that if mental distress is not too remote within the meaning of either limb of the rule in *Hadley v. Baxendale*, it can be compensated in damages.

Recoverability of such damages on the basis of the ordinary remoteness rules is the view taken in the broader modern cases (*e.g. Heywood v. Wellers*; *Cox v. Philips Industries*; *Whelan v. Waitaki Meats*; Gallen J. in *Rowlands v. Collow*; Wilson J. in *Vorvis*, McHugh J. in *The Mikhail Lermontov*). On the other hand, it might be said that the application of such rules cuts both ways, in that, on one view at least, the rule against damages for mental distress 'represents an essentially pragmatic and judicially imposed assumption which is to be made for the purposes of the application of the second limb in *Hadley v. Baxendale*, that is to say, it is to be assumed that disappointment or distress flowing from the breach of contract would not have been in the contemplation of the parties, at the time they made the contract, as a likely result of the breach' (*The Mikhail Lermontov* (1992–1993) 176 C.L.R. 344 at 380–381 *per* Deane and DawsonJJ.). More generally, Professor Clark explains that the common law rule denying such damages emerged from an 'institutional conflict [of] the judges devising a rule of remoteness that took that head of loss out of the reach of the jury'(*Contract Law in Ireland* (3rd ed., Sweet & Maxwell, London, 1992) p 459), so that it might be said that the rule in *Addis* represented a judicial conclusion that mental distress would never come within either limb of *Hadley v. Baxendale*. This is explicit in the speech of Lord Gorell in *Addis*. Many of the narrow modern cases contain similar assertions. For example, there is in the decision of Cooke P. in *Mouat v. Clark Boyce* the assertion that '[o]rdinary commercial contracts are not intended to shelter the parties from anxiety' from which it might be deduced that for Cooke P such anxiety is not reasonably foreseeable and is thus not within the first limb of the rule in *Hadley v. Baxendale*. Indeed, Gallen J. had suggested as much in *Rowlands v. Collow* ('With commercial contracts it is most unlikely that such damage will have been foreseeable or within the parties' contemplation; with contracts of a more personal nature, mental distress could well be a foreseeable consequence and within the contemplation of the parties' ([1992] 1 N.Z.L.R. 178 at 207)). Similarly, in *Kelly v. Crowley*, Murphy J. also held that 'damage of that nature is not reasonably foreseeable'. On the other hand, McHugh J. in *The Mikhail Lermontov*, argued that 'such an explanation does not accord with everyday experience relating to the making of contracts. The parties to many contracts, including many commercial contracts, are fully aware, when they make them, that breach will result in disappointment and sometimes distress to the innocent party' ((1992–1993) 176 C.L.R. 344 at 396). Furthermore, we have seen that the policy underlying such a rule of law does not support it. Consequently, this artificial assumption as to the operation of the rules of remoteness ought to be abrogated, and the rules properly applied to the specific facts of each case; and even if it its rare that the rules are satisfied in one type of case, this rarity ought not to be elevated into a rule which would preclude such damages in a case in which the rules are properly satisfied.

We have already seen that had there been implied into the contract in *Sullivan v. Southern Health Board* a term that the Board would employ a second consultant at the hospital, that would have amounted to a term as to the quality of the plaintiff's working conditions. Applying *Hadley v. Baxendale*, the question would have been whether it was foreseeable that when the Board breached the contract, the plaintiff would have suffered mental distress due to the consequent decline in his working conditions, either because in such circumstances the mental distress was have been reasonably foreseeable within the first limb of the rule, or because it was (or could have been) foreseen by the parties within the second limb of the rule. It would not have been difficult to hold in favour of the plaintiff either on the first limb, or, perhaps, on the second. The mental distress arising out of the decline in the quality of working conditions would almost certainly have been reasonably foreseeable, and it may very well have been (or ought to have been) foreseen by the Board. Hence, damages for mental distress would have been available on the basis of the straightforward application of the remoteness rules to the facts of *Sullivan*. (Indeed, as Professor Burrows points out – though with disapproval – this is likely to be a common conclusion whenever the plaintiff is a person: [1984] *L.M.C.L.Q.* 119 at 121). We have already seen that they would not have been on the basis of the application of the objects of the contract test. Since Murphy J. held that the plaintiff is entitled to recover 'general . . . damage[s]', which would not be available on the basis of an objects test but would be available on the basis of the ordinary remoteness rules, *Sullivan* seems to be another case in favour of the latter test.

In conclusion, the general rule that in an action for breach of contract, a plaintiff is not entitled to recover damages for pain and suffering, emotional upset, mental distress, or the like, occasioned by the breach of contract, is often traced to *Addis v. Gramophone Co Ltd* and, as a matter of Irish law, to *Kinlen v. Ulster Bank*. To this general exclusion, there were exceptions allowing the recovery of such damages in, for example, the case of disastrous holiday (e.g. *Jarvis v. Swans Tours*; *The Mikhail Lermontov*). The exceptions were often expansively applied (e.g. *Heywood v. Wellers*; *Cox v. Philips Industries*; *Perry v. Sidney Philip*) especially in Ireland (*Johnson v. Longleat Property*; *Murphy v. Quality Homes*). However, a retrenchment in England from this expansive view (*Bliss v. South East Thames Regional Health Authority*; *Hayes v. Dodd*; *Watts v. Morrow*) though presaged in Ireland (*Garvey v. Ireland*) has not been followed elsewhere, where the courts adopt either the expansive view of the exceptions (the majority in *Vorvis*, followed in *Wallace*; *The Mikhail Lermontov*) or are prepared to overturn the general rule either in the case of non-commercial contracts (as in New Zealand) or altogether (the minority in *Vorvis*, McHugh J. in *The Mikhail Lermontov*; *Rolands v. Collow*). Given that the only real policy justification for the rule against damages for mental distress, a fear of high damages, can be met by temperate and modest awards, such an overturning is more than justified; and, if it is to come, it has been made easier by the *Malik v. BCCI* reinterpretation of *Addis*. Similar reinterpretations of *Kinlen* and *Garvey* are possible, explaining the absence of a claim for damages for mental distress for breach of contract in those cases as turning on the fact that such distress was too remote. The exceptions to *Addis* may also be explained simply as examples where such distress was not too remote. If the English retrenchment is discounted as turning on the application of authorities and a policy which have been discredited, then the general remoteness rules supply the proper basis for the assessment of damages for mental distress. Indeed, Professor Clark was of the view that Irish law was close to this point in 1978 (see (1978) XIII *Ir. Jur. (ns)* 186). Cases such as *Smith* and *Sullivan* may have ensured that the final step has since been taken. The story has therefore been one of a general rule and its exceptions, collapsing under the weight of the exceptions when the absence of logic at its foundations has been exposed. The best position is the sweeping away of the rule in *Addis* and its exceptions in favour simply of the application of the general remoteness rules. That, in fact, seems to have been the position assumed by McGuinness J. in *Smith* and by Murphy J. in *Sullivan*, but if Irish law has not quite yet reached that destination, in common with the rest of the common law world, it ought soon to do so.

SALE OF GOODS

Definition of 'goods'   The Sale of Goods Act 1893, and the Sale of Goods and Supply of Services, 1980 imply certain consumer protection terms into contracts for the sale of goods, and contracts for the supply of services, (and the Consumer Credit Act 1995 applies similar terms into certain financial contracts). It therefore becomes crucial to know, for example, what are 'goods' for the purposes of the 1893 and 1980 Acts. In this context, by section 62 of the 1893 Act the term 'goods' is defined as 'including all chattels personal other than things in action and money, . . .'. Thus, sales of such choses in action as debts, intellectual property rights, and shares are expressly excluded; and so must also be contracts for the sale of land. On the other hand, planes, boats and automobiles are all goods for the purposes of this definition (see, for example, *Re Blyth Shipbuilding* [1926] Ch. 494; *Bord Iascaigh Mhara v. Scallan* (High Court, unreported, 8 May 1973, Pringle J) *Rogers v. Parish* [1987] 2 All E.R. 135). For the purposes of the sale of goods section of the Act a contract to supply a service does not satisfy the definition. However, it may often be difficult to distinguish between a contract to sell a good or to supply a service. Thus, a contract to *sell* a ship is a contract for the sale of a good and thus within the ambit of the 1893 Act and Part II of the 1980 Act; whereas a contract to *build* a ship is not so clearly a contract to sell a good, though this has ultimately been held in *Re Blyth Shipbuilding* [1926] Ch. 494 also to amount to a contract of sale, not of supply. Furthermore, in *Cammell Laird v. Manganese Bronze & Brass Co* [1934] A.C. 402, the House of Lords held that a contract for the manufacture of propellers to the buyers' design was a contract for the sale of a good. However, the inclusion in Part IV of the Act of 1980 of express terms for services probably renders this distinction largely meaningless in practice, though even there, given that the terms implied into each contract are different, the distinction may yet prove important.

A *dictum* in a recent Supreme Court decision illustrates that discussion of the definition of a good for the purposes of the Acts is not however confined to cases distinguishing goods from services. In *Brosnan v. Leeside Nurseries* [1998] 1 I.L.R.M. 312, Barrington J. held that he 'would have no difficulty in accepting that potted dwarf chrysanthemums on a supermarket shelf are 'goods' for the purposes of the Sale of Goods Act 1893' ([1998] 1 I.L.R.M. 312 at 317). However, the case concerned not the sale of goods but the manufacture of goods for the purposes of tax relief, and Barrington J. (O'Flaherty, Lynch and BarronJJ. concurring) held that the process of cultivation of chrysanthemums was not one of manufacture for the purposes of Part IV of the Corporation Tax Act 1976 or of Part I of the Finance Act 1980. Keane J. delivered a judgment to like effect which did not advert to the Sale of Goods point. Barrington J.'s decision points up yet again that the concept of goods 'is of a very general and quite indefinite import' and, in statutes, the word 'primarily derives its meaning from the context in which it is used' (*The Noordam (No 2)* [1920] A.C. 904 at 909–909).

Coroners

Attorney General's power to re-order inquest   In *Farrell v. Attorney General* [1998] 1 I.L.R.M. 364 (HC & SC), Smyth J. and, on appeal, the Supreme Court, held that the power conferred on the Attorney General to order the conduct of an inquest under section 24 of the Coroners Act 1962 did not apply where a full inquest has already taken place.

The case concerned a deceased person who had died in a Dublin hospital while undergoing a routine operation. The inquest into the deceased's death had been conducted by the applicant, the Dublin Coroner. The widow of the deceased was represented at the inquest. Evidence was given at the inquest that the deceased had been administered with a dosage of penicillin, despite the fact that he was allergic to penicillin. The evidence from the autopsy was that it was unclear whether the penicillin had caused the death of the deceased, since there was also evidence that the deceased had moderately severe coronary arterial disease. There was general disagreement amongst the medical witnesses as to the exact cause of death and the applicant drew this to the attention of the inquest jury during his summing up. The jury returned a verdict that death was possibly due to the administration of the penicillin combined with the deceased's pre-existing heart disease.

The applicant was of the opinion that the verdict reflected the medical evidence given at the inquest. In July 1994, the Attorney General wrote to the applicant expressing the view that there was dissatisfaction at the conduct of the inquest, in particular from the widow of the deceased, who wished the word 'possibly' to be deleted from the signed verdict. At this time, it was clear that the Attorney General was of the opinion that a further inquest was not necessary. But in November 1994, the Attorney General decided that a new, fresh or further inquest should be held, and he directed that a deputy coroner should conduct the inquest pursuant to section 24(1) of the Coroners Act 1962. The applicant successfully contested that direction on judicial review.

Smyth J. held that section 24 of the 1962 Act was an enabling section which conferred on the Attorney General a limited discretionary power in limited circumstances to direct the holding of an inquest, not a new, fresh or further inquest. The section did not, he concluded, empower the Attorney General to direct the holding of an inquest while there was an extant verdict from a concluded inquest. Unless and until that inquest had been quashed, the Attorney General had no right or power to direct the holding of a new, fresh or further inquest. The claim that the jury did not hear all the evidence in the coroner's possession was unsustainable, particularly as the deceased's widow had been represented at the hearing of the inquest. He therefore quashed the purported exercise by the Attorney of the power under section 24(1) of the 1962 Act as being unreasonable in law and *ultra vires* in that there were no circumstances in which he could properly have concluded that the holding of a fresh inquest was necessary. Finally, apart from questions of jurisdiction, Smyth J. suggested that, to alter the form of the jury's verdict in the instant case could have had the effect of denoting an element of civil liability, which is of course prohibited by section 30 of the 1962 Act.

On appeal, the Supreme Court noted that there had been no new material before the Attorney General which would have justified the change of view he had taken from is earlier refusal to order a second inquest. Accordingly, the Court held that Smyth J. had been correct in concluding that the Attorney General had acted irrationally within the meaning of the principles laid down in *O'Keeffe v. An Bord Pleanála* [1993] 1 I.R. 39; [1992] I.L.R.M. 237 (1991 Review, 16-18).

The Court also accepted that the inherent jurisdiction of the courts on judicial review extended beyond errors going to jurisdiction, as had been held in decisions such as *Anisminic Ltd v. Foreign Compensation Tribunal* [1969] 2 A.C. 147 and *The State (Holland) v. Kennedy* [1977] I.R. 193. This confirmed the view it had already taken in *Killeen v. Director of Public Prosecutions* [1998] 1 I.L.R.M. 1 (SC) (discussed in the Criminal Law chapter, 320, below) and supports the views on the scope of judicial review expressed by Costello J. in *Ryan v. Compensation Tribunal* [1997] 1 I.L.R.M. 194 (HC), discussed in the 1996 Review, 5-7.

Nonetheless, the Court accepted that section 24 of the Coroners Act 1962 provided an important protection where new evidence did come to light which required a fresh inquest be held. The Court pointed out that, on judicial review, the High Court would not be empowered to quash a direction under section 24 of the 1962 Act merely on the basis that new evidence had come to light which made a fresh inquest desirable or necessary. However, since there was in fact no new evidence in the instant case the Court, as indicated, upheld the High Court decision to quash the order made by the Attorney General. The additional comments by the Supreme Court will doubtless prove of some comfort in the exercise of the power in section 24 of the 1962 Act in the future.

Criminal Law

ACCESS TO SOLICITOR

Privacy In *The People v. Finnegan*, Court of Criminal Appeal, July 15, 1997, the Court held that the effect of a denial to an accused person of his constitutional right to consult with his solicitor in private was to render his detention illegal. The defendant had been charged with and convicted of handling stolen property, contrary to the Larceny Act 1916, as amended by the Larceny Act 1990 (1990 Review, 229-35). He contended that he was never allowed access to his solicitor in private prior to the conduct of two interviews with the Gardaí, in that the Gardaí were present in the room when he phoned his solicitor. He therefore argued that the details of the two interviews which took place after his over-heard telephone call to his solicitor were inadmissible. The Court of Criminal Appeal agreed, quashed his conviction and did not order a retrial.

The Court re-iterated the view expressed by the Supreme Court in *The People v. Healy* [1990] 2 I.R. 73; [1990] I.L.R.M. 313 (1989 Review, 137-9) that an accused person's right to communicate with his solicitor is a constitutional right, and there is thus a duty on the State to defend and vindicate that right as far as practicable. The Court held that the right to communicate with a solicitor would be of little value unless it carried with it, as a necessary concomitant, the right to consult in private. Although the right to make a telephone call to a solicitor may not be, *per se*, a constitutional right, once it was allowed, the defendant had a constitutional right to make that call in private. The Court held that it was not acceptable that Garda officers assumed that the defendant did not require privacy simply because he did not mention it. and there had thus been a breach of the defendant's constitutional right to communicate with his solicitor in private. Citing the decision in *The People v. Madden* [1977] I.R. 336, the Court concluded that the effect of this denial was to render his detention illegal and that there was no special statutory power that could make admissible any evidence obtained from him after the time he had been denied private access to his solicitor.

APPEAL

Appeals to Court of Criminal Appeal based on transcript of recording
Section 7 of the Criminal Justice (Miscellaneous Provisions) Act 1997 (dis-

cussed generally, 314, below) amended section 33 of the Courts of Justice Act 1924 which provided that in appeals to the Court of Criminal Appeal from trials on indictment, the transcript must be based on the report of an official stenographer present at the trial. Section 7 of the 1997 Act now provides that the transcript before the Court of Criminal Appeal may be derived from a sound recording or other equipment. It also repealed section 97 of the Courts of Justice Act 1924.

Miscarriage of justice: general principles   In *The People v. Pringle*, Supreme Court, March 4, 1997, the Supreme Court dealt with another long-standing *cause celebre* in the Irish canon of alleged miscarriages of justice. The Court also provided important guidance on the application of section 9 of the Criminal Procedure Act 1993 (1993 Review, 210-14), which introduced a new mechanism by which persons wrongly convicted could seek compensation for a miscarriage of justice where a 'newly discovered' fact places their original conviction in doubt. The *Pringle* case itself clearly reflected the basis for the 1993 Act. It concerned a conviction for murder dating back to the early 1980s, a previous appeal against conviction had been dismissed in the mid 1980s (see *The People v. Pringle* (1981) 2 Frewen 57) and the restrictions imposed by the *res judicata* principle had placed severe limitations on civil proceedings for compensation (see *Pringle v. Ireland* [1994] 1 I.L.R.M. 467 (1993 Review, 463-4)). The applicant then sought to use the new route provided for in the Criminal Procedure Act 1993. In the Court of Criminal Appeal, the Court held that a newly discovered fact, which threw doubt on the credibility of crucial evidence given by a detective Garda, showed that there had been a miscarriage of justice in relation to the conviction for murder of the applicant. However, the Court refused to certify that this newly discovered fact showed that there had been a miscarriage of justice within the meaning of section 9(1)(a)(ii) of the 1993 Act. A certificate to that effect is a necessary pre-condition to claiming compensation for the miscarriage of justice. On further appeal to the Supreme Court on a point of exceptional public importance, the Supreme Court held that the case should be remitted to the Court of Criminal Appeal.

The Supreme Court accepted that the mere fact that an applicant's conviction was quashed as being unsafe and unsatisfactory under the 1993 Act could not on its own entitle the person to a certificate that there had been a miscarriage of justice. The Court held that an inquiry as to whether a section 9 certificate should be given was not a criminal trial, but rather an inquiry as to whether there has been a miscarriage of justice, the onus being on the applicant. It was not, the Court held, a trial in which the onus was on the State to prove the guilt of the accused and thus the presumption of innocence had no place in such an inquiry. The Court underlined this by stating that the standard of proof is the same standard as in any civil claim, namely on the balance of probabilities.

In this respect, the Court held that a person applying for a certificate under section 9 of the 1993 Act must establish on the balance of probabilities that there has been a miscarriage of justice in his case and that a newly discovered fact, either on its own or to a significant degree in combination with other matters, shows that there has been such a miscarriage of justice. The primary meaning of miscarriage of justice is that the applicant for a certificate is on the balance of probabilities as established by relevant and admissible evidence innocent of the offence of which he was convicted Even if the court is satisfied that a miscarriage of justice has occurred it must be remembered that a certificate cannot issue unless the court is also satisfied on the balance of probabilities that such miscarriage of justice has been shown to exist by a newly discovered fact either on its own or to a significant degree in combination with other matters.

The Supreme Court added, finally, that it may not have been fully appreciated by Bench or Bar in the Court of Criminal Appeal that an application for a certificate is a distinct and different enquiry from the appeal against conviction, such as to entitle either party to adduce further evidence in addition to making further submissions. Accordingly the Court ordered that the matter be remitted to the Court of Criminal Appeal to determine the matter on the basis of the principles outlined in the decision.

Miscarriage of justice: newly discovered fact In *The People v. Meleady and Grogan*, Supreme Court, March 4, 1997, the Supreme Court delivered judgment on the same date as that in the *Pringle* case, discussed above, in another application under the Criminal Procedure Act 1993 in which the applicants claimed that a newly discovered fact showed that there had been a miscarriage of justice in relation to their convictions. As is clear from the *Pringle* case, a certificate to that effect is a necessary pre-condition to claiming compensation for the miscarriage of justice under the 1993 Act. The convictions dated back to 1985 when the applicants had been convicted of malicious damage and assault arising from the alleged theft of a car, and had been sentenced to five years imprisonment. The case against the applicants rested solely on identification evidence given by the car's owner and his son. Following an appeal, a new trial took place and the applicants were again convicted and given the same sentence. The case had become something of a *cause celebre* in the media at the time, the defendants becoming known as the 'Tallaght Two.' The owner of the car had also been severely traumatised by events arising from the car theft: see *Gavin v. Criminal Injuries Compensation Tribunal*, High Court, February 9, 1996 (1996 Review, 236-8). The applicants then instituted the present application under the 1993 Act. In 1995, the Court of Criminal Appeal quashed their convictions but considered that it was precluded from granting a certificate under section 9 of the 1993 Act that a miscarriage of justice had occurred on the ground that there had been no decision by a jury in a trial in which the non-disclosed material had been available to the accused.

On further appeal to the Supreme Court on a point of law of exceptional public importance the Court remitted the case to the Court of Criminal Appeal to consider again the application for a certificate under section 9 of the 1993 Act. The Supreme Court held that there was no provision in the 1993 Act which supported the conclusion that a certificate should be granted under section 9 only where there has been a trial at which the non-disclosed material was made available. The Court held that, once the condition in section 9(1)(a)(i) of the 1993 Act was satisfied in one or other of three ways, the party who has had a conviction quashed, or has been acquitted on a retrial, is entitled to have the Court enter into an inquiry as to whether he is entitled to a certificate that a newly discovered fact shows that there has been a miscarriage of justice. In this respect, the Court held that no distinction is to be made between persons whose convictions are quashed and those who are acquitted on retrial.

Miscarriage of justice: separate application after conviction quashed   In *The People v. Connell (No.3)*, Court of Criminal Appeal, October 16, 1997, the Court of Criminal Appeal held that where a conviction was quashed by a court on appeal, the successful appellant was later entitled to have the court enter into an inquiry as to whether he was entitled to a certificate that a newly-discovered fact showed that there had been a miscarriage of justice under the 1993 Act. The applicant's conviction for murder had been quashed on appeal to the Court of Criminal Appeal in 1995 and no new trial had been ordered: see *The People v. Connell* [1995] 1 I.R. 244 (1995 Review, 246). He then applied in 1997 for a certificate under section 9(1)(a)(i) and (ii) of the 1993 Act, certifying that a miscarriage of justice had occurred in relation to his conviction. It was agreed that a preliminary issue should be tried as to whether section 9 could apply to an appeal other than one brought pursuant to section 2 of the 1993 Act. The Director of Public Prosecutions maintained that the 1993 Act did not apply to the applicant, as his conviction had been quashed under the provisions of the Courts of Justice Act 1924 rather than in an application under the 1993 Act. The Court of Criminal Appeal rejected this argument.

The Court noted that an appeal against conviction differed from an appeal under section 2 of the 1993 Act. Section 9 of the 1993 Act applied to a person whose conviction had been quashed by the court on an application under section 2 of the 1993 Act, or who had been acquitted in any retrial, and where the appellate court or court of retrial certified that a newly-discovered fact established that there had been a miscarriage of justice. The Court held that the aim of section 9 was to provide for payment of compensation, and it applied to those whose convictions had been quashed by a court and the court certified that a newly-discovered fact showed that there had been a miscarriage of justice, and to a person pardoned and the Minister was of the opinion that a newly-discovered fact showed that there had been a miscarriage of justice. In interpreting section 9(1)(a)(i) and (ii), the Court held that it could take into consideration the provisions which dealt with the meaning of 'newly-discovered fact'. It was clear that it was not the legislature's intention to confine 'appeal' to those taken under section 2, and the provisions of section 9 applied not only to applications under section 2 but to other appeals to the court where it was certified that a newly-discovered fact showed that there had been a miscarriage of justice. Thus, as the applicant's conviction had been quashed by the court on appeal, he was entitled to have the court enter into an inquiry as to whether he was entitled to a certificate that a newly-discovered fact showed that there had been a miscarriage of justice. Whether he was entitled to such a certificate was a matter to be determined by the court hearing the application, in accordance with the principles laid down in the *Pringle* case, discussed above.

ARREST

Detention under 1984 Act   Section 2 of the Criminal Justice (Miscellaneous Provisions) Act 1997 (discussed generally below, 314) amended section 4 of the Criminal Justice Act 1984. It inserted a new section 4(6) into the 1984 Act which provides that where detention for the original offence for which the person was detained is no longer justifiable, the person may be detained on suspicion of another offence. It also provides that, where a person is absent from the place of detention in connection with a challenge to the lawfulness of his or her detention, such absence shall not be reckoned in calculating the period of detention under section 4 of the 1984 Act.

Detention and re-arrest   In *Director of Public Prosecutions v. Early*, High Court, December 2, 1997 McGuinness J. upheld the validity of a re-arrest under section 4 of the Criminal Justice (Drug Trafficking) Act 1996 (1996 Review, 241-4) notwithstanding an infirmity attaching to a previous detention under the 1996 Act. The case involved five accused who had been arrested under the Misuse of Drugs Acts 1977 to 1984 for offences under those Acts. They had been detained under section 2 of the Criminal Justice (Drug Trafficking) Act 1996 for investigation of the alleged offences. District Judge Windle had granted an application for a warrant to extend the period of detention under the 1996 Act. It transpired that only certain judges of the District Court had been nominated by the President of the District Court to extend the period of detention under the 1996 Act and that Judge Windle was not among such judges (we note parenthetically here that, arising from this case, all judges of the District Court are now nominated by the President of the District Court to extend the period of detention under the 1996 Act). The warrant of detention concerning the five accused persons was thus invalid and they were released from detention. The five were then re-arrested under section 25 of the Misuse of Drugs Act 1977 which permits arrest without warrant, and were brought before the respondent judge of the District Court. He discharged the five accused from custody, accepting submissions on their behalf that they had been rearrested under section 4(1) of the 1996 Act (rearrest for the purpose of further detention), but that the requirements of that provision had not been met. The prosecution had argued that the rearrest had been under section 4(5) of the 1996 Act, which allowed for rearrest and immediate charge. Three of the accused were arrested two days later (the other two accused having absconded), following the issue of warrants for their rearrest by a judge who had been nominated to issue such a warrant under the 1996 Act. They appeared before the respondent judge who again ordered that they be discharged from custody. The Director of Public Prosecutions sought an order of certiorari quashing this decision. McGuinness J. granted the order sought.

She held that section 4(1) of the 1996 Act contained a safeguard against repeated detention by the Garda Síochána for the same offence without any new information having come to light. She distinguished this from the situation where a person is released from detention under section 2 of the 1996 Act and at a later stage is charged with an offence. She concluded that section 4(5) of the 1996 Act permitted a further arrest for that purpose only, that is, an immediate charge. Since there was no evidence of any *mala fides* on the part of the Garda Síochána, there was, she held, nothing unlawful in rearresting the accused persons provided they were immediately charged and brought before the court. She summarised the position by noting that a rearrest under section 4(1) was for further detention and questioning and had to be justified by new information, whereas a section 4(5) arrest was a normal arrest for the purposes of charging the person arrested before the District Court.

Proof of arrest and caution by certificate   Section 6 of the Criminal Justice (Miscellaneous Provisions) Act 1997 (see generally, 314, below) makes provision for the giving of evidence relating to the arrest, charging and cautioning of a person and certain other procedural evidence by way of a certificate. Prior to the 1997 Act, such evidence had to be given by oral evidence. The section also provides that the court may require oral evidence to be given of these matters where the interests of justice so require. The Criminal Justice (Miscellaneous Provisions) Act 1997 (Section 6) Regulations 1997 (S.I. No.345 of 1997) prescribe the forms for use in relation to proof of the arrest and caution of a person for a specified offence under section 6 of the 1997 Act.

They came into effect on September 8, 1997. See also the Evidence chapter, 385, below.

Reasons In *Director of Public Prosecutions v. O'Connell*, High Court, October 16, 1997, Geoghegan J. reiterated the well-established requirement that the person arrested should be in general be informed of the reason why he is arrested but that this did not apply if the circumstances were such that he must have known the general nature of the alleged offence for which he was arrested. The issue arose when the defendant was arrested on suspicion of having committed the drink-driving offence in section 49 of the Road Traffic Act 1961. When making the arrest, the arresting Garda had referred to section 49(8) of the Road Traffic Act 1994 rather than section 49(8) of the 1961 Act (section 10 of the 1994 Act had inserted an amended section 49 into the 1961 Act: see the 1994 Review, 217). On a case stated from the District Court, Geoghegan J. held that the arrest was valid notwithstanding this defect.

Geoghegan J. noted that a judge at all times takes judicial notice of the law, and there was only one inference which a judge could draw from the statutory citation given by the Garda, even though he had clumsily and incorrectly given the relevant citation. Thus, the trial judge would have to draw the conclusion that the Garda had intended to effect the arrest pursuant to the correct citation. Citing the leading decision in *Christie v. Leachinsky* [1947] A.C. 573, Geoghegan J. held that the requirement that the person arrested should be informed of the reason why he is arrested did not apply if the circumstances were such that he must have known the general nature of the alleged offence for which he was arrested.

ARRESTABLE OFFENCE (ABOLITION OF FELONY/MISDEMEANOUR)

Felony/misdemeanour distinction abolished The main purpose of the Criminal Law Act 1997 was to abolish the division of offences into felonies and misdemeanours. In this respect, the 1997 Act achieved what had been enacted in the United Kingdom by the Criminal Justice Act 1967 and which had been proposed in this jurisdiction by the ill-fated Criminal Justice Bill 1967. As pointed out by the Minister for Justice in the Oireachtas debate on the 1997 Act, the term 'felony' was formerly used to denote the more serious offences and 'misdemeanour' the less serious. In the course of time however, the distinction between the two became blurred and anomalies crept in, so that some very serious offences were classified only as misdemeanours while some less serious offences were felonies. A number of statutes or parts of statutes related in some way to felonies were also repealed because the part relating to felonies became inoperative. The general effect of the 1997 Act is that the prior law on misdemeanours is now applied to all offences, although the power of arrest without warrant which previously applied to felonies is retained in respect of a new class of serious offences to be designated as 'arrestable offences'. These are offences punishable with five years' imprisonment or more and which corresponded approximately to felonies.

Abolition of obsolete punishments The Criminal Law Act 1997 also introduced certain changes not related to the felony/misdemeanour distinction. The changes comprise principally the abolition of obsolete or unnecessary provisions, but also include the formal abolition of obsolete forms of punishment for prisoners such as penal servitude, hard labour, whipping and prison divisions.

Commencement As provided for in section 1 of the 1997 Act, the 1997 Act came into force on July 22, 1997, that is, three months after its signing into law by the President.

Arrestable offence Section 2 of the 1997 Act defines, *inter alia*, the term 'arrestable offence' as an offence in respect of which a person may be punished by imprisonment for five years or by a more severe penalty. The term 'a more severe penalty' covers offences for which there is a mandatory sentence greater than five years' imprisonment, for example, life imprisonment for treason or murder under section 2 of the Criminal Justice Act 1990. The penalty must be a statutory one. Thus, common law misdemeanours (which are as a matter of law punishable with imprisonment for an unlimited period) are not included. Section 2 also defines the expression 'fixed by law' in relation to the sentence for an arrestable offence. This in effect applies only to offences for which a court is required by law to pass a sentence of imprisonment for life. An attempt to commit an arrestable offence is also an arrestable offence.

Abolition of distinction between felony and misdemeanour Section 3(1) of the 1997 Act abolished all distinctions between felony and misdemeanour and section 3(2) provides that, subject to some exceptions discussed below, the prior law applicable to misdemeanours, including the law and practice as to mode of trial, will apply to all offences, including piracy. The reference to 'mode of trial' is to certain requirements concerning trials for felony, some of which had fallen into disuse, such as the formalities of giving the accused in charge of the jury and asking the accused, after conviction, whether he or she has anything to say why the court should not pass judgment according to law. The reference in section 3 to piracy is because that offence, though generally treated as a felony, had sometimes been treated as an offence of a separate class.

As was pointed out during the passage of the 1997 Act, many of the distinctions between felonies and misdemeanours arise from the Forfeiture Act 1870, which, while it substantially abolished the former forfeitures and disabilities attached to felonies, retained some of them, in particular the following. Section 2 of the 1870 Act provided that any person who had been convicted of treason or felony and sentenced to death or more than twelve months' imprisonment forfeited any of certain public offices which he or she may hold and also forfeited any pension or superannuation allowance payable from public funds to which he or she was entitled. The conviction also disqualified such a person from subsequently holding such office until he or she had served his or her sentence. Section 8 of the 1870 Act provided that a person convicted of treason or felony and sentenced to death or penal servitude (sentences of penal servitude were for at least three years) was generally disqualified from suing in a civil action or making a contract while the sentence remained in force. Under the 1870 Act, the Minister for Justice could appoint an administrator for the convicted person's property, with very wide powers, including power to pay compensation for loss or injury caused by any alleged wrongful act of the convicted person, even where the alleged act has not been proved in any court: see generally *Woods v. Attorney General*, High Court, December 20, 1974, discussed in Byrne, Hogan and McDermott, *Prisoners' Rights* (Co-Op Books, 1981), pp.97-8. Penal servitude was abolished by section 11 of the 1997 Act. The effect of section 3 of the 1997 Act is to render inoperative the disqualifications and disabilities provided for by the 1870 Act, and the 1870 Act was also formally repealed in its entirety by the 1997 Act. Another distinction between felonies and misdemeanours that ceased to be operative is the rule that, in general, an action for tort in respect of a felony could not be brought unless the offender had first been prosecuted or reasonable cause was shown why this had not been done.

Arrest without warrant   Section 4 of the 1997 Act broadly reproduced the common law powers of arrest without warrant for felonies, but applied them to the new form of arrestable offences. Since arrestable offences correspond approximately to felonies, very little change of substance to the powers of arrest was made in the 1997 Act. However, the five year test means that the power to arrest without warrant now applies to some of the more serious misdemeanours. These include obtaining property by false pretences, fraudulent conversion and some sexual offences. During the Oireachtas debate on section 4, some concern was expressed that the power of arrest was drafted too broadly and that it should, in general, be limited to arrest by members of the Garda Síochána. This was done by means of section 4(4) of the 1997 Act.

Section 4(1) provides that, subject to section 4(4) and section 4(5), any person may arrest without warrant anyone who is or whom he or she, with reasonable cause, suspects to be in the act of committing an arrestable offence. This corresponds to the common law rule in relation to felonies. Section 4(2) and (3) confer powers to arrest a person without warrant on suspicion that he or she has committed an arrestable offence. As with the common law provisions, the powers differ according to whether the person arresting is a member of the Garda Síochána or a private person. If the arrestable offence has in fact been committed, any person, whether a member of the Garda Síochána or not, may arrest anyone who is guilty of the offence or whom the person arresting suspects, with reasonable cause, to be guilty of it. But in the case of a member of the Garda Síochána it is not necessary that the offence should in fact have been committed: it is sufficient that the member suspects, with reasonable cause, that it has been committed by the person in question.

Section 4(4), which was added to the Act during the course of the Oireachtas debate, provides:

> 'An arrest other than by a member of the Garda Síochána may only be effected by a person under subsection (1) or (2) where he or she, with reasonable cause, suspects that the person to be arrested by him or her would otherwise attempt to avoid, or is avoiding, arrest by a member of the Garda Síochána.'

It remains to be seen whether section 4(4) will be interpreted in a manner which will preclude the exercise of powers of arrest under section 4 by, for example, security personnel who suspect that an individual has been engaged in 'shoplifting' offences. The wording of section 4(4), and the legislative context within which it was enacted, would appear to indicate that such an arrest would not always, if ever, involve a suspect attempting to avoid arrest by a Garda.

Section 4(5) provides that a person arrested under section 4(4) shall be transferred to the custody of the Garda Síochána 'as soon as practicable.'

Finally, section 4(6) provides that the section shall not affect the operation of any enactment restricting the institution of proceedings for an offence, for instance where an enactment provides that a prosecution may be brought only by or with the consent of the Director of Public Prosecutions. The subsection also provides that the section shall not prejudice any power of arrest conferred by law apart from the section. Examples are the common law power to arrest in order to prevent personal injury or a breach of the peace.

Arrest on warrant or order of committal   Section 5 of the 1997 Act provides that a Garda may arrest on foot of a warrant or order of committal even if the warrant or order is not in his or her possession, subject to production of the warrant or order, as soon as practicable, on demand. Prior to the 1997 Act, apart from some specific statutory exceptions (for example, under the Extradition Act 1965), a Garda was required to have in his or her possession the warrant or order (although, in the case of felony, knowledge of the existence of a warrant could be a sufficient ground for a Garda to exercise the power of arrest without warrant on reasonable suspicion that a felony had been committed).

Entry and search of premises to effect an arrest   Section 6 of the 1997 Act provides that, for the purpose of arresting a person for an arrestable offence or on foot of an order of committal, a member of the Garda Síochána may enter (if need be, by use of reasonable force) and search any place, including a dwelling, where that person is or where the member, with reasonable cause, suspects him or her to be. The prior common law as to when a place could be entered in order to effect an arrest depended on whether the offence in question was a felony. Section 6 applies only to Gardaí; thus a private person would have to obtain the assistance of a Garda if he or she was not in a position to carry out an arrest without entering the place in question (unless the person can justify making an entry on grounds of necessity, for example to prevent personal injury). Section 6 contains specific provisions on entry of a dwelling, without the consent of the owner/occupier.

Penalties for assisting offenders   Section 7 of the 1997 Act replaces the previous categorisation of, and penalties for, those who assist the principal offender in the commission of offences. In the context of felonies, some important distinctions applied between principals in the first degree, principals in the second degree, accessories before the fact and accessories after the fact. A principal in the first degree was a person who himself or herself committed the felony in question. A principal in the second degree was a person who 'aids or abets' the commission of the felony by the principal in the first degree, and an accessory before the fact was a person who 'counsels or procures' that commission, that is, who successfully incites the principal in the first degree to commit the felony. Prior to the 1997 Act, when it was necessary in a statute to refer to being a principal in the second degree or an accessory before the fact, the statute usually referred to these kinds of offences together as 'aiding, abetting, counselling or procuring'. An accessory after the fact to a felony was one who, knowing another to have committed a felony, aided that person in order to enable him or her to escape apprehension or prosecution. In the case of misdemeanours, all those who assisted the principal in the first degree were treated alike as principal offenders. The effect of section 7 of the Criminal Law Act 1997 is to retain the misdemeanour rule and to extend it to cover those offences that were previously felonies.

Section 7(1) provides that any person who aids, abets, counsels or procures the commission of an indictable offence shall be liable to be tried as a principal offender. This replaces section 8 of the Accessories and Abettors Act 1861, which applied to misdemeanours only, and which was repealed by the 1997 Act.

Section 7(2) creates a new offence to replace the common law offence of being an accessory after the fact to a felony, there being no offence of being accessory after the fact to a misdemeanour. section 7(2) provides that, if a person has committed an arrestable offence, any other person who, knowing or believing him or her to be guilty of that or some other arrestable offence does, without reasonable excuse, any act with intent to impede his or her apprehension or prosecution will be guilty of an offence.

Section 7(3) provides that, if on the trial on indictment for an arrestable offence it is proved that the accused is not guilty of the offence charged, he or she may, if the circumstances warrant it, be found guilty of an offence under subsection (2) of doing an act with intent to assist the person who committed the arrestable offence in question. Section 7(4) specifies the penalties for the offence under subsection (2) of acting with intent to impede an offender's apprehension or prosecution. They are graduated according to the gravity of the principal offence. Section 7(5) provides that, where a person is charged with an offence under subsection (2), no further proceedings (except any remand) shall be taken except with the consent of the Director of Public Prosecutions. Section 7(6) adapts sections 13(1) and 29(1)(f) of the Criminal Procedure Act 1967 relating to offences of being accessory before or after the fact so as to bring them into line with section 7 of the 1997 Act. Section 7(7) enables the offence of impeding prosecution under section 7(2) to be tried summarily, by adding that offence to the list in the Schedule of the Criminal Justice Act 1951.

Penalty for concealing offence   Section 8 of the Criminal Law Act 1997 deals with the effect of the abolition of the offences of misprision of felony and of compounding a felony. Misprision of felony consisted of concealing or procuring the concealment of a felony known to have been committed. There was no offence of misprision of misdemeanour. Compounding a felony consisted of agreeing in consideration of any reward not to prosecute for the felony. Whether compounding a misdemeanour was an offence was doubtful.

Section 8(1) created a new offence to replace the offence of compounding a felony (and compounding a misdemeanour, if that was an offence). The new offence applies where an arrestable offence has been committed and a person, knowing or believing that the offence, or some other arrestable offence, has been committed and that he or she has information which might be of material assistance in securing the prosecution or conviction of an offender for it, accepts or agrees to accept any consideration for not disclosing the information. Although under the previous law a person might have been guilty of compounding a felony even if the consideration consisted of the return of stolen property, section 8(1) makes an exception in relation to the new offence where the consideration consists of the making good of loss or injury caused by the offence or the making of reasonable compensation for that loss or injury. The result therefore is that the offence under section 8(1) is in effect one of accepting a bribe not to disclose information. Section 8(2) provides that no proceedings for an offence under the section may be instituted except by or with the consent of the Director of Public Prosecutions. Section 8(3) removes any doubt over the compounding of misdemeanours by providing that the section supersedes the common law offence of compounding. Section 8(4) enables the offence to be tried summarily, by adding it to the list in the Schedule of the Criminal Justice Act 1951.

Trial of indictable offences   Section 9 of the 1997 Act made procedural provisions as to trials on indictment. In particular, it sets out what is to be the general rule as to when a person may be found guilty of a less serious offence than that on which he or she has been arraigned. As was pointed out during the passage of the Act, the need to provide this rule was consequential on the abolition of the distinction between felony and misdemeanour, because the rules about alternative verdicts differ as between them. The effect of section 9 is that in general a person charged with offence A may be convicted of a lesser offence B whose ingredients are included in offence A; but special provision is made as regards charges of murder, corresponding broadly to the position prior to the 1997 Act.

Section 9(1) makes three provisions for trials on indictment. First, it allows the accused to make a plea of not guilty in addition to any demurrer or special plea. This replaced the law as regards felonies but possibly not as regards misdemeanours. Second, it reproduces the rule, previously contained in section 1(2) of the Criminal Justice (Verdicts) Act 1976, that a person may plead guilty to another offence of which he or she could be found guilty on the indictment. Third, it restated the rule under which, where the accused stands mute of malice or will not answer directly to the indictment, he or she is treated as having pleaded not guilty.

Special provision is made in section 9(2) to (4) for convictions of lesser offences in the case of persons found not guilty of murder to which section 3 of the Criminal Justice Act 1990 applies (formerly capital murder) and murder. The provisions correspond broadly to the provisions in the 1990 Act and at common law. These provisions were included because without them a wide range of possible verdicts would be in theory open (including perhaps even a verdict of common assault) and because of the special need for certainty as to the verdicts available to the jury in murder cases. The other offences on which a person may be convicted in the case of a charge of murder after the 1997 Act are: (i) manslaughter, (ii) causing serious bodily harm with intent to do so (section 29 of the Non-Fatal Offences against the Person Act 1997 deleted the reference to causing grievous bodily harm), (iii) an offence of which a person may be convicted under another statute specifically so providing (for example, infanticide or concealment of birth), (iv) the offence under section 7(2) of the 1997 Act of assisting a person guilty of murder, (v) an attempt to commit murder or any of the other offences mentioned above, and (vi) aiding and abetting suicide, under the Criminal Law (Suicide) Act 1993.

Section 9(5) provides that any allegation of an indictable offence shall be taken as including an allegation of attempting to commit that offence (so that a person charged with having committed an indictable offence may, as under the previous law, be convicted of the attempt). It also provides that, if a person is charged on indictment with attempting to commit an offence or with an assault or other act preliminary to an offence, he or she may be convicted of the offence charged notwithstanding that he or she is shown to be guilty of the completed offence. This replicated section 12 of the Criminal Procedure Act 1851 (which was repealed by the 1997 Act) where the completed offence was a felony (an attempt to commit a felony was a misdemeanour except in certain cases where it was made a felony by statute). Where the completed offence was a misdemeanour there was some doubt as to the law but section 9(5) makes it clear for all indictable offences. As with section 12 of the 1851 Act, the 1997 Act also provides that the right to convict is subject to the discretion of the court to discharge the jury with a view to the preferment of a new indictment for the completed offence.

Section 9(6) provides that, if a person pleads not guilty of the offence charged but guilty of another offence and the latter plea is accepted, so that he or she is not tried for the offence charged, the conviction on the plea of guilty will be an acquittal of the offence charged. This was also declaratory and did not make any change of substance. Section 9(7) made similar provision in respect of a person who is convicted after trial for the offence charged. Finally, section 9(8) provides that, in indictments containing more than one count, each count is treated as containing a separate indictment.

Powers of dealing with offenders   Section 10 deals with a number of minor offences created by statute for which no maximum penalty is provided in the statute that created the offence. These consist, mainly, of the making of false statements for the purpose of the particular statute concerned. In theory, they are punishable with imprisonment for an indefinite period, but section 10(1) provides for a maximum limit of two years.

Section 10(2) gives statutory force to the rule of practice that the maximum term of imprisonment or fine for an attempt to commit an offence for which a maximum term of imprisonment or fine is provided by an enactment should not exceed the maximum for the completed offence.

Section 10(3) confers a general power on a court to fine an offender convicted on indictment. In the case of a misdemeanour the court already had the power under common law, but there was no general power to fine in the case of a felony. The power will not apply where the offence is one for which the sentence is fixed by law, such as is the case in murder. The amount of the fine that may be imposed will be unlimited except where there is a statutory limit. The provision is also subject to any statutory requirement to deal with the offender in a particular way, for example disqualification.

Section 10(4) makes clear that a court may bind a person to keep the peace or to be of good behaviour without sentencing that person to imprisonment or fining him or her. Under some statutes a court has power to fine the offender and require the offender to enter into his or her own recognisances for keeping the peace.

Section 10(5) provides that a person sent forward by the District Court for sentence under section 13(2) of the Criminal Procedure Act 1967 following a plea of guilty is deemed to have been convicted on indictment for all purposes including those of section 10(1) to (3).

Abolition of penal servitude, hard labour and prison divisions Section 11(1) formally abolishes penal servitude. There had been no difference in practice between the prison conditions applicable to penal servitude and those applicable to imprisonment. Section 11(2) substitutes imprisonment for penal servitude. It provides that any statutory power of a court to pass a sentence of penal servitude will be treated as a statutory power to pass a sentence of imprisonment subject to the same maximum duration that would apply to a sentence of penal servitude in a particular case at present. The minimum period of penal servitude was three years but, under section 1 of the Penal Servitude Act 1891 (repealed by the 1997 Act), a court could substitute imprisonment for a maximum period of two years. After the 1997 Act, a court may pass a sentence of, for example, two and a half years.

Prior to the commencement of section 1 of the Penal Servitude Act, 1891, some statutes provided for the imposition of penal servitude without specifying any maximum period. Section 1 of the 1891 Act provided that in such cases the maximum term of penal servitude would be five years. While the repeal of that section did not affect the five year maximum which it applied to earlier statutes, it was thought desirable to make it clear that the maximum term of imprisonment corresponding to penal servitude under any enactment passed prior to the enactment of the 1891 Act is five years unless the enactment concerned specifically authorises a greater period.

Section 11(3) abolished sentences of imprisonment with hard labour. There was, in fact, no difference for many years in the prison conditions applicable to persons sentenced to imprisonment and those applicable to persons sentenced to imprisonment with hard labour.

Section 11(4) repealed various obsolete provisions which envisaged that prisoners would be divided into several divisions of varying degrees of severity. Again, such distinctions had not applied for many years.

Abolition of whipping and corporal punishment as penalty   Section 12 formally abolished the obsolete punishment of whipping whether under the sentence of a court or for offences against prison discipline under, for example, the Rules for the Government of Prisons 1947.

Amendment of particular enactments   Section 13 and the First Schedule to the 1997 Act amended a number of enactments which had depended on the difference between felony and misdemeanour. Among the enactments amended were: the Slave Trade Act 1824; the Carriers Act 1830 (amended to exempt common carriers from liability for loss of property in certain circumstances, but not to loss arising from theft, embezzlement or forgery, replacing a reference to 'felonious' acts); the Criminal Law Amendment Act 1885 and the Criminal Law Amendment Act 1935 (both concerning sexual offences involving girls under the age of 17 years); sections 35, 37, 41 and 44 of the Larceny Act 1916; and the Criminal Law (Sexual Offences) Act, 1993.

Amendment of Defence Act 1954   Section 14 and the Second Schedule provides for various modifications to the Defence Act 1954. The principal effect is to keep military law under the 1954 Act in line with the ordinary criminal law by incorporating in that Act such amendments as flow from the abolition of the distinctions between felony and misdemeanour, the abolition of penal servitude and hard labour and related amendments. There is one minor change of substance, relating to the place where a sentence of imprisonment passed by a court-martial is served. The effect of sections 228 and 229 of the Defence Act 1954 was that, if the sentence was one of penal servitude (the minimum term of penal servitude is three years), the sentence was served in a civil prison but, if the sentence was of imprisonment, apart from life imprisonment (that is to say, is for a term of not more than two years), it could be served either in a civil prison or in a military prison or detention barracks or partly in one and partly in another. In consequence of the abolition of penal servitude, the 1954 Act now provides that the sentences which are in all cases to be served in a civil prison shall be those of more than two years' imprisonment. See also the Defence Forces chapter, 351, below.

Savings and other general provisions   Section 15 of the 1997 Act consists chiefly of procedural provisions to enable prosecutions commenced before the Act came into effect to be dealt with on the basis of the law before the abolition of the distinctions between felony and misdemeanour. It also includes some general adaptations and savings.

Repeals   Section 16 and the Third Schedule contain the principal repeals effected by the 1997 Act. These include provisions already referred to, such as those in the Criminal Procedure Act 1851 the Accessories and Abettors

Act 1861 and the Penal Servitude Act 1891. These would have become inoperative as a consequence of the abolition of the distinction between felonies and misdemeanours in the 1997 Act. In addition, a number of obsolete enactments were included because they were linked in some way with the subject matter of the 1997 Act. These included the repeal *in toto* of the following: the Sunday Observance Act 1695, the Forcible Entry Act 1786, the Riot Act 1787, the Whipping Act 1820, the Hard Labour Act 1822, the South Australia Act 1842, The Whipping Act 1862 and the Garrotters Act 1863.

BAIL

General reform of bail law The Bail Act 1997 gave effect to the Sixteenth Amendment of the Constitution Act 1996 (1996 Review, 229) by which Article 40.4 of the Constitution was amended in order to provide that bail may be refused to persons charged with certain serious offences where it is reasonably considered necessary to prevent the commission of a serious offence by that person. The main effect of the Sixteenth Amendment was to reverse the effect of the decision of the Supreme Court in *The People v. O'Callaghan* [1966] I.R. 501 and *Ryan v. Director of Public Prosecutions* [1989] I.R. 399; [1989] I.L.R.M. 333 (1988 Review, 144-7) in so far as serious offences are concerned. The 1997 Act also introduced other administrative changes to the bail regime, which are not limited to serious offences. These include provision for reviews of refusals of bail where the trial has not commenced within four months, requiring cash or cash equivalent to be lodged as part of bail; requiring bailpersons to guarantee the good behaviour of the accused while on bail and allow the forfeiture of bail in this regard; and strengthening the provisions of the Criminal Justice Act 1984 in relation to the imposition of consecutive sentences for offences committed on bail. Prior to the 1997 Act, bail was largely regulated by common law and the decisions in the *O'Callaghan* and *Ryan* cases, so the Act constitutes a fundamental reform of this area, both in substantive and procedural terms. In that respect, some of its provisions reflect those in the United Kingdom Bail Act 1977. At the time of writing (May 1998), the Act had not been brought into force by Ministerial Order.

Definition of serious offence The restrictive bail provisions introduced by the Sixteenth Amendment to the Constitution and the 1997 Act apply to persons charged with serious offences, defined as those specified in the Schedule to the Act (as amended by section 30 of the Non-Fatal Offences against the Person Act 1997, discussed generally below, 304) and in respect of which a person may be punished by a term of imprisonment of five years or more. Thus, while all offences to which the 1997 Act applies must carry a penalty of five years or more, not all such offences will be covered by the legislation -

primarily on the grounds that some offences are unlikely to be ones where the question of re-offending is relevant. Thus, while a 'serious offence' under the Bail Act 1997 is comparable to the definition of an arrestable offence in the Criminal Law Act 1997 (see above, 268), the terms are not identical.

Refusal of bail for serious offence   Section 2 of the Bail Act 1997 provides (in accordance with the Sixteenth Amendment of the Constitution) that where an application is made for bail by a person who is charged with a serious offence, a court may refuse to grant bail if it is 'satisfied that such refusal is reasonably considered necessary to prevent the commission of a serious offence' by the accused. The refusal of bail under section 2 is not, however, automatic in respect of any particular serious offence or category of offence. The court, in deciding whether the refusal of bail is reasonably considered necessary to prevent the commission of a serious offence by the accused, is required by section 2(2) to take into account any or all of the following six factors:

'(a) the nature and degree of seriousness of the offence with which the accused person is charged and the sentence likely to be imposed on conviction,
(b) the nature and degree of seriousness of the offence apprehended and the sentence likely to be imposed on conviction,
(c) the nature and strength of the evidence in support of the charge,
(d) any conviction of the accused person for an offence committed while he or she was on bail,
(e) any previous convictions of the accused person including any conviction the subject of an appeal (which has neither been determined or withdrawn) to a court,
(f) any other offence in respect of which the accused person is charged and is awaiting trial.'

In addition, the court *may* have regard to a seventh factor, namely, that the accused is addicted to a controlled drug within the meaning of the Misuse of Drugs Act 1977. In taking into account these matters the court may hear submissions by or on behalf of the accused and/or the prosecution before making a decision.

Section 2(3) provides that the court, in deciding whether the refusal of bail is reasonably considered necessary to prevent the commission of a serious offence by the accused, does not have to be satisfied that any *specific* offence is likely to be committed by the accused. This is, of course, central to the substantive changes effected by the Sixteenth Amendment and the 1997 Act, since it was expressly noted in the *O'Callaghan* and *Ryan* cases that it was inconsistent with Article 40.4 as it was then worded for the courts to deprive a person of his or her liberty on the basis of predicting future behaviour while on bail. By permitting the courts to refuse bail on the basis of a prediction about possible future behaviour without specifying what that behaviour might be, the Sixteenth Amendment and the 1997 Act involve a substantial diminution of the presumption of innocence, at least in respect of serious offences. Given that the background to the referendum on the Sixteenth Amendment was the murder of investigative journalist Veronica Guerin (1996 Review, 228), it is hardly surprising that there was unanimous political backing for the changes thus effected to the criminal justice system. Sustained opposition to the Sixteenth Amendment and the 1997 Act was expressed by those concerned that the proposals involved a disproportionate response to the perceived problem of crimes committed on bail, but these were not accepted against the political context sketched.

Renewal of bail application   Section 3 of the Bail Act 1997 provides for the review of a refusal of a bail application if the trial has not commenced within four months of the initial refusal. The court may, if it is satisfied that the interests of justice require it, release the person on bail. Before deciding whether to grant or refuse bail in such a case, the court may hear submissions by or on behalf of the accused and/or the prosecution concerning the issue of delay. It is expressly provided that section 3 does not affect the operation of section 24 of the Criminal Procedure Act 1967 concerning the periods of remand, as amended by the Criminal Justice (Miscellaneous Provisions) Act 1997, discussed below, 315. The Minister for Justice pointed out during the passage of the Act in the Oireachtas that it had always been the practice to give priority to trials of accused persons remanded in custody, but that the imposition of a express time limit would highlight the necessity to treat these cases on a priority basis and avoid a situation of an accused spending a long period in prison on remand.

Evidence of previous criminal record   Section 4 of the 1997 Act deals with measures to ensure that a pending trial is not prejudiced through the publication of details of a person's criminal record. Where a court is hearing an application for bail under section 2, the previous criminal record of the accused cannot be referred to in a manner which may prejudice a fair trial subsequently. In order to prevent possible prejudice the court is empowered to direct that the bail application be held *in camera* or to exclude members of the public other than *bona fide* representatives of the media, or any other person whom the court permits to remain. The Act also prohibits the publication or broadcast of any information concerning the criminal record of the accused which was referred to during the bail application and provides that it is an offence for a proprietor, editor, publisher or broadcaster to publish or broadcast any matter in contravention of section 4, in respect of which the penalties are, on summary conviction, a maximum fine of £1,500 and/or imprisonment for up to 12 months and, on conviction on indictment, a maximum fine of £10,000 and/or imprisonment for up to three years.

Payment of moneys in court   Section 5 of the 1997 Act obliges an accused, and his or her sureties, to pay into court at least one third of the amount fixed for bail before the accused is free on bail. Prior to the 1997 Act, there was no formal requirement that an accused person being released on bail, or his or her sureties, must, prior to being released on bail, pay any money into court. In practice in the majority of cases no money (or equivalent security) was in fact paid into court and an accused was released on the promise that the bail money would be paid by him or her or his or her sureties in the event of his or her failure to answer bail.

Section 5 of the 1997 Act provides that it is open to the court to specify an amount which is greater than one third where it considers it appropriate to do so. It also empowers the court to accept some other form of security in lieu of cash in order to comply with the requirement that at least one third of the amount of bail must be paid into court. Most forms of security which could easily be converted to cash may be accepted, including bank, building society, credit union and post office deposit books. Title deeds to land are specifically excluded. Where such securities are accepted, the court will direct that the relevant institution not permit the balance in the amount to be reduced below an amount equal to that required to be paid into court or the current balance, whichever is the lesser. The amount paid into court will be returned to the accused and his or her sureties where the conditions of the recognisance have been duly complied with.

Conditions of bail   Section 6 provides that a court shall attach standard conditions relating to good behaviour and also allow a range of other conditions to be attached to the granting of bail. Section 23 of the Criminal Procedure Act 1967 provides that a person's release on bail will be conditioned for his or her appearance before the court at the end of the period of remand. In granting bail judges had in practice often attached conditions such as a requirement to report to the Gardaí at stated intervals or the surrender of passports. Section 6 of the 1997 Act provides that the recognisance to be entered into by an accused person who is granted bail will be subject to the conditions that he or she:

   (i)   appears before the court at the end of the period of remand,
   (ii) will not commit any offence while on bail and
   (iii) will otherwise be of good behaviour while on bail.

In addition the court may impose any further condition or conditions as appropriate, including a requirement to reside or remain in a particular place in the State, to report to a Garda station at specified intervals, to surrender his or her passport, to refrain from frequenting certain places or having contact with certain persons. The accused and his or her sureties will be given a copy of the recognisance containing the conditions and the accused will be entitled to apply to the court to have the conditions (other than the standard conditions relating to good behaviour) varied, added to or revoked. Where there is an application to vary the conditions the prosecutor will be entitled to be heard in those proceedings.

Section 6 also provides that a surety or a Garda may apply to the court for the issue of a warrant for the arrest of the accused on the ground that he or she is about to contravene any of the conditions attached to his or her bail. In the case of the surety, such an application may be made with the aim of prevention the subsequent estreatment or forfeiture of the amount by which he or she has agreed to be bound if the accused actually breaches a condition. A Garda may then arrest the accused even if he or she does not have the warrant in his or her possession at the time of arrest, but the warrant must be produced and served on the accused subsequently. A person arrested on foot of such a warrant must be brought before the court as soon as practicable where he or she may be either committed to prison pending trial or readmitted to bail on entering a fresh recognisance. These provisions replace those in section 33 of the Criminal Procedure Act 1967, which was repealed by the 1997 Act.

Sufficiency of bailspersons Section 7 of the 1997 Act provides that a court must satisfy itself as to the sufficiency and suitability of proposed bailspersons. In so doing the Court will have regard to that person's financial resources, character and antecedents, any previous convictions and his or her relationship to the accused. For this purpose the court may, if it thinks it necessary, hear evidence or submissions on the matter. Section 7 replaces section 27 of the Criminal Procedure Act 1967 which provided merely that the Court shall in every case be satisfied as to the sufficiency of proposed bailspersons.

Endorsement on warrants as to release on bail Section 8 inserted a new section 30 of the Criminal Procedure Act 1967 and arose from the changes relating to payments into court in section 5 of the 1997 Act and the conditions to be attached to the granting of bail in section 6 of the Act. Section 8 provides that when a warrant is issued for the arrest of a person, the warrant may be endorsed to permit bail to the person, with or without sureties, when he or she is arrested. The endorsement will state the amount in which the accused and his or her sureties are to be bound as well as the conditions of the recognisance. The endorsement will permit the Garda in charge of the Garda Station to which the person is brought on arrest to release him or her where he or she enters into a recognisance and upon the payment of the specified amount of the recognisance. Any money received by the Garda must be deposited with the relevant District Court clerk. These provisions do not apply to persons arrested under section 251 of the Defence Act 1954 on suspicion of being a deserter or an absentee without leave from the Defence Forces.

Estreatment of recognisance and forfeiture of moneys paid into court Section 9 of the 1997 Act is intended to make the process of estreatment or forfeiture of bail money simpler by requiring a court, in cases where an accused breaches a condition of his or her recognisance, and where it issues a warrant for his or her arrest to order, at the same time, the estreatment of the recognisance and forfeiture of the amount paid into court. It will then be for the accused or his or her sureties to demonstrate to the court why there should be no estreatment or forfeiture.

It provides that the court may issue a warrant for the arrest of an accused person where a Garda gives information on oath that the accused has contravened a condition of his or her bail. A Garda may then arrest the accused even if he or she does not have the warrant in his or her possession at the time of arrest, but the warrant must be produced and served on the accused subsequently. A person arrested on foot of such a warrant must be brought before the court as soon as practicable. The accused and his or sureties will remain bound by their recognisances where a warrant has been issued under the section and any money paid into court will not be released until proceedings under section 9 are concluded.

Where the court is satisfied that the accused has contravened a condition of his or her recognisance, it shall order the estreatment of the recognisances of the accused and his or her sureties and the forfeiture of the amount paid into court. Where a court orders estreatment or forfeiture, the accused and his or her sureties may apply within 21 days to have the order varied or discharged and where such an application is made the court will hear representations by or on behalf of the applicant as to why the order of estreatment or forfeiture should be varied or discharged.

Consecutive sentences for offences committed on bail Section 10 of the 1997 Act amended section 11 of the Criminal Justice Act 1984 (which deals with the imposition of consecutive sentences for offences committed while on bail) by inserting a new section 11(4) to provide that a court, in deciding on the penalty to be imposed in respect of an offence committed while the accused was on bail in the context of consecutive sentences required by the section, will treat the fact that the offence was committed while on bail as an aggravating factor and will impose a greater sentence as a result. The amendment will not apply to cases where the sentence for the previous offence is life imprisonment or where the court considers that there are exceptional circumstances to justify not doing so.

Abolition of function of Peace Commissioners in bail   Section 11 of the 1997 Act amended sections 26, 28 (1), 28 (4) and 33 of the Criminal Procedure Act 1967 by deleting references to the power of Peace Commissioners to grant bail. This was described as a tidying up provision, taking account of a number of decisions which had indicated that the power of Peace Commissioners to grant bail might be inconsistent with Article 34 of the Constitution: see, for example, *O'Mahony v. Melia* [1989] I.R. 335; [1990] I.L.R.M. 14 (1989 Review, 92).

Post conviction application for bail   In *The People v. Sweetman*, Court of Criminal Appeal, July 23, 1997, the Court, in an *ex tempore* judgment, emphasised that the criteria applicable in a bail application pending the hearing of an application for leave to appeal to the Court are quite different to those that apply to a pre-trial bail application. The defendant had been convicted of murder in the Central Criminal Court and applied for bail pending the hearing of the application for leave to appeal the conviction. Pursuant to section 32 of the Courts of Justice Act 1924 (as amended by section 3(6) of the Criminal Procedure Act 1993) the Court has a wide discretion whether to grant or refuse bail in any instance. The defendant had been convicted primarily on the basis of a confession. In the application for leave to appeal, he would be challenging its admissibility in evidence on the grounds that it was the fruit of a voice identification which had been ruled inadmissible, that the accused had not signed the statement, and that it had resulted from improper conduct by the Garda Siochana during the period of detention and questioning. The Court of Criminal Appeal refused the defendant bail, noting that the criteria relevant to pre-trial applications for bail are not the same as those that operate post conviction, in particular because a convicted person no longer enjoys the presumption of innocence. In connection with the defendant's inculpatory statement or confession, the Court held that the proper course was to take the statement as it stood with the presumption that the trial had been conducted in accordance with law. In the absence of any contrary evidence, the statement constituted clear evidence on which a jury would be entitled to convict the defendant of murder; and thus the prosecution's case, based on the materials before the Court, was such a strong one that in exercising its discretion, the Court was not justified in admitting the defendant to bail at that stage.

COMMON LAW OFFENCES

Abolition of common law offences by statute   The Interpretation (Amendment) Act 1997 was enacted to deal with the situation where a common law offence is repealed by statute but where prosecutions involving the old common law offences have yet to be heard. Its direct origins can be traced to the abolition by section 28 of the Non-Fatal Offences against the Person Act 1997 of various common law offences, such as assault, false imprisonment and kidnapping and their replacement by offences in the 1997 Act (see below 312). During the passage of the Interpretation (Amendment) Act 1997, the Minister for Justice referred to a number of decisions in the Central Criminal Court and the Special Criminal Court which cast doubt on whether charges of committing the old common law offences could be prosecuted after the coming into force of the Non-Fatal Offences against the Person Act 1997. The Interpretation (Amendment) Act 1997 provides that where a common law offence is abolished by statute, it shall not in general affect pending prosecutions; the Act came into effect on November 1, 1997, on its signature the President. During the debate in the Oireachtas, the Minister for Justice indicated that his advice was that section 28 of the Non-Fatal Offences against the Person Act 1997 operated prospectively only, but he also accepted that the matter should be put beyond doubt. As it transpired, in *Quinlivan v. Governor of Portlaoise Prison (No.3)*, High Court, December 9, 1997, decided after the Interpretation (Amendment) Act 1997 came into effect, McGuinness J. held, in effect, that the Minister's advice was correct.

In *Quinlivan (No.3)*, the applicant was in custody awaiting trial before the Special Criminal Court with false imprisonment contrary to common law (on another aspect of the applicant's detention, see *Quinlivan v. Governor of Portlaoise Prison (No.2)* [1998] 1 I.L.R.M. 294 (SC), 319, below). The Non-Fatal Offences Against the Person Act 1997 created a new statutory offence of false imprisonment and section 28 of the 1997 Act had abolished the common law offence. There was no specific provision in the 1997 Act saving the prosecution of offences of common law false imprisonment allegedly committed prior to the date when the Act came into force on August 19, 1997 and coming to trial after that date. The applicant sought his release from custody under Article 40.4 of the Constitution on the ground that there was now no offence known to the law on which he could be charged. The respondents contended that the general canons of construction of legislation would enable the court to imply that section 28 of the 1997 Act should not operate retrospectively so as to eliminate prosecutions already in being when the Act came into force. In effect, McGuinness J. accepted this argument.

She accepted, as had been done by the Special Criminal Court in *The People v. Kavanagh*, Special Criminal Court, October 29, 1997, that the core offence with which the applicant had been charged remained an offence at common law and could not benefit from the saver in section 21(1)(e) of the Interpretation Act 1937. She then turned to section 28 of the 1997 Act which she held had to be considered not only in the light of the canons of construction, particularly the presumption against retrospective effect (discussed in *Hamilton v. Hamilton* [1982] I.R. 466), but also in the light of the constitutional requirement of non-interference with the judicial process (considered in the leading case *Buckley v. Attorney General* [1950] I.R. 67). In this respect, McGuinness J. held that where two interpretations of section 28 were open, the Court had to adopt that which was not in conflict with the Constitution. She held that the 1997 Act contained no provision for pending cases, nor did it expressly state that the abolition of the common law offence of false imprisonment was to have the effect of halting all prosecutions for the offence before courts. The court had to hold that the intention of the Oireachtas was to act prospectively and not to interfere with prosecutions under common law of which the courts were already seized. As indicated already, the Interpretation (Amendment) Act 1997 had already been enacted to deal with this point, though the decision of McGuinness J. provided a more solid basis on which to proceed with the trials such as those in the instant case.

DEFENCES

Automatism *O'Brien v. Parker* [1997] 2 I.L.R.M. 170 (HC), Lavan J. considered the application of the defence of automatism. Although the case arose in a civil context, the decision is of interest to criminal practitioners. Similarly, although *Doyle v. Wicklow County Council* [1974] I.R. 66 was not a criminal prosecution, the discussion of the defence of insanity in that case proved highly influential to criminal practitioners.

In *O'Brien v. Parker*, the plaintiff had instituted proceedings in the Circuit Court against the defendant for damages arising from a road traffic accident. The defendant claimed that he had suffered an epileptic fit at the time of the accident, and that this absolved him of negligence. The plaintiff's claim was dismissed and he appealed to the High Court. On the re-hearing in the High Court, the defendant agreed that he had no history of epilepsy but that, immediately before the accident, he had experienced an altered state of consciousness, had become aware of a strange smell, became sensitive to light and that the next thing he remembered was the car crash.

Lavan J. accepted for the purposes of the case the defendant's argument that, where a defendant proved that his actions were the result of sudden illness, a defence of inevitable accident was made out. However, he held that, in order for the defence of automatism to apply, a state of unconsciousness in which the defendant was left without control of his actions had to exist. Thus, impaired, reduced or partial control was not sufficient to maintain the defence. this respect, he held that the defendant had not, on the balance of probabilities, established the defence because there had been no total destruction of the defendant's voluntary control. It is notable that the plaintiff had contended that negligence was established in the instant case because the defendant had admitted that there were symptoms which should have led him to stop driving.

For a further discussion of automatism, see *The People v. Courtney*, Court of Criminal Appeal, July 21, 1994 (1994 Review, 167-9), which was not apparently opened to Lavan J. in *O'Brien v. Parker*. On the liability in tort in *O'Brien*, see the Torts chapter, 716–23, below.

Provocation In two cases in 1997, the Court of Criminal Appeal reversed murder convictions on the ground that the trial judge had misdirected the jury in respect of the defence of provocation.

In the first of these cases, *The People v. Mullane*, Court of Criminal Appeal, March 11, 1997, the only issue before the trial jury was whether the applicant was guilty of murder or manslaughter as it was conceded that he had unlawfully killed the deceased, but it was argued that he had been provoked. In directing the jury on the question of provocation, the trial judge twice read two paragraphs from the decision of the Court of Criminal Appeal in *The People v. MacEoin* [1978] I.R. 27. The jury found the defendant guilty. In his application for leave to appeal, the applicant accepted that the *MacEoin* case correctly stated that the test to be applied was a subjective one, but argued that the trial judge had erred in simply quoting the relevant passages from the judgment since they might on their own convey the impression that an objective test still applied in relation to the amount of force used. The applicant contended that it was necessary for the trial judge to explain to the jury that the amount of force used must also be assessed by reference to the accused's state of mind, and whether given his state of mind it was reasonable for him to act in the manner that he did. As indicated, the Court of Criminal Appeal ordered a re-trial.

The Court held that the trial judge obviously meant well in repeating the very words of the *MacEoin* case, but the words of a judgment were not to be used as if they were embodied in a statute and should rather have been used as a guide. The Court accepted that the relevant passage was capable of creating an impression in the minds of a jury that they might approach the matter by reference to the standard of a reasonable person. Since this had not been intended by *MacEoin* case, a trial judge was required to make it clear to the jury at all times that they had to decide matters by reference to the state of mind of the accused. In the instant case, while it did not appear that the applicant had any particular sensitivities above the usual, nonetheless, the jury were the ones who heard him give evidence and had the chance to size up what manner of individual he was, and therefore, it was necessary to emphasise to them the subjective nature of the test. On this basis the Court considered that a re-trial should be ordered.

In the second case on provocation, *The People v. Noonan* [1998] 1 I.L.R.M. 154 (CCA), the Court of Criminal Appeal also reversed the defendant's conviction for murder on the ground that the trial judge had misdirected the jury in respect of the defence of provocation. The defendant contended that the trial judge had opened case law supporting an objective test on the nature of provocation, when the correct test was, as we have already seen, a subjective one. It was accepted that no objections had been raised on requisitions at the trial itself. Nonetheless, as indicated, the Court of Criminal Appeal quashed the defendant's conviction and ordered a re-trial. The only conclusion the Court could reach as to why no objection had been made to the trial judge's charge was that this was due to an oversight and, as the directions had been crucial to a fundamental aspect of the defence, in the interests of justice the Court would deal with the points argued on appeal as to the adequacy of the directions. The Court accepted that, in general terms, the trial judge had made the objective test, derived from English case law, a constituent element of the legal defence of provocation. Although the trial judge had quoted from the relevant Irish case law, in particular the decision in *The People v. MacEoin* [1978] I.R. 28, where a subjective test was applied, the Court held that it was impossible to escape the conclusion that a jury being told about two quite inconsistent tests, namely the English objective test and the Irish subjective one, could be left in confusion. The Court re-iterated the view expressed in *The People v. Berber and Levy* [1944] I.R. 405 that where inconsistent instructions were given to a jury on a vital matter, it was impossible to be sure that a jury did not act on the incorrect direction and that a conviction in such circumstances should be quashed.

DELAY

Assault and larceny In *Connolly v. Director of Public Prosecutions*, Supreme Court, January 17, 1997, the Supreme Court held that the applicant had not established that the delay in finally dealing with various offences against him was sufficient to prohibit his prosecution. In August 1994, the applicant had been charged with namely assault, larceny and demanding money with menaces. His trial was listed for hearing in February 1995, but he sought and was granted an adjournment. The case came on for hearing in May 1995, but after two days the jury was discharged. The matter was next listed for hearing in July 1995. On that occasion the jury were unable to reach a verdict. On the applicant's next trial date in December 1995, no court was available to hear the matter. In the meantime, the Court of Criminal Appeal had ordered a re-trial in another matter involving the accused and he sought an adjournment of the instant case until after the re-hearing in February 1996. The instant case was listed for March 1996, but on the night before the hearing the applicant was injured and was treated in hospital. The case was re-listed for April 1996, by which time the applicant had applied for judicial review.

As indicated, the Supreme Court declined to prohibit the trial from proceeding. Applying the case law arising from *The State (O'Connell) v. Fawsitt*

[1986] I.R. 362, including *Director of Public Prosecutions v. Byrne* [1994] 2 I.R. 236; [1994] 2 I.L.R.M. 91 (1993 Review, 223-6), *Cahalane v. Murphy* [1994] 2 I.R. 262; [1994] 2 I.L.R.M. 383 (1994 Review, 171-3) and *Hogan v. President of the Circuit Court* [1994] 2 I.R. 513 (1994 Review, 173), the Court held that the onus of demonstrating a breach of the right to a trial with reasonable expedition lay at all times on the applicant and that in the instant case, the applicant had not discharged that onus of proof. The Court accepted that the prosecution had moved with reasonable dispatch in charging the applicant with the offences in question and in proceeding to bring him to trial. It also noted that no blame attached to the prosecution for the collapse of the May 1995 trial and that any delay was not so excessive as to raise an inference that the risk of an unfair trial had been established as a reality. While the delay may well have caused the applicant substantial disappointment, the Court concluded that he had not established that he was unfit to stand trial.

Fraud In two separate cases in which Quirke J. delivered judgment on the same date in 1997, he declined to order that trials for fraud be prohibited on the grounds of delay.

In the first such case, *Flynn v. Director of Public Prosecutions*, High Court, October 7, 1997, the applicant and others had been charged with conspiracy to defraud a company by misappropriating its moneys to buy apartments in Spain. He claimed there had been inexcusable and unwarranted delay in the prosecution, and that there had been a failure to bring the proceedings against him to trial with reasonable expedition. He submitted that a result of the lack of expedition and delay was that an essential witness would not be available to testify at trial, and that this would prejudice his capacity to adduce vital evidence in his defence. As indicated, Quirke J. refused the relief sought.

He referred with approval to the factors set out in *B v. Director of Public Prosecutions* [1997] 2 I.L.R.M. 188 (see 289, below), in particular that the court had to have regard to the right of the applicant to a fair trial and to the interests of the community in prosecuting crime. He held that the court had to determine whether on the evidence the applicant's defence had been explicitly prejudiced by the non-availability of a material witness. He accepted that there had been a significant delay in the trial of the charge against the applicant, but he was satisfied that no act or omission on the part of the prosecution caused or contributed to any delay in the trial. He concluded that the prosecution had acted reasonably in all the circumstances and was not guilty of any unreasonable delay in the investigation of the complaint and the prosecution of the proceedings, including the date of the hearing of these proceedings. Quirke J. acknowledged that the applicant had been disadvantaged in his personal and professional life and was restricted in his capacity to earn a livelihood, and that he had suffered substantial anxiety and concern. However, he held that there were valid reasons for the delay, the delay was not unreasonable in the circumstances, and the disadvantage to the applicant was unavoidable in all the circumstances. As to the absence of the testimony of the witness in this case, Quirke J. opined that it could hardly be said to work an injustice on the applicant; indeed, the contrary appeared to be the case. On that basis, the relief sought was refused.

In the second judgment delivered by him in this area, *Keely v. Moriarty*, High Court, October 7, 1997, Quirke J. also declined to order that a trial for fraud be prohibited on the grounds of delay. The applicant had been employed as a financial accountant with a company called Aer Lingus Holdings Ltd, a subsidiary of Aer Lingus Teo the State-owned airline. In May 1990, an investigation was commissioned by the Garda Fraud Squad into the accounting affairs of the company. Between May 1990 and January 1994, exhaustive investigations and enquiries were undertaken and in January 1994 the applicant was arrested and charged on indictment with the offence of conspiracy to defraud contrary to common law. In October 1995, the applicant sought discovery and the date for trial was put back to April 1996 as neither party were then in a position to proceed. The applicant sought an order of prohibition on the ground that, arising from the delay an essential witness was unavailable to testify, thus prejudicing the applicant's capacity to adduce evidence in his defence. As indicated, Quirke J. refused the relief sought. He again referred with approval to the factors set out in *B v. Director of Public Prosecutions* [1997] 2 I.L.R.M. 188 (see below) and that in investigating the reason for the delay regard must be had to both the interests of the applicant and the community. In the instant case, he held that the Gardaí had acted with reasonable expedition having regard to all the circumstances which affected the investigation against the applicant, in particular the complexity of the issues involved in the case, and that there had thus been no unreasonable delay. He also referred to the fact that the applicant had not been incarcerated whilst awaiting trial. Finally, he held that the non-availability of the particular witness referred to by the applicant would not work an injustice or prejudice his capacity to adduce vital evidence in his defence.

Handling stolen goods In *McCormack v. Director of Public Prosecutions*, High Court, March 20, 1997, Budd J. rejected an application for prohibition in respect of delay connected with a prosecution for handling stolen goods.

Sexual abuse Nine judgments delivered in 1997 concerned delays in sexual abuse cases, reflecting the enormous increase in reporting and prosecution of such cases in recent years. In three of these cases the courts ordered that the trial be prohibited arising from the delays in the case.

In the first, *B. v. Director of Public Prosecutions* [1997] 2 I.L.R.M. 188, the applicant had been charged in 1993 with sexual offences against three of his daughters alleged to have been committed between 1963 and 1973. In January 1994, he was returned for trial to the Central Criminal Court on an indictment containing 69 counts alleging rape and indecent assault. That trial was adjourned pending the outcome of the instant judicial review proceedings. The application was dismissed in the High Court and the Supreme Court affirmed this and dismissed the appeal.

The Court accepted that, *prima facie*, the delay of around 20 or 30 years between the alleged offences and the pending trial was an inordinate lapse of time. It also accepted that if the defence had been explicitly prejudiced by the prosecution's delay, for example, by the non-availability of a material witness, then the accused would be entitled, on the delay being unreasonable and prejudicial, to an order prohibiting the trial. The Court should consider the length of any delay, any reason for the delay, the accused's assertion of his right, and the prejudice to the accused by the delay. The Court also accepted that cases involving allegations of sexual abuse of children and young people were in a special category, as had been held in *G v. Director of Pubic Prosecutions* [1994] 1 I.R. 374 (1994 Review, 174). Factors relevant to such cases included, *inter alia*, the interpersonal relationships between the parties, the extent of the dominion exerted, the nature of the offence and the availability of alibis or witnesses. In the instant case, the Court held that it was clear from the evidence (as stated by a psychologist) that the trial judge could, as he did, find that dominion was exercised in the family relationships by the applicant over his daughters and that this dominion placed the case in a special category, as the applicant's actions prevented the daughters from taking steps to allow the prosecution proceed within a more usual time frame. Thus, the applicant was prevented from arguing that the delay was unreasonable while such dominion existed, and any delay which occurred during this time of dominion was reasonable. On that basis, the Court declined to prohibit the trial.

The second case on delay in sexual assault cases in 1997 was *J.J. v. Director of Public Prosecutions*, High Court, February 21, 1997. The applicant was a married man charged with assaulting his eldest daughter in 1987. As a result of a complaint made to a counsellor in 1988, the applicant had attended counselling in relation to the assault. He claimed that the Gardaí compelled him to attend counselling and could not now initiate a prosecution. Barron J. refused the relief sought. He held that he applicant could not rely on a form of estoppel in asserting that the prosecution could not now be entitled to initiate a prosecution. He emphasised that counselling and prosecution were two distinct reactions to the matters complained of. Nor did he accept that this was a case were there was a serious risk that the applicant would not receive a fair trial or that it would otherwise be unconscionable to put him on trial.

The third case in this category was *O'R. v. Director of Public Prosecutions*, High Court, February 27, 1997. Again, Kelly J. took into account the extent to which the accused person may have contributed to the delay in the reporting of the offences alleged to the prosecution authorities. In 1995, the applicant had been charged with ninety offences of a sexual nature, alleged to have been committed between 1976 and 1992 when the applicant was a swimming coach at a swimming club attached to a school. The majority of the charges related to the period between 1976 and 1984. The applicant contended that the earlier charges were inadequately specified and that he had been prejudiced by the delay.

Kelly J. accepted that it was clear that the bulk of the delay in respect of which complaint had been made arose from the failure on the part of the alleged victims to report the matters in question to the Garda Síochána. As in the previous cases already discussed, Kelly J. noted that the onus of demonstrating grounds warranting the intervention of the High Court lay at all times on the applicant, that special considerations arose in the case of charges of the sexual abuse of children and that he had to consider the extent to which the applicant may have contributed to the delay in the reporting to the prosecution authorities of the offences alleged. In this respect, the evidence was to the effect that the relationship between the applicant and the children was not merely one of adult and children, but was a great deal more than that by virtue of the position held by the applicant. In addition, Kelly J. concluded that the evidence did not satisfy him that any actual or particular prejudice had been established by the applicant which would render his trial unfair.

The fourth case in this area was *P.D. v. Director of Public Prosecutions*, High Court, March 19, 1997. Here, the applicant had been sent forward for trial in December 1993 in respect of nine charges of indecent assault alleged to have been committed between 1979 and 1986. The matter had been reported in 1992. McCracken J. dismissed the applicant's claim that the trial be prohibited. He again emphasised that the onus was on the applicant to show that there was a real risk that he would not be able to have a fair trial and that the applicant had not discharged that onus. Having reviewed the particular facts of the case, he concluded that the delay on the part of the complainant's delay in reporting the abuses was reasonable and understandable. He also concluded that no prejudice had been established by the applicant. McCracken J. added that, although the onus was on the applicant to show that there was a real risk that he would not be able to obtain a fair trial, the onus at the trial would be on the prosecution to prove beyond all reasonable doubt that these offences took place, that it would be the duty of the trial judge to warn the jury of any possible prejudice to the applicant arising due to the passage of time and to direct them that this was a matter that they must take into account in assessing the evidence of the respective witnesses.

The fifth case in this area was *P.C. v. Director of Public Prosecutions*, High Court, July 24, 1997 in which McGuinness J. granted an order of prohibition preventing the applicant's prosecution. He had been charged in 1995 with various offences of a sexual nature alleged to have taken place in 1985 and 1986. In 1988, the complainant had informed various people of the alleged abuse, but no action had been taken until 1995. The applicant's claim was based both on grounds of excessive delay, a lack of specificity in the charges alleged against him and that the book of evidence contained impermissible statements.

McGuinness J. held that the element of dominion referred to in the previous cases already discussed should not be presumed to exist automatically in all cases where a person was accused of sexual offences. She accepted that the delay between 1988 and 1995 had been due to the complainant alone and had not been caused in any way by the applicant. There was, in her view, a real risk that, by reason of the delay, the applicant would not obtain a fair trial. Finally, McGuinness J. concluded that the defects in the book of evidence were such that it should be withdrawn and not be left to the Distinct Court judge to rule on in a preliminary examination. We note here that the Supreme Court reversed this decision in judgments delivered on May 28, 1998 and we will discuss that appeal in the 1988 Review.

The sixth case in this area was *D.C. v. Director of Public Prosecutions*, High Court, October 31, 1997 in which Geoghegan J. declined to order prohibition. The applicant, a Roman Catholic priest had been a teacher in a secondary school from September 1963 to July 1991. He was charged with a number of sexual offences against four different males, all of whom were former pupils of his in the college. The first communication of any complaint were in 1991 and ere made anonymously. The allegations in respect of the first complaint were put to the applicant who denied them. In April 1995, the applicant was informed in an interview by the Garda Síochána of further allegations. In January 1996, the applicant was interviewed in respect of additional complaints. As indicated, the application for prohibition against this background was refused. Geoghegan J. held that the applicant's poor health was a factor, but that it had never been accepted that ill health falling short of an inability to appear in court for his trial could be invoked as a ground for prohibiting the trial. Ill health could be relevant where a situation was very finely balanced and the Court was genuinely concerned on other grounds that an accused might not have a fair trial by reason of delay. He distinguished the instant case from then circumstances in *P.C. v. Director of Public Prosecutions*, High Court, July 24, 1997 (291, above) because a senior clinical psychologist had conducted extensive interviews with three of the complainants and therefore he was not relying for his opinion that dominion had existed on statements made to the Garda Síochána. In addition, he held that the decision in *B. v. Director of Public Prosecutions* [1997] 2 I.L.R.M. 188 (289, above) must not be taken as authority for the proposition that in all cases where an accused is charged with sexual abuse of a child or young person which took place some years ago, any claimed prejudice on account of delay can be negatived by a claim that the accused exercised 'dominion' over the complainant, since regard must be had at all times to the presumption of innocence. Nonetheless, he held that no prejudice had been established to justify prohibition and he pointed out that if it emerged at the trial that the delays had genuinely prejudiced the applicant in some way that was not clear at the pre-trial stage it would be open to the trial judge to deal with the matter in whatever way appeared to him or her to be just.

The seventh case in this area was *P.W. v. Director of Public Prosecutions*, High Court, November 27, 1997 in which Flood J. granted an order of prohibition. The applicant had been charged on a number of counts of indecent assault, alleged to have been committed on dates unknown between the years 1977 and 1983. The complainant had also made complaints against another man, who had died before the instant case came before the High Court. Flood J. noted that the delay in this case was not due to any dominance exercised over the complainant by the applicant and the delay had been solely down to the complainant. Having regard to the book of evidence in the case, there was no corroboration of the prosecution case, so that the jury would have to decide the case on its view of the credibility of the complainant and the applicant should he give evidence. Flood J. accepted that in the non-availability of the other man against whom the complainant had also made a complaint, the applicant was deprived of a vital witness. By virtue of the lapse of time, a potentially vital element of the defence no longer existed, and this could constitute a major prejudice to the applicant's defence, while he had not been responsible in any way for the delay. Since the absence of evidence which could be material in a challenge to the complainant's credibility could be a very significant prejudice, Flood J. concluded that the applicant should be granted the relief sought.

The eighth case in this area was *Fitzpatrick v. Director of Public Prosecutions*, High Court, December 5, 1997 in which McCracken J. also granted an order of prohibition. In 1997 the applicant had been charged with the indecent assault and rape of two young sisters in the early 1980s, the offences relating to two alleged incidents in the girls' home. While McCracken J. accepted that special factors had to be considered in cases of sexual abuse of children and young people, he also noted that there was no special relationship of trust between the applicant and the girls in this case and that there was no evidence of dominion. Two witnesses, who would have been available had the complaints been made earlier, were not now available, one having died and the other proving untraceable. Having regard to the presumption of innocence, McCracken J. concluded that the defendant was deprived of two witnesses who could contradict the prosecution evidence. Without that evidence, the sole way he could defend himself was by his own evidence and this was unsatisfactory as that evidence was not independent and since he also had what McCracken J. described as an inherent right not to give evidence. Taking all these factors into account, there was a serious risk that the applicant would not obtain a fair trial due to the delay. See also the Evidence chapter, 412, below.

The ninth case in this area was *F.(S.) v. Director of Public Prosecutions*, High Court, December 17, 1997 in which Geoghegan J. refused an order of prohibition. The applicant, a Roman Catholic priest, faced 66 charges of indecent assault and/or procuring acts of gross indecency, in respect of which there were eight complainants. Geoghegan J. applied the principles in the case law, including *B. v. Director of Public Prosecutions* [1997] 2 I.L.R.M. 188 (289, above) in concluding that the charges should be allowed to proceed. However, he also emphasised that where, as here, there had been a great deal of pre-trial publicity surrounding the case, the trial judge could prevent an unfair trial by appropriate directions to the jury.

DETENTION

Access to custody records under Custody Regulations In *Director of Public Prosecutions v. Dempsey*, High Court, July 2, 1997, Kinlen J. held that a prosecution against the defendant, who had been charged with offences under the Road Traffic Acts 1961 to 1994, had been correctly dismissed for what was described as a fundamental breach of the Criminal Justice Act 1984 (Treatment of Persons in Custody in Garda Stations) Regulations 1987. The defendant's solicitor had requested that copies of relevant custody records be furnished to the defence but that these had been refused. The District Court judge held that there was a conscious and deliberate refusal on the State's part to make the custody records available to the defence and that this entitled the court to dismiss the charges against the defendant. The prosecution conceded that there had been a breach of the 1987 Regulations in refusing to supply a copy of the custody record on request by the defendant's solicitor, but that the District Court should have considered what effect the breach had had on his ability to meet the charges brought against him. McCracken J. did not accept this argument.

He held that 'there was no doubt' that the District Court judge had acted within jurisdiction. He accepted that section 7(3) of the Criminal Justice Act 1984 provided that non-compliance with the 1987 Regulations did not bring about the automatic exclusion of all evidence obtained from an accused in custody and that it was for the court of trial to adjudicate in each case as to the impact of the non-compliance on the prosecution's case. In the instant case, the defendant was entitled to see the custody record. Since there was evidence to support the District Court's findings and the prosecution had accepted that the defendant had been deprived of documents to which he was entitled, he concluded that the District Court judge was entitled to exercise his discretion to dismiss the charges against the defendant on the ground that there had been a failure to comply with the principles of natural justice.

Custody Regulations: juvenile In *The People v. D'Arcy*, Court of Criminal Appeal, July 29, 1997, the Court upheld a conviction based on evidence obtained in circumstances where there had been a breach of the Criminal Justice Act 1984 (Treatment of Persons in Custody in Garda Stations) Regulations 1987. The defendant had been convicted of murder. He was 16 years of age at the time of the offence and had been arrested under section 4 of the 1984 Criminal Justice Act. He was interviewed in the presence of his uncle but in the absence of a solicitor. On arrival at the Garda station he had been given a notice of his rights in the form prescribed under the 1987 Regulations and had been informed of his right to legal advice. The main evidence against the defendant at trial comprised admissions allegedly made by him during the period in custody in the Garda station, which were ruled admissible by the trial judge. The defendant claimed that the relevant interview had been conducted in breach of his constitutional right to legal advice and the 1987 Regulations. It was also claimed that the statements should have been excluded on the ground that the 1987 Regulations had been breached as to the number of Gardaí present. As indicated, the Court of Criminal Appeal dismissed the defendant's application for leave to appeal.

The Court held that there was ample evidence to support the finding of the trial judge that there was nothing in the nature of a conscious and deliberate act on the part of the Gardaí to deprive the defendant of his right of access to a solicitor. The Court accepted that the requirements in the 1987 Regulations as to the number of Gardaí present at interview had not been observed, but there had been no suggestion that the questioning was otherwise oppressive or unfair. It was thus a case in which the trial judge, in the exercise of his discretion, could decide as he did to apply section 7(3) of the 1984 Act, by which failure to observe the 1987 Regulations did not in itself to affect the admissibility in evidence of statements. The Court noted that, in the instant case, the substance of the defendant's rights had been preserved, since he was informed of his right to obtain a solicitor, the attendance of a responsible adult was secured as soon as practicable, the defendant's uncle was aware of the entitlement to legal advice, and no interviewing had been conducted until the uncle was present. On this basis, as indicated, the application for leave to appeal was dismissed. See also the Evidence chapter, 402–4, below.

Electronic recording of interviews The Criminal Justice Act 1984 (Electronic Recording of Interviews) Regulations 1997 (S.I. No.74 of 1997), made under section 27 of the Criminal Justice Act 1984, provide for the electronic recording, including audio and video tapes, of interviews with persons detained in Garda stations under section 4 of the 1984 Act, section 30 of the Offences Against the State Act 1939 or section 2 of the Criminal Justice (Drug

Trafficking) Act 1996 (1996 Review, 241-2). They came into force on March 1 1997. The issue of electronic recording must be seen in the context of the admissibility of admissions in evidence at subsequent trials. Recording of such interviews may assist in determining whether interviews were conducted in accordance with the Criminal Justice Act 1984 (Treatment of Persons in Custody in Garda Stations) Regulations 1987, discussed above and the common law rules on voluntariness as well as the Judges' Rules. However, it remains to be seen whether indications that detained persons are reluctant to have interviews recorded electronically will impact on the efficacy of the 1997 Regulations. The 1997 Regulations are further discussed in the Evidençe chapter, 405–6, below.

DRUG TRAFFICKING

Money laundering Section l4 of the Criminal Justice (Miscellaneous Provisions) Act 1997 (discussed in general below, 314) amended section 32 of the Criminal Justice Act 1994 (1994 Review, 175) to give effect to Article 11 of Council Directive 91/308/EEC on the prevention of the use of the financial system for the purpose of money laundering. The other provisions of the 1991 Directive were implemented in the 1994 Act.

Revenue offences Section l5 of the Criminal Justice (Miscellaneous Provisions) Act 1997 added a new section 56A to the Criminal Justice Act 1994 to ensure that revenue offences were included within the terms of the 1994 Act.

Warrants Section l5 of the 1997 Act also amended section 55 of the Criminal Justice Act 1994 in connection with the issuing of warrants under the 1994 Act.

EVIDENCE
(The general area of Evidence is discussed in the Evidence chapter, below.)

Confession/ inculpatory statement In *The People v. Connolly*, Court of Criminal Appeal, April 14, 1997, the Court held that there was no basis in law for excluding a statement from evidence on the grounds that the person who made the statement was upset at the time it was made. The defendant had been convicted of the murder of a man with whom his wife was having a relationship. The conviction was based primarily on the basis of a statement or confession made by him while he was in Garda custody. In seeking leave to appeal against his conviction he argued that the statement should have been ruled inadmissible as he had made it wile he was upset. In refusing leave to appeal, the Court of Criminal Appeal held that the only basis on which a statement could be ruled out of evidence was if it was an involuntary statement or if there had been oppressive circumstances surrounding the taking of it, or if there had been a breach of the Judges' Rules, in which case it became a matter for the judge's discretion; but the Court held that there was no heading whereby a statement could be excluded because the person who made it was upset. The Court therefore concluded that the ground raised did not affect its admissibility.

Incriminating document   In *The People v. McGavigan*, Court of Criminal Appeal, November 10, 1997, the Court quashed a conviction for possession of an incriminating document under section 12 of the Offences Against the State Act 1939. Section 2 of the Offences Against the State Act 1939 defines an incriminating document as one 'issued or emanating from an unlawful organisation or appearing to be so issued... or appearing to aid and abet any such organisation or calculated to promote the formation of an unlawful organisation'. The applicant had been charged arising from being in possession of a video cassette. The video was a documentary on the Provisional IRA, an unlawful organisation. Prosecution witnesses conceded that the video had not, on the balance of probabilities, been issued by the Provisional IRA and that it had emanated from French television. The Court of Criminal Appeal accepted that the documentary gave the IRA a platform to express certain views but also pointed out that it contained, although not to the same extent, condemnation of the organisation. While within the documentary there was what appeared to be an extract from a document issued by the Provisional IRA, the Court pointed out that it was dealing with a crime which was contained in particularly restrictive legislation, the 1939 Act, which had to be interpreted in a strict manner. In particular the 1939 Act impinged on the constitutional freedom to express opinions in Article 40.6 and the court could not be satisfied on the basis of the evidence placed before it that this was a document which appeared to aid or abet the Provisional IRA. On this basis, it quashed the conviction.

Sexual assault: complaint   In *The People v. Roughan*, Court of Criminal Appeal, June 23, 1997, the defendant had been convicted of rape and sexual assault. The defendant sought leave to appeal, *inter alia*, on the ground that the complaint had not been made within a reasonable period of time. The Court of Criminal Appeal dismissed the application. Citing its decision in *The People v. Brophy* [1992] I.L.R.M. 709 (1992 Review, 253) the Court accepted that such a complaint had to be made as soon as was reasonably possible and that it had to be voluntary in nature. In the instant case, the trial judge had decided that the complainant had been in such a psychological state that it was not in fact reasonably possible for her to make the complaint until she did make it. That was a decision for the trial judge and since there was evidence to support his conclusion, the Court would not interfere with that decision.

The defendant had also argued that the judge had erred in holding that it was not improper for the prosecution in cross-examination to put it to the accused that the complainant was either lying or perjuring herself. The Court accepted that it was 'undesirable' to put such a question. However, it doubted whether it could have had any real impact on the course of the trial.

The defendant had also sought leave to appeal on the basis that the trial judge had permitted the complainant's husband to remain in court when she was giving evidence. The trial judge had relied on section 11(3) of the Criminal Law (Rape)(Amendment) Act 1990 in declining to exclude her husband from court. The Court of Criminal Appeal held that, in the circumstances of the case, this decision had no significance so far as the result of the trial was concerned.

Since there was evidence on which the jury could have convicted the defendant, the Court did not see that there was any ground on which their verdict could be interfered with and, as indicated, it dismissed the application The Court also concluded that none of the points raised constituted a point of law of exceptional public importance on which the Court required the assistance of the Supreme Court. See also the discussion in the Evidence chapter, 407–8, below.

Video link evidence   The Criminal Evidence Act 1992 (Section 29) (Commencement) Order 1997 (S.I. No.371 of 1997) brought section 29 of the Criminal Evidence Act 1992 (see generally the 1992 Review, 262-3) into effect on October 6 1997. Section 29 of the 1992 Act provides for video link evidence to be given from abroad.

Visual identification   In *The People v. Kavanagh*, Court of Criminal Appeal, July 7, 1997, the Court dismissed an application for leave to appeal in which the defendant had challenged identification evidence. The defendant had been charged with murder. The deceased had been shot dead in his family home by one of two men who entered his home wearing balaclavas. The deceased's wife gave evidence that although the murderer wore a balaclava, she recognised him as the accused through his eyes, his build, his height and his voice. The deceased's daughters also identified the accused by his voice. The jury found the defendant guilty.

The Court of Criminal Appeal held that the trial judge should be accorded a wide discretion to express the warning regarding identification evidence, reiterating the view expressed many times that it should not be a mechanical repetition of everything set forth in *The People v. Casey (No.2)* [1963] I.R. 33 but should have regard to the underlying rationale of *Casey*. This was not such a case that the evidence was so thin that the jury should not have been entrusted with it and the case boiled down to what the jury were to make of the evidence tendered. The inexorable conclusion was, the Court held, that they must have been satisfied about the reliability of the testimony and in those circumstances the verdict should stand. See also the Evidence chapter, 420, below.

By contrast, in *The People v. Murphy*, Court of Criminal Appeal, November 3, 1997, the Court quashed a conviction based on identification evidence. The defendant had been charged with unlawful sexual assault. The victim of the assault gave evidence that she had recognised the man who had assaulted her and she could now identify him as the applicant. The defendant appealed on the basis that the trial judge had distinguished between identification and recognition cases and had failed to give the required warning to the jury in relation to the victim's identification evidence. The Court of Criminal Appeal allowed the appeal and declined to order a retrial.

The Court held that whether a case was concerned with identification pure and simple, or recognition, where a witness had previous acquaintance with the person accused, it was necessary to warn the jury where the identification was challenged, as required by the decisions in *The People v. Casey (No.2)* [1963] I.R. 33 and *The People v. Stafford* [1983] I.R. 165. As indicated in *Casey*, the direction should not be a stereotyped formula but should in some cases be stronger than in others. In the instant case, the absence of this direction to the jury had resulted in a fundamental error and the trial was thus rendered unsatisfactory. Bearing in mind the time already served by the defendant, the Court considered that it could not with any justification order a retrial. See also the Evidence chapter, 420, below.

EXTRADITION

Correspondence In *Casey v. Assistant Garda Commissioner*, High Court, April 19, 1997, Morris J. (as he then was) held that the offence for which the applicant was being sought in England, attempting to obtain money by deception, corresponded with attempting to obtain money by false pretences in section 32 of the Larceny Act 1916. In considering in an extradition cases this issue, Morris J. held that a court is not concerned with the construction of English law, but, as indicated in *Wyatt v. McLoughlin* [1974] I.R. 378, its sole concern is to be satisfied that the acts constituting the particular offence for which extradition is sought are acts which, if committed within this jurisdiction, would constitute a criminal offence. In that respect, he concluded that all the ingredients of the offence of attempting to obtaining money by false pretences in this jurisdiction were to be found in the facts alleged in the offence in the warrant n the instant case.

Delay In *Langan v. O'Dea*, High Court, October 10, 1997, Kelly J. held that the applicant was not entitled to object to an extradition request on the ground of delay where the bulk of any delay was attributable to the accused's own criminal conduct and as such it would be extraordinary if a criminal could rely on his own criminal wrong-doing so as to avail himself of the provision concerning delay in section 50(2)(bbb) Extradition Act 1965, inserted by the Extradition (Amendment) Act 1987 (1987 Review, 131-2).

The applicant had escaped from prison hospital in England in 1991 and had come to Ireland. In 1993, he was charged with committing a burglary in Dublin, but he absconded before his case was heard. He was re-arrested four months later. He was sentenced for that offence, and was released in 1996 on condition that he be of good behaviour. Kelly J. noted that he had dishonoured that commitment as he was due to plead guilty to a charge of conspiracy in November 1997. In 1994, the British authorities had commenced extradition proceedings seeking the return of the applicant to England. He was arrested on foot of the warrant in 1996. As indicated the applicant sought his release pursuant to section 50(2)(bbb) of the 1965 Act by reason of the alleged lapse of time, arguing that it would be unjust to return him to England, in particular because his family would not be in a position to visit him.

Kelly J. concluded that the bulk of any delay was attributable to the applicant's own conduct and that it would be 'extraordinary' if a criminal could rely on his own criminal wrongdoing so as to avail himself of section 50(2)(bbb) of the 1965 Act. He held that the authorities in both jurisdictions had acted with reasonable expedition in the way in which they had dealt with the matter. He added that the British authorities were quite entitled not to seek the applicant's extradition pending the determination of criminal proceedings in Ireland. Nor was there any suggestion that any delay was caused by a decision of the British authorities not to seek extradition, as had been the case in *Fusco v. O'Dea* [1994] 2 I.L.R.M. 389 (1994 Review, 376-8). Finally, he held that there was nothing exceptional or unjust in there being difficulties for the applicant's family in seeking to visit him in England.

Evidence to be adduced at trial In *O'Sullivan v. Conroy*, High Court, July 31, 1997, Barr J. rejected a claim that the plaintiff's extradition be refused. His extradition was sought on the charge of having conspired with others to defraud the Secretary of State for Social Security of England and Wales by dishonestly obtaining welfare benefits in the United Kingdom. In the District Court, it was held that the offence specified in the extradition warrant corresponded with an offence under the laws of the State, namely, conspiracy to defraud contrary to common law. The plaintiff applied for his release under section 50 of the Extradition Act 1965, arguing that evidence to support the alleged conspiracy would be admissible in an English court even though such evidence was conditional on the introduction of other evidence of common purpose. He argued that this was in conflict with Irish law, which required that a jury should not receive evidence prejudicial to an accused if the admissibility of that evidence was dependent on other evidence which might not be forthcoming.

As already indicated, Barr J. refused the plaintiff's application. He held that the function of the court under section 50 of the 1965 Act was to examine the procedure to be adopted in connection with the proposed trial in England and consider whether it would be acceptable in Irish law, having regard to the constitutional safeguards provided for the benefit of accused persons in criminal trials in this jurisdiction. He reviewed the relevant English case law, such as *R. v. Donat* (1986) 82 Cr. App. Rep. 173. This indicated that if conditional evidence of a conspiracy was introduced, and it transpired that there was no other evidence of common purpose, the trial judge would be obliged to withdraw the case from the jury and direct an acquittal. The question of an alleged unfair procedure as understood in Irish constitutional law would thus not arise and the plaintiff had failed to establish any ground on which his release could be ordered under section 50 of the 1965 Act.

Revenue In *Byrne v. Conroy* [1997] 2 I.L.R.M. 99 (HC), Kelly J. held that the offence of smuggling grain into the State from Northern Ireland with the intent of defrauding the revenue authorities in Northern Ireland by dishonestly avoiding payments due to the Intervention Board for Agricultural Produce under relevant EC Regulations did not constitute a revenue offence within the meaning of section 50 of the Extradition Act 1965. The Court thus held that plaintiff's extradition to Northern Ireland could proceed. The case is discussed in the European Community law chapter, 380, 382, below.

FIREARMS

Decommissioning of arms and explosives: Northern Ireland The Decommissioning Act 1997 provides, in effect, for a partial amnesty from prosecution in respect of persons engaged in the decommissioning of firearms, ammunition and explosives where they are given to the International Decommissioning Commission established by agreement between the Government of Ireland and the Government of the United Kingdom. The Act is connected with the multi-party negotiations in Northern Ireland, which involved both Governments, and which led to the Belfast Agreement of April 10, 1998, subsequently approved in referendums held in the State and in Northern Ireland on May 22 1998. During these negotiations, the two Governments had agreed to the establishment of such a Commission to deal with the decommissioning of unlawfully held firearms and explosives. The 1997 Act (other than section 3(1) and sections 5 and 6) came into effect on 24 September 1997 when the envisaged Commission was also established: Decommissioning Act 1997 (Commencement) Order 1997 (S.I. No. 397 of 1997) and Decommissioning Act 1997 (Section 3) (Commencement) Order 1997 (S.I. No. 398 of 1997). The Decommissioning Act 1997 (Independent International Commission on Decommissioning) (Privileges and Immunities) Order 1997 (S.I. No. 399 of 1997) conferred extensive immunities on the members of the Commission and the Decommissioning Act 1997 (Independent International Commission on Decommissioning) Regulations 1997 (S.I. No. 400 of 1997) provides detail on the financing of and performance of functions by the Commission.

JURY

Constitution   In *The People v. Morgan*, Court of Criminal Appeal, July 28, 1997, the defendant claimed that the jury in his trial on charges of robbery had been improperly constituted when the trial judge permitted a juror to be added in substitution for another juror after the defendant had been put in charge and the jury foreman elected. The Court of Criminal Appeal, in refusing his application for leave to appeal, held that the issue of the jury's composition was a procedural matter of a trivial nature. The instant case thus came within counsel's entitlement to consent to the course of action that the judge had proposed and the Court also noted that the trial had not started in any real sense.

LARCENY

Handling   In *O'Kelly v. Director of Pubic Prosecutions*, High Court, February 20, 1997, the appellant had been convicted in the District Court of handling stolen property, a wallet, contrary to section 33 of the Larceny Act 1916, as amended by section 3 of the Larceny Act 1990 (1990 Review, 230) after the District Court judge had acquitted the appellant of stealing the wallet. On a case stated, O'Donovan J. quashed the conviction. Citing the decision in *The People v. O'Hanlon*, Court of Criminal Appeal, February 1, 1993 (1993 Review, 236), O'Donovan J. held that before a person could be convicted for handling stolen property there had to be evidence that the goods were stolen by a person other than the accused. He noted that there was no such evidence adduced in the instant case and thus the conviction could not stand.

LEGAL AID

Fees   The Criminal Justice (Legal Aid) (Amendment) Regulations 1997 (S.I. No. 232 of 1997), made under the Criminal Justice (Legal Aid) Act 1962, increased the fees payable under the 1962 Act. The amended fees had some elements of retrospection and prospection, coming into force on various dates between January 1 1994 and October 1 1998.

MISUSE OF DRUGS

Possession In *The People v. Byrne, Healy and Kelleher*, Court of Criminal Appeal, December 17, 1997, the Court upheld convictions against the defendants on charges of the unlawful importation into the state of controlled substances, contrary to the Misuse of Drugs Act 1977. The defendants contended that the prosecution had not discharged the burden of proof on them to prove that they knew that they were handling packets which contained controlled drugs. They submitted that they had no knowledge that they were handling drugs and that the prosecution had failed to prove that they did have such knowledge. The prosecution contended that it had discharged the burden of proof on it by adducing proof that the defendants had reasonable grounds for suspecting that they were in possession of controlled drugs, even in the absence of actual knowledge.

The Court of Criminal Appeal held that there was clearly evidence in this case on which the jury could be satisfied beyond a reasonable doubt that each of defendants was in possession of the bales of drugs in question in the sense of having them physically in their possession or under their control on the date in question. Referring to the decision of the House of Lords in *Warner v. Metropolitan Police Commissioner* [1969] 2 A.C. 256, the Court accepted that it was not sufficient for mere physical possession to be established and a mental element or *animus possidendi* had also to exist. The Court noted that section 29(2)(a) of the Misuse of Drugs Act 1977 had been enacted in order to avoid the injustice of a person being convicted solely because he was in possession of the drugs, where it was clear that he did not know and had not any reason to suspect that he had drugs in his possession. In the instant case, the Court held that there was evidence on which the jury could be satisfied beyond a reasonable doubt that each of the defendants had, and knew that he had, the bales in his control, that the bales contained something and that the bales in fact contained the controlled drug specified in the indictment. On that basis, the Court affirmed the convictions.

MONEY LAUNDERING

Convention countries The Criminal Justice Act 1994 (Section 37(1)) Order 1997 (S.I. No. 63 of 1997) declared a number of States to be Convention countries for the purposes of section 37 of the Criminal Justice Act 1994 (see 1994 Review, 174–5), with effect from March 3, 1997.

Designated countries The following Orders made in 1997 extended various search and seizure powers of the Criminal Justice Act 1994 (1994 Review, 174–5) to Austria, Hungary, Benin, Estonia and Kazakhstan: the Criminal Justice Act 1994 (Section 46(1)) Order 1997 (S.I. No. 104 of 1997); the Criminal Justice Act 1994 (Section 47(1)) Order 1997 (S.I. No. 105 of 1997); the Criminal Justice Act 1994 (Section 46 (1)) (No. 2) Order 1997 (S.I. No. 366 of 1997); the Criminal Justice Act 1994 (Section 47 (1)) (No. 2) Order 1997 (S.I. No. 367 of 1997); the Criminal Justice Act 1994 (Section 55 (1)) Order 1997 (S.I. No. 368 of 1997); and the Criminal Justice Act 1994 (Section 46 (1)) (No. 3) Order 1997 (S.I. No. 463 of 1997).

Financial systems Section 14 of the Criminal Justice (Miscellaneous Provisions) Act 1997 (discussed further, 314, below) amended section 32 of the Criminal Justice Act 1994 (1994 Review, 175) in order to give effect to Article 11 of Directive 91/308/EEC on the prevention of the use of the financial system for money laundering. The remaining provisions of the 1991 Directive had already been implemented by the 1994 Act. Section 14 of the 1997 Act came into force on March 4, 1997.

Police Property Acts *Whitehead v. Garda Commissioner*, Supreme Court, February 27 1997, discussed below, 313, concerned an unsuccessful application for the return of property under the Police Property Acts.

NON-FATAL OFFENCES AGAINST THE PERSON

In 1994, the Law Reform Commission in its Report *Non-Fatal Offences Against The Person* (1994 Review, 192-200) recommended the repeal and replacement of the greater part of the Offences Against the Person Act 1861, in particular those provisions of the 1861 Act concerning assault, assault causing harm, causing serious harm, threats to kill or cause serious injury. The Non-Fatal Offences against the Person Act 1997 largely takes account of these recommendations and section 29 of the 1997 Act repealed the relevant provisions of the 1861 Act to take account of defects and lacunae in the 1861 Act. Certain of these non-fatal offences were also offences at common law and section 28 of the 1997 Act also repealed these, replacing them with new offences. On the prospective effect of these repeals, see the Interpretation (Amendment) Act 1997 and *Quinlivan v. Governor of Portlaoise Prison (No.3)*, High Court, December 9, 1997 (284, above). The main offences dealt with in the 1997 Act are assault, assault causing harm, causing serious harm, threats to kill or cause serious injury, a range of new offences relating to criminal conduct involving syringes, coercion, harassment ('stalking'), demand for payment of debt causing alarm, poisoning, endangerment, false imprisonment and abduction of a child by parents or others. The 1997 Act retained most of the common law defences available in such cases, such as self-defence and other defences associated with, for example, contact sports. As provided for in section 32 of the 1997 Act, sections 6, 7, 8 and 10 of the 1997 Act (which introduced the new offences concerning assaults with syringes and harassment) came into force on May 20, 1997 (the day after its passing) and the remainder of the Act came into force on August 19, 1997 (three months after its passing).

Assault   Section 2 of the Non-Fatal Offences Against the Person Act 1997 replaced the common law offences of assault and battery with a new offence of assault, which combines, in a single offence, the element of inflicting personal violence in 'battery' and the element of causing another to apprehend the immediate infliction of personal violence in 'assault'. As indicated, the common law offences were abolished by section 28 of the 1997 Act. Section 2(3) of the 1997 Act provides that an offence will not be committed in circumstances 'generally acceptable in the ordinary conduct of daily life.' Section 2(4) provides that the offence is punishable on summary conviction by a fine not exceeding £1,500 and/or imprisonment for a term not exceeding 6 months.

Assault causing harm   Section 3 of the 1997 Act replaces the offence of assault causing actual bodily harm, contained in the now repealed section 47 of the 1861 Act, with the offence of assault causing harm. Section 3(2) makes the offence punishable on summary conviction by imprisonment for a term not exceeding 12 months and/or by a fine not exceeding £1,500 or on conviction on indictment by an unlimited fine and/or imprisonment for a term not exceeding 5 years.

Causing serious harm   Section 4 of the 1997 Act creates the offence of 'intentionally or recklessly causing serious harm' and replaced the offences of 'causing grievous bodily harm with intent' and 'inflicting grievous bodily harm with intent' in sections 18 and 20, respectively, of the 1861 Act. Section 4(2) makes the offence punishable on indictment by an unlimited fine and/or imprisonment for life.

Threats to kill or cause serious injury   Section 5 of the 1997 Act creates the offence of threatening to kill or cause serious injury to another. This offence replaces the offence of threatening by writing to kill or murder another in section 16 of the 1861 Act. The new offence covers threats by 'any means' and extends to threats to cause serious harm as well as to threats to kill. Section 5(2) makes the offence punishable on summary conviction by a fine not exceeding £1,500 and/or imprisonment for a term not exceeding 12 months and on indictment by an unlimited fine and/or imprisonment for a term not exceeding 10 years.

Syringe attacks   Sections 6, 7 and 8 of the 1997 Act create a range of new offences relating to criminal conduct involving syringes. These are associated with the recent phenomenon of persons infected with an infectious disease (in particular AIDS) threatening others. Section 6 deals with attacks involving syringes. Section 6(1) creates a new offence of injuring another by piercing the skin with a syringe or threatening to do so, with the intention of causing the person concerned to believe that he or she will become infected with disease as a result of the injury caused or threatened. Section 6(2) creates the offence of spraying, pouring or putting onto another blood or any fluid or substance resembling blood or to threaten to do so, with the intention of causing that person to believe that he or she may become infected with disease as a result of the action taken or threatened. Section 6(3) provides that an offence or attempted offence under section 6(1) or (2) leading to injury to a third party shall be guilty of an offence. Section 6(4) provides that an offence under section 6(1), (2) or (3) shall be punishable on summary conviction by a fine not exceeding £1,500 and/or imprisonment for a term not exceeding 12 months and on indictment by an unlimited fine and/or imprisonment for a term not exceeding 10 years.

Section 6(5) provides for two more offences: (a) intentionally to injure another by piercing the skin of that person with a syringe which contains or has on it contaminated blood or contaminated fluid; and (b) intentionally to spray, pour or put contaminated blood onto another. Both offences are punishable on conviction on indictment by imprisonment for life.

Possession of syringe in certain circumstances   Section 7(1) of the Non-Fatal Offences Against the Person Act 1997 makes it an offence to have in any place a syringe or blood in a container with the intention of causing or threatening injury or intimidating a person. Section 7(6) provides that for the purposes of the section, blood includes any fluid or substance resembling blood. Section 7(7) makes an offence under section 7(1) punishable on summary conviction by a fine not exceeding £1,500 and/or imprisonment for a term not exceeding 12 months and on indictment by an unlimited fine and/or imprisonment for a term not exceeding 7 years. The section also empowers a member of the Garda Síochána, who reasonably suspects a person of committing an offence under section 7 to stop, question and, if necessary using reasonable force, search the person and seize and detain any syringe or container found on or in the immediate vicinity of the person (unless the person has a reasonable excuse). Where a syringe or container is so found the member can require the name and address of the person. It also empowers the Garda to arrest without warrant a person who fails to co-operate with, or obstructs, a Garda in the exercise of such powers and it provides that a person who fails to stop, answer questions, give his or her name and address when required or gives a false or misleading name and address or obstructs or interferes with a member of the Garda Síochána may be arrested without warrant and shall be guilty of an offence punishable on conviction by a fine not exceeding £1,500 and/or 6 months imprisonment. Section 7(5) provides that in prosecuting an offence under section 7, it will not be necessary to prove intent to cause injury to a particular person; and having regard to all the circumstances the court or jury may regard possession of the syringe or container as sufficient evidence of intent.

Placing or abandoning syringe Section 8(1) creates the offence of placing or abandoning a syringe in any place in such a manner that it injures or is likely to injure, cause a threat to or frighten another, but section 8(3) provides that this offence does not apply to persons who place a syringe in any place whilst administering or assisting in lawful medical, dental or veterinary procedures. Section 8(3) provides that where the syringe is placed in a private dwelling where the accused normally resides, it will be a defence to a prosecution under section 8(1) for the accused to show that he or she did not intentionally place the syringe in such a manner that it injured or was likely to injure, cause a threat to or frighten another. Section 8(4) makes an offence under section 8(1) punishable on summary conviction by a fine not exceeding £1,500 and/or imprisonment for a term not exceeding 12 months and on indictment by an unlimited fine and/or imprisonment for a term not exceeding 5 years.

Section 8(2) creates a separate offence of placing a contaminated syringe in any place in such a manner that it injures another. section 8(6) provides that an offence under section 8(2) is punishable on indictment to imprisonment for life.

Coercion Section 9 of the 1997 Act replaces section 7 of the Conspiracy and Protection of Property Act 1875. Section 9(1) makes it an offence for a person, with a view to compelling another to do an act or refrain from doing an act which the person has a lawful right to do or to abstain from doing wrongfully or without lawful authority to:

(a) use violence to or intimidate another person or his or her family, or
(b) injure or damage the property of another, or
(c) persistently follow the person, or
(d) watch or beset any place or the approach to such place, where the person resides, works or carries on business, or happens to be, or
(e) follow the person with one or more others in a disorderly manner in or through a public place.

Section 9(2) provides that attending at a place in order to obtain or communicate information is not deemed to be watching or besetting for the purposes of section 9(1)(d). This reflects, for example, the need to protect activity which might be associated with trade disputes or political activity.

Section 9(3) provides that an offence under the section shall be punishable on summary conviction by a fine not exceeding £1,500 and/or imprisonment for a term not exceeding 12 months and on indictment by an unlimited fine and/or imprisonment for a term not exceeding 5 years.

Harassment ('stalking')   Section 10(1) creates a new offence of harassment where any person by any means, including use of the telephone, harasses another by persistently following, watching, pestering or communicating with him or her. Section 10(2) provides that a person harasses another where the acts involved 'seriously interferes with the other person's peace and privacy or causes alarm, distress or harm to the other' and the acts are such that a reasonable person would realise that this would be the effect of the actions. The section is aimed at behaviour which has come to be known as 'stalking'. Section 10(3) empowers a court to order, for such period as it specifies, a person found guilty of an offence under section 10(1) not to communicate with the other person or not to approach within any distance which the court specifies, of any place of residence or employment of the person, and section 10(4) makes it an offence to fail to comply with the terms of such an order. Section 10(5) provides that the court may make an order under section 10(3) on application to it, if it is satisfied having regard to the evidence that it is in the interests of justice to do so even if the court is not satisfied on the evidence that the person should be convicted of an offence under section 10(1). Section 10(6) makes an offence under this section punishable on summary conviction by a fine not exceeding £1,500 and/or imprisonment for a term not exceeding 12 months and on indictment by an unlimited fine and/or imprisonment for a term not exceeding 7 years.

Demands for payment of debt causing alarm   Section 11(1) of the 1997 Act provides that a person demanding payment for a debt shall be guilty of an offence if:

(a) the demands because of their frequency are calculated to subject the debtor or his or her family to alarm distress or humiliation, or
(b) he or she falsely represents that criminal proceedings lie for non-payment, or
(c) he or she falsely represents that he or she is authorised in some official capacity to enforce payment, or
(d) he or she utters a document falsely represented to have an official character.

Section 11(2) makes an offence under this section punishable on summary conviction by a fine not exceeding £1,500.

Poisoning Section 12(1) makes it an offence for a person intentionally or recklessly to administer to, or cause another to take, a substance which he or she knows to be capable of interfering substantially with the other person's bodily functions and where he or she knows the person does not consent to what is being done. Section 12(2) provides that a substance capable of inducing unconsciousness or sleep is capable of interfering substantially with bodily functions. Section 12(3) makes an offence under the section punishable on summary conviction by a fine not exceeding £1,500 and/or imprisonment for a term not exceeding 12 months and/on indictment by an unlimited fine or imprisonment for a term not exceeding 3 years. This offence replaces the offence of administering poison with intent to injure, aggrieve or annoy in section 24 of the 1861 Act.

Endangerment Section 13 creates a new general offence of endangerment, that is, where a person intentionally or recklessly engages in conduct which creates a substantial risk of death or serious harm to another. Section 13(2) makes the offence punishable on summary conviction by a fine not exceeding £1,500 and/or imprisonment not exceeding 12 months and on indictment by an unlimited fine and/or imprisonment for a term not exceeding 7 years.

Endangering traffic Section 14 creates a new offence of endangering traffic and replaces sections 32 and 33 of the 1861 Act which were limited to endangerment offences related to railways. Section 14(1) creates an offence where a person intentionally places or throws any dangerous obstruction, or interferes with any device for the direction, control or regulation of traffic, or interferes with or throws anything at or on any conveyance, on a railway, road, street, waterway or public place and where he or she is aware that injury to the person or damage to property may be thereby caused or is reckless in that regard. Section 14(3) makes an offence under this section punishable on summary conviction by a fine not exceeding £1,500 and/or imprisonment for a term not exceeding 12 months and on indictment by an unlimited fine and/or imprisonment for a term not exceeding 7 years.

False imprisonment Section 15 of the 1997 Act replaces the common law offence of false imprisonment (repealed by section 28 of the 1997 Act) with an extended offence which covers cases where the false imprisonment is brought about by deception causing the victim to believe that he or she is under legal compulsion to consent. Section 15(1) provides that a person commits the new offence of false imprisonment if he or she intentionally or recklessly takes, detains, causes to be taken or detained or otherwise restricts the personal liberty of another without that person's consent. Section 15(2) provides that the other person does not consent if the consent is obtained by force or threat of force or by deception causing that person to believe that he or she is under legal compulsion to consent. Section 15(3) makes the offence punishable on summary conviction by a fine not exceeding £1,500 and/or imprisonment for a term not exceeding 12 months and on indictment by imprisonment for life.

Abduction of child by parent   Section 16 of the 1997 Act creates a new offence of abduction of a child by his or her parent or guardian. This reflects the provisions of the Hague Convention on Recognition and Enforcement of Child Custody Decisions, the civil aspects of which were implemented by the Child Abduction and Enforcement of Custody Orders Act 1991. Section 16(1) provides that it is an offence for a person to take, send or keep a child under the age of 16 years out of the State or cause a child to be so taken, sent or kept, in defiance of a court order or without the consent of each person who is a parent, guardian or a person granted custody of the child by a court unless a court has consented. Section 16(2) provides that the offence can be committed by a parent, guardian or a person granted custody of the child by a court but does not apply to a parent who is not a guardian of the child. Section 16(3) provides that it will be a defence if the defendant has been unable to communicate with the persons whose consent is required by the section and he or she believes they would consent, or if he or she did not intend to deprive others having rights of guardianship or custody of the child of those rights. Section 16(4) makes the offence punishable on summary conviction by a fine not exceeding £1,500 and/or imprisonment for a term not exceeding 12 months and on indictment by an unlimited fine and/or imprisonment for a term not exceeding 7 years. Section 16(5) provides that proceedings under the section shall only be instituted by or with the consent of the Director of Public Prosecutions.

Abduction of child by other persons   Section 17 provides for an offence of abduction of a child by other persons to replace sections 55 and 56 of the 1861 Act. Section 17(1) makes it an offence for a person other than a person to whom section 16 applies to intentionally take or detain a child under 16 years or cause such a child to be taken or detained, in order to remove the child from, or keep the child out of, the lawful control of any person having such control. Section 17(2) provides for a defence where the defendant believes the child to be 16 years or over. Section 17(3) makes an offence under this section punishable on summary conviction by a fine not exceeding £1,500 and/or imprisonment for a term not exceeding 12 months and on indictment by an unlimited fine and/or imprisonment for a term not exceeding 7 years.

Defence: justifiable use of force in self-defence, protection of property and prevention of crime   Section 18 (1) sets out various situations in which reasonable force may be lawfully used, particularly in self-defence, defence of family, protection of property and the prevention of crime. The force used must be reasonable by reference to the circumstances believed by the person to exist. Where reasonable force is used to protect against trespass to another person or another person's property the force must be with the authority of that other person. Section 20 defines the term 'use of force' for the purposes of section 18. Section 18(3) provides that for the purposes of the section an act is a crime or is criminal although the person committing it would be acquitted on any of a number of grounds which section 18(3) sets out. Section 18(5) provides that whether an act is of a kind mentioned in section 18(1) must be determined according to the circumstances which the person using the force believes them to be. Section 18(6) provides that no defence for the use of force exists if the person using it knows that the force is used against a member of the Garda Siochana acting in the course of duty or against a person assisting such member unless he or she believes the force is immediately necessary to prevent harm to himself or another. Section 18(7) provides that the defence in the section does not apply where a person causes a state of affairs or conduct with a view to using force to resist it but it will apply where the occasion for the use of force arises only because the person does something he or she may lawfully do, knowing that such an occasion will arise.

Defence: justifiable use of force in effecting or assisting lawful arrest Section 19(1) provides that the use of force by a person in effecting or assisting a lawful arrest, if it is only such as is reasonable in the circumstances which he or she believes to exist, is not an offence. 'Use of force' is defined by section 20. Section 19(3) provides that the question as to whether the arrest is lawful shall be determined according to the circumstances as the person using the force believed them to be. On the power of arrest without warrant, see section 4 of the Criminal Law Act 1997, discussed at 269, above.

Defence in criminal damage Section 21 of the 1997 Act amended section 6(2) of the Criminal Damage Act 1991 (1991 Review, 134-6) so that the test in relation to damaging property is the same as the test set out in section 18 of the 1997 Act, namely that the conduct of the defendant must be reasonable given the circumstances as he or she believed them to be.

General defences Section 22 preserves defences available under the common law or statute law in relation to acts which might otherwise attract criminal sanctions under the 1997 Act. Section 22(1) provides for the continuation of any enactment or rule of law providing a defence or providing lawful authority, justification or excuse for an act or omission. Thus, for example, the common law rules under which bodily harm caused with consent in the course of sports, dangerous exhibitions or medical treatments will apply to exempt the actor from criminal liability (as will other general defences such as duress, necessity, lawful excuse for action). Thus section 22 takes account of such activities as contact sports, including the much-beloved Gaelic games, association football and rugby union which occupy much of the time and energy of so many people (including the editors of this work - as least as interested observers). Section 22(2) abolishes the common law defence of necessary defence in conjunction with the provisions of sections 18 and 19.

Consent by minor over 16 years to surgical, medical and dental treatment   Section 23(1) provides that the consent of a minor who has attained the age of 16 years to any surgical, medical or dental treatment which, without consent, would be a trespass to that person shall be as effective a consent as consent by a person of full age. Section 23(2) specifies certain procedures which are included in the term 'surgical, medical or dental treatments'. Section 23(3) provides that nothing in the section shall be construed as making ineffective any consent which would have been effective if the section had not been enacted.

Abolition of common law immunity of teachers   Section 24 of the 1997 Act abolishes the common law rule of immunity for teachers from criminal liability in respect of physical chastisement, that is corporal punishment, of pupils. This formally confirms the abolition of corporal punishment in schools in the State by a 1982 administrative Circular from the Department of Education. See further Farry, *Education and the Constitution* (Round Hall Sweet & Maxwell, 1997).

Evidential value of certain certificates signed by medical practitioners   Section 25(1) provides that in proceedings for an offence alleging the causing of harm or serious harm to a person, the production of a certificate signed by a registered medical practitioner, relating to an examination of that person will, unless the contrary is proved, be accepted as evidence of any fact certified in it without proof of signature or without proof that the signature is that of the practitioner.

Extra-territorial offences and extradition   Sections 26 and 27 of the 1997 Act amended the Schedule to the Criminal Law (Jurisdiction) Act 1976 and the First Schedule of the Extradition (Amendment) Act 1994, respectively, consequent to the abolition of the common law offences and those under the 1861 Act and their replacement by the new offences in the 1997 Act.

Abolition of common law offences   As already indicated, section 28(1) of the 1997 Act provided for abolition of the common law offences of assault and battery, kidnapping and false imprisonment. On the connection with the Interpretation (Amendment) Act 1997, which provides that the abolition of common law offences by legislation operates prospectively only, see 284, above. Section 28(2) provides, notwithstanding section 28(1), for the continuation of the operation of certain provisions of the Criminal Law (Jurisdiction) Act 1976.

Repeal of statutory offences As already indicated, many sections of the Offences against the Person Act 1861 were repealed by section 29 of the 1997 Act. The specific provisions of the 1861 Act repealed were: sections 16 to 26, 28 to 34, 36, 37, 39, 40, 42, 46, 47, 53 to 56, 64, 65 and 73. In addition, the following were repealed: sections 6 and 7 of the Conspiracy and Protection of Property Act 1875; sections 3(3), 7 and 8 of the Criminal Law Amendment Act 1885; section 11 of the Criminal Justice Act 1951 and section 11(2) of the Criminal Law Act 1976.

Common assault In *Director of Public Prosecutions v. Brennan*, High Court, January 16, 1997, McCracken J. declined to prohibit a prosecution of the defendant, who had been charged summarily with common assault, though the particulars alleged assault on a police officer in the execution of his duty. If the charge had been brought under section 19(1) of the Criminal Justice (Public Order) Act 1994 (1994 Review, 214), which expressly provides for such a specific assault, the defendant would have been entitled to elect for trial on indictment. This right had been inserted in section 19 of the 1994 Act during the Oireachtas debate on the basis that to remove the right of election could be deemed in breach of the right to a trial in due course of law under Article 38.1 (1994 Review, 214). Citing the decision in *The People v. McDonagh* [1996] 1 I.R. 565; [1996] 2 I.L.R.M. 468 (1996 Review, 274-8), McCracken J. held he was entitled to examine the reason for the inclusion of the right to election in section 19 of the 1994 Act. Since section 19 of the 1994 Act preserved any other enactments involving assault as well as a police officer, McCracken J. held that this could be taken to include the offence of assault on 'any other person' in section 42 of the Offences against the Person Act 1861 (since replaced by the Non-Fatal Offences against the Person Act 1997, discussed, 304 *et seq.*, above). On this basis, he concluded that the offence of common assault had been preserved and the prosecution against the defendant could proceed. He also added that any prohibition could adversely affect the discretion of the Director as to what charges to bring and would unduly complicate the conduct of prosecutions.

POLICE PROPERTY ACTS

Return of assets In *Whitehead v. Garda Commissioner*, Supreme Court, February 27, 1997, the Supreme Court declined to interfere with an order made in the High Court that property confiscated under the Police Property Acts should not be returned to the applicant. The case concerned a large sum of sterling which the Gardaí had seized in the following circumstances. Two cars under Garda surveillance had been followed from the port of Dun Laoghaire where they had arrived by boat from England. Almost £60,000 in sterling was found in one car and £80,000 in sterling was found in the spare tyre of the second car. Both drivers were then detained under the Criminal Justice Act 1984. Neither claimed to be the owner of the moneys in question but that they had received the moneys in a bag from the applicant for the purpose of bringing it to Sligo where it was to be used to purchase a public house. The trial judge rejected the applicant's evidence along with that of the drivers, as he could not accept that a business man would conduct himself in such an extraordinary way. In addition he was sceptical that a businessman would bring sterling into the State to complete a transaction in Irish punts. The applicant appealed to the Supreme Court on the grounds that the trial judge had erred in holding that he was not the lawful owner of the money. As indicated, the Supreme Court dismissed the appeal.

The Court emphasised that, unlike the trial judge, it did not enjoy the opportunity of seeing and hearing the witnesses and their demeanour. Having regard to the circumstances in which the money had been found, the Court held that the trial judge had been entitled to be sceptical of the entire transaction as outlined before him and to reject the evidence of ownership given by the applicant. In those circumstances, it was not open to the Court to interfere with the findings of the trial judge. The Court added, however, that if the applicant had been in a position to satisfy the trial judge of his ownership of the money, he would have been entitled to an order for its return because no evidence had been adduced before the trial judge to suggest that the respondent was entitled to retain possession. The use of the Police Property Acts must now be regarded as being secondary to the confiscation powers contained in the Proceeds of Crime Act 1996 (1996 Review, 233-4).

PROCEDURE

The Criminal Justice (Miscellaneous Provisions) Act 1997 was concerned primarily with amending the law concerning criminal procedure with a view, in particular, to reducing the amount of time spent by Gardaí on court-related duties. The Act extended the maximum period for which a person may be remanded in custody and provides for the issue of search warrants where specified serious offences have been committed. It also amended the powers of the Director of Public Prosecutions under the Criminal Justice Act 1951. The Act came into force generally on March 4, 1997, but sections 3 to 10, section 12 and section 18 came into effect on April 4, 1997. We will discuss the terms of the 1997 Act and then discuss the case law in 1997 concerning criminal procedure.

Station bail   Section 3 of the 1997 Act amended section 31 of the Criminal Procedure Act 1967 to provide that a person released on 'station' bail must enter a recognisance to appear before the District Court at the next sitting of the District Court or at any subsequent sitting thereof within 30 days after such next sitting. Prior to the 1997 Act, section 31 of the 1967 Act had required that the person enter a recognisance to appear before the District Court at the appropriate time and place.

Extension of remand period   Section 4 of the 1997 Act inserted a new section 24 into the Criminal Procedure Act 1967, which now provides that the District Court may remand a person in custody, on that person's second or subsequent appearance before the Court on a particular charge, for a maximum period of 15 or 30 days with the consent of that person and the prosecutor. The maximum remand period for a first appearance remains at eight days, as was the case prior to the 1997 Act. The new section 24 also provides that where the District Court is of the opinion in all the circumstances that it would be unreasonable to remand the person in custody for period of 15 or 30 days, the Court may remand the person in custody for any lesser period of days.

Remand to Court nearest remand prison   Section 5 of the 1997 Act provides that, notwithstanding section 79(2) of the Courts of Justice Act 1924 and section 27(3) of the Courts of Justice Act 1953, the court before which a person first appears may remand that person in custody to appear before a District Court in the District where the remand prison where that person is held in custody is situated.

Evidence of arrest etc by certificate   Section 6 of the 1997 Act makes provision for the giving of evidence relating to the arrest, charging and cautioning of a person and certain other procedural evidence by way of a certificate. Prior to the 1997 Act, such evidence had to be given by oral evidence. The section also provides that the court may require oral evidence to be given of these matters where the interests of justice so require. The Criminal Justice (Miscellaneous Provisions) Act 1997 (Section 6) Regulations 1997 (S.I. No. 345 of 1997) prescribe the forms for use in relation to proof of the arrest and caution of a person for a specified offence under section 6 of the 1997 Act. They came into effect on September 8, 1997.

Consent of Director for summary trial of all indictable offences   Section 8 of the 1997 Act amended section 2 of the Criminal Justice Act 1951 to provide that the consent of the Director of Public Prosecutions is required before a District Court can try summarily a person charged with any indictable offence contained in the First Schedule to the 1951 Act. Prior to the 1997 Act, the Director's consent was required for only some of the scheduled offences.

Consent of Director to offences being taken into account Section 8 of the Criminal Justice Act 1951 provides that a person convicted of an offence may admit guilt to other offences and ask that they be taken into account by the court in determining sentence. Section 9 of the 1997 Act amended section 8 of the 1951 Act to provide that the Director of Public Prosecutions' consent will be required before offences, which are not the subject of the charges before the court, may be taken into consideration.

Search warrant for serious offences Section 10 of the 1997 Act provides that the District Court may issue a warrant to a Garda to search any place and any person found on that place for evidence relating to the commission of certain serious offences, including (a) an indictable offence involving the death or serious bodily injury to an person, (b) false imprisonment, (c) rape and (d) various sexual offences specified in the First Schedule to the 1997 Act.

Electronic recording of fingerprints and palmprints Section 11 of the 1997 Act provides that any statutory power to take fingerprints and palmprints shall be taken to include the taking of them by electronic means. Section 12 of the 1997 Act substituted a new section 28 of the Criminal Justice Act 1984 in order to empower the taking of fingerprints and palmprints within seven days of conviction or of the making of a probation order under the Probation of Offenders Act 1907.

Sexual offence and evidence generally Section 16 of the 1997 Act amended the definition of sexual offence in the Criminal Evidence Act 1992 (1992 Review, 251-61) to take account of changes made in the Criminal Law (Sexual Offences) Act 1993 (1993 Review, 264-6).

Appearance before court on day following arrest or charge Section 18 of the 1997 Act amended section 15 of the Courts of Justice Act 1951 to provide that a person arrested on a warrant or charged following arrest without a warrant after 5 p.m. may be brought before a court not later than noon on the following day. Prior to the 1997 Act, the 1951 Act had provided that the remanding of a person to appear in court on the following day was restricted to where a person was arrested or charged after 10 p.m.

Adjournment In *Cullen v. Fitzpatrick*, Supreme Court, February 26, 1997, the applicant had been arrested on charges of possession of a controlled drug with intention to supply, contrary to the Misuse of Drugs Acts 1977 and 1984 and been detained in a Garda station under the Criminal Justice Act 1984. At his trial by the respondent judge of the District Court, the applicant wished to cross-examine the Garda who had informed the applicant that he was being detained under the 1984 Act. No argument was made that the applicant's constitutional rights had been in any way violated during the course of his arrest and detention. The respondent declined to adjourn the trial to enable the Garda to be called and proceeded to convict the applicant and to impose a 12-month sentence. The applicant sought to have the conviction quashed on the ground that fair procedures had not been followed and that the respondent should have adjourned the trial. He was successful in the High Court, but on appeal, the Supreme Court held that the respondent had acted within jurisdiction in declining to adjourn. The Court noted that the prosecution did not in any way rely on evidence obtained during the course of the applicant's detention and that no argument was addressed to the District Court that any rights had been infringed during detention. The respondent District Court judge was thus entitled to exercise his jurisdiction as he did by declining to adjourn the proceedings in order to secure the attendance of a witness whose evidence would have been irrelevant to the issues to be determined, thus distinguishing the instant facts from those in *Coughlan v. Patwell* [1992] I.L.R.M. 808 (1991 Review, 147).

Court jurisdiction In a series of cases that attracted considerable public attention, the High Court and Supreme Court held that a defect in charging defendants before an improperly constituted Special Criminal Court could be cured by a subsequent charging before a properly constituted Special Criminal Court. The difficulty in the composition of the Special Criminal Court had arisen because one of its judges had, at his request, been removed as a judge of the Court and the decision of the Government to this effect had been published in *Iris Oifigiúil*. Unfortunately, the judge was not informed of the Government's decision and he continued to sit as a judge of the court after he had, in fact, been removed as a judge of the court. When the problem was ultimately discovered, the Minister for Justice ordered the prison authorities to release the affected defendants from custody and also directed that they immediately be re-arrested by the Gardaí and re-charged before a properly constituted Special Criminal Court. Most of the releases took place as soon as the prison authorities became aware of the Ministerial direction. The question that then arose in a series of the cases was whether the releases, re-arrests and re-charging were permissible. In each of the cases, the High Court and Supreme Court held that no invalidity attached to the procedures adopted.

In *Duncan and Ors v. Governor of Portlaoise Prison (No.2)*, High Court, June 9, 1997 and *Cully v. Governor of Portlaoise Prison*, High Court, June 18, 1997 Kelly J. dealt with a number of these cases. In *Duncan*, the applicants attached importance to the fact that they had been re-arrested on prison property. They further contended that, once the problem with the Special Criminal Court had become known, the State authorities had conspired to keep the applicants in unlawful custody until the State was in a position to release them followed immediately by a purportedly lawful arrest and a recharging before the Special Criminal Court. In *Cully*, the applicant had not been released until some hours after the applicants in *Duncan*. On his release, he was re-arrested at common law on prison property and later re-charged before the Special Criminal Court. In both his judgments, Kelly J. took a common approach to the legal issues raised.

He held that there was nothing unlawful *per se* about an arrest of a person already in custody or detention provided that such arrest was carried out with the consent of the custodian or detainer. In the case of the applicants in *Duncan*, once the respective prison authorities were informed of the Ministerial order for release, everything that they did from that moment on was with a view to bringing their custody of the prisoners to an end. As to the failure to release the applicant in *Cully* at the same time as the other affected prisoners occurred, he held that this had been through inadvertence and was not in any sense deliberate or conscious. Kelly J. rejected the argument that there was any evidence of any agreement on the part of the State authorities to do something unlawful or to do something lawful by unlawful means. As the prison authorities consented to the arrests taking place on prison property, that was sufficient to make the arrests lawful, and relying on the decision in *Re Singer (No. 2)* (1964) 98 I.L.T.R. 112, he concluded that the locus of the arrests had no significance with regard to their lawfulness. Applying the decision in *The People v. McCann and O'Shea* (1981) 2 Frewen 57, he went on to hold that the fact that the arrests in suit were effected after a period of unlawful detention did not affect their legality of efficacy.

When the cases came before the Special Criminal Court, Kelly J. noted that the necessary statement of fact was made that the Director of Public Prosecutions had given the appropriate direction under the Offences against the State Act 1939 to have the charges against the applicants heard in the Special Criminal Court. The mere fact that the Court was not told in express terms until the next day that the charges before it were in substitution for those already made was of no consequence and it had been perfectly lawful for the prosecution and the Court to deal with the new charges as they did. Finally, Kelly J. held that he was not engaged in an exercise of punishing the State but was investigating the lawfulness of the applicants' detention. If there had been unlawful activity, he noted that there had been no fruits from it and the applicants were in the same position had the chapter of accidents in question not taken place.

In another case in this series, *Hegarty v. Governor of Limerick Prison*, Divisional High Court, February 26, 1997 a further argument concerning the alleged conspiracy was rejected. It had been argued that the circumstances in the instant case were similar to those in *The State (Trimbole) v. Governor of Mountjoy Prison* [1985] I.R. 550. Delivering the leading judgment, Geoghegan J. held that, unlike in *Trimbole*, there was no evidence of a scheme deliberately involving an abuse of the process of the courts and, again unlike *Trimbole*, not only was the applicant wanted for offences against the law of this State but a direction had been given by the Director of Public Prosecutions that he was to be prosecuted for those offences in the Special Criminal Court.

In a third case, *Quinlivan v. Governor of Limerick Prison (No.2)* [1998] 1 I.L.R.M. 294 (SC), the Supreme Court affirmed the views which had been taken in the High Court. In the instant case, the applicant had, after the error already described had been discovered, been released from prison through the main gate, where he was immediately arrested, brought before the properly constituted Special Criminal Court and remanded in custody. The High Court and Supreme Court rejected the applicant's claim that he was in unlawful custody in that he had not properly released and that the further arrest was unlawful and an abuse of process.

The Supreme Court agreed with the High Court's findings of fact that the applicant was no longer in the custody of the prison when he was arrested after release. The Court held that the validity of the arrest outside the gate was not affected by the fact that the applicant was not brought to the public street before arrest. The Court also accepted that there had been no concerted plan on the authorities' part constituting a conscious and deliberate violation of the applicant's constitutional rights, by contrast with the situation in *The State (Trimbole) v. Governor of Mountjoy Prison* [1985] I.R. 550 and *R v. Horseferry Road Magistrate's Court, ex p Bennett* [1994] 1 A.C. 42.

The Court added that once it transpired that due to an administrative error a warrant under which the applicant was being detained was invalid, there was a positive duty on the authorities to remedy the situation; this duty had been discharged by the prompt release followed by the applicant's immediate arrest so that he could be brought before a properly constituted court.

Forensic examination In *Dutton v. Director of Public Prosecutions*, High Court, July 9, 1997, Flood J. declined to order that a trial for larceny be prohibited where the applicant claimed there had been no opportunity afforded him to conduct a forensic examination of the stolen property. The applicant had been accused of stealing a car, but had pleaded not guilty. He claimed that he had requested that the car be forensically examined, but the Gardaí asserted that no request was ever been received by them and that the first they heard of such a request was nearly two years after the accident. It was also pointed out that a forensic examination had been carried out y the Gardaí shortly after the car had been stolen. The applicant contended that he had been denied fair procedures. Flood J. disagreed. He noted that no application for an examination had been made until some 23 months after the accident. He considered that some account should be taken of the innocent owner of the car where the deprivation of possession would seriously prejudice or inconvenience him. In addition, he took account of the fact that a forensic examination had been carried out promptly by the Gardaí, and that the applicant did not seek an examination for two and a half months after he had been charged. In those circumstances, he held that there had been no breach of fair procedures or of the terms of the Criminal Procedure Act 1967.

Preliminary examination In *Killeen v. Director of Public Prosecutions* [1998] 1 I.L.R.M. 1 (SC), the Supreme Court declared that a decision of the District Court declining to send the applicant forward for trial was a nullity and did not necessarily preclude a re-hearing of the preliminary examination. The applicant had appeared before the District Court charged with obtaining money by false pretences. The charge stated that the offence was contrary to section 33(1) of the Larceny Act 1916, but the offence had in fact been created by section 32(1) of the 1916 Act. The applicant submitted that the warrant for the applicant's arrest was invalid as the charges were not properly brought on the basis of the statements in the book of documents served on the applicant under the Criminal Procedure Act 1967. The judge of the District Court discharged the applicant under section 8(5) of the Criminal Procedure Act 1967. Fresh summonses were issued charging the applicant with the same offences, save the error as to the correct section of the Larceny Act 1916. The applicant successfully sought judicial review on the ground that since the order of the District Court was made within jurisdiction the prosecution was precluded from instituting fresh proceedings. The Director appealed to the Supreme Court, which reversed the High Court decision and remitted the charges to the District Court.

The Court accepted that, in light of the decision in *Costello v. Director of Public Prosecutions* [1984] I.R. 436, where a judge of the District Court, acting within jurisdiction, formed the opinion that there was not a sufficient case to put the accused on trial and ordered the accused to be discharged under section 8(5) of the 1967 Act, it was not open to the prosecution to institute fresh proceedings in respect of the same offences. The real issue was whether the order made in the instant case had been made within jurisdiction. The Supreme Court reviewed the case law on errors going to jurisdiction, including the judgment of Henchy J. in *The State (Holland) v. Kennedy* [1977] I.R. 193, which appeared to have followed the views expressed by the Privy Council in *Anisminic Ltd. v. Foreign Compensation Commission* [1969] 2 A.C. 147. Thus, the Court confirmed the modern view of jurisdiction that it did not necessarily follow that a court which started a hearing within jurisdiction will be treated as continuing to act within jurisdiction. A similar view had been expressed by Costello J. in *Ryan v. Compensation Tribunal* [1997] 1 I.L.R.M. 194 (HC), discussed in the 1996 Review, 5-7. The Court reiterated this approach in *Farrell v. Attorney General* [1998] 1 I.L.R.M. 364 (HC & SC) (discussed in the Coroners chapter, 259, above).

Thus there are circumstances which could render the decision of a tribunal a nullity, although it had jurisdiction to enter upon the inquiry. The Supreme Court held that the *Killeen* case was one such situation. *Certiorari* could lie if an error of law had the consequence of the making of an order which the court had no jurisdiction to make. If the District Court judge had discharged the applicant because he considered himself precluded from sending him forward for trial due to the defect in the warrant, that was not an error of law within his jurisdiction to make. If the judge was of that view, he had failed to determine the question assigned to the District Court, namely, whether on the materials before the court, there was a sufficient case to put the applicant on trial. If that was his decision it constituted an error of law which rendered his order a nullity. The judge had confined his adjudication to a determination that due to the defective warrant the applicant was entitled to be discharged, and this was based on an erroneous view of his jurisdiction. The Supreme Court made an order of *certiorari* setting aside the order of the District Court, and remitted the charges to the District Court.

Prosecutor discretion In *Landers v. Garda Síochána Complaints Board*, High Court, March 7, 1997, Kelly J. confirmed that the prosecutorial discretion of the Director of Public Prosecutions is rarely amenable to judicial review. The plaintiffs, all members of the Garda Síochána, were alleged by one Derek Fairbrother to have severely assaulted him in June 1988 in the course of an attempted arrest (the incident attracted considerable publicity at the time). The Director made a determination that no prosecutions for assault should proceed against the plaintiffs but Mr Fairbrother made a complaint under the Garda Síochána (Complaints) Act 1986 to the Garda Síochána Complaints Board. In the course of this complaint, the plaintiffs instituted judicial review proceedings by way of plenary summons in which they sought to establish that the Director had acted *ultra vires* his powers under the Prosecution of Offences Act 1974 and in an unconstitutional manner by not prosecuting the plaintiffs on foot of the complaint made against them. Kelly J. struck out the claim against the Director. He accepted that, in principle, decisions of the Director concerning the prosecution or non-prosecution of a person are subject to review by the court, but that as indicated in *The State (McCormack) v. Curran* [1987] I.L.R.M. 225 and *H v. Director of Public Prosecutions* [1994] 2 I.R. 589; [1994] 2 I.L.R.M. 285 (1994 Review, 208-10) such a review can only occur if it can be demonstrated that the Director reached a decision *mala fide* or was influenced by an improper motive or improper policy. He considered that there was nothing in the documents placed before him which demonstrated that the plaintiffs had placed themselves within those categories in which the court would review the Director's decision.

Summons amendment   In *Director of Public Prosecutions v. Doyle* [1997] 1 I.L.R.M. 379 (HC), Geoghegan J. held that the Courts (No.3) Act 1986 had not affected in any way the wide powers of amendment of summonses given to District Court judges under rule 88 of the District Court Rules 1948 (now replaced by the District Court Rules 1997: see the Practice and Procedure chapter, 599, below). The summons against the defendant alleged that, being a person arrested under the Road Traffic Act 1961 and brought to a Garda Station, he had failed to permit a registered medical practitioner to take a specimen of blood or urine at a Garda station at 'Cavendish Row, Dublin 1.' The District Court judge noted that the summons failed to disclose an offence in that there was no Garda station at Cavendish Row. The prosecution requested the judge to permit an amendment to the summons in order to substitute the words 'Fitzgibbon Street Garda Station.' The judge refused to make the amendment being of the opinion that rule 88 had been amended by implication by the Courts (No. 3) Act 1986, which empowered him to make amendments where the particulars of the offence recited in the summons disclosed a valid criminal offence. On case stated, Geoghegan J. held that the judge had erred in law.

Geoghegan J. held that section 1(6) of the 1986 Act provided that a summons duly issued under that Act should be deemed for all purposes to be a summons duly issued pursuant to the law immediately before the passing of the Act. The District Court judge had thus been entitled to treat the summons in exactly the same manner as a summons issued under the pre-1986 system and was free to accede to the application for the amendment under the District Court Rules.

In *Lennon v. Brennan*, High Court, April 30, 1997 Smyth J. affirmed a different type of amendment. In this case, the applicant was summonsed to attend the District Court on a charge of assault. The summons called upon the accused to show cause as to why he ought not be bound to the peace. His solicitor appeared in court objecting to the jurisdiction of the Court. The respondent judge deleted the words 'to show cause' from the summons. On judicial review, Smyth J. held that the respondent had not erred in law. He noted that in the eyes of the law, binding to good behaviour is not a punishment but a precautionary proceeding against misbehaviour. Nonetheless, the applicant was not obliged to come to court 'to show cause' and Smyth J. noted that this was clearly appreciated by the respondent by deleting this from the summons, thus attending to the substance of the complaint which was one of assault only.

Summons application   In *Kelly v. Hamill*, High Court, January 21, 1997, McCracken J. held that since an application for a summons is a purely administrative matter the failure to name the applicant in the summons could not be deemed to affect any substantive element of the prosecution. A number of summonses had been issued against the applicant alleging offences under the Licensing Acts 1824 to 1994. The application for the summons had given the registered number of the prosecuting Garda, but did not state his name. The application was made by and under the signature of a Department of Justice official. When the summonses came before the respondent judge of the District Court, the applicant's solicitor objected to the issuing and service of the summonses and submitted that the respondent had no jurisdiction to determine the matters. The applicant subsequently sought orders of certiorari and prohibition. McCracken J. refused the relief sought.

He noted that as the word 'summons' is not used in any esoteric manner in the Courts Acts and it is simply a document calling upon or summoning the person named to appear in court on a certain date, the application for the summons is a purely administrative matter and any formality or informality in such an application cannot affect or prejudice the accused. McCracken J. held that, although the summons must state the name of the applicant for the summons, there is no provision in either the Courts (No.3) Act 1986 or the District Court (Forms of Summons) Rules 1987 for any particular form of application for a summons, nor is there any reference to who must physically make the application. Thus, the Garda in charge of the investigation is perfectly entitled administratively to request some other person physically to attend at the District Court office and indeed physically to fill in whatever form is necessary.

Summons arrest warrant In *Dunphy v. Crowley*, Supreme Court, February 17, 1997 the applicant had been served with ten summonses alleging insurance and tax offences under the Road Traffic Act 1961. Three days before the hearing of the charges in the District Court, he instructed his solicitor to appear on his behalf. On the morning of the hearing, he telephoned his solicitor and instructed him that he was unable to attend court that day and that his solicitor should seek an adjournment to enable him to locate relevant documentation. When his solicitor sought the adjournment, the respondent judge asked the prosecuting Garda what his attitude was and the latter seemed to indicate that he was leaving the matter in the court's hands. The judge then said that that the applicant should have appeared, particularly in relation to the insurance matter and he then issued a bench warrant for the applicant's arrest. The applicant sought an order of *certiorari* to quash the warrant. Rule 40 of the District Court Rules 1948 empowered a judge of the District Court power to issue a warrant for the arrest of a defendant where a summons was issued requiring the attendance of a defendant who was charged with an offence and the defendant failed to 'appear' at the required time and place. The applicant claimed that he did not fail to appear because he had instructed a solicitor to appear on his behalf. He relied on rule 7 of the District Court Rules 1948 which provided that 'any party to any proceedings in the District Court or the solicitor for such party... may appear and address the court and conduct the proceedings.' In the High Court, Barr J. held that the judge of the District Court had jurisdiction to issue the warrant and on appeal this view was upheld by the Supreme Court.

The Supreme Court held that rule 7 of the 1948 Rules did not deal with the question of whether the summons requires the personal attendance of the defendant. Its purpose was to provides that a solicitor or counsel may appear and address the court and conduct the proceedings on the defendant's behalf, but it is silent on the question of whether the rule operates if the defendant has not come to court in obedience to the summons. The Court relied on the decision in *Great Southern Railway Co. v. Leyden* [1907] 2 I.R. 160 in holding that a summons requires the personal attendance of the defendant, so that being represented by a solicitor was not a sufficient compliance with the summonses. The Court pointed out that the normal meaning in the summons of the words 'and to require you to appear at the said sitting to answer the accusation' was that a defendant was required personally to attend the court. Rule 40 of the 1948 Rules corroborated this meaning since it requires the 'attendance' of the defendant. The Court concluded that it was significant that the rule which gives the judge the power to issue a warrant for the arrest of a defendant if he does not appear is also the rule which describes the summons as requiring the attendance of the defendant, rather than requiring him to appear.

The Court pointed out that this view was supported by section 11 of the Petty Sessions (Ireland) Act 1851, from which rule 40 of the 1948 Rules derived its authority. Section 11 of the 1851 Act confirmed indirectly that a summons requires a personal attendance by the defendant. The Court held that the plain meaning of the form of the summons given in the Schedule to the 1851 Act was that the defendant is commanded personally to attend, and this was supported by the fact that a summons in precisely the same form is used for securing the attendance of a witness. The same meaning should be given to the summons whether it was being used to procure the attendance of a witness or of a defendant, and that meaning was personal attendance. In that respect the applicant's failure to attend amounted to disobedience to the summonses and entitled the judge in the exercise of his discretion to exercise one of three options: he could have adjourned the case, heard the complaint or issued a warrant for the defendant's arrest. As the applicant's solicitor was not briefed to defend the case but to seek an adjournment, the Supreme Court held that the judge was correct in deciding not to hear the case. As he had decided that there were no grounds for granting an adjournment, the only option left was to issue a warrant for the applicant's arrest and this had been a proper exercise of his discretion.

Video evidence: intermediary   The Criminal Evidence Act 1992 (Sections 14 and 19) (Commencement) Order 1997 (S.I. No. 66 of 1997), brought sections 14 and 19 of the Criminal Evidence Act 1992 (1992 Review, 262), which provide for the use of an intermediary in the examination of young persons by video link, into force on March 3, 1997.

PROCEEDS OF CRIME

Procedure   In *M.M. v. D.D.*, High Court, December 19, 1996, Moriarty J. held, in an application under the Proceeds of Crime Act 1996, the courts should apply the established rule that some appreciable measure of hearsay evidence was considered acceptable in affidavits filed on behalf of parties.

The respondent had been restrained by the High Court under section 2 of the 1996 Act from dealing with certain moneys held in his name in a bank account. The order had been granted to the applicant ex parte under section 3 of the 1996 Act, which requires that the court be satisfied that a person is in possession or control of specified property that constitutes directly or indirectly proceeds of crime, or was partly or wholly acquired with or in connection with property that constitutes such proceeds, where the property is not less than £10,000. Pursuant to section 9 of the 1996 Act, the applicant required the respondent to specify on an affidavit of discovery both the property in his possession or control and his income and its sources for the ten years prior to the application. The respondent objected to the application on the grounds that the nature and standard of proof advanced on affidavit against him were unsatisfactory and inadequate to warrant the relief sought, that the hearsay rule was breached, that the relief if granted would offend his privilege against self-incrimination, and that section 9 should not be considered to have retrospective effect.

Moriarty J. found largely in the applicant's favour and granted the order of discovery sought, though he limited the discovery to a period of six years prior to the date of the application, rather than the ten years sought.

He held that while the 1996 Act was silent on the nature of proof sufficient to induce a court to exercise its discretion in any particular case, an initial onus of proof was placed on an applicant and he concluded that the standard of proof was that applicable to civil proceedings. Moriarty J. held that the 1996 Act entrusted the Court with a wide discretion to ensure compliance with the requirements of natural justice and to ensure that injustice was not perpetrated against meritorious persons. He noted that the 1996 Act ad adopted a procedure broadly similar to that in *Mareva* applications. It was, he pointed out, the established usage of the courts in such cases that an 'appreciable measure of hearsay evidence' was considered acceptable in affidavits filed on behalf of parties. He held that the exceptional case could arise where a judicial discretion could be exercised to prefer Garda evidence involving a hearsay element to an applicant's own testimony.

In any event, Moriarty J. held that the combined evidence in the instant case took it beyond the realm of mere hearsay, speculative or otherwise inadequate evidence. He noted that the general averments in the applicant's affidavits were to be coupled with the transcripts of a previous trial in which the respondent had been acquitted by a jury but in which he was recorded as having attributed earnings to activities which were illegal, and the circumstances of a telephone call noted by a Garda. In total, these items merited the relief sought, while natural justice also required that the respondent be afforded the opportunity to cross-examine and challenge the Garda in question insofar as his crucial evidence was tendered on a hearsay basis.

Noting the degree of nexus between the applicant and the Director of Public Prosecutions, Moriarty J. held that it would be necessary, if discovery were ordered, that an undertaking be given by the Director in order to prevent possible prejudice in any future criminal proceedings. He referred in this context to the following English authorities on discovery and disclosure orders: *Bekhor Ltd. v. Bilton* [1981] 1 Q.B. 923, *Re O.* [1991] 2 Q.B. 520, *Istel Ltd. v. Tully* [1993] A.C. 45 and *R v. Thomas (Disclosure Order)* [1992] 4 All E.R. 814.

As to the retrospection argument, Moriarty J. held that it would frustrate the intention of the Oireachtas if the definition of income was confined to that received after the passage of the 1996 Act. While he accepted that there was a presumption that the 1996 Act should be interpreted as being prospective rather than retrospective (as to which, see *Chestvale Ltd v. Glackin* [1993] 3 I.R. 35; [1992] I.L.R.M. 221, discussed in the 1992 Review, 68-73), he concluded that section 9 of the 1996 Act should enable discovery of property or income held or enjoyed for a maximum period of ten years prior to application. However, in the instant case, he held that six years was an adequate period.

ROAD TRAFFIC

Blood specimen   In *Director of Public Prosecutions v. Lynch*, Supreme Court, February 5 1997, the Supreme Court (O'Flaherty, Barrington and Keane JJ.) held that where a member of the Garda Síochána, pursuant to section 13(1)(b) of the Road Traffic (Amendment) Act 1978, requires an arrested person either to permit a designated registered medical practitioner to take a specimen of his blood or to provide a designated registered medical practitioner with a specimen of his urine and where the member of the Garda Síochána informs the arrested person of the statutory basis of the requirement and the penalties for non-compliance, the arrested person is under a duty to facilitate the taking of a such specimens and to comply with any reasonable request which the designated registered medical practitioner may make of him for this purpose.

In the instant case, the defendant had been arrested under section 49(6) of the Road Traffic Act 1961, as amended by section 10 of the Road Traffic Act (Amendment) Act 1978, and brought to a Garda Station where he was introduced to a designated registered medical practitioner. Pursuant to section 13(1)(b) of the 1978 Act, the arresting Garda required the defendant either to permit the doctor to take a specimen of his blood or, at the defendant's option, to provide the doctor with a specimen of his urine. The Garda informed the defendant that if he failed to comply with this requirement he would be guilty of an offence and also informed him of the penalties for such an offence. The doctor informed the defendant that if he opted to give blood, the blood specimen would be taken from his arm and that if he opted to provide a urine sample, he could do so by providing a sample in the container provided for this purpose. The defendant told the doctor that he should take the blood sample from his (the defendant's) big toe. The doctor informed the defendant that there were dangers associated with taking blood from a big toe and he explained these dangers to him. The Garda cautioned the defendant that failure to comply with the doctor's requirement was an offence and repeated the penalties applicable. The defendant was charged with failure to comply with the requirement of a designated registered medical practitioner in relation to the taking of a specimen of blood following a requirement under section 13(1)(b) of the Road Traffic (Amendment) Act 1978, contrary to section 13(3) of the Road Traffic (Amendment) Act 1978.

The defendant submitted at his trial in the District Court that, since he had been charged with failure to comply with the requirement of a designated registered medical practitioner and that there was no evidence that the doctor had informed him of the legal basis of such requirement, he should be acquitted. On a case stated from the Circuit Court, the Supreme Court held that the defendant could be convicted in the circumstances which had arisen.

The Court held that section 13 of the 1978 Act provides for the making of only one formal requirement in relation to the furnishing of a specimen of blood or urine, that is, a requirement by a member of the Garda Síochána pursuant to section 13(1)(b) that a person either permit a designated registered medical practitioner to take a blood specimen or provide for the designated registered medical practitioner a specimen of his urine. There was ample evidence that the defendant was informed of this formal legal requirement and of the statutory basis for it. This formal requirement imposes a duty on the arrested person to facilitate the taking of a blood specimen and to comply with such reasonable requests as the designated registered medical practitioner may make of him for this purpose. The Court held that the term 'requirement' in section 13(3)(1)(b) means such request as the medical practitioner may make of the arrested person in order to take a blood specimen pursuant to the formal requirement made by the member of the Garda Síochána. It is thus neither necessary nor correct for the medical practitioner to refer to the provisions of the statute every time he requests the arrested person to do something for the purpose of the taking of a blood specimen. In the instant case, there was ample evidence that the doctor had required the defendant to co-operate in the taking of a blood specimen and that he had refused to comply with this request.

Stop and search   Section 13 of the Criminal Justice (Miscellaneous Provisions) Act 1997 (discussed generally, 314, above) amended section 8 of the Criminal Law Act 1976 so that it applies to an offence under section 112 of the Road Traffic Act 1961, as amended by section 3(7) of the Road Traffic (Amendment) Act 1994.

SEARCH

Dwelling   In *Director of Public Prosecutions v. Delaney* [1998] 1 I.L.R.M. 507 (SC), the Supreme Court held that a Garda may enter a dwelling where it was required to safeguard life and limb and that such entry was thus not in breach of Article 40.5 of the Constitution. The defendants had been charged with various public order offences relating to a disturbance outside a flat involving a large crowd hostile to those within the flat, including the defendants. The arresting Garda entered the flat in purported exercise of a power he believed he possessed at common law, and the defendants were arrested. The Garda's evidence was that he thought he had the right to enter the dwelling in order to protect the safety of a number of children in the flat and in the interests of the persons inside the flat, having regard to the attitude of the crowd outside. At the defendants' trial in the District Court, their solicitor applied for a direction on the basis that the entry of the flat was illegal and in breach of the defendants' constitutional rights under Article 40.5, and that their consequent arrests were unlawful. It was submitted that the Garda Síochána only have power to arrest without warrant in a person's home where there existed reasonable grounds for suspecting that the person had committed a felony or permission had been given by an appropriate person to enter the premises. On a consultative case stated from the District Court, the High Court held that the entry had been lawful. On further appeal, the Supreme Court affirmed.

The Supreme Court held that the lawfulness of an arrest was only relevant where proof of a valid arrest was an essential ingredient to ground a charge, for example, in a drink-driving prosecution under section 49 of the Road Traffic Act 1961. The Court pointed out that, in the instant case, it was not necessary in the case of any of the charges brought against the defendants to prove a lawful arrest.

Applying the harmonious approach to the Constitution, the Court noted that there was a hierarchy of constitutional rights and there could be a collision of rights where one right might have to yield to another. In the instant case, the arresting Garda was obliged by the circumstances to make his decision in a very fraught situation, and provided he made his choice *bona fide*, he was entitled to enter the premises to protect the persons within. It was irrelevant that he thought he was acting pursuant to some common law power since the Court considered that the safeguarding of life and limb was more important that the inviolability of the dwelling of a citizen. This approach was similar to that taken by the Court in *The People v. Shaw* [1982] I.R. 1.

SENTENCING

Aggregate consecutive in District Court In *Meagher v. O'Leary*, High Court, October 8, 1997, Moriarty J. upheld the constitutional validity of section 5 of the Criminal Justice Act 1951, as amended by section 12(1) of the Criminal Justice Act 1984, which provides for a maximum period of 2 years in consecutive terms of imprisonment imposed by the District Court. The applicant had been convicted in the District Court on 11 summonses charging possession of illegal animal growth promoters (for previous proceedings in the case, see *Meagher v. Minister for Agriculture and Food* [1994] 1 I.R. 329; [1994] 1 I.L.R.M. 1 (1993 Review, 299-304)). The applicant was sentenced on to concurrent terms of eight months, save in respect of the first two summonses heard, in regard to which it was ordered that the eight month terms should operate consecutively. He challenged the constitutional validity of section 5 of the 1951 Act on judicial review.

Moriarty J. held that the applicant was entitled to maintain his constitutional argument in the judicial review proceedings and was not obliged to institute plenary proceedings seeking declaratory relief, citing *The State (Lynch) v. Cooney* [1982] I.R. 337 and *The State (Gallagher, Shatter & Co) v. deValera (No.2)* [1987] I.R. 55; [1987] I.L.R.M. 555 (1987 Review, 280) in this respect.

He went on to state that it was imperative that any maximum aggregate sentence that is set down by the Oireachtas accords with the requirements of fairness and constitutional justice. He accepted that construing the impugned section of the 1951 Act, as amended by the 1984 Act, involved a balancing of conflicting constitutional rights and duties and that he had to determine from an objective stance whether the balance was so contrary to reason and fairness as to constitute an unjust attack on a citizen's rights. Applying the proportionality test in *Heaney v. Ireland* [1996] 1 I.R. 580; [1997] 1 I.L.R.M. 117 (1996 Review, 329-32), he concluded that the limit of two years aggregate maximum of lesser consecutive sentences could not be said to so contravene reason and fairness as to constitute an unjust attack on the applicant's constitutional rights.

Finally, using the rationality test in *The State(Keegan) v. Stardust Victims Compensation Tribunal* [1986] I.R. 642, he held that while the sentence imposed on the applicant was one of appreciable rigour it could not be said to amount to one which was arbitrary, disproportionate and of such dimensions as to be a manifestly unjust punishment warranting the intervention of the Court.

Burglary and criminal damage   In *The People v. O'Shea and Anor*, Court of Criminal Appeal, February 17, 1997 the two defendants had pleaded guilty to charges of burglary and criminal damage, the first defendant receiving a total sentence of six years with the last year suspended, and the second defendant receiving a total of six years. For the first defendant, the sentence for criminal damage was made consecutive on the burglary sentence. On appeal, the Court of Criminal Appeal reduced the first defendant's sentence to four years but affirmed the sentence on the second defendant. As to the first defendant, the Court referred to the decision in *O'Brien v. Governor of Limerick Prison* [1997] 2 I.L.R.M. 349 (SC) (see 333, below) in holding that the courts could not impose a sentence of suspension after a sentence of imprisonment unless the court which imposed the sentence retained seisin of the case. Since this was not possible in the instant case, the court disregarded the final year which was suspended for the first defendant and regard the total sentence as being five years imprisonment. The Court held that, in the first defendant's case, if the trial judge erred in relation to the burglary charges it was in imposing a sentence which was too light. Taking into account the plea of guilty, a four year sentence was more appropriate than the three years imposed. For the criminal damage charges, the offences formed part of the burglary act and the sentences should be concurrent, leaving the defendant's total sentence at four years. As to the second defendant, the Court described his record as 'appalling'. Since he was also older than the first defendant, the Court concluded that there had been no error in principle in the sentence of six years imposed on him.

Drugs: 'street value'   In *The People v. Gannon*, Court of Criminal Appeal, December 15, 1997, the Court affirmed a sentence of nine years' imprisonment for unlawful possession of drugs for sale or supply, contrary to the Misuse of Drugs Act 1977. The defendant was convicted following the making of a full statement and plea of guilty. He appealed the severity of the sentence, claiming that expert evidence was not given as to the 'street value' of the drugs. In affirming the sentence, the Court held that the 'street value' of the drugs was just a factor to which some regard should be had, but it was never central to what a trial judge had to decide finally as punishment. The Court also noted that no objection had been at trial to the evidence which was given. The Court accepted that the defendant's plea of guilty had been taken into account. There was thus no error in principle in the way the judge approached the matter of sentence. Moreover, while the Court noted that it had jurisdiction to increase the sentence, it would not do so in this case, thus indicating that it would certainly have imposed at least the sentence in this case had it considered the matter *res integra*.

Guilty plea: lesser charge   In *The People v. Magee*, Court of Criminal Appeal, July 29, 1997, the defendant had pleaded guilty in the Central Criminal Court to sexual assault and received a sentence of four years imprisonment. He had originally been charged with rape and indecent assault, but the rape charge was not proceeded with following his plea to the sexual assault on arraignment. On appeal against the sentence imposed, the Court of Criminal Appeal reduced the sentence to two years. The Court held that there was a duty on the prosecution where a plea to a lesser charge was accepted to marshall the evidence in such a way as to ensure it remained within the boundaries of the offence before the court. It noted that the description of the events given by the victim in the instant case went beyond what were just matters of sexual assault. The maximum sentence for the offence this case was five years. Since the defendant had pleaded guilty at an early opportunity, the Court concluded that the appropriate sentence was two years imprisonment.

Guilty plea: maximum sentence precluded   In *The People v. F.B.*, High Court (Central Criminal Court), January 24, 1997, Carney J. confirmed his view that the sentencing jurisprudence precludes the imposition of the maximum penalty provided by law where a plea of guilty in entered. We note here that we have previously doubted the correctness of this view (1995 Review, 258) but it has been applied consistently by Carney J.

In the instant case, the defendant had pleaded guilty to counts of rape, indecent assault and incest, the offences being sample counts of numerous offences committed by the defendant over a number of years against his three daughters. The case disclosed that the defendant had operated a 'sexual tariff' by requiring his daughters to submit to a sexual act with him before being allowed leave the house. His wife was completely unaware of what was happening and was out of the house working when the offences occurred. The statutory maximum penalties for most of the offences to which the defendant had pleaded guilty were life imprisonment. Carney J. imposed concurrent sentences of 15 years imprisonment.

He considered that a life sentence would be appropriate given the following factors: the gravity and multiplicity of the offences involved, the cowardly circumstances in which the sexual tariff was extracted from the girls over a period of years, the fact that it would enable release only when those qualified to so decide were satisfied that the defendant would no longer pose a threat, that release from a life sentence was on licence which could be made subject to conditions and was subject to recall, and the deterrent effect of such a sentence. Nonetheless, he concluded that a life sentence was not permissible. He referred to the relevant decisions in this area, including his own judgments in *The People v. D.(J.)*, High Court, April 27, 1995 (1995 Review, 257)and *The*

People v. Bambrick [1996] 1 I.R. 265 (HC) (1996 Review, 272–3). In the instant case, the defendant had surrendered himself to the Gardaí, had volunteered a confession, pleaded guilty and made it clear from an early stage that his daughters would not be called to give evidence, and he felt obliged to impose a determinate sentence which would have to be less that a life sentence as it is actually served.

Sexual assault – indecency In *The People v. Coogan*, Court of Criminal Appeal, July 29, 1997, the Court affirmed a sentence of five years for indecent assault. The defendant had been convicted on one count of indecent assault contrary to section 10 of the Criminal Law (Rape) Act 1981 and subsequently pleaded guilty to a second count. The offences had been committed in 1984 and 1988. The trial judge pointed out that the maximum sentence available to these offences under the 1981 Act was one of 10 years. A change had been introduced into the law by the Criminal Law (Rape) Amendment Act 1990 to distinguish between two types of sexual assault. The trial judge treated the situation as if the law was such at the time the offence was committed and placed in the assault in the less serious of the two categories which carried a five-year maximum sentence. The applicant appealed on the ground, *inter alia*, that the trial judge had not given sufficient regard to his plea of guilty or his hitherto blameless record. The Court held that it had been within the trial judge's power to impose a consecutive sentence but that this would only apply in a very exceptional case which bore a close resemblance to the offence committed and the invariable practice was to impose concurrent sentences. The Court accepted that the trial judge had given consideration to the plea of guilty but this had come after the other case in which the first victim was put through the trauma of giving evidence. The Court was not satisfied that had the offences been brought in 1984 and 1988 a lighter sentence would have been imposed and thus concluded that the sentence imposed should not be interfered with. For a further discussion of this delay issue, see the decision of the Court of Criminal Appeal in *The People v. J.(T.)*, Court of Criminal Appeal, November 6, 1996 (1996 Review, 269-71).

Sexual assault on infant In *The People v. D.(J.)*, High Court (Central Criminal Court), July 29, 1997, Flood J. affirmed that it was only in the most absolutely exceptional circumstances that non-custodial sentences followed from a sexual assault by a paedophile. The defendant had pleaded guilty to counts of rape and sexual assault. It was his first offence and he had co-operated with the Garda Siochana. He indicated that he would leave the country and not return if he received a non-custodial sentence. Flood J. imposed custodial sentences. He held that the offences to which the defendant had pleaded guilty could not be regarded as anything but serious offences. While he took full account of the evidence of the consultant psychiatrist and the treatment options outlined, he could not accede to the proposition that the defendant should leave the jurisdiction without any punishment and it was only in the most absolutely exceptional circumstances that non-custodial sentences followed from what he described as paedophilic acts. He concluded that the appropriate sentences of imprisonment were seven years for rape and five years for sexual assault, to run concurrently. The defendant was, however, granted liberty to apply to the High Court from the year 2000 to review the sentence and Flood J. directed that he receive appropriate sexual therapy at an early date.

Suspended sentence In *O'Brien v. Governor of Limerick Prison* [1997] 2 I.L.R.M. 349 (SC), the Supreme Court held that a sentence, which involves a period of imprisonment remaining suspended over a prisoner's head after his release, is inconsistent with the Prisons (Ireland) Act 1907 and the Rules for the Government of Prisons 1947 and should not be imposed.

The applicant had been sentenced to ten years imprisonment on a count of burglary, to run concurrently with ten years imprisonment on a count of aggravated sexual assault already being served by him. The trial judge went on to order that the last six years of the sentence be suspended on the condition that the applicant enter into a bond to keep the peace and that if the applicant committed a further offence while in custody or during the suspended part of his sentence, he would serve the balance. It was clear that the trial judge intended the applicant to serve the first four years of his sentence without remission. Rule 38 of the Rules for the Government of Prisons 1947 provides that a convicted prisoner shall be eligible by industry and good conduct, to earn a remission of a portion of his sentence, not exceeding one-fourth of the whole sentence, provided that the remission does not result in the prisoner being discharged before he has served one month. The applicant asserted that the custodial part of his sentence should attract the usual remission of one quarter and applied to Court for his release pursuant to Article 40.4 of the Constitution. In the High Court, it was held that the applicant's detention was lawful but on appeal the Supreme Court reversed.

The Supreme Court did pass any general judgment on the desirability of the jurisdiction to pass suspended sentences, except to note that the matter should be left to reside in the individual discretion of the judge of trial, being subject to the appellate jurisdiction of the Court of Criminal Appeal. In the type of suspended sentence in the instant case, which consisted of a period of imprisonment followed by a period during which imprisonment was suspended, the judge was *functus officio* and the executive power to commute under Article 13 of the Constitution remained intact. However the Court found it difficult to see how the executive power of remission could be properly exercised, as it could not be exercised in respect of the initial period; and if it was to be exercised in respect of the whole sentence, a well behaved prisoner might not be in prison long enough to earn any remission;

If the trial judge had used a formula in imposing the sentence, by which he had retained seisin of the matter to himself, then there would have been no implied clash with the executive's entitlement to grant remission. The Supreme Court was satisfied that when the trial judge, having suspended six of the ten years, indicated that that was all the remission the applicant was to receive, he had not intended to pre-empt the executive's power of remission but rather to indicate that the applicant had received every leniency to which he could be entitled. However it remained a fact that the form of order made by the trial judge created difficulties for governors of prisons and other persons who had to administer the system of remission on the grounds of good conduct. The Court noted that the Prisons (Ireland) Act 1907 and the Rules for the Government of Prisons 1947 did not appear to contemplate a sentence of imprisonment where the period of imprisonment was not identical to the period of the sentence. Such a sentence could not reconciled with the legislation and therefore should not be imposed. Thus, the order of the trial judge had to be regarded as valid in so far as it imposed a sentence of four years imprisonment and that accordingly was the period of imprisonment in respect of which remission had to be calculated. In those circumstances the Court was satisfied that the applicant was not being detained in accordance with law and directed his release under Article 40.4 of the Constitution. The decision is also discussed in the 1996 Review, 498-500.

STOP AND SEARCH

Re-arrest In *The People v. Ferris and Vearer*, Court of Criminal Appeal, March 11, 1997, the defendants, coming off a ferry in a vehicle, had been stopped by customs officials acting under the Customs and Excise (Miscellaneous Provisions) Act 1988 and the vehicle was searched. They were detained in order to be searched. Before that took place, they were arrested by a customs officer on a charge of importing prohibited goods into the country. They were also arrested by the Gardaí under the Misuse of Drugs Acts 1977 and 1984 and were detained and interviewed pursuant to section 4 of the Criminal Justice Act 1984. They were convicted on various counts of possessing and importing drugs, contrary to the Misuse of Drugs Acts 1977 and 1984. They appealed unsuccessfully against their convictions.

The Court of Criminal Appeal held that it had been appropriate for the customs officers to have involved the Gardaí, who had exercised their power of arrest when they arrived. The Court cited the decision in *The People v. O'Shea*, [1996] 1 I.R. 556 in holding that it was lawful to have an arrest upon an arrest (as to which, see also *Quinlivan v. Governor of Portlaoise Prison (No.2)* [1998] 1 I.L.R.M. 294, discussed above, 319).

TRIAL OF OFFENCES

Children   In *Director of Public Prosecutions v. Thornton*, High Court, September 24, 1997, McGuinness J. drew a clear distinction between criminal proceedings and care proceedings involving a young person. The defendant, who was 15 years old, had been remanded in custody by the District Court on criminal charges. The defendant was also the subject of a fit person order under the Children Act 1908 and he had been committed to the care of the Eastern Health Board. As part of its order remanding the defendant in custody, the District Court had directed the Board to submit its proposals for a secure residential assessment to confirm a preliminary psychiatric diagnosis and a care programme for the defendant while he remained in the care of the Board. On a consultative case stated to the High Court, the Board argued that it did not have to submit to the District Court's order.

McGuinness J. held that it was clearly open to the District Court to raise the fitness to plead issue of his own motion, and in these circumstances it was correct in so doing. Given the existence of the fit person order, the Board was a guardian as defined by section 131 of the 1908 Act and could be required under section 98 to attend at the court before which the defendant was appearing. Moreover, in order to decide whether the defendant was fit to plead, or fit to elect for summary disposal or trial on indictment, the judge of the District Court was entitled to seek information from the guardian Board through an assessment carried out by the Board.

McGuinness J. held that the primary issue before the District Court was the guilt or innocence of the defendant, and bearing in mind the constitutional right to a reasonably expeditious trial in due course of law, the District Court's order should be limited to an assessment to ascertain whether the defendant had the capacity to follow the proceedings and instruct his legal advisors. The District Court was not entitled, she considered to make any order which extended to diagnosis and the provision of a care programme for the defendant while in the Board's care. She held that in a criminal trial, where there was a clash between the general welfare rights and the rights specifically delineated by the Constitution as relevant to the trial of offences, the provisions concerning a trial in due course of law under Article 38.1 should in general have priority and should prevail. She concluded that there should thus be a clear division between criminal proceedings deciding the guilt or innocence of an accused and child care proceedings which provided for the general welfare and future care and custody of a child.

She went on to state that it was clear from section 98 of the Children Act 1908 that the court could make orders against a guardian who had been required to attend before the court and such orders were binding on the guardian. The Board was bound to carry out an assessment, if so ordered, as to whether the defendant had the capacity to follow proceedings and instruct legal advisors. Once the assessment was received, the District Court should complete the investigation into whether the defendant was fit to understand and follow the proceedings and to give real and valid instructions concerning the defence. If the conclusion was that the defendant was not so fit, the District Court should decline to enter on the criminal proceedings and should make no order of any description with regard to the further attendance or custody of the defendant.

Defence Forces

Ciaran Craven and Gerard Humphreys, Barristers at Law

OVERSEAS MISSIONS

Defence Forces Participation in Overseas Missions – Stabilisation Force (SFOR) Traditionally, the dispatch of members of the Defence Forces overseas has been confined to United Nations-led peace keeping operations. However, participation in peace enforcement missions was sanctioned by the Defence (Amendment) Act 1993 (See Annual Review 1993, 279-280) to allow for the dispatch of troops to serve with the United Nations mission in Somalia (UNOSOM II) in 1993/94. Although the Dáil had also previously approved the dispatch of a contingent to serve with a multinational force planned for Zaire (now the Democratic Republic of the Congo) in late 1996 – the force having a mandate under Chapter VII of the United Nations Charter – the force ultimately was not sent.

As part of this ongoing change, on May 14, 1997, the Dáil, approved the dispatch – pursuant to section 2 of the Defence (Amendment) (No. 2) Act 1960 as applied by section 3 (1) of the Defence (Amendment) Act 1993 – of a contingent of the Permanent Defence Force for service with the United Nations authorised multinational NATO-led Stabilisation Force (SFOR) in Bosnia and Herzegovina. SFOR, the successor to the Implementation Force (IFOR), was authorised for a period of 18 months from December 1996 by Security Council Resolution 1088 of December 12, 1996 to assist in the implementation of the Dayton peace agreement. Like its predecessor, SFOR operates under Chapter VII of the UN Charter. It is entitled to use force to implement its mandate, to separate the parties in the event of a resumption of hostilities and to protect itself.

Both IFOR and SFOR reflect a trend in the United Nations to rely increasingly on regional organisations to help meet security challenges in the post Cold War era. Given the previous failures of the UN particularly in Bosnia and Herzegovina and Rwanda, and given the expense of mounting such operations, such a move was probably inevitable. Furthermore, it is a recognition that large security international peace operations pose military, humanitarian, economic and diplomatic challenges that only the reserves of regional organisations can effectively meet (see: *Dáil Debates*, May 14, 1997 Cols. 520/521).

However, given the UN reliance on NATO and the structure of SFOR, members of the Permanent Defence Force are inevitably subject to NATO command structures within the force overall. Having their troops subject to NATO command structures did not pose particular difficulties for other neutral countries such as Finland, Sweden and Austria or non-NATO countries such as Russia.

However, it was stated that once in the area of operations. the Irish contingent would serve under the operational control of the NATO Supreme Allied Commander in Europe and his designated Force Commander for SFOR. Furthermore, the contingent would be subject to NATO rules of engagement. Although non-NATO nations would retain national command of their contingents, and the Defence Forces, through the contingent commander, would take the necessary measures to ensure the maintenance of proper discipline and retain exclusive criminal jurisdiction for the Irish contingent (see *Dáil Debates*, May 14, 1997 Col. 538) such arrangements failed to address the inherent constitutional limitations. Thus, it was not considered whether or not it was constitutionally permissible to allow members of the Defence Forces to be placed under the operational command of a commander who is not ultimately answerable to Dáil Éireann. There is no provision in statute that permits such a delegation of command. The manner in which this issue was addressed in the Dáil Debates suggests that national command is retained for pay, administration and discipline purposes only. How this can be reconciled with the duty of care imposed on Defence Forces commanders by the decision of the Supreme Court in *Ryan v. Ireland* [1989] I.R. 177 remains to be determined. Questions of Status of Forces Agreements and criminal jurisdiction separate matters.

Unlike in other UN operations, the costs of participation in SFOR are borne by the Government, rather than by the UN. Terms of an exchange of letters between NATO and the Government, clarifying the State's financial responsibility arising from participation in SFOR were approved by the Dáil, as it amounts to an international agreement involving a charge on public funds within the meaning of Article 29 of the Constitution (see *Dáil Debates*, May 14, 1997 Col. 521, advice of the Attorney General). The contingent of Defence Force personnel may not be withdrawn without formal prior notice to the United Nations, unless otherwise agreed and it is envisaged that the commitment to SFOR will expire with the force's mandate in mid-1998.

COMMAND OF THE DEFENCE FORCES

Article 13 of the Constitution vests supreme command of the Defence Forces in the President, the exercise of this command being regulated by law. Section 17 of the Defence Act, 1954 provides that military command, under the direction of the President, is exercisable by the Government and through and by the

Minister (for Defence). Although the President is *de iure* the supreme commander, *de facto* command vests in the Minister for Defence, under the direction of the Government. This contrasts with the pre-Treaty situation when supreme command was vested in a military officer who reported to the Minister for Defence.

Sealed orders from the Government, in turn, authorise the Minister to exercise military command over the Defence Forces and to delegate command. Furthermore, the President, on the advice of the Government, appoints an officer of the Permanent Defence Force to each of the three principal military offices, *i.e.* the Chief of Staff, Adjutant-General and Quartermaster-General, the functions of each being assigned by the Minister, to whom they are directly responsible for the performance of their assigned duties. Although responsible for the day-to-day management of the Defence Forces, none of these officers exercises military command, properly so-called.

In addition to this administrative/executive layer, the Council of Defence is charged with aiding and counselling the Minister for Defence on all matters relating to the business of his department on which they may be consulted. It consists of two civilian members, the Minister of State at the Department of Defence and the Secretary of the Department (who is secretary to the Council) and the holders of the three principal military offices. Meetings are held whenever summoned by the minister.

Thus, there is no provision for a single military commander of the Defence Forces, resulting in a lack of centralised command. This apparently deliberate arrangement has previously been the subject of criticism (particularly by General Lewis McKenzie in his report on the efficiency of the Defence Forces). It might reasonably be surmised that the current command structure reflects the manner in which the State came into being, the effects of the 1924 mutiny and the Government's proper desire to exercise tight control over its Defence Forces.

However, the Public Service Management Act 1997 (see 1, above) it seems, perhaps unwittingly, seeks to unravel the other statutory provisions. Section 1 provides that the Department of Defence means not alone that part of the Department staffed by civil servants but also includes the Principal Military Branches, *i.e.* the military branches for which the Principal Military Officers are responsible. Accordingly, it appears that the newly styled secretary-general of the Department of Defence can purport to exercise command over Defence Forces personnel, in a manner contrary not alone to the Defence Acts and the regulations made thereunder but also the provisions of Article 13 of the Constitution. If the Minister for Defence has a statutory and non-delegable role – other than to military officers – in the command of the Defence Forces, it is unclear, in the absence of an amendment to the contrary, that control can also vest in the secretary-general of his department. Nor does the Act appear to contemplate the fate of the Government's sealed orders and the delegation of *military* command to *military* officers – who receive their commissions from the President. This can hardly be regarded as a matter of simple detail but rather it appears to substitute bureaucratic accountability for the (heretofore) democratic and constitutional accountability of the Defence Forces – and, arguably, in a manner not contemplated by the Constitution.

COURTS OF INQUIRY – JUDICIAL REVIEW

The role of Defence Forces Courts of Inquiry fell to be considered in *Owen Farrell v. Minister for Defence and ors,* High Court, Geoghegan J. December 19, 1997. The Rules of Procedure (Defence Forces) 1954 provide for the convening of a court of inquiry – an assembly of officers – to inquire into any matter and to make such finding and declaration as may be required. Section 174 (1) of the Defence Act 1954 provides that a court of inquiry may be established when a soldier has been absent without leave for a period exceeding 21 days. In the instant case, in accordance with these provisions, a court was convened for the purpose of investigating and recording the applicant's absence without leave and any deficiencies of service equipment arising therefrom. The declaration that a soldier has been absent without leave by a court of inquiry into an illegal absence has the legal effect – if he does not afterwards surrender or is not apprehended – of a conviction by court-martial for desertion. The maximum penalty for desertion (not on active service) is imprisonment for a term not exceeding seven years.

The applicant claimed *inter alia* that the manner in which the court of inquiry was convened and conducted was contrary to the rules of natural and constitutional justice and sought an order of *certiorari* quashing its proceedings and findings. At the time of the convening of the court of inquiry, the applicant's address and whereabouts were well known to the military authorities and his solicitor was in correspondence with them in relation to the applicant's position. No notice of the inquiry of any kind was given to the applicant or his solicitors, nor was any opportunity offered to the applicant of putting any evidence before the inquiry as to whether there might be sufficient cause for his absence. The applicant maintained that his absence was caused by injuries sustained in a road traffic accident and that, accordingly, that although he did not have leave, there was sufficient cause for his absence from duty. The military authorities, for their part, contended that the applicant, by virtue of his being a member of the Defence Forces, had consented to the holding of a court of inquiry in the manner prescribed by statute and the regulations. In those circumstances, it was maintained that the applicant was estopped from alleging that the holding of the court of inquiry was in breach of his rights to natural or constitutional justice. However, Geoghegan J. rejected such a contention. He held:

There is nothing in the Defence Acts or Defence Regulations which absolves the Army authorities from the normal rules of constitutional and natural justice and indeed if there was the constitutionality of any such provision would be in question.

He could not accept that membership of the Defence Forces resulted in a waiver of one's rights to natural and constitutional justice; nor, in his view, did it estop a person from invoking those rights. This approach faithfully follows that of Gavan Duffy J. in *Curran v. Attorney General*, High Court, February 27, 1941, and approved in *C v. Court Martial*, Supreme Court, December 15, 1995. Similar echoes are found in the judgment of the Supreme Court in *Ryan v. Ireland* [1989] I.R. 177.

In a telling observation, Geoghegan J. noted that the military authorities, to some extent, regard a court of inquiry as an evidence gathering exercise, rather than a court of trial, such as a court-martial. Indeed, it might also be observed that the holding of a court of inquiry into the illegal absence of a deserter effectively enables the military authorities to close the book, administratively speaking, on the matter, without necessarily obliging them to process matters further. However, as Geoghegan J. also pointed out, the findings of a court of inquiry can have serious practical consequences. Thus, the findings of a court of inquiry may, if they amount to *prima facie* evidence of an offence having been committed against military law, be used to remand a person for trial by court-martial, without the normal preliminary investigation of the offence charged. In the specific case, a finding by a court of inquiry into an illegal absence had the effect of a conviction by court-martial for desertion (if the soldier did not afterwards surrender or was not apprehended).

That is not to say, however, that a court of inquiry may not be held into any illegal absence without affording the absentee an opportunity to be heard. The court was careful to point out that where a soldier has left, without leaving any address, and he cannot reasonably be located, a court of inquiry could proceed in his absence and without an opportunity for him to give evidence. In such a case, the court was satisfied that a soldier had waived his rights by implication. In the circumstances of the instant case however, *certiorari* of the court of inquiry was granted.

Given those strictures, it now seems that the holding of a court of inquiry *simpliciter* may no longer be used to close the book on illegal absentees and deserters from the Defence Forces. Some attempt to find an absent soldier must surely now be deemed mandatory before a court of inquiry into his absence may be convened. As to when such an absentee cannot "be reasonably located" is a matter of fact to be determined in each individual case. The facts of *Farrell* are somewhat unusual in this regard. There is, in effect, a statutory duty to hold a court of inquiry into the absence of every soldier who has been absent for a period exceeding 21 days. Although section 174 of the Defence

Act 1954 appears merely permissive in tone, and the holding of a court of
inquiry into an illegal absence or desertion is not express in the provisions of
Defence Force Regulation (DFR) A. 5, the provisions of DFR CS 7 contemplates that the provision is directory in nature. In those circumstances, attempts to locate the whereabouts of deserters must now be regarded as
mandatory. Absence without leave and desertion being specific offences against
military law, absentees and deserters must be arrested, charged and duly tried.
It is arguable that, given the current statutory framework, any policy of not
actively seeking out errant soldiers is now unsustainable.

COURTS OF INQUIRY – DISCOVERY OF DOCUMENTS

In *O'Brien v. Minister for Defence,* Supreme Court July 7, 1997, a unanimous
Supreme Court allowed an appeal by the plaintiff against a refusal by O'Hanlon
J. (reported at [1995] I.R. 568) to make an order for further and better discovery of documents in the defendant's possession relating to the death of the
plaintiff's husband. He died in December 1986 in South Lebanon from gun-
shot wounds sustained while stationed with a contingent of the Permanent
Defence Force serving with the United Nations Interim Force in Lebanon
(UNIFIL). The defendant, in the negligence action arising from that death,
sought to maintain a blanket privilege in respect of all documents relating to
both the UNIFIL and the Defence Forces courts of inquiry that were carried
out in relation to the death. The High Court had proceeded in reliance of a
note of an *ex tempore* judgment in *O'Mahoney v. Minister for Defence,* High
Court, Barrington J., June 6, 1989, to the effect that the proceedings of courts
of inquiry enjoy the same type of statutory privilege as applies to documents
given to the Government by the United Nations in circumstances of confidence.

United Nations documents are privileged pursuant to the provisions of the
Diplomatic Relations and Immunities Act 1967 section 9 and Article 11(4) of
the Third Schedule. In the Supreme Court, a challenge to the applicability of
these provisions to the documents arising from a UNIFIL court of inquiry was
not pursued. Defence Forces courts of inquiry, however, are subject to the
Rules of Procedure (Defence Forces) 1954. Briefly, rule 121 provides that the
proceedings of a court of inquiry – and any confession or statement made, or
answer to any question given at the court – is not admissible in evidence against
any person subject to military law. Furthermore, evidence in regard to the
proceedings of a court of inquiry may not be given against any person subject
to military law, save in certain exceptional circumstances. Rule 122 provides
that a finding of a court of inquiry is not admissible in evidence nor may any
questions be asked of any witness in relation to it. Rule 123 goes on to provide

that their disclosure to interested parties is prohibited, except where they are required to be delivered to a person order to be tried by court-martial where he is to be tried in respect of any matter that is the subject of a finding of a court of inquiry, or where his character or military reputation is adversely affected by anything in the proceedings or findings of the court of inquiry. That the findings and recommendations of all courts of inquiry are to be treated as confidential is provided for by Defence Force Regulation (DFR) A. 5 Regulation 11(2).

It was argued that the documents in relation to a Defence Forces court of inquiry do not enjoy the same privilege or immunity as the documents relating to a UNIFIL court of inquiry. It was further submitted that what is protected is only the finding and recommendation of a court of inquiry – which are expressly stated to be confidential. The Supreme Court accepted this contention and rejected the argument that it should extend "the statutory privilege (*sic*) to cover all proceedings and all statements made by witnesses before the court of inquiry."

Noting that claims in relation to other privileges – executive and legal – remain, in the absence of particulars of the relevant documentation and the nature of the privilege being claimed in respect of each document, the Court declined to decide the issue of privilege in respect of any document. They concluded:

> It is not sufficient in the circumstances . . . to claim general privilege in respect of bundles of documents or files as they have been called. . . .

and held that the onus is on the defendant to specify in detail by number each of the relevant documents in his possession – including those in relation to the United Nations court of inquiry – and to specify in detail the nature of the privilege claimed in respect of each document and the basis for that claim. Accordingly, the defendant cannot avoid setting out, in list form, all of the documents put before the courts of inquiry.

The conclusion of the Supreme Court is unexceptional procedurally and merely re-states the law in relation to discovery. However, it nevertheless calls for some brief observations. Firstly, the court seemed prepared to equate the confidential nature of the findings and recommendations of Defence Forces courts of inquiry with statutory privilege. Whereas privileged documents are invariably confidential, it is equally clear that not all confidential documents are privileged. Thus, to take a common example, at common law, medical records are confidential in nature, although not privileged. In the normal course of events, only certain confidential communications with one's legal or spiritual advisers or certain intra-governmental communications attract privilege. The results of other communications, as, for instance take place during other inquiries, *e.g.* tribunals of inquiry and inquests, are public. That an assumption that a similar approach might apply to the findings of a Defence Forces court of inquiry could be regarded as probable, were it not for the exception provided for in Defence Forces Regulations. However, there may be perfectly proper operational and security reasons for maintaining their confidential nature – and even thereby extending the mantle of privilege to them. That said, absent operational or security considerations, there is no compelling reason in logic or principle why confidentiality (or, following from such considerations, privilege) is necessary and might not ordinarily be waived. Rules 121 and 122 of the Rules of Procedure, in respect of the non-admissibility of evidence adduced before a court of inquiry, are unexceptional and effectively echo similar provisions in the Tribunals of Inquiry (Evidence) Acts 1921 and 1979. In the circumstances, the provisions of DFR A. 5 regulation 11 (2) – not expressly noted in the judgment – seem hardly necessary.

Secondly, the exceptions provided for in the Rules of Procedure and Defence Forces Regulations are clearly premised on consideration of the principles of natural and constitutional justice. However, where the central issue in an inquiry is the death on operational duty of a member of the Defence Forces, consideration of the constitutional and natural rights of the deceased's family are arguably also deserving of consideration. Where a death on operational duty takes place in Ireland, a coroner's inquest takes place, the findings being appended to the court of inquiry that is subsequently held. That inquiry is capable of addressing the family's concerns. However, where such a death occurs on overseas service, a domestic inquest is not normally carried out – although there is no apparent reason why one should not be carried out when the body returns to the jurisdiction pursuant to the provisions of the Coroners Act 1962 section 17. In the circumstances, a blanket prohibition on the release of the findings and recommendation of the court of inquiry carried out by the Defence Forces into a death is capable of significantly impacting on the exercise of the rights that would otherwise be exercisable by the family of a deceased where the death occurred here.

Thirdly, it might be suggested that the significant interference with the conduct of litigation that such a blanket prohibition maintains – by the application of a rule of procedure that has its origins in other concerns to situations never contemplated on its formulation – is simply not justifiable on policy grounds. Although it has been reported that *O'Mahoney* decided that rules 121 and 122 of the Defence Forces Rules of Procedure are not *ultra vires* the Defence Act 1954, the constitutionality of DFR A. 5 regulation 11 (2) must remain suspect.

Given that the issue of diplomatic privilege in relation to documents arising from a UNIFIL court of inquiry has yet to be directly considered by the Supreme Court it remains to be seen what attitude will be taken, in an appropriate case, by the court to the question. In this regard, it might be noted that, in such inquiries, some of the documents may have been created entirely by

Defence Forces personnel in situations where command may have been completely maintained by officers of the Defence Forces who remain, at all times, subject to the provisions of the Defence Acts. Although clearly there may be some areas where privilege will be appropriate for reasons of security of the United Nations operations or, perhaps, even diplomatic sensibilities, a blanket prohibition on discovery, in circumstances such as arose in *O'Mahoney* and *O'Brien*, is hardly sustainable on the grounds of necessity. But, DFR CS 7 effectively provides that a Defence Forces court of inquiry into incidents occurring on UN service may not be held unless so directed by one of the Principal Military Officers or the contingent commander. Accordingly, where a national court of inquiry is not held, and diplomatic privilege is upheld in respect of the UN court of inquiry any attack on the constitutionality of DFR A. 5 regulation 11 would not advance the position of a litigant in proceedings in this jurisdiction.

COURTS-MARTIAL

What constitutes an order by a superior to a subordinate fell to be determined by the Courts-Martial Appeal Court in *Re O'Mahony,* Courts-Martial Appeal Court, February 24, 1997. Although a simple case arising from a trivial incident of alleged disobedience to a lawful order, it raises significant policy issues in relation to the Defence Forces and the manner in which the civilian courts approach military matters and procedures.

Here, the appellant, who was detached from his home unit to another unit and service corps failed, because of a domestic commitment, to attend a sporting competition as directed by a superior officer who was a staff officer (as distinct from one in a command position). The direction was later confirmed by a superior officer of the appellant's home unit but not by an officer of the unit to which he was attached. He was duly charged with disobeying a lawful order of a superior officer contrary to the provisions of section 131 of the Defence Acts 1954 to 1990. He was convicted by limited court-martial, of which his former commanding officer was president – and to whom the appellant objected, although the objection was disallowed – and he was fined £190. He appealed to the Courts-Martial Appeal Court against both conviction and sentence.

Relying on the provisions of paragraph 24 (a) of Defence Force Regulation A. 18 – to the effect that a soldier is deemed to belong to the unit to which he is attached – the appellant maintained that that the order had not followed the proper line of command, *i.e.* it had not come through his *commanding* officer. However, the court rejected this argument. Recognising that the command given had perhaps been 'administratively defective' it was satisfied on the evidence that the order had been ratified by an officer of the appellant's home unit. Although accepting the order could have come from one of the appellant's immediate *commanding* officers, the court was satisfied that it would be a severe handicap on the military if a court were to hold that where a soldier had been detached to a different unit, orders could only be given through the officers deemed to be in command of him at that time. Holding that the offence of disobeying a lawful order had been made out, the court noted that that would be too narrow a construction to put on the statutory provisions and rejected that ground of appeal.

Command is not defined in the Defence Acts or the Defence Force Regulations. However, it may be considered to be the control that a person exercises over others by virtue of his/her military rank and appointment. That said, its purpose must be to ensure the orderly conduct of military affairs, the avoidance of confusion as to duty or obligation, and the creation of certainty. To permit orders to be given other than through a recognised chain of command is surely a recipe for the disaster contemplated by the aphorism "order, counter-order, disorder". Nevertheless, the Defence Acts specify the duty to obey the command of a *superior* officer only. Whereas commanding officers are always, by virtue of their rank and appointment, superior officers, the reverse is obviously not always the case. In the context of military operations, properly so called, and which, of their nature, are always evolving, there might well be compelling operational reasons for insisting upon compliance with the orders of the most senior officer present, even one outside the normal chain of command. However, in the context of the instant case where the order at issue related to what was essentially a voluntary sporting, and extra-military, activity such considerations surely do not arise.

Where, in particular, the order involves the absence of a soldier from his unit, one would have considered it mandatory, from the point of view of good organisation, that the assent of the soldier's immediate commander be obtained. At no point was this sought, or obtained, in this case. The court characterised the order that was given as 'perhaps administratively defective' – a description that captures the essence of the irregularity. However, the system depends for its very effectiveness on clarity and certainty, and compliance with regulations and orders. Indeed, the officer giving the initial order must be presumed to have known the requirements of the regulations. And, this was not a situation where the appropriate *commanding* officer could not also have been consulted. In the circumstances, the court's assertion in relation to the handicap that strict conditions would impose on the ability of the military authorities to command seems arguably overstated.

In this regard, the failure of the court to distinguish between orders in relation to essentially military and non-military matters is reminiscent of *Ryan v. Ireland* [1989] I.R. 177 (see Annual Review 1989, 410–8) in relation to the liability of commanders in respect of injuries suffered by their subordinates. It could be strongly argued that in purely administrative matters, the prescribed chain of command must be strictly adhered to – unless there is compelling reason to the contrary, *e.g.* in an emergency where a staff officer effectively sanctions compassionate leave in the absence of the commander. Such considerations cannot, and indeed should not, apply to operational matters. This distinction is far from semantic and well capable of recognition and adherence within the overall structure of the Defence Forces which readily distinguishes pay, administration and disciplinary matters from (military) operational control. However, this begs the wider question, also addressed in one of the other grounds of appeal, as to whether or not an order to take part in a voluntary activity is an order of a type contemplated by the provisions of section 131 of the Defence Act 1954. The participation of members of the Defence Forces in sporting activities on behalf of their units or commands is undoubtedly highly desirable from a management point of view in maintaining morale and *ésprit de corps*. However, it is also arguable that it is more desirable that failure to participate ought not result in the invocation of the full regime of the military justice system by way of limited court-martial. O'Flaherty J. noted:

> [The court] cannot dictate to the army how it should conduct its affairs in the way of deciding that a matter is so minor as not to require the full panoply of a court-martial. That is a detail that the army authorities must work out for themselves. It would be idle . . . for this court to lay down any guidelines in this regard.

Given the use of administrative instructions prescribing new procedures and sanctions in the area of interpersonal behaviour and similar administrative provisions in relation to a new complaints inquiry system – operating in parallel with the statutory provisions in the Defence Acts – it is surely possible to deal with issues such as arose in *O'Mahony* in a less draconian fashion. Although the punishment imposed by the court-martial was deemed by the court to be lenient enough (a fine of £190), it is worth noting that the range of punishment awardable upon conviction by a court-martial under section 131 includes imprisonment for a term not exceeding seven years (see, below).

Although the appellant had objected to the president of the court-martial on the grounds that he had been the appellant's former commanding officer, and that they had had regular contact, the objection was disallowed without any reason being given. In this regard, the court noted that it would have been desirable to give reasons. Nevertheless, the court disposed of the matter thus:

> . . . as against that, no reasonable cause was put forward for the objection. Section 197 of the Act, which gives an entitlement to an accused to challenge the composition of the court-martial, requires that it should be for reasonable cause. Simply to say that the president of the court had some previous contact with the accused does not seem . . . to be a sufficient ground to lodge an objection. . . .

HEARING LOSS

The Defence Acts and the Army Pensions Acts are silent as to the duty owed by commanders to soldiers and by soldiers to fellow soldiers except in respect of discipline and obedience to lawful orders. Defence Force Regulations, however, impose a variety of duties on different military personnel directed at the protection of the health and safety of both members of the Defence Forces and the public. The regulations are silent as to civil liability for their breach – although members of the Defence Forces may be prosecuted for such breaches. Applying the normal canons of constructions, it is at least arguable that such a civil remedy does lie. However, notwithstanding the procedural advantages in pleading such breaches of statutory duty, the difficulties relating to general availability of Defence Force Regulations undoubtedly limit the extent to which such breaches are pleaded in civil actions by serving and former soldiers against the state. In this regard, it is worth noting that the printing and notice of publication of Defence Force Regulations was dispensed with by direction of the Attorney General under the provisions of section 2 (3) of the Statutory Instruments Act, 1947 – a direction not yet rescinded. Their general non-availability was also reflected by a failure of the Defence Forces to effectively disseminate their own internal regulations and circulars.

The regulations governing the issue of hearing protection required the officer in charge of firing to ensure that verbal orders were, in the interests of safety, heard by all those under their command. The apprehension by many that the more immediate danger to soldiers engaged in firing exercises was posed by loss of control by a failure to properly communicate critical orders, seems to have taken precedence over the apparently less immediate dangers of damage to hearing. The balancing of risks that this entailed resulted in a practice of non-adherence to the relevant regulations. Notwithstanding this, the most notable feature in the ongoing saga of claims prosecuted by serving and former members of the Defence Forces in 1997, in respect of hearing impairment allegedly sustained as a consequence of exposure to gunfire noise, was that no case was taken by the Minister for Defence to the Supreme Court which was pursued to a judgment. On the other hand, however, it is also worth noting that the Department of Defence has not sought to avail of the exemptions provided for – in respect of Defence Forces personnel – by the Health Safety and Welfare at Work (General Application) Regulations 1993.

In *Whitely v. Minister for Defence* [1997] 2 I.L.R.M. 416, discussed in the Limitation of Actions Chapter, 542, below, High Court, Quirke J., June 10, 1997, a claim for damages for noise-induced hearing loss, found to have been caused by the defendant's admitted negligence, failed on the ground that the plaintiff had knowledge of his injury, and that it was a significant hearing loss and tinnitus, outside the limitation period. The court did not accept that the relevant date of knowledge depended on a combination of noise-induced hearing loss and the natural decrease in hearing acuity attributable to age. However, many physical injuries may be caused by agents that do not produce immediate permanent effects, but rather result in injury incrementally, and often barely perceptibly over time. In such cases, the injury may not become apparent to the sufferer for many years after exposure – and ongoing damage – has ceased and the effects of ageing are superimposed. On the basis of *Whitely* it seems that first initial sign of the injury itself and its causal connection to the defendant's activities may be sufficient to fix a plaintiff with knowledge for the purpose of the Statute of Limitations (Amendment) Act 1991. That the injury might not strike a plaintiff as significant until the effects of ageing are superimposed may not be relevant.

Amendment of Defence Force Regulations on medical matters   On October 6, 1997 the Minister for Defence amended Defence Forces Regulation (DFR) A. 12 dealing with the medical grading of members of the Defence Forces. It is based on detailed assessment, in substitution for an older, less detailed method. However, whereas previously only a medical board (comprised of not less than two medical officers of the Army Medical Corps) could classify or reclassify the medical grade of Defence Forces personnel, now a single medical officer acting alone may perform this task – except where it is proposed to re-grade a person to Grade X (equivalent to the category previously known as 'below army medical standards'). However, a decision of the medical officer may be appealed to the command medical officer who must then convene a medical board to classify or reclassify the person concerned. The decision of the medical board is deemed to be final. A person's medical classification is critical to his suitability to serve in certain appointments, e.g. on operational, including international, missions.

Although reclassification to Grade X, given its implications – dismissal from the Defence Forces – might ordinarily have been regarded as requiring adherence to the provisions of Administrative Instruction A. 12, implemented following the decision of the High Court in *Motherway v. Minister for Defence,* High Court, Lardner J. May 26, 1989, it is not, however, express on the face of the amended DFR A. 12. Nevertheless, it must be presumed that the procedures the Administrative Instruction prescribes will apply.

That said, the most fundamental change effected by amended DFR A. 12 is in relation to the basis of the medical classification of Defence Forces personnel. The new medical classification code is determined by a combination of age, constitution, military fitness, keenness of vision, colour vision and hearing acuity. The introduction of age and an assessment of colour vision as factors to be considered are new. Military fitness was previously effectively assessed by reference to a person's constitution and an ability to march.

The grading of constitution now involves assessment of physical or mental impairment, disability, handicap, physiological alteration and the level of medical of care required. Four principal grades (1 to 4) are prescribed, along with Grade T (to include personnel recovering from serious illness or those who are temporarily unfit) and Grade X (those who do not fall into any other defined category, i.e. below the Defence Forces standard). A similar grading system also applies to the assessment of military fitness, which includes assessment of fitness for military duties and training and the ability to undergo physical and mental strain and exertion. Acuity of vision (categorised from grades 1 to 7) is assessed using standard Snellen charts, and there is similar provision in relation to Grades T and X, as in the case of constitution and military fitness. However, the Director of the Army Medical Corps may prescribe minimum standards, outside of this grading system, for certain specialist appointments, *e.g.* in the Air Corps. Colour vision (categorised from grades 1 to 3) is assessed using Ishihara's charts and practical tests. Hearing, the categories of which include grades 1 to 5 and T and X, is graded by measurement of air conduction thresholds of hearing levels in decibels [(dB) hearing threshold loss] on a designated audiometer at frequencies between 500 Hz and 8,000Hz in accordance with procedures laid down. A formula is then used to calculate the appropriate hearing grade in respect of each ear – although the system remains the subject of controversy.

The new medical classification system prescribed is based upon a seven digit code derived from the new grading categories. Thus, any assessment, in any category, of grade T, puts the person so graded into an army medical category equivalent to the old Category D. However, it is now provided that the period of time that may be spent in this category may be extended beyond the eighteen months formerly provided and it does not necessarily preclude a member of the Defence Forces from attendance for all military duties. Where a person is classified as Grade X under any heading of assessment, (s)he is deemed to be below Defence Forces medical standards – effectively equivalent to the old Category E – and procedures prescribed for his/her discharge must be followed. The new system is considerably more sophisticated that the one it replaces and appears to provide for greater discretion as far as fitness for service is required.

Amendment to the Defence Acts The Criminal Law Act 1997 discussed in the Criminal Law Chapter, 267, above, apart from abolishing the distinction between felonies and misdemeanours also abolished penal servitude and imprisonment with hard labour as punishments that might be awarded by court-martial. Accordingly, all references to penal servitude, penal servitude prisons, military convicts and hard labour have now been deleted from the Defence Acts 1954 to 1993 – specifically, the provisions dealing with the imposition, commencement and suspension of sentences of penal servitude. The maximum punishment now awardable by a court-martial is imprisonment for life, or any specified period.

Imprisonment for a term not exceeding seven years was substituted for penal servitude as an available punishment in respect of the following offences prescribed by the Defence Act, 1954:

- Damage to property while on active service (section 126 (2) (i)).
- Arising out of being a prisoner of war (section 127).
- Disobedience to the order of a superior officer (section 131).
- Desertion (section 135 (1) (b))
- In relation to interference with persons in custody (section 145)
- In relation to state ships (section 149), aircraft (section 151) and disobedience to the orders of a captain of an aircraft (section 154 (1)).
- Fraud in relation to public property (section 155).
- Bribery, corruption and fraud (section 158).

Imprisonment for life is now provided, instead of penal servitude, in relation to the following offences:

- Mutiny without violence (section 129).
- Conspiracy to mutiny (section 130).
- Striking a superior officer (section 132).
- Desertion on active service (section 135 (1) (a)).
- Manslaughter or rape (section 169 (3) (a) and (b)).

Discharge with ignominy or discharge from the Defence Forces is now mandatory in all cases where a soldier is sentenced by court-martial to imprisonment for a term exceeding two years (whereas previously this provision was only activated upon a sentence of imprisonment for life or penal servitude). The net effect is to lower the threshold for the discharge of soldiers from the Defence Forces. However, a sentence of an officer to any term of imprisonment (other than in respect of contempt of a court-martial) was always sufficient to result in his dismissal as an officer.

However, in relation to the limiting provisions regarding concurrent sentences, a radical change has taken place. Whereas previously it was provided that where a court-martial proposed to pass a sentence in respect of person who was already serving a sentence of imprisonment or detention, to a term of further imprisonment or detention, the new sentence could not exceed two consecutive years including the term then unexpired of the former sentence. This provision did not formerly apply in respect of a sentence of imprisonment for life. However, the Act, which deleted that provision, now further provides that the new sentence shall be served concurrently with the term then unexpired of the former sentence and, on completion of either sentence, any balance of the other sentence must be served. In effect, offences committed in military prisons – wherein prisoners are still subject to military law – may now be punished consecutively.

Insofar as the execution of sentences of imprisonment is concerned, military prisoners sentenced to a term exceeding two years must now be committed, as soon as practicable, to a public (civilian) prison to undergo sentence. Other sentences may still be served, as before, either in a military prison or detention barrack or in other service custody or in a public prison or in any combination thereof.

Education

INSTITUTES OF TECHNOLOGY

DIT: degree conferring   The Dublin Institute of Technology Act 1992 (Assignment of Function) Order 1997 (S.I. No. 224 of 1997) assigned the power of conferring degrees on the DIT with effect from September 1, 1998.

RTCs become ITs   Two Orders made under the Regional Technical Colleges Act 1992 (1992 Review, 312) changed the title of two former Regional Technical Colleges (RTCs) to Institutes of Technology (ITs), thus bringing them within the terms of the 1992 Act. The Regional Technical Colleges Act 1992 (Amendment) (No. 2) Order 1997 (S.I. No. 199 of 1997) changed the name of Waterford RTC to Waterford Institute of Technology with effect from May 7, 1997. The Regional Technical Colleges Act 1992 (Change of Name of College) Order 1997 (S.I. No. 512 of 1997) changed the name of Cork RTC to Cork Institute of Technology with effect from December 18, 1997. These two changes were followed in 1998 by the Regional Technical Colleges Act 1992 (Change of Name of College) Order 1998 (S.I. No. 19 of 1998), which changed the names of the remaining RTCs to ITs: we will further note that Order in the 1998 Review.

NCEA

Designation of institutions   The National Council for Educational Awards Act 1979 (Designation of Institutions) Order 1997 (S.I. No. 159 of 1997), made under the National Council for Educational Awards Act 1979, designated Tipperary Rural and Business Development Institute for the purposes of the 1979 Act, with effect from April 16, 1997.

Renaming of colleges   The National Council for Educational Awards Act 1979 (Designation of Institutions) (Amendment) Order 1997 (S.I. No. 279 of 1997) renamed several of the colleges designated under the 1979 Act with effect from June 18, 1997.

RTC

Designated college   The Regional Technical Colleges Act 1992 (Amendment) Order 1997 (S.I. No. 149 of 1997) amended the schedule of the Regional Technical Colleges Act 1992 to include the Dun Laoghaire College of Art and Design as a recognised RTC with effect from April 1, 1997. The College became an Institute of Technology in 1998: see the Regional Technical Colleges Act 1992 (Change of Name of College) Order 1998 (S.I. No. 19 of 1998).

SCIENCE AND TECHNOLOGY

Funding   The Scientific and Technological Education (Investment) Fund Act 1997 provided for the establishment of a fund (incorporating public and private moneys) for use in capital expenditure on technological, scientific and vocational education and research. The Act, which came into effect on December 24, 1997 on its signature by the President, envisages the expenditure of £250m during the period 1998 to 2000.

UNIVERSITIES ACT 1997

The Universities Act 1997 involved the first all-encompassing legislative measure concerning the university sector since the establishment of the State. It redefined the objects and functions of all universities in the State, revised the composition of their governing authorities and academic councils, provided for the appointment, functions and powers of chief officers of universities and provided new structures of accountability and transparency in their affairs. The Act also reconstituted the colleges of the National University of Ireland (NUI) and St. Patrick's College, Maynooth as constituent universities of the NUI, provided for some amendments to the governance of Trinity College Dublin and also incorporated under its terms the two universities established in 1989, the University of Limerick and Dublin City University. A number of provisions in the original proposal, particularly those concerning the role of the Higher Education Authority (HEA), were substantially amended in the course of the passage of the 1997 Act, resulting in a greater degree of freedom for the universities than originally proposed. A great deal of the amendments were effected through contributions from those senators in Seanad Éireann representing the universities. The Act came into force on June 16, 1997: Universities Act 1997 (Commencement) Order 1997 (S.I. No. 254 of 1997).

Application   Section 4 of the 1997 Act provides that it applies to the constituent colleges of the National University of Ireland, Dublin City University, the University of Limerick and Trinity College Dublin, and to any other universities established under section 9 of the 1997 Act.

NUI Colleges become NUI universities   Section 7 provides for the establishment of the constituent colleges of the National University of Ireland as constituent universities of the National University of Ireland. The NUI colleges, now NUI universities, are the National University of Ireland, Cork (formerly University College Cork), the National University of Ireland, Dublin (formerly University College Dublin), the National University of Ireland, Galway (formerly University College Galway) and the National University of Ireland, Maynooth (formerly St Patrick's College Maynooth).

Incorporation of institution into university   Section 8 provides for the incorporation by Order of an educational institution as part of a university. An Order under this section may be made by the Minister for Education with the consent of the Minister for Finance, the institution concerned and the governing authority of the university and following consultation with the Higher Education Authority (HEA).

Establishment of additional universities by Order   Section 9 provides for the establishment of additional universities. It provides that new universities can be established by Order of the Government, after consideration of the advice of a body of experts and the advice of the HEA. An Order under this section requires a positive resolution of both Houses of the Oireachtas before it becomes effective.

Change of name   Section 10 provides that the Minister for Education may change the name of a university where a university requests this. In the case of a constituent university, the approval of the Senate of the National University of Ireland is required.

Dublin City University and University of Limerick   Section 11 of the 1997 Act amended the Dublin City University Act 1989 and the University of Limerick Act 1989 to confirm that the two universities continue to be corporate bodies with the same powers they possessed before the passage of the 1997 Act.

Objects of a university   Section 12 of the 1997 Act sets out the objects of a university. These are to include the following 11 areas: the advancement of knowledge through teaching, scholarly research and scientific investigation; the promotion of learning in the student body and in society generally; the promotion of the cultural and social life of society and respecting the diversity of the university's traditions; to foster a capacity for independent critical thinking amongst its students; to promote the official languages of the State and Irish culture; to support and contribute to the realisation of national economic and social development; to educate and train higher level professional, technical and managerial personnel; to promote the highest standards in, and quality of, teaching and research; to disseminate the outcomes of its research in the community; to facilitation life-long learning through the provision of adult and continuing education; and to promote gender balance and equality of opportunity among students and employees of the university.

Functions of university   Section 13 provides that a university shall have the powers and functions necessary to further its objects, including: the provision of courses; the conferral of degrees; promotion and facilitating research; establishing companies; collaborating with other relevant interests (including professional bodies, employers and trades unions and cultural organisations) to further the objects of the university; maintaining, managing and disposing of the property and rights of the university; collaborating with graduates; purchasing, holding and disposing of land and other property; and accepting gifts of money or land on such trusts and conditions of the donor as are not inconsistent with the 1997 Act. It also provides that in performing its functions a university shall have regard to accountability and transparency in its affairs.

Academic freedom and interpretation of Act   Section 14 of the 1997 Act, which was inserted into the legislation during its passage through the Oireachtas, provides:

'A university, in performing its functions shall –

(a) have the right and responsibility to preserve and promote the traditional principles of academic freedom in the conduct of its internal and external affairs, and

(b) be entitled to regulate its affairs in accordance with its independent ethos and traditions... and in doing so it shall have regard to-
    (i)   the promotion and preservation of equality of opportunity and access,
    (ii) the effective and efficient use of resources, and
    (iii) its obligations as to public accountability,

and if, in the interpretation of [the 1997] Act, there is a doubt regarding the meaning of any provision, a construction which would promote that ethos and those traditions and principles shall be preferred to a construction that would not so promote.'

The emphasis on academic freedom is extended by section 14(2) to mean that an individual member of the academic staff shall be entitled 'to question and test received wisdom' and to state controversial or unpopular opinions and is not be disadvantaged as a result. No similar freedom is extended to those members of staff who are not members of academic staff. The designation of staff thus becomes of some importance in this respect.

Governing authority Section 15 of the 1997 Act provides that each university shall have a governing authority, which shall perform the functions conferred on a university by the Act, though the title 'governing authority' need not necessarily be used. Section 16 provides for the composition of the governing authorities of the universities. It empowers each university to have a governing authority which best suits its own interests, subject to the parameters set out in the Act. Thus, within a range of between 20 and 40 members, the membership shall include: the chief officer of the university; a chairperson (if other than the chief officer); at least one but no more than two senior administrative staff; not less than two or more than six members of the academic staff at Professor or Associate Professor level; not less than three or more than five permanent academic staff; at least one but not more than three members of the non academic staff; not less than two or more than three students; one post-graduate student; at least one but not more than four persons appointed by the governing authority from bodies in the wider community; and at least one but not more than four nominees of the Minister for Education. The 1997 Act also provides for at least one but not more than two nominees of any local Education Board, if established (since the 1997 Act was enacted, the incoming government has indicated that no such Education Boards would be established). In addition, a governing authority may co-opt up to four other persons as members, having regard to the extent to which cultural and artistic interests are represented, and include up to four graduates of the university as members.

Section 16 also allows for representation on governing authorities of individual universities from bodies which reflect the traditions and history of each university. In the case of the former colleges, now universities, of the National University of Ireland, this includes nominees of County Councils, certain Lord Mayors and Mayors and a nominee of the National University of Ireland. In the case of St Patrick's College Maynooth, nominees of the trustees of St. Patrick's College and a nominee of the Seanad of the National University of Ireland is provided for. In the case of Trinity College Dublin, special provision for fellows is made. Dublin City University and the University of Limerick are given the authority to appoint representatives from their respective local authorities and fund-raising bodies. The Mayor of Limerick may also be a member of the governing authority of the University of Limerick. Section 16 also ensures that there will be a representation of at least two persons from business or industry on each governing authority and that there is gender balance also.

Chair of governing authority   Section 17 provides that each governing authority shall decide whether it is to be chaired by the chief officer (the President or Provost) or a person from outside the university. In the case of the universities which had, prior to the 1997 Act, a chairperson other than the chief officer, this arrangement will continue. Except where the chief officer is the chairperson, the chairperson must not be an employee of the university or a member of the governing authority. Where a chief officer chaired the governing authority prior to the 1997 Act, this situation cannot be altered while the incumbent occupies the office of chairperson. The chairperson, including a chief officer who acts as a chairperson, may be removed from office by the governing authority or the Government. A chairperson appointed under section 17 will not be appointed on a full-time basis and will exercise no executive functions in the university.

Functions of governing authority   Section 18 sets out the functions of the governing authority. It provides that the governing authority will be responsible for controlling the affairs and property of the university and for the appointment of the chief officer and other employees. In carrying out the latter functions, the governing authority shall develop such interview and other procedures as will ensure participation in the selection process by high quality candidates from both within and outside the staff of the university. In carrying out its functions the authority will be required to have special regard to the promotion of the Irish language and cultures, to the attainment of gender balance and equality of opportunity in education and to the promotion of national, economic and social development. The Third Schedule to the Act also provides for a range of other matters relating to the operation and business of a governing authority. It provides, *inter alia*, for a university seal and its legal status, for the term of office of the members, filling of casual vacancies, removal from office, resignation, age limits, eligibility for membership, conflicts of interest, remuneration and the holding and conduct of meetings.

Visitation   Section 19 provides for visitation of a university. Where a university does not have a visitor, the Minister will request the Government to appoint a person or persons to be visitor for the purposes of section 19. The visitor shall be a judge or retired judge of the High Court or Supreme Court. Section 20 provides that where there is *prima facie* evidence that there has been a breach by a university of the laws, ordinances or statutes governing it, the Minister, after allowing a university an opportunity to make its case and with the agreement of Government, may request that the visitor to the university enquire into aspects of the operation of the university. The visitor will proceed with the investigation if he or she is satisfied that there are reasonable grounds for the Minister's opinion. The visitor will be entitled to enter the university to conduct an inspection of the university, its buildings, equipment and records or to enquire into the academic or other affairs of the university. The visitor is to be afforded all reasonable co-operation and facility by the university, its employees and its governing authority.

Suspension of governing authority Section 21 provides for the suspension of a governing authority. Where, after receiving the report of a visitor appointed under section 20, the Minister is of the opinion that a governing authority is not carrying out its functions effectively and the Government agrees, the Government may by Order, but only with the consent of both Houses of the Oireachtas, suspend the membership and appoint another body to carry out their functions for a period of up to one year. Before such an Order can be made a university must be given an opportunity to make representations to the Minister on the stated reasons for the proposed suspension. A new authority must be established within one year of the suspension in the same manner as the first governing authorities are set up under the Act, including the appointment of a commission under section 23: see below.

Transitional arrangements Section 22 provides that a governing authority of a university which held office prior to the commencement of the 1997 Act shall remain in office until the new governing authority has been constituted in accordance with the provisions of the Act and when such an authority has been so constituted the old governing authority shall stand dissolved. Section 21 provides that the Minister must appoint a commission for each university to determine the composition of the first governing authority under the Act and to oversee its appointment. In the case of the constituent universities, Dublin City University and the University of Limerick, the commission comprised the President, the Registrar, two members of the incumbent governing body and the Chairman of the HEA or his or her nominee. In addition the Chancellor of the National University of Ireland or a nominee sat on the commission for the constituent universities. The Provost, Vice-Provost, Chancellor, two members of the Board and the Chairman of the HEA or his or her nominee comprised the commission for Trinity College Dublin. The commissions dissolved when the governing authority holds its first meeting. Note also that a commission would also be required in the event of the dissolution of a governing authority under section 21 of the 1997 Act: see above.

Chief officer of a university Section 24 provides for the appointment of the chief officer of a university (the President or Provost) , the selection of whom will be a function of the governing authority in accordance with procedures determined by the governing authority and set out in a university statute. The chief officer will be the accounting officer of the university and may be called upon to give evidence in that capacity before the Public Accounts Committee of Dáil Éireann. The Fourth Schedule to the 1997 Act describes in further detail the role and function of the chief officer, including the management of the university subject to the policies of the governing authority to which he or she will be responsible for the exercise of his or her powers and functions. It also provides for the delegation of the powers of the chief officer, but in the event of such delegation he or she will remain accountable to the governing authority for the exercise of the powers.

Staff of a university   Section 25 provides for matters relating to staffing, such as appointment, terms, pay, pensions and dismissal. Each university will decide its staffing structures having regard to the efficient use of resources, accountability for public funds, Government pay policy in the public sector, the impact of their decisions on their budgets and guidelines issued by the HEA under section 50 of the Act. The HEA guidelines on the staffing of universities are not binding on the universities and may be departed from. A proposal in the original draft of the 1997 Act to make such guidelines virtually compulsory was deleted from the final version of the 1997 Act after substantial opposition was expressed that this would constitute excessive interference with the independence of the universities. Under section 25 of the 1997 Act, the terms and conditions of staff are a matter for the universities while pay, allowances and pensions remain subject to the approval of the Ministers for Education and Finance.

Dispute resolution   Section 26 of the 1997 Act requires each governing authority to establish procedures for the resolution of disputes, other than industrial relations matters. This provision does not apply to Trinity College Dublin.

Academic council   Section 27 provides that each university shall have an academic council which shall, subject to the financial constraints determined by the governing authority and to review by that authority, control the academic affairs of the university. Section 28 provides for the composition of the academic council, the majority of the members of which shall be academic staff in the university drawn from a range of academic disciplines and a range of levels. Membership must also include students, the number to be determined by the governing authority. The numbers, composition, selection, appointment and terms of office of members shall be provided for in a statute of each university. The section also provides that the terms of office of members who are first appointed under the Act will be determined in consultation with members of the academic council holding office at the coming into force of the Act. The chief officer and the senior officer responsible for academic affairs shall be, *ex officio,* a member of the academic council. Section 29 provides that an academic council will hold such number of meetings as it thinks necessary to perform its functions and may regulate its own procedure. The chief officer will be entitled to preside over meetings of the academic council or a committee of the council if he or she chooses to do so. An academic council may establish committees to assist in the performance of its functions. Such a committee may consist of members and non-members of the academic council. Section 30 provides for transitional arrangements for existing academic councils.

Charters and Statutes   Section 31 provides that a university may have a charter providing for: the objects and functions of the university in respect of its academic and administrative affairs; arrangements the university has for the promotion of the Irish language and cultures; the composition of the governing authority; the rights of the employees and students of the university, their responsibility to the university and the responsibility of the university to them; arrangements for review of, or appeals against, decisions of the governing authority and the academic council which affect employees or students; the university's policy on the promotion of equality of opportunity among students and employees; the university's policy in relation to adult and continuing education; and any other matters that the governing authority may consider relevant. Charters are to be prepared following appropriate consultation within the university and will be supplemental charters where a university is already governed by charter, as was the case with the National University of Ireland and Trinity College Dublin.

Section 32 provides that the Government may, by Order, following the application of a university, amend the charter of a university in the manner agreed with the university. It had been originally proposed that this provision would also provide that the charter of the National University of Ireland, the charter of any of its constituent colleges and the charter of Trinity College would remain in force after the coming into force of the 1997 Act only to the extent that they were not in conflict with the Act. This was abandoned in the face of opposition criticism.

Section 33 provides that a university may make statutes which may regulate the affairs of the university. Having made a statute, a governing authority will be required to publish it in *Iris Oifigiúil* and to inform the HEA and the Minister.

Planning and evaluation   Section 34 provides that the governing authority will require its chief officer to prepare a strategic development plan setting out the medium to long-term goals for the university and detailing the plans for achieving them. The plan which will then be submitted to the HEA and the Minister.

Section 35 requires each governing authority, through the chief officer, to establish procedures for evaluating the quality of teaching and research at the university. Procedures will include evaluation of all departments and faculties of the university not less than once every ten years. They will also involve evaluation by university staff in the first instance followed by evaluation by people from outside the university, including people who are competent to make national and international comparisons on quality issues at university level The findings arising from these evaluations will be published. In addition, assessment by students is provided for. The universities will be required to implement the findings of evaluations where it is practical to do so.

Section 36 provides that each university will set out its policies on access and equality in its activities. In determining these policies a university will have regard to Ministerial policies. Universities shall implement the policies set out in their policy statement.

Finance, property and reporting   Section 37 provides that each university will be obliged to seek approval annually from the HEA for its recurrent budget. The HEA will determine the amount of moneys to be allocated to the university for the financial year and that amount together with other expected income of the university, as agreed with the HEA, will be the budget of the university for the financial year. The chief officer will have the responsibility of ensuring that the budget is carried into effect. If a governing authority exceeds its budget in a manner which cannot be met from its own resources, any such excess shall be the first charge on the university's budget for the next financial year. It had been proposed in the original draft of the 1997 Act that any departure from the annual budget could only be agreed with the consent of the HEA and that a university could not, without the consent of the Minister for Education and the Minister for Finance, increase its budget by borrowing. These proposals were deleted from the Act after substantial opposition was voiced as to their intrusive nature.

Section 38 provides that a university may borrow on such conditions as to the terms of borrowing as may from time to time be determined within a framework by the HEA, in consultation with the university and with the consent of the Minister for Education and the Minister for Finance.

Section 39 provides that accounts relating to receipt and expenditure of moneys must be kept in a form prescribed by the HEA. The Comptroller and Auditor General will decide which accounts are to be submitted for audit by that Office. The audited accounts, together with the Comptroller and Auditor General's report, will be made available to the Minister and to the HEA and laid before each House of the Oireachtas.

Section 40 provides that a university may charge fees for their services of such amounts as the governing authority sees fit. In fact, by the time the 1997 Act came into force, undergraduate fees had been abolished by the then Minister for Education. Section 36 also provides that the may advise the universities on the fees charged by a university. A proposal that the Minister could make a determination that certain fees were excessive, in line with the recommendations of the HEA, was abandoned during the passage of the Act.

Section 41 provides for the submission of a report at least every three years from a university on its activities to the Minister for Education. This report will place the operations of the university in the context of the university's strategic development plan. The reports will be laid before the Houses of the Oireachtas. A proposal to have annual reports prepared and submitted to the HEA and the Minister was abandoned.

Section 42 provides that a university may dispose of its land and buildings. Where the land and buildings have been funded from public moneys after the 1997 Act came into effect, such sale or other disposal will be subject to the terms and conditions agreed by the Minister and the governing authority. It also provides that, where a university becomes a privately funded body, the grants paid to the university after the passing of the Act through which property was acquired, refurbished or developed must be repaid on terms agreed between the governing authority and the Minister. Where agreement cannot be reached, section 42(4) provides for arbitration by a court appointed arbitrator under the Arbitration Acts 1954 and 1980.

National University of Ireland, Maynooth   Section 43 establishes the Recognised College at St. Patrick's College, Maynooth, as a constituent university of the National University of Ireland to be known as the National University of Ireland, Maynooth. Section 44 provides for the transfer of the staff employed in St. Patrick's College, Maynooth, to the new university. Where staff were paid from public funds they became employees of the university automatically on the coming into force of the Act. Where staff were paid partly from public funds, they remained the staff of St. Patrick's College, Maynooth, unless and until agreement is reached between the two institutions that they should be employees of the new university.

National University of Ireland   Section 45 amends the Charter of the National University of Ireland in so far as it relates to the Senate of the National University of Ireland. In providing for the composition of a new Senate, the section provides for an equal number of representatives from each of the constituent universities of the National University of Ireland including the National University of Ireland, Maynooth, and follows the previous statutory provisions relating to the composition. It also provides for gender balance in the composition of the Senate of the National University of Ireland.

Section 46 amends the Irish Universities Act 1908 by deleting provisions which are no longer relevant, including those which prohibited the imposition of tests of religious belief in relation to lecturers and students of a constituent college. It also removed the restriction on the public funding of the teaching of religion or theology in a constituent college.

Section 47 sets out the relationship between the National University of Ireland and the constituent universities. The role of the National University of Ireland will include establishing the basic matriculation requirements for the constituent universities, in addition to which the constituent universities may set other requirements. The National University of Ireland will also have a role in reviewing academic standards and in the appointment, with the agreement of the universities, of external examiners.

Section 48 sets out the membership of the constituent universities of the National University of Ireland. The membership of each university will include the members of its governing authority and its academic council, its employees, its students, its graduates and other persons that the governing authority may appoint.

HEA   Sections 49 to 51 specify various functions of the Higher Education Authority (HEA). They replace the much more extensive provisions proposed in the original draft of the legislation in, for example, sections 34 to 35 and 50, already referred to above. Under section 49, the Authority may review the various universities plans and procedures prepared under sections 34 to 36 and 50 of the Act. Any such reviews may be published. Section 50 empowers the Authority to issue guidelines on the numbers or grades of university employees and the proportion of budgets to be applied to different activities. If a university departs from such guidelines, no restrictions or conditions may be applied to a university. Section 50 requires universities to provide information to the Authority regarding staff levels and other related matters.

Use of title university restricted   Section 52 provides that the title 'university' may not be used to describe an educational establishment or facility without the approval of the Minister for Education except in relation to an educational establishment or facility established or described as such before 30 July 1996, the date on which the 1997 Act was first introduced in the Dáil. It also provides that the Minister may apply to the High Court for an injunction to restrain any person from using the title 'university' in contravention of this section.

Repeals   Section 6 and the First Schedule to the 1997 Act repealed the National Institute for Higher Education, Limerick, Act 1980 and the National Institution for Higher Education, Dublin, Act 1980, sections 3, 4 and 5 of the University of Limerick Act 1989 and section 3, 4 and 5 of the Dublin City University Act 1989 which became obsolete on the passing of the Act.

VOCATIONAL EDUCATION

Amalgamation of Areas   The following Orders, made under section 100 of the Vocational Education Act 1930, brought about a number of amalgamations in vocational educational areas: Vocational Education (Borough of Wexford Vocational Education Area and County Wexford Vocational Education Area) Amalgamation Order 1997 (S.I. No. 88 of 1997); Vocational Education (Urban District of Tralee Vocational Education Area and County Kerry Vocational Education Area) Amalgamation Order 1997 (S.I. No. 89 of 1997); Vocational Education (Borough of Drogheda Vocational Education Area and County Louth Vocational Education Area) Amalgamation Order 1997 (S.I. No. 90 of 1997); Vocational Education (Urban District of Bray Vocational Education Area and County Wicklow Vocational Education Area) Amalgamation Order 1997 (S.I. No. 91 of 1997); Vocational Education (Borough of Sligo Vocational Education Area and County Sligo Vocational Education Area) Amalgamation Order 1997 (S.I. No. 92 of 1997). The Orders all came into effect on January 1, 1998.

YOUTH WORK

Education boards and grants   The Youth Work Act 1997 provided for the functions of the Education Boards in relation to youth work (defined as programmes of activity designed to provide developmental and education training) and establishes a Youth Work Committee within each local Education Board and a National Youth Work Advisory Committee. The Act also provides for grants for youth work. The Youth Work Act 1997 (Commencement) Order 1997 (S.I. No. 260 of 1997) brought the Act into force on June 19 1997. The Youth Work Act 1997 (Section 22) Regulations 1997 (S.I. No. 271 of 1997) prescribes the National Youth Council of Ireland as a nominating body to the Advisory Committee under section 11 of the 1997 Act. Since the 1997 Act envisaged the establishment of local Education Boards as the means for distributing the funds for youth work, and since the government elected in June 1997 committed itself not to establishing such Boards, it appears at the time of writing (May 1998) that the Act is, in effect, inoperable and that further amending legislation will be required. The Act is further discussed in the Labour and Employment Law chapter, 518, below.

Electricity and Energy

Bord Gáis   The Energy (Miscellaneous Provisions) Act 1995 (Section 140) Order 1997 (S.I. No. 71 of 1997) vested the assets of certain gas companies in Bord Gáis Éireann with effect from February 4 1997. The Gas (Amendment) Act 1987 (Section 2(7)) (Amendment) Order 1997 (S.I. No. 119 of 1997) extended the areas where the functions of Bord Gáis Éireann may be exercised with effect from March 11, 1997.

Offshore installation   The Continental Shelf (Protection of Installations) (Connemara Field) Order 1997 (S.I. No. 267 of 1997) and the Continental Shelf (Protection of Installations) (Connemara Field) (Amendment) Order 1997 (S.I. No. 317 of 1997), made under the Continental Shelf Act 1968, established a 500m safety or exclusion zone surrounding the Connemara gas exploration field. In effect, ships are excluded from this area, except for those in distress. The first Order came into effect on July 1, 1997, the amended Order on July 10, 1997.

MINING LICENCE

Procedure   In *Cobh Fishermen's Association Ltd v. Minister for the Marine and Natural Resources*, High Court, August 29, 1997, O'Sullivan J. held that the applicants had failed to establish that the respondent Minister had acted in breach of the rules of natural justice in connection with considering its objections to the grant of a mining licence under the Foreshore Act 1933. The applicants had sought to quash an extraction licence granted by the Minister under the 1933 Act. They argued that the extraction of minerals from certain areas posed a threat to fish stocks which were the basis of their livelihood and that the operation actually being conducted by the licensee, particularly concerning dredging operations associated with the licence, was very different to that described in the Environmental Impact Statement prepared under the European Communities (Environmental Impact Assessment) Regulations 1989 (which had amended the 1933 Act) to the extent that they contended that the licence had been procured by a misrepresentation. They also argued that the Minister should have availed of the power in section 19 of the 1933 Act to publish a notice of the granting of a licence and to afford the applicants the opportunity to make representations to the Minister. As indicated, O'Sullivan J. dismissed the application.

He noted that all the information before the Minister was available to the applicants and that natural justice did not require the Minister to call for and consider additional material which came to hand after the relevant period for objection. He also pointed out that the Minister had a discretion whether or not to publish a notice under section 19 of the 1933 Act, and to suggest hat there was an obligation to reopen the closed phase of the application procedure or to duplicate it would greatly diminish the object and value of the statutory procedures themselves. As to the Environmental Impact Statement, O'Sullivan J. concluded that it did not lay down a specific phasing for the carrying out of the dredging operation to the extent that it could not be altered or modified in any way. In that respect, he held that the extraction was, in general, in line with the licence granted.

PETROLEUM

Licensing   In *Lough Neagh Explorations Ltd v. Morrice and Ors*, High Court, August 8, 1997, Laffoy J. declined to grant a mandatory interlocutory injunction since the instant case did not manifest such circumstances as would justify an the making of an order which in reality would finally determine the dispute between the parties at the interlocutory stage. The plaintiff unsuccessfully applied to prevent the Minister for Energy from granting a mineral exploration licence under the Petroleum and other Minerals Development Act 1960. It had been alleged that certain information had been misappropriated by one of the defendants. Laffoy J referred to *Dublin Port and Docks Board v. Britannia Dredging Company Ltd* [1968] I.R. 136 in determining where the balance of convenience lay. She concluded that the misappropriation or misuse of the reports for a limited period in conjunction with a party who had a licence from the Minister would not result in a loss to the plaintiff which could not be compensated by an award of damages, nor could the defendants be adequately safeguarded by the plaintiff's undertaking as to damages.

Whitegate offtake   The Petroleum Oils (Regulation or Control of Acquisition, Supply, Distribution or Marketing) (Continuance) Order 1997 (S.I. No. 487 of 1997), made under the Fuels (Control of Supplies) Act 1971, continued in force the Whitegate offtake regime established in 1983 for a further year from January 1, 1998: see the 1996 Review, 288.

Equity

Hilary Delany, Trinity College Dublin

EQUITABLE REMEDIES

Interlocutory injunctions The principles which are applied by the courts to situations where relief in the form of an interlocutory injunction is sought are well settled, as being those laid down by the House of Lords in *American Cyanamid Co. v. Ethicon Ltd* [1995] A.C. 396 as applied by the Supreme Court in *Campus Oil Ltd v. Minister for Industry and Energy (No. 2)* [1983] I.R. 88, namely that the plaintiff must establish that there is a serious question to be tried and that the balance of convenience favours the granting of relief. These principles were applied by the Supreme Court in *Connolly v. Byrne,* Supreme Court, January 23, 1997 which concerned an application for an interlocutory injunction in relation to certain works which it was proposed to carry out at Carlow Cathedral, including the removal of altar rails and a pulpit as well as the covering of a mosaic floor. In a judgment delivered on January 13, 1997, Barron J. held that the plaintiff had not made out any arguable case that he was entitled to the relief sought and dismissed the application. On appeal to the Supreme Court, O'Flaherty J. was satisfied that the plaintiff had at least made an arguable point in relation to the lack of applicability of section 51 of the Charities Act 1961 which would have required the consent of the Attorney General to the bringing of such proceedings. The Supreme Court reached the conclusion that the plaintiff had established a fair question to be determined at the trial of the action concerning the existence of the right which he sought to protect by injunction and O'Flaherty J. stated that the principles laid down in *Campus Oil* expressly precluded the Court from looking at the probability of success from the plaintiff's point of view. However, as regards the balance of convenience, the Court had no doubt that this lay with the defendants. A contract to carry out the proposed works had already been entered into with contractors and if the parish did not comply with its contractual obligations, it would be exposed to a substantial claim for damages. In addition O'Flaherty J. referred to the fact that the cathedral administrator had deposed that it was the defendants' intention to retain the altar rails and the pulpit and if the plaintiff was ultimately successful, they could be reinstated. In the circumstances the Supreme Court was satisfied that the plaintiff's application for an interlocutory injunction should be refused.

While it has been acknowledged that the *American Cyanamid* principles should be regarded as guidelines rather than rules which must be strictly adhered to, they have tended to be applied except where departure from them is justified in certain exceptional circumstances. The most common of these is where the parties agree that the hearing of the interlocutory application will constitute the trial of the action or where the trial of the action is unlikely to take place. Recently an attempt has been made in *Symonds Cider and English Wine Co. Ltd. v. Showerings (Ireland) Ltd* [1997] 1 I.L.R.M. 481 (HC) to further extend the list of situations in which the *American Cyanamid* principles should not be applied.

The plaintiff has sold 'Scrumpy Jack' cider on the Irish market since 1991 and the can in which the product was sold in June 1996 was a shiny gold colour bearing the name 'Scrumpy Jack' in large brown script. The defendant introduced a new brand of cider to the market in June 1996 called 'Annerville Golden Scrumpy' which was also sold in a gold coloured can with the name 'Golden Scrumpy' appearing in large brown script on the centre of the can. The plaintiff instituted proceedings alleging trade mark infringement and passing off against the defendant and sought an interlocutory injunction restraining the defendant from selling its cider under the mark 'Golden Scrumpy' in cans so similar to their own. In August 1996, the plaintiff launched a new 'Scrumpy Jack' can which was still gold in colour but which had a matt appearance and incorporated a number of other minor changes. It was submitted on the plaintiff's behalf that the principles by which the Court should be guided in determining the application for interlocutory injunctions were those set out by the House of Lords in *American Cyanamid* as adopted by the Supreme Court in *Campus Oil*. However, counsel for the defendant submitted that the *American Cyanamid* guidelines had been significantly refined particularly in the field of intellectual property. He pointed to the fact that in a passing off action such as this, the outcome of the interlocutory proceedings often determined the final outcome of the action and submitted that in such circumstances the court is justified in considering the substantive case. It was also submitted on the defendant's behalf that if its product were removed from the market in compliance with an interlocutory injunction there would be no point in subsequently seeking to re-introduce the brand and so the plaintiff should be required to show that it had a real substantial and forceful case to make at the trial. Laffoy J. rejected that contention and said that having regard to the decision of the Supreme Court in *Westman Holdings Ltd v. McCormack* [1992] 1 I.R. 151 – which applied the *American Cyanamid* principles – it was not open to her, assuming that the plaintiff established that there was a fair and *bona fide* question to be tried, to express any view on the strength of the contending submissions. Laffoy J. was satisfied that the plaintiff had shown that there were fair issues to be tried in this case and then turned to the question of assessing the balance of convenience of which whether damages would be an adequate remedy was an important element. She concluded that damages would not be an adequate remedy for the plaintiff if it was refused an interlocutory injunction and that equally damages would not adequately compensate the defendant if an interlocutory injunction were granted against it but it was successful at the trial. In assessing the overall balance of convenience, Laffoy J. was satisfied that the detriment which would accrue to either party was qualitively the same, being damage to reputation and goodwill, but she concluded that the prevalence of the plaintiff's new can on the market tipped the balance of convenience in favour of refusing the interlocutory relief. In her view it had not been established that there was a fair question to be tried as to the likelihood of confusion between this new can and defendant's product.

The approach adopted by Laffoy J. in *Symonds* shows that the courts in this jurisdiction are still anxious to adhere to the *American Cyanamid / Campus Oil* guidelines unless there is good reason for departing from them. Laffoy J. certainly showed a reluctance to extend the list of recognised exceptions to an entire class of proceedings, namely intellectual property disputes, although undoubtedly there may be individual cases falling under this heading in which the facts may warrant the conclusion being reached that the trial of the action is unlikely to be take place and that a wider consideration of the merits of both parties' cases is therefore justified.

ESTOPPEL

In delivering the judgment of the Supreme Court in *McCarron v. McCarron,* Supreme Court, February 13, 1997, Murphy J. made a number of interesting comments of an *obiter* nature about the ambit of the doctrine of proprietary estoppel. The plaintiff had for a period of about 16 years helped his father's cousin with the management and operation of the latter's farm. After the cousin's death the plaintiff contended that the deceased had entered into an oral agreement with him during that time that he would compensate him for the work which he was carrying out on the farm by ultimately devising the property to him. The plaintiff brought proceedings claiming an order of specific performance of this agreement or alternatively argued that he was entitled to relief on the basis of proprietary estoppel arising from the statements of intention made by the deceased and the actions which the plaintiff had taken in reliance on these statements.

Carroll J. upheld the claim of the plaintiff which was based on contract and the Supreme Court concluded that she had been correct in holding that there was evidence of a sufficient degree of certainty of a contract between the parties to the effect that the deceased had agreed to devise his property to the plaintiff. However, Murphy J. went on to express his opinion on that aspect of the plaintiff's claim based on proprietary estoppel. He commented that most cases, and in particular the Irish decisions of *Cullen v. Cullen* [1962] I.R. 268 and *McMahon v. Kerry County Council* [1981] I.L.R.M. 419, concerned disputes in which a plaintiff had or would suffer detriment as a result of spending money on the erection of premises on lands owned by the defendant in circumstances in which it would be unjust to deprive the plaintiff of his money or assets. Murphy J. stated that in principle he could see no reason why the doctrine should be confined to the expenditure of money or the erection of premises on the lands of another and that in a suitable case it might be argued that a plaintiff suffers as severe a loss or detriment by providing his own labour or services in relation to another's lands which should equally qualify for recognition in equity. This principle would seem eminently fair and it will be interesting to see whether the courts will embrace it if a similar situation arises in the future.

PART PERFORMANCE

Often where an oral agreement is reached between parties, there may be no sufficient note or memorandum to satisfy the requirements of the Statute of Frauds and equity is faced with the dilemma of insisting on strict compliance with the formalities or allowing alternative evidence of the agreement in order to prevent the perpetration of a fraud. It is a well established principle that a statute may not be used as an instrument of fraud and in the exercise of this equitable jurisdiction, the courts will prevent a defendant from relying on non-compliance with the statutory formalities where to do so would amount to fraud. Equally, a plaintiff may be able to obtain specific performance in the absence of a sufficient note or memorandum of an agreement by invoking the equitable doctrine of part performance which allows a plaintiff to rely on his own actions as evidence of the existence of an agreement. While the equitable doctrine of part performance is no longer recognised in England and section 2(1) of the Law of Property (Miscellaneous Provisions) Act 1989 now provides that contracts for the sale of land must be in writing, it still has a role to play in this jurisdiction.

Detailed consideration was given by Barron J. to the doctrine of part performance in delivering the judgment of the Supreme Court in *Mackey v. Wilde* [1998] 1 I.L.R.M. 449 (SC). The plaintiff and the first named defendant were the owners of a joint fishery on rivers in Co. Donegal. The original rules for the operation of the fishery had been laid down in an indenture but the plaintiff was dissatisfied with the arrangements relating to the number of people who could fish on the rivers and the parties met with a view to reaching agreement about the number of annual licences and daily tickets which would be issued. Subsequently correspondence took place between the parties in which the plaintiff sought to obtain the defendant's written agreement to the limiting of the number of licences for the fishery. The plaintiff then instituted proceedings claiming that there was a binding agreement that each party would be limited to the granting of 25 annual licences and submitted that there had been part performance on foot of the agreement. Costello P. held that a concluded agreement to this effect had been reached and that an additional term relating to the number of day tickets which could be granted had also been agreed upon. He therefore ordered that the first named defendant be restrained from issuing more than 25 annual licences and ten day tickets and this finding was appealed to the Supreme Court. The defendants submitted that the trial judge had been incorrect in finding that there had been a concluded agreement and that there were no sufficient acts of part performance to make the agreement enforceable. Barron J. accepted the first submission and held that there had not been a concluded agreement reached. It remained for him to consider whether there had been sufficient acts of part performance. He quoted extensively from the speech of Lord Simon in *Steadman v. Steadman* [1976] A.C. 536 and from those of Lord O'Hagan and the Earl of Selborne LC in *Maddison v. Alderson* (1883) 8 App. Cas. 467 in relation to the nature of the doctrine and of the acts which could be relied upon to constitute part performance. Barron J. stated that ultimately the court is seeking to ensure that a defendant is not, in relying upon statute, 'breaking faith' with the plaintiff. He stated that the doctrine of part performance is based in three things; the acts on the part of the plaintiff which are said to have been in part performance of the concluded agreement, the involvement of the defendant with respect to such acts and the oral agreement itself. Barron J. stated that ultimately what is essential is that (1) there was a concluded oral contract (2) the plaintiff acted in such way which showed an intention to perform that contract (3) the defendant induced such acts or stood by while they were being performed and (4) it would be unconscionable and a breach of good faith to allow the defendant to rely on the terms of the Statute of Frauds to prevent performance of the contract. Barron J. stated that it is more logical to find out what the parties agreed since in the absence of a concluded agreement there is no point in seeking to find acts of part performance. In summary he stated that the doctrine requires that the acts relied upon as being acts of part performance should be such that on an examination of the contract which has been found to have been concluded and to which they are alleged to refer, they show an intention to perform the contract. He also said that in the earlier cases it had been assumed that the acts of part performance must necessarily relate to and affect land and nothing which he had said should be taken to suggest a modification of that position. Applying these principles to the facts of the case before him, Barron J. concluded that there was nothing in what was alleged which would in any way be a breaking of faith by the defendant with the plaintiff for the defendant to plead the Statute of Frauds. He therefore held that even if there had been a concluded oral agreement as claimed, there were no acts on the part of the plaintiff which showed an intention to perform the alleged contract.

European Community Law

Ubaldus de Vries, Dublin City University

EUROPEAN PARLIAMENT ELECTIONS

The European Parliament Elections Act 1997 gives effect to Council Directive 93/109/EC and together with the Electoral Act 1992 (1992 Review, 141-4) provides for the electoral procedures for election of members to the European Parliament. It repeals the European Parliament Elections Act 1993 (1993 Review, 309) and other relevant legislation (see the First Schedule to the 1997 Act). The 1997 Act and Parts II, III, IV and XXIII of the 1992 Act are construed as one Act and may be cited as the European Parliament Elections Acts 1992-1997. Rules for the conduct of the elections are set out in the Second Schedule to the 1997 Act. For the purpose of European elections there are four constituencies: Connacht-Ulster, entitled to three representatives, and Dublin, Leinster and Munster, each entitled to four representatives (Third Schedule to the 1997 Act). The form of the ballot paper is set out in the Fourth Schedule to the 1997 Act.

Nationals of all Member States are entitled to vote in Ireland (sections 6 and 8). The nationals must be eighteen or over. Nationals of Ireland and the United Kingdom, resident in the State, are automatically entitled to vote, subject to registration. All other nationals resident in Ireland are entitled to vote in a constituency if such a person applies to the Minister to be registered and provides a statutory declaration. This declaration must contain the person's nationality, address in the State, the constituency of his or her home Member State (if so registered in the Home Member State) and his or her intention to exercise his or her right to vote in Ireland only. This declaration is also sent to the national's home Member State. In doing so, the Act aims at preventing possible abuse of voting rights. Nationals who are already registered prior to 1994 remain so registered and are not obliged to fulfil the above requirements.

Every person over 21 and who is a citizen of Ireland or a national of another Member State resident in Ireland is entitled to stand for the European Parliamentary elections (section 11). Such a person may nominate him or herself or be nominated, with his or her consent, by any elector registered to vote in the constituency for which the elector proposes to nominate that person (section 12). Candidates cannot be nominated for more than one constituency. The relevant candidates must deposit a sum of £1,000 to give effect to the nomination (section 13). Persons who are excluded include persons disqualified under section 41(f)-(k) of the 1992 Act, judges, the Comptroller and the Auditor General, Irish citizens standing for election in another Member State, and nationals of other Member States, other than the United Kingdom, disqualified under domestic law of their home State. Persons who are elected to the European Parliament but, at the time, hold the office of Attorney General, of Chairman or Deputy Chairman of the two Houses of the Oireachtas, or of Minister of State, must cease to hold that office. Likewise, persons who are members of the European Parliament must cease to be a representative upon becoming holder of the office of judge, Comptroller, Auditor General, Attorney General, Chairman or Deputy Chairman of the two Houses of the Oireachtas, Minister of State, or upon becoming disqualified under section 41(f)-(k) of the 1992 Act.

The election takes place according to the principle of proportional representation, each elector having one transferable vote (section 7). A transferable vote means to indicate the elector's preference for the candidates in order and which is capable of being transferred to the next choice. The voting is by secret ballot. Only persons whose name is on the register of European electors of the appropriate constituency are entitled to vote at the poll in that constituency (section 8). Voting can only take place in person, unless the elector is put on the postal voters list or special voters list (section 9). Only a limited category of persons are entitled to be put on the postal voters list or special voters list.

For many other persons, when election day comes, the physical ability to vote may be hampered as they, for example, work or study outside the constituency they reside in. In the past this has led to protests and accusations against the government of the day for maximising the government's change of a successful outcome of the vote, it being an election or referendum under Article 47 of the Constitution. It may, therefore, be welcome to introduce a system whereby people are entitled to vote by way of a proxy. The person unable to vote may authorise another (a spouse or other relative entitled to vote for example) to vote on his or her behalf. Safeguards can be built in to prevent abuse. This possibility is not unusual in other Member States, both for European and local elections (see for example, Article L.1 of the Dutch Election Act 1909).

The Act further regulates for the function of the returning officers and local returning officers (section 16-18), casual vacancies (section 19), the inspection of ballot papers and other documents (section 20), and the method by which the outcome of the elections can be questioned (section 21).

EUROPOL

Article K.3 of the Treaty of the European Union (the Maastricht Treaty: see the 1992 Review, 326-31) aims to set up a European police force. To this end, the Member States signed up to the Convention on the Establishment of a European Police Office (the Europol Convention) in July 1995. The Europol Act 1997 gives force of law to the Convention. The Act and the Convention pay specific attention to the European Convention on Automatic Processing of Personal Data 1981, transposed in Ireland in the Data Protection Act 1988 (1988 Review, 390-9), to provide for a degree of confidentiality in relation to data collected by Europol and national police authorities.

Aim and scope The need for the European Police Office (Europol) was influenced by the increasing problems relating to terrorism, drugs and other forms of international crime. Its objective is to combat these crimes and to improve the protection of security and public order (Article 1 of the Europol Convention). To this end, it aims at improving co-operation between police authorities in the Member States if there are factual indications that an organised criminal structure is involved and two or more Member States are affected in such a way as to require a common approach. Its scope will initially be limited to crimes, including illegal money laundering, relating to drug trafficking, nuclear and radioactive substances, illegal immigrant smuggling, trade in human beings and motor vehicle crime (Article 2). Crimes relating to terrorist activities are also included. At any time, the Council may instruct Europol to deal with other forms of crime, not listed in Article 2 of the Convention.

Europol does not have any powers of investigation, prosecution or detention. As of yet it must be viewed as an information source and a service provider for the Member States' national police forces. It centralises information and it will enable these forces to effectively co-operate to combat and prevent crime. Serious issues though will arise when Europol is given powers of a similar nature to those of the Member States' national police forces. This is presently not anticipated. However, if the need arises to provide Europol with such powers, stringent guarantees must be put in place to protect the interests of the accused and the public at large. In relation to the accumulation of data, these stringent guarantees are laid down in the European Convention on Automatic Processing of Personal Data (1981) and, more recently, in the Council Directive (95/46/EC) regarding the protection of individuals in relation to the processing of personal data and on the freedom of movement of such data. The latter refers to both automated data and manually processed data (see Article 2(b) of the Council Directive).

One commentator pointed out that international police co-operation has expanded rapidly over the past two decades, and that this development has left judicial co-operation behind. To combat this apparent gap, the commentator discussed the idea of a future European judicial network, working alongside Europol and suggests a model for organising and managing transnational criminal investigations in the European Union (see Vermeulen, 'A European Judicial Network linked to Europol? In Search of a Model for Structuring Trans-National Criminal Investigations in the EU', (1997) 4 *Maastricht Journal of European and Comparative Law*, 346-372).

Tasks Europol's tasks are set out in Article 3 of the Europol Convention. These tasks include the facilitation of the exchange of information between Member States, to obtain and process information and intelligence, to notify the competent authorities of the Member States of information concerning them and of connections between criminal offences, to aid investigations in the Member States and to set up and maintain a computer information system. To improve the co-operation between the police forces of the Member States, Europol will develop specialist knowledge of the investigative procedures of the Member States and to provide advice on investigations, and will provide for strategic intelligence so to effectively use resources available at national level. It may also assist Member States through advice and research with training of members of the police forces, organising and equipping these forces, crime prevention and other policing methods.

Organisation Europol will be established in the Netherlands, its head office located in The Hague (Article 26). It will have a Management Board delegated with specific tasks as set out in Article 28. The Board is the main decision-making body. Europol is headed by a Director with a tenure of four years (once renewable). The Director is assisted by Deputy Directors and is responsible for the performance of Europol's tasks, the day-to-day administration and other tasks assigned to him or her under the Convention or by the Management Board (Article 29).

Liaison between Europol and the competent national authorities or police forces takes place through national units, set up and regulated by national law (Article 4). These units supply Europol with all relevant information, respond to requests from Europol for information, intelligence and advice, keep information up to date and supply Europol with this information for storage. Information that may be against national security interests, jeopardise current investigations or the safety of individuals, or involve information regarding State security need not to be provided to Europol. The national units each appoint at least one liaison officer to Europol to represent the interests of the national unit (Article 5).

Data One of Europol's functions is to set up and maintain a computer information system to enable it to perform its tasks. The rules in relation to this system are set out in Articles 7 - 25. The system includes an information system containing data from the national units, provided to it in accordance with national procedures, and data obtained by Europol from third parties. This data is directly accessible by the national units, liaison officers, the Director and other nominated officials. Only persons or units that have entered data into the system may modify, correct or delete such data. Data relates to persons who are suspected of committing or having committed or having taken part in a criminal offence, or have been convicted of an offence for which Europol is competent. Data is distinguished between personal data and other data. Personal data may only include the person's name, date and place of birth, nationality, sex and other relevant characteristics, including objective physical characteristics. Other data referring to these persons include criminal offences, alleged crimes and when and where they were committed, the means used, the national departments handling the case, suspected memberships of criminal organisations and convictions.

The system further includes work files and an index system. The former are files established for a variable period of time for the purpose of analysing particular criminal activities. They contain comprehensive information in addition to data stored in the information system. The opening of such a file is subject to an order approved by the Management Board. The data may include data listed in the first sentence of Article 6 of the European Convention on Automatic Processing of Personal Data (1981), but only if this is strictly necessary for the purposes of the file concerned. This data refers to racial origin, political opinions religious beliefs, health and sexual orientation. The index system contains points of reference from the work files.

Data protection The Member States are required to have in place measures to provide a sufficient standard of data protection similar to that set out in the European Convention on Automatic Processing of Personal Data (1981) (Article 14 of the Europol Convention). This Convention was transposed in Ireland in the Data Protection Act 1988. The Europol Convention itself provides for provisions as to the use of data (Article 17), its communication to third States and other third bodies (Article 18), correction and deletion of data (Article 20), and time limits for storage and deletion of files (Article 21). It also provides that each Member State sets up an independent supervisory body (Article 23). This body must monitor, in accordance with national law, the permissibility of the input, retrieval and communication of personal data, and to examine whether rights of data subjects are violated. It also has supervisory powers as regards other activities of the national units and liaison officers. In addition, a joint supervisory body will be set up (Article 24). Its role is to review all activities of Europol to ascertain as to whether the rights of individuals are not violated by the storage, use and transmission of data.

Individuals may exercise their right to access data, including non-automated data relating to that person (Article 19). A request must be dealt with by

Europol within three months, in accordance with the law of the Member State where the right to access is claimed. For Ireland, and most other States this will be the law as laid down in European Convention on Automatic Processing of Personal Data (1981) and subsequent Community legislation such as the Council Directive (95/46/EC) on the protection of individuals in relation to the processing of personal data and on the freedom of movement of such data. Access to data may be refused if the refusal is necessary to enable Europol to fulfil its duties properly, to protect the security and public order in the Member State or to prevent a crime, or to protect the rights and freedoms of third parties.

The grounds for refusal are broadly stated and allow Europol to exercise a large degree of discretion as to its decision to allow individuals access to data. In addition, the very nature of the data held by Europol, and the purpose for which this data is held, will make it difficult for persons to gain access to data relevant to him or her. However, a refusal can be appealed to the joint supervisory body (Article 19(7)).

Europol Act 1997 The Europol Act 1997 gives effect to the Europol Convention and provides for related matters. It amends certain sections of the Garda Síochána Act 1989. It allows the Minister for Justice to set up a national unit within the Garda Síochána, under the control and general superintendence of the Commissioner of the Garda Síochána (section 3). The Commissioner will appoint a liaison officer (section 4). The national unit itself will be headed by a person not below the rank of Chief Superintendent. The Act makes further provisions for the application of the Data Protection Act 1988 and designates the Data Protection Commissioner as the national supervisory organ for the purpose of Article 23 of the Convention. Finally, the Official Secrets Act 1963 applies to all facts or information that come or have come to the knowledge of all persons under a particular obligation of discretion or confidentiality under the Europol Act or Europol Convention (section 9). However, access to information, held in Ireland, is also guaranteed in the Freedom of Information Act 1997. The latter also amends the Official Secrets Act 1963. Section 4 of the 1963 Act provides that only persons duly authorised to do so, may communicate official information to other persons. This section is amended by section 48 of the Freedom of Information Act 1997 stating that persons duly authorised to pass on information under the 1963 Act will also be authorised to do so under the Freedom of Information Act 1997. The extent of the application of the Freedom of Information Act 1997 in relation to data held by the national unit in Ireland remains as of yet unclear. (For a further discussion on the Freedom of Information Act 1997, see 2–8, above, in the Administrative Law chapter).

IMPLEMENTATION OF COMMUNITY LAW

Other relevant European Community law, both legislation and case law, are discussed in other individual chapters of this Review. In addition, readers are referred to the Table of European Community Legislation Implemented by Statutory Instrument in the *Irish Current Law Monthly Digest*. The Digest provides for a comprehensive listing of Community law implemented during 1997.

IRISH CASE LAW CONCERNING THE NATURE OF COMMUNITY LAW, THE OBLIGATIONS OF THE STATE AND THE ROLE OF THE NATIONAL COURTS

Two Irish cases are discussed here because they illustrate the nature of Community law, the obligations of the State and the role of the national courts. These cases are *Murphy v. Minister for the Marine* [1997] 2 I.L.R.M. 523 (HC) and *Byrne v. Conroy* [1997] 2 I.L.R.M. 99 (HC).

In both cases, the High Court discussed the extent of the State's obligations under Community law irrespective of the purpose or meaning of the legislation that was brought into question. The question became as to whether the relevant legislation could be interpreted or used to execute Community policy, even if the legislation was not initially designed to execute Community policy. As regards the interpretation of legislation (*Byrne v. Conroy*), it is a common rule that the literal or strict interpretation is used if the legislation concerns or inhibits on someone's liberty. Can the court use a more harmonious or schematic approach if this is necessary to avoid the State breaching its obligations under Community law? Likewise, if legislation affords a degree of discretion to a competent authority, for example, a Departmental Minister (*Murphy v. Minister for the Marine*), can or must that discretion be used for the purpose of Community policy notwithstanding the initial purpose of that piece of legislation?

Ministerial discretionary powers and Community law   The decision in *Murphy v. Minister for the Marine* [1997] 2 I.L.R.M. 523 (HC), concerned the licensing of sea fishing vessels. Under relevant domestic legislation, in particular the Fisheries (Consolidation) Act 1959 and the Fisheries (Amendment) Act 1983, the Minister has a discretion to refuse or grant such a licence (section 222B of the 1959 Act (as amended by section 2 of the 1983 Act)). The applicant's licence, after a long delay and change of Government, and a change of licensing policy, was so refused. The applicant had failed to demonstrate that his vessel met the Department's policy guidelines, set out in a letter in

June 1990. (Under the old policy the applicant would have been granted a licence). The new policy was designed to execute Ireland's obligations under the EU common fisheries policy. The applicant argued that the refusal to grant him a licence was unfounded. The question arose as to what extent the Minister, in exercising his discretion in this case had to have regard to the State's obligations under Community law and the common fisheries policy (taking into account that the licensing legislation pre-dated the common fisheries policy).

The Court first emphasised that it had a duty under Articles 5 and 189 of the EC Treaty, Article 29.4.5° of the Constitution and the European Communities Act 1972 to give precedence to Community law over national law. This meant that national legislation had to be interpreted in a manner consistent with the provisions of Community law to which a case is subjected. In addition, Member States were refrained from doing any act that may breach their obligations under the Treaties. The national courts must have regard to these obligations in interpreting national legislation.

In relation to the common fisheries policy, the Court pointed out that Articles 38-43 of the EC Treaty provided for a framework of a common fisheries policy. Part of the policy was to reduce the fishing fleet of the EU Member States. It required Member States to implement a programme or policy to give effect to this reduction. Ireland submitted such a programme. It was approved by the Commission by its decision of December 11, 1987 (88/142/EEC). The policy was referred to as "tonnage replacement policy". Under this policy, an applicant must be able to show that his application involved tonnage replacement in order to obtain a licence to fish at sea.

The Court, however, also stated that in its view the licensing rules laid down in the Fisheries (Consolidation) Act 1959 and the Fisheries (Amendment) Act 1983 were not initially designed to give effect to the common fisheries policy or aspects thereof. Section 222B of the 1959 Act was designed only to eliminate flags of convenience from the Irish fishing fleet. Section 224B suggested that any obligations under the common fishing policy ought to be discharged by way of Ministerial regulation, not by licence. The question, then, was whether the Government was obliged to grant or refuse the licence by the existing legislation alone, or whether it was entitled, if not obliged, to use the existing legislation for the purpose of Community policy (the common fisheries policy). Was it justified to change its policy under the legislation for the purpose of its European obligations, and so to refuse the licence to the applicant?

The Court held that the discretionary powers of the Minister could be set aside by the court in a number of circumstances. Among them were the principles of natural justice. The court relied on the decision in *Carrigaline Community Television Broadcasting Co Ltd v. Minister for Transport, Energy and Communications* [1997] 1 I.L.R.M. 241 (1996 Review, 181). Keane J. stated there that a decision must be set aside if, *inter alia*, the competent authority (the Minister) took into account factors which it should have excluded. Was the Minister in the *Murphy* case entitled to have regard to the new policy in taking the decision to refuse the licence?

The Court stated that the Minister was obliged to have regard to the new policy. This policy, approved by the Commission, created an obligation for Ireland, not a mere aspiration, to reduce the fishing fleet. The policy was an appropriate measure that ensured the fulfilment of Ireland's obligations under the common fisheries policy. The Court, in determining the legality of the State's actions in executing its obligations was to 'refrain from interpreting the 1983 legislation in a manner inconsistent with the provisions of [C]ommunity law' ([1997] 2 I.L.R.M. 523 at 539). The Court was obliged by Community law to do so. It was irrelevant whether or not those EU obligations pre-dated or post-dated the national legislation.

Thus, the decision in the *Murphy* case indicates that existing legislation designed to give effect to a policy that was not European in nature and gives a Minister certain discretionary powers can be used by the relevant Minister to give effect to Community policy of a later date. The court's role is to examine whether the Minister exercises his or her discretion properly in furtherance of Community policy. The decision also indicates that it is irrelevant whether the policy is implemented by Ministerial regulation, as suggested from section 224B of the 1959 Act. The decision illustrates again the supremacy of Community law. Not only does Community law take precedent over domestic law, the latter must also be interpreted to be in line with Community law and Community policy. The end result may be that a particular piece of domestic legislation can be interpreted in two different ways depending as to whether the legislation must be used to further the goals and aims of the European Union. This became also apparent in the second case: *Byrne v. Conroy*.

Legislative interpretation and Community policy   In *Byrne v. Conroy* [1997] 2 I.L.R.M. 99 (HC) the applicant was arrested in the State on foot of a warrant issued in Northern Ireland for the alleged offence of conspiring to defraud the Intervention Board for Agricultural Produce and to subvert the Agricultural Levies (Export Control) Regulations 1983 (UK). These Regulations were implemented pursuant to European law in relation to the Common Agricultural Policy (Article 38, 39 and 235 of the EC Treaty and Council Directives 729/70/EEC and 974/71/EEC, consolidated by Council Regulation 677/85/EEC, and Council Directive 81/77/EEC). The Regulations provide for a scheme to ensure that farmers across the European Union would be selling the same agricultural produce at the same price irrespective of exchange rate fluctuations. This was achieved by adjusting the price of agricultural produce crossing the borders of the Member States through the operation of so-called "Green Rates". These rates allow the Intervention Board to compensate farmers when they lose out on the sale of their produce due to a negative exchange rate and they allow the Intervention Board to levy farmers who profit from a distortion in the exchange rate. The applicant was alleged to have conspired to defraud by not paying these levies in relation to grain transports from Northern Ireland to Ireland.

The authorities in the UK sought the applicant's extradition. However, the applicant claimed that the offence was a revenue offence and for that matter, he ought to be released under section 50 of the Extradition Act 1965 (as amended by the Extradition (Amendment) Act 1994).

The Court first pointed out that section 50 of the Extradition Act 1965 demanded a strict or literal construction as to the meaning of "revenue offence". The Act concerned or inhibited the applicant's liberty. The Court referred to *The State (McFadden) v. Governor of Mountjoy Prison* [1981] I.L.R.M. 113. The phrase must be given its ordinary and natural meaning and no gloss should be placed on it. In doing so, the court could conclude that the offence was a revenue offence.

However, in its determination as to whether the offence constituted a revenue offence the Court also had to take account of the State's obligations under Community law since the alleged offence stood in relation to the Common Agricultural Policy (CAP). The Court pointed out that the compensation and levy scheme found its origins in Community law and the CAP. The latter aimed at harmonising the prices of agricultural produce throughout the European Union.

Under the decision by the Court of Justice of the European Communities in *Marleasing SA v. La Commercial Internacional de Alimentacionsia SA* [1991] E.C.R. 1 4135; [1992] 2 C.M.L.R. 247, national courts are required to interpret their national laws in the light of the wording and purpose of European law if this is necessary to achieve the result set out in the Treaties. This was again emphasised in *Faccini Dore v. Recreb* [1994] E.C.R. 1 3325; [1994] 1 C.M.L.R. 665. As regards fraud, Article 209A of the EC Treaty (as amended by Article E(77) of the EU Treaty) points out that Member States are required to take the same measures to counter fraud affecting the financial interests of the Community as they would to counter fraud affecting their national financial interests. Similarly, under Council Regulation 729/70/EEC Member States were obliged to take measures, in relation to the operation of the scheme, to deal with irregularities and to recover sums lost as a result of these irregularities or as a result of negligence.

The Court then reviewed two cases of the Court of Justice of the European Community (*Nordgetreide v. Hauptzollamt Hamburg Jonas* [1985] E.C.R. 3127 and *SA Roquette Frères v. French State* [1980] E.C.R. 3333) to conclude that section 50 of the Extradition Act must be construed in a manner consistent with Community law. In doing so, the court pointed out that one of the obligations of the State, as a Member State, was to protect the financial interests of the European Union. This left the court to conclude that to construe the offence as a revenue offence would impede this obligation, as it would prevent the applicant's extradition and subsequent prosecution in another State of the European Union. The offence was not a revenue offence. It was not one connected with taxes, duties or exchange controls. Rather the offence was connected with monetary compensation afforded to farmers as an implication of the Common Agricultural Policy.

Thus, whereas legislation, such as the Extradition Act 1960 is normally interpreted literally or grammatically, a harmonious or teleological interpretation can be used if the legislation stands in connection with European policy and such an interpretation can enhance the furtherance of such policy in the State. Again, it shows that the courts can interpret legislation differently, depending on whether the legislation stands in connection with Community law.

The two cases show that in addition to a body of common law case law and constitutional case law, both judicial decisions for the purpose of the development of domestic law, that a new body is emerging in the jurisdictions of the Member States. This body of law is a result of judicial decisions made for the purpose of giving effect to Community law and Community policy. As the two cases illustrate, this body of law and the judicial decisions that flow from it may bare a different outcome than the outcome in the former categories, irrespective of the applicable domestic legislation. Domestic legislation can be interpreted differently if this is necessary to give effect to Community law and policy.

Evidence

Declan McGrath, Trinity College Dublin

BURDEN OF PROOF

Standard of proof in civil cases   A number of 1997 decisions have advanced further the process of the crystallisation of the standard of proof in civil cases around the unitary, though contextually variable standard, of proof on the balance of probabilities.

Since the decision of the Supreme Court in *Banco Ambrosiano SpA v. Ansbacher & Co. Ltd.* [1987] I.L.R.M. 669 (1987 Review, 165), the orthodox view has been that there is only one standard of proof applicable in civil cases, that of proof on the balance of probabilities. However, this standard incorporates a degree of flexibility and where grave allegations are made or an adverse finding would have serious consequences for a party, a court will be careful to ensure that the burden of proof has been discharged.

Straightforward applications of this orthodoxy can be seen in *Chanelle Veterinary Ltd. v. Pfizer Ltd.* [1998] 1 I.L.R.M. 161 discussed in the Commercial Law chapter, 54, above and *O'Keefe v. Ferris* [1997] 2 I.L.R.M. 161, see the Company Law chapter, 118, above. In *Chanelle*, O'Sullivan J. endorsed Keane J.'s conclusion in *Masterfoods Ltd. v. HB Ice Cream Ltd.* [1993] I.L.R.M. 145, at 183 (1994 Review 152), as to the standard of proof to be applied in competition cases:

> These are civil proceedings and it follows that the applicable standard of proof is that appropriate in such cases, *i.e.*, proof on the balance of probabilities. It may well be that that standard should be applied with some degree of flexibility and that the court should require allegations of particular gravity to be clearly established in evidence.

Similarly, in *O'Keefe v. Ferris*, it was held by the Supreme Court that proof of fraud under section 297(1) of the Companies Act 1963 was to the civil standard though O'Flaherty J. pointed out that 'the more serious the allegation made in civil proceedings, then the more astute must the judge be to find that the allegation in question has been proved.'

It was argued last year (at 310) that implicit in this approach was the idea of degrees of probability propounded by Denning L.J. in *Bater v. Bater* [1951]

P. 35, at 36. It may be remembered that in that case, he said that:

> [I]n civil cases the case must be proved by a preponderance of probability, but there may be degrees of probability within that standard. The degree depends on the subject-matter. A civil court, when considering a charge of fraud, will natrually require for itself a higher degree of probability than that which it would require when asking if negligence is established. It does not adopt so high a degree as a criminal court, even when it is considering a charge of a criminal nature; but still it does require a degree of probability which is commensurate with the occasion.

It would now appear that this idea has been expressly endorsed by the Supreme Court.

In *Georgopoulus v. Beaumont Hospital Board*, Supreme Court, June 4, 1997, the appellant was challenging the respondent's finding of professional misconduct against him. One of the grounds for impugning the decision of the Board was that it had applied the wrong standard of proof, namely proof on the balance of probabilities rather than proof beyond a reasonable doubt.

However, the Supreme Court, in a judgment delivered by Hamilton CJ, held that the application of the criminal standard of proof was confined to criminal trials and had no application to the proceedings before the Board which were of a civil nature. Hamilton C.J. acknowledged that the complaints against the appellant involved grave charges with serious implications for his reputation but stated that they could be dealt with using the civil standard. He did, however, enter the caveat that 'the degree of probability required should always be proportionate to the nature and gravity of the issue to be investigated.'

The Chief Justice went on to quote with approval a passage from the judgment of Lord Scarman in *Redge v. Home Secretary, ex p. Khawaja* [1984] A.C. 74, at 112 to the effect that:

> My Lords, I have come to the conclusion that the choice between the two standards is not one of any great moment. It is largely a matter of words. There is no need to import into this branch of the civil law the formula used for the guidance of juries in criminal cases. The civil standard as interpreted and applied by the civil courts will meet the ends of justice.

The question of the standard of proof required to prove an allegation of professional misconduct was also raised in *O'Laoire v. Medical Council*, Supreme Court, July 25, 1997. The appellant had been found guilty of a number of charges of professional misconduct by the Fitness to Practice Committee.

Sanctions were imposed by the Medical Council on foot of the Committee's report and the appellant issued a special summons seeking an order cancelling the decision of the Council.

Keane J. in the High Court had applied the criminal standard in rehearing the charges and the Supreme Court dealt with the appeal from his decision on that basis. Therefore, it was unnecessary to deal with the question of the appropriate standard of proof and (somewhat surprisingly in view of the Court's earlier decision in *Georgopoulus*) a majority of the Court left this issue open for future resolution. However, O'Flaherty J. availed of the opportunity to make some *obiter* comments on this question.

He was of the view that the criminal standard was peculiarly suited to the structure of the criminal trial, especially trials by jury, and should be confined thereto. Thus, the appropriate standard in civil cases was the civil standard subject to the rider that 'the degree of probability required should always be proportionate to the nature and gravity of the issue to be investigated'. He went on to cite the passage from the judgment of Lord Scarman in *Ex parte Khawaja* set out above as support for the proposition that as a practical matter, there is often little difference between the two standards of proof. He also approved the statement of Woolf L.J. in *R. v. Wolverhampton Coroner, ex p. McCurbin* [1990] 2 All E.R. 759, at 763, that:

> [J]udges (and, I would add, all tribunals) should be cautious not to create problems for themselves by approaching the question of burden of proof in an artificial manner. From a practical point of view, where a serious allegation is being made, obviously, a high standard of proof is required, however technically you define that burden.

Citing a number of commonwealth cases in support (*Rizzo v. Hanover Insurance Co.* (1990) 68 D.L.R. 4th 420, *Neat Holdings Pty Ltd. v. Karajan Holding Pty Ltd.* [1992] A.L.R. 170 and *Beck v. National Insurance Company of New Zealand Ltd.* [1996] 3 N.Z.L.R. 363), he concluded that:

> The common law panorama at this time gives the impression that there is but one standard of proof in civil cases though, of necessity, it is a flexible one. This flexibility will ensure that the graver the allegation the higher will be the degree of probability that is required to bring home the case against the person whose conduct is impugned.

It is clear from these cases that the difference between the criminal and civil standards may be merely semantical in some instances. Thus, where serious allegations are made in civil proceedings, the courts will, as a practical matter, require clear and convincing proof before they find that the allegation has been proved on the balance of probabilities. Bearing in mind that the consequences of a civil case may be as serious as that of a criminal case, the courts will be careful to apply the standard of proof with sufficient stringency to ensure that justice is done and that an adverse finding is not made without satisfactory proof.

Ultimately, if the standard of proof in civil proceedings is contextualised in this fashion, then it would appear that the proposition that there is a single unitary standard is essentially illusory. However, as was pointed out last year (at 310), this approach does have the merit of avoiding the technicalities and anomalies attendant upon the task of expressly delineating categories where an accentuated standard of proof is to be applied. Thus, whilst it may be difficult to defend intellectually, it is justifiable in pragmatic terms.

Failure to discharge the civil burden   In *Buckley v. Motor Insurers Bureau of Ireland*, Supreme Court, *ex tempore*, November 12, 1997, the plaintiff was appealing from the dismissal of his claim for damages by the High Court. The claim arose out of an accident in which the car which the plaintiff was driving left the road and crashed. He alleged that the accident was caused by an unidentified car coming in the opposite direction on the wrong side of the road which had forced him off the road.

Lynch J., delivering the judgment of the Court, adverted to the fact that the defendant was unable to call any witness to the accident and said that because of this, it was important to bear in mind and apply the rules as to the onus of proof. The trial judge had not been satisfied that the accident had occurred in the manner alleged by the plaintiff who had therefore failed to prove his case on the balance of probabilities. This was a conclusion which the judge was entitled to reach on the evidence and the Court declined to interfere with it.

Presumption of innocence   In *Rock v. Ireland*, Supreme Court, November 19, 1997 (which is examined below, 430–3), the Supreme Court rejected a challenge to sections 18 and 19 of the Criminal Justice Act 1984 on the ground that they infringed the presumption of innocence. Using the same analytical approach as *O'Leary v. Attorney General* [1995] 2 I.L.R.M. 259 (1995 Review 181, 243), the Court concluded that the provisions did not interfere in any way with the presumption of innocence or the obligation of the prosecution to prove the guilt of the accused beyond a reasonable doubt because the inferences which can be drawn under the sections are evidence only, not proof of anything. In addition, a person cannot be convicted of an offence solely on the basis of such inferences which may only be used as corroboration of any other evidence in relation to which the failure or refusal is material.

Proceeds of crime   In *Gilligan v. Criminal Assets Bureau*, High Court, June 26, 1997 (discussed in the Constitutional Law chapter, 195, above), one of the grounds on which the plaintiff impugned the constitutionality of the Proceeds

ceeds of Crime Act 1996 was that, pursuant to section 8(2) the standard of proof to be applied in forfeiture proceedings was proof on the balance of probabilities. However, McGuinness J. concluded that the proceeding are not criminal in nature and therefore it is permissible for the standard of proof to be set at the civil standard.

She also rejected the contention that by requiring the plaintiff to establish that property frozen pursuant to sections 2 and 3 was not the proceeds of crime, there has been a breach of Article 38.1 because the burden of proof had shifted to him. Once it was accepted that the proceedings are civil in nature, there is no constitutional infirmity in a procedure whereby the onus is placed on a person seeking property to negative the inference from evidence adduced that a criminal offence has been committed.

Article 38.1 is, of course, confined to criminal proceedings. However, this does not mean that the Oireachtas has *carte blanche* to shift the burden of proof in civil proceedings. It may well be that, in an appropriate case, shifting the burden of proof would constitute a breach of the State's duty under Article 40.3.1° to defend and vindicate, as far as practicable, the personal rights of the citizen.

Charge to the jury   In *The People v. Rawley* [1997] 2 I.R. 265, the appellant had been convicted of robbery and possession of a knife. He had been stopped by gardaí shortly after the offence took place and found to be in possession of purses taken at the time of the robbery and a sum of money. His explanation was that he had found the purses and the money had been given to him by his girlfriend to buy wallpaper.

In the course of his summing up, the trial judge instructed the jury, more than once, that they had to be convinced beyond a reasonable doubt before convicting the accused. On appeal, it was submitted that the charge was inadequate in that the trial judge ought to have told the jury that if they had any reasonable doubt as to the truth of the accused's explanation they should have given him the benefit of that doubt and acquitted him. Although no authority is given for this submission, it is supported by *The People v. Byrne* [1974] I.R. 1, at 9, where the Court of Criminal Appeal, in a judgment delivered by Kenny J., held that it was 'essential . . . that the jury should be told that the accused is entitled to the benefit of the doubt and that when two views on any part of the case are possible on the evidence, they should adopt that which is favourable to the accused unless the State has established the other beyond reasonable doubt.'

However, the Court of Criminal Appeal was of the view that the jury had been properly charged and they had not been left in any doubt that they could not convict if taking all the evidence as a whole they were left with any reasonable doubt as to the accused's innocence. Thus, it seems that the formula laid down in *Byrne* does not have to be repeated parrot-like at the risk of a misdirection and that it will suffice if it is made clear to the jury that the accused should be given the benefit of any reasonable doubt.

The Court also rejected the contention that the trial judge had breached the interdiction laid down in *The People v. Oglesby* [1966] I.R. 162, against conveying to the jury the impression that there is an onus on the accused to give an explanation and that if he fails to do so or that if they do not believe it, they are entitled to convict.

A challenge to the charge of the trial judge also failed in *The People v. Byrne*, Court of Criminal Appeal, December 17, 1997. One of the points taken by the applicant was that in the course of his charge, the trial judge said to the jury 'you are people of the world, you know what goes on'. It was argued that this expression unfairly weighted his charge in favour of the prosecution. However, the Court held that the expression was merely a legitimate reminder to the jury that they were entitled to use their common sense and knowledge of the world in assessing whether they were satisfied that the prosecution had established the case beyond a reasonable doubt.

It is clear from both these cases that the Court of Criminal Appeal will not engage in an overly-forensic examination of a charge. It will not dissect every word and phrase used but will take a more global view. Thus, if the charge as a whole adequately conveys to the jury the correct principles, the Court will not interfere.

CHARACTER EVIDENCE

Evidence of bad character	In *Director of Public Prosecutions v. Keogh* [1998] 1 I.L.R.M. 72, the accused was charged under section 8(2) of the Criminal Law (Sexual Offences) Act 1993 with failure to comply with a direction issued by a garda under section 8(1). This subsection provides that a garda who has reasonable cause to suspect that a person is loitering in a street or public place in order to solicit persons for the purposes of prostitution may direct the person to leave that street or public place immediately. At the hearing before the District Court, the garda gave evidence that he had formed the requisite suspicion because of the character of the area which was well known as a 'red light' area and because he had personally known the accused for a period of two and a half years and had seen her approach cars in the area previously.

A case was stated to the High Court as to whether evidence of this type was admissible. It was accepted by counsel for the accused that evidence of the character of the area was admissible and therefore, the issue was whether evidence of the previous character and activities of an accused was admissible. Kelly J. answered this question in the negative.

He quoted from the judgment of McWilliam J. in *King v. Attorney General*

[1981] I.R. 233, at 241-42, where he said that:

> One of the concepts of justice which the Courts have always accepted is that evidence of character or of previous convictions shall not be given at a criminal trial except at the instigation of the accused, as that could prejudice the fair trial of the issue of the guilt or innocence of the accused.

He pointed out that in formulating this principle based on the constitutional concept of justice, McWilliam J. was reiterating a principle which was well established at common law (see, for example, *R. v. Harris* [1951] 1 K.B. 107, at 113 and *R. v. Goodwin* [1944] K.B. 518, at 523-24). Kelly J. therefore concluded that adducing such evidence 'would run counter to the basic concept of justice inherent in our legal system'. In addition, he pointed out that the evidence of the garda in this case was vague, imprecise and exceedingly difficult to rebut. Thus, it would place the accused person at a considerable disadvantage and would be inconsistent with the constitutional conception of fair procedures.

Addressing the argument that section 8(1) permitted the admission of such evidence, Kelly J. said that if the section were to render admissible evidence of prior character, it would have to do so in very explicit terms. Construing the statute strictly, he did not find in section 8 any warrant for suggesting that the well established common law rule was to be departed from. He also rejected the argument that the evidence was admissible because the accused was not in danger of being convicted because of her character. Although the offence was failure to comply with a direction, before such a direction could lawfully be given, the garda had to have a reasonable suspicion. Thus, evidence had to be adduced as to the basis upon which the suspicion was formed. Therefore, although an accused would not in peril of conviction directly because of her character, such evidence would be relevant in the proceedings.

The admission of evidence of bad character in criminal trials carries with it a serious risk of prejudice to the accused. This prejudice may arise for many reasons. There is a natural tendency for the jury to reason from the bad character of the accused to his guilt on the charge before them because of the premise that a 'bad' person is more likely to commit an offence than a 'good' person. Therefore, there is a risk that the accused may be convicted on the basis of his character, not the evidence. In addition, what Eggleston (Sir Frederick Eggleston, *Proof and Probability*, chapter 7) referred to as the 'regret factor' is reduced where the jury are exposed to evidence of bad character. Thus, the jury may discharge their duties less conscientiously and convict more readily because they believe the consequences of a mistaken conviction to be less serious.

The net effect is that the introduction of bad character evidence may cause the jury to ignore, either consciously or unconsciously, a reasonable doubt in favour of the accused. Thus, the admission of such evidence undermines the presumption of innocence which is guaranteed by Article 38.1 (see *O'Leary v. Attorney General* [1995] 2 I.L.R.M. 259 (1995 Review, 181, 243)). Indeed, the threat to the presumption of innocence was recognised by McWilliam J. in the passage set out above. It may well be that in the aftermath of *Keogh*, we can add to the penumbra of rights protected by Article 38.1, (see the list enumerated by the Constitutional Review Group), the right to trial by a jury which has not been exposed to evidence of bad character.

The problem in *Keogh* was not that the garda had relied on his knowledge of the previous activities of the accused in order to form the suspicion that she was soliciting but placing this knowledge before the tribunal of fact with its inevitable potential for prejudice. However, it should be noted that the quantum of the risk varies in accordance with the nature of the offence before the court and the nature of the discreditable conduct disclosed. Thus, if the charge before the court had been one of soliciting, there would have been a very clear risk of prejudice, in the sense of reasoning from past conduct to present guilt, attendant upon the admission of evidence that the accused had previously engaged in soliciting. However, there was considerably less scope for such prejudice where the evidence was given, not as direct proof of the offence itself, but in order to establish the condition precedent of the reasonableness of the garda's direction.

In *Keogh*, the balance of evidence was sufficient to ground the suspicion of the garda. However, the decision will make it more difficult for gardai to enforce section 8 in areas less renowned for their nocturnal activities.

Misconduct evidence in criminal cases   The question of the admissibility of misconduct evidence arose peripherally in *The People v. Byrne*, Court of Criminal Appeal, December 17, 1997. The applicants were convicted of various offences arising out of an attempt to import a large amount of drugs into the State at a remote beach in Connemara. At the trial, evidence was given that two of the applicants and another man were already known to gardaí when they were seen in a car near the place where the attempted importation took place. The trial judge concluded that the probative value of this evidence outweighed its prejudicial effect and the Court agreed with this conclusion.

Because of the brevity with which this point is dealt, it is difficult to assess whether the balancing test was actually satisfied in the case. However, what is of interest is the apparent acceptance by the Court of the balancing test which is now used by throughout the common law world and was endorsed by Budd J. in *B.(C.) v. Director of Public Prosecutions*, High Court, October 9, 1995.

In *The People v. Kavanagh*, Court of Criminal Appeal, *ex tempore*, July 7, 1997 (the facts of which are set out below), the question arose as to the appropriate course of action where the jury had been exposed to inadmissible misconduct evidence. The applicant had been convicted of murder. During the course of her evidence, the wife of the deceased, Mrs. Craig, referred to an incident where the applicant had allegedly assaulted his wife who was a sister of Mrs. Craig. The Court agreed that this was inadmissible evidence of previous misconduct but rejected the submission that the jury should have been discharged as a result. It was stated that a jury should only be discharged for some happening or dereliction of a grave nature in the course of a trial. Here, there were a number of avenues open to the trial judge to cure any prejudice caused. One such avenue, and the one which was implicitly adopted by the trial judge in his charge, was to instruct the jury to disregard the evidence. However, the Court pointed out that it was often better not to refer to evidence which had been wrongly but incidentally admitted because to do so might only attach an importance to it which it does not deserve.

In *People (D.P.P.) v. Marley* [1985] I.L.R.M. 17, the Court of Criminal Appeal decided that the appropriate course of action to be taken where the jury was exposed to inadmissible misconduct evidence was to discharge the jury. However, the divergence between the two cases is explicable on the basis of the difference between the relative gravity of the misconduct revealed in the two cases. In *Kavanagh*, the applicant was charged with murder and the misconduct which was revealed was the assault of his wife. In contrast, the applicant in Marley was charged with forgery and the misconduct revealed was that he had previously been tried for, though acquitted, of murder. Comparing the comparative gravity of the misconduct revealed in both cases, it is clear that the risk of prejudice was relatively high in *Marley*, necessitating the discharge of the jury, but relatively low in *Kavanagh*. Hence, in *Kavanagh*, the case could properly continue.

Misconduct evidence in civil cases The question of the admissibility of misconduct evidence in civil cases was raised in *Smyth v. Tunney*, Supreme Court, *ex tempore*, April 8, 1997. The Court did not find it necessary to deal with the question but it did indicate that where there is a question of intent or motive in a civil case, then misconduct evidence might be admissible in the same way as it is in criminal trials.

The question of the admissibility of misconduct evidence in civil cases has given rise to a contrariety of opinion as to whether the exclusionary rule applied in criminal cases also applies to civil cases in the same or a modified fashion or whether the admission of such evidence can be adequately dealt with using the ordinary notion of relevance. The trend of modern authority is to establish something of a middle ground between these two views. The risk of prejudice is much reduced in civil cases because of the nature of the proceedings and the fact that most civil actions are heard by a judge sitting alone. Thus, in many cases, the probative force required to outweigh this risk of prejudice will approach the level of mere relevance. However, everything will depend on the facts and issues in the case and where the admission of misconduct evidence could potentially cause prejudice or injustice, a heightened requirement of probative force will be imposed.

The leading English authority is *Mood Music Publishing Co. Ltd. v. De Wolfe Publishing Ltd.* [1976] Ch. 119. Evidence was admitted by the trial judge in a copyright infringement action which showed that the defendants had, on other occasions, produced musical works which bore a close resemblance to copyrighted works. Lord Denning M.R. outlined the position as follows (at 127):

> The criminal courts have been very careful not to admit [misconduct] evidence unless its probative value is so strong that it should be received in the interests of justice; and its admission will not operate unfairly to the accused. In civil cases the courts have followed a similar line but have not been so chary of admitting it. In civil cases the courts will admit evidence of similar facts if it is logically probative, that is if it is logically relevant in determining the matter which is in issue; provided that it is not oppressive or unfair to the other side; and also that the other side has fair notice of it and is able to deal with it.

On the facts, it was held that the evidence had been properly admitted to rebut the defence of coincidence.

It remains to be seen what approach the Irish courts will take should the matter arise for express decision.

CHILDREN'S EVIDENCE

Part III of the Children Act 1997, which will come into force on such day as is fixed by the Minister, introduces sweeping changes regarding the admission of children's evidence in civil proceedings.

The first provision of note is section 28(1) which provides that in any civil proceedings, 'the evidence of a child who has not attained the age of 14 years may be received otherwise than on oath or affirmation if the court is satisfied that the child is capable of giving an intelligible account of events which are relevant to the proceedings.' Subsection (3) extends the application of subsection (1) to persons with a mental disability who are aged 14 or over. This section which is drafted in virtually identical terms to section 27 of the Criminal Evidence Act 1992, thereby equalises the position between civil and criminal cases and cures the anomaly whereby unsworn evidence of children was admissible in criminal but not in civil proceedings (see *Mapp v. Gilhooley* [1991] 2 I.R. 253 (1991 Review, 348)).

Section 28 applies to all civil proceedings but the application of the balance of Part III is restricted to proceedings concerning the welfare of a child or a person of full age who has a mental disability to such an extent that it is not reasonably possible for the person to live independently. Such proceedings include those relating to the care, custody or guardianship of a child.

Section 21 makes provision for evidence to be given by live television link. It is noteworthy that the leave of the court is required and that a child does not benefit from the presumption of trauma which a person 17 years of age giving evidence in criminal proceedings enjoys (see section 13(1) of the 1992 Act). No guidelines are given as to when such leave should be granted and it seems as if a trial judge will enjoy considerable discretion in this regard. However, it would seem that, at a minimum, some evidential basis that a child would suffer trauma if required to testify, will have to be presented.

Section 22 allows questions to be put by an intermediary where a child is giving evidence via television link. Section 22(1) provides that 'the court may, of its own motion or on the application of a party to the proceedings, if satisfied that, having regard to the age or mental condition of the child, any questions to be put to the child should be put through an intermediary, direct that any such question be so put.' One point of departure between this section and its equivalent in the 1992 Act, section 14, is that under section 22(1), the court may direct questions to be put through an intermediary of its own motion. This reflects the more inquisitorial nature of many child care proceedings (cf. the comments of Costello P. in *Re K. (Infants)* (reported *sub nom. Re M., S. and W. Infants* [1996] 1 I.L.R.M. 370 (1996 Review 315).

Sections 21 and 22 essentially replicate the scheme for giving evidence established in the criminal sphere by sections 13 and 14 of the 1992 Act. However, section 23 of the 1997 Act goes well beyond anything contained in the 1992 Act. It provides that:

(1) Subject to subsection (2), a statement made by a child shall be admissible as evidence of any fact therein of which direct oral evidence would be admissible in any proceeding to which this Part applies, notwithstanding any rule of law relating to hearsay, where the court considers that –
(a) the child is unable to give evidence by reason of age, or
(b) the giving of oral evidence by the child, either in person or under section 21, would not be in the interest of the welfare of the child.

(2)(a) Any statement referred to in subsection (1) or any part thereof shall not be admitted in evidence if the court is of the opinion that, in the interests of justice, the statement or that part of the statement ought not to be so admitted.
(b) In considering whether the statement or any part of the statement ought to be admitted, the court shall have regard to all the

circumstances, including any risk that the admission will result in unfairness to any of the parties to the proceedings.

The section applies in two situations. The first is where the child is not competent as a witness by reason of age. However, since a child can now give unsworn evidence if he or she is capable of giving an intelligible account of events (s.28), then it would seem that it is only in exceptional circumstances that a hearsay statement should be admitted under this head because it will necessarily be the statement of a child who is incapable of giving an intelligible account of events. It is worth noting that the Law Reform Commission (*Report on the Rule Against Hearsay in Civil Cases* (LRC 25-1990), p.22), recommended that an out of court statement of a child who is not competent to give evidence should not be admissible.

The second scenario provided for in the section is where the giving of oral evidence by the child, either in person or under section 21, would not be in the best interests of the child. This caters for the situation where a child might suffer trauma even if the live television procedure was used. This procedure greatly reduces the stress and trauma associated with requiring children to testify in court. However, it is of little avail where the welfare of a child could be injured merely by requiring the child to recount a distressing experience such as child abuse. Hence, the need for section 23(1)(b) as a fall back measure.

In order to prevent surprise, section 23(3) introduces a notice obligation. A party proposing to introduce hearsay evidence under the section is obliged to give such notice and particulars as is reasonable and practicable in the circumstances for the purpose of enabling the other parties to deal with any matter arising from its being hearsay. Under subsection (4), the parties, by agreement, may disregard subsection (3). It is noteworthy that the notice obligation is drafted in flexible terms being couched in terms of reasonableness. It thus eschews the strict and complicated notice requirements for the admission of business records in section 7 of the 1992 Act.

The drafting of section 23 and especially the stipulation that notice 'shall' be given suggests that notice is a mandatory requirement and that, if it is not given, then the evidence will be inadmissible. However, because of the broad terms in which the section is drafted, in practice a trial judge will enjoy considerable discretion to decide whether adequate notice has been given. In some circumstances, he or she might decide that it was not reasonable or practicable to give any notice, *e.g.* if such evidence is introduced at an ex parte or interlocutory hearing.

With concession of the principle of the admissibility of hearsay statements, the main question becomes one of the weight to be attributed to such statements. This is a difficult question and guidance is provided by section 24:

(1) In estimating the weight, if any, to be attached to any statement admitted in evidence pursuant to *section 23*, regard shall be had to all the circumstances from which any inference can reasonably be drawn as to its accuracy or otherwise.

(2) Regard may be had, in particular, as to whether -
   (a) the original statement was made contemporaneously with the occurrence or existence of the matters stated,
   (b) the evidence involves multiple hearsay,
   (c) any person involved has any motive to conceal or misrepresent matters,
   (d) the original statement was an edited account or was made in collaboration with another for a particular purpose, and
   (e) the circumstances in which the evidence is adduced as hearsay are such as to suggest an attempt to prevent proper evaluation of its weight.

The drafting of this section owes a fairly obvious debt to section 4 of the English Civil Evidence Act 1995 and it would seem that the case law under that section, of which there is currently very little, will be of considerable relevance to the interpretation of section 24.

As to the factors specified in subsection (2), factors (a) and (b) have an obvious bearing on the reliability of any hearsay statement. With regard to factor (c), the phrase 'any person involved' is broad enough to encompass not just the child declarant but the person hearing/reading/seeing the statement and where multiple hearsay is involved the person giving evidence of the statement and any intermediaries. This factor is likely to prove particularly important in situations where there is some form of custody dispute involving the child and it is contended that allegations of child sexual abuse are being fabricated at the instigation of one of the parties seeking custody. Indeed, the phrase is wide enough such that it would seem to cover any person who may have prompted the child to make the statement.

The purpose for which a statement was made will, as acknowledged by factor (e), have an important bearing on its reliability. Where a statement was made at a point before the proceedings in which it was sought to admit it had commenced or were contemplated, then this reduces the risk that it is being made at the suggestion of a third person for a motive connected with the proceedings.

Section 25 (which is drafted in virtually identical terms to section 9 of the 1992 Act) makes provision for the admission of evidence as to the credibility of the hearsay declarant. The purpose of the section is to place the child whose hearsay statement is admitted in the same position, for the purpose of impeaching credibility as if he or she had been called as a witness.

CONDITIONAL ADMISSIBILITY

Sometimes, a fact may not be relevant in and of itself but only when it is considered in conjunction with another fact. However, it may be necessary to adduce it before the second fact and where this occurs, the court will admit the fact conditional on its subsequently proving to be relevant.

This procedure was challenged as constitutionally impermissible in *O'Sullivan v. Conroy*, High Court, July 31, 1997. The applicant argued that evidence could not be introduced to a jury while there was any qualification as to its admissibility. He asserted the principle that a jury should not receive evidence prejudicial to an accused, the admissibility of which is dependent on other evidence which may not be forthcoming. He grounded this submission on the decision of the Supreme Court in *The People v. Conroy* [1986] I.R. 460, and in particular on a passage from the judgment of Finlay C.J. where he stated (at 472):

> It seems to me clear that the constitutional right of a person charged with anything other than a minor offence to a trial with a jury does not involve nor does the decision in the *Lynch Case* [1982] I.R. 64 suggest that it involved a right that issues of fact arising with regard to the admissibility of evidence should be tried by the jury. I am, however, satisfied that the constitutional right to a trial in due course of law as interpreted by this Court would involve as a fundamental matter the right to trial by a jury from whose knowledge there is excluded any evidence of guilt which is inadmissible at law. For this reason I have the greatest possible difficulty in conceiving circumstances under which, with justice it would be possible to leave to a jury at the conclusion of the case, evidence the admissibility of which is being challenged, simply giving to them a direction on the issue of fact which is involved and a warning that if they should resolve that issue in favour of the accused they should ignore the incriminating evidence which they had heard. Experience as a judge indicates that even as a trained lawyer there is a very significant difficulty in excluding from one's mind incriminating evidence on the trial of a criminal case which is inadmissible. In my view, it would be an unreal task to seek to impose on a jury of law persons, and the risk of real injustice flowing from it would be great.

Barr J. did not find it necessary on the facts of the case to address the correctness of this submission. However, he did express doubt as to whether the principle enunciated in *Conroy* extends to include the concept of conditional admissibility and it is submitted that his doubts are well-founded.

As is clear from the passage set out above, the essential problem identified in *Conroy* was that of a jury adjudicating on the innocence or guilt of an accused after being exposed to inadmissible and prejudicial evidence. In any given case, it would not be possible to know whether the jury had been exposed to inadmissible evidence or not. Hence, the entire procedure was tainted by unconstitutionality. However, this is not the case with conditional admissibility. At the point where the case is left to the jury, it will be apparent whether the evidence admitted *de bene esse* is relevant or not. If it is, then it can be left to the jury. If it is not, then the judge will have to decide whether the matter can be cured by a warning to disregard the evidence or whether it will be necessary to discharge the jury. Where there is a substantial risk of prejudice to the accused, then on the authority of *Conroy*, it would seem that discharge of the jury would be the proper option.

CONFESSIONS

Right to a solicitor   In *The People v. Finnegan*, Court of Criminal Appeal, July 15, 1997, it was confirmed that the constitutional right to obtain legal advice carries with it a concomitant right to obtain such legal advice in private.

The appellant was arrested on suspicion of larceny and while in custody, he asked to speak to his solicitor. He was permitted to telephone him. However, a number of gardaí stayed in the room while he made the call and the conversation took place in the hearing of at least one garda.

The Court held that the right to a solicitor 'necessarily implies, except in the most exceptional circumstances, a right to consult with the Solicitor in private, in the sense of out of the hearing of police officers or prison warders. Indeed the right to consult a Solicitor would usually be of little value unless it carried with it, as a necessary concomitant, the right to consult him in private'. Therefore, when the appellant asked to speak with his solicitor by telephone, that request carried with it the necessary implication that he wished to speak to his solicitor in private. The gardaí were not entitled to assume that he did not require privacy simply because he did not mention it.

Thus, the Court concluded that there had been a breach of the appellant's constitutional right to consult a solicitor in private. The request of the appellant to consult with his solicitor, although made in the early hours of the morning, was not unreasonable in view of the fact that the gardaí made no complaint and had no difficulty in contacting the solicitor. In addition, the denial of privacy was unreasonable in view of the fact that the member in charge had said he would have made arrangements for the applicant to consult with his solicitor in private had he asked for privacy. The fact that the remarks overheard by the gardaí were relatively innocuous was irrelevant because the circumstances was not such as to permit a free interchange between the appellant and his solicitor.

The conclusion that the right to a solicitor entails a right to consult that solicitor in private follows inevitably from the purpose of the right. This was outlined by Finlay C.J. in *The People v. Healy* [1990] 2 I.R. 73, at 81; [1990] I.L.R.M. 313, at 320 (1989 Review 137) as follows:

> The undoubted right of reasonable access to as solicitor enjoyed by a person who is in detention must be interpreted as being directed towards the vital function of ensuring that such person is aware of his rights and has the independent advice which would be appropriate in order to permit him to reach a truly free decision as to his attitude to interrogation or to the making of any statement, be it exculpatory or inculpatory. The availability of advice from a lawyer must, in my view, be seen as a contribution, at least, towards some measure of equality in the position of the detained person and his interrogators.

It has long been recognised in the sphere of legal professional privilege that confidential communication is essential so that a client may make a 'clean breast' of it to his or her legal adviser and receive the appropriate legal advice (see *Anderson v. Bank of British Columbia* (1876) 2 Ch. D. 644, at 649 (*per* Jessel M.R.)). Similarly, if a suspect in custody is to make a free and full informed decision as to whether to make a statement (as envisaged by *Healy*), then it is essential that he or she should be able to consult and put all the facts before his or her solicitor in private so that the appropriate legal advice can be received.

The next question was the effect of the breach and the Court took the view that it was to render the detention of the appellant illegal. No evidence was adduced to show that this unlawful detention came to an end at any particular time. Thus, the trial judge had no discretion to admit any statements made during this time.

In reaching that conclusion, the Court relied on an *obiter dictum* in *The People v. Madden* [1977] I.R. 326, at 355, to the effect that:

> A person held in detention by the Garda Síochána whether under the provisions of the Act of 1939 or otherwise, has got a right to reasonable access to his legal advisers and that a refusal of a request to give such reasonable access would render his detention illegal.

The Court also relied upon the decision of the Supreme Court in *Healy*. There, it will be remembered, it was held that there was a breach of the accused's constitutional right of reasonable access to a solicitor where the accused who was in the course of making a statement was not informed of the arrival of his solicitor at the garda station. The Court regarded the following passage from the judgment of Finlay C.J. as being of significance (at 82, 321):

> I am satisfied that the conclusion reached by the learned trial Judge that it was impossible, on the evidence before him, for him to be satisfied beyond a reasonable doubt or, as he expressed it in his Ruling, even as a matter of probability, that the significant incriminating statements which were contained in the tendered written statement were made prior to the arrival of the Solicitor at 4pm was a conclusion of fact which he was entitled to make and cannot be disturbed on appeal by this Court.

In the opinion of the Court, the implication of this passage was 'that any statement made after 4 p.m. would have been inadmissible presumably because the prisoner was from that hour in unlawful detention because of the denial of his constitutional right of access to his solicitor and any statement obtained from him was therefore inadmissible.' However, this does not follow. Rather, it seems that both the trial judge and Finlay C.J. were simply applying the concept of causation. This was flagged by the Chief Justice as a crucial issue (at 81, 320):

> The vital issue which arises . . . if a breach of the right of access to a solicitor has occurred as a result of a deliberate and conscious act of a member of the Garda Síochána, is as to whether there is a causative link between that breach and the obtaining of an admission.

Thus, the trial judge's conclusion was simply that he could not be satisfied beyond a reasonable doubt that the incriminating statements had been made before the breach of the right of access to a solicitor. If they had, then applying the concept of causation, they would have been admissible because they would not have been obtained as a result of the breach. As regards statements obtained after the breach, then the requirement of causation was satisfied because the solicitor would very likely have advised the accused not to say anything and he, therefore, would not have made those statements. Thus, both the trial judge and Finlay C.J. were merely seeking a causative link and this passage is no authority for the view that a breach of the right to a solicitor renders an accused's custody illegal.

Indeed, the whole line of cases applying causation where there has been a breach of the right of reasonable access to a solicitor (including *Walsh v. O'Buachalla* [1991] 1 I.R. 56 (1990 Review, 150), *The People v. Cullen*, Court of Criminal Appeal, March 30, 1993 (1993 Review 214), and *Director of Public Prosecutions v. Spratt* [1995] 2 I.L.R.M. 117 (1995 Review, 244)) are based on the premise that the breach does not render the detention of the accused unlawful. If this was the case, then the question would simply be whether there had been a breach of the right or not. If there was, then any evidence obtained after that time would be automatically inadmissible because it was obtained while the accused was in illegal custody. The requirement of a causative link only makes sense if the accused is not in illegal custody.

The right to liberty and the right to a solicitor are two separate rights protected by two different constitutional provisions and the breach of one does not automatically entail a breach of the other. Where the breach of the right to a solicitor while a suspect is in custody is *mala fides*, then applying the transactional approach adopted in *Madden*, there might well be scope for arguing that the breach should render the detention of the suspect illegal such that any evidence obtained will be excluded. However, in the normal run of cases, a breach of the right to a solicitor will not, of itself, render custody illegal.

The right to a solicitor, in both its legal and constitutional manifestations, was also raised in *The People v. Darcy*, Court of Criminal Appeal, July 29, 1997. The applicant had been detained under section 4 of the Criminal Justice Act 1984 in the early hours of Saturday morning in connection with the murder of a youth. He was sixteen at the time and the gardaí having ascertained that he was a juvenile tried to contract his parents. They were in the States at the time but an uncle, Mr. Bermingham was contacted, and thereafter the applicant was questioned in his presence. He requested a solicitor and unsuccessful attempts were made to contact three solicitors until eventually a solicitor was contacted who agreed to act. He arrived at 12.15pm on Saturday and after consultation with him, the applicant refused to answer any further questions. Later, a memorandum of the entire interview was read over to the applicant in the presence of his solicitor and he was asked if the notes were correct. He made one objection but refused to sign the notes.

Counsel for the applicant submitted that the decision of the gardaí to interview the applicant in the absence of a solicitor constituted a breach of his constitutional right to a solicitor. However, the Court rejected this ground of appeal on the basis that the gardaí had acted properly and reasonably in the circumstances:

> [T]here was ample evidence to support the finding of the learned trial judge that there had been nothing in the nature of a conscious and deliberate act on the part of the gardaí to deprive the Applicant of his right of access to a solicitor. Given that the Applicant was detained in the early hours of Saturday morning, it could not seriously be said that, despite their having got in touch with a number of solicitors, it was not possible to obtain the attendance of one until midday on the Saturday, constituted a denial of the Applicant's constitutional rights. In addition, the gardaí acted perfectly properly in deferring the interviewing of the Applicant until the arrival of Mr. Bermingham, gave Mr. Bermingham and the Applicant the opportunity of a discussion in private and complied with Mr. Bermingham's request that nothing in the form of a written statement should be taken from the Applicant until his solicitor arrived. It is

to be noted that the Applicant was not invited to sign the record of his answers, including those which might be regarded as being of an incriminating nature, until such time as his solicitor arrived.

This case emphasises once more that the constitutional right established by *The People v. Healy* [1990] 2 I.R. 73; [1990] I.L.R.M. 313 (1989 Review, 137), is one of *reasonable* access to a solicitor (cf. *Barry v. Waldron*, High Court, *ex tempore*, May 23, 1996 (1996 Review, 337)). Thus, provided that reasonable attempts are made by the gardaí to contact a solicitor if asked to do so, this is sufficient. This decision also confirms that it is not necessary for the gardaí to refrain from questioning a suspect until such time as his or her solicitor arrives. Indeed, to hold otherwise could greatly undermine the utility of section 4 because the time limit under the section would run from the time of the arrest but the gardaí would be unable to question until such time as the solicitor had arrived and conferred with his or her client.

A submission that there had been a breach of the applicant's legal right to a solicitor under Articles 8(1) and 9(1)(a)(i) of the Custody Regulations was also rejected. While there was no evidence of detailed compliance with the requirements of these provisions, the Court was of the view that it was clear that the substance of the applicant's rights had been preserved. He had been informed of his right to obtain a solicitor, the attendance of a responsible adult was secured as soon as practicable, the latter was aware of the Applicant's entitlement to legal advice and no interviewing had taken place until he was present.

The Custody Regulations and the Judges' Rules Another ground of appeal in *The People v. Darcy*, Court of Criminal Appeal, July 29, 1997, was that the trial judge had erred in not excluding the statements of the applicant under section 7(3) of the 1984 Act on the ground that there had been a breach of Article 12(3) of the Regulations. This Article provides that not more than two members should question an arrested person at any one time. It was argued that the trial judge should have exercised his discretion to exclude the statements because the breach was particularly important in this case in view of the fact that the case against the Applicant depended crucially on the admissions made by him while in custody. It also had to be borne in mind that he was a juvenile and that he was a person of low intelligence. The Court, however, rejected this submission. It was pointed out that although Article 12(3) was breached, the questioning was not otherwise oppressive or unfair and concluded that this was clearly a case in which the trial judge could, in the exercise of his discretion, decide to admit the statements.

A number of decisions including *The People v. Connell* [1995] 1 I.R. 244, have laid emphasis on the key phrase 'of itself' in section 7(3) to hold that a breach of the Custody Regulations is insufficient, on its own, to warrant exclusion. In order to succeed an accused will have to show a breach plus something extra. That something extra is, of its nature indefinable, but in *Darcy*, there is a hint that it must be something that would render the admission of the accused's statement oppressive or unfair.

A point was also raised in *Darcy* as to the relationship between the Judges' Rules and the Custody Regulations. It was argued that there was a lack of harmony between the two because the Judges' Rules envisaged the making, by a person in custody, of a written statement in narrative form. No further questioning is permitted in respect of that statement save to resolve any ambiguities or doubts. By way of contrast, the Regulations provide for the interviewing of a person detained thereunder.

However, the Court confirmed that the Custody Regulations do not in any way deprive a person detained in custody of the protection of the Judges' Rules. The Rules apply with full force to persons detained under the Regulations but are broader in that they apply also to persons questioned by the police who were not actually in custody.

Rule 7 of the Judges' Rules does provide that a suspect making a voluntary statement must not be cross-examined and that no questions should be put to him about it except for the purpose of removing ambiguity. However, it is clear that the Rules, as a whole, do envisage the questioning of suspects in custody. Thus, there is no incompatibility between the Rules and the Regulations. Indeed, the Rules can be viewed as a judicially created forerunner to the Custody Regulations because they were 'so framed as to try and ensure that . . . statements . . . [made] in police custody as a result of interrogation, are not admitted into evidence when their admission would be unsafe or when it would be unfair' (*per* Finlay C.J. in *The People v. Kavanagh* (1989) 3 Frewen 243, at 347).

In *The People v. Morgan*, Court of Criminal Appeal, *ex tempore*, July 28, 1997, the accused sought to exclude an admission made by him on the basis of a breach of the Judges' Rules. The accused had been questioned by gardaí and was cautioned at least once, perhaps twice, in accordance with the Judges' Rules. An identification parade was then held and after the parade, interviewing recommenced. The accused was told by a garda that he was still under caution and, according to the garda, the accused indicated that he understood this. However, he later challenged an admission made by him during the course of this interview on the basis that he had not been cautioned.

The Court concluded that there had not been any breach of the Judges' Rules. O'Flaherty J. said that it is not necessary for the police officers 'to repeat in parrot like fashion' the words of the caution on every occasion. The point of giving the caution is the person should understand what it is about. The accused had been under caution originally and understood it. He had also had the benefit of legal advice while in custody so he knew his rights.

The caution required by the Judges' Rules is not an end of itself but is merely the preferred method of informing a suspect of his right to silence. In fact, despite judicial warnings that 'the sense of the caution and of every limb of it must be conveyed to the mind of the person to whom it is addressed, otherwise it ceases to be a caution' (*per* Kennedy C.J. in *Attorney General v. Cleary* (1934) 1 Frewen 14, at 17), it is clear that often the administering of the caution is a mere formality. It is commonly the case that the gardaí give the required caution which informs the suspect of his right to silence and immediately begin to question him in terms designed to ensure that he does not exercise that right. Thus, the Court is correct to focus on the substantive question of the degree to which the accused was aware of his rights rather than on the formalistic question of whether a caution had been given.

Electronic recording of interviews   The electronic recording of interviews was first mooted in the report of the O'Briain Committee (*Report of the Committee to Recommend Certain Safeguards for Persons in Custody and for Members of An Garda Síochána* (1978), paragraph 67) and section 27(1) of the Criminal Justice Act 1984 provided that the Minister for Justice could introduce regulations providing for the recording of interviews by electronic or other means. Such regulations have now been promulgated in the Criminal Justice Act 1984 (Electronic Recording of Interviews) Regulations 1997.

Article 4(1) of the Regulations provides that interviews with persons to whom the Regulations apply shall be electronically recorded. These persons are those detained under the various detention provisions, namely, section 4 of the Criminal Justice Act 1984, section 30 of the Offences Against the State Act 1939 and section 2 of the Criminal Justice (Drug Trafficking) Act 1996 (Article 3(2)). Electronic recording is defined in Article 2(1) to include both audio tape and video tape recording (with or without a soundtrack).

However, the Regulations contain a number of exceptions that restrict their application and effectiveness. Article 3(1) contains the caveat that the Regulations shall only apply to stations where electronic recording equipment has been provided and installed. This is a major loophole because, at the moment, very few stations have the appropriate equipment installed. This leaves open the possibility that the gardaí could circumvent the Regulations by the simple stratagem of bringing a suspect to a station where recording equipment has not been installed. If it could be established that this had been deliberately done, then it is submitted that any inculpatory statements made ought to be excluded as being taken in breach of fundamental fairness because the accused would have been deprived of a procedural protection to which he or she would otherwise have been entitled (see the test set out by Griffin J. in *The People v. Shaw* [1982] I.R. 1, at 61). In addition, pursuant to Article 4(3), an interview or part of an interview does not have to be electronically recorded where the equipment is not working or it is in use at the time that the interview is to commence or where it is not practicable to record an interview.

On the whole though, the introduction of these regulations is a welcome development. One of the main problems with the voluntariness test (as extended by the concept of oppression) is that its application is crucially dependent on accurate information as to what went on in the interview room and frequently resolves itself into a 'swearing contest' between the suspect and the gardaí. The recording of interviews by providing such information is the best way of ensuring that the rights of the suspect are respected and that he or she is not subjected to illegitimate pressure. Indeed, recording of interviews also has advantages from the viewpoint of the gardaí because the experience of Australasian jurisdictions has been that the advent of recording has been accompanied by a drop in the number of challenges made to the admission of confession evidence.

The introduction of electronic recording also has an important bearing on the corroboration warning in respect of confessions introduced by section 10 of the Criminal Procedure Act 1993. Section 10(1) provides that where 'at a trial of a person on indictment evidence is given of a confession made by that person and that evidence is not corroborated, the judge shall advise the jury to have due regard to the absence of corroboration.' If, and this is a question yet to be resolved, the section requires corroboration of the confession itself rather than the accused's participation in the offence, then such corroboration would be provided by the record of the interview. Thus, where the interview had been recorded, there would be no necessity to give a corroboration warning.

Section 27(4) of the 1984 Act provides that any failure to comply with a provision of the regulations shall not, without prejudice to the power of the court to exclude evidence at its discretion, by itself render inadmissible in evidence anything said during such questioning. This section is drafted in very similar terms to section 7(3) which deals with breaches of the Custody Regulations and so, presumably, a similar approach will be taken to its interpretation. Thus, the courts are unlikely to exclude statements made by an accused merely because of a breach of the Electronic Recording Regulations. An accused will have to go further and show that some form of unfairness has flowed from the breach.

Distress of the accused In *The People v. Connolly*, Court of Criminal Appeal, *ex tempore*, April 14, 1997, the applicant, apparently unable to bring himself within one of the traditional grounds for exclusion, sought to argue that a statement made by him should be excluded on the ground that he was upset at the time he made it. The Court gave short shrift to this argument saying that this 'would be quite an absurd departure for the law to make'.

Implication of a co-accused A confession is only evidence against the person who made it and is not evidence against a co-accused (*The People v. Keane* (1976) 110 I.L.T.R. 1). However, there is a serious danger that the jury will so regard it. Therefore, it is incumbent upon a trial judge to direct the jury that statements by an accused tending to incriminate a co-accused cannot be used as evidence in deciding the guilt of that co-accused (*The People v. Sherlock* (1975) 1 Frewen 383). This obligation was reiterated by the Court of Criminal Appeal in in *The People v. Ferris*, Court of Criminal Appeal, *ex tempore*, March 11, 1997. However, the Court went on to specify that 'when what is said is simply background material which is equivocal – which does not point to the guilt of the accused on its own – we cannot see that there is any need to give a warning in that situation'. Indeed, it was pointed out that giving a warning in that situation might well do more harm than good from the co-accused's point of view.

COMPLAINTS IN SEXUAL CASES

The law regarding the admission of complaints in sexual cases as laid down by the Court of Criminal Appeal in *The People v. Brophy* [1992] I.L.R.M. 709 (1992 Review, 252), was endorsed and applied by the Court in *The People v. Roughan*, Court of Criminal Appeal, *ex tempore*, June 23, 1997.

The facts are not very clear but it appears that the prosecutrix and her husband visited the home of the accused and her husband's sister on a Sunday and stayed the night. The prosecutrix alleged that she had been raped and sexually assaulted by the applicant that evening but she did not tell either her husband or his sister of the assault. Neither did she tell her husband when they were driving home the next morning but waited until later in the day.

Brophy requires a complaint to be made as speedily as could reasonably be expected and therefore, the question arose as to whether the delay in making the complaint rendered it inadmissible. Her explanation for the delay was that the assault had had a profound psychological effect upon her which made it difficult for her to talk about it. She found it hard to make a complaint to the partner of the man who had been guilty of the assault and she found it hard to complain to her husband in circumstances where, had she complained to him in the house, there might have been a violent confrontation between him and the accused. This explanation was accepted by the trial judge who took the view that the prosecutrix was in such a psychological state that it was not reasonably possible for her to make the complaint until she did. The Court of Criminal Appeal declined to interfere with the decision of the trial judge, which was supported by the evidence.

This decision fits in with the trend in recent years to take a more flexible attitude towards delay by a complainant in making a complaint. There is now a greater appreciation of the complex cocktail of emotions and feelings including shock, fear, distress, remorse, shame, embarrassment and denial which may result from a sexual assault, the effect of which may be to inhibit a complainant from making a complaint even to a trusted friend or close relative (see Úna Ní Raifeartaigh, "The Doctrine of Fresh Complaint in Sexual Cases" (1994) 12 *ILT* 160).

It was also argued that the complaint was not voluntary because it was made in response to questioning by the husband. The prosecutrix and the husband had a conversation in the garden which commenced with her telling him that 'Denis is no gentleman' and the husband then asked a question which resulted in the story coming out. The Court was satisfied that this was not a case of the husband interrogating her and that he merely assisted her in saying something which she herself wished to say.

In *Brophy*, it was also stipulated that a complaint had to be voluntary and not the result of any inducements or exhortations. This does not mean that a complaint in answer to questions is inadmissible *per se* though it is an important factor in determining the voluntariness of a complaint. Perhaps, the dividing line between legitimate and illegitimate questioning was best drawn by Ridley J. in *R. v. Osborne* [1905] 1 K.B. 551, at 556:

> If the circumstances indicate that but for the questioning there probably would have been no voluntary complaint, the answer is inadmissible. If the question merely anticipates a statement which the complainant was about to make, it is not rendered inadmissible by the fact that the questioner happens to speak first.

The facts of *Roughan* fell into the latter category and so, the complaint was admissible.

CORROBORATION

In *The People v. Murphy*, Court of Criminal Appeal, *ex tempore*, November 3, 1997, the appellant had been convicted of the sexual assault of a woman and on appeal, a point was taken as to the trial judge's direction on corroboration. He had defined corroboration along classic *Baskerville* lines as something that tends to implicate the accused in a material way in the crime with which he is involved but he then went on to describe dirt on the complainant's clothes and body as corroborating evidence which supported her account.

It is patently clear that such evidence could not constitute corroboration because it failed to implicate the accused in the offence (see *James v. R.* (1970) 55 Cr. App. Rep. 299). However, the Court held that there had been no misdirection on this point. It was clear that the judge had given a very limited importance to the corroborating evidence and as O'Flaherty J. noted, '[t]he modern law does not require a judge to say anything about corroboration if he is of such a mind.'

Although it is difficult to draw any conclusions from the Court's very brief treatment of the corroboration point, this decision may signal a change in direction from the decision in *The People v. Molloy*, Court of Criminal Appeal, July 28, 1995. There, it was stated that 'where the charge is essentially supported by the evidence of the Complainant alone without collateral forensic evidence or any other form of corroboration, it is a prudent practice for the trial Judge to warn the jury that unless they are very satisfied with the testimony of the Complainant that they should be careful not to convict in the absence of corroborative evidence'. By way of contrast, *Murphy* seems to emphasise the discretion of a trial judge not to give a corroboration warning if he so decides.

This decision leaves a number of questions unanswered and we still await definitive guidance as to the effect of section 7 of the Criminal Law (Rape) (Amendment) Act 1990 and the nature of the obligation, if any, on trial judges to give a corroboration warning in sexual cases.

DOCUMENTARY EVIDENCE

In *In re Article 26 and the Employment Equality Bill 1996* [1997] E.L.R. 132 (discussed in the Labour Law chapter, 485, below), the Supreme Court concluded that section 63(3) of the Bill, which provided for certification of the circumstances of an offence under the section, was repugnant to the provisions of the Constitution.

Section 63(1) created the offences of obstructing or impeding the Labour Court, the Director or an equality officer in the exercise of powers under Part V of the Bill, or failing to comply with a requirement of the Court, Director or an equality officer. Section 63(3) went on to provide that in any proceedings for an offence under the section 'a document purporting to be certified by the Director or to be sealed with the seal of the Court and relating to the circumstances in which the offence is alleged to have occurred shall be received as prima facie evidence of the facts stated therein.'

Following an examination of the wording of the subsection, the Court concluded that it was clear that, in the case of a document purportedly certified by the Director, it could be certified whether or not the Director had direct knowledge of the information being certified. In addition, such certificate could relate to all the circumstances in which the offence is alleged to have occurred.

Hamilton CJ, delivering the decision of the Supreme Court, was of opinion that the subsection raised a fundamental matter touching on the essence of a criminal trial. He pointed out that it is a cardinal principle in our criminal justice system that, in general, trials are conducted on viva voce evidence (citing *In re Haughey* [1971] I.R. 217, 261). Statutory exceptions could be made to this principle but only in relation to specific issues of a scientific or technical nature. This limitation of viva voce evidence is reasonable in circumstances where the evidence is technical and by its form appropriate to certification because this means that many technicians and officials are not required to be called to court in each case. However, the question of whether an offence had been committed under section 63 fell into a different category. It was likely to give rise to a sharp conflict of evidence and was not amenable to proof by certification:

> The idea that a criminal trial could proceed from beginning to end concluding with a verdict of guilty on the production of a document is inconsistent with the concept of trial in due course of law. The use of a certificate as proposed in section 63(3) is to do more than prove evidence of certain technical matters by certificate. It is a document which may be certified by a person with no personal knowledge of or involvement in the events in issue. It purports to relate to all the facts of the offence. No other evidence may be anticipated.

Counsel for the Attorney General sought to rely on *Hardy v. Ireland* [1994] 2 I.R. 550 (1995 Review, 182), to support the proposition that the section was constitutional but it was distinguished by the Court on the basis that to hold 'that there may be documentary evidence from which inferences may be drawn is not to say that the proof of a case may be by certificate.' The Court also rejected purported reliance on *O'Leary v. Attorney General* [1991] I.L.R.M. 454 (HC) (1991 Review, 133); [1995] 2 I.L.R.M. 259 (SC) (1995 Review, 181, 243). Again it did not address the issue raised by section 63 of the entire case being provide on a single certificate where the certifying person may have been informed of the incident only and not have been a party thereto. Indeed, O'Flaherty J. spoke to the very antithesis of such a circumstance when he stated that the courts would not act as 'automatons' in the assessment of evidence.

The Court then considered whether the interference with the right to trial in due course of law was proportional. The Court applied the test of proportionality laid down by the Canadian Supreme Court in *R. v. Oakes* [1986] 1 S.C.R. 103 and *Chaulk v. R.* [1990] 3 S.C.R. 1303 and asked: (a) was the section rationally designed to meet the objective of the legislation? (b) did it intrude into constitutional rights as little as is reasonably possible? (c) was there a proportionality between the section and the right to trial in due course of law and the objective of the legislation?

The Chief Justice concluded that the section failed the first test because the process of certification was not rationally connected to the objective of the Bill. The objective of equality in employment did not require that the offence in section 63 be tried in the manner set out in section 63(3). Thus, there was no rational reason why the process of certification was necessary in this type of case.

In passing, it might be noted the equivalent section in the Equal Status Bill 1997, section 40(3) was found to be unconstitutional for the same reasons in *In re Article 26 and the Equal Status Bill 1997* [1997] E.L.R. 185 (discussed in the Labour Law chapter, 492, below),

The number of provisions providing for certain matters to be proved by certificate have multiplied in recent years. The cumulative effect of these has been a gradual erosion of the orality of the criminal trial. These decisions, however, reaffirm that basic principle of orality and should stand as a bulwark against this creeping certification. The decisions are also welcome in providing a fairly workable test for assessing the constitutionality of certification provisions. These will be held to be a proportionate interference with the principle of *viva voce* evidence where they relate to minor or technical issues in a case which are unlikely to give rise to a conflict of evidence.

A section which would seem to easily pass the test posited in the *Employment Equality Bill Case* is section 6 of the Criminal Justice (Miscellaneous Provisions) Act 1997. This section allows certain evidence of a formalistic nature to be given via certificate. Thus, section 6(1) provides that on the first appearance of a person arrested without a warrant before the District Court, a signed certificate stating that a garda arrested, charged or cautioned a person with regard to a specified offence shall be admissible as evidence of the matters stated in the certificate. Section 6(2) which applies in any criminal proceedings allows evidence to be given on certificate, *inter alia*, that a garda commenced duty, or replaced a specified member on duty, at a specified time at a place (i) where the offence to which such proceedings relate is alleged to have been committed, (ii) adjacent to such a place, or (iii) containing evidence of the offence to which the proceedings relate. The type of evidence to which both of these subsections relate is of the formalistic variety and the use of certification will prevent the waste of scarce garda resources in giving evidence of these matters which are unlikely to give rise to contention. If a conflict of evidence as to any of these matters, then section 6(4) can be invoked. This provides that the court may, if it considers that the interests of justice so require, direct that oral evidence of the matters stated in a certificate should be given, and the court may for the purpose of receiving oral evidence adjourn the proceedings to a later date.

Regulations for the form of the certificate have been made and are to be found in the Criminal Justice (Miscellaneous Provisions) Act 1997 (Section 6) Regulations 1997 (S.I. No. 345 of 1997).

EXAMINATION OF WITNESSES

In *The People v. Roughan*, Court of Criminal Appeal, *ex tempore*, June 23, 1997, the applicant had been convicted of rape and sexual assault. One of the grounds of appeal advanced was that the trial judge had erred in holding that it was not improper for the prosecution in cross-examination to put it to the accused that the complainant was either lying or perjuring herself. The Court agreed that a question 'put in that particular form implying that either the prosecutrix is a perjuress or the accused guilty of rape is one which is inherently unfair to the accused in that the jury might take the view that if they acquitted the accused they would be implying that the prosecutrix was a perjuress.'

There were many reasons why a jury might acquit an accused short of concluding that the prosecutrix was lying. Thus, while counsel may clearly suggest that a witness is not telling the truth or is not reliable, the Court was of the view that 'the advancement of justice in a trial is not helped by forcing a witness to take up so extreme an attitude particularly in relation to a question like perjury'.

EXPERT EVIDENCE

In *Fitzpatrick v. Director of Public Prosecutions*, High Court, December 5, 1997 (see the Criminal Law chapter, 293, above), the complainants were two sisters who had allegedly been sexually abused on a regular basis over a long period by members of their family. They also alleged incidents of abuse by the applicant who was a neighbour and he was charged with two sexual offences.

The applicant brought judicial review proceedings seeking an order of prohibition preventing his trial on the ground of delay. One of the affidavits filed by the respondent was sworn by a senior clinical psychologist. The purpose of this affidavit was to give expert evidence to explain why such a long period had elapsed between the alleged offences and the ultimate complaints. In the affidavit, he failed to mention the abuse of the complainants by members of their family or the psychological effect which this might have had on them. Under cross-examination, he sought to explain this omission on the basis that did not know of the allegations against the members of the family and he did not think that the fact that the complainants had been abused by someone else should form part of his report.

Speaking of this failure, which he characterised as 'astonishing', McCracken J. said that:

> It is my strongly held view that where a witness purports to give evidence in a professional capacity as an expert witness, he owes a duty to

dence in a professional capacity as an expert witness, he owes a duty to ascertain all the surrounding facts and to give that evidence in the context of those facts, whether they support the proposition which he is being asked to put forward or not.

He did not accept that the background of abuse of the complainants was not relevant and as a consequence, he gave little weight to the evidence of the psychologist.

Because the opinion evidence of experts is likely to carry great weight, it is natural that higher standards of impartiality and research should be required. An expert's duties and responsibilities in this regard have been articulated in other jurisdictions, most notably by Cresswell J. in *National Justice Cia Naviera S.A. v. Prudential Assurance Co. Ltd.* [1993] 2 Lloyd's Rep. 68, at 81. He enumerated a list of duties which included the following:

1. Expert evidence presented to the Court should be, and should be seen to be, the independent product of the expert uninfluenced as to form or content by the exigencies of litigation.
2. An expert witness should provide independent assistance to the Court by way of objective unbiased opinion in relation to matters within his expertise. An expert witness should never assume the role of advocate.
3. An expert witness should state the facts or assumptions upon which his opinion is based. He should not omit to consider material facts which could detract from his concluded opinion.
4. An expert witness should make it clear when a particular question or issue falls outside his expertise.
5. If an expert's opinion is not properly researched because he considers that insufficient date is available, then this must be stated with an indication that the opinion is no more than a provisional one.

In seems likely, on the strength of *Fitzpatrick*, that this catalogue of duties would meet with approval in this jurisdiction.

FALSE EVIDENCE

In *Curran v. Gallagher*, Supreme Court, May 7, 1997, the members of the Court disagreed as to the inferences which could be drawn where the plaintiff gave false evidence.

The plaintiff was injured when the car in which he was travelling collided with a wall and lamp post late at night. He sued the driver of the car (the first named defendant), the owner of the car (the second named defendant) and the

Motor Insurers Bureau of Ireland. A default judgment was obtained against the first and second named defendants and the M.I.B.I. denied liability to satisfy this judgment on the basis that the plaintiff either knew, or should reasonably have known, that the use of the vehicle was not covered by insurance.

On the night in question, the plaintiff, the first named defendant and a number of others had been out drinking. At 1 a.m., they left one licensed premises with the intention of going to another but while en route, the car in which they were travelling broke down. As it happened, the mother of the first named defendant worked at an Old Folks home nearby and the family car was parked outside. The first named defendant took the car and shortly afterwards the accident occurred.

There was a dispute about the circumstances surrounding the taking of the car which bore on the question as to whether the first named defendant had permission to drive the car. Her evidence was to the effect that the car was unlocked and that the key was under the mat. She simply retrieved the key, got into the car and drove off. However, the evidence of the plaintiff was that the first named defendant had knocked on a window of the Old Folks Home and that her mother had handed her the keys.

In the High Court, Carroll J. accepted the first named defendant's account in preference to that of the plaintiff and concluded that the circumstances surrounding the taking of the car were suspicious and that the plaintiff ought to have known that she was not insured. One of the matters which she took into account in reaching this conclusion was her finding that the plaintiff had lied about the circumstances attending the taking of the car.

A majority of the Supreme Court allowed the appeal. Lynch J., with whom Keane J. concurred, pointed out that the test of knowledge was subjective and the onus of proof was on the defendants (*Kinsella v. Motor Insurers Bureau of Ireland*, Supreme Court, April 2, 1993). Bearing that in mind, he took the view that if the evidence of the first named defendant had stood uncontradicted, it would not have established knowledge on the part of the plaintiff that the first defendant did not have authority to take the car. As to the question of the inference to be drawn from the plaintiff's false account, Lynch J. pointed out that it is 'a regrettable and reprehensible fact that litigants sometimes exaggerate and even grossly exaggerate their cases'. In this case, the plaintiff had fabricated evidence in an effort to strengthen his case. However, while the fact that he lied tended to suggest and did suggest to the trial judge the inference that he knew more than he admitted, it did not establish as matter of probability that he knew that the first named defendant did not have authority to take the car.

Murphy J. dissenting, took a different view. He opined that while there were different reasons why the plaintiff might have concocted his account, 'the proper inference to draw from the fact that he was prepared to give and did give untruthful evidence was that he was understandably apprehensive that a court of law would draw the same conclusions as he had drawn from the facts as they truly were.'

The significance of the lie in this case depended on the motive for it and the divergence of opinion as to the proper inference to be drawn from the plaintiff's lie reflected an underlying divergence of opinion as to the motive for the lie. A majority of the Court took the view that the plaintiff gave false evidence simply in an effort to bolster his case while Murphy J. was of the opinion that the plaintiff knew that the first defendant did not have permission and was worried that if he told the truth the court would realise that.

In most cases, there will not be reliable information available to the court as to the motive for the lie and it will fall to the court to infer from the facts what it was. This is not an easy task and will depend on wider issues of credibility. Therefore, when such an inference falls to be reviewed by a higher court, considerable weight should be given to the conclusion reached by the trial judge.

HEARSAY

Opinion polls In *Hanafin v. Minister for the Environment* [1996] 2 I.R. 321, the petitioner sought to adduce evidence of opinion polls taken before the Divorce Referendum in order to establish the voting intentions of the people. The respondents objected to the admissibility of the opinion polls on the ground that they were hearsay evidence.

The Divisional High Court held, in a judgment delivered by Murphy J., that evidence obtained by a properly conducted research survey was admissible proof of the fact that the opinions obtained had in fact existed and was therefore, not hearsay. Alternatively, even if the opinion polls were hearsay, they were admissible by way of an exception to the hearsay rule as evidence of the state of mind of the public.

In reaching this conclusion, extensive reliance was placed on the judgment of Mahon J. in *Customglass Boats Ltd. v. Salthouse Brothers Ltd.* [1976] 1 N.Z.L.R. 36; [1976] R.P.C. 589. The learned judge was of the opinion that:

> The evidence obtained by research survey is in my view legitimate proof of the fact the opinions obtained had in fact existed, whether rightly held or not, and on that view of the matter it is my opinion that such evidence is not hearsay at all and that, even if it did fall within the technical concept of hearsay or [sic] representing a collation of individual statements made out of court, then the evidence would still be admissible by way of exception to the hearsay rule because it exhibits the existence of a state of mind shared in common by a designated class of persons.

Survey evidence is treated as admissible throughout the common law world. However, a considerable difference of opinion exists as to the basis on which such evidence is admissible. Indeed, there is a clearly an element of *ex post facto* reasoning to the admission of such evidence. Survey evidence is regarded as the best evidence available of public opinion. The alternative is the impractical one of calling the respondents surveyed to give their opinions first hand. Furthermore, if the survey is properly conducted according to generally recognised standards, then such evidence is quite reliable. Therefore, the question becomes one, not of whether such evidence should be admitted, but of finding a satisfactory basis on which to admit it.

One approach is to say that such evidence is not hearsay at all. This, as we have seen, was the opinion of Mahon J. in *Customglass* and was also the view taken by Falconer J. in *Lego Systems Aktienelskab v. Lego M. Lemelstrich Ltd.* [1983] F.S.R. 155, at 179, who concurred that survey evidence 'is not hearsay at all, but is evidence proving an external fact, namely, that a particular opinion was held by the public or class of public'. This approach proceeds on the basis that the survey evidence is adduced merely to prove the fact that the opinions found actually existed, rather than to prove that such opinions are correct. Thus, such evidence falls outside the scope of the hearsay rule and is admitted as original evidence of the fact that the persons surveyed held the opinions expressed.

However, the problem with this approach is that while the correctness of the opinions is not in issue, the question of whether they were genuinely held or not is. The survey evidence is adduced to prove that the section of the public surveyed held a certain opinion. Yet, it can only do this if the persons surveyed actually held those views. Therefore, the answers of the respondents to the survey fall squarely within the scope of the hearsay rule.

This leaves the question of whether survey evidence is admissible under an exception to the hearsay rule. The applicable exception propounded by Mahon J. in *Customglass* was the state of mind exception. This is a limb of the inclusionary doctrine of *res gestae* whereby statements by a person as to his contemporaneous state of mind or emotion are admissible as evidence of the existence of that state or mind or emotion. Authority to support the view that survey evidence can be admitted under this head can be found in *R. v. Vincent* (1840) 9 C. & P. 275. A question arose as to whether a particular public meeting had caused alarm and a police officer was called to prove that a number of people had complained to him that the meeting had made them fearful and apprehensive. The objection that this evidence was hearsay was overruled on the basis that in order to prove the state of mind of the public, it is permissible for a witness to give evidence of the feelings and emotions expressed to him by members of the public. With regard to opinion polls which elicit voting intentions, it is clear that this exception also covers declarations of intention which are admissible as evidence of the existence of that intention at the time

Mellish L.J.)).

On balance, it would seem that the better view is that survey evidence is admissible hearsay. However, such evidence does potentially suffer from hearsay dangers such as inaccuracy and insincerity so it is necessary that it be admitted subject to certain safeguards. This was recognised by Mahon J. who cautioned that the weight of such evidence would depend on the circumstances and that care must be taken in the way that the questions asked were drawn up and in how the survey was conducted:

> There must be a formulation of questions cast in such a way as to preclude a weighted or conditioned response, there must be clear proof that the answers were faithfully and accurately recorded, and there must be evidence that the answers were drawn from a true cross-section of that class of the public or trade whose impression or opinion is relevant to the matter in issue.

Murphy J. in *Hanafin* endorsed these safeguards and also stated that the weight to be attached to such evidence would be a matter for the court to decide.

Proceeds of crime   Section 8 of the Proceeds of Crime Act 1996 (1996 Review 321) renders admissible the opinion evidence of a garda or authorised officer in applications under sections 2 and 3 of the Act. Such evidence is likely to contain a significant hearsay element and concern on this account was expressed by Moriarty J. in *M.M. v. D.D.*, High Court, December 10, 1996 (see the Criminal Law chapter, 325, above), and McGuinness J. in *Gilligan v. Criminal Assets Bureau*, High Court, June 26, 1997 (see the Constitutional Law chapter, 195, above).

In *M. v. D.*, Moriarty J. was satisfied that the proofs adduced merited the relief sought but he specifically reserved 'to another occasion consideration of the hypothesis of how a case in which hearsay proof of suspicion alone is tendered, particularly if likely to be substantiated by a plea of privilege on challenge, should be addressed by the Court'. Moreover, he acknowledged 'concern that significant circumspection and care for such a respondent's entitlements may require to be exercised, and that a generalised advertance to "the innocent who have nothing to fear" would not appear to in any realistic sense satisfy the requirements of Section 2 or 3 of the Proceeds of Crime Act 1996'.

Moriarty J.'s concern about the prospect of making orders under sections 2 or 3 of the 1996 Act on hearsay proof of suspicion alone was echoed by McGuinness J. in *Gilligan*. She was of the view that a court should be slow to make orders under section 3 on the basis of such evidence without other corroborating evidence. She said that, although the courts would undoubtedly conduct the procedures of the 1996 Act in accordance with constitutional justice, in dealing with the type of evidence allowed under section 8, any Court would have to take special care to protect the rights of a Respondent.

Tribunals An objection to the admission of hearsay evidence in disciplinary proceedings was considered in *Maher v. Irish Permanent plc*, High Court, October 7, 1997 (see the Labour Law chapter, 517, below).

IDENTIFICATION EVIDENCE

In-court identifications In *The People v. Cooney* [1998] 1 I.L.R.M. 321, the appellant had been arrested on suspicion of murder and while he was in custody, two identification parades were held in which a number of witnesses identified the appellant as the perpetrator. At the trial, the judge concluded that the appellant had been in unlawful custody at the time these parades were held and therefore, he excluded evidence of both of them. He did, however, allow the witnesses to identify the accused in court.

The appellant applied to the Court of Criminal Appeal for leave to appeal on the ground that the trial judge had erred in law, or alternatively in the exercise of his discretion, in allowing the identification evidence of the witnesses to go to the jury. The Court refused leave to appeal but certified, pursuant to section 29 of the Courts of Justice Act 1924, that its decision involved a point of law of exceptional public importance and that it was desirable in the public interest that an appeal should be taken to the Supreme Court.

The Court, in a decision delivered by Keane J., accepted that in-court identification was an undesirable and unsatisfactory procedure:

> Our criminal law has for a long time recognised that so called 'dock identifications' are undesirable and unsatisfactory. The reason is obvious: save in what are called 'recognition' cases (where the identifying witness knew the suspect before seeing him or her commit the alleged offence), the identification of the accused for the first time when he or she is sitting in the place normally reserved for the accused and usually flanked by prison officers is of limited probative value.

Therefore, in cases where the identification of the accused is likely to be an issue, the appropriate procedure is to hold an identification parade or, if that is impracticable, to afford the witness some other opportunity of identifying the accused. However, even where such procedures were not adopted, evidence of a dock identification could still be admitted in exceptional circumstances at the discretion of the trial judge.

Keane J. was of the view that the facts of the instant case provided an example of where a trial judge could exercise his or her discretion to admit example of where a trial judge could exercise his or her discretion to admit such identifications:

> Once it had been established to his satisfaction that a formal identifica-
> tion parade had been held, that it had complied with the normal require-
> ments as to the holding of such a parade and that the fact that it was held
> at a time when the appellant was in unlawful custody was not the result
> of any action taken *mala fide* by the gardaí, the court is satisfied that it
> was within his discretion to allow evidence of an identification in court,
> unless he was of the view that its prejudicial value [*sic*] would outweigh
> any probative value it might have.

Having held that the dock identification evidence was admissible, the other question was whether the trial judge had adequately warned the jury of the dangers of relying on it. Proceeding by analogy with *The People v. McDermott* [1991] 1 I.R. 359 (1991 Review 154), Keane J. held that where such evidence was given, in addition to the normal Casey warning, it was also necessary to warn the jury of the particular and accentuated dangers attendant upon in-court identification evidence. The warning given by the trial judge in this case met the required standard because he had 'not only warned the jury in express terms of the dangers inherent in every form of identification evidence, but specifically directed the attention of the jury to the particular dangers associ-ated with a 'dock identification' and the necessity for additional caution be-cause of that factor alone'.

The Court also rejected the submission of the appellant that the defence had been unfairly inhibited in the cross-examination of the identification wit-nesses. This was the unavoidable consequence of the exclusion of the evi-dence, at the instance of the defence, of the identification parades. In addition, the defence was in a position to lay stress, when addressing the jury, on the absence of any pre-trial identification procedures.

This case emphasises, once more, the importance of identification proce-dures to the reliability and probative value of identification evidence. An in-court identification which is not preceded by any form of pre-trial identification procedure is very unreliable and thus should normally be excluded on the basis that its prejudicial effect outweighs its probative value. This is because, as pointed out by Keane J., the procedure is inherently suggestible because of the circumstances in which it takes place. In addition, a witness may feel some pressure to identify the accused and may do so even if he or she has some residual doubts on the basis that the Gardaí must have arrested the right per-son. The effect of these factors has been that in some cases, witnesses have purported to identify a defendant in-court despite having failed to do so at an earlier identification parade (see, for example, *The People v. Bond* [1966] I.R. 225).

However, the balance alters significantly in favour of admission where an in-court identification has been preceded by a properly conducted identification parade. It is this factor which was crucial in *Cooney*. Although, the identification parades themselves were not admissible, the fact that the witnesses had picked out the appellant in such parades greatly lessened the suggestibility of the in-court identification and strengthened its probative value. If such parades had not been conducted, then it is unlikely that the evidence would have been admitted.

Recognition evidence In *The People v. Murphy*, Court of Criminal Appeal, *ex tempore*, November 3, 1997, it was held that the trial judge erred in failing to give a *Casey* warning with regard to recognition evidence which was challenged by the defence. The Court thus confirmed what was implicit in *The People v. Casey* [1963] I.R. 33 and made explicit in *The People v. Stafford* [1983] I.R. 165, namely that the *Casey* warning applies equally to recognition evidence though a stronger warning may be required where there is no previous acquaintance between the witness and the defendant. The reason for extending the cautionary instruction to recognition evidence was pinpointed by Lord Widgery C.J. in *R. v. Turnbull* [1977] Q.B. 224; [1976] 3 All E.R. 549: 'Recognition may be more reliable than identification of a stranger; but even when the witness is purporting to recognise someone whom he knows, the jury should be reminded that mistakes in recognition of close relatives and friends are sometimes made.'

Withdrawal of identification evidence from the jury In *The People v. Kavanagh*, Court of Criminal Appeal, *ex tempore*, July 7, 1997, the applicant failed in his submission that the trial judge had erred in refusing to grant an application for a direction at the end of the prosecution case.

The applicant was convicted of the murder of Patrick Craig. On the night of the murder, the Craig family had been watching television in their house in Neilstown when two men burst into the living room wearing balaclavas. One of the men said 'Don't anyone move' and he shot Patrick Craig in the head.

Crucial to the prosecution case was the identification evidence of the deceased's wife Mrs. Craig and three of her daughters. She said that she recognised the accused, who was married to her sister, through his eyes, his build, his height and his voice. The three girls also identified him to varying degrees but all stated that they recognised his voice.

On appeal, it was argued that the identification evidence of the accused was very frail and that it was incumbent upon the prosecution to have arranged for some form of identification parade to find out whether the evidence of the Mrs. Craig and her daughters could be relied upon. However, the Court agreed with the prosecution that the holding of a parade was not practical. The Court was of the view that this would be an 'unreal' exercise and expressed its scepticism that the applicant would have used his authentic voice if invited to speak at such a parade. The Court then considered the question of whether the evidence should have been withdrawn from the jury:

> [T]he Court is convinced that it was not such a case that the evidence was so thin that the jury should not have been entrusted with it. It became at the end of the day, after most careful directions at every stage by the learned trial judge, a matter for the jury to decide whether they could be convinced beyond all reasonable doubt of the guilt of the accused.

It is clear that although the holding of an identification parade may render admissible weak identification evidence which would otherwise be excluded, the mere failure to hold a parade does not render inadmissible identification evidence which is strong enough to leave to the jury. Here, the evidence was certainly not strong but it seems as if it was not weak enough to withdraw it from the jury. A very important factor was that the applicant was well known to Mrs. Craig and thus, her evidence fell into the category of recognition evidence rather than mere identification evidence. This had the effect of strengthening her evidence sufficiently to justify its admission in the same way as the profession of the security guard did in *The People v. O'Callaghan*, Court of Criminal Appeal, July 30, 1990 (1990 Review 209).

In this case, it is not clear whether the holding of an identification parade was as impracticable as suggested. Certainly, with regard to having the participants speak the words spoken at the time of the shooting, there was a danger of the applicant frustrating the parade by putting on a false voice. However, it seems that it would have possible to test the visual identification evidence. In view of the fact that the assailant was wearing a balaclava, it would have added considerably to the reliability and probative value of Mrs. Craig's evidence had she been able to pick out the accused wearing a balaclava in a suitably arranged identification parade.

The Court also had to consider whether the trial judge had given the jury an adequate warning of the dangers of acting on the identification evidence in the case. O'Flaherty J. referred to the comment of Kingsmill Moore J. in *The People v. Casey (No.2)* [1963] I.R. 33, 40, that the direction is 'not meant to be a stereotypical formula' and said that:

> The Court rejects the idea that there should be a mechanical repetition of everything that is set forth in the *Casey* judgment. On the contrary, a judge should be accorded a wide discretion to express the warning in the way that he thinks best – having regard to the underlying rationale of the *Casey* decision.

In *Casey*, it was stipulated that one witness could not corroborate another and that it was necessary to examine the identification evidence of each witness separately. The Court here was satisfied that the trial judge had not contravened this prohibition against mutual corroboration by telling the jury that where more than one person recognised the accused, the case is stronger. This was logical.

The stress which the Court placed on the flexibility of the *Casey* warning and the need to tailor it to the circumstances of the case is welcome and should help to prevent the calcification of the warning into a ritualistic formula with attendant technicalities. One surprising point though, especially in light of the Court's invocation of the free-flowing form of the *Casey* warning is that there is no statement of the need for a particularly strong warning in light of the weakness of the identification evidence in the case. The actual terms of the trial judge's direction on corroboration are not set forth in the judgment of the Court of Criminal Appeal so it is difficult to know how far the trial judge went in emphasising the weakness of the identification evidence but at a minimum a warning as to the special difficulties in the case due to the fact that the assailant had been wearing a balaclava and because no identification parade had been held would have been required.

IMPROPERLY OBTAINED EVIDENCE

In *The People v. Cooney* [1998] 1 I.L.R.M. 321, the facts of which are set out above, the Supreme Court also rejected the submission, based on *The State (Trimbole) v. Governor of Mountjoy Prison* [1985] I.R. 550; [1985] I.L.R.M. 465, that the in-court identifications were irremediably tainted because of their association with the earlier identification parades and thus, should have been excluded as the fruits of an unconstitutional procedure. Keane J. stated that:

> The identification procedures were held by [the gardaí] in accordance with recognised procedures which ensured fairness to the appellant. The infringement by the garda officers of the appellant's constitutional rights was not *mala fide*: his unlawful detention was the result of their misunderstanding of the true legal position. The application by the learned trial judge of the strict exclusionary principle as to evidence obtained during such an unlawful detention led, on the application of the defence, to the ruling as inadmissible of any evidence in relation to the identification procedures. The appellant's constitutional rights were thus upheld in full and it was not in any sense a necessary consequence of their vindication that the further identification by the witnesses of the appellant in court, with all its attendant frailties, should be excluded.

It was the absence of *mala fides* which distinguished this case from *Trimbole* and it seems to be implicit in the decision that, if *mala fides* had been present, the Court might have reached a different conclusion. It therefore appears that, although the presence of absence of *mala fides* is irrelevant to the application of the exclusionary rule, it will be a very important factor in determining whether a breach of the constitutional rights of the accused will have any consequences beyond the exclusion of any evidence obtained as a result thereof. Thus, where it is present, the courts may well take a transactional approach which eschews the strict causation requirement applied as an adjunct to the exclusionary rule and exclude evidence obtained following, and not just because of, a breach of the accused's constitutional rights.

Thus, in *Cooney*, even though the evidence of the identification parades was not admissible, the fact that witnesses has picked out the appellant in them added probative force to their in-court identifications and had an important bearing on their admissibility. To that extent, the evidence of the parades was not totally discounted although it was not admissible as such. However, if the gardaí had acted *mala fides*, then the Court might well have taken a different approach and held that evidence of the identification parades could not be used or considered for any purpose.

PRIVILEGE

Attorney General   Judgment in three companion cases, *Duncan v. Governor of Portlaoise Prison, O'Neill v. Governor of Mountjoy Prison* and *Quinlivan v. Governor of Portlaoise Prison*, arising out of the 'Judge Dominic Lynch affair' was delivered by Kelly J. on January 23, 1997. In each of the cases, discovery of certain documentation pertaining to the detention of applicants was sought from the respondents and notice parties and this was resisted on the grounds of legal professional privilege and executive privilege.

In *Duncan v. Governor of Portlaoise Prison* [1997] 1 I.R. 558; [1997] 2 I.L.R.M. 296, a claim of legal professional privilege was made in respect of a number of documents. The legitimacy of the claim was not disputed but it was submitted that the Court should direct the production of the documents with a view to the court reading them and extracting from them the factual content, in respect of which legal professional privilege would not apply. However, Kelly J. rejected this 'unprecedented' proposition:

> It appears to me that the proposition advanced by [counsel] to the effect that the Court ought in this case to direct the production of the documents in respect of which legal professional privilege is claimed and then, in effect, edit them so as to make factual matter in them disclosable to him, would be to dilute in very considerable measure the whole notion and effect of legal professional privilege. It would, in my view, be

an unwarranted and dangerous course to embark upon and would amount to a serious interference with what the then Lord Chief Justice of England described [in *R. v. Derby Magistrates' Court, ex p. B.* [1995] 3 W.L.R. 681, at 695] as "a fundamental condition on which the administration of justice as a whole rests".

He went on to point out the practical difficulties attendant upon the proposition:

> If [counsel] is correct in his submission, any case in which legal professional privilege is claimed may, on the simple request of the opponent, result in the court being called upon to go through the entire of the documents with a view to ascertaining, not the validity of the claim to legal professional privilege, but rather to engage in the work of editing the documents with a view to extracting from them factual material to be disclosed to the other side. This exercise would have to be conducted at a time in advance of the trial when no judge can be fully apprised of the entire factual matrix against which the action is brought. The conduct of such an exercise would, in my view, be much more likely to work against the administration of justice than in its favour.

He did state that in a rare case where cogent evidence was adduced to suggest that a claim of legal professional privilege was being wrongfully asserted, a court could direct production of the documents for inspection. However, this would solely be for the purpose of ascertaining whether or not the documents were truly privileged.

It should be noted that, apart from the objections voiced by Kelly J., there was a more fundamental problem with the contention of the applicant. It seems to proceed on the basis that legal professional privilege only applies to legal advice passing between a legal adviser and client and, therefore, that it would be possible to separate any factual information communicated from the advice element. However, legal privilege not only protects legal advice, it also protects the communication of factual information. Indeed, one of the limbs of legal privilege, namely litigation privilege, is expressly designed to protect the communication of factual information in anticipation of litigation. Even with regard to legal advice privilege, any factual information in a communication giving or seeking legal advice is likely to be so inextricably intertwined with that advice, that it would be difficult, not to say unfair, to try to separate one from the other. Therefore, to hold that factual information contained in privileged documents could be edited and disclosed would be to totally emasculate legal privilege as we know it. How could a client 'make a clean breast of it' (*per* Jessel M.R. in *Anderson v. Bank of British Columbia* (1876) 2 Ch. D. 644, at 649) if he or she knew that any factual information communicated to his or her legal adviser was liable to disclosure?

Similar submissions to those advanced in *Duncan* were also made in *O'Neill* and *Quinlivan*, and were disposed of in the same manner. However, in *Quinlivan*, an additional submission was made that the claim of legal professional privilege made by the notice parties ought to be disallowed because of the existence of a conspiracy between the Director of Public Prosecutions, the Minister for Justice and the Attorney General to deprive the applicant of his right to liberty. This submission was summarily rejected by Kelly J. because there was no evidence at all to support it. He characterised the claim as one of "extravagant speculation" and said that in the absence of any evidence to support it, should not have been made.

In each of the three cases, the applicants also challenged the claim made of executive privilege made in respect of the documents. However, because in each of the cases the claim of legal professional privilege had not been upset, Kelly J. declined to address the arguments made regarding executive privilege as it would be otiose to do so.

An appeal by the applicants to the Supreme Court *sub nom. Quinlivan v. Governor of Portlaoise Prison*, Supreme Court, March 5, 1997, was dismissed. At the hearing of the appeal, only one document was disputed, a letter written by the Attorney General to the Minister for Justice, in respect of which legal professional privilege was claimed.

Although the Attorney General has other functions, the Court was satisfied that the letter was written by the Attorney General pursuant to his position as legal advisor to the Government under Article 30 and was therefore privileged. Hamilton C.J. said:

> There is no doubt whatsoever but that communications containing legal advice are privileged documents by virtue of the long-held principles of the common law relating to the privilege attaching to communications between legal advisers and their clients which has always been regarded by the Courts as absolutely essential to and of paramount importance in the administration of justice. People should be entitled to communicate with their legal advisers with a certain and considerable degree of confidentiality and that is the position which was accepted by the learned trial judge.

The Court also rejected the submission that it would be open to it to edit the document and discover purely factual information. Keane J. said that this proposition 'is unsupported by authority, is clearly incorrect in principle and, if admitted, would undermine the whole basis of legal professional privilege.'

The Court also rejected the submission that privilege should be pierced because of a conspiracy between certain organs and officers of the State. There was no evidence to substantiate this claim and the trial judge had been correct to dismiss it.

Legal professional privilege In *Gallagher v. Stanley*, Supreme Court, December 18, 1997, the defendants claimed privilege in respect of certain documents on the basis that they were created in contemplation of litigation.

The infant plaintiff had a very difficult birth in the National Maternity Hospital, as a result of which he was severely disabled. The documents in question were statements made by nurses on duty the night of the birth. They had been requested to make these the following morning by the Matron of the hospital. In her affidavit, the Matron stated that she had requested the statements because she anticipated litigation and intended to furnish them to the legal secretary of the hospital.

The claim of privilege was rejected by Moriarty J. who concluded, in view of the fact that the statements had been made very near the time of the birth, that the suggestion that the statements had come into existence in anticipation of proceedings was unwarrantedly premature. On appeal, the Supreme Court agreed that the documents were not covered by privilege.

The leading judgment was delivered by O'Flaherty J. He stated that the purpose of legal professional privilege is 'to aid the administration of justice; not to impede it. In general, justice will be best served where there is the greatest candour and where all relevant documentary evidence is available.' With regard to litigation privilege, he said that 'it is essential that litigation should be reasonably apprehended at the least before a claim of privilege can be upheld.'

In assessing the purposes behind the genesis of the statements, he used the dominant purpose test laid down by the House of Lords in *Waugh v. British Railways Board* [1980] A.C. 521, and endorsed by O'Hanlon J. in *Silver Hill Duckling Ltd. v. Minister for Agriculture* [1987] I.R. 289 (1987 Review, 280) in preference to the sole purpose test formulated by the High Court of Australia in *Grant v. Downs* (1976) 135 C.L.R. 674. Thus, the test to be applied was whether the dominant purpose for which the documents came into being was apprehension or anticipation of litigation.

He accepted that, in view of the increasingly litigious nature of society, apprehension of litigation was a consideration in the Matron requesting the statements. However, it was not the sole purpose nor the dominant purpose. He was satisfied that the main concern of the Matron was that she should be in a position to account for the events of the night in question and how the staff under her control had conducted themselves. Thus, this information was required for the proper management and running of the hospital. He said:

> Both principles, full disclosure on the one hand and legal professional privilege on the other, are there to advance the cause of justice. Sometimes they may be on a collision course, but not, I think, here. This is not like a case where a client is expected to deal with his lawyer with the utmost disclosure so that the case will be properly presented. It is rather

a case where both sides are entitled to know what exactly happened before and at the birth of the infant. After all the nurses are the mother and the child's nurses as well as being hospital employees. I believe it is likely to help the course of the trial if these documents are made available to the plaintiff's advisers now and I do not see that the principle of legal professional privilege suffers in any way.

He had read the documents since preparing his judgment and this confirmed his belief that they were essentially straightforward accounts of events and conversations, and did not contain any element that should attract an entitlement to legal professional privilege.

In their concurring judgments, Lynch J. and Barron J. also endorsed the dominant motive test. Lynch J. pointed out that people often act for mixed motives and therefore the sole purpose test set too high a threshold for the application of privilege. The true test is that anticipation and/or contemplation of litigation should have been the dominant motive or reason. Barron J. stressed that it was the Court's view as to the motive for the statements, not that of the hospital which was important. Bare assertion on the part of the hospital was not enough without anything to back it up. If there were good reasons why there was no need to take statements from the nurses in relation to hospital administration, there was no reason why such should not have been put on affidavit. In the circumstances, the view of the Court that the threat of legal proceedings was not the predominant reason was a proper one. He also criticised the defendants for seeking to suppress innocuous documents.

This decision is important because it gives the *imprimatur* of the Supreme Court to the dominant motive test which had previously been endorsed by O'Hanlon J. in *Silver Hill Duckling*. However, it is clear that the Court will apply the test in quite a rigorous manner. Such an approach is justified because, in cases where there are multiple motives, a party is inevitably going to claim that preparation for litigation was the dominant motive. Thus, in order to keep litigation privilege within reasonable bounds, it will be necessary for a court to go behind the affidavits of the party resisting discovery and ascertain, objectively, what the dominant purpose for the genesis of the documents was. Here, the Supreme Court did this and concluded that hospital administration was the dominant motive.

Indeed, one of the striking features of this case is the obvious desire of the Supreme Court to circumscribe the potentially wide orbit of litigation privilege. As pointed out, society has become increasingly litigious. Therefore, whenever any sort of mishap occurs, litigation is always a possibility. To accept privilege merely on this basis would be to greatly expand the potential scope of legal privilege to the detriment of the administration of justice. Therefore, the scepticism of the Court towards claims of this type is both welcome and necessary.

Statutory privilege In *O'Brien v. Minister for Defence*, Supreme Court, July 7, 1997, the plaintiff, whose husband had been killed serving with UNIFIL in the Lebanon, instituted proceedings claiming damages in respect of the death of her husband. She brought a motion for further and better discovery in respect of the reports and documentation generated in the course of two inquires into the death of her husband: (i) a United Nations Inquiry, and (ii) a Court of Inquiry held under the Defence Act 1954. The relief sought was refused by O'Hanlon J. (*sub nom. O'Brien v. Ireland* [1995] 1 I.L.R.M. 22 (1994 Review, 375)) and she appealed to the Supreme Court.

At the hearing of the appeal it was conceded that the documentation relating to the United Nations Inquiry was privileged and therefore, the Court only examined the question as to whether the documents relating to the Court of Inquiry were privileged. The claim of privilege in respect of these documents was based primarily on Regulation 11(2) of the Defence Forces Regulations 1982 (No. A5) which provides that the findings and recommendations of all courts of inquiry shall be treated as confidential and shall not be disclosed to interested parties except as provided in section 181(2) of the Defence Act 1954, the Rules of Procedure (Defence Forces) 1954 and the Defence Forces Regulations (No. A8).

It was submitted by the defendant that the Court should extend this statutory privilege to cover all proceedings and all statements made by witnesses before the Court of Inquiry. However, the Court agreed with the submission of the plaintiff that the privilege granted extended only to the findings and recommendations of the Court of Inquiry.

The Court availed of the opportunity to make some comments as to the form in which privilege should be claimed. Hamilton C.J. stated that it is not sufficient to claim general privilege in respect of bundles of documents or files:

> The onus is on the Defendant to specify in detail by number each of the documents in their possession relating to matters the subject matter of the proceedings and to specify in detail the nature of the privilege claimed in respect of each document and the basis for such privilege.

This statement repeats the direction given by Finlay C.J. in *Bula Ltd. v. Crowley* [1991] 1 I.R. 220, at 222; [1990] I.L.R.M. 756, at 758 (1990 Review, 432), that what is required is 'an individual listing of the documents with the general classification of privilege claim in respect of each document indicated in such fashion by enumeration as would convey to a reader of the affidavit the general nature of the document concerned in each individual case together with the broad heading of privilege claimed for it.' He opined that this was necessary in order to comply with the principles laid down by the Court in *Smurfit Paribas Bank Ltd. v. A.A.B. Export Finance Ltd.* [1990] 1 I.R. 469;

[1990] I.L.R.M. 558 (1990 Review, 435).

A claim of statutory privilege was also rejected by the Supreme Court in *Skeffington v. Rooney* [1997] 1 I.R. 22; [1997] 2 I.L.R.M. 56 (which is considered further, 436–8, below). It was argued that documents in possession of the Garda Síochána Complaints Board relating to a claim made by the plaintiff were privileged by reason of section 12 of the Garda Síochána (Complaints) Act 1986, which provides that:

> (1) A person shall not disclose confidential information obtained by him while performing functions as a member of the Board, a tribunal or the Appeal Board, or as a member of the staff of the Board, unless he is duly authorised to do so.
>
> (2) In this section –
> 'confidential' means that which is expressed to be confidential either as regards particular information or as regards information of a particular class or description. . . .

However, after examining statutory provisions which had been held to ground privilege in other cases (including section 8 of the Adoption Act 1976 discussed in *P.B. v. A.L.* [1996] 1 I.L.R.M. 154), Keane J. concluded that the drafting of section 12 was markedly different:

> [Section 12] does not purport to confer any form of statutory privilege or immunity from disclosure: it does no more than prohibit members of the Board or its employees from disclosing information expressed to be confidential (or categories expressed to be such) to anyone else without the authority of the Board. That is not in any sense a prohibition on the production to a court in the interests of justice of documents in the Board's possession which are relevant to proceedings before that court. If the Oireachtas had intended to confer a privilege or immunity on such documents, it would have used language similar to that contained in the other statutes to which I have referred.

It seem that, while it is open to the Oireachtas to confer statutory privilege upon certain documentation or categories of documentation, subject of course to constitutional limitations, the courts lean against a finding that such privilege has been conferred. Therefore, very clear language will be required before privilege will be found to exist.

PRIVILEGE AGAINST SELF-INCRIMINATION

Inferences from silence   In *Rock v. Ireland*, Supreme Court, November 19, 1997, the Supreme Court affirmed the decision of Murphy J. (High Court, November 10, 1995 (1995 Review, 243)) upholding the constitutionality of sections 18 and 19 of the Criminal Justice Act 1984.

Section 18(1) provides that where:

(a) a person is arrested without warrant by a member of the Garda Síochána, and there is –
    (i) on his person, or
    (ii) in or on his clothing or footwear, or
    (iii) otherwise in his possession, or
    (iv) in any place in which he is at the time of his arrest,

any object, substance or mark, or there is any mark on any such object, and the member reasonably believes that the presence of the object, substance or mark may be attributable to the participation of the person arrested in the commission of the offence in respect of which he was arrested, and

(b) the member informs the person arrested that he so believes, and requests him to account for the presence of the object, substance or mark, and

(c) the person fails or refuses to do so,

then if, in any proceedings against the person for the offence, evidence of the said matters is given, the court, in determining whether to send forward the accused for trial or whether there is a case to answer and the court (or subject to the judge's directions, the jury) in determining whether the accused is guilty of the offence charged (or of any offence of which he could lawfully be convicted on that charge) may draw such inferences from the failure or refusal as appear proper; and the failure or refusal may, on the basis of such inferences, be treated as, or as capable of amounting to, corroboration of any other evidence in relation to which the failure or refusal is material, but a person shall not be convicted of an offence solely on an inference drawn from such failure or refusal.

Section 19, which is drafted in very similar terms provides that inferences may be drawn from an accused's failure to account for his presence at a particular place at or about the time the offence in respect of which he was arrested is alleged to have been committed.

As noted above, the plaintiff attacked the provisions on the basis that they infringed the presumption of innocence but his main submission was that they infringed the privilege against self-incrimination. It seems to have been common case that the sections did infringe the privilege and therefore, debate centred on whether the infringement was constitutionally permissible.

Unsurprisingly, the State placed great reliance on the decision in *Heaney v. Ireland* [1996] 1 I.R. 580; [1997] 1 I.L.R.M. 117 (Supreme Court) (1996 Review, 329); [1994] 3 I.R. 593; [1994] 2 I.L.R.M. 420 (High Court) (1994 Review, 128), where the constitutionality of section 52 of the Offences Against the State Act 1939 was upheld. Indeed, in the High Court, Murphy J. had expressed the opinion that section 52 was 'far more draconian than the 1984 Act and entrenches to a far greater extent on the right on the right to silence at the investigative stage of a criminal trial'.

However, the Court pointed out two significant differences between section 52 and the impugned provisions. First, as was acknowledged by the Supreme Court in *Heaney*, Part V of the 1939 Act (which includes section 52) is an exceptional provision which is intended to deal with circumstances where there is an extraordinary threat to public order and perhaps, even to the security of the state. In contrast, the 1984 Act is a piece of ordinary criminal legislation. Secondly, the consequences of non-compliance with sections 18 & 19 are potentially more serious than those of non-compliance with section 52. Although, an accused is liable to imprisonment for up to six months for failure to comply with section 52, no adverse inferences can be drawn at his trial. However, failure to comply with sections 18 or 19 can lead to the drawing of an inference which could result in an accused being convicted of an offence (carrying a sentence of anything from 5 years to life) in circumstances where there might otherwise have been insufficient evidence. Thus, the Court concluded that the decision in *Heaney* did not dispose of the issues in the case.

Dealing with the contentions of the plaintiff, the Court quickly disposed of the plaintiff's submission that his privilege against self-incrimination was not in conflict with the State's right to investigate crime and protect the public. Hamilton C.J., delivering the judgment of the Court, stated:

> The protection of citizens from attacks on their person or property is, to some degree, an aim of all criminal legislation. It is a constitutional duty which is imposed on the State; and the State is entitled to act on it, as long as due regard is had for the constitutional rights of accused persons. To suggest, therefore, as counsel for the Applicant did in this case, that there is no conflict of rights in this instance, is misleading.

In testing the constitutionality of the sections, Hamilton C.J. stated that the question to be considered by the Court was whether the restrictions which the impugned sections placed on the privilege were any greater than necessary to enable the State to fulfil its constitutional obligation. Although, he set forth the proportionality test expounded by Costello J. in *Heaney*, he seems to have actually examined the provisions by reference to the test set forth in *Tuohy v. Courtney* [1994] 3 I.R. 1, at 47 (1994 Review, 336), that where the Oireachtas balances constitutional rights, 'the role of the courts is not to impose their view of the correct or desirable balance in substitution for the view of the legislature as displayed in their legislation but rather to determine from an objective stance whether the balance contained in the impugned legislation is so contrary to reason and fairness as to constitute an unjust attack on some individual's constitutional rights'. Applying this test, the Court concluded:

> It is the opinion of this Court that, in enacting sections 18 and 19 of the 1984 Act the legislature was seeking to balance the individual's right to avoid self-incrimination with the right and duty of the State to defence and protect the life, person and property of all its citizens. In this situation, the function of the Court is not to decide whether a perfect balance has been achieved, but merely to decide whether, in restricting individual constitutional rights, the legislature have acted within the range of what is permissible. In this instance, the Court finds they have done so, and must accordingly uphold the constitutional validity of the impugned statutory provisions.

While Hamilton C.J. accepted that the sections could lead to the conviction of an accused of a serious offence in circumstances where he or she might otherwise have been acquitted, there were two important, limiting factors at work. Firstly, an inference cannot form the basis for a conviction in the absence of other evidence. Secondly, an inference adverse to the accused can only be drawn where the court deems it proper to do so.

The ultimate decision of the Court is unsurprising but the level of analysis is disappointing. The Court does little more than state a conclusion without engaging in any in-depth analysis, either of the privilege against self-incrimination or the application of sections 18 and 19. In particular, it is disappointing that the Court, after setting out the proportionality test propounded by Costello J. in *Heaney* did not actually employ it.

It is also regrettable that the Supreme Court did not avail itself of the opportunity presented by *Rock* to provide guidance as to what inferences can be legitimately drawn under the sections. Such guidance is required because the degree to which provisions such as sections 18 and 19 actually entrench upon constitutionally protected rights and values depends to a considerable extent on their practical application by the courts. However, the Court confined itself to observing that:

> In deciding what inferences may properly be drawn from the accused person's failure or refusal, the Court is obliged to act in accordance with the principles of constitutional justice and having regard to an accused

person's entitlement to a fair trial must be regarded as being under a constitutional obligation to ensure that no improper or unfair inferences are drawn or permitted to be drawn from such failure or refusal.

This still leaves unanswered the question of what is a proper inference although Hamilton C.J. did give one example of an improper inference – where the prejudicial effect of the inference would outweigh its probative value as evidence.

It is doubtful whether trial judges, on whose shoulders the decision as to what inferences can be drawn and the task of directing the jury accordingly falls, will find their job any easier after reading *Rock*.

Proceeds of crime   One of the main submissions advanced by the plaintiff in *Gilligan v. Criminal Assets Bureau*, High Court, June 26, 1997, in his constitutional challenge to the Proceeds of Crime Act 1996, was that the provisions of the Act infringed the privilege against self-incrimination. He argued that the structure of the Act forced him to give evidence in regard to the property affected by Orders under sections 2 and 3 and that this evidence could be self-incriminating.

In reply, the defendants submitted that a respondent to proceedings under the Act is not in any way forced to give evidence which could be self-incriminating. He has the options of giving evidence and seeking to realise his assets, or declining to say anything that might incriminate him, or giving evidence omitting any particulars that might incriminate him. Furthermore, even though an obligation is imposed on a respondent to displace the evidence which has been adduced by the applicant in proceedings under the Act there is no obligation *per se* on the respondent himself to give evidence. He can seek to displace the evidence that has been tendered by the applicant by means of cross-examination, by means of third party evidence, or by means of real evidence.

McGuinness J. criticised the defendant's argument as a sophisticated version of 'the innocent have nothing to fear' argument which she did not accept as sufficient, in itself, to offset a threat to the privilege against self-incrimination. She also pointed out that, as a practical matter, a failure by the respondent to give evidence will, in all probability, result in the disposal of the respondent's assets. However, she did not hold the Act to be unconstitutional on this ground.

The scheme of the 1996 Act is such that it does exert pressure on a respondent to give evidence or else risk losing his property. However, there is no direct or indirect element of compulsion in the Act. Therefore, it does not seem to infringe the privilege against self-incrimination.

McGuinness J. next considered whether section 9 of the Act infringed the privilege. This section provides that:

At any time during proceedings under section 2 or 3 or while an Interim Order or an Interlocutory Order is in force, the Court or, as appropriate, in the case of an appeal in such proceedings, the Supreme Court may by Order direct a Respondent to file an Affidavit in the Central Office of the High Court specifying –

(a) the property of which the Respondent is in possession or control, or
(b) the income, and the sources of the income, of the Respondent during such period (not exceeding ten years) ending on the date of the application for the Order as the Court concerned may specify.

or both.

The construction and application of this section had previously been considered by Moriarty J. in *M.(M.) v. D.(D.)*, High Court, December 10, 1996. In that case, the applicant sought an order requiring the respondent to file an affidavit in the terms set out in section 9. The application was resisted on the ground, inter alia, that the relief sought, if granted, would infringe the respondent's privilege against self-incrimination.

Moriarty J. considered a number of English authorities where the interaction between the privilege and disclosure orders had been considered. In *In re O.* [1991] 1 All E.R. 330, a disclosure order had been made in aid of a restraint order under section 77 of the Criminal Justice Act 1988. It was held by the Court of Appeal that the disclosure order was subject to the common law rule against self-incrimination. Thus, the appellants would be entitled to refuse to comply with the disclosure order made, in and in so far as to so might tend to incriminate them. However, this would frustrate the purpose of the order and therefore the preferable solution was to make the order subject to the condition that no disclosure made in compliance with the order could be used as evidence in the prosecution of an offence alleged to have been committed by the person required to make that disclosure or by his or her spouse.

The decision in *Re O.* was approved by the House of Lords in *A.T. & T. Istel Ltd. v. Tully* [1993] A.C. 45; [1992] 3 All E.R. 523. The case arose out of a large fraud as a result of which the plaintiffs commenced civil proceedings and a criminal investigation was also initiated. The plaintiffs applied for and were granted a wide ranging order for Mareva injunctions and discovery against some of the defendants. The order required the first and second defendants to file an affidavit setting out with full particularity all dealings with regard to certain monies but also contained a condition identical to that imposed in *Re O.*

The House of Lords held that there was no absolute privilege against self-incrimination in civil proceedings and a defendant was only entitled to rely on the privilege if and so far as compliance with a disclosure order would provide evidence against him in a criminal trial. In order to prevent the defendants exploiting the privilege to deprive the plaintiffs of their civil rights and remedies, the courts were entitled to substitute a different protection in place of the privilege if the person required to divulge information could be adequately protected against being exposed to the risk of the information divulged being used in a criminal prosecution. In this case, unlike *Re O.*, the Crown Prosecution Service was not a party to the proceedings and therefore could not be bound by the condition contained in the order. However, it had written to the plaintiffs indicating that it did not wish to intervene in the proceedings or to make use of any material divulged as a result of the disclosure order. In the view of their Lordships, this undertaking by the CPS not to make use, directly or indirectly, of the divulged material coupled with the condition in the order conferred sufficient protection and they restored the order.

Applying these decisions, Moriarty was satisfied that, in view of the degree of nexus between the applicant and the Director of Public Prosecutions, it was necessary that an undertaking be given by the Director of Public Prosecutions, in the terms given by the CPS in *Istel*, in order to prevent possible prejudice in future criminal proceedings.

In *Gilligan*, McGuinness J. said that in order to minimise any encroachment on constitutional rights and in order to operate the procedures under the 1996 Act in a way which is in accordance with constitutional justice, the Court would have to take particular care in deciding whether to make an order under section 9 requiring disclosure. She was of the opinion that the type of undertaking sought by Moriarty in *M. v. D.* would be essential in virtually every case where an order under section 9 is granted. Even then, there might well be difficulty in operating such an undertaking in a secure and watertight manner.

It is interesting that in both these decisions, the concept of what Keane (*Modern Law of Evidence* (4th ed.) (1996), p.518) has termed 'substituted protection' was accepted. This is the mechanism which courts in England have used to deal with statutory provisions which require disclosure of information but do not either expressly abrogate the privilege against self-incrimination or provide protection for it by stipulating that any information obtained cannot be used in any subsequent criminal proceedings. Substituted protection allows the courts to give maximum efficacy to the disclosure provisions whilst, at the same time, providing equivalent protection to the privilege.

However, in the context of disclosure orders under section 9, it is perhaps doubtful whether an undertaking from the D.P.P. can provide effective substitute protection. Apart from use in criminal prosecutions, such information could also be of utility in suggesting lines of inquiry to the gardaí. In view of the very close nexus between the Criminal Assets Bureau and the gardaí, it is perhaps not unrealistic to expect that despite the undertaking there might be some 'inadvertent' pooling of information.

PUBLIC INTEREST IMMUNITY

In *Skeffington v. Rooney* [1997] 1 I.R. 22; [1997] 2 I.L.R.M. 56, the plaintiff sought discovery of documents in the possession of the Garda Síochána Complaints Board concerning a complaint made by him against the first two defendants. In the High Court ([1994] 1 I.R. 480 (1993 Review, 457)), Barr J. had taken the view that his function was 'to resolve the conflict . . . between the public interest in the production of evidence . . . and the public interest in the confidentiality of documents relating to the exercise of quasi-judicial statutory power'. He examined the documents and concluded that there was nothing in the statements of a confidential nature, nor anything to suggest that any of the persons who made the statements did so on a confidential basis. Therefore, he did not consider that the functions of the Board would be compromised in any way by disclosure of the documents to the plaintiff.

On appeal, the defendants argued that the documents fell into a category which should be accorded privilege merely on the basis of a description of their nature and contents. It was contended that it was essential for the effective exercise by the Board of its statutory functions that both members of the public and of the gardaí could be assured of the confidentiality of any statement made by them to the Board. Such an argument had been accepted in England in *Neilson v. Laugharne* [1981] Q.B. 736, where the Court of Appeal accepted a class claim in respect of statements made to the Police Complaints Authority.

Keane J. acknowledged the importance of the functions of the Board under the Garda Síochána (Complaints) Act 1986 and the public policy considerations behind the Act which, he said, should be accorded due weight in assessing the claim of immunity. Thus, 'there had be weighed against the public interest in the disclosure of the documents relating to the complaint to the Board, the public interest in ensuring that the statutory functions of the Board are not frustrated.' However, he endorsed the principles laid down by Finlay C.J. in *Ambiorix Ltd. v. Minister for the Environment (No.1)* [1992] 1 I.R. 277; [1992] I.L.R.M. 209 (1991 Review 338) and reiterated that:

> Since the decision in *Murphy v. Dublin Corporation* [1972] I.R. 215, our law has taken a different course from English law in declining to recognise any right of the Executive to prevent the judicial arm of Government from examining particular documents or categories of documents in order to ascertain whether they should be admitted in evidence in civil or criminal proceedings. While it is always open to the Executive, as it is to any citizen, to claim that specific documents are privileged, if that claim is opposed, the issue as to whether the documents must be produced can only be decided by the court having seisin of the proceedings.

In some cases, the question of whether the documents were privileged from production could be resolved by the judge by reference to the description of the documents contained in the affidavit of discovery. More frequently, it would involve an examination of some or all of the disputed documents. The procedure to be adopted would depend to some degree upon the circumstances of each case and the nature and extent of the disputed documentation. Therefore, in this case, Barr J. had been correct in holding that the documents were not privileged by reason of their nature and in proceeding to examine them before deciding whether to uphold the claim of public interest immunity.

The claim of the Board that immunity was necessary for the discharge by it of its statutory functions, proceeded on the basis of the candour argument. However, the problem with the candour argument is that it requires a class claim to be recognised because it is only where such protection is conferred that the desired candour will be achieved. However the courts, since *Murphy*, have consistently set their face against class claims. As Walsh J. said in that case, '[t]o grant or withhold the production of a document simply by reason of the class to which it belongs would be to regard all documents as being of equal importance notwithstanding that they may not be.' Thus, the decision of the Court in *Skeffington* in refusing to accept a class claim is in line with well-established jurisprudence.

Because of the way in which the appeal was argued, it was unnecessary for the Supreme Court to consider whether a contents claim in respect of the disputed documentation could be made out. Barr J. in the High Court considered that it could not. He concluded that there was nothing in the statements of a confidential nature, nor anything to suggest that any of the persons who made the statements did so on a confidential basis. Therefore, he did not consider that the functions of the Board would be compromised in any way by disclosure of the documents to the plaintiff. One point which both he and the Supreme Court regarded as significant was that it was the complainant who was seeking the documentation.

Different considerations would apply where documents relating to a complaint to the Board were sought by a party to litigation other than the complainant. In such a case, Keane J. said that 'depending entirely on the particular circumstances, the court might be justified in declining to allow the inspection of documents forwarded in confidence by a complainant to the chief executive or even the identity of a complainant'. There are a number of other points worth noting about the decision. First, although class claims could not be accepted, Keane J. said that this did not preclude the courts from identifying particular categories of evidence such as the identity of informers, which, in general, will be regarded as privileged. These 'categories of public interest are not closed and must alter from time to time whether by restriction or extension as social conditions and social legislation develop' (*per* Lord Hailsham in *D. v. N.S.P.C.C.* [1978] A.C. 171, at 230).

Secondly, although he held that the fact that documents were furnished in confidence to the party against whom the order of discovery is sought does not of itself make them privileged, he left open the question of whether the Court might refrain from requiring members of professions other than the legal profession to disclose confidential communications where it did not appear essential in the interests of justice in the particular case that they should be so disclosed.

Thirdly, with regard to nomenclature, Keane J. seemed to indicate a willingness to abandon the term 'executive privilege' which is singularly inappropriate to this category of case where a claim of public interest immunity may be made by a body which is not exercising any of the executive powers of the State.

RES JUDICATA

Estoppel *per res judicatam* precludes a party from reopening a matter that has previously been determined by the final decision of a judicial tribunal of competent jurisdiction. The doctrine therefore promotes the maxim *interest rei publicae ut sit finis litium* and in view of the rising tide of litigation, it is unsurprising that 1997 saw increased invocation of this doctrine in its many manifestations.

Issue estoppel   The constituent elements of issue estoppel are, by now, well established and in *McCauley v. McDermot* [1997] 2 I.L.R.M. 486, at 492, Keane J., delivering the decision of the Supreme Court, endorsed the following enumeration by Lord Guest in *Carl Zeiss Stiftung v. Rayner & Keeler Ltd.* [1967] 1 A.C. 853, at 935:

> The requirements of issue estoppel still remain (1) that the same question has been decided; (2) that the judicial decision which is said to create the estoppel was final; and, (3) that the parties to the judicial decision or their privies were the same persons as the parties to the proceedings in which the estoppel is raised or their privies.

In order to aid clarity of exposition, it is proposed to examine the cases under the criteria identified by Lord Guest, namely (1) identity of issue; (2) identity of the parties; and (3) finality of decision.

Identity of issue In *McCauley v. McDermot* [1997] 2 I.L.R.M. 486, the plaintiff was the passenger in a car that was involved in a collision with a tractor. The car owner had previously instituted proceedings in the District Court against the tractor owner claiming damages for damage to his car and, on appeal, it was held by the Circuit Court that the collision was due to the negligence of the tractor driver and that there was no contributory negligence on the part of the car driver.

The instant proceedings were instituted by the plaintiff against the tractor owner claiming damages for personal injuries. The tractor owner was granted liberty to issue and serve a third party notice against the car driver and a motion was subsequently brought to strike out the third party notice on the grounds that the issues arising between the tractor owner and the car driver were *res judicata*.

In order to determine whether the same issue was involved in both proceedings, Keane J. examined the issues in both cases. In the earlier Circuit Court proceedings, the issues as to liability to be determined were: (1) Was the damage to the car caused by the negligent driving of the tractor driver? (2) If so, was the damage also caused or contributed to by the negligence of the car driver? (3) If the court found that both the car driver and the tractor driver were negligent, in what degrees should their liability be apportioned? In the instant proceedings, the only issue as to liability was whether the injuries suffered by the passenger were caused by the negligence of the tractor driver. In the event of her succeeding in that issue, the issues which would arise in the third party proceedings would be: (1) Were the injuries allegedly sustained by the passenger contributed to by the negligence of the car driver? (2) If so, in what degrees should liability be apportioned as between the car driver and the tractor driver? Thus, the two questions to be determined in the third party proceedings were the same as the second and third questions previously determined in the Circuit Court proceedings and therefore, the requirement of identity of subject matter was met.

It is submitted, however that this analysis is not supported by the terms of the Circuit Court decision. This was to the effect that the collision was due to the negligence of the tractor driver and that there had been no *contributory negligence* on the part of the car driver. In *Donohue v. Browne* [1986] I.R. 90, it was held by Gannon J. that there was a distinction in law between the nature of the duty of care, the breach of which is imputed by a plea of contributory negligence, and the duty of care to all road users, imputed in a plea of ordinary negligence. Thus, the finding by the Circuit Court judge that the car driver had not been contributorily negligent did not dispose of the issue of whether the car driver had been negligent.

It may be that this case heralds a shift from the narrow technical approach of earlier cases to identity of issues towards a broader, more common sense approach. According to the narrow approach, there is a bright line distinction between negligence and contributory negligence. Therefore, a finding of contributory negligence on the part of a plaintiff in one action does not create an estoppel on the issue of his negligence in a later action. The broad approach looks past the technicalities of the various duties of care and asks whether the issue in the later case was substantially determined in the earlier case.

In *Belton v. Carlow County Council* [1997] 2 I.L.R.M. 405, the third parties to the action were the directors and shareholders of a company. A factory owned by the company was destroyed by fire and it brought a claim for compensation under the Malicious Injuries Act 1981. It was common case that the fire had been started deliberately, the only question was by whom. The County Council contended that it had been started by the third parties and on appeal to the High Court, the claim was dismissed on the basis that the company had failed to satisfy the onus of proof that the fire was started by the malicious act of a third party.

The fire had also caused damage to adjoining premises owned by the applicant and the instant proceedings had been instituted by him seeking compensation. Liability was not disputed by the County Council but they claimed an indemnity from the third party, arguing that they were estopped by the decision of the High Court from denying that they had deliberately started the fire.

Keane J. relied on the judgment of Dixon J. in *Blair v. Curran* (1939) 62 C.L.R. 464, at 531-2, to hold that issue estoppel would arise where a party sought to litigate an issue which had necessarily and fundamentally been determined in previous proceedings if those proceedings could be regarded as having been between the same parties or their privies. Applying this test, Keane J. concluded that the issue as to whether the fire had been caused by the third parties or someone else, had been a necessary and fundamental basis of the High Court judgment.

Identity of parties In *McGuinness v. Motor Distributors Ltd.* [1997] 2 I.R. 171 (HC), Supreme Court, *ex tempore*, July 17, 1997, the plaintiff was suing the defendants for breach of contract in supplying him with an unroadworthy bus. The bus had been involved in an accident and in earlier proceedings taken by a passenger on the bus, the plaintiff had joined the defendants as third parties alleging that the accident was caused by defects in the bus supplied to him. At the hearing of the action, the plaintiff was found to be liable and the issue between him and the defendants was dismissed. The defendants relied on this finding as raising an estoppel in the instant case but the plaintiff sought to resist the plea on the basis that although it had been a party to the previous proceedings, he had not been a real party to the earlier proceedings and that in reality, it was his insurance company, not he, who had been in control of the proceedings.

In the High Court, Barron J. accepted that the earlier proceedings had been controlled by the insurance company but refused to hold that the plaintiff had not been a party by virtue of this fact. His conclusion was upheld on appeal by the Supreme Court on the basis that there was a clear privity of interest between the parties.

Some support for the contention advanced by the plaintiff can be garnered from the judgment of Lowry L.C.J. in *Shaw v. Sloan* [1982] N.I. 393, at 397, who said that 'there is, so far as policy can be relevant, an argument against allowing a party to be prejudiced in later proceedings by the way in which his insurers have in their own interest conducted the earlier proceedings.' However, although unfairness may sometimes result, it is submitted that there are strong policy reasons in favour of the conclusion reached in *McGuinness*.

First, it would be productive of complexity and uncertainty if, in each case that involved an insurance company, the courts were prepared to go behind the identity of parties in order to ascertain who were the 'real' parties. Secondly, because so much litigation is effectively fought out between insurance companies, the policy goal of finality of litigation would be greatly undermined if a party could escape the binding force of a previous decision on that basis.

A person will also be bound by a previous decision where, although not a party to it, they are in privity with a party to it. In both *McCauley* and *Belton*, Keane J. adopted the definition of privity advanced by Lowry L.C.J. in *Shaw v. Sloan* [1982] N.I. 393, at 396, namely that '[a] party is the privy of another by blood, title or interest when he stands in his shoes and claims through or under him.' By far the most important category is that of privity by interest and it is with that that both *Belton* and *McCauley* were concerned.

In *Belton*, it was held that privity was absent. The first proceedings had been between the company and the County Council whilst the instant proceedings were between the County Council and the third parties. Applying the doctrine of separate legal personality, the third parties and the company were separate legal entities and thus, the third parties were not bound by proceedings to which the company was a party. Next, it had to be considered whether there was sufficient privity of interest between the company and the third parties.

Keane J. decided that there was not. While the interests of the company and its controlling shareholders would often coincide, that would not always be the case. He fortified his conclusion by reference to an application for compensation for malicious damage. If such an application was successful, the proceeds would become the assets of the company and would fall to be dealt with in accordance with the memorandum and articles. Similarly, in the event of the application being unsuccessful, the consequent liability for costs would be that of the company alone and not that of the third parties personally. By contrast, in the instant proceedings, the third parties alone would be liable, in the event of the County Council's claim succeeding and the company had no interest, present or contingent, in the outcome.

This conclusion was correct in the instant case because there was no identity of interest with regard to the malicious damages application between the company and the third parties. However, shareholders and directors of a company may be privies in an appropriate case (see *Effem Foods Pty. Ltd. v. Trawl Industries Pty. Ltd.* (1993) 43 F.C.R. 510, at 542).

In *McCauley*, it was argued that sufficient privity of interest arose by virtue of section 118 of the Road Traffic Act 1961 which provides that a car owner is vicariously liable for the negligence of a person driving the car with his consent. However, Keane J. declined to hold that it followed from the section that there was sufficient identity of interest between the owner and driver of a car.

Although this decision seems unduly narrow, an equally narrow approach had been adopted in a number of previous decisions including *Reamsbottom v. Rafftery* [1991] 1 I.R. 531 (1990 Review, 449) and *Lawless v. Bus Éireann* [1994] 1 I.R. 474 (1995 Review, 412). However, these decisions were concerned with situations where it was sought to bind a party by a previous decision *against* them to which they were allegedly privy. Hence, a narrow approach had been adopted in order to avoid the potential injustice of holding a party to be bound by a previous decision to which they had not been a party. Here, this factor was absent because the tractor driver against whom the determination was made had been the defendant in the Circuit Court proceedings. Nevertheless, Keane J. held that privity did not exist.

It is clear that an important factor in reaching this conclusion was adherence by the Court to the requirement of mutuality. Keane J. cited Alderson B. in *Petrie v. Nuttall* (1856) 11 Ex. 569, 575-76, to the effect that: 'It is essential to an estoppel that it be mutual, so that the same parties and privies may both be bound and take advantage of it'. Thus, if the Circuit Court had decided the issue in the previous proceedings against the car owner and in favour of the tractor owner, the car driver would not have been estopped because he was not party or privy to the earlier proceedings. That being so, he could not take advantage of the decision against the tractor owner.

Therefore, mutuality dictated that in order to prevent a person being unfairly bound by previous decisions by reason of being found to be a privy of one of the parties, an equally narrow approach was required where a person sought to take advantage of a determination on the ground of privity.

The principle of mutuality has stymied any attempt in this jurisdiction to follow the U.S. lead in developing a doctrine of non-mutual preclusion. However, there is a strong case to be made for such an innovation because the reasons, rooted in fairness, which lie behind the non-preclusion of a person who was not a party or privy to the earlier proceedings do not arise where it is sought to raise estoppel against a person who was party or privy to the earlier proceedings. It is not unfair to hold a person bound by a decision to which they were party or privy and it undermines the policy goal of finality of litigation to allow an issue which has been determined against a party to be reopened merely by changing defendants.

Finality of Decision In *Director of Public Prosecutions v. Gray*, Supreme Court, *ex tempore*, November 10, 1997, it was held that the doctrine of *res judicata* does not apply where there has been a change in circumstances. Thus, the applicant, who had been refused bail, was entitled to renew his application to the High Court on that basis. Although no cases are cited, this proposition is clearly supported by authority including the decision of the Court in *O'B. v. O'B.* [1984] I.R. 182.

One noteworthy aspect of the decision in *Gray* is that it seems to leave open the possibility that a plea of *res judicata* might succeed in the absence of a change of circumstances. However, it is submitted that the doctrine has no application in the context of bail applications because one of constituent elements namely, that of finality of the previous determination, is missing. This is because a bail application is interlocutory in nature and the dismissal of an interlocutory application does not bar a further application (see, for example, *Kinex Exploration Pty. Ltd. v. Tasco Pty. Ltd.* [1995] 2 V.R. 318). Thus, although a further application is unlikely to succeed in the absence of a change in circumstances or further evidence, it is not precluded by the doctrine of *res judicata*. Hence, the traditional view has been that an unsuccessful applicant can renew his application to the High Court for bail on an indefinite number of occasions (Ryan and McGee, *The Irish Criminal Process* (1983), p.201).

Abuse of process In *McCauley*, the Supreme Court also demonstrated a willingness to employ the doctrine of abuse of the process of the court in order to uphold the decision of a court of competent jurisdiction when a plea of *res judicata* would not be successful. Keane J. outlined the policy considerations underlying this area as follows:

> In cases of this nature, the courts are concerned with achieving a balance between two principles. A party should not be deprived of his or her constitutional right of access to the courts by the doctrine of *res judicata* where injustice might result, as by treating a party as bound by a determination against his or her interests in proceedings over which he or she had no control. *Res judicata* must be applied in all its severity, however, where to do otherwise would be to permit a party bound by an earlier judgment to seek to escape from it, in defiance of the principles that there should ultimately be an end to litigation and that the citizen must not be troubled again by law suit which has already been decided.

Having concluded that issue estoppel did not apply on the facts, Keane J. acknowledged that it remained the case that the tractor owner was 'seeking to relitigate an issue which was conclusively and finally determined against him in the Circuit Court proceedings, the very mischief which the doctrine of issue estoppel was intended to prevent.' In fact, it was conceded on behalf of the tractor owner that the only reason for not joining the car owner in the later proceedings was that he would have been met with an unanswerable plea of *res judicata*. In these circumstances, Keane J. concluded that '[t]o allow that party to bring about the same result by the stratagem of suing the [car driver] rather than the car owner would be to ignore the maxim *interest rei publicae ut sit finis litium* and facilitate an abuse of process.'

It is clear from *Belton* that the doctrine of abuse of process will only be deployed against parties who seek to evade determinations against them in previous decisions. In *Belton*, it was also argued that to allow the third parties to controvert the previous finding of the High Court would be an abuse of process. However, Keane J. pointed out that the third parties had not initiated the proceedings for the purpose of mounting any form of attack upon the High Court decision. Rather, the proceedings had been initiated by the local authority and "their invocation of the abuse of process principle is intended to deprive the defendants of a defence, which they might otherwise have upon the merits, to the present claim.

In *Bula Ltd. v. Crowley*, High Court, April 29, 1997, Barr J. effectively conflated issue estoppel and abuse of process to create such a doctrine of non-mutual preclusion. The plaintiffs in this case wished to controvert findings that had been made against them in separate proceedings in which they were also the plaintiffs. Barr J. acknowledged that issue estoppel did not apply because there was no identity between the defendants in the instant case and any of the parties in the other proceedings. Thus, the question of whether the plaintiffs were bound by the findings in the other proceedings depended on whether 'it would be unjust in all the circumstances and an abuse of the process of the court' to allow such findings to be re-visited in the instant action. Relying on the decisions of Blayney J. in *Breathnach v. Ireland (No. 2)* [1993] 2 I.R. 448 (1989 Review, 358), and the House of Lords in *Hunter v. Chief Constable of West Midlands* [1982] A.C. 529; [1981] 3 All E.R. 727, he held that when 'an issue has been finally determined by a court of competent jurisdiction it is an abuse of the process of the court to seek to have it relitigated in new proceedings'.

So far his judgment is in chartered waters, but he then went on to quote with approval an enumeration of the elements of issue estoppel by Dixon J. in *Blair v. Curran* (1939) 62 C.L.R. 464, at 531-2, and stated that it applied where the plaintiffs but not the defendants were the same in both actions. He concluded that there were three questions to be addressed by a court in determining whether a party was bound by findings of fact or law by a court of competent jurisdiction in earlier proceedings: (i) is the party seeking to re-open an issue of fact or law which was decided against them in the earlier proceedings? (ii) was the finding in question necessary to the determination, in the earlier proceedings, of the issue to which it relates? (iii) is the finding relevant to an issue raised by that party in the instant proceedings? Applying these tests to the facts of the case, he held that they were satisfied and that the plaintiffs were precluded from controverting the findings against them in the earlier proceedings.

We can see in *McCauley* and *Bula*, a willingness on the part of the courts to use the doctrine of abuse of the process of the courts to achieve a partial doctrine of non-mutual preclusion. However, it would be preferable if this were achieved by a dilution or abandonment of mutuality accompanied by the development of a principled approach within the parameters of *res judicata* rather than through invocation of the amorphous doctrine of abuse of process. Instead, that doctrine should be confined to egregious cases where one party seeks to obtain an unfair advantage or to in some way manipulate the requirements of *res judicata* to his own ends.

Indeed, *Bula* indicates the practical desirability of developing such a doctrine. The earlier proceedings, *Bula Ltd. v. Tara Mines*, had run for 277 days and the findings which the plaintiffs sought to challenge had been reached by Lynch J. after assessment of a huge volume of evidence. If re-opened, they would have added greatly to the duration and expense of the instant proceedings. It is easy to sympathise with the opinion of Barr J. that there 'was no acceptable reason in justice to revisit such findings and to permit the plaintiffs to challenge them'.

Family Law

At the introduction to the Chapter, we welcome the publication in 1997 of the fourth edition of Alan Shatter's *Family Law*. This new edition, of well over a thousand pages, presents a comprehensive, clear and authoritative analysis by an author whose long experience as a practitioner and a legislator gives him an unrivalled perspective on the subject.

NULLITY OF MARRIAGE

Formal requirements   Section 32 of the Family Law Act 1995 introduced the requirement of three months' notice of intention to marry to the Registrar for the District in which the marriage is to be solemnised. See the 1995 Review, 322. It transpired that a number of couples gave notice in error to a Registrar for a District other than where they intended to marry. Section 3(1) of the Family Law (Miscellaneous Provisions) Act 1997 remedies the position, retrospectively and prospectively. Section 3(2) affords retrospective validation to judicial exemptions under section 33 to the three-month notice requirement under section 32 or the minimum age requirement under section 31 of the 1995 Act (as to which, see the 1995 Review, 32–3) where the judge of the Circuit Family Court who granted the exemption was not the appropriate judge having regard to section 38 (4) of the 1995 Act, which prescribes the relevant jurisdictional limits. Section 2(2) prospectively removes these jurisdictional limits for applications for exemption under section 33. For analysis of these legislative changes, see Shatter, *op. cit.*, 152–3, 159–61, and Brian Gallagher's Annotation of the 1997 Act, *ICLSA*.

This is not the first time that a legislative measure has conferred retrospective validation on a marriage. The previous instance was section 2 of the Marriages Act 1972, which did so in relation to marriages that had been celebrated in Lourdes in religious ceremonies without having previously gone through a civil ceremony, as French law required. See W. Binchy, *Irish Conflicts of Law*, 223–7 (Butterworths, 1988).

Some interesting questions arise as to the effect of retrospective legislative validation of marriage on a second marriage by one of the parties with a third party which took place in the interim, where that party to the original marriage was proceeding, correctly, on the basis of the invalidity of the first marriage. The second marriage, prior to the legislation, was entirely valid. Perhaps, from a jurisprudential standpoint, it is necessary to categorise all marriages as voidable in the sense that they are susceptible to subsequent retrospective invalidation by implication. That somewhat unsatisfactory conclusion seems preferable to the idea that legislative provisions such as section 3 of the 1997 Act or section 2 of the 1972 Act should have the effect of creating a novel mode of lawful bigamy.

One suspects that the Constitution casts a shadow over this area of the law, in terms of respect for the principles of autonomy and reliance, on the one hand, and a lack of sympathy for those seeking to take advantage of a legal technicality in defiance of their own previous undertakings, on the other. One should have a sense of realism about this problem in the context of section 3 of the 1997 Act. The timeframe was very short, in contrast to the Lourdes marriages, where the practice of marrying without a prior civil ceremony had gone back several years.

Consent

Absence of informed consent and incapacity to maintain a normal marital relationship The limitations of a short law report are evident in *M.J. v. D.P.M.* (1997) 16 *ILT* 126 (Circuit Court, Judge Buckley, 1997). As one reads the summary of Judge Buckley's judgment, there is a strong desire to have access to the full text, because of the questions and doubts which it raises.

The petition for annulment was brought by a woman who became free of hepatitis at the age of thirty. Before then, as a result of her medical condition, she had felt precluded from entering into any serious relationships. She met the respondent, a divorced person. They married in March 1993. The respondent's work kept them apart for periods of several months. The petitioner spent some time abroad with the respondent, but in August 1995 she returned to Ireland. The parties lived together briefly thereafter but, the reports notes, at this time 'they really only shared occupation'. The respondent later went to London.

Judge Buckley granted an annulment, apparently on two grounds: the petitioner's lack of consent and the respondent's inability to sustain a normal marital relationship with the petitioner. As to the former, Judge Buckley is reported as saying that the court had to determine whether the petitioner's consent had been an informed one – 'a consent based on adequate knowledge.' The test to be applied was a subjective one: whether the petitioner had 'adequate knowledge of every circumstance relevant to the decision she was making, so that her consent could truly be said to be an informed one.'

Judge Buckley went on to find that the petitioner had had little experience of serious relationships with men and had not had regular personal contact with the respondent during the relationship. She had been unaware of his drinking and gambling. The marriage had been 'thrust upon the petitioner with inordinate haste.' The respondent had showed classical signs of immaturity. If the petitioner had recognised them, she would not have consented to the marriage. Accordingly, the petitioner 'did not have adequate knowledge of every circumstance relevant to the decision she was making, and her consent was not an informed one.'

On the evidence, the respondent had been unable to sustain a normal marital relationship with the petitioner by reason of incapacity 'deriving from lack of emotional maturity and psychological weakness'.

It would take a bold lawyer to articulate with any conviction and clarity the principles underlying this ground, which made its first appearance in *R.S.J. v. J.S.J.* [1982] I.L.R.M. 263. For a sceptical analysis, see Fergus Ryan, '"When Divorce Is Away, Nullity's At Play': A New Ground for Annulment, Its Dubious Past and Its Uncertain Future', 1 *Trinity College Law Review* 15 (1998).

Parental consent requirements The new version of section 19 of the Marriages (Ireland) Act 1844, as inserted by section 7 of the Marriages Act 1972, requires parental consent (or in default, a judicial exemption) for a marriage ceremony by a person between the ages of sixteen and twenty-one. It has been accepted by all who have commented on this provision that it is directory only and that a marriage, otherwise valid, is not rendered invalid by reason of failure to comply with it.

In *D.C. v. N.M. (falsely known as N.C.),* High Court, June 26, 1997, the petitioner sought an annulment on the basis (*inter alia*) of non-compliance with section 19. The respondent was aged nineteen at the time of the ceremony, in a Catholic Church, in 1978. It appeared that a scheme had been devised whereby the respondent's brother forged her father's consent, with the successful aim of misleading the priest. Both parties were aware of the forgery.

Geoghegan J. refused to grant a decree of nullity on this ground. He noted that the decision of *Rex v. Inhabitants of Birmingham*, 8 B & Cr. 29 (1829), holding the equivalent English provision directory only, was still cited in modern times as authority for the same proposition in relation to the original section 19 of the 1844 Act. The new version, in the 1972 Act, did not contain any alternation on foot of which a different interpretation could be maintained.

The fact that there had been a knowing breach of the section did not alter matters. This had been a crucial factor in *I.E. v. W.E.* [1985] I.L.R.M. 691, but there the relevant provision, section 49 of the 1844 Act, was drafted in such a way as to make it clear that a knowing and wilful breach of it would render the marriage void.

Similarly, nothing in section 19 rendered the marriage automatically invalid by reason of the fact that the consent had been forged. For the petitioner to succeed, he would have to satisfy the court that, 'independently of the section, though of course having regard to it as part of the surrounding circumstances', the forged consent rendered the marriage voidable. Since both parties were aware of the forgery, this ground was unsustainable.

What Geoghegan J. seems to have in mind here is the fact that the grounds of fraud and mistake can in appropriate circumstances render a marriage invalid (voidable, in the case of fraud). The idea that the presence or absence of parental consent could play such a crucial role as to invalidate a marriage of a nineteen-year-old seems implausible, though it could perhaps be argued that duplicity on such a matter might go to the root of a person's character. These considerations may well explain Geoghegan J.'s view that, if the petitioner had not been aware of the forgery, the marriage would not have been invalidated unless the petitioner could establish that, 'to the knowledge of the respondent, he relied on that consent in entering into the marriage and would not have entered into it had he known of the forgery.' This suggests that the only ground relevant in the context of forged parental consent is fraud rather than mistake. Otherwise the knowledge of the respondent would not be a crucial factor.

Duress In *D.C. v. N.M. (falsely known as N.C.)*, High Court, June 26, 1997, Geoghegan J. gave a helpful summary of the proper scope of the ground of duress when dismissing a petition for nullity brought by the petitioner who claimed that his consent to enter the marriage had been obtained 'by the undue influence and or duress exerted upon him by the respondent by reason of her alleged pregnancy by him.' At the time of the ceremony, in 1978, the petitioner was twenty one years old, the respondent nineteen.

Geoghegan J. noted that, for some years previously, it had been quite common for a nullity decree to be granted in a case where a young girl became unexpectedly pregnant and parental or external pressure had been exerted on one or both of the parties to marry. If that pressure was 'excessive so as to prevent them forming an independent mature decision of their own', the court had no hesitation in declaring the marriage invalid.

That was not the situation in the instant case. There had been no evidence of any pressure from the parties' parents or other external source. The pregnancy had not arisen from a single night's passion: 'this was a couple in a loving relationship' with a long term plan to marry, though no date had been fixed. It was true that their decision to marry at the actual time they did had been related to the pregnancy and 'to a certain extent each felt a sense of duty to each other to get married.' It was also fair to say that the respondent did not want to be an unmarried mother. But Geoghegan J. found nothing in the petitioner's evidence to indicate that he was under any undue or excessive pressure by the respondent or anyone else, though he appeared to have been 'under pressure to some extent from his own conscience.'

The couple were 'not particularly young' at the time of the marriage. The respondent had been 'in a sense a mature nineteen in that she had been leading an independent life for a considerable period.' If a decree of nullity were granted in a case such as this, it would effectively mean that no marriage arising out of an unwanted pregnancy could ever be upheld. None of the previous decisions supported that proposition and in Geoghegan J.'s view there was no justification for adopting such an approach. It was 'quite a different matter, of course,' where there was parental or external pressure which a young immature person might be unable properly to withstand.

Geoghegan J.'s indifference as to the significance of labels of duress or undue influence is worth noting. It reflects O'Hanlon J.'s approach in *M.K. v. F. McC.* [1982] I.L.R.M. 277 and that of McCarthy J. in *N. (otherwise K.) v. K.* [1986] I.L.R.M. 75; [1985] I.R. 733.

DIVORCE

In *R.C. v. C.C.*, [1997] 1 I.LR.M. 401, Barron J. was called on to determine whether the new Article 41.3.2° of the Constitution, inserted by the Fifteenth Amendment, required the enactment of legislation as a precondition to a constitutional entitlement to divorce. Article 41.3.2° provides as follows:

A Court designated by law may grant a dissolution of marriage where, but only where, it is satisfied that –

1. at the date of the institution of the proceedings, the spouses have lived apart from one another for a period of, or periods amounting to, at least four years during the previous five,
2. there is no reasonable prospect of a reconciliation between the spouses,
3. such provision as the court considers proper having regard to the circumstances exists or will be made for the spouses, any children of either or both of them and any other person prescribed by law,
4. any further conditions prescribed by law are complied with.

The Family Law (Divorce) Act 1996 came into effect on February 27, 1997. A few weeks before then, the plaintiff sought a dissolution of marriage on the basis of Article 41.3.2°. He was terminally ill and apprehended that he might die before he had the opportunity to apply for a divorce under the terms of the legislation. There were three children of the marriage, all of whom were adults.

Barron J, following *R. v. R.* [1984] I.R. 296 and *Tormey v. Ireland* [1985] I.R. 289, held that the High Court was for the purposes of Article 41.3.2° a court designated by law and that the jurisdiction granted by the provision might be exercisable by the High Court:

There is nothing in that provision which limits the powers of this Court to exercise the jurisdiction created nor is there any statutory provision in force based upon any other provision of the Constitution which takes away such jurisdiction.

Having established that the Court had jurisdiction to determine the application for divorce, Barron J. went on to consider the matters on which he had to be satisfied before he could grant a decree. The requirement of four years' separation presented no difficulties (though the judgment lacks specificity on how long the parties had been living apart). Barron J. concluded on the evidence that there was no prospect of reconciliation between the spouses. He was also satisfied that the economic provision proposed for the spouses and children was 'in the overall circumstances of the family' proper. Accordingly, being satisfied that there was no collusion between the spouses, Barron J. made an order for the dissolution of the marriage.

Barron J. noted a distinction between clause 3 of Article 41.3.2°. which requires that:

> such provision as the court considers proper having regard to the circumstances exists or will be made for the spouses, any children of either or both of them and any other person prescribed by law,

and section 5(1)(c) of the Family Law (Divorce) Act 1996, which provides for:

> such provision as the court considers proper having regard to the circumstances exists or will be made for the spouses and any dependent members of the family.

Barron J. observed that:

> [s]ince the jurisdiction invoked is that contained in the Constitution and not that amplified by the Act, it is necessary for the Court to consider the position of the children. While I do not purport to determine that non-dependent children should necessarily have provision made for them, I am satisfied that in the particular circumstances of the present case it is proper that certainly the two daughters of the marriage [who were not dependent children – eds.] should have provision made for them in the interests of the family as a whole.

Barron J. was surely correct to address the position of non-dependent children since clearly the limitation contained in the 1996 legislation had no application to an application for divorce grounded on Article 41.3.2°. A question must arise as to whether the legislation is constitutional in view of the fact that it is on its face more limited than the explicit language of Article 41.3.2°.

In defence of the constitutional validity of the legislation it can be argued that the definition of 'dependent child' contained in section 2(1) of the 1996 Act extends the parental obligation into the adulthood of the children of divorcing parents in certain circumstances.

As against this it can be argued, with some force, that the 1996 Act fails to give full effect to the requirements of Article 41.3.2° in that it is very easy to envisage situations in which an adult non-dependent child may be deserving of provision on the divorce of his or her parents. The radical significance of section 117 of the Succession Act 1965 is that it embraces the value-judgment that a testator may in some cases owe a moral duty to provide for an adult non-dependent child by will. While it is true that adult non-dependent children have no entitlement to obtain a maintenance order from either of their parents or to obtain any other order for their financial provision, Article 41.3.2° accepts the value-judgment that there may be circumstances where such a moral obligation can arise. It requires the court, when addressing a divorce application, not to grant a decree unless satisfied that such provision as it considers proper having regard to the circumstances exists or will be made for any children of either or both of the spouses. While it is true that the children of divorced parents have no less entitlement to make an application under section 117 of the 1965 Act, in contrast to a divorced spouse, whose rights under the 1965 Act are transformed by the divorce, the fact remains that Article 41.3.2° requires the court at the time of the divorce proceedings to address the issue of proper provision for non-dependent adult children, in contrast to the 1996 Act.

Does this mean that the 1996 legislation is unconstitutional? Not necessarily. It would seem open to the courts to save the constitutional validity of the Act by holding that the Act is constitutional *so far as it goes*, but that, by way of supplementary constitutional duty, the court is obliged to address the question whether proper provision has been or will be made to the non-dependent adult children. There is, however, something untidy and unconvincing about having to fall back on the residual jurisdiction of the court to salvage the poorly framed legislation.

The new law is analysed in detail by Muriel Walls and David Bergin, *The Law of Divorce in Ireland* (1997) and by Kieron Wood and Paul O'Shea, *Divorce in Ireland* (1997).

JUDICIAL SEPARATION

Grounds   In *J.D. v. D.D.*, High Court, May 14, 1997, where the wife sought a decree for judicial separation on (*inter alia*) grounds (a) and (f) of section

2(1) of the Judicial Separation and Family Law Reform Act 1989, McGuinness J. addressed the question whether the fact that the marriage relationship had broken down 'a long time' before the husband's adultery should be a reason for the court's not granting a decree on ground (a) if satisfied that the facts warranted the granting of a decree on the basis of ground (f). McGuinness J. disposed on the matter as follows:

> I accept that the wife, in hindsight, believes that the marriage had broken down for some years before the actual separation of the parties but I feel that some slight hope of reconciliation remained up to the time that the husband embarked on his extramarital relationship in the summer of 1994. The husband's adultery put the nail in the coffin of the marriage and I am not, therefore, prepared to ignore it as a ground for a decree of judicial separation. I will therefore grant a decree pursuant to section 2(1)(a) and section 2(1)(f) of the 1989 Act.

This passage would seem to suggest that, if the adultery had taken place after the marriage had broken down or the parties had separated, it would not be appropriate for the court to grant a decree on the basis of ground (a). The manner in which section 2(1) is drafted does not support this interpretation. The 1989 legislation, in contrast to the English divorce legislation, does not identify the basis of the decree as the breakdown of the marriage but rather the proof by the applicant of one or more of specific facts. In its original manifestation, Deputy Alan Shatter's Bill had so provided but this was dropped as a result of negotiations between Deputy Shatter and the Minister for Justice, Mr. Collins, at a sensitive stage of the passage of the legislation: see Binchy, 'Recent Development in Family Law', 5 *Dlí* 38, at 39 (1991).

Financial provision In *J.D. v. D.D.*, High Court, May 14, 1997, McGuinness J. gave a most insightful judgment on the policies underlying the Judicial Separation and Family Law Reform Act 1989, the Family Law Act 1995 and the Family Law (Divorce) Act 1996. At the heart of her analysis was the concept of the 'clean break' as a guiding principle for the court in making orders for financial provision in family litigation.

There are strong arguments in favour of a 'clean break' approach if a society with open eyes embraces the 'no fault' philosophy of divorce by agreement or on unilateral demand. If we should exclude from our understanding of marriage any notion of permanent commitment and if, during the joint lifetimes of spouses, there should be the opportunity of two or more relationships carrying the name of marriage, then the idea of attaching lifelong responsibilities and entitlements to marriage in this context would contradict the logic of impermanency of commitment; a 'clean break' philosophy harmonises with the notion of moving on and disengaging from the ongoing responsibilities of the first marriage.

Of course, the implication of a 'clean break' philosophy is that it hurts spouses who have invested in the idea that marriage is for life. Most obviously, it damages the economic position of wives (or, more rarely, husbands) who have sacrificed career prospects in order to bring up their children in the family home. As McGuinness J. observed, 'over-reliance on the "clean break" policy has been criticised as causing future hardship to dependent wives.'

The legislative history on this issue has been curious. The 1989 Act encouraged a 'clean break' philosophy: section 15(2) provided that in general a court could grant a property adjustment order once and once only. Section 9 of the 1995 Act contained no such restriction. McGuinness J., surely correctly, decided that there was no limit on when a court could grant a property adjustment order within the joint lifetimes of the spouses, provided the spouse against whom the order was sought had not remarried. The divorce legislation of 1996 had retained this flexibility.

What is striking about *J.D. v. D.D.* is the fact that the wife in proceedings for judicial separation was unusual in that her circumstances indicated that a 'once and for all' resolution of her financial relationship with her husband would be better for her than a solution based on simply a periodical maintenance order, coupled with short-term financial provision solutions. This was because the spouses both came from rich families, they were in their middle age and the wife's options for employment, having been a home-maker, were extremely limited.

McGuinness J. solved the problem by ordering the husband to pay a lump sum by way of maintenance of £200,000 to his wife in addition to financing his wife's residence and to make a periodical payment of £20,000 per annum gross (as the husband had offered). She made an order under section 14 of the 1995 Act extinguishing the share of each spouses in the other's estate under the Sussession Act 1965.

It is worth recording McGuinness J.'s unhappiness with the statutory policy of 'tota[l] oppos[ition]' to the concept of the "clean break"'. McGuinness J. stated:

> This policy is not only clear on the face of the statutes but was most widely discussed, referred to and advocated in the considerable debate that surrounded the enactment of divorce legislation. Such an approach unfortunately not only renders the Court's task in making financial and property orders more difficult; it also, I fear, will create considerable difficulties for parties and their legal advisers when endeavouring to reach a settlement and avoid costly court proceedings.

Separation agreement as a bar to proceedings Irish family law is in a state of some incoherence as to how best to balance the values of spousal autonomy, paternalism and public policy. It will be recalled that the value of spousal autonomy was considered by the Supreme Court to be so strong that it wrecked reforming legislation in relation to ownership of the family home, in *In re Matrimonial Homes Bill* [1994] 1 I.L.R.M. 241; [1994] 1 I.R. 305.

The potential for a clash between these three values is particularly strong in the context of judicial separation. This possibility is enhanced by the changing social attitudes to marriage. Formerly, when marriage involved a mutual commitment for life, backed by proceedings for restitution of conjugal rights, the courts regarded separation agreements with some hostility. Thus, in *Mortimer v. Mortimer*, 2 Hagg Cons. R. 310 (1820), Sir W. Scott stated that the Ecclesiastical Court of the Church of England:

> considers a private separation as an illegal contract, implying a renunciation of stipulated duties, a dereliction from those mutual offices which the parties are not at liberty to desert – an assumption of a false character in both parties contrary to the real *status personae* – and to the obligations which both of them have contracted in the sight of God and man, to live together 'till death do them part' and on which the solemnities both of civil society and of religion have stamped a binding authority from which the parties cannot release themselves by any private act of their own, or for causes which the law itself has not pronounced to be sufficient and sufficiently proved. These courts, therefore, to which the law has appropriated the right of adjudicating upon the nature of the matrimonial contract, have uniformly rejected such convenants as insignificant in a plea of bar, and leave it to other Courts to enforce them so far as they think proper upon a more favourable view, if they entertain it, of their consistency with the principles of the matrimonial contract.

Judicial attitudes on this issue gradually softened. Early this century, Palles CB could state in *MacMahon v. MacMahon* [1913] 1 I.R. 422, at 442, that contracts providing for immediate separation were 'not against the policy of the law', since the rights of the spouses in respect to cohabitation had 'since the Reformation been no more than private rights which the spouses can validly renounce.'

In *Courtney v. Courtney* [1923] 2 I.R. 31, the Court of Appeal of the Irish Free State held that a valid separation agreement constituted a bar not merely to actions for the restitution of conjugal rights but also to petitions for divorce *a mensa et thoro*. In *K. v. K.* [1988] I.R. 161, McKenzie J. endorsed this approach. See the 1988 Review, 243–4.

In *F. v. F.* [1995] 2 I.R. 354, which we analysed in the 1995 Review, 287–91, an application in 1986 for a divorce *a mensa et thoro* and a barring order had been settled and stayed on the basis that the respondent would remain away from the family residence and that neither spouse would molest and interfere with one another. In 1992, three years after the enactment of the Judicial Separation and Family Law Reform Act 1989, the applicant instituted new proceedings seeking a decree of judicial separation under that legislation, as well as a permanent exclusion order, a property adjustment order and an order extinguishing the succession rights of the respondent in relation to the applicant's estate. The Supreme Court, on a Consultative Case Stated, held that the earlier proceedings for a divorce *a mensa et thoro* precluded the taking of separate proceedings for judicial separation. Blayney J. observed that:

> the whole effect of the consent entered into in the proceedings in 1987 was to satisfy and discharge the applicant's claim to a divorce *a mensa et thoro* so that she was barred thereafter from bringing such a claim. And this continued to be the position after the Act of 1989 became law as it did not introduce a new cause of action but altered the title of the procedure to judicial separation.

This fact, in Blayney J.'s view, also distinguished *F. v. F.* from the earlier Supreme Court decision of *H.D. v. P.D.,* May 8, 1978 (extracted in W. Binchy, *A Casebook on Irish Family Law* 313 (1984)) as the Court in *D. v. D.* had been 'dealing with a completely new right which had been introduced by section 5 of the Family Law (Maintenance of Spouses and Children) Act 1976. (We shall come back to *D. v. D.* presently).

In *P. O'D. v. A. O'D.* [1998] 1 I.L.R.M. 543, the Supreme Court returned to the theme, in a Consultative Case Stated by Circuit Court Judge McGuinness (as she then was). The spouses had entered into a separation agreement in 1979. In 1986, the wife had successfully taken proceedings under section 12 of the Married Women's Status Act 1957 for a declaration that she was sole beneficial owner of the family home. In 1988, she obtained an order under section 4 of the Family Home Protection Act 1976, dispensing with her husband's consent for the raising of a mortgage on the house.

In 1995, the husband took proceedings under the 1989 Act, applying for a decree of judicial separation, orders for the transfer or sale of the family home, an award of a lump sum and an order extinguishing his wife's share in his estate as a legal right or intestacy or otherwise. The wife sought by motion to have this application dismissed, on the ground, *inter alia*, that the court could not grant a decree of judicial separation in circumstances where the parties were already relieved of the duty to cohabit with each other by reason of the separation agreement. Judge McGuinness, who had considered the same issue in *N.(C). v. N.R.* [1995] 1 I.F.L.R. 14, held (as she had done in the earlier decision) that the existence of a separation agreement did not in itself bar a subsequent application for judicial separation under the 1989 Act. See Annual Review 1995, 291. The Supreme Court held that this was not correct.

Keane J. (Lynch and Barron JJ. concurring), considered that *F. v. F.* supplied 'an authoritative answer' to the question. It was true that the grounds on which a decree of judicial separation could be granted had been widened by the 1989 Act and a more elaborate range of ancillary reliefs had been provided, but the nature of the primary relief remained precisely the same. After the Act, as before it, the husband and wife by entering into a binding agreement to live separate and apart from each other could render superfluous the granting of a divorce *a mensa et thoro* or a decree of judicial separation. Since the Oireachtas had made it clear that the new and more elaborate reliefs which were now available could only be obtained as ancillary to proceedings where a decree of judicial separation was being claimed, it followed that an applicant could not, by instituting such proceedings in a case where he had already been granted a divorce *a mensa et thoro*, or had entered into a separation agreement, obtain the ancillary reliefs.

Unlike the instant case, a petition had actually been issued in *F. v. F.* seeking a divorce *a mensa et thoro* but there was no reason to suppose that the decision would have been any different if proceedings had not actually been instituted, as was made clear by the following passage from the judgment of Blayney J.:

> For the reasons I gave earlier I am satisfied that the applicant is not entitled to continue her proceedings under the [1989 Act]. There is an additional reason also. The applicant does not need a judicial separation. She has been lawfully separated from her husband for the last seven years. The proceedings she has instituted are not for the purpose of obtaining a judicial separation but are an attempt on her part to get such an order so that she can ask the court to make various ancillary orders in her favour. So she is asking the court to give her relief she does not need with a view to being in a position to obtain other orders that she would like to have. It seems to me that this is not a form of proceeding to which the court could lend its support.

That reasoning was fully applicable to the position of the husband in the instant case.

Keane J. identified two reasons for treating a separation agreement as a bar to subsequent proceedings for judicial separation. First, where the agreement provided (as it invariably did) that the parties were to live separate and apart, the granting of such a decree would be superfluous. Secondly, where parties had entered into a binding contract to dispose of differences that had arisen between them as husband and wife, it would be unjust to allow one party unilaterally to repudiate that agreement, irrespective of whether it took the form of a compromise of proceedings actually instituted.

It might seem harsh to deprive a person who had entered into a separation agreement on the basis of the law formerly applicable to proceedings under the Married Women's Status Act 1957 of the right to avail himself or herself of the more flexible jurisdiction to grant property transfer orders introduced by the 1989 Act. As against this,

> it was for the Oireachtas to balance the possible injustice that might arise in some cases against the desirability of ensuring the finality and certainty in settlements of family law disputes and discouraging parties from re-litigating matters with the consequent trauma for all involved, particularly the children of the marriage. By providing, as it did, that the new reliefs are only to be available where a decree of judicial separation is obtained, the Oireachtas has determined that the last mentioned considerations outweigh any possible injustice that may arise to parties who entered into settlements before the enactment of the 1989 Act.

This judicial emphasis on spousal autonomy and finality is hard to reconcile with other developments in Irish family law. First, the policy in relation to family support obligations is to enable 'applicant spouses' – usually wives – to apply for maintenance for themselves and their children under the Family Law (Maintenance of Spouses and Children) Act 1976, even where they have expressly contracted in a separation agreement not to do so. Section 27 of the 1976 Act makes this plain. It is significant that the Supreme Court, in *D. v. D.,* came to the same conclusion without express reference to section 27.

Secondly, the policy of the law in relation to ancillary orders in the context of judicial separation decrees is opposed to finality. Section 9 of the Family Law Act 1995 makes this clear: See our discussion, above, of McGuinness J.'s judgment in *J.D. v. D.D.*, High Court, May 14, 1997. If a spouse who has made a separation agreement in which he or she has contracted not to seek a court order for maintenance is nonetheless entitled to do so and if a spouse, having been awarded a decree of judicial separation, is always entitled to return to court seeking a further order for maintenance or other ancillary order, what policy justifies excluding a spouse from applying for proceedings for judicial separation simply because he or she has previously made a separation agreement?

The Supreme Court in *J.D. v. D.D.* and in *P. O'D. v. A. O'D.* has identified two rationales. The first this that a separation agreement accomplishes the goal of judicial separation proceedings, which is to entitle the spouses to live apart, and that judicial separation proceedings are therefore otiose. This seems an entirely formalistic justification. There never was a law, enforceable by the State or indeed anyone other than the spouses themselves, requiring spouses to live with each other. Desertion *per se* was neither an offence nor a ground for divorce *a mensa et thoro*. The action for restitution of conjugal rights, for many years unused and for practical purposes a bargaining counter for a spouse to obtain financial support from a deserting husband, had been abolished by the Family Law Act 1988. To interpret the 1989 legislation as being essentially concerned with establishing the right of one spouse to live from the other is unconvincing.

The second rationale identified by the Supreme Court is that it would be *unjust* to enable a spouse who had made a separation agreement prior to the 1989 Act to obtain a decree of judicial separation order to get access to the entitlement to the range of ancillary orders that the court may make on or after the granting of a decree of judicial separation. If this is so, then it must be unjust for a spouse who made a separation agreement before the enactment of the Family Law (Maintenance of Spouses and Children) Act 1976 to seek to obtain its new wide-ranging orders, yet the Supreme Court in *D. v. D.*, without express reliance on section 27 of that Act, held to the contrary, In *F. v. F.*, Blayney J. sought to distinguish that case from *D v. D* on the basis that in *D. v. D.* The Court 'was dealing with a completely new right which had been introduced by section 5 of the Family Law (Maintenance of Spouses and Children) Act 1976'. It would be hard to argue convincingly that, in the context of the wife in *D. v. D.*, the remedy afforded by section 5 of the 1976 Act had any greater novelty than the array of ancillary orders created by the 1989 Act for spouses in relation to whom a decree of judicial separation is made.

DOMESTIC VIOLENCE

Under section 3 of the Domestic Violence Act 1996, a cohabitee who applies for a barring order must have lived with the respondent for at least six months in aggregate during the nine months immediately prior to the application. This requirement gave difficulty where applications for renewals or extensions of barring orders came before the courts. Accordingly, section 4 of the Family Law (Miscellaneous Provisions) Act 1997 removes the uncertainty by providing in unambiguous terms that where, by reason only of a barring order or interim order, the parties have not lived together for the requisite period prescribed by section 3 of the 1996 Act, they are deemed to have done so for the purposes of section 3.

FAMILY HOME PROTECTION ACT 1976

The Supreme Court decision in *Allied Irish Banks v. Finnegan* [1996] 1 I.L.R.M. 401 continues to reverberate. It will be recalled that the Court held that, where a bank was alleging that a mortgage was valid by reason of section 3(3) of the Family Home Protection Act 1976, the burden of proof rested upon it and that the issue whether the bank had actual or constructive notice of the possible invalidity of the non-owning spouse's consent was one that could not be decided on affidavit.

In *ICC Bank plc v. Treacy*, High Court, March 10, 1997, Laffoy J. applied *Finnegan* in a case where the non-owning wife sought to block an order for possession of land including the family home on foot of a mortgage where her husband had failed to make the necessary repayments. The wife filed an affidavit in which she asserted that she had never been involved in the administration of her husband's business, that he had obtained previous loans from the plaintiff which had never affected the family home, that at no stage was she aware that the family home was being used as security for her husband's business dealings and that she had not been aware of the fact that a mortgage had been granted 'nor of the implications thereof'.

Before the mortgage was executed, the wife had made a statutory declaration to the effect that she was the spouse of the mortgagor, that she consented to the creation of the charge and that she had no beneficial interest in the premises being charged. She subsequently averred in her affidavit that she had been in no way advised as to the implications of that documentation or her entitlement to the family home.

Laffoy J. considered that the circumstances arising in the instant case were 'not materially distinguishable' from those in *Finnegan*. On the question of the wife's consent to the mortgage, there was only one version of the circumstances, and this impugned the validity of the consent. The question could be resolved only on oral evidence. Accordingly Laffoy J. made the necessary order joining the wife as a defendant and requiring that the issues of the validity of her consent to the mortgage and of the plaintiff's status as *bona fide* purchaser for value without notice of the invalidity (if such it was) should be tried on oral evidence.

Treacy can be contrasted with *ICC Bank plc v. Gorman*, High Court, March 10, 1997, another judgment of Laffoy J., handed down on the same day as the *Treacy* judgment. In *Gorman*, the case again involved an issue as to the validity of the consent by a non-owning wife to the mortgage of the family home by her husband, in proceedings for possession by the mortgagee for non-repayment of the mortgage instalments. The difference was that, in *Gorman*, the husband and not the wife was seeking to raise the validity of the wife's consent as an issue. He argued that the proceedings for possession should be adjourned because his wife might swear an affidavit.

Laffoy J. noted that the characteristics of a non-owning spouse's consent for the purposes of section 3 of the 1976 Act had been considered by the Supreme Court in *Bank of Ireland v. Smyth* [1995] 2 I.R. 459. In his judgment, Blayney J. had stated as follows:

> The consequences of a consent under section 3 are not as far reaching as the consequences of a consent to marry or to place a child for adoption

but one of the elements required for the validity of the consent in each of these cases is in my opinion applicable in the case of a consent under section 3 also. This is the requirement that the consent must be an 'informed consent' . . .

In my opinion, a consent under section 3 must satisfy this requirement. It must be a fully informed consent. The spouse giving it must know what it is that she or he is consenting to. Since giving one's consent means that one is approving of something, obviously a pre-condition is that one should have knowledge of what it is that one is approving."

In support of its claim for possession, the plaintiff has produced the original of the mortgage on which there was endorsed a form of consent esd signed by the wife. By its terms, the consent was a 'prior consent' to the mortgage. There was no requirement in law that a spouse who was giving a consent for the purposes of section 3 must have the benefit of independent legal advice in the sense of advice from a legal practitioner who was not acting for the mortgagor spouse or the mortgagee. What was required was that the consent should be a 'fully informed consent'. A solicitor had witnessed the giving of the wife's consent and attested her signature. In the circumstances, in the absence of evidence to the contrary, the court was entitled to assume that the wife had given her consent voluntarily and on the basis of adequate knowledge of what she was doing. The wife had been served with the proceedings and had been put on notice of the reliance of the plaintiff on the fact that she consented in writing to the mortgage. Given that she had not challenged the validity of the mortgage, the court was entitled to assume that she accepted its validity.

The circumstances which arose in the instant proceedings, were in Laffoy J.'s view distinguishable from those of *Finnegan*, in which the non-owning spouse presented affidavit evidence as to her lack of knowledge of the true nature of the consent she had signed. Here, there was just a bald statement by the defendant, 'unsupported by any, not to mention any credible, evidence that the mortgage was executed without the prior consent in writing of [his wife]'.

Accordingly, on the evidence before the court, Laffoy J. was satisfied that the mortgage was valid.

CHILDREN

The provisions of Part III of the Children Act 1997 are discussed in the Evidence chapter, 394, above.

NON-MARITAL CHILD

In *L.M. v. Devally* [1997] 2 I.L.R.M. 369, in judicial review proceedings for *certiorari*, Carroll J. addressed an important issue of social policy, where principles of autonomy and paternalism come into conflict. That issue concerns the question of finality in relation to maintenance entitlements of children whose parents did not marry each other. In the context of families based on marriage, legislative policy for the past couple of decades has generally favoured the principle of paternalism. This will be clear from our discussion of *J.D. v. D.D.*, High Court, May 14, 1997 and *P. O'D. v. A. O'D.*, Supreme Court, December 18, 1997, above, 452–4 and 456–9. Section 27 of the Family Law (Maintenance of Spouses and Children) Act 1976 provides that an agreement is void in so far as it would have the effect of excluding or limiting the operation of any provision of the Act. Under section 5, there is a right to apply for a maintenance order on the basis that a spouse has not provided proper maintenance for the family, even in cases where the spouses may have agreed in a separation agreement not to go to the court seeking a maintenance order. In these circumstances, the existence and terms of such a separation agreement will be a circumstance – possibly a very potent one – to which the court has regard when deciding whether to make a maintenance order and, if so, its amount; but there is not way of preventing the court from hearing the application. The Supreme Court came to this conclusion, even without an overt reference to section 27, in *D. v. D.*, May 8,1978, extracted in Binchy, *A Casebook on Irish Family Law*.

The position regarding non-marital children was somewhat different. The woman's affiliation action under legislation of 1930, seeking maintenance for her child, used to be a grim affair, with stringent requirements for corroboration of her evidence and a pressingly short limitation period. The 1976 Act eased some of these restrictions but it preserved the possibility for the father to make a once-off payment in replacement of his ongoing obligation to maintain his child.

Section 10(3) of the 1930 Act, as amended by the 1976 Act, provided that a District Court judge approve voluntary agreements between parties to make provision for a non-marital child only if of the opinion that the provision was substantially as beneficial to the child and his or her mother as the benefits which could be obtained under the Act. Section 10(4) made such an order of approval by the District Court judge a complete bar to any further proceedings under the Act.

The Status of Children Act 1987 greatly integrated the maintenance entitlements of children regardless of the marital status of their parents. It inserted section 5A into the 1976 Act, giving the court power in respect of a dependant child whose parents are not married to each other, on application to it by either parent, to order the other parent to make periodical payments to the applicant parent for the support of the child. As with section 5, in deciding whether to do so and, if so, determining the amount of the order, the court is to have regard to all the circumstances.

In *L.M. v. Devally*, the parties, four years before the statutory changes brought about by the 1987 Act, had compromised a claim for maintenance in relation to a non-marital child. Their agreement had been approved by the court, whose order stated that in 'full and final settlement of all and any claims between the parties', the father would pay the mother £2000 on the date of the order and a further £5,500 within a year. After the 1987 legislation was enacted, the applicant sought an order for maintenance for her child under section 5A of the 1976 Act. The Circuit Court judge dismissed the proceedings on the basis tht the earlier agreement constituted a bar to jurisdiction. Carroll J. granted an order of *certiorari* and remitted the proceedings to the Circuit Court to hear the application on the merits.

Carroll J. reasoned as follows. The 1987 Act had involved a new regime for non-marital children. Since the immunity given by section 10(4) of the 1930 Act related only to proceedings under that Act, it, did not extend to the new regime. When the 1987 Act inserted section 5A into the 1976 Act, it became 'an integral part' of that Act and was subject to section 27. While the court in maintenance proceedings under section 5A was required to take into account all the circumstances of the case, including the lump sum payment, the ultimate issue was whether the father had failed to provide such maintenance for the child as was proper in the circumstances. Accordingly Carroll J. granted an order for *certiorari* and sent the matter back to the Circuit Court to hear the application on its merits.

GUARDIANSHIP OF CHILDREN

The Children Act 1997, which is not yet in force, updates the law on guardianship and custory of children and on aspects of evidence by and relating to children in civil proceedings. Declan McGrath, in the Chapter on Evidence, above 394, discusses these evidential changes. We shall analyse the changes in relation to Guardianship and Custody of Children in the 1998 Review if the Act has come into force by the end of 1998.

Fisheries and Harbours

AQUACULTURE

1997 Act and commencement   The Fisheries (Amendment) Act 1997 provided for the establishment of an Aquaculture Licences Appeals Board and provides a new framework for the licensing and regulation of aquaculture. The Board replaces the Minister for the Marine as the licensing authority for aquaculture. For difficulties which arose under the Ministerial regime, see *Courtney v. Minister for the Marine* [1989] I.L.R.M. 605 (1988 Review, 256) and *Madden v. Minister for the Marine* [1993] I.L.R.M. 436 (HC); [1997] 1 I.L.R.M. 136 (1992 Review, 377–9 and 1996 Review, 386–7). The Fisheries (Amendment) Act 1997 (Commencement) Order 1998 (S.I. No. 46 of 1998) brought sections 2-3, 4(in part), 5(2), 10, 23, 63-64, 65(2) and (3) and 66-67 of the 1997 Act into effect on February 26, 1998 with a view to establishing the new regime by April 1998. Richard Hewitt's annotation, *Irish Current Law Statutes Annotated*, provides a comprehensive overview of the Act.

Regulation of aquaculture   Section 6 of the 1997 Act provides that it is an offence for a person to engage in aquaculture save in accordance with a licence under the Act or under prior statutory authority. Section 9 empowers the Minister to grant a non-renewable trial licence, for a maximum period of two years, for the purpose of investigating the suitability of a site or for experimental purposes and to make the licence subject to conditions. Section 12 provides for the determination of licence applications, notification of the decision to the applicant, and decision publication.

Aquaculture Licences Appeals Board   Section 22 provides for the establishment of an Aquaculture Licences Appeals Board by Order of the Minister. It was estimated during the passage of the 1997 Act that the establishment and operation of the Aquaculture Licences Appeals Board would be in the region of £100,000 per annum. Section 23 provides for the composition of the Board, while section 24 provides for the tenure of office of Chairperson and members of the Board. Section 40 provides that aggrieved persons may appeal against licensing decisions, including revocations and amendments, and details the procedures for lodging appeals and deciding upon them. Sections 44 and 45 provide that in relation to an appeal the Minister, other parties and any person who is not a party, may make submissions or observations within a time limit of one month as specified. Section 49 provides that the Board shall have absolute discretion to hold an oral hearing and prescribes the procedure for requesting such a hearing. Section 58 provides that the Board may refer questions of law to the High Court.

Ministerial directives Section 62 provides that the Minister may issue general policy directives on aquaculture and obliges the licensing authority to have regard to any such directive in performing its functions and prescribes that directives be publicised.

Fees Sections 63 and 64 provide for a fees regime for applications licences and appeals.

Unauthorised installations Section 67 amends section 12 of the Foreshore Act 1933 to enable the removal of unauthorised aquaculture installations and makes it an offence not to comply with an order to do so.

Revocation etc. of licences Section 68 provides that the Minister may revoke or amend an aquaculture licence, the procedures to be followed and compensation provisions where appropriate. Section 69 provides for automatic cessation of licences and a provision for revocation of licences by Minister for reasons of non-operation. Section 70 provides for review of licences on application after three years.

FISHERIES COMMISSION

Membership The Fisheries (Commissions) Act 1997 continued the membership of the Fisheries Commission of a named person and validated orders and actions of the Commission including the named person. The Act came into effect on February 12 1997 on its signature by the President.

HARBOURS

Dublin port harbour The Harbours Act 1996 (Limits of Dublin Port Company) Order 1997 (S.I. No. 98 of 1997), made under the Harbours Act 1996 (1996 Review, 390–6), altered the limits of the Dublin Port harbour with effect from March 4, 1997.

Dun Laoghaire The Harbours Act 1996 (Staff of Dun Laoghaire Harbour Company) Regulations 1997 (S.I. No. 188 of 1997), made under the Harbours Act 1996 (1996 Review, 390–6), enables the transfer of staff from the Department of the Marine to the Dun Laoghaire Harbour Company established under the 1996 Act, with effect from March 3, 1997.

Harbour and port companies   The Harbours Act 1996 (Commencement) Order 1997 (S.I. No. 95 of 1997) and the Harbours Act 1996 (Companies) (Vesting Day) Order 1997 (S.I. No. 96 of 1997) brought many of the harbour and port companies envisaged by the Harbours Act 1996 (1996 Review, 390–6) into existence on March 3, 1997.

Light dues   The Merchant Shipping (Light Dues) Order 1997 (S.I. No. 138 of 1997), made under the Merchant Shipping (Light Dues) Act 1983, prescribed revised fees for vessels calling at ports in the State with effect from April 1, 1997.

Pilotage   The Harbours Act 1996 (Commencement) (No. 2) Order 1997 (S.I. No. 253 of 1997) and the Harbours Act 1996 (Commencement) (No. 3) Order 1997 (S.I. No. 324 of 1997) brought the provisions of the Harbours Act 1996 (1996 Review, 390–6) relating to pilotage into force on June 15, 1997 and July 26, 1997. The Harbours Act 1996 (Initial Organisation of Pilotage Services) Regulations 1997 (S.I. No. 325 of 1997) provides for the provision of pilotage services by the harbour companies and port companies established by the 1996 Act, with effect from July 26, 1997.

LICENCES

Bye-law   In *Guiry v. Minister for the Marine*, High Court, July 24, 1997, Laffoy J. upheld the validity of a bye-law made under section 11(1)(d) of the Fisheries (Consolidation) Act 1959. The Salmon and Trout Conservation (Close Season and Close Time) Bye-law 1997 (Bye-law No. 729 of 1997) which came into operation in January 1997, restricted the use of drift-net and other net fishing. The plaintiffs, drift-net salmon fishermen, sought a declaration that the bye-law was invalid. Section 11 of the Fisheries (Consolidation) Act 1959 provides that an appeal against the making of a bye-law can be brought before the High Court which can confirm or annul the bye-law and that the decision is final. Order 93 of the Rules of the Superior Courts 1986 provides that such appeal shall be brought by special summons which shall state the bye-law concerned and the grounds of appeal.

Citing *Dunne v. Minister for Fisheries* [1984] I.R. 230 and *Needham v. Western Regional Fisheries Board*, High Court, November 6, 1996 (1996 Review, 388–9), Laffoy J. held that the Court's function in an appeal under section 11 of the 1959 Act was to consider the appeal on the merits, notwithstanding the terms in which the relief sought by the plaintiffs was framed in the special summons. She stated that the central issue for the Court was whether, having regard to the evidence before the court, the bye-law was expedient for the more effectual government, management, protection and improvement of the fisheries of the state. In this respect, she was not satisfied that the Minister had failed to take proper account of the recommendations of any report of a particular task force on the fisheries sector, as had been alleged by the plaintiffs. The bye-law did not reflect any deliberate policy to eliminate any sector or to favour any sector over another and Laffoy J. could not come to any conclusion other than that the bye-law was expedient for the good of the State's fisheries and that in making the bye-law the Minister had acted within the ambit of the stated objects of the 1959 Act. She thus affirmed the bye-law.

Registration of fishing boats   The Merchant Shipping (Registry, Lettering and Numbering of Fishing Boats) Regulations 1997 (S.I. No. 294 of 1997) were made under section 373 of the Merchant Shipping Act 1894, as amended by the Fisheries (Amendment) Act 1994: see the 1994 Review, 277. They provide for a new register of fishing boats and for procedures in relation to registration, certificates of registration and the particulars to be registered. The 1997 Regulations revoked and replaced the 1989 register provided for in the Merchant Shipping (Registry, Lettering and Numbering of Fishing Boats) Regulations 1989 (1989 Review, 274). The Regulations were deemed to come into force on August 1, 1994, when the Fisheries (Amendment) Act 1994 came into force.

Salmon trader   In *Tiernan v. North Western Regional Fisheries Board*, High Court, May 12, 1997, Barr J. made an order of *certiorari* quashing the respondent Board's refusal to grant the applicant a salmon trader's licence. Section 158 of the Fisheries (Consolidation) Act 1959 empowers the Board to grant a licence to engage in salmon dealing. Section 159 of the 1959 Act provides that a certificate of fitness to hold such a licence must be obtained from the District Court judge assigned to the area where the applicant carries on or proposes to carry on business and provides that where such a certificate has been obtained, the applicant should, within 28 days, apply to the Board sending the certificate and application fee. Having obtained a certificate and duly applied to the Board for a licence, the applicant filled out the standard application form and submitting the required fee. The Board ultimately refused a licence and indicated that a certificate of fitness did not automatically entitle him to a licence and that the Board had been entitled to take into account all relevant matters, including the presence of a number of other licensees in the area. In the judicial review application, the Board stated it had a policy of restricting the number of licences granted, particularly because it had limited resources to monitor those persons whose were licensed. In the applicant's case, the Board stated that its strongest reason for refusing the application was that there were a number of other dealers in the applicant's area and that the applicant was not involved in the food retail business but the sale of fishing equipment.

Barr J. noted that the primary objective of the 1959 Act was to protect fisheries on a regional basis and the reason that a certificate of fitness was required before a salmon dealers licence could be granted, was to ensure that the applicant would not engage in or facilitate salmon poaching and similar unlawful activity. He stated that the Board's function in dealing with an application for a licence was far from being a mere 'rubber stamp' exercise following the obtaining by an applicant of a certificate of fitness. The statutory purpose of licensing salmon dealers was to provide a public benefit and not to confer a benefit on licensees to sell fish. He accepted that the requirement in the interest of the common good that salmon traders had to be licensed was a potential interference with and restriction of their right to carry on a lawful business. Accordingly, in exercising its function to grant or refuse a licence, the Board was required to perform its duty fairly and reasonably. Citing the decision in *International Fishing Vessels Ltd v. Minister for the Marine* [1989] I.R. 149 (1988 Review, 18), he held that this entailed, *inter alia*, inviting the applicant to specify the case which he wished to make in support of his application and allowing him liberty to respond to any adverse information which might have been furnished to the Board. In considering applications for licences, he held that the Board was engaged in a quaS.I. judicial process and was not entitled to refuse an application on the ground that it did not have the manpower or resources to monitor an applicant's business if granted a licence. Since the applicant had been given no opportunity to make his case and the Board had made its decision without any knowledge of that case and since the applicant had been given no opportunity to respond to the fact that there were already three dealers in his area or to the fact that he had no involvement in the food retail business, the Board had failed in its duty to act fairly and reasonably in ruling on the applicant's application.

Sea fishing boat In *Murphy v. Minister for the Marine* [1997] 2 I.L.R.M. 523, Shanley J. dismissed the plaintiff's claim that the refusal by the Minister of his licence application under section 222B(2) of the Fisheries (Consolidation) Act 1959, inserted by the Fisheries (Amendment) Act 1983, was invalid. Section 222B(2) provides that 'a sea fishing boat to which this section applies shall not be used for sea fishing . . . save under and in accordance with the licence granted for the purpose of this section and in relation to the boat by the Minister'. Section 222B(3)(c) provides that the Minister may allow or refuse an application for a licence subject to section 222B(4)(a) which provides that the Minister shall not grant a licence unless the sea fishing boat is wholly owned by an Irish Citizen or a body corporate established under and subject to the law of the state and having its principal place of business in the state.

Section 224(B)(1) of the 1959 Act, also inserted by the Fisheries (Amendment) Act 1983, provides that 'the Minister may by regulations make provision to give effect within the exclusive fishery limits of the state to any provision either of the treaties or any act adopted by an institution of the European Communities which authorises any or all of the member states of the European Communities to restrict, or otherwise regulate in the manner specified in the provision, fishing in waters or in part of waters, under its or their sovereignty of jurisdiction'.

In January 1989, the plaintiff had applied for a licence when he was negotiating the purchase of a third sea fishing boat. In the event, the sale did not proceed and the plaintiff entered into negotiations for the purchase of another boat. The plaintiff submitted a revised application in March 1989. The plaintiff contacted a Senator who made representations on his behalf to the Minister. The Senator reported to the plaintiff that the Minister would issue the licence and in July 1989 the plaintiff concluded the purchase of the boat. In the wake of a general election in June 1989 and a change of Minister in the Department, the plaintiff was informed by letter in August 1989 that the Minister had established a licensing review group to make recommendations on sea fishing policy and that consideration of all sea fishing boat licence applications had been suspended. The letter invited the plaintiff to submit his views in writing to the Department. By a further letter in June 1990, the Department informed the plaintiff that preference would be given to applicants who had proposed tonnage replacement and requested him to indicate whether his application involved tonnage replacement. The plaintiff did not respond to this letter and fished with the boat until January 1991 when it was arrested. In November 1991, the Minister refused the plaintiff's application on the grounds that he had failed to demonstrate that his application involved tonnage replacement.

Shanley J. heard evidence on behalf of the Minister that section 222B of the Fisheries (Consolidation) Act 1959 was initially inserted by the Fisheries (Amendment) Act 1983 to control Spanish flagship registrations but had come to be used as a convenient tool for quota management. This should be seen against the background of Article 3 of (EC) Regulation 4028/86 on Community measures to improve and adopt structures in the fisheries and aquaculture sector, which required Member States to submit to the Commission a programme concerning, *inter alia*, their fishing fleet. Article 1 required such programmes to include measures for 'the adjustment of fishing capacity by the temporary or permanent withdrawal of certain vessels from fishing activities'. In 1988, the State had submitted a programme having the objective of reducing the size of the Irish fishing fleet to 43,941 gross registered tonnage by 1991 and the programme was approved, subject to certain conditions, by Commission Decision 88/142/EEC. In accordance with the approved programme, by April 1989 the Department was advocating an interim policy in relation to applications for licences based on tonne for tonne replacement. The plaintiff's application (among others) was deferred pending a decision on full review of the licensing policy. A review group was set up within the Department, which reported in February 1990 and advocated that licenses should generally issue only on a replacement basis. The Minister decided to adopt the recommendations and announced this policy in a Dáil Statement in May 1990; the letter to the plaintiff in June 1990 followed from this Statement.

As indicated, Shanley J. rejected the applicant's arguments that the Minister had *acted ultra vires*. He accepted the applicant's case that section 222B of the Fisheries (Consolidation) Act 1959 appeared to have been designed solely to eliminate flags of convenience from the Irish fishing fleet as the only express restriction on the grant of a licence was based on nationality. It did not appear to have been intended to serve as a mechanism to enforce any obligations arising from the Common Fisheries Policy and the terms of section 224B suggested that the legislature had intended that such obligations would be fulfilled by way of statutory Regulations. Despite these initial comments which appeared to favour the applicant, Shanley J. had regard to Articles 5 and 189 of the EC Treaty and Article 29.4.5° of the Constitution, which (together with the European Communities Act 1972) obliged the courts of the State to give precedence to Community law over national law and to construe national legislation in a manner consistent with Community law. He held that the programme submitted by the State pursuant to (EC) Regulation 4028/86 and approved by Decision 88/142/EEC created obligations which the State was bound to discharge. Thus, the adoption of a policy restricting the grant of licences to applications involving tonnage replacement was an appropriate measure to ensure the State's fulfilment of its obligations. Accordingly, the Minister was bound to have regard to the State's obligations under the Common Fisheries Policy in considering the plaintiff's application and was entitled to take into account the policy of restricting the grant of licences to applications involving tonnage replacement.

He held that the decision to refuse a licence to the plaintiff on the grounds that his application did not involve tonnage replacement had not been taken in breach of fair procedures as the plaintiff had been informed of the Department's intention to develop a policy and his views were sought on such a policy. While he accepted that there had been inordinate delay in dealing with the application, there was no evidence that the delay in itself resulted in any prejudice to the plaintiff which would entitle him to an order setting aside the decision. Finally, Shanley J. did not accept the plaintiff's averment that an official in the Department had assured the plaintiff that the licence would issue and there was no admissible evidence that the Minister had made any representation to the plaintiff sufficient to give rise to a legitimate expectation that the Minister would grant the licence. See further the discussion of the case in the European Community chapter, 380, above.

Gaming and Lotteries

PRIZE BONDS

The Prize Bonds (Amendment) Regulations 1997 (S.I. No. 431 of 1997), made under the National Treasury Management Agency Act 1990, amended the period set out in Regulation 19 of the Prize Bonds Regulations 1993, with effect from October 13, 1997.

Garda Síochána

ADMISSION

Bias   In *McAuley v. Keating (No.2)*, High Court, July 8, 1997, O'Sullivan J. held that no bias had been established in the conduct of disciplinary proceedings involving the applicant, a student Garda, under the Garda Síochána (Admissions and Appointments) Regulations 1988 (1988 Review, 259). In previous proceedings, he had successfully challenged certain aspects of these proceedings, but the Supreme Court refused an order prohibiting the Garda Commissioner from taking further disciplinary proceedings, provided that such proceedings were conducted in accordance with the disciplinary code and the requirements of natural and constitutional justice: *McAuley v. Garda Commissioner*, High Court, July 4, 1995; Supreme Court, Febuary 15, 1996 (1995 Review, 337, and 1996 Review, 403–4). The applicant unsuccessfully challenged the subsequent decision to prevent him from progressing to the next phase of his training: *McAuley v. Keating*, High Court, April 24, 1997. In the instant application, the reconstituted investigation into the applicant's conduct was challenged on the grounds that there was unconscionable delay, and that the first respondent, the officer appointed to investigate the alleged breach of the code, had exhibited bias in the sense of pre-judgment against the applicant. O'Sullivan J. dismissed the claim.

He held that, in light of the decision in *McNeill v. Garda Commissioner* [1995] 1 I.L.R.M. 321 (HC); Supreme Court, July 30, 1996 (1994 Review, 281–3, and 1996 Review, 401–2), the applicant was not entitled to any relief on the ground that the procedure adopted by the respondents was either in breach of the 1988 Regulations or his procedural rights by reason of delay. As to bias, he followed the decisions of the Supreme Court in *O'Neill v. Beaumont Hospital Board* [1990] I.L.R.M. 419 (1989 Review, 8–9) and *Dublin Well Woman Centre Ltd. v. Ireland* [1995] 1 I.L.R.M. 408 (1994 Review, 109–110) that the appropriate test of pre-judgment bias was objective in nature, namely, whether a reasonable person would apprehend that his chance of a fair and independent hearing did not exist by reason of the pre-judgment of the issues involved. Applying that test, he concluded that the first respondent was not culpable of pre-judgment bias.

Minimum requirements   The Garda Síochána (Admissions and Appointments) (Amendment) Regulations 1997 (S.I. No. 470 of 1997), made under the Police Forces Amalgamation Act 1925, amended the Garda Síochána (Admissions and Appointments) Regulations 1988 (1988 Review, 259) and prescribe revised minimum educational requirements for entry to the Garda Síochána with effect from May 8, 1997.

COMPLAINTS BOARD

Discovery The decision in *Skeffington v. Rooney* [1997] 2 I.L.R.M. 56 (SC), in which discovery of certain documents held by the Garda Síochána Complaints Board was claimed, is discussed in the Practice and Procedure chapter, 587, below.

Reasons for decision In *McCormack v. Garda Síochána Complaints Board* [1997] 2 I.L.R.M. 321 (HC), Costello P. declined to hold that there was a general duty on the Board to give reasons for its decisions: see the discussion in the Administrative Law chapter, 16–18, above. The decision was followed by Kelly J. in *Flood v. Garda Síochána Complaints Board*, High Court, October 8, 1997.

GARDA COMMISSIONER

Disclosure In *Church v. Garda Commissioner*, High Court, March 18, 1997, Costello P. held that the plaintiffs were obliged to disclose certain sources to the Garda Commissioner in the following circumstances. The plaintiffs were members of the Garda Síochána who, in 1988, as members of the Drug Squad had carried out a search of an hotel along with a search of the home of the one of the hotel employees. The searches were made pursuant to a warrant which had been issued following confidential information received from an informant. Nothing was recovered on foot of these searches and proceedings were later instituted against the plaintiffs and the State claiming damages for what was alleged to be an illegal search. The first plaintiff had written a report within three days of the search in which he stated that the information which he had received might have been given in a deliberate attempt to discredit the parties involved. In 1988, the hotel had asked for the identity of the informant but this request was refused. An investigation was carried out to see whether or not a crime had been committed by maliciously giving false information to the Gardaí. During this investigation, the plaintiffs had refused to reveal the name of their informant and were threatened with disciplinary proceedings. However, the Commissioner later directed that no such proceedings should be commenced unless he so authorised. In 1991, the hotel wrote to the Commissioner stating that new information was available to show that the information had been given maliciously. A new investigation was authorised in 1993 with a view to seeing whether or not a criminal offence had been committed.

By an official circular of May 1993, the Assistant Garda Commissioner dealt expressly with the question of the disclosure of an informant's identity by members of the force. This stated, *inter alia*, that though the identity of an informant did not have to be disclosed save as required by law, it had to be remembered that information in relation to the commission of crime which came into the possession of a Garda, was not his personal property, to be dealt with him as he would. In the course of the new investigation the plaintiffs again refused to reveal their informant's identity. By an order made in December 1993, the Commissioner required both plaintiffs to name the informant, stating that any refusal would be considered to be of such gravity as to merit seeking their dismissal from the Gardaí, pursuant to Regulation 40 of the Garda Síochána (Discipline) Regulations 1989 (1989 Review, 278). The plaintiffs objected to the proposal to operate the summary procedures contained in Regulation 40 and issued the instant proceedings claiming that the Order made in December 1993 was *ultra vires*. They also indicated that they would abide by an order of the High Court should it direct them to disclose the identity. The plaintiffs relied on a manual entitled 'Crime Investigation Techniques' which had been issued on the authority of the Commissioner in 1979 and which stated that to divulge the name of an informant was to act in bad faith. As indicated, Costello P. ordered the plaintiffs to disclose the identity of their informant.

Costello P. held that the plaintiffs had wrongly construed the manual 'Crime Investigation Techniques' because this was a guideline only which did not purport to interpret the law. He held that it did not entitle a member of the Gardaí to disobey orders of a superior or to ignore official circulars. In addition the evidence had established that, notwithstanding the guidelines, in practice in certain circumstances, superior officers did seek the name of informants form Gardaí and this information was given. He considered that the law of evidence and the rules on discovery (as indicated by his own decision in *Director of Consumer Affairs v. Sugar Distributors Ltd* [1991] 1 I.R. 225; [1991] I.L.R.M. 395 (1990 Review, 434-5) and of the Supreme Court in *Burke v. Central Independent Television Plc* [1994] 2 I.R. 61; [1994] 2 I.L.R.M. 161 (1993 Review, 455-7) had no application when considering whether or not an order of the Commissioner was *ultra vires*.

REPRESENTATIVE ASSOCIATIONS

Bias   *Bane v. Garda Representative Association*, High Court, June 27, 1997 involved an aspect of a long simmering dispute concerning the expulsion procedures of the Garda Representative Association (GRA). The GRA had been established under the Garda Síochána Acts 1923 to 1977 and the Garda Síochána (Associations) Regulations 1978 to represent members of the Garda Síochána in matters affecting their welfare and efficiency. A standing committee had power to regulate the membership of the GRA. A serious dispute arose when some members of the GRA took issue with its representation of its members, and in judicial review proceedings in 1994, Morris J. dismissed a case brought against the GRA by several applicants, who included those bringing the present action.

The applicants in the present case were members of the GRA's central executive committee when the earlier case was brought. They had resigned from membership of the GRA following notification from the standing committee that oral hearings would be held concerning charges that they had acted prejudicially to the interests of the GRA and its members. Some of the charges related to evidence given in the earlier court case. At the oral hearings the standing committee found that all charges were proven and imposed penalties relating to membership of the GRA. When these adjudications were made, the second to fifth respondents were members of the committee and each of them had given evidence for the GRA in the earlier proceedings before Morris J. The applicants sought judicial review on the grounds that the expulsion decision was *ultra vires* in that it was inappropriate that persons who had given evidence against them in earlier proceedings should sit to determine whether or not the evidence given by the applicants in those proceedings were false. Kelly J. granted the relief sought.

He held that judicial review lay because the functions of the GRA and its members came within the public domain of the State. He referred in this context to the Supreme Court decisions in *Beirne v. Garda Commissioner* [1993] I.L.R.M. 1 (1992 Review, 382-3), *Geoghegan v. Institute of Chartered Accountants in Ireland* [1995] 3 I.R. 86 (1995 Review, 132) and *Walsh v. Irish Red Cross Society*, Supreme Court, March 7, 1997 (Administrative Law chapter, 14–16, above). The standing committee was obliged to act fairly and in accordance with the principles of natural justice in deciding on the guilt or innocence of members and the penalties to be imposed in the event of wrongdoing being found against them, particularly since a finding against a member could have serious consequences. As to the question of bias, Kelly J. agreed that the hearings were infirm by reason of perceived bias. Applying the objective test of bias in *O'Neill v. Beaumont Hospital Board* [1990] I.L.R.M 419 (1989 Review, 7-9), he concluded that it was inappropriate that many of the charges against the applicants had been instigated by the standing committee itself. For this reason too the adjudications of the committee were vitiated. Indeed, in the circumstances, he held that the charges would not be remitted to the standing committee for further consideration.

Health Services

AGEING AND OLDER PEOPLE

National Council The National Council on Ageing and Older People (Establishment) Order 1997 (S.I. No. 120 of 1997), made under the Health (Corporate Bodies) Act 1961, established the National Council on Ageing and Older People to advise the Minister for Health on this area. The Order came into effect on March 19, 1997.

CANCER REGISTRY

Information The Health (Provision of Information) Act 1997 enabled the provision of personal information to the National Cancer Registry Board, the Minister for Health and Health Boards for the purposes of the national cancer screening programmes. It was considered that, in the absence of such legislation, the passing of personal information would be regarded as being in breach of confidentiality duties and the Data Protection Act 1988 (1988 Review, 390-9). The 1997 Act came into effect on April 1, 1997, on its signature by the President.

CHILD CARE

The Child Care (Pre-School Services) (Amendment) Regulations 1997 (S.I. No. 268 of 1997), made under the Child Care Act 1991 (1991 Review, 232-52) amended the Child Care (Pre-School Services) Regulations 1996 in connection with the forms for notifying health boards that fire safety requirements have been complied with, with effect from June 20, 1997.

HEALTH BOARD

Common contract In *Sullivan v. Southern Health Board*, Supreme Court, July 30, 1997, the Supreme Court reversed a finding that the plaintiff, a consultant doctor, was entitled to damages for breach of his 'common contract' with the defendant Board. Nonetheless, the Court remitted the case to the

High Court for a re-assessment of damages. The plaintiff had been appointed as medical consultant in Mallow Hospital in 1981. He claimed that the Board was in breach of the 'common contract' in that (a) he had been consistently required over a period of years to work hours far in excess of those contracted for; (b) the Board had failed to make available to him reasonable facilities or resources for the proper discharge of his duties; (c) he had not been afforded his annual entitlement to 30 days leave; and (d) the Board was in breach of an implied term in the common contract to appoint and engage a second consult-ant physician from 1988. In the High Court, the plaintiff was awarded £92,966 in damages for breach of contract, £35,654 being for losses sustained by the plaintiff for the failure of the Board to appoint a second physician, £42,312 for loss to the plaintiff of fees from private practice and £15,000 for damages for stress and anxiety caused to the plaintiff in his professional and domestic life.

On appeal by the Board, the Supreme Court allowed the appeal and di-rected a retrial on the quantum of damages for the breach of contract arising from the failure to provide proper resources to the plaintiff. The Court held that it was clear from the course of the High Court action that the claim for £35,654 was not based on the failure of the Board to appoint a second perma-nent physician but was in fact a claim for moneys payable on foot of the con-tract, and that this had not been made in the pleadings or formally presented at any time before the commencement of the proceedings and could not, there-fore, be sustained as damages for breach of the contract. The Court also felt that the plaintiff's claim for general and special damages caused to him by the failure of the Board to provide him with resources for the proper discharge of his duties was inextricably bound up with his unsustainable claims to dam-ages for the alleged breach of contract in failing to appoint a permanent medi-cal consultant and thus had to be overturned.

Nonetheless, as indicated, the Court accepted that the Board was in breach of the terms of the common contract it had entered into with the plaintiff and accordingly was clearly liable to him in damages. The Court thus remitted the claim to the High Court for a re-assessment of damages on that basis. It is also notable that the Court rejected another ground of appeal of the Board, namely that its liability to damages be calculated after deduction of the plaintiff's liability to tax. The Supreme Court held that it would not be proper for any Court to do so without a convincing case having been made for the adoption of that course. On the reduction of damages to take account of tax liability, see *Glover v. BLN Ltd (No. 2)* [1973] I.R. 432.

Financial accountability   The Health (Amendment) (No.3) Act 1996 (Com-mencement) Order 1997 (S.I. No. 209 of 1997) brought ss.1 (in part), 5 to 10 and 12 of the Health (Amendment) (No. 3) Act 1996 (1996 Review, 405–6) into force on January 1, 1998.

HEPATITIS C TRIBUNAL

Establishment and procedure The Hepatitis C Compensation Tribunal Act 1997 provided for the establishment of a statutory Tribunal to compensate persons who had contracted Hepatitis C from Anti-D or blood transfusion or blood products, and their spouses, children, carers or dependants, the background to which was discussed in the 1996 Review, 408. The Act provides for the payment of damages, both general and special and for exemplary or aggravated damages. The non-statutory Hepatitis C Tribunal, which had been established in 1996, stood dissolved on the formal establishment of the statutory Tribunal. This occurred on October 20, 1997, in accordance with the Hepatitis C Compensation Tribunal Act 1997 (Establishment Day) Order 1997 (S.I. No. 443 of 1997). The Hepatitis C Compensation Tribunal Act 1997 (Reparation Fund) (Appointed Day) Order 1997 (S.I. No. 444 of 1997) provided for the statutory reparation fund under the 1997 Act, also with effect from October 20, 1997. The Hepatitis C Compensation Tribunal Act 1997 (Number of Ordinary Members of Tribunal) Regulations 1997 (S.I. No. 441 of 1997) prescribed the number of ordinary members of the Tribunal. Finally, the Hepatitis C Compensation Tribunal Regulations 1997 (S.I. No. 440 of 1997) specified the procedure for applications to the Tribunal, and came into effect on October 30, 1997.

HOSPITALS

Charges The Health (Out-Patient Charges) (Amendment) Regulations 1997 (S.I. No. 509 of 1997), made under section 5 of the Health Act 1947, increased the charges for out-patient hospital services to £20 with effect from January 1, 1998. The Health (In-Patient Charges) (Amendment) Regulations 1997 (S.I. No. 510 of 1997), also made under section 5 of the 1947 Act, increased the hospital charges for in-patient hospital services to £25 per day subject to a maximum of £250, also with effect from January 1, 1998.

LICENSING OF HUMAN MEDICINES

Procedure In *Genmark Pharma Ltd v. Minister for Health*, High Court, July 11, 1997, Carroll J. granted the applicant company judicial review of a decision of the Minister for Health refusing a product authorisation for a drug which the applicant had planned to manufacture in Ireland under the Medical Preparations (Licensing Advertisement and Sale) Regulations 1984. The applicant had argued that the Minister had acted in breach of natural and constitutional justice and that he failed to properly apply Directives 65/65/EEC and

75/318/EEC, which the 1984 Regulations had implemented in Irish law. It was further alleged that the Minister had failed to exercise independent judgment in that he had sought advice from the National Drug Advisory Board (the NDAB).

Carroll J. accepted that while the NDAB had issued guidelines for applications for authorisations under the 1984 Regulations, it had not made Regulations. It had thus been proper for the Minister to seek advice on the application from the NDAB as the latter was a body which had been established by legislation in 1966 to give advice in such situations. But while the Minister had been entitled to seek advice from the NDAB, he was not entitled to rely on the advice in the form of conclusions without reference to the basic material on which those conclusions were based, citing the decision of Barron J. in *Flanagan v. University College Dublin* [1988] I.R. 724; [1989] I.L.R.M. 469 (1988 Review, 14-15) and of the Privy Council in *Jeffs v. New Zealand Dairy Production and Marketing Board* [1967] 1 A.C. 551 in this context. n particular, the Minister had failed to evaluate the advice he had received based on relevant documentation submitted. Applying the decision in *Geraghty v. Minister for Local Government* [1976] I.R. 153, she concluded that the applicant had been entitled to know the final grounds put forward by the NDAB so that it could respond to them before the Minister had made his decision and it was not enough to say that the applicant was aware of the main ground of objection. Finally, Carroll J. noted that the Minister was specifically required to give reasons for his decision by Directive 65/65/EEC.

We should note that the functions discussed in the *Genmark Pharma* case have since been taken over by the Irish Medicines Board, established under the Irish Medicines Board Act 1995: see the 1995 Review, 339-40.

MEDICAL PRACTITIONERS

The decisions in *Georgopoulus v. Beaumont Hospital Board*, Supreme Court, June 4, 1997 and *O'Laoire v. Medical Council*, Supreme Court, July 25, 1997 are discussed in the Evidence chapter, 386–8, above.

REGISTRATION OF BIRTHS AND DEATHS

Amalgamation The amalgamation of registration areas continued in 1997: the Registration of Births And Deaths (Ireland) Act 1863 (Section 18) (Laois) Order 1997 (S.I. No. 134 of 1997); the Registration of Births and Deaths (Ireland) Act 1863 (Section 17 and Section 18) (Mid-Western) Order 1997 (S.I. No. 414 of 1997); the Registration of Births and Deaths (Ireland) Act 1863 (Section 17) (Western) Order 1997 (S.I. No. 416 of 1997); the Registration of Births and Deaths (Ireland) Act 1863 (Section 17 and Section 18) (North Eastern) Order 1997 (S.I. No. 417 of 1997); the Registration of Births and Deaths (Ireland) Act 1863 (Section 17 and Section 18) (South Eastern) Order 1997 (S.I. No. 418 of 1997); the Registration of Births and Deaths (Ireland) Act 1863 (Section 17 and Section 18) (Eastern) Order 1997 (S.I. No. 419 of 1997); the Registration of Births and Deaths (Ireland) Act 1863 (Section 17 and Section 18) (Midland) Order 1997 (S.I. No. 420 of 1997); and the Registration of Births and Deaths (Ireland) Act 1863 (Section 17 and Section 18) (Southern) Order 1997 (S.I. No. 421 of 1997). For previous Orders, see the 1993 Review, 348, 1994 Review, 290–1, 1995 Review, 341, and 1996 Review, 412.

SOCIAL WORK

Qualifications   The National Social Work Qualifications Board (Establishment) Order 1997 (S.I. No. 97 of 1997), made under the Health (Corporate Bodies) Act 1961, established the National Social Work Qualifications Board which will advise the Minister for Social Welfare as to the recognition of social work qualifications. The Order came into effect on February 27, 1997.

WOMEN

Health council   The Women's Health Council (Establishment) Order 1997 (S.I. No. 278 of 1997), made under the Health (Corporate Bodies) Act 1961, established a Women's Health Council to advise the Minister for Health on all aspects of women's health. The Order came into effect on June 24, 1997.

Labour Law and Employment Law

Dr Ubaldus de Vries, Dublin City University

This Chapter deals with labour and employment law matters concerning 1996 and 1997.

CONTRACT OF EMPLOYMENT: IMPLIED TERMS

Employer's liability insurance In *Sweeney v. Duggan* [1997] 2 I.L.R.M. 211, the plaintiff had been awarded damages for injuries he sustained operating a drill at the defendant's quarry. At the time of the award, however, the company had gone into voluntary liquidation and was unable to pay its creditors. The defendant was the managing director and effectively sole shareholder of the company. He was also the quarry manager and as such he had a duty to observe the provisions of the Mines and Quarries Act 1965 regarding the safety, health and physical welfare of persons in quarrying operations. The plaintiff initiated proceedings against the defendant claiming that the defendant had a personal duty to ensure that the company would have an employer's liability insurance or, alternatively, to warn employees that the company had no such policy in existence. The plaintiff argued that this duty derived primarily from his contract of employment and had to be implied having regard to the exceptional nature of quarry work, the company's financial situation and the plaintiff's own small insurance against work-related injuries.

Both the High Court and Supreme Court dismissed the plaintiff's claim. Murphy J. (with whom Hamilton C.J. and Barrington J. concurred) stated that the Courts will imply terms under common law only if such a term can be inferred on the basis of the presumed intention of both parties (see *Shirlaw v. Southern Foundries (1926) Ltd* [1939] 2 K.B. 206; *The Moorcock* (1889) 14 P.D. 64). Alternatively, in certain circumstances a term can be derived from the nature of the contract, regardless of the intention of the parties, as a necessary legal incident of a definable category of contracts. It is not enough that it is reasonable to infer a term, it must also be necessary to give effect to a contract. In the underlying case, Murphy J. stated that to imply the term as to insurance did not hold under the *Moorcock* doctrine. The contract operated effectively without the term and the term would, if suggested by the "officious bystander", be rejected. An employer's liability insurance was primarily beneficial to the company. The term would not have been accepted without considerable negotiations and discussion as to its value to both the employee and employer. As regards whether the term as to insurance was a necessary legal incident, the Court found that the term was not necessary, either as a matter of law or logic, to enable the provisions of the contract to have operative effect.

Neither could the duty of the defendant be found in tort. Referring to English case law (*Scally v. Southern Health and Social Services Board* [1992] 1 A.C. 294), Murphy J. stated that the obligations which exist between employer and employee in the underlying case are to be found in contract alone.

As the contract of employment was between the company and the plaintiff, and no term as to insurance could be implied, the corporate veil could not be lifted to impose liability in contract to the defendant, Mr Duggan, as shareholder or managing director. The Court stated that no duty on the part of a shareholder to an employee could be more extensive than that of the corporation itself.

Notice period In *Smith v. Custom House Docks Development Authority*, High Court, March 20, 1997, the plaintiff carried out work for the defendant as a quantity surveyor in relation to the development of the Custom House Docks. He commenced providing his services in 1987. The contract was a contract for services. The plaintiff argued that the contract for services included an express or implied term that his services would be retained for the entire period of the construction and development of the Custom House Docks (which included the development of the International Financial Services Centre) as set out in the Master Project Agreement Building Programme. The defendant argued that the contract for services was for services "as and when required". This meant that the services of the plaintiff could be terminated at any time when his services were no longer required. In 1992 the plaintiff was informed that his services were no longer required. At no time did the defendant issue a letter of appointment setting out clearly the terms of the plaintiff's appointment. McGuinness J. stated that as there was an unresolvable conflict about the contents and meaning of the contract between the two parties, she had to interpret the contract from the documentation and the available facts. On this basis, the judge concluded that the plaintiff was contracted to carry out work, from time to time, for the period of the Master Project Agreement. As long as this work was performed professionally, 'it was not open to the [d]efendant unilaterally to terminate the contract and employ another quantity surveying firm'. As to what was the precise period of the Master Project Agreement, the judge stated that this was the period as initially set out in the Agreement: five years. She could not come to any longer period given an area so uncertain as the building industry. The judge awarded damages accordingly. Perhaps *obiter*, McGuinness J. also stated that:

A public body such as the CHDDA [Custom House Docks Development Authority], which is acting on behalf of citizens and taxpayers, should be most careful and scrupulous in going through the proper formalities in regard to employment, appointments, and contracts. It was most undesirable that the appointment of the [p]laintiff to carry out an important part of the crucial task of monitoring the MPA [Master Project Agreement] should have been carried out in such a confused and informal manner, without any form of advertising or tendering process or any formal written contract or letter of appointment.

CONTRACT OF SERVICE OR CONTRACT FOR SERVICES

In *Henry Denny & Sons (Ireland) Ltd trading as Kerry Foods v. Minister for Social Welfare* [1996] 1 I.L.R.M. 418, [1996] E.L.R. 43 (High Court); Supreme Court, 12 December 1997 (see Social Welfare chapter, 693, below), the Supreme Court got an opportunity to mark a clear distinction between an employee and an independent contractor for the purpose of determining the legal status of persons who perform work for others. (See also Lanford "The Classification of Workers: Employees and Independent Contractors" (1998) *CLP* 63). This distinction is important because it determines, among other things, the applicability of employment legislation. A worker, for example, who works under a contract for services cannot rely on the Social Welfare Acts 1993-1997, nor has, for example, the Employment Appeals Tribunal jurisdiction to hear disputes arising out of a contract for services (see *O'Hara v. Radio 2000 Ltd* [1997] E.L.R. 61).

In the *Denny* case, a worker was hired as an in-house demonstrator by the applicant. The worker underwent a brief induction as to what she was required to do. She worked approximately 28 hours a week at a basic rate of £85.00 for 48-50 weeks a year. Although she could refuse to work, she could not, save in exceptional circumstances, have others do the work for her. The demonstration stand, products and uniform were supplied to her and she was required to abide by the directions and regulations of the supermarket. She received no holiday pay or pay for illness, nor was she member of the company's pension scheme. She signed a yearly contract. It stipulated that each time she worked for the applicant it was a separate contract and that she was free to do other work. When her yearly contract ended in 1988 she continued to do work for the applicant under separate agreements for another five years. These agreements set out that she was an independent contractor, not an employee, and that nothing would be construed as creating a master-servant or principal-agent relationship. In 1992, the worker and the company were required to fill in a form to determine whether she was an insurable person under the Social

Welfare Acts 1993 to 1997. The social welfare officer decided she was an insurable person. The company appealed this decision which was rejected by the appeals officer. The latter stated that the worker was under a contract of service as she was subject to the control and direction of and dismissal by the company. This decision was reviewed and upheld by the chief appeals officer who found the decision consistent with the law. The applicant company appealed to the High Court.

In the High Court, Carroll J. dismissed the appeal, stating that merely labeling the contract as one for services was not enough (see *Massey v. Crown Life Insurance Co* [1978] 1 W.L.R. 676). To determine whether a contract of service or a contract for services existed, Carroll J. applied a number of tests: the control test (can the company direct the demonstrator as to what is to be done and how?; see *Roche v. Patrick Kelly & Co Ltd* [1969] I.R. 100), the integration test (is the work done an integral part of the company's business?), the economic reality test (does the worker provide her own work for a remuneration and agrees to be subject to the company's control?; see *Readymix Concrete Ltd v. Minister of Pensions* [1968] 2 Q.B. 497) and the entrepreneurial test (is the worker who has engaged herself to perform the services performing them as a person in business on her own account?; see *Market Investigations Ltd v. Minister for Social Security* [1969] 2 Q.B. 173). On the facts of the case, Carroll J. concluded that a contract of service existed. The appeals officer had applied the law correctly and sufficient evidence existed for him to reasonably draw the conclusion that a contract of service existed. The worker was an employee and, thus, an insurable person. The company appealed to the Supreme Court.

In the Supreme Court, Keane J., dismissed the appeal. He stated first that the trial judge was correct in holding that merely describing the worker in the written agreement as an "independent contractor" was not conclusive. The appeals officer was right not to confine himself solely to what was contained in the contract but also to consider all the circumstances of the worker's employment. The High Court was correct in concluding it could not interfere with these findings on appeal. The second question was whether the appeals officer had erred in law. To this end, Keane J., by reference to English and Irish case law, discussed the criteria used to consider whether a particular employment was to be regarded as a contract of service or a contract for services. Each case had to be considered on its own particular facts. In addition certain general principles applied. The first principle related to the extent and degree of control exercised by one party over the other in the performance of the work. Keane J. pointed out that this may not always be of use. He referred to a master of ship, although clearly employed under a contract of service, the ship's owners are not entitled to tell the master how to navigate the ship (see *Cassidy v. Ministry of Health* [1951] 2 K.B. 343). Second, the Courts had developed the so-called entrepreneurial test: is the person who engages himself to perform certain services performing them as a person in business on his or her own account? (see *Market Investigations Ltd v. Minister of Social Security* [1969] 2 Q.B. 173; Keane J. also referred to a decision of the Supreme Court of the Irish Free State, *Graham v. Minister for Industry and Commerce* [1933] I.R. 156). If so, the contract is a contract for services; if not, the contract is a contract of service. Considerations that determine this are necessarily non-exhaustive (and depend on the circumstances of the case). They include, however, the extent of control exercised, provision of own equipment, taking of financial risks or investments, employing other persons, etc. Applying this test, Keane J. held that the appeals officer had not erred in law; the worker was employed under a contract of service.

EMPLOYMENT EQUALITY

The Employment Equality Bill 1996   On April 3, 1997, the then President, President Robinson, referred the Employment Equality Bill 1996 to the Supreme Court in accordance with Article 26 of the Constitution for a decision as to whether the Bill or any of its provisions were repugnant the Constitution or certain provisions of the Constitution: *In re the Employment Equality Bill 1996* [1997] E.L.R. 132. The judgment was delivered by the Chief Justice, Hamilton C.J.

The chief aim of the Bill was to outlaw discrimination in employment and to promote equality between employed persons. The Bill also was to give effect to two Council Directives: Council Directive (75/177/EEC) on equal pay between men and women, and Council Directive (76/20/EEC) on the equal treatment between men and women as regards access to work, vocational training and promotion and working conditions. The Bill purported further to provide for rules in relation to harassment at work, and the name and constitution of the Employment Equality Agency. It would have repealed the Anti-Discrimination (Pay) Act 1974 and the Employment Equality Act 1977. (See also Barry "Employment Equality Bill 1996" [1996] E.L.R. xvii-xxv).

It was felt that certain exceptions as to what amounted to discrimination, for example, the religious ground exception, could be unconstitutional. It was also argued that the exceptions on the grounds of age or disability and the employer's duty to provide for extra facilities or special treatment to disabled employees could be deemed to be unconstitutional. The President decided to refer the whole Bill to the Supreme Court, rather than these specific provisions. This led the Chief Justice to remark that the Supreme Court's function in this particular case was a 'formidable one' ([1997] E.L.R. 132 at 142). The Bill consisted of 74 sections and affected 33 other Acts. The Bill was a novel and wide-ranging reformist measure. This meant that the Court could not restrict itself to reviewing one or some provisions that had been argued to be unconstitutional. The Bill, and the referral procedure under Article 26, demanded that the Court had to review the entire Bill upon its constitutionality. If otherwise, the questions posed to the Court by the President would not be fully answered and the Bill might continue to cause concern to the President. The Supreme Court concluded that eight aspects of the Bill demanded particular attention. These aspects related to:

- provisions relating to the age ground: sections 6(3), 33 and 37(6);
- provisions relating to the religious ground: sections 12 and 37;
- provisions relating to the disability ground: sections 6(2)(g), 16 and 35;
- provisions relating to the employers' vicarious liability: sections 14 and 15;
- provisions in relation to unlawful sexual behaviour: section 16(4);
- certification of the offence set out in section 63 (obstruction/non-compliance);
- provisions in relation to the inviolability of the dwelling: section 58;
- provisions in relation to the right of silence: section 59(3).

Age Section 6(3) of the Bill provided that treating persons under 18 or over 65 less favourably than others did not constitute discrimination on the age ground. Section 33 provided that the provisions of the Bill were not to prevent measures to ensure integration into employment of people of 50 years old or older. Section 37(6) provided that the anti-discrimination measures in relation to age did not apply to members of the Garda Síochána, the Defence Forces or the prison service.

It was argued that these sections were unconstitutional, violating Article 40.1. (equality) and Article 40.3. (right to work and the right to earn a livinghood). Counsel assigned by the Court argued that that the cut-off ages of 18 and 65 in relation to section 6(3) was arbitrarily achieved and in itself discriminatory in the absence of any rational justification. Counsel also argued that section 6(3), as well as sections 33 and 37(6) did not provide an objective justifiable ground. The object of section 33, for example, could be achieved more reasonably by referring to the time of unemployment rather than the age of the unemployed person, it was submitted. Section 37(6) clearly discriminated between persons working in the public sector and persons working in the private sector. Finally, the sections were unconstitutional from the employers' perspective in that they unjustifiably and disproportionately interfered with their right to earn a livinghood and their right to property. The provisions would prevent them from taking into account the suitability of prospective employees for the work in question having regard to their age. Counsel on behalf of the Attorney General pointed out that in construing the relevant provisions of the Bill, one had to take into account the overriding objective of the Bill: to promote equality between workers.

The Supreme Court first pointed out that Article 40.1 of the Constitution guarantees that all citizens are held equal before the law but that the State may have regard to "differences of capacity, physical and moral, and of social function". Discrimination between groups of persons in relation to, for example, their age, was not *prima facie* a violation of those persons' rights to equality before the law (the Court referred to, for example, *Brennan v. Attorney General* [1983] I.L.R.M. 449 and *The People v. Quilligan (No.3)* [1993] 1 I.R. 305, 1992 Review, 234-39). As regards Article 40.3, the Court recognised that people have an unenumerated right to work and to earn a livinghood. The State may, however, impose restrictions 'where that is required by the exigencies of the common good' ([1997] E.L.R. 132 at 151). The Court concluded that the provisions in relation to age were not repugnant to the Constitution. Article 40.1 allows the State to treat citizens or classes of citizens differently. Any other interpretation would defeat the purpose of Article 40.1. Where the Oireachtas does categorise persons into different categories for the purpose of legislation, nothing will stop it to do so on age, as long as this is not arbitrary or irrational. The age limits chosen in section 6(3) were not arbitrary or irrational, as they properly reflect the thresholds at which employees normally enter or leave the work force. As regards section 33, the cut-off age of fifty was also not arbitrary or irrational, nor was it unrelated to the purpose of reducing long-term unemployment. As long as the method chosen by the Oireachtas is not irrational or arbitrary, the Court must accept this method, even though other methods are also available. As regards section 37(6), the Court stated that discrimination on the grounds of age falls into a different category than discrimination on the grounds of sex or race. Taking into account the specific nature of the employment and the relatively narrowly defined class of employees in question in section 37(6) the decision of the Oireachtas was understandable and justified. Finally, the Court held that the provisions did not violate the employers' right to earn a livinghood and to property. Although the provisions may be burdensome to employers, particularly smaller firms, the Bill had sought, as far as practicable, to balance the conflicting interests. As this has been proven not to be arbitrary or irrational, the provisions were not unconstitutional.

Religion Section 12 set out that persons offering vocational training cannot discriminate against persons (who are not statutorily obliged anymore to attend school) in relation to the terms by which they offer courses, refusing or omitting to afford access to such courses and the manner in which they provide courses. Subsection 12(4), however, stated that discrimination based on religious belief or outlook may be exercised to ensure the availability of nurses and primary school teachers, but only to the extent to preserve the religious ethos of the institution that promotes in the exercise of its services certain religious values. Section 37 allowed for religious, educational and medical institutions to discriminate in relation to employing staff on the basis of the religion ground, as long as the institution was established for religious purposes or the institution provides services in an environment which promotes certain religious values. In effect, these institutions may treat certain persons (employees or prospective employees) more favourably than others in order to maintain the religious ethos of the institution or to prevent persons to undermine the religious ethos. Discrimination, here, can relate to marital status, family status, sexual orientation, religion, race or being a member of the traveling community.

Counsel assigned by the Court argued that these provisions violated Articles 40.1 and 44.2 of the Constitution. The provisions purported to legalise religious discrimination and to endow certain religions contrary to Article 40.2.2°. The provisions would allow employers to make religion a criterion to employ, dismiss, or allow employees to undergo vocational training. Furthermore, it was submitted that the provisions would have a far more far-reaching effect than envisaged by Article 44 and be disproportionate to it. The provisions would allow institutions to define their own (religious) ethos and, in doing so, dictate the institutions' employment policy. This could undermine the right of persons who practice a "minority" religion or who do not practice a religion at all, to earn a livinghood. A final point made by counsel was that "institutions" were not further defined in the Bill. Counsel for the Attorney General claimed that the discrimination allowed under sections 12 and 37 amounted in effect to positive discrimination. They were necessary to give effect to Article 44. Counsel also submitted that the State did engage in aiding institutions and that this is authorised by the Constitution. The distinctions made in the Bill were, subsequently, authorised by implication.

The Court stated that the Bill validly balanced the constitutional rights at stake. On the one hand, there was a general prohibition to discriminate or even distinguish between citizens on the basis of religion, as set out in Article 44. However, on the other hand, Article 44.2 of the Constitution provided for free profession and practice of religion. This could, in limited circumstances allow for discrimination to give life and reality of free profession and religion. In addition, the right to earn a livinghood and the right to equality should be taken into account. Section 37 – permitting to discriminate to maintain the religious ethos of a institution where it is reasonable to do so or is reasonably necessary to prevent a (prospective) employee to undermine the ethos of the institution – represented a reasonable balance between the right to free profession and practice of religion on the one hand and the right of equality before the law and the right to earn a livinghood on the other hand. The test as to what was "reasonable" is an objective test and must be resolved on a case to case basis. As to what amounted to "ethos", although an institution should define its own ethos, was also a matter to be resolved, on final analysis, by the Courts on a case-by-case basis. By analogy, section 12 on vocational groups and the provision of training, represented a reasonable balance between the competing constitutional rights and was, also, not unconstitutional.

In practice, section 37 of the Bill gave the religious institutions the benefit of the doubt. The Court thought it appropriate to safeguard the religious ethos of an institution in favour of the basic rights of employees or prospective employees. These persons will not be allowed to or will fear not to be allowed to fully express their individuality if this is not similar to the ethos of the institution they work in or apply to. The conflicts that may stem from this difference in outlook or propensity, will always undermine the relationship between employer and employee, and will always be more disadvantageous for the latter.

Disability The cumulative effect of sections 6(2)(g), 16 and 35 of the Bill meant that an employer should bear all relevant costs associated with extra facilities or special treatment to enable disabled persons to carry out their work, unless these costs would cause undue hardship for the employer. It was argued that in effect, the provisions would limit the employer's right to carry on a business and earn a livinghood. The provisions were an unjust attack on a person's property rights under Article 40.3, unless the provisions were reconciled with the exigencies of the common good and social justice (the promotion of equality in the work place between the disabled and other workers).

The Court agreed with counsel appointed by the Court that the provisions and the constitutional guarantees could not be reconciled and formed an unjust attack on a person's property rights and, therefore, were repugnant to the Constitution. First, the Court found that society should bare the costs to promote this equality. The provisions attempted to require employers to employ disabled people, but also to shift the costs of what was essentially a societal problem to a particular group. Second, the provisions did not allow for exemptions for small or medium-sized companies. However, the Court allowed the Defence Forces, the Garda Síochána and the prison service to be exempt from the provisions although it found it difficult to understand why, for example, the clerical and civilian wings of these services should be exempt. In effect, the Court stated that it would be impermissible to impose any cost burden in this area on employers. The Court found that this was a matter for the State.

An editorial in (1997) 15 *ILT* 109 pointed out that this part of the judgment was hard to reconcile with Regulations made in pursuance of the Safety, Health and Welfare at Work Act 1989 and European Health and Safety Directives, requiring employers to organise places of work to take account of handicapped employees, if necessary. It depended, however, as to whether these provisions of the Bill could be referred to as being health and safety legislation and being subject to health and safety Directives as defined under Article 118a of the EC Treaty. If so, the Supreme Court's decision may be contrary to European law.

Vicarious liability   The vicarious liability provisions of the Bill were perceived as the most controversial (section 15). The provisions attempted to make employers vicariously liable for discriminating acts done by employees in the course of their employment or as the employers' agents. These acts could amount to serious criminal offences. Employers would have only one defence: they can show that they have taken steps that were reasonably practicable to prevent such persons to carry out discriminatory acts.

Is it fair and reasonable to make employers vicariously liable for such acts carried out by their employees or agents? The general principle in the context of criminal proceedings is that persons are responsible for their own acts, and not for the acts done by their servants or agents unless the former has authorised such criminal acts. Statutory exceptions to this rule are made in relation to offences which are essentially regulatory in nature and apply to persons who have a particular privilege or duty to uphold public standards. The Court referred to this end to health and safety legislation, environmental legislation and consumer protection legislation. The Court, however, stated that section 15 would impose liability on an employer for offences carried out by his or her employees that could potentially lead to severe criminal sanctions for which the employer may be devoid of any guilty intent. The offences referred to were far from regulatory in character. To impose liability would be so unjust, irrational and inappropriate that any court trial deriving from section 15 would not be one that could be held in due course of law, and would be contrary to Articles 38.4 and 40.1 of the Constitution. In addition, the Court stated that section 15 would constitute a radical departure from present criminal law and be disproportionate to the social policy behind section 15, which was to make the Bill more effective.

Unlawful sexual behaviour   Section 16(4) stated that none of the Bill's provisions required an employer to recruit or promote any person if he or she had a past criminal conviction for unlawful sexual behaviour or that person was considered, based on reliable information, to be engaged in or had a propensity to engage in unlawful sexual behaviour. Counsel assigned by the court argued that the provision could violate a person's right to equality as identified in *King v. Attorney General* [1981] I.R. 233, on the grounds that a person could be singled out on the basis of "reliable information". The language used, "reliable information", was uncertain and against the requirement that laws, such as this should be certain. Counsel for the Attorney General pointed out that the provision was an exemption an employer can avail of, and did not affect an employee's existing legal and Constitutional remedies against his or her employer for, *e.g.*, unfair dismissal.

The Court pointed out that the provision was a matter of policy and was justified to be included in the Bill on the grounds of safety and prudence. As to what amounted to "reliable information" or "the propensity to engage in unlawful sexual behaviour" would be decided by the relevant tribunal. The Court also stated that it is important that an employer confronted with a problem, must make a *bona fide* judgement and give due regard to all the relevant circumstances.

It is regrettable that the Court did not take the opportunity to define "reliable information" or "the propensity to engage in unlawful sexual behaviour". It would give subsequent tribunals some point of references, and certainty. This would benefit all parties involved. It could have prevented better the unnecessary damage to a person's reputation if the allegations are subsequently found to be unfounded.

Other issues The Supreme Court addressed three other constitutional challenges unrelated, to an extent, to labour and employment law.

First, section 63 made it an offence to obstruct or impede the court, the Director of Equality Investigations or equality officers in the exercise of their functions and made it an offence to fail to comply with their requirements under Part V of the Bill. Subsection 63(3) allowed to this end, a document certified by the Director or sealed by the court that stood in relation to the alleged offence to be *prima facie* evidence of the facts stated therein. It was argued that it was unconstitutional that a criminal procedure could be conducted, on the part of the prosecution, on a certificate alone, and to require the accused to give evidence or suffer the consequences. The certificate may have been drawn up by a person who may not have been the person involved in the events and certify information he or she received from others. The net effect was that it shifted the burden of proof. To this end, subsection 63(3) constituted a violation of an accused right to a trial in due course of law. The Court agreed with counsel and stated that the right to a fair trial implied that it is a fundamental principle that criminal procedures are conducted on *viva voce* evidence. It referred to the decision in *In Re Haughey* [1971] I.R. 217. Proof by certification is only appropriate when it is proportionate to the ends it wants to achieve. The Court referred to, for example, scientific or technical matters. The scope, however, of the certification process was too wide under section 63(3). It included matters which were not amenable to resolution in that manner and the certifying person may not have had direct knowledge of these matters. In addition, the process envisaged a conclusion of a guilty verdict simply on the basis of the certificate because it may refer to all circumstances in which the offence was alleged to have occurred. The certification process interfered with the right to a fair trial because the interference was disproportionate, intruded too much on the accused constitutional rights and the interference was not rationally designed to meet the objectives of the Bill.

Second, it was argued that section 58 of the Bill was repugnant to the Constitution as it allowed, among other things, the forcibly entry into a dwelling. The Court stated that the powers contained in this section were reasonably necessary to enable the Minister, the Director of Equality Investigations or the Labour Court to carry out their functions for the purpose of enforcing the provisions of the Bill. The provisions were surrounded by express limitations, including the mandatory search warrant to be authorised by the District Court. The provisions were not repugnant to the Constitution.

Finally, it was submitted that section 59(3), which required persons to answer truthfully any questions put to them by the Director or chairman of the Labour Court, was also repugnant to the Constitution as it would violate a citizen's privilege against self-incrimination. Again, the Court stated that the provisions contained in the section were reasonably necessary to enable the Director or the Labour Court to carry out their function for the purpose of enforcing the provisions of the Bill. They did not encroach, having also regard to the saver contained in subsection 3(a), on any privilege against self-incrimination.

The Employment Equality Act 1998 which takes account of the decision of the Supreme Court, will be discussed in the 1998 Review.

The Equal Status Bill 1997   In *In re the Equal Status Bill 1997* [1997] E.L.R. 185, the Supreme Court struck down sections 40(3) and 71 of the Equal Status Bill 1997, as these were similar to the provisions which were declared unconstitutional in *In re the Employment Equality Bill 1996* [1997] E.L.R. 132. Given this, the Court stated that there was no presumption for counsel assigned by the Court to rebut and no justiciable issue to try. Section 40(3) of the Equal Status Bill 1997 related to the admission in criminal proceedings of a certificate relating to the circumstances of the offence as *prima facie* evidence of the facts stated in the certificate. All material aspects were similar to subsection 63(3) of the Employment Equality Bill 1996. Section 71 provided for the vicarious liability of employers in relation to criminal offences and was similar in terms to section 15 of the Employment Equality Bill 1996.

Unlike the decision in *In re the Employment Equality Bill 1996*, in *In re the Equal Status Bill 1997* the Supreme Court did not consider the constitutionality of any other provisions. The Court held that it was established jurisprudence that if one provision of a referred Bill under Article 26 was held to be unconstitutional, the Court should remain silent in respect of the constitutionality of other provisions (see *In re the Housing (Private Rented Dwellings) Bill 1981* [1983] I.R. 186 and *In re the Matrimonial Home Bill 1993* [1994] I.R. 305). This was contested by counsel for the Attorney General, claiming that the Supreme Court had modified its view since its previous decision in *In re the Employment Equality Bill 1996*. The Court pointed out that in *In re the Equal Status Bill 1997* the referral of the Employment Equality Bill 1997 was of a different nature and not to review other provisions that were of concern to the President could have led to an unnecessary series of referrals under Article 26. The reference concerning the Equal Status Bill

1997 was different. First, section 40(3) and 71 were clearly repugnant to the Constitution, so there was no need to review other provisions. Second, large portions of the Bill were inoperable because they depended on the implementation of the Employment Equality Bill 1996.

Adoptive leave In *Telecom Éireann v. O'Grady* [1996] 2 I.L.R.M. 374, the respondent submitted that his employer, the appellant, discriminated against him in not allowing him adoptive leave. Sections 2 and 3 of the Employment Equality Act 1977 provide that an employer cannot discriminate against an employee by reason of the employee's sex. Section 16 of the Act allows employers to put in place special provisions for women in connection with pregnancy and child birth. The Act gave force to a Council Directive on the implementation of the principle of equal treatment for men and women as regard access to employment, vocational training and promotion, and working conditions (76/207/EEC). The Directive states in Article 2(3) that the Directive 'shall be without prejudice to provisions concerning protection of women, particularly as regards pregnancy and maternity'.

The respondent applied for adoptive leave. This was refused as this was only made available under the company' scheme to women. The respondent claimed that the words "pregnancy" and "childbirth" were applicable to a biological relationship between mother and child and were not wide enough to include a non-biological relationship as is the case in an adoption. The equality officer disagreed and favoured the broader interpretation of the two words. The respondent successfully appealed to the Labour Court. This Court stated that section 16 of the Act must receive a narrow interpretation and, therefore, did not justify discriminatory treatment in relation to adoptive leave. The employer appealed to the High Court. It argued that the teleological and purposive approach, as normally used in interpreting EU Directives justified the broader meaning of "childbirth".

The High Court dismissed the appeal. Murphy J. held that the scheme as operated by the applicant was only available for women and that the respondent was discriminated against was *prima facie* well-founded. The question, however, was whether section 16 of the Act would allow for such discrimination. Murphy J. stated that the 1977 Act gave effect to Ireland's obligations under EC law. To this end, the national legislation had to be construed in accordance with the purpose of the Council Directive (see *Marleasing SA v. La Commercial Internacional de Alimentacionsia SA* [1990] E.C.R. 4156). Article 2(3) of the Directive aimed at protecting women in two ways. First, to ensure the safety of a (pregnant) woman's biological condition and, second, to protect the special mother-and-child relationship following the pregnancy and birth. To this end, maternity leave could legitimately be reserved for the mother alone. The Directive left Member States with sufficient discretion as to implement measures to give effect to the framework of the Directive, as directives normally do (see *Hofmann v. Barmer Ersatzkasse* [1984] E.C.R. 3047). The 1977 Act allowed for special treatment in relation to "pregnancy" and "childbirth". The Oireachtas decided not to refer to the terminology used in the Directive: "pregnancy" and "maternity". The word "maternity" would include, contrary to "childbirth", adoption. In this context, Murphy J. stated that a narrow interpretation had to be given to the words used that allow for exemptions under the 1977 Act and the Directive (section 16 and Article 2(3) respectively). In doing so, the goal of the Council Directive, to avoid discrimination, was better achieved. Accordingly, Murphy J. concluded that the discrimination was not permitted by the statutory exemption and that the respondent would be entitled to adoptive leave.

This case was appealed to the Supreme Court (*Telecom Éireann v. O'Grady*, [1998] E.L.R. 61). The Court dismissed the appeal. A full discussion of the Supreme Court's decision will take place in the 1998 Annual Review.

Equal pay   In *Flynn and Others v. Primark (trading as Penneys Ltd) and the Minister for Equality and Law Reform* [1997] E.L.R. 218, the plaintiffs brought an equal pay claim under the Anti-Discrimination (Pay) Act 1974. Most plaintiffs were female and employed as clerical or sales assistants. The comparators were all male store men. The Equality Officer found no discrimination on sex as other factors justified the difference in pay. The Labour Court rejected the appeal (*Sales and Clerical Assistants v. Penneys Ltd* [1996] E.L.R. 78). (See also: Bolger [1996] E.L.R. iv-ix "A History of Inequality in the Law on Equal Pay"). It upheld the decision of the Equality Officer. She had found that although the work of the plaintiffs and their comparators was of equal value (the plaintiffs were doing like work under section 3(c) of the Act), the nature of the work was not similar, (the plaintiffs were not performing like work under section 3(b) of the Act), and other factors had determined the rate of pay. (As regards work of equal value, see also: *C & D Food Ltd v. Cunnion and Others*, High Court, July 30, 1996). The rates of pay were achieved through different industrial routes and were both unisex rates even though one group consisted of predominantly female workers and the other group consisted of predominantly male workers.

On appeal, the High Court had to consider whether the Labour Court had used the appropriate principles to determine whether the plaintiffs were discriminated against. Barron J. argued that the Labour Court had applied the wrong principle. It was established European law that where a practice existed that affects significantly more members of one sex than the other, *prima facie* discrimination existed which was prohibited under Article 119 of the EC Treaty. The proper principle, then, to be applied was whether the difference in pay was objectively justified on economic grounds (cf: *Jenkins v. Kingsgate* [1981] E.C.R. 911). The onus was on the employer to show it did. The National Court, *i.e.* the Labour Court, had to determine as a matter of fact whether the pay policy was discriminatory on the grounds of sex, cf. *Enderby v. Frenchay Health Authority* [1994] I.C.R. 112. It was not sufficient for the Labour Court only to consider whether there were other reasons unconnected with sex for the difference in pay. Instead, the Court had to consider whether such findings had been made and, if so, whether they would objectively justify the difference in pay. That the rates of pay were determined through different industrial routes did not *per se* objectively justify the difference in pay. (See also *8 Male Workers v. Eastern Health Board* [1997] E.L.R. 1 and *24 Female Employees v. Spring Grove Services* [1996] E.L.R. 147).

The case was remitted to the Labour Court to apply the objective justification principle (as to how the Equality Officers assessed "like work" under sections 3(a) and 3(b) of the Anti-Discrimination Act 1974): *Penneys Ltd v. MANDATE* [1998] E.L.R 94. The Labour Court found that the difference was justified, objectively, on economic grounds. The difference in payment went back as far as 1970 and, at the time, was economically justified. The changes in work practices of the comparator group generated economic and industrial benefits. The differences remained justified for three reasons. First, to alter the work practices would mean increased costs and a reduction of productivity. Second, if the additional pay given to the comparator group had to be removed, serious industrial consequences could follow. Third, it is normal industrial practice that benefits which have been required are retained.

The Editorial in the Employment Law Reports (Volume 9, Issue 2) points out that the respondent gained industrial peace for the extra payments to the comparator group, and that this is a valuable consideration and justified the differential in pay. The decision of the Labour Court is once again under appeal to the High Court.

In *Minister for Transport Energy and Communications v. Campbell* [1996] E.L.R. 106, the defence of "red circling" was raised to justify the difference in the rate of pay between two groups of employees doing like work. The claimants, female employees working in the accounts unit processing charges levied on users of the communications services of the Minister ("communications assistants"), claimed they were entitled to the same rate of pay as two male employees, graded as "radio officers" (the comparators). They claimed they were doing like work relying on section 2(1) of the Anti-Discrimination (Pay) Act 1974. They claimed that a case for discrimination on grounds other than sex was not made out (section 2(3) of the 1974 Act). In the Labour Court, the Minister justified the difference in rate of pay on the basis of the "red circling" defence. Red circling is used to re-assign an individual or group of individuals to other duties for specific reasons, for example, health reasons, as was the case in *Campbell*. These duties would normally attract a lower rate of pay but the re-assigned male workers fell in a protected pay category and were entitled to their "old" and higher rate of pay. The consequential apparent discrimination that followed was based on other grounds than sex (health) and was justified under section 2(3) of the 1974 Act. The Labour Court did not accept this defence. The Court stated that the Minister had failed to show the reasons that had given rise to "red circling" and had also failed to show that 'a recognized, factual and acknowledged position of red circling existed' ([1996] E.L.R. 106 at 107). The Minister would only satisfy the second criterion if all parties concerned were fully aware of the circumstances which brought the procedure of red circling in operation and the manner of its operation. The Minister appealed to the High Court, arguing that the Labour Court could not rely on the second criterion to determine the justification to pay different rates of pay for like work. Keane J. allowed the appeal. The judge stated that the Labour Court had erred in law to apply the second criterion. Keane J. stated that this criterion would:

> introduce a precondition to the operation of the subsection [subsection 2(3)] which has not been enacted by the Oireachtas and may prevent the application of the subsection in a case where the discrimination was based on grounds other than sex, although the object of the subsection is precisely to exclude the operation of subsection (1) in such a case ([1996] E.L.R. 106 at 113).

See also *O'Leary v. Minister for Transport Energy and Communications*, High Court, February 14, 1997 (Barron J.).

Access to employment In *Nathan v. Bailey Gibson Ltd, the Irish Print Union and the Minister for Labour* [1996] E.L.R. 114, the employer (the first named defendant) had entered into a "closed-shop" agreement with the second named defendant, the Irish Print Union (IPU), to the extent that if a vacancy arose it would first be offered to employed or unemployed members of the IPU. If no such person could fill the vacancy, a non-union worker so employed would be offered union membership without distinction on the basis of sex. In the printing industry, the IPU was a union for craftworkers only. Non-craftworkers in the printing industry were organised in general unions on a gender basis. In the *Nathan* case the appellant was a female non-craft worker employed in the first named defendant company as an assistant to a machine operator (a craft worker and member of IPU). This operator retired and she applied for the vacancy that subsequently arose. The employer wanted to employ her as a machine operator but the IPU refused to waive the terms of the closed-shop agreement. The employer, eventually, employed an unemployed IPU member to the post. The appellant initiated proceedings. The case was eventually decided by the Supreme Court on a point of law.

The relevant sections were section 2(a), (c) and section 3 of the Employment Equality Act 1977. The Act gives effect to the Council Directive on employment equality (76/207/EEC). The Directive prohibits any form of direct or indirect discrimination on the basis of sex or marital status, including selection criteria for access to employment regardless the sector or branch of activity (see: Articles 2.1, 3.1 and 5.1). This meant that the national courts must interpreted the relevant national provisions that give effect to European law, in the light of the wording and purpose of European law; here: the Council Directive on employment equality. The Court referred to *Von Colson and Kamann v. Land Nordrhein Westfalen* [1994] E.C.R. 1891 and *Marleasing SA v. La Commercial Internacional de Alimentacionsia SA* [1991] E.C.R. 1 4135; [1992] 2 C.M.L.R. 247. See also: *supra, Telecom Éireann v. O'Grady* [1996] 2 I.L.R.M. 374.

Section 2 refers to discrimination under the Act where by reason of his or her sex a person is treated less favourable than a person of the opposite sex (section 2(a)) or where a person, because of his or her sex or marital status is obliged to comply with a particular requirement which is not essential to the employment of such person or the membership of such person to a particular organisation, and in respect of which persons of the opposite sex or different marital status are able to comply is much higher (section 2(c)). Section 3(1) states that employers cannot discriminate against a (prospective) employee in relation to access or conditions of employment, training, promotion or re-grading. By reference to the Directive, the Supreme Court stated that "discrimination" must refer to both direct and indirect discrimination. Section 3(2) provides that an employer has a clear and primary obligation 'not to have rules or instructions which would discriminate either directly or indirectly against an employee'. The Supreme Court considered whether to interpret section 2(c) and section 3 of the 1977 Act as to oblige:

> the Labour Court to consider the question, as to whether the requirement that the appellant be a member of IPU before being appointed to the post which she sought constituted indirect discrimination against her contrary to the provisions of the Directive.

In the High Court, the trial judge agreed with the interpretation of the Labour Court of section 2(c) and section 3. The latter stated that section 2(c) required a causal connection between the sex or marital status of a person and the treatment afforded to him or her. The 1977 Act did not regard as discrimination the fact that historical factors (other than sex or marital status) had limited eligible candidates to a pool containing more males than females. Historically more male workers were employed as craftworkers in the printing industry and, thus, member of the IPU.

The Supreme Court disagreed. It first stated that section 2(c) in no way limited the general obligations not to discriminate imposed by sections 3(1) and 3(2). Section 2(c) rather was a separate and specific obligation imposed on employers. It only applied in relation to discrimination because of a person's sexual or marital status. If the obligation was imposed for other reasons, it had to be considered in the light of the provisions of the Directive and the provisions in section 3 of the 1977 Act. In doing so, the Court stated that:

> [a] requirement, relating to employment or membership of a body which is not an essential requirement for such employment or membership and in respect of which the proportion of persons of the other sex or (as the case may be) of a different marital status but of the same sex able to comply is substantially higher may amount to indirect discrimination even when a person is obliged to comply therewith for reasons other than a person's sex or marital status.

Consequently, the appellant was not required to show a causal connection between the practice and her sex. All she has to show was that the practice 'bears more significantly more heavily on members of the complainant's sex than on members of the other sex'.

INDUSTRIAL RELATIONS

Ballot   The decision of the Supreme Court in *G&T Crampton Ltd v. Building and Allied Trade Union* [1998] 1 I.L.R.M. 43 is discussed in the Torts chapter, 781–3, below.

Disciplinary procedures   The Industrial Relations Act 1990, Code of Practice on Disciplinary Procedures (Declaration) Order 1996 (S.I. No. 117 of 1996) provides for a code of practice for the purpose of section 42 of the Industrial Relations Act 1990. The code is set out in the Schedule to the Order. The purpose of the code is to provide guidelines for employers and employees as how to conduct disciplinary hearings. It sets out certain general principles in this regard (section I). The guidelines must be applied unless alternative procedures exist and these are agreed upon by both the employees and employer. The general principles include that the procedure must be rational and fair, its basis clear, the penalties well-defined and that the procedure must provide for an internal appeal mechanism. The procedures should be periodically reviewed and up-dated, if so required. In addition, the established rules of natural justice and fair procedures must be adhered to. The procedures should be in writing and presented in clear intelligible language and provided to all employees. Disciplinary action may range from an oral warning to dismissal. Finally, it emphasises that disciplinary proceedings can only operate efficiently if proper records are kept and when all members of management are familiar with and adhere to the terms of the procedure.

Protection of Employment Order 1996 The Protection of Employment Order 1996 (S.I. No. 370 of 1996) amended certain sections of the Protection of Employment Act 1977 for the purposes of implementing the Council Directive (92/56/EEC) (amending Council Directive (75/129/EEC)) on the approximation of the laws of the Member States in relation to collective redundancies. It amends section 2(1) as regards the meaning of a "contract of employment". It further amends section 6 as regards collective redundancies, section 7(2)(e), section 9(1) and 9(2)(a), section 10(2), section 12 and section 14.

INTERVIEW BOARDS

In *O'Dwyer v. McDonagh and Others* [1997] E.L.R. 91, Limerick Regional Technical College had advertised vacancies for Grade V and Grade VII non-academic positions. To this end a four person selection board was set up as required under section 21(1)(b) of the Regional Technical Colleges Act 1992. The board consisted of two internal and two external members. The merits and suitability of each candidate would be considered after all candidates were interviewed. The appellant already held a Grade IV position, while applying to these positions. She was not successful in relation to the Grade VII position but was for the Grade V position. The Grade VII position was given to another employee who had previously held a Grade III position. The appellant sought to squash the decision not to give her the Grade VII position. She also sought declarations that the decision was null and void and against the principles of natural and constitutional justice and fair procedures. She also sought an order for mandamus against Limerick RTC to take all necessary steps to hold proper interviews for the Grade VII position and, if necessary, constitute a new interview board. Although counsel for the applicant conceded that there had been no *mala fides* on the part of the internal interview board members, he argued however that the views expressed by them to the external members at the selection meeting mounted to an unfair interference with the end-decision of the board. He also argued that the attitude of the internal members indicated that the position was already named and that the grounds as to his client's suitability for the post should have been put before her for her to have an opportunity to answer them.

In the High Court, Barr J. refused the relief sought by the applicant. He first stated that the *bona fides* of the internal members was without question, relying on the evidence of one of the external board members. He also stated that the board, although required under statute, did not exercise a judicial or quasi-judicial function. This meant that the board was not required to provide reasons for its decision. Furthermore, in the absence of *mala fides*, the Court was not entitled to investigate whether opinions expressed by the internal members were well founded. The conduct of the board was not such that would give "'reasonable persons an apprehension of bias having regard to all the surrounding circumstances'" (following *O'Reilly v. Cassidy* [1995] 1 I.L.R.M. 306, 1994 Review, 10). Barr J. also stated that it was not for him to decide whether the interview procedure adopted by Limerick RTC was the best one, as long as the procedure was not 'so flawed as to vitiate the validity of the interview process' ([1997] E.L.R. 91 at 102).

LEGAL STATUS OF CIVIL SERVANTS

In *Gilheany and Meehan v. Revenue Commissioners* [1996] E.L.R. 25, the Court was asked to determine the legal status of civil servants. Were the applicants holders of office or employees under contract of service? This determination was important to establish whether their employer could be accused of having breached their contract of employment. The applicants were employed as executive officers and applied internally to a higher position. Although unsuccessful they were informed that they were put on the panel of candidates for future promotion (first circular). One year later a decision was made not to fill vacancies by promotion of (lower level) staff. This was set out in the second circular. Instead, the respondents opted for lateral transfer. This decision was justified according to the respondents, due to a surplus of Dublin-based staff at higher executive officer level. They were also obliged to adhere to an inter-departmental promotion scheme. This scheme obliged them to fill a certain amount of vacancies each year from an inter-departmental panel. The applicants argued that the decision was a breach of their contract of employment and sought declaratory relief and an injunction restraining the respondents from operating the second circular. The applicants sought declarations stating that they had a right to the promotion arising from their conditions of service and that they held a legitimate expectation that appointments would be made in accordance with the first circular. The decision to transfer employees laterally was *ultra virus*, it being unreasonable and irrational.

Costello P dealt first with the contract issue. He stated that under section 17(1) of the Civil Service Regulation Act 1956 civil servants are holders of an office to which they are appointed by the Minister. These appointments are the result of an administrative act in pursuance of the Minister's statutory powers. For the purpose of section 17(1), the Minister may make arrangements as he thinks fit (section 17(2)). Counsel for the applicants pointed out that this subsection had been interpreted as allowing the Minister to enter into contractual arrangements (cf: *McMahon v. Minister for Finance*, High Court, May 13, 1963 (Kenny J.)). Did the Minister enter into a contractual relationship when he initially appointed the applicants or did the appointment result from the Minister's statutory powers? Costello P., in applying the basic principles of contract law, stated that the Minister did not enter into a contract due to the absence of any intention to do so. He supported this finding, pointing out that the Minister cannot appoint an officer for a fixed term (this is prohibited under section 5 of the 1956 Act), nor can he enter into legally binding arrangements as regards future terms and conditions, as this would fetter his discretion under section 17 of the 1956 Act. In addition, many other terms and conditions are already regulated in the 1956 Act. The legal basis for the applicants' appointment was an administrative act made by the exercise of the Minister's statutory powers.

Did a contract arise by virtue of the first circular and the applicants' subsequent application? Similarly, Costello P. pointed out that this depended on the intention to create a legally binding agreement. Under section 17, the Minister could vary and cancel arrangements in relation to promotion; a discretion that could not be fettered with and restricted the Minister's freedom to contract. The President of the High Court could not find any evidence of such an intention. He stated *obiter* that this did not necessarily mean that the applicants have no legal rights that could be enforced in Court . He stated:

> It seems to me that when a statute confers a power on a [M]inister to grant a benefit to some person and that power is exercised it also confers a corresponding right on that person to receive the benefit. This means that there is a statutory right which the Court will enforce to the benefits contained in the terms and conditions of appointment of a civil servant [...] as well as to those benefits arising from the terms and conditions relating to promotion contained in administrative acts, until such time as the right is canceled or varied by the valid exercise of a power in that behalf contained in section 17 ([1996] ELR 25 at 38).

Was there an implied term in the conditions of service of the applicants in relation to promotion as set out in the first circular? As no contract existed, Costello P. stated that this issue had to fail. Moreover, the first circular was an administrative act, allowed to be canceled or varied under statute.

Did the applicants have a legitimate expectation to expect that promotion would be made from the panel in accordance with the first circular? Costello P. pointed out that the doctrine cannot be used to limit the exercise of a discretionary statutory power. He referred to remarks he made in *Tara Prospecting Ltd v. Minister for Energy* [1993] I.L.R.M. 771 (1993 Review, 23–5). There he stated that if a legitimate expectation existed under these circumstances, it was merely conditional. It meant that a benefit will be given if the Minister considered it a proper exercise of the statutory power in the light of the current policy. In the light of the discretionary powers set out in section 17 the applicants could not rely on the principle of legitimate expectation.

Was the decision not to make the appointment from the panel unreasonable and irrational and, thus, *ultra virus*? Did it constitute an abuse of discretionary power? The applicable test, according to Costello P. was whether the decision "'plainly and unambiguously flies in the face of fundamental reason and common sense'" (relying on *The State (Keegan) v. Stardust Victims Compensation Tribunal* [1986] I.R. 642). Costello P. found the Minister's decision not unreasonable nor irrational. The reason to change the policy towards promotion on a lateral basis was due to a surplus of Dublin-based staff at higher executive officer level. The respondents were also obliged to adhere to an inter-departmental promotion scheme.

ORGANISATION OF WORKING TIME

The Organisation of Working Time Act 1997 gives force to the Council Directive on certain aspects of the organisation of working time (93/104/EC). The Directive is a consequence of the overall Community policy to provide for minimum requirements to encourage improvements in the working environment to ensure better protection of the health and safety of workers. It refers specifically to the Community Charter of Fundamental Social Rights of Workers 1989. The Charter points out that the completion of the internal market must go hand in hand with improved working conditions. These include a minimum weekly rest period, annual paid leave and satisfactory health and safety conditions in the working environment. To this end, the Directive aims at providing regulations for both adequate breaks on a daily and weekly basis and for annual paid leave, as well as setting limits on the weekly working hours. It pays particular attention to night work. It acknowledges herewith that night work can be more detrimental to the human body. Thus, the Directive sets out guidelines as to the organisation of working time in the work place. The Directive also points out, however, that it should not impose administrative, financial or legal constraints to prevent the further development of small and medium-sized undertakings.

The Organisation of Working Time Act 1997 is divided into four parts. Part I sets out general and preliminary provisions and provides for certain definitions. Part II refers to minimum rest periods and other matters relating to working time. Part III refers to annual leave and other holidays, including public holidays. Part IV provides for miscellaneous provisions including provisions not provided for in the Council Directive. It refers to the role of the Labour Court, codes of practice, complaints procedures and offences and penalties for non-compliance with the Act. Six Schedules are attached to the Act setting out certain transitional arrangements and the text of the Council Directive (Sixth Schedule). The Act came fully into operation on March 1, 1998 (see the Organisation of Working Time Act 1997 (Commenement) Order 1997 (S.I. No. 392 of 1997)). (See also Boyle "The Organisation of Working Time Act 1997 – An Overview" (1997) 15 *ILT* 130.)

The scope of the Act   The Act applies to all persons who have entered into a contract of employment in the private or public sector (including civil servants). A contract of employment refers to any contract of service or apprenticeship and contracts of employment through an employment agency (section 2). The Act does not apply to members of the Garda Síochána and members of the Defence Forces (section 3(1)). Part II of the Act, in relation to minimum rest periods, does not apply to persons employed for work at sea (including sea fishing), doctors in training, persons employed by a relative and that person is a member of the relative's household or farm, and persons who enjoy a certain degree of autonomy of decision-making as regards his or her working time (section 3(2)). Here, the scope of the Act is wider than that of the Directive. The Minister has, however, the discretion to apply the provisions of the Act to the categories of persons mentioned in section 3(1) & (2) (section 3(4)). The Act does apply to all persons employed in the transport sector and other civil protection services. However, the Minister has the discretion, under section 3(3) of the Act to exclude these categories of persons from the Act.

Three further general points are worth noting. First, the Council Directive allows Member States to derogate from certain provisions in some instances. Ireland has not availed of all of the derogations afforded to it. In particular, it has not availed of the general "opt-out" provision allowing collective agreements to ignore the 48 hour work week. Second, certain provisions go further than the Directive, such as the limited provisions in relation to Sunday work and zero hour contracts. Third, although the Act refers to certain general health and safety provisions, it has not transposed the detailed provisions on health and safety provided for in the Council Directive. It was decided that these provisions will be dealt with by detailed Regulations under the Safety, Health and Welfare at Work Act 1989. This may have certain implications. As the health and safety provisions in the Council Directive will not be implemented in time (November 23, 1996; see; Article 18(1) of the Council Directive)) the Council Directive may have horizontal direct effect. It may allow an employee to sue the State for its failure to transpose those parts of the Council Directive in time (as long as the employee fulfills the criteria set out in *Francovich v. Italian Republic* [1991] E.C.R. I-5357)). In addition, we may pose the question as to whether the employer or the industry has a duty to anticipate on these health and safety provisions as, for one reason, the Directive is attached to the Act in the Sixth Schedule.

Minimum rest periods   Section 11 provides for the daily rest period. It sets out that an employee is entitled to a minimum rest period of no less than 11 consecutive hours in each 24 hour period he or she works for his or her employer. Daily rest breaks are provided for in section 12. Employees are not required to work for more than four and a half hours without a fifteen minute break. A thirty minute break is required for employees working for six consecutive hours. The weekly rest period is set out in section 13. Per seven days, an employee is entitled to a period of 24 hours of rest preceded by the 11 hours daily rest. In effect, the worker is entitled to at least 35 hours of weekly rest. An employer may grant the employee two consecutive rest periods of 24 hours over 14 days. The employer may also decide that the weekly rest period is not immediately preceded by the daily rest period if this is not possible due to considerations of a technical, organisational or other objective nature relating to the work.

Sunday work   Supplementary provisions apply in relation to Sunday work. Section 14 points out that persons who work on Sundays must be compensated for this by the payment of an allowance, an increase of the employee's rate of pay, by extra time off, or a combination of increased payment and time off.

Weekly working hours   Ireland has not availed of the opt-out clause in relation to the 48 hour working week. This means that no employer can demand from his or her employees to work more than an average of 48 hours in each period of seven days (section 15). This average is calculated over a period (referred to as "reference period") of four months, or six months where the worker's place of work and residence or places of work are distant from one another, the work concerns security or surveillance work that requires permanent presence, the work demands continuity of service or production, or where it concerns work where there is a foreseeable surge of activity, for example, agriculture and tourism. The reference period is determined by collective agreement in relation to work of which the hours vary on a seasonal basis or where a reference period of four or six months is not practical due to considerations of a technical, organisational or other objective nature.

The 48 hour work week may be phased in over a period of three years. If so, the Act allows for a maximum working week of 60 hours in year one and 55 hours in year two. This phasing-in must be approved of by collective agreement. The Fifth Schedule to the Act points out that the agreement must be consented to in writing by each employee who is affected by it. The employee must be named in the agreement and the agreement itself must be approved of by the Labour Court.

Night work   Night work is work carried out between midnight and seven o'clock in the morning (section 16). A night worker is a worker who works at least three hours of his or her daily work between midnight and 7 am, and his or her total number of hours of night work equals or exceeds 50% of the total of hours worked by him or her that year. The Act further distinguishes "special category night worker" from other night workers. The former means a night worker subjected to an assessment under section 28(1) of the Safety,

Health and Welfare at Work Act 1989 in relation to risks attached to the work. The work involves special hazards or a heavy physical or mental strain (section 16(3) of the 1997 Act). Employers cannot require these workers to work for more than 8 hours at any given time. In relation to other night workers, the maximum daily working time is an average of 8 hours. The average is calculated over a reference period of no more than two months, or more if so specified in a collective agreement which is approved of by the Labour Court under section 24 of the 1997 Act.

Information The employer is obliged to inform his or her employees at least 24 hours in advance about the times they are required to work in each week, unless these times are set out in the contract of employment, an Employment Regulation Order, a registered employment agreement or a collective agreement (subsection 17(1)). In any event, the employer must notify his or her employers about any additional hours they are required to work in a particular week (subsection 17(2)).

Zero hours contracts Special provisions apply for persons working under a zero hour contract (section 18). It is a contract of employment that requires the employee to work in a week (i) a certain number of hours (the contract hours), (ii) as and when so required by his or her employer or (iii) both. However, the requirement is not one that can merely arise by virtue of the fact that the employee has done work of a casual nature for his or her employer on occasions prior to the said week. The employee is not required to be "on call" (section 18(5)).

These employees are entitled to specific provisions depending on the actual time they have been asked to work for the employer. At all times, the employees are entitled to payment even if they have not been asked to work in a particular week or have only been asked to work for no more than 25% of the total contract hours or 25% of the time the employee would have been required to make himself or herself available for the employer. In these circumstances, the employee is entitled to either 15 hours of payment or the percentage of hours (up to 25%) he or she was or would have been required to work, which ever is less (section 18(2)(i)). If the employee was required to work in that week less than that percentage (and that percentage is less than 15 hours), his or her pay is calculated by reference to that percentage (section 18(2)(ii)). Section 18(2) does not apply if the employee was not required to work the percentage of hours due to him or her being laid-off, kept on "short-time" for that week or due to exceptional or emergency circumstances, or due to illness or any other reason the employee would not have been available to work (section 18(3)).

Derogations The Act has availed of a number of derogations set out in the Council Directive. Employers who employ persons in shift work or in an activity consisting of work being spread out over the day, are exempt from sections 11 & 13, if those persons cannot avail of the daily or weekly rest period (subsections 4(1) & (2)).

Subsection 4(3) allows, after consultation between the Minister and representatives of employers and employees, for exemptions of sections 11 (daily rest), 12 (breaks) 13 (weekly rest), 16 (night work) and 17 (information) in relation to work:

- where the place of work and place of residence of the employee are distant from one another, or where the places of work are distant from one another.
- where work concerns security or surveillance activities.
- where activities need continuity of service or production, for example, in hospitals, airports, the media or agricultural sector.
- where there is a foreseeable surge in activity in, for example, agriculture, tourism or the postal services (see further: Article 17, paragraph 2, point 2.1. of the Council Directive (Schedule Six to the 1997 Act).

Subsection 4(5) allows for an exemption of sections 11, 12 or 13 where a collective agreement (approved of by the Labour Court), a registered employment agreement or an Employment Regulation Order (ERO) provides that any or all of the sections will not apply. It shows that the Act provides for flexibility as to the implementation of the rules contained in it.

Finally, section 5 allows an employer not to comply with sections 11, 12, 13, 16 or 17 in exceptional circumstances, emergency situations, or any other unusual or unforeseeable circumstances beyond the employer's control.

Derogations or exemptions availed to in subsections 4(1), (2) & (3) are subject to section 6. This section obliges employers to provide for compensatory rest periods. If this is not possible, the employer is obliged to compensate his or her employees with any other provisions, other than monetary compensation, for example, a benefit which improves the physical conditions under which his or her employees work or which improves the amenities or services available to the employee at work.

Holidays Each worker is entitled to paid annual leave. The leave is either equal to four working weeks in one leave year in which the worker has worked at least 1,365 hours, or one-third of a working week for each month in the leave year in which the employee worked at least 117 hours, or 8% of the hours the employee works in a leave year but to a maximum of 4 working weeks (subsection 19(1)). An employee who falls ill on an annual leave day and furnishes to his or her employer a medical certificate may disregard that day as an annual leave day (subsection 19(2)). The annual leave must include an unbroken period of two weeks if the employee has worked for eight months or more in a leave year, unless otherwise decided in any Employment Regulation Order, registered employment agreement or collective agreement or any other agreement between employer and employee (subsection 19(3)). The times an employee can take his or her annual leave shall be determined by his or her employer. The employer takes into account the work requirements and other considerations such as family responsibilities and recreational opportunities. The employer must also have consulted the employee or trade union, if any, of which the employee is a member (subsection 20(1)). Payment can take place in advance of the employee taking the leave or at the normal rate (subsection 20(2)). Specific regulations in relation to the determination of holiday payments are set out in the Organisation of Working Time (Determination of Pay for Holidays) Regulations 1997 (S.I. No 475 of 1997).

The annual leave provisions can be phased in over a period of three years. Transitional provisions are set out in the First Schedule to the Act.

In respect of Public Holidays, the employee is entitled to a paid day off on that day or within a month of that day, an additional day to his annual leave, or to an additional day's pay (see further section 21).

Inspectors   The Act provides for Inspectors, appointed by the Minister, to carry out inspections of places of employment to ascertain that the provisions of the Act are complied with. To this end, the Inspectors have right of access to all relevant records and may seek information from persons as they may reasonably request (section 8). To this end, employers are obliged to keep records that can show whether the provisions of the Act are complied with in relation to the individual employees. These records must be retained for at least three years from the date of their making (section 25).

Complaints   An employee or the trade union of which he or she is a member may present a complaint to a rights commissioner that his or her employer has contravened a relevant section of the Act (section 6, 11-23, 26 and paragraph 9 of Schedule Six) (section 27). The complaint must be presented within six months of the contravention and must be presented in writing. The rights commissioner can decide that the complaint was or was not well founded. If the complaint was well founded, the rights commissioner can direct the employer to comply with the relevant provisions and may require the employer to pay the employee compensation. The decision can be appealed to the Labour Court (section 28). Its decision can be further appealed, on a point of law, to the High Court whose decision will be final and conclusive.

Repeals   The Act repeals previous legislation in relation to working hours, notably the Conditions of Employment Act 1936 and 1944, the Shops (Conditions of Employment) Acts 1938 and 1942, the Night Work (Bakeries) Acts 1936 and 1981, the Holiday (Employees) Act 1973 and the Worker Protection (Regular Part-Time Employees) Act 1991. In addition, the Organisation of Working Time Act 1997 applies without prejudice to the provisions of the Protection of Young Persons (Employment) Act 1996 (1996 Review, 543–5), and amends section 22(2) of that Act.

Common law rules Common law rules for poor organisation of working time (typically involving stress and repetitive strain injury) remain in operation. The exclusions and limitations relied upon by employers will not create a defence to any compensation claim. Thus, the common law rules in relation to, for example, a personal injury claim arising from excessive working hours remain applicable alongside the 1997 Act.

Collective agreements The 1997 Act appears to give a greater role to collective agreements, contrary to other employment legislation. They provide employers and employees greater flexibility for the operation and implementation of the provisions of the Act. This is particularly well illustrated in relation to collective agreements on the weekly working hours (regulated in Schedule Five to the Act). For such agreements to work, however, they must comply with strict criteria. This may indicate that a breach of an employer of the collective agreement can be regarded as a breach of contract between the employer and an individual employee, particularly so as the agreement must obtain the names and signatures of all of the individual employees. If this is so, it is a move away from the common law position that normally a collective agreement cannot be legally enforced (see also *O'Rourke v. Talbot (Irl) Ltd* [1984] I.L.R.M. 587). This common law position reflects the idea of voluntarism or exclusion from Court perusal which is perceived to be central to collective bargaining and industrial relations practice in Ireland.

TRANSNATIONAL INFORMATION AND CONSULTATION OF EMPLOYEES ACT 1996

The Transnational Information and Consultation of Employees Act 1996 aims at improving the right of employees in Community-scale undertakings or group of undertakings to be informed and consulted by the central management of the undertaking about certain matters relating to the undertaking's business. The Act gives effect to the Council Directive 94/45/EC and came into force on September 22, 1996 (S.I. 276/1996). The Act applies to Community-scale undertakings with at least 1,000 employees within the Member States and at least 150 employees in each of at least two Member States. It applies to Community-scale groups of undertakings with at least 1,000 employees within the

Member States, and two group undertakings with no less than 150 employees in two Member States (section 3). The workforce thresholds are set out in section 4.

The Act does not apply to those undertakings that already had in force an agreement providing for transitional information and consultation of employees. The Act shall, however, apply if such an agreement expires and is not renewed (section 6).

Section 8 sets out the general obligations for a Community-scale undertaking or group of undertakings. The undertakings are required to set up a European Works Council or establish arrangements for an information and consultation procedure. If a Community-scale group of undertakings consists of one or more undertakings or group of undertakings that in themselves are Community-scale undertakings or group of undertakings, the group is required to set up a European Employees' Forum at group level. The groups or undertakings that form part of the mother group set up themselves a European Works Council or establish arrangements for the information and consultation of employees, if so requested by their respective employees or their representatives. Such a Forum need not to be established if an agreement to provide otherwise has been entered into by the Special Negotiating Body (section 11(1)).

The central management of the respective undertaking is required to put in place the conditions and means necessary for creating an arrangement for information and consultation (section 9). To this end, it must establish a Special Negotiating Body (section 10). This Body consists of 3 to 17 members. They may be employees and trade union officials (section 3). It negotiates with central management to come to an agreement for the establishment of the European Employees' Forum if the undertaking consists of one or more undertakings or group of undertakings that in themselves are Community-scale undertakings or group of undertakings. It negotiates for the establishment of an information and consultation procedure, including a European Employees Works Council, in respect to other undertakings (see also section 11). The negotiations must take place in a spirit of co-operation; both parties having regard to their respective rights and obligations (section 16).

The agreement for the arrangement for information and consultation, whatever form it takes, must determine the structure of the undertaking, the duration of the arrangement and the procedure for its re-negotiation, and the method by which information and consultation is conveyed to all employees and their opinions are recorded (section 12(3)). If the agreement requires the establishment of an information and consultation procedure, it also determines the procedure, the issues for information and consultation, the methods by which representatives of the employees can meet and exchange views and the allocation of financial and other resources (section 12(5)). In relation to the European Employees' Forum, the agreement also determines the Forum's composition, venue, and allocation of resources, as well as the procedure for information and consultation (section 12(4)). The European Works Council is subject to subsidiary requirements set out in the Second Schedule to the Act. These requirements relate to the Council's competence, function, composition, procedure and election. Although these requirements are specific to the Council they may also apply to any other agreement entered into under subsections 12(4) or (5).

The employees' representatives, whether on the Special Negotiating Body, the Forum or Council, or in relation to an information and consultation procedure, are elected or appointed by the employees, or appointed, in agreement with the employees, by central management (section 15(1)). Further rules on the election of representatives are set out in the First Schedule of the Act. Representatives cannot be dismissed or otherwise unfavourably treated or suffer any other action prejudicial to their employment because of their status or duty as a representative (section 17(1)).

The representatives to an information and consultation procedure, or other members to the Special Negotiating Body, Council or Forum, whether past or present, are required to keep confidential information provided to them in the exercise of their function (section 15(1) & (2)). Central management may withhold from the above organs information that is deemed commercial sensitive if disclosure would or could prejudice the economic or financial situation of the undertaking or if this information is of a kind that meets objective standards for determining that it should be withheld, and this is agreed between central management and the relevant organ (section 15(3)).

The Act further provides for certain offences and prosecution and penalties for these offences (sections 18 and 19). It also provides for arbitration in the event of a dispute between central management and employees or their representatives about the disclosure of information, the withholding of commercial sensitive information (section 20), and about the interpretation of an agreement entered into under section 11(1) of the Act.

UNFAIR AND WRONGFUL DISMISSALS

Application of the Unfair Dismissals Act 1977   In *Central Bank of Ireland v. Gildea* [1997] 2 I.L.R.M. 391; [1997] E.L.R. 238, the Employment Appeals Tribunal found that the respondent had been unfairly dismissed by his employer, the Central Bank. On appeal of this decision in the Circuit Court, a preliminary issue arose as to whether the Unfair Dismissals Act 1977 was applicable to the respondent's employment. The Court stated a case to the Supreme Court to determine the matter. Was the employee employed 'by or under the State' within the meaning of section 2(1)(h) of the 1977 Act? If so, the respondent's employment would be outside the provisions of the Act. The Central Bank argued that it was an integral part of Government and performed functions essential to the operation of the State. For this reason, its employees were properly described as civil servants employed 'by or under the State'. In addition, section 23(3) of the Central Bank Act 1942 provided that the Civil Service Regulations Acts 1924-1926 did not apply to its directors and, thus, by implication did apply to its other employees. The respondent, on the contrary, argued that the bank was a separate legal entity and did not form part of the Government. It could not have been the intention of the legislature that the bank's employees would be in a similar position as civil servants. To the latter a self-contained legislative code for their employment existed. Moreover, section 15(2) of the Central Bank Act 1989 set out that officers and servants employed by the bank hold office under terms determined by the bank itself. The bank's employees were in a similar position as the employees in, for example, Telecom Éireann and An Post. Finally, the bank recognised in the respondent's terms of employment that normal industrial relations procedures would apply in accordance with the Unfair Dismissals Act 1977.

Keane J. (with whom Hamilton C.J. and Barrington J. concurred) stated that the respondent was not employed "by or under the State". Relying on the decision by Walsh J. in *Byrne v. Ireland* [1972] I.R. 241, Keane J. pointed out that persons are either employed "by the State", such as persons employed in the office of the Attorney General, the Auditor and Comptroller General or are "employed under the State". The latter category referred to persons employed in, for example, the Ministerial Departments. The respondent, according to Keane J, did not fall into either category. He was not a member of any State organ created by the Constitution and accorded with a role separate and distinct from the three organs of government. Nor was he an employee in any of the Ministerial Departments, responsible to the individual Minister and thus, not employed "under the State".

It appears from the judgment and the decisions in *Byrne v. Ireland* [1972] I.R. 241 and *McCloughlin v. Minister for Social Welfare* [1958] I.R. 1 that Keane J. defined civil servants as employees who are either subject or responsible to a person carrying political responsibility, such as a Departmental Minister, and as such these employees are civil servants of the Government and, thus, of the State, or employees who work in any of the State organs set up under the Constitution other than the legislative, executive and judiciary. Keane J. referred to, for example, the office of the Attorney General.

Keane J. stated that the respondent employee was employed by a body created by Statute. Although the bank performed functions that are essential to the operation of the State, it had separate legal entity and its powers could be removed by the Oireachtas. To this end, it could be compared with other so-called "semi-State" bodies. In the absence of specific legislation, employees of such bodies could not be regarded as civil servants. The employee was not subject to detailed legislation as it applied to civil servants. His contract of employment was solely governed by the terms of employment set out by the bank itself. Accordingly, the Court found that the respondent was not employed "by or under the State". The provisions of the 1977 Act were applicable to his employment.

Discretion of EAT In *Carney v. Balkan Tours Ltd*, [1997] E.L.R. 102, the appellant was dismissed as she had failed to adhere to procedures in relation to dealing with revenue and lodgements to the respondent's bank. The Employment Appeals Tribunal (EAT) decided that she was unfairly dismissed but had contributed substantially to her dismissal and awarded her a mere £200.00 under section 7 of the Unfair Dismissals Act 1977. The appellant argued that the Tribunal could not have taken into account the contribution to her dismissal in determining the amount of redress she was entitled to for unfair dismissal. The respondent claimed that section 7 states to take account of "all the circumstances" leading to a dismissal. The Supreme Court rejected the appellant's claims and stated that the Tribunal was entitled to take into account the appellant's contribution to her dismissal. It also stated that the Tribunal's discretion in this regard is wide-ranging. Subsections 7(1) and (2) are to be interpreted, and intended to be so by the legislature, as allowing the Tribunal to take into account all circumstances in determining the redress including the parties conduct prior to the dismissal. The Court referred to the decision of Ellis J. in *McCabe v. Lisney & Son*, High Court, March 16, 1981, and subsequent jurisprudence based thereon.

Common law or statutory relief In *Parsons v. Iarnod Éireann/Irish Rail* [1997] E.L.R. 203, the plaintiff was dismissed in 1989 and claimed redress under section 7 of the Unfair Dismissal Act 1977. The Rights Commissioner who first heard the claim recommended that the plaintiff should attend the next stage of the defendant's internal disciplinary procedure. This procedure was an *ad misericordian* meeting. However, the dismissal was confirmed by the defendant. Subsequently, the plaintiff initiated proceedings in the High Court. There, he claimed declaratory orders to the effect that the defendant's decision to dismiss him and other decisions were null and void. He also sought a mandatory injunction to be re-instated and sued for damages for breach of contract and unfair/wrongful dismissal, and damages for loss of earnings and mental distress. The defendant claimed, however, that the claim should be struck out. It argued that the plaintiff's claim was contravening section 15(2) of the Unfair Dismissal Act. This section states (prior to its amendment by the Unfair Dismissal Act 1993):

> Where an employee gives a notice in writing under section 8(2) of this Act in respect of the dismissal to a Rights Commissioner or the Tribunal, he shall not be entitled to recover damages at common law for wrongful dismissal in respect of that dismissal.

Section 15(1) states that, subject to subsection 15(2), nothing shall prevent a person to recover damages at common law for wrongful dismissal.

The High Court agreed with the defendant. The plaintiff appealed to the Supreme Court. The Court dismissed the appeal. It simply stated that section 15 provided employees with an additional remedy to the remedy at common law in the High Court. It gave employees a choice: to sue under common law or to claim relief under the Act. The Act did not intend to oust the jurisdiction of the High Court. As regards the plaintiff's declaratory order, the Court stated they these cannot exist independently from the common law remedy but were in aid to this remedy, which the plaintiff had waived seeking redress to the Rights Commissioner under the Unfair Dismissal Act 1977.

The Unfair Dismissals Amendment Act 1993 changes the position of affected employees in this regard. Under the Amendment Act, an employee is deemed not to have elected either remedy until a recommendation under the Act is made by the Rights Commissioner or until the hearing by a Court for a claim for damages at common law has commenced.

Notice period   In *Lyons v. M.F. Kent & Co (International) Ltd* [1996] E.L.R. 103, the issue arose as to what was the proper notice period for dismissal. The plaintiff had worked for the defendant since 1989 on a number of projects throughout Europe. His original appointment had been oral but in subsequent memoranda details of his remuneration package were set out. No express agreement as regards notice of termination of employment had been discussed or set out in any agreement. In 1994 the defendant informed the plaintiff that no further position was available and offered him a settlement. The plaintiff rejected this and sued the defendant for wrongful dismissal and sought payment in arrears of remuneration. The defendant conceded that the plaintiff was wrongfully dismissed before the date of the trial. What remained to be tried was the appropriate length of notice (so as to determine the appropriate amount of remuneration in arrears). The plaintiff submitted he was entitled to twelve month's notice based on his remuneration and his responsibilities within the defendant's company. Alternatively, he submitted he was entitled to twelve month's notice on the basis of a so called "general hiring for one year". The defendant argued that in the absence of any express agreement regarding notice, the appropriate length of notice could be determined in three ways. First, it could be determined by reference to the custom or trade. This did not hold as there was no evidence of such custom or trade, according to the defendant company. Second, as regards "general hiring for one year", the defendant argued that there were no modern authorities supporting it, and, in any event, the presumption would be easily rebutted. Third, to determine the appropriate length of notice, all circumstances had to be taken into account as to what was a reasonable period. In doing so, the defendant argued that the length of service (5 years) warranted a notice period of two weeks as required under the

Minimum Notice and Terms of Employment Act 1973 (as amended). A notice period of one year was deemed to be too excessive.

Costello P. agreed with the defendant company that no custom existed within the company as regards a reasonable length of notice. He also agreed that the doctrine of general hiring of one year may be obsolete and could be rebutted as the period of hiring had been indefinite. As regards the third point, Costello P. stated that the appropriate notice period had to be decided on what was reasonable in all circumstances. These circumstances included the plaintiff's status and level of responsibility within the company. Further relevant factors were the plaintiff's professional qualification (chartered accountant) and the fact that he had carried out his profession independently prior to taking up a position in the defendant's company. The most important factor, however, was that the plaintiff was required to work abroad. Costello P. referred to the officious bystander and what the parties might have said had he or she drawn their attention to it. What would they have considered reasonable? Costello P. thought it unlikely that a person would leave his profession in Ireland to work abroad if the contract had a notice period of six months. Taking all these circumstances into account, Costello P. decided that a twelve month's period was indeed warranted.

Interlocutory relief and damages   In *Fennelly v. Assicurazioni Generali Spa* (1985) 3 I.L.T.R. 73, the question arose as to whether damages was an adequate remedy at the interlocutory stage pending the determination of the issue at the trial in first instance. The Court stated in that case that, in relation to interlocutory relief, there is a general principle that the Courts do not give specific performance of an employment contract save to exceptions as expressed by, for example, Lord Denning in *Hill v. C.A. Parsons Ltd* [1972] Ch. 305 (CA). Considering the circumstances in this case, Costello J. (as he then was) decided that it would be appropriate for the plaintiff to be continued to be paid his salary. The balance of convenience was in the plaintiff's favour. He should not be left in a virtually destitute situation between now and the action at first instance. At the same time, the plaintiff gave an undertaking to perform such duties his employer asked him to do.

The decision was followed in both *Boland v. Phoenix Shannon Plc* [1997] E.L.R. 113 and *Harte v. Kelly, Anderson and HKC Ltd* [1997] E.L.R. 125. In *Boland*, the plaintiff was the operations director and vice-president of the defendant company. The company was acquired by an American company but failed to perform adequately. During this time the plaintiff was under investigation for alleged misconduct and was suspended. Some time later he was stopped paid his salary without any notice. The plaintiff sought interlocutory relief, including an order to be paid his salary pending the trial. Barron J. decided on the facts that damages would not be appropriate as the inevitable delay that will occur pending trial would leave the plaintiff without income;

the plaintiff has an entitlement to earn a living. In the *Harte* case, the plaintiff was director, employee and minority shareholder of the defendant company. It was alleged by the company he had been involved with covert negotiations with one of the defendant's clients. He was subsequently dismissed by the company. The plaintiff claimed he was wrongfully dismissed. He sought orders restraining the defendants from interfering with him in relation to his conduct and functions as an employee and executive of the company. He also sought reinstatement to his employment and an order to be continued to be paid his salary and expenses pending the trial at first instance. Laffoy J. granted him the order that he should be paid his salary and expenses. It would be unjust to leave a person without his salary pending the trial of the action who alleges he has been wrongfully dismissed. Laffoy J. added that such an order 'is not limited to situations in which the plaintiff can establish that he will face penury if such an order is not made' ([1997] E.L.R. 125 at 130).

Fair procedure In *Georgopoulus v. Beaumont Hospital Board*, Supreme Court, June 4, 1997, the plaintiff was appointed a neurosurgical registrar in October 1989. In June 1991 his appointment was terminated after an investigation of complaints made against him. The complaints included that he had been uncooperative with medical staff and that this had put the patients' care at risk. He was given no opportunity to deal with these complaints. At an interlocutory hearing it was decided between the parties that a new disciplinary hearing would be conducted and that the plaintiff could be represented by counsel or solicitor. The decision to terminate the plaintiff's contract was suspended. At the new hearing, the defendant Board concluded that the decision to terminate the contract was warranted. It concluded that the plaintiff had failed to fulfill his contractual duties to a satisfactory standard. Against this decision, the plaintiff initiated the underlying proceedings. The plaintiff claimed that the decision to dismiss him was *ultra virus* and that the defendant Board had violated the rules of natural and constitutional justice. The High Court dismissed the claim; the plaintiff appealed.

The Supreme Court first set out that the requirements of natural justice (and the extent of its application) depended on the nature of the inquiry, the circumstances of the case, the rules to which the hearing itself is subjected and the subject matter that is being dealt with (the Court referred to Keane J. in *The State (Boyle) v. General Medical Services (Payment) Board* [1981] I.L.R.M. 14, who relied on the *dictum* of Tucker LJ in *Russell v. Duke of Norfolk* [1949] 1 All E.R. 109). The nature of the inquiry was civil, not criminal, and arose from a settlement entered in between the parties after the interlocutory hearing. It dealt with alleged non-performance of the plaintiff's contractual duties. Such an inquiry should be conducted fairly and a decision fairly reached. This was an implied term of the contract (cf. Walsh J. in *Glover v. BLN Ltd* [1973] I.R. 388). The fair procedures included providing the plaintiff with all relevant particulars and notice of the complaints made against him and to give him the opportunity to hear the evidence in support of the complaints, to test the evidence in cross-examination, and to give or call evidence on his behalf. These requirements were not breached.

However, the plaintiff argued that others were: Was the Board entitled to receive legal advice without providing the plaintiff the particulars of such advice? Was it wrong to preclude the plaintiff's legal representatives from making submissions analogous to a plea in mitigation subsequent to the decision of the Board? Finally, should the defendant's decision be based on the standard of proof as required in a criminal charge, that is, beyond reasonable doubt?

The Court first dealt with the third issue. It again emphasised that the inquiry was civil in nature. Regardless the seriousness of the allegations and the possible implications for the plaintiff's reputation, the allegations can be dealt with on the balance of probabilities as long as the probability required is proportionate to the nature and gravity of the allegations under investigation. The Court relied on the decision in *R. v. Home Secretary, ex p. Khawaja* [1984] A.C. 74.

As regards the second issue – absence of mitigation of penalty (termination of employment) after the Board's decision – the Court stated that appropriate sanctions were discussed by the parties in the course of the plaintiff's council's submissions to the Board. The plaintiffs relied on O'Hanlon J.'s decision in *Graham v. The Racing Board*, High Court, November 22, 1983. There, O'Hanlon J. stated that 'there was an onus on the [Racing Board] to inquire as to whether any further submissions were sought to be made in mitigation of penalty once they had decided the issue of guilt or innocence' (at p. 7 of the unreported judgment). The Court rejected this argument as, contrary to the proceedings in the *Graham* case, the issue of penalty had already been raised during the proceedings. The rules of natural justice do not require that such a plea should take place only after a decision as to the guilt of innocence of the person was made.

As regards the first issue – legal advice – the Court stated that it was appropriate for the Board to seek legal advice regarding procedural and substantive issues that may arise in the course of the proceedings. The need for legal advice would ensure that the Board – a lay body – would be acquainted with the requirements of natural justice. It is not the function of the legal adviser to advise the Board on matters of fact. Should this advice have been disclosed to the plaintiff? The latter argued that the Irish Courts have accepted that non-disclosure of information by a decision-maker such as the Board amounts to a breach of natural justice (cf. *Killiney and Ballybrack Developments Ltd v. Minister for Local Government* (1978) I.L.T.R. 9 and *The State (Polymark Ltd) v. ITGWU* [1987] I.L.R.M. 357. However, although the argument does carry merit, disclosure of information related only to information on the facts of the case. Information as to the proper conduct of an inquiry need not to be disclosed. There was no evidence that the legal adviser participated or intended to participate in a discussion as to the issue of facts.

In *Maher v. Irish Permanent Plc (No. 1)* [1998] E.L.R. 77, the plaintiff, a branch manager for the defendant, faced allegations of sexual harassment. He was suspended during the investigation and was later informed that a decision to dismiss him was warranted. He was also told that the decision would not be finalised for one week within which he could make representations. The plaintiff initiated proceedings seeking an order to restrain the defendant from taking further steps unless they were in accordance with the defendant's internal disciplinary procedures and the rules of natural justice. He claimed that the procedure lacked fairness. He pointed to a lack of representations at crucial stages at the procedure as well as his suspension without notice of the charges brought against him, and a failure to provide him with copies of statements made by the complainant to him. Laffoy J. granted the order. She first pointed out that an agreement regulating the relationship between an employer and employee is subject to the rules of natural justice as it is an agreement that affects rights or imposes liabilities (cf: *Glover v. BLN Ltd* [1973] I.R. 388 and *Gunn v. Bord na Choláiste Náisiúnta Ealáine is Deartha* [1990] 2 I.R. 168). Under the rules of natural justice, the plaintiff was entitled to be furnished with copies of the statements, he was entitled to legal representation and that, in the absence of legal representation, the oral hearing could and did not provide a fair result.

The defendant proceeded with the disciplinary proceedings into the allegations of sexual harassment in accordance with Laffoy J.'s judgement. This time, the plaintiff sought an interlocutory injunction to restrain the defendant from proceedings with the proceedings: *Maher v. Irish Permanent Plc (No. 2)* [1998] E.L.R. 89. The plaintiff claimed that the proceedings would not be followed or be in breach of the rules of natural justice, particularly in the light of the previous proceedings deemed in breached of the rules of natural justice by Laffoy J. in *Maher v. Irish Permanent Plc (No. 1)* [1998] E.L.R. 77. He also argued that the defendant could not investigate allegations based on hearsay or admit hearsay evidence at the hearing. Finally, the plaintiff argued that the defendant was no entitled to consider allegations of serious misconduct prior to the final written warning he received before he was informed that his dismissal was warranted. Costello P. rejected the application. He first stated that the defendant was entitled to proceed with the proceedings as long as they were in accordance with the rules of natural justice (see also: *Mooney v. An Post*, Supreme Court, March 20, 1997). He also stated that past conduct could be considered and that this was not a breach of the rules of natural justice. As regards the use of hearsay evidence, the former President of the High Court stated that the rules of natural justice did not prevent the defendant's own internal proceedings from taking into account or consider hearsay evidence. He stated that it would not be appropriate to assume that, in relation to hearsay evidence, the defendant 'is going to act in a grossly unfair manner' ([1998] E.L.R. 89 at 93).

In *Frizelle v. New Ross Credit Union Ltd*, High Court, July 30, 1997, Flood J. clearly spelled out the premises which must be established or adhered to, where a question of unfair dismissal is at issue, to support a decision to terminate a contract of employment for misconduct. It meant that the principles of natural justice must be unequivocally applied. These include that the complaint must be *bona fide* and unrelated to some other agenda of the complainant. The complaint should be stated factually, clearly and fairly where the complainant is a person or body of intermediate authority. The complaint must be without innuendo or hidden inferences or conclusions. The employee against whom the complained is addressed should be interviewed and his version should accordingly be noted and handed over to the relevant decision-making authority. This must be done contemporaneously with the complaint and without comment. The decision of the authority should be based on the balance of probabilities and be based on the factual evidence available and in the light of the explanation offered. Finally, the decision as to whether the employee should be dismissed should be proportionate to the gravity of the complaint, and also of the gravity and effect the dismissal may have for the affected employee. As to the rules of natural justice and fair procedure; see also: *Corcoran and Others v. Electricity Supply Board*, Supreme Court, February 6, 1997.

YOUTH WORK AND YOUNG PERSONS IN EMPLOYMENT

Youth Work Act 1997 This Act aims at extending the function of educational boards in relation to youth work and to make provisions for the making of grants and the establishment of voluntary youth councils, youth work programmes and services and other related issues. It also aims to establish a National Youth Work Advisory Committee. It defines "youth work" as a programme or activity designed for the purpose of providing developmental and educational training. In doing so, it aims at assisting the personal and social development of young persons. Such programmes must require the young person's voluntary participation and are complementary to academic or vocational training. (section 2). The Act came into operation on June 19, 1997 (S.I. No. 260 of 1997).

Section 3 obliges the Minister for Education to develop and co-ordinate policies in relation to youth work, to co-ordinate youth work programmes and services with education programmes, to provide the financial resources, to carry out necessary and relevant research, and to monitor and assess these programmes and services. The Minister must also establish a National Youth Work Council. In carrying out his or her function the Minister must have regard to the treatment of male and female young persons in relation to access to work, the number of male and females young persons likely to participate in the programmes and services, as well as to young persons who are socially or economically disadvantaged.

In addition to functions conferred to educational boards under any other Act, the Youth Work Act 1997 obliges educational boards, in section 4, to carry out the policies developed by the Minister to ensure the provision of youth work programmes or services. To this end, the boards co-ordinate these programmes and services in co-operation with national and local voluntary youth work organisations, and provides for assistance, including financial assistance to these organisations. The boards must pay specific attention to youth work requirements of persons between 10 and 21 years old and are socially or economically disadvantaged. The Minister may remove from a board the functions under this Act if the Minister thinks the board has failed to perform its functions properly or effectively (section 6). Each board is required to submit to the Minister a Youth Work Budget estimating the expenditures and income for the purposes of this Act (section 12). The Budget must be approved by the Minister and may be amended. The implementation of the Budget must be supervised by the board to avoid it from exceeding the expenditure approved by the Minister (section 13).

One of the functions of an educational board is to develop, every three years, a Youth Work Development Plan (section 6). Such a Plan must be approved of by the Minister and must specify the youth work requirements of the relevant education region, the measures required to meet the requirements and financial estimates. The board is required to comply with directions, if any, from the Minister and must consult the youth work committee. The plan must be reviewed each year (section 7).

The Minister must, under section 10, set up a National Youth Work Advisory Committee. Its role is to advise and consult with the Minister in relation to youth work generally and youth work programmes and services in particular. The Committee consist of no less than 22 and no more than 24 members (section 11). The Minister appoints the chairperson and three other persons. The Committee further consists of members from the various Government Departments, and the National Youth Council of Ireland (set up under section 22 of the Act and the Youth Work Act 1997 (section 22) Regulations (S.I. No. 271 of 1997)). More rules in relation to the Committee are set out in the Schedule to the Act.

The Minister also appoints a Voluntary Youth Council for each functional area (section 15). The Council advises the educational board in that area in relation to the development and implementation of the Youth Work Development Plan. No more than thirty and no less than ten persons are to be elected to the Council (section 15). The education boards set out directions as to the election procedures. However, persons eligible are persons who work in a voluntary capacity and are not employees of a prescribed national or local voluntary youth work organisation. Persons for elections must include persons under 25 and persons engaged in the provision of youth work programmes within the traveling community.

Each educational board must appoint a youth work committee (section 17). The committee makes recommendations to the board on its performance and may advise the board on any matter the board has requested such advise. On the difficulties with implementing the 1997 Act, see the Education chapter, 365, above.

Protection of young persons   The Protection of Young Persons (Employment) Act 1996 (1996 Review, 543-5) provides for a better protection of young persons in employment. It gave effect to the Council Directive on the protection of young people at work. The Act requires from employers to display the prescribed Abstract of the 1996 Act. The Abstract is provided for in the Protection of Young Persons (Employment) (Prescribed Abstract) Regulations 1997 (S.I. No. 3 of 1997). The Abstract sets out in for young persons understandable language the main rules of the Act, such as the age limit, the maximum working hours per week, including early morning and night work and rest breaks. It also sets out the exceptions to the Act, the duties of employers and how a complaint can be made in respect of breaches of the Act.

Section 6 provides that employers cannot employ young persons for any work unless certain working time requirements are adhered to. However, the Minister may, under section 8 of the 1996 Act decide otherwise. The Minister may by Regulation permit an employer to employ a young person if the requirements set out in section 6 prove impractical because of the seasonal nature of the work, the technical or organisational requirements for the work or any other substantial reason. The Minister must, however, be satisfied that the health, welfare and safety of the young employee will not be endangered. The Minister has permitted this for employers in the fishing and shipping sector: Protection of Young Persons (Employment) (Exclusion of Workers in the Fishing or Shipping Sector) Regulations 1997 (S.I. No. 1 of 1997). The Minister has regulated, under section 9 of the 1996 Act, that sections 3, 5, 6(1)(a) and 11 of the 1996 Act do not apply to the employment of close relatives: Protection of Young Persons (Employment of Close Relatives) Regulations 1997 (S.I. No. 2 of 1997).

Employment information   The Terms of Employment (Information) Act 1994 (Section 3(6)) Order 1997 (S.I. No. 4 of 1997) requires an employer, who employs a child or young person within the meaning of the Protection of Young Persons (Employment) Act 1996, to provide, within a month of employment, that person with a copy of the prescribed abstract of the Protection of Young Persons (Employment) Act 1996. The prescribed abstract is set out in the Protection of Young Persons (Employment) (Prescribed Abstract) Regulations 1997 (S.I. No. 3 of 1997).

Apprenticeship Rules The Labour Services Act 1987, Apprenticeship Rules 1997 (S.I. No. 168 of 1997) revoked all previous Apprenticeship Rules made under the Apprenticeship Act 1959, the Industrial Training Act 1967 and the Labour Services Act 1987 in relation to classes of apprenticeships set out in Rule 1(4). The Rules set out the minimum age at which a person can enter in to an employment of apprenticeship (16) and the minimum educational requirements (Rule 3). Rule 6 specifically prohibits employers from bargaining for or accept any premium, fine, fee or any other consideration in respect of the employment of any person as an apprentice. Rule 7 states that an apprentice can only be dismissed in strict accordance with the relevant applicable legislation. In the case of inevitable redundancy the employer must notify An Foras Áiseanna Saothoir (FAS) and take all reasonable steps to have the apprenticeship transferred to another employer. Finally, a contract of apprenticeship is automatically terminated if the apprentice fails to reach, after three attempts, the required minimum qualifying standard as specified by FAS.

Land Law

Paul Coughlan, Trinity College Dublin

ADMINISTRATION OF ESTATES

Application to set aside entry of caveat   In *In re Nevin*, High Court, March 13, 1997, the deceased had been murdered. The deceased died intestate and his widow applied for letters of administration to his estate. However, when an application was made on her behalf it was discovered that the deceased's mother had entered a caveat in the Probate Office of the High Court. A caveat is a warning which prevents grants of probate or letters of administration being granted without notice to the person entering the caveat. Once a warning has been given to the person entering the caveat that person must either abandon their claim to a grant of probate or letters of administration, or bring proceedings in order to establish their claim to the grant. The deceased's mother refused to withdraw the caveat until a decision had been made by the Director of Public Prosecutions concerning prosecution in relation to the deceased's death. Accordingly, the deceased's widow applied for an order setting aside the caveat and restraining the deceased's mother from lodging any further caveats on the ground that the lodgment of the caveat amounted to an abuse of the process of the court.

Shanley J. held that to uphold such a claim, the court would have be satisfied that the lodgment of the caveat amounted to conduct which in all the circumstances no reasonable person could properly treat as bona fide. The evidence here did not establish such a want of bona fides and so the caveat would not be set aside. But while the deceased's mother had not abused the process of the court in lodging the caveat and had an undisputed interest in maintaining a caveat, Shanley J. pointed out that the deceased's spouse should not be under any legal disability merely because she had been interviewed by the Gardaí in relation to her husband's death and she was entitled to her good name and the benefit of the presumption of innocence. The interest which the deceased's mother had sought to protect could be protected while at the same time allowing a grant of letters of administration to the deceased's spouse. This could be done by limiting the grant to the gathering in and preservation of the estate of the deceased without distributing it. If the deceased's spouse wished for such an order to be made it would be done on terms allowing her to seek an unlimited grant at the expiration of a period of nine months. Shanley

J. emphasised that the court's refusal to clear off the caveat was based on the interest of the deceased's mother and the fact that she was not wanting in bona fides. It did not reflect upon the innocence of the deceased's spouse.

ADVERSE POSSESSION

Onus of proof and need for sufficient evidence of adverse possession In *Fanning v. Jenkinson*, High Court, July 2, 1997, the plaintiff claimed title by adverse possession over part of a river bank the paper title to which was vested in the defendants, who were neighbouring landowners. Kinlen J. pointed out that the onus was on the plaintiff to show that he dispossessed the true owner or that the true owner discontinued his possession, and that the plaintiff had been in adverse possession. Mere abandonment or leaving land vacant was not enough because until someone else goes into adverse possession, the true owner has no right of action against anyone. After reviewing at length evidence given by both sides concerning the use, repair and fencing off of the land in dispute, Kinlen J. found that the evidence of the defendants was to be preferred to that of the plaintiff and accordingly dismissed his claim.

EQUITABLE INTEREST

Indirect contributions not related to acquisition of land in respect of which equitable interest claimed In *C.D. v. W.D.*, February 5, 1998, the plaintiff, who was the wife of the first named defendant, claimed that she was entitled to a beneficial interest in certain farm land which was in her husband's sole name. She also asserted that any claim to security over the land by Barclays Bank plc, the second named defendant, was confined to her husband's share in the lands. The plaintiff's husband was registered as full owner of the land on July 21, 1972. On May 26, 1986 he executed a deed of charge over the lands in favour of Barclays Bank plc in order to secure present and future advances, along with interest thereon, and on September 8, 1989 the charge was registered. The family home of the plaintiff was not located on the land. When the plaintiff's husband defaulted on the loan Barclays Bank plc obtained an order for possession on October 14, 1991. At no stage prior to the commencement of the plaintiff's proceedings in June 1995 did she indicate to the bank that she was asserting a proprietary interest in the land.

The plaintiff gave evidence that she had contributed approximately £25,000 towards the cost of building and furnishing the family home occupied by herself, her husband and their three children. This home was in fact an extension added on to a house occupied by the plaintiff's mother and other family members. The plaintiff's claim, which was not resisted by her husband, was based on her contribution to the building of the extension, the fact that she had used her earnings as a nurse to run the household with very little financial assistance from her husband, who used his money to run the farming business, and an undertaking on the part of her husband at an early stage in their marriage that he would put the lands in question into their joint names. While no steps had been taken to arrange a formal transfer, the plaintiff claimed that she had relied upon her husband's statement and regarded herself as a joint owner of the land.

It was clear that the plaintiff did not make a direct contribution to the acquisition of the land. While she had contributed to what Finlay P. in *W. v. W.* [1981] I.L.R.M. 202, at 204-205, had called a 'general family fund' by using her own earnings on household expenditure and thereby allowing her husband to use any earnings of his own in the farming business, McGuinness J. held that this did not amount to an indirect contribution towards the acquisition of the land in question. Any contributions had been directed to the acquisition or furnishing of the family home. The farm land had been acquired by her husband in 1972 and between their marriage in 1983 and the creation of the charge in favour of the bank in 1986 the lands had been unencumbered. Accordingly, if the plaintiff had no proprietary rights in the land in 1986 when the bank acquired its charge, the entire legal and beneficial ownership had been available to the husband to use as security. As to the claim that her husband had undertaken to transfer the land into their joint names, McGuinness J. found that there was no serious intention to do so on the part of the husband and it was clear that in 1986 he regarded himself as sole owner of the land. Equally, the plaintiff had shown little interest when the bank had moved to take possession and, in the view of McGuinness J., this was not the attitude of a joint owner of the land.

In any event, any beneficial interest which the plaintiff would have had in the land was unregistered and she had not been in actual occupation or in receipt of the rents and profits of the land when the charge was created in favour of the bank. Accordingly, no reliance could be placed on section 72(1)(j) of the Registration of Title Act 1964 and so the bank's charge would have had priority. Furthermore, acquiescence on the part of the plaintiff from the time when the charge was created would have barred her from asserting any beneficial interest that might be vested in her against the bank. Similarly, it could be said that she was estopped from doing so.

LANDLORD AND TENANT

Exclusion of right to reversionary lease where buildings destroyed by fire reinstated by lessee pursuant to covenant In *Fenlon v. Keogh*, High Court, February 10, 1997, the plaintiff was the lessee of premises consisting of a hay barn, tarmacadam forecourt and market garden. The lease contained a covenant that if the premises were destroyed or damaged by fire during the term of the lease monies received in respect of fire insurance cover should be expended in repairing and reinstating the demised premises to the satisfaction of the landlord. The premises were totally destroyed by fire in 1990. The plaintiff had carried on the business of a car repairer from the premises. He proposed to reinstate the premises as they had been, but ran into difficulties with the local planning authority. Accordingly, he decided to replace the premises with a much more elaborate custom built garage which he built using his own labour at a cost of around £90,000. All of this was done with the approval of the lessor. However, a question arose as to whether the plaintiff was entitled to a reversionary lease.

In the High Court O'Flaherty J. found that the plaintiff satisfied conditions (a)-(d) in section 9(1) of the Landlord and Tenant (Ground Rents) (No. 2) Act 1978. Condition (d) stipulates that one of the alternative conditions set out in section 10 must be satisfied and O'Flaherty J. found that the first of these was satisfied in that the permanent buildings on the land were erected by the person who at the time of their erection was entitled to the lessee's interest under the lease. However, O'Flaherty J. felt constrained to find that section 9(4) of the Act effectively disqualified the plaintiff from relying on the first condition in section 10. Section 9(4) provides:

> Permanent buildings erected by a lessee in pursuance of a covenant in his lease to reinstate the buildings comprised in the lease in the event of their destruction by fire or otherwise shall be deemed to have been erected by the person who erected the original buildings.

Although the plaintiff had replaced the premises with a much more elaborate structure, the fact remained that the new building had been erected in pursuance of the plaintiff's obligation under the lease to provide at least as good a building. Therefore section 9(4) applied and the plaintiff could not be regarded as having erected the buildings. Consequently, he was not entitled to a reversionary lease. This left him with an entitlement to a new lease under Part II of the Landlord and Tenant (Amendment) Act 1980.

Distinction between leases and licences In *Kenny Homes & Co. Ltd v. Leonard*, High Court, December 11, 1997 the second named defendant had claimed a new tenancy under Part II of the Landlord and Tenant (Amendment) Act 1980 in respect of premises comprising a filling station, garage and car park in the city of Cork. The plaintiff, which bought the premises from Irish Shell Ltd and intended building apartments and commercial units on it, brought proceedings in the High Court seeking to restrain the defendants from trespassing on the site. The second named defendant, which had taken a transfer of the purported interest of the first named defendant, argued that the Circuit Court in Cork had exclusive jurisdiction to hear its application under the 1980 Act and, as section 28 of the Act gave it the right to retain possession pending the determination of its claim to a new tenancy, the injunction claimed by the plaintiff could not be granted. However, Costello P. held that while the Circuit Court had exclusive jurisdiction to hear and determine claims for a new tenancy, the 1980 Act did not deprive the High Court of jurisdiction to hear an application for an injunction based on the claim that the defendants were trespassers. Ordinarily, where a claim to a new tenancy was resisted on the grounds that a tenancy did not exist or that the premises did not constitute a tenement, those issues should be determined in the Circuit Court and the High Court should stay proceedings before it pending such a determination. However, given the urgency of the matter these issues could be determined in the High Court and, if it was decided that there was a tenancy and the premises constituted a tenement, the injunction proceedings would be dismissed and the Circuit Court would then have to determine whether a new tenancy should be granted.

Costello P. then turned to the series of agreements with Irish Shell Ltd under which the first named defendant and his brothers had occupied the site since 1960. At first the agreements were yearly and then for periods of three years. Each agreement conferred a right to enter the site for the purpose of using equipment that had been hired out to the first named defendant, such as petrol pumps and storage tanks. It was expressly provided that he was not entitled to an interest in the land or exclusive possession, and that the relationship of landlord and tenant did not exist between the parties. However, the first named defendant and not Irish Shell Limited had held the keys to the property. Applying the principles laid down by the Supreme Court in *Irish Shell and BP Ltd v. John Costello Ltd* [1981] I.L.R.M. 66, Costello P. rejected the claim that the site was held under a lease or contract of tenancy. Indeed, he held that the agreements which excluded this could not have been in clearer terms. Moreover, it did not follow that because the landowner had no keys the first named defendant's possession of the premises must be regarded as exclusive. Likewise, the fact that the first named defendant and his brothers had occupied the site for over 27 years was irrelevant in determining the nature of the agreements under which such occupation had been enjoyed.

On the question as to whether the premises were a 'tenement' within the meaning of section 5 of the 1980 Act, the key issue was whether the portion of the land not covered by buildings was subsidiary and ancillary to the buildings. Costello P. found that there were two businesses being conducted on the site, namely the business of supplying motor fuel to the public and a car park business. He accepted that part of the car park under which the fuel tanks were located had to be treated as associated with the first business. Furthermore, it was accepted that the fuel storage tanks were buildings within the meaning of the 1980 Act. However, approximately two thirds of the site was associated with the car park business and the land surrounding the small office which received payments and the keys to cars being parked on the site could not be regarded as ancillary to the office. On the contrary, the office was ancillary to the business of parking cars. Costello P. rejected the defendants' argument that the car park was ancillary to the business of selling motor fuel because persons parking their cars also purchased petrol when arriving or leaving, and that the whole area was a 'tenement' for the purposes of the 1980 Act. Accordingly, Costello P. found that the premises were not a 'tenement' and so no right to a new tenancy arose on this ground also.

REGISTERED LAND

Location of constituent offices of central office outside Dublin   Section 1 of the Registration of Title (Amendment) Act 1997 amended section 7 of the Registration of Title Act 1964 so as to facilitate decentralisation of the Land Registry. In particular, section 7(1) of the 1964 Act now provides that the central office of the Land Registry will consist of one or more than one constituent offices situated in the county borough of Dublin and in such area or areas as the Minister for Justice, Equality and Law Reform may designate. By means of the Registration of Title Act 1964 (Central Office) Order 1997 (S.I. No. 340 of 1997) the minister designated Waterford as an area within which one or more of the constituent offices of the central office shall be located.

RIGHTS OF WAY

Extinguishment of public right of way over park   In *Smeltzer v. Fingal County Council* [1998] 1 I.L.R.M. 24 Dublin County Council had compulsorily acquired Swords House and its gardens in 1978. The compulsory purchase order had been made on 20 January 1975 and stated that it had been made 'pursuant to section 10 of the Local Government (No. 2) Act 1960 as substituted by section 86 of the Housing Act 1966.' The order provided that Dublin County Council were authorised to acquire the land compulsorily 'for the purpose of providing Town Square development.' After its acquisition the land was left derelict and the house was destroyed by fire in 1982. As a result of pressure from local residents Dublin County Council decided to develop the land as a public park. The management of the land was taken over by the parks department of Dublin County Council which demolished the remains of Swords House and began to lay out the site in 1985. The public park was officially opened on 8 June 1986. The parks department of Dublin County Council produced an official brochure which referred to the 'Swords Town

Park' and included a map showing the pathways within the park and the entrances leading in to it. The brochure also contained the statement 'It is appropriate that the last remnant of the large estate, Swords Demesne should be developed as a Town Centre park for the use and enjoyment of all the people of Swords.' The 1985 development plan for the area provided that the site was zoned as an amenity open space.

By virtue of the Local Government (Dublin) Act 1993 Dublin County Council was divided into three local authorities, namely Dun Laoghaire/Rathdown, South Dublin and Fingal. It was decided that each of the new councils should have new administrative offices and in the case of Fingal County Council it was decided on September 11, 1995 that the county hall should be located on the town park in Swords. The plans for the new offices were such that the construction of the building would deprive the residents of Swords of the use of the town park which had existed since 1986 and prevent them from using the pathways within it. The plaintiff, who was a resident of Swords, sought an interlocutory injunction preventing the county council from carrying out any development on the town park unless and until there was compliance with all necessary statutory procedures. She also sought an interlocutory injunction requiring the county council to comply with all statutory procedures relating to the extinguishment of all public rights relating to the lands. Section 73 of the Roads Act 1993 provides that where a local authority proposes to extinguish a public right of way, a notice of the proposed extinguishment must be advertised in a newspaper, objections to the proposed extinguishment must be considered and, should the local authority consider it appropriate to do so, persons making objections or representations may be given an oral hearing where they have requested this in writing. The plaintiff accepted that the county council had the statutory power to carry out the proposed development. However, she claimed that in respect of the park there was a public right to enjoy the land as a park arising from a trust created at the time when the land was acquired. She also argued that the county council, as owners of the land, had dedicated public rights of way over the lands when they laid out and opened the park to the public in 1986.

Before addressing the substantive issues Costello P. considered the question of *locus standi*. It was well established that only the Attorney General or a person specially injured can sue in respect of an obstruction of a public right of way. A member of the public who has not been specially injured can bring proceedings in the name of the Attorney General in a relator action provided that the leave of the Attorney General has been obtained. In this case the plaintiff had not obtained the leave of the Attorney General, but the defendants had not challenged the plaintiff's *locus standi*. Costello P. felt that in the absence of such an objection it was appropriate for the court to adjudicate upon the matter.

Costello P. noted that the council had not acquired Swords House under any express statutory power relating to acquisition for the purpose of establishing a public park, but under section 10 of the Local Government (No. 2) Act 1960. Furthermore, the compulsory purchase order declared that the purpose of the purchase was to develop a town centre and did not specify that it would be a public park. Accordingly, Costello P. held that the plaintiff had failed to establish that when acquiring the lands under statutory powers a trust in favour of the public was thereby created, or that by the expenditure of public money on their acquisition did such a trust come into existence. The plaintiff had also relied upon section 10 of the Open Spaces Act 1906 which provides that where an agreement has been entered into by a local authority by which the local authority acquired an open space and undertook the management and control of the open space, the local authority holds the land in trust for the public to enjoy it as an open space. However, Costello P. held that the 1906 Act did not provide statutory public rights as regards the park. Under section 71(d) the Act did not apply to county councils in Ireland. Furthermore, in this case there was no agreement whereby the local authority acquired the open space and agreed to manage it as laid down in section 10 of the 1906 Act, and it had not been proved that the land was acquired as an open space as defined in section 20 of the Act.

Costello P. accepted that the law does not recognise a public right in the nature of a *jus spatiendi*, that is to say a right to wander and remain on land (see *Attorney General v. Antrobus* [1905] 2 Ch. 188 and *Giant's Causeway Co. v. Attorney General* (1905) 5 N.I.J.R. 301). However, the public can have a right of way over land. In order to establish that a public right of way was created, it has to be proved that there was an intention on the part of the owner to dedicate his land to the public, there was an actual dedication and the public accepted the dedication. In this case the evidence established that Dublin County Council had done more than merely give the public a mere licence to enter their land. It was intended that the pathways would be dedicated to the public in the sense that the public and not the local authority would enjoy their use indefinitely into the future. There had been an intention to dedicate public rights of way over the lands in the park on the pathways laid out on them, an actual dedication and an acceptance of the rights so dedicated by the use of the park. The evidence also showed that those rights were about to be infringed. Accordingly, Costello P. made an order prohibiting the defendants from carrying out the proposed development until there was compliance with the statutory proceedings relating to the extinguishment of a public right of way.

SALE OF LAND

Determination as to whether there is a concluded agreement prior to ex-

amination by court of acts alleged to amount to part performance In *Mackey v. Wilde* [1998] 1 I.L.R.M. 449 the plaintiff and the first named defendant were the owners of a joint fishery on the River Finn and the River Reelan in County Donegal. The rules for the operation of the fishery had been laid down in an indenture dated March 29, 1920. The plaintiff was unhappy with the provisions of the indenture concerning the number of people who could fish on the rivers and by letter dated October 11,1985 he suggested to the first named defendant that they could agree new terms governing the fishery which would supersede the indenture. The plaintiff claimed that he met the first named defendant prior to 15 January 1986 and it was agreed that each would be limited to the granting of 25 annual licences and a few daily tickets. Following the meeting the plaintiff issued a circular to persons who had received tickets in the past which stated that for the year 1986 it was proposed that the number of annual licences would be limited to 25 for each owner of the fishery and that some daily tickets would be sold. Subsequently correspondence took place between the plaintiff and the first named defendant in which the plaintiff sought to obtain a written agreement limiting the number of fishing licences for the fishery. Ultimately the plaintiff instituted proceedings claiming that there was a binding agreement that each would be limited to the granting of 25 annual licences and that there had been part performance on foot of this agreement. In the High Court Costello P. held that at the end of 1985 or the start of 1986 a concluded agreement had been reached that each would be limited to the granting of 25 annual licences. He further held that a term relating to additional day tickets had been included and this entitled each party to issue up to ten day tickets. Accordingly, the first named defendant was restrained from issuing more than 25 annual licences and ten day tickets.

The Supreme Court unanimously allowed the defendants' appeal. Barron J. accepted that a valid binding agreement can be found to exist notwithstanding that the full terms of the contract are not set out precisely. For instance, a term may be implied, there may be a formula for determining the apparent uncertainty with precision, or a term may be determined upon the basis of what is reasonable or by reference to custom or trade usage. Even if none of these methods can be applied, an agreement can be upheld where the court is satisfied that the term which is still to be settled is a subsidiary one and the parties intended to be bound in any event by the main agreement. The essential question is whether the parties have left over some matter to be determined which can only be determined by themselves. An agreement to enter into an agreement is not a concluded contract.

Having said all this, Barron J. held that here the agreement could not be saved because the parties did not intend to be limited to 25 annual licences without any day tickets. The number of day tickets could not be determined by what was reasonable. While Costello P. held that ten day tickets would be reasonable, equally any other number between two and ten could also be described as reasonable. By using the word 'few' to denote the number of day tickets the parties had left over for agreement something which only they could settle and the court could not make the agreement for the parties by saying what would be reasonable. It followed that there was no concluded agreement.

Barron J. then took the opportunity to discuss the doctrine of part performance. He noted that the doctrine requires consideration of the acts on the part of the plaintiff which are said to have been in part performance of the concluded agreement, the involvement of the defendant with respect to those acts and the oral agreement itself. In order to succeed under the doctrine of part performance it must be shown that:

(a) There was a concluded contract;

(b) The plaintiff acted in such a way that showed an intention to perform the contract;

(c) The defendant induced such acts or stood by while they were being performed; and

(d) It would be unconscionable and a breach of good faith to allow the defendant to rely upon the terms of the Statute of Frauds to prevent performance of the contract.

Barron J. was of the view that if the terms of the contract could not be considered until the acts of the plaintiff have been found capable of being acts of part performance, there is the possibility, albeit not a very strong one, that the acts might well have been inconsistent with the terms of the contract and in fact not carried out in pursuance of it, but instead for a different reason. In his view it was more logical to find out what the parties agreed because, in the absence of a concluded agreement, there is no point in seeking to find acts of part performance. Only then can the court begin its determination as to whether the behaviour of the parties justified the application of the equitable doctrine to modify the legal rule. Furthermore, the equitable doctrine required that the acts relied upon as being acts of part performance should be such that, on an examination of the contract which has been found to have been concluded and to which they are alleged to refer, they show an intention to perform that contract. The acts of part performance must necessarily relate to and affect land.

The detriment to the plaintiff must be the result of what the plaintiff does with the defendant standing by, and not the detriment to the plaintiff as a result of what the defendant does with the plaintiff standing by. In the present case the only detriment to the plaintiff was the lessening in value of the fishery through over-fishing. There was nothing in what was alleged which would in any way be a breaking of faith by the defendant with the plaintiff for the defendant to plead the Statute of Frauds. Accordingly, even if there had been a concluded agreement as claimed, there were no acts on the part of the plaintiff which showed an intention to perform the alleged contract.

Part performance of contract to devise land In *McCarron v. McCarron*, Supreme Court, February 13, 1997, the deceased owned farms in County Monaghan. As a result of an accident he became disabled and unable to work the farms. The plaintiff's father was a first cousin of the deceased. The plaintiff's father sent him to assist the deceased with the running of his farms and on a number of occasions over the years the deceased assured the plaintiff that he would receive the farms as compensation for the work he had done. After the death of the deceased a question arose as to whether the conversations which had taken place between him and the plaintiff constituted a contract to devise the farms to the plaintiff. The defendant, who was the personal representative of the deceased, did not raise any issue regarding the absence of a note or memorandum in writing for the purposes of the Statute of Frauds (Ireland) 1695. In the High Court Carroll J. held that there was a contract and granted a decree of specific performance. This was unanimously affirmed by the Supreme Court where Murphy J. pointed out that in determining whether the evidence supported the existence of a contract significance had to be given to the fact that the plaintiff had worked on the farms for long hours over a period of sixteen years without reward. The work was not done on a neighbourly or charitable basis, nor was it done in the vague hope that the deceased might in his discretion remember the kindness if and when he made a will. It was reasonably clear that in consideration of work done and to be done by the plaintiff the deceased would give the farms to him. There was a sufficient degree of certainty supporting a contract of which specific performance could be decreed.

Murphy J. also addressed the plaintiff's alternative argument that he was entitled to the farms by reason of the doctrine of proprietary estoppel. He observed at p.13:

> In principle I see no reason why the doctrine should be confined to the expenditure of money or the erection of premises on the lands of another. In a suitable case it may well be argued that a plaintiff suffers a severe loss or detriment by providing his own labours or services in relation to the lands of another and accordingly should equally qualify for recognition in equity. In practice, however, it might be difficult to determine the extent of the estate or interest in land for which a plaintiff might qualify as a result of his personal efforts. Perhaps a claim of that nature would be adequately compensated by a charge or lien on the lands for a sum equivalent to reasonable remuneration for the services rendered.

Indeed, one only needs to look at the English case of *Re Basham* [1986] 1 W.L.R. 1498 to find proprietary estoppel being employed to uphold a claim to the entire estate of the deceased, and not merely a lien securing reasonable remuneration, in circumstances similar to those in *McCarron v. McCarron.*

Stipulation as to time for payment of deposit   In *Kramer v. Arnold,* Supreme Court, April 24, 1997, the defendant granted the plaintiff an option to acquire the fee simple in certain commercial premises. The plaintiff exercised the option on March 15, 1994 and, because the parties could not agree on a price, in accordance with the terms of the option agreement it was fixed by an independent surveyor at £92,000. The valuer acting for the plaintiff received notification of the price from the independent surveyor between 5.30 p.m. and 6.00 p.m. on Friday March 31, 1995. The option agreement provided that 'immediately the purchase price shall have either been agreed . . . or shall have been determined by such valuer in accordance with the provisions hereinbefore contained. . . .' the plaintiff should pay a deposit of 10% to the defendant's solicitors as stakeholders. By letter dated April 3, 1995 the defendant's solicitor sought immediate payment of the deposit of £9,200. On April 12, 1995 the defendant's solicitor delivered a letter to the plaintiff's solicitors purporting to terminate the option agreement on the ground that the deposit had not been paid. On the same day the plaintiff's solicitor delivered a cheque for £9,200 to the defendant's solicitor, but this was returned and the plaintiff instituted proceedings seeking specific performance.

In the High Court McGuinness J. held that while the word 'immediately' was used there was no exact measure of time and the deposit had been paid within a reasonable time. Furthermore, given the lack of an exact measure of time it was incumbent on the defendant to notify the plaintiff of his intention to rescind if the deposit was not paid by a particular date, in which circumstances time would have been of the essence. Accordingly, she found for the plaintiff and granted a decree of specific performance. However, this decision was unanimously reversed by the Supreme Court.

It had been conceded by the defendant that the plaintiff could not be expected to deliver the deposit on the Friday evening that notification of the price was received. However, Keane J. observed that the parties had chosen to use the word 'immediately' and so it had to be given some significance. It suggested that while the plaintiff would not be under an obligation to pay the deposit within a time limit compliance with which was impossible or impracticable, the deposit should be paid as soon as it was practicable after he or his agent received notification of the price. Applying the reasoning of McVeigh J. in the Northern Irish case of *Morrow v. Carty* [1957] N.I. 147, Keane J. pointed out that the payment of a deposit in the context of a contract for the sale of land was an important matter as it demonstrated that the purchaser had the means and willingness to complete the contract and so, when the parties stipulated that it was to be paid 'immediately,' this required that it should be paid as soon as practicable. After receiving notification of the price the plaintiff set about organising finance for raising the deposit with his bank. However, Keane J. held that this could have been done earlier, especially as the plaintiff was aware that the defendant had been looking for £150,000 for the property and so he might be required to pay anything up to £15,000 by way of a deposit. It followed that the plaintiff was in breach of the clause governing the payment of the deposit. Keane J. held that a condition of this nature was at least a fundamental term of the contract and so the defendant was entitled to treat the contract as discharged.

As the parties themselves had stipulated expressly that the deposit was to be made immediately and the condition was a fundamental term of the contract, there was no basis for invoking any equitable principle which would tend towards a more liberal approach to stipulations as to time in contracts. Keane J. distinguished the decision of Warner J. in *Millichamp v. Jones* [1983] 1 All E.R. 267, where it was held that it would be inequitable to allow the vendor to rely upon a failure to pay the deposit on time. The principal distinction between that case and the present was that here there was no oversight on the plaintiff's part. He knew that the defendant was dissatisfied with the valuation of the property and the need for meticulous compliance with the condition as to the payment of the deposit was evident from the letter sent by the defendant's solicitors on April 3, 1995. Furthermore, there was no question of the defendant belatedly taking advantage of the non-payment of the deposit on time, as had occurred in *Millichamp v. Jones*.

SUCCESSION

Automatic entitlement to legal right share where spouse left nothing in deceased's will   In *Re Cummins; O'Dwyer v. Keegan* [1997] 2 I.L.R.M. 401 Thomas Cummins died on February 2, 1995. At the time of his death his wife, Kathleen Cummins, was comatose. She died twelve hours after her husband. Both husband and wife died testate and without children. The husband made no provision for his wife in his will. The wife had not renounced her legal right in an ante-nuptial contract or in writing after marriage and during the life of her husband as she was entitled to do under section 113 of the Succession Act 1965. The defendant, who was a residuary legatee under the wife's will, argued that on the death of the husband, the wife automatically became entitled to one half of his estate by virtue of section 111(1) and so when she died twelve hours later her estate had been enhanced by having added to it one half of her husband's estate. The plaintiffs, who were the executors of the wife's will, argued that section 111(1) did not effect an automatic transfer but merely created a right to one half of her husband's estate exercisable by the wife if she so wished and as she had not exercised that right her estate did not include one half of her husband's.

This argument was supported by the notice parties who were the husband's next of kin. In a judgment delivered on July 12, 1996 ([1997] 1 I.L.R.M. 102) Kelly J. held that the wife's estate did not include one half of the husband's estate. This decision was unanimously reversed by the Supreme Court. According to Barron J., it was clear from sections 3, 111 and 112 of the 1965 Act that the surviving spouse has a right to share in the estate and this right has the same quality as an interest arising under a will or a share arising on intestacy. Just as an interest arising under a will or a share arising on intestacy vests on death, so also does the legal right share of the surviving spouse. The absence of any procedure whereby the surviving spouse could be notified of the right and given the opportunity to exercise it was fatal to the plaintiffs' argument that section 111(1) merely created a right to one half of her husband's estate exercisable by the wife if she so wished. It was on this basis that *Re Cummins; O'Dwyer v. Keegan* could be distinguished from the earlier Supreme Court decision in *Re Urquhart* [1974] I.R. 197. There the deceased died one day after his wife without becoming aware of her death. His wife's will left part of her estate to him provided that he survived her for a period of one month. Although his entitlement under the will lapsed because he did not survive for the requisite period, the Revenue Commissioners claimed estate duty calculated on the basis that his estate included half of his wife's estate on the grounds that he had been competent to dispose of this property given his legal right under section 111. The Supreme Court, by a majority, rejected this argument because the deceased had not elected to take his legal right share instead of the gift under the will. In this situation, unlike *Re Cummins; O'Dwyer v. Keegan*, there was by virtue of section 115 of the 1965 Act a statutory right of election of which the personal representatives were bound to inform the surviving spouse. Section 115 does not cater for a situation in which the will leaves nothing whatsoever to the surviving spouse and so the personal representatives are not bound to notify the spouse.

Barron J. concluded by observing that in the present case it had to be presumed that in the absence of a renunciation of the legal right under section 113, both spouses realised that the survivor of them would be entitled to the legal right and, even accepting that this was an interest conditional on acceptance, so could distribute the relevant assets as he or she wished. Barron J. felt that it was important that the law should be certain so that those who rely upon it when they make their wills should be in no doubt as to how their assets will be distributed not only in expected circumstances but in unexpected circumstances also.

Consequences of disclaiming entitlement on intestacy   Section 6 of the Family Law (Miscellaneous Provisions) Act 1997 amended the Succession

Act 1965 by inserting section 72A which provides:

> Where the estate, or part of the estate, as to which a person dies intestate is disclaimed after the passing of the Family Law (Miscellaneous Provisions) Act, 1997 (otherwise than under section 73 of this Act), the estate or part, as the case may be, shall be distributed in accordance with this Part–
> (a) as if the person disclaiming had died immediately before the death of the intestate, and
> (b) if that person is not the spouse or a direct lineal ancestor of the intestate, as if that person had died without leaving issue.

The effect of this amendment is remove any doubt concerning the consequences of disclaiming an entitlement on intestacy and to make it clear that all disclaimed shares do not pass to the State as ultimate intestate successor. Instead, having left the disclaiming party out of the order of entitlement, one proceeds to ascertain who would next qualify under Part VI of the 1965 Act.

Construction of will to avoid partial intestacy   In *Re Lefroy; Williams v. Shuel*, High Court, May 6, 1997 a question arose as to how a clause in the testator's will governing the entitlement to a share of his residuary estate should be construed. After providing that the residue should be invested by the trustees and the income paid to his wife for life and then, as to one moiety, to one of his sisters for life and after her death 'upon trust to divide such moiety into twelve equal shares and to divide such shares among the children of [the sister] in the following proportions ...' which were then specified as regards the two nephews and three nieces named, the will went on to declare that as regards the share of the residuary estate:

> which is hereinbefore expressed to be given to each of my said nephews and nieces, children of my said sister ... shall not vest absolutely in him or her but shall be retained by my Trustees and held by them upon trusts as follows, namely:
> (a) the income thereof shall be paid to such nephew or niece during his or her life.
> (b) from and after his or her decease, such share and the income thereof shall be held upon trust for all or any of the children or child of such nephew or niece who being male shall attain the age of 21 years or being female shall attain that age or previously marry and if more than one in equal shares as tenants in common.

The will then provided:

In the event of the failure or determination of the trusts hereinbefore declared concerning the share of my residuary estate hereby given to any niece or nephew of mine, the share of such niece or nephew including any share accruing to him or her by virtue of this present provision shall go and accrue to the others or other of my said nephews or nieces to whom my residuary estate is hereinbefore given, if more than one in the same share or proportion to which my residuary estate is hereinbefore made devisable and be added to and devolve with their and his or her original share or shares.

Three of the surviving nieces and nephews died unmarried and without issue. The applicants argued that the will failed to provide for this eventuality and accordingly a partial intestacy occurred. However, Morris J. held that the scheme envisaged by the testator was that should one of his five nephews or nieces fail, by reason of death or otherwise, to enjoy the benefits acquired under the will, the share allocated to that nephew or niece should be divisible among the surviving nephews or nieces and should pass on their death to their sons who reached the age of 21 years or their daughters who married before that time. It was never the intention of the testator to die intestate insofar as such a share was concerned. It was also the testator's intention that if a nephew or niece died leaving no children, the children of other nephews and nieces should benefit notwithstanding that his or her parent was dead as they would have done on his or her death had they been living at the date when the nephew or niece died without issue. Morris J. drew support for this interpretation from the fact that one of the persons who would have benefited from a partial intestacy was a named nephew of the testator. The will provided that the trustees should set aside £1,000 and pay the income thereof to that nephew for his life and after his death to the benefit of his son or sons who attained the age of 21 or his daughters who attained that age or married. Morris J. felt it unlikely that the testator would have specifically provided for that nephew in that manner while at the same time intending a further benefit to accrue to him by way of partial intestacy.

Licensing

COMBATING DRUG ABUSE AT DANCES

The Licensing (Combating Drug Abuse) Act 1997 provides for the disqualification of persons convicted of drugs offences from holding intoxicating liquor, public dancing or public music and singing licences. The Act also increases the power of Gardaí to intervene in cases of unlicensed dances, particularly 'rave' dances. In accordance with section 22 of the Act, it came into effect on June 21, 1997, one month after the date of its passing. Marc McDonald's comprehensive annotation to the 1997 Act (*Irish Current Law Statutes Annotated*) suggests that a number of provisions in the 1997 Act, for example, those involving permanent disqualification from holding a drinks licence on foot of a conviction under the 1997 Act, may be open to constitutional challenge.

Definitions Section 1 defines 'drug trafficking offence' as in the Criminal Justice Act, 1994. It also includes offences under any regulations made under section 5 of the Misuse of Drugs Act 1977 involving the manufacture, production, preparation, importation, exportation, supply, offering to supply, distribution or transportation of a controlled drug; an offence under section 15 of the 1977 Act concerning the possession of a controlled drug for unlawful sale or supply; certain offences under the Customs Act or an offence under section 31 of the 1994 Act in relation to the proceeds of drug trafficking. The most important elements in the definition of 'unlicensed dance' are that there must be a gathering of persons open to the public at which a member of the Garda Síochána not below the rank of superintendent reasonably believes the primary purpose of which will be to entitle people to dance and will be an occasion for the sale, supply or distribution of any controlled drug.

Disqualification Section 2 disqualifies without limit as to time any person who has been convicted of a drug trafficking offence from holding any intoxicating liquor licence, any public dancing licence or any public music and singing licence. A 'public dancing licence' is defined as a licence granted by the District Court that permits a person to use a particular place, whether licensed or not licensed for the sale of intoxicating liquor, for public dancing. A 'public music and singing licence' is also granted by the District Court and it permits a person to use a house, room, garden or other place, whether licensed or not for the sale of intoxicating liquor, for singing, music or other public entertainment of the like kind.

Revocation of licence   Section 3 empowers the District Court to revoke a public dancing licence or a public music and singing licence where the holder of the licence has been convicted of a drug trafficking offence or an offence under section 19(1)(g) of the Misuse of Drugs Act 1977, which makes it an offence for a person who is the occupier or is in control or is concerned in the management of any land (which includes buildings) knowingly to permit or suffer the sale, supply or distribution on the land of a controlled drug in contravention of regulations made under section 5 of the 1977 Act. Where a licence is revoked under this section the premises to which the licence attached will be prohibited from again having such a licence attached to it. An application may be made to the court by the owner of the premises, where the owner was not the licence holder, to allow the premises to again have a licence attached to it. Section 4 permits the District Court to revoke a public dancing licence or a public music and singing licence where it is satisfied that the holder of the licence permitted or suffered the use of the dance hall or other place for the sale, supply or distribution of any controlled drug or did not exercise proper control over the dance hall or other place to prevent such sale, supply or distribution. As the licence holder himself or herself has not been convicted of a drugs offence, the revocation under this section will be for a period of five years and for the same period the premises to which the licence attached will be prohibited from having a licence attached to it.

Dances indoors or outdoors   Section 5 amends the definition of 'place' in section 1 of the Public Dance Halls Act 1935 in order to ensure that a public dancing licence will be required for all public dances, whether held indoors or out of doors.

Licensing of dances   Section 6 amends section 2 of the 1935 Act so that a judge of the District Court is obliged to have regard to the arrangements, where appropriate, that have been made to ensure that there will not be any drug abuse at a public dance. Section 7 inserts a new section 4 into the 1935 Act to ensure that when a public dancing licence is granted it will, where appropriate, contain a condition that the person to whom the licence is being granted will make all reasonable arrangements to prevent drug abuse at the dance. Section 8 amends section 9 of the 1935 Act by giving a right of appeal to the Circuit Court to the holder of a licence that was revoked under sections 3, 4 or 21 of the 1997 Act or the owner of a place who was not the holder of the licence who unsuccessfully applied pursuant to sections 3(5), 4(3) or 21(4). Section 9 inserts a new section 10 into the 1935 Act to ensure that no place can be used for public dancing unless a public dancing licence is in force in respect of the place. The penalties for organising a public dance without a licence or permitting a place to be used for that purpose were increased from £10 for every day during which such place is used for public dancing to a fine not exceeding £1,500 or to a 12 months imprisonment, or both, or a fine not exceeding £10,000 or a term of imprisonment not exceeding 3 years, or both, on conviction on indictment. Section 10 of the 1997 Act inserts a new section 11 into the 1935 Act and obliges a judge of the District Court to revoke a public dancing licence where the condition on the licence relating to the prevention of drug abuse has been contravened. The penalty generally for contravention of a public dancing licence was increased from £5 for every day during which the place is used for public dancing to a fine not exceeding £1,500. Section 11 extends the provisions relating to the conditions end restrictions contained in public dancing licences to public music and singing licences granted under section 51 of the Public Health Acts Amendment Act 1890.

Garda powers Section 12 of the 1997 Act empowers a member of the Garda Síochána not below the rank of superintendent the power to give a direction to persons preparing for an unlicensed dance, who are present at an unlicensed dance which is in progress and who prepared or organised that dance, or are using the sound equipment at an unlicensed dance, to leave the place and to remove any sound equipment or other property which they have with them at that place. This empowers the Gardaí to intervene to halt an unlicensed dance at which they reasonably believe controlled drugs are being sold, supplied or distributed. It is primarily aimed at 'rave' dances, whether held out of doors or indoors in places such as warehouses. Section 13 provides a mechanism for preventing an unlicensed dance taking place by giving the Gardaí power to stop persons from proceeding towards the unlicensed dance. This power can only be used within two miles of the place where the Gardaí believe the dance is to take place unless it is to be held on one of the offshore islands, in which case there will be no distance restriction. Section 14 empowers the Gardaí to enter without warrant any place which is being used for public dancing without a public dancing licence (or at any other reasonable time) if the Gardaí consider that the place requires an inspection, or examination for the prevention or detection of a drug trafficking offence, or for the purpose of being able to give a direction under section 12 of the 1997 Act. Section 15 empowers the District Court to order the forfeiture of any sound equipment that has been seized under section 14. Section 16 empowers the Garda Síochána to retain any sound equipment removed under section 14 until the conclusion of proceedings against the person from whom it was seized for an offence under section 12.

Intoxicating liquor licences Section 17 of the 1997 Act extends the provisions of section 3 of the 1997 Act relating to the revocation of a public dancing licence or a public music and singing licence to the forfeiture of intoxicating liquor licences. Section 18 extends the provisions of section 4 relating to the temporary disqualification from holding a public dancing licence or a public music and singing licence to intoxicating liquor licences. In this case the holder of an intoxicating liquor licence may have the licence suspended, for up to five years and during that time the person will be disqualified from holding any intoxicating liquor licence. During that time the premises, to which the licence is attached cannot again be licensed under the Licensing Acts before the annual licensing sessions of the fourth year following the date of the suspension. Section 19 amended section 4 of the Courts (No.2) Act 1986 to provide a mechanism whereby a suspended licence may be re-activated at the end of the period of suspension. Section 20 provides for an appeal to the Circuit Court against the forfeiture or suspension of an intoxicating liquor licence. Until an appeal has been heard a temporary licence may attach to the premises.

'Shadow' licence holder Section 21 of the 1997 Act introduces a novel concept into licensing law, namely the 'shadow' licence holder. Any person who has been disqualified under the 1997 Act from holding an intoxicating liquor licence, a public dancing licence or a public music and singing licence is prohibited by section 21 from enjoying or being entitled to any gain or profit deriving from the operation of the licence or from controlling or conducting the activities under any such licence during the period of disqualification.

HORSE RACING

Tote *Madden v. Irish Turf Club*, [1997] 2 I.L.R.M. 148 (SC), in which the Supreme Court held that no liability in negligence attached to the Turf Club arising from unsuccessful bets placed on the tote, is discussed in the Torts chapter, 700, below.

Limitation of Actions

PERSONAL INJURIES

In the 1991 Review, 299–302, we analysed the Statute of Limitations (Amendment) Act 1991, which, following the recommendations of the Law Reform Commission in its Twenty-First Report (cf. the 1987 Review, 253-5), introduces the 'discoverability' test for personal injury litigation. The limitation period does not begin to run until the injured plaintiff 'first had knowledge' of the injury, the fact that the injury in question was significant, the fact that the injury was attributable to the defendant's conduct and the identity of the defendant: section 2(1). Section 2(2) provides that a person's knowledge includes knowledge which he might reasonably have been expected to acquire from facts ascertainable by him or from facts ascertainable by him with the help of medical or other appropriate expert advice which it is reasonable for him to seek.

Whitely v. Minister for Defence [1997] 2 I.L.R.M. 416 was concerned with the problem of hearing loss among the defence forces. The plaintiff had enlisted in the army in 1957 and served until 1978. During this period of twenty one years he was exposed to excessive noise without adequate protection. This was conceded by the defendant.

The crucial question was whether the plaintiff's claim, initiated in 1995, fell foul of the limitation period of three years after the 'date of knowledge' (section 2(1)).

The plaintiff's evidence was to the effect that, while he was in the army, he noticed that he was encountering a problem with his hearing and a ringing in his ears immediately after he had been exposed to high levels of noise. After he was voluntarily discharged from the army in 1978, he suffered from tinnitus and difficulty with speech discrimination in the presence of background noise.

Quirke J. dismissed the plaintiff's claim on the basis that it was statute-barred. He was of the view that as early as 1978 or 1980 the plaintiff would have considered his hearing loss and his tinnitus sufficiently serious to justify his instituting proceedings for damages against 'a defendant who did not dispute liability and was able to satisfy a judgment.' This was the criterion for determining whether the plaintiff regarded the injury as significant which is prescribed by English legislation and which, not commanding the support of the Law Reform Commission, had been ommitted from the 1991 Act. Quirke J. accepted that, in these circumstances, the English criterion was not the appropriate one. A 'broader and more subjective test' had to be applied. In the light of the evidence, he concluded that there were no particular circumstances existing between 1978 and 1993 which would have interfered with the plaintiff's capacity to understand the nature and extent of his injury. The 'more objective dimension' of the test was contained in section 2(2). Quirke J. was of the view that the plaintiff knew or ought reasonably to have known from facts which were observable or ascertainable by him alone that he had sustained an injury which was significant; accordingly it was not necessary for Quirke J. to consider paragraph (B) of section 2(2).

While there are references in Quirke J's judgment to the subjective quality of the test prescribed by the 1991 Act, in truth the effect of section 2(2) is to render it largely an objective one. The test is, however, centred on the circumstances of the plaintiff in determining whether *this* plaintiff, in the light of his or her experience ought to have known of the facts which are deemed crucial by section 2(1).

In *Gallagher v. Minister for Defence*, High Court, February 25, 1998, O'Higgins J., in similar litigation, 'had regard' to Quirke J.'s judgment in *Whitely*. Even if the more restrictive test of the British leglislation were applicable, O'Higgins J., on the evidence in *Gallagher*, did not believe that the plaintiff had the required knowledge that the injury was significant; *a fortiori*, therefore, applying the broader criteria which Quirke J. had set down in *Whiteley*. We shall examine *Gallagher* in detail in the 1998 Review.

BREACH OF CONSTITUTIONAL RIGHTS

In the 1996 Review, 86, we analysed *McDonnell v. Ireland* [1996] 2 I.L.R.M. 222, where Carroll J. held that section 11(2) of the Statute of Limitations 1957 applies to actions founded on the breach of a constitutional right. In taking this approach, she applied the same reasoning as that which she had adopted in *Tate v. Minister for Social Welfare* [1995] I.L.R.M. 507.

The Supreme Court, on July 23, 1997, affirmed Carroll J.'s holding. It will be recalled that in *McDonnell* the plaintiff sought compensation for infringement of his constitutional right to earn a livelihood and his property rights by reason of having forfeit his office as a clerk with the former Department of Posts and Telegraphs in 1974 on being convicted of membership of the Irish Republican Army. This fate followed inexorably from section 34 of the offences Against the State Act 1939, which many years later was struck down by the Supreme Court in *Cox v. Ireland* [1992] 2 I.R. 503: see the 1992 Review, 211. The plaintiff's claim was that, having been dismissed under a constitutionally invalid statutory provision, and not having been reinstated subsequently, he had suffered considerable economic loss.

The case raised the problem, first apparent in *Murphy v. Attorney General* [1982] I.R. 241, of how the courts should deal with the opening of the flood-gates by a holding that a long-established statutory provision with serious negative impact on many citizens has no constitutional force. We need not deal with this issue here as it does not impact directly on the limitation question save to the extent that it offers a useful pragmatic ancillary long-strop to widespread claims.

The leading judgment was delivered of Keane J., whose thorough analysis of the juridical character of the action for infringement of constitutional rights merits close attention.

Keane J. proceeded on the basis that the plaintiff had 'some form of action, however loosely defined and conceptually uncertain, for breach of his constitutional rights.' Noting the broad definition of a tort in Salmond & Heuston's *Law of Torts*, (20th ed., 1992) as 'some act done by the defendant whereby has had without just cause or excuse caused some form of harm to the plaintiff, Keane J. observed:

> Manifestly, as this and other leading textbooks demonstrate, the law, as it has evolved, has staked out the territory within which the law of torts holds sway with more precision. For a variety of reasons, damage which at first sight may seem to have been wrongfully inflicted may not be properly remediable in tort. Even where remediable, the proceedings may still require to be brought within the constraints of a different form of action, most conspicuously in the case of actions for breach of contract, with significant consequences in areas such as the assessment of damages. But, subject to these limitations, which do not require exploration in the context of the present case, it may well be said that the English law of tort has, as a matter of history, demonstrated over the centuries a flexibility and a capacity to adapt to changing social conditions, even without legislative assistance, which made it the obvious instrument for the righting of civil wrongs when the Constitution was enacted in 1937.
>
> The dynamic nature of the tort action was well understood when the 1957 Act was enacted. It had been graphically illustrated by the manner in which the action for negligence outgrew the medieval constraints of the action for 'trespass on the case'. The law had seen new species of tortious principles, such as the rule in *Rylands v. Fletcher*, impose novel forms of liability on defendants. I see no reason to suppose that the Oireachtas legislated in 1957 on the basis that the law of tort was at that stage petrified for all time. It may be, however, – and surmise on the topic would be both unjustifiable and unprofitable – that the draughtsman did not envisage the extent to which the developing constitutional jurisprudence of the High Court and the Supreme Court in later decades

would powerfully reinforce the progressive development of the law of civil wrongs.

Keane J. took by way of example the unenumerated constitutional right of privacy upheld in *Kennedy and Arnold v. Ireland* [1987] I.R. 587. While it was true that English court had been hesitant in recognising the existence of such a tort, as was evident from *R. v. Khan (Sultan)* [1996] 3 All E.R. 289, such a novel growth, even in the absence of a written constitution, might, for all one knew, have flourished sturdily in Ireland. The fact that it did so in the form of an action for infringement of a constitutional right did not prevent it from being classified as a civil wrong, which was not a breach of contract but which was remediable by an action for unliquidated damages and/or an injunction.

Legislative intervention such as the Civil Liability Act 1961 apart, the law of torts – including the categorisation by name of specific forms of wrongdoing as torts – had been evolved by the courts; there was thus no obstacle to an action for damages for breach of a constitutional right being identified as such.

Keane J. considered that the famous passage from Walsh J.'s judgment in *Meskell v. Coras Iompair Eireann* [1973] I.R. 121, at 132, to the effect that constitutional rights carry within them their own entitlement to a remedy for their enforcement, was perfectly consistent with their being protected 'by a new form of action in tort, provided, of course, the form of action thus fashioned sufficiently protects the constitutional right in question.' Nor was there anything in Henchy 's judgment in *Hanrahan v. Merck Sharp & Dohme (Ireland) Ltd* [1988] I.L.R.M. 629, to suggest that, where a plaintiff was obliged to have recourse to an action for breach of a constitutional right, because the existing corpus of tort law afforded him no remedy, or an inadequate remedy, that action could not in turn be described as an action in tort, albeit a tort not hitherto recognised by the law, within the meaning of, and for the purpose of, the 1957 Act.

The reference by Finlay C.J. in *Conway v. INTO* [1991] 2 I.R. 305 to 'damages in tort or for breach of a constitutional right' did not assist the plaintiff. The Chief Justice had been solely concerned at that point in his judgment with considering the differing headings of damages recoverable in Irish law, whether in an action for tort in the conventional sense or in an action for breach of a constitutional right. Whether the second category – actions for breaches of constitutional rights – could approximately be grouped under the heading of 'actions in tort' in other contexts, such as the 1957 Act, was not under consideration in *Conway*.

Keane J. acknowledged that, in considering whether other features of the general corpus of tort law apply to actions in protection of constitutional rights, questions might arise which were not relevant in the instant proceedings. Whatever might be the position in regard to other possible defences, no one had been able to identify in the instant case any ground for supposing that an action for breach of a constitutional right which had all the *indicia* of an action in tort should have a different limitation period from that applicable to actions in tort generally – or indeed no limitation period at all – other than its origin in the Constitution itself, which was a classically circular argument. Nor could it be seriously argued that the fact that the action for breach of a constitutional right frequently took the form of proceedings against organs of the State was of itself a reason for treating a limitation statute as inapplicable. Even if it were, it had to be borne in mind that, as was made clear by *Meskell v. CIE*, the defendant in such actions need not necessarily be an organ of the State.

Noting the policy considerations underlying statutes of limitation such as the 1957 Act, which had been 'succinctly and comprehensively stated' by Finlay C.J. in *Tuohy v. Courtney* [1994] 3 I.R. 1 (noted in the 1994 Review, 336–8) Keane J. admitted that he could:

> see no reason why an actress sunbathing in her back garden whose privacy is intruded upon by a long-range camera should defer proceedings until her old age to provide her with a nest egg, while a young man or woman rendered a paraplegic by a drunken motorist must be cut off from suing after three years. The policy considerations identified by [Finlay C.J.] in [*Tuohy v. Courtney*] are applicable to actions such as the present as much as to actions founded on tort in the conventional sense.

Keane J.'s judgment on the limitations issue received the overt support of O'Flaherty J., who expressed his 'total agreement' with it. Hamilton C.J. also concurred. Barrington J. did not think it necessary to decide, for the purposes of the case, whether all breaches of constitutional rights are torts within the meaning of the Statute of Limitations. His analysis as to the character and scope of the action for breach of constitutional rights appears to follow closely that of Henchy J. in *Hanrahan* and, indeed, to adopt a narrower view of the circumstances in which such an action will be available.

It may be useful to quote *in extenso* what Barrington J. had to say on this question:

> The general problem of resolving how constitutional rights are to be balanced against each other and reconciled with the exigencies of the common good is, in the first instance, a matter for the legislature. It is only when the legislature has failed in its constitutional duty to defend or vindicate a particular constitutional right pursuant to the provisions of Article 40, section 3 of the Constitution that this Court, as the Court of last resort, will feel obliged to fashion its own remedy. If, however, a practical method of defending or vindicating the right already exists, at

common law or by statute, there will be no need for this Court to interfere. . . .

There is no doubt that constitutional rights do not need recognition
by the legislature or by common law to be effective. If necessary the
courts will define them and fashion a remedy for their breach. There
may also be cases where the fact that a tort is also a breach of a constitutional right may be a reason for awarding exemplary or punitive damages.

But, at the same time, constitutional rights should not be regarded as
wild cards which can be played at any time to defeat all existing rules. If
the general law provides an adequate cause of action to vindicate a constitutional right it appears to me that the injured party cannot ask the
Court to devise a new and different cause of action. Thus the Constitution guarantees the citizen's right to his or her good name but the cause
of action to defend his or her good name is the action for defamation.
The injured party, it appears to me, has to accept the action for defamation with all its incidents including the time limit within which the action must be commenced. Likewise the victim of careless driving has
the action for negligence by means of which to vindicate his rights. But
he must, generally, commence his action within three years. He cannot
wait longer and then bring an action for breach of his constitutional
right to bodily integrity.

So it was with the plaintiff in the instant case. If the State had purported to
forfeit his office without having authority to do so, the law offered him a
relief; but he could not wait indefinitely before claiming this relief, particularly as the case was one concerning an officer holder. In such a case the
situation did not remain the same. An innocent third party might be appointed
to the office. Moreover, had the plaintiff's claim been successful, the Government might have wished to consider the question of dismissal. In fact the
situation changed radically with the establishment of An Post in 1983. In the
unlikely event of the plaintiff's claim still subsisting as a validly enforceable
claim in 1983 it had changed radically then.

Barron J. took a different approach. In his view the plaintiff's case was not
grounded on breaches of constitutional rights because section 34 of the 1939
Act, being null and void on account of its constitutional invalidity, had never
applied to the plaintiff and therefore could not have infringed his constitutional rights. His position had never been forfeited. The refusal to reinstate
him was breach of the terms of his contract. This was the true basis of his
claim, which was clearly barred by section 11(1) of the Statute of Limitations
1957, which applies to actions for breach of contract. Any claim the plaintiff
had in relation to any right guaranteed by the Constitution would be co-extensive with his right of action for breach of contract; once the 1957 Act applied

to the latter it equally applied to any co-extensive right in relation to the Constitution.

Noting that the instant case was not one where the cause of action stemmed solely from the provisions of the Constitution itself, Barron J. reserved for another time the question whether such cause of action would be barred under the Statute of Limitations.

The judgments of Keane, Barrington and Barron JJ. raise interesting questions. There is much to be said for Keane J.'s view that an action for damages or an injunction for breach of a constitutional right is capable of juridical classification as a tort but this is so only because of the breadth and virtual vacuity of so many traditional definitions of a tort.

It would seem quite mistaken to proceed from the fact that the action for breach of a constitutional right is capable of being juridically characterised as a tort to the automatic conclusion that a judicial and statutory corpus of law which has developed over centuries under the rubric of the law of torts should be applied, without further deep reflection, to this newly-named tort. To do so would lead to shallow solutions which are unworthy of the formidable challenge which creating a system of compensation by way of damages for breaches of constitutional rights invokes.

Accepting that there are good policy reasons for having a limitation period or periods for actions for breaches of constitutional rights, this does not mean that the reasons are identical with those applying to (other) torts. The Statute of Limitations 1957 does not treat all torts identically: it prescribes different periods for certain different torts. Moreover the Statute of Limitations (Amendment) Act 1991 prescribes a new, and potentially far longer, period for certain types of litigation. There is no basis for assuming that a single period of limitation will do justice to the complexity of circumstances that can arise in respect of breaches of constitutional rights. The constitutional right that is broken can vary enormously: it can have a limited focus – the right to earn a livelihood, for example – or it can be entirely lacking in specificity – the right to property is one instance. The manner of breach can also vary, and our courts have yet to provide any clear guidance on this crucial aspect of the action for breach of constitutional rights. A right may be breached intentionally, in the sense that the defendant intended to act as he or she did, but with no intent to act in a manner that detrimentally affects the victim's right. It may be breached intentionally in the sense that the defendant did indeed intend to affect the right detrimentally. In the latter case, the court would surely look for what might be called factual rather than legal intent: so, in an action for infringment of a plaintiff's right to privacy of communications, it would be sufficient to base liability on the actor's intention to eavesdrop without requiring proof that the actor sought, at a conscious level, to violate the plaintiff's unspecified personal right under Article 40.3 of the Constitution. Snoopers are rarely experts in constitutional law; their liability for intentional breaches of constitutional rights should depend on their intent to engage in conduct which they know to be detrimental to the plaintiff's interests in the broad sense.

Presumably it is possible that a constitutional right can be breached negligently: the acceptance by the courts that the tort of negligence presents part of the panoply of legal remedies available to protect the constitutional rights suggests that this is so. It is true that the tort of negligence does not require that the defendant acted inadvertently: a conscious decision to act in a way that is lacking in due care to the plaintiff can constitute negligence just as much as a heedless act. Nothing the courts have said so far would suggest that the inadvertent character of a defendant's conduct should defeat a claim for damages for breach of a constitutional right. This indicates that, in relation to claims for breach of constitutional rights, the courts will be obliged to develop some concept equivalent of the duty of care in negligence, the standard of care and the foreseeability of injury to the plaintiff. It will not always be possible to find, as Costello P. did in *W. v. Ireland, the Attorney General and the Government of Ireland (No. 2)* [1997] 2 I.R. 141, that the limits of the common law duty of care in negligence are co-extensive with the limits of actionability for breach of a constitutional right. See further our discussion of *W.*, in the Torts chapter, below, 709–14.

When we come to conduct lacking in the intent or negligence required to violate a constitutional right, the question arises as to whether there are any circumstances in which a claim for 'no-fault' invasion of the constitutional right might be sustainable. One could not reject such a possibility *a priori*: after all there are many torts involving strict liability of this kind.

To raise these basic uncertainties regarding the scope of liability for damages for breach of constitutional rights reinforces one's anxiety about a single limitation period for all of these breaches. If there are sound policy reasons for shortening or extending periods of limitation for particular torts, it is hard to see why similar policy considerations should not apply to particular actions for breaches of particular constitutional rights.

DISMISSAL FOR WANT OF PROSECUTION

In *Private Motorists Protection Association Ltd (in liquidation) v. Private Motorists Provident Society Ltd (in liquidation)*, High Court, February 20, 1997, Costello P. had to deal with another chapter of the litigation relating to P.M.P.S. We examined the earlier decision of the Supreme Court in *Primor v. Stokes Kennedy Crowley*, December 19, 1995 (1995 Review, 401). That case made it plain that there is an inherent judicial jurisdiction to strike out proceedings on the ground of delay causing prejudice, not just where delay is attributable to the prosecution of the proceedings but also where there has been delay in instituting them.

In the instant cases, a scheme was initiated in 1976 by which the Provident Society made loans to the Insurance Company and paid the amounts of the loans to the Insurance Company. In 1979 the Provident Society agreed to assign debts then due by motorists to it amounting to around £970,000 to the Protection Association. In September of that year, the Protection Association paid £250,000 in part discharge of the purchase price to the Provident Society and, in March 1980, it paid a further £200,000.

The group collapsed in 1983. In 1986, for the first time a claim was made by the official liquidator of the Provident Society against the administrator of the Insurance Company in relation to the operation of the scheme prior to May 1978. The administrator repudiated the claim and the matter was then dropped.

In 1992, the Protection Association issued a plenary summons against the Provident Society claiming a declaration that its agreement to purchase for £970,000 the motorists' debts to the Provident Society was *ultra vires*, null and void and claiming the return of the £450,000 paid under the agreement.

In July 1993, the High Court gave liberty to the Provident Society to issue and serve a third party notice on the Insurance Company. The following year, a plenary summons was issued by the Provident Society against the Insurance Company, which shortly afterwards were discontinued. The Provident Society consented to judgment in favour of the Protection Association for £450,000.

In 1995 the Provident Society served a summons on the Insurance Company. In the same year the Insurance Company instituted proceedings against the company's former auditors and accountants; as we have noted already, the Supreme Court on December 19, 1995 ordered their dismissal by reason of delay.

In the instant cases, Costello P. also ordered their dismissal for the same reason. The scheme whose lawfulness was being questioned had been made twenty one years previously. The claim that it was invalid, made by the liquidator of the Provident Society in 1986, had not been pressed. The first action had been commenced in 1992, seventeen years after the scheme had come into operation; the second action had been commenced in 1995, nineteen years after it had done so. The directors who had been involved in establishing and administering the scheme were either deceased or very elderly. It was clear from the *Primor* case that the period of delay was to be calculated by reference to the date on which the alleged wrong was committed rather than when the Society's liquidator was appointed in 1983.

On the matter of prejudice, Costello P. did not consider that the evidence of the elderly witnesses was otiose because the issue was essentially one of law, whereby the loans, if *ultra vires*, were recoverable as a matter of law. In *In re P.M.P.A. Garages Ltd. (No. 2)*, [1992] 1 I.R. 332, Murphy J. had laid down the principles relating to the power of a lender who had made an *ultra vires* loan to recover it from the borrower by way of a tracing action *in rem* or in an action for monies had and received. That was not the situation in the instant cases, where the borrowers, the motorists, had directed the Provident Society to pay the monies they had borrowed to discharge debts due by them to a third party, the Insurance Company. Thus, the transaction had not created a debt by the Insurance Company to the Provident Society.

It seemed to Costello P. that different considerations might well apply when determining whether or not it would be unconscionable and inequitable to allow the Insurance Company to retain the money it had received than in a case where a lender claimed the return of monies lent to a borrower. The issues arising in the instant cases could be determined properly only by evidence relating to the entire transaction and 'in particular' the evidence of the persons involved in the scheme.

In *Reidy v. National Maternity Hospital*, High Court, July 31, 1997, Barr J, applying the principles laid down by the Supreme Court in *Ó Domhnall v. Merrick* [1984] I.R. 151 and in *Primor Plc v. Stokes Kennedy Crowley and Oliver Freaney & Co.*, December 19, 1995, held that the plaintiff's action should not be struck out for inordinate and inexcusable delay in its prosecution. The plaintiff was born by way of breach delivery in 1976. She alleged that she suffered from a congenital dislocation of her hips which had not been diagnosed by the defendant's medical staff who attended the birth and that she had not received appropriate treatment when under the care of the defendant's medical and nursing staff, whereby a condition that initially was remediable became permanent.

Detailed hospital records made it clear that a problem in the plaintiff's hips had been diagnosed at birth. There was divided opinion as to its cause. The plaintiff was not referred to an orthopaedic surgeon for assessment.

When the plaintiff began to walk in 1978 it became evident that she had difficulty in doing so. Her parents then first realised that she might have a hip problem. She came under the care of an orthopaedic surgeon at Crumlin hospital who wrote to the consultant pediatrician in the hospital where she had been born and who 'was the expert in that sphere who had charge of the plaintiff while she was in the defendant's care'. The letter noted that the plaintiff had been found to have widely displaced hips and added: 'I thought you would been interested to know about this.'

The plaintiff's mother deposed that she and her husband had been reassured at Crumlin that the plaintiff's treatment would be successful; it was not until around 1989 that they realised the fact that she would not make a complete recovery and would always have difficulties associated with the original congenital dislocation of her hips. The plaintiff's mother sought information in relation to her continuing physical disability and ultimately approached her solicitors for advice. In September 1990 the solicitors gave notice to the defendant that they intended to pursue a claim in negligence against it.

Twelve months elapsed before the hospital furnished all of the records and related information which the solicitors had sought. The solicitors then set about obtaining orthopaedic advice on behalf of the plaintiff. All of the experts in Ireland whom they approached either refused to provide their services or failed to respond to the solicitors' request. Eventually an English consultant pediatrician reviewed copies of hospital records and other correspondence relating to the plaintiff, as well as a medical report from her general medical practitioner and a statement from her mother. He swore an affidavit in which he expressed the view that early orthopaedic intervention would probably have been fully effective in enabling the plaintiff's hips to develop normally and that the failure to refer her to an orthopaedic surgeon was 'totally inexplicable and inappropriate even by the standards prevailing at the time.'

The defendant sought an order striking out the plaintiff's proceedings on account of inordinate and inexcusable delay in their institution and prosecution. Barr J. distilled from *Ó Domhnaill v. Merrick* and *Primor* the following four propositions:

> (1) The test is whether the delay is inordinate and inexcusable without countervailing circumstances which would justify a disregard of such delay and [whether] by reason of its duration and the consequences for the defendant it would not be fair and reasonable to compel the latter to defend the plaintiff's claim.
>
> (2) The function of the court is to strike a balance between the plaintiff's need to carry on his or her delayed claim against a defendant and the defendant's basic right not to be subjected to a claim which by reason of delay he or she could not reasonably be expected to defend.
>
> (3) The plaintiff's action may be struck out by reason of inordinate and inexcusable delay in bringing or prosecuting his or her claim even though the right to proceed is not statute barred.
>
> (4) In reviewing the circumstances the court should have regard to the conduct of both parties, including delay by the defendant.

Barr J. was not satisfied that there had been an inordinate and inexcusable delay on the part of the plaintiff in initiating and prosecuting her claim against the hospital. An eminent orthopaedic surgeon had sworn an affidavit on behalf of the defendant in which he expressed grave doubt about the suggestion that the surgeons who had been looking after the plaintiff at Crumlin hospital had not indicated to her parents the potential gravity of their daughter's condition. Barr J. commented:

> Be that as it may and, of course, I do not doubt the *bona fides* of the views expressed by [the eminent orthopedic surgeon], senior surgeons are not always informative and may have little, if any, personal contact

with the parents of non-fee paying patients. [The plaintiff's mother]'s informants may have been junior medical or surgical personnel or nursing staff and they may have expressed more optimistic views than the realities warranted.

In Barr J's view, it would have been 'irresponsible and an abuse of the process of the court' for the parents to have launched a professional negligence action against the hospital without first ascertaining that there were reasonable grounds for doing so. The unwillingness of the Irish experts to advise the plaintiff had led to the delay occasioned by the need to obtain the services of an English pediatrician.

Even if there had been culpable delay, which Barr J. did not accept, there were countervailing circumstances which justified disregarding it. Sufficient hospital records were in existence to establish the facts essential to a determination of the issue of negligence. The defence of the hospital was not dependent on the actual recollection of the plaintiff by any member of the hospital staff.

RENEWAL OF PLENARY SUMMONS

In what circumstances should the court make an order under Order 8, rule 1 of the Rules of the Superior Courts 1986 renewing a plenary summons that has expired twelve months after it was issued? The Supreme Court addressed this issue in two decisions, one in 1987, the other in 1998, in both of which it declined to renew. For an excellent discussion of the subject, see David McGrath SC, 'Renewal of a Summons under Order 8 of the Rules of the Superior Court (1997) 3 *Bar Review* 36.

In *O'Brien v. Fahy t/a Greenhills Riding School*, Supreme Court, March 21, 1997 (*ex tempore*), the plaintiff, 'a young girl', had been injured when at the defendant's riding stables in 1988. The plenary summons was issued in 1991, on the last day of the limitation period. (Barrington J.'s judgment makes no reference to an extension of the limitation period to take account of the plaintiff's minority.) Eleven months later the plaintiff's solicitors gave the defendant its first intimation that proceedings were contemplated against it. Within ten days of the forthcoming expiry of the period of twelve months from the time the plenary summons was issued the plaintiff's solicitors informed the defendant's insurers of the proceedings and requested them to nominate solicitors to accept service. This was done three days after the period had expired.

Barr J. refused to discharge an order of Carney J. extending the time within which the plenary summons could be served, but the Supreme Court reversed. Barrington J. (Lynch and Barron JJ. concurring) did not think that the plaintiff had shown a 'good reason', as Order 8, rule 1 required.

The 'good reason' which the plaintiff advanced was that, if the summons was not renewed, she would lose her right of action and that this would be an injustice to her. Barrington J. acknowledged that this was 'a matter to which it appears the Court must give a very great weight'; nevertheless, applying the principle in *McCooey v. Minister for Finance* [1971] I.R. 159, it was not the only matter to which the Court must pay attention. One of the factors in *McCooey* was that the defendants had known right from the beginning that a claim would be made against them. In the instant case, even though the defendant was aware of the accident and the fact that the plaintiff had been removed to hospital, the defendant had not been given any warning for a period of four years that a claim would be made against her. Her solicitor had sworn an affidavit saying that, as a result, were a claim to be now made, the plaintiff would be greatly prejudiced in the defence of the case as it was now nearly four and a half years since the alleged accident and it was extremely difficult, if not impossible to investigate all the circumstances surrounding the accident

It appeared to Barrington J. that the balance of justice in the circumstances of the case was in favour of refusing to extend the time for service of the summons.

In *Roche v. Clayton,* Supreme Court, May 8, 1998 (*ex tempore*), the principles stated in *O'Brien v. Fahy* were applied. The plaintiff had been involved in personal injury litigation in which the defendant firm of solicitors had represented him. A settlement was reached, with the advice of 'very able counsel', in 1990. The plaintiff in 1995 wrote to the defendant firm complaining that the amount of the settlement had been too low, stating that he was now consulting new solicitors, and giving notice of his intention to have proceedings issued against the defendant firm.

It appeared on the plaintiff's evidence that the plaintiff had been in contact with another solicitor, to whom he paid money for the issue of the plenary summons. When this solicitor failed to do so, the plaintiff had issued it himself.

O'Flaherty J. (Keane and Lynch JJ. concurring) reversed Johnson J.'s refusal to set aside Carney J.'s renewal of the summons on an *ex parte* application. Referring to *O'Brien v. Fahy* and the earlier cases of *Baulk v. Irish International Insurance Company Ltd.* [1969] I.R. 66 and *McCooey v. Minister for Finance* [1971] I.R. 159, he stated:

> The upshot of those three decisions is clear: that there is certainly a wide discretion in the judge of the High Court to renew a summons. But there must be some good reason. Here we really have got no good reason at all. The only reason advanced by [the plaintiff] is that he was let down by [the other solicitor]. That has nothing to do with the defendants. We

must make an order that renders justice between the two immediate parties to the litigation. It seems to me that no good reason has been advanced at all. He did know that he had to serve the summons. In a sense (if he is correct), he had been let down by [the other solicitor] before he ever issued the summons because he says he gave money to [him] to issue the summons and he did not issue it.

I cannot detect that here is any good reason. It is not a good reason in the light of *O'Brien v. Fahy* to renew a summons simply to prevent the defendant availing of the Statute of Limitations. The Statute of Limitations must be available on a reciprocal basis to both sides of any litigation.

These two Supreme Court decisions may be contrasted with *Foran v. O'Connell*, High Court, May 6, 1997, where Morris J. made an order renewing a plenary summons which had expired after twelve months, in April 1995. The plaintiff had claimed damages for the alleged negligence of the defendant, her doctor, in prescribing steroids in 1991 after the doctor should have apprehended that this was improper in view of a reaction that the plaintiff had had to an earlier prescription of steroids by the defendant. The defendant had frankly acknowledged that she had available to her all her records, all referrals to hospital and all discharge summaries and that she remembered most things about her treatment of the plaintiff. She had agreed with counsel for the plaintiff that, if the matter were to go to a hearing, she would be under 'no disadvantage.'

Morris J., while accepting that to have the matter reawakened after such a long period was 'a distressing and disagreeable experience' for the defendant, nevertheless considered that the renewal of the summons would not work an injustice on her.

In *Baulk v. Irish National Insurance Company Ltd.* above, Walsh J. referred to the earlier case of *Armstrong v. Callaghan*, February 5, 1967, in which the Supreme Court had decided that the fact that the Statute of Limitations would defeat any new proceedings 'could in itself be a good cause to move the Court to grant the renewal'. Morris J. noted that one of the features of the instant case was that, since the issue of the summons might well have post-dated the last treatment by a period in excess of three years, the summons might well be outside the relevant period of limitation. This was, however, a matter which 'might fall to be decided on another occasion.'

ADVERSE POSSESSION

In *Fanning v. Jenkinson*, High Court, in a Circuit Court appeal, July 2, 1997, Kinlen J. rejected the plaintiff's claim to have acquired title to part of a garden by adverse possession. There was a strong conflict of evidence. Kinlen J. considered that the plaintiff had been confused about some of his dates and that his evidence differed from that of his wife. The defendants' evidence, which covered a longer period, had been much clearer. The plaintiff had agreed that certain acts indicative of possession, including the placing of lights and the construction of a waterfall, had not started until about 1987.

Local Government

BUILDING CONTROL

Building Control Regulations   The Building Control Regulations 1997 (S.I. No. 496 of 1997), made under the Building Control Act 1990 (1990 Review, 404-6), consolidated with amendments the Building Control Regulations 1991 and 1994 (1991 Review, 307, and 1994 Review, 339) and came into force on July 1, 1998. Like the 1991 and 1994 Regulations, which the 1997 Regulations replace, they require that advance notice be given to a building control authority (in effect, large local authorities) of the commencement of any building works covered by the 1990 Act, in the form set out in the Second Schedule to the 1997 Regulations. This includes not merely new building but also material alterations to existing buildings (that is, buildings in use before June 1, 1992, when the 1991 Regulations came into force). They also require that a fire safety certificate be obtained from a building control authority before building works commence. The form of application for a certificate is included in the Third Schedule to the 1997 Regulations and the certificate itself in the Fourth Schedule. Such a fire certificate can only be granted by the authority if the building plans comply with the fire safety requirements of the Building Regulations 1997 (S.I. No. 497 of 1997), discussed below. Fees payable to the building control authority are also prescribed. The building control authority must maintain a register of applications for fire certificates and of decisions on such applications. Finally, they also provide for appeals to An Bord Pleanála against decisions made by the building control authority.

Building Regulations   The Building Regulations 1997 (S.I. No. 497 of 1997), also made under the Building Control Act 1990 (1990 Review, 404–6), consolidated with amendments the Building Regulations 1991 to 1994 (1991 Review, 307, and 1994 Review, 339) and came into force on July 1, 1998. Like the 1991 and 1994 Regulations, which the 1997 Regulations replace, they are a statutory code of building standards for the entire State. They require compliance with specified building standards in respect of building works commenced on or after July 1 1998 both in respect of new buildings and also in respect of material alterations to existing buildings. As with the 1991 Regulations, the text of the 1997 Regulations is relatively short. The explanation for this is that the detail of the relevant technical standards to which buildings should conform are incorporated into the 1997 Regulations by reference to what they describe as 'Technical Guidance Documents.' These are, in effect, the documents which set out the technical standards, whereas the 1997 Regulations set out the basic framework around which such documents are built. Revised Technical Guidance Documents were published by the Department of the Environment and Local Government to coincide with the promulgation of the 1997 Regulations, as had also been the case with the 1991 Regulations. The advantage of such documents is that they may be updated as necessary to take account of new standards without the need to change the structure of the 1997 Regulations.

The Second Schedule to the 1997 Regulations also contains the basic headings in relation to which the Technical Guidance Documents provide information on standards to which building works must comply. These fall under the following headings:

Part A: Structure
Part B: Fire Safety
Part C: Site Preparation and Resistance to Moisture
Part D: Materials and Workmanship
Part E: Sound
Part F: Ventilation
Part G: Hygiene
Part H: Drainage and Waste Water Disposal
Part J: Heat Producing Appliances
Part K: Stairways, Ladders, Ramps and Guards
Part L: Conservation of Fuel and Energy
Part M: Access for Disabled People.

While these headings are broadly similar to those in the 1991 Regulations, many changes in technical specification have been made in the Technical Guidance Documents published by the Department of the Environment and Local Government which deal with each of these headings in turn. Like the Building Control Regulations 1997, above, the Building Regulations 1997 apply both to new building works and also to material alterations of existing buildings. However, Regulation 13 provides that materials changes of use to existing buildings need only comply with certain elements of Parts A, B, C, F, G, H, J and L of the Second Schedule. Finally, it should be mentioned that Regulation 8 provides for a number of exemptions from the provisions of the 1997 Regulations.

CITY AND COUNTY MANAGEMENT

Employment   The Local Government (Appointment of Officers) (Amendment) Regulations 1997 (S.I. No. 262 of 1997), made under the Local Government Act 1941, amended the Local Government (Appointment of Officers) Regulations 1974 to enable local authorities to admit local authority officers or employees to confined competitions. The Regulations came into effect on July 1, 1997.

Manager   In *O'Reilly v. O'Sullivan*, Supreme Court, February 26, 1997, the Supreme Court held invalid an aspect of an 'emergency works' order purportedly made by the respondent, a County Manager, under section 2 of the City and County Management (Amendment) Act 1955. The Order had been made in June 1995 with a view to carrying out works on a site for the purpose of providing a temporary halting site for six travelling families. The respondent had formed the view that the Order was required in the interests of the personal health and safety of the families involved and of the public health generally, as provided for in section 2 of the 1955 Act, and such an Order entitled him to proceed with the works without formal notification to the elected members of the Council. Each of the families to whom sites were to be made available had been offered but had refused accommodation by the Council. The applicants, residents in the area, strenuously objected to the site and engaged consultants to examine various aspects of the proposal, who concluded that the site was unsuitable for the intended purpose. The applicants sought to quash the Order made under section 2 of the 1955 Act on the grounds that it was unreasonable and irrational and was *ultra vires*. The claim was dismissed in the High Court by Laffoy J. but, on appeal to the Supreme Court, the Court allowed the appeal on one ground.

The Court accepted that Laffoy J. had fully evaluated the considerable volume of evidence before her in concluding that the applicants had not discharged the onus resting on them of establishing that the Manager had acted irrationally within the meaning of *O'Keeffe v. An Bord Pleanála* [1993] 1 I.R. 39; [1992] I.L.R.M. 237 (1991 Review, 16-8) in making his Order under the 1955 Act. The Court held that the Manager's powers under the 1955 Act were not restricted to situations that were 'emergencies' in the ordinary meaning of that word and, the provisions of section 2 of the 1955 Act became operative if the Manager was bona fide of the view that the provision of a halting site was required as a matter of urgency to provide a reasonable standard of accommodation for the travelling families involved, in the interests of their personal health and safety and of the public health generally. Since it was clear that he had formed such an opinion in the instant case, his invocation of the relevant powers was not vitiated by the absence of an 'emergency situation' in the conventional sense.

The Court noted that a housing authority is obliged under the Housing Act 1988 (1988 Review, 302-6) to have regard to the needs, not merely of those who are 'homeless' within the meaning of section 2 of the 1988 Act, but also of those in the travelling community who are living in unacceptable conditions but who do not wish to abandon their traditional way of life. The Manager was thus entitled to provide a halting site for members of the travelling community who were not 'homeless' within the meaning of section 2 of the 1988 Act but who did not wish to be accommodated in local authority housing. Ironically, on this aspect of the case, the Manager had treated the travelling families as 'homeless' for the purposes of the 1988 Act, and had thus erred in law and to that extent the Order made under the 1955 Act could not be regarded as having been validly made in the exercise of the powers conferred on the Manager. As indicated, on that basis the Supreme Court reversed the High Court decision and quashed the Order made.

CONTROL OF ANIMALS

Horses The Control of Horses Regulations 1997 (S.I. No. 171 of 1997), made under the Control of Horses Act 1996 (1996 Review, 443-5), prescribe the forms and fees for fine notices and licences and the use of a microelectronics system for the identification of horses. They came into force on April 24, 1997.

FINANCING

The Local Government (Financial Provisions) Act 1997 can be seen against the background of the 1995 White Paper on financing local government, *Better Local Government – A Programme for Change*, which had proposed a new financing system for local authorities including a new funding base. The 1997 Act implemented three elements of the White Paper, namely, assigning the proceeds of motor tax to local authorities, with provision for equalisation of financial resources between local authorities, abolishing charges for water and sewerage services to domestic consumers and introducing value for money auditing in local authorities. Other elements of the White Paper have been overtaken by new proposals implemented by the government elected in 1997 and introduced in 1998, which we will discuss in the 1998 Review. The Local Government (Financial Provisions) Act 1997 (Commencement) Order 1997 (S.I. No. 263 of 1997) brought all provisions of the Act, other than section 7, into force on July 1, 1997. The Local Government (Local Variation of Car Tax Rates) Regulations 1997 (S.I. No. 265 of 1997) established the consultation procedures to be followed under the 1997 Act in making a variation decision on the rate of car tax, with effect from June 19, 1997. The Local Government (Equalisation) Fund (County Clare) Order 1997 (S.I. No. 266 of 1997), made under section 5 of the 1997 Act, provided that County Clare shall pay 45% of the car tax collected by it into the Equalisation Fund. The Local Government (Value for Money) Unit (Establishment) Order 1997 (S.I. No. 264 of 1997) made under section 14 of the 1997 Act, established the Local Government (Value for Money) Unit with effect from July 1, 1997.

HOUSING

Exclusion orders The Housing (Miscellaneous Provisions) Act 1997 amended the Housing Acts 1966 to 1992, and the Social Welfare Acts 1993 to 1997 to enable local authorities to make excluding orders against individual occupants of local authority housing who are involved in anti-social behaviour, including drug dealing. It also empowers local authorities to refuse to let or sell dwellings on the grounds of anti-social behaviour or good estate management and enables the withdrawal by health boards of supplementary allowance from persons excluded from local authority housing due to anti-social behaviour. The Act also provides for the deduction of rent arrears from social welfare payments and provides new court procedures for the eviction of squatters. Blanaid Clarke's Annotation, *Irish Current Law Statutes Annotated*, provides a comprehensive analysis of the Act, which came into operation on July 1, 1997: Housing (Miscellaneous Provisions) Act 1997 (Commencement) Order 1997 (S.I. No. 247 of 1997).

MALICIOUS INJURIES

Res judicata In *Belton v. Carlow County Council* [1997] 2 I.L.R.M. 405 (SC), the Supreme Court held that the principle of *res judicata* did not apply in the following circumstances. The owner of a factory destroyed by fire had been unsuccessful in a claim for damages under the Malicious Injuries Act 1981 brought against the respondent Council. It had been accepted in those proceedings that the fire had been started deliberately but the Council successfully maintained in the High Court (on appeal from the Circuit Court) that it had not been caused by a third party and thus the factory owner was not entitled to a claim under the 1981 Act. The fire had also caused damage to an adjoining premises, owned by the applicant. The Council did not deny liability to the applicant and he was awarded £4,500 in the Circuit Court. The directors of the company which owned the factory premises were third parties in the instant proceedings and the Council claimed to be entitled to be indemnified by them under the 1981 Act. In the High Court, Johnson J. stated a case for the Supreme Court as to whether the directors were estopped by the *res judicata* principle from adducing facts in the instant proceedings as to the cause of the fire. The Supreme Court held they were not.

The Court referred to the decision of the High Court of Australia in *Hoystead v. Taxation Commissioner* (1921) 29 C.L.R. 537; [1926] A.C. 155 in holding that an issue estoppel would arise only if the directors sought to litigate an issue which necessarily and fundamentally formed the basis of previous proceedings and if those previous proceedings could be regarded as having been between the same parties or their privies who were party to the present proceedings The Court referred to the leading authority on the status of a company, *Salomon v. Salomon & Co.* [1897] A.C. 22 in concluding that, even assuming that the directors were the owners of all the shares in the company and were its only directors, there was no privity of interest between them and the company and their interests were not identical with the company's.

The Court held that the invocation by the Council of the abuse of process principle was intended to deprive the directors of a defence on the merits which they might otherwise have to the present proceedings. The Court held that this was not a necessary consequence of the maxim *interest rei publica ut sit finis litium* and to accede to the Council's submission would unjustly deprive the directors of their rights as litigants to resist the claim now being made.

Interest In *Cleary & Co (1941) Plc. v. Dublin Corporation*, High Court, January 14, 1997, Barr J. held that since section 5(4) of the Malicious Injuries Act 1981 specifically limited a claim for compensation to an assessment of the actual damage done, the question of interest on the compensation award could not arise. He held that a claim for interest was a consequential claim and not a claim in monetary terms as to the actual malicious damage, and was expressly excluded by section 5(4) of the 1981 Act. While he accepted that interest was recoverable on malicious injury awards prior to the enactment of the 1981 Act, section 5(4) had extinguished that right.

PLANNING

Change of use: sign In *Dublin Corporation v. O'Dywer Bros. (Mount Street) Ltd*, High Court, May 2, 1997, Kelly J. granted the plaintiff planning authority orders to restrain the defendant company from carrying out or continuing to carry out allegedly unauthorised developments at a licensed premises and to restrain it from making or continuing to make any unauthorised use of those premises.

It was claimed that the defendant had replaced part of the original frontage of the premises with a large plastic gargoyle with the lettering 'Howl at the

Moon' and doors to a night-club in the basement, that this area's former use was as a restaurant on foot of planning permission granted in 1990, that the plaintiff had no record of planning permission for the change of use, and that various signs had been erected and affixed on the outside of the premises. The plaintiff had received complaints from members of the public concerning the changes to parts of the premises and the facade of the night-club.

Section 4(1)(g) of the Local Government (Planning and Development) Act 1963 provides that certain developments shall be exempted developments and includes 'development consisting of the carrying out of works for the maintenance, improvement or other alteration of any structure, being works which affect only the interior of the structure or which do not materially affect the external appearance of the structure so as to render such appearance inconsistent with the character of the structure or of neighbouring structures'.

Kelly J. took account of a photograph of what he described as the offending sign, and held that the defendant company was not entitled to rely on section 4(1)(g) of the 1963 Act as the erection of the sign materially affected the external appearance of the structure and did so in a way as to render it inconsistent with the character of neighbouring structures. The simple assertion that there had been no unauthorised change of use was unsatisfactory and it appeared to Kelly J. that there was sufficient evidence of the premises being used as a night-club and an injunction would be granted in the absence of a more satisfactory response. A stay was, however, granted to allow the removal of the sign.

Change of use: concerts on sports ground   In *Mahon v. Butler (Irish Rugby Football Union)*, High Court, July 28, 1997; [1998] 1 I.L.R.M. 284 (SC), the Supreme Court reversed Costello P. in the High Court and held that it had not been established that the holding of a rock concert in a sports ground constituted a material change of use within the meaning of section 4 of the Local Government (Planning and Development) Act 1963, thus requiring planning permission. The defendants were the trustees of the Irish Rugby Football Union (IRFU) and owners of the sports ground at Lansdowne Road and the plaintiffs were local residents of the area. The plaintiffs sought relief pursuant to section 27 of the Local Government (Planning and Development) Act 1976 seeking to restrain the defendants from using the lands at Lansdowne Road for a concert by U2, one of Ireland's most successful rock groups, on August 30 and 31, 1997. The plaintiffs claimed, *inter alia*, that the holding of concerts amounted to a material change in the use of the lands.

The High Court made an order restraining the holding of the concerts in Lansdowne Road on the August 30 and 31, 1997 finding no 'exceptional circumstances' which would justify him in refusing relief under the section.

In allowing the appeal, the Supreme Court held that section 27 of the 1976 Act gave powers to members of the public over land whether or not they had interest in the land. Delivering the Court's decision, Denham J. held that the clear omission of the reference to future events was consistent with a legislative intention to limit to the public the right to intervene only in present or established events. On the facts, Denham J. concluded that the plaintiffs had not made out the case that a continuous unauthorised use recommenced at the concert earlier that year. She added that there was no statutory power in section 27 of the 1976 Act to make an order in relation to an anticipated breach. Section 27 was a statutory injunction which was distinct from the general equitable jurisdiction of the High Court and the Court had no jurisdiction to extend the statute by invoking the court's equitable jurisdiction.

Denham J. noted that the High Court order, if upheld, would determine in a final, peremptory and irreversible fashion a *bona fide* dispute between the parties as to whether the holding of the concerts at the end of August required planning permission. The final and irreversible nature of the High Court order was graphically illustrated by the fact that the plaintiffs had refused at any stage to give an undertaking to be responsible for the damages sustained by the trustees. The failure to give any such undertaking was consistent with the order being an order of a final, as opposed to an interlocutory, nature. As there were very complex issues of fact and law to be resolved, she held that the plenary hearing was the appropriate process in which to resolve them. It was unnecessary, Denham J. held, to express any view as to whether the holding of such an event constituted a development within the meaning of section 3 of the 1963 Act.

Conditions: harbour authority required to carry out road works   In *Drogheda Port Company v. Louth County Council*, High Court, April 11, 1997 Morris J. (as he then was) upheld the applicant's contention that it was entitled to seek judicial review where the Council had required the applicant, a harbour authority, to carry out road works or pay a contribution to the cost of improving a road as part of a development being planned and in respect of which the Council had given planning permission. Morris J. accepted that 'substantial grounds' within the meaning of section 19 of the Local Government (Planning and Development) Act 1992, as interpreted in *Scott v. An Bord Pleanála* [1995] 1 I.L.R.M. 426 (1994 Review, 352) and *McNamara v. An Bord Pleanála* [1995] 2 I.L.R.M. 125 (1995 Review, 374), had been established to satisfy the Court that the requirement was invalid and should be quashed. Since the applicant were not empowered to carry out road works it had discharged the onus of proof that leave to seek judicial review should be given. However, Morris J. added that section 26 of the Local Government (Planning and Development) Act 1963 contained no provision which would make a condition requiring payment of a contribution to another planning authority improper. Indeed, he noted that it clearly envisaged an entitlement to require payment of a contribution to a neighbouring local authority.

Dublin docklands The Dublin Docklands Development Authority Act 1997 provided for the establishment of the Dublin Docklands Development Authority for the purposes of the renewal and the development of the Dublin docklands area. The Act provides for the functions, powers and appointment of members of the Authority, which replaces the Customs House Docks Development Authority, established by the Urban Renewal Act 1986. The Dublin Docklands Development Authority Act 1997 (Commencement) Order 1997 (S.I. No. 135 of 1997) brought most of the provisions of the Act into force on March 27, 1997 and the remainder on May 1, 1997. The Dublin Docklands Development Authority Act 1997 (Establishment Day) Order 1997 (S.I. No. 136 of 1997) appointed May 1, 1997 as the day on which the Authority was formally established. The Dublin Docklands Development Authority Act 1997 (Council) Regulations 1997 (S.I. No. 164 of 1997) prescribed the organisations for selecting members of the Council to be appointed by the Minister and came into effect on April 21, 1997.

Dublin transport The Local Government (Planning and Development) (No.2) Regulations 1997 (S.I. No. 121 of 1997) amended the Local Government (Planning and Development) Regulations 1994 (1994 Review, 350) and provided that any draft development plans impacting on transport must be forwarded to the Dublin Transportation Office, established under the Dublin Transportation Office (Establishment) Order 1995. The 1997 Regulations came into effect on April 1, 1997.

Locus standi: **company** In *Malahide Community Council Ltd v. Fingal County Council*, Supreme Court, May 14, 1997, discussed below, 566, the majority of the Court (Hamilton CJ reserving his position on this point) expressed doubts as to whether a limited company, such as the applicant, was an appropriate body to litigate matters under the Local Government (Planning and Development) Acts 1963 to 1993 and it doubted whether the applicant had sufficient *locus standi* to maintain the proceedings. The doubts expressed were made *obiter* since the issues raised in the case were fully canvassed, but the views expressed nonetheless place some doubts on the use of such corporate bodies as vehicles for such challenges.

Mobile telephones The Local Government (Planning and Development) Regulations 1997 (S.I. No. 78 of 1997) amended the Local Government (Planning and Development) Regulations 1994 (1994 Review, 350) and provided that the addition or replacement of mobile telegraphy antennae or masts is, subject to certain conditions, exempted development under section 4 of the Local Government (Planning and Development) Act 1963. The Regulations came into effect on February 13, 1997. The Regulations were made against the background of public concern that the microwaves generated by the erection of mobile telephone masts in locations such as Garda stations (an agreement having been reached between the Garda authorities and a mobile telephone operator to that effect) could involve health damage to those in close proximity to the masts.

Re-zoning In *Malahide Community Council Ltd v. Fingal County Council*, Supreme Court, May 14, 1997, the Supreme Court held that where the courts found that a planning authority had exceeded its powers in re-zoning property from recreational to residential such as to invalidate a decision it had made, they were confined to quashing that decision and directing that the planning authority reconsider the matter and decide the question at issue in a lawful and regular manner. The Court thus reversed the High Court decision in the instant case in which the trial judge had purported to re-instate the recreational zoning of the property in question. The Supreme Court emphasised that any court must be very slow to interfere with the democratic decision of the local elected representatives entrusted with making planning decisions by the legislature. It accepted that the provision of amenities was a proper matter to be considered by the Council, but they were not bound to include in any Development Plan every possible knock on benefit or detriment which may be hoped for or feared

Right of way In *Smeltzer v. Fingal County Council* [1998] 1 I.L.RM. 24 (HC), Costello P. accepted that the respondent Council had failed to comply with relevant statutory procedures in extinguishing a public right of way. The Council intended to erect their new administrative offices on the site of an existing park in Swords, a town within their administrative area. After construction, only one-third of the park would be left as an amenity. The applicant contended that where the Council undertook a new development they had to have regard to acquired and public rights over the land they proposed to develop, and that they had failed to do so in this case. In particular, it was claimed that by virtue of section 10 of the Open Spaces Act 1906, the Council held the park in trust for the public to enjoy it as an open space.

Costello P. accepted that it had not been proved that the park was an open space as defined by section 20 of the 1906 Act and hence no public rights had been acquired under that Act. Citing *Attorney General v. Antrobus* [1905] 2 Ch. 188, he held that there was no common law right in the public or customary right in the inhabitants of a particular place to stray over an open space and that in that respect no *jus spatiendi* had been established.

As to whether a public right of way had been established, Costello P. held that what had to be proved was an intent on the part of the owner to dedicate his land to the public, an actual dedication, and an acceptance by the public of the dedication. In the instant case, the Council was the owner of the property in question and the evidence established that it was doing a lot more than giving the public a mere licence to enter their land, as it had contended. He noted that the 1985 Development Plan for the area in question had zoned the park as an amenity open space; and that it appeared that the Council had intended that the pathways in the park would be dedicated to the public in the sense that the public would enjoy their use indefinitely into the future. The evidence thus established that the proposed development would infringe these public rights and he ordered that the Council be restrained from carrying out the proposed development until the necessary statutory procedures relating to the extinguishment of a public right of way had been complied with. The relevant procedures are contained in section 73 of the Roads Act 1993 (1993 Review, 592).

Sewage plant In *McBride v. Galway Corporation*, High Court, July 31, 1997, Quirke J. dismissed a claim that the respondent Council had acted *ultra vires* in its proposed development of a sewage plant in its administrative area. The Council was the sanitary and planning authority for Galway City and its environs and sought to locate a sewage station for the purposes of pumping sewage from the City out to sea at Mutton Island, in Galway Bay. An interim licence was granted to the Council by the Minister for the Environment in September 1990 to commence work on the drainage system. In August 1993, an area of the foreshore was leased to the Council by the Minister for the Marine although at no time had the Council made a formal application to the Minister for such a lease under the Foreshore Act 1933. The applicant sought judicial review of the various actions connected with the proposed development.

As to the application for a lease pursuant to section 2 of the Foreshore Act 1933, Quirke J. held that it need not, of necessity, comprise a single formal request. He was satisfied that the Council had by a combination of letters clearly and unambiguously made known to the Minister for the Marine that it was applying for a lease or a licence.

Quirke J. went on to consider the effect of the 1985 Environmental Impact Assessment Directive. Citing the decision of the Court of Justice in *Marleasing SA v. La Commercial International de Alimentacion SA* [1990] E.C.R. I-4135, he held that the 1985 Directive did not have direct effect within this jurisdiction as it was not 'unconditional and sufficiently precise' to be relied upon by an individual against the State. We note that this issue had been left for further consideration by Barron J. in *Browne and Ors v. An Bord Pleanála* [1989] I.L.R.M. 865 (1989 Review, 201-3 and 331). Quirke J. was of the view that there were difficulties in the direct application of the Directive in the absence of implementing legislation.

The 1985 Directive had, belatedly, been implemented (in the wake of the *Browne* case) by the European Communities (Environmental Impact Assessment) Regulations 1989 (1989 Review, 331-2), which came into force on February 1, 1990. The 1989 Regulations had amended a number of Acts, including the Foreshore Act 1933, requiring that Environmental Impact Statements (EISs) be prepared for the various developments mentioned in the Regulations. The development in the instant case would be such a development, but the next issue considered by Quirke J. was whether the 1989 Regulations had retrospective effect to the development in the instant case. Quirke J. cited the leading decision in *Hamilton v. Hamilton* [1982] I.R. 466 in support of the view that, unless a contrary intention appears therefrom, the provisions of a statute are presumed to have prospective and not retrospective effect. He could not find anything in the 1989 Regulations which would be sufficient to displace the presumption against the retrospective construction of the 1933 Act as amended by the 1989 Regulations. In any event, however he considered that the applicant's complaint was more one of form rather than substance in failing to comply with the provisions of the 1985 Directive. In so far as the requirements of the 1985 Directive could be identified with any degree of precision, he concluded that they appeared to have been complied with in at least as broad a manner as their somewhat general terms appeared to warrant.

He similarly found against the applicant in connection with the 1977 Habitat Directive, namely that it could not be regarded as 'unconditional and sufficiently precise' to allow an individual to rely on it against the State nor was there anything in either its Preamble or substantive provisions which suggested that it was intended to extend to projects which had commenced prior to the date of its implementation in Irish law.

The decision of Quirke J. was upheld by the Supreme Court in March 1998 and we will discuss that decision in the 1998 Review.

Waste management   The Local Government (Planning and Development) (No.3) Regulations 1997 (S.I. No. 261 of 1997) amended the Local Government (Planning and Development) Regulations 1994 (1994 Review, 350) and transferred from the Minister for the Environment to the Environmental Protection Agency the consideration of environmental impact statements for local authority developments requiring waste management licences. They also exempt developments carried out in compliance with the Waste Management Act 1996 from planning permission. They came into effect on June 24, 1997.

RATING (VALUATION)

Actual state: greyhound stadium   In *Shelbourne Greyhound Stadium Ltd. v. Commissioner of Valuation*, High Court, January 22, 1997, McGuinness J. largely upheld the approach taken by the Commissioner and the Valuation Tribunal to the valuation of the applicant's greyhound stadium in Shelbourne Park, Dublin. The questions raised before her were: whether the tribunal was correct in having regard to the current investment in the hereditament in question by Bord na gCon (the Greyhound Racing Board), and whether it was correct in accepting the that the non-profit elements of the hereditament had been taken into consideration by the Commissioner in determining the rateable valuation.

McGuinness J. stated that while section 11 of the Valuation (Ireland) Act 1852 required a determination as a question of fact of the rent which a hypothetical tenant would pay for the hereditament in determining rateable valuation, the decision in *Irish Management Institute v. Commissioner of Valuation* [1990] 2 I.R. 409 (1990 Review, 423-4) confirmed that there was no one way in which the issue should be resolved. The valuation of the hereditament in the instant case presented difficulties because the standard of ordinary market value for office blocks, apartment blocks or private housing was absent, and the hereditament appeared comparable only with other greyhound tracks, but that none of the suggested tracks was satisfactorily comparable with the stadium in issue. She held that the Valuation Tribunal's decision to reject attendances, turnover and other income as a basis for valuation was a mixed question of fact and law and should not be disturbed unless it was unreasonably reached, based on an erroneous interpretation of documents or on a wrong view of the law and since it was reasonably based she would not interfere with it.

In considering the net annual value of a hereditament, she noted that section 11 of the 1852 Act required that the estimated rent was the rent for which, one year with another, it might 'in its actual state' be reasonably expected to let from year to year. In this respect she accepted the company's contention that any planned investment in a future development should not be taken into account in deciding the current net annual value for 1993. This did not resolve the issue in the company's favour however, because she was prepared to hold that the Tribunal had been correct in law if the amount of current investment taken into account in the valuation referred to the estimated capital value of the hereditament.

As to whether the Commissioner had taken into account the non-profit element, McGuinness J. concluded that, in light of the evidence available to the Tribunal, it had been correct in accepting the Commissioner's claim in that regard.

Machinery In *P.W.A. International Ltd v. Commissioner of Valuation*, Supreme Court, July 22, 1997, the issue before the Valuation Tribunal was whether two furnaces and a box oven were rateable plant fell within the meaning of section 7 of the Annual Revision of Rateable Property (Ireland) Amendment Act 1860. The High Court upheld the Tribunal's finding that the items were not rateable plant. On further appeal to the Supreme Court, the Court held that since there was evidence which entitled the Tribunal to reach the decision which it did, the Court would not interfere with that construction.

REORGANISATION

Libraries The Local Government (An Comhairle Leabharlanna) Regulations 1997 (S.I. No. 499 of 1997), made under the Local Government Act 1994 (1994 Review, 342-7), provided for the continued establishment and operation of An Comhairle Leabharlanna (the Library Council), with effect from January 1, 1998.

Practice and Procedure

Hilary Delany and Raymond Byrne

ABUSE OF PROCESS/NO REASONABLE CAUSE OF ACTION

Order 19, rule 28 of the Rules of the Superior Courts 1986 provides that a court may order a pleading to be struck out on the grounds that it discloses no reasonable cause of action or in any case where the action is shown by the pleadings to be frivolous or vexatious. It has been accepted that the court can only make an order under Order 19, rule 28 where the statement of claim discloses on its face no reasonable cause of action and in addition, the court has an inherent jurisdiction to strike out a plaintiff's claim where the proceedings are frivolous or vexatious or clearly unsustainable. In *Doe v. Armour Pharmaceutical Inc*, High Court, July 31, 1997 the third named defendant sought an order dismissing the plaintiffs' claim pursuant to Order 19, rule 28 and the inherent jurisdiction of the Court. The plaintiffs were amongst a group of haemophiliacs who had received treatment with blood products prepared by the first three named defendants. The third named defendant argued that the plaintiffs had no evidence whatever to establish that they were treated with a product for which it was responsible. Morris J. (as he then was) referred to the principles identified in *Barry v. Buckley* [1981] I.R. 306 and *Sun Fat Chan v. Osseous Ltd* [1992] 1 I.R. 425 (1991 Review, 325–6) that the inherent jurisdiction of the Court to dismiss a claim 'should be exercised with great caution' and to the fact that the Court would only exercise this jurisdiction in cases where it was clear beyond doubt that the plaintiffs could not succeed. Such circumstances would clearly envisage that no dispute could arise on issues of fact. If there was such a dispute it could only be determined by the trial judge at the hearing of the action. Neither the plaintiffs nor the remaining defendants accepted as matters of fact the facts relied on by the third named defendant in reaching its conclusion that none of the plaintiffs were treated with its product. Until such time as the facts were established Morris J. stated that it was not open to the court to make the order sought.

A similarly cautious approach to this issue was taken by the Supreme Court in *Harrington v. J.V.C. (UK) Ltd*, Supreme Court, February 21, 1997. O'Flaherty J. reiterated that the courts have an inherent jurisdiction to dismiss an action where to allow it to continue would constitute an abuse of the process of the court, although he stressed that the *dicta* of McCarthy J. in *Sun Fat Chan v. Osseous Ltd* [1992] 1 I.R. 425 at 428, namely, that the Court should be slow to entertain an application of that kind, should be borne in mind. O'Flaherty J. concluded that while he could see the force in the argument that the plaintiff's case against the third named defendant was very tentative at that time, he held that it would be preferable that this defendant should remain in the proceedings. This approach seems to confirm that the courts will be very slow to exercise their inherent jurisdiction to dismiss a claim on this basis and to establish that the *dicta* of McCarthy J. in *Sun Fat Chan* to the effect that 'experience has shown that the trial of an action will identify a variety of circumstances perhaps not entirely contemplated at earlier stages in the proceedings' is still being followed.

The courts also dealt with a number of claims that proceedings should be dismissed using the courts' inherent jurisdiction to dismiss on the grounds of abuse of the process of the court. In *Southern Mineral Oil Co Ltd. v. Cooney*, Supreme Court, July 22, 1997 the applicant companies had been put into liquidation in November 1988. In August 1994 a notice of motion was served on behalf of the companies claiming that the respondents had been knowingly carrying on the business of the companies with intent to defraud their creditors contrary to section 297 of the Companies Act 1963. In December 1994 the respondents sought an order dismissing the claim on the grounds of abuse of the process of the court. Murphy J. refused the application and the Supreme Court dismissed their appeal. Keane J. stated that it is clear that the jurisdiction to strike out proceedings can be exercised even though proceedings have been instituted within the relevant limitation period and referred to the decisions of the Supreme Court in *Ó Domhnaill v. Merrick* [1984] I.R. 151 and *Toal v. Duignan (No. 1)* [1991] I.L.R.M. 135 (1990 Review, 394) and *Toal v. Duignan (No. 2)* [1991] I.L.R.M. 140 (1990 Review, 394–8). Keane J. said however that different considerations apply to the normal limitation period in respect of actions in contract and tort, where the risk of possible injustice is significantly less. In such cases where the proceedings are instituted within the limitation period, the fact that the plaintiff has been guilty of inordinate and inexcusable delay may not of itself be sufficient to justify the striking out of a claim. However, if a plaintiff is thereafter guilty of such delay in the prosecution of proceedings, it is clear from the authorities that the court may exercise its jurisdiction to strike out and may take into account the delay which occurred prior to the institution of the action. Keane J. went on to say that it is clear that even where a delay has been both inordinate and inexcusable, the court must proceed to consider whether the balance of justice is in favour of or against the striking out of proceedings. He stated that a delay of five years and nine months is undoubtedly significant but in terms of both its length and its consequences for the possibility of a fair trial it could not be regarded as in any way comparable to the delays in *Ó Domhnaill* and *Toal*. The case depended on whether the period of delay which had ensued since the issuing of the notice of motion could properly be described as inordinate and inexcusable and if so, whether the balance of justice required the striking out of proceedings. Keane J. concluded that there had not been any inordinate and inexcusable delay subsequent to the institution of the proceedings and that it did not appear that the respondents had been unduly hampered in their defence by the lapse of time which had occurred since the winding up. Both Lynch and Barron JJ. delivered separate judgments in which they essentially agreed with the principles and conclusions set out in the judgment of Keane J.

APPELLATE COURT

Fresh evidence   In *Pat O'Donnell & Co Ltd v. Truck & Machinery Sales Ltd* [1997] 1 I.L.R.M. 466 (SC), the Supreme Court refused leave to adduce additional evidence relating to an appeal before it. The broad background to the application concerned the terms of a settlement of proceedings relating to defective equipment. The plaintiff had claimed interest on foot of the settlement and, in the High Court, the thrust of the case appeared to centre on the rate of interest rather than the issue as to whether interest was due and owing. The defendant sought, in its appeal, to dispute that interest was owing.

The Supreme Court was of the view that what was being described as new or additional evidence was not new in the sense of having become available to the defendant since the hearing. At all times, the defendant's managing director had been able to instruct his legal advisers as to what had occurred at his meetings with the plaintiff. The Court considered that it was inconceivable that the defendant had failed adequately to advert to the substantial claim for interest, and indeed it had expressly admitted the claim to interest. It also noted that the run of the case in the High Court had concerned evidence and argument as to the rate of the interest charged rather than whether interest was owing.

The Court then adverted to the case law in this area, including *Lynagh v. Mackin* [1970] I.R. 180, *Murphy v. Minister for Defence* [1991] 2 I.R. 161 (1991 Review, 327–8) and *Smyth v. Tunney (No. 3)* [1993] 1 I.R. 451 (1992 Review, 469–70). It noted that three conditions were necessary before it would receive further evidence on an appeal from a final judgment or order, namely: (i) it must be shown that the evidence could not have been obtained with reasonable diligence for use at the trial; (ii) the evidence was such that if given it would probably have an important, if not decisive, influence on the result of the case, and (iii) the evidence must be apparently credible, though not necessarily incontrovertible.

The Court indicated that it had misgivings as to whether the second and third conditions had been fulfilled, but the real issue was whether the first condition had been met. The Court emphasised the need to ensure finality in the legal system and that it was in the interest of society that there should be some end to litigation (citing the *Ampthill Peerage* case [1977] A.C. 547 in this context). Having regard to the run of the case in the High Court, and the absence of any 'sharp practice' by the plaintiff, the Court was satisfied that justice would not require or permit the court to deprive the plaintiff of the judgment already obtained so as to afford the defendant the opportunity of making a case now which it had not sought to make at the relevant stage.

CASE STATED

Refusal In *McKenna v. Deery*, Supreme Court, December 11, 1997, the Supreme Court declined to interfere with the respondent judge's decision refusing the applicant to appeal by way of case stated to the Supreme Court. The applicant owned and operated an amusement arcade in Donegal and acquired an amusement machine licence for the premises. Gaming under the Gaming and Lotteries Act 1956 was prohibited in Donegal, but the use of amusement machines was not. In 1994, the applicant was convicted in the District Court on six summonses alleging, *inter alia*, that he had provided facilities for unlawful gaming. Evidence at the hearing was to the effect that two customs and excise officials played machines at the applicant's premises, sought to recover and were paid sums in excess of the amount which they had put into the machine during the last game. The applicant had argued that the customs and excise officers had acted in breach of section 11 of the Gaming and Lotteries Act 1956 and, in claiming the sums of money on their winnings had obtained money by false pretences, thus tainting their evidence in the prosecution against the applicant. These arguments were rejected in the District Court and, on appeal, in the Circuit Court where the convictions were affirmed by the respondent Circuit Court judge. As indicated, he also refused an application for leave to appeal by case stated under section 16 of the Courts of Justice Act 1936; the issues in such an appeal would have concerned the issues raised unsuccessfully by the applicant in the District Court and Circuit Court. The applicant sought judicial review of this refusal and was successful in the High Court, but on appeal the Supreme Court reversed and dismissed the application for judicial review.

The Court pointed out that section 16 of the Courts of Justice Act 1947 conferred a discretion on the Circuit Court judge to accede to or refuse an application for a consultative case stated and that the section did not qualify that discretion in any way. It held that consultative cases stated were primarily for the guidance and assistance of the judge who was asked to state such a case and if the judge was quite clear in his own mind as to the proper decision in the case, *prima facie* he would be entitled to refuse the application and to go ahead and decide the case in accordance with his firm and positive views. The Court added that the Superior Courts should be slow to interfere with a decision of a judge who refuses a consultative case stated and should only do so if there was not merely an arguable case but substantial, weighty and solid grounds calling for a decision by the Supreme Court on the question or questions of law the subject matter of the application.

Nonetheless, the Supreme Court addressed the issues raised by the applicant. As to the alleged unlawfulness of the conduct of the customs and excise officers in the manner in which they obtained the evidence, the Court found that they had not breached section 11 of the Gaming and Lotteries Act 1956. As to whether the officers had obtained money with intent to defraud, the Court concluded that it could not be reasonably said that they were acting with intent to defraud or cheat in carrying out as they were doing the duties of their offices in relation to the prevention of unlawful gaming. Even if it could be said that there was a technical offence to be discerned from the conduct of the officers, the Supreme Court quoted with approval the view of the respondent judge 'that in the balancing of the matter of the public interest as against any resulting harm against the individual in the getting of such evidence at all times the public interest must be considered'.

CONSOLIDATION/SEPARATE TRIALS

In *Murphy v. Times Newspapers Ltd*, Supreme Court, October 21, 1997, the Supreme Court affirmed a High Court order that the plaintiff's libel action be tried separately from that of his brother, applying the principles in *Duffy v. News Group Newspapers Ltd* [1992] 2 I.R. 369 (1992 Review, 476–7).

COSTS

Agreement on fees: whether 'no foal, no fee' In *Hickey v. Carlyon*, Supreme Court, October 24, 1997, the Supreme Court affirmed the High Court in concluding that the agreement on fees in the instant case had not been of the 'no foal, no fee' variety. The defendant had lost a High Court action in which he had alleged certain wrongdoing by the Garda Siochana. He appealed that decision to the Supreme Court (the appeal was ultimately dismissed). While that appeal was pending, the plaintiff, his solicitor, wrote to him stating that the legal costs of the appeal would be £50,000 plus VAT, and that this was in addition to amounts paid earlier, which had come to £15,900. The defendant signed the letter to signify his agreement to its terms. The agreement was not honoured, and the plaintiff then instituted the instant proceedings seeking specific performance of its terms. In the High Court, the defendant contended that the original agreement on the case was that it was to be 'no foal, no fee'. He also argued that since he had been suffering from stress when he signed the letter, he should not be bound by it. The defendant's arguments were rejected in the High Court and, on appeal, in the Supreme Court.

The Supreme Court noted that the central issue in such a case was that it had to be satisfied that any sums claimed by a solicitor from his client were fair and reasonable. The Court ultimately concluded that nothing had been advanced to show that the High Court was not entitled to make the findings which it did. The Court was thus not required to express any findings on the validity of a 'no foal no fee' arrangement.

Brief fee In *Commissioners of Irish Lights v. Maxwell, Weldon & Darley*, High Court, May 15, 1996; [1998] 1 I.L.R.M. 421 (SC), the Supreme Court reversed the decision of Barron J. in the High Court (1996 Review, 471–2) in which he had declined to review a brief fee. The respondent firm of solicitors had acted on the Commissioner's behalf in a planning appeal and had instructed a senior counsel. The firms' instructions fee and counsel's brief fee and refresher fees were allowed in full by the taxing master and in the High Court, Barron J. had dismissed the Commissioner's application for a review of the taxation. The only disputed item on appeal was the brief fee allowed to counsel. The Supreme Court applied the general test, as outlined in the most recent decision in this area, *Smyth v. Tunney (No. 3)* [1993] 1 I.R. 451 (1992 Review, 469–70), namely whether it was reasonable for a reasonably careful and reasonably prudent solicitor to have agreed the fee. Delivering the Court's decision, Keane J. held that, in the light of other brief fees in cases of comparable magnitude, the fee here of 30,000 guineas failed the objective test and should be reduced to £15,000. The Court referred to the fee of £12,600 allowed by Barrington J. in *Crotty v. An Taoiseach (No. 2)* [1990] I.L.R.M. 617 (1989 Review, 346-7).

Security for costs: company The provisions of section 390 of the Companies Act 1963 which deal with the circumstances in which an order for security for costs should be made against a limited company were considered in *Irish Press plc v. E.M.Warburg Pincus & Co.* [1997] 2 I.L.R.M. 263 (HC). The defendants brought a motion seeking an order requiring the plaintiff in an action for negligent misrepresentation to provide security for costs. The defendants accepted that the plaintiff company had an arguable case but contended that they had reason to believe that the plaintiff company would be unable to meet the defendants' costs if successful as the plaintiff was no longer trading and had substantial continuing costs. The plaintiff asserted that it would be in a position to pay the costs or alternatively, that any impecuniousity suffered by it had been caused by the wrongful acts of the defendants.

McGuinness J. refused the application for security for costs. She stated that the Court should deal first with the question of the plaintiff's inability to pay and secondly, if there was such inability, with whether there were special circumstances justifying the refusal of an order. The onus was on the defendant to establish the first point and on the plaintiff to establish the existence of any special circumstances. She stated that in determining the question of ability to pay, the costs of the High Court proceedings alone should be considered. McGuinness J. also stated that on reading the authorities, she had gained the impression that on balance the courts had tended to lean against the making of orders for security. She concluded that while the company's assets appeared to be diminishing, it was not insolvent and continued to have some investment income and its future costs would not be large. In addition, the company continued to hold reasonably substantial assets through its subsidiary companies which were under the complete control of the plaintiff. On balance McGuinness J. concluded that the plaintiff had sufficient resources to meet any order for costs.

The provisions of section 390 were also considered in *Harrington v. J.V.C. (UK) Ltd*, Supreme Court, February 21, 1997. Both sides accepted that the *dicta* of Murphy J. in *Bula Ltd v. Tara Mines Ltd (No. 3)* [1987] I.R. 494 (1987 Review, 279) represented a correct summary of the position where a claim is made that a plaintiff company's financial problems were brought about by the conduct of the defendants, as had been claimed in this case. Therefore the onus lay on the plaintiff to establish a *prima facie* case that its financial problems were caused by conduct of the defendant which is the subject matter of litigation. O'Flaherty J. was satisfied that the trial judge had been justified in holding that the plaintiff against which security was sought had not established circumstances which would bring it outside the requirement to furnish such security. He stated that while the Supreme Court undoubtedly had jurisdiction to exercise its own discretion, in a case where it appeared clear that the trial judge had applied the correct principles, he believed that the Court should not interfere with the exercise of this discretion.

Security for costs: form   Another aspect of the circumstances in which security for costs should be given was considered by Morris J. in his judgment in *Lancefort Ltd v. An Bord Pleanála* [1997] 2 I.L.R.M. 508 (HC). The applicant had obtained leave to apply by way of judicial review seeking an order that the respondent's decision to grant permission to the notice party to develop a site in Dublin was invalid and a declaration that section 14(8) of the Local Government (Planning and Development) Act 1976 was repugnant to the Constitution. The second named respondent and the notice party brought an application for security for costs and counsel for the applicant made the point that no demand for security had been made in accordance with Order 29, rule 1 of the Rules of the Superior Courts 1986. Morris J. stated that while undoubtedly the party requiring security is obliged to make the appropriate demand, failure to make such demand would only be relevant if it transpired that the applicant was prepared to give security for costs and never had the opportunity to do so by reason of the failure of the moving party to make the demand. In the circumstances, Morris J. concluded that a failure to make a demand of that nature did not invalidate the application.

Another point raised by the applicant was that by obtaining leave to apply for judicial review, it had established a 'substantial case' within the meaning of the Local Government (Planning and Development) Act 1963 Act as amended and submitted that the case was one which raised a question of law of public importance and therefore was one in which the court should not grant an order for security for costs. This submission was based on the *dicta* laid down by the Supreme Court in *Midland Bank v. Crossley Cooke* [1969] I.R. 26 to the effect that the Court should not ordinarily entertain an application for security for costs if it is satisfied that the matter at issue is a question of law of public importance. Morris J. stated that while he was of the view that a challenge to the constitutionality of a section which permits An Bord Pleanála to materially contravene a development plan must be regarded as of importance, he was unable to conclude that the point was of such gravity and importance that it transcended the interests and considerations of the parties actually before the Court. A further factor in his view was the fact that the applicant company appeared to have been formed to avoid the risk of financial ruin to individual plaintiffs should their application fail and Morris J. felt that these individuals could now demonstrate their commitment by providing the necessary funds to support the company's application. Morris J. concluded that he would make an order requiring the applicant to pay sufficient security for the costs of the respondents and the notice party.

Security for costs: general principles The well-established principles which apply to an application for an order for security for costs under Order 29 of the 1986 Rules as well as under section 390 of the Companies Act 1963 were restated in *Lough Neagh Exploration Co. Ltd v. Morrice* [1998] 1 I.L.R.M. 205 (HC) in which the plaintiff was a limited company incorporated outside the jurisdiction. As Laffoy J. stated, in the case of an application under section 390 where it is established that a plaintiff company would be unable to meet the costs of a successful defendant, the onus lies on the plaintiff to establish special circumstances which would justify refusal of the order. In relation to an application pursuant to Order 29, Laffoy J. said that a defendant who establishes a *prima facie* defence to a claim made by a plaintiff residing outside the jurisdiction has a *prima facie* right to an order for security for costs. However, this right is not an absolute one and the court has a discretion to be exercised according to the facts of each case. In exercising its discretion the court may have regard to whether the plaintiff has made out a *prima facie* case that its financial state flows from the wrong alleged to have been committed by the defendant.

In the instant case the defendants sought orders for security for costs in relation to proceedings brought by the plaintiff company against them. It was acknowledged on behalf of the plaintiff that there was reason to believe that it would be unable to pay the defendants' costs if they were successful, but it was argued that this financial position had arisen because of the very actions for which the defendants were being sued. It was also submitted on the plaintiff's behalf that it had intangible assets such as information and expertise in relation to oil and gas exploration and a licence to prospect in Northern Ireland which were not adequately reflected on its balance sheet and that these factors should be taken into account. Laffoy J. was satisfied that there was no evidence that the intangible assets referred to could ever be converted into assets of substance to meet an award of costs made and concluded that the plaintiff had not made out a *prima facie* case that its financial position flowed from the defendants' wrongdoing. She therefore decided to make an order that the plaintiff furnish security for the costs of the defendants.

COURT COSTS

District Court   The District Court (Fees) Order 1997 (S.I. No. 369 of 1997), made under the Courts of Justice Act 1936, prescribed revised fees chargeable in the District Court with effect from October 1, 1997.

COURT OFFICERS

Appointment: delegation of function   In *Devanney v. Shields* [1998] 1 I.L.R.M. 81 (SC), the Supreme Court held that it was permissible for the appointment of District Court clerks by the Minister for Justice to be delegated to officials in the Department of Justice. The applicants had been summonsed to appear in the District Court charged with various offences under the Road Traffic Acts 1961 to 1994. The summonses had been signed by a District Court clerk. The applicants instituted judicial review proceedings claiming that the clerk in question had not been validly appointed by the Minister for Justice pursuant to section 46(1) of the Court Officers Act 1926, since the relevant letters of appointment had been signed by officers in the Department of Justice rather than by the Minister personally. The respondents relied on the delegation principle outlined in the leading English case *Carltona Ltd v. Commissioners of Works* [1943] 2 All E.R. 560. In the High Court, it was held that the *Carltona* principle did no apply in view of the express wording of section 46(1) of the 1926 Act. This decision cast doubt on many appointments of District Court clerks and, of course, many decisions of the District Court. On appeal, however, the Supreme Court reversed and dismissed the application for judicial review.

The Court referred to the House of Lords decision in *R v. Home Secretary, ex p. Ladehindie* [1991] 1 A.C. 255, and noted that the *Carltona* principle was, in effect, a convention of English constitutional law which could either be negatived or confirmed by express statutory provision. While the Court did not advert expressly to its decision in *Cityview Press Ltd v. An Chomhairle Oiliúna* [1980] I.R. 281, it must have intended to indicate that the delegation of power in a specific instance must also, in Irish constitutional law comply with the 'principles and policy test in the *Cityview* case (see also the Constitutional Law chapter, 192, above).

The Court accepted that the appointment of District Court clerks was an important matter. However it compared their role to that of the civil servants in the Department of Justice exercising the functions of the Minister for Justice under the Aliens Act 1935. It noted that, in its decision in *Tang v. Minister for Justice* [1996] 2 I.L.R.M. 46, the Court had concluded that the delegation of the Minister's functions to civil servants was a permissible delegation. In the instant case, the Court held that a similar delegation thought not strictly necessary, was permissible and, the Court opined, conducive to efficient administration of functions within the Department.

It is worth noting that a more extensive power of delegation of functions is now authorised by the Public Service Management Act 1997: see the Administrative Law chapter, 1–2, above.

Civil servant status   In *Sexton and Ors v. Minister For Justice*, High Court, February 26, 1997, Morris J. (as he then was) held that District Court Clerks, although office holders under the Court Officers Act 1926 were civil servants and were subject to the power of the Minister for Justice to remunerate them accordingly under the Civil Service Regulation Act 1956.

The applicants, District Court clerks assigned to districts outside the Dublin and Cork areas, claimed that under the Courts Officers Act 1926, as amended, they were entitled to be regarded as holding the independent statutory office of District Court Clerk. They sought a declaration to that effect and an order of mandamus directed to the Minister that she assign to them their correct statutory status in accordance with the 1926 Act. They claimed that the Minister had acted *ultra vires* in attempting to incorporate them or 'servicize' them into the general civil service and to remunerate them accordingly and in linking their rate of remuneration with the amount of cases handled by each District Court clerk.

Section 46 of the 1926 Act provides, *inter alia*, that every District Court clerk is to be appointed by and hold office at the will of the Minister for Justice. Section 48 provides, *inter alia*, that each clerk shall be assigned to one or more areas as the Minister directs. Section 60 of the 1926 Act provides that the Civil Service Regulations Act 1924 and amending Acts 'shall apply to every office and situation under this Act'. The 1924 Act was replaced by the Civil Service Regulations Act 1956 and section 17 of the 1956 Act provides that the Minister is responsible for the remuneration of civil servants and for the fixing of the terms and conditions of service and promotion of civil servants.

Morris J. accepted that while there were certain aspects of a District Court clerk's duties which required the exercise of an independent judgment and discretion in relation to the clerk's functions and in the carrying out of the duties of that office, this was not an independent office in the sense claimed by the applicants. Section 46 of the 1926 Act was clear that a clerk held office at the will of and may be removed by the Minister. He noted that section 48 empowered the Minister to assign a clerk to more than one area and, since the District Court Rules 1948 contained clear authority for the proposition that there could be more than one clerk in any given area, he rejected the claim that there could only be one clerk per District Court area.

He also held that there was no doubt that, in the light of section 17 of the Civil Service Regulations Act 1956, the Minister was vested with the power to regulate the remuneration of clerks and that the applicants had at all times been civil servants. He was also satisfied that on a correct reading of section 60 of the Courts Officers Act 1926 all clerks appointed under the 1926 Act were appointed as civil servants and there was no question of their having been 'servicized'. He added that the appointment of clerks from the ranks of civil servants was in complete accordance with the scheme of the 1926 Act.

He then held that the Minister, being responsible for fixing the terms and conditions of service of civil servants and their remuneration, had acted within the scope of her powers in entering into the productivity and realignment agreements. He noted that there had been full representation on both the official and staff sides in the negotiations leading up to these agreements and the agreements were freely negotiated and binding on the applicants. In any event, he did not accept that any unfair differentials would arise in remuneration where the system was based on a 'case count'.

DELAY

Inherent power In *P.M.P.A. Ltd. (In Liquidation) v. P.M.P.S. Ltd. (In Liquidation)*, High Court, February 20, 1997, Costello P. dismissed certain actions arising from complex and long-running proceedings involving two parties. The plaintiff and defendant were part of a large group of companies which dominated the Irish motor insurance market but which collapsed at the end of 1983. The defendant was registered as an industrial and provident society and was ordered to be wound up in December 1983. The plaintiff was ordered to be wound up almost a year later. The companies were associated with an insurance company, PMPA Insurance Ltd, which provided insurance cover on certain conditions, based on a scheme developed in 1976. The 1976 scheme included a requirement that they become members of the plaintiff company and to pay it a membership fee. The motorist then obtained a loan from the defendant of the balance and as security completed a promissory note in the defendant's favour for the loan plus interest and charges. PMPA Insurance Ltd then issued an insurance certificate to the motorist. The defendant then made the loan by issuing the loan cheque to PMPA Insurance Ltd to discharge the balance on the premium and the defendant was given the promissory note signed by the motorist.

The plaintiff commenced proceedings against the defendant in November 1992, in which PMPA Insurance Ltd was joined as a third party. In a second action commenced in August 1995, the defendant sued the insurance company. Both actions involved complex claims that, arising from the operation of the 1976 scheme up to 1983, certain sums of money were due and owing by PMPA Insurance Ltd to the plaintiff in the first action and to the defendant company, the plaintiff in the second action. PMPA Insurance Ltd applied to have both sets of proceedings against it dismissed on the ground of delay. It claimed that the delay in instituting and prosecuting the proceedings resulted in prejudice and made a fair trial impossible. Costello P. concurred in this view.

Costello P. noted that the relevant scheme which was the subject matter of the proceedings had been developed in 1976 and that one of the claims in the second action related to a balance due for loans made in that year, 21 years prior to the delivery of his judgment. He also noted that the official liquidator of the defendant company had initiated a claim in 1986 that the 1976 scheme was invalid, but that this had not been proceeded with. He also pointed out that the first action had been initiated in 1992 and the claim in those proceedings that the scheme was *ultra vires* the defendant's powers and that PMPA Insurance Ltd should indemnify the defendant in respect of the plaintiff's claim had been made in a third party notice served 17 years after the scheme had first operated.

Citing the decision in *Primor plc v. Stokes, Kennedy Crowley*, Supreme Court, December 19, 1995 (1995 Review, 401–4), Costello P. stated that the principles to be applied concerning the Court's exercise of its inherent jurisdiction to dismiss for want of prosecution were well-settled. The judge had a discretionary power to strike out an action for want of prosecution if two preconditions were satisfied: the plaintiff was guilty of inordinate and inexcusable delay, and such delay gave rise to a substantial risk that it was not possible to have a fair trial, or was likely to cause or have caused serious prejudice to the defendant. He added that the Court's inherent jurisdiction was not just to strike out proceedings in which there was prejudicial delay in prosecuting, but also where there was delay in instituting the proceedings;

In the instant case, he held that the delay in instituting the claim for indemnity which was made in the third party proceedings and the delay in prosecuting that claim, and the delay in instituting the second action, were both inordinate and inexcusable. In his view, the delays in initiating the third party claim 16 years after the first alleged *ultra vires* loan, and the delay in initiating the second action 19 years after the first alleged *ultra vires* loan, were inordinate by any standard and no plausible reason had been advanced as to why such delays should be excused by the Court. The delay had deprived the insurance company of the opportunity to obtain the attendance of witnesses whose evidence would certainly be admissible and might be decisive in determining the issues in the case, in particular whether they could be deemed to have had constructive knowledge as to whether the loans were in fact *ultra vires*. On this basis, as already indicated, he struck out the actions.

DISCOVERY

General principles In *Irish Nationwide Building Society v. Charlton*, Supreme Court, March 5, 1997, some notable general comments were made by Murphy J. about the nature of the discovery process in delivering the judgment of the Supreme Court. The case concerned an appeal from a decision of Costello P. refusing the defendants' application for further and better discovery of documents. The action concerned a claim by the plaintiff for damages for negligence or breach of duty by the defendants of a solicitors' undertaking in relation to the provision of security for an advance by the plaintiff to another company. Murphy J. stated that he was satisfied that the secretary of the plaintiff, who had sworn affidavits of discovery, had misconceived the principles upon which discovery should be made or else misconceived the issue as to damages in the matter. He therefore concluded that if the deponent had correctly understood the obligations imposed upon him, he would have disclosed further documents and directed that the plaintiff make a full affidavit of discovery in substitution for those already sworn on its behalf. Murphy J. stated as follows:

> Discovery of documents is an extremely valuable legal procedure. On the other hand it can be a very burdensome one. Perhaps this burden has been accentuated by the proliferation of documentary records and the improvement in recent years of photocopying equipment. There is a danger that this valuable legal procedure may be invoked unnecessarily or applied oppressively. It will always involve delay and expense. In virtually every commercial case it is the greatest single cause of delay in

obtaining a judicial determination on the real issues between the parties.

Murphy J. also added some comments about the meaning of the word 'documents' and the circumstances in which they may be relevant for the purposes of Order 31, rule 12 of the Rules of the Superior Courts 1986 and referred to the frequently quoted *dicta* set out in *Compagnie Financiere Du Pacifique v. Peruvian Guano Co.* (1882) 11 Q.B.D. 55, 62. However, he stated that as the case before him illustrated, there may be a difficulty in applying that definition to the circumstances of any particular action and said that while a deponent may be familiar with documents in his possession or within his power, he may have little understanding of the manner in which the contents of any document may advance or damage the case of either party. Murphy J. stated that it is this problem which imposes on the solicitor to the party making discovery the duty to take positive steps to ensure that his client appreciates the extent of the obligation imposed by an order of discovery. The solicitor owes a duty to the court to go through the documents disclosed by the client carefully to make sure that as far as possible, no relevant documentation has been withheld from disclosure. However, Murphy J. stressed that a deponent cannot abdicate his duty in relation to disclosure to his legal advisers nor could a lawyer accept the responsibility of inspecting all of the documents in the possession of his clients.

The Court concluded that sufficient, though limited, time should be allowed the plaintiff in the instant case to appreciate, with the benefit of legal advice, the extent of the discovery actually required in order to comply fully with the discovery order made.

Contemplation of proceedings   In *Gallagher v. Stanley*, Supreme Court, December 17, 1997, a medical negligence claim, the Court ordered discovery of statements made by three nurses on duty at the relevant time. The defendants claimed that they had been made solely for the purpose of or in contemplation of litigation and were not ordinary medical or treatment records as they were not made in the ordinary course of treatment. The Supreme Court referred to the leading cases, *Silver Hill Duckling Ltd v. Minister for Agriculture* [1987] I.R. 289; [1987] I.L.R.M. 516 (1987 Review, 280) and *Waugh v. British Railways Board* [1980] A.C. 521, in holding that the issue was whether the defendants' dominant reason or motive for obtaining the statements was the anticipation or contemplation of litigation. If not, privilege did not apply to the statements. As to the statements in question, the Court noted that they were straightforward accounts of events and conversations and did not contain any element that would attract an entitlement to legal professional privilege. It thus held that it was likely to aid the course of the trial if the statements were made available to the plaintiff's advisors. See further the discussion in the Evidence chapter, 426–7, above.

Cross-examination   In *Duncan and Ors v. Governor of Portlaoise Prison* [1997] 2 I.L.R.M. 296 (HC), Kelly J. emphasised that the circumstances in which it may be permissible to cross-examine on an affidavit of discovery are extremely rare. The applicant had been detained on foot of an order of the Special Criminal Court which it subsequently transpired was invalid. He was released and re-arrested and remanded in custody in Portlaoise Prison. An application was made for an inquiry pursuant to Article 40.4.2° of the Constitution into the lawfulness of his detention and in the course of these proceedings the applicant sought discovery against the respondent and a number of notice parties. The notice parties made affidavits of discovery which included claims of legal professional and executive privilege. The applicant sought, *inter alia*, an order directing an oral hearing of the claims of privilege and served a notice of intention to cross-examine in respect of the notice parties' affidavits of discovery, claiming that he was entitled to test the claim of privilege by way of cross-examination. Kelly J. refused the relief sought. He stated that as a general principle the courts should have the ability to adjudicate fully on the adequacy and accuracy of an affidavit of discovery, which in exceptional cases may involve cross-examination of the deponent of an affidavit. He stated that he did not accept that 'in Irish law an affidavit of discovery must be considered as conclusive and can never be the subject of cross-examination.' However, he said that the circumstances in which it might be permissible to cross-examine on an affidavit of discovery were extremely rare because of the variety of other remedies which are available with a view to testing matters contained in an affidavit of discovery, namely, orders for further and better discovery, the delivery of interrogatories and the inspection by the court itself of documents referred to in an affidavit. Kelly J. stated that the rare circumstances in which cross-examination may be merited need not be specified, but it appeared this should only be permitted where it was both necessary and where other remedies proved inadequate. He concluded that cross-examination on the affidavits which had been made was neither necessary nor appropriate in the circumstances of the present case. If the court was satisfied as to the inadequacy of the discovery already made, it might instead make an order requiring further and better discovery. On the substantive issues in the case, see *Duncan and Ors v. Governor of Portlaoise Prison (No. 2)*, High Court, June 9, 1997 (Criminal Law chapter, 317, above).

Privilege: legal professional and Attorney General   In *Quinlivan v. Governor of Limerick Prison*, Supreme Court, March 5 1997 (further discussed in the Evidence chapter, 423–5, above), the Supreme Court held that communications between the Minister for Justice and the Attorney General fell within the rules concerning legal professional privilege. The Court declined, in the instant case, to hold that it would be permissible to order discovery of edited versions of communications that were, *prima facie*, privileged. This may be contrasted with the editing process approved by Murphy J. in *Gormley v. Ireland* [1993] 2 I.R. 75 (1991 Review, 339–40). The Court held that there was no evidence in the instant case that the organs of State had acted in a conspiracy to defeat the applicant's constitutional rights; it was accepted that the organs of State might have acted in concert with one another, but that was far from evidence of he conspiracy alleged. On the detailed circumstances of the case, see *Quinlivan v. Governor of Limerick Prison (No. 2)* [1998] 1 I.L.R.M. 294, discussed in the Criminal Law chapter, 319, above.

Privilege: UN inquiry   In *O'Brien v. Minister for Defence* [1995] 1 I.L.R.M. 22 (HC); [1998] 2 ILRM 156 (SC), the Supreme Court reversed the High Court finding that certain UN-related materials were not discoverable, though without making a definitive determination on the issue. The plaintiff's deceased husband, a member of the Defence Forces, had received injuries in the course of his duties in the United Nations peacekeeping force in the Lebanon which resulted in his death. The plaintiff instituted proceedings against the defendants claiming that the injuries were occasioned by the negligence of the defendant. The plaintiff sought discovery of, *inter alia*, documents and findings of both a United Nations Inquiry held in the Lebanon and a Court of Inquiry held in the State. The High Court refused the relief sought, *sub nom. O'Brien v. Ireland* [1995] 1 I.L.R.M. 22 (1994 Review, 375–6).

On appeal, the Supreme Court reversed. The Court held that it was not open to the Court to decide on questions of privilege in the absence of having available to it particulars of the documentation in the possession of the defendants relating to the matter and without having particulars with regard to the nature of the privilege claimed in respect of each document. It was not sufficient in the circumstances to claim general privilege in respect of bundles of documents of files and the Court held that the onus was on the defendants to specify in detail each of the documents in their possession relating to the matters the subject matter of the proceedings and to specify in detail the nature of the privilege claimed in respect of each document and the basis for such privilege. The Court thus declined to rule that these documents should be produced but it concluded that they should have been enumerated and the basis of the privilege claimed in respect thereof be set forth. See further the Evidence chapter, 428, above.

Privilege: public interest   The principle laid down in *Murphy v. Dublin Corporation* [1972] I.R. 215 and *Ambiorix Ltd v. Minister for the Environment* [1992] 1 I.R. 277; [1992] I.L.R.M. 209 (1992 Review, 214–5) was that where a conflict arises during the exercise of the judicial power between the aspect of public interest involved in the production of evidence and the aspect of public interest involved in the confidentiality or exemption from production of documents pertaining to the exercise of the executive power of the State, it is the judicial power which will decide which public interest shall prevail. This principle was reaffirmed by the Supreme Court in *Skeffington v. Rooney* [1997] 2 I.L.R.M. 56 (SC) in which the plaintiff brought a claim for personal injuries which he alleged had been sustained as a result of an assault by gardaí, which was also the subject of a complaint before the Garda Complaints Board. The plaintiff sought third party discovery against the board and Barr J, having inspected the documents, held that the plaintiff was entitled to such discovery and that the functions of the board, which was the notice party would not be compromised by the disclosure. The Supreme Court dismissed the appeal of the board. The court stressed that neither a minister nor any other person in the public service can prevent the court from embarking on an inquiry by certifying that the public interest requires that documents should not be produced. However, the fact that the decision as to whether documents should be discovered was exclusively an issue for determination by the judiciary did not preclude the courts from identifying particular categories of evidence which in general will be regarded as privileged. Here the fact that the documents were furnished in confidence to the party against whom discovery is sought did not make them privileged. The documents did not come within a category identified as being privileged even without examination by the court and the Supreme Court concluded that Barr J. had been correct to examine them before deciding on a claim of privilege. See further the Evidence chapter, 429, 436–8, above.

Substantive relief   In *Doyle v. Garda Commissioner* [1998] 1 I.L.R.M. 229 (HC), Laffoy J. declined to order discovery against the defendant Commissioner in what amounted to a claim for substantive relief by discovery. The plaintiff's daughter and two granddaughters were three of the victims of car bombings which had taken place in Dublin and Monaghan on May 17, 1974. The plaintiff claimed that the Royal Ulster Constabulary (RUC) had failed to take appropriate action to prevent the bombings. He had lodged an application with the European Commission of Human Rights claiming to have been to be an indirect victim of a violation by the United Kingdom of Article 2 of the Council of Europe Convention for the Protection of Human Rights and Fundamental Freedoms. The plaintiff had instituted the instant proceedings against the Commissioner seeking a declaration that he was entitled to access to information within the control of the Commissioner concerning the investigation of the bombings. Laffoy J. refused the relief claimed.

Applying the decision in *Megaleasing U.K. Ltd v. Barrett (No. 2)* [1993] I.L.R.M. 497 (1992 Review, 479-80), Laffoy J. held that the jurisdiction of the Court to grant relief in an action for discovery only arose where there was very clear proof of the existence of wrongdoing. In the instant case, the wrong-doing alleged was the inadequate investigation of criminal activity in Northern Ireland. The purpose of the proceedings was not to identify the perpetrators of wrongdoing, since there was very clear proof that wrongdoing, in the form of the car bombings, had plainly occurred. Laffoy J. held that the plaintiff had not adduced any proof of a violation of Article 2 of the Convention. Accordingly, she concluded that the jurisdiction of the Court did not extend to granting the remedy sought.

She also held that the non-existence of a jurisdiction in the State which empowered the Court to make an order for discovery against a person, namely the Commissioner, who was not a party to a complaint before the Commission, could not be regarded as a hindrance of the right of individual complaint to the Commission. This was in the context of her reference to the presumption that Irish law was in conformity with the European Convention, as discussed in such cases as *Ó Domhnaill v. Merrick* [1984] I.R. 151, *The State (D.P.P.) v. Walsh* [1981] I.R. 412 and *Desmond v. Glackin* [1993] 3 I.R. 1; [1992] I.L.R.M. 490 (1992 Review, 239-42).

Third party The principles relating to an application for third party or notice party discovery were considered by O'Donovan J. in *Ulster Bank Ltd v. Byrne*, High Court, July 10, 1997. The respondents appealed against an order for notice party discovery made by the Master of the High Court under Order 31, rule 29 of the Rules of the Superior Courts 1986. The plaintiff's claim against the defendant arose from the countermanding of cheques. O'Donovan J. referred to the judgment of the Supreme Court in *Allied Irish Banks plc v. Ernst & Whinney* [1993] 1 I.R. 376 (1992 Review, 483-4) and reiterated that it had been laid down there that there was an onus on an applicant for discovery pursuant to Order 31, rule 29 to establish first that the party from whom discovery is sought is likely to have had the documents sought to be discovered in his possession, custody or power and secondly that the documents are relevant to an issue arising or likely to arise out of the cause or matter of which discovery is sought. Further, even if this is established, the court still has a discretion to refuse the application if it considers that particular oppression or prejudice will be caused to the person called upon to make discovery which is not capable of being adequately compensated by the payment by the party seeking discovery of the costs of the making thereof. Whatever discretion the court may have, the basic purpose and reason for the procedure of discovery is to ensure as far as possible that the full facts concerning any matter in dispute before the court is capable of being presented to the court.

Counsel for the plaintiff referred to *Murphy v. Kirwan* [1993] 3 I.R. 501; [1994] 1 I.L.R.M. 293 (1992 Review, 480-2, and 1993 Review, 449-51) and suggested that when, in an application for third party discovery a party to the cause or matter has been guilty of fraud or other malpractice, then the application for discovery should be granted irrespective of the relevance of the documents sought to be discovered or of any oppression or prejudice which may be caused to the person called on to make the discovery. O'Donovan J. rejected that suggestion and said that in his opinion, *Murphy* did not in any way alter the principles laid down in *Allied Irish Banks* that documents sought to be discovered were to be relevant to the issue in respect of which those documents are sought to be discovered, notwithstanding that one of the parties may be alleging fraud.

In *Kennedy v. Law Society of Ireland*, Supreme Court, November 28, 1997, the Supreme Court, reversing the High Court, ordered partial third party discovery from a firm of accountants who had taken on what the Court described as something of an investigative role for the Law Society arising from proceedings involving the applicant, a solicitor. The Court considered that there was no need for the limited third party discovery order to go beyond requiring the third party to make an affidavit within whatever period would be reasonable and in so limiting the order, the Court considered that it was doing justice both to the applicant and the third party.

DISTRICT COURT

A large number of Orders made by the Minister for Justice in 1997 under section 26 of the Courts of Justice Act 1953 and section 16 of the Courts Act 1971 provided for the re-organisation of District sittings and District Court areas. These are part of an overall plan to rationalise court sittings and to ensure that District Court sittings are held in appropriate accommodation. They also reflected concern that decisions of certain District Court judges had been challenged on the basis that the sittings had been held in locations, such as ballrooms and licensed premises which were, a least arguably, impermissible.

Re-organisation of courts and areas: Donegal The following Orders concerned Donegal: the District Court Areas (Alteration of Place) (No. 1) Order 1997 (S.I. No. 6 of 1997), the District Court Areas (Alteration of Place) (No. 2) Order 1997 (S.I. No. 7 of 1997), the District Court Areas (Alteration of Place) (No. 3) Order 1997 (S.I. No. 8 of 1997), the District Court Areas (Alteration of Place) (No. 4) Order 1997 (S.I. No. 9 of 1997), the District Court Areas (Alteration of Place) (No. 5) Order 1997 (S.I. No. 10 of 1997), the District Court Areas (Alteration of Place) (No. 6) Order 1997 (S.I. No. 11 of 1997), the District Court Areas (Alteration of Place) (No. 7) Order 1997 (S.I. No. 12 of 1997), the District Court Areas (Alteration of Place) (No. 8) Order 1997 (S.I. No. 13 of 1997), the District Court Areas (Alteration of Place) (No. 9) Order 1997 (S.I. No. 14 of 1997), the District Court Areas (Alteration of Place) (No. 10) Order 1997 (S.I. No. 15 of 1997), the District Court Areas

(Alteration of Place) (No. 11) Order 1997 (S.I. No. 16 of 1997), the District Court Areas (Alteration of Place) (No. 12 Order 1997 (S.I. No. 17 of 1997), the District Court Districts and Areas (Section 26) Order 1997 (S.I. No. 20 of 1997), the District Court Districts and Areas (Section 26) (No. 2) Order 1997 (S.I. No. 22 of 1997), the District Court Districts and Areas (Section 26) (No. 3) Order 1997 (S.I. No. 23 of 1997), the District Court Districts and Areas (Section 26) (No. 4) Order 1997 (S.I. No. 24 of 1997), the District Court Districts and Areas (Section 26) (No. 5) Order 1997 (S.I. No. 25 of 1997), the District Court Districts and Areas (Section 26) (No. 9) Order 1997 (S.I. No. 34 of 1997), the District Court Districts and Areas (Section 26) (No. 10) Order 1997 (S.I. No. 35 of 1997), the District Court Districts and Areas (Section 26) (No. 11) Order 1997 (S.I. No. 36 of 1997), the District Court Districts and Areas (Section 26) (No. 12) Order 1997 (S.I. No. 37 of 1997) and the District Court Districts and Areas (Section 26) (No. 13) Order 1997 (S.I. No. 38 of 1997).

Re-organisation of courts and areas: Kildare The following Orders concerned Kildare: the District Court Districts and Areas (Section 26) (No. 16) Order 1997 (S.I. No. 41 of 1997) and the District Court Districts and Areas (Section 26) (No. 17) Order 1997 (S.I. No. 42 of 1997).

Re-organisation of courts and areas: Leitrim The following Orders concerned Leitrim: the District Court Districts and Areas (Section 26) (No. 14) Order 1997 (S.I. No. 39 of 1997), the District Court Districts and Areas (Section 26) (No. 15) Order 1997 (S.I. No. 40 of 1997) and the District Court Areas (Alteration of Place) (No. 13) Order 1997 (S.I. No. 167 of 1997).

Re-organisation of courts and areas: Meath The following Order concerned Meath: the District Court Districts and Areas (Section 26) (No. 6) Order 1997 (S.I. No. 26 of 1997).

Re-organisation of courts and areas: Monaghan The following Order concerned Monaghan: the District Court Districts and Areas (Section 26) (No. 8) Order 1997 (S.I. No. 27 of 1997).

Re-organisation of courts and areas: Tipperary The following Order concerned Tipperary: the District Court Districts and Areas (Section 26) (No. 7) Order 1997 (S.I. No. 28 of 1997).

Seal of District Court Section 20 of the Criminal Justice (Miscellaneous Provisions) Act 1997 (discussed generally in the Criminal Law chapter, 314, above) inserted a new section 13A into the Courts Act 1971 to require that a seal of the District Court be provided for each District Court Area and for the Dublin Metropolitan District.

ENFORCEMENT OF ORDERS

Examination of debtors The Courts (No. 2) Act 1986 (Commencement) Order 1997 (S.I. No. 106 of 1997) bought sections 1 and 9 of the Courts (No. 2) Act 1986 into force on May 1, 1997. These provisions of the 1986 Act had amended the Enforcement of Court Orders Act 1926 concerning the examination of debtors.

EXTRA-TERRITORIAL LAWS OF NON-EC STATES

Jurisdiction of courts The European Communities (Extra-territorial Application of Legislation Adopted by a Third Country) Regulations 1997 (S.I. No. 217 of 1997) gave full effect to (EC) Regulation No. 2271/96. They conferred jurisdiction on the High Court in respect of actions for compensation arising from the extra-territorial application of legislation adopted by the UNited States in connection with its trade embargo with Cuba. The 1997 Regulations also provide penalties for non-compliance with their terms. They came into effect on May 23, 1997.

FAIR PROCEDURES

Discretion of judge In *Fagan v. Wong*, Supreme Court, May 7, 1997, the Supreme Court dismissed an appeal in a personal injuries action. The Court held that, having read the transcript of the trial, it was satisfied that any interventions by the trial judge were manifestly within the proper competence of the trial judge to make in the running of the trial and did not give any valid grounds of appeal, applying the principles laid down in *Donnelly v. Timber Factors Ltd* [1991] 1 I.R. 553 (1991 Review, 344-5). The Court accepted that a judge was bound to listen carefully to the evidence as it was being given and on a continuing basis to form views as to its reliability or otherwise. In this context a judge might and sometimes should indicate his reaction to the evidence presented with a view to clarifying ambiguities or to provide an opportunity to resolve misunderstandings which could arise and that if a judge did not believe a witness he was entitled to say so. Indeed, the Court considered that there was no reason why a bystander should not gain an impression of how a case was running. Judges had a large measure of discretion as to how they conducted their courts and the trials which they heard, provided that all the parties were allowed to present their respective cases fully and fairly.

INTERROGATORIES

Leave to apply The comprehensive summary of the principles relating to the circumstances in which leave should be granted to deliver interrogatories set out in by Costello J. in his judgment in *Mercantile Credit Co. of Ireland v. Heelan* [1994] 2 I.R. 105 (1994 Review, 381-2) was approved and applied by Shanley J. in *Woodfab Ltd v. Coillte Teo* [1998] 1 I.L.R.M. 381 (HC). The action concerned a claim by the plaintiff that the defendants were in breach of the provisions of sections 4 and 5 of the Competition Act 1991 and Articles 85, 86 and 92 of the EC Treaty. The plaintiff sought leave to deliver interrogatories for the examination of the first named defendant, which argued that these interrogatories were vague and imprecise and that they had not been shown to be essential in the interests of justice. Counsel for the plaintiff argued that leave to deliver the interrogatories should be given because it claimed, it had been established on affidavit evidence that the answering of the interrogatories was necessary for disposing fairly of the action or for the purposes of saving costs, and that a special exigency existed by reason of the claim of anti-competitive behaviour which made it necessary to adduce evidence of the internal workings of the first named defendant. Counsel for the first named defendant relied on the decision of the English Court of Appeal in *Hall v. Sevalco Ltd* [1996] T.L.R. 183 in which Lord Bingham MR had stated that interrogatories had to be necessary either for disposing fairly of the cause of action or for saving costs, and that 'necessity' was a stringent test in that context. Lord Bingham MR had stated that it must be shown that the interrogatories would serve a clear litigious purpose and that they 'should not be regarded as a source of ammunition to be routinely discharged as part of an interlocutory bombardment preceding the main battle'. Shanley J. stated that no party has a right to have interrogatories delivered and answered and all the cases to which he had been referred identified the delivery of interrogatories as an unusual step in an action commenced by plenary summons. Once a party satisfied the court that such delivery would serve a clear litigious purpose then the court should allow them unless to do so would work an injustice upon the party interrogated. Shanley J. adopted the criteria set out by Costello J. in *Mercantile Credit Co. of Ireland v. Heelan* [1994] 2 I.R. 105 and stated that he was satisfied that all the questions which he proposed to allow were ones which met the criteria laid down in that case. While he concluded that the fact that the case before him was one concerning the application of the Competition Act 1991 did not constitute a 'special exigency' warranting the delivery of interrogatories, he was satisfied that the answers to the questions which he proposed to allow to be delivered would undoubtedly save costs.

JUDICIARY

Numbers: High Court   The Courts Act 1997 provided for an increase in the maximum permissible number of ordinary judges of the High Court from 19 to 22 and that if a judge of the High Court is appointed Chair of the Law Reform Commission the number of ordinary judges of the High Court shall be not more than 23. The Act came into force on March 20, 1997, on its signature by the President. The Courts (No. 2) Act 1997, which came into effect on December 18, 1997, further increased the number of ordinary judges of the High Court to 24, with the consequential change that if a judge of the High Court is appointed Chair of the Law Reform Commission the number of ordinary judges of the High Court shall be not more than 25. The Explanatory Memorandum published with the legislation provided the helpful information that the estimated annual cost at 1997 levels of a High Court judge, including salary, pension and administrative assistance was £131,000.

Presidents of courts   The Courts (No. 2) Act 1997, which came into force on December 18, 1997, provided that appointments, from its coming into force, of Presidents of the courts, namely the Chief Justice, President of the High Court, President of the Circuit Court and President of the District Court, will be for a seven year non-renewable term. The Act also inserted a new section 9 into the Courts of Justice Act 1924 describing the new precedence between judges of the different courts, taking into account the new possibility of former Presidents of courts continuing as ordinary judges of their courts after their seven year term of office as President has expired. The Act gave effect to a recommendation of the Denham Working Group on the courts: see the 1996 Review, 481-2.

JURY DISTRICTS

Leitrim   The Jury Districts Order 1997 (S.I. No. 129 of 1997), made under section 5 of the Juries Act 1976, had the effect of making County Leitrim into a one jury district with effect from March 25, 1997.

PERSONAL INJURY ACTIONS: DISCLOSURE AND ADMISSION

The Rules of the Superior Courts (No. 7) 1997 (S.I. No. 348 of 1997), which provide for the disclosure and admission of reports in High Court personal injuries actions, deserve separate discussion from the other Rules of Court made in 1997 in view of their general importance. The 1997 Rules came into effect on September 1, 1997. For a comprehensive overview, see Robert Pierce's article, 'New Superior Courts Rules on Disclosure and Admission of Reports and Statements' (1997) 15 *ILT* 190 which we have followed closely in the discussion following.

1995 Act   The 1997 Rules were made under section 45 of the Courts and Courts Officers Act 1995 (1995 Review, 401) and inserted new rules in Order 39 of the Rules of the Superior Courts 1986, which deals with the procedure for giving evidence. In essence, the 1997 Rules require the parties to a High Court personal injuries action to disclose to each other any report or statement from any expert intended to be called to give evidence of medical or para-medical opinion in relation to an issue in the case or from any other expert of the evidence intended to be given by that expert in relation to an issue in the case. They also require disclosure of a written statement from the Department of Social Welfare showing all payments made to a plaintiff subsequent to an accident. Section 45 of the 1995 Act provides that the Rules made pursuant to it will reverse the effect of any rule of law against the admission of hearsay evidence and the privilege attached to documents prepared for the purpose of pending or contemplated civil proceedings.

Reports defined   As indicated, the new Order 39, rule 46 of the Rules of the Superior Courts 1986, inserted by the 1997 Rules, imposes on the plaintiff, defendant and other parties various duties to disclose reports and statements, within certain prescribed time limits. Order 39, rule 45 of the 1986 Rules, also inserted by the 1997 Rules, defines 'reports' thus:

'(e) 'reports' includes reports (including reports in the form of a letter), statements from accountants, actuaries, architects, dentists, doctors, engineers, occupational therapists, psychologists, psychiatrists, scientists or any other expert whatsoever intended to be called to give evidence in relation to an issue in an action and shall also include any maps, drawings, photographs, graphs, charts, calculations or other like matter referred to in any such report.

(f) The following shall also be deemed to be reports for the purposes of this rule:

(i) any copy report (including a copy report in the form of a letter), copy statement or copy letter however made, recorded or retained and originating from any such expert referred to above the original of which has been concealed, destroyed, lost, mislaid, or is not otherwise readily available; and

(ii) any report, or statement or note or letter made by any person who is not an expert but which reports, records, notes or con-

veys any relevant opinion from any expert intended to be called to give evidence in relation to an issue in an action.
(g) Any report, statement or letter from any private investigator shall not be deemed to be a report within the meaning of these rules.'

This definition emphasises the scope of the changes effected by the 1997 Rules to High Court personal injuries litigation.

Duties of plaintiff   The duties on the plaintiff under Order 39, rule 46(1) to (3) of the 1986 Rules, as inserted by the 1997 Rules, are as follows:

(1) to deliver to the defendant or his solicitor every report and statement mentioned in section 45(1)(a)(i) and (ii) of the 1995 Act (that is, medical, paramedical and other experts reports or statements) within three months of the service of notice of trial in respect of the action;
(2) to deliver to the defendant or his solicitor the information and statements referred to in section 45(1)(a)(iii), (iv) and (v) of the 1995 Act (that is, names and addresses of all witnesses intended to be called, a full statement of special damages with vouchers or statements of loss and a statement of social welfare payments or authority to obtain that information) within two months of the case being first listed for hearing; and
(3) to deliver to the defendant or his solicitor a copy of any report or statement within the meaning of section 45 or the name and address of any further witness obtained subsequent to the delivery of the documents mentioned under (1), above, within 28 days from the receipt thereof by the plaintiff of any such report or statement or details of the name and address of any such witness, as the case may be.

Duties of defendant   Similar duties are imposed on the defendant under Order 39, rule 46(4) to (6) of the 1986 Rules, as inserted by the 1997 Rules, from the date of receipt of the plaintiff's documents. These are as follows:

(1) when the documents referred to in section 45(1)(a)(i) and (ii) of the 1995 Act (that is, medical, paramedical and other experts reports or statements) are delivered by the plaintiff or his solicitor, the defendant must disclose to the plaintiff every like report or statement within three months;
(2) on the plaintiff delivering the information and statements referred to in section 45(1)(a)(iii), (iv) and (v) of the 1995 Act (that is, names and addresses of all witnesses intended to be called, statements of special damages and social welfare payments), the defendant has the duty of disclosing within two months from the date of service of those

documents the information required by section 45(1)(a)(iii) and (v) of the Act, that is, names and addresses of all witnesses intended to be called and social welfare payments, but not statements of special damages; and

(3) as with the plaintiff, the defendant must deliver to the plaintiff or his solicitor a copy of any report or statement within the meaning of section 45 or the name and address of any further witness obtained subsequent to the delivery of the documents mentioned under (1), above, within 28 days from the receipt thereof by the defendant of any such report or statement or details of the name and address of any such witness, as the case may be.

Service Order 39, rule 46(7) of the 1986 Rules, also inserted by the 1997 Rules, provides that service of any of the reports, statements or information can be effected by letter in writing.

Withdrawal Order 39, rule 46(8) of the 1986 Rules, also inserted by the 1997 Rules, provides that any party who has delivered any report, statement or details of a witness may withdraw such information by confirming by letter that he does not intend to call the author of such report or statement or such witness to give evidence in the action.

Notices to admit reports and statements Order 39, rule 47 of the 1986 Rules, also inserted by the 1997 Rules, provides that either party may serve a notice on the party to whom such reports or statements have been delivered requiring that party to admit in evidence any report or statement without requiring that the expert who has supplied such report or statement be called to give *viva voce* evidence of such at the trial of the action. If the notice party does not agree in writing to admit the statement or report in evidence within 28 days of service the request will be deemed to have been refused. The Rules also provide for a consent to admit, in a form contained in the Schedule to the 1997 Rules.

Failure to comply and orders for costs against solicitors Order 39, rule 48 of the 1986 Rules, also inserted by the 1997 Rules, provides that a party may bring a motion for directions when that party alleges that another party to the action has failed to comply with the requirements concerning disclosure and/or admission. It also provides that if the court is satisfied that the solicitor for any party concerned has acted unreasonably or has unduly delayed in failing to comply with a requirement under section 45 of the 1995 Act or in failing to comply with any request contained in a notice served under the 1997 Rules or who has otherwise been in default without reasonable excuse therefor, 'the Court may order that such solicitor personally bear any of the costs incurred as a result of such failure, delay or default as have or may be awarded to any such party.' This exceptional provision providing that the solicitor rather than the client must bear the relevant costs, is a significant change in the practice and procedure applicable in High Court personal injury actions.

In addition, Order 39, rule 49 of the 1986 Rules, also inserted by the 1997 Rules, provides that if at any stage of the hearing of an action it appears to the court that there has been non-compliance with any of the provisions in the 1997 Rules, the court may make such order as it deems fit, including an order prohibiting the adducing of evidence in relation to which such non compliance relates.

Objections Order 39, rule 50 of the 1986 Rules, also inserted by the 1997 Rules, provides that in any case in which objection is taken by a party to the admission in evidence of any report or statement or to which section 45 of the 1995 Act applies and such objection is based on the ground that such document contains hearsay evidence, the parties may by agreement exclude such part of the document to which the objection is taken. In default of such agreement the party objecting to the admission of such evidence may apply to the court either prior to or at the trial of the action by motion on notice seeking an order that the portion of the report or statement to which the objection relates be excluded from being admitted in evidence under the Rules or for an order that such matter to which objection is taken be proved by admissible evidence in the ordinary way at the trial of the action.

Exceptions Order 39, rule 52 of the 1986 Rules, also inserted by the 1997 Rules, now provides that in any case application may be made to the court *ex parte* by any party for an order that in the interest of justice the provisions of Order 39. rule 46, that is, the rule requiring disclosure of reports and statements, shall not apply in relation to a particular report or statement or portion thereof. In dealing with that application the court may make such order as to it seems just and may adjourn such application in order that notice of the application in a form and manner to be determined by the court be given to the party who will be effected by the order that is proposed and may make such further order in relation to costs as appear just.

1997 Rules not retrospective The question arose as to whether the 1997 Rules applied retrospectively to actions in being at the time they came into operation on September 1, 1997. Costello P. had issued a Practice Direction on September 15, 1997 indicating that the obligation on the plaintiff in the new Order 39, rule 46(1) did not apply to pending actions in which notice of trial was served prior to June 1, 1997 and that the obligation under Order 39, rule 46(2) did not apply to actions which were first listed for hearing prior to July 1, 1997. In respect of actions in which notice of trial had been served after June 1, 1997, the Practice Direction had provided that delivery of the statements or reports could be effected without the need to apply to court to extend the time for so doing. This limited element of retrospection was not regarded as administratively workable and some concerns were expressed that the retrospection might not be compatible with the right of access to the courts under Article 40.3 of the Constitution. Whatever the merits of such arguments, they were in effect accepted by the Superior Courts Rules Committee and the Department of Justice. The Rules of the Superior Courts (No. 8) (Disclosure and Admission of Reports and Statements) (Amendment) 1997 (S.I. No. 471 of 1997) amended the Order 39, rule 53 inserted by the No. 7 Rules to provide that the rules relating to disclosure or reports and statements only apply to proceedings initiated and reports coming into existence after September 1, 1997. As a result, therefore, the 1997 Rules apply prospectively only.

Rules for Circuit Court   It is envisaged that comparable Rules for the Circuit Court will emerge in the near future, and we will discuss any such Rules in a future Review.

PRECEDENT

Supreme Court   In *Society for the Protection of Unborn Children (Irl) Ltd v. Grogan and Ors. (No. 3)*, Supreme Court, March 6, 1997, the Court considered to what extent it was prepared to overrule one of its previous decisions: see the Constitutional Law chapter, 178, above.

RES JUDICATA

General   The general caselaw on *res judicata* is discussed in the Evidence chapter, 438–45, above.

Jurisdiction to stay   In *McCauley v. McDermot* [1997] 2 I.L.R.M. 486 (SC), the Supreme Court applied the principles in *Reamsbottam v. Rafferty* [1991] 1 I.R. 53 (1990 Review, 449) and *Lawless v. Bus Éireann* [1994] 1 I.R. 474 in holding that the defendant was precluded from litigating issues in third party proceedings arising from a road traffic accident. The Court concluded that the proceedings would seek to relitigate an issue which had been conclusively and finally determined against him in Circuit Court proceedings arising out of the same incident and that this was the very mischief which the doctrine of issue estoppel had been intended to prevent. The Court also held that the inherent jurisdiction of the courts to stay proceedings which were an abuse of the process of the court, while only exercised with great caution, could be invoked in a case such as the present where there was a difficulty in treating the matter as *res judicata*. See further the Evidence chapter, 438–40, above.

RULES OF COURT

Circuit Court: adoptive leave   The Circuit Court Rules (No. 2) 1997 (Adoptive Leave Act 1995) (S.I. No. 118 of 1997) inserted Order 63B into the Rules of the Circuit Court 1950 to provide for the enforcement of decisions of a rights commissioner or the Employment Appeals Tribunal made under section 39 of the Adoptive Leave Act. They came into effect on March 24, 1997.

Circuit Court: civil bills   The Circuit Court Rules (No. 3) 1997 (S.I. No. 500 of 1997) inserted a new Order 10 into the Rules of the Circuit Court 1950 to provide for a new form of issuing and service of civil bills. They came into effect on December 22, 1997.

Circuit Court: Family   The Circuit Court Rules (No. 1) 1997 (S.I. No. 84 of 1997) inserted a new Order 78 into the Rules of the Circuit Court 1950 to specify the procedures and forms to be used in applications under the Judicial Separation and Family Law Reform Act 1989, the Family Law Act 1995 and, in particular, the Family Law (Divorce) Act 1996, with effect from February 27, 1997. We noted in the 1996 Review, 357, that the High Court had held that the divorce jurisdiction of the High Court could be exercised prior to the coming into force of Rules of Court: see *R.C. v. C.C.* [1997] 1 I.L.R.M. 401, discussed further in the Family Law chapter, 450, above.

District Court Rules: Consolidated and Revised   The District Court Rules 1997 (S.I. No. 93 of 1997) consolidated, with revisions, the District Court Rules 1948, as amended, which have been revoked by the 1997 Rules. It is not possible to describe in the present context all the amendments effected by the 1997 Rules, save to note one or two of the more significant. On the civil side, the Civil Process has been replaced by the Civil Summons and the 1997 Rules provide for the first time that a formal defence to a claim may be entered. While the 1948 Rules did not make provision for a defence to a civil process, the practice had grown up in recent years that in many instances the defendant would send to the plaintiff a formal letter, amounting in effect to a defence. The 1997 Rules have formally recognised this practice. On the criminal side, by contrast, provision is not made for the defence to seek a statement from the prosecution of the material it seeks to rely on, in accordance with the guidelines developed in the wake of the decision of Barr J. in *Cowzer v. Kirby*, High Court, February 11, 1991 (1991 Review, 145–6) and subsequent leading decision of the Supreme Court in *Director of Public Prosecutions v. Doyle* [1994] 1 I.L.R.M. 529 (SC) (1994 Review, 210–11). The 1997 Rules came into effect on May 1, 1997. We should also welcome the initiative of the Government Publications Office in publishing the 1997 Rules in convenient loose-leaf form, with a view to the easy incorporation of future amendments.

Rule-making authority In *Kerry County Council v. McCarthy* [1997] 2 I.L.R.M. 481 (SC), the Supreme Court held that it was within the remit of the District Court Rules Committee, acting under section 91 of the Courts of Justice Act 1924, to provide that a District Court clerk should be empowered to issue a summons in a civil case, in this instance an action for possession by the Council under section 62 of the Housing Act 1966. The Court emphasised that the proceedings in the instant case were of a civil, not a criminal, nature.

Superior Courts: disclosure and admission The Rules of the Superior Courts (No. 7) 1997 (S.I. No. 348 of 1997) and the Rules of the Superior Courts (No. 8) 1997 (S.I. No. 471 of 1997), which provide for the disclosure and admission of reports in personal injuries actions, are considered separately above, 593–8.

Superior courts: family The Rules of the Superior Courts (No. 3) 1997 (S.I. No. 343 of 1997) insert a revised Order 70A into the Rules of the Superior Courts 1986 and make provision for family law proceedings, including provision for divorce under the Family Law (Divorce) Act 1996. They came into force on September 1, 1997. We noted in the 1996 Review, 352, 357, that the High Court had held that the divorce jurisdiction of the High Court could be exercised prior to the coming into force of Rules of Court: see *R.C. v. C.C.* [1997] 1 I.L.R.M. 401, discussed further in the Family Law chapter, 450, above.

Superior Courts: minors The Rules of the Superior Courts (No. 1) 1997 (S.I. No. 52 of 1997) amended Order 22 of the Rules of the Superior Courts 1986 to provide for applications to approve awards proposed to be made to minors by compensation tribunals, in particular the Hepatitis C Compensation Tribunal (see the Health Services chapter, 478, above). The Rules came into effect on February 11, 1997.

Superior courts: payment out The Rules of the Superior Courts (No. 4) 1997 (S.I. No. 344 of 1997) amended Order 77, rule 21 of the Rules of the Superior Courts 1986 to facilitate the payment out of funds lodged in Court where there is consent or a lodgement has been accepted. They came into force on September 1, 1997.

Superior courts: recognition of qualifications   The Rules of the Superior Courts (No. 5) 1997 (S.I. No. 345 of 1997) amended Order 113A of the Rules of the Superior Courts 1986 providing for appeals to the Court pursuant to the European Communities (General System for the Recognition of Higher Education Diplomas) Regulations 1991 (1991 Review, 187) and the European Communities (Second General System for the Recognition of Professional Education and Training) Regulations 1996 (1996 Review, 284). They came into force on September 1, 1997.

Superior courts: subpoenas   The Rules of the Superior Courts (No. 2) 1997 (S.I. No. 166 of 1997) amended Order 39, rule 30 of the Rules of the Superior Courts 1986 so that a Court Order need not be obtained in order to issue certain subpoenas in High Court personal injuries actions. They came into force on April 28, 1997.

Superior courts: transfer of prisoners   The Rules of the Superior Courts (No. 6) 1997 (S.I. No. 347 of 1997) inserted a new Order 128 into the Rules of the Superior Courts 1986 to provide for applications under the Transfer of Sentenced Persons Act 1995 (1995 Review, 418). hey came into effect on September 1, 1997.

SERVICE OF PROCEEDINGS

Residence in jurisdiction   In *Uwaydah v. Nolan*, High Court, February 21, 1997, Barron J. (sitting as a judge of the High Court) deemed good service of proceedings under Order 9, rule 15 of the Rules of the Superior Courts 1986 in the following circumstances. The plaintiff had instructed a private investigator to serve proceedings on the defendant. The private investigator duly rang the telephone number listed for the address as set out on the summons. The person who answered said that the defendant was not there at that time and was not sure if he would be back. The investigator travelled down to the residence in question and spoke to the same person over the intercom. On this occasion he was told that the defendant was not there and that the person did not when he would be home. The following day the investigator called to the house again. Eventually a woman drove up who said that she was the defendant's wife and stated that she thought the defendant was in Germany. The summons was served on her. Although there was some dispute about these events, Barron J. held that there was *prima facie* evidence of the defendant's presence within the jurisdiction on the dates in question since neither the defendant or his wife had made any specific denial as to the defendant's presence on those dates and there had been no suggestion by the defendant's wife that he had gone to Germany as she had stated.

Barron J. accepted that service within the jurisdiction could not in general be effected when the defendant sought to be served was not within the jurisdiction. He adverted to the decision of the High Court of Australia in *Laurie v. Carroll*, 98 C.L.R. 310 which had established that an exception to this could arise when the defendant had left the jurisdiction to avoid service. However, on the facts as found above, it was not necessary to determine whether this principle applied in this jurisdiction, though Barron J's general approach would appear to indicate that he was amenable to its application. He held that once there was *prima facie* evidence of the defendant's presence in the jurisdiction, the onus to disprove this passed to him and this onus had not been discharged.

THIRD PARTY PROCEDURE

Section 27(1)(b) of the Civil Liability Act 1961 provides that any party who wishes to make a claim for contribution under the Act shall, if the person from whom he wishes to claim contribution is not already a party to the action, serve a third party notice 'as soon as is reasonably possible'. The meaning of this phrase was considered in two decisions in 1997. In *McElwaine v. Hughes*, High Court, April 30, 1997 the plaintiff's claim was for damages arising out of the consumption of shellfish at the defendant's hotel premises. The proceedings were commenced by plenary summons issued on April 16, 1993 but it was not until the replies to notices for particulars were furnished on April 5, 1994 that confirmation was received by the defendant that the plaintiff was relying on the oysters as the cause of his injuries. The defendant's solicitor was advised by counsel to seek the opinion of a microbiologist which was not received until January 18, 1995 and notices of motion for liberty to serve third party notices were issued on February 21, 1995 and the orders made on May 8 of that year. Applications were then brought to have the notices set aside on the grounds that they had not been served as soon as was reasonably possible within the meaning of section 27(1)(b) of the Civil Liability Act 1961.

Barron J. referred to the *dicta* of O'Keeffe J. in *Gilmore v. Windle* [1967] I.R. 323 to the effect that section 27 was clearly intended to ensure that as far as possible all questions relating to the liability of concurrent wrongdoers should be tried in a single proceeding. He stated that setting aside a third party notice would have two serious consequences: that the defendant would be at risk of circumstances arising which would justify the Court in refusing him relief in fresh proceedings and that the overall policy of the Act to have all claims heard together in one proceeding would be defeated. He therefore stated that while a court should not construe 'as soon as is reasonably possible' too liberally, it should not at the same time be too astute to set aside a third party notice on such grounds. Barron J. stated that although the words clearly denote that there should be as little delay as possible, nevertheless the use of the word 'reasonable' indicates that circumstances may exist which would justify some delay in the bringing of proceedings. He also stated that since the obligation is on the defendant to serve the notice within a reasonable time it seemed to him that the onus of showing that the delay was not unreasonable lay on the defendant. Barron J. concluded that in his opinion the defendant was entitled to decide whether the proceedings should be defended and if so on what basis and whether to institute third party proceedings. Such time should be allowed as was reasonably necessary to reach such decisions and to obtain any evidence that might be required on which to base them. In the circumstances Barron J. concluded that the third party proceedings had been brought as soon as reasonably possible.

In the second case on this area, *S.F.L. Engineering Ltd v. Smyth Cladding Systems Ltd*, High Court, May 9, 1997 Kelly J. stated that it seemed to follow from the interpretation given by Finlay C.J. in *Kelly v. St Laurence's Hospital* [1990] 2 I.R. 31; [1989] I.L.R.M. 877 (1989 Review, 354–5) that in considering applications of this nature, the court is not concerned with any question of prejudice arising as a result of the delay in applying for liberty to join the third party but is rather concerned with whether the application has been made as soon as is reasonably possible.

The third and fourth named third parties applied to have the third party notices served on them set aside. The action was commenced by plenary summons on February 19, 1994. It was alleged by the defendant that the general manager of the third named third party had given an assurance that it would stand behind the defendant although he would not commit his company to providing a written indemnity, and letters from the companies in March and April 1994 suggested otherwise. In November 1995 solicitors for the defendant wrote to the companies calling on them to admit liability and to undertake to indemnify the defendant and they refused. A notice of motion was issued dated February 8, 1996 and the orders were made on March 4, 1996 joining the third parties. Kelly J. concluded that the solicitors for the companies had made it plain by the end of April 1994 that they would not provide indemnity and he did not accept the explanation of continued reliance on the oral assurance. In these circumstances he held that the notices had not been served as soon as reasonably possible and should be set aside.

On this area, see also the 1991 Review, 352–4, and the 1996 Review, 495–6.

Prisons

INTERNATIONAL TRANSFER

Delay In *Duffin v. Minister for Justice*, High Court, February 28, 1997, Carney J. held that there had been no unconscionable delay in dealing with an application for a transfer pursuant to the Transfer of Sentenced Persons Act 1995 (1995 Review, 418, and below). In November 1995, the applicant, who was serving a sentence of imprisonment in this State, applied to the Minister for a transfer to a prison in Northern Ireland pursuant to the 1995 Act, which came into force on November 1, 1995. The Minister had received another 28 applications in or around the same time. In June 1996, the Minister forwarded the application to the Northern Ireland Office and also requested that the NIO reply to certain issues raised by the Minister; no reply had been received from the NIO by October 1996. In October 1996, the applicant obtained leave to apply for an order of *mandamus* on the grounds that the delay in processing his application was unconscionable.

Carney J. held that, taking into account the complexity of the new legislation, the number of applications and the extensive enquiries involved, the delay in processing the applicant's application between November 1995 and June 1996 had not been unconscionable. As to the delay after June 1996, he noted that the processing of the application had been delayed because the information sought by the Minister had not been furnished by the NIO. Carney J. held that it was not appropriate for the Court to enquire into or comment on the processing of the application in Northern Ireland.

Maximum sentence in transferring State The Transfer of Sentenced Persons (Amendment) Act 1997 amended section 7 of the Transfer of Sentenced Persons Act 1995 (1995 Review, 418) in order to facilitate the transfer into the State of persons who have been sentenced to periods of imprisonment greater than the maximum penalties permissible in this jurisdiction. The 1995 Act had implemented the 1983 Council of Europe Convention on the Transfer of Sentenced Persons. Section 7 of the 1995 Act provides for the issue of a warrant by a Court in this State authorising the continued enforcement by the State of the sentence imposed by the sentencing State. In accordance with Article 10 of the 1983 Convention, section 7 of the 1995 Act empowers a court to adapt the sentence to a sentence prescribed by the law of the State for an offence similar to the offence for which the sentence was imposed where the sentence concerned is in its legal nature or duration incompatible with the law of the State. The changes effected to section 7 of the 1995 Act by the 1997 Act empowers a court to adapt a sentence that is incompatible by its duration with the law of the State only where an application in this regard is made by the Minister for Justice, Equality and Law Reform. It was explained during the passage of the Act that this would facilitate the negotiation of transfers with States which insist that there can be no question of the sentence imposed in the sentencing State being reduced, while at the same time allowing a mechanism for the adaptation of the duration of sentences where the States in question have no objection to this procedure. The Act came into effect on December 17, 1997 on its signature by the President.

RULES OF PRISON AND PLACES OF DETENTION

Privilege restrictions The Detention of Offenders (Restrictions on Privileges) Regulations 1997 (S.I. No. 116 of 1997), made under section 3 of the Prisons Act 1970, amend certain restrictions on privileges for prisoners being detained in a prison or other place of detention. The amendments concern restrictions on visits, communications and any other privileges. The 1997 Regulations amended, *inter alia*, the Detention of Offenders (Unit A Castlerea) Regulations 1996 (1996 Review, 500) and the Detention of Offenders (The Curragh) Regulations 1996 (1996 Review, 500). The 1997 Regulations came into effect on March 12, 1997.

Rule-making authority Section 19 of the Criminal Justice (Miscellaneous Provisions) Act 1997 (discussed generally in the Criminal Law chapter, 314, above) introduced a new power of the Minister for Justice to make Regulations for the regulation and good government of prisons. The rule-making power includes provisions concerning: (a) the duties and conduct of the governor and officers of the prison, (b) the classification of persons detained, (c) the treatment of persons detained, including diet, clothing, maintenance, employment, instruction, discipline and correction, (d) the provision of services, including educational facilities and medical services, (e) the imposition of penalties, (f) remission for good conduct and (g) the taking of fingerprints and palmprints. Section 19 also amended section 3 of the Prisons (Visiting Committees) Act 1925 to provide that an appeal will lie to a visiting committees from a punishment inflicted by a governor pursuant to rules made under the 1997 Act. It also continues in force current rules, including the Rules for the Government of Prisons 1947. Section 19 repealed the previous statutory basis for rule-making, namely section 12 of the General Prisons (Ireland) Act 1877, section 8 of the Penal Servitude (Ireland) Act 1891 and section 1 of the Prisons (Ireland) Act 1907. The enactment of section 19 of the 1997 Act paves the way for the making of modern rules of prison to take account of the State's international obligations in this area, in particular compliance with the Council of Europe's minimum standards on prison conditions.

SENTENCE REMISSION

Delegation of power by Order   Section 17 of the Criminal Justice (Miscellaneous Provisions) Act 1997 (discussed generally in the Criminal Law chapter, 314, above) amended section 23 of the Criminal Justice Act 1951 to provide that the Government may, by Order, delegate to the Minister for Justice the power of remission of punishment. While such power has been delegated to the Minister, the 1951 Act had not specified by what instrument the power was to be delegated.

Suspended sentence and remission   The decision of the Supreme Court in *O'Brien v. Governor of Limerick Prison* [1997] 2 I.L.R.M. 349 (HC) is discussed in the Criminal Law chapter, 333, above.

TRANSFER FROM ST PATRICK'S INSTITUTION TO PRISON

The Prisons Act 1970 (Section 7) Order 1997 (S.I. No. 257 of 1997) continued section 7 of the Prisons Act 1970 in operation for a further two years from June 28, 1997. On the effect of section 7 of the 1970 Act, see the 1995 Review, 418.

Restitution

Eoin O'Dell, Trinity College, Dublin

The unification of the formerly dispersed elements of the law of restitution under the guidance of the principle against unjust enrichment has many advantages. It means, for example, that the similarities between otherwise disparate matters can be perceived, and anomalies between them can be addressed: it allows like cases to be treated alike, and therefore allows arguments by analogy from one issue to a related other. Conversely, if the restitutionary essence of a doctrine is recognised, an attempt to deploy such a doctrine beyond the confines of the law of restitution immediately and obviously fails. Thus, it is obvious that a cause of action in restitution does not generate a cause of action outside the law of restitution; and a defence to an action in restitution is not a defence to a claim in another area of the law. Such matters ought to be so obvious that they went without saying, but they need saying because such obvious matters eluded the Supreme Court not once but twice this year; once in relation to the cause of action in mistake (in *Duff v. Minister for Agriculture (No.2)* [1997] 2 I.R. 22), and once in relation to the defence of change of position (in *McDonnell v. Ireland,* Supreme Court, July 23, 1997. Each is discussed below. Most of the other cases are interesting more for the issues which they implicate rather than for any resolution of such issues which they offer; but the possible contours of such resolution are sketched below.

The key phrases "restitution" and "unjust enrichment" should be used with precision. For example, Birks and Swadling insisted upon "careful use of the word 'restitution'. Unnecessary difficulty is caused if 'restitution' is allowed to overlap with 'compensation'.... It is convenient, indeed essential for clear thinking, that a terminological line be drawn between compensation for losses and restitution of gains. To use 'restitution' for 'compensation' is to court confusion, and confusion is no court's friend." (Birks and Swadling [1997] All E.R. 385 at 385 (discussing at pp.385 to 387 *Swindle v. Harrison* [1997] 4 All E.R. 705 (CA))). Similarly, it is essential to make a plea for the more careful use of the phrase "unjust enrichment". It is not a synonym for "undeserved windfall", it is not a broad conception of palm tree justice, nor is it a vehicle for individual judicial discretion. It is a precise and technical term of art which represents a conclusion that a defendant received a quantifiable benefit (an enrichment) which for a specific reason (an "unjust" factor, such as the plaintiff's mistake, or the defendant's free acceptance) ought to be returned to the plaintiff. Hence, to use "unjust enrichment" to mean something like "undeserved windfall" is also to court confusion, "and confusion is no court's friend". There are examples of sensitive discussions of non-technical uses of these words, (*e.g.* Friedmann "Valid, Voidable, Qualified and Non-existing Obligations" in A Burrows (ed.) *Essays on the Law of Restitution* (Oxford, 1991) 247 at 251 discussing non-technical usages of the phrase "unjust enrichment"). Nevertheless, problems arise when such phrases are used in a loose and non-technical way in a context which demands precision and accurate usage. It may be that the decision of McCracken J. in *Burke v. The Revenue Commissioners*, High Court, February 4, 1997 represents such a non-technical usage in a context which required accuracy. Here, the applicant had sought to challenge the Revenue's assessment that more VAT was payable by him. He failed before McCracken J., who remarked that if he "were to grant the applicant relief . . . there would appear to be a considerable element of unjust enrichment in favour of the applicant". Clearly, the applicant would have received an undeserved windfall. But, in the absence of any analysis of whether there were on the facts an unjust factor and a consequential enrichment, it cannot properly be said that the applicant had received an unjust enrichment. Such non-technical usages of the term are therefore better avoided.

In the case concerning *The Bricklayers' Hall*, Keane J. in the Supreme Court predicated the obligation to make restitution upon four "essential preconditions": whether there was (i) an enrichment to the defendant (ii) at the expense of the plaintiff, (iii) in circumstances in which the law will require restitution (*i.e.* the 'unjust' phase of the enquiry), (iv) where there is no reason why restitution will be withheld. (*Dublin Corporation v. Building and Allied Trade Union* [1996] 2 I.R. 468 at 483; [1996] 2 I.L.R.M. 547, 558). Since they are all described as essential, all four enquiries will have to be answered in the plaintiff's favour before an order for restitution can be made. Consequently, the light sketch of the law of Restitution in last year's Review was organised around these four enquiries, as is the analysis below of this year's crop of cases.

ENRICHMENT

Keane J. observed in the *Bricklayers' Hall* case that there is seldom any problem in ascertaining whether a defendant has received an enrichment ([1996] 2 I.R. 468, 483; [1996] 2 I.L.R.M. 547 at 558). This is most clear where the defendant has been enriched by the receipt of money: it "has the peculiar character of a universal medium of exchange. By its receipt, the recipient is inevitably benefited." (*BP v. Hunt* [1979] W.L.R. 783 at 799 *per* Goff J.). Problems might arise where the plaintiff has conferred not money but a service. Nevertheless, where the service has enriched the defendant as a matter of fact, it is as much an enrichment as the receipt of money. This has often been judicially recognised. In *Delgman v. Guaranty Trust Co of Canada and Constantineau* [1953] 3 D.L.R. 785, the nephew of the deceased had lived with her whilst at college, and claimed that she promised that if he helped out at home, she would leave him some property. He helped out for six months, then left and never returned. The nephew sued the deceased's estate, alleging that he had a contract with her to that effect; the Supreme Court of Canada held that in the absence of a note or memorandum in writing, or sufficient part performance, any such contract was unenforceable. Nevertheless, the Court held that an action in restitution for the value of services rendered to the deceased was open to the nephew, and the Statute of Frauds

> in such a case does not touch the principle of restitution against what would otherwise be an unjust enrichment of the defendant at the expense of the plaintiff. This is exemplified in the simple case of part or full payment in money as the price under an oral contract; it would be inequitable to allow the promise to keep both the land and the money and the other party to the bargain is entitled to recover what he has paid. *Similarly is it in the case of services given.* (*Delgman v. Guaranty Trust Co of Canada and Constantineau* [1953] 3 D.L.R 785 at 788 *per* Rand J., Rinfert C.J.C. and Taschereau J. concurring, emphasis added.)

The deceased was enriched as much by the nephew's services as she would have been had she received money; and in each case comes under a similar duty to make restitution.

An excellent Irish example of such an equation between money and services is provided by *Premier Dairies v. Jameson,* High Court, March 1, 1983, McWilliam J. In November 1980, the parties conducted negotiations to execute a written agreement under which the plaintiff would give the defendant (who was already an independent milkman) a further milk round, in return for £ 2,000 from the plaintiff and an undertaking from the defendant that he would take all of his supplies of milk from them. The plaintiff introduced the defendant to customers taking a total of 20 crates of milk a day on the round, and supplied the milk to the defendant on credit; but after 10 days, the defendant discontinued the arrangement in favour of a different supplier. McWilliam J. held that the parties had not concluded a contract, but that "the acceptance by the defendant of the additional customers and the renewal of supplies to him could only be attributed to an expectation of the completion of the proposed agreement and I was of opinion that this created a liability on the part of the defendant to restore the parties to their previous positions to the best of his ability" (at pp.7-8) that is, to make restitution. He went on to observe that

> [d]uring the course of the arguments I asked counsel of the defendant if

the plaintiff would have been entitled to a return of the sum of £ 2,000 if it had been paid before the proposed contract was abandoned and he agreed that it would. Although the expression was not used by either of us, I assume that he meant that the money would be recoverable as money which had been paid for a consideration which had failed. I find it difficult to see any difference in principle between such a situation and the situation which actually arose, that is, that *benefits* were given to the defendant at a cost to the plaintiff, . . . (at pp.10-11 of the transcript, emphasis added).

The defendant was enriched as much by the benefits provided by the plaintiff as he would have been had the plaintiff provided the £2,000; and in each case comes under a similar duty to make restitution.

A *dictum* of Murphy J. in *McCarron v. McCarron,* Supreme Court, February 13, 1997, might come to be seen in a similar light. Here, the Supreme Court enforced an agreement that the deceased would leave his farm to the plaintiff as remuneration for his work on the it, but Murphy J. (Hamilton C.J., Keane J. concurring) nevertheless went on briefly to refer to the availability of further remedies had the agreement been unenforceable. For example, he could see no reason in principle why the doctrine of proprietary estoppel

should be confined to the expenditure of money or the erection of premises on the land of another. In a suitable case it may well be argued that a plaintiff suffers as severe a loss or detriment by providing his own labours or services in relation to the lands of another and accordingly should equally qualify for recognition in equity.

Here, Murphy J. is equating the receipt of the benefit of the plaintiff's labours or services with the receipt of money or property. It might be taken as a general indication of the equation of value between services and money. But it might also be more than that: the proprietary estoppel in *McCarron* (and in the earlier and similar *Smyth v. Halpin* [1997] 2 I.L.R.M. 38 (HC, Geoghegan J.)) might be seen as raised to prevent unjust enrichment. In both of those cases, as in *Delgman* (above), the estate had the benefit of the plaintiff's work, and the remedy is concerned to make restitution to the plaintiff for the value of the work done. Thus, even if the prevention of unjust enrichment cannot provide a complete explanation for the doctrine of proprietary estoppel, it certainly provides an explanation of many of the cases within it (see *e.g.* Treitel *The Law of Contract* (9th ed., Stevens/ Sweet & Maxwell, London, 1995) p.126) and, it is submitted, explains the proprietary estoppel contemplated in *McCarron* and established in *Smyth*. If so, then Murphy J's *dictum* is another example of the judicial acceptance of the enriching quality of services.

AT THE PLAINTIFF'S EXPENSE

In the 1996 Review, 504–505, the requirement that the defendant have derived his enrichment at the expense of the plaintiff was described as the equivalent of a causation requirement, linking in any given case this particular defendant with this particular plaintiff. Where that enrichment is demonstrated by a benefit which passed directly from the plaintiff to the defendant, it can be said that the defendant's enrichment was by subtraction from the plaintiff. Similarly, where that enrichment is demonstrated by a benefit intended by a third party to reach the plaintiff, but which instead reached the defendant, it can be said that the defendant's enrichment by interception was not so much by direct subtraction from the plaintiff as by interceptive subtraction. This notion of interceptive subtraction seems to be embodied as a matter of Irish law in the decisions of Costello J. in *HKN Invest OY v. Incotrade PVT Ltd* [1993] 3 I.R. 152, 162 and of Carroll J. in *Shanahan v. Redmond* (High Court, June 21, 1994).

An early example is provided by *McMechan v. Warburton* [1896] 1 I.R. 435 at 441. Mrs Warburton intended to settle her property by voluntary deed; certain shares were to have been settled upon trust for Mr McMechan, but the solicitor in error omitted this from the deed. Upon her death, the plaintiff sought the shares from the recipient. Chatterton V.C. had "no doubt that she intended to declare such a trust as to them; that she never changed her intention that they should be effectually subjected to the trusts of the deed; and that she always to her death believed that this had been done" ([1896] 1 I.R. 435 at 439). He held that though a court would not rectify a voluntary deed against a donor, it could of course have ordered rectification at the suit of the donor, and upon her death could do so in favour of the donor's intention which had not been carried out due to mistake. The Court of Appeal simply affirmed the decision of the Vice-Chancellor ([1896] 1 I.R. 435 at 441). Here, the defendant recipient was enriched at the expense of the plaintiff intended beneficiary, and the defendant's enrichment at the plaintiff's expense demonstrates the concept of interceptive subtraction. A more recent example is provided by the decision of Lynch J. in *In re PMPA Insurance Co Ltd* [1986] I.L.R.M. 524. The Company and the Society were members of the same group of companies. They shared the same bank. The bank, having received cheques, standing orders, bank giros and so forth, validly filled in with respect to the Company, nonetheless paid them to the Society. The bank had therefore misdirected to the defendant Society money intended for the plaintiff Company. Lynch J. held that the Company could recover from the Society: "It was never intended by the owner or payer of these moneys that they should be paid to the Society. . . . The bank made these errors and put the moneys into the name of the Society instead of the Company. In these circumstances, it seems to me that there is no sense in which such moneys could be regarded as assets of the

Society." Hence the Society was enriched at the expense of the Company, and the defendant's enrichment at the plaintiff's expense demonstrates the concept of interceptive subtraction.

This concept of interceptive subtraction explains the result in one aspect of *Behan v. Bank of Ireland,* High Court, August 15, 1997, Morris J. The plaintiff had made various claims against the bank, and was for the most part unsuccessful in his contract and tort claims. Credits supplied by the Minister for Agriculture to the bank to give interest relief to the plaintiff were applied by the bank to reduce another liability which it claimed the plaintiff owed it. However, that liability had been settled by an agreement by the bank to accept a reduced amount; Morris J. held that having made that agreement, "the bank were not entitled to apply these monies in the manner in which they did". Hence, the bank had simply misapplied to itself money intended for the plaintiff, and the plaintiff was "entitled to receive these amounts as money had and received to his use". To explain the plaintiff's success in the action for money had an received requires that the terms of the principle against unjust enrichment be fulfilled. As to whether it can be said that the bank's enrichment was at the expense of the plaintiff, since it can be said that had all gone as it ought to have, the credits in question "would certainly have arrived in the plaintiff if had not been intercepted by the defendant *en route* from the third party, it is true to say that the plaintiff has lost by the defendant's gain" (Birks, 133-134), and the concept of interceptive subtraction explains the defendant bank's enrichment at the plaintiff's expense.

As a result of cases like *McMechan, PMPA Insurance, HKN, Shanahan,* and now *Behan,* the concept of interceptive subtraction seems securely supported by authority as a matter of Irish law. Nevertheless, it has been argued that it is suspect in principle. For example, Smith's ". . . Critique of Birks' Theory of Interceptive Subtraction" (1991) 11 *OJLS* 481 argues that it is difficult in fact to be sure that the enrichment would certainly have reached the plaintiff (pp.486-487); and that in such three party configurations, where the defendant receives from the third party, in most such cases the third party is the proper plaintiff (the recipient "has been enriched at the expense of the donor, not of the intended beneficiary" (p. 517)). On this view, many of the key cases are wrongly decided, unless they can be reanalysed and "explained as simple direct subtractions" (p. 493). For example, in cases where a debtor pays a third party instead of his creditor plaintiff, where Birks (pp. 132, 142-143) perceives an interceptive subtraction and a claim against the third party by the plaintiff, Smith argues that the third party is enriched at the expense of the plaintiff only where the payment discharged the debt, in which case the plaintiff may sue the third party. But if the payment did not discharge the debt, it is the debtor who paid at whose expense the third party is enriched.

Furthermore, Burrows argues that "subject to wide-ranging exceptions, the plaintiff is not entitled to the restitution of benefits conferred by a third party rather than by himself" (p.46). This he describes as a general privity restriction. As with Smith, Burrows regards enrichments received by the defendant from the third party as enrichments at the expense of the third party rather than of the intended recipient plaintiff. Nevertheless, Burrows does accept that the arguments from practicality and principle "are finely balanced" so that "there is no overwhelming case against privity" and "one can readily understand the courts' preference for developing exceptions rather than departing from the general restriction" (p.48). Hence, he accepts that there are several important exceptions to what he regards as the general privity restriction.

First, if the plaintiff actually owns the property received by the defendant from the third party, then the defendant's enrichment is at the plaintiff's expense. Second, if the third party is the agent of the plaintiff in conferring the benefit upon the defendant, then clearly the defendant's enrichment is at the expense of the plaintiff as the third party agent's principal. *Behan* might be forced to fit this pattern, by arguing that the department was the agent of the plaintiff in paying to the bank. But this would probably be to force the facts of these cases too much.

The case of the payment by third party to the defendant as the plaintiff's agent is different: as Smith points out (in the context of breaches of fiduciary duty (1991) 11 *OJLS* 481, 514-516) the failure of the agent to account to his principal would render the agent unjustly enriched at the expense of the plaintiff, but this would be an example of unjust enrichment by wrongdoing, rather than of unjust enrichment by subtraction (for which, since it is an alternative to unjust enrichment by subtraction, no such subtraction need be shown (Smith, p.482); and this exclusion of the general notion of subtraction necessarily requires the exclusion of its subset, interceptive subtraction). *HKN* might be forced to fit this pattern: the promoter of a company received in advance commissions for services which the company was to render, but retained the advances, and was held liable to the company for them. Clearly he received as agent for the company, and if the failure to account constituted a wrong, then the liability would be an example of unjust enrichment by wrongdoing. Nevertheless, Costello J. held that the promoter's liability would accrue even if the retention not wrongful since "he has received the commission for the benefit of the company which is to be incorporated and not for his own benefit" ([1993] 3 I.R. 152, 162). Hence, the decision is, like *Behan*, an example of liability in unjust enrichment by subtraction to make restitution of money intercepted en route to the plaintiff.

Third, Burrows (pp.53-54) points to *dicta* of Lord Romilly MR in *Lister v. Hodgson* (1867) LR 4 Eq. 30, 34 which seem to establish that where a deed of gift is mistakenly drawn up by the third party in favour of the defendant rather than the plaintiff, the plaintiff can have rectification of the deed if the third party died without realising the mistake. On the other hand, Smith (p.518) argues that there is no such exception, and that the enrichment of the defendant is always at the expense of the third party donor and not of the intended beneficiary (cp. *Hill v. van Erp* (1996-1997) 188 C.L.R. 159 (HCA) 225-227 *per* Gummow J.) Nevertheless, the doctrine seems well established as a matter of Irish law. *McMechan v. Warburton* was a case of this type in which *Lister* was expressly relied upon by Chatterton V.C. So also is *Shanahan v. Redmond* (where a donor had instructed a life assurance company to name the plaintiff as beneficiary, but the company had failed to do so and paid out to the defendant who was the beneficiary originally named in the policy, the defendant's enrichment was at the expense of the plaintiff) which moreover illustrates that the doctrine applies not only to mistake but to other unjust factors as well (*in casu*, ignorance) (on this case, see generally, O'Dell [1997] *LMCLQ* 197). But, in these terms, the exception is confined to rectification of gifts, and does not explain the liability of the Society to the Company in *In re PMPA Insurance* in respect of the payments through cheques, standing orders, bank giros and so forth which were plainly not gifts to the Company by the payors.

Fourth, where a plaintiff holds an office which carries with it the right to receive payments from third parties, and the defendant usurps that office and therefore intercepts those payments, the defendant's enrichment is at the expense of the plaintiff. For Birks, such cases are prime examples of interceptive subtraction (p.134). For Smith, on the other hand, there is an old rule of law ("designed to protect people who pay fees to office holders" (p.494)) by which the payments by the third parties extinguished their obligations, in which case, the receipt by the defendant was at the expense of the plaintiff. Burrows finds that explanation "an appealing one" (p.51) but goes on to argue that "a closely linked alternative approach to Smith's . . . [which is] equally open on the authorities, is to say that [the plaintiff] has the choice whether to treat the debt as discharged or not. That choice is exercised by [the plaintiff] electing to sue either [the third party] in contract for the original debt (in which case [that] debt . . is not discharged) or [the defendant] in restitution (in which case [that] debt . . . is discharged). . . . Either of [these] alternatives seems a more satisfying explanation of the usurpation of office and related cases than does the idea of interceptive subtraction" (p.51).

It is also possible to characterise the actions of the usurper as a wrong. In the old Irish case of *Lawlor v. Alton* (1874-1875) I.R. 8 CL 160, Whiteside C.J. held that plaintiff succeeded not upon the count for money had and received, but in tort ((1874-1875) I.R. 8 CL 160, 163), and so focussed simply upon the plaintiff's loss (two quarters' salary) rather than upon the defendant's gain (the first quarter's salary; that for the second had been paid to neither party). If, however, the court had characterised the defendant's actions as a wrong, and then went on to calculate the plaintiff's recovery by reference to the defendant's gain, then it would have supplied an example of unjust enrichment by wrongdoing. Nevertheless, in the great majority of the usurpation of office cases, the remedies are based on the defendant's gain, and so would be open to be explained on the basis of unjust enrichment by wrongdoing rather than by (interceptive) subtraction. Nevertheless, the vast majority of the cases (the leading case is *Arris v. Stukely* (1677) 2 Mod. 260; 86 E.R. 1060) take the view that the defendant would liable for his gain even if he had not wrongfully deprived the plaintiff of the office (and in *Lawlor v. Alton* itself, where the parties had been the candidates for the office of Surgeon to the Infirmary of the County of Kerry, the defendant been elected to the office, and the plaintiff had subsequently successfully challenged the validity of that election, it seems harsh to characterise the defendant's occupation of the office as a usurpation or wrongful). Thus, as with *HKN* above, any attempt to explain these cases as turning upon wrongs committed by the defendants founders on the fact that the cases allow recovery even where the defendants' actions were not wrongful.

The question which must be posed is this: which is more sound in principle and capable of giving a coherent explanation to the various cases discussed above: Birks' theory of interceptive subtraction; Smith's outright rejection of the theory; Burrows' similar rejection in favour of a pragmatic privity requirement subject to wide-ranging exceptions? (For the sake of completeness, it should be noted that there may in any event be a defence on the facts in many of the cases (*e.g.* Tettenborn "Lawful Receipt – A Justifying Factor ?" [1997] *RLR* 1), but the presence of the subsequent defence is irrelevant to the prior question of liability). Birks' theory of interceptive subtraction seems to provide an elegant explanation for the enrichment of the defendants at the expense of the plaintiffs in the Irish cases of *McMechan*, *PMPA Insurance, HKN, Shanahan*, and now *Behan*. Burrows' alternative of a strict rule requiring privity subject to wide exceptions is not appealing, since although some of the cases (*McMechan, Shanahan*) can be accommodated within the exceptions, the others cannot. Further, Burrows nowhere explains why he chooses to represent the law as composed of a privity restriction subject to wide-ranging exceptions. Certainly there is no argument in principle deployed to justify this position; it seems largely pragmatic. But there is at least one strong argument against this pragmatic position: the law of restitution has long suffered from the importation of contract notions (consider in particular the pernicious influence of the implied contract theory of restitutionary liability, see *e.g.* O'Dell "The Principle Against Unjust Enrichment" (1993) 15 *DULJ* (*ns*) 27). If Burrows' notion of "privity" is derived from the contractual context, this is a sufficient reason to be wary of it. Furthermore, it may be said to totter under the weight of the exceptions which it already recognises, and it certainly provides no guide for the consideration of the legitimacy of further exceptions which would have to be crafted to explain cases like *PMPA Insurance, HKN* and *Behan*.

As to Smith's even more sceptical approach, I have argued elsewhere against his essential position that it is too difficult in fact to determine that the enrichment which has been intercepted by the defendant on the way from the third party would certainly have arrived with the plaintiff ((1991) 11 *OJLS* 481, 485-487) on the basis that that difficulties of fact should never impugn the validity of a principle (any principle), such factual problems merely serve to limit the number of successful cases (O'Dell [1997] *LMCLQ* 197). Whilst it may be that such factual problems if they were insurmountable would call the principle into question, nevertheless in cases such as *McMechan* and *Shanahan*, Chatteron VC and Carroll J. specifically held that the respective donors' intentions were certainly to benefit the respective intended beneficiaries, thereby demonstrating that though it might be difficult to make such a finding, it is by no means impossible, so that the problems perceived by Smith are not insurmountable. Of course, many of the cases which Smith argues are properly examples of direct subtraction almost certainly are. And others are susceptible of reanalysis in terms of unjust enrichment by wrongdoing. That still leaves those cases in respect of which he argues that the third party was the appropriate plaintiff (since the enrichment of the defendant is at his expense and not that of the intended beneficiary). This would have the effect of denying recovery to many successful plaintiffs (such as in *HKN* and *Behan*), and, in the first instance, a theory (such as that of interceptive subtraction) which explains the results in the decided cases is more attractive than one which posits that they are wrong.

On the other hand, Birks' theory of interceptive subtraction is derived from and consistent with the principle against unjust enrichment which underpins the law of restitution; and it explains and unites the various cases referred to above, and those comprised in the various contexts from which Birks derived and in what Burrows regards as exceptions to the privity rule). Since the theory of interceptive subtraction is supported by a principle which explains a significant body of Irish authority, it ought to be expressly adopted as a matter of Irish law; certainly it explains why, in *Behan*, the plaintiff was entitled to sue the bank for restitution of money paid by the Department to the bank.

UNJUST FACTORS

Mistake "Restitution is the response which consists in causing one person to give up to another an enrichment received at his expense . . ." (Birks *An Introduction to the Law of Restitution* (Rev ed., Clarendon Press, Oxford, 1989) p.13). An enrichment will be "unjust" if its conferral was not voluntary, as where the plaintiff paid the defendant by mistake; thus, the plaintiff's mistake renders the enrichment involuntary and the defendant's receipt "unjust". On this scheme, mistake is a cause of action in restitution which allows the recovery of an enrichment conferred pursuant to a mistake. Its contours have been well mapped out in the case law (see, *e.g.* 1996 Review, 507-510; discussing *National Bank v. O'Connor & Bowmaker* (1969) 103 I.L.T.R. 73; *Barclays Bank v. Simms* [1980] Q.B. 677; *David Securities v. Commonwealth Bank of Australia* (1992) 175 C.L.R. 353). Thus, if "a person pays money to another under a mistake of fact which *causes* him to make the payment, he is *prima facie* entitled to recover it as money paid under a mistake of fact" ([1980] Q.B. 677 at 695 *per* Goff J.).

Hence, a bank which pays a defendant on foot of fraudulent drafts, mistakenly believing them to be valid, may recover their mistaken payment (*O'Connor*); a bank which mistakenly pays on foot of a cheque, forgetting a stop order, may recover their mistaken payment (*Simms*); and a client who pays interest to a bank, believing that the loan contract so required when in fact the relevant clause was void, can recover this mistaken payment (*David Securities*). It is obvious that, in every case, the plaintiff is mistaken, and that mistake generates a cause of action in restitution.

It was at one time thought that this cause of action only lay for mistakes of fact; so that it would not be available for mistakes of law. As a limitation without essential logic, it was in time revealed to be "a rule built on inadequate foundations, lacking in clarity (the distinction between mistake of fact and mistake of law can best be described as a fluttering, shadowy will-o'-the-wisp), and whose harshness had led to a luxuriant growth of exceptions" (*Air Canada v. British Colombia* (1989) 59 D.L.R. (4th) 161, 191*per* La Forest J., approving the dissenting judgment of Dickson J. in *Hydro Electric Commission of Nepean v. Ontario Hydro* (1982) 132 D.L.R. (3d) 193 esp. at 201-211). One of the main threads with which the courts busied themselves "weaving a complicated web of exceptions and qualifications" (*Nepean* (1982) 132 D.L.R. (3d) 193, 203 *per* Dickson J.) was that first spun by Lord Denning giving the advice of the Privy Council in *Kiriri Cotton v. Dewani*:

> The true proposition is that money paid under a mistake of law, by itself and without more, cannot be recovered back. . . . If there is something more in addition to the mistake of law – if there is something in the defendant's conduct which shows that, of the two of them, he is the one primarily responsible for the mistake – then it may be recovered back. Thus, if as between the two of them, the duty of observing the law is placed on the shoulders of the one rather than the other – it being imposed upon him specially for the protection of that other – then they are not *in pari delicto* and the money can be recovered back. . . . Likewise, if the responsibility for the mistake lies more on the one than on the other – because he has misled the other when he ought to know better – then again they are not *in pari delicto* and the money can be recovered back . . ." ([1960] A.C. 192, 204)

Thus, a plaintiff who had paid customs duty on imported drink, and then successfully challenged the basis of assessment, had paid the duty under the mistaken belief in the validity of the duty. Though this was a mistake of law, nonetheless, "money paid by one person because of a mistake of law can be recovered by him if the cause of the mistake were the statements about the law made to him by the party receiving the money, or if the parties were not on equal terms at the time when the payment was made." Hence, the "payment of . . . duty . . . was caused by the error made by [the defendants]: they were solely responsible for the mistake and they ought to have known better . . . the plaintiff would, in my opinion, be entitled to recover the moneys overpaid by him because they were paid under a mistake of law caused entirely by the defendant". (*Dolan v. Neligan* [1967] I.R. 247, 259, 260 *per* Kenny J. in the High Court, who however held that the plaintiff should have made that argument in the earlier proceedings which challenged the basis of the assessment; the Supreme Court reversed and found a remedy under the Customs Consolidation Act 1876). The Supreme Court approved and expressly applied this analysis in *Rogers v. Louth County Council* [1981] I.R. 265; [1981] I.L.R.M. 143. Rogers, as administrator of a deceased's estate, redeemed an annuity upon property payable to the defendant. However, the basis upon the Council had calculated it was subsequently successfully challenged: under the correct method of calculation, the estate had overpaid, and Rogers began an action to recover back the overpayment. Although the mistake was a mistake of law, nonetheless, the defendants were primarily responsible for the mistake and the plaintiff administrator was entitled to recover the overpayment. There have been many other important approvals of the *Kiriri Cotton* exception in Ireland (including *East Cork Foods v. O'Dwyer Steel* [1978] I.R. 103, 108 *per* Henchy J.; *Carey v. Ryan* [1982] I.R. 179 at 186; [1982] I.L.R.M. 121, 124 *per* Henchy J; *Dublin Corporation v. Trinity College Dublin* [1984] I.L.R.M. 84; [1985] I.L.R.M. 283 at 286 *per* Hamilton J. (*reversed* on a different point on appeal: [1985] I.L.R.M. 283); *Dublin Corporation v. Building and Allied Trades Union,* High Court, March 6, 1996 at pp.24 at 30-31 *per* Budd J.; on appeal to similar effect (though reversing the court below on another point) [1996] 2 I.R. 468 at 484; [1996] 2 I.L.R.M. 547, 558 *per* Keane J.; *cp. Pine Valley v. Minister for Environment* [1987] I.R. 23 at 42 *per* Henchy J.) and it was interpreted in a similarly expansive manner by the Supreme Court of Canada (in *Eadie v. Brantford Township* (1967) 63 D.L.R. (2d) 561) before that court abolished the mistake of law limitation (*Air Canada*).

Thus, although money paid pursuant to a mistake of fact can be recovered, money paid pursuant to a mistake of law was thought irrecoverable, unless the defendant was more at fault than the plaintiff in the matter of the plaintiff's mistake (*Kiriri Cotton*); in which case, though one of law, the mistake nonetheless was sufficient to allow restitution. However, as the analysis in the 1996 Review demonstrated (pp.509-510) the distinction between a mistake of fact and a mistake of law collapsed under the weight of its exceptions, and it is now clear that an enrichment conferred under "a mistake of fact *or law*" is recoverable (*Dublin Corporation v. Building and Allied Trades Union* [1996] 2 I.R. 468 at 484; [1996] 2 I.L.R.M. 547 at 558 *per* Keane J. (emphasis added)).

Although the "mistake of law" rule has now been relegated to the level of historical absurdity rather than current doctrine, nonetheless, it seemed to push its way centre stage in curious fashion in the decision of the Supreme Court in *Duff v. Minister for Agriculture (No.2)* [1997] 2 I.R. 22. *Duff* arises out of the impact upon Irish agriculture of membership of the European Economic Community and its successors since 1972. Under Council Regulation 857/84 EEC, implemented in Ireland by the Minister for Agriculture, the EEC milk quota scheme allowed farms to produce milk to a quota based on their 1983 production. The Minister had previously instituted another EEC scheme to improve significantly the output of under-performing farms (under Directive 72/159 EEC); but on many farms that development plan continued after 1983. Diary farmers taking advantage of the scheme, whose milk production increased after 1983, were thereby exceeding their 1983-based quota, and were thus potentially liable to be left without a market for their surplus milk or to superlevy penalties for its sale. The Regulation provided (in Article 3(1)) for special or additional quotas for exceptional events (broadly at the Minister's discretion, though farmers with diseased herds in 1983 would be entitled to "obtain, on request" an additional quota); provided that these additional quotas were "drawn from a reserve constituted by the Member State within" the total quota allocated to that Member State (Article 5). After widespread consultation, the Minister decided not to constitute any reserve, and thus not to make special provision for the needs of the development plan farmers, but instead resolved to meet their needs by redistributing any unused quotas (the 'flexi-milk' scheme). After the national quota had been allocated, however, the Commission pointed out that the Minister was obliged to constitute some reserve (for the diseased herd farmers), and could not use the flexi-milk scheme to grant permanent additional quotas. So the Minister bought back some of the quota, and constituted a tiny reserve, inadequate to meet the needs of the development plan farmers, to be applied exclusively to "exceptional events" such as the needs of the diseased herd farmers; and he resolved to meet the needs of the development plan farmers by allocating flexi-milk quotas on a temporary rather than permanent basis.

When they did not obtain a permanent quota for their increased milk production, the development plan farmers sought declarations that they were entitled either to additional quotas to take account of their increased production or to damages.

In the High Court, Murphy J. dismissed their application. The plaintiffs' essential argument was that the discretion in Article 3 of the Regulation was in principle subject to judicial review, and could be reviewed on the grounds that the Minister failed to take the farmers' legitimate expectations into account. Murphy J. found as a fact that all of the development plan farmers believed "that their position was protected by the fact that they were expanding production in accordance with a scheme which was approved and in part financed by the Department of Agriculture" and with its agents' "advice and assistance" ([1997] 2 I.R. 22 at 31, 32; [1993] 2 C.M.L.R. 969 at 975 *per* Murphy J.). Hence, Murphy J. was prepared to hold that the farmers had a legitimate expectation of bringing their plans to fruition ([1997] 2 I.R. 22 at 32; [1993] 2 C.M.L.R. 969 at 975 *per* Murphy J., citing *inter alia* Case 120/86 *Mülder v. Minister van Landbouw en Visserij* [1988] E.C.R. 2321). Nevertheless, he held that "the discretion was granted to each Member State to be exercised in accordance with the national policy of that State" and that it would be "impossible for the courts to review decisions based on questions of national policy" ([1997] 2 I.R. 22 at 43; [1993] 2 C.M.L.R. 969, 984-985). Furthermore, even if the decision were *ultra vires* and judicially reviewable, damages would only have been available if the Minister "had acted negligently, or with malice (in the sense of spite, ill-will or suchlike improper motive), or in the knowledge that the decision would be in excess of the authorised power" ([1997] 2 I.R. 22 at 45; [1993] 2 C.M.L.R. 969, 986 *per* Murphy J., citing *Pine Valley Developments v. The Minister for the Environment* [1987] I.R. 23 at 40 *per* Henchy J.); and the plaintiffs' claim in negligence against the Minister's agents was not made out on the facts.

The plaintiffs appealed. The Supreme Court sought a preliminary ruling from the ECJ; which held that Article 3 of the Directive was valid and that neither it nor general principles of European law such as the legitimate expectations of the farmers imposed upon the State an obligation to grant an additional quota to the development plan farmers (Case C-63/93 [1996] E.C.R. I–569). Although those of the plaintiffs' claims which were based on European law therefore failed, the Supreme Court, by a majority (O'Flaherty, Blayney and Barrington JJ.; Hamilton C.J. and Keane J. dissenting), allowed the appeal on a point of national law.

For the majority, O'Flaherty J. pointed out that the Regulation provided that, whatever the position in European law, as "a matter of national law . . . the plaintiffs had a legitimate expectation that the Minister would honour" his commitment to see the development farmers right if they developed their farms. "The fulfilment of that promise would have required only that the Minister would exercise his discretion in a particular way". ([1997] 2 I.R. 22 at 74). Consequently, since "the Minister, through his mistake of law, put himself in a position where he could not come to exercise a discretion . . . the persons entitled to expect that a discretion might be exercised in their favour are unable to get the benefit of that to which they had a legitimate expectation" ([1997] 2 I.R. 22, 74, 75) and the plaintiffs were entitled to have the matter remitted to the High Court for an enquiry as to the appropriate remedy. Similarly, Barrington J. described the "principle of legitimate expectation [as] one of the principles of Community law [which] provides, *inter alia*, that those who in good faith act under representations of the State shall not be frustrated in their expectations" ([1997] 2 I.R. 22 at 90). Although the ECJ had made clear that the principle, as a matter of European law, "could not be invoked to deny the community legislature the right to change the law, or to force an agent given a discretion by community law to exercise that discretion in any particular way" nevertheless, Barrington J. held that, as a matter of national law, "the plaintiffs are entitled to assume that their expectations will not be frustrated by a mistake of law made by a Minister of State" ([1997] 2 I.R. 22 at 91). He, too, remitted the case to the High Court for the assessment of damages. Blayney J. was simply content to indicate his agreement with both O'Flaherty and Barrington JJ.

For the minority, although Hamilton C.J. seemed to cite with approval the views of Murphy J. in the court below to the effect that the Minister's discretion on a matter of national policy was unreviewable ([1997] 2 I.R. 22 at 60-63), he nevertheless held that the Minister's decisions to distribute the full national quota, without a reserve for the development plan farmers, taken after wide consultations including representations from those farmers, and representing the industry consensus, were not unreasonable (within the meaning of Henchy J's test in *The State (Keegan) v. The Stardust Victims Compensation Tribunal* [1986] I.R. 642 at 658). At most, he thought, the plaintiffs' "legal entitlement was to have their situation taken into account by the Minister" ([1997] 2 I.R. 22 at 71); as this was done, the plaintiff's claim failed. The other dissentient, Keane J., characterised the plaintiff's claim as one in which they claimed that "the Minister should have foreseen that his initial proposals were unlawful in terms of European Union law and should, accordingly, have taken the . . . option . . . of creating a national reserve by an across-the-board reduction in the national quota, the quotas being freed then used to meet the special situations." ([1997] 2 I.R. 22 at 98). For him, the plaintiffs' argument "that the only reserve which the Minister could properly have created was one which also met their special needs . . . [wa]s totally irreconcilable with the finding of the Court of Justice that the Regulations imposed no obligation on the Minister to meet the special needs of producers such as the plaintiffs out of a national reserve . . ." ([1997] 2 I.R. 22, 99). There being no remedy available to the plaintiffs as a matter of European law, Keane J., referring to the views of Murphy J. and Hamilton C.J., also held that there was no remedy available to the plaintiffs as a matter of national law, as they had not discharged the onus placed upon them by *Keegan* ([1997] 2 I.R. 22 at 103).

Although the majority crafted a remedy for plaintiffs who had been hard done by, nevertheless, they were treated badly by a political decision, and there is a certain attractiveness in Murphy J's observation that "it was a decision based on national policy for which the Minister like all politicians in a democratic society is answerable politically and not to the courts . . ." ([1997] 2 I.R. 22 at 44; [1993] 2 C.M.L.R. 969 at 985). Thus, in the Supreme Court, for the minority, Hamilton C.J. held that the plaintiff's expectations were satisfied by the Minister considering their position in making his decision, and both he and Keane J. held that the decision was not unreasonable. On the other hand, the majority held that the plaintiffs' legitimate expectation generated a ground for judicial review of the Minister's exercise of his discretion, and that this of itself justified an enquiry as to damages. Nevertheless, as Murphy J. had pointed out in the Court below, for an award of damages, it is not enough that a decision be susceptible of judicial review, it must also fulfill the *Pine Valley* requirements, *e.g.* negligence or malice. If this is so, then, either the majority decision is unsound on the basis of having omitted this enquiry; or, the *Pine Valley* requirements are an incomplete statement of the bases upon which damages are available, and breach of legitimate expectations ought to be added to the list (envisaging the latter option, *cp.* Hogan and Morgan *Administrative Law in Ireland* (3rd ed., Round Hall, Sweet & Maxwell, Dublin, 1998) 811; for other examples, see *Duggan v. An Taoiseach* [1989] I.L.R.M. 710 at 731 *per* Hamilton P.; *Cannon v. Minister for the Marine* [1991] I.L.R.M. 261 at 265-267 *per* Barr J. (*semble*)).

On the other hand, despite what the majority said, Hogan and Morgan think it "likely that the claim based on legitimate expectations was rejected on the ground that a legitimate expectation cannot prevail against the exercise of a statutory power, still less a change of law" (p.843, and see the case turning on operational negligence (*id*, see below)). With respect, the majority did base their decision on legitimate expectations; in which case, either the principle cited by Hogan and Morgan demonstrates that it is wrong, or the decision constitutes an exception to that principle. Here, it is necessary to consider the decision of the majority insofar as both O'Flaherty and Barrington JJ tied their decisions on the frustration of the plaintiffs' legitimate expectations to what they described as the Minister's "mistake of law" ([1997] 2 I.R. 22 at 73-75 *per* O'Flaherty J., 90-91 *per* Barrington J.).

For example, for O'Flaherty J., everything flowed from the initial and "fundamental mistake of law . . . on the part of the Minister" ([1997] 2 I.R. 22 at 73) not to constitute a national reserve. Hence, in his view "the question posed for resolution" was: "if a public officer, through a mistake of law on his part, is debarred from exercising a discretion at all, is his situation any different from a public officer who declares that, while he has a discretion, he debars himself from exercising it ?" ([1997] 2 I.R. 22 at 74; referring on the latter point to *The State (McGeough) v. Louth County Council* (1956) 107 I.L.T.R. 12). And he concluded that just "as money paid under a mistake of law can be recovered if the responsibility for the mistake lies more on the one party than the other and the one with the responsibility is in a more powerful position (*Rogers v. Louth County Council* [1981] I.R. 265), so I believe should the plaintiffs be entitled to a remedy at the hands of the Minister for the wrongs they have suffered" ([1997] 2 I.R. 22 at 75). Reflecting this, Barrington J. held that if "the plaintiffs have suffered loss and damage as a result of the Minister's mistake of law it appears to me just and proper in the circumstances of this case, that the Minister should pay them compensation" ([1997] 2 I.R. 22 at 90). It is odd, to say the least, first, to see life being breathed into a doctrine which has been abolished in many jurisdictions and is on its last legs in many others, and then to see the rejuvenated doctrine transmuted from a bar into a cause of action. In these passages, their lordships seem more concerned to state an argument from justice than to state one from legal principle: hence, it appeared to Barrington J. "that the court would be doing less than its duty if it failed to vindicate [the plaintiffs'] right to compensation in the circumstances of this case" (*ibid.*; compare his similar willingness to "fashion a remedy on the principle of *ubi jus ibi remedium*" in *McDonnell v. Ireland*, Supreme Court, July 23, 1997 at p.8; but contrast the decision of Barron J. in *Campbell v. Minister for Agriculture,* High Court, October 8, 1997). Consequently, the analogy which they draw with mistake of law needs to be treated with care; in particular, the terms in which O'Flaherty J. stated it seem to fail on many levels.

First, and generally, the distinctions which made it meaningful to speak in terms of "mistake of law" were unsound in principle have been abolished not only all over the common law world but also in Ireland. If a doctrine in its context is regarded as unsound and has consequently been abrogated, then in principle it must be dangerous to draw an analogy with it to generate a liability in another area of the law. The decline of the mistake of law rule in the law of restitution must make O'Flaherty J.'s reliance upon it (whether directly, or as seems more likely, by way of comparative analogy) more than suspect.

Second, recall the conclusion above that, in every case of mistake in the law of restitution, the *plaintiff* is mistaken, and that mistake generates a cause of action in restitution. Thus, in *Rogers v. Louth County Council*, to which O'Flaherty J. refers, the plaintiff had mistakenly overpaid the defendant, and recovered the overpayment. There was no question of an analysis of whether the defendant was mistaken. Thus, if *Duff* is to be taken seriously as a mistake case, any relevant mistake would have to have been that of the plaintiff farmers (if any), not of the defendant Minister. Third (and similarly), mistake is a cause of action in *restitution*; it is concerned with the recovery of benefits transferred. The plaintiff farmers had conferred no benefit upon the defendant Minister; they did not seek restitution from him; mistake therefore had no role to play on the facts.

Fourth, recall further the conclusion above that the law precluded such a cause of action where the mistake was one of law. Thus, the role of the former "mistake of law" rule was to bar a cause of action in restitution based upon mistake. It is therefore odd, to say the least, both to perceive the rejuvenation of an otherwise universally excoriated doctrine, and then to see the rejuvenated doctrine transmuted from a bar into a cause of action. It is so odd that it ought not to be.

Fifth, recall also the further conclusion above that, where a plaintiff had paid pursuant to a mistake of law, nevertheless, if the defendant was more at fault than the plaintiff in the matter of the plaintiff's mistake, the plaintiff could have restitution. Thus, in *Rogers v. Louth Co Council*, although the plaintiff's mistake in overpaying the defendant was one of law, nonetheless, since the defendant was at fault in the plaintiff's making it, the plaintiff could recover the overpayment. In mistake cases, the fault of the defendant, such as the Minister in *Duff*, is relevant only in displacing the bar which precludes a plaintiff's claim in mistake as being one of law. That fault does not constitute a cause of action in its own right. *Duff* should not be read as suggesting otherwise.

In summary, there is no true analogy between a mistakenly overpaying plaintiff, on the one hand, and an erroneous defendant, on the other. Consequently, the so-called "mistake of law" rule does not state a cause of action in the terms seemingly applied by O'Flaherty and Barrington JJ. However, that analysis does not preclude the possibility that the mistake was relevant as an element of some other cause of action. It might, for example, demonstrate negligence on the part of the Minister, and if the plaintiffs could have demonstrated that he owed them a duty of care, then the mistake – constituting negligence – would have amounted to a breach of that duty of care. Thus, for Hogan and Morgan "the plaintiffs seem to have succeeded on the ground of something like a negligent error of law in that the Minister had misunderstood the EC Directive which he was applying. This may be classified as special case of operational negligence as opposed to the negligent exercise of a discretionary power" (pp.843-844). Similarly, arising out of the various EC instruments in play, there might have been a duty akin to a statutory duty arising upon the Minister, and the mistake – constituting negligence – would have amounted to a breach of that (statutory) duty. Similarly, O'Flaherty and Barrington JJ. considered that the plaintiffs' legitimate expectations generated a duty on the part of the Minister to meet those expectations; the Minister's mistake precluded him from meeting them. The mistake was therefore relevant as an element of the plaintiffs' cause of action in legitimate expectations; it should not be taken as independently stating a cause of action in its own right on the facts. Thus, the decision of the majority in the Supreme Court in *Duff* ought to be read as giving a remedy for the plaintiffs' legitimate expectations frustrated by the error of the Minister: it is therefore, a legitimate expectations case, and not one on "mistake of law" properly understood. It should now be clear that any more extensive interpretation of their lordships' *dicta* on the issue of mistake of law would be bizarre and absurd.

Ignorance The unjust factors of the family which contains mistake, duress and failure of basis are united by the idea that the plaintiff did not intend the defendant to have the enrichment. By the ordinary processes of legal reasoning, if there are other categories in which it can also be said that the plaintiff likewise did not so intend, it becomes difficult to resist the conclusion that any such unintentional transfer should also be characterised as unjust and trigger restitution. In the 1996 Review, 519-520, it was therefore argued that where a plaintiff does not intend to enrich because he is unaware of (ignorant of) the defendant's enrichment, that enrichment should likewise be characterised as unjust. For example, the victim of a theft is unaware of (ignorant of) the thief's enrichment at the plaintiff-victim's expense, but can obviously have restitution from the thief. Again, where a bank is paid money intended for one company in a group (the Company), but it misdirects the money to another company in the group (the Society), the Company is unaware of (ignorant of) the Society's enrichment at its expense, and can have restitution from the Society. This is what happened in *In re PMPA Insurance Co Ltd* [1986] I.L.R.M. 524. in which Lynch J. came close to articulating judicially the rationale for the unjust factor of ignorance as a matter of Irish law. In regard to the cheques, standing orders, bank giros and so forth, validly filled in with respect to the Company, which constituted the payments received by the bank and paid to the Society, it seemed to Lynch J. that:

> the owners of the moneys never intended that the Society should have possession of those moneys, much less their ownership. I think these monies have come into the name or possession of the Society in a way different from what is usually understood by moneys paid under a mistake of fact. Where moneys are paid under a mistake of fact as is usually understood by that expression the payer really intends to pay the moneys to the payee. He would not pay the moneys if he were not under some misapprehension but nevertheless being under some misapprehension his intention is that the moneys shall go from him to the payee. When he discovers his mistake of fact, he has, of course, a right to reclaim payment of the moneys from the payee but that right ranks as a simple contract debt.
>
> That is not what happened in regard to the sums with which I am now dealing however.

According to Lynch J., when a plaintiff is mistaken, in one sense it can be said that he consents ("he really intends to pay") but that his consent is vitiated ("would not pay the moneys if he were not under some misapprehension"); but here it seems that when the bank paid the Company's money to the Society, he held that the Company was not mistaken in that sense. Though he does not reach the conclusion, this aspect of the judgment of Lynch J. is the first part of the argument in favour of ignorance as an unjust factor. Certainly, he seems to have held that mistake is not the relevant cause of action, and yet the Company succeeded. The best explanation for the success of the Company's cause of action in restitution is that it did not consent to the Society's enrichment not so much because it was mistaken as because it was unaware of (ignorant of) the Society's enrichment. Hence, this would seem to constitute a good Irish authority in favour (at least) of setting off down the road to ignorance as an unjust factor. On the other hand, Goff and Jones *The Law of Restitution* (4th ed., Sweet & Maxwell, London, 1993) p.107 reject ignorance as an unjust factor, subsuming it within mistake; and Mason and Carter *Restitution Law in Australia* (Butterworths, Sydney, 1995) para.409, pp.117-118 cautiously treat ignorance cases in the context of mistake. Nevertheless, it is submitted first, that the argument in principle from the absence of the plaintiff's consent in favour of the recognition of the unjust factor of ignorance, distinct from mistake, is compelling, and second, that *PMPA Insurance* is not a case on mistake but on ignorance.

Hence, in *PMPA Insurance*, the Company is as ignorant of the Society's enrichment at its expense as the victim of a theft is of the thief's enrichment at his expense. As a matter of authority, an action in restitution lies against not only the thief, but also the recipient from the thief: thus, in *Lipkin Gorman v. Karpnale* [1991] 2 A.C. 548 (HL) a partner of a law firm gambled at the Playboy club with money stolen from the firm, and the firm recovered the money from the club in an action for money had and received at common law. However, in such circumstances, the remote recipient will often have the benefit of the defence of change of position (as in *Lipkin Gorman v. Karpnale* itself) or of the defence of *bona fide* purchase for value without notice (unsuccessful on the facts of *Lipkin Gorman v. Karpnale*). In *Lipkin Gorman*, the money was directed from the plaintiff to the remote recipient by a thief; but the action lies where the plaintiff is unaware of the direction of the money from him to a remote defendant even by a non-fraudulent hand. Hence, in *Re Diplock* [1948] Ch. 465, *affd* [1951] A.C. 251, where the administrators of the deceased's estate directed payments to beneficiaries under a will which was later set aside, the beneficiaries on the intestacy recovered from the original recipients. In all such cases, the plaintiff is unaware of (ignorant of) the defendant's enrichment, and since he did not intend to enrich the defendant, the enrichment is unjust.

In the 1996 Review, 519, it was speculated that if the personal equitable duty to account as constructive trustee for receipt of trust funds is to be explained on restitutionary grounds (*Royal Brunei Airlines v. Tan* [1995] 2 A.C. 378, 386f *per* Lord Nicholls), then, the fact that the plaintiff whose funds were misdirected was unaware of the misdirection to the defendant means that the appropriate unjust factor is ignorance, (a view long espoused by Professor Birks; see, *e.g.*: (1989) 105 *LQR* 352; (1989) 105 *LQR* 528; [1989] *LMCLQ*

296; [1991] *LMCLQ* 473; [1993] *LMCLQ* 218; *Restitution. The Future* (Federation Press, Sydney, 1992) chapter 2; "Trusts in the Recovery of Misapplied Assets" in McKendrick (ed.), *Commercial Aspects of Trusts and Fiduciary Relationships* (Oxford, 1992) p.149; "Gifts of Other People's Money" in Birks (ed.), *Frontiers of Liability* (Vol. 1, Oxford, 1994) p.31). The action for money had and received lay at the heart of the decision of the House of Lords in *Lipkin Gorman*; this liability to account as a constructive trustee "is the counterpart in equity of the common law action for money had and received" (*El Ajou v. Dollar Land Holdings* [1993] 3 All E.R. 717, 736 *per* Millett J.); on this view, the common law and equitable actions both have the aim of achieving restitution to prevent unjust enrichment.

However, equity has not yet unequivocally committed itself to this view, and there has been no case similar to *Tan* in which its consequences have been comprehensively explored. Hence, in this year's crop, the decision of Laffoy J. in *Ulster Factors v. Entoglen,* High Court, February 21, 1997, reflected the pre-*Tan* non-restitutionary orthodox approach to the question of the liability of the recipient.

Here, pursuant to a factoring agreement between the plaintiff factor and the plaintiff company, the plaintiff, at the request of one of the company's directors, had made a payment of Stg£35,000 on behalf of the company to a firm of solicitors. The factor subsequently debited Ir£37,839.83 from the company's current account with it (representing the amount paid plus interest). When the company was wound up, the plaintiff sought to recover moneys outstanding to it; but the liquidator retained Ir£37,839.83 contending that he was entitled to reverse that debit and so recover the money paid by the company to the factor, on the grounds that the payment was made either without authority or was *ultra vires*. On the authority point, Laffoy J. held that the director who had requested the payment by the factor had ostensible authority to bind the company. On the *ultra vires* point, the liquidator argued that the money paid by the factor had discharged the debt not of the company but of a third party, which, on the authority of *In re Frederick Inns* [1994] 1 I.L.R.M. 387 (SC), would have been *ultra vires* the company; but Laffoy J. held that the evidence did not support the argument.

Furthermore, she held that even if the liquidator had established that as between the company and the firm of solicitors the payment was *ultra vires*, the liquidator had "not established any basis on which the plaintiff, which was merely the medium through which the payment was made, should be required, in effect, the make restitution for the *ultra vires* payment" (p.7). The legal basis which the liquidator had advanced was "the principle enunciated in *Belmont Finance v. Williams (No.2)* [1980] 1 All E.R. 393 (CA) applied by Blayney J. in *In re Frederick Inns* that, if the directors of a company in breach of their fiduciary duties misapply the funds of their company so that they come into the hands of some stranger to the trust who receives them with knowledge (actual or constructive) of the breach, he cannot conscientiously retain those funds against the company . . ." (pp.7-8). Laffoy J. held that

> [u]nder the *Belmont* principle, as applied by the Supreme Court, what renders the recipient of or the dealer with funds which are being misapplied in breach of fiduciary duties of the directors of a company liable as a constructive trustee is knowledge, actual or constructive, of the breach of trust.

She held that the plaintiff did not have such knowledge. The plaintiff had simply paid the £35,000 to the firm of solicitors pursuant to the director's request, as they were contractually obliged to do. It was "clear from the evidence that [the plaintiff] did not have actual knowledge of the purpose for which the payment was being made or of the breach" (p.9) of fiduciary duty being committed by the *ultra vires* payment. Nor did the plaintiff have constructive notice: "[t]here was no obligation on the plaintiff to enquire as to the purpose for which any payment which the company requested the plaintiff to make to a third party was being made or to satisfy itself that the payment was intra vires the company, and even if the payment was *ultra vires*, constructive knowledge of a breach of trust cannot be imputed to the plaintiff for failure to make such enquiries" (*id*).

Hence, in an action by the plaintiff for moneys due under the factoring agreement, the defendant could not set-off £37,839.83 on the grounds that it had been paid to the plaintiff *ultra vires* and in breach of the directors' fiduciary duties. This was so for three reasons. First, the defendant could not establish as a matter of fact that the payment had been applied to the *ultra vires* purpose of the payment of the debt of a third party. Second, the plaintiff did not have actual or constructive knowledge of the defendant's lack of *vires* and thus of the breach of fiduciary duty. Third, even if they had, the plaintiffs should not be liable because they were "merely the medium through which the payment was made". The first reason states that the claim failed on the facts; the second states that the terms of the cause of action were not made out; and third states that even it were, there would be a defence.

The cause of action which was not made out was described as imposing liability upon "the recipient of or the dealer with" funds misapplied in breach of fiduciary duty. At least two issues arise here: the first relates to whether the payments were in fact made in breach of fiduciary duty; the second relates to the cause of action arising if they had been.

First, it seems that Laffoy J. treated *In re Frederick Inns* as authority for the proposition that an *ultra vires* payment by a company is automatically made in breach of the directors' fiduciary duties. And that seems to be a fair reading of Blayney J.'s judgment: the payments "being *ultra vires* . . . constituted as misapplication by the directors of the companies' funds . . . The misapplication was a breach by the directors of their fiduciary duties" ([1994] 1 I.L.R.M. 387, 399). However, that would seem to conflate two quite distinct issues in principle. In the leading similar English authorities, where *ultra vires* payments were also payments in breach of fiduciary duties, this occurred not because the latter followed from the former, but because whilst the payments were *ultra vires*, they were also *independently* breaches of the directors' fiduciary duties to the companies not to let duty and interest conflict, and so on (see *e.g. International Sales v. Marcus* [1982] 3 All E.R. 551; *Rolled Steel Products v. British Steel* [1985] 3 All E.R. 52 (CA)). Indeed, in *In re Frederick Inns*, Blayney J. expressly held that directors owe fiduciary duties to creditors at least when the company is insolvent, and that the (*ultra vires*) payments in question were paid in breach of those fiduciary duties. Hence, it is submitted that *In re Frederick Inns* should not be read as holding that every *ultra vires* act, of itself and without more, amounts to a breach of directors' fiduciary duties. On the facts of *Ulster Factors v. Entoglen*, therefore, there would seem to have been no breach of fiduciary duty in the payment. Laffoy J. stated the cause of action comprised in "the *Belmont* principle" to be based upon payments made in breach of fiduciary duty, and since the mere fact that the payments were *ultra vires* should not mean that they were made in breach of fiduciary duty, that element of "the *Belmont* principle" as Laffoy J. understood it was also not made out.

Second, for Laffoy J., that principle imposes liability upon "the recipient of or the dealer with" misapplied funds. Equity has traditionally treated such liability as one example of the liability of strangers receiving with or dealing with trust property: Delany, *Equity and the Law of Trusts in Ireland* (Round Hall Sweet & Maxwell, Dublin, 1996) p.186; cp. Keane, *Equity and the Law of Trusts in the Republic of Ireland* (Butterworths, Dublin, 1988) p.184, paragraph 13.08-09 (iv); an excellent, orthodox, analysis and critique of the issues is to be found in Harpum, "The Stranger as Constructive Trustee" (1986) 102 *LQR* 114 (Part I), 217 (Part II); see also Harpum, "The Basis of Equitable Liability" in Birks (ed.) *Frontiers of Liability* (Vol. 1, Oxford, 1994) p.9 (hereafter: Harpum "Basis"). Delany, Harpum and Keane distinguish three categories: (a) an intermeddler in the trust who takes it upon himself to act as trustee by doing acts with trust property which it is the business of the trustee to do, thereby makes himself a (constructive) trustee *de son tort*; (b) an accessory who dishonestly assists in a breach of trust will become liable to account to the beneficiary; and (c) a receiver of trust property with knowledge that he is receiving trust property, thereby makes himself a (constructive) trustee of the property. For the purposes of this discussion, let us call these various strangers, respectively, the intermeddler, the accessory and the recipient.

On the facts of *Entoglen*, the factors were not intermeddlers in the sense of being trustees *de leurs torts*. Whether by distinguishing between "the recipient of *or* the dealer with" misapplied funds, Laffoy J. was seeking to distinguish between liability for recipients and for accessories is difficult to discern. It is certainly more than possible, for three reasons; first, Laffoy J's use of the disjunctive "or"; second; dealing inconsistently with trust property does in fact constitute a form of accessory liability (see. *e.g. Agip v. Jackson* [1990] Ch. 265 at 292-292 *per* Millett J; *affd* [1991] Ch. 547 (CA); Harpum, "Basis" pp.16-17; an example is the old Irish case of *Sheridan v. Joyce* (1844-1845) 7 I.R. Eq. Rep. 115); and third, "dealer" could be used to mean "accessory" so that "knowing dealing" could mean "knowing assistance". On the other hand, rather confusingly, the traditional description of the recipient's liability in equity has been described both as "knowing receipt *or* dealing" (*e.g. Baden Delvaux* (1982) [1983] B.C.L.C. 325, 404; [1992] 4 All E.R. 161, 231 *per* Peter Gibson J., citing *Snell's Principles of Equity* (28th ed., 1982) pp.194-195, compare (29th ed., 1990) pp.193-194)) and as knowing receipt *and* dealing (*e.g.* Delany, p.197). Much confusion has been sown by the various shorthands which have been deployed in the cases and in the books, so much so that such time-honoured phrases can easily admit of many meanings (and clarity may on occasion be best achieved by avoiding them and their ambiguities altogether; hence for example whilst Hanbury and Martin, *Modern Equity* in its 14th ed. (Sweet & Maxwell, London, 1993) uses the phrase "knowing receipt and dealing" (p.304), the 15th ed. (1997) does not). However, the whole tenor of the judgment of Laffoy J. in *Ulster Factors v. Entoglen*, in particular her reference to *Belmont Finance* as it was deployed in the Supreme Court in *In re Frederick Inns* strongly suggest that she was only concerned with the liability of the recipient. Although *Belmont Finance* concerned both recipient and accessory liability, only the claim against the defendant as recipient succeeded, and it was on this point that it was considered in *Frederick Inns* which only concerned recipient liability. It is to avoid just such ambiguities that in this discussion the three species of strangers whose liability is discussed by Delany, Harpum and Keane are here called respectively, the intermeddler, the accessory and the recipient.

On the account presented by Delany, Harpum and Keane, there are two different liabilities which might be visited on such strangers: a personal liability to make good the pecuniary loss suffered by the trust, and a proprietary liability to return to the trust the very property *in specie* which it has lost. (cp. Hanbury and Martin, *Modern Equity* (15th ed., Sweet & Maxwell, London, 1997) p.298). In principle, the standard for the imposition of personal liability need not be as high as that for the imposition of proprietary liability.

Furthermore, on the account presented by Delany, Harpum and Keane, the reasons for the imposition of liability upon the various strangers differ. The liability of the intermeddler is a primary liability, "because the intermeddler is the person who actually commits the breach of trust" (Harpum, "Basis" p.10); he is liable "by reason of his wrong" (Keane, p.184), and it seems that since he holds the trust property, he is *proprietarily* liable to hold that very property on constructive trust. The liability of the accessory is a secondary liability (Harpum, "Basis" p.10; *Tan* [1995] 2 A.C. 378, 386 *per* Lord Nicholls). We now know from the fundamental restatement in *Tan* (above) that it is imposed because of the accessory's dishonest inducement of or assistance in a breach of trust. And it seems that (at least where he simply assists in the breach of trust) since he does not in fact hold the trust property, he is *personally* liable to account to the trust the amount the trust has lost as a consequence of his dishonesty. Prior to *Tan*, much was made of the fact that equity had traditionally characterised the action as one for "*knowing* assistance", and debate focussed on the level of knowledge required to make the accessory liable. Hence, in *Baden Delvaux* [1983] B.C.L.C. 325 at 407; [1992] 4 All E.R. 161, 235, Peter Gibson J. (adopting the submission of counsel) (in)famously posited a scale of five types of knowledge which could suffice: "(i) actual knowledge; (ii) wilfully shutting one's eyes to the obvious; (iii) wilfully and recklessly failing to make such inquiries as an honest and reasonable man would make; (iv) knowledge of circumstances which would indicate the facts to an honest and reasonable man; (v) knowledge of circumstances which would put an honest and reasonable man on inquiry". Gardner, in an article which provides a superb map through the thicket of the relevant authorities, observed that "knowledge and notice are often defined by reference to these categories. Knowledge is often identified with the first three, notice with the remaining two. This may be supportable as regards knowledge, but it is incorrect as regards notice. Categories (iv) and (v) have the defendant knowing evidence from which the reasonable person would have drawn the crucial inferences, but (*scirelicet*) himself failing to draw them, albeit that this failure is not 'wilful' or 'reckless.' True notice, however, extends further, to the case where the reasonable person would have discovered or inferred the crucial facts, regardless of whether the defendant himself did or was aware of any evidence from which to do so. . . . [The *Baden* scale] does not therefore, offer a definition of knowledge and notice, but a (wide) view as to the meaning of knowledge" (Gardner, "Knowing Assistance and Knowing Receipt: Taking Stock" (1996) 112 *LQR* 56, 57-58). Later cases have largely concerned themselves which the details of this scale, and with discerning which degree of knowledge was made out on the facts, and whether the lesser degrees of knowledge were properly included. In his speech in *Tan*, Lord Nicholls has now of course displaced this focus upon (or even obsession with) knowledge in favour of a focus simply on the *dishonesty* of the accessory.

As to whether the standard in *Tan* forms part of Irish law, the runes are decidedly difficult to read. On the one hand, if, in *Ulster Factors v. Entoglen*, Laffoy J. did indeed intend to include both recipients and accessories in referring to the liability of "the recipient of *or* the dealer with" misapplied funds as being based upon actual or constructive knowledge, then *Entoglen* is authority in favour of the proposition that the liability of the accessory is based not upon dishonesty but upon constructive knowledge. On the other, in *Taxback v. The Revenue Commissioners,* High Court, January 21 1997, McCracken J. declined to accept that the Revenue, in making repayments to the plaintiff VAT refund agency as agents for those statutorily entitled to VAT refunds, might be said to have assisted in any dishonesty on the part of the plaintiffs. He seems to have considered *Tan* in coming to that conclusion. Neither of these cases is decisive on this point. Nevertheless, Laffoy J. probably did not intended to include the liability of the accessory in her statement of principle, and *Taxback* might well constitute the Irish adoption of the principle in *Tan.* (If it does, then it provides a further reason why *Ulster Factors v. Entoglen* ought to be understood as a case solely on the liability of the recipient). In any event, if Irish law is not already to that effect, it is submitted (cp. Delany, p.192) that it ought to come into line with the speech of Lord Nicholls in *Tan* at the first opportunity.

As to the liability of the recipient, much has here also been made of the fact that equity had traditionally characterised the action as one for "*knowing receipt*", and debate focussed on the level of knowledge (on the *Baden* scale, above) required to make the recipient liable. The cases are divided. Some of the divisions are recounted in the next paragraph. However, not only are the cases divided, but some of the decisions are also sufficiently delphic that it is difficult to be sure as to which position the judges have taken.

Many cases favour a dishonesty standard for the liability of the recipient (similar to that postulated for the accessory in *Tan*) and those cases *post-Baden* often describe it as encompassing the first three points on the *Baden* scale (*e.g. Carl-Zeiss Stiftung v. Herbert Smith (No.2)* [1969] 2 Ch. 276 (CA); *Competitive Insurance v. Davies* [1975] 1 W.L.R. 1240 (Goff J.); *Re Montagu's Settlement Trusts* (1985) [1987] Ch. 264, [1992] 4 All E.R. 308 (Megarry VC); *Lipkin Gorman v. Karpnale* [1987] 1 W.L.R. 987 (Alliott J.), the matter was dealt with as an aspect of a breach of contract claim by the majority in the Court of Appeal [1989] 1 W.L.R. 1340 (though May LJ reached the same conclusion as Alliott J. on this point) and the claims in equity were not pursued in the House of Lords: [1991] 2 A.C. 548; *Barclays Bank v. Quinecare* (1988) [1992] 4 All E.R. 363 (Steyn J.); *Eagle Trust v. SBC Securities* [1992] 4 All E.R. 488 (Vinelott J.); *Cowan de Groot v. Eagle Trust* [1992] 4 All E.R. 700 (Knox J.); *Polly Peck v. Nadir (No.2)* [1992] 4 All E.R. 769 (CA); *Eagle Trust v. SBC Securities (No.2)* [1996] 1 B.C.L.C. 121 (Arden J.)). Other cases favour a negligence standard for the liability of the recipient, and those cases *post-Baden* often describe it either as encompassing all five points on the *Baden* scale, or as encompassing notice, or as both (though we have seen that the *Baden* scale properly relates only to a wide view of knowledge and not to notice). (The old Irish case of *O'Hehir v. Cahill* (1912) 97 ILTR 274 (Dodd J. and CA) is probably of this negligence standard ("*Scienter* is not necessary, but it exists here and makes the case stronger" (1912) 97 I.L.T.R. 274, 276 *per*

Gibson J.); the leading modern cases include *Nelson v. Larholt* ([1948] 1 KB 339; *Belmont Finance v. Williams (No.1)* [1979] Ch. 250; *(No.2)* [1980] 1 All E.R. 393 (CA); *International Sales v. Marcus* [1982] 3 All E.R. 551 (Lawson J.); *Rolled Steel Products v. BSC* [1982] 3 All E.R. 1057 (Vinelott J.); [1985] 3 All E.R. 52 (CA); *Westpac Banking v. Savin* [1985] 2 N.Z.L.R. 41; *Agip (Africa) v. Jackson* [1990] Ch. 265, (Millett J.) *(semble)*; *affd* [1991] Ch. 547 (CA)); *El Ajou v. Dollar Land Holdings* [1993] 3 All E.R. 717 (Millett J. *(semble)*); *rvsd* on the application of this principle to the facts [1994] 2 All E.R. 688 (CA); *Equitcorp Industries v. Hawkins* [1991] 3 N.Z.L.R. 700; *Marshall Futures v. Marshall* [1992] 1 N.Z.L.R. 315 (and cp. *Equiticorp v. R* [1996] 3 N.Z.L.R. 586 (summary))) *Gold v. Rosenberg* (1997) 152 C.L.R. (4th) 385 (SCC); *Citadel General Assurance v. Lloyds' Bank Canada* (1997) 152 C.L.R. (4th) 411 (SCC)). Since Blayney J. in *In re Frederick Inns* [1994] 1 I.L.R.M. 387 (SC) and Laffoy J. in *Ulster Factors v. Entoglen* both purport to follow *Belmont*, Irish law would seem to have adopted this view (though this point will be returned to below).

Since the authorities are divided (or unclear), this is a debate which cannot resolved simply by reference to authority. The precedential value of a decision favouring one position, without explaining why that position is to be preferred, must be weak. And that is the case with *Frederick Inns* (by which Laffoy J. in *Ulster Factors* was bound). Furthermore, much of that debate had long overlooked the fact that the liability of the accessory and of the recipient are in essence two different things: the liability of the recipient aims to return the property or its value to the trust; the liability of the accessory aims to punish the accessory for his dishonesty. The actions serve different policies, and it is these policies which dictate the principles upon which the different strangers are to be made liable (cp. Gardner (1996) 112 *LQR* 56, 70-93); in terms of the *Baden* scale, it is these policies which will determine whether it is meaningful to speak the language of knowledge in this context, and if so, what level is necessary for liability.

This has been overlooked in the confusion which arises because many of the cases contain claims against both recipients and accessories. In a few cases, it is difficult to discern whether the plaintiff is seeking to make the defendant liable as a recipient or as an accessory (as in *Ulster Factors v. Entoglen*, as a consequence of the ambiguity identified above in the distinction which Laffoy J. seemed to draw between "the recipient of *or* the dealer with" misapplied funds). In some cases, the plaintiff seeks to make the same defendant liable either as a recipient or as an accessory (as in *Belmont Finance v. Williams (No.1)* [1979] Ch. 250; *(No.2)* [1980] 1 All E.R. 393 (CA) where a company was made liable as a recipient but not as an accessory). In most cases, the plaintiff seeks to make one defendant liable as a recipient and another (or others) liable as accessories, *e.g. Lipkin Gorman v. Karpnale* at first instance ([1987] 1 W.L.R. 987 and in the Court of Appeal ([1989] 1 W.L.R. 1340, though not in the House of Lords ([1991] 2 A.C. 548 where only the claim against the recipient was pursued. In some such cases, the positions of the recipients and the accessories are equated and the same standards applied (as in the judgment of Ungoed Thomas J. in *Selangor v. Craddock (No.3)* [1968] 1 W.L.R. 1555 and in that of Alliott J. at first instance in *Lipkin Gorman v. Karpnale* [1987] 1 W.L.R. 987 followed in this by Steyn J. in *Barclays' Bank v. Quinecare* (1988) [1992] 4 All E.R. 363. *Ulster Factors v. Entoglen* might be another example: Laffoy J. was prepared to impose liability on the basis of actual or constructive knowledge upon "the recipient of *or* the dealer with" misapplied funds: if she did indeed intend by that phrase to distinguish between recipients and accessories, then her statement of principle imposes liability upon both on the basis of the same standard). Since some cases equate the standards of accessory and recipient liability, subsequent cases cite earlier authorities on either standard interchangeably (as in the judgment of Knox J. in *Cowan de Groot v. Eagle Trust* [1992] 4 All E.R. 700, who seems to have inter-mingled the authorities on both species of liability in a recipient liability case). In other cases, the issues of law relating to recipients and accessories are first clearly separated, but then the separate issues are regarded as interchangeable illustrations of a more general standard such as want of probity (as in the judgment of Edmund Davies LJ in *Carl-Zeiss Stiftung v. Herbert Smith (No.2)* [1969] 2 Ch. 276 (CA)) or unconscionability (as in the judgment of Thomas J. in *Powell v. Thompson* [1991] 1 N.Z.L.R. 597). In others, the issues are properly separated and kept separate, but the same standards of liability applied (as in *Baden Delvaux*). And in still yet others, the issues are properly separated and kept separate, and different standards of liability applied (as in *Agip (Africa) v. Jackson* [1990] Ch. 265, 292 *per* Millett J. (the "basis of liability in the two types of case is quite different; there is no reason why the degree of knowledge required should be the same, and good reason why it should not"); *affd* [1991] Ch. 547 (CA)). It is only this last approach which will avoid difficulty. Thus, as Lord Nicholls put it in *Tan*, as between the liability of the accessory and the recipient, "[d]ifferent considerations apply to the two heads of liability"

Once the two types of liability are clearly separated, analysis can proceed as to the most appropriate standards of liability for each. Lord Nicholls in *Tan* conducted that analysis for the liability of the accessory. He also suggested that "recipient liability is restitution-based" ([1995] 2 A.C. 378, 386f; distinguishing it from accessory liability, which is not). The restitutionary basis of the liability of the recipient was also recognised by Edmund Davies L.J. in *Carl-Zeiss Stiftung v. Herbert Smith (No.2)* [1969] 2 Ch. 276, 300h (CA), by Thomas J. in *Powell v. Thompson* [1991] 1 N.Z.L.R. 597, 607, and, following him, by Smellie J. in *Equiticorp v. R* [1996] 3 N.Z.L.R. 586 (summary) at p.604; and by the Supreme Court of Canada in *Gold v. Rosenberg* (1997) 152 C.L.R. (4th) 385, 396 *per* Iacobucci J; *Citadel General Assurance v. Lloyds'*

Bank Canada (1997) 152 C.L.R. (4th) 411, 424-425 *per* La Forest J; on both of these cases, see Smith (1998) 114 *LQR* 394). It may even have been so by Laffoy J. in *Ulster Factors v. Entoglen*, since she characterised the action by the liquidator in seeking to reverse the debit on the company's account with the factor as one by which the factor would be "required, in effect, to make restitution for the *ultra vires* payment" (p.7).

The separation of accessory and recipient liability (and the recognition of the restitutionary nature of the latter) has also been achieved by Budd J. in the High Court in the *Bricklayers' Hall* case, March 6, 1996). Budd J. considered the nature of liability in restitution, held that the plaintiff had a cause of action in restitution, and that the defendant could not raise the defence of *res judicata*. On appeal, Keane J. for the Supreme Court ([1996] 2 I.R. 468; [1996] 2 I.L.R.M. 547) also considered the nature of liability in restitution, but did not consider whether the plaintiff had a cause of action in restitution since he held that the defendant could rely on the defence of *res judicata*. Those aspects of Budd J's judgment which therefore remain undisturbed contain many useful hints as to the possible future evolution of Irish law of restitution. His comments on this issue are just one such hint. In dealing with *Lipkin Gorman* Budd J. explained that the firm whose funds had been gambled at the club by the partner by means of converted cheques claimed both against the club which had received the funds (in an action for money had and received and for knowing receipt) and the bank which had converted the cheque (in knowing assistance). Then he characterised the "action against the club . . . [as] restitutionary in charac-ter; being an action to recover back misdirected funds, and [it] was argued both at common law and in equity. By contrast, the action against the bank was not restitutionary, since it was not an action to recover back misdirected funds" (p.51; *cp.* O'Dell (1993) 15 *DULJ* (*ns*) 27, 44). This is a recognition, as a matter of Irish law, that the action in knowing receipt, the claim in equity against the club, is "restitutionary in character", whereas the action in know-ing assistance is not. The position on this point is therefore the same as that of Lord Nicholls in *Tan*.

If the lead - suggested by Lord Nicholls in *Tan*, by Edmund-Davies LJ in *Carl Zeiss Stiftung*, by Thomas J. in *Powell v. Thompson*, by Smellie J. in *Equiticorp v. R*, by Iacobucci J. in *Gold v. Rosenberg*, by La Forest J. in *Cita-del v. Lloyds*, and by Budd J. in the *Bricklayers' Hall* case, as well as perhaps by Laffoy J. in *Ulster Factors* - is taken, and the liability of the recipient is characterised as restitutionary, the question arises as to whether it is meaning-ful to continue to speak the language of knowledge in this context. If the liability of the recipient is properly to be characterised as restitutionary, then it must fulfill the terms of the four enquiries of the principle against unjust en-richment: whether there was (i) an enrichment to the defendant (ii) at the ex-pense of the plaintiff, (iii) in circumstances in which the law will require restitution (*i.e.* the 'unjust' phase of the enquiry), (iv) where there is no reason why restitution will be withheld.

There is often little difficulty with the first enquiry as to whether the defendant has been enriched: in all of the above cases, it is money which has been misdirected from the plaintiff, which inevitably had the effect of enriching the recipient. On the other hand, Swadling argues that whilst property in a mistaken payment will usually pass confining the mistaken payor to a personal restitutionary claim, where the plaintiff is ignorant of the transfer, "[t]here being no consent whatsoever to the transaction, there is no question of property passing from such a person, with the result that the 'ignorant' payor can still bring claims based on his continuing retention of property rights" (1996] *LMCLQ* 63, 65). But, unless title has passed from the plaintiff to the defendant, "the payor has lost nothing" (*id*) and thus the defendant has not been enriched at his expense (*cp.* Bant [1998] *LMCLQ* 18; *cf.* Grantham and Rickett [1996] *LMCLQ* 465). That raises the question of whether enrichment is confined to circumstances where the defendant has obtained title, or whether it includes circumstances where the defendant might have the use and benefit of it (even if that does not amount to title). The defence of ministerial receipt (below), in denying enrichment, denies it not because the defendant does not have title, but because he does not have use and benefit. Conversely, therefore, if he does have use and benefit, he should be regarded as having being enriched: the defendant is enriched by receipt of the money, not just by ownership.

As to the second enquiry as to whether that enrichment is at the plaintiff's expense, with two party cases, as where the plaintiff is suing a thief directly, there is likewise little difficulty. Similarly with three-party cases where the plaintiff has had the enrichment and it is misdirected to the defendant (as where a fraudster misdirects money from the plaintiff's account to the defendant). However, some of the three-party cases raise the issue of interceptive subtraction discussed above, where the enrichment is *en route* to the plaintiff but is misdirected to the defendant, (as where a fraudster alters the name of the payee on a cheque from that of the plaintiff because that of the defendant). The view expressed above is that it is correct to regard the defendant's enrichment as at the plaintiff's expense. On Smith's sceptical view, the proper plaintiff is the third party payor, not the intended recipient; on Burrows' view, although there is no privity between the plaintiff and the recipient, there is, for him, an exception by which, if the plaintiff actually owns the property received by the defendant from the third party, then the defendant's enrichment is at the plaintiff's expense. However, this might not work in the face of Swadling's argument (in [1996] *LMCLQ* 63) that if the plaintiff continued to own the money, the defendant was not enriched. Nevertheless, the views expressed above were that it is correct to regard the defendant in such circumstances as having been enriched (simply by the receipt of the enrichment) at the plaintiff's expense (by interceptive subtraction from the plaintiff).

Furthermore, where the money has passed down a chain to a remote recipient, to show that the money which the remote recipient received was that which was directly or interceptively subtracted from the plaintiff requires recourse to the rules on the tracing and following of value (see, generally, Smith *The Law of Tracing* (Oxford, 1997)) in so far as they establish that the remote recipient had received value at the expense of the plaintiff. Thus, in *Banque Belge v. Hambrouk* [1921] 1 K.B. 321 (CA), the plaintiff bank had been defrauded by Hambrouk who paid the money on to his mistress; in the Court of Appeal, the bank succeeded in a claim for money had and received against the mistress, and the rules of tracing were invoked to establish that she had received the plaintiff's money. Similarly, in *Lipkin Gorman v. Karpnale*, the plaintiff firm had been defrauded by Cass who paid the gambled the money away at the defendant club; in the House of Lords, the firm succeeded in a claim for money had and received against the club (subject to a partial defence of change of position), and the rules of tracing were invoked to support this claim by establishing that the club had received the firm's money. The plaintiff's claim in this respect was aided by the defendant's seemingly overgenerous concession that any mixing of the plaintiff's money with that of Cass did not bar tracing and prevent the identification of the plaintiff's value in the defendant's hands.

Consequently, if a plaintiff needs to fall back upon the rules of tracing to establish that the remote defendant's receipt was at the plaintiff's expense, and those rules do not allow such an identification to be made, then one aspect of the claim for restitution is not made out. In *Agip v. Jackson*, the plaintiff firm had been defrauded by Zdiri who misdirected some its funds to a puppet company called Baker Oil he had set up to receive them. Millett J. held that the plaintiff's action for money had and received against Baker Oil's bank failed, since the payment could not be followed or traced from Agip though the electronic clearing system to the bank ([1990] Ch. 265, 286 (all that passed was "a stream of electrons"); *affd* [1991] Ch. 547 (CA); criticised on this point in Smith, pp.250-252, and see now Smith "Tracing and Electronic Fund Transfers" in Rose (ed.) *Restitution and Banking Law* (Hart, 1998, forthcoming); the plaintiffs also failed in equity against the bank since they had received as agents for Baker Oil, but succeeded in making the accountants who had assisted Zdiri's fraud liable as accessories). If right, *Agip* is an example of a case where the plaintiff's claim for restitution from the remote recipient failed because the plaintiff could not prove that the remote recipient's enrichment was at the plaintiff's expense.

As to the third enquiry, the analysis here has been that the cases within the traditional rubric of knowing receipt are for the most part examples of ignorance as an unjust factor: an enrichment is unjust if the plaintiff did not consent to the defendant's enrichment, and here, the plaintiff did not so consent because he did not know of (was ignorant of) the enrichment. Of course, in principle, the facts could disclose any unjust factor, and readings of many of the cases have been offered which discern other unjust factors. For example, in *Agip v. Jackson* (above), both Millett J. and the Court of Appeal seemed to treat the plaintiff's claim as based upon the unjust factor of mistake (though McKendrick [1991] *LMCLQ* 378, 381-382 argues that it would have been better to treat it as ignorance). Further, as Birks and Swadling ([1997] *All E.R. Rev* 385, 389) read *Hillsdown Holdings v. Pensions Ombudsman* [1997] 1 All E.R. 862 (esp. at 903 *per* Knox J.) it is an example of duress. Again, the speculation is advanced below that incapacity might have been available as an unjust factor on the facts of *Entoglen* and of the possible recipient liability case of *PMPA v. PMPS and Primor,* High Court, February 20, 1997). Be that as it may. Most of the so-called "knowing receipt" cases are probably examples of ignorance as the unjust factor. The explicit acceptance of these cases as restitutionary may very well supply occasion of the explicit acceptance of the unjust factor of ignorance which best explains them.

As to the fourth enquiry, although in principle the full panoply of defences recognised by the law of restitution is available, *Lipkin Gorman* teaches us that the defences of change of position and *bona fide* purchase for value without notice are appropriate on the facts and often potentially available to the recipient. So also will be the defence of ministerial receipt. As to change of position (which is also discussed in more detail in the Defences section, below), in *Lipkin Gorman,* a partner of a law firm gambled at the Playboy club with money stolen from the firm, and the firm recovered the money from the club in an action for money had and received at common law, subject to the club's defence of change of position, by which their liability for their receipt was discounted by the amount which they had *bona fide* paid out to the gambling partner. It is an open question as a matter of Irish law whether the factor in *Ulster Factors v. Entoglen* who paid the solicitor and then received the payment from the company would have had the defence of change of position. Though the line between those payments out which do not qualify, *e.g. Goss v. Chilcott* [1996] A.C. 788, 799, and those which do (as in *Lipkin Gorman*) is not easy to draw, principle suggests that the defence ought to be so available, but the misconceived decision of Clarke J. in *South Tyneside MBC v. Svenska* [1995] 1 All E.R. 545 suggests that payments out *in advance* do not qualify.

As to *bona fide* purchase, a recipient who *bona fide* gives value for the receipt without notice of the plaintiff's claim will have a complete defence. Hence, in *Polly Peck v. Nadir (No.2)* [1992] 4 All E.R. 769 (CA) at 781-782, Scott L.J. held that a bank receiving sterling and exchanging it for foreign currency receives the sterling for its own use and benefit, but the bank's *bona fide* purchase of the foreign currency without notice of the plaintiff's claim afforded the bank a defence. And those "knowing" receipt cases where the defendant did not have the requisite degree of knowledge (or notice) can be seen as cases where the defendant was *bona fide*. On the other hand, Swadling has argued that there is no general defence of *bona fide* purchase in the law of restitution, since it is confined to the perfection of titles and is thus an aspect of the law of property, so that those "cases in which the defence of *bona fide* purchase was properly applied, in all of which the unjust factor was 'ignorance', are not . . . restitution cases at all; being concerned with the vindication of property rights, they are properly part of the law of property" ("Restitution and *Bona Fide* Purchase" in Swadling (ed.), *The Limits of Restitutionary Claims* (BIICL, 1997) 79at 79; cp. Swadling, "Some Lessons from the Law of Tort" in Birks (ed.), *Frontiers of Liability* (Vol. 1, Oxford, 1994) p.41 at, 46). He therefore argues that the defence of *bona fide* purchase ought not to be available in the law of restitution; and since that defence has been seen as crucial to many ignorance cases, those cases which seems seemed to turn it on must therefore either be property cases (or restitution cases which turn on some other defence such as change of position). On the other hand, the policy underlying the need for a defence of *bona fide* purchase in the law of restitution is that it is necessary for "promoting commercial certainty", as "the need for security in commercial exchange-transactions is currently perceived (rightly or wrongly) to be so important that it will prevail even where the receipt of money under such a transaction has precipitated no unfairness upon the recipient". (Barker, "After Change of Position: Good Faith Exchange in the Modern Law of Restitution" in Birks (ed.), *Laundering and Tracing* (Oxford, 1995) 191 at p.198; cp. Burrows, p.472); and if it is therefore admitted as a general defence in the law of restitution it is not of course confined to ignorance case, but extends to claims based on other unjust factors, such as coercion: see *e.g.* O'Dell ,"Restitution, Coercion by a Third Party, and the Proper Role of Notice" [1997] *CLJ* 71.

As to the defence of ministerial receipt (see the 1995 Review, 203-204), since the liability is based upon receipt, if the defendant did not receive the money "for his own use and benefit", he is not enriched and cannot be liable in restitution. This is the defence of ministerial receipt. And it is "why neither the paying nor the collecting bank can normally be brought within" the terms of the cause of action, since "[i]n paying or collecting money for a customer the bank acts only as his agent" ([1990] Ch. 265 at 292). The banks in such situations act simply as the conduits for the money. Hence, in *Agip v. Jackson* [1990] Ch. 265; *affd* [1991] Ch. 547 (CA) the plaintiff firm had been defrauded by Zdiri who misdirected some its funds to a puppet company called Baker Oil he had set up to receive them. Millett J. held that the plaintiff's action to make Baker Oil's bank liable as a recipient failed, as the bank had not received the money for its own use and benefit, but acted only as agent (see Tan [1991] *LMCLQ* 357; Rickett [1995] *NZLJ* 78; Bryan [1996] *JBL* 165).

However, Millett J. held that "it is otherwise . . . if the collecting bank uses the money to reduce or discharge the customer's overdraft" since, in doing so "it receives the money for its own use and benefit" (*id*); the decision of La Forest J. in the Supreme Court of Canada in *Citadel General Assurance v. Lloyds' Bank Canada* (1997) 152 C.L.R. (4th) 411 at 422-423 is to the same effect. In this respect, it almost amounts to saying that payments out by the agent in anticipation of payments in do not count, so that only payments out subsequent to receipt can attract the defence of ministerial receipt (cp. *South Tyneside MBC v. Svenska* [1995] 1 All E.R. 545 (anticipated payments do not constitute changes of position)). Of course, the bank will often have the benefit of the defence of *bona fide* purchase in such a situation (see *Polly Peck v. Nadir (No.2)* (above)), but the distinction seems suspect. On the one hand, it seems that strictly speaking the bank receives beneficially whenever *any* lodgment is made to an account (Smith (1998) 114 L.Q.R. 394, 397). On the other, if there is room for the argument that it does not take beneficially but as an agent in some situations, then it might have received as agent even where the deposit reduced an overdraft: if I instruct my bank to pay out to a third party an amount which I will later pay them to meet their payment, the position is exactly the same as if I had paid the bank first and then instructed it to pay out. If the bank received as agent in the second case, why does it not in the first ? In the first case, the bank, as agent, had already incurred the liability which the subsequent payment discharged, and the subsequent payment is to its use and benefit only in so far as it had previously incurred the liability as agent. Indeed, in *Ulster Factors v. Entoglen*, since the factor was "merely the medium through which the payment was made" to the firm of solicitors, Laffoy J. held that no basis for restitution had been made out. This comes close to saying that even though the factor had first paid and then received, it was still the conduit through which the money passed. This seems eminently sensible, and it suggests that if the exclusion by Millett and La Forest JJ. of overdrafts from the defence of ministerial receipt is not wrong, it is at least in need of qualification.

To demonstrate that the money out corresponds with the money in may require a tracing identification exercise; in particular to demonstrate that that a prior payment out was in substance the payment on of a subsequent payment in may well require what Scott VC (in *Foskett v. McKeown* [1997] 3 All E.R. 392 at 405) referred to as "backwards tracing" by which the tracer can trace back from a loan paid off into the asset previously purchased with the money lent. That tracing exercise is intended to do no more than to identify as a matter of fact the route the money took, which Laffoy J. was able to do in *Ulster Factors v. Entoglen* simply by observing that the Stg£35,000 paid out became the Ir£37,839.83 debited from the company's account with the plaintiff. If such an identification exercise demonstrates that the bank or factor was no more than the conduit, then they did not receive for their own use and benefit, and the terms of the defence are made out.

The analysis so far has attempted to demonstrate how the principles of equitable liability for "knowing" receipt might be recast in terms of the principle of unjust enrichment as it has been recognised in Ireland (and, it seems in Australia, England and New Zealand as well). It might be said that the principle is descriptive, at least in so far as it simply states the conclusion that the four enquiries have been answered in the plaintiff's favour. Thus, to answer the question whether the enrichment is unjust, Irish law requires that there be an unjust factor, a cause of action in restitution; it is only if there is that it may be said that an enrichment is "unjust". And if it is, liability in restitution is personal. The Canadian approach is different, in at least two ways. First, the Canadian version of the principle (derived from *Pettkus v. Becker* (1980) 117 D.L.R. (3d) 257) is capable of being more prescriptive; in particular, whilst in the Irish version, "unjust" simply states the conclusion that there is an unjust factor on the facts, in the Canadian scheme of things, that notion is much more at large. In consequence, conclusions from Canada on the notion of "unjust" must be treated with caution in jurisdictions not sharing the prescriptive view of the principle. And second, (again deriving from *Pettkus v. Becker* (1980) 117 D.L.R. (3d) 257) liability in restitution is often proprietary by means of a constructive trust. Even though *Gold v. Rosenberg* (1997) 152 C.L.R. (4th) 385 and *Citadel General Assurance v. Lloyds' Bank Canada* (1997) 152 C.L.R. (4th) 411, accept that recipient liability is restitutionary, the manner by which they accommodate such liability within the terms of the Canadian principle against unjust enrichment reflects both of the issues by which that principle differs from its Irish counterpart. Thus, as to the first difference, whilst *Gold* and *Citadel* argue that the reason why from a Canadian perspective such a receipt is unjust is because the defendant was culpable in its receipt (*Citadel v. Lloyds* (1997) 152 C.L.R. (4th) 411 at 434: "lack of enquiry . . . renders the recipient's enrichment unjust") thus making restitutionary liability fault-based, they do so because of the very different emphasis placed upon the role of "unjust" in Canadian law, a role which is not shared by the descriptive principle against unjust enrichment which is the law outside Canada. As to the second, it is not clear whether the liability at issue in *Gold v. Rosenberg* and *Citadel v. Lloyds* was a proprietary constructive trust rather than a personal liability, though the former seems probable from a reading of the judgments. Hence, whilst the Canadian cases may be good authorities for the view that the law can accommodate the recipient's liability within the terms of the principle against unjust enrichment, nevertheless, because they then go on to accommodate it within a prescriptive principle and impose a proprietary liability, they ought not to be treated as good authorities for the manner of its accommodation within the terms of a descriptive principle which contemplates personal liability.

The cause of action in restitution is complete when the four enquiries have been satisfied. Once there has been an unjust enrichment of the defendant at the plaintiff's expense, in the absence of defences, the defendant is liable.

There is no further or other enquiry; in particular, there is no further enquiry as to whether the defendant is at fault in his receipt, or whether he knew of the plaintiff's claim at the time of the receipt. In other words, liability in restitution (where the unjust factor is from the family of consent-related unjust factors, so that the plaintiff's cause of action is based upon the impairment of his consent) is not fault-based, but strict. (See, *e.g.*, Birks (1989) 105 *LQR* 352, 353; Millett (1991) 107 *LQR* 71, 85 (changing his mind from the view which he had expressed in *Agip v. Jackson* [1990] Ch. 265 at first instance); Birks, "Gifts of Other People's Money" in Birks (ed.), *Frontiers of Liability* (Vol. 1, Oxford, 1994) p.31, 34; Swadling "Some Lessons from the Law of Tort in Birks" (ed.), *Frontiers of Liability* (Vol. 1, Oxford, 1994) p.41, 45; Burrows, chapter 4). Furthermore, as with contract and tort, liability in restitution is personal, in the sense that it is a liability to pay an amount of money (rather than a duty to transfer specific property). For example, in *Agip v. Jackson* [1990] Ch. 265, 282 Millett J. held that the cause of action in restitution is personal, and complete when the money is received. This is what Lynch J. meant in *In re PMPA Insurance Co Ltd* [1986] I.L.R.M. 524 when he held that the action in restitution to recover money paid under mistake (and, by implication the action to recover money paid in ignorance) ranked as a personal "simple contract debt" rather than as a proprietary constructive trust. The point that restitutionary liability is, in the first instance, both personal and strict was summed up as follows by Lord Goff in *Lipkin Gorman v. Karpnale* in the House of Lords:

> "the action for money had and received is not usually founded upon any wrong of the [defendant] . . . It is founded simply on the fact that, as Lord Mansfield C.J. said, the [defendant] cannot in conscience retain the money – or as we say nowadays, for the [defendant] to retain the money would result in his unjust enrichment at the expense of the [plaintiff] . . . [the] claim for money had and received is nevertheless a personal claim, it is not a proprietary claim . . ." ([1991] 2 A.C. 548, 572).

Hence, if the liability of the stranger receiving trust property is to be understood as restitutionary, it must be understood as personal and strict. In which case, it would not be meaningful from the perspective of the cause of action to enquire into the plaintiff's knowledge. However, that is not to say that such language is entirely irrelevant, since the defendant's knowledge would be relevant on the issue of defences: it would determine whether he was *bona fide* for the purposes of the defences of change of position and *bona fide* purchase; and it would determine whether he had notice or not for the purposes of that latter defence.

On the other hand, Chancery lawyers, even where they accept the characterisation of the liability as restitutionary (*e.g.* Harpum, "Basis" pp.10 at 17 *et seq.*) can point to the force of precedent in favour of some level of knowledge for liability (Burrows (1990) 106 *LQR* 20, 23-24; Harpum, "Basis" pp.19-21, though cf. 24) even if the courts have divided over what that level of knowledge should be and "have not evinced much enthusiasm for resolving the matter one way or the other" (Harpum, "Basis" p.19).

It would therefore seem that the position advocated from a restitutionary perspective and that described from an orthodox chancery perspective are irreconcilable. Appearances may be deceptive, for at least four reasons. First, it might be said that the principle against unjust enrichment simply rearranges the order of the enquiries, so that the traditional primary focus on knowledge is displaced in favour of an analysis of whether there was an enrichment (receipt for own use and benefit) which was unjust (not consented to, due to ignorance, mistake, and so on), and received by the defendant at the expense of the plaintiff (direct or interceptive subtraction, possible demonstrated by tracing), but in which the question of knowledge becomes relevant to the potential defences of change of position and *bona fide* purchase. The order of the enquiries might change, as might the language, but the substance is not radically altered.

Second, at least as a matter of Irish law, the older authorities are ambiguous as to whether there is in fact a knowledge requirement, and in recent authorities, it has often been so diluted that the cases almost read as examples of strict liability. Thus in *O'Hehir v. Cahill* , Gibson J. held that "[s]*cienter* is not necessary, but it exists here and makes the case stronger" ((1912) 97 I.L.T.R. 274 at 276). This clearly envisages the scope of liability extending beyond "*scienter*", but much turns on what Gibson J. meant by that word. There are at least three possibilities. First, if "*scienter*" means knowledge confined to the first three points on the *Baden* scale, then extending liability beyond that at least includes the remaining two points. Second, if, however, "*scienter*" means knowledge on all five points on the *Baden* scale, then extending liability beyond that at least includes notice properly so called. And, third, if "*scienter*" were to encompass both knowledge (widely defined) and notice, extending liability beyond that might even reach strict liability. Though none can be ruled out, the second possibility is the most likely from the context of the judgment. The leading recent authority is *In re Frederick Inns* [1994] 1 I.L.R.M. 387 (SC) where Blayney J. held that the Revenue Commissioners had received funds "with constructive knowledge" (399) of the fact that they were being paid *ultra vires* and in breach of directors' duties, since they could have consulted the relevant memoranda of association. First, if, as was argued above, the relevant breach of fiduciary duty is not in the fact that the payment was *ultra vires*, but in the fact that it was made in breach of the directors' fiduciary duties to the company's creditors, then knowledge of the memoranda is beside the point, and the real question ought to have been whether the Revenue Commissioners had such knowledge of the companies' insolvency and thus of the directors' duties to the creditors (and on this point, Blayney J. had earlier held that at "the time the payments were made, all four companies were insolvent and were known by the Revenue Commissioners to be insolvent" ([1994] 1 I.L.R.M. 387, 395)). Second, "constructive knowledge" of the memoranda was held to be sufficient knowledge to render the Revenue liable. This was followed by Laffoy J. in *Ulster Factors v. Entoglen*. Knowledge on the *Baden* scale is primarily concerned with failures to *infer*; whereas what was at issue in *Frederick Inns* was a failure to *enquire*. Notice properly so called is concerned with such failures to enquire, and it is more accurate to say that such documents of public record confer "constructive *notice*" rather than "constructive knowledge" (cp. Forde, *Company Law* (Round Hall Sweet & Maxwell, Dublin, 1992) p.76). Hence, Blayney J.'s application of the *Belmont* principle would seem to go further than even the fifth point on the *Baden* scale and reach failures to enquire. Hence, even if the *Baden* scale does not reach notice properly so called, *Frederick Inns* certainly seems to (cp. Delany, ". . . the approach adopted by the Supreme Court . . . was effectively to accept that constructive notice suffices . . ." (p.200)). This makes the traditional 'knowledge' requirement very easy to satisfy; it is tantamount to emptying it of all content, and comes close to the imposition of strict liability. On this view, the express adoption of a restitutionary analysis would not work a large change in the law, and indeed, the concomitant recognition of defences would mitigate any perceived harshness of the move.

Third, Birks has long maintained that *Re Diplock* illustrates that equity does contemplate imposing personal liability upon recipients strictly because of their receipts, in so far as the personal representatives of the testator had distributed the deceased's estate to beneficiaries in accordance with an invalid bequest, and the beneficiaries had to make personal restitution to the next of kind who became entitled upon the failure of that gift (this is a point he has made in all of his articles cited in this section; see *e.g.* "Gifts of Other People's Money" in Birks (ed.), *Frontiers of Liability* (Vol. 1, Oxford, 1994) p.31 at 33-34, and most recently [1997] N.Z.L.R. 623 at 651-653; *cp.* Burrows, pp.156 -158; *cf.* Harpum, "Basis" pp.22-24). Furthermore, the judgment of Thomas J. in *Powell v. Thompson* [1991] 1 N.Z.L.R. 597 at 608 demonstrates that a strict liability standard is capable of being accommodated within traditional equitable principles: he "would not preclude the possibility that in certain circumstances a Court of Equity could be persuaded to examine the equities of competing claims . . . Because liability in this class of case stems from [unjust enrichment] . . . and not any particular conduct or misconduct . . . knowledge may not be necessary".

Fourth, recall that the traditional descriptions of the liabilities of strangers distinguished between a personal liability to make good the pecuniary loss suffered by the trust, and a proprietary liability to return to the trust the very property *in specie* which it has lost. It is the difference between a personal liability to account to the beneficiaries for receipts and a proprietary liability to hold the property on trust for the beneficiaries. The principles being developed under the influence of the law of restitution are what give content to the personal liability to account. The traditional equitable principles based upon the recipient's knowledge might with profit be deployed to give content to the proprietary liability to hold the property on constructive trust. There are traces of this in the cases, and since the defendant is to be fixed with a high degree of liability (proprietary liability) it may be appropriate to require a high degree of fault (such as the *Tan* standard of dishonesty, or the first the three elements on the *Baden* scale if it is to be retained; compare the position of Lord Browne-Wilkinson in the House of Lords in *Westdeutsche Landesbanke Girozentrale v. Islington LBC* [1996] A.C. 669 (HL) that a constructive trust would require that the recipient be aware of the facts which constitute him a constructive trustee). Hence, insofar as the Supreme Court of Canada in *Gold v. Rosenberg* (1997) 152 C.L.R. (4th) 385 and *Citadel v. Lloyds* (1997) 152 C.L.R. (4th) 411 has recently seemed to treat the liability of the recipient as properly holding the receipt on constructive trust, it is appropriate that such proprietory liability was imposed on the basis of fault (constructive knowledge). If it is accepted that, if the various tests are satisfied, a recipient can come under either a personal or a proprietary liability, the description of constructive trust adds nothing to the personal liability but is precisely descriptive of the propri-etary liability; (perhaps the phrase "constructive trust" ought therefore to be avoided in the context of the recipient's personal liability and confined the context of the recipient's proprietary liability ?)

All of this is entirely speculative. Academic discourse has raced well ahead of the caselaw, and might well be exploring routes which as the law develops may not even open up. Nevertheless, the speech of Lord Nicholls in *Tan* clearly owed much to the academic literature (a debt acknowledged in the wealth of academic citation in the speech). Writing extra-judicially, he has recently called for a clarification of the principles underlying the liability of the recipient ("Knowing Receipt: The need for a new Landmark" in Cornish, *et al* (eds.), *Restitution. Past, Present and Future* (Hart, 1998, forthcoming)) and proposed both a strict personal restitutionary equitable liability to account for receipts, and a parallel personal liability to compensate the trust for losses sustained. (On the latter point, two matters must be considered, first the extent to which equity can properly be said to be able to award such compensation (see *e.g.* O'Dell, "When Two Tribes Go To War: Privacy Interests and Media Speech" in McGonagle (ed.) *Essays on Law and Media* (Round Hall, Sweet & Maxwell, Dublin, 1997) p.181 at 216-218, nn.215-228 considering equitable damages both in general and in the specific context of breach of confidence), and second, the extent to which such a liability to compensate is no more than an element of the liability of the accessory considered in *Tan*, in that the recipient has by his receipt aided in the breach and is therefore an accessory). Resolution of these issues, and all of the other issues canvassed here, must, however, await Lord Nicholl's hoped-for landmark. It ought to establish the liability of the recipient as restitutionary. Whether it does or not, if it is as logical, clear, coherent and compelling as his speech in *Tan*, it cannot come quickly enough.

Incapacity   The unjust factors of the family which contains ignorance, mistake, duress and failure of basis are united by the idea that the plaintiff did not intend the defendant to have the enrichment. By the ordinary processes of legal reasoning, if there are other categories in which it can also be said that the plaintiff likewise did not so intend, it becomes difficult to resist the conclusion that any such unintentional transfer should also be characterised as unjust and trigger restitution. The discussion above has focussed on the admissibility of ignorance as a member of that family. Some of this year's cases raise the possibility of incapacity as another member of that family. Where a party suffers an incapacity, a disability as a matter of law, for example, where a company acts *ultra vires*, or where a person is below the age of majority, or is suffering from a mental incapacity or intoxication, such a party has no capacity to contract (see, *e.g.*, *Treitel*, chapter 13): as a matter of law, such a party cannot consent to the relevant transaction. A mistaken plaintiff claims restitution on the basis that the mistake meant that he did not properly consent to the defendant's enrichment; a plaintiff unaware of (ignorant of) the defendant's enrichment claims restitution on the basis that he did not consent to the defendant's enrichment because he did not know (was unaware or ignorant) of it; similarly, the plaintiff suffering an incapacity makes a bid for restitution based upon the argument that he could not have consented at all to the defendant's enrichment. The pattern of such plaintiffs' claims is thus: I did not consent because I was mistaken; I did not consent because I was unaware/ignorant; I could not consent because I was an incapax. Thus, logic dictates the admission of incapacity to the family of unjust factors based upon the impairment of consent, since such incapacity – where law provides that the plaintiff could not consent - constitutes the ultimate impairment of consent.

Hence, incapacity is justified by the terms of the principle against unjust enrichment. It is also justified as a matter of precedent. For example, the High Court of Australia has held that if the Commonwealth, pursuant to an *ultra vires* contract, had made a payment, the fact that the Commonwealth "exceeded the limits of its constitutional powers . . . [or] capacity . . . that would have been considered a reason for paying it back . . ." (*In re KL Tractors* (1961) 106 C.L.R. 334-335 *per* Dixon C.J., McTiernan and Kitto JJ.). To like effect is the decision of the Supreme Court of Canada in *Breckenridge Speedway v. The Queen in Right of Alberta* (1967) 64 D.L.R. (2d) 480 (Alb); (1970) 9 D.L.R. (3d) 142 (SCC) reaffirmed in *Communities Economic Development Fund v. Canadian Pickles Corpn* (1992) 85 D.L.R. (4th) 88 (SCC). Furthermore, it has been expressly held that a company can have restitution of an *ultra vires* gift: in *International Sales v. Marcus* [1982] 3 All E.R. 551, Lawson J. held that the defendants held the gift on trust but would have reached "the same conclusion if the plaintiffs' claims were based solely on the defendants' receipt . . . of the moneys paid *ultra vires*" ([1982] 3 All E.R. 551, 560). Similar sentiments were expressed in Ireland by Lardner J. in the High Court in *In re Frederick Inns* [1991] I.L.R.M. 583, (though varied by the Supreme Court in [1994] 1 I.L.R.M. 387, which did not consider this particular issue): according to Lardner J., the effect of payments made to the Revenue *ultra vires* the paying company was "unjustly to enrich . . . the Revenue Commissioners who received the payments". As a consequence, "an action for money had and received [lay] against the Revenue Commissioners . . . [who] have become improperly enriched" ([1991] I.L.R.M. 583 at 591 and 593).

There are also many cases where restitution on the basis of the incapacity has been assumed, and the remedies granted are predicated upon it. In *O'Hehir v. Cahill* (1912) 97 I.L.T.R. 274, the liquidator of one society recovered a loan made *ultra vires* to another; Dodd J. at first instance holding that the recipients were liable both in equity (on a constructive trust similar to that discussed above) and at law "on the common indebitatus count for money had and received by the defendants to the use of the plaintiffs. . . ." ((1912) 97 I.L.T.R. 274, 276). In this he was affirmed on appeal. Similarly, in *In re Irish Provident Assurance Co* [1913] 1 I.R. 352 (CA Ir.) the Court of Appeal assumed the availability of restitution of payments made *ultra vires,* and predicated restitution to the company of payments made *ultra vires* the assurance company upon counter-restitution by the company of benefits it had received in exchange. And in the important decision of Murphy J. in *In re PMPA Garage (Longmile) Ltd (No.2)* [1992] 1 I.R. 332; [1992] I.L.R.M. 337, one of the cases arising out of the collapse of the PMPA group of companies, he held that the guarantors of a loan *ultra vires* the payor were estopped from denying the validity of the guarantee, and in the course of his analysis he confirmed that the lender was entitled to restitution of the *ultra vires* loan. (See, generally, O'Dell "Estoppel and *Ultra Vires* Contracts" (1992) 14 *DULJ* (*ns*) 123). In this regard, he was guided by the decisions in *KL Tractors* and *Breckenridge*, and this right to restitution was conceded in subsequent cases in the same litigation (see *e.g. PMPA v. PMPS,* High Court, June, 27 1994, Murphy J.).

So much for the cases of companies acting *ultra vires*. There are similar lines of authority stating or assuming such a right to restitution in the contexts of minority (see, *e.g. Pearse v. Brain* [1929] 2 K.B. 310, 314 *per* Swift J. and the Canadian cases discussed Percy (1975) 53 *Can Bar Rev* 1, 22-26, 32-34; McCamus (1979) *UNBLJ* 89, 99-104) and mental incapacity (*McLaughlin v. Daily Telegraph* (1903-04) 1 C.L.R. 243 (HCA) affd [1904] A.C. 776 (PC); *Wilson v. R* [1938] 3 D.L.R. 433 (SCC); *Scott v. Wise* [1986] 2 N.Z.L.R. 484 (NZ CA)).

The essence of these authorities is summed up in an old Canadian case: in

Goodfellow v. Robertson (1871) 18 Gr. 572, Robertson claimed that he had
paid $1,200 to the testator whilst suffering from a mental disability, and in his
action to recover the money from the testator's estate, Spragge C concluded
that

> If Robertson was at that time a lunatic, he *could not have assented* to the
> advance and application of the money, and so the testator had in his
> hands $1,200 of the moneys of the lunatic ... [and is under] a liability to
> account for it, and that money is still due from his estate. ... If this be a
> correct view, Robertson is a creditor of the testator's estate for the amount
> in question, being for so much money received for his use ... ((1871) 18
> Gr. 572, 576 emphasis added).

It is time to recognise the essential unity of these and similar cases, constituting a strong body of authority embodying the right to restitution for incapacity. (An extended argument to that effect, considering the above authorities
and many others in detail, and concluding that principle, precedent and policy
favour such an unjust factor, is to be found in O'Dell, "*Swaps* and the Reason
for Restitution. A *Coda* Upon Incapacity" in Birks (ed.), *Implications of the
Swaps Litigation* (Mansfield, 1998/1999 forthcoming)).

At least four of this year's cases can be seen as embodying this unjust
factor. It was suggested above that there are traces of it in the High Court
judgment in *In re Frederick Inns*. Similarly, if an unjust factor is to be discerned on the facts of *Ulster Factors v. Entoglen* (above) and if ignorance is
unavailable (either because it is simply not properly made out on the facts, or
because the contrary arguments have prevailed) then the fact that the payments were *ultra vires* itself states the unjust factor of incapacity. It was also
observed above that in the litigation arising out of the collapse of the PMPA
group of companies, the right of *ultra vires* payors to restitution of such payments was established in *In re PMPA Garage (Longmile) Ltd (No.2)*, and has
been conceded in subsequent cases. That concession figured in the decision
of Costello P. in this year's *PMPA v. PMPS and Primor,* High Court, February
20, 1997).

A motor insurance company, a provident society and a protection association were members of the PMPA Group of companies. Under a scheme operated by the group from early 1976 to mid 1978, motorists could get loans from
the provident society for 75% of their annual insurance premia, which the
society would pay directly to the insurance company. The motorist would then
repay the loan to the society. Many such loans remained unpaid. So, in 1979
and 1980, the society assigned those debts to the association, for which it paid
the society a total of £450,000. In late 1983, the Group collapsed. In 1992, the
association commenced proceedings against the society seeking restitution of
the £450,000 as having been paid *ultra vires*. In June 1994, the society con-

sented to judgment in favour of the association. Given that the association had paid the £450,000 *ultra vires*, that incapacity was the unjust factor - the basis of the association's cause of action in restitution against the society which had received the money. Nevertheless, *quaere* whether such a claim was statute barred by a six year limitation period ? (Section 11(1)(b) of the Statute of Limitations, 1957 provides a six-year limitation period for claims in "quasi-contract", that is to personal claims to restitution at common law, and it also applies by analogy to personal claims to restitution in equity (cp. *Westdeutsche Landesbank Girozentrale v. Islington LBC* [1994] 4 All E.R. 890, 943) not least because the personal equitable liability of the recipient is properly described as a liability to account, for which s11(4) of the Statute of Limitations, 1957 also prescribes a six-year limitation period).

However, the society, having had to repay to the association, sought an indemnity from the insurance company. The society argued, first, that *it* too had acted *ultra vires* in the *making* of the loans in the first place so that the sums advanced to the motorists and paid to the insurance company on their behalf "remained the property" (p.9) of the society; and, second, that the directors of the insurance company knew that the loans were *ultra vires* and so held them on trust for the society. Hence, during the action by the association against the society, the society joined the insurance company (in July 1993) as a third party in those proceedings. When the society consented to judgment in favour of the association, the society commenced proceedings directly against the insurance company (first in June 1994, and again in August 1995 when the 1994 proceedings were discontinued). In May 1996 the insurance company sought to have the society's claims against them dismissed on the grounds of delay.

Costello P., applying *Primor v. Stokes Kennedy Crowley,* Supreme Court, December 19, 1995; see the 1995 Review, 401), dismissed the society's claims against the insurance company on the grounds of delay in instituting the proceedings. The society's claims as pleaded were based on the knowledge of the directors in 1976, two of whom (including the central figure in devising the scheme) were dead, and three of whom were very elderly and ill (on this aspect of the case, see the Practice and Procedure chapter, below, 581–3). The delay caused the detriment of the unavailability of these directors' evidence to controvert the plaintiff's assertions: Costello P. could not "agree that a fair trial could now be held. It seems to me that the delay has deprived the Insurance Company of the opportunity of obtaining the attendance of witnesses whose evidence would certainly be admissible and perhaps decisive for determining the issues in the case. . . . The issues that arise in the present cases could only be properly be determined by evidence relating to the entire transaction and in particular to the evidence of the persons involved in the 'scheme'" (pp.25–26).

For Costello P., the principles of a direct action in restitution between an *ultra vires* lender and a borrower were settled in *In re PMPA Garage (Longmile) (No.2)* (above); but in the three-party case where the lender seeks to recover not from the borrower but from a third party recipient, "different considerations may well apply when considering whether or not it would be unconscionable or inequitable to allow the Insurance Company to retain the money they received than in a case where a lender claims the return of monies lent to a borrower" (pp.25-26), and such different considerations would require the now substantially unavailable evidence of the persons in the group involved in the scheme. It was argued above that where a company pays money *ultra vires*, the unjust factor of incapacity states the basis of a cause of action in restitution to recover the *ultra vires* payment, and that the restitution action recognised in *In re PMPA Garage (Longmile) (No.2)* is an example of that unjust factor. Similarly, Costello P.'s adoption of *In re PMPA Garage (Longmile) (No.2)* means that *PMPA v. PMPS and Primor* ought to be understood as another example of that unjust factor. Certainly, it is easy to understand how the action in restitution can apply in the two-party case where the payor is the plaintiff and the recipient is the defendant. However, Costello P. distinguished between this straightforward two-party case, and a three-party scenario to which he felt "different considerations may well apply". But he gave no indication as to precisely what such "different considerations" in the three-party scenario might be. In an application to dismiss for delay, it may not be necessary to define precisely what the contours of the relevant cause of action might be, but their broad outline must be understood, so that the matters on which evidence must be led might be appreciated. Hence, in *Primor v. Stokes Kennedy Crowley*, the leading case on dismissal for delay, O'Flaherty J. considered the terms of the cause of action in negligence to determine what the plaintiffs would have to prove and what the defendants would necessarily have to dispute so as to understand precisely the detriment which the delay would have caused. Similarly, here, Costello P. ought to have defined the "different considerations" with rather greater particularity so that it would be clear what the plaintiffs would have to prove and what the defendants would necessarily have to dispute so as to understand precisely the detriment which the delay would have caused.

For example, in a two-party case of direct enrichment, where the plaintiff claims restitution on the basis of the defendant's unjust enrichment at his expense, the cause of action is complete when the plaintiff demonstrates an unjust factor and an enrichment of the defendant at the plaintiff's expense, and it would then be for the defendant to plead any defences which might be open to it. Indeed, on the facts before Costello P., he was not dealing with money paid by the society to borrowers who then paid it to the insurance company, but with money paid by the society directly to the insurance company (albeit at the direction of the borrowers), which seems to be a straightforward two-party case of direct enrichment. In which case, the society can demonstrate an unjust factor (incapacity arising from *ultra vires*) and an enrichment of the insurance company (here, the receipt of the £450,000) at the its expense, and it would then be for the defendant insurance company to plead any defences which might be open to it. If so, there was substance in the society's argument that the evidence of the directors was unnecessary (and hence there was no prejudice to the insurance company arising from the delay) since if the society could have established that the loans were *ultra vires* they were *prima facie* recoverable. It would then have been for the insurance company to plead defences and to demonstrate that the knowledge of the directors was relevant to the pleaded defences. That may have been the case, in that the insurance company might have been able to argue that since it had given value to the motorists on foot of the insurance policies without notice of the society's claim in return for the receipt of the money, it had the benefit of the defence of *bona fide* purchase for value without notice; plainly, the knowledge of the directors would have been relevant to the question of the insurance company's *bona fides* and notice of the plaintiff's *ultra vires*. But even here, the fact that the statutes and other constituent documents of the society were documents of public record might mean that the insurance company could be fixed with notice of the society's lack of *vires* (*Northern Bank Finance v. Quinn and Achates* [1979] I.L.R.M. 221; *In re Frederick Inns* [1994] 1 I.L.R.M. 387 (SC)) in which case the defence would not be available, and the knowledge of the directors would again be irrelevant.

If, contrary to the position in the previous paragraph, the payment by the society directly to the insurance company, at the direction of the borrowers, is not a straightforward two-party case of direct enrichment, but is instead a three-party scenario, the question then arises as to whether in fact "different considerations" do apply, as Costello P. held without further elaboration. More particularly, the question arises as to whether the directors' knowledge was relevant to such "different considerations". This can be tested by reference to the plaintiff's pleadings. The society argued, first, that the *ultra vires* payments to the insurance company "remained [its] property". As in *Lipkin Gorman v. Karpnale* [1991] 2 A.C. 548, the plaintiffs might have been content to vindicate that property right by means of the personal action for money had and received (in much the same way as the plaintiff whose property has been converted vindicates his property right in the converted property by means of the personal tort action for conversion). If that is so, since *Lipkin Gorman* (above) indicates that liability in such an action is personal and strict and founded upon the principle against unjust enrichment, the question arises as to whether the four enquiries of the principle are fulfilled: whether there was (i) an enrichment to the defendant, (ii) at the expense of the plaintiff, (iii) which was 'unjust', (iv) where there are no defences. Answering the enquiries, it seems that (i) the £450,000 was the enrichment received by the defendants; (ii) it was paid by the plaintiff to the defendant so that the enrichment was by direct subtraction from the plaintiff and thus was at the plaintiff's expense (and no question of tracing the route of the value to identify this receipt seems to arise here as it often does in other three party situations); (iii) *Lipkin Gorman* suggests that the retention of the plaintiff's property by the defendant is a sufficient unjust factor; and (iv) no defences seem open; in particular, the analysis above suggests that the defendant's constructive notice of the plaintiff's incapacity forecloses the defence of *bona fide* purchase for value without notice. In other words, in an action for money had and received to vindicate any property right the plaintiff might have had to the money, no "different considerations" arise; in particular, none based upon the directors' knowledge arises.

Though it would have been a matter for the trial if the claim had not been dismissed, the question arises as to whether in fact the retention of the plaintiff's property by the defendant without the plaintiff's consent is a sufficient unjust factor (see, generally, Burrows chapter 13). For example, recall Swadling's argument ([1996] *LMCLQ* 63, discussed above) that if the plaintiff continued to own the money, the defendant was not enriched, though it was suggested above that it is correct to regard the defendant in such circumstances as having been enriched. More fundamentally, the mere fact that the payment of the money was *ultra vires* would not have prevented the property from passing (*e.g.* Swadling (1996) 16 *Leg Stud* 133; *Westdeutsche Landesbanke Girozentrale v. Islington LBC* [1996] A.C. 669 (HL)), and if property had passed, then the unjust factor would not have been made out, and the basis of the action would have fallen away. Furthermore, it has been doubted whether the House of Lords were correct to regard the unjust factor in *Lipkin Gorman* as based upon the retention by the defendant of the plaintiff's property. For example McKendrick (1992) 55 *MLR* 377 argues that the retention by the defendant of the plaintiff's property does not state a consent-related unjust factor, whereas ignorance does; so that the unjust factor ought to have been regarded as ignorance. On the other hand, Virgo ((1996) 10 *TLI* 20) argues that a restitutionary response can indeed be triggered to vindicate the plaintiff's proprietary interest, and that argument may be taken one step further: the family of consent-related unjust factors includes incapacity, ignorance, mistake, duress, and failure of consideration. In the context of failure of consideration, consent is said to be qualified (see the 1996 Review, 515-516, 518); in the context of mistake and duress, consent is said to be vitiated (*ibid.*); in the context of incapacity and ignorance, where the plaintiff (respectively) could not consent or did not know, it might be said that the consent of the plaintiff is absent. Hence, absence, vitiation and qualification of consent are the three types of impairment of consent which trigger restitution (see, *e.g.* Birks and Chambers *Restitution Research Resource* (2nd ed., Mansfield Press, 1997) p.2). Where the defendant has retained the plaintiff's property without his consent, it might be regarded as a strong form of absence of consent. If that is so, then the unjust factor in *Lipkin Gorman* does relate to the impairment of the plaintiff's consent, and does constitute an unjust factor in the consent-related family of unjust factors. Hence, *pace* Virgo, *Lipkin Gorman*, even on a "vindication of property" reading, remains a case of restitution for unjust enrichment. (Though the unjust factor stated in *Lipkin Gorman* might thus be accommodated, it is still an open question as to whether it or ignorance would have been a more appropriate unjust factor on the facts of the case itself).

If any of these objections were to prove fatal, and the defendant insurance company's retention of money which was the property of the plaintiff society is not understood to state an unjust factor, a replacement is to hand in incapacity. Since the payments were *ultra vires* the society, that incapacity states a consent-related unjust factor, and as the analysis above has demonstrated that other three enquiries required by the principle against unjust enrichment seem to come down in favour of the plaintiff, the society would seem to have had a complete cause of action in restitution against the insurance company. It would then have been an open question as to the extent to which a claim based on the incapacity would properly have been open on the pleading that the payments "remained the property" of the society. If it had been, or if the *Lipkin Gorman* unjust factor were made out, then liability in such an action would have been founded upon the principle against unjust enrichment and thus personal and strict. In substance, this is exactly the action in *In re PMPA Garage (Longmile) (No.2)* the correctness of which Costello P. acknowledged. Hence, there was no difference between that and the action before him, and no "different considerations" seem to arise.

Such "different considerations", based upon the directors' knowledge, seem however to arise out of the society's alternative pleading that the insurance company *knew* that the loans were *ultra vires* and thus held them on trust. This pleading probably amounts to an allegation of "knowing receipt" by the insurance company. The discussion of this topic above in the context of the unjust factor of ignorance, *inter alia*, (i) observed the traditional debate about what constitutes sufficient knowledge; (ii) distinguished between the recipient's personal liability to account and proprietary liability to hold the property on trust; and (iii) argued that the principles being developed under the influence of the law of restitution are what ought to give content to the personal liability to account, whilst the traditional equitable principles based upon the recipient's knowledge might with profit be deployed to give content to the proprietary liability to hold the property on constructive trust.

If the plaintiff's pleading was directed to the former personal liability, then it reflected the traditional view that such liability is predicated upon the defendant's knowledge. Nevertheless, if the liability to account as a constructive trustee for knowing receipt does come to be seen as a personal restitutionary liability, then the analysis ought to proceed on the basis of the four enquiries of the principle against unjust enrichment, and, if there are no defences, the

liability is strict and personal. Hence, the knowledge of the defendant's directors is irrelevant to the plaintiff's claim, and, whilst it might have been relevant to the defence of *bona fide* purchase for value without notice, the analysis
above suggests that the defendant's constructive notice of the plaintiff's incapacity forecloses it on the facts. Furthermore, as to the other three elements of
the plaintiff's unjust enrichment claim, the £450,000 was the enrichment received by the defendants; it was paid by the plaintiff to the defendant so that
the enrichment was by direct subtraction from the plaintiff and thus was at the
plaintiff's expense (no question of tracing the route of the value to identify
this receipt seems to arise here as it often does in other three party situations);
and the incapacity arising from the *ultra vires* nature of the payment provided
the unjust factor. In other words, on the personal claim, no "different considerations" arise if pleading that the insurance company knew that the loans
were *ultra vires* and thus held them on trust is no more than an allegation
"knowing receipt" against the insurance company and that in turn is no more
than a personal equitable liability to make restitution.

If, on the other hand, the plaintiff's pleading was directed to the latter
proprietary liability, then the knowledge of the defendants might properly have
been in issue, and it was the detriment arising from the unavailability of the
directors' evidence as to their knowledge which led Costello P. to dismiss the
plaintiff's claim on the grounds of delay. As to how knowledge might be relevant to that claim, it was suggested above that the *Tan* standard of dishonesty
was the appropriate basis for such liability, and Lord Nicholls explained that
"the standard of what constitutes honest conduct is not subjective. Honesty is
not an optional scale, with higher or lower values according to the moral standards of each individual. . . . Honest people do not intentionally deceive others
to their detriment. Honest people do not knowingly take other people's property. Unless there is a very good and compelling reason, an honest person
does not participate in a transaction if he knows it involves a misapplication of
trust assets to the detriment of the beneficiaries. Nor does an honest person in
such a case deliberately close his eyes and ears, or deliberately not ask questions, lest he learn something he would rather not know, and then proceed
regardless" ([1995] 2 A.C. 378, 389). In any event, if the unavailability of the
directors' evidence as to their knowledge prejudiced the defendants' case,
their unavailability would be likewise prejudicial where what could have been
in issue was not so much their knowledge as their honesty. Furthermore, if the
plaintiff's first pleading that the *ultra vires* payments to the insurance company "remained [its] property" in equity, that would have been a claim that
whilst property in the money might have passed at law, the insurance company held it upon trust for the society. As the speech of Lord Browne-Wilkinson
in the House of Lords in *Westdeutsche Landesbanke Girozentrale v. Islington
LBC* [1996] A.C. 669 (HL) demonstrates (if it is correct), no resulting trust
arises in such circumstances from a retention or separation of title, and a con-

structive trust would require that the recipient be aware of the facts which constitute him a constructive trustee. This is in substance exactly the same enquiry as that already suggested as appropriate to make the recipient proprietarily liable. And since it is predicated upon the recipient's awareness of the facts, the prejudice which Costello P. derived from the unavailability of the directors' evidence still arises.

In summary, Costello P. identified the prejudice caused by the delay as the unavailability of the evidence of the directors as to what they knew at the time of the relevant transactions. To the extent that the plaintiff's statement of claim properly disclosed issues of proprietary liability to which that knowledge was relevant, then that prejudice arose. However, it is more than arguable that the plaintiff's statement of claim in substance pleaded the personal restitutionary liability of the defendants – we have seen that all of the personal claims ultimately reduced to the question whether the terms of the principle against unjust enrichment were fulfilled – and since such liability is in effect strict, it is a matter to which the knowledge of the defendants is irrelevant. If that is so, then the prejudice identified by Costello P. does not seem to arise. (However, what is afforded to the plaintiff by the fact that the defendants could not be said to have suffered prejudice in meeting the personal claims, might be taken away again by the fact that the personal claims attract a limitation period of six years (see the discussion of section 11(1)(b) of the Statute of Limitations 1957 above), so that the claims would be barred not by delay but by limitation).

Finally, it is for the plaintiff to plead and prove its case. It seems that Costello P. regarded the plaintiff's claims as based upon the knowledge of the defendants' directors; and if the absence of these directors prevents the plaintiff from establishing a factual basis for its claims, it seems that as a matter of logic that it would be the plaintiff – rather than the defendants – who could potentially be prejudiced. In other words, it seems that what the defendants proposed – and Costello P. accepted – as a vice to them was in fact a virtue. Of course, the defendants' allegation would have substance if the directors' knowledge was relevant to a defence, as it might be to that of change of position, or *bona fide* purchase (though the analysis above suggests that the defendants would have had constructive notice of the plaintiff's incapacity, thus precluding the defence).

On the same day that Costello P. handed down his judgment in *PMPS v. PMPA and Primor*, the Supreme Court handed down their decision on an appeal from another decision of Costello P. in another long running saga. In *In re Greendale Developments,* Supreme Court, February 20, 1997, Keane J. (Blayney and Murphy JJ. concurring) delivered the third of this year's judgments which raised issues relating to incapacity. The appellant had caused the company to make gratuitous payments to him or to third parties on his behalf, and the company sought restitution of the payments. Costello P. had given judgment in favour of the company, and the appellant appealed. Keane J. held that the payments were *ultra vires* and recoverable by means of the procedure prescribed in section 298(2) of the Companies Act 1963 as substituted by section 142 of the Companies Act 1990. However, it is important to notice that section 298(2) does not create a substantive cause of action, it is merely the procedural vehicle by which an already existing cause of action might be maintained (see *e.g. Coventry and Dixon's Case* (1880) 14 Ch. D 660, 670 *per* James L.J., 673 *per* Bramwell L.J.; *Cavendish-Bentick v. Fenn* (1887) 12 A.C. 652 (HL), 661 *per* Lord Herschell, 669 *per* Lord Macnaghten; *In re Irish Provident Assurance Co* [1913] 1 I.R. 352, 373-375, 378 *per* Cherry L.J., Holmes L.J. concurring; *Greendale* at p.29 of the transcript of Keane J.'s judgment). The question therefore arises as to what was the cause of action against the appellant which was being maintained by means of section 298(2), and the answer is that the company was seeking restitution of the payments. An action in restitution must fulfill the four enquiries of the principle against unjust enrichment, in particular it must be based upon an unjust factor. Running throughout the judgment of Keane J. is the assumption that the fact that the payments were *ultra vires* rendered them recoverable; that is an assumption that if the company did not have the capacity to make them, they were recoverable. Thus, *Greendale* can be added to the list above of cases in which incapacity was assumed as an unjust factor.

Three points remain. First, it may be that Keane J. concluded too readily that a gratuitous payment not to the benefit of the company must be *ultra vires* (compare his Lordship's own doubts, as a high court judge, in *Northern Bank Finance v. Quinn and Achates* [1979] I.L.R.M. 221, 227, and *cf. Rolled Steel Products v. BSC* [1982] 3 All E.R. 1057 (Vinelott J.); [1985] 3 All E.R. 52 (CA); as to this, see the Company Law chapter, 126, above). Second, at one stage in his judgment, Keane J. commented that the payments "were *ultra vires* the company and their fundamental illegality cannot be cured by the fact that . . . all the shareholders assented . . . (pp.27-28). This equation of incapacity and illegality is to be regretted; the two matters had been kept distinct in the earlier decision of Egan J. in the Supreme Court in *FAS v. Abbott and Ryan* (1994-1995) *JISLL* 311 (see the 1995 Review, 204-209); and it is a distinction which has long been recognised and maintained (*e.g. Ashbury Railway Carriage and Iron Co v. Riche* (1875) LR 7 HL 653 (HL) 672-673 *per* Lord Carins LC; *O'Hehir v. Cahill* (1912) 97 ILTR 274, 276 *per* Dodd J.; *Hydro Electric Commission of Nepean v. Ontario Hydro* (1982) 132 D.L.R. (3d) 193 (SCC) 238-239 *per* Estey J.; *First City Developments v. Durham* (1989) 67 O.R (2d) 665 (Ont. HC) 686 *per* Craig J.). Finally, in a further instalment in the Greendale saga, Laffoy J. in the High Court (*In re Greendale Developments: McQuaid v. Malone and Fagan,* High Court, July 2, 1997) gave another defendant leave to counterclaim against the liquidator on the grounds of subrogation.

The fourth of this year's cases raising incapacity issues in the decision of McCracken J. in *CH (Ireland) v. Credit Suisse Canada,* High Court, December 12, 1997; also discussed in the Company Law chapter, 107, above). The plaintiff sold shares in itself for Stg£18.8m, and then placed that money on deposit with one bank as security for a loan which had already been made by a lender (the defendant) to a company called Castor. The money lent to Castor had changed hands and then been used by the purchaser of the shares in the plaintiff for that purpose. The defendant-lender eventually executed against the plaintiff's deposit with the bank. In effect, the plaintiff had deposited funds with the bank, which had then been withdrawn by the lender, in return for which the lender had lent money to Castor which was eventually used by the purchaser to purchase the plaintiff's own shares. When the company was being wound up, the liquidator commenced proceedings against the bank and the lender; but the proceedings against the bank had been stayed. Thus, no order could be made against it in the liquidator's present proceedings against the lender, in which McCracken J. declared void the lender's payment obligation as against the bank.

By the terms of section 60(1) of the Companies Act 1963 it is unlawful for a company to give any financial assistance to another party for the purchase of its own shares, and by section 60(14) any such transaction is voidable at the instance of the company against any person who had notice of the relevant facts. It was quite clear that the company had provided the finance for the purchase of its own shares, and the defendant lender had (actual) notice of the nature of the transaction (*Bank of Ireland v. Rockfield* [1979] I.R. 21 (SC) applied). Nevertheless, the "only transaction which [could] be attacked under subsection 14 is a transaction directly involving the company" (p.17), here the deposit by the company with the bank. McCracken J. made it clear that he had "no real doubt but [the bank] were aware of all the facts" (p.21). Thus, if the stayed proceedings against them could be revived, transactions with them would also be voidable by the terms of section 60(14). If the plaintiff company is then entitled to restitution from them of the money it had placed on deposit with the bank, the question arises as to what the relevant unjust factor is. It is unlikely that the plaintiffs mistakenly believed in the validity of the transaction. There may very well have been a failure of consideration, but that is unlikely to have been total, and the law currently insists upon a *total* failure of consideration. The fact that the court declared the payment "void" could form the basis of a claim in *absence* of consideration (as in *Westdeutsche* at first instance [1994] 4 All E.R. 890) but this ground for restitution is open to serious doubt (see McKendrick "Swaps and the Reason for Restitution" in Birks (ed.) *Lessons of the* Swaps *Litigation* (Mansfield Press, forthcoming)). As to whether incapacity is available as an unjust factor here, recall the distinction above between illegality and incapacity; it may be that since section 60 renders it unlawful and section 60(14) allows the court to declare that the transaction is "void", there is no issue of incapacity or *vires* at all (and hence no space for the unjust factor of incapacity), but rather one of illegality.

However, even if there were an unjust factor, the illegality might become relevant as a defence, since the policy which renders the contract unlawful and void might nevertheless continue on to deny restitution (*Morgan v. Ashcroft* [1938] 1 K.B. 49; *Boissevain v. Weil* [1950] A.C. 327; cf. *Equiticorp v. R* [1996] 3 N.Z.L.R. 586 (summary) (HC Smellie J.)).

Even if the illegality of the transaction does not preclude restitution, the bank may very well have the benefit of the defence of ministerial receipt. If so, the question arises as to whether the transmission of the money to each subsequent recipient can be traced, so that the party who is enriched at the plaintiff's expense can be identified. For example, the funds deposited with the bank had been withdrawn by the lender: it had clearly received them for its own use and benefit and the defence of ministerial receipt is thus precluded; it gave value for that receipt in the form of the loan to Castor, but the defence of *bona fide* purchase for value without notice of the plaintiff's claim is precluded because McCracken J. held that the lender had actual notice of the nature of the transaction. McCracken J. concluded his judgment with doubts as to the utility of his findings of fact, but this analysis demonstrates that they lay the foundations of a possible cause of action in restitution. (Finally, and parenthetically, *quaere* whether the lender might also be liable in equity as an accessory to the company's breach of trust on foot of the principle in *Tan* (above, 163)

Failure of consideration   In *In re Edenfell Holdings,* High Court, July 30, 1997) Laffoy J. held that a receiver was in breach of his statutory duty to "exercise all reasonable care to obtain the best price reasonably obtainable for the property as at the time of the sale" (imposed by section 321A of the Companies Act 1963 as inserted by section 172 of the Companies Act 1990). She granted an injunction restraining the completion of the contract for sale (*Holohan v. Friends Provident* [1966] I.R. 1 (SC) applied) and ordered that the purchaser's deposit was to be returned. Looking at the return of the deposit from the perspective of the purchaser's cause of action to recover it in such circumstances, the question arises as to whether the purchaser would have a cause of action in restitution.

If the injunction amounted to a frustration of the contract, consideration would have failed and the deposit would therefore have been recoverable on the grounds of the unjust factor of failure of consideration (*Fibrosa v. Fairbairn* [1943] A.C. 32 (HL)).

Rather more difficult is the position if the injunction had merely resulted in a breach on the part of the vendor. There are many cases in which consideration has been held not to have failed at all, even though there has been a breach of contract (*e.g. Hyundai v. Papadopoulos* [1980] 1 W.L.R. 1129 (HL);

Stocznia v. Latvian Shipping [1998] 1 All E.R. 883 (HL)). On the other hand, if the breach does amount to a failure of consideration, the deposit would again be recoverable on the ground (cp. *Foran v. Wight* (1989-1990) 168 C.L.R. 385 (HCA *per* Brennan, Deane Dawson, and Gaudron *JJ.*)). In some cases, such a recovery of the deposit is cast in terms of relief against forfeiture (*e.g. Coyle v. Central Trust* [1978] I.L.R.M. 211 (HC: McWilliam J.) where it was assumed that if the defendant could not forfeit, the plaintiff could recover; cp. *Workers Trust v. Dojap* [1993] A.C. 537 (PC)) though strictly speaking in such cases the failure of the right to forfeit is the failure of the right to retain the money and is thus the relevant failure of consideration.

Even if there has been a failure of consideration, and thus a cause of action, there might be a defence. For example, the contract might have provided (*Union Eagle v. Golden Achievement* [1997] 2 All E.R. 215 (PC)) or the parties might have intended (*e.g. Dojap* deposit not such 'an earnest') that the deposit be non-returnable and thus remain with the defendant 'at all events' (by analogy with *Barclays Bank v. Simms* [1980] Q.B. 677, 695; and cp. *Birsbane v. Dacres* (813) 5 Tanut 143; *Maskell v. Horner* [1915] 3 K.B. 106 (voluntary submission)), so that the defendant would have the benefit of the defence of 'voluntary enrichment' (see the 1996 Review, 526).

Thus, the right of the purchaser in *Edenfell* to restitution of the deposit might not have been as straightforward as the order of Laffoy J. might suggest, since there ought to have been an enquiry as to whether the order to restrain the sale amounted to a failure of consideration consequent upon the frustration or breach of the contract, and as to whether there were any defences open on the facts.

DEFENCES

Defences to a claim of unjust enrichment can be grouped into three broad categories: (i) those which deny an essential element of the principle against unjust enrichment, *i.e.*, those which answer one of the first three enquiries in the defendants' favour; (ii) those which would deny restitution even if the terms of the first three enquiries were answered in the plaintiff's favour; and (iii) those which reflect defences more generally in the law. The defence of change of position is of the first kind, in that it denies that a defendant has been relevantly enriched on the basis that the enrichment is no longer in the defendant's hands. It has been recognised as a matter of Canadian law (*Storthoaks v. Mobil Oil Canada* (1975) 55 D.L.R. (3d) 1), Australian law (*David Securities v. Commonwealth Bank of Australia* (1992) 175 C.L.R. 353, 385-386), and English law (*Lipkin Gorman v. Karpnale* [1991] 2 A.C. 548 (HL); note that in the discussion of that case in the 1996 Review, 253 a typographical error caused the principle that "that the defence should not be available to a wrongdoer" ([1991] 2 A.C. 548, 579 *per* Lord Goff) to appear without the crucial "not"; apologies !).

The analysis of defences in the 1996 Review concluded (at 528-529) with the argument that any tendency to import palm tree justice on the fourth enquiry (defences) having forcibly ejected it on the third (unjust) must be resisted. Thus, it is because a plaintiff is mistaken, for example, that a defendant's enrichment can be characterised as unjust, not for reasons of judicial discretion. Likewise, it ought to be understood that it is because of the existence of a recognised defence that a plaintiff's claim fails, not for reasons of judicial discretion: hence the defence of change of position renders it "inequitable to compel [the defendant] to make full restitution" ([1982] I.R. 241, 319 *per* Henchy J.) because the *bona fide* expenditure in reliance upon the receipt means that the defendant is no longer enriched in the amount so expended. As Lord Goff argued in *Lipkin Gorman v. Karpnale*, a "claim to recover money at common law is made as a matter of right; and, even though the underlying principle of recovery is the principle of unjust enrichment, *nevertheless, where recovery is denied, it is denied on the basis of legal principle. . . .*" ([1991] 2 A.C. 548, 578 emphasis added; for more detail on the nature of the defence as related to enrichment rather than "unjust" – especially not to a discretionary view of justice – see Nolan "Change of Position" in Birks (ed.), *Laundering and Tracing* (Oxford, 1995) 135 at pp.172-175; Birks, "Overview: Tracing, Claiming and Defences" in *ibid.* 289, at pp.321-332; Birks, "Change of Position" in McInnes (ed.) *Restitution: Developments in Unjust Enrichment* (LBC, Sydney 1996) 49 at pp.62-64).

The full details of the defence remain to be worked out, but it is clear that merely paying the money out in the ordinary course of business is insufficient to fulfill the terms of the defence (*Storthoaks v. Mobil Oil Canada* (1975) 55 D.L.R. (3d) 1; *Lipkin Gorman v. Karpnale* [1991] 2 A.C. 548, 570-580 *per* Lord Goff; *Goss v. Chilcott* [1996] A.C. 788, 799 *per* Lord Goff; *State Bank of New South Wales v. Swiss Bank Corp* (1995-1996) 39 N.S.W.L.R. 350 (NSW CA)). Gallen J. in *National Bank of New Zealand v. Waitaki International Processing* [1997] 1 N.Z.L.R. 724 has recently explained that the "cases which establish that a mere spending of funds held in the ordinary of course of business does not amount to a change of position, need to be read now in the light of the broader comments in *Lipkin Gorman*, but can also be explained that in such cases a benefit has been retained, albeit in some different form" ([1997] 1 N.Z.L.R. 724, 732-333). This reason therefore explains why a defendant from whom the money has been stolen can have the benefit of the defence (compare, *e.g.* Birks, "Overview. Tracing, Claiming and Defences" in Birks (ed.), *Laundering and Tracing* (Oxford, 1995) 289 at p.330, "Change of Position" in McInnes (ed.) *Restitution: Developments in Unjust Enrichment* (LBC, Sydney 1996) 49 at pp.61-62, and "Change of Position and Surviving Enrichment" in Swadling (ed.), *The Limits of Restitutionary Claims* (BIICL, 1997)

36 at pp.48-51; changing his mind from *Restitution. The Future* (Federation Press, Sydney, 1992) pp.142-143). In *National Bank of New Zealand v. Waitaki International Processing* itself, the plaintiffs had mistakenly paid $500,000 to the defendants (on the mistake in that case, see Grantham and Rickett [1997] *RLR* 83). Pending resolution of whether it was in fact due, the defendants deposited the money with a finance company. The finance company went into liquidation and the deposit was lost. Gallen J. held that the defendant did not derive a benefit from the money "because it has been lost by the failure of the ultimate recipient. There is no question of it having been spent or used by the defendant" (*id*). Hence, the defendants were entitled to rely on the defence of change of position.

However, this excellent point is marred somewhat by other remarks of Gallen J. treating the defence change of position as a vehicle for discretionary judicial reduction of the amount of the enrichment to be returned: he treated *Lipkin Gorman* as an authority which requires "a process of balancing the competing equities" and held that "overall in the round" ([1997] 1 N.Z.L.R. 724, 734) the plaintiff bank was entitled to recover 10% of the mistaken payment. No further explanation of the figure is given. If, as it seems to have been, it represents a judicial discretion, then this is to misunderstand the nature of the defence of change of position, which denies restitution to the extent that the defendant is no longer relevantly enriched, and for that reason. If all of the money on deposit was lost in the finance company's insolvency, then the defendants ought to have had a complete defence. If 10% of it remained, or if the defendants were entitled to recover 10% in the insolvency, then the defendants would have remained enriched in the amount of that 10%. But neither of these reasons was given; and the defence of change position should not have been used as a vehicle for discretion.

The place of the defence of change of position as a matter of Irish law is secure as a consequence of the decision of Henchy J. in *Murphy v. AG* [1982] I.R. 241 (SC). Gallen J's interpretation of the speech of Lord Goff in *Lipkin Gorman* demonstrates that the terms of the defence are open to misinterpretation; so also is the judgment of Henchy J. in *Murphy*. It was considered in the Supreme Court in *McDonnell v. Ireland*, July 23, 1997).

The plaintiff's contract of employment had been terminated in July 1975 pursuant to the terms of a statute declared unconstitutional in *Cox v. Ireland* [1992] 2 I.R. 503 (SC); the plaintiff sued for damages for that termination, and in the belief that the limitation period for actions at common law had expired, the plaintiff's claim was framed as one arising under the constitution. Keane J. (Hamilton C.J. and O'Flaherty J. concurring) analogised the plaintiff's claim to one in tort, and held that the six year limitation period for tort (in section 11(2)(a) of the Statute of Limitations 1957) barred the plaintiff's claim. Barron J. held that the plaintiff's claim was for a breach of contract, but that the six year limitation period for contract (in section 11(1)(a) of the Statute of

Limitations 1957) barred the plaintiff's claim. These aspects of the decision are considered elsewhere in this Review (though it may be questioned why the mistaken belief of all concerned in the validity of the statute was not a sufficient mistake within the terms of section 72(1) of the Statute of Limitations 1957 to stop time from running until the mistake was discovered by the declaration of unconstitutionality of the relevant statute in *Cox*; and if it is objected that the mistake was a mistake of law and thus irrelevant, the abrogation of that bar (as described above) is a sufficient answer). For present purposes, other *dicta* of Keane and Barron JJ. raise profound structural questions for the relationship of the law of restitution with other areas of the law; while another aspect of the judgment of Barron J. may supply an example of the misinterpretation of that aspect of the judgment of Henchy J. in *Murphy* which deals with the defence of change of position as instead a vehicle for individual judicial discretion.

By way of background to the structural questions raised by the case, take the example of a contract under which the plaintiff paid in advance, and before the defendant could perform, the contract is frustrated. Whether the contract is frustrated is a matter which is determined by the law of contract. Once the contract has been discharged, there may be then a further enquiry as to whether the plaintiff can have restitution of the advance payment on the ground of failure of consideration. (See *e.g. Fibrosa Spolka Ackyjna v. Fairbarin Lawson Combe Barbour* [1943] A.C. 32 (HL) where their lordships considered both questions in a single case). Similarly, when a contract is void for *ultra vires*, it is a matter of company law (in the case of a company; or of public law in the case of a public body) as to whether the contract is *ultra vires*. If it is, then the payor under the contract can seek restitution of money paid. For example, in *Hazell v. Hammersmith and Fulham London Borough Council* [1992] 2 A.C. 1 (HL) the House of Lords held that a local authority did not have the power to enter into speculative swaps contracts. And in a large series of subsequent litigation, the courts have held that the net payors on the swaps were entitled to restitution of the net payments (*e.g. Westdeutsche Landesbanke Girozentrale v. Islington LBC* [1994] 4 All E.R. 890 (Hobhouse J. and CA) [1996] A.C. 669 (HL)). Similarly, in Ireland, Murphy J. held that certain loans were *ultra vires* the PMPS (*In re PMPA Garage (Longmile) Ltd (No.1)* [1992] 1 I.R. 315; [1992] I.L.R.M. 337 (HC)) and then in subsequent proceedings held that, in principle, the lender could have restitution of monies so lent (*In Re PMPA Garage (Longmile) Limited (No.2)* [1992] 1 I.R. 332; [1992] I.L.R.M. 349 (HC); *PMPA v. PMPS,* High Court, unreported, June 27, 1994, Murphy J.) (at p.1 of the transcript); and see now also *PMPA v. PMPS and Primor* (High Court, February 20, 1997, Costello P., above). Thus, when a contract goes off - for any reason of contract law, company law, public law, equity, and so on – there is then the occasion for possible restitution on the basis of the application of the principle against unjust enrichment. The absence of the contract, on this view, is merely the occasion upon which an enquiry as to a cause of action in restitution is conducted. Had the contract not gone off, the occasion would never have arisen, but all the absence of the contract does is provide that occasion for a restitutionary enquiry.

Take the case of a statute which requires the payment of a tax but is then found to be unconstitutional. In *Air Canada v. British Columbia* (above) the Supreme Court of Canada held that a taxing statute was unconstitutional, and then held that since the plaintiffs had paid in the mistaken belief in the validity of the tax, the plaintiffs' mistake gave rise to a cause of action in restitution. Similarly, in *Murphy v. Attorney General* (above), the Supreme Court held that a taxing statute unconstitutional, and then held that since the plaintiffs had paid under duress (duress *colore offici*), the duress gave the plaintiffs a cause of action in restitution. The unconstitutionality of the statute, on this view, is merely the occasion upon which an enquiry as to a cause of action in restitution is conducted. Had the statute not been declared unconstitutional, the occasion would never have arisen, but all its absence does is provide that occasion for a restitutionary enquiry. Thus, in *McDonnell*, Keane J. held that as was made clear in *Murphy v. Ireland*, the fact that the provisions struck down were invalid *ab initio* does not have, as a necessary consequence, the vesting of a cause of action in the plaintiff' (p.25 of the transcript of his judgment; *cp.* Barron J. at p.11 of the transcript of his judgment). The cause of action arose, not because the statute was invalid *per se*, but because the defendant was consequently unjustly enriched.

A similar sensitivity to the nuances of the judgment of Henchy J. in *Murphy* was not, however, shown by Barron J. on another issue in *McDonnell*:

> [h]aving considered various equitable principles related *inter alia* to laches, estoppel and restitution, Henchy J. concluded this aspect of his judgment [in *Murphy*] at p. 320 as follows:

> > Whether the taxpayer's action be framed as a common law action in quasi-contract for money had and received, or as an equitable claim for restitution of money by which the State was unjustly enriched, there is ample authority for the conclusion that the radical change in circumstances of the kind I have indicated would be sufficient to defeat, at least in part, the taxpayers' claim: see Jones's 'Change of Circumstances in Quasi-Contract' (1957) 73 *LQR* 48.

> In this case, whether the claim be treated as one in quasi-contract or as one in equity, I would consider the enforceable cause of action to have arisen at the beginning of the tax year 1978-9.

> In the instant case, apart from the basic finding of invalidity *ab initio* there are other facts which existed in *Murphy's* case. Admittedly, that

case in its conclusion limited the date at which the cause of action to remedy what had occurred was found to have arisen. But the same principles should be applied to limit the period within which equitable relief should be permitted after such a cause of action has arisen. There was a *bona fide* belief on the part of the defendants' predecessors in title that the plaintiff was no longer entitled to be employed in the postal service, a belief fostered by the absence of any claim to the contrary. (at pp.6-7 of the transcript).

Barron J. went to consider whether laches would bar the plaintiff's claim, by analogy with Henchy J's treatment of laches in *Murphy*. However, the *ratio* of Barron J.'s judgment in *McDonnell* is to be found in the following sentence: "[a]ccepting the cause of action as being one for breach of contract, it has clearly been barred by the provisions of section 11(1) of the Statute of Limitations 1957" (p.11). Thus, all of his comments on *Murphy* are *obiter*, and this is probably just as well. The judgment of Henchy J. in *Murphy* holds that, following upon the unconstitutionality of the taxing statute, the plaintiffs had a *prima facie* cause of action in restitution to which the defence of change of position provided the government with a defence. The defence arises where a party receives, and *bona fide* in reliance on that receipt, spends, what would otherwise be an unjust enrichment. Thus, the government was unjustly enriched by the overpaid taxes, but since it had *bona fide* in reliance upon that receipt, spent that enrichment, it had a defence. And it had this defence except as against the instant plaintiffs from the tax year in which they had commenced their action (1978-9), since in respect of receipts after those dates it was on notice that it might be unjustly enriched by those receipts, it was not therefore *bona fide*, and one element of the defence was not fulfilled.

It is important to notice that the element of good faith is simply one element of the defence of change of position, and that the defence of change of position in turn is simply a defence to a cause of action in restitution. It cannot be stressed enough that, in *Murphy*, Henchy J. did not carve out a general power on the part of the Supreme Court to ignore or cure the consequences of unconstitutionality if the relevant defendant acted in good faith. He simply did not; his focus on good faith was in the context of a defence (of which it formed an element) to a cause of action in *restitution* which arose on the occasion of the unconstitutionality of the taxing statute.

In *McDonnell*, the plaintiff was not alleging that the defendant had been unjustly enriched at his expense; there was thus no basis for the deployment of the defence of change of position. Hence, Barron J's reliance upon it here is as misconceived as O'Flaherty J's analogy with mistake of law in *Duff*. Furthermore, Barron J. in *McDonnell*, (by attaching significance to the "*bona fide* belief on the part of the defendants' predecessors in title that the plaintiff was no longer entitled to be employed"), seems however to regard Henchy J. as focussing on good faith as a general defence to causes of action arising out of unconstitutionality. If that is so, then it is seriously to misconstrue the import of the judgment of Henchy J., and provides another reason why this aspect of the decision of Barron J. ought not to be followed.

Safety and Health

CHEMICAL SAFETY

Chemical weapons   The Chemical Weapons Act 1997 implemented the United Nations Convention on the Prohibition of the Development, Production, Stockpiling and Use of Chemical Weapons and their Destruction (CWC). The 1997 Act prohibits the production, development, use, retention or transfer of chemical weapons and restricts the use of certain toxic chemicals. It provides that the National Authority for Occupational Safety and Health (the Health and Safety Authority) is the designated national authority for the purposes of the Convention, thus conferring substantial inspection and enforcement powers on the Authority. The Act came into effect on July 1, 1997: Chemical Weapons Act 1997 (Commencement) Order 1997 (S.I. No. 269 of 1997).

Cosmetics   The European Communities (Cosmetic Products) Regulations 1997 (S.I. No. 87 of 1997) consolidated with amendments the legislative provisions on cosmetic products and give effect to a number of Directives in this area, in particular the principal Directive on cosmetic products, 76/768/EEC, as amended by no less than 26 Directives listed in Regulation 4 of the 1997 Regulations, the most recent being Directive 97/1/EC. They prohibit placing on the market of cosmetic products which, under normal conditions of use, are liable to cause damage to human health. In that respect, the 1997 Regulations complement the Product Directives on manufacturing standards discussed below, 672. The 1997 Regulations either prohibit or severely restrict the use of certain ingredients in cosmetics. A list of certain colouring agents, antimicrobial preservatives and ultraviolet sun-screen filters is also included in the 1997 Regulations. Requirements concerning packaging and labelling and also specified. Full ingredient labelling was introduced by the 1997 Regulations with effect from March 1, 1997. In addition, express reference to whether the cosmetic involved animal testing must also be included. Testing on animals is, in principle, prohibited from January 1, 1998, but may be used where it is required in order to comply with the 1997 Regulations. In effect, this is subject to progress in the development of a satisfactory alternative method of testing. The Regulations also prescribe information to be kept by the relevant enforcement authorities in particular the Department of Health. Finally, a fine of up to £1,000 may be imposed on summary prosecution for non-compliance with the Regulations. The Regulations, which also revoked the European Communities (Cosmetic Products) Regulations 1990 to 1996 (1996 Review, 530), came into effect on various dates between March 1, 1997 and July 1, 1998.

Explosives The Sale Of Explosives Order 1997 (S.I. No. 364 of 1997), made under section 43 of the Explosives Act 1875, provides that explosives to which the Order applies shall not be sold without the appropriate certificate from the Garda Síochána that the material is required for immediate industrial or agricultural use. The Order applies to ammonium nitrate, sodium chlorate, nitrobenzene, potassium nitrate and sodium nitrate, all of which had previously been deemed by various Orders made under the 1875 Act to be explosives for the purposes of the 1875 Act. The Order came into effect on September 1, 1997. The Ammonium Nitrate Mixtures Exemption Order 1997 (S.I. No. 365 of 1997) made under sections 50 and 83 of the Explosive Substances Act 1875 exempts the manufacture of ammonium nitrate or mixtures thereof from the provisions of the 1875 Act, subject to a licence being obtained from the Minister for Justice. The Order came into effect on September 1, 1997.

Transport The Dangerous Substances (Conveyance of Scheduled Substances by Road (Trade or Business) (Amendment) Regulations 1997 (S.I. No. 458 of 1997) amended the Dangerous Substances (Conveyance of Scheduled Substances by Road) (Trade or Business) (Amendment) Regulations 1996 (1996 Review, 629) so that they apply to vehicles registered before January 1, 1997.

ENVIRONMENTAL SAFETY

Air pollution The Environmental Protection Agency Act 1992 (Ozone) Regulations 1997 (S.I. No. 132 of 1997) gave effect to Directive 92/72/EEC. They lay down provisions in relation to tropospheric ozone and the information and monitoring role of the EPA and came into effect on April 1, 1997.

Eco labelling The European Communities (Energy Labelling of Household Electric Washing Machines) (Amendment) Regulations 1997 (S.I. No. 208 of 1997) added an additional category to the list of machines excluded by the European Communities (Energy Labelling of Household Electric Washing Machines) Regulations 1996 (1996 Review, 532) with effect from May 13, 1997. The European Communities (Energy Labelling of Household Combined Washer-Dryers) Regulations 1997 (S.I. No. 319 of 1997) gave effect to Directive 96/60/EC and prohibit the placing on the market, for sale, for hire or reward, of combined washer dryers (excluding second-hand and models production of which has ceased) unless accompanied by certain information relating to electrical energy consumption. They came into effect on August 1, 1997. The European Communities (Energy Efficiency Requirements for Household Electrical Refrigerators, Freezers and Combinations Thereof) Regulations 1997 (S.I. No. 482 of 1997) gave effect to Directive 96/57/EC and set out the energy efficiency requirements for household fridges and freezers and prohibit placing models on the market which do not comply with the energy efficiency requirements laid down. They become fully operational on September 3, 1999.

EPA and judicial review   In *Ni Éili v. Environmental Protection Agency* [1997] 2 I.L.R.M. 458 (HC), Kelly J held that the time limit for reviewing decisions of the Environmental Protection Agency in section 85 of the Environmental Protection Agency Act 1992 is to ensure that such proceedings are instituted at an early date so that uncertainty about the decision can be disposed of. Thus, he declined to permit the applicant to amend the grounds for seeking judicial of a decision of the Agency since these would amount to an additional and entirely new case and raised in effect a new cause of action. Citing the decision in *KSK Enterprises Ltd v. An Bord Pleanála* [1994] 2 I.R. 128; [1994] 2 I.L.R.M. 1 (1994 Review, 359-60), which dealt with the time limits introduced into the planning code in 1992, he concluded that the amendments, if permitted, would run contrary to the intention of the legislature when enacting section 85 of the 1992 Act. He also opined that, even if the provisions of section 85(8) of the 1992 Act were not rigid and did not fall to be construed in such a strict manner amendments to the grounds for judicial review could be made as a matter of judicial discretion but that in the instant case, he would not have been prepared to allow such an alteration when it took into account the particular circumstances in the case.

GMOs   The Genetically Modified Organisms (Amendment) Regulations 1997 (S.I. No. 322 of 1997), made under section 111 of the Environmental Protection Agency Act 1992 amended the Genetically Modified Organisms Regulations 1994 (1994 Review, 397-8). They introduced additional requirements to be complied with in order to obtain approval for genetically modified organisms and came into effect on July 30, 1997.

IPC   The Environmental Protection Agency Act 1992 (Established Activities) Order 1997 (S.I. No. 140 of 1997) sets out the dates on or after which a further list of activities set out in the Order are required to have applied for integrated pollution control (IPC) licences by the various dates specified in the Order.

Litter   The Litter Pollution Act 1997 introduced increased controls over litter and repealed the Litter Act 1982. The 1997 Act introduced new powers and functions for local authorities in relation to litter control including requiring occupiers, promoters of public events, operators of mobile outlets selling produce, food or drink and occupiers of certain classes of premises, to take remedial or precautionary measures in connection with litter. Local authorities are also required to have litter management plans and are given powers to make bye-laws to implement these. Among the novel provisions in the 1997 Act are extended duties on occupiers to keep land free of litter and to keep footpaths adjoining their property (including retail premises) free of litter. The Act also provided that failure to clear up dog foul is an offence. The 1997 Act also provided for increases in the fines for litter offences by comparison with the 1982 Act and also empowers the Garda Síochána to impose on the spot fines for offences. The Litter Pollution Act, 1997 (Commencement) Order 1997 (S.I. No. 213 of 1997 brought the 1997 Act into force on July 1, 1997. The Litter Pollution Regulations 1997 (S.I. No. 214 of 1997) prescribed the forms for on the spot fines under the Act.

Petrol emissions   The Environmental Protection Agency Act 1992 (Control of Volatile Organic Compound Emissions Resulting from Petrol Storage and Distribution) Regulations 1997 (S.I. No. 374 of 1997) gave effect to Directive 94/63/EC and introduced controls by way of permit from the EPA on volatile organic compound emissions from petrol storage and distribution at terminals. They came into effect on October 1, 1997. The Air Pollution Act 1987 (Petroleum Vapour Emissions) Regulations 1997 (S.I. No. 375 of 1997) also gave effect to Directive 94/63/EC and provide for monitoring of compliance of service stations and mobile container operators by local authorities of controls on petroleum storage emissions. They also came into effect on October 1, 1997.

Waste management   The Waste Management (Licensing) Regulations 1997 (S.I. No. 133 of 1997), made under the Waste Management Act 1996 (1996 Review, 546-55) gave effect to a number of Directives in the area of waste management, including 75/442/EEC, 80/68/EEC, 91/689/EEC and 94/62/EC as envisaged by the 1996 Act. They set out the detailed procedures for the operation of a licensing system for waste disposal, whose provisions come into effect on various dates from 1997 to 1999. The Waste Management (Planning) Regulations 1997 (S.I. No. 137 of 1997), also made under the 1996 Act, set out the matters to be addressed in a waste management plan made under section 22 of the 1996 Act. They came into effect on March 27, 1997. The Waste Management (Register) Regulations 1997 (S.I. No. 183 of 1997) prescribe the entries to be made in the registers to be maintained by local authorities and the Environmental Protection Agency under the 1996 Act and came into effect on April 30, 1997. The Waste Management (Packaging) Regulations 1997 (S.I. No. 242 of 1997) imposed obligations on persons who supply packaging to the Irish market with an exemption for persons who participate in approved packaging waste recovery schemes. They came into effect on July 1, 1997. The Waste Management (Farm Plastics) Regulations 1997 (S.I. No. 315 of 1997) lays down a scheme for the recovery of farm plastics, with effect from August 1, 1997. As is clear from these Regulations, many of their mandatory provisions may be avoided where the duty holders, for example, industrial waste generators or the farming community, enter into collective waste management schemes alluded to in the Regulations. Such schemes have already been put in place, aided by grant schemes from industry and government. The Local Government (Planning and Development) (No. 3) Regulations 1997 (S.I. No. 261 of 1997) amended the Local Government (Planning and Development) Regulations 1994 (1994 Review, 350) and transferred from the Minister for the Environment to the Environmental Protection Agency the consideration of environmental impact statements for local authority developments requiring waste management licences. They also exempt developments carried out in compliance with the Waste Management Act 1996 from planning permission. They came into effect on June 24, 1997.

FIRE SAFETY

The Child Care (Pre-School Services) (Amendment) Regulations 1997 (S.I. No. 268 of 1997), made under the Child Care Act 1991 (1991 Review, 232-52) amended the Child Care (Pre-School Services) Regulations 1996 in connection with the forms for notifying health boards that fire safety requirements have been complied with, with effect from June 20, 1997.

FOOD SAFETY

Additives The European Communities (Detailed Provisions on the Control of Additives other than Colours and Sweeteners for use in Foodstuffs) Regulations 1997 (S.I. No. 128 of 1997) gave effect to Directive 95/2/EC and set out detailed provisions as to the use of additives other than sweeteners and colouring in food, in effect listing the permitted 'E numbers' in foodstuffs. They came into effect on March 25, 1997 and complement the European Communities (General Provisions on the Control of Additives in Particular Colours and Sweeteners for use in Foodstuffs) Regulations 1995 (1995 Review, 441).

Bananas   The European Communities (Bananas) Regulations 1997 (S.I. No. 67 of 1997) gave full effect to Regulation (EC) No. 404/93 and Regulation (EC) No. 2898/95 They provide the necessary enforcement powers and prescribe offences for non-compliance with quality standards for fresh green bananas. They came into effect on February 5, 1997.

Food Safety Authority   The Food Safety Authority of Ireland (Establishment) Order 1997 (S.I. No. 524 of 1997), made under the Health (Corporate) Bodies Act 1961, established the Food Safety Authority of Ireland with effect from January 1, 1998. The Authority's remit includes advising the government on food safety standards and the legislative regime in place. It is envisaged that the Authority will be empowered in the future to enforce food safety standards, but this will require the enactment of a Food Safety Authority Act. The Food Safety Advisory Board (Revocation) Order 1997 (S.I. No. 523) dissolved the Food Safety Advisory Board, the Authority's predecessor, also with effect from January 1, 1998.

Fruit and vegetables   The European Communities (Fruit and Vegetables) Regulations 1997 (S.I. No. 122 of 1997) gave full effect to Regulation (EC) No. 2200/96. They provide the necessary enforcement powers and prescribe offences for non-compliance with quality standards for fruit and vegetables. They came into effect on March 19, 1997. The European Communities (Pesticide Residues) (Fruit and Vegetables) (Amendment) Regulations 1997 (S.I. No. 218 of 1997) gave effect to Directive 96/32/EC and amended the levels of pesticide residues permitted in fruit and vegetables with effect from May 22, 1997.

Labelling   The European Communities (Labelling, Presentation and Advertising of Foodstuffs) (Amendment) Regulations 1997 (S.I. No. 151 of 1997) gave effect to Directive 93/102/EEC and require a specific indication on labelling of foodstuffs of the presence of sweeteners and/or added sugars. They came into effect on July 1, 1997.

Materials in contact with foodstuffs   The European Communities (Materials and Articles Intended to Come into Contact with Foodstuffs) (Amendment) Regulations 1997 (S.I. No. 335 of 1997) gave effect to Directive 96/11/ EC and specify further requirements concerning materials, including plastics, which come into contact with food, in particular as covering. They came into effect on July 28, 1997.

Meat products   The European Communities (Fresh Poultrymeat) Regulations 1997 (S.I. No. 125 of 1997) gave further effect to Directives 91/494/ EEC and 93/121/EEC and provide for animal health conditions governing intra-community trade in and imports from third countries of poultry meat. They came into effect on March 31, 1997. The European Communities (Meat Products and other Products of Animal Origin) (Amendment) Regulations 1997 (S.I. No. 175 of 1997) amended the European Communities (Meat Products and other Products of Animal Origin) Regulations 1995 (1995 Review, 16) to give effect to Directive 95/68/EC with effect from May 8, 1997. The European Communities (Fresh Meat) Regulations 1997 (S.I. No. 434 of 1997) gave effect to Directives 91/497/EEC, as amended, and 91/498/EEC. They specify updated standards for the hygienic production and placing of fresh meat on the market for human consumption and for its health marking. They came into effect on November 10, 1997.

Pistachios   The European Communities (Suspension of Imports of Pistachios and Certain Products Derived From Pistachios Originating on or Consigned From Iran) Regulations 1997 (S.I. No. 432 of 1997) gave effect to Decision 97/613/EC and suspended the import of pistachios from Iran into the State with effect from October 15, 1997.

GENERAL PRODUCT SAFETY

The European Communities (General Product Safety) Regulations 1997 (S.I. No. 197 of 1997) implemented the Directive on General Product Safety (92/ 59/EEC). Because the specific EC Product Directives (the 'CE' Marking Directives), such as those referred to below, 678, necessarily apply to specified items, it was accepted that a General Product Safety Directive was required to lay down at least a minimum standard of protection even where no specific Directive or technical standard applied. The 1992 Directive was approved in response to this. It was due to have been implemented in June 1994. The 1997 implementing Regulations came into effect on May 25, 1997, the day they were signed by the Minister for Enterprise and Employment.

Connection with the Product Liability Directive   Article 13 of the 1992 General Product Safety Directive provides that it is without prejudice to the Product Liability Directive, 85/374/EEC, transposed by the Liability for Defective Products Act 1991 (1991 Review, 420-34). Regrettably, the 1997 Regulations contain no reference to the 1991 Act; such reference would have facilitated a clearer understanding of the interaction between the two legislative provisions.

Definition of product and general application of Regulations   Regulation 2(1) of the 1997 Regulations defines 'product' as:

any product intended for consumers or likely to be used by consumers, supplied whether for consideration or not in the course of a commercial activity and whether new, used or reconditioned.

Nonetheless, Regulation 3 goes on to provide that the Regulations do not apply to the following two categories:

- second-hand products supplied as antiques or as products to be repaired or reconditioned prior to being used, provided that the supplier clearly informs the person to whom he supplies the product to that effect; or
- any product where there are specific provisions in Product Directives governing all aspects of the safety of the product or any enactment or any Regulation made under section 3 of the European Communities Act 1972 giving effect to any such rules, such as those discussed below; the 1997 Regulations will apply where a specific Directive or implementing Regulations do not make specific provision for an aspect of the safety of the product.

Duties of producer and distributor   The main obligations under the 1997 Regulations fall on producers and distributors.

Regulation 2 defines 'producer' as:

- (a) the manufacturer of the product, when the manufacturer is established in the Community, and any other person presenting himself as the manufacturer by affixing to the product his name, trade mark or other distinctive mark, or the person who reconditions the product, or
- (b) the manufacturer's representative, when the manufacturer is not established in the Community or, if there is no representative established in the Community, the importer of the product, or
- (c) other professionals in the supply chain, insofar as their activities may affect the safety properties of a product placed on the market.

This definition is wider than the definition in the 1985 Product Liability Directive and the 1991 Act.

Regulation 2 defines distributors, as 'any professional in the supply chain whose activity does not affect the safety properties of a product.'

Prohibition on producers placing unsafe products on market   Regulation 4 of the 1997 Regulations provides that a producer 'shall not place or attempt to place on the market a product unless it is a safe product.'

Duty of producers to give relevant information Regulation 5 provides that a producer must provide consumers with all relevant information relating to the product to enable them to assess the risks inherent in the product throughout the normal or reasonably foreseeable period of its use, where such risks are not immediately obvious without adequate warnings.

Duty of producers to withdraw unsafe products: product recall Regulation 5 also provides that, if necessary, the producer must take appropriate follow-up action, including, withdrawing the product in question from the market to avoid those risks. This emphasises the need to have effective product recall arrangements, including where required advertisements directed at members of the public and other notices to distributors and retailers.

Other duties of producers Regulation 6 of the Regulations provides that, in addition, a producer must, where appropriate:

(a) mark the product or product batches in such a way they can be identified,
(b) carry out sample testing of the product,
(c) investigate any complaints made about marketed products, and
(d) keep distributors informed about any risks in the product.

Again, the Director may issue a direction to a producer in relation to compliance with this Regulation.

Duties of distributor Regulation 7 provides that a distributor 'shall act with due care' to ensure that any product he supplies is a safe product. In particular, it also provides that a distributor 'shall not supply or attempt to supply a product which he knows or it is reasonable to presume that he should know is a dangerous product.'

A distributor must also monitor the product's safety, and must inform the producer and consumers of 'any defects in [a product] or risks it may pose to consumers that he becomes aware of.'

General definition of safe product Regulation 2 defines a 'safe product' as 'any product which, under normal or reasonably foreseeable conditions of use, including duration, does not present any risk or only the minimum risks compatible with the product's use considered as acceptable and consistent with a high level of protection for the safety and health of persons.'

Regulation 4 of the 1997 Regulations provides that, in determining whether a product is safe, the following must be taken into consideration:

(a) the characteristics of the product, including its composition, packaging, instructions for assembly and maintenance;

(b) the effect on other products, where it is reasonably foreseeable that it will be used with other products;

(c) the presentation of the product, the labelling, any instructions for its use and disposal and any other indication or information provided by the producer; and

(d) the categories of consumers at serious risk when using the product, in particular children.

Regulation 4 also provides that merely because higher levels of safety might be feasible or because other products presenting a lesser degree of risk are available 'shall not constitute grounds for considering a product to be unsafe or dangerous.'

These general provisions must also be seen in the context of Regulation 8, which deals with compliance with technical standards.

Products deemed safe if in compliance with standards   Regulation 8 provides that a product is deemed to be a safe product if it conforms with any national safety standards, provided these are deemed compatible with the EC Treaty.

Where no national safety standards exist, the 1997 Regulations state that the general safety of a product is to be assessed 'taking into account' the following:

(a) voluntary national standards giving effect to a European standard, or

(b) Community standards, or

(c) if there are no such voluntary national or Community standards:

    (i) standards drawn up in the State, or

    (ii) 'codes of good practice in the product sector concerned, or

    (iii) 'the state of the art and technology, and the safety which consumers may reasonably expect.'

Clearly, this hierarchical approach to standards reflects the approach at common law in negligence and also under the 1991 Act, namely that, if a standard exists it should be applied, in default of which 'best practice' and the 'state of the art' will be taken in to account. This should also be seen in the context of the principles in *Roche v. Peilow* [1985] I.R. 232, which require that regard be had to whether standards are inherently safe or involve inherent defects. Doubtless, however, compliance with legislative standards will in virtually all instances prove sufficient at common law and under the 1991 Act and 1997 Regulations.

Director's role in relation to dangerous products   In addition to the power
to issue directions already referred to, Regulation 9 of the 1997 Regulations
also empowers the Director of Consumer Affairs, where there is evidence it is
dangerous to the health and safety of consumers, to direct a producer or distributor to take positive action to enforce the terms of the 1997 Regulations.
These regulatory elements mark a clear difference between the civil liability
focus of the 1991 Act and the combined civil liability and public enforcement
and (as we shall see) criminal aspect of the 1997 Regulations. Regulation 9 of
the 1997 Regulations empowers the Director of Consumer Affairs to:

(a) prohibit or impose such restrictions as specified in a direction on the
    product or product batch being placed on the market, or
(b) require the withdrawal of the product or product batch from the mar-
    ket and, if necessary, its destruction under such conditions as may be
    specified in the direction.

Regulation 10 empowers the Director to direct a producer or distributor to:

(a) affix to a product or to any packaging of the product such warnings as
    may be specified in the direction regarding the risks which the prod-
    uct may present, or
(b) publish, in such form and manner and on occasions specified in the
    direction, a warning about any risks in any product, or
(c) give to consumers such information or to take such action concerning
    the product as specified in the direction, where the Director considers
    that a producer has not given relevant information to consumers or
    taken appropriate action in relation to risks referred to in Regulation
    5.

Regulation 11 requires the Director, where feasible, to give an opportunity to
any person to whom he is considering making a direction under the Regulations to submit their views on the proposed direction before the adoption of
the measure. If not feasible before the direction is issued, because of the urgency of the measures to be taken, the opportunity must be given by the Director in due course after the direction takes effect.

Regulation 11 also specifies the form which such a direction is to take.
Regulation 12 provides that an appeal lies to the Circuit Court against the
making of a direction, within 21 days of receipt of the direction. Regulation
13 provides for the appointment and powers of authorised officers of the Director for the purposes of enforcement of the Regulations. These include powers
of entry, inspection and detention common in such regulatory legislation. Regulation 16 provides for applications to the District Court for the release of goods
detained under Regulation 13.

Injunctions and forfeitures Regulation 14 provides that, where a person fails to comply with a direction of the Director under the Regulations, the Director may institute High Court proceedings for an order requiring the person to comply with the terms of the direction. Regulation 15 provides that the Director may apply to the District Court for a forfeiture order, by which any product may be seized on behalf of the Director by an authorised officer.

Prohibition on disclosure of information Regulation 17 provides that it is an offence for a person to disclose information obtained for the purposes of the Regulations or the 1992 Directive which by its nature is confidential, other than information relating to the safety properties of any product in order to protect the safety and health of consumers.

Offences and penalties Contraventions of the mandatory provisions of the Regulations, including those concerning placing unsafe products on the market and refusing to obey a direction from the Director, are offences.

Regulation 20 provides that a person guilty of an offence under the Regulations is liable to a maximum fine of £1,500 and/or 3 months imprisonment.

Regulation 22 contains the common provisions to the effect that where an offence under the Regulations is committed by a corporate body and is proved to have been so committed with the 'consent, connivance or approval of, or to have been facilitated by any neglect on the part of any director, manager, secretary or any other officer of such body or a person who was purporting to act in any such capacity, such person shall also be guilty of an offence.'

Prosecutions by Director Regulation 18 would ordinarily not give rise to much comment, but it is worded in a most unfortunate manner. It provides that:

> An offence under this Act may be prosecuted summarily by the Director.

It is patently the case that the 1997 Regulations may not be described as 'this Act'. It remains to be seen whether the original text signed by the Minister carries this misprint, or, if it does, whether this would give rise to difficulties in any prosecutions which might be contemplated under the 1997 Regulations: see the discussion of typographical errors in *The State (Murphy) v. Johnson* [1983] I.R. 235 and *The State (Rollinson) v. Kelly* [1984] I.R. 248, where the Supreme Court declined to 'correct' patent drafting errors.

MANUFACTURING STANDARDS

As in previous Reviews, we note here Regulations which gave effect to further 'New Approach' EC Directives linked to the CE technical conformity marking and European Norms (ENs), that is technical manufacturing standards.

Electrical sockets and plugs   The National Standards Authority of Ireland (Section 28) (13 A and Conversion Adaptors For Domestic Use) Regulations 1997 (S.I. No. 525 of 1997), made under the National Standards Authority of Ireland Act 1996 (1996 Review, 538-41), introduced new requirements and standards for 13 Amp plugs. They revoked the Industrial Research and Standards (Section 28) (13 A and Conversion Adaptors For Domestic Use) Regulations 1969 and the Industrial Research and Standards (Section 28) (13 A and Conversion Adaptors For Domestic Use) Regulations 1987. The 1997 Regulations came into effect on June 18, 1997. The National Standards Authority of Ireland (Section 28) (Electrical Plugs, Plug Similar Devices and Sockets for Domestic Use) Regulations 1997 (S.I. No. 526 of 1997), also made under the 1996 Act introduced new provisions on manufacturing standards for electrical plugs, plug similar devices and sockets for domestic use. They provide that manufacturers may comply with Irish (IS), British (BS) or European (EN) standards, replacing a previous emphasis on Irish standards alone. They came into effect on December 18, 1997.

General product safety   The European Communities (General Product Safety) Regulations 1997 (S.I. No. 197 of 1997), which gave effect to Directive 92/59/EEC the General Product Safety Directive, is discussed separately above, 672.

NSAI   The National Standards Authority of Ireland Act 1996 (Commencement and Establishment Day) Order 1997 (S.I. No. 176 of 1997) established the eponymous Authority on April 14, 1997 and brought the remainder of the 1996 Act (1996 Review, 538-41) into effect on January 1, 1997.

Personal Protective Equipment   The European Communities (Personal Protective Equipment) (Amendment) Regulations 1997 (S.I. No. 81 of 1997) amended the European Communities (Personal Protective Equipment) Regulations 1993 (1993 Review, 480-1) to give effect to Directive 95/58/EC. They removed the requirement to indicate the year the CE marking was affixed to personal protective equipment and came into effect on February 10, 1997.

OCCUPATIONAL SAFETY & HEALTH

Dangerous goods   The European Communities (Training for Drivers Carrying Dangerous Goods by Road) Regulations 1997 (S.I. No. 311 of 1997) gave effect to Directive 94/55/EC and specify standards of training and certification for drivers of vehicles carrying dangerous goods by road. They came into effect on July 10, 1997 and replace the European Communities (Vocational Training for Drivers of Vehicles Carrying Dangerous Goods) Regulations 1992 (1992 Review, 540).

Extractive industries   The Safety, Health and Welfare at Work (Extractive Industries) Regulations 1997 (S.I. No. 467 of 1997), made under the Safety, Health and Welfare at Work Act 1989 (1989 Review, 379-93), gave effect to Directives 92/91/EEC and 92/104/EEC. They prescribe detailed duties on employers in the extractive industries, which includes mining, quarrying and onshore and offshore mineral exploration activities. Many provisions of the 1997 Regulations state that they are in addition to provisions in the Mines and Quarries Act 1965 and the Safety, Health and Welfare (Offshore Installations) Act 1987 (1987 Review, 299), and Regulations made under the 1965 and 1987 Acts, respectively. It is notable (and regrettable) that where there are clear overlaps between the 1997 Regulations and the existing statutory provisions in this area, no repeal or revocation of the pre-1997 legislation has been effected. The 1997 Regulations came into effect on November 21, 1997.

Fishing   The European Communities (Minimum Safety and Health Requirements for Improved Medical Treatment on Board Vessels) Regulations 1997 (S.I. No. 506 of 1997) gave effect to Directive 92/29/EC, which requires the provision of certain medical facilities on specified sea-going vessels. The 1997 Regulations came into effect on December 31, 1997.

SEA POLLUTION

The Sea Pollution (Harmful Substances in Packaged Form) Regulations 1997 (S.I. No. 513 of 1997), made under the Sea Pollution Act 1991 (1991 Review, 366), gave effect to Annex III of the 1973 International Convention for the Prevention of Pollution from Ships and prohibited the carriage of harmful substances by sea unless done in accordance with provisions with regard to packing, marking and labelling, documentation and stowage. Similarly, the Sea Pollution (Prevention of Oil Pollution) (Amendment) Regulations 1997 (S.I. No. 514 of 1997), also made under the 1991 Act, amended the Sea Pollution (Prevention of Oil Pollution) Regulations 1994 (1994 Review, 398) and gave effect to amendments to Annex I of the 1973 Convention. The Sea Pollution (Prevention of Pollution by Noxious Liquid Substances in Bulk) (Amendment) Regulations 1997 (S.I. No. 515 of 1997), also made under the 1991 Act, amended the Sea Pollution (Prevention of Pollution by Noxious Liquid Substances in Bulk) Regulations 1994 (1994 Review, 398) to give effect to amendments to Annex II of the 1973 Convention. Finally, the Sea Pollution (Prevention of Pollution by Garbage from Ships) (Amendment) Regulations 1997 (S.I. No. 516 of 1997), also made under the 1991 Act, amended the Sea Pollution (Prevention Of Pollution By Garbage From Ships) Regulations 1994 (1994 Review, 398) to give effect to amendments to Annex v. of the 1973 International Convention for the Prevention of Pollution from Ships. These Regulations all came into effect on January 30, 1998.

Social Welfare Law

Gerry Whyte, Trinity College, Dublin

SOCIAL WELFARE ACT

In addition to providing for the annual increases in welfare payments, the Social Welfare Act 1997 provided, *inter alia,* for the introduction of a new means-tested payment for sick people, improved the entitlements of the self-employed and continued the process of removing gender discrimination from the social welfare code.

Part I contains the usual provisions for short title and construction and definitions.

Part II provides for the annual changes in welfare rates and in the calculation of social insurance contributions. Section 7 also provides for the continued payment of child dependant allowances for up to 13 weeks to people who, immediately before taking up insurable employment or insurable self-employment, were engaged in Community Employment and to people who take up employment under the Jobs Initiative Scheme administered by FÁS.

Part III introduces changes in relation to a number of social insurance schemes. Sections 10 and 11 provide for the extension of Maternity Benefit and Adoptive Benefit respectively to self-employed contributors. (These provisions were brought into effect on June 9, 1997 by S.I. No. 248 of 1997, see below. See also S.I. No. 249 of 1997.) Section 12 empowers the Minister to provide for the payment of reduced rate Old Age (Contributory) Pension or reduced rate Retirement Pension to persons who have a yearly average of less than 48 contributions from when they first became insured until the end of the contribution year before reaching age 66, provided that, where the yearly average is less than 20, they have a minimum of 260 paid contributions. (This provision was brought into effect on November 21, 1997 by S.I. No. 490 of 1997. See also S.I. No. 489 of 1997.) The section also provides for increases in the number of qualifying contributions which will be required of claimants for both pensions in the future. Those qualifying for either pension on or after April 6, 2002 will have to show that they have at least 250 paid contributions, while those claiming on or after April 6, 2012 will require 520 qualifying contributions or an aggregate of 520 qualifying and voluntary contributions of which at least 260 must be qualifying contributions. In addition, from April 6, 2012, a person with a mixed insurance record, *i.e.* with contributions paid at both full and modified rate, who wishes to qualify for a pro-rata mixed insurance Old Age (Contributory) Pension will be required to have an aggregate of 520 full rate and modified contributions of which not more than 260 may be paid at the modified rate. Finally, section 12 also increases the number of paid contributions required for the purpose of becoming a voluntary contributor from 156 to 260 with effect from April 6, 2002. Section 13 changes, for the better, the conditions for requalifying for Unemployment Benefit. Now a claimant may requalify where s/he has paid 13 contributions after the first six months of unemployment rather than after the first fifteen months of unemployment as heretofore was the case. Section 14 abolishes the gender discrimination that existed as between widowers and widows claiming Death Benefit under the Occupational Injuries Code (see the 1993 Review), though curiously the opportunity was not taken to abolish comparable discriminatory provisions governing the entitlement to the same benefit of mothers and fathers of deceased workers. The section also makes Death Benefit payable where the deceased worker had been entitled, immediately before the date of death, to Disablement Pension in respect of a disablement assessed at 50% or more.

Part IV deals with payments to the sick. Sections 15 and 16 provide for the introduction of a new means-tested payment, Sickness Allowance, which will be payable to people who are incapable of work but not entitled to Disability Benefit because of an inadequate social insurance record and not entitled to Disability Allowance because they are not substantially handicapped in undertaking employment. Section 17 provides for the renaming of Disability Benefit as Sickness Benefit and of Invalidity Pension as Disability Pension while section 18 provides that the provisions of this Part shall be brought into effect by ministerial order.

Part V continues the process of purging the social welfare code of any gender discrimination in respect of new claimants by providing for a new means-tested payment for widowers on the same terms as the Widow's (Non-Contributory) Pension is available to widows. (Heretofore childless widowers did not qualify for any specially designated welfare payment, unlike childless widows – see the 1996 Review, 556). This Part was brought into effect on October 17, 1997 by S.I. No. 437 of 1997 – see below. (See also S.I. No. 438 of 1997.)

Part VI effects a number of miscellaneous changes to various social assistance schemes which, by virtue of section 27, require ministerial orders in order to be brought into effect. Section 22 empowers the Minister to extend entitlement to Disability Allowance to persons who reside in an institution on a part-time basis, though in such cases the allowance will be payable at a reduced rate – see further S.I. No. 251 of 1997. The section also provides that where one of a couple is in receipt of Disability Allowance and the other is in receipt of the Old Age (Non-Contributory) Pension or Invalidity Pension, each of the couple may receive the full personal rate of payment. It also empowers the Department to meet the cost of medical certificates issued for the purpose of claiming Disability Allowance or Sickness Allowance. (Sub-sections 1 and 2 of section 22 were brought into effect on June 4, 1997 by S.I. No. 250 of 1997 – see below.) Section 23 provides for the payment of up to 150% of the standard rate of Carer's Allowance to a person caring for more than one incapacitated person and also empowers the Minister to prescribe the circumstances and conditions under which a person is to be regarded as providing full-time care and attention to a relevant pensioner. (See further S.I. No. 333 of 1997.) Section 24 provides that claimants who cease to be entitled to One-Parent Family Payment or Carer's Allowance may qualify for Pre-Retirement Allowance without first having to have been in receipt of unemployment payments for 15 months. This section was brought into effect on April 10, 1997 by S.I. No. 162 of 1997 – see below, 686. Section 25 continues the process of standardising the provisions for the assessment of capital by extending the new provisions applying in the case of Disability Allowance and One-Parent Family Payment to Old Age (Non-Contributory) Pension, Blind Pension, Widow's (Non-Contributory) Pension, Widower's (Non-Contributory) Pension, Orphan's (Non-Contributory) Pension and Carer's Allowance, while section 26 consolidates the provisions relating to amounts disregarded in the assessment of means and also provides for the disregard of rental income from the assessment of means for Old Age (Non-Contributory) Pension where the income is in respect of a person who lives with and pays rent to the pensioner. (Sections 25, 26(1)(c) and 26(1)(d) were brought into effect on October 17, 1997 by S.I. No. 435 of 1997 – see below.)

Part VII effects a number of miscellaneous changes to the social welfare code. Section 28 provides that on the introduction of tapered adult dependant allowances, a person in receipt of such an allowance will be assessed with only half the joint means of the couple. Moreover the term "adult dependant" in now replaced in the social welfare code by the term "qualified adult". (See further S.I. No. 492 of 1997). Section 29 provides that decisions requiring a person to maintain a relative who is in receipt of One-Parent Family Payment or Supplementary Welfare Allowance shall in future be made by Deciding Officers as opposed to executive officers which is currently the position. One important consequence of this change is that the person affected now has a right of appeal to the Social Welfare Appeals Office. Section 29 also empowers the Minister to prescribe, by way of regulation, the basis on which the contribution which a person is required to pay in these circumstances is to be calculated and further provides that a divorced person will remain liable to contribute towards the cost of any such allowance or Deserted Wife's Benefit paid to his or her former spouse until such time as that spouse remarries. This section will be brought into effect by ministerial order. Section 30 provides that the requirement of "waiting days" (whereby a person is not paid for the first three days of a claim for Unemployment Benefit) will not apply in the case of a claim for benefit made following a claim for Disability Benefit in the same period of interruption of employment. The section also empowers the Minister to make regulations dispensing with this requirement in relation to claims for Unemployment Assistance in certain circumstances and also specifying the circumstances in which a person will be regarded as being available for and genuinely seeking employment for the purposes of entitlement to Unemployment Benefit or Unemployment Assistance. It further provides that people who were in receipt of either Unemployment Benefit or Unemployment Assistance prior to their participation in the European Voluntary Service Initiative may immediately resume such entitlement on completion of the programme. Section 31 provides that where a person is convicted of an offence under section 32 of the Larceny Act 1916, by virtue of having received any social welfare payment by way of personation, the amount involved may be recovered from any social welfare payment to which the person is or becomes entitled. Section 32 incorporates into primary legislation the existing regulatory provisions governing the payment of arrears on foot of late claims, thus avoiding the argument cogently put by the Ombudsman in his *Report of Investigation of Complaints against the Department of Social Welfare regarding Arrears of Contributory Pensions in cases where the pension claim is late* (14 March 1997) that the then existing law did not authorise the Minister to restrict the arrears of welfare payable where a claim had been put in late. It also extends from six to twelve months the period in respect of which arrears may be paid in the case of certain prescribed payments. This section was brought into effect on April 8, 1997 by S.I. No. 161 of 1997 – see below. Section 33 empowers the Department to collect P.R.S.I. from certain categories of self-employed contributors who are exempt from tax liability. It also provides for the refunding of the Old Age (Contributory) Pension element of self-employment contributions to a person who, previously having been insured as an employee, became insured as a self-employed contributor after reaching age 56 and provided s/he does not qualify for the Old Age (Contributory or Non-Contributory) Pension. The section also provides for regulatory powers to refund part of the employer's portion of contributions paid in respect of seafarers. (See further S.I. No. 291 of 1997). Section 34 amends the social welfare appeals system by enabling the Chief Appeals Officer to divert an appeal from an appeals officer to the Circuit Court where the Chief Appeals Officer certifies that the ordinary appeals procedures are inadequate to secure the effective processing of the particular appeal. Section 35 amends a number of references to regulatory provisions in the Social Welfare (Consolidation) Act 1993, consequential on the consolidation of regulations relating to contributions and insurability in 1996. The section also deletes section 212(7) of the 1993 Act, which provides that a person shall not be required to give any evidence or answer any questions tending to incriminate himself in the course of an inspection by a Social Welfare Inspector, on the ground that such a provision is unnecessary having regard to the common law right against self-incrimination. Section 36 provides for the continuity of Regulations made under the provisions of the 1993 Act which are amended by the 1997 Act.

In Part VIII, section 37 amends the functions of the National Social Service Board, in the light of the transfer of responsibility for the Board from the Minister for Health to the Minister for Social Welfare, to reflect more accurately the role of the Board in promoting and supporting independent information, advice and advocacy services throughout the country.

Sections 38 and 39, in Part IX, increase the weekly earnings below which employees are exempt from liability for the Health Contributions and the Employment and Training Levy and also increase the annual income limit below which self-employed people are exempt from these levies. They also exempt from liability for the levies any payment made pursuant to a maintenance arrangement within the meaning of section 3 of the Finance Act 1983 relating to a marriage for the benefit of the other party to a marriage (unless the provisions of section 4 of the 1983 Act apply in respect of such payment) or any distribution from an Irish resident company received by a person who is not an Irish resident.

Finally, section 40, in Part X, empowers the Minister to exclude external schemes or certain categories of external schemes from the application of some or all of the provisions of the Pensions Act 1990 and/or regulations made pursuant to that Act.

REGULATIONS

Thirty two regulations relating to income maintenance schemes were promulgated during 1997. They are as follows:

Social Welfare (Consolidated Contributions and Insurability) (Amendment) (Defence Forces) Regulations 1997 (S.I. No. 154 of 1997) – These regulations provide for the reduction of the modified social insurance rate applying to NCOs and enlisted personnel in the Defence Forces.

Social Welfare (Miscellaneous Control Provisions) Regulations 1997 (S.I. No. 155 of 1997) – These regulations consolidate existing regulations relating to control provisions and amend those provisions by (a) extending the requirement to notify the Department of the commencement of employment to the meat processing industry; (b) requiring institutions of education to provide details of PLC students to the Department; and (c) requiring nursing homes to provide details of recipients of social welfare payments.

Social Welfare (Consolidated Payments Provisions) (Household Budgeting) Regulations 1997 (S.I. No. 156 of 1997) – These regulations provide for the extension to One-Parent Family Payment and Deserted Wife's Benefit of the Household Budgeting facility whereby claimants of certain welfare payments can arrange to have deductions made from their weekly payments in respect of regular household expenses and paid over to specified bodies such as the ESB, Telecom Éireann and local authorities.

Social Welfare Act 1997 (Section 32) (Commencement) Order 1997 (S.I. No. 161 of 1997) – This Order brings section 32 of the 1997 Act into effect on 8 April 1997.

Social Welfare Act 1997 (Section 24) (Commencement) Order 1997 (S.I. No. 162 of 1997) – This Order brings section 24 of the 1997 Act into effect on April 10, 1997.

Social Welfare (No. 2) Act 1995 (Sections 2, 3, 4, 5, 6, 7, 8, 9, 10(1) and 10(2)) (Commencement) Order 1997 (S.I. No. 194 of 1997) – This Order brings sections 2, 3, 4, 5, 6, 7, 8, 9, 10(1) and 10(2) of the 1995 (No. 2) Act, providing that claimants will not be disadvantaged in terms of welfare entitlements as a result of obtaining a divorce, into effect on April 21, 1997.

Social Welfare Act 1996 (Sections 20 and 28) (Commencement) Order 1997 (S.I. No. 195 of 1997) – This Order brings sections 20 and 28 of the 1996 Act providing that claimants of One-Parent Family Payment, Widow's (Contributory) Pension or Widower's (Contributory) Pension shall not be disadvantaged in terms of welfare entitlement by virtue of having obtained a divorce, into effect on April 21, 1997.

Social Welfare (Occupational Injuries) (Amendment) Regulations 1997 (S.I. No. 235 of 1997) – These regulations provide for increases in the reduced rates of certain Occupational Injuries Benefits.

Social Welfare (Rent Allowance) (Amendment) Regulations 1997 (S.I. No. 236 of 1997) – These regulations provide for increases in the amount of means disregarded for the means test for rent allowance and for the minimum rent payable under this scheme.

Social Welfare (Consolidated Payments Provisions) (Amendment) (No. 2) (Increase in Rates) Regulations 1997 (S.I. No. 237 of 1997) – These regulations provide for increases in the reduced rates of certain social insurance payments.

Social Welfare Act 1997 (Sections 10 and 11) (Commencement) Order 1997 (S.I. No. 240 of 1997) – This Order provides that sections 10 and 11 of the 1997 Act will come into effect on June 9, 1997.

Social Welfare (Consolidated Payments Provisions) (Amendment) (No. 4) (Maternity and Adoptive Benefit) Regulations 1997 (S.I. No. 249 of 1997) – These regulations increase the minimum rate of Maternity and Adoptive Benefit and also prescribe the manner of calculating the reckonable weekly earnings, reckonable weekly emoluments and reckonable weekly income of a claimant of either benefit.

Social Welfare Act 1997 (Section 22(1) and (2)) (Commencement) Order,

1997 (S.I. No. 250 of 1997) – These regulations bring section 22(1) and (2) into effect from June 4, 1997.

Social Welfare (Consolidated Payments Provisions) (Amendment) (No. 3) (Disability Allowance) Regulations 1997 (S.I. No. 251 of 1997) – These regulations provide for payment of Disability Allowance at half-rate to persons who reside in an institution for between 2 and 3 days of each week and for the payment of the allowance to persons who are temporarily resident outside of an institution while on holidays. They also provide for an increase in the amount of weekly earnings derived from employment of a rehabilitative nature disregarded in the assessment of means for Disability Allowance.

Social Welfare (Consolidated Contributions and Insurability) (Amendment) (No. 2) (Refunds) Regulations 1997 (S.I. No. 291 of 1997) – These regulations provide for refunds to certain employers in the shipping industry in respect of the employer's portion of the social insurance contributions paid in respect of seagoing employees. They also provide that a person who became insured as a self-employed contributor on or after April 6, 1988 and had attained 56 years on that date will be entitled to a refund in respect of the Old Age (Contributory) Pension element of their self-employment contribution provided that they do not qualify for Retirement or Old Age (Contributory or Non-Contributory) Pension.

Social Welfare (Consolidated Contributions and Insurability) (Amendment) (No. 3) (Homemakers) Regulations 1997 (S.I. No. 292 of 1997) – These regulations provide that homemakers shall be awarded credited contributions in respect of (a) each week from the week in which the person becomes a homemaker to the end of that contribution year or until the person ceases to be a homemaker, whichever occurs first or (b) where the insured person was a homemaker in the previous contribution year, from the beginning of the contribution year in which the person ceases to be a homemaker up to the end of the contribution week in which the said cessation occurs. These credited contributions are reckonable for Old Age (Contributory) Pension only.

Social Welfare (Consolidated Payments Provisions) (Amendment) (No. 5) (Homemakers) Regulations 1997 (S.I. No. 293 of 1997) – These regulations provide for the application to become a homemaker for the purposes of the Old Age (Contributory) Pension where a person is not in receipt of Child Benefit or Carer's Allowance. Such an application must be made before the end of the contribution year following the contribution year in which the person became a homemaker or, where someone became a homemaker between April 6, 1994 and April 5, 1997, before April 5, 1999. The regulations also provide for the submission of such documents or information as may be necessary to decide on an application.

Social Welfare (Alteration of Name of Department and Title of Minister) Order 1997 (S.I. No. 307 of 1997) – This Order changes the name of the Department of Social Welfare to that of the Department of Social, Community and Family Affairs and the title of the Minister for Social Welfare to that of the Minister for Social, Community and Family Affairs.

Social Welfare (Consolidated Payments Provisions) (Amendment) (No. 6) (Carer's Allowance) Regulations 1997 (S.I. No. 333 of 1997) – These regulations provide for the relaxation of the 'full-time care' requirement to extend entitlement to Carer's Allowance to carers of those attending rehabilitation courses or day-care centres.

Social Welfare (Consolidated Supplementary Welfare Allowances) (Amendment) Regulations 1997 (S.I. No. 334 of 1997) – These regulations provide that budgetary increases in social welfare payments shall not have the effect of reducing Dietary Supplements where such supplements are already being paid. They also provide that compensation payments awarded to people who either have contracted Hepatitis C from certain blood products or have disabilities attributable to Thalidomide shall be disregarded in the calculation of means for the Supplementary Welfare Allowance scheme.

Social Welfare (Consolidated Payments Provisions) (Amendment) (No. 7) (Treatment Benefit) Regulations 1997 (S.I. No. 390 of 1997) – These regulations extend entitlement to optical and medical Treatment Benefits by abolishing income limit provisions for such benefits, providing for the retention of benefits where the spouse qualifies for Old Age Pension, providing for the retention of benefits for spouses who take up employment with income in excess of £60 p.w. until they establish entitlement on their own insurance, and extending entitlement to medical appliance benefit to enlisted personnel of the Defence Forces paying reduced PRSI.

Social Welfare Act 1997 (Sections 25, 26(1)(c) and 26(1)(d)) (Commencement) Order 1997 (S.I. No. 435 of 1997) – This Order provides that sections 25, 26(1)(c) and 26(1)(d) of the 1997 Act shall come into effect on October 17, 1997.

Social Welfare (Consolidated Payments Provisions) (Amendment) (No. 8) Regulations 1997 (S.I. No. 436 of 1997) – These regulations provide for the payment of Constant Attendance Allowance with Disablement Pension to those in receipt of a social insurance payment. They also continue the process of standardising the various methods of assessing capital by extending the revised capital assessment provisions for long term social assistance payments to Pre-Retirement Allowance.

Social Welfare Act 1997 (Part V) (Commencement) Order 1997 (S.I. No. 437 of 1997) – This Order brings Part V of the 1997 Act, providing for the introduction of the Widow's and Widower's (Non-Contributory) Pension, into effect on 17 October 1997.

Social Welfare (Consolidated Payments Provisions) (Amendment) (No. 9) (Widow's and Widower's (Non-Contributory) Pension) Regulations 1997 (S.I. No. 438 of 1997) – These regulations provide for consequential amendments to existing provisions relating to the making of claims and payments of

Widow's (Non-Contributory) Pension on the introduction of the new Widow's and Widower's (Non-Contributory) Pension.

Maintenance Allowances (Increased Payment) Regulations 1997 (S.I. No. 479 of 1997) – These regulations provide for the payment of the Christmas bonus to claimants of Infectious Diseases Maintenance Allowance.

Social Welfare (Consolidated Payments Provisions) (Amendment) (No. 10) (Pensions) Regulations 1997 (S.I. No. 489 of 1997) – These regulations enable a person who has a yearly average of 10 to 19 social insurance contributions to qualify for a reduced rate of Old Age (Contributory) Pension provided he or she has 260 qualifying contributions. They also provide that the increase for people aged 80 or more may be divided for the purposes of separate payments in the case of Retirement Pension, Old Age (Contributory) Pension, Old Age (Non-Contributory) Pension and Invalidity Pension.

Social Welfare Act 1997 (Section 12(1)(b)) (Commencement) Order 1997 (S.I. No. 490 of 1997) – This Order brings section 12(1)(b) of the 1997 Act into effect on November 21, 1997.

Social Welfare (Temporary Provisions) Regulations 1997 (S.I. No. 293 of 1997) – These regulations provide for the payment of the Christmas bonus to long-term social welfare claimants.

Social Welfare (Consolidated Payments Provisions) (Amendment) (No. 11) (Increase for Qualified Adult) Regulations 1997 (S.I. No. 492 of 1997) – These regulations provide for the introduction of tapered increases in respect of qualified adults for claimants of Disability Benefit, Unemployment Benefit, Injury Benefit, Unemployability Supplement, Unemployment Assistance, Pre-Retirement Allowance and Disability Allowance.

Social Welfare Act 1995 (Section 15) (Commencement) Order 1997 (S.I. No. 493 of 1997) – This Order provides that section 15 of the Social Welfare Act 1995 will come into effect on November 26, 1997.

Social Welfare (Consolidated Payments Provisions) (Amendment) (No. 13) (Treatment Benefit) Regulations 1997 (S.I. No. 530 of 1997) – These regulations extend entitlement to Dental Benefit by abolishing income limit provisions and also consolidate the existing regulatory provisions relating to Treatment Benefit.

EQUAL TREATMENT

In the 1993 Annual Review, the present writer argued that the ruling of the Court of Justice in *Marshall v. Southampton and South West Hampshire Area Health Authority (No. 2)*, Case 271/91, August 2, 1993, [1993] E.C.R. I–4367, to the effect that the payment of interest as part of an award of damages was an essential component of full compensation for the purposes of article 6 of Directive 76/207, had obvious implications for Directive 79/7/EEC, article 6 of which is framed in identical terms to its counterpart in the earlier Directive. Certainly the practice of the State in settling claims for equality arrears taken by Irish women was to adjust the amount due in line with increases in the Consumer Price Index. However, in *R. v. Secretary of State for Social Security, ex parte Sutton*, Case C-66/95, April 22, 1997, [1997] E.C.R. I–2163, the Court of Justice held that no interest is payable on arrears of welfare due under Directive 79/7/EEC. The Court held that *Marshall II* applied only to compensation payable as a remedy for loss and damage sustained as a result of discrimination and that arrears of welfare payments did not constitute such compensation. However, this rather formalistic view of the situation arguably does not fully meet the argument that where a person has suffered delay in obtaining welfare to which he or she is entitled because of the discriminatory action of the State, the only way in which to ensure that the State does not benefit from its wrongdoing is to oblige it to pay the full value of the sum originally due. The Court went on to hold that under the *Francovich* principle – see *Francovich v. Italy* [1996] E.C.R. I–1029 – whereby the State may be held liable for loss and damage caused to an individual as a result of breaches of Community law for which the State can be held responsible, it is the national law on liability which provides the framework within which the State must make reparation.

In another case decided during 1997 on Directive 79/7/EEC, *Balestra v. INPS,* Case C-139/95, January 30, 1997; [1997] E.C.R. I–549, the Court of Justice held that a difference in the calculation of early-retirement benefits was objectively and necessarily linked to the setting of pensionable ages which differ for men and women and therefore permissible discrimination having regard to article 7 of the Directive.

APPEALS

The case of *Galvin v. Chief Appeals Officer*, High Court, June 27, 1997, raised two different issues for consideration, the first of which was to identify when an oral hearing of an appeal should be held.

The claimant's appeal against a refusal to pay him an Old Age (Contributory) Pension had been disallowed by an appeals officer (whose decision was subsequently confirmed by the Chief Appeals Officer) on the ground that the claimant did not have the requisite minimum yearly average of twenty paid or credited social insurance contributions between January 5, 1953 and April 3, 1992. This decision was based on the Department's own records of the claimant's social insurance contributions over that period. However the evidence before the court indicated that, at an earlier stage in the processing of this claim, different officers in the Department had made two different errors in the case based on these records, indicating their fallibility. The particular decision challenged in the High Court proceedings implicitly assumed that no contributions had been made by the claimant while working for a particular company between 1948 and 1961, an assumption which was contested by the claimant.

The claimant's first line of attack was to argue that, in failing to give him an oral hearing, both the appeals officer and the Chief Appeals Officer had acted in breach of natural/constitutional justice. Under the social welfare code, the appeals officer has a discretion as to whether or not to hold an oral hearing of an appeal. According to Costello P., there were no hard and fast rules for determining when such a hearing is required; rather each case has to be decided "on the circumstances pertaining, the nature of the inquiry being undertaken by the decision-maker, the rules under which the decision-maker is acting, and the subject matter with which he is dealing and account should also be taken as to whether an oral hearing was requested." In the instant case, the judge concluded that an oral hearing was necessary for a number of reasons. First, the relevant contribution period under consideration began nearly 50 years ago and finished about 36 years ago, increasing the possibility that records might have been mislaid, misfiled or destroyed. Second, as already noted, the court had evidence of the fallibility of the Departmental records in this particular case. Third, the proper resolution of the dispute required an assessment of the strength of the case advanced by the claimant and yet the evidence suggested that the Department operated a policy of relying on its own records as conclusive evidence of a person's contribution record. Accordingly, Costello P. concluded that the appeals officer should have conducted an oral hearing in this case and that his failure to do so amounted to an error of law which the court would quash.

This decision is in line with the earlier Supreme Court case of *Kiely v. Minister for Social Welfare* [1977] I.R. 267 in which the Court stated, *per* Henchy J. at p.278, that:

> an oral hearing is mandatory unless the case is of such a nature that it can be determined without an oral hearing, that is, summarily. An appeal is of such a nature that it can be determined summarily if a determination of the claim can be made fairly on a consideration of the documentary evidence. If, however, there are unresolved conflicts in the documentary evidence as to any matter essential to a ruling of the claim, the intention of the Regulations is that those conflicts shall be resolved by an oral hearing.

WELFARE CLAIMS AND THE DOCTRINES OF ESTOPPEL AND LEGITIMATE EXPECTATION

The second issue raised in *Galvin* was whether a claimant could rely on a mistaken representation made by the welfare authorities in order to establish a claim to a benefit to which the claimant would not otherwise be entitled. The representation in the instant case was contained in a letter from the Department in 1987 indicating that the claimant would qualify for an Old Age (Contributory) Pension. However Costello P. held that the doctrine of estoppel did not apply here for two reasons. First, the claimant did not suffer any detriment as a result of the representation as even if he had been properly advised by the Department in 1987 of the inadequacies in his insurance record, he could not have improved that record in order to qualify for a pension. Second, applying the Supreme Court decision in *In re Greendale Building Company* [1977] I.R. 256, the doctrine of estoppel did not apply where the claimant was not entitled by statute to the benefit claimed. This ground was also sufficient to dispose of the claimant's argument based on the doctrine of legitimate expectation.

TAXATION OF WIDOW'S (CONTRIBUTORY) PENSION

In *Ó Síocháin v. Neenan*, High Court, April 4, 1997, the High Court was asked to rule on whether the increase in respect of qualified children paid with the Widow's (Contributory) Pension was, for income tax purposes, the income of the widow. Holding that it was not assessable for tax, Smyth J. followed a similar decision of Lynch J. in *Ó Coindealbhán (Inspector of Taxes) v. O'Carroll* [1989] IR. 229 in relation to pensions payable under the Garda Síochána Pensions Order 1981 (even though that Order expressly provides for a children's contributory pension whereas the Social Welfare Acts, in contrast, provide for an increase in the widow's pension, albeit that in both cases the sums involved are paid directly to the widow.) Applying a purposive approach to the interpretation of the Social Welfare Acts, the judge concluded that the increase in respect of qualified children payable with the Widow's (Contributory) Pension, although payable to the widow, was clearly intended and destined for the child. He also noted that whereas section 15 of the Finance Act 1992 sought to make certain social welfare benefits chargeable to tax, section 10 of the Finance Act 1995 expressly excluded from such liability increases in such benefits payable in respect of qualified children.

This decision was subsequently appealed to the Supreme Court and the Supreme Court decision will be reviewed in the 1998 Annual Review.

SCOPE OF SOCIAL INSURANCE

In *Henry Denny & Sons (Ireland) Ltd v. Minister for Social Welfare*, December 1, 1997, the Supreme Court upheld Carroll J.'s decision in the High Court – [1996] 1 I.L.R.M. 418; E.L.R. 43 – in which she refused to set aside an appeals officer's decision classifying a demonstrator in a supermarket as an employee of the company whose product she was promoting.

Two issues arose for consideration in the case. The first was to clarify the role of the High Court in reviewing a decision of an administrative tribunal. Following its earlier decision in *Mara (Inspector of Taxes) v. Hummingbird Ltd* [1982] I.L.R.M. 421, the Supreme Court, *per* Keane J., held that the High Court could set aside the findings of a tribunal if they were based on an incorrect interpretation of documents or on a mistaken view of the law or, in the case of findings on primary facts, if there was no evidence whatever to support them.

Arising from the ruling, the second issue in the case was whether the conclusions reached by the appeals officer were based on an erroneous view of the law. On this question of how to distinguish an employee from an independent contractor, Keane J. said:

> . . . [W]hile each case must be determined in the light of its particular facts and circumstances, in general a person will be regarded as providing his or her services under a contract of service and not as an independent contractor where he or she is performing those services for another person and not for himself or herself. The degree of control exercised over how the work is to be performed, although a factor to be taken into account, is not decisive. The inference that the person is engaged in business on his or her own account can be more readily drawn where he or she provides the necessary premiums or equipment or some other form of investment, where he or she employs others to assist in the business and where the profit which he or she derives from the business is dependent on the efficiency with which it is conducted by him or her.

In the instant case, the Court held that the appeals officer was entitled to hold that the demonstrator was an employee on the facts as found by him.

PUBLICATIONS

Finally it is worth noting the special *Report of Investigation of Complaints against the Department of Social Welfare regarding Arrears of Contributory Pensions in cases where the pension claim is late*, published by the Office of the Ombudsman in March 1997. This report contains a close analysis of the statutory provisions regulating late claims and argues cogently that regulations allowing the Minister to restrict the amount of arrears payable to claimant who make late claims are *ultra vires*. (However note section 32 of the Social Welfare Act 1997 which clearly protects the Minister's powers in this regard for the future.)

Solicitors

LIEN

Title deeds In *Ring v. Kennedy*, High Court, July 18, 1997, Laffoy J. held that the common law lien only applied to costs incurred by the client against whom it was claimed. In the instant case, the plaintiffs were directors of companies which admittedly owed fees to the defendant, a solicitor. The plaintiffs had discharged their personal indebtedness to the defendant. They successfully sought an order directing the defendant to deliver the title deeds to their property, over which the defendant had claimed a lien pending resolution of the dispute concerning the costs owed to him by the companies of which the plaintiffs were directors. As indicated, Laffoy J. held that the common law lien did not extend to the circumstances of the instant case and ordered the delivery sought.

MAINTENANCE

In *O'Keeffe v. Scales* [1998] 1 I.L.R.M. 393 (SC), the plaintiffs sought damages in negligence from the defendant, a solicitor, who had acted for them in connection with a financial transaction which, it transpired, was wholly unsuccessful and caused them financial ruin. Included in the claim for damages against the defendant was a claim for £275,620, due and owing by the plaintiffs to another solicitor who had been instructed by the plaintiff during the period n which the defendant had also been instructed by the plaintiffs. A substantial part of this sum remained due and owing during the currency of the instant proceedings. The defendant sought an order seeking to stay the plaintiffs' action on the ground that the proceedings smacked of maintenance.

The defendant argued that the inclusion in the proceedings of sums owing by the plaintiffs to the other solicitor amounted to the other solicitor having an interest in the outcome of the action inconsistent with his position as solicitor for the plaintiffs. The defendant argued that the proceedings were an abuse of process and should be stayed until such time as the matters giving rise to the abuse of process had been brought to an end. The argument was rejected in the High Court and, on appeal, by the Supreme Court.

The Supreme Court accepted that it was clear from the authorities that the law relating to maintenance and champerty still existed in the State. But although the law still applied, the Court held that it could not be extended in such a way as to deprive people of their constitutional right of access to the courts under Article 40.3 to litigate reasonably stateable claims. The Court considered that, even if the other solicitor was maintaining the plaintiffs' action in a champertous and unlawful manner, it was doubtful that that in itself would amount to a defence to the plaintiffs' negligence claim much less entitle the defendant to 'stifle' the plaintiffs' claim *in limine* on the motion to stay or dismiss in advance of a plenary trial.

By way of some potential consolation to the defendant, the Court added that, if at the plenary hearings the defendant was successful in her defence to the claim in negligence, and it was established that the other solicitor had maintained the proceedings in a champertous fashion, it would be open to the defendant (citing the decision in *Alabaster v. Harness* [1894] 2 Q.B. 897) to sue that solicitor directly for all the damage suffered by her. Such a claim could include any costs awarded to her and not recovered or recoverable from the plaintiffs.

Finally, the Court held that the inclusion in the plaintiffs' claim of the items of special damage in respect of costs due to the other solicitor did not contravene section 68 of the Solicitors (Amendment) Act 1994, which regulates the manner in which solicitors charge clients (1994 Review, 430). The decision is further discussed in the Torts chapter, 784–5, below.

RETAINER

Written retainer rule *Mackey v. Wilde and Longin*, Supreme Court, January 15, 1997 involved a complex dispute concerning whether a solicitor had been properly retained and instructed to act on behalf of his client. It was alleged at one point during the proceedings in the High Court that a written retainer had not been obtained by the solicitor in question. It was contended that the law imposed upon a solicitor an obligation to obtain a written retainer from his client, and that if he failed to do so, and if the client subsequently disputed the terms of the retainer, the client's evidence had to be supported in preference to that of the solicitor. In the High Court, Morris J. (as he then was) declined to follow this line of authority and proceeded to hear evidence from the client and the solicitor as to whether instructions had been issued. He concluded that there had. On appeal, the Supreme Court affirmed.

The Court held that Morris J. had been correct in refusing to follow the line of authority with regard to written retainers (such as *Allen v. Bone* (1841) Beav. 493 and *Griffiths v. Evans* [1953] 2 All E.R. 1364) because any practice which required the courts to prefer the evidence of one party to a dispute to that of another would not be in compliance with its obligation to observe fair procedures. Such a rule as the one with regard to a written retainer was to be regarded as a rule of prudence rather than as a rule of law, and in the circumstances of this case, it would be absurd if the Court were prevented from getting at the truth by any rule of private law, if such existed, which was designed to regulate the private relations between solicitor and client.

The Court was satisfied that despite the procedural difficulties of a solicitor issuing a motion in his own name, he was entitled to do so where there was the possibility that the client had misled the Court when he represented that the solicitor had no authority to act on his behalf. Having being put on notice of such grave allegations, the Court held that Morris J. was entitled to launch his own enquiry. Acting on the principles in such cases as *Hay v. O'Grady* [1992] 1 I.R. 210; [1992] I.L.R.M. 689 (1992 Review, 470-3), the Court held that since Morris J. had seen the witnesses being cross-examined, and was able to form a clear view as to who was telling the truth, the Supreme Court could not interfere with his findings where there was ample evidence for them.

For the substantive issues in the case see *Mackey v. Wilde and Longin (No. 2)* [1998] 1 I.L.R.M. 449 (SC) in the Contracts chapter, 204, above.

REGULATIONS

Admission: US attorneys   The Solicitors Act 1954 (Section 44) Order 1997 (S.I. No. 241 of 1997) provides for the admission as solicitors in Ireland of attorneys qualified in New York and Pennsylvania. The Order came into effect on June 13, 1997.

Apprenticeship   The Solicitors Acts 1954 to 1994 (Apprenticeship and Education) Regulations 1997 (S.I. No. 287 of 1997) consolidate with amendments the provisions for the education and training of persons seeking to be admitted to practice as solicitors, with effect from July 1, 1997. While the 1997 Regulations expressly revoke and replace, *inter alia*, the Solicitors Acts 1954 to 1994 (Apprenticeship and Education) Regulations 1991, they also provide that Regulation 26 of the 1991 Regulations continues to have full force and effect to the extent required. Regulation 26 of the 1991 Regulations was central to the outcome in *Bloomer and Ors v. Incorporated Law Society of Ireland* [1995] 3 I.R. 14 (HC); Supreme Court, February 6, 1996 (1995 Review, 464) and *Abrahamson and Ors v. Law Society of Ireland* [1996] 1 I.R. 403; [1996] 2 I.LR.M. 481. It is worth noting that the 1997 Regulations no longer contain the exemption for law graduates from the FE-1 examination; the exemption contained in the 1991 Regulations had been declared invalid in the *Bloomer* case.

Compensation fund   The Solicitors (Adjudicator) Regulations 1997 (S.I. No. 406 of 1997) provides for the appointment of an adjudicator, as envisaged by section 15 of the Solicitors (Amendment) Act 1994 (1994 Review, 419) to administer the Compensation Fund and sets out the powers, functions and duties of the adjudicator. The Regulations came into effect on October 1, 1997.

Misconduct: sale of land   The Solicitors (Professional Practice, Conduct and Discipline) Regulations 1997 (S.I. No. 85 of 1997) provide that it would constitute misconduct for a solicitor to act for the vendor and purchaser in the sale and purchase of a new residential unit where the vendor is also the builder. The Regulations came into effect on April 1, 1997.

Practising certificates   The Solicitors (Practising Certificates 1998) Regulations 1997 (S.I. No. 507 of 1997) prescribed the form for applications for 1998 practising certificates, while the Solicitors (Practising Certificates 1998 Fees) Regulations 1997 (S.I. No. 508 of 1997) prescribed the fees for 1998 applications. Both sets of Regulations came into effect on January 1, 1998.

Statutory Interpretation

ABOLITION OF COMMON LAW OFFENCES

The origins and effect of the Interpretation (Amendment) Act 1997 is discussed in the Criminal Law chapter, 283, above.

OIREACHTAS BILL

In *An Blascaod Mór Teo v. Commissioners of Public Works*, High Court, July 1, 1997, Budd J. held that the Court was entitled to examine the text of the Bill which had become An Blascaod Mór National Historic Park Act 1989 in order to assist in the interpretation of the words 'lineal descendant' in section 4(4) of the 1989 Act. The order was made under section 5 of the Documentary Evidence Act 1925. The instant proceedings involved a constitutional challenge to the validity of the 1989 Act. Budd J. noted that the court was entitled to examine in this context the policy behind the 1989 Act, and in that context was entitled to look at what was the mischief sought to be addressed by the passing of the 1989 Act. In that respect, the wording of the Bill, as opposed to the parliamentary records of the debates on the passage of the legislation, could assist the Court in framing a statement of the purpose of the Act. For an earlier similar (unsuccessful) application, see *An Blascaod Mór Teo v. Commissioners of Public Works*, High Court, November 27, 1992 (1992 Review, 483). Finally, we note here that, in a judgment delivered in 1998, the High Court found the 1989 Act to be in conflict with the Constitution. We will examine that decision in the 1998 Review.

OIREACHTAS DEBATES

In *Director of Public Prosecutions v. Brennan*, High Court, January 16, 1997, (discussed in the Criminal Law chapter, 313, above), McCracken J. followed the decision in *The People v. McDonagh* [1996] 1 I.R. 565; [1996] 2 I.L.R.M. 468 (1996 Review, 274-8) in holding he was entitled to examine the reason giving during the Oireachtas debate for the inclusion of a particular provision in section 19 of the Criminal Justice (Public Order) Act 1994 (1994 Review, 214).

Torts

DUTY OF CARE

Introduction　In 1997, the Irish courts addressed the question of the nature and scope of the duty of care in negligence. The most comprehensive conceptual analysis was in the High Court; there are strands of evidence that the centre of gravity of judicial thought in the Supreme Court is shifting in a more conservative direction but well short of what McGechan J. in *Trevor Ivory Ltd v. Anderson* [1992] 2 N.Z.L.R. 517, at 530 described as the 'medieval retreat' of the House of Lords in *Murphy v. Brentwood DC* [1991] 1 A.C. 398.

Contract as a barrier to generation of a duty of care　In the 1993 Review, 531-3, we analysed Morris J.'s decision in *Madden v. Irish Turf Club*, High Court, April 2, 1993. Briefly, the case concerned a race at Punchestown won by an ineligible horse that was later disqualified on account of its failure to fulfil the necessary qualifications to compete in the race. The plaintiff had bet on the horse that had come second but was elevated to first place on the disqualification of the ineligible horse. The rules of the totalisator, where he had placed the bet, were that payment was made after the 'All right' had been declared and that no subsequent disqualification would affect his. The plaintiff, who would have won over £18,000 if his horse had come first, sued the Irish Turf Club, which administers flat racing in Ireland, and the Irish National Hunt Steeple Chase Committee, which has a similar function in relation to steeple chasing, both of these defendants sharing facilities and employees; he argued that, in carelessly permitted an ineligible horse to run in the race, they had breached their duty of care in negligence to him.

This argument commended itself to Morris J., but not to the Supreme Court, which allowed the defendants' appeal: [1997] 2 I.L.R.M. 148, O'Flaherty J. (Blayney and Murphy JJ. concurring), after summarising the earlier holdings of the Court in *Ward v. McMaster* [1988] I.R. 337; [1989] I.L.R.M. 400 and *Sunderland v. Louth County Council* [1990] I.L.R.M. 658 as well as Blayney J.'s decision, when in the High Court, in *McMahon v. Ireland* [1988] I.L.R.M. 610, reasoned as follows. The betting aspect of race meetings was separate from the defendants' 'essential function', which was to regulate and control horse races at various courses throughout the country. The Rules of Racing and the Irish National Hunt Steeple Chase Rules expressly provided, in rules 19 and 23, that stewards were to take no cognisance of any disputes or claims with respect to bets. Further,

> the plaintiff's contractual relationship was with the tote management
> and that erected a barrier so as to prevent such close and direct relations
> to occur as is necessary to give rise to any duty of care between the
> plaintiff and the defendants.

Emphasising the words 'ought reasonably to have them in contemplation' in
Lord Atkin's classic answer in *Donoghue v. Stevenson* [1932] A.C. 562, at
580, to the question of 'Who . . . in law, is my neighbour?', O'Flaherty J.
considered it clear from rules 19 and 23 that the defendants had not contemplated having any liability in respect of betting mishaps and, instead, had expressly provided that they were to have nothing to do with them. While the
instant case was not about a betting dispute, nonetheless the rules were 'relevant in indicating that the betting aspect of race meetings must be kept in a
separate compartment.'

The defendants' chief function was to administer horse racing in as orderly a fashion as possible and carry out their system of checks and balances
in relation to owners, trainers and jockeys as well as horses in accordance
with their rules. The matter of how gambling, on the tote or otherwise, was
conducted belonged to a different regime for which they had no responsibility.

The Supreme Court holding is not perhaps surprising. As we indicated in
the 1993 Review, 531–3, it would be curious if gamblers, whose wagering
contracts are not legally enforceable, could claim the benefit of a duty of care
in negligence. Claims for negligently caused pure economic loss are generally
hard to sustain; this particular kind of claim was scarcely the most compelling
one. Nevertheless there are aspects to O'Flaherty J.'s analysis that are surprising and worthy of comment.

The first is his assertion that the plaintiff's contractual relationship was
with the tote management and that 'that erected a barrier so as to prevent such
close and direct relations to occur as is necessary to give rise to a duty of care
between the plaintiff and the defendants.' The idea that the existence of a
contractual relationship between A and B should prevent the genesis of a duty
of care between C and A may seem to some to reflect a judicial approach more
hostile to the duty of care than was apparent in *Winterbottom v. Wright* (1842)
10 M & W 109, 152 ER 402. That was precisely the philosophy rejected by
Donoghue v. Stevenson, yet O'Flaherty J. could draw support from a phrase in
Lord Atkin's speech in that decision to justify his approach.

In the 1996 Review, 579, we noted that O'Flaherty J. adopted the same
approach in *McCann v. Brinks Allied Ltd and Ulster Bank Ltd.* [1997] 1
I.L.R.M. 461 in the more alarming context of protection of bodily integrity,
whereby the defendant bank could immunise itself from a duty of care to

protect employees of a security firm transporting the bank's moneys by the insertion of a provision in its contract with the security firm. At least *Madden* was concerned only with the fate of a bet.

Perhaps the best justification for invoking the contract as a reason for arguing that no duty of care arose is not that the contract erected a barrier to the existence of a duty of care but rather that, in the light of the contract's terms, the plaintiff should not be regarded as having relied in any way on the careful execution by the defendants of their functions. The plaintiff, when betting on the tote, knew that the prize would attach to the winner at the 'All right' and that it would not be affected by a subsequent disqualification. The possibility that the defendants might act carelessly, leading to such a disqualification, was a foreseeable part of the wager, the risk of which was open to assessment by any wagerer. There was, on this view, no basis for reliance on their careful performance in the sense that such reliance could generate a duty of care on the defendants' part. This would seem to be the import of the argument of counsel for the defence, summarised by O'Flaherty J; [1997] 2 I.L.R.M. at 152.

O'Flaherty J.'s analysis of the conceptual aspect of the duty of care is of some interest. He noted that Mr. Kevin Feeney S.C., counsel for the defendants, who had not appeared in the High Court, had drawn attention to the wide ramifications attendant on imposing liability in circumstances such as the instant case in regard to horse races as well as sporting events in general. This public policy argument had not been advanced in the High Court. Since it had not been debated there and it was 'not necessary for any decision' in the instant case, O'Flaherty J. left over consideration of that point to a case where it would be necessary for resolution.

It is clear, therefore, that the plaintiff's case failed because of lack of proximity rather than on policy grounds. It will be recalled that, in *Ward v. McMaster*, above, McCarthy J., having referred to Lord Wilberforce's 'two-step' test in *Anns v. Merton London Borough* [1978] A.C. 728, at 751–752 and the 'just and reasonable' proviso tagged on in *Governors of the Peabody Donation Fund v. Sir Lindsay Parkinson Ltd.* [1985] A.C. 210, at 241, said that he would:

> prefer to express the duty as arising from the proximity of the parties, the foreseeability of the damage, and the absence of any compelling exemption based upon public policy. I do not, in any fashion, seek to exclude the latter consideration, although I confess that such a consideration must be a very powerful one if it is to be used to deny an injured party his right to redress at the expense of the person or body that injured him.

It seem that, in *Madden*, the plaintiff fell at the first of these fences. This is worth emphasising in the context of the question whether the Irish courts will follow the lead of the House of Lords in *Murphy v. Brentwood DC*, above, in repudiating Lord Wilberforce's 'two-step' test in *Anns*. That famous test was expressed as follows:

> First one has to ask whether, as between the alleged wrongdoer and the person who has suffered damage, there is a sufficient relationship of proximity or neighbourhood such that, in the reasonable contemplation of the former, carelessness on his part may be likely to cause damage to the latter, in which case a *prima facie* duty of care arises. Secondly, if the first question is answered affirmatively, it is necessary to consider whether there are any considerations which ought to negative, or to reduce or limit the scope of, the duty or the class of person to whom it is owed or the damages to which a breach of it may give rise.

What ultimately discredited this test was, not that the first step *required* courts to answer in the affirmative in response to factual situations where injury was reasonably foreseeable, but that trial courts frequently erroneously interpreted the first step as requiring them to do so. If we assume that McCarthy J.'s test in *Ward v. McMaster*, quoted above, broadly echoes the *Anns* two-step test, then it is clear from O'Flaherty J.'s approach in *Madden* that it is quite possible for a plaintiff to fail the first hurdle, even where the injury or damage is entirely foreseeable, on the basis of lack of proximity of relationship between the parties.

It is interesting that O'Flaherty J. made no reference to *Murphy v. Brentwood DC* or *Caparo plc v. Dickman* [1990] 2 A.C. 605 where the House of Lords exploded the metaphysical character of the language of the duty of care. In *Caparo* ([1990] 2 A.C., at 628), Lord Roskill counselled that:

> phrases such as 'foreseeability', 'proximity', 'neighbourhood,' 'just and equitable', 'fairness' .... are not precise definitions. At best they are but labels or phrases descriptive of the very different factual situations which can exist in particular cases and which must be carefully examined in each case before it can be pragmatically determined whether a duty of care exists and, if so, what is the scope and extent of that duty.

In *Madden*, O'Flaherty J. was content to use the language of neighbourliness and proximity without embarrassment or apology.

It is worth noting the possible eclipse of the Supreme Court decisions of *Purtill v. Athlone Urban District Council* [1968] I.R. 205 and *McNamara v. Electricity Supply Board* [1975] I.R. 1, which laid such a strong emphasis on proximity language, to the extent that the well-established immunity of occupiers of property from a duty of care in negligence to trespassers was capable of being defeated by the 'proximity of relationship' between the parties.

O'Flaherty J.'s only reference to these decisions (on which Morris J. had relied) was in the context of summarising the argument of counsel for the defendants to the effect that they should be sidelined as cases dealing with personal injury or physical damage rather than economic loss. Of course, the particular context of those cases has been radically altered by the Occupiers Liability Act 1995, which restores the old draconian law regarding trespassers which was set out seventy years ago in *Addie (Robert) & Sons (Collieries) Ltd v. Dumbreck* [1929] A.C. 358. This unfortunate and retrograde step is no reason why the principles stated in *Purtill* and *McNamara*, which are of the greatest generality, should be ignored in contemporary litigation relating to the duty of care.

Sweeney v. Duggan [1997] 2 I.L.R.M. 211 represents a further example of the Supreme Court's aversion to recognising a duty of care in negligence in the overall context of a contractual relationship. It is, perhaps, the converse of *Madden*, where the existence of a contractual relationship between the defendant and others was seen as erecting a barrier to the establishment of a duty of care towards the plaintiff. In *Sweeney v. Duggan*, the Court reasoned that, if the defendant did *not* owe a contractual duty to the plaintiff, it would be wrong to look to the law of tort to find a duty of care in negligence.

We have already discussed the facts of *Sweeney v. Duggan* in the 1991 Review, 386, in our analysis of Barron J.'s judgment, dismissing the plaintiff's claim: [1991] 2 I.R. 274. The case concerned a now liquidated company, which had been involved in quarrying limestone. Its managing director, who owned all but one of the shares, was the defendant in the litigation. The plaintiff was an elderly labourer who had been injured when working for the company. He successful sued the company for damages for negligence and breach of statutory duty, but was able to enforce only part of the judgment against the company as it had no employers' liability insurance and at the time of liquidation was unable to pay all its creditors in full.

The plaintiff sued the defendant, arguing that the company ought to have procured employers' liability insurance or, failing that, to have warned him that no such policy was in existence. The plaintiff also claimed that the defendant had had a duty to ensure that the company obtained such insurance or, if not, to warn him that it had not done so.

It was contended on behalf of the plaintiff that the obligations, so far as they fell on the company, derived primarily, and perhaps exclusively, from the contractual relationship between the employer and employee. The particular duty to insure against liability was, it was argued, an implied term of the contract.

Murphy J. (Hamilton C.J. and Barrington JJ. concurring) gave a detailed analysis of the latter issue, concluding that such a term could not be implied, in spite of the great danger to employees working in quarries where the accident rate was about eight times s bad as on building sites generally. Murphy J.

placed considerable emphasis on British decision, in particular *Scally v. Southern Health and Social Services Board* [1992] 1 A.C. 294, in support in his view that 'the obligation[s] as between the employer and employee in a case such as the present are to be found in contract and not in tort.'

If the company had no liability in contract to the plaintiff, then neither had the defendant. It was true that the defendant had a variety of duties to the plaintiff as 'a fellow workman' and in his capacity as quarry manger, the breach of which would involve him in tortious liability, but in the instant case the plaintiff had not alleged that any of these duties had been neglected nor would the breach of any of them provide the remedy which the plaintiff sought to assert.

Murphy J. found it:

> difficult to accept that a director or shareholder as such has the necessary relationship with an employee of his company to give rise to any duty on the part of the director/shareholder for the economic welfare of the employee. I find it inconceivable that any such duty on the part of a corporator, if it did exist, could be more extensive than that of the corporation itself.

Accordingly, the Supreme Court dismissed the plaintiff's appeal.

Sweeney v. Duggan throws little light on the juridical relationship between contractual and delictual claims. It appears to hold that the limits of liability in negligence on the part of an employer are broadly co-extensive with those of contractual liability. It is true that Murphy J. does not go quite so far, since he restricts his remarks to 'a case such as the present.' His judgment gives no clear guidance on what particular distinguishing features of the instant case made it appropriate to restrict the employer's liability to the contractual aspects of its relationship with its employee.

It is, of course, true that very many of the breaches by an employer of its duty of care in negligence to an employee will also generate contractual liability: see Michael Forde, *Employment Law* (The Round Hall Press, 1992), p. 4–5. This does not mean, however, that the starting and finishing point for judicial analysis should be in the field of implied contractual terms. Where the plaintiff's case centres on two matters in particular, it seems that the courts should give the right of way to the negligence action.

The first of these matters is whether the employer has acted as a reasonable employer ought to have acted in relation to the employee. It is better for the courts to deal with this question by reference to the standard criteria appropriate to actions for negligence rather than to ask whether it is possible to fashion an implied contractual term. It is not the case that every employment contract contains an implied term that the employer will comply with the requirements of the standard of care in every aspect of the employment relationship.

The second matter is one that was raised in *Sweeney v. Duggan*; this concerns the duty of care in negligence. A characteristic of the law of negligence is that it allows a plaintiff to assert that the defendant owed a duty of care in totally novel circumstances, where no court previously held there to be such a duty. The court may, of course, reject the claim: in 1997 there are plenty of examples of courts doing precisely this. But equally a court, whether applying McCarthy J.'s test in *Ward v. McMaster* or otherwise, may hold that, in spite of the novelty of the claim, a duty of care did indeed arise. There is simply no way in which the same outcome could be reached by the route of an implied contractual term. It would be implausible to suggest that a novel duty of care could pass the *Moorcock* test: (1889) 14 PD 64; nor could it often be convincingly claimed that an implied term to this effect derives from the nature of the contract itself.

The limits of paternalism In *McKenna v. Best Travel Ltd t/a Cypriano Holidays*, Supreme Court, November 18, 1997, the Supreme Court, reversing Lavan J., held that a travel agent and tour operator had not been guilty of negligence in failing to warn the plaintiff, who booked a holiday in Cyprus and indicated her desire to go on a mini-cruise to Israel and Egypt, that a state of unrest existed in the Bethlehem area. The brochure produced by the tour operator contained details of the mini-cruise, which had to be booked in Cyprus. The plaintiff was injured by a stone thrown at the coach in which she was travelling close to Bethlehem. Tension in the area had been heightened by the Iraqi invasion of Kuwait some weeks previously.

Barron J. (Hamilton C.J. and Keane J. concurring) approached the issue by stating that the duty of care in tort arose 'from the proximity created by the contractual relationship.' That duty extended to 'all matters concerning the safety, well-being and comfort of the tourists which by the nature of the relationship between the tourists and those providing the service would or should be known to the latter but not to the former.' The standard of knowledge to be attributed to the tourists was 'that of someone who, having decided to go on holiday to a particular country, or area or place within that country, might be expected to have gained from advertisements or news items relating thereto.' The standard of knowledge to be attributed to someone in the travel industry was 'that of the person on the spot providing the service.'

In the instant case, the fact that there was tension in the area did not of itself mean that tourists coming into the area would be at any particular risk. There was no evidence to suggest that the managing director of the travel agency had any particular knowledge of the circumstances on the ground at that time. She had given evidence that during the period concerned she would have advised her staff to advise any customers who asked them about tours to Israel and Egypt not to go on them. Barron J. commented:

No doubt she genuinely wished to ensure that her customers did not get involved in what she believed was an area of unrest. Nevertheless it was a policy personal to her. There was no evidence that it was advice offered by any other travel agents in Ireland nor was there any circular from the Travel Agents Association dealing with that area or persons travelling to it.

Evidence was given to the effect that the bus company providing the service would make enquiries daily as to whether it was safe to run the service. Counsel for the plaintiff suggested that this was an indication of something which should have been subject of a warning to the plaintiff. Barron J. thought not, saying:

> Unfortunately, there are very many risks and dangers associated not only with foreign travel but with day to day living. The security industry is growing ever bigger. It cannot be suggested that persons providing services to the public have an obligation to inform the public not only that they provide security but the extent and nature of that security. To do so would be to make life practically impossible both for those providing the services and those accepting them.

The defendants were not insurers that nothing would happen to injure the plaintiff. Their obligation stopped at taking all reasonable steps to ensure the safety and well-being of their customers. The fact of unrest in certain parts of Israel at the material time was well known and a tour operator was entitled to assume such knowledge on the part of its customers. What it was not entitled to assume was knowledge on the part of its customers which it acquired in its capacity as a tour operator.

The test was what a reasonably prudent tour operator exercising reasonable care would consider it necessary to inform those travelling with it. The evidence was that large numbers of tour buses had been bringing tourists to Bethlehem daily without incident. The best case for the plaintiff was that there had been an incident involving a tourist nine months before. That did not warrant any particular knowledge of danger which required passing on to a tourist, who must be presumed to be aware of the general conditions in the area to which she was travelling.

The *McKenna* judgment was invoked in a private international law context in *McGee v. JWT Ltd and Société Holding Imberte*, High Court, March 27, 1998 where the plaintiff alleged that the first defendant, as travel agent, ought to have ensured that a group of invalids and elderly people on a pilgrimage to Lourdes would have a non-slip surface on the bathroom floors of their hotel and that the showers would be equipped with curtains to prevent spillage. O'Sullivan J. considered that the plaintiff's case passed the test set by the

Supreme Court in *Gannon v. British and Irish Steam Packet Company Ltd.*, [1993] 2 I.R. 359 (analysed in the 1992 Review, 127–8). He considered that an affirmative answer had to be given to the question whether there were 'any plausible grounds of any descriptiion for suggesting that the hotel was of such kind or was in such condition as it would be unsafe for the plaintif[f].' We shall analyse *McGee* in the 1998 Review.

In *O'Flynn v. Balkan Tours Ltd,* Supreme Court, April 7, 1997 (*ex tempore*) the Supreme Court upheld Flood J.'s finding of negligence against the defendant company, which specialised in providing skiing holidays, where the plaintiff was injured when travelling down a dangerous part of a mountain, having missed the last chair-lift because of a sequence of events traceable to the fact tht the defendant had failed to have an effective system for communicating to those going on skiing holidays the time of a preliminary orientation meeting. Such a meeting, which was critical for people who were skiing for the first time, would have given details as to times of ski-lifts and ski runs which would have protected the plaintiff from the injury he sustained.

It appeared that some information may possibly have been given to the plaintiff, when he was travelling in a bus on the way to the hotel, about the orientation meeting, which was held at 9 a.m, regardless of the time that those on holiday arrived. The plaintiff had not reached his hotel until 3.30 a.m. Regardless of this, Flood J., and the Supreme Court, considered that this level communication was inadequate; it should have been provided in documentary form.

Flood J. also held that the defendant had been under a duty of care to its clients, including the duty to advise them of the details of ski runs and their chair lifts, most critically the time of the final departure of the chair-lift from the summit.

Flood J. reduced the plaintiff's damages by 75% to take account of his contributory negligence. He considered that the plaintiff was guilty of 'an unbelievable want of care' for his own safety, since the hotel where the defendant was staying, the depot at the bottom of the chair-lift and the chair-lift centre at the top were all festooned with copies of a map setting forth a more sensible route by which to descend, as well as stating the time of departure of the last chair-lift.

O'Flaherty J. (Keane and Barron JJ. concurring) was not certain that he would have reached exactly the same conclusion as Flood J. if he had been trying the case, but nonetheless he considered that his findings should not be disturbed.

O'Flynn can be contrasted with *McKenna* in terms of the stringency of the duty of care each case involves. It is true that the risk which arose in *McKenna* was a small one that might be considered peripheral to the holiday which the plaintiff selected, whereas the orientation meeting was more central to the plaintiff's concerns in *O'Flynn*. Nevertheless, *O'Flynn* tends towards a mollycuddling culture for holidaymakers. Whatever its merits, such culture strains the duty of care in negligence to serve goals for which is not best designed to accomplish. The law of contract or consumer protection legislation are more suitable vehicles for doing so. That the law of negligence can provide a remedy in cases such as *O'Flynn v. Balkan Tours Ltd* and fail to do so in cases such as *Sweeney v. Duggan*, above, should lead us to reflect on what social values the duty of care shold seek to foster.

Public officials   In *W. v. Ireland, the Attorney General and the Government of Ireland (No. 2)* [1997] 2 I.R. 141, Costello P. gave important guidance on the circumstances in which a duty of care in negligence may arise. For an incisive analysis of the decision, see Noel Gaughran, 'Tort, Public Policy and the Protection of Constitutional Rights' (1998) 16 *ILT* 88. The plaintiff, a victim of Father Brendan Smyth, a convicted paedophile, the delay in whose extradition led to the fall of the Government in 1994, sought compensation from the State, the Attorney General and the Irish Government for the continuing emotional shock, distress and consequential psychiatric problems she suffered resulting from the delay. She based her claim of negligence and breach of constitutional rights.

The parties were agreed that the issue of negligence at common law was to be determined in accordance with the principles established in *Ward v. McMaster* [1988] I.R. 337, and in particular the test approved by McCarthy J. Costello P. referred to the House of Lords decision in *Murphy v. Brentwood DC* [1991] A.C. 389 at 457, departing from *Anns* 'insofar as it affirmed a private law duty of care to avoid damage to property which causes present or imminent danger to the health and safety of owners or occupiers, resting upon local authorities in relation to their function of supervising compliance with building by-laws or regulations. . . .'

Irish law had therefore parted company with English law but Costello P. was by 'no means certain' that the departure was a major one. The view of the Irish courts had been that *Anns* was a 'confirmation' of the long established principles of the law of tort contained in *Donoghue v. Stevenson* and was not (as some commentators in England seemed to consider) a major innovation in the law of tort.

Moreover, as *Ward v. McMaster* made it clear, when the court was required to consider whether a duty of care at common law arose in the exercise of statutory duties, powers or functions, the issue was largely determined by the scope and nature of the relevant statutory provisions. This had been underlined in two decisions in which the principles established in *Ward v. McMaster* were considered in the Supreme Court: *Sunderland v. Louth County Council* [1990] I.L.R.M. 658 and *Convery v. Dublin County* Council, Supreme Court, 12 November 1996.

After summarising the judgments in these cases, Costello P. referred to the

Supreme Court decision in *Madden v. The Irish Turf Club* [1997] 2 I.L.R.M.
148, Blayney J.'s judgment in *McMahon v. Ireland* [1988] I.L.R.M. 610 and
J.C. Doherty Timber Ltd. v. Drogheda Harbour Commissioners [1993] 1 I.R.
315.

Turning to the instant case, Costello P. noted that the Extradition Act 1965
(as amended) imposed a statutory *function* rather than *duty* on the Attorney
General in relation to victims of the crimes referred to in the warrant which he
was required to consider. This function was (a) to consider whether or not
there was a clear intention on the part of the authorities in Northern Ireland to
prosecute the person named in the warrant for the offences with which he was
charged and if so, (b) to consider whether such an intention was founded on
sufficient evidence. Having satisfied himself on these points he was then required to decide whether to give a direction to the Commissioner under section 44(A). His function was one which the Oireachtas required him to perform
as part of the extradition process in relation to persons accused of crimes
committed in Northern Ireland.

In considering whether or not there was a clear intention to prosecute the
person named in the warrant, and whether or not the intention to prosecute
was founded on the existence of sufficient evidence, the circumstances of the
victim were in no way relevant:

> The statute conferred a public professional function on the Attorney
> General which created no relationship of any sort between him and the
> victims of the crimes referred to in the warrants he was considering.
> This is in striking contrast to the statutory provisions of the Housing Act
> 1966 which were designed to assist a class of persons and which the
> Supreme Court held in *Ward* conferred a special relationship between
> them and the housing authority which resulted in imposition of a com-
> mon law duty of care.

In the absence of any relationship between the plaintiff and the Attorney General, Costello P. concluded that the Extradition Acts imposed no common law
duty of care on the Attorney General in relation to the plaintiff.

Costello P. considered that there was a further and compelling reason why
the court should decide that no common law duty of care existed in the instant
case. Even if there had been a sufficient relationship of proximity between the
Attorney General and the plaintiff and even if the kind of injury of which the
plaintiff complained was reasonably foreseeable, it would be contrary to public policy to impose a duty of care on the Attorney General.

The principles in *Ward v. McMaster* (and indeed in the pre-*Ward* law of
torts) recognised that on the grounds of public policy the law might not recognise the existence of a duty of care. Clearly, it was only in exceptional cases
that the court should deny a right of action to a person who had suffered loss

on the ground that it would not be in the public interest to allow it. In considering whether the Attorney General should be protected from actions of negligence, the court was balancing the hardship to individuals which such a rule would produce against the disadvantage to the public interest if such a rule existed.

In the very first significant discussion by an Irish court of the issue of advocates' immunity from a duty of care, Costello P. stated:

> How the court carries out this balancing exercise is illustrated in the judgments in the House of Lords in *Rondel v. Worsley* ([1969] 1 A.C. 191) in which the long established immunity from actions for negligence which barristers enjoyed was re-considered and justified on the grounds of public policy. In the course of his judgment Lord Reid pointed out that every counsel has a duty to his client to act fearlessly in his interests but that as an officer of the court concerned in the administration of justice he has an overriding duty to that court to the standards of his profession and to the public. A barrister must not mislead the court, nor cast aspersions on the other party for which there was no basis in the information in his possession, must not withhold authorities or documents which may tell against his client but which the law or the standards of his profession require him to produce. Because the barrister is required to put his public duty before the apparent interest of his client the public interest requires that on the grounds of public policy the barrister's immunity from suit be maintained.

For similar reasons judges were immune from actions for negligence. In *Garnett v. Ferrand*, 6 B & C 611, at 625–626, 108 E.R. 576, at 581 (1827) Lord Tenterden C.J. had stated:

> This freedom from action and question at the suit of an individual is given by the law to the judges, not so much for their own sake as for the sake of the public, and for the advancement of justice, that, being free from actions, they may be free in thought and independent in judgment, as all who are to administer justice ought to be.

This case had been quoted with approval and applied in *Deighan v. Ireland* [1995] 2 I.R. 56.

The principle had again been applied in England in *Hill v. Chief Constable of West Yorkshire* [1989] A.C. 53, holding that on the grounds of public policy a duty of care ought not to be imposed on police investigating a crime. Of particular relevance to the issues in the instant case, the English Court of Appeal, in *Elguzuoli-Daf v. Commissioner of Police of the Metropolis* [1995] 1 All E.R. 833 had held that on the grounds of public policy the Crown Prosecution Service could not be sued in negligence. Steyn L.J. had observed:

> While it is always tempting to yield to an argument based on the protec-
> tion of civil liberties, I have come to the conclusion that the interests of
> the whole community are better served by not imposing a duty of care
> on the CPS. In my view such a duty of care would tend to have an inhib-
> iting effect on the discharge of the CPS of its central function of pros-
> ecuting crime. It would in some cases lead to a defensive approach by
> prosecutors to their multifarious duties. It would introduce a risk that
> prosecutors would act so as to protect themselves from claims of negli-
> gence. . . .

The question of prosecutorial immunity from suit in an action for malicious
prosecution had been considered by the Supreme Court of Canada in *Nelles v.
Ontario* 60 D.L.R. (4th) 103 (1989). Whilst referring to the authorities in
Canada and in the United States in which immunity from actions of *negligence* was conferred by the courts on prosecutorial authorities, the Court held
that immunity from an action for *malicious prosecution* should not be granted.
The case, however, did not decide that such an immunity would not exist in
relation to actions for negligence.

Turning to the facts of the instant case, it seemed to Costello P. that the
denial of a right of claim for damages for negligence on the grounds of public
policy arose from the functions which the Attorney General was called upon
to perform in the public interest and the consequences on his ability properly
to perform them should the alleged duty exist. By conferring an important role
on him in the extradition process the Oireachtas had involved him in a significant way in ensuring that a proper compliance with the State's international
obligations in the field of extradition was achieved. The statute required him
to weigh the information made available to him relating both to the intention
to prosecute the person named in the warrant and also the evidence on which
the intention to prosecute was based and should the information he obtained
not be sufficient he was required to request further information. If in carrying
out this function he were also under a duty of care to the victim of the crime
referred to in the warrant not to delay, there was a risk, which it was not in the
public interest that he should be asked to run, that a conflict might arise between the proper exercise of his public function and the common law duty of
care to the victim which might result in an improper exercise of his statutory
functions.

There were further compelling reasons why in the public interest the duty
claimed by the plaintiff should not be allowed. If a duty under the 1965 Act
existed it must logically follow, first, that the Attorney General would be under a similar duty in respect of any prosecutorial functions conferred on him
by section 5 of the Prosecution of Offences Act 1974 and, secondly, that, in

exercising his prosecutorial functions, under that Act, the Director of Public Prosecutions would owe a like duty to all victims of crimes in the cases in which he was considering the institution of prosecution. Because of the inhibiting effect on the proper exercise by the Attorney General and the Director of Public Prosecutions of their prosecutorial functions it would be contrary to the public interest that a duty of care at common law be imposed on them. So to conclude was not to submit to a 'floodgates' argument of doubtful validity; it was to accept the logical consequences of imposing the duty of care at common law on the Attorney General in the execution of his functions under the 1965 Act.

Costello P. distinguished the Supreme Court decision of *Ryan v. Ireland* [1989] I.R. 177 where the issue had been whether under Irish common law an immunity from suit by a serving soldier in respect of operations consisting of armed conflict existed. The court held that it did not. Such an immunity would be inconsistent with the State's guarantees to respect and vindicate the personal rights of the citizen under Article 40 of the Constitution. The Supreme Court had not decided that in no case could the law confer immunity from suit on a constitutional officer and, in this context, the Irish courts had recognised the validity of such a rule in relation to judges carrying out their judicial functions:

> Laws may limit the exercise of protected rights and in each case when the claim is raised it is a question for the court to decide where, in the interests of the common good, the balance should lie.

The plaintiff further argued that, even if the *Attorney General* was immune from suit on the grounds of public policy, this did not necessarily deprive the plaintiff of a claim for damages against the *State* arising from his negligent act. Costello P. rejected this contention on the basis that, even if not himself personally subject to liability, '[t]he Attorney General would still be conscious that he owed a duty of care to the victim, that the State could be sued if he breached it and . . . this knowledge would have the same disabling effect as a law which conferred personal liability on him for damages.'

Finally it was urged on behalf of the plaintiff that the court should not follow the English decisions mentioned by Costello P. in his judgment because they were decided after the House of Lords had overruled *Anns* in *Murphy v. Brentwood DC*. In an important passage, Costello P. rejected this argument, stating that:

> the reversal of *Anns* had no effect on the principles to be applied when the court considers a claim for immunity from suit. They were applied by the courts in England in the cases to which I have referred without any reference to *Anns* and whilst, of course, they are not binding on this

court they serve usefully to illustrate one of the principles which *Ward*
concluded should be applied in this country when considering whether
or not it would be proper for the court to impose a private duty of care on
the exercise of a public function.

Costello P. went on to consider, and reject, the plaintiff's second substantive
argument that she was entitled to damages for infringement of her constitutional rights under Article 40.3. We discuss this part of Costello P.'s judgment
later in the Chapter, under the heading 'Infringement of Constitutional Rights',
below, 790–4.

Costello P.'s analysis of the duty of care issue is the most thorough of any
Irish decision on the subject. It is noteworthy that he was content to use the
doctrinal language of the duty of care at the same time as identifying clearly
practical considerations. The judgment gives no indication of the warfare between doctrine and pragmatism which has characterised British litigation on
the duty of care over the past decade. As far as Costello P. is concerned, there
is simply no clash between them. For him, Lord Wilberforce's two-step test
was merely the culmination of what had gone before; not having created anything new, there was no question of having to pause before accepting it.

Costello P.'s analysis is faithful to both of these steps and to McCarthy J.'s
version in *Ward v. McMaster*. His express reference, not only to proximity, but
also to public policy, reflects closely to McCarthy J.'s language.

Of course, if Costello P. is right and Lord Wilberforce's 'two step' test
contained nothing new, then the British debate over the past decade was a
redundant and misconceived exercise. Yet we know that matters of substance
have been at issue. What Costello P.'s reference to *Anns* makes plain is that
the British retreat is not merely from what was said by Lord Wilberforce in
1977 but is far more radical, ultimately challenging the conceptual coherence
of Lord Atkin's 'neighbour' test in *Donoghue v. Stevenson*. If pragmatism is
to replace principle, as *Murphy* and *Caparo* suggest, then not only *Anns* must
go, but also all the earlier decisions based on general principle. Clearly, Irish
decisions such as *Purtill* and *McNamara* were not dependent on *Anns*, having
been decided years beforehand.

As regards Costello P.'s assessment of the impact of imposing a duty of
care toward victims of crime on the Attorney General and the Director of
Public Prosecutions, it is worth recalling that Costello P. was himself Attorney General two decades previously and had been instrumental in establishing the position of Director of Public Prosecutions. His analysis of the issue
was thus firmly rooted in practical experience rather than based on mere academic speculation.

The Gardaí, searches and privacy from media intrusion   In *Hanahoe v.
Hussey, The Commissioner of An Garda Síochána, Ireland and the Attorney*

General, High Court, November 14, 1997, Kinlen J. awarded the plaintiff firm of solicitors £100,000 where the Gardaí, in the course of obtaining and acting on a warrant under section 64 of the Criminal Justice Act 1994 to search the plaintiff's offices, created 'a media circus' by carelessly allowing a leak of information regarding the proposed search to emanate from a Garda source. A client of the plaintiff firm was suspected of serious wrongdoing as a drug dealer. Although the actual search had been conducted 'with discretion, efficiency and courtesy,' by the time the Gardaí left the premises, ten or twelve reporters and photographers had gathered there.

It appears that Gardaí conceded that disclosure emanating from careless conduct on the part of one or more of their members would amount to negligence under the principle set out by McCarthy J. in *Ward v. McMaster* [1988] I.R. 337, at 349. They nonetheless sought to argue that the fact that the search had taken place would inevitably have become public knowledge in due course; the statutory obligation to secrecy, they contended, was designed to avoid prejudice to the State's interest in secrecy generally and the integrity of prosecutions in particular. This duty, therefore, was owed, 'not to the public but to the State.' They did not accept that any member of the Gardai owed a duty of care towards the citizen in relation to the premature emergence of information of matters which would in any event have come into the public domain in the fullness of time. Kinlen J. disposed of the argument in a single sentence:

This Court does not accept such a proposition.

It has to be said that it is hard to see how the argument that no duty of care arose could have been made consistently with the concession that McCarthy J.'s principle in *Ward v. McMaster* applied to the case, once carelessness by a member of the Garda Síochána was established. There are, however, formidable arguments that police forces should not be required to work under a wide-ranging duty of care towards prospective victims, suspects, witnesses and the general public. This is clear from Costello P.'s judgment in *W.*, which we have analysed above, 709. English courts have addressed the general issue in several contexts. A broad distinction can be drawn between positive acts of carelessness by members of the police forces which create new dangers, on the one hand, and the failure by members of the police force to take effective steps to protect particular people or the general public, on the other. In the former category of cases, courts are willing to find a duty of care which has been broken: see, *e.g.*, *Knightley v. Johns* [1982] 1 All E.R. 851, *Rigby v. Chief Constable of Northamptonshire* [1985] 2 All E.R. 985, *Frost v. Chief Constable of the South Yorkshire Police* [1997] 1 All E.R. 540. In the latter category of cases, public policy considerations have been held to prevent a duty of care from arising. Thus, in *Hill v. Chief Constable of West Yorkshire* [1989] A.C. 53, the House of Lords held that police officers should not be under a duty of care towards prospective victims when investigating crime.

In *Hanahoe*, the carelessness of a member of the Garda Siochána in contributing to the disclosure of the information would appear clearly to fall within the former category.

THE STANDARD OF CARE

Automatism and 'the reasonable person' In *O'Brien v. Parker* [1997] 2 I.L.R.M. 170 (Circuit Court Appeal), Lavan J. addressed the important question of how objective the standard of care should be in an action for negligence. It is easy to find judicial utterances emphasising the objectivity of the test: Lord Macmillan in *Glasgow Corporation v. Muir* [1943] A.C. 448, at 457, observed that, in negligence cases, the law 'eliminates the personal equation'. Quite clearly, a person may be found guilty of negligence even where he or she intended no harm and was doing his or her incompetent best. But does this mean that the court should have no regard for the individual circumstances of the defendant? The answer has to be that the issue of negligence can properly be determined only in the particular context in which the defendant has acted. The level of care that the parents of infant triplets can be expected to give to them must be somewhat more diluted in some instances than that which they could give to a single child.

Of course the courts must not slip into an unduly subjective approach. An inexperienced doctor, recently qualified, will not be able to invoke his or her lack of experience in treating a patient any more than a driver can seek to be judged by a lower standard of care simply because he or she passed the driving test a few days ago.

The courts have traditionally had regard to physical disability in negligence litigation. A person who is unable to hear or to see, for example, will not be judged by the same standard as those who are fully able to hear and see. Instead, the courts judge that person's conduct by the standard of *the reasonable person with the particular disability*. This does not give a *carte blanche* to the disabled person to act as he or she wishes. Reasonable care demands that a person who cannot see should not engage in conduct for which sight is an essential prereqisite if the task is to be performed safely.

In the context of driving cars, the law of negligence requires of the reasonable driver that he or she should have due regard to any physical disability, or propensity to such a disability, before deciding whether to engage in the activity of driving in the first place. Of course, this requirement is backed up by legislation in relation to the granting of driving licences but, even if there were no such legislation, a reasonable driver with, for example, the knowledge that he or she has a serious medical condition which could result in a heart attack or other seizure at any time should not drive a car.

O'Brien v. Parker was an appeal from the dismissal by the President of the Circuit Court of the plaintiff's action. The defendant had been involved in a traffic accident in which he had crashed into the plaintiff's vehicle. There was no dispute that, if no particular individuating circumstances were taken into account, the defendant's driving would be considered negligent. The defence lodged by the defendant, however, asserted that he had 'suffered an attack of epilepsy without prior indication or warning' and that '[i]n the circumstances the defendant was not negligent.'

According to the doctor's reports, based on an interview with the defendant, it appeared that the defendant, who had never previously been treated for epilepsy and who had no family history of that condition, had on the fateful day, when driving his car, experienced 'an altered state of consciousness'. He first had become aware of a strange smell and had noticed colours to be unusually vivid. The next thing he remembered was his car crashing.

The medical report of another medical witness, a consultant neurologist, differed somewhat from the first report in that the defendant had told him that, *before he got into his car*, he had developed a ringing in his ears and there was then an alteration of his vision. Lavan J. noted that the defendant had told the consultant neurologist that

> [h]e got images of intense light which came and went a little bit. He still felt able to get into his car. He was not quite sure what was happening. Possibly he was getting some sort of migrainous episode. This seemed to settle down. But while he was driving he said he felt peculiar: as though he was not quite fully there and his consciousness was in some slight way impaired. He described this by saying that, although he knew that there were cars on the other side of the road, he had to keep reminding himself of this fact. It is not known if he lost consciousness or not at this stage, but he actually struck three cars. He was stopped by the Garda Síochána who thought he was either drunk or on drugs, neither of which pertained. He settled down and was obviously concerned about what had actually happened to him.

The defendant, in evidence, said that he had 'certain experiences at home', before driving. He was able to get into his car, but when he was driving he had 'some sense of smell' and felt unwell as he approached the junction where the collusion took place. He had no further recollection of the final hundred yards before the collision.

It transpired that a condition of temporal lobe epilepsy had manifested itself 'out of the blue'. The consultant neurologist was of the opinion that the plaintiff suffered from a complex partial seizure. This would 'allow for some consciousness on an objective basis [and] would allow a person suffering from this condition to make a decision. There was a degree of awareness. . . .'

Counsel for the defendant argued that, where a defendant proved that his or her actions were the result of a sudden illness, the defence of inevitable accident as made out. He conceded that the illness in the case had to result in automatism or a state of unconsciousness in which the respondent had been left without control of his actions.

Lavan J., after a review of some British authorities on the defence of automatism in *criminal prosecutions*, concluded that it seemed clear that 'strict limits' had been emphasised in these decisions before the defence could succeed. It was necessary to establish 'a total destruction of voluntary control on the defendant's part.' Impaired, reduced or partial control was not sufficient to maintain the defence.

Applying this test to the instant case, Lavan J. was not satisfied that the defendant had established this defence on the balance of probabilities. Notwithstanding having experienced 'some difficulties' at home, the defendant had been able to make a decision to drive and had in fact driven some distance. He had been conscious of experiencing some symptoms before the accident had occurred. There had not been a total destruction of voluntary control; impaired, reduced or partial control, of which evidence had been given in the case, was not sufficient to enable the defendant to succeed. Accordingly Lavan J. vacated the order of the President of the Circuit Court and gave judgment in favour of the plaintiff.

The judgment raises a number of issues of general interest. Lavan J.'s conclusions are understandable in the light of the parameters of the defence put forward in the case, but the question can be raised as to whether the scope of any defence in a civil action should be determined on the basis of judicial authorities dealing with criminal responsibility. In England, in *Roberts v. Ramsbottom* [1980] 1 W.L.R. 823, Neill J. thought it appropriate to make such a transposition but the Court of Appeal, in *Mansfield v. Weetabix Ltd.*, [1997] P.I.Q.R. 526, roundly criticised this approach.

It seems that two different issues need to be separated when a court is assessing the question of liability for negligence in a case where the defendant's conduct has been affected by some emergency. The first of these issues is whether it can truly be said that the defendant engaged in any conduct at all, for which he or she may be called to answer. If the defendant has not engaged in any conduct that is legally cognisable, then, unless the case is one of a limited range of omissions for which a person may be liable in negligence, no question of holding the defendant responsible will arise, not because the defendant acted reasonably in all the circumstances, but because, so far as the law is concerned, the defendant has not engaged in any conduct that should activate the attention of the law. In *Mansfield v. Weetabix Ltd.*, above, at 528, Leggatt L.J., considered that the question of automatism could not arise in a civil case but in truth it can, not as the sole issue governing liability but rather as a threshold issue before going on to consider the issue of negligence.

This second issue, of negligence, can arise only where the defendant has engaged in legally cognisable conduct. In such circumstances, the plaintiff alleges that the defendant's conduct was unreasonable. Often the situation will be such as to give rise to the operation of the *res ipsa loquitur* principle. The defendant replies that, in the light of all the circumstances, what looks like unreasonable conduct was not in fact so because of some emergency, which caused the defendant to act as he or she did. This emergency could be generated from within, as it were, by an epileptic episode or a heart attack, for example, but it could equally be caused from without, as where a driver is stung by a bee or blinded by some object going into his or her eye.

The point to note here is that, even if a driver is engaging in conscious, non-insane, non-automatic, conduct, an emergency can arise. In these circumstances, if the plaintiff cannot show that the defendant was acting unreasonably, the proceedings must be dismissed because negligence has not been established. Thus, in the instant case, the issue was not merely whether the defendant had been rendered incapable of exercising *any* voluntary control over his actions. If he was affected by the sudden unforeseeable onset of a medical emergency which interfered with his control, and his reaction could not be stigmatised as unreasonable in the circumstances, then the plaintiff simply had not established negligence on his part.

Of course, if a driver has reason to believe that his or her driving will be affected by the onset of a sudden medical condition, he or she will be held negligent if, in spite of that risk, he or she starts (or continues) to drive. Perhaps the defendant in the instant case had sufficient premonition to render his decision to drive or his failure later to *stop* driving negligent. The symptoms were probably sufficiently bizarre to justify a finding that it was negligent on his part to embark on the journey or, having done so, not to stop earlier. There is plenty of authority throughout the common law world supporting the imposition of liability in these circumstances. Lavan J.'s observations are consistent with the view that this aspect of the defendant's conduct was culpable, but he does not identify it in express terms as the basis of his holding, which appears limited to the issue of automatism.

It is worth reflecting on where, and how, the line should be drawn between so-called subjective and objective factors when determining whether conduct should be stigmatised as negligent. The answer is a good deal more difficult than it may first appear.

The essence of negligence is that it involves a value-judgment by the court on what is called an 'objective' question of whether the defendant acted reasonably or unreasonably. The courts traditionally invoked a hypothetical creature – 'the reasonable man' or, more recently, 'the reasonable person' – to emphasise the objectivity and generality of the test. This language encourages the notion that the court in some way distances itself from the flesh-and-blood reality of the particular defendant. The truth is that it does so in some but by no means all respects. The challenge for analysis is to identify whether there is any principled basis for, in one instance, having regard to the defendant's particular circumstances and, in another instance, not doing so.

One should note that the courts have never had any difficulty in taking into account the particular circumstances *surrounding* the defendant's conduct. Thus, for example, in litigation resulting from road traffic accidents, the fact that the road was slippy on the fateful day will be taken into account in deciding whether a reasonable driver should have avoided the accident.

When it comes to the defendant's own personal circumstances, however, the courts have favoured an eclectic approach, from which it possible to discern, if not a principled basis, at least a basis that can be understood in terms of a mixture of humanitarianism, concern for protection of life and bodily integrity and sheer pragmatism.

As to the humanitarian basis, we have already noted that the courts have modified the generality of the 'reasonable person' test in cases of physical disability, so that the relevant standard becomes that of the reasonable person with the particular disability that affected the defendant. Perhaps it might be considered that humanitarianism is not the appropriate basis for this modification, since the constitutional principle of equality under Article 40.1 envisages that appropriate attention will be paid to differences of physical or moral capacity. This rationale, however meritorious, does not, however, explain why, in negligence cases, courts have regard to some differences of physical or moral capacity but not to others.

Perhaps the most striking personal characteristic which the courts ignore in tort litigation is that of mental incapacity, whether deriving from lack of intellectual capacity or mental illness. In criminal law, the issue of insanity has generated thousands of decisions, reflecting the fact that a finding of insanity was in practice (and in some states still is) the only way of avoiding capital punishment. In stark contrast, there are less than a dozen significant decisions throughout the common law world dealing with the question of the negligence of the mentally disabled. The pragmatic policy adopted by the courts, with only minimal modifications, is that mental incapacity should not be taken into consideration.

The spectre of the unrecompensed victim has encouraged the courts to ignore the issue of the defendant's mental incapacity where they will not ignore physical incapacity. Why should this be so? One can only speculate as to the true reason but the answer may well be found in the instinctive sympathy the court has for the blind, deaf and immobilised people and the lack of a similar sympathy for the mentally disabled, compounded by an anxiety that, if mental incapacity were to be a ground for not imposing liability in negligence, it would be abused, at the expense of victims.

It is interesting to note that, when dealing with the issue of a plaintiff's contributory negligence, courts tend to be more sensitive to the question of mental incapacity. Thus, in *Armstrong v. Eastern Health* Board, High Court, October 5, 1990, where the plainitff attempted suicide, Egan J. held that she was not guilty of contributory negligence because she had 'not [been] really in control of her thoughts' at the time. See the 1990 Review, 523–6.

One should bear in mind in this context that the issue of the negligence or (more usually) the contributory negligence of *children* is judged by a subjective test, which takes into account, not only the particular child's age, but also his or her mental development and experience. There is, perhaps, an argument in favour of taking into account the mental development of a child on the basis that children do not mature intellectually at a constant age; but the sad fact of life is that, regardless of the variable pace of intellectual development, some children are, and will continue into adulthood to remain, less intelligent than others. The regard that the courts pay to the mental development of the particular child therefore goes further than ensuring that the variable process of maturation is given due attention; it means that children who are now, and are destined as adults to be, less intelligent than others are treated more leniently than they will be when they reach adulthood, at which point the inflexible standard of 'the reasonable person' will be applied to them, at all events where the issue of their negligence arises, with no regard to their lack of intellectual capacity.

Could it be that the courts treat children subjectively because of a positive sentiment towards the idea of childhood? Whatever may be the answer to this question, it is worth noting that the present subjective approach does not always result in a benefit for the child, since the reference to the particular child's experience is a two-edged sword. A child with unusually extensive experience will be judged by a sterner standard than that of the 'average' child. This can work hardship and injustice in some instances as, for example, in *Brennan v. Savage Smyth Ltd* [1982] I.L.R.M. 223, where the Supreme Court raised from 5% to 25% the attribution of contributory negligence against an [eleven-year-old] child playing at the base of a tower of flats in Ballymun who was injured when 'scutting' on a lorry. He was, said O'Higgins C.J., 'a child of his environment. . . .'

When one comes to consider the activity of driving a motor vehicle, the courts will generally approach the task of assessing the issue of negligence on the basis of the generalised test of 'the reasonable driver'. Nonetheless, they will sometimes have regard to individuating factors. Thus, in *McComiskey v. McDermott* [1974] I.R. 75, the Supreme Court, by a majority, held that the appropriate test to apply to a rally driver who crashed his car, injuring his navigator, was not that of 'the reasonable driver' but rather that of the reasonable rally driver who had a navigator as a passenger. The effect of individuating the duty was to deny a remedy to the navigator which would have been available had the former characterisation been applied. The explanation may well be that Irish courts, no less than their English counterparts, do not have much sympathy for a legislative circumscription of the defence of *volenti non fit injuria.* Cf. *Pitts v. Hunt* [1991] 1 Q.B. 24, *Morris v. Murray* [1991] 2 Q.B. 6.

The courts will sometimes take into account the particular knowledge or experience of a driver in assessing the question of his or her negligence or contributory negligence. So it has been held that regard should be had to the fact that the driver knew a particular stretch of the road particularly well as he had driven down it many times previously: *Copaz v. Louth County Council* [1997] Irish Law Log Weekly 402. The test thus becomes, not 'the reasonable driver', but rather 'the reasonable driver who knows the road as well as the driver in the present case did.'

In contrast, a driver's lack of experience will not be taken into account in mitigation. A driver who is on the road for the first time will be judged by the generalised standard of 'the reasonable driver'. The court will not individuate the standard to that of 'the reasonable driver with no previous experience of the road in question.'

The same lack of indulgence applies to professionals or others engaging in business or trade who lack experience. The courts take the view that such subjective factors have no place in modifying the generality of the negligence test.

We now arrive at the kind of individuating factor that arose in *O'Brien v. Parker.* This is a sudden emergency which affects the ability of the driver of a motor vehicle to drive safely. If the emergency arises *ab extra*, as, for example, where a young child steps in front of the vehicle, the driver who swerves and crashes into another car will be allowed to invoke the emergency in having the issue of his or her due care assessed. This will be so even where the driver's response is largely instinctive. Similarly a driver on whose car a boulder falls or who is stung by a wasp in the eye can invoke the emergency.

So why should a driver not be permitted to invoke an emergency whose source comes from within rather than outside? The sudden onset of an epileptic attack is in principle no different from the sudden attack of a wasp and the appropriate test should be that of the reasonable driver affected by the attack. This is not to suggest that in *O'Brien v. Parker* the defendant should have been exempted from responsibility on the evidence in the case: the epileptic condition did not occur in an instant; it unfolded over a reasonably extensive period of time which gave the defendant the opportunity to desist from driving. Perhaps it could be argued that, by the time the defendant became aware of the problem, he was already so affected by his changed medical condition as to be unable to exercise a coherent choice. If the Garda investigating the accident concluded that he was under the influence of alcohol or drugs, the defendant scarcely had the cogency to make a rational response to the onset of his condition. A *via media*, which may appeal to the more pragmatic temperament, is proposed by the Law Reform Commission in its *Report on the Liability in Tort of Mentally Disabled Persons* (LRC 18–1985).

No doubt it will seem very unfair to the victim of a driver affected by the sudden onset of a physical condition that there should be no compensation but, as long as the law of negligence requires the existence of fault, courts should not hold liable those who have not acted in a faulty way.

Air carriers   In *S. Smyth & Co. Ltd. v. Aer Turas Teo*, Supreme Court, February 3, 1997 an interesting question regarding the scope of the duty of care of air carriers fell for consideration. The plaintiff company was a livestock exporter. Italy was the principal market. The calves were exported on flights operated by the defendant carrier between Dublin and the airport of Malpensa in Milan. Every consignment was accompanied by the necessary documentation, carried in the plane's pouch.

On arrival at Malpensa Airport the bag containing the documents was given by the crew load master to an official of S.E.A. (Societa' P.A.S. Estercizi Aeroportuali), an Italian organisation which had a monopoly on providing ground services at Malpensa Airport for all aircraft except those operated by T.W.A.

The bag containing the documentation was brought by the S.E.A. official to the S.E.A. office in the airport building and from there the documents were distributed to their appropriate destinations. The cargo manifest and general declaration were delivered to the civil aviation authorities to obtain authorization to unload the aircraft and a copy of these documents was delivered to Customs. The air weighbill, the invoice and an E.C. document known as a T5 form were given to the consignee or his clearing agent. The most important document was the plaintiff's invoice to the consignee. An original and six copies were prepared and were furnished to the Customs at Dublin Airport with the rest of the documentation. One copy was retained by the Irish Customs, the original and four copies were included with the documents in the bag carried on the plane, and the remaining copy was held by the plaintiff.

Payment for each consignment was normally made by the consignee's bank within about three weeks. Under Italian Exchange Control Regulations a consignee could not import any consignment without first obtaining a document from his bank confirming that he had adequate funds to pay for the consignment. On the arrival of the consignment, this document would be presented to the Customs at Malpensa Airport together with the consignor's invoice and, when stamped by the Customs authorities would be presented to the consignee's bank and payment would then be duly made by the bank.

During the period between February and June 1978, forty consignments of calves were carried to Malpensa Airport by the defendant on behalf of the plaintiff, but the plaintiff received no payment for any of them. It was subsequently discovered that this was due to a fraud which had been perpetrated in Italy. No one employed by the defendant had been involved in any way.

The nature of the fraud was that between the time the bag containing all the documentation was given by the load master to the S.E.A. official, on the arrival of the plane, and the presentation of the relevant documents to the Customs, a different invoice was substituted for the plaintiff's invoice. This was an invoice purporting to be from a firm called "Livestock Forwarding Agencies" having an address in Surrey. While the consignees initially claimed that their failure to pay the plaintiff was due to difficulties encountered with the Italian Exchange Control Regulations, ultimately they relied on the substituted invoices and claimed that the calves had been supplied to them by "Livestock Forwarding Agencies" and not by the plaintiff. The plaintiff recovered judgment in Ireland for £361,607 against the consignee of thirty four consignments, but it was not possible to recover anything on foot of this judgment.

In these circumstances the plaintiff instituted proceedings against the respondent claiming damages for negligence and breach of duty and/or misrepresentation in and about the handling of the necessary Customs arrangements at Malpensa Airport. The trial judge, dismissing the claim, said that the case made on behalf of the plaintiff was that there was an implied condition in each contract of carriage that the defendants' personnel would be responsible for the safe delivery of the relevant documentation for each consignment to the Italian Customs, that S.E.A. was its agent for this purpose and the defendant was vicariously liable. He held that there was no evidence to support such an implied term. He was satisfied that the extent of the defendant's liability regarding the documentation was its safe delivery to the S.E.A. representative, and its obligation in this regard had been duly performed in the case of each consignment. While the officials of S.E.A. might have had an opportunity to tamper with the consignment documentation, there was no evidence to establish a probability that they did do so. It was more likely that the switch of documents was made after the relevant documents were handed over by S.E.A. to the consignees of their representative, and in handing over the documents in that way S.E.A. were following an established practice and were not negligent. He was satisfied that S.E.A. was not acting as agent for the defendant in distributing the flight documentation.

The Supreme Court affirmed. Blayney J. noted that the plaintiff's claim in the High Court had rested on the argument that the defendant had breached an implied term of its contract. On appeal, 'a totally different case' had been made. The plaintiff had sought to establish that the defendant had been negligent, in failing to observe the duty of care which it owed to the plaintiff in performing the contracts of carriage which it had entered into with the plaintiff, or alternatively, that S.E.A. had been negligent and that the defendant was vicariously liable for its negligence.

As to the first argument, counsel for the plaintiff contended that,

> in circumstances where it was necessary to make Customs entry of freight or goods at any place, the carrier was under the duty to take reasonable

care to furnish to the Customs authorities all the relevant documents relating to the goods furnished by the consignor to the carrier.

He did not cite any authority in support of this formulation and Blayney J. was satisfied that none could be found to support it.

The essential issue in the case was what the duty of care which the respondent undertook in regard to the documents which accompanied each consignment. Blayney J. considered that it was a duty to perform whatever was required in a normal competent manner. It was clear from the evidence that the universal practice at Malpensa Airport was to deliver the pouch containing the documents to S.E.A. who were the handling agents at the airport.

Blayney J. was satisfied that, in using the services of S.E.A., the defendants had been in no way in breach of the duty of care which they owed to the appellant:

They were following what was the universal practice of airlines using the Malpensa Airport and could not be faulted for that.

The defendants could not have foreseen any risk of damage by using the services of S.E.A. They had been using their services without incident for at least two years before the frauds which gave rise to the proceedings were perpetrated and they had no reason to think that there could be any risk in continuing to use them.

Blayney J. agreed with the trial judge's holding that S.E.A. had not been guilty of negligence. It was clear from the evidence that S.E.A. had no duty in regard to the invoice except to give it to the consignee or his clearing agent, who would present it to the Italian Customs, 'so once this had been done their duty to the [plaintiff] or the [defendant] was fulfilled. They owed no duty to either as to what happened to the invoice subsequently.' It was not part of S.E.A.'s function to examine the documents to see what they were in order. Their sole function was to deliver the documents to the appropriate destinations.

Since the S.E.A. was not negligent, the issue of the defendant's vicarious liability for their acts did not arise.

Horse-riding establishments In *Baldwin v. Foy and Forest Way Riding Holidays Ltd.*, High Court, July 1, 1997, Laffoy J., held that the defendant horse-riding establishment was guilty of negligence in letting the plaintiff, an inexperienced rider, loose on a cross-country course adjacent to boggy land that was overgrown with gorse bushes. On 'a cold, wet, miserable day' in November, the plaintiff was thrown from her horse during a sudden hailstorm. Had there been a fence segragating the cross-country course from the unsafe terrain, the likelihood was that the horse would have stayed within a safer environment.

Prison authorities	Over the past decade there has been a significant amount of litigation where prisoners who have been attacked by other prisoners have sought to implicate the prison authorities in negligence in failing in their duty of care to protect them from the risk of assault. The courts have taken the view that a system of control and inspection which would guarantee protection against assaults of this kind would be so oppressive as to defeat other important goals relating to the morale of prisoners and the encouragement of rehabilitation.

Bolger v. Governor of Mountjoy Prison, High Court, November 12, 1997, represents the most difficult fact situation so far. The plaintiff, a prisoner in Mountjoy, had been the victim of an attack by a fellow prisoner, who threw a bucket of scalding water over him. The fellow prisoner had a known history of violent behaviour. Seven years previously, when he was in St. Patrick's Institution at the age of sixteen, 'he had been caught fighting on a couple of occasions and ... damaging prison property' and had assaulted another prisoner with boiling water. A month before the incident in which the plaintiff was injured, the fellow prisoner had thrown a dinner plate at another prisoner, having, shortly before then, threatened a prison officer.

O'Donovan J. held that the prison authorities were not liable. The incident involving an assault with boiling water had been when the fellow prisoner 'was only sixteen years of age'. Over the next six years he had not been involved in any similar occurrence.

Admittedly, the fellow prisoner had a history of fighting other prisoners and of damaging prison property but none of those incidents had warranted more by way of punishment than either an warning as to his future behaviour or his having to forfeit a few days' recreation. That history did not suggest that he was so dangerous that, in the interests of the safety of other prisoners in their custody, the prison authorities should have recognised a need to segregate him from the other prisoners. Segregation was tantamount to solitary confinement and, given that the fellow prisoner was serving a ten year sentence, it seemed to Flood J. that it would have been 'an entirely excessive precaution were he to be segregated from other prisoners on account of his past history.' The fact that six years previously, when he was only sixteen years of age, the fellow prisoner had attacked another prisoner with boiling water did not mean that it was incumbent on the prison authorities to deny him access to hot water 'which, of course, he would require for the purpose of washing himself and, perhaps, for making himself a cup of tea, which, apparently, is a facility which is available to all prisoners.' To punish an adult prisoner in that way for an offence which he had committed when only a boy would, in O'Donovan J.'s view, be grossly excessive.

In the 1998 Review, we shall analyse *Bates v. Minster for Justice*, Supreme Court, March 4, 1998, in which the prison authorities were held not to have been negligent when a fellow prisoner threw a jug of hot water containing sugar in the plaintiff's face. Murphy J. (Lynch and Barron JJ. concurring) said:

> Whilst it might be possible to devise some system under which prison-
> ers could obtain tea of reasonable quality and temperature without en-
> dangering the safety of other inmates there is no obvious means by which
> this can be achieved without excessive hardship on the prisoners or an
> excessive burden on the prison authorities. No doubt prison manage-
> ment is a constant battle between the need to preserve security and safety
> on the one hand and, on the other hand, the obligation to recognise the
> constitutional rights of the prisoners and their dignity as human beings.
> Procedures for the provision of food and hot drink and the means by and
> the location in which it will be provided will require to be reviewed
> from time to time but it would seem unfortunate if the requirement of
> safety precluded access to tea or necessitated further restrictions on com-
> munal eating and social intercourse between the inmates. It is a difficult
> balance to achieve but it is in that context that the duty of care owed by
> the defendants to the plaintiff must be tested.

In the instant case, the prison warders had been unaware of any antagonisms between the aggressor and the plaintiff. Whilst obviously there had been a danger that boiling water could be thrown, 'there was no evidence to suggest that there was any particular risk to inmates from such conduct; only to ward-ers [*sic*].'

PROFESSIONAL NEGLIGENCE

Lawyers

Litigation strategy In *Lopes v. Walker*, Supreme Court, July 28, 1997, the important issue of solicitors' duties in relation to strategy as to court jurisdiction fell for consideration. The Court, by a majority (Lynch and Barron JJ., Murphy J. dissenting) overturned a verdict against the plaintiff by Morris J. in the High Court.

The plaintiff was involved in a traffic accident in 1988. He had worked previously in the merchant navy, but at the time of the accident was owner of a newsagent's business. The accident was attributable to the negligence of an intoxicated driver. Within three weeks, and before medical reports were received, the plaintiff's original solicitor had issued a civil bill in the Circuit Court. The plaintiff wished to have the case transferred to the High Court. Counsel advised against this. The plaintiff changed from his original solicitor to the defendant solicitor on March 1, 1991. The defendant had for many months been aware of the plaintiff's dissatisfaction with the proceedings continuing in the Circuit Court. The case was heard on May 14, 1991. the plaintiff was awarded £10,000 general damages and just over £2,000 special damages. The Circuit Court judge awarded nothing for loss of earnings.

The threshold for the High Court jurisdiction at the time of the litigation was £15,000.

The plaintiff sued the defendant for negligence, contending that he should not have let the case proceed to judgment in the Circuit Court without further adjournment. The essence of his claim was that the defendant ought to have sought another expert medical opinion when the neurologist who examined the plaintiff regarded an arachnoid cyst on the left side of his brain as congenital rather than as being attributable to the accident. The plaintiff also contended that greater attention should have been paid to his claim for loss of earnings. He argued that his injuries were such as to prevent him returning to his career as a merchant seaman, which yielded an income of £18,000 per annum.

Morris J. dismissed the claim but, as has been mentioned, the Supreme Court, by a majority upheld the plaintiff's appeal.

Barron J., one of the two judges upholding the appeal, considered that the defendant ought to have arranged through the neurologist for a second opinion. Moreover, although the evidence of the neurologist, an orthopedic surgeon and a psychiatrist had been fairly presented, the reports of the neurologist and psychiatrist had contained provisos, to which no attention appeared to have been paid. These might have been asked about them but they never had been. Furthermore, a certificate by a doctor approved by the Minister for Communications to the effect that he had examined the plaintiff and found him unfit for seafaring, had not been followed up. It was true that counsel's opinion as to the value of the case was in favour of remaining in the Circuit Court, but his assessment was clearly affected by his view of the medical evidence and it was hard to see how he had taken such a strong view of it. Contrary to his assertion that there was no positive evidence of physical injury, there was in fact such evidence 'albeit soft tissue injury and not boney injury'. In addition, counsel's view as to loss of earnings seemed to be based on the proposition that, since the plaintiff had not been earning a seaman's wages at the date of his accident, he could not then claim such a loss:

> Undoubtedly, counsel's opinion was supported by the assessment of damages by the trial judge. But that is not really the true test of what the plaintiff could or should have recovered as of that date. It is merely an assessment of what was the proper sum to award to the plaintiff on the basis of the manner in which his case was presented to the Court.

Even if the plaintiff had never expressed any intention before the accident of returning to sea and even if his newsagent's business would have failed anyway, the fact still remained that, had he still been in full health, he would have been in a position to return to sea.

The plaintiff had been happy to proceed in the Circuit Court provided he could subsequently sue the neurologist. It must, however, have been obvious to the defendant that a hypothetical action against a doctor, which was highly unlikely to be successful, was no remedy for proceeding in a court and under a jurisdiction which the plaintiff did not want. The defendant's failure to tell him so meant that the plaintiff could not make an informed decision to let the case proceed in the Circuit Court.

Lynch J., the other judge in the majority, expressed the defendant's failure somewhat more narrowly in terms of not having sought an adjournment of the case as soon as he received the file on March 1, 1991 to give him 'breathing space to sort the matter out properly one way or the other.'

Murphy J., dissenting, pointed to a number of potent factors weighing against liability. In relation to the reports of the neurologist and the orthopedic surgeon, the defendant had expressly advised his client in writing that he was entitled to obtain a second expert medical opinion if he wished. During the pre-trial consultation at the courthouse, counsel had made the position clear to the plaintiff. A memorandum kept by the defendants' assistant recorded counsel advising the plaintiff as follows:

> In his estimation the valuation based on [his] knowledge of the Judge and on the knowledge of what the doctors would say was about £10,000. He reiterated that Mr. Lopes must be absolutely satisfied that he was happy to go into Court today for a maximum of £15,000. He did not have to follow the opinion of his legal advisors. If he was not happy he must bring the case in another Court and this decision must be made today. If he felt that the compensation was not adequate then he should tell us today and go to another Court. Mr. Lopes said that it would be silly of him to go to the High Court if no more damages would [be] awarded in that Court.

On the issue of loss of earnings, the memorandum recorded that counsel had pointed out that there was:

> no proof of loss of earnings. The court would compensate Mr. Lopes on the basis of what he was actually working at at the time. The test was one of probabilities and not possibilities and the probability was that he would not be working at sea.

In the plaintiff's later case against the defendant, counsel gave evidence before Morris J. to similar effect. The medical reports did not paint a picture of a person who would have been incapable of carrying on the business of a shopkeeper; moreover, since the plaintiff had not been engaged as a ship's officer for some years before the accident and had no immediate plans of taking up that occupation before the accident, it could not be used as the basis for calculating his loss. Such a claim was in fact made before the Circuit Court Judge who had expressly rejected it. Morris J. had not merely upheld counsel's advice as a tenable, competent, professional opinion but had confirmed that it represented his own assessment of the interpretation of the medical evidence available to the legal advisor on the date of the hearing of the personal injury action.

As regards the medical evidence, there had been no suggestion that the plaintiff had relied upon any guidance from the defendant as to what doctors he should consult. While the plaintiff had wished for the neurologist to be called as a witness in order to be cross-examined by the plaintiff's counsel as to the provenance of the cerebral cyst, such a course would have been 'extremely imprudent', in Murphy J.'s view.

Murphy J. concluded by noting that the proceedings had been issued, particulars delivered and all of the medical examinations conducted before the defendant came on record as the plaintiff's solicitor. Furthermore, and even more importantly, the fundamental responsibility as to the witnesses to be called and as to the advice to be given to the client in relation to the valuation of the claim was a matter for counsel. The defendant had, therefore, a more limited role in the proceedings and Morris J. had been entirely correct in concluding that there was no evidence that he had failed to discharge those duties.

Conflict of interest In *Phelan Holdings (Kilkenny) Ltd v. Hogan, carrying on practice under the style and title of Poe Kiely Hogan,* High Court, October 15, 1996, Barron J. imposed liability in negligence on the defendant solicitor who allowed a conflict of interest to develop between himself and the plaintiff, his client. The plaintiff, a building contractor, sought to develop property by purchasing land and building houses on it. Part of the project involved buying a right of way over a strip of land from a company of which the defendant was beneficial owner. The defendant also acted for him as his solicitor. The development ran into local opposition, planning problems and financial difficulties, which resulted in the plaintiff having to abort his plans, at a financial loss.

Barron J. considered that, when the defendant agreed to grant to the plaintiff the right of way over the green strip, he should have advised him to be represented by a different solicitor:

> It was not just a case of a solicitor acting for both parties; one of the parties was in reality the solicitor himself. Once this transaction had been completed there would have been no bar *per se* to his acting in relation to the purchase of the site or in relation to any other legal matter.

As the development strategy proceeded, the conflict of interest should have become apparent to the defendant. By the time that local residents were threatening proceedings, the defendant 'had no alternative but to advise the plaintiff that he could no longer act for him. The likelihood of prejudice to the plaintiff if he continued to do so was all too clear.'

Barron J. noted that '[u]nfortunately the facts . . . in the proceedings by [the residents] were such that the conflict was no technical breach of a technical rule.' The defendant was in a position where he was quite incapable of dealing objectively with the situation which presented itself. When he sought advice from senior counsel, he had professed to do so on behalf of the plaintiff. The problem was in reality his own, since his company would have been liable in damages to the plaintiff if he could not have used the right of way which had been agreed, through the defendant, to be granted to him. If senior counsel had known the defendant's real involvement, they would have pointed out the conflict and required separate representation for each defendant.

It had been submitted on behalf of the defendant that the conflict of interest was potential only. Barron J. could not accept that this was so. The defendant had been 'in clear breach of the duty as a solicitor towards his client.' He had deprived him of the opportunity to obtain proper independent advice in relation to all his various problems.

Assessing damages was a somewhat complicated and tentative process since several factors combined to make this determination uncertain. In particular, the plaintiff's financial capacity to succeed fully in the development project as originally designed was not entirely clear. Barron J. accepted that the plaintiff would have been required to obtain an equity partner. One would definitely have been available; what was less clear were the terms on which that partner would have been willing to invest. The opposition of the residents, with probable consequential delay in the commencement of the development, was another factor affecting the assessment of damages.

In making these determinations, Barron J. proceeded on the basis of the principle of the balance of probabilities. He noted that counsel for the defendant had referred to *Davies v. Taylor* [1974] A.C. 207 and *Allied Maples Group v. Simmons* [1995] 1 W.L.R. 1602, which supported the concept of a reduction in the amount of damages proportionate to the chance that particular events would have occurred; on this approach, a plaintiff deprived of a 40% chance of gaining £1,000 should be awarded £400. In the instant case, neither counsel had made any submissions as to the validity of this approach and accordingly Barron J. left the issue unresolved.

In addition to financial loss, the plaintiff claimed damages for the anxiety and depression which he suffered as the result of the defendant's default. Barron J. noted that, in *Kelly v. Crowley* [1985] I.R. 212 Murphy J. had refused to grant damages for mental distress arising from the negligence of a solicitor in the purchase of a public house for the plaintiffs.

The recent Supreme Court case of *Kelly v. Hennessy* [1995] 3 I.R. 253 had set out the principles relating to mental injury, distinguishing between nervous shock, which was the expression used to include any psychiatric illness, and mental distress without any such illness. According to Hamilton C.J. (at 259), to obtain damages for nervous shock, the nervous shock sustained by the plaintiff had to be by reason of actual or apprehended physical injury to the plaintiff or a person other than the plaintiff. Hamilton C.J. had approved the following passage from the judgment of Brennan J. in the Australian case of *Jaensch v. Coffey* (1984) 155 C.L.R. 549:

> A plaintiff may recover only if the psychiatric illness is the result of physical injury inflicted on him by the defendant or if it is induced by shock. Psychiatric illness caused in other ways attracts no damages, though it is reasonably foreseeable that psychiatric illness might be a consequence of the defendant's carelessness.

Barron J. accepted that the plaintiff's mental illness was nervous shock within the meaning of that term as used in *Kelly v. Hennessy*. He further accepted that it had been caused by the negligence of the defendant and was something which was a reasonably foreseeable consequence of that negligence. The defendant had known of the fact that the plaintiff had been to a psychiatric hospital during the course of events and must have been aware of his increasing agitation as proceedings by the residents for judicial review of planning permission awarded the plaintiff approached. Nevertheless the negligence of the defendant did not cause any physical injury to the plaintiff. 'Accordingly,' Barron J. stated, 'no damages are recoverable for the nervous shock which he sustained.'

This conclusion is difficult to support. Certainly, it seems inconsistent with what the Supreme Court held, and what the Chief Justice and Denham J. said, in *Kelly v. Hennessy* and what the High Court of Australia decided in *Jaensch v. Coffey*. In *Kelly v. Hennessy*, the defendant had neither caused nor risked any physical injury to the plaintiff, who was some miles away from the place of the accident at the time the accident occurred. Brennan J., in the passage from *Jaensch v. Coffey* quoted by Barron J., made it plain that the infliction of physical injury on the plaintiff was not a precondition of entitlement to recover damages for psychiatric illness. Perhaps the explanation for Barron J.'s holding lies in the fact that the plaintiff's illness was attributable in increasing apprehension about future events rather than to some earlier precipitating event.

For a thorough analysis of the subject, see Gillian Kelly, 'Post Traumatic Stress Disorder: A Recognisable Psychiatric Illness' (1998) 16 *ILT* 10, 26, 38 and Ken Bredin, 'Nervous Shock and the Secondary Victim' (1997) 3 *Bar Review* 133.

Doctors

Paediatric treatment In *Lynch v. O'Connor*, High Court, June 28, 1996, Kinlen J. acquitted a pediatrician, the second defendant, of negligence in his treatment of the plaintiff, who was born in 1980. The plaintiff's brother had been born with an extreme case of spina bifida in 1979 and had lived for only a month. The plaintiff had a skin tag when she was born. The pediatrician successfully ligated it. He did not, however, seek the assistance or advice of a neurologist, neurosurgeon or orthopedic surgeon; nor did he have an x-ray taken. (Kinlen J. considered it 'extremely doubtful whether anything material would have been discovered by the use of such expertise.') In fact it appears that the plaintiff probably had a minor form of spina bifida occulta.

There was some evidential confusion surrounding the sending by the pediatrician of a letter to the plaintiff's mother's general practitioner raising the possibility of an x-ray in the future and the receipt by the general practitioner of this letter. There was a conflict of evidence as to whether the pediatrician had warned the plaintiff's mother to return for an examination six weeks after the birth: the pediatrician 'gave very clear and positive evidence' to this effect but the plaintiff's mother had no recollection of any such conversation. As the case unfolded nothing hinged on these issues.

The plaintiff's mother took her to a post-natal clinic for a six-weeks check. A ten-month examination similarly failed to unearth any problem. When the plaintiff first went to school, at the age of four and a half, her teacher noticed that she had a problem when gripping pens in her hand. Medical investigation revealed that she had a condition of spina bifida.

The plaintiff received occupational therapy and some time later a surgical intervention was carried out successfully. The plaintiff did not relate happily with her occupational therapist.

The plaintiff's claim for negligence against the pediatrician failed because she did not establish negligence on his part and also on account of lack of causation. Applying the test for professional negligence laid down by the Supreme Court in *Dunne v. National Maternity Hospital* [1989] I.R. 91, Kinlen J. considered that 'as of 1980 . . . [the pediatrician] was [not] negligent.' Although his treatment of the skin tag did not have universal support, it had been conceded that it was not negligent. In 1980 there was no scheme of recall – Kinlen J. added: 'although perhaps there should be' – and the hospital where the plaintiff was born was the only hospital in Dublin at the time which sent out letters to the general practitioner and the obstetrician of the findings of the pediatrician. The pediatrician would probably have come to the same conclusions as had been reached by those who in fact examined the plaintiff after six weeks and ten months.

The delay in the plaintiff's receiving occupational therapy did not, on the evidence, cause the plaintiff injury.

Delay in provision of antibiotics In *Fitzpatrick v. The Midland Health Board*, High Court, May 1, 1997, Johnson J. addressed two issues: the adequacy of the treatment regime adopted by a surgeon employed by the hospital where the plaintiff went with a pain and swollen finger and the manner in which a report of a medical test should have been communicated to the surgeon so that he could act upon it expeditiously. On the first visit to the hospital, the plaintiff was placed on antibiotics; his finger was operated on by the surgeon; a culture was taken and sent for analysis. It was found to be sterile and the plaintiff was discharged, his finger now in a satisfactory condition. He was seen again two days later and told to return after a week. When he did so, it was found that he was suffering from a severe pulp space infection of the right index finger.

The surgeon operated on the plaintiff for a debridgement of the finger; he removed the tissue from the distal phalanx, took a swab and sent it for culturing. He decided at this stage not to give the plaintiff any antibiotics.

The result of the culturing did not return until three days later. It as not seen by the surgeon for a further two days. He then prescribed antibiotics, which were not given to the plaintiff until yet another day had passed. The condition of the finger deteriorated. The tip of the index finger proved to be necrotic. The surgeon removed two millimetres of bone. The care of the patient was transferred to another surgeon, because the first surgeon was going on vacation. The second surgeon, responding to the fact that osteomyelitis had set in, amputated the distal phalanx.

The essence of the plaintiff's case was that the first surgeon ought to have prescribed antibiotics earlier. There was a conflict of opinion as to whether it would have been appropriate to have treated the plaintiff with broad spectrum antibiotics before the swab was taken and cultured or whether it would have been preferable to wait until the swab had been cultured and the specific antibiotic which ought to be used identified. There was no disagreement among the medical witnesses, however, that the delay in starting the antibiotics after the culture had been taken was unreasonable.

Johnson J., in the light of the division of professional opinion on the first issue, held that one could 'not say that the failure to apply the broad spectrum antibiotics immediately was negligent'. But he was satisfied that the delay in starting the treatment after the culture had been taken was negligent and that this had exacerbated the plaintiff's injuries, meriting an award of £20,000 general damages.

Johnson J. reiterated the fact that:

> it is essential where a course is adopted by the [treating doctor] not to apply broad spectrum antibiotics . . . that (a) a report be delivered regarding the culture of the swab as soon as it is practicable to the treating doctor, (b) that it is brought to his attention and (c) that he is therefore

enabled to act upon it as soon as is possible.

The question of internal communications between doctors, technicians, scientists, nurses and administrators in a hospital setting is sometimes perceived as a matter to be resolved by the *Dunne* test. In the instant case, this was not problematical as there was no dispute among the professional witnesses. In truth, practical strategic questions as to how medical services are delivered to the patient should not be determined by the *Dunne* test but rather on the basis of straightforward negligence principles.

Informed consent to treatment   In the 1994 Review, 454–5, we discussed Geoghegan J.'s decision in *Bolton v. Blackrock Clinic Ltd.*, High Court, December 20, 1994, dismissing proceedings for negligence against the defendants, a cardio-thoracic surgeon and a consultant thoracic physician. The gravamen of the plaintiff's claim was that the doctors had failed to obtain her informed consent to sleeve resection surgery. Applying the test favoured by O'Flaherty and Hederman JJ. in *Walsh v. Family Planning Services Ltd* [1992] 1 I.R. 496, which did 'not depend on any general and approved practice of the profession without defects' but rather was 'to be determined by the trial Judge on the ordinary established principles of negligence...', Geoghegan J. held that the doctors had not failed in their duty of disclosure to their patient.

The plaintiff appealed unsuccessfully to the Supreme Court, which delivered its judgment on January 23, 1997. Hamilton C.J. (Barrington and Murphy JJ. concurring) held that Geoghegan J.'s finding that the plaintiff had given 'a fully informed consent' was supported by the evidence. He quoted from Finlay C.J.'s judgment in *Walsh* ([1992] 1 I.R. 496, at 510), which includes the passage where Finlay C.J. stated that the question of disclosure of risk should be determined by the test laid down by the Supreme Court in *Dunne v. National Maternity Hospital* [1989] I.R. 91. In essence, this test defers to the customary practices of the medical profession, while reserving to the court the entitlement to stigmatise as negligent a practice containing inherent defects which ought to have been obvious to any person giving the matter due consideration.

Hamilton C.J. made no reference to the fact that Geoghegan J. had applied the more stringent test preferred by O'Flaherty and Hederman JJ. It seems clear from Hamilton C.J.'s judgment, which is largely composed of extracts from the transcript of the evidence given at trial, that the Chief Justice supported the test set down by Finlay C.J. in *Walsh*. It is unfortunate that the radical division of judicial opinion apparent in *Walsh* has not been resolved, one way or the other, by a thorough analysis of the competing approaches. It would still seem open to a litigant to argue that O'Flaherty and Hederman JJ.'s approach retains vitality since Hamilton C.J. made no critical references to it or to the fact that Geoghegan J. had adopted it, and the Chief Justice did not expressly state his preference for the approach favoured by Finlay C.J.

and (it would seem) McCarthy J. in *Walsh*. Hamilton C.J. ignored, not only O'Flaherty J.'s judgment (with which Hederman J. concurred) but also the judgments of McCarthy and Egan JJ. It would be hard to argue that *Bolton* has definitively resolved the debate. For analysis of *Bolton* and a more wide-ranging discussion of the subject, see John Healy, 'Duties of Disclosure and the Elective Patient: A Case for Informed Consent' (1996) 4 *MLJI* 25 (1998).

In *Mordaunt v. Gallagher and McPartland*, High Court, July 11, 1997, Laffoy J. confronted the problem which was first addressed by the Irish courts forty four years ago in *Daniels v. Heskin* [1954] IR 73, concerning the duty of a medical practitioner to disclose to the patient the fact that a particular treatment has turned out less satisfactory than was intended, with a consequent risk of detriment for the patient.

In *Daniels v. Heskin*, the situation involved a home birth, where a needle had broken without any negligence on the part of the doctor. In *Mordaunt*, the plaintiff, aged fifty nine, had had a hip replacement operation which resulted in the failure to remove fully the trochenteric wires. This failure was in no way attributable to any party involved in the operation. The result for the plaintiff was pain for a number of months until the situation was remedied.

Laffoy J. acquitted the defendant of negligence. Even if he had made an error of judgment this was not necessarily negligence. In her view, having regard to the risks inherent in prolonging the procedure and in particular the risk of exposing the plaintiff's hip to infection, the doctor, in deciding not to explore further for the inaccessible end of the remaining wire and not to bring an x-ray machine into the theatre to try to obtain a later exposure of the plaintiff's hip, had not been guilty of negligence.

Dentists Later in the Chapter, in the Section on Damages, we examine *Cooper v. O'Connell*, Supreme Court, June 5, 1997, which, in the context of proceedings for professional negligence against a dentist, analysed the circumstances in which it may be appropriate to award exemplary or aggravated damages. On the facts of the case, the Supreme Court, upholding Barron J., held that an award under either heading was not justified.

EMPLOYERS' LIABILITY

Safe system, proper equipment and statutory duty In *Matthews v. The Irish Society for Autism and the National Autistic Association*, High Court, April 18, 1997, the plaintiff was the office manager of the defendant corporations, of which she and her husband were founding members, her husband being their executive director. On a wet afternoon, when she was carrying fifty information packs in her arms and a large briefcase over her shoulder, she rushed across the footpath at O'Connell Street, Dublin, towards her husband's car. As she did so, an unidentified woman who was coming along the footpath to her left slipped and fell. In falling, she grabbed the plaintiff who, in turn, lost her balance and fell heavily on her arm and shoulder, fracturing her neck.

The plaintiff claimed that the defendants were negligent in failing to provide a safe system of working for her and in failing to provide appropriate equipment for the task she was required to so. She further contended that the defendants were in breach of their statutory duty under section 12 of the Safety, Health and Welfare at Work Act 1989 in failing to prepare a safety statement. Had they done so, she argued, the hazard to which she was subjected would have been identified and appropriate steps taken to avoid it.

The essence of the plaintiff's claim regarding failure to provide a safe system and proper equipment was that, under the system in place at the time, she was required to handle manually an excessive load or weight of material and that the environment through which she had to carry it exposed her to risk. The weight she was carrying – forty three pounds – exceeded the limit prescribed for female employees under Article 3 of the Factories Act 1955 (Manual Labour) (Maximum Weights and Transport) Regulations 1972. These regulations had no application to the instant case but the plaintiff nonetheless contended that the load was too heavy for one female. Her counsel argued that requiring her to cradle loose information packs in her arms when crossing a busy urban footpath on a wet afternoon, when pedestrians tended to rush, was not a safe way to transport the material, even if the weight was acceptable.

Laffoy J. dismissed the plaintiff's case. The accident was 'entirely attributable' to the fact that the unidentified female pedestrian had collided with the plaintiff. The fact that the plaintiff was carrying a heavy and an awkward load had not contributed to her fall. There was 'a high degree of probability' that the accident would have happened in the same way, with the same consequences, if the plaintiff had not been encumbered by the information packs or the briefcase and if she had not been rushing. It was probable that the same result would have ensued if she had been going with the flow of pedestrian traffic in front of the woman who collided with her. The hazard which the accident had highlighted was not of a type that would reasonably be anticipated by the defendants' employee who had responsibility for preparing a safety statement and not something which would have been required to have been identified and addressed in the formulation of such a safety statement, had there been one.

Laffoy J.'s decision is of interest for a number of reasons. First, her characterisation of the kind of accident that occurred was of crucial relevance to the outcome of the proceedings. The essence of the event was that the plaintiff had been knocked down by another person whose fall would have brought about the plaintiff's accident regardless of what she was carrying. The heavy load that she was bearing had not in Laffoy J.'s view, increased the prospects of an accident occurring. Laffoy J., although describing in detail the plaintiff's argument that the defendants had been negligent in failing to provide a safe system of work, or proper equipment, never specifically held that the defendants had in fact been guilty of negligence. The general tenor of her discussion of this argument, however, suggests that she did not demur from the proposition that they had been negligent.

The reason why the plaintiff lost her case was, thus, not (necessarily) that the defendants were not negligent, but that any such negligence could not have been the cause of the plaintiff's injuries. It is true that in *Hughes v. Lord Advocate* [1963] A.C. 837, the House of Lords held that a negligent defendant will be liable, even where the precise circumstances of an accident are unforeseeable, if the injury is of a *kind* that was foreseeable. This case could not assist the plaintiff, however, since Laffoy J. did not simply hold that the accident was not of a different kind from that which was foreseeable: on her analysis the cause of the injury was the unidentified woman's fall, so the defendants simply had not caused the plaintiff's injury, whether foreseeable or otherwise.

The unforeseeability of the accident was, however, the reason why Laffoy J. held that the defendants were not in breach of section 12 of the Safety, Health and Welfare at Work Act 1989. Laffoy J. went so far as to hold that a collision with *any* pedestrian 'coming along the pavement' was not so foreseeable as to warrant being addressed in the formulation of a safety statement. The fact that the plaintiff was knocked down by a pedestrian who was herself already falling was not a relevant factor in determining the plaintiff's action for breach of statutory duty, in contrast to her common law action for negligence. It is perhaps surprising that a safety statement should not have to address the risk of an employee's colliding with another pedestrian when the employee was as encumbered as the plaintiff.

Finally, it is worth noting that Laffoy J. referred to the plaintiff's argument that common law liability in negligence could be inspired by a regulation or standard narrower in its terms than the asserted liability at common law. She recorded the plaintiff's invocation of regulations relating to maximum weights for female employees which admittedly had no application to the instant case. Laffoy J. neither accepted nor rejected this argument and her failure to reject it can scarcely be treated too seriously in view of the fact that the plaintiff could not have succeeded on this point in view of the lack of causal relationship between the alleged negligence and the plaintiff's injury. Nevertheless, one may record that in *Duffy v. Rooney and Dunnes Stores (Dundalk) Ltd.*, High Court, June 23, 1997, which we discuss in detail in the section on Products Liability, below 745-52, Laffoy J. interpreted a standard of particular, limited, scope as contributing to the generation of a more wide-ranging duty of care in negligence at common law.

The decision of *Dunne v. Dublin Cargo Handling Ltd (in liquidation)*,

Supreme Court, August 30, 1997 (*ex tempore*) throws light on the relationship between common law negligence and breach of statutory duty in employers' liability litigation.

The plaintiff, a sixty-year-old employee, was injured in a night-time accident involving a mobile crane when he was unloading a boat at the Port of Dublin. The crane was moving on tracks on the deck of the vessel. Its driver could not see the movement of the plaintiff when he emerged onto the deck of the vessel, and the crane struck him.

The former practice had been to have a person known as singer-out on or near the deck who communicated with the crane driver by shouting and later, as technology improved, by walkie-talkie. The singer-out had given way to a system which required employees to avoid the crane rather than the crane driver to take care to avoid them. The crane was provided with a flashing light and a loud siren; if it came in contact with some other body, there was an automatic cut-out so that it moved no further. (As Murphy J. acknowledged, this latter device would only mitigate rather than prevent injury.)

Johnson J. held that this was a safe system. The Supreme Court dismissed the appeal. Murphy J. (Lynch and Barron JJ. concurring) observed:

> Of course an employer could do more. Ingenuity could of course devise more complex or even simple [–] perhaps inexpensive [–] systems. Other things could be done and could be devised. There could be a combination of perhaps the original system of singer-out plus the technical innovations and perhaps a combination of the two with the use of walkie talkies for the singer-out. This all could be done. But the issue is to decide what was reasonable and I think it is proper to note that this is an area . . . which is covered by stringent statutory regulations none of which apparently require a singer-out to be provided or a person performing such functions. At the end of the day the learned trial Judge was performing the function of deciding what was reasonable. He had the views of the witnesses and the views of two engineers, one called on behalf of the plaintiff and one on behalf of the defendant. With that he reached a conclusion that what the plaintiff had in the circumstances did not constitute negligence. He concluded that the device and the system represented the view that the employers had exercised reasonable care for their employee. In my view he was amply justified in reaching that conclusion, a conclusion which this Court would not be justified in disturbing.

In his concurring judgment, Barron J. thought it 'significant' that there was 'no contest but that [the statutory] regime [regulating the work] was being followed.'

The implications for plaintiffs in future litigation seems clear. The Supreme Court apparently regarded the statutory regime in relation to safety in the work environment as being so wide-ranging and protective of employees as to generate, in effect, a presumption that the statutory duties represent the outer limit of what should be expected of employers. An employee alleging that an employer was negligent at common law in failing to provide a particular kind of protection will have to overcome the judicial assumption that, if there is merit in the argument, the Oireachtas would already have incorporated the particular protection in its statutory code.

In the context of the particular facts of the instant case, this is a particularly unfortunate mind-set. Clearly the days of the singer-out are over; contemporary thinking on safety practices no longer favours shouts as a viable means of communication. Yet the old system had the merit of placing the burden of protection on the source of the danger rather than on those imperiled by the danger. Our courts should hesitate before approving a system which makes employees' bodily integrity depend solely on their own constant vigilance.

Causation   In the 1993 Review, 543–5, we analysed Murphy J.'s decision in *O'Leary v. Cork Corporation*, High Court, 19 May 1993, rejecting the plaintiff's claim that he had developed multiple sclerosis as a result of a work-related accident. The Supreme Court dismissed the plaintiff's appeal on July 4, 1997. Lynch J. (O'Flaherty, Barrington, Keane and Barron JJ. concurring) held that there was 'ample evidence' to support Murphy J.'s conclusions on whether the trauma suffered by the plaintiff precipitated the onset of multiple sclerosis. In this case there had been 'a carefully conducted trial lasting seven days followed by a reserved judgment dealing logically and clearly with the issues arising [there]in. . . .'

The respondent had not sought to question Murphy J.'s finding that trauma *is capable* of being a precipitating factor in the onset of multiple sclerosis. One suspects that, on this contested issue of medical science, the Supreme Court must have been relieved that it was not called on to act as referee. In the 1992 Review, 611, we noted the judicial embarrassment evident in *Best v. Wellcome Foundation Ltd.* [1992] I.L.R.M. 609; [1993] 3 I.R. 421 where the Court was called on to resolve to somewhat similar disputed medical issue. Finlay C.J.'s attempt to deny that the Court was actively entering fully into the scientific issue was less than convincing.

OCCUPIERS' LIABILITY

McCracken J.'s decision in *Thomas v. Leitrim County Council* [1998] 2 I.L.R.M. 74, is on one view a matter of only historical interest, since it dealt with the common law position prevailing before the Occupiers' Liability Act

1995 came into effect on July 17, 1995: see the 1995 Review, 518, McNamee, 'The Occupiers' Liability Act 1995: A Farewell to *McNamara v. E.S.B*' (1997) 1 *Irish Insurance Law Rev.* 3. Nevertheless, it is of some significance for future litigation in giving an indication of the extent to which a court may attach significance to indirect economic purposes of occupiers of land when assessing the scope of their responsibilities to entrants onto their property.

In *Thomas*, the plaintiff, an English visitor to Sligo who had come there to attend a hot air balloon festival, took the opportunity to go sightseeing when the event was cancelled because of strong winds. She and her husband and their friends went to Glencar Waterfall in County Leitrim, as they had read about it in the Michelin Guide.

The area around Glencar Waterfall had been purchased by the defendants in 1986 for development as a tourist amenity. They had erected a car park and toilet block at the main road adjacent to the waterfall, and renewed pathways leading up to the top of the waterfall. The pathway consisted of stone slabs four feet in width. It led from the road up the side of the waterfall to a viewing platform at the top of the waterfall. The pathway then continued at a sharp angle to the left and rose to its highest point. From there it descended again quite steeply by way of steps, turned to the left and rejoined the original pathway, thus creating a loop, which was in the shape of a triangle.

The defendants employed a local woman as a part-time caretaker, but her functions were limited to ensuring that the toilet block was properly kept and that there were no problems in the car parking area. She had no responsibility for the pathway up to the top of the waterfall. There was also no system of regular inspections of this area by the defendants. The engineer responsible for roads and amenities had visited the site four weeks previously.

When the plaintiff and her friends visited the site, they walked up the path to the top of the waterfall and descended back down again on the loop pathway. Towards the bottom of the step part of that pathway they encountered a tree fallen across the path, completely blocking it. To the right of the path where the tree had fallen was a row of trees, and it would have been quite impossible to pass on that side. To the left had side of the path there was a very steep bank leading downwards towards the bottom of the path on the road. This had been grassed; it had been used as a shortcut to some considerable degree and there were two distinct bare tracks on it, one on each side of a tree stump. These tracks showed a considerable amount of bare earth where the grass had been worn away.

The plaintiff's party were walking in a single file down the pathway when they came to the fallen tree. There was no discussion about what ought to be done before the various members of the party stepped off the path on to the bank at slightly different places. The plaintiff was the last in the file. The bank was very steep and it was necessary to side step down the bank to keep one's balance. The plaintiff's husband slipped shortly after stepping off the path, although he did not hurt himself. Just as he was getting up, the plaintiff stepped off the path higher up, and she slipped and suffered serious injuries to her ankle.

Applying the pre-legislation common law, McCracken J. had to decide whether to abolish the traditional distinction between the duties owed to invitees and licensees, respectively. McCarthy J. had favoured this approach in *Rooney v. Connolly* [1987] I.L.R.M. 768, at 786, but McCracken J. observed that McCarthy J.'s judgment was 'quite clearly *obiter*' and that the other members of the Supreme Court had specifically declined to consider the point, which had not been argued before the court.

Adopting the definition of invitee and licensee set out in McMahon & Binchy, *op. cit.*, 213, 216, McCracken J. concluded that the plaintiff was an invitee, since there was a material benefit to the defendants in having Glencar Waterfall open to the public:

> This is not a park being provided as an open space in an urban area by a local authority: this is a scenic attraction in a rural area. I very much doubt if the defendant county council spent considerable sums of money on building a car park and toilet block and on building a path of some length simply for the residents of Co. Leitrim. This is clearly a tourist amenity, and is designed to attract tourists into Co. Leitrim. The plaintiff and her party in fact went to the area because they read of it in a book dealing with tourist attractions.
>
> The question remains whether attracting tourists is a sufficient material interest to bring entrants into the area under the heading of [invitees]. On balance, I think it is. One of the main purposes, if not the principal purpose, of attracting tourists into an area is that they bring financial benefits to the area. While these benefits may initially put money in the pockets of local shopkeepers, nevertheless there is, at lest indirectly, a benefit to the local authority as well. Accordingly, in my view, the plaintiff entered the area of Glencar Waterfall as an invitee.

The traditional duty owed by a occupier to an invitee had been expressed by Willes J. in *Indermaur v. Dames* (1866) L.R. 1 C.P. 274, at 287, to the effect that:

> with respect to such a visitor, at least, we consider it settled law that he, using reasonable care on his part for his own safety, is entitled to expect that the occupier shall on his part use reasonable care to prevent damage from unusual danger which he knows or ought to know.

In the Supreme Court decision of *Foley v. Musgrave Cash and Carry Ltd.*, on December 20, 1985 (extracted in McMahon & Binchy's *Casebook on the Irish*

Law of Torts (2nd ed., 1991), 164), Griffin J. had expressed the view that:

> [i]n modern times . . . the duty owned by the occupier to an invitee could best be said to be to take reasonable care in all the circumstances to see that the premises are reasonably safe for the invitee. Nowadays in a case of this kind it seems to matter little whether this test is used or whether the test of foresight and proximity enunciated by Mr. Justice Walsh in *Purtill v. Athlone UDC* [1968] I.R. 205 or that of the neighbour principle stated by Lord Atkin in *Donoghue v. Stevenson* [1932] A.C. 862 is applied.

McCracken J. accepted this passage as 'restating the test' laid down by Willes J. more than a century previously. Applying the *Foley* test to the facts, he held the defendants guilty of 'a clear lack of reasonable care' in not ensuring, through an adequate system of inspection of the public area, that the pathway was kept clear and passable, particularly in an area where there was a steep and possibly dangerous bank at the side of the path. He reduced the plaintiff's damages by two-thirds, however, to take account of her contributory negligence in 'show[ing] a total disregard for her own safety. . . .'

It is interesting to speculate on how the plaintiff would have fared under Willes J.'s test. It is debatable whether a fallen tree in a public area is an 'unusual danger'. The controversial aspect of *Indermaur v. Dames*, in modern discussion at least, is that, in laying down a threshold requirement of proof of an unusual danger, it relieved occupiers of liability to invitees in cases where they had clearly shown a lack of reasonable care but where the plaintiff could not point to any particular danger that could be characterised as unusual. Perhaps one could in the instant case characterise the tree as constituting an unusual danger, not because of the fact that it fell but rather having fallen some considerable time previously, it remained as a dangerous obstacle which the plaintiff had a right to expect not to have been thus neglected by the defendants.

It is difficult to assess the full impact of *Thomas v. Leitrim County Council* on litigation occurring under the Occupiers Liability Act 1995. Entrants are now categorised as *visitors, recreational users* and *trespassers*. A person may be classified as a visitor even when he or she does not confer a material benefit on the occupier. Visitors are owed a duty of care similar to that expressed by Griffin J. in *Foley* relative to invitees. It appears, however, that an entrant such as Mrs. Thomas would have to be characterised as a recreational user of the defendants' property to whom no duty of care would be owed. The legislation, controversially, reduces the legal protection for recreational users to the limited entitlement not to be injured intentionally by the occupier nor exposed to injury from acts done by the occupier with reckless disregard for their presence. It is ironic that the indirect material benefit to the occupier which McCracken J. discerned in *Thomas v. Leitrim County Council*, in terms of encouraging local tourism, was the very factor that underlay the *reduction* of the protection of recreational users, many thousands of whom will be tourists, to a shamefully low level.

In the section on Vicarious Liability, below, 787, we discuss Laffoy J.'s decision in *Duffy v. Rooney and Dunnes Stores (Dundalk) Ltd*, High Court, June 23, 1997. An issue of occupier's liability arose in this case. For the reasons we mention, we do not consider that much significance should be attached to this aspect of the case.

ROAD TRAFFIC

In *O'Brien v. Armstrong*, Supreme Court, March 19, 1997 (*ex empore*), the Supreme Court, affirming Budd J., held that the defendant had not been guilty of negligence when driving his cattle truck along a country road. Shortly before a sharp and dangerous corner, the road narrowed from twenty three feet to twenty and a half feet, so that, on the defendant's side of the road, he had only just over ten feet. Assuming his truck was eight feet wide, 'almost inevitably some part of it would be over the continuous white line' (*per* O'Flaherty J). The defendant was conscious that there were cars behind him, which he checked periodically. The plaintiff attempted to pass the defendant but found that there was not sufficient space and an accident occurred.

O'Flaherty J. based his analysis on lack of foreseeability:

> The defendant was approaching this blind bend which was known as an accident black spot with one of those signs that so indicated, so is it to be thought right that the law should impose a duty on him to foresee that someone should attempt this very dangerous mission of passing him out at this particular place – which is what the plaintiff attempted?

Lynch J., concurring, added a further point:

> [T]he real question is whether [the defendant] should have been watching in his mirror as the plaintiff came up along side. He most certainly should not. [The defendant] in his cattle truck was approaching a blind corner with a continuous white line and a large accident black spot sign at the corner. His duty in those circumstance was to watch very carefully ahead of him and that was the one place where he could not be expected to be watching in his mirror to the rear. His duty was to concentrate on the road ahead. There was no negligence in [the defendant's] not being aware that the plaintiff was coming alongside him, ignoring the white line, ignoring the blind corner and ignoring the black spot if it were visible to him.

PRODUCT LIABILITY

General product safety   The European Communities (General Products Safety) Regulations 1997 (S.I. No. 197 of 1997), which implemented the 1992 Directive on General Products Safety, 92/59/EEC, are discussed in the Safety and Health chapter, 672, above.

The duty to warn

Retailers   In *Duffy v. Rooney and Dunnes Stores (Drogheda) Ltd.*, High Court, June 23, 1997, Laffoy J. gave the most comprehensive analysis thus far in Ireland of the issue of duty to warn of dangers inhering in products. The most significant previous decision is that of the Supreme Court in *O'Byrne v. Gloucester*, November 3, 1988 (extracted in McMahon & Binchy's *Casebook on the Irish Law of Torts*, 22 (2nd ed., 1991)). The Supreme Court, on April 23, 1998, affirmed Laffoy J.'s judgment, which had been appealed on only a narrow issue relating to the causal connection between the second defendant's negligence and the plaintiff's injuries.

In *Duffy*, the plaintiff, a girl aged two years and ten months, was seriously burned when a coat she was wearing on a visit to her grandparents' home came in contact with an open fire in the sitting room. The coat had been purchased in the second defendant's store. Later in the chapter, in the section on Vicarious Liability, below, 787 we consider the issue of the liability of the first defendant, the child's grandfather, for negligent supervision. Here we concentrate on the issue of product liability.

The accident took place in 1992. The coat, which had been manufactured in 1991, was designed and sold as a hooded raincoat. It was made of an outer fabric which was a brightly coloured printed woven cotton/polyester mix, with an inner lining of woven 100% polyester, intended for insulation purposes. This wadding was sewn to the lining at the hem and at the seams and in a quilted fashion in lines four to five inches apart. The coat was buttoned down the front. The outer fabric was a full flared skirt, which was designed to stand out from the body in a bell shape. The lining with the attached wadding was neither as long nor as full as the outer fabric, leaving a gap for air to circulate between the outer fabric and the lining.

The coat had two labels sewn into it. One had the words 'St Bernard Aged 3 – 4 approx' on one side and 'Made in U.K. Dry clean or hand wash 40⁰C' on the other side. The other label set out the constituents of the fabrics. The coat contained no warning that the fabrics were flammable or that it should be kept away from fire.

The coat was one of a range of over five thousand sold by companies in the Dunnes Stores Group which were manufactured for the Group by an English Company. This company was a large reputable manufacturer specialising in children's outer wear for many of the leading multiple chain stores in Britain and Ireland as well as North America and other countries. Its annual turnover was three million pounds and it manufactured 120,000 garments a year. The fabrics for the raincoat that the plaintiff wore had been sourced by the manufacturer from a large reputable British supplier. The coats were of a standard design and style popular in the market at the time of manufacture. In 1991 there were no standards or regulations in force in Britain in relation to the manufacture or assembly of outer garments for children. The manufacturer did not carry out flammability testing on the fabrics. No warning label was attached to the coats and there was no standard or regulation requiring warning labels to be affixed. From 1992 onwards the Dunnes Stores Group put warning labels on all children's garments.

The plaintiff's case did not involve any suggestion that the coat she wore was a 'rogue' one: her complaint impugned 'the whole genus of which [her] coat formed part.'

In 1991, the only Irish standard in force in relation to the children's apparel was I.S. 148: 1988, under which EOLAS (now the National Standards Authority of Ireland) prescribed the flammability and labeling requirements of fabrics and fabric assemblies used in children's nightwear. Children's nightdresses, dressing gowns and pyjamas fell within the scope of these requirements but there was no dispute that the plaintiff's coat did not come within their remit. Had it done so, the fabrics of which it was made up would not have been used; the words 'Keep away from Fire' would have been necessary if the fabrics had been permitted to be used.

Laffoy J. approached the issue of the second defendant's liability as follows. It was not in issue that that, as retailer of the coat, the second defendant owed a duty of care to the plaintiff, the ultimate user of the coat. The question was whether the second defendant had observed the standard of care required of it.

After detailed reference to the Supreme Court decisions of *Bradley v. Coras Iompair Eireann* [1976] I.R. 217 and *Roche v. Peilow* [1985] I.R. 232, which, in her view, posited 'fundamentally the same test' as to whether the appropriate standard of care has been observed . . . , albeit in different factual contexts', Laffoy J. sought to translate that test into the factual context of the instant case as raising the question:

> whether, irrespective of the prevailing practice amongst manufacturers and retailers in 1991, a reasonable and prudent retailer, giving due consideration to the fabric composition, the design and the construction of [the plaintiff]'s coat and the fact that it was intended to be worn by a three year old child, would have realised that the child would be exposed to the risk of serious injury if the garment was put into circulation at all or, alternatively, if it was put into circulation without being treated

with flame retardant or, alternatively, without having a warning label affixed to it.

Laffoy J., referred to the Supreme Court decision of *O'Byrne v. Gloucester* and to the decision of *Browne v. Primark t/a Pennys*, High Court, December 10, 1990, where Lardner J., in an *ex tempore* judgment, had acceded to the defendants' application for a non-suit in a case where a five-year-old boy, wearing pyjamas with a warning label, 'Keep away from Fire,' as required by I.S. 148: 1988, had been burned when playing with matches. Lardner J. was:

> not persuaded that a reasonable careful retailer, or maker of the garments of this kind, should, in 1986, in this country, have used only flame resistant fabrics in children's pyjamas. Public standards, which are declared by the Institute which is set up by statute and which are under the control of the Department of State, do not require it and there is no evidence that such standards were commonly applied here and I am not satisfied that a reasonably careful trader should, as a matter of legal duty at common law, have observed the higher standard of safety claimed on behalf of the plaintiff. It may well be that such a higher duty should be required by law but, if that is the case, it is a matter for the legislature.

In the instant case, Laffoy J. noted that I.S. 148: 1988 was not directly relevant, since the coat worn by the plaintiff was not a garment to which the standard applied. Nevertheless, this standard was relevant insofar as it evidenced:

> an official awareness of the risk inherent in using fabric other than fabric of low flammability for lightweight, long, loose garments such as night-dresses, pyjamas, and dressing gowns intended primarily for indoor wear and an official determination that, insofar as it is not necessary to proscribe the use of fabrics other than fabrics of low flammability in the manufacture of such garments, a warning, by means of labeling, of that risk is necessary to protect the public, as evidenced by the requirement of a warning label on pyjamas and terry-toweling bathrobes. It is also of relevance in that official awareness was communicated to the public, and, in particular, to manufacturers and retailers through publication of I.S. 148: 1988 and, indeed, through publication of the standards and the enactment of the regulations which preceded it.

Applying these principles to the facts of the case, Laffoy J. was not satisfied that the plaintiff's coat was so inherently dangerous that it should not have been put in circulation. The court was required to have regard to 'demands of the market place and the popularity of this type of garment', which was 'entirely understandable in the light of its attractiveness and utility', and to weigh these factors against the risks the coat presented and the manner in which those risks might adequately be addressed.

Moreover, Laffoy J. was not satisfied on the evidence that in 1991 a reasonable and prudent manufacturer or retailer, if it had addressed the issue, would have considered it necessary to substitute a low flammability fabric, such as nylon, for the cotton/polyester outer layer of the plaintiff's coat. The resulting garment would have been of a different type from the one that found favour with customers. To have treated the outer fabric with flame retardant would have detracted from the attractiveness and comfort of the coat because it would have rendered the fabric stiffer and less comfortable where it met the body.

Laffoy J. was, however, of the view that a reasonably prudent manufacturer or retailer, if it had properly addressed the issue, would have affixed a label on the coat warning that it should be kept away from the fire, taking into account the following seven factors:

(a) that the trend in recent times had been to use lighter weight and more flammable fabrics for garments intended for wear by children out of doors than had formerly been the case;

(b) that in design terms there were many similarities between a coat of the type worn by the plaintiff and a night-dress or dressing gown, particularly in terms of length and looseness and the fact that frequently with garments such as raincoats and wintercoats the child wore a size bigger than was appropriate to the child's age (as was the situation in the instant case);

(c) that very young children had to be dressed by a parent or other adult and that even a garment primarily designed for outdoor wear was normally put on the child in the house and might be worn around the house for some time before the child went out;

(d) that open fires and gas heaters were a common feature of domestic life in Ireland;

(e) that young children were unpredictable and lacked a sense of danger;

(f) the gravity of the consequences of fire accidents;

and

(g) the relatively low cost of labeling garments.

It was not enough, however, for the plaintiff to establish that the second defendant had been guilty of negligence in failing to affix a warning label to the coat; it was essential for her to show that this negligence had resulted in her injuries. This, in Laffoy J.'s judgment, the plaintiff had failed to do. The plaintiff's grandmother, who had bought the coat in 1991 and given it to her as a Christmas present, gave evidence, that if there had been a warning label, she would have adverted to it and been hesitant to buy something which would have been dangerous, particularly for her granddaughter. While Laffoy J. had no doubt that the grandmother honestly believed this, she considered that the belief was 'informed by more than a modicum of hindsight' and was not satisfied that the grandmother would not in fact have bought the coat if the warning had been attached. Similarly Laffoy J. rejected the plaintiff's mother's belief that she would not have dressed her daughter in the coat if it contained a warning. On the fateful day, the plaintiff was wearing trousers and a sweatshirt to which warning labels were attached.

Neither did Laffoy J. consider that, if the warning label had been affixed, affairs in the household on the day in question would have been conducted in such a way that the plaintiff's coat would not have come in contact with the fire. Accordingly the plaintiff's action against the second defendant was dismissed.

The first defendant appealed unsuccessfully to the Supreme Court, his appeal concentrating on the issue of the causal connection between the second defendant's negligence and the plaintiff's injuries. The Supreme Court, delivering its judgment on April 23, 1993, rejected the argument that the onus on the causation question should rest on the second defendant.

Laffoy J.'s judgment is a model of lucidity, clarity and depth of analysis. It is likely to have considerable influence in the development of the Irish law of products liability. Several aspects of the case call for comment.

First, Laffoy J. had no difficulty in recognising that a retailer can have a duty of care towards a user of a product. That duty rests in tort, though of course it is also capable of being based in contract, at all events where the plaintiff is a party to the contract. In some instances of retail sales, where one member of a family buys an item and then gives it to another member of the family, a court may be willing to regard the purchaser as the agent of the ultimate user, but cases involving such a straining of the privity rule are not easy to find (cf. *Jackson v. Horizon Holidays* [1975] 3 All E.R. 92, doubted in *Woodar v. Wimpey* [1980] 1 W.L.R. 277) and there are authorities to the contrary: see, *e.g.*, *Sigurdson v. Hillcrest Service Ltd.*, 73 D.L.R. (3d) 132 (Sask. Q.B., 1977). In the instant case it would not be credible to contend that the plaintiff's grandmother had bought the coat as her agent. She had purchased it 'in the spring or early summer' of 1991 and had given it to the plaintiff the following Christmas. Cf. *Kirby v. Burke and Holloway* [1944] I.R. 207; *Priest v. Last* [1903] 2 K.B. 148.

There is a well-established judicial authority in favour of holding that a retailer or other distributor can owe a duty of care in negligence to the ultimate user of a product which the retailer or other distributor sells: see, *e.g. Andrews v. Hopkinson* [1957] 1 Q.B. 229, *Fisher v. Harrods* [1966] 1 Lloyd's

Rep. 500. Nonetheless, Professor Waddams (*Products Liability*) (2nd ed., 1980), p. 17) is surely right to suggest that:

> there is a practical difference between the standard imposed on a manufacturer and that imposed on other business distributors. . . . [S]omething like a presumption operates against a manufacturer who supplies a defective product, but no such presumption is applicable to a retailer or wholesaler who may have no reason to suspect the presence of the defect and no means of avoiding it. So, although the courts speak of a single standard, that of due care, as being applicable to manufacturer, other business supplier, and non-business supplier, the practical effect of the application of the standard varies in each case.

In the context of the facts of *Duffy*, it is also worth heeding the qualifications expressed by *Winfield & Jolowicz on Tort* (14th. ed., by WVH Rogers, 1994), 254–6:

> The manufacturer's duty extends to taking steps (for example, warnings) concerning dangers which are discovered only after the product has gone into circulation. A mere distributor or supplier has not actively created the danger in the same way as a manufacturer but he, too, may be under a duty to make inquiries or carry out an inspection of the product and if it is dangerous for some reason of which he should have known, his failure to warn of it will then amount to negligence. . . . [A] retail grocer, for example, cannot be expected to institute inspections to discover whether his tinned food is contaminated. He may be obliged to satisfy himself as to the reputation of his supplier and he must certainly follow proper practices in keeping his wares but otherwise unless the contamination was caused by his negligence or he actually knew of it, his only liability is to the actual purchaser under the contract of sale. If a third party becomes ill on eating the contaminated food, his remedy, if any, is against the manufacturer.

In *Duffy*, as we have seen, the second defendant did not dispute that, as retailer of the coat, it owed a duty of care to the plaintiff, as the ultimate user of the coat. The only question was whether it had 'observed the standard of care in retailing that product which the law required of it.' Nowhere in her judgment does Laffoy J. address the proposition that the scope of a retailer's duty may be narrower than, or at all events different in scope from, that of a manufacturer. Instead, one finds an elision between the two. Thus, for example, Laffoy J. was not satisfied on the evidence that in 1991 'a reasonable or prudent *manufacturer or retailer*, if he had addressed the issue, would have considered it necessary to substitute a low flammability fabric . . . in order to protect the plaintiff' (emphasis added). A similar elision may be noted in Laffoy J.'s observation that 'a reasonably prudent *manufacturer or retailer*, had he properly addressed the issue would have, and the second defendant ought to have, affixed a label to [the plaintiff]'s coat warning that it should be kept away from fire' (emphasis added). On Laffoy J.'s approach there is, in effect, an identical duty resting on the manufacturer and the retailer to ensure that a product is made of safe ingredients and to ensure that the consumer is adequately warned as to any dangers inherring in the product. Perhaps there is justification for expanding the duty of the retailer to meet that of the manufacturer in a case where the retailer is a huge commerial organisation with adequate resources to engage in close scrutiny of products that it actually commissions, but nothing in Laffoy J.'s judgment confirms that this is why she articulated the respective duties of manufacturer and retailer in identical terms.

It is worth noting that the manufacturer in this case was a large and reputable one. The evidence was to the effect that the Irish standards as to warnings followed rather than led those in England. Yet there is no suggestion in Laffoy J.'s judgment that the second defendant, as retailer, might be entitled to assume that the manufacturer had addressed the requirements as to warning. As against this, it may be responded that the case was not comparable to one where a retailer sells contaminated tinned food. Here the second defendant had full information as to the constituent fabrics in the coat. The question of formulating an appropriate warning was not more difficult, and no less urgent, for the second defendant to address than it was for the manufacturer.

We have noted that Laffoy J. considered that 'fundamentally the same test as to whether the appropriate standard of care has been observed is posited in *Bradley v. Coras Iompair Eireann* [1976] I.R. 217 and *Roche v. Peilow* [1985] I.R. 232, albeit in different factual contexts'. She came to this conclusion having been invited by the counsel for the second defendant to find an analogy with the principles applied to employers' liability litigation where the plaintiff argues that the employer is guilty of a culpable omission as to safety and by counsel for the first defendant to find an analogy with the principles applicable to professional negligence. When one closely examines the British and Irish decisions in these two areas we finds a significant degree of cross-fertilisation (cf. *Winfield & Jolowicz on Tort, op. cit.*, 128 -32) but the position at which the Irish courts ultimately arrived, in *Bradley* and *Roche*, was that a straightforward negligence test is applied to employers' liability cases, even where omissions as to safety are alleged (cf. McMahon & Binchy, *op. cit.* 319–21) whereas in professional negligence litigation considerable deference continues to be afforded to customary practice: only where the particular practice has inherent defects which ought to be obvious to any person giving the matter due consideration, will it be impugned. These two approaches are far from identical. Laffoy J. has rightly analogised with *Bradley* rather than *Roche*

v. Pielow in the context of product liability. Whatever justification there may
be for deference to professional customary practices – and this is a controversial judicial stance – there is surely none for doing so in the context of product
liability.

Laffoy J.'s interpretation of the significance of I.S. 148: 1988 is of much
interest. It might perhaps have been thought that its limited scope and the fact
that it applied only to children's nightwear might have led to the conclusion
that the prevailing standard did not require a warning label for other garments.
Instead, Laffoy J. drew from the existence of I.S. 148: 1988 evidence of 'an
official awareness' of a risk that *went further* than the garments falling within
the standard: the list of garments that it covered represented, in her view, only
particular instances of the category of 'lightweight, long, loose garments.'

Finally, it is worth noting that, although the plaintiff in her statement of
claim had sought to impose liability on the second defendant under the Liability for Defective Products Act 1991, Laffoy J. was not disposed to investigate
this avenue of liability since it was 'common case' that the plaintiff's grandmother had purchased the coat before the Act came into force. No mention
was made of the possibility of maintaining an action against the Irish Government for its delay in implementing the European Product Liability Directive:
see McMahon, 'Liability for Defective Products Act 1991' in A. Schuster
(ed.), *The New Product Liability Regime*, at p. 17 (1992); Shuster, 'Review of
Caselaw under Directive 85/374/EEC on Liability for Defective Products'
(1998) 6 *Consumer L.J.* 195. On this broad theme see Niamh Hyland, 'State
Liability for Non-Implementation of Directives – Further and Better Particulars' (1997) 3 *Bar Review* 40.

NEGLIGENT MISREPRESENTATION

Auctioneer   In *McCullagh v. PB Gunne (Monaghan) plc*, High Court, January 17, 1997, Carroll J. gave important guidance on the legal position of auctioneers. Briefly, the case concerned the purchase of licensed premises by a
naive married couple with no business experience, where the price of £125,000
was just beyond their means. The business venture 'was a disaster'. (Carroll J.
did not expand on this.) When the property was put up for resale, in spite of
the earlier representation by the defendant auctioneer's employee at the time
of purchase that he could get the plaintiffs a profit of £10,000 to £20,000 if
they resold, the highest offer received was only £85,000. There were 'problems' with the licence. Because there was no money to stamp the deed of
conveyance, it could not be produced at the annual licensing sessions.

The facts thus stated, while unfortunate, would not necessarily involve
any question of liability on the part of the auctioneer. In the particular circumstances of the case, however, it appeared that the employee of the defendant

auctioneer had taken a proactive role. The plaintiffs had told him that they had never previously bought property and they asked him to keep them straight. He had told them not to worry and that he could arrange finance. He sold their farm for £35,000 sterling. He kept the deposit of (IR£11,657) in the clients' account. He arranged to open an account with a building society for the balance of the purchase money of the farm in the name of the plaintiffs c/o Gunnes. This employee later told the plaintiffs that the licensed premises which they subsequently bought was ideal for them. He said he was not going to advertise because, if he did, the phone would never stop ringing and they would not get a chance to buy. In fact the owner of the premises had asked him to put the property on the market but to keep it very quiet. The plaintiffs inspected the premises and decided they were happy with it. They asked him to buy it at the best price, as cheaply as possible. Having bought the premises for £125,000, he kept telling the plaintiffs not to worry about money and that he could get a loan of 60% to 65% from a financial institution.

The plaintiffs claimed that Gunnes had held itself out to find them premises at a price they could afford and that it would arrange finance. Mr McCullagh acknowledged that he was aware that Gunne's employee had been acting as an auctioneer and had been paid a commission by the vendor but he said that the employee had never told him that he could not also act for the McCullaghs or advise them. Mr McCullagh 'did not understand figures, [nor] what turnover meant' and the plaintiffs had put their trust in the auctioneer's employee.

Carroll J. imposed liability for negligent misrepresentation on the defendant auctioneer. She noted that the defendant's employee had told the plaintiffs that he was not advertising the property and that, if he did, the phone would not stop ringing:

> This gave the impression that he was on the McCullaghs' side and that they were on some kind of inside track compared to other prospective purchasers. This may be a ploy of auctioneers but, if it is, it is wholly unjustified. An auctioneer is employed by a vendor to get the best price and should always make it clear that the vendor is his only client, not the purchaser as well. Auctioneers cannot be all things to all men.

Carroll J., having referred to the English decision of *Hedley Byrne & Co. Ltd. Heller and Partners Ltd* [1964] A.C. 465, *Esso Petroleum Co Ltd v. Mardon* [1976] Q.B. 801, *Yianni v. Edwin Edmonds & Son* [1981] 3 All E.R. 592, *Smith v. Eric Section Bush* [1982] 2 All E.R. 514, *Gran Gelator Ltd v. Richcliff* [1992] 1 All E.R. 865 and *McCullagh v. Lane Fox & Partners Ltd*, [1994] 1 EGLRR 48 as well as the Irish decisions of *McAnarney v. Hanrahan* [1993] 3 I.R. 492 and *I.P.B.S. v. O'Sullivan* [1990] I.L.R.M. 598, concluded that, in the circumstances of the instant case, the auctioneer's employee had taken over the burden of assisting the McCullaghs to arrange adequate finance in their quest for a suitable business. He had sold the farm for them and opened an account for them in the building society; he had not demurred when they said they wanted him 'to keep them straight' nor when they asked him to buy the licensed premised at the best price. He had supplied the turnover and projections to the building society. He had found the plaintiffs not one but two solicitors. He had encouraged them by telephone to believe they would get as much money as they needed for the purchase. He had got them to sign the loan approval form without solicitor's advice.

It must have been obvious to him that the plaintiffs were depending on him and his expertise to get them adequate finance. He had done nothing to disabuse them of the reliance which they had obviously placed in him. Even after he got them a second solicitor, he had not sent them off to him for advice on the loan application which showed the purchase price inaccurately at £130,000 and the promoters' input at £65,000. As late as at the stage of post contract/ preclosing, he had promised them as much as they needed. Even at that point they probably could have refused to close:

> The plaintiffs are naive but they impressed me as very straight honest people. They did not deserve the treatment they had [received from the defendant's employee] and this was certainly a case where it is fair, just, equitable and reasonable that a duty of care be recognised by the Court.

The plaintiffs were simply claiming their money back. Carroll J. awarded them £50,000 (increased by reference to the Consumer Price Index).

Bank manager   In *Forshall v. Walsh*, High Court, June 18, 1997, the facts of which we state in more detail in the Section of this Chapter headed 'Deceit', below, 769, Shanley J. held that Michael McSweeney, a bank manager, who failed to exercise due care to the plaintiff in making representations that the company of which his brother Timothy was director was a concessionaire of Lamborghini Motor Cars, was liable for negligent misrepresentation and negligent misstatement to her when she gave moneys to the company, which she would not otherwise have done, to her detriment. Shanley J. made it clear that he did not believe that the bank manager was guilty of telling conscious untruths to the plaintiff.

Shanley J. proceeded on the basis that a party seeking damages for negligent misrepresentation had to establish that the representor had failed to exercise due care in making the representation, as a result of which the representee 'was induced to enter into the particular agreement and suffered damage in consequence of the inaccurate representation'. Closely aligned to the claim of negligent misrepresentation was the wider tort of negligent misstatement. In relation to this latter tort, the plaintiff had to establish that the defendant owed him or her a duty of care. In this context, Shanley J. noted that, in *Ward v.*

McMaster [1989] I.L.R.M. 400, McCarthy J. had considered that the duty of care arose from the proximity of the parties, the foreseeability of the damage and the absence of any compelling exemption based on public policy. In *Caparo Industries plc v. Dickman* [1990] 2 A.C. 605, at 617–618, Lord Bridge had stated:

> What emerges is that, in addition to the foreseeability of damage, necessary ingredients in any situation giving rise to a duty of care are that there should exist between the party owing the duty and the party to whom it is owed a relationship characterised by the law as one of 'proximity' or 'neighbourhood' and that the situation should be one in which the Court considers it fair, just and reasonable that the law should impose a duty of a given scope on the one party for the benefit of the other.

Lord Bridge had observed, in relation to decided cases in which a duty of care in respect of negligent misstatement had been held to exist, that the limit on the liability of a wrongdoer towards those who had suffered economic damage:

> . . . rested on the necessity to prove, in this category of the tort of negligence, as an essential ingredient of the 'proximity' between the plaintiff and the defendant, that the defendant knew that his statement would be communicated to the plaintiff, either as an individual or as a member of an identifiable class, specifically in connection with a particular transaction or transactions of a particular kind (*e.g.* in a prospectus inviting investment) and that the plaintiff would be very likely to rely on it for the purpose of deciding whether or not to enter on that transaction or upon that transaction or upon a transaction of that kind. *Id.,* at 621.

Shanley J. considered that in the instant case there had been 'clearly a most exceptional relationship' between Michael McSweeney and the plaintiff:

> It started with the fact that she was doing business with a customer of the bank. It was compounded by the fact that the Managing Director of the customer of the bank was a brother of Michael McSweeney. That the relationship was exceptional is illustrated, first by the number of unsolicited phone calls made by Michael McSweeney to [the plaintiff] and that, when in trouble, [the plaintiff] phoned Michael McSweeney, not just at his office, but at his home, using a number which he himself had given her.

Whether one adopted McCarthy J.'s test in *Ward v. McMaster* or Lord Bridge's test in *Caparo*, all the necessary ingredients which might give rise to a duty of care existed in relation to the bank and the plaintiff:

> [T]here was a relationship which can undoubtedly be characterised as one of the 'proximity' or 'neighbourhood', a relationship of such a nature that the bank, in the person of Michael McSweeney, was aware that statements he might make would most likely be relied upon by [the plaintiff] and that carelessness in making such statements might cause her damage. There can be no doubt in my mind that in such circumstances it is fair, just and reasonable that the law should impose a duty of care on the bank in relation to the representations it made to [the plaintiff].

CAUSATION

Housing authority In *Felloni v. Dublin Corporation* [1998] 1 I.L.R.M. 133, Morris J. dismissed an action for negligence brought by a fifteen-year-old girl who lived with her aunt in a flat of which the defendant was landlord. The plaintiff had lost the tip of her finger when closing the front door. The principal means of closing the door originally had been a knocker, which with the passage of time 'became defective'.

Morris J. placed emphasis on the fact that the plaintiff's aunt had not informed the defendant of the defect and had not perceived the situation as a problem. Even if the defendant had been negligent, that negligence would have been overtaken by the negligence of the plaintiff and her aunt and her aunt's husband in allowing the state of affairs to continue 'whereby presumably a number of times a day they would voluntarily expose themselves to what must have been a risk of injury in the slamming of the door when the remedy was available to them at little or no expense, to remedy the problem by fixing some sort of handle onto the door at minimal expense.

Morris J. considered that the Supreme Court decisions of *Crowley v. Allied Irish Bank* [1987] I.R. 382; [1988] I.L.R.M. 225 (1987 Review, 326–29) and *Conole v. Redbank Oyster Co.*, [1976] I.R. 91 applied. These cases involved the defence of *novus actus interveniens*. In the instant case, such doctrine seems to be somewhat harsh. The relationship between landlord and tenant is ongoing; it does not consist of an initial provision of premises to the tenant, for which the tenant must thereafter take over responsibility. No one would wish to encourage a dependency culture but Morris J.'s resolution is out of harmony with earlier caselaw and appears somewhat indulgent to the defendant. A reduction for contributory negligence would seem a sufficient sanction.

CONTRIBUTORY NEGLIGENCE

'Slippery slope' arguments   In *Thomas v. Leitrim County Council* [1998] 2 I.L.R.M. 74, which we discuss in detail in the Section on Occupiers' Liability, above, 000-00, McCracken J. made a swingeing reduction of two-thirds of the plaintiff's damages to take account of her contributory negligence when, on a walk at Glencar Waterfall, she encountered a fallen tree in her path and decided to go down a steep bank rather than retrace her steps to the top of the waterfall and go down a path that she knew to be safe.

McCracken J. was of the view that the plaintiff had shown 'a total disregard for her own safety' in trying to side-step down the bank. She had taken a calculated risk in the knowledge that there was a danger of falling.

In *O'Flynn v. Balkan Tours Ltd* Supreme Court, April 7, 1997, (*ex tempore*), which we discuss in the Section on Duty of Care, above, 708, the Supreme Court upheld a reduction of 75% for the contributory negligence of the plaintiff skier, where, having missed the last chair-lift because of a sequence of events traceable to the defendant's negligence, he showed 'an unbelieveable want of care' for his own safety in proceeding down a dangerous part of a mountain. The real difficulty with this case is the holding that the defendant was guilty of negligence. A significant reduction from the award to take account of contributory negligence does not really remove, or even mitigate, the difficulty.

Train passengers   In *Forde v. Iarnród Eireann v. Irish Rail*, Supreme Court, November 4, 1997 (*ex tempore*), the Supreme Court reduced to 30% from 75% a finding of contributory negligence against a passenger, aged sixteen, who was injured when on his way back to Galway, after that country had just won the All-Ireland hurling final. The train had stopped at Ballinasloe. Of its eight carriages, nearly two had been parked so far away from the platform as to render it impossible for passengers to alight onto the platform. The plaintiff had been obliged to get out of the rear passenger cars, which were not at the platform. When the guard blew his whistle twice, the plaintiff tried to return, found the door of carriage closed, advanced up the train and 'climbed onto the running board of the carriage whilst also grasping an overhead rail.' The door was closed from the inside, the train moved off, the plaintiff slipped down and his leg came into contact with the platform, causing him severe injuries.

O'Flaherty J. (Barrington and Lynch JJ. concurring) considered that the defendant company ought to have organised activities so that, on an occassion of crowds, excitement and celebration, a member of its staff would have gone down from the platform to ensure that there was no one in the vicinity of the train when it was pulling off. Had this been done, no accident would have happened. Whilst the plaintiff ought to have realised that he was taking some risk in attmepting to re-enter the train in the unorthodox manner he had adopted, the preponderence of blame ought to be placed on the defendant.

Road traffic accidents In *O'Brien v. Armstrong*, Supreme Court, March 19, 1997 (*ex tempore*), which we discussion the Road Traffic section of this Chapter, above, 744, the Supreme Court affirmed Budd J.'s dismissal of proceedings brought by a driver whose vehicle came in contact with the defendant's cattle truck as the plaintiff was attempting to pass the defendant at a dangerous bend. The road had narrowed to just over twenty feet. The defendant's vehicle was around eight feet wide. O'Flaherty J. considered that 'almost inevitably some part of it would be over the continuous white line', which was rather faded.

O'Flaherty J. considered that the accident was not foreseeable. Lynch J. added that the defendant was not under an obligation to check his mirror as he was negotiating the bend. O'Flaherty J. observed:

> This is one of those cases where one has to hold that the mishap was due to the exclusive negligence of one of the parties. The introduction of a power in a court to apportion fault between two negligent parties introduced for the first time into our law by the Civil Liability Act, 1961, should not cause us to lose sight of the fact that there is an onus on a plaintiff to establish negligence. There are cases where a court will come to the conclusion that the mishap in question was due to the exclusive fault of one of the parties and if the evidence is clear to that effect the duty that devolves on the particular judge is to make that finding. That is what Mr. Justice Budd did in this case.

Failure to mitigate damages In *Baldwin v. Foy and Forest Way Riding Holidays Ltd.*, High Court, July 1, 1997, which we discuss earlier in this Chapter in the Section on the Standard of Care, above, 725, Laffoy J. held that the plaintiff, who had been injured in a horse-riding accident caused by the defendants' negligence, had failed to mitigate her damages, and was accordingly guilty of contributory negligence, in deciding not to continue to pursue a career in catering but instead to take training courses in skills related to 'the advertising business – copywriting and graphics and such like'. The evidence in the case was to the effect that, three years after the accident, the plaintiff would have been able to obtain employment in the catering business. Her losses thereafter, in Laffoy J.'s view, were attributable to her decision to engage in a career change.

VOLUNTARY ASSUMPTION OF RISK

The defence that the plaintiff 'voluntarily assumed the risk' of injury is a rarity in modern Irish litigation. A simple, but unconvincing explanation is that defence lawyers are so intimidated by the terms of section 34(1)(b) of the Civil Liability Act 1961 that they regard the defence as a hopeless one. This can hardly be the reason as the jurisprudence surrounding section 34(1)(b) is so meagre. Far from foreclosing adversarial debate, it cries out for questions to be asked and answered.

It will be recalled that section 34(1)(b) provides that section 34(1), which deals with contributory negligence,

> shall not operate to defeat any defence arising under a contract or the defence hat the plaintiff before the act complained of agreed to waive his legal rights in respect of it, whether or not for value, but, subject as aforesaid, the provisions of this subsection shall apply notwithstanding that the defendant might, apart from this subsection, have the defence of voluntary assumption of risk.

In *O'Hanlon v. E.S.B.* [1969] I.R. 75, at 90, Walsh J. observed that, since section 34(1)(b) had been enacted, 'what used to be called the defence of *volenti non fit injuria* . . . can now properly be described in the words of th[e 1961] Act . . . as "the defence that the plaintiff before the Act complained of agreed to waive his legal rights in respect of it."'. In *O'Hanlon*, the Supreme Court (*per* Walsh J) made it clear that the 'agreement' contemplated by section 34(1)(b) contemplated 'some sort of intercourse or communication between the plaintiff and the defendan[t] from which it could be reasonably inferred that he waived any right of action he might have in respect of the negligence of the defendan[t]. A one-sided secret determination on the part of the plaintiff to give up his right of action for negligence would not amount to an agreement to do so.'

Subsequent to *O'Hanlon v. E.S.B.*, there has been almost no judicial elaboration on the requisite scope of this 'intercourse or communication between the parties.'

In *Baldwin v. Foy and Forest Way Riding Holidays Ltd.*, High Court, July 1, 1997, the issue fell for consideration. We set out the facts in greater detail earlier in this Chapter, in the section on the Standard of Care, above, 725. Briefly, the plaintiff, a novice horse-rider, succeeded in her action for negligence against the horse-riding establishment for exposing her to danger by letting her ride on a cross-country course adjacent to boggy land, resulting in her being thrown from her horse during a sudden hailstorm.

The defendants invoked section 34(1)(b), unsuccessfully. Laffoy J. expressed the view, laconically, that it was 'not possible to draw an inference from the evidence that the plaintiff agreed to waive any right of action she might have in respect of negligence on the part of the defendants.' Laffoy J. made no reference to *O'Hanlon v. E.S.B.*, although of course that decision, of the Supreme Court, bound her.

The defendants also sought to avoid liability on the basis of disclaimer notices displayed at their premises. Both were headed 'A.I.R.E. Association of Irish Riding Establishments'. The first read as follows:

The Association of Riding Establishments Schemes for the registration of riding establishments is a voluntary non-statutory scheme under which the Association has set up and maintains a register of riding establishments which have been inspected by the Association and the owners of which have been advised of A.I.R.E.'s minimum requirements in relation to the provision of facilities, equipment, supervision, safety requirements, insurance, etc. Non-compliance by a riding establishment with these standards would automatically result in cancellation of the registration of that riding establishment. The A.I.R.E. wishes to make it clear that it cannot accept legal liability in respect of any accident, however caused, arising out of the operation of any riding establishment.

The second notice was in the following terms:

Riding is a risk sport. Your choice to ride is voluntary. We take care to provide suitable and safe horses and ponies for our customers, but all animals can be unpredictable. We strongly advise you to take out full personal accident cover.

Laffoy J.'s view, neither of the above notices was open to the construction that the defendants, as distinct from A.I.R.E., were disclaiming liability for negligence and breach of duty.

NUISANCE

The duty of occupiers to abate nuisance created on their property In *Vitalograph (Ireland) Ltd. v. Ennis Urban District Council and Clare County Council*, High Court, April 23, 1997, Kelly J. granted an interlocutory injunction in favour of companies carrying on business at an industrial estate in Ennis against Clare County Council, the owner of a strip of land at the entrance to the estate which was occupied by members of the Travelling community, requiring it to restrain acts of nuisance by those in occupation of the land. It appeared that a number of caravans had forced their way onto the land, which was a former car park. Further caravans had arrived later. The plaintiffs complained of the existence of large amounts of scrap metal, the steady accumulation of litter, the presence of horses and dogs, and the 'total lack of any sanitary facilities on the site'. They expressed concern also about the safety of

Traveller children who played in the vicinity of manufacturing facilities.

The County Council sought to deny responsibility on the basis that those in occupation of their land had entered it without their express or implied consent and remained there without any authorisation. The only step it had taken to remove them, however, was to write a letter, after the proceedings had begun, asking them to leave.

Kelly J. was satisfied that the County Council had in these circumstances adopted the nuisance. Lord Wright's speech in *Sedleigh-Denfield v. O'Callaghan* [1940] A.C. 880 and the English Court of Appeal decision in *Page Motors Ltd v. Epson and Ewell Borough Council* (1982) 80 L.G.R. 337 supported his view that the County Council had not taken appropriate steps within a reasonable period to bring the nuisance to an end:

> Whilst it has never given its permission for either the trespass or the tortious activities which are going on on its lands, neither has it done anything to bring them to an end in an effective way. In my view, the County Council has with knowledge left the nuisance occurring on its lands.

Kelly J. did not accept that the plaintiffs should be refused an injunction because they had a remedy against 'the occupiers of the lands' (the Travellers). The plaintiffs were entitled to choose the remedy they considered to be the more suitable one for their requirements. Whilst they might obtain an injunction to restrain nuisance against 'the occupiers', they could not obtain an order for possession of the site as they had no entitlement to it. An injunction against the County Council might, in the circumstances, be the only practical and effective way of terminating the nuisance. The policing and enforcement of an injunction prohibiting nuisance alone 'would probably be difficult'.

It appears from Kelly J.'s judgment that the County Council had made attempts over the years to provide appropriate accommodation for members of the Travelling community. In October 1995, it had been restrained from using lands at Drumcliffe, Ennis, as a halting site. It later obtained another site, at Erinaghmore, Fountain, Ennis, with a view to providing a temporary halting site on it. Once this became known, immediate objections were raised by a number of local residents. Kelly J. noted that there were 'allegations of intimidation and threats being made towards the servants or agents of the County Council and its contractors concerning the site.' The County Council had also identified a site at Erinagh Beg as a possible permanent halting site, but '[s]uch was the level of protest concerning tests to be carried out on that site that the Council itself had to apply to the High Court and it obtained injunctions restraining trespass on the lands.' In later proceedings for judicial review in the High Court, on December 18, 1996, Barron J. had restrained the County Council from developing the Erinaghmore site as the development was a material contravention of the County Development Plan. On this issue generally, see Simons, 'Travellers Planning Issues', (1997) 4 IPELJ 8.

In *Lind v. Tipperary (North Riding) County Council*, High Court, November 9, 1990 (judgment circulated in January 1997), Carroll J., modifying the terms which had governed an earlier interlocutory injunction, granted a permanent injunction against the defendant local authority and those using a halting site restraining them from acting or permitting others to act so as to be a nuisance. The order permitted each family on the site to have two caravans. If any member of a family was in breach of the local authority's rules for the operation of the site, the injunction required all of the family to leave.

Carroll J. also thought that 'in particular the exclusion of animals from the site is essential' and she so ordered. She further ordered the local authority to keep the open verges adequately fenced off, on the basis that:

> as long as the other families can come and camp in the neighbourhood it intensifies the nuisance. The only hope the local settled population have where a halting site is erected is that the itinerant population will be limited to those on that halting site and that those who used to camp in that area will be excluded to the best ability of the local authority . . .'

The local authority had argued that, long before the halting site was opened, there had always been a gathering of Travellers in the area for significant periods during the year. The same type of depredations had been referred to in evidence at an inquiry held in 1977 when the local authority was in the process of acquiring the lands. It claimed that it would cast an unfair burden on local authority which was trying to ameliorate the position by opening a site to be responsible for acts occurring after it was opened where the same acts had been committed before then.

Carroll J. rejected this argument on the evidence, holding that matters had greatly worsened after the site was opened and that supervision was totally inadequate. She also observed that the local authority was in breach of its statutory duty in that it had provided only five places for a Traveller population of forty-one (1989 figures), of whom nineteen were transient. She emphasised that the issue in the case was nuisance rather than breach of statutory duty.

Carroll J. considered that the local authority, by providing the site, had intensified the nuisance which had already existed. It was responsible in so far as this intensification had occurred.

On the basis that blame should equally apportioned to those living within the site and those living outside it, Carroll J. awarded damages against the local authority to the extent of 50% of what the plaintiffs had claimed. This included the loss of silage, damage to a wall, the loss of stock and 'mental distress and upset [to the plaintiffs, a married couple] by having to move out'.

(The judgment does not elaborate further on this aspect of the claim.) Carroll J. did not, however, think that the theft of an antique bell could be laid at the hands of the local authority:

> [i]t was a simple criminal act and I do not think it is possible to make the County Council liable even for 50% of that.

In *Daly v. McMullan* [1997] 2 I.L.R.M. 232, Judge Buckley, in the Dublin Circuit Court, held that the principles set out by the Privy Council in *Goldman v. Hargrave* [1967] A.C. 645 and adopted by the English Court of Appeal in *Leakey v. National Trust* [1980] 1 Q.B. 485 were in accord with the law in the State. He was comforted to find that a similar view had been take on the law in Northern Ireland by McDermott L.J. in *Neill v. Department of the Environment for Northern Ireland* [1990] N.I. 84. The essence of these principles is that an occupier may be liable for the tort of private nuisance, even though not the creator of the nuisance, if he or she, with means of knowledge of its existence, suffers it to continue without taking reasonable steps to abate it within a reasonable time. The source of the nuisance is not important: the occupier will have a duty of abatement whether the nuisance was created by some third party or arose from a natural cause.

In *Daly v. McMullan*, the parties, who lived beside each other, had both derived title from the Howth Estate. They lived on an embankment. A number of falls of soil had previously taken place from the defendant's part of the embankment into the plaintiffs' property. In August 1996 a considerable quantity of soil came down from the defendant' part of the embankment. The plaintiffs issued an equity civil bill in November 1996, seeking an order compelling the defendant to undertake works to render the embankment safe and to protect the plaintiffs from further spillage: see [1997] 2 I.L.R.M. 232 at 233 (headnote). The plaintiffs contended that the defendant was liable for negligence and nuisance.

It appeared that the plaintiffs' house had been cut out of the embankment. Judge Buckley did not consider that this fact was of any strategic advantage to the defendant. It seemed to him that:

> whatever might have been the position of the plaintiffs' predecessors in title *vis-à-vis* the Howth Estate in relation to the creation of the unstable bank, the unstable bank was in existence when the defendant took the lease of his property and the defendant must have had notice of the existence of the bank, if not precise knowledge that it was unstable. The fact that both the plaintiffs and the defendant derive title from the Howth Estate seems to me to leave the position that no claim of third party alteration of the natural contour is relevant since any such alteration was ... carried out [either] by or with the consent of the Howth Estate to

which the defendant are successor in title in the plaintiffs' case and lessee in the defendant's case.

Acknowledging that the defendant had a duty to ameliorate the nuisance once
he had been put on notice of its existence when the first spill had occurred,
Judge Buckley then was faced with the question of the extent to which
individuating factors relating to the defendant should be taken into account.
In *Goldman v. Hargrave* [1967] 1 A.C. 645, at 663, the Judicial Committee of
the Privy Council had been of the view that:

> [i]n such situations the standard ought to be to require of the occupier
> what it is reasonable to expect of him in his individual circumstances.
> Thus less must be expected of the infirm that of the able bodied; the
> owner of a small property where a hazard arises which threatens a neigh-
> bour with substantial interests should not have to do so much as one
> with larger interests of his own at stake and greater resources to protect
> them: if the small owner does what he can and promptly calls on his
> neighbour to provide additional resources he may be held to have done
> his duty; he should not be liable unless it is clearly proved that he could,
> and reasonably in his individual circumstances, should, have done more.

In *Neill v. Department of the Environment* [1990] N.I. 84, at 92, McDermott
L.J. said that he would not:

> read this passage as meaning that the duty varies with, for instance, the
> affluence of the occupier. Rather, I think the various factors considered
> in this passage are those which may well be very relevant when deciding
> if the occupier has been in breach of this duty.

In *Leakey v. National Trust* [1980] 1 Q.B. 485, at 525 Megaw L.J. observed:

> The defendants' duty is to do that which it is reasonable for him to do.
> The criteria of reasonableness include, in respect of a duty of this na-
> ture, the factor of what the particular man – not the average man – can
> be expected to do, having regard, amongst other things where a serious
> expenditure of money is required to eliminate or reduce the danger, to
> his means. Just as, where the physical effort is required to avert an im-
> mediate danger, the defendants' age and physical condition maybe rel-
> evant in deciding what is reasonable, so also logic and good sense require
> that, where the expenditure of money is required, the defendants' capac-
> ity to find the money is relevant. But this can only be in the way of a
> broad, and not a detailed, assessment; and, in arriving at a judgment on
> reasonableness, a similar broad assessment may be relevant in some cases

as to the neighbour's capacity to protect himself from damage, whether by way of some form of barrier on his own land or by way of providing funds for expenditure on agreed works on the land of the defendant.

Judge Buckley noted that, although indications had been given to him during the course of the hearing of the *defendant's* financial strength, he had been given no similar indications of the *plaintiffs'* financial strength. Equally, although indications of the respective values of the properties of the plaintiffs and defendant had been given, they were not professional valuations and Judge Buckley did not think that it would be appropriate for him to rely on them. He added that, while it was obvious that the plaintiffs' house might be most adversely affected by the existence of the unstable bank, it was now also the case that, once he had found that there was a duty on the defendant in respect of the amelioration of the nuisance, this would have the effect of diminishing the value of the defendants' property.

Judge Buckley adjourned matters, pending the carrying out of further investigations to identify the most suitable method of ameliorating the nuisance and the giving of further information to him of the values of the respective properties.

Daly v. McMullan is of interest for a number of reasons. First, it presents in stark form the closeness of the relationship between the tools of negligence and private nuisance. Judge Buckley was of the view that, since both torts had been pleaded, he did 'not even have to consider whether in the words of Megaw LJ in the *Leakey* case [[1980] 1 Q.B. 485, at p. 514], there could be 'a regrettable modern instance of the forms of action successfully clanking their spectral chains'. Certainly, in situations where the occupier is not the author of the nuisance and the issue is whether he or she has taken reasonable steps to abate it, the test is essentially identical to that adopted by the courts in negligence actions. Negligence requires a degree of individuation in certain instances, as we have seen in our discussion of *O'Brien v. Parker*, [1997] 2 I.L.R.M. 170, earlier in the Chapter, above, 716.

Whilst Judge Buckley took no concluded position on the precise extent to which such individuation would be appropriate in the case before him, the extracts of judgments from earlier cases which he quoted suggests that he was reluctant to afford primacy to the financial circumstances of the occupier. This caution is surely soundly based. One can envisage some cases where the occupier's resources will play a crucial role in determining whether or not he or she has acted reasonably on the question of abatement. Such cases will include sudden emergencies which call on a quick response from the occupier. If he or she simply has not the financial ability to respond effectively, that should be a good reason for regarding his or her response as not being unreasonable. But cases will arise where the nuisance can be predicted and the defendant, in deciding whether to become, or to remain as, an occupier may be perfectly aware that he or she may be called on to abate the future nuisance at some time. It would seem unjust if a person of modest means could be permitted to make such a decision on the basis that his or her indigency will be able to trump his or her potential liability.

Finally, it is worth noting that, in *Daly v. McMullan*, Judge Buckley considered it 'extremely clear' that the doctrine in *Rylands v. Fletcher* had no application to the case since there was 'no question of any unnatural user of land'.

Who may sue for private nuisance?	In *Royal Dublin Society v. Yates*, High Court, July 31, 1997, Shanley J. addressed an important issue regarding the nature of the tort of private nuisance. Traditionally, this tort was associated with protecting the interests of owners and occupiers of land against unneighbourly conduct by adjoining occupiers that caused injury to the land or interfered with its beneficial user. Thus, in *Malone v. Laskey* [1907] 1 K.B. 517, the English Court of Appeal held that the wife of the occupier of premises who was injured by a bracket falling from the wall, allegedly caused by vibrations for next door, had not right to use for private nuisance as she had no interest in the premises and was 'a mere licensee'.

As time went by, private nuisance began to look more like the tort of negligence. Remoteness of damage came to be determined by a foreseeability test and the right to sue was gradually extended to persons who were not owners or occupiers.

In Canada, in *Motherwell v. Motherwell*, 73 D.L.R. (3d) 62 (Alberta Supreme Court, 1976), Clement J. held that a wife who had a right to live in the family home was entitled to sue for nuisance. In *Devons Lumber Co. Ltd v. MacNeill*, 45 D.L.R. (4th) 300 (New Brunswick Court of Appeal, 1987), Rice J.A., dissenting considered that this right should extend to children of the family. In England, in *Khorasandjian v. Bush* [1993] Q.B. 727, the Court of Appeal granted an injunction against harassing telephone calls to an eighteen year old young woman living with her mother, who owned the house.

In Ireland, until the instant decision, Irish courts made no elaborate analysis of the issue. It is striking, nonetheless, that in *Hanrahan v. Merck Sharp & Dohme (Ireland) Ltd* [1988] I.L.R.M. 629, the Supreme Court had no difficulty with a nuisance action taken by Mrs Hanrahan who was the registered owner of the premises, her son and his wife, neither of whom had any right to the exclusive position of the premises. Henchy J., in his judgment, with which other members of the Court concurred, made it clear that he considered that all the plaintiffs had the right to sue for negligence. Contrasting the respective circumstances in which proceedings might be brought for nuisance and under the rule in *Rylands v. Fletcher*, he said that 'in some cases liability requires to be determined under *Rylands v. Fletcher* [only], such as where the plaintiff is not an occupier of land . . .'

In England, in *Hunter v. Canary Wharf Ltd.*, [1997] 2 W.L.R. 685, the House of Lords firmly re-established the rule that generally only a person with an interest in the land or premises may sue for private nuisance. Their Lordships regarded this limitation as essential to the true character of the tort which involved, in their view, an interference with the ownership or occupation of land rather than wrongful conduct directed at, or affecting, individuals as such. Thus, personal discomfort from noise or smells, for example, should be compensated on the basis of the diminution in the amenity value of the premises rather than by reference to damages in an action for personal injury: see *id.*, at 708 (*per* Lord Hoffman). For analysis of *Hunter*, see Steele, 'Being There is Not Enough – The House of Lords puts the Brakes on Nuisance in the Home,' 9 J. of Environmental L 345 (1997); McIntyre, 'Television Interference and Non-Proprietary Rights in Nuisance,' 4 IPELJ 119 (1997).

In *Royal Dublin Society v. Yates*, the plaintiff society sought an injunction and damages against the defendant for (*inter alia*) the tort of nuisance. The essence of its case was that the defendant had engaged in harassing and intimidating a female and a male employee of the plaintiff. The defendant strongly contested the claim and counterclaimed for several torts.

After a detailed review of the evidence, which included quotation from communications sent by the defendant to the female employee and her father, Shanley J. addressed the legal issues. He referred to the English developments culminating in *Hunter* and to the Irish decision of *Hanrahan*. Since the Royal Dublin Society was not just the owner, but also the occupier, of the lands at Ballsbridge and entitled to the exclusive possession of them it was 'unnecessary to consider the difference of approach which appear[ed] to have emerged between the Irish Supreme Court as exemplified by the judgment of Mr. Justice Henchy in *Hanrahan* ... and in the House of Lords in the speeches of the majority ... in ... *Hunter*. ...' Shanley J. thus left the question open for future debate.

Applying the test as to what constitutes a nuisance which Gannon J. had propounded in *Halpin v. Tara Mines Ltd*, High Court, February 16, 1976, Shanley J. considered that certain occasions when the defendant was on the plaintiff Society's premises and when 'there were verbal altercations (at the least) between him and the officers and members of the Society' were such as to constitute a private nuisance to the Society and had required the Society to deploy staff to observe the defendant whenever he had been on its premises. While the Society had not sought to lead evidence as to the quantum of damage caused by the nuisance, Shanley J. was nonetheless satisfied that damage had been caused:

> [The defendant's] presence on the premises of the Society cannot be considered in isolation. That presence must be considered in the context of the acrimonious and offensive correspondence he was having with

[the female employee] together with the threatening correspondence he
was having with other parties. I believe that the presence of [the defend-
ant] upon the premises of the Society at these various events did indeed
constitute an interference with the ordinary comfort and enjoyment by
the Society of its property. That interference amount to nuisance.

Shanley J. made an order restraining the defendant from attending at or entering on the Society's Ballsbridge premises and from communicating or attempting to communicate with the Society's staff or employees 'in any manner
whatsoever'. Shanley J. did not, however, award any damages in respect of
the private nuisance of which the defendant was guilty. He did not enlarge on
why he took this course.

The public interest   In *Clifford v. The Drug Treatment Centre Board*, High
Court, November 7, 1997, McCracken J. addressed the issue of the relevance
of the public interest to granting or refusing an interlocutory injunction. The
plaintiffs, owners or occupiers of business premises in the Pearse Street area
of Dublin, sought two interlocutory injunctions. The first was to restrain the
defendant from using its premises in Pearse Street as a centre for referral for
drug addicted patients in numbers in excess of that for which the premises had
been used prior to January 1992. The second was to restrain the defendant
from operating the premises so as to be a nuisance to the plaintiffs.

The Centre provided an out-patient drug treatment service. The plaintiffs
claimed that the presence of a large number of drug addicts attending the
premises had led to harassment, theft and violence and threats of violence
involving syringes. They contended that the incidence of such anti-social conduct had increased substantially in the previous five years and was having a
serious effect on their businesses. It appeared that the defendant intended to
increase the service it provided in the near future.

The defendant argued that the problems of which the plaintiffs complained
were no different from those encountered by business people anywhere in the
inner city and that the incidence of crime in the Pearse Street area was less
than in many other inner city areas.

McCracken J. had no doubt that the plaintiffs had made out a good arguable case that the actions of those visiting the defendant's Centre were such as
to seriously affect them in the conduct of their businesses and in their use of
their premises and also that this was a nuisance caused by the numbers attending the Centre. He considered that the defendant had not discharged the onus
of establishing the defence of legislative authority under the principles stated
in *Alan v. Gulf Oil Refining Ltd* [1981] 1 All E.R. 353 and *Manchester Corporation v. Farnworth* [1930] A.C. 171.

Turning to the question of whether damages would be an adequate remedy
for the plaintiffs, McCracken J. concluded that it 'quite clearly would not', as

the plaintiffs had suffered personal inconvenience and trauma as well as merely pecuniary losses. Equally he did not think that the defendant could be compensated by an award of damages should the interlocutory injunction be wrongly granted, since '[t]he loss would not so much be a pecuniary loss to the defendant but a loss to persons being treated by [it]'. This is an interesting approach for McCracken J. to have adopted: a more hard-hearted judge might well have taken the view that, since the defendant itself would not suffer the loss, its concern about the loss suffered by those whom it treated should not be characterised as irreparable loss on its part.

Finally, on the question of the balance of convenience, McCracken J. considered tht he was required to take into account, not only the convenience of the defendant, but also the convenience or damage to those who attended the Centre, 'and indeed the public at large'. If the numbers attending the Centre were reduced to the 1992 level, as the plaintiffs requested, the immediate result would be that less drug addicts would be treated, which was 'clearly against the public interest, besides depriving possibly hundreds of individuals of badly needed treatment'. McCracken J. 'certainly' did not think that he would be justified in taking such a step at the interlocutory stage of the proceedings.

McCracken J. did however grant an interlocutory injunction restraining the defendant from *increasing* the number of drug addicted patients. He noted that this would not affect the existing patients.

Clifford represents a clear contradiction to what Maguire C.J. and Murnaghan J. said in *Bellew v. Cement Ltd*, [1948] I.R. 61 regarding the public interest. This is to be welcomed. The idea that courts operate in a social vacuum is abhorrent.

DECEIT

In *Forshall v. Walsh*, High Court, June 18, 1997, Shanley J. imposed liability for the tort of deceit on of the defendants, Timothy McSweeney, who caused loss to the plaintiff by representing falsely that the company of which he was a director was concessionaire of Lamborghini Motor Cars. The representation was made with a view to inducing the plaintiff to enter into an agreement for the purchase of Lamborghini Diablo cars. This defendant had also prepared a statement of affairs which he was aware would be shown to people interested in dealing with his company, such as the plaintiff. That statement of affairs falsely represented the company as a financially healthy one. The effect of the statement of affairs was that the plaintiff, believing that the company was financially sound and a concessionaire of Lamborghini, invested her money in a way that she would not otherwise have done, to her detriment.

Shanley J. noted that no argument had been made at trial that the statement of affairs failed to meet the requirements of section 6 of the Statute of Frauds

Amendment Act 1868, which provides that:

> No action shall be brought whereby to charge any person upon or by
> reason of any representation or assurance made or given concerning or
> relating to the character, conduct, credit, ability, trade or dealings of any
> other person, to the intent or purpose that such other person may obtain
> credit, money or goods upon, unless such representation or assurance be
> made in writing signed by the person to be charged therewith.

The somewhat anomalous aspect of this provision is that, while an injured
may sue on a *negligent* oral misrepresentation relating to a third party's cred-
itworthiness no action will lie for a *fraudulent* misrepresentation of this kind
unless it is in writing. Shanley J. considered it 'arguable' that the statement of
affairs did indeed fail the requirements of section 6 but, in the absence of
argument, did not express a view on the matter other than to observe that, even
if this defence had succeeded, Mr. McSweeney would still have been liable to
the plaintiff on the basis of his false representation that the company of which
he was a director was concessionaire of Lamborghini.

PASSING OFF

The subject of passing off is excellently analysed by Robert Clark and Shane
Smyth in *Intellectual Property Law in Ireland*, published in 1997 (Butterworths), and by John Healy in 'The Tort of Passing Off' (1997) 15 *ILT* 196,
218.

Names In *Radio Limerick One Ltd v. Treaty Radio Ltd*, High Court, November 13, 1997, Costello P. declined to grant an interlocutory injunction restraining an alleged passing off. The plaintiff's contract with the Independent Radio
and Television Commission to broadcast on FM channel and on the 95 wavelength in the Limerick area had been terminated by the Commission for serious and persistent breaches of the contract. The plaintiff took unsuccessful
legal proceedings challenging the termination as far as the Supreme Court:
[1997] 2 I.R. 291. The plaintiff also had a license to broadcast on the Astra
satellite granted by the BBC. There were around 7,000 satellite dishes in the
Limerick area capable of receiving what the plaintiff transmitted. The plaintiff
also sold advertising space on its broadcast service. It used different call signs
on its radio broadcast and is promotional literature: these were 'Limerick 95
FM', 'Limerick 95' and Radio Limerick'.

The plaintiff claimed that the defendant was not entitled to use the word
'Limerick' in its style or in its call signal, or the figure and letters '95 FM' in
its call or promotional literature.

Costello P. gave a helpful definition of the tort of passing off, stating that its nature was:

> perfectly clear and long established. It is an actionable wrong for a defendant to represent that his business is that of a plaintiff. The representation can be made by using some of the badges by which a plaintiff's business is known or by colourably resembling them. So if a plaintiff is known by descriptive material or a slogan, provided that it is part of the goodwill of a plaintiff, this material can be protected by means of an injunction should it be shown that a defendant has committed the actionable wrong of passing off (citing the *Pub Squash* case [1981] R.P.C. 429-490).

In the instant case the defendant had merely represented that it was broadcasting on a certain wavelength on a certain waveband in a certain area. It was not representing that it was carrying on the plaintiff's business but rather that it was now broadcasting on the wavelength on which the plaintiff had formerly broadcast and in the same area. There was no misrepresentation involved in what the defendant was doing and in Costello P.'s opinion no tort had been established.

Costello P. considered that there was a further reason why injunctive relief should be refused. The plaintiff had lost its licence to broadcast in the Limerick area because it had been in serious breach of the conditions of its licence. It would now be illegal for the plaintiff to broadcast in the Limerick area. In these circumstances the plaintiff had no longer any goodwill in the business of sound broadcasting on the FM wavelength which the Court could protect. Although the plaintiff had apparently applied to the Minster for a licence to re-transmit the signal from the Astra satellite this licence had not yet been obtained. The Court could not exercise its discretion on the basis of a possibility that a licence might be granted by the Minister.

The balance of convenience also tilted towards refusing interlocutory relief. If an injunction was wrongly granted, there is no evidence to suggest that the uncompensatable damage which the plaintiff would suffer would be in any way material. It would be easy to calculate the figures for advertising revenue which the plaintiff would lose. If an injunction was wrongly refused, however, 'considerable damage' would be done to the defendant, in Costello P.'s view.

In *O'Neills Irish International Sports Co Ltd. v. O'Neills Footwear Dryer Co. Ltd.*, High Court, April 30, 1997, two aspects of the law of passing off fell for consideration. The plaintiffs manufactured and sold sports goods under the name O'Neills. The defendant company was formed in 1995 by one John O'Neill. In 1994, he obtained a patent for an electrically operated shoe dryer. He sought to interest sports manufacturers, including the plaintiffs, in his invention but without success. One manufacturer suggested that it might be interested if he could establish sales in the product. Not being able financially to manufacture the product for commercial purposes, he imported from the Far East a similar product for the sole purpose of establishing sales figures.

The product, as imported, was packaged in a box about the same size and shape as a normal shoe box. The sides of the box showed pictures of different types of shoes and of the dryer and generally indicated the nature of the product. Before putting the product on sale the defendant company had labels printed which were placed over the two main sides of the box. These labels showed that the product was 'O'Neill's Footwear Dryer', and referred to Cellbridge, Co Kildare, Ireland. Elsewhere on the box were the words 'made in China'. There was no other indication as to the person putting the product on the market.

The product as so labeled was on sale in several department stores and other stores around the country. In the main it was sold through sports outlets. In addition to the packaging, the product was also sold by means of a large advertising panel headed 'O'Neills Footwear Dryer', which was generally similar to the overprinted labels on the box.

From the evidence, Barron J. was satisfied that the word O'Neills was associated with the plaintiffs in relation to sports goods and that they had built up a considerable reputation in the name. The manner in which the defendant's product was being marketed was calculated to lead persons seeing that product and its advertising panel to believe that the product was the product of the plaintiff.

Barron J. observed:

> No doubt John O'Neill believed that since his name was O'Neill he could form a company with O'Neill in its name and market the product under that name. In that belief he was wrong. While a person may use his name in the course of trade and cannot be faulted on that ground alone, that does not entitle him to use his own name in such a way as is calculated to lead others to believe his goods are those of another. That is the case here.
>
> The nature of this tort is to be found in its name. The wrong is that of passing-off ones goods as those of another. This can be done by similarity of name, appearance, get-up or any other similarity which achieves the same purpose. How it is done is immaterial so long as the similarity is calculated to deceive those who might buy or otherwise deal in the goods. Deliberate intention is not necessary.

The defendant argued, secondly, that there was no evidence of any damage to the plaintiff since the plaintiff did not deal with the particular goods and could not, therefore, have lost any sales. Barron J. rejected this contention. Cases such *as C. & A. Modes v. C. & A. (Waterford Ltd.)*, [1976] I.R. 198,

Falcon Travel Ltd v. The Owners Abroad Group plc [1991] 1 I.R. 175 and *Spalding v. Gamage* (1915) 32 R.P.C. 273 had identified the damage as being the violation of the plaintiffs' property rights in its *reputation or goodwill*. Accordingly, Barron J. granted the injunction sought by the plaintiffs, who had not sought damages in the proceedings.

Interlocutory injunction In *Symonds Cider & English Wine Co. Ltd. v. Showerings (Ireland) Ltd.* [1997] 1 I.L.R.M. 481, Laffoy J. was called on to deal with the issue of the proper test for determining applications of interlocutory injunctions in relation to passing off. Some decisions of Costello J. – *Three Stripe International v. Charles O'Neill* [1989] I.L.R.M. 124 and *Benchkiser Gmbtt v. Fibrisol Service Ltd.*, High Court, May 13, 1988, analysed in the 1988 Review, 199–203 – favour the view that, if the interlocutory injunction is likely to represent the end of the road for the parties, with no prospect of proceedings going on to a plenary hearing, the court should seek to determine the merits of the substantive legal issue rather than proceed immediately to address the questions of irreparable damage and the balance of convenience once satisfied that there is a serious question to be tried. Support for this general approach is also apparent in Laddie J.'s judgment in *Series 5 Software Ltd. v. Clarke* [1996] F.S.R. 273.

It will be recalled that the Supreme Court decision of *Holdings Ltd v. McCormack* [1991] I.L.R.M. 833, at 838; [1992] 1 I.R. 151, at 157-8. Finlay C.J. expressed the view that, having regard to the Court's earlier decision in *Campus Oil Ltd. v. Minister for Industry and Energy (No. 2)* [1983] I.R. 88 and in particular O'Higgins C.J.'s judgment in that case, the position was that, once the plaintiff had raised a fair question to be tried, the court should not express *any* view on the strength of the contending submissions, but should proceed to consider the issues of irreparable damage and balance of convenience.

In *B. & S. Ltd v. Irish Auto Trader Ltd.*, [1995] 2 I.L.R.M. 152, at 156; [1955] 2 I.R. 142, at 145, a case dealing with an application for an injunction for passing off, McCracken J., echoing the approach favoured by the House of Lords in *American Cyanamid Co. v. Ethicon Ltd* [1975] A.C. 396, acknowledged that consideration of the respective strengths of the competing arguments should be allowed, after the court had established that there was a fair issue to be tried. As one of five matters the court should there address, McCracken J. stated that:

> where the arguments are finely balanced, the court may consider the relative strength of each party's case as revealed by the affidavit evidence adduced at the interlocutory stage where the strength of one party's case is disproportionate to that of the other.

In *Symonds Cider*, Laffoy J. quoted McCracken J.'s five point test in *B. & S. Ltd v. Irish Auto Trader Ltd* with apparent approval. She went on to say that she was satisfied that, having regard to the *Westman Holdings* decision of the Supreme Court, it was not open to the High Court, where the plaintiff had established a fair and *bona fide* question to be tried, to express any view on the strength of the contending submissions on this issue. Even if this were permissible, it would be impossible to do so in the instant case, which was 'bristling with difficult issues of fact arising from conflicting affidavit evidence and difficult issues of law.'

Briefly, the facts were as follows. The plaintiff was an English company, part of the HP Bulmer group, the world's largest cider maker. Since the early 1980s, it had been selling cider in England under the trade mark 'Scrumpy Jack'. This had come onto the Irish market in 1991, reaching 17% of the canned cider market in 1995. It was widely advertised in Ireland.

Originally, the product was marketed and sold in Ireland in a gold coloured can with the name 'Scrumpy Jack' in large brown script and a logo whose dominant feature was a display of red apples on either side of an old-fashioned cider press, with the words 'strong cider' below. A newly designed can was put on the Irish market in the late summer of 1996. The gold colour was darker and more matt in appearance; the cider press logo appeared without the display of apples; the product was described as 'traditional' rather than 'strong' cider.

The plaintiff sought, *inter alia*, an interlocutory injunction against passing off. The proceedings were instituted about a month before the new product was launched on the Irish market. The new product quickly replaced the old product in Irish retail outlets.

Although the thrust of the plaintiff's case was that the defendant had imitated its *old* can, the plaintiff contended that it had, and would continue to have, a residual and persistent reputation in the get-up of the old can and in the name of 'Scrumpy Jack' which was sufficient to found an action for passing off.

The defendant argued that the word 'Scrumpy' was part of the common-age of the English language, being a descriptive term denoting rough dry cider. It could not be monopolised by any trader. The plaintiff contested the accuracy of this assertion in respect of Ireland, contending that the word 'scrumpy' was only of dialectal significance in certain parts of England and that, before the Irish launch of 'Scrumpy Jack', it had no particular significance in Ireland.

Laffoy J. had no difficulty in holding that there was a fair question to be tried. Nor was there any doubt that damage would not adequately compensate either party if an interlocutory injunction were, or were not, granted as the case might be. The respective detriments to the parties were 'evenly balanced in terms of nature and degree' but for one factor. This was that the plaintiff's new cans were by now on the Irish market. The plaintiff's case had focused on its old can and Laffoy J. was not satisfied that the plaintiff had shown on the affidavit evidence before the court that there was a fair issue to be tried as to the likelihood of confusion between the plaintiff's new can and the defendant's can or that there had been actual confusion.

Accordingly Laffoy J. declined to grant an interlocutory injunction.

DEFAMATION

Qualified privilege In *Dawson and Dawson t/a A.E. Dawson & Sons v. Irish Brokers Associations*, Supreme Court, February 27, 1997, the circumstances in which the defence of qualified privilege may be put forward were considered. The plaintiff's insurance brokers sued the defendant association for defamation in relation to a letter it sent to nineteen insurance companies, the Minister for Industry and Commerce and the Insurance Compliance Bureau, advising the recipients that, as from April 21, 1992, the plaintiffs' membership of the defendant organisation 'was terminated due to non-compliance with the requirements of the Insurance Act 1989'. This was not true. The defendant accepted that the statement was defamatory and did not plead justification but argued that it was protected by the defence of qualified privilege. Barron J. rejected this argument, and the jury awarded the plaintiffs over half a million pounds damages.

The Supreme Court dismissed the appeal, so far as the issue of qualified privilege was concerned, holding that, since the defendant Association had not acted in accordance with its own rules, the defence was not available to it. O'Flaherty J. (Hamilton C.J. and Barrington J. concurring) considered that the question for resolution could be shortly stated:

> [I]t is that for a claim of qualified privilege to succeed, arising as it does where there is a duty or common interest on one person to make a report to another, the person making the report cannot be held to have had such a common interest as the law requires unless . . . the Council of the Association acted in accordance with the Association's own rules. In other words, if it is in breach of its own rules in the circumstances of the publication of which complaint is made, it has no entitlement to make a report to anyone at all.

O'Flaherty J. cited *Reilly v. Gill* (1946) 85 I.L.T.R. 165 and *Green v. Blake* [1948] I.R. 242 in support. For analysis of these decisions see Marc McDonald, *Irish Law of Defamation* (2nd ed., Round Hall Press, 1989) and McMahon & Binchy, *op. cit.*, 652.

After a detailed review of the defendant Association's rules, it seemed clear to O'Flaherty J. that the defendant had breached them when in effect, it had expelled the plaintiffs from membership of the Association and that therefore no occasion of qualified privilege had arisen.

Interrogatories *Conlon v. Times Newspaper Ltd.*, Supreme Court, July 28, 1997, concerned interrogatories in the defamation action taken by Gerard Conlon, one of the 'Guildford Four', arising from an article in which the author wrote of the plaintiff that '[h]is awe-inspiring pacifist father never forgave him for implicating him in his forced confession (which Gerard doesn't do here) and he died before there was a reconciliation'. The plaintiff also complained about the words 'after Guiseppe has been thrown into jail on his churlish son's account'.

The gravamen or sting of the alleged libel was alleged by the plaintiff to be that the plaintiff was a churlish son who betrayed his own father and that that betrayal was such that, even though made in the course of a forced confession, his father, an exceptionally kind and good man, never forgave the plaintiff before his own death in prison.

In its defence the defendant admitted that it was untrue to say that the plaintiff had implicated his father in his forced confession and accordingly, that it was untrue to say that the plaintiff's father had never forgiven him for doing so. The defendant nonetheless denied that what it published had been done so maliciously or recklessly as to whether they were true or false. It claimed that the factual error in stating that the plaintiff had implicated his father in his forced confession and that his father had never forgiven him for this, was an innocent error by the defendant as to the detail of historical events.

The appellant further pleaded that having regard to the widespread public knowledge of the injustice done to innocent people, including the Guildford Four by the extraction of forced confessions and by their wrongful conviction and imprisonment, what it had published could not have been damaging to the plaintiff's reputation and accordingly was not defamatory of the plaintiff. What it had published should be understood to mean that an innocent person had been implicated in the forced confession of the plaintiff and thereafter wrongly imprisoned. This was the sting of the allegations and what was published, so understood, was true in substance and in fact.

The three interrogatories sought to be delivered for examination of the plaintiff were as follows:

1. Was not the plaintiff while in custody in Godalming Police Station, Surrey, England between the 30th November and the 4th December 1974 forced to make and sign two written statements to the Surrey Constabulary concerning the Guildford pub bombings on the 5th October 1974?

2. Was not the plaintiff in course in making the said statements caused to implicate the following persons in the said Guildford pub bombings and/

or in other serious subversive criminal activity?

(a) Paul Hill:
(b) Patrick Armstrong:
(c) Carole Richardson:
(d) Anne Maguire.

3. Are not the statements set out at appendix E of the Return to an Address of the Honourable the House of Commons dated 30th June 1994 for a report of the inquiry into the circumstances surrounding the convictions arising out of the bomb attacks in Guildford and Woolwich in 1974 (the May report) as being the statements of the plaintiff (copies of which are annexed hereto) true and accurate transcriptions of the two written statements so made and signed by the plaintiff between the 30th November and the 4th December 1974 at Godalming Police Station?

Costello P. found however that these interrogatories were not relevant to any of the issues in the case and on that basis refused leave to deliver them.

The Supreme Court reversed. Lynch J. (Murphy and Barron JJ. concurring), considered that questions 1 & 2 were relevant to a number of issues. The first and second were whether the publication was defamatory and whether it was justified in the limited form pleaded, to the effect that what the defendant had stated meant no more than that the plaintiff implicated innocent people in forced confessions and that no one would think the worse of him for that because they were forced confessions. The third issue, not fully clarified in Lynch J.'s judgment, concerned the question of justification in the light of 'the true meaning or sting of the words', as characterised by the defendant.

Different considerations applied to question 3. The statements appended to the May report were typewritten, including typewritten signatures. They were not manuscript nor a photostat of the original manuscript statements. They had been taken some twenty three years previously 'in circumstances of oppression and impropriety.' That being so, Lynch J. thought that 'it would be quite unreasonable' to expect the plaintiff to answer this question, which was accordingly disallowed.

Separate trials   In *Murphy v. Times Newspapers Ltd.*, Supreme Court, October 21, 1997 (*ex tempore*), the Supreme Court ordered separate trials where two brothers sued for defamation. Applying the test set out by McCarthy J. in *Duffy v. News Group Newspapers Ltd.* [1992] 2 I.R. 369, which supported a joint trial where there is a common question of law or fact of sufficient importance, a substantial saving of expense or inconvenience and a likelihood of confusion or miscarriage of justice, O'Flaherty J. (Keane and Murphy JJ. concurring) was of the view that each plaintiff would be 'mounting quite a distinct case and met with quite a separate and distinct form of defence.'

A complicating feature of the litigation was that, in relation to one of the brothers, the defendants argued that they had not intended to refer to him but that if he persuaded the jury, on the basis of the famous decision of the House of Lords in *Hulton v. Jones* [1910] A.C. 20 that the article could be taken to refer to him, they would seek to establish that he was in any event guilty of impugned conduct and should recover no damages. O'Flaherty J. commented:

> I am not saying that in principle such a case cannot be made. (In a sense, it is but the converse of *Hulton v. Jones*.) I am simply saying that I have never heard of it being done in the past.

It is hard to see any objection in principle to such a defence. *Hulton v. Jones* extends potential liability widely, by enabling people to whom a defendant did not intend to refer to sue successfully for defamation. It would be doubly oppressive if a defendant were prevented from making the argument that, even though there had been no intent to refer to the particular plaintiff, the defamatory propositions are, by way of happenstance, true in relation to that plaintiff.

Damages   In *Dawson and Dawson t/a A.E. Dawson & Sons v. Irish Brokers Association*, Supreme Court, February 27, 1997, an award of £515,000 in favour of the plaintiffs was set aside on appeal. We have outlined the facts earlier in the chapter in the Section on Qualified Privilege, above. Very briefly the plaintiffs complained that a defamatory letter circulated by the defendant Association to many insurance companies as well as the Minister for Industry and Commerce and the Insurance Compliance Bureau had gravely damaged their insurance brokerage business. Their father had founded the business thirty years previously. It had enjoyed the confidence of a burgeoning population in Raheny. A modest claim for special damages in the sum of £6,000 was abandoned in the course of the litigation. No evidence was adduced at the trial that anyone shunned the plaintiffs or thought the worse of them after the publication of the circular letter. The plaintiffs had, however, been put to the trouble of replying to three or four hundred queries once the circular had gone out.

The plaintiffs on appeal persisted in suggesting that the award was appropriate and, indeed, was, if anything, on the light side, but O'Flaherty J. (Hamilton C.J. and Barrington J. concurring) considered that they had advanced no rational basis that that assertion. The award was wholly disportionate to any injury the plaintiffs had suffered.

O'Flaherty J. went on to observe:

> The approach to the assessment of damages in a defamation action is in essence no different from any other type of proceeding. The jury should, in the first instance, be told that their first duty is to try to do essential justice between the parties. There may be cases where the circumstances

of the case will call for the consideration of an award of aggravated or exemplary damages. But this was not such a case. The damages, as far as this case is concerned, could be compensatory only. The jury were entitled to award damages for loss of reputation, as well as for the hurt, anxiety, trouble and bother to which the plaintiffs had been put. However, the defendants in defamation cases should never be regarded as the custodians of bottomless wells which are incapable of ever running dry. The opposite has proved true in the publishing sphere in this and other countries – with sad consequences for those who lost employment as a result of untoward awards. Further, unjustifiably large awards as well as the cost attendant on long trials, deals a blow to the freedom of expression entitlement that is enshrined in the Constitution.

Deriving support from Henchy J.'s comments in *Barrett v. Independent Newspapers Ltd.* [1986] I.R. 13, at 23, O'Flaherty J. noted that, in the instant case it was clear that no evidence had been given that the plaintiffs had been shunned by any right thinking members of the community; the impugned publication had been made to 'a fairly limited and quite sophisticated class of person' and the plaintiffs had demonstrated that they were well able to put their side of the case. This was evident, in particular, from the consideration that they had received from the insurance companies who had been circulated during the six months before they became aligned with the other body that could certify to their compliance with the Act:

> Whether they were obdurate and difficult or not would be a matter to put in the scales, as would the conduct of the defendant for being in breach of its own rules; acting rather precipitately and perhaps prolonging the litigation unduly and persisting (as [it] did up to this Court) with the allegation that the plaintiffs had not complied with the legislation in question.

Giving the case the most favourable construction in regard to the plaintiffs, in the sense of asking himself what damages the plaintiffs had made out 'in regard to loss of reputation etc.,' and taking their case at the high water mark, O'Flaherty J. was nonetheless of the view that the award must be regarded as so excessive that it could not stand.

The Supreme Court ordered a retrial confined to the question of damages. When the case returned to the High Court, the defendant applied successfully for an order for particulars of damage and/or discovery: High Court, June 23, 1997. Moriarty J. was guided by Holroyd Pearce L.J.'s observations in *Lewis v. Daily Telegraph Ltd.*, [1963] 1 Q.B.D. 340, at 376 and Russell L.J.'s observations in *Calvet v. Tomkies* [1963] 3 All E.R. 610, at 613, to the effect that, if large losses are to be attributed to a business resulting from a libel, it was plainly desirable that, in the absence of a claim for special damage, these losses should be identified and, so far as possible, supported by evidence.

In the instant case, the plaintiffs had explained their failure to persist in a claim for special damage, in spite of suffering substantial and ongoing losses of clients, by stating that it was embarrassing to seek to procure the testimony of these lost clients and impossible to speculate as to the identity of potential new clients whom they had lost.

Transnational defamation In the Chapter on Conflicts of Law, above, 140, we discuss *Ewins v. Carlton U.K. Television Ltd and Ulster Television plc* [1997] 2 I.L.R.M. 223, which deals with important aspects of transnational defamation, where European Community law is having increasing influence.

TORT AFFECTING BUSINESS RELATIONSHIPS

In *Bula v. Tara Mines Ltd.*, High Court, February 6, 1997, Lynch J. dismissed the plaintiffs' claim for damages resulting from several torts affecting business relationships, including conspiracy and intimidation. The case arose from the ongoing conflict between the two companies in relation to their mining developments, which adjoined each other. In a judgment extending over 188 pages, Lynch J. noted (at p. 187) that he had been supplied by counsel with eight volumes of copies of reported cases. He said that, whilst he had listened attentively to those cases that had been opened to him and he had considered them and borne them in mind in preparing the judgment, he did not find it necessary to summarise the legal arguments or to discuss the authorities, since the csae was 'really one of fact and having found the facts the legal consequences are clear.' This is a surprising judicial strategy. The legal principles relating to torts affecting business relationships are so complex and difficult to apply to factual situations with any degree of confidence that the conslusion that the case could be reduced to issues solely of fact seems hard to fathom.

INDUSTRIAL RELATIONS

In the 1990 Review, 347–56, we examined the Industrial Relations Act 1990, Part II of which sought to adopt a pragmatic reform of the tort law relating to industrial relations. It gave certain new advantages to employees and trade unions, especially in regard to their exposure to the risk of injunctions, but it enacted a price, in terms of imposing a requirement of seven days' prior notice of a strike or other industrial action as well as due compliance with secret ballot processes.

Section 19(2) provides that:

[w]here a secret ballot has been held in accordance with the rules of a trade union as provided for in section 14, the outcome of which or, in the case of an aggregation of ballots, the outcome of the aggregated ballots favours a strike or other industrial action and the trade union participating in the strike or other industrial action gives notice of not less than one week to the employer concerned of its intention to do so, the court shall not grant an injunction restraining the strike or other industrial action where the respondent establishes a fair case that he was acting in contemplation or furtherance of a trade dispute.

In *G. & T. Crampton Ltd. v. Building & Allied Trades Union* [1998] 1 I.L.R.M. 430, the Supreme Court, in an *ex tempore* judgment, grappled with the meaning of this provision. It is of the nature of much of the industrial relations litigation, especially in the context of trade disputes and applications for injunctions, that the Supreme Court is called on to make highly significant rulings. This was apparent in the Court's earlier decision in *Talbot (Ireland) Ltd. v. A.T.G.W.U.*, April 30, 1981, reported in *The Irish Times*, May 1, 1981.

It is perhaps unfortunate that in *Crampton* the Court did not adopt the strategy of giving its ruling without delay and producing considered supporting judgments some time afterwards.

In *Crampton*, the defendants had placed a picket on the plaintiff's premises. Laffoy J. granted an interlocutory injunction. She held that a fair case had been made out by the defendants that they had been acting in contemplation or furtherance of a trade dispute. She concluded that there was 'no evidence whatever before the court' as to the outcome of the secret ballot conducted by the union and in particular that there was no evidence that its outcome favoured picketing the site. On this ground alone she was satisfied that there was no evidence before the court that one of the preconditions stipulated in section 19(2) had been complied with.

The defendants were, 'to say the least of it, aggrieved by this particular finding' by Laffoy J. They argued on appeal that this issue had not been raised in the affidavit filed on behalf of the plaintiff and that they had not the opportunity of dealing satisfactorily with the point in view of the shortness of time and the manner in which the case was dealt with.

Hamilton C.J. (O'Flaherty and Barrington JJ. concurring) noted that a question arose by way of interpretation of the legislation as to whether a notice relating to 'strike or other industrial action', without purporting to particularise the nature the industrial action sought to be taken, had sufficient specificity to comply with the terms of sections 14 and 19. On this issue alone there was a fair question to be tried. There was also a fair question to be tried as to the need for all of the circumstances the ballot to be investigated for the purpose of ascertaining whether or not the members whom it was reasonable to expect at the time would be called on to engage in the strike or other industrial action had been given a fair opportunity of voting. The ballot papers had not contained the proposal on which the members were being called to ballot. Whether the ballot paper was adequate to comply with the requirements of section 14 or the rules of that trade union was also a relevant issue that arose in the case. Hamilton C.J. also noted that Laffoy J. had found that here was a fair issue to be tried as to whether two trade unionist picketers were entitled to the protection of section 2(1) even though the plaintiff was not their employer in the context of which the expression was used in section 11.

Hamilton C.J. invoked Finlay C.J.'s judgment in *Westman Holdings Ltd v. McCormack*, [1991] I.L.R.M. 833, at 838; [1992] 1 I.R. 151, at 157, to the effect that, once the court was satisfied that the plaintiff had raised a fair question to be tried, the court should not express any view on the strength of the contending submissions on that question but should proceed to consider the other matters then arising in regard to the granting of an interlocutory injunction.

Hamilton C.J. was satisfied that the affidavits disclosed a fair question to be tried on the issue whether the provisions of section 11(1) applied to the defendants and also that 'a number of questions' stood to be determined with regard to the interpretation of sections 14 and 19 regarding the specificity of the terms of the notice and the absence of an actual proposal on the ballot paper. That being so, Laffoy J. was entitled to come to the conclusion that the condition precedent to the implementation of section 19 had not been complied with. Moreover, she had been entitled to come to the conclusion that damages would not be an adequate remedy and that the balance of convenience was in favour of granting the injunction. Accordingly the appeal was dismissed.

The outcome of the appeal seems well justified but the basis on which the Chief Justice came to his decision can be questioned. Section 19(2) *requires* the court to refuse an injunction where (a) the respondent establishes a fair case that he was acting in contemplation of or furtherance of a trade dispute *and* (b) a secret ballot has been held in accordance with the rules of the trade union which favours the strike or other industrial action *and* (c) the requisite period of one week's notice has been given. It says nothing about the court having to concern itself as to whether there is a fair question to be tried as to compliance with requirements (b) and (c). Only if the court is satisfied that these requirements have in fact been complied with is it required to refuse to grant an injunction. In the instant case, Laffoy J. had come to the firm conclusion to the contrary: that there was 'no evidence whatever' before the court as to the outcome of the secret ballot; there was thus 'no evidence before the court that one of the preconditions stipulated in section 19(2) ha[d] been complied with'. It was mistaken for the Supreme Court to try to read into requirements (b) and (c) the 'fair case' test appropriate to requirement (a). Laffoy J.'s finding should have been let stand undiluted by a 'fair case' modification which finds no basis in the provisions of section 19(2). If the finding was wrong, it should have been overturned on appeal and, if necessary the case remitted to the High Court for further evidence on the issue. Murphy J.'s observations on this general question in *Nolan Transport (Oaklands) Ltd v. Halligan*, Supreme Court, May 15, 1998 are instructive. We shall examine that decision in some detail in the 1998 Review.

INTIMIDATION

The tort of intimidation consists of a threat delivered by the defendant of a person whereby the defendant intentionally causes that person to act or refrain from acting in a manner which he or she is entitled to act either to his or her own detriment or to the detriment of another person: McMahon & Binchy, *op. cit.*, 570. It is essential that the person thus threatened actually *complied* with the demand: if he or she successfully resisted the threat then, although the defendant may have acted reprehensibly, and may in some circumstances be guilty of anther tort, such as intentional infliction of emotional suffering, the defendant will not be guilty of the tort of intimidation: *Whelan v. Madigan* [1978] I.L.R.M. 136.

In *Royal Dublin Society v. Yates*, High Court, July 31, 1997, which we discuss in detail earlier in the Chapter, above, 766, in the Section on Nuisance, both parties claimed that the other had been guilty of intimidation. The Royal Dublin Society contended that the defendant had intimidated a male and female employee of the Society. The defendant counterclaimed that employees and members of the Society had intimidated him.

The Society's claim failed on two grounds: any 'threats' the defendant may have made had not been complied with by the employees and, even if they had been, it was clear that the *Society* had not succumbed to any of his threats. The defendant's claim failed on the evidence, Shanley J. being satisfied that none of the actions by the members or employees of the Society of which the defendant complained 'could colourably constitute the tort of intimidation ...' The actions taken by the Society against the defendant on certain of his visits to their premises had been 'no more than consistent with the discharge of th[e] duty of care owed by it to its employees.'

MAINTENANCE AND CHAMPERTY

The torts and crimes of maintenance and champerty, which had provoked no litigation in Ireland for many years, generated controversy in two decisions in quick succession: *McElroy v. Flynn* [1991] I.L.R.M. 294, which we discuss in the 1992 Review, 114–8 and *Fraser v. Buckle*, [1996] 2 I.L.R.M. 34; [1996] 1 I.R. 1, discussed in the 1996 Review, 131–2. See also Eoin O'Dell's analysis of the subject in the 1994 Review, 184–8. The effect of these decisions is that the torts of maintenance and champerty still exist in Irish law.

In *O'Keeffe v. Scales* [1998] 1 I.L.R.M. 393, the Supreme Court returned to the subject once more. The plaintiffs, a married couple, had in 1983 invested their life savings, backed by extensive borrowings, in a hotel and time share development. Over the next six years the investment failed and the plaintiffs were financially ruined. The plaintiffs had engaged the defendant to act as their solicitor to advise and assist them in the legal management of their affairs from March 1988 to May 1989. They sought damages against her for breach of contact and negligence. During the course of the period between 1983 and 1993, the plaintiffs had incurred a substantial liability to another solicitor, of £275,620. Of this sum, £164,3000 was due on foot of a High Court decision in 1993 by that solicitor and the balance was due on foot of further work he had done for the plaintiffs in proceedings instituted by other parties against the plaintiffs. The sum of £275,620 was included in the plaintiffs' statement of claim in their proceedings against the defendant on special damages. The other solicitor was the solicitor on record for the plaintiffs in their action against the defendant.

The defendant unsuccessfully sought to have the action stayed or dismissed on the basis that the inclusion of the items amounting to £275,620 involved the other solicitor in having an interest in the outcome of the action inconsistent with his position as solicitor for the plaintiff. The essence of the defendant's argument was that their inclusion operated to alter the other solicitor's position as solicitor for the plaintiffs into a position of maintenance and champerty in that he was assisting in the promotion and conduct of the plaintiffs' litigation from which he had an interest to receive a share of the award if they were successful in repayment of the debts due to him as distinct from his proper costs as solicitor for the plaintiffs in the particular action.

Lynch J. (Barrington and Murphy JJ. concurring) was of the view that, while the law relating to maintenance and champerty 'undoubtedly' still subsisted in the jurisdiction, it should not be extended in such as way as to deprive people of their constitutional right of access to the courts to litigate reasonably stateable claims. For the defendant to succeed in stifling the plaintiffs' action before any plenary hearing, she would have to make out a clear case, analogous to the onus resting on a party bringing a motion to dismiss an action on the basis that the statement of claim disclosed no cause of action or that the proceedings were frivolous and vexatious.

Judicial authorities in other jurisdictions are divided on the question of *in limine* disposition of claims for maintenance and champerty. Against such an approach are *Hilton v. Woods* (1867) L.R. 4 Eq. 432, *Martell v. Consett Iron Co. Ltd.*, [1995] 1 Ch. 363 and the Canadian decision of *Pioneer Machinery (Rental) Ltd v. El-Jay Inc.* (1979) 93 D.LR. 3d 726. In its favour in the recent English case of *Grovewood Holdings plc v. James Capel & Co. Ltd* [1994] 4

All E.R. 417.

Lynch J. noted that, in both *McElroy v. Flynn* and *Fraser v. Buckle*, the agreements between the parties had involved maintenance and champerty on the part of the plaintiffs but nobody had suggested that the defendants were not entitled to make and succeed in their claims to a share in the respective deceaseds' estates even though their knowledge and ability to do so arose in a manner contrary to the law of maintenance and champerty. Assuming in the instant case that the plaintiffs had a reasonably stateable cause of action, and it had not been suggested that they had not, Lynch J. did not consider that it would be a valid ground for stifling their cause of action before a plenary hearing even if it could be said that the action was being maintained in a champertous fashion by the other solicitor, which Lynch J. was 'not satisfied in the case.' Nor did the inclusion in the claim of the items of special damage in respect of costs due to the other solicitor contravene section 68 of the Solicitors (Amendment) Act 1994: see the 1994 Review, 430–1.

EURO-TORT

In *Emerald Meats Ltd v. The Minister for Agriculture (No. 2)* [1997] 1 I.R. 1, the Supreme Court clarified the scope of damages awards against the State, under the *Francovich* principle, for breach by the State of a duty under European Community law. Commission Regulation 4024/89/EEC required that 90% of the GATT meat quota should be apportioned among the importers who had imported GATT meat within the previous three years. Member States were required to forward to the Commission a list of qualified applicants. The Minister for Agriculture failed to include the plaintiff on the list. Costello P. in the High Court, 9 July 1991, and the Supreme Court on appeal ([1997] 1 I.R. 1) held that this failure was a breach of duty which was, in effect a breach of statutory duty. Costello P. was satisfied that the plaintiff's failure to obtain the quota to which it was entitled had severely disrupted its business and its relationship with other traders. He awarded the plaintiff special damages of £385,922 plus interest and costs but declined to award general damages, stating tersely:

> I accept the submission made to me by counsel on behalf of the plaintiff that the breach of duty by the Minister is analogous to a breach of statutory duty under national law. I do not believe that, for such a breach of statutory duty, general damages would be awarded by an Irish court against the Minister. For that reason, I refuse to award any general damages to the plaintiff.

The Supreme Court reversed Blayney J. (Hamilton C.J. and Denham JJ. concurring) commented that:

> In taking the view that general damages would not be awarded against
> the Minister for Agriculture by an Irish court for a breach of statutory
> duty, the learned trial judge was making a distinction between damages
> awarded for special damage and damages awarded for general damage,
> and was concluding that damages for the latter type of damage, *i.e.* gen-
> eral damage, would not be awarded against the Minister. I have been
> unable to find any authority to support this view. And I do not think that
> this is surprising. All damage suffered as a result of a tort is divided into
> 'special damage' and 'general damage' and the plaintiff is entitled to
> recover damages under each head.

The distinction between these two heads of damage had been described as
follows by Bowen L.J. in *Ratcliffe v. Evans* [1892] 2 Q.B. 524 at 528:

> [I]t is desirable to recollect that the term 'special damage', which is found
> for centuries in the books, is not always used with reference to similar
> subject matter, nor in the same context. At times (both in the law of tort
> and of contract) it is employed to denote that damage arising out of the
> special circumstances of the case which, if properly pleaded, may be
> super-added to the general damage which the law implies in every breach
> of contract and every infringement of an absolute right: see *Ashby v.
> White* 2 Ld. Raym. 938. In all such cases the law presumes that some
> damage will flow in the ordinary course of things from the mere inva-
> sion of the plaintiff's rights, and particular damage (beyond the general
> damage), which results from the particular circumstances of the case,
> and of the plaintiff's claim to be compensated, for which he ought to
> give warning in his pleadings in order that there may be no surprise at
> the trial.

Since 'general damage' was damage which the law implied in every infringement of an absolute right, and special damage meant particular damage beyond general damage, Blayney J. found it difficult to see how the Minister
could be liable for the former and not for the latter. Furthermore, since both
were equally caused by the wrongful act, there was no reason why the Minister should not be liable for both. Blayney J. adopted as a correct statement of
the law the following passage from Hogan and Morgan, *Administrative Law
in Ireland* (2nd ed.) at p 634:

> As a general proposition, it is true to say that neither State nor any other
> public authority enjoys any special position in the law of torts. The gen-
> eral law – trespass, negligence, nuisance, breach of statutory duty etc. –

applies in substantially the same way as to private person.

Blayney J. was satisfied in the circumstances that the plaintiff was entitled to general damages, in addition to the special damages already awarded to it. The action was remitted to the High Court for assessment of damages.

The Supreme Court holding that the State should be liable for general damages as well as special damages is undoubtedly sound so far as it seeks to refute the proposition that a breach by it of a statutory duty under European Community law should never expose the State to liability for general damages. Such a proposition would clearly be mistaken. But was not Costello P., albeit with striking succinctness, putting forward a far narrower proposition, namely, that, for breach of *this particular* statutory duty, only special damages should be allowed.' He said that he did not believe that, 'for *such* a breach of statutory duty, general damages would be awarded by an Irish court against the Minister'. Costello P. was scarcely contending that, in Irish domestic tort law, a breach of statutory duty by a Minister warrants an award of only special damages. There is a respectable (though far from coercive) argument that the particular duty breached by the Minister was so clearly related to a narrow well-defined entitlement to a specific quota, well capable of economic calculation, that the damages should be restricted to the loss of this specific, ascertainable benefit.

VICARIOUS LIABILITY

In Ireland, for over two decades the courts have emphasised the notion of control as being at the base of vicarious liability in tort. The Supreme Court decision in *Moynihan v. Moynihan* [1975] I.R. 192 clearly so held. Whilst this approach has much to commend it, its application to the facts of the case in *Moynihan* was controversial and unconvincing. The majority (Walsh and O'Higgins C.J.; Henchy J. dissenting) imposed liability on a grandmother whose adult daughter negligently exposed the plaintiff, the two year old granddaughter of the defendant, to the danger of being burnt when the plaintiff pulled a teapot down on her. The plaintiff was at the time visiting her grandmother's home, where her adult daughter lived with her. The majority of the Court rationalised the holding on the basis that the mother was offering hospitality, that 'the nature and limits of this hospitality were completely under [her] control' and that the daughter was 'in the *de facto* service of her mother'. The characterisation of the daughter's role has disturbing echoes of the fiction of *de facto* service which is a feature of the torts of seduction, enticement of harbouring children: see McMahon & Binchy, *op. cit.* 600–603.

In *Duffy v. Rooney and Dunnes Stores (Dundalk) Ltd*, High Court, June 23, 1997, Laffoy J. wisely declined the invitation to apply *Moynihan* to another situation where a grandchild was injured when visiting a grandparents' home. The plaintiff, aged two years and ten months, was injured when her coat ignited as she was passing the fire in her grandparent's sitting room. Her grandfather had earlier put a fireguard against the fire but it was not in place on the hearth when the plaintiff was injured. The grandfather believed that one of his adult daughters must have removed it.

Laffoy J. held that the grandfather was personally rather than vicariously liable for negligence. He had responsibility for the plaintiff's care and protection during the vital moments before the accident took place. He had failed in his duty of care to her by allowing her to enter and cross a room in which there was an unguarded open fire.

Laffoy J., also imposed liability on the grandfather on the basis of his position as occupier. Her discussion of this aspect of the case is brief. The plaintiff's case in this regard had been expressed in terms of failure to insure that the plaintiff, as a guest and a very young child, was 'adequately protected from the dangers of an unguarded open fire.' Since the accident happened several years before the enactment of the Occupiers Liability Act 1995, the case would have proceeded on common law principles. There is no discussion as to whether the traditional characterisation of the plaintiff as a licensee was appropriate. Undoubtedly the fire would be consider a 'hidden danger' to a child of the plaintiffs age: *Rooney v. Connolly* [1987] I.L.R.M. 768, *Boughton v Bray U.D.C.* [1964] Ir. Jur. Rep. 57, *Bohane v. Driscoll* [1929] I.R. 428. Equally clearly, a warning of the danger given to an infant would be unlikely to be effective. Laffoy J. appears to have proceeded on the basis that the appropriate test was that of negligence, unencumbered by the traditional refinements. Since the grandfather was in any event liable in negligence on the basis of his inadequate care of the child, it would seem unwise to attach too much significance to the disposition of the occupier's liability issue.

Laffoy J. rejected the plaintiffs argument that the grandfather should be held vicariously liable on the basis of *Moynihan v. Moynihan.* The evidence had not established that his adult daughter was in his *de facto* service when she removed the fireguard, if that is in fact what she did. (At no stage in her judgment did Laffoy J. make a finding that the daughter had done so.) Even if she did remove it, the evidence was to the effect that, 'in doing so she acted totally independently of [her father] and not in any sense in pursuance of the performance of a gratuitous service for [him] . . .'

CLUBS

In *Walsh v. Butler* [1997] 2 I.L.R.M. 81, Morris J. confronted the rule that members of a club are not entitled to sue each other in tort. See McMahon and Binchy, *op. cit.*, 709–11. The plaintiff had been injured while playing rugby for Bandon Rugby Football Club. The Club was founded around a hundred and fifty years ago. Before 1979, it had no constitution or rules. In that year, when the Club acquired a premises, it was decided to apply for a club licence for the sale of intoxicating liquour. Another rugby club provided a copy of its rules for use as a precedent. In due course the appropriate order was made for the granting of the certificate under the Registration of Clubs (Ireland) Act 1904.

The Club continued to operate successfully, but its members 'paid virtually no regard to the rules', save for the creation of 'various' committees and the holding of an annual general meeting. The procedure prescribed by Rule 9 for the election of members was never followed. Instead, the Club operated on an informal basis by attracting young people directly onto the pitch, training them and absorbing them into one of the teams. Although as team members, they were required to pay an annual subscription, no sanction resulted from failure to do so.

The plaintiff, born in 1968, had started to play rugby with the Club in 1982. In 1989 he was elected vice-captain of the first team; he took over as team captain shortly afterwards. He had paid his subscription in the 1987–88 season and again in 1988–9 but not, it seemed, for the 1989–90 season. The accident took place in early 1990.

The defendants sought to avoid liability, as a preliminary issue, on the basis that the plaintiff was a member of the Club. They argued that it was within the capacity of all the members of the Club to accept a member into the Club without having to follow the formal procedure provided for by the rules. They further contended that the plaintiff was estopped by his conduct from seeking to establish that he was not a member of the Club as he had held himself out to be such a member for a number of years.

Morris J. held in favour of the plaintiff. It had not been possible for him to acquire membership of the Club in defiance of Rule 9 of the rules which required the names and addresses of the persons proposed as ordinary members to be displayed in the club premises for at least two weeks before election and provided that '[a]ll members shall be elected by the general committee'.

Morris J. considered it:

> clear beyond doubt that the only route by which one may join the club is by election to the general committee. To hold otherwise would give rise to a situation where the committee of the club would have lost all control over affairs of the club. Members could be assumed into the club and shed from the club without the knowledge of the general committee. The contractual relationship as between members regulated by their acceptance of the general committee as the regulating authority would be varied without their approval and consent.

Even if it was within the capacity of the universal membership of the Club to set aside the formal election provision and assume a candidate into the Club as a member, there was no evidence that this had occurred. No question of estoppel could arise as 'the mere act of holding oneself out as a member without adverse consequence to a third party, cannot give rise to estoppel.'

Morris J. identified 'a further fundamental point': even if the plaintiff had been a member of the Club, his membership would have lapsed when his subscription remained unpaid on the date of the annual general meeting in May 1989, under Rule 8 of the Club's Rules.

INFRINGEMENT OF CONSTITUTIONAL RIGHTS

Earlier in the Chapter, in the section on the Duty of Care, above, 709–14, we discuss *W. v. Ireland, the Attorney General and the Government of Ireland (No. 2)* [1997] 2 I.R. 141, in which Costello P. rejected a claim for damages by a victim of Father Brendan Smyth, a convicted paedophile for shock and distress and consequent psychiatric problems resulting from the delay in his extradition. Costello P. rejected the plaintiff's claim in negligence. He then turned to consider, and reject, her claim for damages for infringement of her constitutional rights under Article 40.3, in particular her right to bodily integrity.

Just as the Extradition Act 1965 (as amended) did not impose a duty of care on the Attorney General towards the plaintiff, for similar reasons it did not impose a duty on him (or on any of the other defendants) not to infringe the plaintiff's right to bodily integrity:

> The Act created no relationship of any sort between any of the defendants and the plaintiff and no circumstances of any sort existed by which a duty to take into consideration the plaintiff's bodily integrity (and to speedily consider the extradition warrants) existed.

Costello P. considered that the second reason why the Attorney General at common law owed no duty of care to the plaintiff, arising from considerations of *public policy*, applied also when considering the claim based on the Constitution:

> The rights guaranteed under the Constitution are not absolute rights (with the exception of an implied right not to be tortured, which must be regarded as an absolute right which can never be abridged) and their exercise and enjoyment may be, and frequently are, limited by reason of the exigencies of the common good. I concluded, applying well established principles of the law of tort, that it would be contrary to public policy in this case to impose on the Attorney General a duty of care towards the

plaintiff. The reasons why no common law duty existed also meant that no constitutional duty existed, because the exigencies of the common good (that is, in this case the need to allow the Attorney General carry out his important public functions without the threat of an action for damages for negligence at the suit of a private individual) justifies the court in depriving the plaintiff of a claim for damages for breach of duty not to infringe her right to bodily integrity. This means that none of the defendants owed under the Constitution the right asserted on the plaintiff's behalf.

These two grounds were sufficient to dispose the of plaintiff's claim but Costello P. thought it appropriate to express his views on the broader issue of compensation for infringement of constitutional rights. In approaching this issue he considered that constitutionally guaranteed rights might be divided into two distinct classes: *first* those which, independently of the Constitution, were regulated and protected by law (common law and/or statutory law) and *secondly*, those that were not so regulated and protected. In the first class were all those fundamental rights which the Constitution recognised that man had by virtue of his rational being antecedent to positive law and were rights regulated and protected by law in every State which valued human rights.

In Ireland there existed a large and complex body of laws which regulated the exercise and enjoyment of these basic rights, protected them against attack and provided compensation for their wrongful infringement. Thus, for example, the right to private property was protected by laws against trespass; its enjoyment was regulated by laws against the creation of nuisance; remedies for breach of the right to private property (by way of injunctive relief and actions for damages) were available; limitation on its exercise was provided by law, allowing for its compulsory acquisition and limiting the power to dispose of it by will. The right to liberty was protected by *habeas corpus* Acts and laws against wrongful imprisonment, whilst the exercise of the right was limited by provisions of the criminal code and legal powers of arrest and imprisonment. The right of freedom of expression was regulated by defamation laws and laws to protect public morality. And the right which was in issue in the instant case, the right to bodily integrity, was protected by the extensive provisions in the law of tort.

The courts had, however, pointed out that the Constitution guaranteed the exercise and enjoyment of other rights which were not regulated by law and for which no legal provision existed either to prohibit an anticipated infringement or to compensate for a past one. It was now established that for this class of rights the Constitution was to be construed as providing a separate cause of action for damages for breach of a constitutional right. Costello P. reviewed the decision of *Meskell v. CIE* [1973] I.R. 121, *Kearney v. The Minister for Justice* [1986] I.R. 116, *McHugh v. Commissioner of Garda Siochana* [1986]

I.R. 228 and *Kennedy v. Ireland* [1987] I.R. 587, all of which involved damages awards, and *Lovett v. Gogan* [1995] 3 I.R. 132, where the Supreme Court held that the defendant's activities constituted an actual or threatened interference with the plaintiff's constitutional right to earn an living by lawful means and it granted an injunction to protect him from the threatened invasion of those rights.

What fell for consideration in the instant case was not a guaranteed right of this second class but a right (the right of bodily integrity) in respect of which there is a large body of law (both common law and statutory), which regulated its exercise, protected it against infringment and compensated its holder should the right be breached. The question, therefore, was whether the Constitution should be construed as conferring a discrete cause of action for damages for breach of the plaintiff's right to bodily integrity notwithstanding the existence of the law of tort and statutory provisions which conferred a right of action for damages for personal injuries sustained by the negligent act of omission of another.

Echoing the approach he had adopted in *Hosford v. Murphy* [1988] I.L.R.M. 300, Costello P. stated:

> The question can be posed this way, should the Constitution be construed so as to confer on a pedestrian injured by an army lorry a right to claim damages against the State for infringement of the right to bodily integrity in addition to, or as an alternate to, an action for damages for negligence?
>
> I am satisfied that it should not be so construed.

Article 40.3.1° did not require the Oireachtas to enact specific laws protecting constitutionally protected rights and the State's duty under this Article was implemented by the existence of laws (common law and statutory) which conferred a right of action for damages (or a power to grant injunctive relief) in relation to acts of omissions which might constitute an infringement of guaranteed rights. Henchy J.'s remarks in *Hanrahan v. Merck Sharp and Dome (Ireland) Ltd.* [1988] I.L.R.M. 629 at 635–636 supported this proposition. Thus, if the law of torts made provision for an action for damages for bodily injury caused by negligence and if the law also adequately protected the injured pedestrian's guaranteed right to bodily integrity, then the State's Article 40 duties were fulfilled.

The courts were required by the Constitution to apply the law and the causes of actions it conferred and when these adequately protected guaranteed rights the courts were not called upon to establish a new cause of action; indeed, it would be contrary to their constitutional function to do so. Furthermore, it would be otiose. If a cause of action for damages for infringement of the constitutional right of bodily integrity were granted to the injured plaintiff in the hypothetical example of the accident involving the army lorry, the court would have to consider whether there was any breach of the duty which the driver of the lorry owed to the pedestrian, since the right was not an absolute one, and, in considering the nature and scope of the duty, would decide whether the lorry driver had failed to take proper care of the plaintiff's safety, whether the pedestrian failed to take care of his own safety, apportion liability as required by the Civil Liability Act 1961, assess damages in accordance with established principles, and in certain circumstance consider whether the claim was statute barred – 'in other words apply the law of tort to the new cause of action.'

There was therefore no need to construe the Constitution as conferring a new and discrete cause of action for damages in those cases in which the acts or omissions which constituted the alleged infringement also constitute an actionable wrong at law for which damages were recoverable. Costello P. acknowledged that a provision of the law to be applied might not in a given case adequately protect the guaranteed right: for example, the law might contain a limitation period which in the particular circumstance trenched unfairly on the guaranteed right and thus deprive the plaintiff of a right to compensation, as in *O'Brien v. Keogh* [1972] I.R. 144. In such a case, the law would be applied without the provision rendered invalid by the Constitution.

Costello P. noted that his conclusions were consistent with and followed from the views of the Supreme Court in *Hanrahan v. Merck Sharp and Dohme (Ireland) Limited* [1988] I.L.R.M. 629. They were also consistent with the views expressed in *Meskell* which, by holding that a new and distinct cause of action for damages for breach of a constitutional right when the existing law failed to confer any right of damages implied that, when it *did* so, no new cause of action should be created.

Counsel for the plaintiff had sought to argue that the crucial passage of Blayney J.'s judgment in *Hanrahan* was *obiter*, that the number of authorities supporting the plaintiff's contentions were more numerous and that *Hanrahan* was inconsistent with the decision of the Supreme Court in *Lovett v. Gogan* [1995] 3 I.R. 132.

It had been perfectly clear since *Meskell* that the courts would award damages and grant injunctions for breach of constitutionally protected rights but, in each of the cases where that occurred, *Meskell* was either explicitly or implicitly applied and damages were awarded, and in the case of *Lovett v. Gogan* an injunction was granted, where *no* remedy at law existed. None of those cases had decided that an action for damages for breach of a guaranteed right would lie in cases where the *existing* law protected the right. Costello P. was satisfied that the law of tort which was applicable in the instant case was not ineffective to protect the plaintiff's constitutionally guaranteed rights:

It does not follow that because a plaintiff does not recover damages under the applicable law (in this case, the law of torts) that it must be ineffective in protecting guaranteed rights. It is necessary to consider why the plaintiff's claim has failed. As already explained, the applicable principles of the law of torts established that there was neither a duty owed to the plaintiff by the defendants under the law of torts or the Constitution to process the extradition warrants speedily and so by applying the principles of the law of torts the plaintiff was not deprived of a remedy to which she was entitled under the Constitution.

Costello J.'s judgment is convincing in its explanation of how there would be an intolerable internal legal dissonance if a plaintiff whose action for negligence was defeated by a considered judicial determination that no duty of care arose in the particular context could nonetheless obtain damages by reframing his or her action as one for infringement of constitutional rights. But, if this is undoubtedly correct, it does not follow that the limits of the duty of care in the tort of negligence should represent the outer circle for recovery of damages for all infringements of constitutional rights. There is no logical reason why the range of recovery should be identical. Indeed it would be remarkably curious if the judges around the common law world who developed the corpus of the law of negligence over the centuries should miraculously have constructed a system of liability that coincides with the range of recovery for infringement of constitutional rights under the Irish Constitution. Costello P.'s attempt to seek such an identity between the positive legal system and fundamental rights based on natural law is unconvincing. It finds no support in Henchy J.'s judgment in *Hanrahan*. Indeed, one might have expected a natural law rationale to justify the second, rather than the first, of the two categories established by Henchy J. and endorsed by Costello P.

DAMAGES

Negligent misrepresentation and misstatement   In *Forshall v. Walsh*, High Court, June 18, 1997, the facts of which we have stated above, 769, Shanley J. took the unprecedented step of adopting the test set out by Henchy J. in *Northern Bank Finance Corporation Ltd v. Charlton* [1979] I.R. 149, at 199 in relation to claims for fraudulent misrepresentation as 'the appropriate guide to the measure of damage for negligent misrepresentation and misstatement. . . .' In *Charlton*, Henchy J. had considered it:

> well settled that the measure of damages is based on the actual damage directly flowing from the fraudulent inducement and that the award may, in an appropriate case, . . . include consequential damages representing

what was reasonably and necessarily expended as a result of acting on the inducement. . . .

This test had already been applied in *Hindle v. O'Dwyer*, Supreme Court, February 14, 1954 and *Leyden v. Malone*, Supreme Court, May 13, 1968. No Irish decision prior to *Forshall v. Walsh* had suggested that the directness test should apply in cases of negligent misrepresentation or misstatement. The Privy Council case of *Overseas Tankship (U.K.) Ltd v. Morts Dock and Engineering Co Ltd (The Wagon Mound (No 1))*, [1961] A.C. 338 and subsequent Irish decisions, including *Burke v. John Paul & Co Ltd.*, [1967] I.R. 277 and *Egan v. Sisk* [1986] I.L.R.M. 283, would suggest that a directness criterion is not appropriate to negligence claims. See McMahon and Binchy, *op. cit.*, chapter 3.

Defamation Earlier in the Chapter, in the Section on Defamation, above, 775, we examine *Dawson and Dawson t/a A.E. Dawson & Sons v. Irish Brokers Association*, Supreme Court, February 27, 1997, which deals with the issue of damages in defamation proceedings.

Loss of consortium In *McKinley v. The Minister for Defence (No. 2)* [1997] 2 I.R. 176, Carney J. had to deal with the reference back to the High Court from the Supreme Court, on July 27, 1992, of the question whether the wife of a person whose sexual faculties were damaged as a result of the defendant's negligence was entitled to sue for impairment to, as opposed to total loss of, her husband's consortium. See [1992] 2 I.R. 333; 1992 Review, 151–2, 220–1, 613–8. Carney J. was satisfied that no assistance could be derived from the older judicial authorities in relation to the determination of rights in this area 'under a democratic constitution committed to the determination of rights and obligations on the basis of equality, including sexual equality.' Echoing the views of Maguire C.J. (dissenting) in *Spaight v. Dundon* [1961] I.R. 201 and McCarthy J. in the plaintiff's earlier appeal to the Supreme Court on July 27, 1992, Carney J. held that the common law action for loss of consortium extended to a wife's claim for partial as well as total loss or impairment of consortium.'

Carney J. expressed gratitude for the guidance that O'Flaherty J. had given on the question of assessment of damages in the Supreme Court [1992] 2 I.R. 333 at 358) to the effect that:

a benchmark might be sought and found in the level of damages that are awarded for mental distress under the Civil Liability Acts in the case of the death of a spouse. It would seem clear in principle, that damages for loss of consortium should be related to those recoverable for the death of a spouse.

In *Coppinger v. Waterford County Council* [1996] 2 I.L.R.M. 427, Geoghegan
J. had interpreted O'Flaherty J.'s remarks as not limiting his discretion to the
artificial statutory maximum of £7,500 which had been set by the Oireachtas
in 1981.

Carney J. noted that '[i]t so happen[ed]' that the sum of £7,500 had just
been updated by Ministerial Order to £20,000 (under the Civil Liability
(Amendment) Act 1996: see the 1996 Review, 600–1). He accepted O'Flaherty
J.'s guidance by assessing damages 'in this updated sum'. He noted that the
significantly higher award which Geoghegan J. had made in *Coppinger* was
based on a finding that the injuries to Mrs Coppinger by reason of loss of
consortium had been 'infinitely worse than the mental distress which she would
have suffered if her husband had died in the accident.' No such case had been
made in the instant proceedings.

We are somewhat less than sure that a helpful analogy can be drawn with
damages in wrongful death litigation, for reasons we set out in the 1996 Review, 615–6.

Loss of earnings   In *McDermott v. Gargan*, High Court, January 24, 1997,
the plaintiff, when aged 47 in 1992, was kicked by a cow in an accident for
which the defendant was 85% liable. He complained of persistent significant
back pain. On medical advise he took early retirement. He claimed that the
injury was so serious as to prevent him working again. Flood J. was of opinion
that there was no evidential foundation that the injury he sustained would
have such long-lasting consequences. Under the heading of loss of future wages,
Flood J.'s award represented a period of one and a half years.

Collateral benefits   Geoghegan J.'s decision in *Greene v. Hughes Haulage
Ltd.*, [1998] 1 I.L.R.M. 34; [1997] 3 I.R. 109 is the first authoritative judicial
interpretation of section 2 of the Civil Liability (Amendment) Act 1964, which
deals with the non-deductibility of certain payments to the plaintiff where
assessing damages. It provides that:

> [i]n assessing damages in an action to recover damages in respect of a
> wrongful act (including a crime) resulting in personal injury not causing
> death, account shall not be taken of:
> (a) any sum payable in respect of the injury under any contract of insur-
>   ance,
> (b) any pension, gratuity or other like benefit payable under statute or
>   otherwise in consequence of the injury.

Section 2 of the 1964 Act mirrors the language of section 50 of the Civil
Liability Act 1961, which provides for equivalent non-deductions in fatal accident claims. A curious dissonance had existed at a statutory level for fifty

six years, since the passage of the Fatal Accidents (Damages) Act 1908: fatal accident claims were through this period governed by a statutory principle of non-deductibility while personal injury claims had had no equivalent, although the courts had developed their own principle of non-deductibility for these claims which was less generous to the plaintiff than the fatal accident provisions.

In *Greene v. Hughes Haulage Ltd.*, the plaintiff, injured in an accident caused by the defendant's negligence, was in receipt of a disability payment under a contract of insurance made by her employer for her benefit. It was well established in respect of fatal accident payments that the fact that the deceased was not himself or herself a party to the insurance contract should not prevent the application of the principle of non-deductibility: *Bowskill v. Dawson (No 2)* [1955] 1 Q.B. 13; *Green v. Russell* [1959] 2 Q.B. 226. Geoghegan J. considered that the same principle should apply in respect of personal injury litigation. He speculated that it might well have been that the judicial confusion apparent in British decisions regarding the scope of the common law principle of non-deductibility for personal injury claims prompted the Oireachtas to enact section 2 of the 1964 Act, 'simplifying the position and in effect applying to personal injury actions the same rules as to non-deductibility as already applied to fatal injury actions under section 50 of the Civil Liability Act 1961.' In each case, the expression 'under any contract of insurance' was used and Geoghegan J. therefore saw no reason why the broad interpretation which had always been given to that expression in the fatal accident cases should not also be applied to personal injury actions. He stressed, however, that this did not mean that a simple *indemnity* policy indemnifying an employer against some contractual undertaking by it to continue making salary payments to an employee who had become incapacitated would come within section 2. Hamilton P.'s ruling in *Dennehy v. Nordic Cold Storage*, High Court, May 8, 1991 could be distinguished on this ground.

Loss of a chattel In *Murphy v. De Braam*, Supreme Court, December 12, 1997, which was an appeal by the defendant against the amount of damages awarded against him for an accident involving his aircraft striking a helicopter, liability being based on section 21 of the Air Navigation and Transport Act 1936, which does not require proof of negligence, Barron J., in an *ex tempore* judgment (O'Flaherty and Keane JJ. concurring), gave a very clear statement of how damages for loss of a chattel are computed in tort litigation. (The plaintiff had conceded that the amount awarded by the trial judge in relation to the helicopter should be reduced by £10,500.)

Barron J. said that:

> The evidence in relation to the loss sustained by reason of the loss of the helicopter was based upon the price originally paid for it and evidence

that it would not have depreciated in value. Damages for the loss of a vehicle as a motor car in the ordinary case or as a helicopter in the present case should not be based upon what it was worth to its owner at the time the damage was incurred. Damages in tort are intended to place the plaintiff back in the position in which he would have been but for the wrong committed against him. That does not mean that he should be put in the position of the owner of the chattel with a particular value. That does not restore him to the position in which he was before the tort was committed. He was the owner of such chattel and in a position to use it.

He had not intention to dispose of it. To be put back into the position in which he was at the date of tort it is necessary to replace his chattel for him by the cost likely to be incurred in the purchase of a similar chattel. This figure would not be the same as the value of the chattel lost since there is always a significant difference between buying and selling prices. The position is different from the case of a claim under a contract of insurance where the amount recoverable is dependent upon the relevant contractual provision.

The plaintiff is entitled to what it would have cost him to replace his helicopter in the condition in which it was when the accident occurred. That condition included the items which he had added to it since he purchased it.

General damages   In *Forde v. Iarnrod Éireann-Irish* Rail, Supreme Court, November 4, 1997 (*ex tempore*), O'Flaherty J. (Barrington and Lynch JJ. concurring) expressed a preference for a somewhat robust approach at appellate level to the computation of damages. Barron J., at trial, had awarded the plaintiff £60,000 general damages for a very serious injury to his legs; £30,000 represented the damages to the date of trial, £30,00 was for future pain and suffering.

Raising the total figure to £80,000, O'Flaherty J. observed that,

> [w]hile we expect trial courts to provide the way damages are computed, past and future, as the court of final appeal we do not find it necessary to engage in that exercise here.

In *Fagan v. Wong and Wong t/a the Pearl River Restaurant and Fagan v. Leahy,* Supreme Court, May 7, 1997, the Supreme Court rejected appeals by the plaintiff in two personal injury actions against low awards by Flood J. in the High Court on July 6, 1995, in which he awarded her £7,500 in the first action and £13,500 in the second. Lynch J. (O'Flaherty and Barron JJ. concurring) placed considerable reliance on the evidence of a highly qualified and experienced neurologist, who was in no doubt that the plaintiff had been malingering. The plaintiff's general practitioner, when asked to explain the inconsistency between what the plaintiff had told the doctors and her ability to do housework, lift objects, drive cars and do gardening, had replied : 'I certainly have none'.

The Supreme Court also rejected the plaintiff's contention that Flood J. had so conducted himself by his interventions that a disinterested bystander would have gained the impression of unfairness and for bias. He stated:

> A judge is bound to listen carefully to the evidence as it is being given and on a continuing basis to form views as to its reliability or otherwise. A judge may and sometimes should indicate his reaction to or provisional decision on evidence presented or arguments made with a view to clarifying ambiguities or to provide an opportunity to resolve misunderstandings which might otherwise arise. . . .
>
> There is no reason why a bystander should not gain an impression of how the case is running and the impression which he gets may of course be correct or completely incorrect. It would not be in keeping with common sense for a judge to remain totally impassive throughout the trial and then to give a judgment based possibly on the misconstruction of something which had been put before him when if he had given an indication of his thinking he would have been disabused of such misconstruction. Judges have a large measure of discretion as to how they conduct their courts and the trials which they hear in them provided always that all parties are allowed to present their respective cases fully and fairly. Indeed if one thinks back over the years it was always common practise when a notable trial was at hearing whether with or without a jury that word would come back to the Law Library that the plaintiff was ten lengths ahead of the field and still gaining ground or was trailing badly and losing more and more ground the longer the case went on. It is quite in order that a disinterested bystander would gain some impression as to which party seemed to be doing well and vice versa whether the trial was before a judge and jury or before a judge alone.

In *Golden v. Cahill*, High Court, July 29, 1997, Flood J. awarded the plaintiff £20,000 general damages for pain and suffering from the time of the accident in 1992 to the time of trial and £12,000 for future pain and suffering. The plaintiff was thirty-seven years old when the accident occurred. The injuries of which she complained included pain in her right shoulder, her neck and her back, as well as deep fatigue. A pre-existing bulge in a disc exacerbated her pain. Flood J. was satisfied that, although the plaintiff 'had a fine sense of her own rights and entitlements', she was a good and forthright witness, active and 'conscientious in the performance of her duties', who might well have been extremely frustrated by the degree of ache and general distress that flowed from her injuries when she compared her existing position to what it had been before the accident.

Exemplary and aggravated damages In *Cooper v. O'Connell*, Supreme Court, June 5, 1997, some light was thrown on the circumstances in which awards of exemplary or aggravated damages are appropriate. The case concerned a course of dental treatment carried out by the defendant dentist on the plaintiff between 1988 and 1991. In spite of having over a hundred and eighty appointments with the plaintiff during this period, the defendant finally accepted that he had failed the plaintiff and indicated that he would send him to another dentist, who would be capable of remedying he situation. When the plaintiff went to this dentist, it transpired that he had not been told about the case. The plaintiff went back to the defendant, who told him that he had made a mistake and that 'everybody was entitled to one mistake.' He also advised the plaintiff that he could not afford to pay for the remedial treatment and that, as the plaintiff had a good case against him, he should go to see his solicitor.

The plaintiff received treatment from another dentist and in due course sued the defendant for negligence. Barron J. imposed liability and awarded damages of £105,000 for pain and suffering and £50,000 for loss of earnings. He rejected as speculative the plaintiff's claim for far higher damages for loss of earnings. The plaintiff had contended that he would have resumed profitable business ventures if he had not had such serious problems resulting from the defective dental treatment. Barron J. considered that there was a paucity of evidence as to these projects; no evidence had been given as to the finance necessary to implement them; its sources and the return that the plaintiff might receive.

The plaintiff appealed unsuccessfully to the Supreme Court against the relatively low award of damages for loss of earnings. Keane J. (Hamilton CJ, O'Flaherty, Barrington and Murphy JJ. concurring) could find no error in principle on Barron J.'s part in arriving at his assessment.

Barron J. had also declined to award the plaintiff exemplary or aggravated damages. The plaintiff appealed against this refusal, arguing that the defendant had abused a relationship of trust and that, in initially admitting his responsibility and then withdrawing that admission when a defence was delivered on his behalf denying liability, he, or those standing in his shoes, had been guilty of conduct which merited an award of exemplary or aggravated damages.

Keane J. quoted from Finlay C.J.'s judgment in *Conway v. Irish National Teachers Organisation* [1991] 2 I.R. 305:

> In respect of damages in tort or for breach of a constitutional right, three headings of damages in Irish law are, in my view potentially relevant to any particular case. They are:

(1) Ordinary compensatory damages being sums calculated to recompense a wronged plaintiff for physical injury, mental distress, anxiety, deprivation of convenience, or other harmful effects of a wrongful act and/or for monies lost or to be lost and/or expenses incurred or to be incurred by reason of the commission of the wrongful act.

(2) Aggravated damages, being compensatory damages increased by reason of

   (a) The manner in which the wrong was committed, involving such elements as oppressiveness, arrogance or outrage, or

   (b) The conduct of the wrongdoer after the commission of the wrong such as the refusal to apologise or to ameliorate the harm done or the making of threats to repeat the wrong or

   (c) Conduct of the wrongdoer and/or his representatives in the defence of the claim of the wronged plaintiff, up to and including the trial of the action.

   Such a list of the circumstances which may aggravate compensatory damages until they can properly be classified as aggravated damages is not intended to be in any way finite or complete. Furthermore the circumstances which may properly form an aggravated feature in the measurement of compensatory damages must, in many instances, be in part a recognition of the added hurt or insult to a plaintiff who has been wronged, and in part also a recognition of the cavalier or outrageous conduct of the defendant.

(3) Punitive or exemplary damages arising from the nature of the wrong which has been committed and/or the manner or its commission which are intended to mark the court's particular disapproval of the defendant's conduct in all the circumstances of the case, and its decision that it should publicly be seen to have punished the defendant for such conduct by awarding such damages, quite apart from its obligation, where it may exist in the same case, to compensate the plaintiff for the damage which he or she has suffered. I have purposely used the above phrase 'punitive *or* exemplary damages' because I am forced to the conclusion that, notwithstanding relatively cogent reasons to the contrary, in our law punitive and exemplary damage must be recognised as constituting the same element.

It was clear that in the instant case no grounds existed for the award of the third of these categories, namely punitive or exemplary damages. While the Supreme Court in *Conway* had rejected the view of Lord Devlin in *Rookes v. Barnard* [1964] A.C. 1129, that awards of such damages should be confined to the three categories referred to in his speech, it was also clear from the judgments of Finlay C.J. and Griffin and McCarthy JJ. that (in the words of McCarthy J):

> The purpose of awarding such damages is truly to make an example of the wrongdoer so as to show others that such wrongdoing will not be tolerated and, more to the point, will not be relieved on payment of merely compensatory damages.

Thus, such damages might be awarded in some, but not all, cases where there was an invasion of the plaintiff's constitutional rights, as in *Conway*. It was unnecessary to explore the precise limitations of the circumstances in which such awards might be made; in the context of the instant case it was sufficient to say that the conduct of the defendant and those standing in his shoes did not come within any of the categories which the courts regarded as of such seriousness as to justify an award of exemplary damages:

> In developing the law as to such damages, the courts in this jurisdiction, as in other common law jurisdictions, have essentially been concerned with the principles of public policy which demand that, in a literal sense, an example should be made of the defendant. The fact that a medical practitioner has been admittedly guilty of negligence and that his defence society or insurers have initially put the plaintiff on proof of liability could not conceivably be regarded as circumstances justifying the invocation of this drastic, although essential, rule grounded on public policy.

As to the aggravated damages, Keane J acknowledged that it might be legitimate to refer to negligent conduct on the part of a medical practitioner as a breach of the trust necessarily reposed by the patient in the practitioner and to say that, to that extent, in common with other forms of professional negligence, it was distinguishable from the general run of actions in negligence. That consideration, however, of itself, did not bring every case of medical negligence within paragraph 2(a) of the circumstances which, in the view of Finlay C.J. in *Conway*, justified the award of aggravated damages namely 'the manner in which the wrong was committed, involving such elements as oppressiveness, arrogance or outrage. . . .'

Keane J. thought that, in this respect, the instant case might usefully be contrasted with the English decision of *Appelton v. Garrett* [1996] P.I.Q.R. 1, where the defendant dentist carried out large scale unnecessary treatment of the plaintiffs, deliberately withholding from them the information that the treatment was unnecessary because he knew that they would not have consented had they known the true position. In holding that the plaintiffs were entitled to aggravated damages, Dyson J. said:

I have no difficulty in finding that the plaintiffs must have suffered mental distress, injured feelings and a heightened sense of injury or grievance when they discovered what Mr. Garrett had done to them, namely that he had carried out treatment which was to his knowledge unnecessary, that he had deliberately concealed the truth from them at the time so as to ensure that they did not withdraw their consent, and all this for financial gain.

No considerations of this or a like nature arose in the instant case. So far as the manner, admittedly and seriously negligent, in which the defendant conducted the treatment was concerned, there was nothing to distinguish his conduct from that of any other defendant in an action for professional negligence. Indeed, unlike many other defendants, he had frankly conceded that he had been negligent and advised the plaintiff to seek legal advice.

Keane J. was also satisfied that the decision of the defendant's insurers or defence union initially to put liability in issue could not possibly be a ground for the award of aggravated damages:

Under our law of tort, a defendant is entitled to put the plaintiff on proof of his allegation that an actionable civil wrong has been committed. To hold that, because the plaintiff's case appears to be of particular cogency, a defendant who elects to put liability in issue exposes himself to an award of aggravated damages would be to create a novel deterrent for defendants which is contrary to fundamental principle and devoid of any support in the decided cases.

Transport

AIR NAVIGATION

Air accidents   The Air Navigation (Notification and Investigation of Accidents and Incidents) Regulations 1997 (S.I. No. 205 of 1997), made under the Air Navigation and Transport Act 1936, provides for the notification and investigation of accidents and incidents by the Air Accident Investigation Unit (AAIU) of the Department of Public Enterprise (formerly Transport). They replaced the Air Navigation (Investigation of Accidents) Regulations 1957 and came into effect on July 25, 1997.

Aircraft performance   The Air Navigation (Operations) (Amendment) Order 1997 (S.I. No. 220 of 1997), made under the Irish Aviation Authority Act 1993 (1993 Review, 584) amended the Air Navigation (Operations) Order 1986 to reflect revised requirements with respect to area navigation performance and reduced vertical separation minima, in order to reduce the risk of mid-air near collisions. They also reflect requirements concerning Joint Aviation Requirements at EC level, as required by Regulation (EEC) No. 3922/91. They came into effect on May 27, 1997.

Aircraft registration   The Irish Aviation Authority (Nationality and Registration of Aircraft) (Amendment) Order 1997 (S.I. No. 219 of 1997) amended the Irish Aviation Authority (Nationality and Registration of Aircraft) Order 1996 (1996 Review, 624) and removed the requirement that the nationality of the company chairman be a deciding factor in the suitability for registration as an aircraft owner. They came into effect on May 27, 1997.

Airworthiness of aircraft   The Irish Aviation Authority (Airworthiness of Aircraft) (Amendment) Order 1997 (S.I. No. 102 of 1997) amended the Irish Aviation Authority (Airworthiness of Aircraft) Order 1996 (1996 Review, 624) to reflect that certain Joint Aviation Requirements at EC level, as required by Regulation (EEC) No. 3922/91, are applicable in the State. They came into effect on March 3, 1997.

Carrier liability   In *S. Smyth & Co Ltd v. Aer Turas Teo*, Supreme Court, February 3, 1997, the Supreme Court affirmed the dismissal in the High Court of the plaintiff company's action against the defendant for damages in negligence and breach of contract. The plaintiff exported calves to Italy on flights operated by the defendant between Dublin Airport and Malpensa Airport, Milan. Each consignment was accompanied by various documents including the consignor's invoice to the consignee. On arrival at Malpensa Airport a bag containing the documents was given by the crew load master to an official of an organisation (SEA), which provided ground services at the airport. In the normal course of events, SEA would give the invoice to the consignee or his clearing agent who would then present them to customs. Fraudulent invoices were substituted for the plaintiff's invoices in relation to certain consignments at some point between the time the invoices were given by the defendant to SEA and the presentation of the invoices to customs. The consignee refused to pay the plaintiff for the consignments.

The plaintiff claimed that the defendant was in breach of its duty of care in and about the handling of the customs arrangements at Malpensa Airport. Alternatively the plaintiff claimed that it was an implied term of each contract of carriage that the defendant would be responsible for the safe delivery of the relevant documents to customs and that SEA was its agent for this purpose. The defendant counterclaimed for the sum of £121,246 in respect of moneys due for the carriage of the calves.

The High Court dismissed the plaintiff's claim and gave judgment for the defendant on the counterclaim. On appeal, the Supreme Court (O'Flaherty, Blayney and Keane JJ.) affirmed.

The Court accepted that the defendant was under a duty of care to deal with the customs formalities in a normal competent manner. Since it was the universal practice at Malpensa Airport for carriers of goods to deliver all necessary documents including invoices to SEA and since the defendant could not have foreseen that any damage would arise through the use of that organisation's services, the defendant had discharged its duty of care to the plaintiff in delivering the invoices to SEA.

The Court considered that the evidence indicated that the sole function of SEA was to deliver invoices to the consignee or his clearing agent and was under no duty to examine the invoices. Accordingly, SEA had not been negligent and the issue of the defendant's vicarious liability for the negligence of SEA did not arise.

Finally, the Court noted that a party to a contract for the international carriage of goods by air may be confined to the remedies contained in the Warsaw Convention on International Carriage by Air, implemented by the Air Navigation and Transport Act 1965. However, as the defendant had not raised this issue it was unnecessary to decide the issue in these proceedings; the Court pointed out that a similar approach had been taken in *Sidhu v. British Airways Plc* (1996) Times L.R. 721. See further the decision in the Torts chapter, 723, above.

Equipment The European Communities (Air Traffic Management Equipment and Systems) (Standards) (Amendment) Regulations 1997 (S.I. No.481 of 1997) amended the European Communities (Air Traffic Management Equipment and Systems) (Standards) Regulations 1996 (1996 Review, 625) to give effect to Directive 97/15/EC which amended the specifications for equipment used in air traffic control. They came into effect on December 4, 1997.

Fees The Irish Aviation Authority (Fees) Order 1997 (S.I. No. 295 of 1997) increased the fees payable to the Irish Aviation Authority for aeronautical licences, certificates and permits. They came into effect on September 1, 1997.

Personnel licensing The Air Navigation (Personnel Licensing) (Amendment) Order 1997 (S.I. No. 101 of 1997) amended the Air Navigation (Personnel Licensing) (Amendment) (No. 2) Order 1996 (1996 Review, 624) to reflect the requirement that certain Joint Aviation Requirements, as required by Regulation (EEC) No. 3922/91, are applicable in the State. They came into effect on March 3, 1997.

Route charges The Irish Aviation Authority (Eurocontrol) (Route Charges) (Amendment) Regulations 1997 (S.I. No. 44 of 1997) adjust the method of applying the ECU exchange rate to route unit rates with effect from January 21, 1997.

State aircraft The Air Navigation and Transport (Application of Regulations to State Aircraft) (Government) Order 1997 (S.I. No. 198 of 1997) and the Air Navigation and Transport (Application of Regulations to State Aircraft) (Ministerial) Order 1997 (S.I. No. 206 of 1997) applies section 60 of the Air Navigation and Transport Act 1936 Act to State aircraft, with effect from May 6, 1997 and May 12, 1997, respectively.

MERCHANT SHIPPING

Liability of ship owners The Merchant Shipping (Liability of Shipowners and Others) Act 1996 (Commencement) Order 1997 (S.I. No. 215 of 1997) brought the Merchant Shipping (Liability of Shipowners and Others) Act 1996 (1996 Review, 626-7) into force on February 6, 1997.

Navigational aids The Merchant Shipping (Commissioners of Irish Lights) Act 1997 was enacted to reverse the effect of the decision in *Keane v An Bord Pleanála (No.2)*, Supreme Court, July 18, 1996 (1996 Review, 458–60), in which the Supreme Court had held (by a 3-2 majority) that the Commissioners' powers under the Merchant Shipping Act 1894 did not extend to the provision of radio-based aids to marine navigation which were unknown at the time of the enactment of the 1894 Act. Section 2 of the Act vests the superintendence and management of all maritime radio navigation systems in the Commissioners. Section 3 empowers the Commissioners to construct, operate and maintain radio navigation systems and allows the Commissioners to buy land for this purpose. It also confers on the Commissioners all necessary ancillary powers in this regard and ensures that the constitutional rights of any person are not affected by powers given under the section. Section 4 empowers the Commissioners to co-operate with other agencies in the provision of radio navigation systems and services relating to maritime navigation. Section 5 empowers the Commissioners to make financial contributions to bodies concerned with maritime navigational assistance, subject to the consent of the Minister for the Marine. Section 6 empowers the Commissioners to enter into agreements for the provision of maritime navigation systems on behalf of harbour authorities and for the performance of services relating to maritime navigation and other matters, again subject to Ministerial consent. Section 7 provides that the Minister may, by Order, and with the consent of the Minister for Finance, give the Commissioners appropriate additional functions in relation to maritime navigational matters and make any necessary provision arising from these functions. The Act came into effect on November 18, 1997, on its signature by the President.

ROAD TRANSPORT

Emission control The European Communities (Mechanically Propelled Vehicle Emission Control) Regulations 1997 (S.I. No. 518 of 1997) further extended the transitional period for giving effect to Directive 94/12/EC and came into force on January 1, 1998.

Insurance policy In *Scanlon v. McCabe and PMPA Insurance plc* [1997] 2 I.L.R.M. 337 (SC), the Supreme Court held that the insurance policy in the instant case did not cover the circumstances of the traffic accident in the instant case. The plaintiff had been travelling on the cargo platform of the first defendant's pick-up truck. The truck had collided with another vehicle and the plaintiff was seriously injured. It was not disputed that the first defendant was solely responsible for the accident. In the High Court, it was held that the carriage of the plaintiff was covered by the insurance policy which the first defendant had obtained from the second defendant, an insurance company. The second defendant successfully appealed that decision to the Supreme Court.

The insurance policy was a standard commercial vehicle policy containing an endorsement providing an indemnity for any accidents befalling passengers carried in the cab of the vehicle. Such cover was not compulsory under the Road Traffic Act 1961, but neither was it sufficient to cover the accident that befell the plaintiff. The plaintiff argued that the insurance certificate issued by the second defendant described a policy which permitted the carriage of passengers generally, so that in the circumstances it was the operative document having regard to section 67(1)(b) of the Road Traffic Act 1961. The second defendant argued that the carriage of passengers was permissive only and did not bear the construction that the insurers were to provide an indemnity for liability for injury sustained by a passenger carried on the cargo platform of the vehicle.

The Supreme Court concurred in the construction contended for by the insurance company It accepted that the provisions on limitations as to use were purely permissive in tenor. Since the policy was silent about providing an indemnity for liability to compensate such passengers carried permissively, there was no contradiction between the policy and the certificate. The Court concluded, therefore, that the insurance certificate did not go any further than the insurance policy.

Licenses   The Road Traffic (Licensing of Drivers) (Amendment) Regulations 1997 (S.I. No. 511 of 1997) require that, in applying for second or subsequent provisional driving licences, the applicant must provide information that she or he has applied for a driving licence test. They came into effect on December 18, 1997.

Manufacturing standards   The European Communities (Motor Vehicles Type Approval) Regulations 1997 (S.I. No. 147 of 1997) and the European Communities (Motor Vehicles Type Approval) (No. 2) Regulations 1997 (S.I. No. 476 of 1997) gave effect to a further series of Directives dealing with, *inter alia*, measures against air pollution by emissions, vehicle towing devices and protection of occupants from frontal impact. They came into effect on April 4, 1997 and December 3, 1997, respectively. The Road Traffic (Construction, Equipment and Use of Vehicles) (Amendment) Regulations 1997 (S.I. No. 404 of 1997) implemented Directive 96/53/EC, which increased the maximum width and length of certain heavy vehicles. They came into effect on September 30, 1997.

On-the-spot fines   The Local Authorities (Traffic Wardens) Act 1975 (Section 5) (Offences) Regulations 1997 (S.I. No.395 of 1997) prescribe a further series of offences to which on the spot fines may be imposed by traffic wardens pursuant to section 3 of the 1975 Act applies and prescribe a form of notice for those offences. They came into effect on October 1, 1997. Similarly, the Road Traffic Act 1961 (Section 103) (Offences) Regulations 1997 (S.I. No.396 of 1997) prescribe a further series of offences to which on the spot fines may be imposed pursuant to section 103 of the 1961 Act applies and prescribe a form for the notice to be affixed to vehicles pursuant to section 103. They also came into effect on October 1, 1997.

Road tax   The Road Vehicles (Registration and Licensing) (Amendment) Regulations 1997 (S.I. No. 405 of 1997), made under the Roads Act 1902, prescribe a method of calculating arrears of road tax, with effect from November 1, 1997.

Signs   The Road Traffic (Signs) Regulations 1997 (S.I. No. 181 of 1997) consolidated with amendments the signs to be used under the Road Traffic Acts 1961 to 1994 and came into force on October 1, 1997.

Taxis   The Road Traffic (Public Service Vehicles) (Amendment) Regulations 1997 (S.I. No. 193 of 1997) amended the provisions relating to wheelchair accessible taxis, with effect from May 8, 1997.

Tractors   The European Communities (Agricultural or Forestry Tractors Type Approval) Regulations 1997 (S.I. No. 446 of 1997) gave effect to Directive 96/63/EC and concern braking devices on tractors. They came into effect on October 30, 1997.

Traffic and Parking Regulations   The Road Traffic Act 1994 (Commencement) Order 1997 (S.I. No. 180 of 1997) brought the provisions of sections 35 and 36 of the Road Traffic Act 1994 (1994 Review, 221), which concern he procedures for making Traffic and Parking Regulations, into operation on May 1, 1997 and October 1, 1997, respectively. The 1997 Order also repealed the former provisions in this area, namely sections 89 and 90 the Road Traffic Act 1961 and section 60 of the Road Traffic Act 1968. The Road Traffic (Traffic and Parking) Regulations 1997 (S.I. No. 182 of 1997) were made under sections 35 and 36 of the 1994 Act and consolidated with amendments the arrangements for making traffic and parking bye-laws on a county basis by the Garda Commissioner. They came into effect on October 1, 1997.

Index